BROWNLIE'S DOCUMENTS
ON HUMAN RIGHTS

BROWNLIE'S DOCUMENTS ON HUMAN RIGHTS

SIXTH EDITION

Edited by

SIR IAN BROWNLIE, CBE, QC

and

GUY S. GOODWIN-GILL

OXFORD
UNIVERSITY PRESS

Great Clarendon Street, Oxford OX2 6DP

Oxford University Press is a department of the University of Oxford.
It furthers the University's objective of excellence in research, scholarship,
and education by publishing worldwide in

Oxford New York

Auckland Cape Town Dar es Salaam Hong Kong Karachi
Kuala Lumpur Madrid Melbourne Mexico City Nairobi
New Delhi Shanghai Taipei Toronto

With offices in

Argentina Austria Brazil Chile Czech Republic France Greece
Guatemala Hungary Italy Japan Poland Portugal Singapore
South Korea Switzerland Thailand Turkey Ukraine Vietnam

Oxford is a registered trade mark of Oxford University Press
in the UK and in certain other countries

Published in the United States
by Oxford University Press Inc., New York

First edition 1971
Second edition 1981
Third edition 1992
Fourth edition 2002
Fifth edition 2006
Sixth edition 2010

British Library Cataloguing in Publication Data

Data available

Library of Congress Cataloging in Publication Data

Data available

Typeset by Newgen Imaging Systems (P) Ltd
Printed in Great Britain
on acid-free paper by
CPI Group (UK) Ltd, Croydon, CRO 4YY

ISBN 978-0-19-956404-0

5 7 9 10 8 6 4

CONTENTS

PART ONE

STANDARD-SETTING BY THE UNITED NATIONS ORGANIZATION

PART TWO

IMPLEMENTATION AND STANDARD-SETTING IN
CONVENTIONS SPONSORED BY THE UNITED NATIONS

PART THREE

CONTRIBUTION OF THE INTERNATIONAL
LABOUR ORGANIZATION

PART FOUR

CONTRIBUTION OF THE UNITED NATIONS
EDUCATIONAL, SCIENTIFIC, AND CULTURAL
ORGANIZATION

PART FIVE

EUROPE

5.1 Council of Europe

5.2 European Union

5.3 Conference on Security and Co-operation in Europe (CSCE)/Organization for Security and Co-operation in Europe (OSCE)

PART SIX

AMERICAS

PART SEVEN

AFRICA

PART EIGHT

ARAB AND OTHER ISLAMIC STATES

PART NINE

ASIA

PART TEN

THE CONCEPT OF EQUALITY

Contents

GUIDE TO THE ONLINE RESOURCE CENTRE

This book is accompanied by an Online Resource Centre – an open-access website which has been designed to support the book. The ORC can be found at:

www.oxfordtextbooks.co.uk/orc/brownliehuman6e/

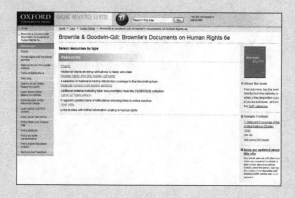

- A regularly updated table of ratifications and sources provides a useful reference resource and includes links to online sources.

- Additional charts showing ratifications by treaty and State.

- Materials moved from earlier editions, including fuller documentation from the CSCE/OSCE collection.

- A selection of material relating to human rights and the human genome provides introductory coverage to this fascinating topic and to the emerging literature.

- A selection of useful web links to sites containing further relevant information helps you to efficiently direct your online research.

PREFACE TO THE SIXTH EDITION

The aim of this work remains to provide a single collection of the most useful sources on human rights in a single volume, together with brief introductions on the background and pointers to the literature. The challenge lies in remaining as comprehensive as possible in face of the continuing and exponential growth in the range of relevant material. We have nevertheless attempted to be careful in selection and to avoid duplication, and in several instances we have compensated for cuts by transferring materials to the *Online Resource Centre*, where they can be accessed directly and/or downloaded.

The arrangement of materials generally follows that adopted in the two previous editions. Part One brings together 'non-treaty instruments', adopted within the United Nations Organization, while UN-sponsored treaties figure in Part Two. The work of two specialized agencies, the International Labour Organization and UNESCO, are covered separately, as are the regions. The 'European' materials in Part Five, are subdivided into Council of Europe, European Union and CSCE/OSCE, while one further instrument—the 1995 Commonwealth of Independent States Convention on Human Rights and Fundamental Freedoms—has been placed in the *Online Resource Centre*. Regional coverage of the Americas, Africa, and Arab and other Islamic States continues as before, and a new section on Asia has been added. Part Ten from the fifth edition— Human Rights and the Human Genome—has been updated and moved in its entirety to the *Online Resource Centre*.

In each Part, the various instruments are organized in chronological order, save that additional or amending protocols are grouped for the sake of convenience and ease of use with the principal instrument.

This edition incorporates some eighteen new items, including those dealing with the Human Rights Council, which replaced the Commission on Human Rights in 2006 (Nos. 2 and 3); the 2007 Declaration on the Rights of Indigenous Peoples (No. 39); two UN conventions from 2006—on the Rights of Persons with Disabilities (No. 63) and on the Protection of All Persons from Enforced Disappearance (No. 64); Protocol No. 14*bis* to the European Convention on Human Rights (No. 87—now largely for historical reasons); three further Council of Europe Conventions (Nos. 102, 103 and 104); three African Union instruments (Nos. 120, 122 and 123); and the 2009 Terms of Reference for the ASEAN Inter-Governmental Commission on Human Rights (No. 127).

We continue to leave declarations, reservations and objections to reservations outside this collection, but have updated the Chart of ratifications, numbers of States parties, and official sources to 31 May 2010. The Web addresses (URLs) here should allow relatively easy cross-checking for readers with Internet access.

We are grateful to Matthew Albert for extensive bibliographic research, particularly on Parts One and Two, and again we have benefited from the courtesy, co-operation and strong support of Oxford University Press. We are especially appreciative of the efficiency with which Tom Young and Rekha Summan have guided the work through to publication in hard copy, and on the Web.

IAN BROWNLIE
BLACKSTONE CHAMBERS
TEMPLE, LONDON

GUY S. GOODWIN-GILL
ALL SOULS COLLEGE
OXFORD

POSTSCRIPT

In December 2009, Ian and I finalized most of the text and introductions for this sixth edition. A month later, he died tragically in a car accident in Egypt. Over the years, we had watched, somewhat ruefully, as this volume grew way beyond its origins as a 'basic' collection. Ian thought we should seriously consider an alternative, *Truly Basic Documents on Human Rights*, but sadly we could find no takers. It seems appropriate, then, that this edition should be re-titled, *Brownlie's Documents on Human Rights*, remembering the great international lawyer that he was, and his pioneering role in making sure that the basic building blocks of international law could be within arm's reach of student and practitioner.

GUY S. GOODWIN-GILL
ALL SOULS COLLEGE
OXFORD
JUNE 2010

TABLE OF RATIFICATIONS AND SOURCES

This Table shows ratifications at 31 May 2010. The treaties are numbered by reference to their order in this 6th edition. The source (treaty series, documentary), also includes the URL (or Universal Resource Locator)—a website providing details of ratifications, reservations, declarations, etc. The resources listed include the United Nations treaty collection: **http://treaties.un.org/**, as well as those of other UN agencies (including the Office of the United Nations High Commissioner for Human Rights (see **http://www.ohchr.org/** and **http://www2.ohchr.org/english/law/index.htm**), the International Labour Organization (**http://www.ilo.org/ilolex/**), UNESCO (**http://portal.unesco.org/**), and of regional organizations.

Since the last edition of this work in 2006, the most significant changes have included the entry into force of the Optional Protocol to the Convention against Torture and Other Cruel, Inhuman or Degrading Treatment or Punishment, 2002 (Number 58 below), with States parties increasing from 16 to 51. There have also been significant increases in the number of parties to the Optional Protocol to the Convention on the Elimination of Discrimination against Women, 1999 (Number 56 below—from 76 to 99), and to the two optional protocols to the 1989 Convention on the Rights of the Child (Number 60—from 106 to 132; Number 61—from 103 to 137).

Charts providing further details of ratifications by State and treaty are available in the *Online Resource Centre.*

Number	Treaty	Date of signature	Date of entry into force	Number of States party	Source
41	Convention on the Prevention and Punishment of the Crime of Genocide, 1948	09/12/48	12/01/51	141	78 *UNTS* 277 **http://treaties.un.org/ http://www2.ohchr. org/english/law/ index.htm**
42	Convention Relating to the Status of Refugees, 1951	25/07/51	22/04/54	144	189 *UNTS* 137 **http://www.unhcr.org/ http://treaties.un.org/ http://www2.ohchr. org/english/law/ index.htm**
	[Protocol relating to the Status of Refugees, 1967]	31/01/67	04/10/67	144	660 *UNTS* 267
43	Convention on the Political Rights of Women, 1953	31/03/53	07/07/54	121	193 *UNTS* 135 **http://treaties.un.org/ http://www2.ohchr. org/english/law/ index.htm**
44	Slavery Convention, 1926, amended by Protocol, 1953	07/12/53	07/07/55	99	60 *LNTS* 253, 212 *UNTS* 17 182 *UNTS* 51 **http://treaties.un.org/ http://www2.ohchr. org/english/law/ index.htm**

Number	Treaty	Date of signature	Date of entry into force	Number of States party	Source
45	Supplementary Convention on the Abolition of Slavery, the Slave Trade, and Institutions and Practices Similar to Slavery, 1956	07/09/56	30/04/57	123	266 *UNTS* 3 http://treaties.un.org/ http://www2.ohchr. org/english/law/ index.htm
46	Convention Relating to the Status of Stateless Persons, 1954	23/09/54	06/06/60	65	360 *UNTS* 117 http://treaties.un.org/ http://www2.ohchr. org/english/law/ index.htm
47	Convention on the Reduction of Statelessness, 1961	30/08/61	13/12/75	37	989 *UNTS* 175 http://treaties.un.org/ http://www2.ohchr. org/english/law/ index.htm
48	International Convention on the Elimination of All Forms of Racial Discrimination, 1966	07/03/66	04/01/69	173	660 *UNTS* 195 http://treaties.un.org/ http://www2.ohchr. org/english/law/ index.htm
49	International Covenant on Economic, Social and Cultural Rights, 1966	16/12/66	03/01/76	160	993 *UNTS* 3 http://treaties.un.org/ http://www2.ohchr. org/english/law/ index.htm
50	Optional Protocol to the International Covenant on Economic, Social and Cultural Rights, 2008	10/12/08	–	–	UNGA Res. 63/117, 10 December 2008 http://treaties.un.org/ http://www2.ohchr. org/english/law/ index.htm
51	International Covenant on Civil and Political Rights, 1966	16/12/66	23/03/76	165	999 *UNTS* 171 http://treaties.un.org/ http://www2.ohchr. org/english/law/ index.htm
52	Optional Protocol to the International Covenant on Civil and Political Rights, 1966	16/12/66	23/03/76	113	999 *UNTS* 171 http://treaties.un.org/ http://www2.ohchr. org/english/law/ index.htm

Number	Treaty	Date of signature	Date of entry into force	Number of States party	Source
53	Second Optional Protocol to the International Covenant on Civil and Political Rights, aiming at the Abolition of the Death Penalty, 1989	15/12/89	11/07/91	72	1642 *UNTS* 414 **http://treaties.un.org/ http://www2.ohchr. org/english/law/ index.htm**
54	International Convention on the Suppression and Punishment of the Crime of Apartheid, 1973	30/11/73	18/07/76	107	1015 *UNTS* 243 **http://treaties.un.org/ http://www2.ohchr. org/english/law/ index.htm**
55	Convention on the Elimination of All Forms of Discrimination against Women, 1979	18/12/79	03/09/81	186	1249 *UNTS* 13 **http://treaties.un.org/ http://www2.ohchr. org/english/law/ index.htm**
56	Optional Protocol to the Convention on the Elimination of Discrimination against Women, 1999	10/12/99	22/12/00	99	2131 *UNTS* 83 **http://treaties.un.org/ http://www2.ohchr. org/english/law/ index.htm**
57	Convention against Torture and Other Cruel, Inhuman or Degrading Treatment or Punishment, 1984	10/12/84	26/06/87	146	1465 *UNTS* 85 **http://treaties.un.org/ http://www2.ohchr. org/english/law/ index.htm**
58	Optional Protocol to the Convention against Torture and Other Cruel, Inhuman or Degrading Treatment or Punishment, 2002	Adopted 18/12/02, opened for signature 04/02/03	22/06/06	51	UNGA Res. 57/199, 18 December 2002 **http://treaties.un.org/ http://www2.ohchr. org/english/law/ index.htm**
59	Convention on the Rights of the Child, 1989	20/11/89	02/09/90	193	1577 *UNTS* 3 **http://treaties.un.org/ http://www2.ohchr. org/english/law/ index.htm**

Number	Treaty	Date of signature	Date of entry into force	Number of States party	Source
60	Optional Protocol to the Convention on the Rights of the Child on the Involvement of Children in Armed Conflict, 2000	25/05/00	12/02/02	132	UNGA Res. 54/263, 25 May 2000 **http://treaties.un.org/ http://www2.ohchr. org/english/law/ index.htm**
61	Optional Protocol to the Convention on the Rights of the Child on the Sale of Children, Child Prostitution and Child Pornography, 2000	25/05/00	18/01/02	137	UNGA Res. 54/263, 25 May 2000 **http://treaties.un.org/ http://www2.ohchr. org/english/law/ index.htm**
62	International Convention on the Protection of the Rights of All Migrant Workers and Members of Their Families, 1990	18/12/90	01/07/03	42	UNGA Res. 45/158, 18 December 1990 **http://treaties.un.org/ http://www2.ohchr. org/english/law/ index.htm**
63	Convention on the Rights of Persons with Disabilities, 2006 Optional Protocol	Adopted 13/12/06, opened for signature 30/03/07	03/05/08 03/05/08	87 54	UNGA Res. 61/106, 13 December 2006 **http://treaties.un.org/ http://www2.ohchr. org/english/law/ index.htm**
64	International Convention for the Protection of All Persons from Enforced Disappearance, 2006	Adopted 20/12/06, opened for signature 06/02/07	[30 days after twentieth ratification: Article 39]	18	UNGA Res. 61/177, 20 December 2006 **http://treaties.un.org/ http://www2.ohchr. org/english/law/ index.htm**
66	Convention Concerning Forced or Compulsory Labour, 1930	10/06/30	01/05/32	174	ILO No. C29 39 *UNTS* 55 **http://www.ilo.org/ ilolex/ http://www2.ohchr. org/english/law/ index.htm**
67	Freedom of Association and Protection of the Right to Organize Convention, 1948	09/07/48	04/07/50	150	ILO No. C87 68 *UNTS* 17 **http://www.ilo.org/ ilolex/ http://www2.ohchr. org/english/law/ index.htm**

Number	Treaty	Date of signature	Date of entry into force	Number of States party	Source
68	Right to Organize and Collective Bargaining Convention, 1949	01/07/49	18/07/51	160	ILO No. C98 96 UNTS 257 http://www.ilo.org/ilolex/ http://www2.ohchr.org/english/law/index.htm
69	Equal Remuneration Convention, 1951	29/06/51	23/05/53	168	ILO No. C100 165 UNTS 304 http://www.ilo.org/ilolex/ http://www2.ohchr.org/english/law/index.htm
70	Convention Concerning the Abolition of Forced Labour, 1957	25/06/57	17/01/59	169	ILO No. C105 320 UNTS 291 http://www.ilo.org/ilolex/ http://www2.ohchr.org/english/law/index.htm
71	Discrimination (Employment and Occupation) Convention, 1958	25/06/58	15/06/60	169	ILO No. C111 363 UNTS 31 http://www.ilo.org/ilolex/ http://www2.ohchr.org/english/law/index.htm
73	Minimum Age Convention, 1973	26/06/73	19/06/76	155	ILO No. C138 1015 UNTS No. 14862 http://www.ilo.org/ilolex/ http://www2.ohchr.org/english/law/index.htm
74	Convention concerning Employment Promotion and Protection against Unemployment, 1988	21/06/88	17/10/91	7	ILO No. C168 http://www.ilo.org/ilolex/ http://www2.ohchr.org/english/law/index.htm
75	Convention Concerning Indigenous and Tribal Peoples in Independent Countries, 1989	27/06/89	05/09/91	20	ILO No. C169 http://www.ilo.org/ilolex/ http://www2.ohchr.org/english/law/index.htm

Number	Treaty	Date of signature	Date of entry into force	Number of States party	Source
77	Worst Forms of Child Labour Convention, 1999	17/06/99	19/11/00	172	ILO No. C182 **http://www.ilo.org/ ilolex/ http://www2.ohchr. org/english/law/ index.htm**
79	Convention Against Discrimination in Education, 1960	14/12/60	22/05/62	97	429 *UNTS* 93 **http://portal.unesco. org/ http://www2.ohchr. org/english/law/ index.htm**
82	Convention on the Protection and Promotion of the Diversity of Cultural Expressions, 2005	20/10/05	18/03/07	110 [plus the European Community]	**http://portal.unesco. org/ http://www2.ohchr. org/english/law/ index.htm**
83	European Convention for the Protection of Human Rights and Fundamental Freedoms, 1950, together with its Protocols, as amended by	04/11/50	03/09/53	47	*ETS* No. 5 **http://conventions. coe.int/**
	Protocol No. 11 Protocol No. 1 Protocol No. 4 Protocol No. 6 Protocol No. 7	11/05/94 20/03/52 16/09/63 28/04/83 22/11/84	01/11/98 18/05/54 02/05/68 01/03/85 01/11/88	47 45 43 46 42	*ETS* No. 155 *ETS* No. 9 *ETS* No. 46 *ETS* No. 114 *ETS* No. 117 **http://conventions. coe.int/**
84	Protocol No. 12 to the European Convention for the Protection of Human Rights and Fundamental Freedoms, 2000	04/11/00	01/04/05	17	*ETS* No. 177 **http://conventions. coe.int/**

Number	Treaty	Date of signature	Date of entry into force	Number of States party	Source
85	Protocol No. 13 to the European Convention for the Protection of Human Rights and Fundamental Freedoms, concerning the Abolition of the Death Penalty in All Circumstances, 2002	03/05/02	01/07/03	42	*ETS* No. 187 **http://conventions. coe.int/**
86	Protocol No. 14 to the European Convention for the Protection of Human Rights and Fundamental Freedoms, amending the control system of the Convention, 2004	13/05/04	01/06/10	47	*CETS* No. 194 **http://conventions. coe.int/** [See also the Madrid Agreement of 12 May 2009 on the provisional application of certain provisions of Protocol No. 14 pending its entry into force]
87	Protocol No. 14*bis* to the European Convention for the Protection of Human Rights and Fundamental Freedoms, amending the control system of the Convention, 2004	27/05/09	01/10/09	12	*CETS* No. 204 **http://conventions. coe.int/** [This protocol ceased to be in force or applied on a provisional basis with the entry in to force of Protocol No. 14 on 01/06/10]
88	European Social Charter, 1961	18/10/61	26/02/65	27	*ETS* No. 35 **http://conventions. coe.int/**
89	Additional Protocol to the European Social Charter, 1988	05/05/88	04/09/92	13	*ETS* No. 128 **http://conventions. coe.int/**
90	Protocol amending the European Social Charter, 1991	21/10/91	[On ratification by all the Parties to the Charter]	23	*ETS* No. 142 **http://conventions. coe.int/**

Number	Treaty	Date of signature	Date of entry into force	Number of States party	Source
91	Additional Protocol to the European Social Charter Providing for a System of Collective Complaints, 1995	09/11/95	01/07/98	12	ETS No. 158 http://conventions. coe.int/
92	European Social Charter (Revised), 1996	03/05/96	01/07/99	30	ETS No. 163 http://conventions. coe.int/
93	European Convention on the Legal Status of Migrant Workers, 1977	24/11/77	01/05/83	11	ETS No. 93 http://conventions. coe.int/
94	European Convention for the Prevention of Torture and Inhuman or Degrading Treatment or Punishment, 1987	26/11/87	01/02/89	47	ETS No. 126 http://conventions. coe.int/
	Protocol No. 1	04/11/93	01/03/02	47	ETS No. 151 http://conventions. coe.int/
	Protocol No. 2	04/11/93	01/03/02	47	ETS No. 152 http://conventions. coe.int/
95	European Convention on the Participation of Foreigners in Public Life at Local Level, 1992	05/02/92	01/05/97	8	ETS No. 144 http://conventions. coe.int/
96	European Charter for Regional or Minority Languages, 1992	05/11/92	01/03/98	24	ETS No. 148 http://conventions. coe.int/
97	European Framework Convention for the Protection of National Minorities, 1995	01/02/95	01/02/98	39	ETS No. 157 http://conventions. coe.int/

Number	Treaty	Date of signature	Date of entry into force	Number of States party	Source
98	European Convention on the Exercise of Children's Rights, 1996	25/01/96	01/07/00	14	*ETS* No. 160 **http://conventions. coe.int/**
99	European Convention on Nationality, 1997	06/11/97	01/03/00	19	*ETS* No. 166 **http://conventions. coe.int/**
100	European Convention on Contact concerning Children, 2003	15/05/03	01/09/05	6	*ETS* No. 192 **http://conventions. coe.int/**
101	European Convention on Action against Trafficking in Human Beings, 2005	16/05/05	01/02/08	27	*CETS* NO. 197 **http://conventions. coe.int/**
102	European Convention on the Avoidance of Statelessness in Relation to State Succession, 2006	19/05/06	01/05/09	4	*CETS* No. 200 **http://conventions. coe.int/**
103	European Convention on the Protection of Children against Sexual Exploitation and Sexual Abuse, 2007	25/10/07	01/07/10	5	*CETS* No. 201 **http://conventions. coe.int/**
104	European Convention on Access to Official Documents, 2009	18/06/09	[After ratification by 10 Member States]	3	*CETS* No. 205 **http://conventions. coe.int/**
109	American Convention on Human Rights, 1969	22/11/69	18/07/78	24	OAS *Treaty Series* No. 36 (1969) **http://www.oas.org/ juridico/english/ treaties.html**

Number	Treaty	Date of signature	Date of entry into force	Number of States party	Source
110	Additional Protocol to the American Convention on Human Rights in the Area of Economic, Social and Cultural Rights, 1988	17/11/88	16/11/99	15	OAS *Treaty Series* No. 69 (1988) **http://www.oas.org/ juridico/english/ treaties.html**
111	Protocol to the American Convention on Human Rights to Abolish the Death Penalty, 1990	08/06/90	[Between ratifying States on ratification]	11	OAS *Treaty Series* No. 73 (1990) **http://www.oas.org/ juridico/english/ treaties.html**
112	Inter-American Convention to Prevent and Punish Torture, 1985	12/09/85	28/02/87	18	OAS *Treaty Series*, No. 67 (1985) **http://www.oas.org/ juridico/english/ treaties.html**
113	Inter-American Convention on the Prevention, Punishment and Eradication of Violence against Women, 1994	09/06/94	05/03/95	32	33 *ILM* 1534 (1994) **http://www.oas.org/ juridico/english/ treaties.html**
114	Inter-American Convention on Forced Disappearance of Persons, 1994	09/06/94	28/03/96	14	33 *ILM* 1529 (1994) **http://www.oas.org/ juridico/english/ treaties.html**
115	Inter-American Convention on the Elimination of All Forms of Discrimination Against Persons with Disabilities, 1999	06/08/99	14/09/01	18	**http://www.oas.org/ juridico/english/ treaties.html**
117	Convention governing the Specific Aspects of Refugee Problems in Africa, 1969	10/09/69	20/06/74	45	1000 *UNTS* 46 **http://treaties.un.org/ http://www. africa-union.org/**
118	African Charter on Human and Peoples' Rights, 1981	17/06/81	21/10/86	53	1520 *UNTS* No. 26,363 **http://treaties.un.org/ http://www. africa-union.org/**

Number	Treaty	Date of signature	Date of entry into force	Number of States party	Source
119	Protocol to the African Charter on Human and Peoples' Rights on the Rights of Women in Africa, 2003	11/07/03	25/11/05	27	http://www. africa-union.org/
120	Protocol on the Statute of the African Court of Justice and Human Rights, 2008	01/07/08	[30 days after receipt of 15 ratifications]	2	http://www. africa-union.org/
121	African Charter on the Rights and Welfare of the Child, 1990	11/07/90	29/11/99	45	http://www. africa-union.org/
123	AU Convention for the Protection and Assistance of Internally Displaced Persons, 2009	23/10/09	[30 days after receipt of 15 ratifications]	1	http://www. africa-union.org/
126	Arab Charter on Human Rights, 2004	22/05/04	15/03/08	10	http://www. arableagueonline. org/ (official Arabic version)

SELECTED ABBREVIATIONS

AJIL	*American Journal of International Law*
AU	African Union
BYIL	*British Yearbook of International Law*
CETS	Council of Europe Treaty Series (replaces *ETS* from No. 194)
CSCE	Conference on Security and Co-operation in Europe
ECOWAS	Economic Community of West African States
EJIL	*European Journal of International Law*
ETS	European Treaty Series
EU	European Union
ICJ	International Court of Justice
ICLQ	*International and Comparative Law Quarterly*
IJRL	*International Journal of Refugee Law*
ILM	International Legal Materials
LNTS	League of Nations Treaty Series
NGO	Non-Governmental Organization
OAS	Organization of American States
OAU	Organization of African Unity
OSCE	Organization for Security and Co-operation in Europe
UN	United Nations
UNGA	United Nations General Assembly
UNTS	United Nations Treaty Series

USEFUL WEBSITES

African Commission on Human and Peoples' Rights: **http://www.achpr.org/**

African Union: **http://www.africa-union.org/**

Council of Europe Treaty Office: **http://conventions.coe.int/**

European Committee for the Prevention of Torture and Inhuman or Degrading Treatment: **http://www.cpt.coe.int/**

European Court of Human Rights: **http://www.echr.coe.int/echr/**

European Union Human Rights Activities: **http://europa.eu/pol/rights/index_en.htm**

Inter-American Commission on Human Rights: **http://www.cidh.org/**

Inter-American Court of Human Rights: **http://www.corteidh.or.cr/**

International Court of Justice: **http://www.icj-cij.org/**

International Labour Organization: **http://www.ilo.org/**

Joint United Nations Programme on HIV/AIDS: **http://www.unaids.org/**

League of Arab States: **http://www.arableagueonline.org/**

Organization for Security and Co-operation in Europe: **http://www.osce.org/**

Organization of American States Department of International Legal Affairs: **http://www.oas.org/dil/**

United Nations Children's Fund (UNICEF): **http://www.unicef.org/**

United Nations Conference on Trade and Development (UNCTAD), Programme on Transnational Corporations: **http://unctc.unctad.org/**

United Nations Documentation Centre: **http://www.un.org/documents/**

United Nations Educational, Social and Cultural Organization (UNESCO): **http://portal.unesco.org/**

United Nations High Commissioner for Human Rights: **http://www.ohchr.org/**

United Nations High Commissioner for Refugees: **http://www.unhcr.org/**

United Nations Inter-Agency Network on Women and Gender Equality: **http://www.un.org/womenwatch/**

United Nations Treaty Collection: **http://treaties.un.org/**

PART ONE

STANDARD-SETTING BY THE UNITED NATIONS ORGANIZATION

INTRODUCTION

A major achievement of the drafters of the Charter of the United Nations was the emphasis of the provisions on the importance of social justice and human rights as the foundation for a stable international order. The Organization, and especially the General Assembly and the Economic and Social Council, has given impetus to the development of standards concerning human rights. The United Nations has undertaken both general propaganda work and the burden of drafting legal instruments containing detailed provisions.

Over a period of some sixty years, from 1946–2006, the body most closely concerned with human rights was the creation of the Economic and Social Council, namely, the Commission on Human Rights. This in turn set up two Sub-Commissions: The Sub-Commission on Freedom of Information and of the Press, and the Sub-Commission on the Promotion and Protection of Human Rights (which had formerly been known as the Sub-Commission on the Prevention of Discrimination and the Protection of Minorities); and a Commission on the Status of Women was also established by ECOSOC in 1946. To these institutions there was eventually added the Office of the High Commissioner for Human Rights in 1993, which took over responsibility from the Division of Human Rights of the United Nations Secretariat.

In 2005, the Secretary-General proposed that the Commission be replaced by a Human Rights Council, a standing body able to meet when necessary rather than for only six weeks each year. See *Report of the Secretary-General, In Larger Freedom: Towards Development, Security and Human Rights for All* (2005); *2005 World Summit Outcome*: UN doc. A/60/1 (2005), paras. 157–9. The Council was duly created in 2006 and is discussed below at pp. 20–38

Certain of the specialised agencies associated with United Nations are also concerned with human rights, the International Labour Organization being the most prominent in this respect. On the ILO and UNESCO, see further below. The specialised agencies make periodic reports on human rights, which are forwarded to the Human Rights Council and other bodies by the UN Secretary-General.

The instruments reproduced in this section reflect in particular the work of United Nations Charter-based organs, including the General Assembly, the Economic and Social Council, the Commission on Human Rights, and the Human Rights Council, as well as conclusions and declarations adopted in international conferences, where these have been endorsed by the UN. Where their standard-setting activities have resulted in specific treaties, these are included in Part Two.

Further reading

KÄLIN, W. and KÜNZLI, J., *The Law of International Human Rights Protection*, Oxford: Oxford University Press, 2009.

KAMMINGA,, M. T. and SCHEININ, M., eds., *The Impact of Human Rights Law on General International Law*, Oxford: Oxford University Press, 2009.

TOMUSCHAT, C., *Human Rights: Between Idealism and Realism*, Oxford: Oxford University Press, 2nd edn., 2008.

1. RELEVANT PROVISIONS OF THE UNITED NATIONS CHARTER, 1945

The Charter of the United Nations was signed on 26 June 1945, in San Francisco, at the conclusion of the United Nations Conference on International Organization, and came into force on 24 October 1945. The Statute of the International Court of Justice is an integral part of the Charter. Of the articles included below, Article 61 has been amended twice, increasing membership of the Economic and Social Council from eighteen to twenty-seven (General Assembly Resolution 1991 (XVIII), 17 December 1963; in force 31 August 1965); and from twenty-seven to fifty-four (General Assembly Resolution 2847 (XXVI), 20 December 1971 (105–2–15); in force 24 September 1973).

Further reading

FASSBENDER, B., *The United Nations Charter as the Constitution of the International Community*, The Hague: Brill Academic Publishing, 2009.

SIMMA, B., ed., *The Charter of the United Nations: A Commentary*, Oxford: Oxford University Press, 2nd edn., 2002.

TEXT

WE THE PEOPLES OF THE UNITED NATIONS DETERMINED

to save succeeding generations from the scourge of war, which twice in our lifetime has brought untold sorrow to mankind, and

to reaffirm faith in fundamental human rights, in the dignity and worth of the human person, in the equal rights of men and women and of nations large and small, and

to establish conditions under which justice and respect for the obligations arising from treaties and other sources of international law can be maintained, and

to promote social progress and better standards of life in larger freedom,

AND FOR THESE ENDS

to practise tolerance and live together in peace with one another as good neighbours, and

to unite our strength to maintain international peace and security, and

to ensure by the acceptance of principles and the institution of methods, that armed force shall not be used, save in the common interest, and

to employ international machinery for the promotion of the economic and social advancement of all peoples,

HAVE RESOLVED TO COMBINE OUR EFFORTS TO ACCOMPLISH THESE AIMS

Accordingly, our respective Governments, through representatives assembled in the City of San Francisco, who have exhibited their full powers found to be in good and due form, have agreed to the present Charter of the United Nations and do hereby establish an international organization to be known as the United Nations.

CHAPTER I
PURPOSES AND PRINCIPLES

Article 1

The Purposes of the United Nations are:

1. To maintain international peace and security, and to that end: to take effective collective measures for the prevention and removal of threats to the peace, and for the suppression of acts of aggression or other breaches of the peace, and to bring about by peaceful means, and in conformity with the principles of justice and international law, adjustment or settlement of international disputes or situations which might lead to a breach of the peace;

2. To develop friendly relations among nations based on respect for the principle of equal rights and self-determination of peoples, and to take other appropriate measures to strengthen universal peace;

3. To achieve international co-operation in solving international problems of an economic, social, cultural, or humanitarian character, and in promoting and encouraging respect for human rights and for fundamental freedoms for all without distinction as to race, sex, language, or religion; and

4. To be a centre for harmonizing the actions of nations in the attainment of these common ends.

Article 2

The Organization and its Members, in pursuit of the Purposes stated in Article 1, shall act in accordance with the following Principles.

1. The Organization is based on the principle of the sovereign equality of all its Members.

2. All Members, in order to ensure to all of them the rights and benefits resulting from membership, shall fulfill in good faith the obligations assumed by them in accordance with the present Charter.

3. All Members shall settle their international disputes by peaceful means in such a manner that international peace and security, and justice, are not endangered.

4. All Members shall refrain in their international relations from the threat or use of force against the territorial integrity or political independence of any State, or in any other manner inconsistent with the Purposes of the United Nations.

5. All Members shall give the United Nations every assistance in any action it takes in accordance with the present Charter, and shall refrain from giving assistance to any State against which the United Nations is taking preventive or enforcement action.

6. The Organization shall ensure that States which are not Members of the United Nations act in accordance with these Principles so far as may be necessary for the maintenance of international peace and security.

7. Nothing contained in the present Charter shall authorize the United Nations to intervene in matters which are essentially within the domestic jurisdiction of any State or shall require the Members to submit such matters to settlement under the present Charter; but this principle shall not prejudice the application of enforcement measures under Chapter VII.

Article 10

The General Assembly may discuss any questions or any matters within the scope of the present Charter or relating to the powers and functions of any organs provided for in the present Charter, and, except as provided in Article 12, may make recommendations to the Members of the United Nations or to the Security Council or to both on any such questions or matters.

Article 13

1. The General Assembly shall initiate studies and make recommendations for the purpose of:

   (a) promoting international cooperation in the political field and encouraging the progressive development of international law and its codification;

   (b) promoting international cooperation in the economic, social, cultural, educational, and health fields, and assisting in the realization of human rights and fundamental freedoms for all without distinction as to race, sex, language, or religion.

2. The further responsibilities, functions and powers of the General Assembly with respect to matters mentioned in paragraph 1(b) above are set forth in Chapters IX and X.

Article 16

The General Assembly shall perform such functions with respect to the international trusteeship system as are assigned to it under Chapters XII and XIII, including the approval of the trusteeship agreements for areas not designated as strategic.

CHAPTER IX
INTERNATIONAL ECONOMIC AND SOCIAL CO-OPERATION

Article 55

With a view to the creation of conditions of stability and well-being which are necessary for peaceful and friendly relations among nations based on respect for the principle of equal rights and self-determination of peoples, the United Nations shall promote:

   (a) higher standards of living, full employment, and conditions of economic and social progress and development;

   (b) solutions of international economic, social, health, and related problems; and international cultural and educational co-operation; and

   (c) universal respect for, and observance of, human rights and fundamental freedoms for all without distinction as to race, sex, language, or religion.

Article 56

All Members pledge themselves to take joint and separate action in co-operation with the Organization for the achievement of the purposes set forth in Article 55.

Article 57

1. The various specialized agencies, established by intergovernmental agreement and having wide international responsibilities, as defined in their basic instruments, in

economic, social, cultural, educational, health, and related fields, shall be brought into relationship with the United Nations in accordance with the provisions of Article 63.

2. Such agencies thus brought into relationship with the United Nations are hereinafter referred to as specialized agencies.

Article 58

The Organization shall make recommendations for the coordination of the policies and activities of the specialized agencies.

Article 59

The Organization shall, where appropriate, initiate negotiations among the States concerned for the creation of any new specialized agencies required for the accomplishment of the purposes set forth in Article 55.

Article 60

Responsibility for the discharge of the functions of the Organization set forth in this Chapter shall be vested in the General Assembly and, under the authority of the General Assembly, in the Economic and Social Council, which shall have for this purpose the powers set forth in Chapter X.

CHAPTER X
THE ECONOMIC AND SOCIAL COUNCIL

Composition

Article 61

1. The Economic and Social Council shall consist of fifty-four Members of the United Nations elected by the General Assembly.

2. Subject to the provisions of paragraph 3, eighteen members of the Economic and Social Council shall be elected each year for a term of three years. A retiring member shall be eligible for immediate re-election.

3. At the first election after the increase in the membership of the Economic and Social Council from twenty-seven to fifty-four members, in addition to the members elected in place of the nine members whose term of office expires at the end of that year, twenty-seven additional members shall be elected. Of these twenty-seven additional members, the term of office of nine members so elected shall expire at the end of one year, and of nine other members at the end of two years, in accordance with arrangements made by the General Assembly.

4. Each member of the Economic and Social Council shall have one representative.

Functions and Powers

Article 62

1. The Economic and Social Council may make or initiate studies and reports with respect to international economic, social, cultural, educational, health, and related matters and

may make recommendations with respect to any such matters to the General Assembly, to the Members of the United Nations, and to the specialized agencies concerned.

2. It may make recommendations for the purpose of promoting respect for, and observance of, human rights and fundamental freedoms for all.

3. It may prepare draft conventions for submission to the General Assembly, with respect to matters falling within its competence.

4. It may call, in accordance with the rules prescribed by the United Nations, international conferences on matters falling within its competence.

Article 63

1. The Economic and Social Council may enter into agreements with any of the agencies referred to in Article 57, defining the terms on which the agency concerned shall be brought into relationship with the United Nations. Such agreements shall be subject to approval by the General Assembly.

2. It may coordinate the activities of the specialized agencies through consultation with and recommendations to such agencies and through recommendations to the General Assembly and to the Members of the United Nations.

Article 64

1. The Economic and Social Council may take appropriate steps to obtain regular reports from the specialized agencies. It may make arrangements with the Members of the United Nations and with the specialized agencies to obtain reports on the steps taken to give effect to its own recommendations and to recommendations on matters falling within its competence made by the General Assembly.

2. It may communicate its observations on these reports to the General Assembly.

Article 65

The Economic and Social Council may furnish information to the Security Council and shall assist the Security Council upon its request.

Article 66

1. The Economic and Social Council shall perform such functions as fall within its competence in connection with the carrying out of the recommendations of the General Assembly.

2. It may, with the approval of the General Assembly, perform services at the request of Members of the United Nations and at the request of specialized agencies.

3. It shall perform such other functions as are specified elsewhere in the present Charter or as may be assigned to it by the General Assembly.

Voting

Article 67

1. Each member of the Economic and Social Council shall have one vote.

2. Decisions of the Economic and Social Council shall be made by a majority of the members present and voting.

Procedure

Article 68

The Economic and Social Council shall set up commissions in economic and social fields and for the promotion of human rights, and such other commissions as may be required for the performance of its functions.

Article 69

The Economic and Social Council shall invite any Member of the United Nations to participate, without vote, in its deliberations on any matter of particular concern to that Member.

Article 70

The Economic and Social Council may make arrangements for representatives of the specialized agencies to participate, without vote, in its deliberations and in those of the commissions established by it, and for its representatives to participate in the deliberations of the specialized agencies.

Article 71

The Economic and Social Council may make suitable arrangements for consultation with non-governmental organizations which are concerned with matters within its competence. Such arrangements may be made with international organizations and, where appropriate, with national organizations after consultation with the Member of the United Nations concerned.

Article 72

1. The Economic and Social Council shall adopt its own rules of procedure, including the method of selecting its President.

2. The Economic and Social Council shall meet as required in accordance with its rules, which shall include provision for the convening of meetings on the request of a majority of its members.

CHAPTER XI
DECLARATION REGARDING NON-SELF-GOVERNING TERRITORIES

Article 73

Members of the United Nations which have or assume responsibilities for the administration of territories whose peoples have not yet attained a full measure of self-government recognize the principle that the interests of the inhabitants of these territories are paramount, and accept as a sacred trust the obligation to promote to the utmost, within the system of international peace and security established by the present Charter, the well-being of the inhabitants of these territories, and, to this end:

    (a) to ensure, with due respect for the culture of the peoples concerned, their political, economic, social, and educational advancement, their just treatment, and their protection against abuses;

(b) to develop self-government, to take due account of the political aspirations of the peoples, and to assist them in the progressive development of their free political institutions, according to the particular circumstances of each territory and its peoples and their varying stages of advancement;

(c) to further international peace and security;

(d) to promote constructive measures of development, to encourage research, and to co-operate with one another and, when and where appropriate, with specialized international bodies with a view to the practical achievement of the social, economic, and scientific purposes set forth in this Article; and

(e) to transmit regularly to the Secretary-General for information purposes, subject to such limitation as security and constitutional considerations may require, statistical and other information of a technical nature relating to economic, social, and educational conditions in the territories for which they are respectively responsible other than those territories to which Chapter XII and XIII apply.

Article 74

Members of the United Nations also agree that their policy in respect of the territories to which this Chapter applies, no less than in respect of their metropolitan areas, must be based on the general principle of good-neighbourliness, due account being taken of the interests and well-being of the rest of the world, in social, economic, and commercial matters.

CHAPTER XII
INTERNATIONAL TRUSTEESHIP SYSTEM

Article 75

The United Nations shall establish under its authority an international trusteeship system for the administration and supervision of such territories as may be placed thereunder by subsequent individual agreements. These territories are hereinafter referred to as trust territories.

Article 76

The basic objectives of the trusteeship system, in accordance with the Purposes of the United Nations laid down in Article 1 of the present Charter, shall be:

(a) to further international peace and security;

(b) to promote the political, economic, social, and educational advancement of the inhabitants of the trust territories, and their progressive development towards self-government or independence as may be appropriate to the particular circumstances of each territory and its peoples and the freely expressed wishes of the peoples concerned, and as may be provided by the terms of each trusteeship agreement;

(c) to encourage respect for human rights and for fundamental freedoms for all without distinction as to race, sex, language, or religion, and to encourage recognition of the interdependence of the peoples of the world; and

(d) to ensure equal treatment in social, economic, and commercial matters for all Members of the United Nations and their nationals and also equal treatment for the latter in the administration of justice without prejudice to the attainment of the foregoing objectives and subject to the provisions of Article 80.

Article 77

1. The trusteeship system shall apply to such territories in the following categories as may be placed thereunder by means of trusteeship agreements:

(a) territories now held under mandate;

(b) territories which may be detached from enemy States as a result of the Second World War; and

(c) territories voluntarily placed under the system by States responsible for their administration.

2. It will be a matter for subsequent agreement as to which territories in the foregoing categories will be brought under the trusteeship system and upon what terms.

Article 78

The trusteeship system shall not apply to territories which have become Members of the United Nations, relationship among which shall be based on respect for the principle of sovereign equality.

Article 79

The terms of trusteeship for each territory to be placed under the trusteeship system, including any alteration or amendment, shall be agreed upon by the States directly concerned, including the mandatory power in the case of territories held under mandate by a Member of the United Nations, and shall be approved as provided for in Articles 83 and 85.

Article 80

1. Except as may be agreed upon in individual trusteeship agreements, made under Articles 77, 79, and 81, placing each territory under the trusteeship system, and until such agreements have been concluded, nothing in this Chapter shall be construed in or of itself to alter in any manner the rights whatsoever of any States or any peoples or the terms of existing international instruments to which Members of the United Nations may respectively be parties.

2. Paragraph 1 of this Article shall not be interpreted as giving grounds for delay or postponement of the negotiation and conclusion of agreements for placing mandated and other territories under the trusteeship system as provided for in Article 77.

Article 81

The trusteeship agreement shall in each case include the terms under which the trust territory will be administered and designate the authority which will exercise the administration of the trust territory. Such authority, hereinafter called the administering authority, may be one or more States or the Organization itself.

Article 82

There may be designated, in any trusteeship agreement, a strategic area or areas which may include part or all of the trust territory to which the agreement applies, without prejudice to any special agreement or agreements made under Article 43.

Article 83

1. All functions of the United Nations relating to strategic areas, including the approval of the terms of the trusteeship agreements and of their alteration or amendment, shall be exercised by the Security Council.

2. The basic objectives set forth in Article 76 shall be applicable to the people of each strategic area.

3. The Security Council shall, subject to the provisions of the trusteeship agreements and without prejudice to security considerations, avail itself of the assistance of the Trusteeship Council to perform those functions of the United Nations under the trusteeship system relating to political, economic, social, and educational matters in the strategic areas.

Article 84

It shall be the duty of the administering authority to ensure that the trust territory shall play its part in the maintenance of international peace and security. To this end the administering authority may make use of volunteer forces, facilities, and assistance from the trust territory in carrying out the obligations towards the Security Council undertaken in this regard by the administering authority, as well as for local defence and the maintenance of law and order within the trust territory.

Article 85

1. The functions of the United Nations with regard to trusteeship agreements for all areas not designated as strategic, including the approval of the terms of the trusteeship agreements and of their alteration or amendment, shall be exercised by the General Assembly.

2. The Trusteeship Council, operating under the authority of the General Assembly, shall assist the General Assembly in carrying out these functions.

CHAPTER XIII
THE TRUSTEESHIP COUNCIL

Composition

Article 86

1. The Trusteeship Council shall consist of the following Members of the United Nations:

(a) those Members administering trust territories;

(b) such of those Members mentioned by name in Article 23 as are not administering trust territories; and

(c) as many other Members elected for three-year terms by the General Assembly as may be necessary to ensure that the total number of members of the Trusteeship Council is equally divided between those Members of the United Nations which administer trust territories and those which do not.

2. Each member of the Trusteeship Council shall designate one specially qualified person to represent it therein.

Functions and Powers

Article 87

The General Assembly and, under its authority, the Trusteeship Council, in carrying out their functions, may:

    (a) consider reports submitted by the administering authority;

    (b) accept petitions and examine them in consultation with the administering authority;

    (c) provide for periodic visits to the respective trust territories at times agreed upon with the administering authority; and

    (d) take these and other actions in conformity with the terms of the trusteeship agreements.

Article 88

The Trusteeship Council shall formulate a questionnaire on the political, economic, social, and educational advancement of the inhabitants of each trust territory, and the administering authority for each trust territory within the competence of the General Assembly shall make an annual report to the General Assembly upon the basis of such questionnaire.

Voting

Article 89

1. Each member of the Trusteeship Council shall have one vote.

2. Decisions of the Trusteeship Council shall be made by a majority of the members present and voting.

Procedure

Article 90

1. The Trusteeship Council shall adopt its own rules of procedure, including the method of selecting its President.

2. The Trusteeship Council shall meet as required in accordance with its rules, which shall include provision for the convening of meetings on the request of a majority of its members.

2. FROM THE COMMISSION ON HUMAN RIGHTS (1946–2006) TO THE HUMAN RIGHTS COUNCIL (2006–)

The Commission on Human Rights (1946–2006) initially played a minimal role in handling complaints of human rights violations. From 1967 onwards, however, it was authorized to consider information relevant to gross violations and to make a thorough study of and report on situations revealing a consistent pattern of human rights violations: ECOSOC Resolution 1235 (XLII). It also began to carry out regular operational fact-finding activities, and, in 1970, ECOSOC devised an improved procedure for handling communications (complaints) from individuals and non-governmental organizations relating to violations of human rights (the '1503 Procedure': ECOSOC Resolution 1503 (XLVIII); for this and related texts, see the 5th edition of this work). Although promising in outline and inception, the procedure proved generally ineffective.[1]

The Secretary-General's 2002 report to the General Assembly, 'Strengthening of the United Nations: An agenda for further change' (UN doc. A/57/387), emphasized the importance of the work on human rights, and the need to build on its achievements and strengthen the UN machinery. Particular attention was paid to the 'special procedure mechanisms' of the Commission, which it was considered could be made more effective. In resolution 57/300, adopted on 20 December 2002, the General Assembly requested the Commission, with the support of the UN High Commissioner for Human Rights, to undertake the necessary review. See 'Report of the United Nations High Commissioner for Human Rights and Follow-Up to the World Conference on Human Rights: Effective Functioning of Human Rights Mechanisms', UN doc. E/CN.4/2004/4, 5 August 2003. This was largely overtaken by the Secretary-General's proposal that the Commission be replaced by a Human Rights Council, a standing body, able to meet when necessary rather than for only six weeks each year. See Report of the Secretary-General, *In Larger Freedom: Towards Development, Security and Human Rights for All*, UN doc. A/59/2005, 21 March 2005, Add. 1.

The United Nations Millennium + 5 Summit approved in principle the proposal to create a Human Rights Council to replace the Commission on Human Rights; and in Resolution 60/251, adopted on 15 March 2006, the General Assembly, 'recognizing the work undertaken by the Commission and the need to preserve and build on its achievements',[2] decided to set up the Council as a subsidiary organ under Article 22 of the Charter. A week later, the Economic and Social Council voted to dissolve the Commission (ECOSOC res. 2006/2, 22 March 2006), and the Human Rights Council held its first session in Geneva from 9 to 30 June 2006; for details of this and subsequent sessions, see: **http://www2.ohchr.org/english/bodies/hrcouncil/.**

---

[1] See van Boven, T., in Cassese, A., ed., *U.N. Law/Fundamental Rights – Two Topics in International Law*, Aalphen aan den Rijn: Sijthoff Noordhoff, 1979, 119 at 124.

[2] Those achievements, of course, included drafting the 1948 Universal Declaration of Human Rights, as well as a substantial record of standard-setting through the work of the Sub-Commission on the Promotion and Protection of Human Rights, the Special Rapporteurs, Representatives and Working Groups, and through the special procedures described above. Those procedures have been continued, as has the competence to receive and respond to complaints of serious violations of human rights; see further below.

In Resolution 60/251, reproduced below, the General Assembly identifies the Council's mandate as 'promoting universal respect for the protection of all human rights and fundamental freedoms for all, without distinction of any kind and in a fair and equal manner' (paragraph 2). It sets out a number of guiding principles (universality, impartiality and non-selectivity, constructive international dialogue and co-operation: paragraph 4), decides that the Council 'should address situations of violations of human rights, including gross and systematic violations, and make recommendations thereon' (paragraph 3), and 'contribute through dialogue and co-operation to the *prevention* of human rights violations and respond promptly to human rights emergencies' (paragraph 5(f)).

The Human Rights Council is an intergovernmental body comprising representatives of forty-seven States (paragraph 7; the Commission had fifty-three). As its name seems to imply, it was considered that the Council might have the same status within the UN as the other Councils, and this option remains open, as and when the HRC is reviewed in 2011. At present, however, its enhanced status as a subsidiary organ of the General Assembly may enable it to acquire a standing and authority which escaped the Commission, particularly in its final years. By contrast with the Commission, the Council is also a standing body, is required to meet for at least ten weeks a year over at least three sessions, and may hold special sessions at the request of one-third of the membership (UNGA res. 60/251, paragraph 10). When electing members of the Council, States are called upon to take into account candidates' human rights record and the voluntary pledge they make on improving human rights protection (UNGA res. 60/251, paragraph 8).

A major innovation is the new mechanism known as the 'Universal Periodic Review' (UPR). All UN Member States, including all elected Council members (UNGA res. 60/251, paragraphs 5(e), 9), will now submit to a periodic review of their human rights performance, to be conducted within the Council over a four-year cycle. The *universal* requirement is intended to ensure that no State can now avoid attention, but the methodology is also intended to be more co-operative than confrontational, although a Council member found to be responsible for gross and systematic violations could be suspended by the General Assembly. In principle, the UPR is intended to 'complement and not duplicate the work of the treaty bodies'. It is not immediately clear how this is to be achieved, particularly as the 'basis for review' includes the UN Charter, the Universal Declaration of Human Rights, human rights treaties to which States are party, voluntary pledges and commitments made by States when presenting themselves as candidates for membership of the Council, and applicable international humanitarian law (HRC Resolution 5/1, Universal Periodic Review Mechanism, paragraph 1).

Also not entirely clear is the relationship between the Council and the Office of the High Commissioner for Human Rights. The High Commissioner is an Under-Secretary-General of the United Nations, appointed by the Secretary-General with the approval of the General Assembly. The Office is a department of the Secretariat, and not an independent body, although it has the right to make recommendations on policy and action. The High Commissioner reports annually to the Human Rights Council and the General Assembly, but also provides significant services to the Council, particularly in the management and implementation of the UPR process. Resolution 60/251 refers to the Council assuming, 'the role and responsibilities of the Commission on Human Rights relating to the Office of the United Nations High Commissioner for Human Rights as decided by the General Assembly in its Resolution 48/141 of 20 December 1993', on which see further below, p. 201.

Paragraph 5(h) provides that the Council is to work with a variety of stakeholders, including governments, regional organizations, national human rights institutions and civil society. Here, the 1993 Paris Principles relating to the Status and Functioning of National Institutions for the Promotion and Protection of Human Rights (see below, p. 205) are important, so far as accreditation as being in compliance with these principles enables National Human Rights Institutions (NHRIs) to submit documentation and to contribute orally to Council sessions.

Paragraph 6 provides expressly that the Council, 'shall assume, review and, where necessary, improve and rationalize all mandates, mechanisms, functions and responsibilities of the Commission... in order to maintain a system of special procedures, expert advice and a complaint procedure'. The Council thus retains the competence of the Commission to address any situation of human rights violations in the world on its permanent agenda: see HRC Resolution 5/1 on 'Institution Building', which is reproduced below at p. 20; it deals in some detail with the UPR (paragraphs 1–38), special procedures (paragraphs 39–64), complaints procedures (paragraphs 85–109— the process remains confidential, however, focusing on situations rather than individual violations), the agenda (Part V), methods of work (paragraphs 110–28), and rules of procedure. The former Sub-Commission on the Promotion and Protection of Human Rights has been replaced by an Advisory Committee, intended to work at the Council's direction and to be its 'think-tank'. It comprises eighteen expert members elected by secret ballot based on allocation by geographical region; see paragraphs 65–84. Unlike its predecessor, the Advisory Committee may not adopt resolutions or decisions.

Resolution 60/251, which follows below, was adopted by the General Assembly on 15 March 2006, by a recorded vote of 170 in favour, 4 against (Israel, Marshall Islands, Palau, United States of America), and 3 abstentions (Belarus, Iran, Venezuela). For debate and explanations of vote, see UNGAOR, Sixtieth sess., 72nd plenary meeting, 15 March 2006: UN doc. A/60/PV.72.

Further reading

ALSTON, P. AND MÉGRET, F., eds., *The United Nations and Human Rights: A Critical Appraisal*, New York: Oxford University Press, 2nd edn., 2008.

ALSTON, P., 'Reconceiving the UN Human Rights Regime: Challenges Confronting the New UN Human Rights Council' (2006) 7 *Melbourne Journal of International Law* 185.

BERNAZ, N., 'Reforming the UN Human Rights Protection Procedures: A Legal Perspective on the Establishment of the Universal Periodic Review Mechanism', in BOYLE, K., ed., *New Institutions for Human Rights Protection*, 2009, 75–92.

BOYLE, K., ed., *New Institutions for Human Rights Protection*, Oxford: Oxford University Press, 2009.

BOYLE, K., 'The United Nations Human Rights Council: Origins, Antecedents, and Prospects', in BOYLE, K., ed., *New Institutions for Human Rights Protection*, 2009, 11–47.

EUDES, M., 'De la Commission au Conseil des droits de l'homme: vraie réforme ou faux-semblant?' (2006) 52 *Annuaire Français de droit international*, 599.

GHANEA, N., 'From UN Commission on Human Rights to UN Human Rights Council: One Step Forwards or Two Steps Sideways?' (2006) 55 *ICLQ* 695.

RODLEY, N. S., 'The United Nations Human Rights Council, Its Special Procedures, and Its Relationship with the Treaty Bodies: Complementarity or Competition?', in BOYLE, K., ed., *New Institutions for Human Rights Protection*, 2009, 49–73.

—— 'United Nations Human Rights Treaty Bodies and Special Procedures of the Commission on Human Rights—Complementarity or Competition?' (2003) 25 *Human Rights Quarterly* 882–908.

SCHRIJVER, N., 'The UN Human Rights Council: A New "Society of the Committed" or Just Old Wine in New Bottles?' (2007) 20 *Leiden Journal of International Law* 809.

'Special Issue: Reform of the UN Human Rights Machinery', (2007) 7 *Human Rights Law Review*, 1–273.

SWEENEY, G. and SAITO, Y., 'An NGO Assessment of the New Mechanisms of the UN Human Rights Council', (2009) 9 *Human Rights Law Review* 203.

TARDU, M., 'Le nouveau conseil des droits de l'homme aux Nations Unies: décadence ou résurrection?' *Revue trimestrielle de droits de l'homme* (2007) 967.

UNITED NATIONS HIGH COMMISSIONER FOR HUMAN RIGHTS: **http://www.ohchr.org/**.

UPR INFO: **http://www.upr-info.org**.

TEXT

General Assembly Resolution 60/251, 'Human Rights Council' 15 March 2006

The General Assembly,

Reaffirming the purposes and principles contained in the Charter of the United Nations, including developing friendly relations among nations based on respect for the principle of equal rights and self-determination of peoples, and achieving international cooperation in solving international problems of an economic, social, cultural or humanitarian character and in promoting and encouraging respect for human rights and fundamental freedoms for all,

Reaffirming also the Universal Declaration of Human Rights and the Vienna Declaration and Programme of Action, and recalling the International Covenant on Civil and Political Rights, the International Covenant on Economic, Social and Cultural Rights and other human rights instruments,

Reaffirming further that all human rights are universal, indivisible, interrelated, interdependent and mutually reinforcing, and that all human rights must be treated in a fair and equal manner, on the same footing and with the same emphasis,

Reaffirming that, while the significance of national and regional particularities and various historical, cultural and religious backgrounds must be borne in mind, all States, regardless of their political, economic and cultural systems, have the duty to promote and protect all human rights and fundamental freedoms,

Emphasizing the responsibilities of all States, in conformity with the Charter, to respect human rights and fundamental freedoms for all, without distinction of any kind as to race, colour, sex, language or religion, political or other opinion, national or social origin, property, birth or other status,

Acknowledging that peace and security, development and human rights are the pillars of the United Nations system and the foundations for collective security and well-being, and recognizing that development, peace and security and human rights are interlinked and mutually reinforcing,

Affirming the need for all States to continue international efforts to enhance dialogue and broaden understanding among civilizations, cultures and religions, and emphasizing that States, regional organizations, non-governmental organizations, religious bodies and the media have an important role to play in promoting tolerance, respect for and freedom of religion and belief,

Recognizing the work undertaken by the Commission on Human Rights and the need to preserve and build on its achievements and to redress its shortcomings,

Recognizing also the importance of ensuring universality, objectivity and non-selectivity in the consideration of human rights issues, and the elimination of double standards and politicization,

Recognizing further that the promotion and protection of human rights should be based on the principles of cooperation and genuine dialogue and aimed at strengthening the capacity of Member States to comply with their human rights obligations for the benefit of all human beings,

Acknowledging that non-governmental organizations play an important role at the national, regional and international levels, in the promotion and protection of human rights,

Reaffirming the commitment to strengthen the United Nations human rights machinery, with the aim of ensuring effective enjoyment by all of all human rights, civil, political, economic, social and cultural rights, including the right to development, and to that end, the resolve to create a Human Rights Council,

1. *Decides* to establish the Human Rights Council, based in Geneva, in replacement of the Commission on Human Rights, as a subsidiary organ of the General Assembly; the Assembly shall review the status of the Council within five years;

2. *Decides* that the Council shall be responsible for promoting universal respect for the protection of all human rights and fundamental freedoms for all, without distinction of any kind and in a fair and equal manner;

3. *Decides also* that the Council should address situations of violations of human rights, including gross and systematic violations, and make recommendations thereon. It should also promote the effective coordination and the mainstreaming of human rights within the United Nations system;

4. *Decides further* that the work of the Council shall be guided by the principles of universality, impartiality, objectivity and non-selectivity, constructive international dialogue and cooperation, with a view to enhancing the promotion and protection of all human rights, civil, political, economic, social and cultural rights, including the right to development;

5. *Decides* that the Council shall, inter alia:

   (a) Promote human rights education and learning as well as advisory services, technical assistance and capacity-building, to be provided in consultation with and with the consent of Member States concerned;

   (b) Serve as a forum for dialogue on thematic issues on all human rights;

   (c) Make recommendations to the General Assembly for the further development of international law in the field of human rights;

   (d) Promote the full implementation of human rights obligations undertaken by States and follow-up to the goals and commitments related to the promotion and protection of human rights emanating from United Nations conferences and summits;

   (e) Undertake a universal periodic review, based on objective and reliable information, of the fulfilment by each State of its human rights obligations and commitments in a manner which ensures universality of coverage and equal treatment with respect to all States; the review shall be a cooperative mechanism, based on an interactive dialogue, with the full involvement of the country concerned and with consideration given to its capacity-building needs; such a mechanism shall complement and not duplicate the work of treaty bodies; the Council shall develop the modalities and necessary time allocation for the universal periodic review mechanism within one year after the holding of its first session;

(f) Contribute, through dialogue and cooperation, towards the prevention of human rights violations and respond promptly to human rights emergencies;

(g) Assume the role and responsibilities of the Commission on Human Rights relating to the work of the Office of the United Nations High Commissioner for Human Rights, as decided by the General Assembly in its resolution 48/141 of 20 December 1993;

(h) Work in close cooperation in the field of human rights with Governments, regional organizations, national human rights institutions and civil society;

(i) Make recommendations with regard to the promotion and protection of human rights;

(j) Submit an annual report to the General Assembly;

6. *Decides* also that the Council shall assume, review and, where necessary, improve and rationalize all mandates, mechanisms, functions and responsibilities of the Commission on Human Rights in order to maintain a system of special procedures, expert advice and a complaint procedure; the Council shall complete this review within one year after the holding of its first session;

7. *Decides further* that the Council shall consist of forty-seven Member States, which shall be elected directly and individually by secret ballot by the majority of the members of the General Assembly; the membership shall be based on equitable geographical distribution, and seats shall be distributed as follows among regional groups: Group of African States, thirteen; Group of Asian States, thirteen; Group of Eastern European States, six; Group of Latin American and Caribbean States, eight; and Group of Western European and other States, seven; the members of the Council shall serve for a period of three years and shall not be eligible for immediate re-election after two consecutive terms;

8. *Decides* that the membership in the Council shall be open to all States Members of the United Nations; when electing members of the Council, Member States shall take into account the contribution of candidates to the promotion and protection of human rights and their voluntary pledges and commitments made thereto; the General Assembly, by a two-thirds majority of the members present and voting, may suspend the rights of membership in the Council of a member of the Council that commits gross and systematic violations of human rights;

9. *Decides also* that members elected to the Council shall uphold the highest standards in the promotion and protection of human rights, shall fully cooperate with the Council and be reviewed under the universal periodic review mechanism during their term of membership;

10. *Decides further* that the Council shall meet regularly throughout the year and schedule no fewer than three sessions per year, including a main session, for a total duration of no less than ten weeks, and shall be able to hold special sessions, when needed, at the request of a member of the Council with the support of one third of the membership of the Council;

11. *Decides* that the Council shall apply the rules of procedure established for committees of the General Assembly, as applicable, unless subsequently otherwise decided by the

Assembly or the Council, and also decides that the participation of and consultation with observers, including States that are not members of the Council, the specialized agencies, other intergovernmental organizations and national human rights institutions, as well as non-governmental organizations, shall be based on arrangements, including Economic and Social Council resolution 1996/31 of 25 July 1996 and practices observed by the Commission on Human Rights, while ensuring the most effective contribution of these entities;

12. *Decides also* that the methods of work of the Council shall be transparent, fair and impartial and shall enable genuine dialogue, be results-oriented, allow for subsequent follow-up discussions to recommendations and their implementation and also allow for substantive interaction with special procedures and mechanisms;

13. *Recommends* that the Economic and Social Council request the Commission on Human Rights to conclude its work at its sixty-second session, and that it abolish the Commission on 16 June 2006;

14. *Decides* to elect the new members of the Council; the terms of membership shall be staggered, and such decision shall be taken for the first election by the drawing of lots, taking into consideration equitable geographical distribution;

15. *Decides also* that elections of the first members of the Council shall take place on 9 May 2006, and that the first meeting of the Council shall be convened on 19 June 2006;

16. *Decides further* that the Council shall review its work and functioning five years after its establishment and report to the General Assembly.

3. HUMAN RIGHTS COUNCIL
INSTITUTION-BUILDING, 2007

The document reproduced below is annexed to Resolution 5/1 adopted without a vote by the Human Rights Council on 18 June 2007. Part VII on the Rules of Procedure, Appendix I (renewed mandates until reconsideration by the Council), and Appendix II (terms of office of mandate holders) are omitted, while the footnotes are from the original document. By the same resolution, the Human Rights Council also decided to submit the text to the UN General Assembly, which in turn endorsed Resolution 5/1 (and Resolution 5/2 on a 'Code of Conduct for Special Procedures Mandate-holders of the Human Rights Council'), together with their annexes and appendices; see Resolution 62/219, 'Report of the Human Rights Council', 22 December 2007, adopted by a vote of 150 in favour, 7 against (Australia, Canada, Israel, Marshall Islands, Micronesia, Palau, United States of America), and 1 abstention (Nauru). For debate and explanations of the vote, see UNGAOR, Sixty-second sess., 79th plenary meeting, 21–22 December 2007: UN doc. A/62/PV.79, 10–11.

TEXT

I. UNIVERSAL PERIODIC REVIEW MECHANISM

A. BASIS OF THE REVIEW

1. The basis of the review is:

   (a) The Charter of the United Nations;

   (b) The Universal Declaration of Human Rights;

   (c) Human rights instruments to which a State is party;

   (d) Voluntary pledges and commitments made by States, including those undertaken when presenting their candidatures for election to the Human Rights Council (hereinafter 'the Council').

2. In addition to the above and given the complementary and mutually interrelated nature of international human rights law and international humanitarian law, the review shall take into account applicable international humanitarian law.

B. PRINCIPLES AND OBJECTIVES

1. Principles

3. The universal periodic review should:

   (a) Promote the universality, interdependence, indivisibility and interrelatedness of all human rights;

(b) Be a cooperative mechanism based on objective and reliable information and on interactive dialogue;

(c) Ensure universal coverage and equal treatment of all States;

(d) Be an intergovernmental process, United Nations Member-driven and action oriented;

(e) Fully involve the country under review;

(f) Complement and not duplicate other human rights mechanisms, thus representing an added value;

(g) Be conducted in an objective, transparent, non-selective, constructive, non confrontational and non politicized manner;

(h) Not be overly burdensome to the concerned State or to the agenda of the Council;

(i) Not be overly long; it should be realistic and not absorb a disproportionate amount of time, human and financial resources;

(j) Not diminish the Council's capacity to respond to urgent human rights situations;

(k) Fully integrate a gender perspective;

(l) Without prejudice to the obligations contained in the elements provided for in the basis of review, take into account the level of development and specificities of countries;

(m) Ensure the participation of all relevant stakeholders, including non-governmental organizations and national human rights institutions, in accordance with General Assembly resolution 60/251 of 15 March 2006 and Economic and Social Council resolution 1996/31 of 25 July 1996, as well as any decisions that the Council may take in this regard.

2. Objectives

4. The objectives of the review are:

(a) The improvement of the human rights situation on the ground;

(b) The fulfilment of the State's human rights obligations and commitments and assessment of positive developments and challenges faced by the State;

(c) The enhancement of the State's capacity and of technical assistance, in consultation with, and with the consent of, the State concerned;

(d) The sharing of best practice among States and other stakeholders;

(e) Support for cooperation in the promotion and protection of human rights;

(f) The encouragement of full cooperation and engagement with the Council, other human rights bodies and the Office of the United Nations High Commissioner for Human Rights.

C. PERIODICITY AND ORDER OF THE REVIEW

5. The review begins after the adoption of the universal periodic review mechanism by the Council.

6. The order of review should reflect the principles of universality and equal treatment.

7. The order of the review should be established as soon as possible in order to allow States to prepare adequately.

8. All member States of the Council shall be reviewed during their term of membership.

9. The initial members of the Council, especially those elected for one or two-year terms, should be reviewed first.

10. A mix of member and observer States of the Council should be reviewed.

11. Equitable geographic distribution should be respected in the selection of countries for review.

12. The first member and observer States to be reviewed will be chosen by the drawing of lots from each Regional Group in such a way as to ensure full respect for equitable geographic distribution. Alphabetical order will then be applied beginning with those countries thus selected, unless other countries volunteer to be reviewed.

13. The period between review cycles should be reasonable so as to take into account the capacity of States to prepare for, and the capacity of other stakeholders to respond to, the requests arising from the review.

14. The periodicity of the review for the first cycle will be of four years. This will imply the consideration of 48 States per year during three sessions of the working group of two weeks each.[1]

D. PROCESS AND MODALITIES OF THE REVIEW

1. Documentation

15. The documents on which the review would be based are:

   (a) Information prepared by the State concerned, which can take the form of a national report, on the basis of general guidelines to be adopted by the Council at its sixth session (first session of the second cycle), and any other information considered relevant by the State concerned, which could be presented either orally or in writing, provided that the written presentation summarizing the information will not exceed 20 pages, to guarantee equal treatment to all States and not to overburden the mechanism. States are encouraged to prepare the information through a broad consultation process at the national level with all relevant stakeholders;

   (b) Additionally a compilation prepared by the Office of the High Commissioner for Human Rights of the information contained in the reports of treaty bodies, special procedures, including observations and comments by the State concerned, and other relevant official United Nations documents, which shall not exceed 10 pages;

   (c) Additional, credible and reliable information provided by other relevant stakeholders to the universal periodic review which should also be taken

---

[1] The universal periodic review is an evolving process; the Council, after the conclusion of the first review cycle, may review the modalities and the periodicity of this mechanism, based on best practices and lessons learned.

into consideration by the Council in the review. The Office of the High Commissioner for Human Rights will prepare a summary of such information which shall not exceed 10 pages.

16. The documents prepared by the Office of the High Commissioner for Human Rights should be elaborated following the structure of the general guidelines adopted by the Council regarding the information prepared by the State concerned.

17. Both the State's written presentation and the summaries prepared by the Office of the High Commissioner for Human Rights shall be ready six weeks prior to the review by the working group to ensure the distribution of documents simultaneously in the six official languages of the United Nations, in accordance with General Assembly resolution 53/208 of 14 January 1999.

2. Modalities

18. The modalities of the review shall be as follows:

   (a) The review will be conducted in one working group, chaired by the President of the Council and composed of the 47 member States of the Council. Each member State will decide on the composition of its delegation;[2]

   (b) Observer States may participate in the review, including in the interactive dialogue;

   (c) Other relevant stakeholders may attend the review in the Working Group;

   (d) A group of three rapporteurs, selected by the drawing of lots among the members of the Council and from different Regional Groups (troika) will be formed to facilitate each review, including the preparation of the report of the working group. The Office of the High Commissioner for Human Rights will provide the necessary assistance and expertise to the rapporteurs.

19. The country concerned may request that one of the rapporteurs be from its own Regional Group and may also request the substitution of a rapporteur on only one occasion.

20. A rapporteur may request to be excused from participation in a specific review process.

21. Interactive dialogue between the country under review and the Council will take place in the working group. The rapporteurs may collate issues or questions to be transmitted to the State under review to facilitate its preparation and focus the interactive dialogue, while guaranteeing fairness and transparency.

22. The duration of the review will be three hours for each country in the working group. Additional time of up to one hour will be allocated for the consideration of the outcome by the plenary of the Council.

23. Half an hour will be allocated for the adoption of the report of each country under review in the working group.

24. A reasonable time frame should be allocated between the review and the adoption of the report of each State in the working group.

25. The final outcome will be adopted by the plenary of the Council.

---

[2] A Universal Periodic Review Voluntary Trust Fund should be established to facilitate the participation of developing countries, particularly the Least Developed Countries, in the universal periodic review mechanism.

E. OUTCOME OF THE REVIEW

1. Format of the outcome

26. The format of the outcome of the review will be a report consisting of a summary of the proceedings of the review process; conclusions and/or recommendations, and the voluntary commitments of the State concerned.

2. Content of the outcome

27. The universal periodic review is a cooperative mechanism. Its outcome may include, inter alia:

(a) An assessment undertaken in an objective and transparent manner of the human rights situation in the country under review, including positive developments and the challenges faced by the country;

(b) Sharing of best practices;

(c) An emphasis on enhancing cooperation for the promotion and protection of human rights;

(d) The provision of technical assistance and capacity-building in consultation with, and with the consent of, the country concerned;[3]

(e) Voluntary commitments and pledges made by the country under review.

3. Adoption of the outcome

28. The country under review should be fully involved in the outcome.

29. Before the adoption of the outcome by the plenary of the Council, the State concerned should be offered the opportunity to present replies to questions or issues that were not sufficiently addressed during the interactive dialogue.

30. The State concerned and the member States of the Council, as well as observer States, will be given the opportunity to express their views on the outcome of the review before the plenary takes action on it.

31. Other relevant stakeholders will have the opportunity to make general comments before the adoption of the outcome by the plenary.

32. Recommendations that enjoy the support of the State concerned will be identified as such. Other recommendations, together with the comments of the State concerned thereon, will be noted. Both will be included in the outcome report to be adopted by the Council.

F. FOLLOW-UP TO THE REVIEW

33. The outcome of the universal periodic review, as a cooperative mechanism, should be implemented primarily by the State concerned and, as appropriate, by other relevant stakeholders.

34. The subsequent review should focus, inter alia, on the implementation of the preceding outcome.

---

[3] A decision should be taken by the Council on whether to resort to existing financing mechanisms or to create a new mechanism.

35. The Council should have a standing item on its agenda devoted to the universal periodic review.

36. The international community will assist in implementing the recommendations and conclusions regarding capacity-building and technical assistance, in consultation with, and with the consent of, the country concerned.

37. In considering the outcome of the universal periodic review, the Council will decide if and when any specific follow up is necessary.

38. After exhausting all efforts to encourage a State to cooperate with the universal periodic review mechanism, the Council will address, as appropriate, cases of persistent non-cooperation with the mechanism.

II. SPECIAL PROCEDURES

A. SELECTION AND APPOINTMENT OF MANDATE-HOLDERS

39. The following general criteria will be of paramount importance while nominating, selecting and appointing mandate-holders: (a) expertise; (b) experience in the field of the mandate; (c) independence; (d) impartiality; (e) personal integrity; and (f) objectivity.

40. Due consideration should be given to gender balance and equitable geographic representation, as well as to an appropriate representation of different legal systems.

41. Technical and objective requirements for eligible candidates for mandate-holders will be approved by the Council at its sixth session (first session of the second cycle), in order to ensure that eligible candidates are highly qualified individuals who possess established competence, relevant expertise and extensive professional experience in the field of human rights.

42. The following entities may nominate candidates as special procedures mandate-holders: (a) Governments; (b) Regional Groups operating within the United Nations human rights system; (c) international organizations or their offices (e.g. the Office of the High Commissioner for Human Rights); (d) non-governmental organizations; (e) other human rights bodies; (f) individual nominations.

43. The Office of the High Commissioner for Human Rights shall immediately prepare, maintain and periodically update a public list of eligible candidates in a standardized format, which shall include personal data, areas of expertise and professional experience. Upcoming vacancies of mandates shall be publicized.

44. The principle of non-accumulation of human rights functions at a time shall be respected.

45. A mandate-holder's tenure in a given function, whether a thematic or country mandate, will be no longer than six years (two terms of three years for thematic mandate-holders).

46. Individuals holding decision-making positions in Government or in any other organization or entity which may give rise to a conflict of interest with the responsibilities inherent to the mandate shall be excluded. Mandate-holders will act in their personal capacity.

47. A consultative group would be established to propose to the President, at least one month before the beginning of the session in which the Council would consider

the selection of mandate-holders, a list of candidates who possess the highest quali-fications for the mandates in question and meet the general criteria and particular requirements.

48. The consultative group shall also give due consideration to the exclusion of nomi-nated candidates from the public list of eligible candidates brought to its attention.

49. At the beginning of the annual cycle of the Council, Regional Groups would be invited to appoint a member of the consultative group, who would serve in his/her per-sonal capacity. The Group will be assisted by the Office of the High Commissioner for Human Rights.

50. The consultative group will consider candidates included in the public list; however, under exceptional circumstances and if a particular post justifies it, the Group may consider additional nominations with equal or more suitable qualifications for the post. Recommendations to the President shall be public and substantiated.

51. The consultative group should take into account, as appropriate, the views of stakeholders, including the current or outgoing mandate-holders, in determining the neces-sary expertise, experience, skills, and other relevant requirements for each mandate.

52. On the basis of the recommendations of the consultative group and following broad consultations, in particular through the regional coordinators, the President of the Council will identify an appropriate candidate for each vacancy. The President will present to member States and observers a list of candidates to be proposed at least two weeks prior to the beginning of the session in which the Council will consider the appointments.

53. If necessary, the President will conduct further consultations to ensure the endorse-ment of the proposed candidates. The appointment of the special procedures mandate-holders will be completed upon the subsequent approval of the Council. Mandate-holders shall be appointed before the end of the session.

B. REVIEW, RATIONALIZATION AND IMPROVEMENT OF MANDATES

54. The review, rationalization and improvement of mandates, as well as the creation of new ones, must be guided by the principles of universality, impartiality, objectivity and non-selectivity, constructive international dialogue and cooperation, with a view to enhancing the promotion and protection of all human rights, civil, political, economic, social and cultural rights, including the right to development.

55. The review, rationalization and improvement of each mandate would take place in the context of the negotiations of the relevant resolutions. An assessment of the mandate may take place in a separate segment of the interactive dialogue between the Council and special procedures mandate-holders.

56. The review, rationalization and improvement of mandates would focus on the relevance, scope and contents of the mandates, having as a framework the internation-ally recognized human rights standards, the system of special procedures and General Assembly resolution 60/251.

57. Any decision to streamline, merge or possibly discontinue mandates should always be guided by the need for improvement of the enjoyment and protection of human rights.

58. The Council should always strive for improvements:

    (a) Mandates should always offer a clear prospect of an increased level of human rights protection and promotion as well as being coherent within the system of human rights;

    (b) Equal attention should be paid to all human rights. The balance of thematic mandates should broadly reflect the accepted equal importance of civil, political, economic, social and cultural rights, including the right to development;

    (c) Every effort should be made to avoid unnecessary duplication;

    (d) Areas which constitute thematic gaps will be identified and addressed, including by means other than the creation of special procedures mandates, such as by expanding an existing mandate, bringing a cross-cutting issue to the attention of mandate-holders or by requesting a joint action to the relevant mandate-holders;

    (e) Any consideration of merging mandates should have regard to the content and predominant functions of each mandate, as well as to the workload of individual mandate-holders;

    (f) In creating or reviewing mandates, efforts should be made to identify whether the structure of the mechanism (expert, rapporteur or working group) is the most effective in terms of increasing human rights protection;

    (g) New mandates should be as clear and specific as possible, so as to avoid ambiguity.

59. It should be considered desirable to have a uniform nomenclature of mandate-holders, titles of mandates as well as a selection and appointment process, to make the whole system more understandable.

60. Thematic mandate periods will be of three years. Country mandate periods will be of one year.

61. Mandates included in Appendix I, where applicable, will be renewed until the date on which they are considered by the Council according to the programme of work. [4]

62. Current mandate-holders may continue serving, provided they have not exceeded the six-year term limit (Appendix II). On an exceptional basis, the term of those mandate-holders who have served more than six years may be extended until the relevant mandate is considered by the Council and the selection and appointment process has concluded.

63. Decisions to create, review or discontinue country mandates should also take into account the principles of cooperation and genuine dialogue aimed at strengthening the capacity of Member States to comply with their human rights obligations.

64. In case of situations of violations of human rights or a lack of cooperation that require the Council's attention, the principles of objectivity, non-selectivity, and the elimination of double standards and politicization should apply.

III. HUMAN RIGHTS COUNCIL ADVISORY COMMITTEE

65. The Human Rights Council Advisory Committee (hereinafter 'the Advisory Committee'), composed of 18 experts serving in their personal capacity, will function

---

    [4] Country mandates meet the following criteria: There is a pending mandate of the Council to be accomplished; or There is a pending mandate of the General Assembly to be accomplished; or The nature of the mandate is for advisory services and technical assistance.

as a think-tank for the Council and work at its direction. The establishment of this subsidiary body and its functioning will be executed according to the guidelines stipulated below.

A. NOMINATION

66. All Member States of the United Nations may propose or endorse candidates from their own region. When selecting their candidates, States should consult their national human rights institutions and civil society organizations and, in this regard, include the names of those supporting their candidates.

67. The aim is to ensure that the best possible expertise is made available to the Council. For this purpose, technical and objective requirements for the submission of candidatures will be established and approved by the Council at its sixth session (first session of the second cycle). These should include:

   (a) Recognized competence and experience in the field of human rights;

   (b) High moral standing;

   (c) Independence and impartiality.

68. Individuals holding decision-making positions in Government or in any other organization or entity which might give rise to a conflict of interest with the responsibilities inherent in the mandate shall be excluded. Elected members of the Committee will act in their personal capacity.

69. The principle of non-accumulation of human rights functions at the same time shall be respected.

B. ELECTION

70. The Council shall elect the members of the Advisory Committee, in secret ballot, from the list of candidates whose names have been presented in accordance with the agreed requirements.

71. The list of candidates shall be closed two months prior to the election date. The Secretariat will make available the list of candidates and relevant information to member States and to the public at least one month prior to their election.

72. Due consideration should be given to gender balance and appropriate representation of different civilizations and legal systems.

73. The geographic distribution will be as follows:

   African States: 5

   Asian States: 5

   Eastern European States: 2

   Latin American and Caribbean States: 3

   Western European and other States: 3

74. The members of the Advisory Committee shall serve for a period of three years. They shall be eligible for re-election once. In the first term, one third of the experts will

serve for one year and another third for two years. The staggering of terms of member-ship will be defined by the drawing of lots.

C. FUNCTIONS

75. The function of the Advisory Committee is to provide expertise to the Council in the manner and form requested by the Council, focusing mainly on studies and research-based advice. Further, such expertise shall be rendered only upon the latter's request, in compliance with its resolutions and under its guidance.

76. The Advisory Committee should be implementation-oriented and the scope of its advice should be limited to thematic issues pertaining to the mandate of the Council; namely promotion and protection of all human rights.

77. The Advisory Committee shall not adopt resolutions or decisions. The Advisory Committee may propose within the scope of the work set out by the Council, for the latter's consideration and approval, suggestions for further enhancing its procedural efficiency, as well as further research proposals within the scope of the work set out by the Council.

78. The Council shall issue specific guidelines for the Advisory Committee when it requests a substantive contribution from the latter and shall review all or any portion of those guidelines if it deems necessary in the future.

D. METHODS OF WORK

79. The Advisory Committee shall convene up to two sessions for a maximum of 10 working days per year. Additional sessions may be scheduled on an ad hoc basis with prior approval of the Council.

80. The Council may request the Advisory Committee to undertake certain tasks that could be performed collectively, through a smaller team or individually. The Advisory Committee will report on such efforts to the Council.

81. Members of the Advisory Committee are encouraged to communicate between sessions, individually or in teams. However, the Advisory Committee shall not establish subsidiary bodies unless the Council authorizes it to do so.

82. In the performance of its mandate, the Advisory Committee is urged to establish interaction with States, national human rights institutions, non-governmental organiza-tions and other civil society entities in accordance with the modalities of the Council.

83. Member States and observers, including States that are not members of the Council, the specialized agencies, other intergovernmental organizations and national human rights institutions, as well as non-governmental organizations shall be entitled to participate in the work of the Advisory Committee based on arrangements, including Economic and Social Council resolution 1996/31 and practices observed by the Commission on Human Rights and the Council, while ensuring the most effective contribution of these entities.

84. The Council will decide at its sixth session (first session of its second cycle) on the most appropriate mechanisms to continue the work of the Working Groups on Indigenous Populations; Contemporary Forms of Slavery; Minorities; and the Social Forum.

IV. COMPLAINT PROCEDURE

A. OBJECTIVE AND SCOPE

85. A complaint procedure is being established to address consistent patterns of gross and reliably attested violations of all human rights and all fundamental freedoms occurring in any part of the world and under any circumstances.

86. Economic and Social Council resolution 1503 (XLVIII) of 27 May 1970 as revised by resolution 2000/3 of 19 June 2000 served as a working basis and was improved where necessary, so as to ensure that the complaint procedure is impartial, objective, efficient, victims-oriented and conducted in a timely manner. The procedure will retain its confidential nature, with a view to enhancing cooperation with the State concerned.

B. ADMISSIBILITY CRITERIA FOR COMMUNICATIONS

87. A communication related to a violation of human rights and fundamental freedoms, for the purpose of this procedure, shall be admissible, provided that:

(a) It is not manifestly politically motivated and its object is consistent with the Charter of the United Nations, the Universal Declaration of Human Rights and other applicable instruments in the field of human rights law;

(b) It gives a factual description of the alleged violations, including the rights which are alleged to be violated;

(c) Its language is not abusive. However, such a communication may be considered if it meets the other criteria for admissibility after deletion of the abusive language;

(d) It is submitted by a person or a group of persons claiming to be the victims of violations of human rights and fundamental freedoms, or by any person or group of persons, including non-governmental organizations, acting in good faith in accordance with the principles of human rights, not resorting to politically motivated stands contrary to the provisions of the Charter of the United Nations and claiming to have direct and reliable knowledge of the violations concerned. Nonetheless, reliably attested communications shall not be inadmissible solely because the knowledge of the individual authors is second-hand, provided that they are accompanied by clear evidence;

(e) It is not exclusively based on reports disseminated by mass media;

(f) It does not refer to a case that appears to reveal a consistent pattern of gross and reliably attested violations of human rights already being dealt with by a special procedure, a treaty body or other United Nations or similar regional complaints procedure in the field of human rights;

(g) Domestic remedies have been exhausted, unless it appears that such remedies would be ineffective or unreasonably prolonged.

88. National human rights institutions, established and operating under the Principles Relating to the Status of National Institutions (the Paris Principles), in particular in regard to quasi-judicial competence, may serve as effective means of addressing individual human rights violations.

C. WORKING GROUPS

89. Two distinct working groups shall be established with the mandate to examine the communications and to bring to the attention of the Council consistent patterns of gross and reliably attested violations of human rights and fundamental freedoms.

90. Both working groups shall, to the greatest possible extent, work on the basis of consensus. In the absence of consensus, decisions shall be taken by simple majority of the votes. They may establish their own rules of procedure.

1. Working Group on Communications: composition, mandate and powers

91. The Human Rights Council Advisory Committee shall appoint five of its members, one from each Regional Group, with due consideration to gender balance, to constitute the Working Group on Communications.

92. In case of a vacancy, the Advisory Committee shall appoint an independent and highly qualified expert of the same Regional Group from the Advisory Committee.

93. Since there is a need for independent expertise and continuity with regard to the examination and assessment of communications received, the independent and highly qualified experts of the Working Group on Communications shall be appointed for three years. Their mandate is renewable only once.

94. The Chairperson of the Working Group on Communications is requested, together with the secretariat, to undertake an initial screening of communications received, based on the admissibility criteria, before transmitting them to the States concerned. Manifestly ill-founded or anonymous communications shall be screened out by the Chairperson and shall therefore not be transmitted to the State concerned. In a perspective of accountability and transparency, the Chairperson of the Working Group on Communications shall provide all its members with a list of all communications rejected after initial screening. This list should indicate the grounds of all decisions resulting in the rejection of a communication. All other communications, which have not been screened out, shall be transmitted to the State concerned, so as to obtain the views of the latter on the allegations of violations.

95. The members of the Working Group on Communications shall decide on the admissibility of a communication and assess the merits of the allegations of violations, including whether the communication alone or in combination with other communications appear to reveal a consistent pattern of gross and reliably attested violations of human rights and fundamental freedoms. The Working Group on Communications shall provide the Working Group on Situations with a file containing all admissible communications as well as recommendations thereon. When the Working Group on Communications requires further consideration or additional information, it may keep a case under review until its next session 'and request such information from the State concerned. The Working Group on Communications may decide to dismiss a case. All decisions of the Working Group on Communications shall be based on a rigorous application of the admissibility criteria and duly justified.

2. Working Group on Situations: composition, mandate and powers

96. Each Regional Group shall appoint a representative of a member State of the Council, with due consideration to gender balance, to serve on the Working Group on Situations. Members shall be appointed for one year. Their mandate may be renewed once, if the State concerned is a member of the Council.

97. Members of the Working Group on Situations shall serve in their personal capacity. In order to fill a vacancy, the respective Regional Group to which the vacancy belongs, shall appoint a representative from member States of the same Regional Group.

98. The Working Group on Situations is requested, on the basis of the information and recommendations provided by the Working Group on Communications, to present the Council with a report on consistent patterns of gross and reliably attested violations of human rights and fundamental freedoms and to make recommendations to the Council on the course of action to take, normally in the form of a draft resolution or decision with respect to the situations referred to it. When the Working Group on Situations requires further consideration or additional information, its members may keep a case under review until its next session. The Working Group on Situations may also decide to dismiss a case.

99. All decisions of the Working Group on Situations shall be duly justified and indicate why the consideration of a situation has been discontinued or action recommended thereon. Decisions to discontinue should be taken by consensus; if that is not possible, by simple majority of the votes.

D. WORKING MODALITIES AND CONFIDENTIALITY

100. Since the complaint procedure is to be, inter alia, victims-oriented and conducted in a confidential and timely manner, both Working Groups shall meet at least twice a year for five working days each session, in order to promptly examine the communications received, including replies of States thereon, and the situations of which the Council is already seized under the complaint procedure.

101. The State concerned shall cooperate with the complaint procedure and make every effort to provide substantive replies in one of the United Nations official languages to any of the requests of the Working Groups or the Council. The State concerned shall also make every effort to provide a reply not later than three months after the request has been made. If necessary, this deadline may however be extended at the request of the State concerned.

102. The Secretariat is requested to make the confidential files available to all members of the Council, at least two weeks in advance, so as to allow sufficient time for the consideration of the files.

103. The Council shall consider consistent patterns of gross and reliably attested violations of human rights and fundamental freedoms brought to its attention by the Working Group on Situations as frequently as needed, but at least once a year.

104. The reports of the Working Group on Situations referred to the Council shall be examined in a confidential manner, unless the Council decides otherwise. When the Working Group on Situations recommends to the Council that it consider a situation in a public meeting, in particular in the case of manifest and unequivocal lack of cooperation, the Council shall consider such recommendation on a priority basis at its next session.

105. So as to ensure that the complaint procedure is victims-oriented, efficient and conducted in a timely manner, the period of time between the transmission of the complaint to the State concerned and consideration by the Council shall not, in principle, exceed 24 months.

E. INVOLVEMENT OF THE COMPLAINANT AND OF THE STATE CONCERNED

106. The complaint procedure shall ensure that both the author of a communication and the State concerned are informed of the proceedings at the following key stages:

   (a) When a communication is deemed inadmissible by the Working Group on Communications or when it is taken up for consideration by the Working Group on Situations; or when a communication is kept pending by one of the Working Groups or by the Council;

   (b) At the final outcome.

107. In addition, the complainant shall be informed when his/her communication is registered by the complaint procedure.

108. Should the complainant request that his/her identity be kept confidential, it will not be transmitted to the State concerned.

F. MEASURES

109. In accordance with established practice the action taken in respect of a particular situation should be one of the following options:

   (a) To discontinue considering the situation when further consideration or action is not warranted;

   (b) To keep the situation under review and request the State concerned to provide further information within a reasonable period of time;

   (c) To keep the situation under review and appoint an independent and highly qualified expert to monitor the situation and report back to the Council;

   (d) To discontinue reviewing the matter under the confidential complaint procedure in order to take up public consideration of the same;

   (e) To recommend to OHCHR to provide technical cooperation, capacity building assistance or advisory services to the State concerned.

V. AGENDA AND FRAMEWORK FOR THE PROGRAMME OF WORK

A. PRINCIPLES

Universality

Impartiality

Objectivity

Non-selectiveness

Constructive dialogue and cooperation

Predictability

Flexibility

Transparency

Accountability

Balance

Inclusive/comprehensive

Gender perspective

Implementation and follow-up of decisions

B. AGENDA

Item 1.   Organizational and procedural matters

Item 2.   Annual report of the United Nations High Commissioner for Human Rights and reports of the Office of the High Commissioner and the Secretary General

Item 3.   Promotion and protection of all human rights, civil, political, economic, social and cultural rights, including the right to development

Item 4.   Human rights situations that require the Council's attention

Item 5.   Human rights bodies and mechanisms

Item 6.   Universal Periodic Review

Item 7.   Human rights situation in Palestine and other occupied Arab territories

Item 8.   Follow-up and implementation of the Vienna Declaration and Programme of Action

Item 9.   Racism, racial discrimination, xenophobia and related forms of intolerance, follow-up and implementation of the Durban Declaration and Programme of Action

Item 10. Technical assistance and capacity-building

C. FRAMEWORK FOR THE PROGRAMME OF WORK

Item 1.   Organizational and procedural matters

Election of the Bureau

Adoption of the annual programme of work

Adoption of the programme of work of the session, including other business

Selection and appointment of mandate-holders

Election of members of the Human Rights Council Advisory Committee

Adoption of the report of the session

Adoption of the annual report

Item 2.   Annual report of the United Nations High Commissioner for Human Rights and reports of the Office of the High Commissioner and the Secretary General

Presentation of the annual report and updates

Item 3.   Promotion and protection of all human rights, civil, political, economic, social and cultural rights, including the right to development

Economic, social and cultural rights

Civil and political rights

Rights of peoples, and specific groups and individuals

Right to development

Interrelation of human rights and human rights thematic issues

Item 4. Human rights situations that require the Council's attention

Item 5. Human rights bodies and mechanisms

Report of the Human Rights Council Advisory Committee

Report of the complaint procedure

Item 6. Universal Periodic Review

Item 7. Human rights situation in Palestine and other occupied Arab territories

Human rights violations and implications of the Israeli occupation of Palestine and other occupied Arab territories

Right to self-determination of the Palestinian people

Item 8. Follow-up and implementation of the Vienna Declaration and Programme of Action

Item 9. Racism, racial discrimination, xenophobia and related forms of intolerance, follow-up and implementation of the Durban Declaration and Programme of Action

Item 10. Technical assistance and capacity-building

VI. METHODS OF WORK

110. The methods of work, pursuant to General Assembly resolution 60/251 should be transparent, impartial, equitable, fair, pragmatic; lead to clarity, predictability, and inclusiveness. They may also be updated and adjusted over time.

A. INSTITUTIONAL ARRANGEMENTS

1. Briefings on prospective resolutions or decisions

111. The briefings on prospective resolutions or decisions would be informative only, whereby delegations would be apprised of resolutions and/or decisions tabled or intended to be tabled. These briefings will be organized by interested delegations.

2. President's open-ended information meetings on resolutions, decisions and other related business

112. The President's open-ended information meetings on resolutions, decisions and other related business shall provide information on the status of negotiations on draft resolutions and/or decisions so that delegations may gain a bird's eye view of the status of such drafts. The consultations shall have a purely informational function, combined with information on the extranet, and be held in a transparent and inclusive manner. They shall not serve as a negotiating forum.

3. Informal consultations on proposals convened by main sponsors

113.   Informal consultations shall be the primary means for the negotiation of draft resolutions and/or decisions, and their convening shall be the responsibility of the sponsor(s). At least one informal open-ended consultation should be held on each draft resolution and/or decision before it is considered for action by the Council. Consultations should, as much as possible, be scheduled in a timely, transparent and inclusive manner that takes into account the constraints faced by delegations, particularly smaller ones.

4. Role of the Bureau

114.   The Bureau shall deal with procedural and organizational matters. The Bureau shall regularly communicate the contents of its meetings through a timely summary report.

5. Other work formats may include panel debates, seminars and round tables

115.   Utilization of these other work formats, including topics and modalities, would be decided by the Council on a case-by-case basis. They may serve as tools of the Council for enhancing dialogue and mutual understanding on certain issues. They should be utilized in the context of the Council's agenda and annual programme of work, and reinforce and/or complement its intergovernmental nature. They shall not be used to substitute or replace existing human rights mechanisms and established methods of work.

6. High-Level Segment

116.   The High-Level Segment shall be held once a year during the main session of the Council. It shall be followed by a general segment wherein delegations that did not participate in the High-Level Segment may deliver general statements.

B. WORKING CULTURE

117.   There is a need for:

(a) Early notification of proposals;

(b) Early submission of draft resolutions and decisions, preferably by the end of the penultimate week of a session;

(c) Early distribution of all reports, particularly those of special procedures, to be transmitted to delegations in a timely fashion, at least 15 days in advance of their consideration by the Council, and in all official United Nations languages;

(d) Proposers of a country resolution to have the responsibility to secure the broadest possible support for their initiatives (preferably 15 members), before action is taken;

(e) Restraint in resorting to resolutions, in order to avoid proliferation of resolutions without prejudice to the right of States to decide on the periodicity of presenting their draft proposals by:

(i) Minimizing unnecessary duplication of initiatives with the General Assembly/Third Committee;

(ii) Clustering of agenda items;

(iii) Staggering the tabling of decisions and/or resolutions and consideration of action on agenda items/issues.

C. OUTCOMES OTHER THAN RESOLUTIONS AND DECISIONS

118. These may include recommendations, conclusions, summaries of discussions and President's Statement. As such outcomes would have different legal implications, they should supplement and not replace resolutions and decisions.

D. SPECIAL SESSIONS OF THE COUNCIL

119. The following provisions shall complement the general framework provided by General Assembly resolution 60/251 and the rules of procedure of the Human Rights Council.

120. The rules of procedure of special sessions shall be in accordance with the rules of procedure applicable for regular sessions of the Council.

121. The request for the holding of a special session, in accordance with the requirement established in paragraph 10 of General Assembly resolution 60/251, shall be submitted to the President and to the secretariat of the Council. The request shall specify the item proposed for consideration and include any other relevant information the sponsors may wish to provide.

122. The special session shall be convened as soon as possible after the formal request is communicated, but, in principle, not earlier than two working days, and not later than five working days after the formal receipt of the request. The duration of the special session shall not exceed three days (six working sessions), unless the Council decides otherwise.

123. The secretariat of the Council shall immediately communicate the request for the holding of a special session and any additional information provided by the sponsors in the request, as well as the date for the convening of the special session, to all United Nations Member States and make the information available to the specialized agencies, other intergovernmental organizations and national human rights institutions, as well as to non-governmental organizations in consultative status by the most expedient and expeditious means of communication. Special session documentation, in particular draft resolutions and decisions, should be made available in all official United Nations languages to all States in an equitable, timely and transparent manner.

124. The President of the Council should hold open-ended informative consultations before the special session on its conduct and organization. In this regard, the secretariat may also be requested to provide additional information, including, on the methods of work of previous special sessions.

125. Members of the Council, concerned States, observer States, specialized agencies, other intergovernmental organizations and national human rights institutions, as well

as non-governmental organizations in consultative status may contribute to the special session in accordance with the rules of procedure of the Council.

126. If the requesting or other States intend to present draft resolutions or decisions at the special session, texts should be made available in accordance with the Council's relevant rules of procedure. Nevertheless, sponsors are urged to present such texts as early as possible.

127. The sponsors of a draft resolution or decision should hold open-ended consultations on the text of their draft resolution(s) or decision(s) with a view to achieving the widest participation in their consideration and, if possible, achieving consensus on them.

128. A special session should allow participatory debate, be results-oriented and geared to achieving practical outcomes, the implementation of which can be monitored and reported on at the following regular session of the Council for possible follow-up decision.

4. UNIVERSAL DECLARATION OF HUMAN RIGHTS, 1948

The references to human rights in the Charter of the United Nations (see preamble, Articles 1, 13, 55, 56, 62, 68, and 76) have provided the basis for elaboration of the content of standards and of the machinery for implementing protection of human rights. On 10 December 1948 the General Assembly of the United Nations adopted a Universal Declaration of Human Rights: Resolution 217 (III). The voting was forty-eight for, none against, and the following eight abstentions: Byelorussian S.S.R., Czechoslovakia, Poland, Saudi Arabia, Ukrainian S.S.R., U.S.S.R., Union of South Africa, and Yugoslavia. The Declaration is not a legally binding instrument as such, and certain of its provisions depart, or departed, from then existing and generally accepted rules. Nevertheless some of its provisions either constitute general principles of law (see the Statute of the International Court of Justice, Article 38(1)(c)), or represent elementary considerations of humanity. More important is its status as an authoritative guide, produced by the General Assembly, to the interpretation of the Charter. In this capacity the Declaration has considerable indirect legal effect, and it is regarded by the Assembly and by some jurists as a part of the 'law of the United Nations'.

The Declaration has its own importance and cannot be regarded as having merely a histori-cal significance. In particular, many States are not yet parties to the International Covenants (see below). The Universal Declaration is also given prominence in, among others, the Proclamation of Tehran, adopted by the United Nations Conference on Human Rights: see the Final Act of the International Conference on Human Rights, Tehran, 22 April–13 May 1968: UN doc. A/CONF. 32/41; the Vienna Declaration and Programme of Action, adopted by the World Conference on Human Rights on 25 June 1993: UN doc. A/CONF.157/23, 12 July 1993 (below, p.151); and the Beijing Declaration and Platform of Action adopted by the Fourth UN World Conference on Women, Beijing, 4–15 September 1995: UN doc. A/CONF.177/20, 17 October 1995 (below, p. 211). See also the General Assembley's Declaration on the Sixtieth Anniversary of the Universal Declaration of Human Rights, 2008, below, p.304.

Further reading

ALFREDSSON, G. and EIDE, A., *The Universal Declaration of Human Rights: A Common Standard of Achievement*, The Hague: Martinus Nijhoff, 1999.

GLENDON, M. A., *A World Made New: Eleanor Roosevelt and the Universal Declaration of Human Rights*, New York: Random House, 2002.

JAICHAND, V. and SUKSI, M., *60 Years of the Universal Declaration of Human Rights in Europe*, Antwerp: Intersentia, 2009.

OPPENHEIM, *International Law* (LAUTERPACHT, H., ed., London: Longmans, Green, 8th edn., 1956), vol. I, 744–6 (JENNINGS, R.Y.A. and WATTS, A., eds., Harlow: Longman, 9th edn., 1992), vol. I, 1000–5.

VON BERNSTORFF, J., 'The Changing Fortunes of the Universal Declaration of Human Rights: Genesis and Symbolic Dimensions of the Turn to Rights in International Law', (2008) 19 *EJIL* 903.

WALDOCK, H., 'General Course on Public International Law', 106 *Recueil des Cours* (1962-II), 198–200.

TEXT

PREAMBLE

Whereas recognition of the inherent dignity and of the equal and inalienable rights of all members of the human family is the foundation of freedom, justice and peace in the world,

Whereas disregard and contempt for human rights have resulted in barbarous acts which have outraged the conscience of mankind, and the advent of a world in which human beings shall enjoy freedom of speech and belief and freedom from fear and want has been proclaimed as the highest aspiration of the common people,

Whereas it is essential, if man is not to be compelled to have recourse, as a last resort, to rebellion against tyranny and oppression, that human rights should be protected by the rule of law,

Whereas it is essential to promote the development of friendly relations between nations,

Whereas the peoples of the United Nations have in the Charter reaffirmed their faith in fundamental human rights, in the dignity and worth of the human person and in the equal rights of men and women and have determined to promote social progress and better standards of life in larger freedom,

Whereas Member States have pledged themselves to achieve, in cooperation with the United Nations, the promotion of universal respect for and observance of human rights and fundamental freedoms,

Whereas a common understanding of these rights and freedoms is of the greatest importance for the full realization of this pledge,

Now, therefore,

THE GENERAL ASSEMBLY

Proclaims this Universal Declaration of Human Rights as a common standard of achievement for all peoples and all nations, to the end that every individual and every organ of society, keeping this Declaration constantly in mind, shall strive by teaching and education to promote respect for these rights and freedoms and by progressive measures, national and international, to secure their universal and effective recognition and observance, both among the peoples of Member States themselves and among the peoples of territories under their jurisdiction.

Article 1

All human beings are born free and equal in dignity and rights. They are endowed with reason and conscience and should act towards one another in a spirit of brotherhood.

Article 2

Everyone is entitled to all the rights and freedoms set forth in this Declaration, without distinction of any kind, such as race, colour, sex, language, religion, political or other opinion, national or social origin, property, birth or other status.

Furthermore, no distinction shall be made on the basis of the political, jurisdictional or international status of the country or territory to which a person belongs, whether it be independent, trust, non-self-governing or under any other limitation of sovereignty.

Article 3

Everyone has the right to life, liberty and security of person.

Article 4

No one shall be held in slavery or servitude; slavery and the slave trade shall be prohibited in all their forms.

Article 5

No one shall be subjected to torture or to cruel, inhuman or degrading treatment or punishment.

Article 6

Everyone has the right to recognition everywhere as a person before the law.

Article 7

All are equal before the law and are entitled without any discrimination to equal protection of the law. All are entitled to equal protection against any discrimination in violation of this Declaration and against any incitement to such discrimination.

Article 8

Everyone has the right to an effective remedy by the competent national tribunals for acts violating the fundamental rights granted him by the constitution or by law.

Article 9

No one shall be subjected to arbitrary arrest, detention or exile.

Article 10

Everyone is entitled in full equality to a fair and public hearing by an independent and impartial tribunal, in the determination of his rights and obligations and of any criminal charge against him.

Article 11

1. Everyone charged with a penal offence has the right to be presumed innocent until proved guilty according to law in a public trial at which he has had all the guarantees necessary for his defence.

2. No one shall be held guilty of any penal offence on account of any act or omission which did not constitute a penal offence, under national or international law, at the time when it was committed. Nor shall a heavier penalty be imposed than the one that was applicable at the time the penal offence was committed.

Article 12

No one shall be subjected to arbitrary interference with his privacy, family, home or correspondence, nor to attacks upon his honour and reputation.

Everyone has the right to the protection of the law against such interference or attacks.

Article 13

1. Everyone has the right to freedom of movement and residence within the borders of each State.

2. Everyone has the right to leave any country, including his own, and to return to his country.

Article 14

1. Everyone has the right to seek and to enjoy in other countries asylum from persecution.

2. This right may not be invoked in the case of prosecutions genuinely arising from non-political crimes or from acts contrary to the purposes and principles of the United Nations.

Article 15

1. Everyone has the right to a nationality.

2. No one shall be arbitrarily deprived of his nationality nor denied the right to change his nationality.

Article 16

1. Men and women of full age, without any limitation due to race, nationality or religion, have the right to marry and to found a family. They are entitled to equal rights as to marriage, during marriage and at its dissolution.

2. Marriage shall be entered into only with the free and full consent of the intending spouses.

3. The family is the natural and fundamental group unit of society and is entitled to protection by society and the State.

Article 17

1. Everyone has the right to own property alone as well as in association with others.

2. No one shall be arbitrarily deprived of his property.

Article 18

Everyone has the right to freedom of thought, conscience and religion; this right includes freedom to change his religion or belief, and freedom, either alone or in community with others and in public or private, to manifest his religion or belief in teaching, practice, worship and observance.

Article 19

Everyone has the right to freedom of opinion and expression; this right includes freedom to hold opinions without interference and to seek, receive and impart information and ideas through any media and regardless of frontiers.

Article 20

1. Everyone has the right to freedom of peaceful assembly and association.

2. No one may be compelled to belong to an association.

Article 21

1. Everyone has the right to take part in the government of his country, directly or through freely chosen representatives.

2. Everyone has the right to equal access to public service in his country.

3. The will of the people shall be the basis of the authority of government; this will shall be expressed in periodic and genuine elections which shall be by universal and equal suffrage and shall be held by secret vote or by equivalent free voting procedures.

Article 22

Everyone, as a member of society, has the right to social security and is entitled to realization, through national effort and international co-operation and in accordance with the organization and resources of each State, of the economic, social and cultural rights indispensable for his dignity and the free development of his personality.

Article 23

1. Everyone has the right to work, to free choice of employment, to just and favourable conditions of work and to protection against unemployment.

2. Everyone, without any discrimination, has the right to equal pay for equal work.

3. Everyone who works has the right to just and favourable remuneration ensuring for himself and his family an existence worthy of human dignity, and supplemented, if necessary, by other means of social protection.

4. Everyone has the right to form and to join trade unions for the protection of his interests.

Article 24

Everyone has the right to rest and leisure, including reasonable limitation of working hours and periodic holidays with pay.

Article 25

1. Everyone has the right to a standard of living adequate for the health and well-being of himself and of his family, including food, clothing, housing and medical care and necessary social services, and the right to security in the event of unemployment, sickness, disability, widowhood, old age or other lack of livelihood in circumstances beyond his control.

2. Motherhood and childhood are entitled to special care and assistance. All children, whether born in or out of wedlock, shall enjoy the same social protection.

Article 26

1. Everyone has the right to education. Education shall be free, at least in the elementary and fundamental stages. Elementary education shall be compulsory. Technical and professional education shall be made generally available and higher education shall be equally accessible to all on the basis of merit.

2. Education shall be directed to the full development of the human personality and to the strengthening of respect for human rights and fundamental freedoms. It shall promote

understanding, tolerance and friendship among all nations, racial or religious groups, and shall further the activities of the United Nations for the maintenance of peace.

3. Parents have a prior right to choose the kind of education that shall be given to their children.

Article 27

1. Everyone has the right freely to participate in the cultural life of the community, to enjoy the arts and to share in scientific advancement and its benefits.

2. Everyone has the right to the protection of the moral and material interests resulting from any scientific, literary or artistic production of which he is the author.

Article 28

Everyone is entitled to a social and international order in which the rights and freedoms set forth in this Declaration can be fully realized.

Article 29

1. Everyone has duties to the community in which alone the free and full development of his personality is possible.

2. In the exercise of his rights and freedoms, everyone shall be subject only to such limitations as are determined by law solely for the purpose of securing due recognition and respect for the rights and freedoms of others and of meeting the just requirements of morality, public order and the general welfare in a democratic society.

3. These rights and freedoms may in no case be exercised contrary to the purposes and principles of the United Nations.

Article 30

Nothing in this Declaration may be interpreted as implying for any State, group or person any right to engage in any activity or to perform any act aimed at the destruction of any of the rights and freedoms set forth herein.

5. STANDARD MINIMUM RULES FOR THE TREATMENT OF PRISONERS, 1955

These rules were adopted by the First United Nations Congress on the Prevention of Crime and the Treatment of Offenders, held at Geneva in 1955, and approved by the Economic and Social Council by its resolution 663 C (XXIV) of 31 July 1957 and 2076 (LXII) of 13 May 1977. The UN has subsequently adopted a wide range of principles, guidelines, and codes of conduct relevant to the administration of justice, only a small number of which are included in the present volume; among others, see below, pp. 105, 114, 116.

Further reading

RODLEY, N. S. and POLLARD, M., *The Treatment of Prisoners under International Law*, Oxford: Oxford University Press, 3rd edn., 2009.

RODRIGUEZ, S. A., 'The Impotence of Being Earnest: Status of the United Nations Standard Minimum Rules for the Treatment of Prisoners in Europe and the United States', (2007) 33 *New England Journal on Criminal and Civil Confinement* 61.

TEXT

Preliminary Observations

1. The following rules are not intended to describe in detail a model system of penal institutions. They seek only, on the basis of the general consensus of contemporary thought and the essential elements of the most adequate systems of today, to set out what is generally accepted as being good principle and practice in the treatment of prisoners and the management of institutions.

2. In view of the great variety of legal, social, economic and geographical conditions of the world, it is evident that not all of the rules are capable of application in all places and at all times. They should, however, serve to stimulate a constant endeavour to overcome practical difficulties in the way of their application, in the knowledge that they represent, as a whole, the minimum conditions which are accepted as suitable by the United Nations.

3. On the other hand, the rules cover a field in which thought is constantly developing. They are not intended to preclude experiment and practices, provided these are in harmony with the principles and seek to further the purposes which derive from the text of the rules as a whole. It will always be justifiable for the central prison administration to authorize departures from the rules in this spirit.

4. (1) Part I of the rules covers the general management of institutions, and is applicable to all categories of prisoners, criminal or civil, untried or convicted, including prisoners subject to 'security measures' or corrective measures ordered by the judge.

(2) Part II contains rules applicable only to the special categories dealt with in each section. Nevertheless, the rules under section A, applicable to prisoners under sentence, shall be equally applicable to categories of prisoners dealt with in sections B, C and D, provided they do not conflict with the rules governing those categories and are for their benefit.

5. (1) The rules do not seek to regulate the management of institutions set aside for young persons such as Borstal institutions or correctional schools, but in general Part I would be equally applicable in such institutions.

(2) The category of young prisoners should include at least all young persons who come within the jurisdiction of juvenile courts. As a rule, such young persons should not be sentenced to imprisonment.

PART I
RULES OF GENERAL APPLICATION

Basic principle

6. (1) The following rules shall be applied impartially. There shall be no discrimination on grounds of race, colour, sex, language, religion, political or other opinion, national or social origin, property, birth or other status.

(2) On the other hand, it is necessary to respect the religious beliefs and moral precepts of the group to which a prisoner belongs.

Register

7. (1) In every place where persons are imprisoned there shall be kept a bound registration book with numbered pages in which shall be entered in respect of each prisoner received:

(a) Information concerning his identity;

(b) The reasons for his commitment and the authority therefor;

(c) The day and hour of his admission and release.

(2) No person shall be received in an institution without a valid commitment order of which the details shall have been previously entered in the register.

Separation of categories

8. The different categories of prisoners shall be kept in separate institutions or parts of institutions taking account of their sex, age, criminal record, the legal reason for their detention and the necessities of their treatment. Thus,

(a) Men and women shall so far as possible be detained in separate institutions; in an institution which receives both men and women the whole of the premises allocated to women shall be entirely separate;

(b) Untried prisoners shall be kept separate from convicted prisoners;

(c) Persons imprisoned for debt and other civil prisoners shall be kept separate from persons imprisoned by reason of a criminal offence;

(d) Young prisoners shall be kept separate from adults.

Accommodation

9. (1) Where sleeping accommodation is in individual cells or rooms, each prisoner shall occupy by night a cell or room by himself. If for special reasons, such as temporary

overcrowding, it becomes necessary for the central prison administration to make an exception to this rule, it is not desirable to have two prisoners in a cell or room.

(2) Where dormitories are used, they shall be occupied by prisoners carefully selected as being suitable to associate with one another in those conditions. There shall be regular supervision by night, in keeping with the nature of the institution.

10. All accommodation provided for the use of prisoners and in particular all sleeping accommodation shall meet all requirements of health, due regard being paid to climatic conditions and particularly to cubic content of air, minimum floor space, lighting, heating and ventilation.

11. In all places where prisoners are required to live or work,

   (a) The windows shall be large enough to enable the prisoners to read or work by natural light, and shall be so constructed that they can allow the entrance of fresh air whether or not there is artificial ventilation;

   (b) Artificial light shall be provided sufficient for the prisoners to read or work without injury to eyesight.

12. The sanitary installations shall be adequate to enable every prisoner to comply with the needs of nature when necessary and in a clean and decent manner.

13. Adequate bathing and shower installations shall be provided so that every prisoner may be enabled and required to have a bath or shower, at a temperature suitable to the climate, as frequently as necessary for general hygiene according to season and geographical region, but at least once a week in a temperate climate.

14. All parts of an institution regularly used by prisoners shall be properly maintained and kept scrupulously clean at all times.

Personal hygiene

15. Prisoners shall be required to keep their persons clean, and to this end they shall be provided with water and with such toilet articles as are necessary for health and cleanliness.

16. In order that prisoners may maintain a good appearance compatible with their self-respect, facilities shall be provided for the proper care of the hair and beard, and men shall be enabled to shave regularly.

Clothing and bedding

17. (1) Every prisoner who is not allowed to wear his own clothing shall be provided with an outfit of clothing suitable for the climate and adequate to keep him in good health. Such clothing shall in no manner be degrading or humiliating.

   (2) All clothing shall be clean and kept in proper condition. Underclothing shall be changed and washed as often as necessary for the maintenance of hygiene.

   (3) In exceptional circumstances, whenever a prisoner is removed outside the institution for an authorized purpose, he shall be allowed to wear his own clothing or other inconspicuous clothing.

18. If prisoners are allowed to wear their own clothing, arrangements shall be made on their admission to the institution to ensure that it shall be clean and fit for use.

19. Every prisoner shall, in accordance with local or national standards, be provided with a separate bed, and with separate and sufficient bedding which shall be clean when issued, kept in good order and changed often enough to ensure its cleanliness.

Food

20. (1) Every prisoner shall be provided by the administration at the usual hours with food of nutritional value adequate for health and strength, of wholesome quality and well prepared and served.

(2) Drinking water shall be available to every prisoner whenever he needs it.

Exercise and sport

21. (1) Every prisoner who is not employed in outdoor work shall have at least one hour of suitable exercise in the open air daily if the weather permits.

(2) Young prisoners, and others of suitable age and physique, shall receive physical and recreational training during the period of exercise. To this end space, installations and equipment should be provided.

Medical services

22. (1) At every institution there shall be available the services of at least one qualified medical officer who should have some knowledge of psychiatry. The medical services should be organized in close relationship to the general health administration of the community or nation. They shall include a psychiatric service for the diagnosis and, in proper cases, the treatment of states of mental abnormality.

(2) Sick prisoners who require specialist treatment shall be transferred to specialized institutions or to civil hospitals. Where hospital facilities are provided in an institution, their equipment, furnishings and pharmaceutical supplies shall be proper for the medical care and treatment of sick prisoners, and there shall be a staff of suitable trained officers.

(3) The services of a qualified dental officer shall be available to every prisoner.

23. (1) In women's institutions there shall be special accommodation for all necessary pre-natal and post-natal care and treatment. Arrangements shall be made wherever practicable for children to be born in a hospital outside the institution. If a child is born in prison, this fact shall not be mentioned in the birth certificate.

(2) Where nursing infants are allowed to remain in the institution with their mothers, provision shall be made for a nursery staffed by qualified persons, where the infants shall be placed when they are not in the care of their mothers.

24. The medical officer shall see and examine every prisoner as soon as possible after his admission and thereafter as necessary, with a view particularly to the discovery of physical or mental illness and the taking of all necessary measures; the segregation of prisoners suspected of infectious or contagious conditions; the noting of physical or mental defects which might hamper rehabilitation, and the determination of the physical capacity of every prisoner for work.

25. (1) The medical officer shall have the care of the physical and mental health of the prisoners and should daily see all sick prisoners, all who complain of illness, and any prisoner to whom his attention is specially directed.

(2) The medical officer shall report to the director whenever he considers that a prisoner's physical or mental health has been or will be injuriously affected by continued imprisonment or by any condition of imprisonment.

26. (1) The medical officer shall regularly inspect and advise the director upon:

(a) The quantity, quality, preparation and service of food;

(b) The hygiene and cleanliness of the institution and the prisoners;

(c) The sanitation, heating, lighting and ventilation of the institution;

(d) The suitability and cleanliness of the prisoners' clothing and bedding;

(e) The observance of the rules concerning physical education and sports, in cases where there is no technical personnel in charge of these activities.

(2) The director shall take into consideration the reports and advice that the medical officer submits according to rules 25(2) and 26 and, in case he concurs with the recommendations made, shall take immediate steps to give effect to those recommendations; if they are not within his competence or if he does not concur with them, he shall immediately submit his own report and the advice of the medical officer to higher authority.

Discipline and punishment

27. Discipline and order shall be maintained with firmness, but with no more restriction than is necessary for safe custody and well-ordered community life.

28. (1) No prisoner shall be employed, in the service of the institution, in any disciplinary capacity.

(2) This rule shall not, however, impede the proper functioning of systems based on self-government, under which specified social, educational or sports activities or responsibilities are entrusted, under supervision, to prisoners who are formed into groups for the purposes of treatment.

29. The following shall always be determined by the law or by the regulation of the competent administrative authority:

(a) Conduct constituting a disciplinary offence;

(b) The types and duration of punishment which may be inflicted;

(c) The authority competent to impose such punishment.

30. (1) No prisoner shall be punished except in accordance with the terms of such law or regulation, and never twice for the same offence.

(2) No prisoner shall be punished unless he has been informed of the offence alleged against him and given a proper opportunity of presenting his defence. The competent authority shall conduct a thorough examination of the case.

(3) Where necessary and practicable the prisoner shall be allowed to make his defence through an interpreter.

31. Corporal punishment, punishment by placing in a dark cell, and all cruel, inhuman or degrading punishments shall be completely prohibited as punishments for disciplinary offences.

32. (1) Punishment by close confinement or reduction of diet shall never be inflicted unless the medical officer has examined the prisoner and certified in writing that he is fit to sustain it.

(2) The same shall apply to any other punishment that may be prejudicial to the physical or mental health of a prisoner. In no case may such punishment be contrary to or depart from the principle stated in rule 31.

(3) The medical officer shall visit daily prisoners undergoing such punishments and shall advise the director if he considers the termination or alteration of the punishment necessary on grounds of physical or mental health.

Instruments of restraint

33. Instruments of restraint, such as handcuffs, chains, irons and strait-jacket, shall never be applied as a punishment. Furthermore, chains or irons shall not be used as restraints. Other instruments of restraint shall not be used except in the following circumstances:

(a) As a precaution against escape during a transfer, provided that they shall be removed when the prisoner appears before a judicial or administrative authority;

(b) On medical grounds by direction of the medical officer;

(c) By order of the director, if other methods of control fail, in order to prevent a prisoner from injuring himself or others or from damaging property; in such instances the director shall at once consult the medical officer and report to the higher administrative authority.

34. The patterns and manner of use of instruments of restraint shall be decided by the central prison administration. Such instruments must not be applied for any longer time than is strictly necessary.

Information to and complaints by prisoners

35. (1) Every prisoner on admission shall be provided with written information about the regulations governing the treatment of prisoners of his category, the disciplinary requirements of the institution, the authorized methods of seeking information and making complaints, and all such other matters as are necessary to enable him to understand both his rights and his obligations and to adapt himself to the life of the institution.

(2) If a prisoner is illiterate, the aforesaid information shall be conveyed to him orally.

36. (1) Every prisoner shall have the opportunity each week day of making requests or complaints to the director of the institution or the officer authorized to represent him.

(2) It shall be possible to make requests or complaints to the inspector of prisons during his inspection. The prisoner shall have the opportunity to talk to the inspector or to any other inspecting officer without the director or other members of the staff being present.

(3) Every prisoner shall be allowed to make a request or complaint, without censorship as to substance but in proper form, to the central prison administration, the judicial authority or other proper authorities through approved channels.

(4) Unless it is evidently frivolous or groundless, every request or complaint shall be promptly dealt with and replied to without undue delay.

Contact with the outside world

37. Prisoners shall be allowed under necessary supervision to communicate with their family and reputable friends at regular intervals, both by correspondence and by receiving visits.

38. (1) Prisoners who are foreign nationals shall be allowed reasonable facilities to communicate with the diplomatic and consular representatives of the State to which they belong.

(2) Prisoners who are nationals of States without diplomatic or consular representation in the country and refugees or stateless persons shall be allowed similar facilities to communicate with the diplomatic representative of the State which takes charge of their interests or any national or international authority whose task it is to protect such persons.

39. Prisoners shall be kept informed regularly of the more important items of news by the reading of newspapers, periodicals or special institutional publications, by hearing wireless transmissions, by lectures or by any similar means as authorized or controlled by the administration.

Books

40. Every institution shall have a library for the use of all categories of prisoners, adequately stocked with both recreational and instructional books, and prisoners shall be encouraged to make full use of it.

Religion

41. (1) If the institution contains a sufficient number of prisoners of the same religion, a qualified representative of that religion shall be appointed or approved. If the number of prisoners justifies it and conditions permit, the arrangement should be on a full-time basis.

(2) A qualified representative appointed or approved under paragraph (1) shall be allowed to hold regular services and to pay pastoral visits in private to prisoners of his religion at proper times.

(3) Access to a qualified representative of any religion shall not be refused to any prisoner. On the other hand, if any prisoner should object to a visit of any religious representative, his attitude shall be fully respected.

42. So far as practicable, every prisoner shall be allowed to satisfy the needs of his religious life by attending the services provided in the institution and having in his possession the books of religious observance and instruction of his denomination.

Retention of prisoners' property

43. (1) All money, valuables, clothing and other effects belonging to a prisoner which under the regulations of the institution he is not allowed to retain shall on his admission to the institution be placed in safe custody. An inventory thereof shall be signed by the prisoner. Steps shall be taken to keep them in good condition.

(2) On the release of the prisoner all such articles and money shall be returned to him except in so far as he has been authorized to spend money or send any such property out of the institution, or it has been found necessary on hygienic grounds to destroy any article of clothing. The prisoner shall sign a receipt for the articles and money returned to him.

(3) Any money or effects received for a prisoner from outside shall be treated in the same way.

(4) If a prisoner brings in any drugs or medicine, the medical officer shall decide what use shall be made of them.

Notification of death, illness, transfer, etc.

44. (1) Upon the death or serious illness of, or serious injury to a prisoner, or his removal to an institution for the treatment of mental affections, the director shall at once inform the spouse, if the prisoner is married, or the nearest relative and shall in any event inform any other person previously designated by the prisoner.

(2) A prisoner shall be informed at once of the death or serious illness of any near relative. In case of the critical illness of a near relative, the prisoner should be authorized, whenever circumstances allow, to go to his bedside either under escort or alone.

(3) Every prisoner shall have the right to inform at once his family of his imprisonment or his transfer to another institution.

Removal of prisoners

45. (1) When the prisoners are being removed to or from an institution, they shall be exposed to public view as little as possible, and proper safeguards shall be adopted to protect them from insult, curiosity and publicity in any form.

(2) The transport of prisoners in conveyances with inadequate ventilation or light, or in any way which would subject them to unnecessary physical hardship, shall be prohibited.

(3) The transport of prisoners shall be carried out at the expense of the administration and equal conditions shall obtain for all of them.

Institutional personnel

46. (1) The prison administration, shall provide for the careful selection of every grade of the personnel, since it is on their integrity, humanity, professional capacity and personal suitability for the work that the proper administration of the institutions depends.

(2) The prison administration shall constantly seek to awaken and maintain in the minds both of the personnel and of the public the conviction that this work is a social service of great importance, and to this end all appropriate means of informing the public should be used.

(3) To secure the foregoing ends, personnel shall be appointed on a full-time basis as professional prison officers and have civil service status with security of tenure subject only to good conduct, efficiency and physical fitness. Salaries shall be adequate to attract and retain suitable men and women; employment benefits and conditions of service shall be favourable in view of the exacting nature of the work.

47. (1) The personnel shall possess an adequate standard of education and intelligence.

(2) Before entering on duty, the personnel shall be given a course of training in their general and specific duties and be required to pass theoretical and practical tests.

(3) After entering on duty and during their career, the personnel shall maintain and improve their knowledge and professional capacity by attending courses of in-service training to be organized at suitable intervals.

48. All members of the personnel shall at all times so conduct themselves and perform their duties as to influence the prisoners for good by their example and to command their respect.

49. (1) So far as possible, the personnel shall include a sufficient number of specialists such as psychiatrists, psychologists, social workers, teachers and trade instructors.

(2) The services of social workers, teachers and trade instructors shall be secured on a permanent basis, without thereby excluding part-time or voluntary workers.

50. (1) The director of an institution should be adequately qualified for his task by character, administrative ability, suitable training and experience.

(2) He shall devote his entire time to his official duties and shall not be appointed on a part-time basis.

(3) He shall reside on the premises of the institution or in its immediate vicinity.

(4) When two or more institutions are under the authority of one director, he shall visit each of them at frequent intervals. A responsible resident official shall be in charge of each of these institutions.

51. (1) The director, his deputy, and the majority of the other personnel of the institution shall be able to speak the language of the greatest number of prisoners, or a language understood by the greatest number of them.

(2) Whenever necessary, the services of an interpreter shall be used.

52. (1) In institutions which are large enough to require the services of one or more full-time medical officers, at least one of them shall reside on the premises of the institution or in its immediate vicinity.

(2) In other institutions the medical officer shall visit daily and shall reside near enough to be able to attend without delay in cases of urgency.

53. (1) In an institution for both men and women, the part of the institution set aside for women shall be under the authority of a responsible woman officer who shall have the custody of the keys of all that part of the institution.

(2) No male member of the staff shall enter the part of the institution set aside for women unless accompanied by a woman officer.

(3) Women prisoners shall be attended and supervised only by women officers. This does not, however, preclude male members of the staff, particularly doctors and teachers, from carrying out their professional duties in institutions or parts of institutions set aside for women.

54. (1) Officers of the institutions shall not, in their relations with the prisoners, use force except in self-defence or in cases of attempted escape, or active or passive physical resistance to an order based on law or regulations. Officers who have recourse to force must use no more than is strictly necessary and must report the incident immediately to the director of the institution.

(2) Prison officers shall be given special physical training to enable them to restrain aggressive prisoners.

(3) Except in special circumstances, staff performing duties which bring them into direct contact with prisoners should not be armed. Furthermore, staff should in no circumstances be provided with arms unless they have been trained in their use.

Inspection

55. There shall be a regular inspection of penal institutions and services by qualified and experienced inspectors appointed by a competent authority. Their task shall be in particular to ensure that these institutions are administered in accordance with existing laws and regulations and with a view to bringing about the objectives of penal and correctional services.

PART II
RULES APPLICABLE TO SPECIAL CATEGORIES
A. Prisoners under Sentence

Guiding principles

56. The guiding principles hereafter are intended to show the spirit in which penal institutions should be administered and the purposes at which they should aim, in accordance with the declaration made under Preliminary Observation I of the present text.

57. Imprisonment and other measures which result in cutting off an offender from the outside world are afflictive by the very fact of taking from the person the right of self-determination by depriving him of his liberty. Therefore the prison system shall not, except as incidental to justifiable segregation or the maintenance of discipline, aggravate the suffering inherent in such a situation.

58. The purpose and justification of a sentence of imprisonment or a similar measure deprivative of liberty is ultimately to protect society against crime. This end can only be achieved if the period of imprisonment is used to ensure, so far as possible, that upon his return to society the offender is not only willing but able to lead a law-abiding and self-supporting life.

59. To this end, the institution should utilize all the remedial, educational, moral, spiritual and other forces and forms of assistance which are appropriate and available, and should seek to apply them according to the individual treatment needs of the prisoners.

60. (1) The regime of the institution should seek to minimize any differences between prison life and life at liberty which tend to lessen the responsibility of the prisoners or the respect due to their dignity as human beings.

(2) Before the completion of the sentence, it is desirable that the necessary steps be taken to ensure for the prisoner a gradual return to life in society. This aim may be achieved, depending on the case, by a pre-release regime organized in the same institution or in another appropriate institution, or by release on trial under some kind of supervision which must not be entrusted to the police but should be combined with effective social aid.

61. The treatment of prisoners should emphasize not their exclusion from the community, but their continuing part in it. Community agencies should, therefore, be enlisted wherever possible to assist the staff of the institution in the task of social rehabilitation of the prisoners. There should be in connection with every institution social workers

charged with the duty of maintaining and improving all desirable relations of a prisoner with his family and with valuable social agencies. Steps should be taken to safeguard, to the maximum extent compatible with the law and the sentence, the rights relating to civil interests, social security rights and other social benefits of prisoners.

62. The medical services of the institution shall seek to detect and shall treat any physical or mental illnesses or defects which may hamper a prisoner's rehabilitation. All necessary medical, surgical and psychiatric services shall be provided to that end.

63. (1) The fulfilment of these principles requires individualization of treatment and for this purpose a flexible system of classifying prisoners in groups; it is therefore desirable that such groups should be distributed in separate institutions suitable for the treatment of each group.

(2) These institutions need not provide the same degree of security for every group. It is desirable to provide varying degrees of security according to the needs of different groups. Open institutions, by the very fact that they provide no physical security against escape but rely on the self-discipline of the inmates, provide the conditions most favourable to rehabilitation for carefully selected prisoners.

(3) It is desirable that the number of prisoners in closed institutions should not be so large that the individualization of treatment is hindered. In some countries it is considered that the population of such institutions should not exceed five hundred. In open institutions the population should be as small as possible.

(4) On the other hand, it is undesirable to maintain prisons which are so small that proper facilities cannot be provided.

64. The duty of society does not end with a prisoner's release. There should, therefore, be governmental or private agencies capable of lending the released prisoner efficient after-care directed towards the lessening of prejudice against him and towards his social rehabilitation.

Treatment

65. The treatment of persons sentenced to imprisonment or a similar measure shall have as its purpose, so far as the length of the sentence permits, to establish in them the will to lead law-abiding and self-supporting lives after their release and to fit them to do so. The treatment shall be such as will encourage their self-respect and develop their sense of responsibility.

66. (1) To these ends, all appropriate means shall be used, including religious care in the countries where this is possible, education, vocational guidance and training, social casework, employment counselling, physical development and strengthening of moral character, in accordance with the individual needs of each prisoner, taking account of his social and criminal history, his physical and mental capacities and aptitudes, his personal temperament, the length of his sentence and his prospects after release.

(2) For every prisoner with a sentence of suitable length, the director shall receive, as soon as possible after his admission, full reports on all the matters referred to in the foregoing paragraph. Such reports shall always include a report by a medical officer, wherever possible qualified in psychiatry, on the physical and mental condition of the prisoner.

(3) The reports and other relevant documents shall be placed in an individual file. This file shall be kept up to date and classified in such a way that it can be consulted by the responsible personnel whenever the need arises.

Classification and individualization

67. The purposes of classification shall be:

    (a) To separate from others those prisoners who, by reason of their criminal records or bad characters, are likely to exercise a bad influence;

    (b) To divide the prisoners into classes in order to facilitate their treatment with a view to their social rehabilitation.

68. So far as possible separate institutions or separate sections of an institution shall be used for the treatment of the different classes of prisoners.

69. As soon as possible after admission and after a study of the personality of each prisoner with a sentence of suitable length, a programme of treatment shall be prepared for him in the light of the knowledge obtained about his individual needs, his capacities and dispositions.

Privileges

70. Systems of privileges appropriate for the different classes of prisoners and the different methods of treatment shall be established at every institution, in order to encourage good conduct, develop a sense of responsibility and secure the interest and co-operation of the prisoners in their treatment.

Work

71. (1) Prison labour must not be of an afflictive nature.

(2) All prisoners under sentence shall be required to work, subject to their physical and mental fitness as determined by the medical officer.

(3) Sufficient work of a useful nature shall be provided to keep prisoners actively employed for a normal working day.

(4) So far as possible the work provided shall be such as will maintain or increase the prisoners' ability to earn an honest living after release.

(5) Vocational training in useful trades shall be provided for prisoners able to profit thereby and especially for young prisoners.

(6) Within the limits compatible with proper vocational selection and with the requirements of institutional administration and discipline, the prisoners shall be able to choose the type of work they wish to perform.

72. (1) The organization and methods of work in the institutions shall resemble as closely as possible those of similar work outside institutions, so as to prepare prisoners for the conditions of normal occupational life.

(2) The interests of the prisoners and of their vocational training, however, must not be subordinated to the purpose of making a financial profit from an industry in the institution.

73. (1) Preferably institutional industries and farms should be operated directly by the administration and not by private contractors.

(2) Where prisoners are employed in work not controlled by the administration, they shall always be under the supervision of the institution's personnel. Unless the work is for other departments of the government the full normal wages for such work shall be paid to the administration by the persons to whom the labour is supplied, account being taken of the output of the prisoners.

74. (1) The precautions laid down to protect the safety and health of free workmen shall be equally observed in institutions.

(2) Provision shall be made to indemnify prisoners against industrial injury, including occupational disease, on terms not less favourable than those extended by law to free workmen.

75. (1) The maximum daily and weekly working hours of the prisoners shall be fixed by law or by administrative regulation, taking into account local rules or custom in regard to the employment of free workmen.

(2) The hours so fixed shall leave one rest day a week and sufficient time for education and other activities required as part of the treatment and rehabilitation of the prisoners.

76. (1) There shall be a system of equitable remuneration of the work of prisoners.

(2) Under the system prisoners shall be allowed to spend at least a part of their earnings on approved articles for their own use and to send a part of their earnings to their family.

(3) The system should also provide that a part of the earnings should be set aside by the administration so as to constitute a savings fund to be handed over to the prisoner on his release.

Education and recreation

77. (1) Provision shall be made for the further education of all prisoners capable of profiting thereby, including religious instruction in the countries where this is possible. The education of illiterates and young prisoners shall be compulsory and special attention shall be paid to it by the administration.

(2) So far as practicable, the education of prisoners shall be integrated with the educational system of the country so that after their release they may continue their education without difficulty.

78. Recreational and cultural activities shall be provided in all institutions for the benefit of the mental and physical health of prisoners.

Social relations and after-care

79. Special attention shall be paid to the maintenance and improvement of such relations between a prisoner and his family as are desirable in the best interests of both.

80. From the beginning of a prisoner's sentence consideration shall be given to his future after release and he shall be encouraged and assisted to maintain or establish such relations with persons or agencies outside the institution as may promote the best interests of his family and his own social rehabilitation.

81. (1) Services and agencies, governmental or otherwise, which assist released prisoners to re-establish themselves in society shall ensure, so far as is possible and necessary, that released prisoners be provided with appropriate documents and identification papers, have suitable homes and work to go to, are suitably and adequately clothed having regard to the climate and season, and have sufficient means to reach their destination and maintain themselves in the period immediately following their release.

(2) The approved representatives of such agencies shall have all necessary access to the institution and to prisoners and shall be taken into consultation as to the future of a prisoner from the beginning of his sentence.

(3) It is desirable that the activities of such agencies shall be centralized or co-ordinated as far as possible in order to secure the best use of their efforts.

B. Insane and Mentally Abnormal Prisoners

82. (1) Persons who are found to be insane shall not be detained in prisons and arrangements shall be made to remove them to mental institutions as soon as possible.

(2) Prisoners who suffer from other mental diseases or abnormalities shall be observed and treated in specialized institutions under medical management.

(3) During their stay in a prison, such prisoners shall be placed under the special supervision of a medical officer.

(4) The medical or psychiatric service of the penal institutions shall provide for the psychiatric treatment of all other prisoners who are in need of such treatment.

83. It is desirable that steps should be taken, by arrangement with the appropriate agencies, to ensure if necessary the continuation of psychiatric treatment after release and the provision of social-psychiatric after-care.

C. Prisoners under Arrest or Awaiting Trial

84. (1) Persons arrested or imprisoned by reason of a criminal charge against them, who are detained either in police custody or in prison custody (jail) but have not yet been tried and sentenced, will be referred to as 'untried prisoners', hereinafter in these rules.

(2) Unconvicted prisoners are presumed to be innocent and shall be treated as such.

(3) Without prejudice to legal rules for the protection of individual liberty or prescribing the procedure to be observed in respect of untried prisoners, these prisoners shall benefit by a special regime which is described in the following rules in its essential requirements only.

85. (1) Untried prisoners shall be kept separate from convicted prisoners.

(2) Young untried prisoners shall be kept separate from adults and shall in principle be detained in separate institutions.

86. Untried prisoners shall sleep singly in separate rooms, with the reservation of different local custom in respect of the climate.

87. Within the limits compatible with the good order of the institution, untried prisoners may, if they so desire, have their food procured at their own expense from the outside, either through the administration or through their family or friends. Otherwise, the administration shall provide their food.

88. (1) An untried prisoner shall be allowed to wear his own clothing if it is clean and suitable.

(2) If he wears prison dress, it shall be different from that supplied to convicted prisoners.

89. An untried prisoner shall always be offered opportunity to work, but shall not be required to work. If he chooses to work, he shall be paid for it.

90. An untried prisoner shall be allowed to procure at his own expense or at the expense of a third party such books, newspapers, writing materials and other means of occupation as are compatible with the interests of the administration of justice and the security and good order of the institution.

91. An untried prisoner shall be allowed to be visited and treated by his own doctor or dentist if there is reasonable ground for his application and he is able to pay any expenses incurred.

92. An untried prisoner shall be allowed to inform immediately his family of his detention and shall be given all reasonable facilities for communicating with his family and friends, and for receiving visits from them, subject only to restrictions and supervision as are necessary in the interests of the administration of justice and of the security and good order of the institution.

93. For the purposes of his defence, an untried prisoner shall be allowed to apply for free legal aid where such aid is available, and to receive visits from his legal adviser with a view to his defence and to prepare and hand to him confidential instructions. For these purposes, he shall if he so desires be supplied with writing material. Interviews between the prisoner and his legal adviser may be within sight but not within the hearing of a police or institution official.

D. Civil Prisoners

94. In countries where the law permits imprisonment for debt, or by order of a court under any other non-criminal process, persons so imprisoned shall not be subjected to any greater restriction or severity than is necessary to ensure safe custody and good order. Their treatment shall be not less favourable than that of untried prisoners, with the reservation, however, that they may possibly be required to work.

E. Persons Arrested or Detained Without Charge

95. Without prejudice to the provisions of article 9 of the International Covenant on Civil and Political Rights, persons arrested or imprisoned without charge shall be accorded the same protection as that accorded under Part I and Part II, section C. Relevant provisions of Part II, section A, shall likewise be applicable where their application may be conducive to the benefit of this special group of persons in custody, provided that no measures shall be taken implying that re-education or rehabilitation is in any way appropriate to persons not convicted of any criminal offence.

6. DECLARATION ON THE GRANTING OF INDEPENDENCE TO COLONIAL COUNTRIES AND PEOPLES, 1960

The Declaration below was adopted by the United Nations General Assembly in Resolution 1514 (XV) on 14 December 1960. Eighty-nine States voted for the resolution and none against, but there were nine abstentions: Portugal, Spain, Union of South Africa, United Kingdom, United States, Australia, Belgium, Dominican Republic, and France. The Declaration relates the normative development in the field of human rights to the rights of national groups, and, in particular, the right of self-determination. The Declaration, in conjunction with the United Nations Charter, supports the view that self-determination is now a legal principle, and, although its precise ramifications are still to be finally determined, the principle has great significance as a root of particular legal developments. See also the Declaration on the Inadmissibility of Intervention in Resolution 2131 (XX) of 21 December 1965. Generally on self-determination, see Whiteman, M. M., 5 *Digest of International Law*, Washington: US Department of State, 1968, 38–87; Brownlie, I., *Principles of Public International Law*, Oxford: Oxford University Press, 7th edn., 2008, 579–82. Resolution 1514 (XV) is in the form of an authoritative interpretation of the Charter rather than a recommendation. For comment see Waldock, H., 106 *Recueil des Cours* (1962 – II), 29–34; and Jennings, R. Y., *The Acquisition of Territory in International Law*, Manchester: Manchester University Press, 1963, 78–87; also, Higgins, R., *Problems and Process: International Law and How We Use It*, Oxford: Clarendon Press, 1994, 111–28. For earlier resolutions see Resolutions 637 A (VII) of 16 December 1952 and 1314 (XIII) of 12 December 1958.

The General Assembly established, as a subsidiary organ, a Special Committee on the Situation with regard to the Implementation of the Declaration on the Granting of Independence by Resolution 1654 (XVI) of 27 November 1961. This consisted at first of seventeen and later of twenty-four States. In 1964 the Special Committee examined situations and made recommendations in respect to fifty-five territories. In 1963 the General Assembly decided to discontinue the Committee on information from non-self-governing territories and to transfer its functions to the Special Committee. As a result, apart from the Trusteeship Council, the Special Committee is the only body responsible for matters relating to dependent territories. See 'Report of the Special Committee on the Situation with regard to the Implementation of the Declaration on the Granting of Independence to Colonial Countries and Peoples on its work during 2001': UN doc. A/56/23, 16 July 2001.

Further reading

BUCHANAN, A., *Justice, Legitimacy, and Self-Determination: Moral Foundations for International Law*, Oxford: Oxford University Press, 2004.

CASSESE, A., *Self-Determination of Peoples: A Legal Reappraisal*, Cambridge: Cambridge University Press, 1995.

CRAWFORD, J., 'State practice and international law in relation to secession', (1998) 69 *BYIL* 85–117.

HIGGINS, R., *Problems and Process: International Law and How We Use It*, Oxford: Clarendon Press, 1994, 111–28.

KNOP, K., *Diversity and Self-Determination in International Law*. Cambridge: Cambridge University Press, 2008.

KOSKENNIEMI, M., 'National Self-Determination Today: Problems of Legal Theory and Practice', (1994) 43 *ICLQ* 241–69.

McCORQUODALE, R., 'Self-Determination: A Human Rights Approach', (1994) 43 *ICLQ* 857–85.

McWHINNEY, E., *Self-Determination of Peoples and Plural-Ethnic States in Contemporary International Law*, Leiden, Boston: Martinus Nijhoff, 2007.

—— 'Declaration on the Granting of Independence to Colonial Countries and Peoples, New York, 14 December 1960': **http://untreaty.un.org/cod/avl/ha/dicc.html**.

MUSGRAVE, T. D., *Self-Determination and National Minorities*, Oxford: Clarendon Press, 2000.

RIGO SUREDA, A., *The Evolution of the Right of Self-determination: A Study of United Nations Practice*, Leiden: AW Sijthoff, 1973.

XANTHAKI, A., *Indigenous Rights and United Nations Standards: Self-Determination, Culture and Land*, Cambridge: Cambridge University Press, 2008.

TEXT

The General Assembly,

Mindful of the determination proclaimed by the peoples of the world in the Charter of the United Nations to reaffirm faith in fundamental human rights, in the dignity and worth of the human person, in the equal rights of men and women and of nations large and small and to promote social progress and better standards of life in larger freedom,

Conscious of the need for the creation of conditions of stability and well-being and peaceful and friendly relations based on respect for the principles of equal rights and self-determination of all peoples, and of universal respect for, and observance of, human rights and fundamental freedoms for all without distinction as to race, sex, language or religion,

Recognizing the passionate yearning for freedom in all dependent peoples and the decisive role of such peoples in the attainment of their independence,

Aware of the increasing conflicts resulting from the denial of or impediments in the way of the freedom of such peoples, which constitute a serious threat to world peace,

Considering the important role of the United Nations in assisting the movement for independence in Trust and Non-Self-Governing Territories,

Recognizing that the peoples of the world ardently desire the end of colonialism in all its manifestations,

Convinced that the continued existence of colonialism prevents the development of international economic co-operation, impedes the social, cultural and economic development of dependent peoples and militates against the United Nations ideal of universal peace,

Affirming that peoples may, for their own ends, freely dispose of their natural wealth and resources without prejudice to any obligations arising out of international economic co-operation, based upon the principle of mutual benefit, and international law,

Believing that the process of liberation is irresistible and irreversible and that, in order to avoid serious crises, an end must be put to colonialism and all practices of segregation and discrimination associated therewith,

Welcoming the emergence in recent years of a large number of dependent territories into freedom and independence, and recognizing the increasingly powerful trends towards freedom in such territories which have not yet attained independence,

Convinced that all peoples have an inalienable right to complete freedom, the exercise of their sovereignty and the integrity of their national territory,

Solemnly proclaims the necessity of bringing to a speedy and unconditional end colonialism in all its forms and manifestations;

And to this end

Declares that:

1. The subjection of peoples to alien subjugation, domination and exploitation constitutes a denial of fundamental human rights, is contrary to the Charter of the United Nations and is an impediment to the promotion of world peace and co-operation.

2. All peoples have the right to self-determination; by virtue of that right they freely determine their political status and freely pursue their economic, social and cultural development.

3. Inadequacy of political, economic, social or educational preparedness should never serve as a pretext for delaying independence.

4. All armed action or repressive measures of all kinds directed against dependent peoples shall cease in order to enable them to exercise peacefully and freely their right to complete independence, and the integrity of their national territory shall be respected.

5. Immediate steps shall be taken, in Trust and Non-Self-Governing Territories or all other territories which have not yet attained independence, to transfer all powers to the peoples of those territories, without any conditions or reservations, in accordance with their freely expressed will and desire, without any distinction as to race, creed or colour, in order to enable them to enjoy complete independence and freedom.

6. Any attempt aimed at the partial or total disruption of the national unity and the territorial integrity of a country is incompatible with the purposes and principles of the Charter of the United Nations.

7. All States shall observe faithfully and strictly the provisions of the Charter of the United Nations, the Universal Declaration of Human Rights and the present Declaration on the basis of equality, non-interference in the internal affairs of all States, and respect for the sovereign rights of all peoples and their territorial integrity.

7. DECLARATION ON SOCIAL PROGRESS AND DEVELOPMENT, 1969

Adopted by General Assembly Resolution 2542 (XXIV) of 11 December 1969.

TEXT

The General Assembly,

Mindful of the pledge of Members of the United Nations under the Charter to take joint and separate action in co-operation with the Organization to promote higher standards of living, full employment and conditions of economic and social progress and development,

Reaffirming faith in human rights and fundamental freedoms and in the principles of peace, of the dignity and worth of the human person, and of social justice proclaimed in the Charter,

Recalling the principles of the Universal Declaration of Human Rights, the International Covenants on Human Rights, the Declaration of the Rights of the Child, the Declaration on the Granting of Independence to Colonial Countries and Peoples, the International Convention on the Elimination of All Forms of Racial Discrimination, the United Nations Declaration on the Elimination of All Forms of Racial Discrimination, the Declaration on the Promotion among Youth of the Ideals of Peace, Mutual Respect and Understanding between Peoples, the Declaration on the Elimination of Discrimination against Women and of resolutions of the United Nations,

Bearing in mind the standards already set for social progress in the constitutions, conventions, recommendations and resolutions of the International Labour Organisation, the Food and Agriculture Organization of the United Nations, the United Nations Educational, Scientific and Cultural Organization, the World Health Organization, the United Nations Children's Fund and of other organizations concerned,

Convinced that man can achieve complete fulfilment of his aspirations only within a just social order and that it is consequently of cardinal importance to accelerate social and economic progress everywhere, thus contributing to international peace and solidarity,

Convinced that international peace and security on the one hand, and social progress and economic development on the other, are closely interdependent and influence each other,

Persuaded that social development can be promoted by peaceful coexistence, friendly relations and co-operation among States with different social, economic or political systems,

Emphasizing the interdependence of economic and social development in the wider process of growth and change, as well as the importance of a strategy of integrated development which takes full account at all stages of its social aspects,

Regretting the inadequate progress achieved in the world social situation despite the efforts of States and the international community,

Recognizing that the primary responsibility for the development of the developing countries rests on those countries themselves and acknowledging the pressing need to narrow and eventually close the gap in the standards of living between economically more advanced and developing countries and, to that end, that Member States shall have the responsibility to pursue internal and external policies designed to promote social development throughout the world, and in particular to assist developing countries to accelerate their economic growth,

Recognizing the urgency of devoting to works of peace and social progress resources being expended on armaments and wasted on conflict and destruction,

Conscious of the contribution that science and technology can render towards meeting the needs common to all humanity,

Believing that the primary task of all States and international organizations is to eliminate from the life of society all evils and obstacles to social progress, particularly such evils as inequality, exploitation, war, colonialism and racism,

Desirous of promoting the progress of all mankind towards these goals and of overcoming all obstacles to their realization,

Solemnly proclaims this Declaration on Social Progress and Development and calls for national and international action for its use as a common basis for social development policies:

PART I—PRINCIPLES

Article 1

All peoples and all human beings, without distinction as to race, colour, sex, language, religion, nationality, ethnic origin, family or social status, or political or other conviction, shall have the right to live in dignity and freedom and to enjoy the fruits of social progress and should, on their part, contribute to it.

Article 2

Social progress and development shall be founded on respect for the dignity and value of the human person and shall ensure the promotion of human rights and social justice, which requires:

    (a) The immediate and final elimination of all forms of inequality, exploitation of peoples and individuals, colonialism and racism, including nazism and apartheid, and all other policies and ideologies opposed to the purposes and principles of the United Nations;

    (b) The recognition and effective implementation of civil and political rights as well as of economic, social and cultural rights without any discrimination.

Article 3

The following are considered primary conditions of social progress and development:

    (a) National independence based on the right of peoples to self-determination;

    (b) The principle of non-interference in the internal affairs of States;

    (c) Respect for the sovereignty and territorial integrity of States;

    (d) Permanent sovereignty of each nation over its natural wealth and resources;

    (e) The right and responsibility of each State and, as far as they are concerned, each nation and people to determine freely its own objectives of social development, to

set its own priorities and to decide in conformity with the principles of the Charter of the United Nations the means and methods of their achievement without any external interference;

(f) Peaceful coexistence, peace, friendly relations and co-operation among States irrespective of differences in their social, economic or political systems.

Article 4

The family as a basic unit of society and the natural environment for the growth and well-being of all its members, particularly children and youth, should be assisted and protected so that it may fully assume its responsibilities within the community. Parents have the exclusive right to determine freely and responsibly the number and spacing of their children.

Article 5

Social progress and development require the full utilization of human resources, including, in particular:

(a) The encouragement of creative initiative under conditions of enlightened public opinion;

(b) The dissemination of national and international information for the purpose of making individuals aware of changes occurring in society as a whole;

(c) The active participation of all elements of society, individually or through associations, in defining and in achieving the common goals of development with full respect for the fundamental freedoms embodied in the Universal Declaration of Human Rights;

(d) The assurance to disadvantaged or marginal sectors of the population of equal opportunities for social and economic advancement in order to achieve an effectively integrated society.

Article 6

Social development requires the assurance to everyone of the right to work and the free choice of employment.

Social progress and development require the participation of all members of society in productive and socially useful labour and the establishment, in conformity with human rights and fundamental freedoms and with the principles of justice and the social function of property, of forms of ownership of land and of the means of production which preclude any kind of exploitation of man, ensure equal rights to property for all and create conditions leading to genuine equality among people.

Article 7

The rapid expansion of national income and wealth and their equitable distribution among all members of society are fundamental to all social progress, and they should therefore be in the forefront of the preoccupations of every State and Government.

The improvement in the position of the developing countries in international trade resulting among other things from the achievement of favourable terms of trade and of equitable and remunerative prices at which developing countries market their products is necessary in order to make it possible to increase national income and in order to advance social development.

Article 8

Each Government has the primary role and ultimate responsibility of ensuring the social progress and well-being of its people, of planning social development measures as part of comprehensive development plans, of encouraging and co-ordinating or integrating all national efforts towards this end and of introducing necessary changes in the social structure. In planning social development measures, the diversity of the needs of developing and developed areas, and of urban and rural areas, within each country, shall be taken into due account.

Article 9

Social progress and development are the common concerns of the international community, which shall supplement, by concerted international action, national efforts to raise the living standards of peoples.

Social progress and economic growth require recognition of the common interest of all nations in the exploration, conservation, use and exploitation, exclusively for peaceful purposes and in the interests of all mankind, of those areas of the environment such as outer space and the sea-bed and ocean floor and the subsoil thereof, beyond the limits of national jurisdiction, in accordance with the purposes and principles of the Charter of the United Nations.

PART II—OBJECTIVES

Social progress and development shall aim at the continuous raising of the material and spiritual standards of living of all members of society, with respect for and in compliance with human rights and fundamental freedoms, through the attainment of the following main goals:

Article 10

(a) The assurance at all levels of the right to work and the right of everyone to form trade unions and workers' associations and to bargain collectively; promotion of full productive employment and elimination of unemployment and under-employment; establishment of equitable and favourable conditions of work for all, including the improvement of health and safety conditions; assurance of just remuneration for labour without any discrimination as well as a sufficiently high minimum wage to ensure a decent standard of living; the protection of the consumer;

(b) The elimination of hunger and malnutrition and the guarantee of the right to proper nutrition;

(c) The elimination of poverty; the assurance of a steady improvement in levels of living and of a just and equitable distribution of income;

(d) The achievement of the highest standards of health and the provision of health protection for the entire population, if possible free of charge;

(e) The eradication of illiteracy and the assurance of the right to universal access to culture, to free compulsory education at the elementary level and to free education at all levels; the raising of the general level of life-long education;

(f) The provision for all, particularly persons in low income groups and large families, of adequate housing and community services.

Social progress and development shall aim equally at the progressive attainment of the following main goals:

Article 11

   (a) The provision of comprehensive social security schemes and social welfare services; the establishment and improvement of social security and insurance schemes for all persons who, because of illness, disability or old age, are temporarily or permanently unable to earn a living, with a view to ensuring a proper standard of living for such persons and for their families and dependants;

   (b) The protection of the rights of the mother and child; concern for the upbringing and health of children; the provision of measures to safeguard the health and welfare of women and particularly of working mothers during pregnancy and the infancy of their children, as well as of mothers whose earnings are the sole source of livelihood for the family; the granting to women of pregnancy and maternity leave and allowances without loss of employment or wages;

   (c) The protection of the rights and the assuring of the welfare of children, the aged and the disabled; the provision of protection for the physically or mentally disadvantaged;

   (d) The education of youth in, and promotion among them of, the ideals of justice and peace, mutual respect and understanding among peoples; the promotion of full participation of youth in the process of national development;

   (e) The provision of social defence measures and the elimination of conditions leading to crime and delinquency especially juvenile delinquency;

   (f) The guarantee that all individuals, without discrimination of any kind, are made aware of their rights and obligations and receive the necessary aid in the exercise and safeguarding of their rights.

Social progress and development shall further aim at achieving the following main objectives:

Article 12

   (a) The creation of conditions for rapid and sustained social and economic development, particularly in the developing countries; change in international economic relations; new and effective methods of international co-operation in which equality of opportunity should be as much a prerogative of nations as of individuals within a nation;

   (b) The elimination of all forms of discrimination and exploitation and all other practices and ideologies contrary to the purposes and principles of the Charter of the United Nations;

   (c) The elimination of all forms of foreign economic exploitation, particularly that practised by international monopolies, in order to enable the people of every country to enjoy in full the benefits of their national resources.

Social progress and development shall finally aim at the attainment of the following main goals:

Article 13

   (a) Equitable sharing of scientific and technological advances by developed and developing countries, and a steady increase in the use of science and technology for the benefit of the social development of society;

(b) The establishment of a harmonious balance between scientific, technological and material progress and the intellectual, spiritual, cultural and moral advancement of humanity;

(c) The protection and improvement of the human environment.

PART III—MEANS AND METHODS

On the basis of the principles set forth in this Declaration, the achievement of the objectives of social progress and development requires the mobilization of the necessary resources by national and international action, with particular attention to such means and methods as:

Article 14

(a) Planning for social progress and development as an integrated part of balanced overall development planning;

(b) The establishment, where necessary, of national systems for framing and carrying out social policies and programmes, and the promotion by the countries concerned of planned regional development, taking into account differing regional conditions and needs, particularly the development of regions which are less favoured or under-developed by comparison with the rest of the country;

(c) The promotion of basic and applied social research, particularly comparative international research applied to the planning and execution of social development programmes.

Article 15

(a) The adoption of measures, to ensure the effective participation, as appropriate, of all the elements of society in the preparation and execution of national plans and programmes of economic and social development;

(b) The adoption of measures for an increasing rate of popular participation in the economic, social, cultural and political life of countries through national governmental bodies, non-governmental organizations, co-operatives, rural associations, workers' and employers' organizations and women's and youth organizations, by such methods as national and regional plans for social and economic progress and community development, with a view to achieving a fully integrated national society, accelerating the process of social mobility and consolidating the democratic system;

(c) Mobilization of public opinion, at both national and international levels, in support of the principles and objectives of social progress and development;

(d) The dissemination of social information, at the national and the international level, to make people aware of changing circumstances in society as a whole, and to educate the consumer.

Article 16

(a) Maximum mobilization of all national resources and their rational and efficient utilization; promotion of increased and accelerated productive investment in

social and economic fields and of employment; orientation of society towards the development process;

(b) Progressively increasing provision of the necessary budgetary and other resources required for financing the social aspects of development;

(c) Achievement of equitable distribution of national income, utilizing, *inter alia*, the fiscal system and government spending as an instrument for the equitable distribution and redistribution of income in order to promote social progress;

(d) The adoption of measures aimed at prevention of such an outflow of capital from developing countries as would be detrimental to their economic and social development.

Article 17

(a) The adoption of measures to accelerate the process of industrialization, especially in developing countries, with due regard for its social aspects, in the interests of the entire population; development of an adequate organization and legal framework conducive to an uninterrupted and diversified growth of the industrial sector; measures to overcome the adverse social effects which may result from urban development and industrialization, including automation; maintenance of a proper balance between rural and urban development, and in particular, measures designed to ensure healthier living conditions, especially in large industrial centres;

(b) Integrated planning to meet the problems of urbanization and urban development;

(c) Comprehensive rural development schemes to raise the levels of living of the rural populations and to facilitate such urban-rural relationships and population distribution as will promote balanced national development and social progress;

(d) Measures for appropriate supervision of the utilization of land in the interests of society.

The achievement of the objectives of social progress and development equally requires the implementation of the following means and methods:

Article 18

(a) The adoption of appropriate legislative, administrative and other measures ensuring to everyone not only political and civil rights, but also the full realization of economic, social and cultural rights without any discrimination;

(b) The promotion of democratically based social and institutional reforms and motivation for change basic to the elimination of all forms of discrimination and exploitation and conducive to high rates of economic and social progress, to include land reform, in which the ownership and use of land will be made to serve best the objectives of social justice and economic development;

(c) The adoption of measures to boost and diversify agricultural production through, *inter alia*, the implementation of democratic agrarian reforms, to ensure an adequate and well-balanced supply of food, its equitable distribution among the whole population and the improvement of nutritional standards;

(d) The adoption of measures to introduce, with the participation of the Government, low-cost housing programmes in both rural and urban areas;

(e) Development and expansion of the system of transportation and communications, particularly in developing countries.

Article 19

(a) The provision of free health services to the whole population and of adequate preventive and curative facilities and welfare medical services accessible to all;

(b) The enactment and establishment of legislative measures and administrative regulations with a view to the implementation of comprehensive programmes of social security schemes and social welfare services and to the improvement and co-ordination of existing services;

(c) The adoption of measures and the provision of social welfare services to migrant workers and their families, in conformity with the provisions of Convention No. 97 of the International Labour Organisation and other international instruments relating to migrant workers;

(d) The institution of appropriate measures for the rehabilitation of mentally or physically disabled persons, especially children and youth, so as to enable them to the fullest possible extent to be useful members of society—these measures shall include the provision of treatment and technical appliances, education, vocational and social guidance, training and selective placement, and other assistance required—and the creation of social conditions in which the handicapped are not discriminated against because of their disabilities.

Article 20

(a) The provision of full democratic freedoms to trade unions; freedom of association for all workers, including the right to bargain collectively and to strike; recognition of the right to form other organizations of working people; the provision for the growing participation of trade unions in economic and social development; effective participation of all members in trade unions in the deciding of economic and social issues which affect their interests;

(b) The improvement of health and safety conditions for workers, by means of appropriate technological and legislative measures and the provision of the material prerequisites for the implementation of those measures, including the limitation of working hours;

(c) The adoption of appropriate measures for the development of harmonious industrial relations.

Article 21

(a) The training of national personnel and cadres, including administrative, executive, professional and technical personnel needed for social development and for overall development plans and policies;

(b) The adoption of measures to accelerate the extension and improvement of general, vocational and technical education and of training and retraining, which should be provided free at all levels;

(c) Raising the general level of education; development and expansion of national information media, and their rational and full use towards continuing education

of the whole population and towards encouraging its participation in social development activities; the constructive use of leisure, particularly that of children and adolescents;

(d) The formulation of national and international policies and measures to avoid the 'brain drain' and obviate its adverse effects.

Article 22

(a) The development and co-ordination of policies and measures designed to strengthen the essential functions of the family as a basic unit of society;

(b) The formulation and establishment, as needed, of programmes in the field of population, within the framework of national demographic policies and as part of the welfare medical services, including education, training of personnel and the provision to families of the knowledge and means necessary to enable them to exercise their right to determine freely and responsibly the number and spacing of their children;

(c) The establishment of appropriate child-care facilities in the interest of children and working parents.

The achievement of the objectives of social progress and development finally requires the implementation of the following means and methods:

Article 23

(a) The laying down of economic growth rate targets for the developing countries within the United Nations policy for development, high enough to lead to a substantial acceleration of their rates of growth;

(b) The provision of greater assistance on better terms; the implementation of the aid volume target of a minimum of 1 per cent of the gross national product at market prices of economically advanced countries; the general easing of the terms of lending to the developing countries through low interest rates on loans and long grace periods for the repayment of loans, and the assurance that the allocation of such loans will be based strictly on socio-economic criteria free of any political considerations;

(c) The provision of technical, financial and material assistance, both bilateral and multilateral, to the fullest possible extent and on favourable terms, and improved co-ordination of international assistance for the achievement of the social objectives of national development plans;

(d) The provision to the developing countries of technical, financial and material assistance and of favourable conditions to facilitate the direct exploitation of their national resources and natural wealth by those countries with a view to enabling the peoples of those countries to benefit fully from their national resources;

(e) The expansion of international trade based on principles of equality and non-discrimination, the rectification of the position of developing countries in international trade by equitable terms of trade, a general non-reciprocal and non-discriminatory system of preferences for the exports of developing countries to the developed countries, the establishment and implementation of general and comprehensive commodity agreements, and the financing of reasonable buffer stocks by international institutions.

Article 24

(a) Intensification of international co-operation with a view to ensuring the inter-national exchange of information, knowledge and experience concerning social progress and development;

(b) The broadest possible international technical, scientific and cultural co-operation and reciprocal utilization of the experience of countries with different economic and social systems and different levels of development, on the basis of mutual advantage and strict observance of and respect for national sovereignty;

(c) Increased utilization of science and technology for social and economic develop-ment; arrangements for the transfer and exchange of technology, including know-how and patents, to the developing countries.

Article 25

(a) The establishment of legal and administrative measures for the protection and improvement of the human environment, at both national and international level;

(b) The use and exploitation, in accordance with the appropriate international regimes, of the resources of areas of the environment such as outer space and the sea-bed and ocean floor and the subsoil thereof, beyond the limits of national jur-isdiction, in order to supplement national resources available for the achievement of economic and social progress and development in every country, irrespective of its geographical location, special consideration being given to the interests and needs of the developing countries.

Article 26

Compensation for damages, be they social or economic in nature—including restitution and reparations—caused as a result of aggression and of illegal occupation of territory by the aggressor.

Article 27

(a) The achievement of general and complete disarmament and the channelling of the progressively released resources to be used for economic and social progress for the welfare of people everywhere and, in particular, for the benefit of develop-ing countries;

(b) The adoption of measures contributing to disarmament, including, *inter alia*, the complete prohibition of tests of nuclear weapons, the prohibition of the devel-opment, production and stockpiling of chemical and bacteriological (biological) weapons and the prevention of the pollution of oceans and inland waters by nuclear wastes.

8. DECLARATION ON THE RIGHTS OF MENTALLY RETARDED PERSONS, 1971

Proclaimed by General Assembly Resolution 2856 (XXVI) of 20 December 1971.

Further reading

HERR, S. S., *et al.* eds., *The Human Rights of Persons with Intellectual Disabilities: Different But Equal*, Oxford: Oxford University Press, 2003.

OWEN, F. and GRIFFITHS, D., *Challenges to the Human Rights of People with Intellectual Disabilities*, London: Jessica Kingsley Publishers, 2009.

TEXT

The General Assembly,

Mindful of the pledge of the States Members of the United Nations under the Charter to take joint and separate action in co-operation with the Organization to promote higher standards of living, full employment and conditions of economic and social progress and development,

Reaffirming faith in human rights and fundamental freedoms and in the principles of peace, of the dignity and worth of the human person and of social justice proclaimed in the Charter,

Recalling the principles of the Universal Declaration of Human Rights, the International Covenants on Human Rights, the Declaration of the Rights of the Child and the standards already set for social progress in the constitutions, conventions, recommendations and resolutions of the International Labour Organisation, the United Nations Educational, Scientific and Cultural Organization, the World Health Organization, the United Nations Children's Fund and other organizations concerned,

Emphasizing that the Declaration on Social Progress and Development has proclaimed the necessity of protecting the rights and assuring the welfare and rehabilitation of the physically and mentally disadvantaged,

Bearing in mind the necessity of assisting mentally retarded persons to develop their abilities in various fields of activities and of promoting their integration as far as possible in normal life,

Aware that certain countries, at their present stage of development, can devote only limited efforts to this end,

Proclaims this Declaration on the Rights of Mentally Retarded Persons and calls for national and international action to ensure that it will be used as a common basis and frame of reference for the protection of these rights:

1. The mentally retarded person has, to the maximum degree of feasibility, the same rights as other human beings.

2. The mentally retarded person has a right to proper medical care and physical therapy and to such education, training, rehabilitation and guidance as will enable him to develop his ability and maximum potential.

3. The mentally retarded person has a right to economic security and to a decent standard of living. He has a right to perform productive work or to engage in any other meaningful occupation to the fullest possible extent of his capabilities.

4. Whenever possible, the mentally retarded person should live with his own family or with foster parents and participate in different forms of community life. The family with which he lives should receive assistance. If care in an institution becomes necessary, it should be provided in surroundings and other circumstances as close as possible to those of normal life.

5. The mentally retarded person has a right to a qualified guardian when this is required to protect his personal well-being and interests.

6. The mentally retarded person has a right to protection from exploitation, abuse and degrading treatment. If prosecuted for any offence, he shall have a right to due process of law with full recognition being given to his degree of mental responsibility.

7. Whenever mentally retarded persons are unable, because of the severity of their handicap, to exercise all their rights in a meaningful way or it should become necessary to restrict or deny some or all of these rights, the procedure used for that restriction or denial of rights must contain proper legal safeguards against every form of abuse. This procedure must be based on an evaluation of the social capability of the mentally retarded person by qualified experts and must be subject to periodic review and to the right of appeal to higher authorities.

9. UNIVERSAL DECLARATION ON THE ERADICATION OF HUNGER AND MALNUTRITION, 1974

Adopted on 16 November 1974 by the World Food Conference convened under General Assembly Resolution 3180 (XXVIII) of 17 December 1973; and endorsed by General Assembly Resolution 3348 (XXIX) of 17 December 1974.

In resolution 2000/10, the Commission on Human Rights requested the Special Rapporteur on the Right to Food (Jean Ziegler, 2000–2008; Olivier De Schutter, 2008–) to submit a report at its annual sessions and to report also to the General Assembly on the activities, themes identified and studies undertaken; see **http://www2.ohchr.org/english/issues/food/annual.htm**.

Further reading

COMMITTEE ON ECONOMIC, SOCIAL AND CULTURAL RIGHTS, General Comment 12, 'The right to adequate food', UN doc. E/C.12/1999/5, 12 May 1999.
ALSTON, P. and TOMASEVSKI, K., eds., *The Right to Food*, Boston: M. Nijhoff, 1984.
NARULA, S., 'The Right to Food: Holding Global Actors Accountable under International Law', (2006) 44 *Columbia Journal of Transnational Law* 691.

TEXT

The World Food Conference,
Convened by the General Assembly of the United Nations and entrusted with developing ways and means whereby the international community, as a whole, could take specific action to resolve the world food problem within the broader context of development and international economic co-operation,
    Adopts the following Declaration:

UNIVERSAL DECLARATION ON THE ERADICATION OF HUNGER AND MALNUTRITION

Recognizing that:

(a) The grave food crisis that is afflicting the peoples of the developing countries where most of the world's hungry and ill-nourished live and where more than two thirds of the world's population produce about one third of the world's food—an imbalance which threatens to increase in the next 10 years—is not only fraught with grave economic and social implications, but also acutely jeopardizes the most fundamental principles and values associated with the right to life and human dignity as enshrined in the Universal Declaration of Human Rights;

(b) The elimination of hunger and malnutrition, included as one of the objectives in the United Nations Declaration on Social Progress and Development, and the elimination of the causes that determine this situation are the common objectives of all nations;

(c)   The situation of the peoples afflicted by hunger and malnutrition arises from their historical circumstances, especially social inequalities, including in many cases alien and colonial domination, foreign occupation, racial discrimination, apartheid and neo-colonialism in all its forms, which continue to be among the greatest obstacles to the full emancipation and progress of the developing countries and all the peoples involved;

(d)   This situation has been aggravated in recent years by a series of crises to which the world economy has been subjected, such as the deterioration in the international monetary system, the inflationary increase in import costs, the heavy burdens imposed by external debt on the balance of payments of many developing countries, a rising food demand partly due to demographic pressure, speculation, and a shortage of, and increased costs for, essential agricultural inputs;

(e)   These phenomena should be considered within the framework of the on-going negotiations on the Charter of Economic Rights and Duties of States, and the General Assembly of the United Nations should be urged unanimously to agree upon, and to adopt, a Charter that will be an effective instrument for the establishment of new international economic relations based on principles of equity and justice;

(f)   All countries, big or small, rich or poor, are equal. All countries have the full right to participate in the decisions on the food problem;

(g)   The well-being of the peoples of the world largely depends on the adequate production and distribution of food as well as the establishment of a world food security system which would ensure adequate availability of, and reasonable prices for, food at all times, irrespective of periodic fluctuations and vagaries of weather and free of political and economic pressures, and should thus facilitate, amongst other things, the development process of developing countries;

(h)   Peace and justice encompass an economic dimension helping the solution of the world economic problems, the liquidation of under-development, offering a lasting and definitive solution of the food problem for all peoples and guaranteeing to all countries the right to implement freely and effectively their development programmes. To this effect, it is necessary to eliminate threats and resort to force and to promote peaceful co-operation between States to the fullest extent possible, to apply the principles of non-interference in the internal affairs of other States, full equality of rights and respect of national independence and sovereignty, as well as to encourage the peaceful co-operation between all States, irrespective of their political, social and economic systems. The further improvement of international relations will create better conditions for international co-operation in all fields which should make possible large financial and material resources to be used, inter alia, for developing agricultural production and substantially improving world food security;

(i)   For a lasting solution of the food problem all efforts should be made to eliminate the widening gaps which today separate developed and developing countries and to bring about a new international economic order. It should be possible for all countries to participate actively and effectively in the new international economic relations by the establishment of suitable international systems, where appropriate, capable of producing adequate action in order to establish just and equitable relations in international economic co-operation;

   (j) Developing countries reaffirm their belief that the primary responsibility for ensuring their own rapid development rests with themselves. They declare, therefore, their readiness to continue to intensify their individual and collective efforts with a view to expanding their mutual co-operation in the field of agricultural development and food production, including the eradication of hunger and malnutrition;

   (k) Since, for various reasons, many developing countries are not yet always able to meet their own food needs, urgent and effective international action should be taken to assist them, free of political pressures,

Consistent with the aims and objectives of the Declaration on the Establishment of a New International Economic Order and the Programme of Action adopted by the General Assembly at its sixth special session,

The Conference consequently solemnly proclaims:

1. Every man, woman and child has the inalienable right to be free from hunger and malnutrition in order to develop fully and maintain their physical and mental faculties. Society today already possesses sufficient resources, organizational ability and technology and hence the competence to achieve this objective. Accordingly, the eradication of hunger is a common objective of all the countries of the international community, especially of the developed countries and others in a position to help.

2. It is a fundamental responsibility of Governments to work together for higher food production and a more equitable and efficient distribution of food between countries and within countries. Governments should initiate immediately a greater concerted attack on chronic malnutrition and deficiency diseases among the vulnerable and lower income groups. In order to ensure adequate nutrition for all, Governments should formulate appropriate food and nutrition policies integrated in overall socio-economic and agricultural development plans based on adequate knowledge of available as well as potential food resources. The importance of human milk in this connection should be stressed on nutritional grounds.

3. Food problems must be tackled during the preparation and implementation of national plans and programmes for economic and social development, with emphasis on their humanitarian aspects.

4. It is a responsibility of each State concerned, in accordance with its sovereign judgement and internal legislation, to remove the obstacles to food production and to provide proper incentives to agricultural producers. Of prime importance for the attainment of these objectives are effective measures of socio-economic transformation by agrarian, tax, credit and investment policy reform and the reorganization of rural structures, such as the reform of the conditions of ownership, the encouragement of producer and consumer co-operatives, the mobilization of the full potential of human resources, both male and female, in the developing countries for an integrated rural development and the involvement of small farmers, fishermen and landless workers in attaining the required food production and employment targets. Moreover, it is necessary to recognize the key role of women in agricultural production and rural economy in many countries, and to ensure that appropriate education, extension programmes and financial facilities are made available to women on equal terms with men.

5. Marine and inland water resources are today becoming more important than ever as a source of food and economic prosperity. Accordingly, action should be taken to promote a rational exploitation of these resources, preferably for direct consumption, in order to contribute to meeting the food requirements of all peoples.

6. The efforts to increase food production should be complemented by every endeavour to prevent wastage of food in all its forms.

7. To give impetus to food production in developing countries and in particular in the least developed and most seriously affected among them, urgent and effective international action should be taken, by the developed countries and other countries in a position to do so, to provide them with sustained additional technical and financial assistance on favourable terms and in a volume sufficient to their needs on the basis of bilateral and multilateral arrangements. This assistance must be free of conditions inconsistent with the sovereignty of the receiving States.

8. All countries, and primarily the highly industrialized countries, should promote the advancement of food production technology and should make all efforts to promote the transfer, adaptation and dissemination of appropriate food production technology for the benefit of the developing countries and, to that end, they should *inter alia* make all efforts to disseminate the results of their research work to Governments and scientific institutions of developing countries in order to enable them to promote a sustained agricultural development.

9. To assure the proper conservation of natural resources being utilized, or which might be utilized, for food production, all countries must collaborate in order to facilitate the preservation of the environment, including the marine environment.

10. All developed countries and others able to do so should collaborate technically and financially with the developing countries in their efforts to expand land and water resources for agricultural production and to assure a rapid increase in the availability, at fair costs, of agricultural inputs such as fertilizers and other chemicals, high-quality seeds, credit and technology. Co-operation among developing countries, in this connection, is also important.

11. All States should strive to the utmost to readjust, where appropriate, their agricultural policies to give priority to food production, recognizing, in this connection the interrelationship between the world food problem and international trade. In the determination of attitudes towards farm support programmes for domestic food production, developed countries should take into account, as far as possible, the interest of the food-exporting developing countries, in order to avoid detrimental effect on their exports. Moreover, all countries should co-operate to devise effective steps to deal with the problem of stabilizing world markets and promoting equitable and remunerative prices, where appropriate through international arrangements, to improve access to markets through reduction or elimination of tariff and non-tariff barriers on the products of interest to the developing countries, to substantially increase the export earnings of these countries, to contribute to the diversification of their exports, and apply to them, in the multilateral trade negotiations, the principles as agreed upon in the Tokyo Declaration, including the concept of non-reciprocity and more favourable treatment.

12. As it is the common responsibility of the entire international community to ensure the availability at all times of adequate world supplies of basic food-stuffs by way of

appropriate reserves, including emergency reserves, all countries should co-operate in the establishment of an effective system of world food security by:

— Participating in and supporting the operation of the Global Information and Early Warning System on Food and Agriculture;

— Adhering to the objectives, policies and guidelines of the proposed International Undertaking on World Food Security as endorsed by the World Food Conference;

— Earmarking, where possible, stocks or funds for meeting international emergency food requirements as envisaged in the proposed International Undertaking on World Food Security and developing international guidelines to provide for the co-ordination and the utilization of such stocks;

— Co-operating in the provision of food aid for meeting emergency and nutritional needs as well as for stimulating rural employment through development projects.

— All donor countries should accept and implement the concept of forward planning of food aid and make all efforts to provide commodities and/or financial assistance that will ensure adequate quantities of grains and other food commodities.

— Time is short. Urgent and sustained action is vital. The Conference, therefore, calls upon all peoples expressing their will as individuals, and through their Governments, and non-governmental organizations, to work together to bring about the end of the age-old scourge of hunger.

The Conference affirms:

The determination of the participating States to make full use of the United Nations system in the implementation of this Declaration and the other decisions adopted by the Conference.

10. DECLARATION ON THE PROTECTION OF WOMEN AND CHILDREN IN EMERGENCY AND ARMED CONFLICT, 1974

Adopted by General Assembly resolution 3318 (XXIX), 14 December 1974. See generally, **http://www.un.org/children/conflict/english**.

Further reading

ARTS, K. and POPOVSKI, V., eds., *International Criminal Accountability and the Rights of Children*, Cambridge: Cambridge University Press, 2006.

BENNOUNE, K., 'Do we need international law to protect women in armed conflict?' (2006–2007) 38 *Case Western Reserve Journal of International Law* 363.

COOMARASWAMY, R., 'Machel Study 10-Year Strategic Review', Report by the Special Representative of the Secretary-General for Children and Armed Conflict': UN doc. A/62/228, 13 August 2007.

MACHEL, G., 'Impact of armed conflict on children. Note by the Secretary-General', Report requested in 1993 by the UN Committee on the Rights of the Child and the General Assembly: UN doc. A/51/306, 26 August 1996; see also, 'The Machel Review 1996–2000': UN doc. A/55/749, 26 January 2001.

VAN BUEREN, G., 'The International Legal Protection of Children in Armed Conflicts', (1994) 43 *ICLQ* 809.

TEXT

The General Assembly,

Having considered the recommendation of the Economic and Social Council contained in its resolution 1861 (LVI) of 16 May 1974,

Expressing its deep concern over the sufferings of women and children belonging to the civilian population who in periods of emergency and armed conflict in the struggle for peace, self-determination, national liberation and independence are too often the victims of inhuman acts and consequently suffer serious harm,

Aware of the suffering of women and children in many areas of the world, especially in those areas subject to suppression, aggression, colonialism, racism, alien domination and foreign subjugation,

Deeply concerned by the fact that, despite general and unequivocal condemnation, colonialism, racism and alien and foreign domination continue to subject many peoples under their yoke, cruelly suppressing the national liberation movements and inflicting heavy losses and incalculable sufferings on the populations under their domination, including women and children,

Deploring the fact that grave attacks are still being made on fundamental freedoms and the dignity of the human person and that colonial and racist foreign domination Powers continue to violate international humanitarian law,

Recalling the relevant provisions contained in the instruments of international humanitarian law relative to the protection of women and children in time of peace and war,

Recalling, among other important documents, its resolutions 2444 (XXIII) of 19 December 1968, 2597 (XXIV) of 16 December 1969 and 2674 (XXV) and 2675 (XXV) of 9 December 1970, on respect for human rights and on basic principles for the protection of civilian populations in armed conflicts, as well as Economic and Social Council resolution 1515 (XLVIII) of 28 May 1970 in which the Council requested the General Assembly to consider the possibility of drafting a declaration on the protection of women and children in emergency or wartime,

Conscious of its responsibility for the destiny of the rising generation and for the destiny of mothers, who play an important role in society, in the family and particularly in the upbringing of children,

Bearing in mind the need to provide special protection of women and children belonging to the civilian population,

Solemnly proclaims this Declaration on the Protection of Women and Children in Emergency and Armed Conflict and calls for the strict observance of the Declaration by all Member States:

1. Attacks and bombings on the civilian population, inflicting incalculable suffering, especially on women and children, who are the most vulnerable members of the population, shall be prohibited, and such acts shall be condemned.

2. The use of chemical and bacteriological weapons in the course of military operations constitutes one of the most flagrant violations of the Geneva Protocol of 1925, the Geneva Conventions of 1949 and the principles of international humanitarian law and inflicts heavy losses on civilian populations, including defenceless women and children, and shall be severely condemned.

3. All States shall abide fully by their obligations under the Geneva Protocol of 1925 and the Geneva Conventions of 1949, as well as other instruments of international law relative to respect for human rights in armed conflicts, which offer important guarantees for the protection of women and children.

4. All efforts shall be made by States involved in armed conflicts, military operations in foreign territories or military operations in territories still under colonial domination to spare women and children from the ravages of war. All the necessary steps shall be taken to ensure the prohibition of measures such as persecution, torture, punitive measures, degrading treatment and violence, particularly against that part of the civilian population that consists of women and children.

5. All forms of repression and cruel and inhuman treatment of women and children, including imprisonment, torture, shooting, mass arrests, collective punishment, destruction of dwellings and forcible eviction, committed by belligerents in the course of military operations or in occupied territories shall be considered criminal.

6. Women and children belonging to the civilian population and finding themselves in circumstances of emergency and armed conflict in the struggle for peace, self-determination, national liberation and independence, or who live in occupied territories, shall not be deprived of shelter, food, medical aid or other inalienable rights, in accordance with the provisions of the Universal Declaration of Human Rights, the International Covenant on Civil and Political Rights, the International Covenant on Economic, Social and Cultural Rights, the Declaration of the Rights of the Child or other instruments of international law.

11. DECLARATION ON THE PROTECTION OF ALL PERSONS FROM BEING SUBJECTED TO TORTURE AND OTHER CRUEL, INHUMAN OR DEGRADING TREATMENT OR PUNISHMENT, 1975

This Declaration is annexed to General Assembly Resolution 3452 (XXX), UN doc. A/10034 (1975), adopted by consensus on 9 December 1975. While General Assembly resolutions are not legislative in effect, they provide evidence of the evolution of principles of general international law. The Declaration annexed to the resolution constitutes evidence for the view that the prohibition of torture is an existing principle of international law: see the consideranda in the preamble and note the terms of article 2.

Further reference should be made to Resolutions 3448 and 3453 adopted by the General Assembly on the same date; and to Resolution 31/85 adopted on 13 December 1976.

The adoption of the Declaration was the prelude to the drafting of a Convention against torture (see further below). However, it must be emphasized that the Declaration is declaratory of existing legal norms. The prohibition of torture is enhanced by the appearance of the Convention but the legality of torture does not depend upon the existence of a Convention. The Resolution to which the Declaration is annexed refers to the 'obligation of States under the Charter'; see Brownlie, I., *Principles of Public International Law*, Oxford: Oxford University Press, 7th edn., 2008, 592–7.

In 1982, taking note of this Declaration and of the adoption by the Assembly of the World Medical Association of the 1975 Declaration of Tokyo and Guidelines for Medical Doctors concerning Torture, the General Assembly adopted the 'Principles of medical ethics relevant to the role of health personnel, particularly physicians, in the protection of prisoners and detainees against torture and other cruel, inhuman or degrading treatment or punishment'; see further below, p.92.

For judicial notice and discussion of the 1975 Declaration, see the following decisions of the International Criminal Tribunal for the former Yugoslavia: *Furundžija* (IT-95-17/1) (Lašva Valley), 10 December 1998, paras. 144, 147, 151–3, 159–64; *Mucić* (IT-96-21) (Čelebići Camp), 16 November 1998, paras. 447, 453–9, 464; *Kunarac* (IT-96-23 and 23/1) (Foča), 22 February 2001, paras. 465–76: **http://www.icty.org/**. See also the judgments of the European Court of Human Rights in *Al-Adsani v United Kingdom* (2002) 34 EHRR 11, para. 28; and *Ireland v United Kingdom*, (1978) 2 EHRR 25, para. 167; and, in the United Kingdom, the judgments of the House of Lords in *A and Others (No. 2) v Secretary of State for the Home Department* [2005] UKHL 71, [2005] 3 WLR 1249, paras. 31, 35; and *R v Bow Street Stipendiary Magistrate, ex parte Pinochet Ugarte (No. 3)* [2000] 1 AC 147, 197–9.

Further reading

PEEL, M. and IACOPINO, M., *The Medical Documentation of Torture*, London: Greenwich Medical Media, 2002.

BRUIN, R., RENEMAN, M. and BLOEMEN, E., eds., *Care Full. Medico-legal reports and the Istanbul Protocol in asylum procedures*, Amsterdam: Pharos, Amnesty International, Dutch Council for Refugees, 2006.

UNITED NATIONS HIGH COMMISSIONER FOR HUMAN RIGHTS, *Istanbul Protocol: Manual on the Effective Investigation and Documentation of Torture and Other Cruel, Inhuman or Degrading Treatment or Punishment*, New York and Geneva: United Nations, 2004.

WORLD MEDICAL ASSOCIATION, 1975 Declaration of Tokyo on Medical Ethics and Torture: **http://www.wma.net**.

TEXT

Article 1

1. For the purpose of this Declaration, torture means any act by which severe pain or suffering, whether physical or mental, is intentionally inflicted by or at the instigation of a public official on a person for such purposes as obtaining from him or a third person information or confession, punishing him for an act he has committed or is suspected of having committed, or intimidating him or other persons. It does not include pain or suffering arising only from, inherent in or incidental to, lawful sanctions to the extent consistent with the Standard Minimum Rules for the Treatment of Prisoners.

2. Torture constitutes an aggravated and deliberate form of cruel, inhuman or degrading treatment or punishment.

Article 2

Any act of torture or other cruel, inhuman or degrading treatment or punishment is an offence to human dignity and shall be condemned as a denial of the purposes of the Charter of the United Nations and as a violation of the human rights and fundamental freedoms proclaimed in the Universal Declaration of Human Rights.

Article 3

No State may permit or tolerate torture or other cruel, inhuman or degrading treatment or punishment. Exceptional circumstances such as a state of war or a threat of war, internal political instability or any other public emergency may not be invoked as a justification of torture or other cruel, inhuman or degrading treatment or punishment.

Article 4

Each State shall, in accordance with the provisions of this Declaration, take effective measures to prevent torture and other cruel, inhuman or degrading treatment or punishment from being practised within its jurisdiction.

Article 5

The training of law enforcement personnel and of other public officials who may be responsible for persons deprived of their liberty shall ensure that full account is taken of the prohibition against torture and other cruel, inhuman or degrading treatment or punishment. This prohibition shall also, where appropriate, be included in such general rules or instructions as are issued in regard to the duties and functions of anyone who may be involved in the custody or treatment of such persons.

Article 6

Each State shall keep under systematic review interrogation methods and practices as well as arrangements for the custody and treatment of persons deprived of their liberty in its territory, with a view to preventing any cases of torture or other cruel, inhuman or degrading treatment or punishment.

Article 7

Each State shall ensure that all acts of torture as defined in Article 1 are offences under its criminal law. The same shall apply in regard to acts which constitute participation in, complicity in, incitement to or an attempt to commit torture.

Article 8

Any person who alleges that he has been subjected to torture or other cruel, inhuman or degrading treatment or punishment by or at the instigation of a public official shall have the right to complain to, and to have his case impartially examined by, the competent authorities of the State concerned.

Article 9

Wherever there is reasonable ground to believe that an act of torture as defined in Article 1 has been committed, the competent authorities of the State concerned shall promptly proceed to an impartial investigation even if there has been no formal complaint.

Article 10

If an investigation under Article 8 or Article 9 establishes that an act of torture as defined in Article 1 appears to have been committed, criminal proceedings shall be instituted against the alleged offender or offenders in accordance with national law. If an allegation of other forms of cruel, inhuman or degrading treatment or punishment is considered to be well founded, the alleged offender or offenders shall be subject to criminal, disciplinary or other appropriate proceedings.

Article 11

Where it is proved that an act of torture or other cruel, inhuman or degrading treatment or punishment has been committed by or at the instigation of a public official, the victim shall be afforded redress and compensation in accordance with national law.

Article 12

Any statement which is established to have been made as a result of torture or other cruel, inhuman or degrading treatment or punishment may not be invoked as evidence against the person concerned or against any other person in any proceedings.

12. DECLARATION ON THE RIGHTS OF
DISABLED PERSONS, 1975

This Declaration was adopted by General Assembly Resolution 3447 (XXX), 9 December 1975. See also 'Standard Rules on the Equalization of Opportunities for Persons with Disabilities, 1993', below, p.175; General Assembly Resolution 48/99, 'Towards full integration of persons with disabilities into society: a continuing world programme of action' 20 December 1993: General Assembly Resolution 49/153, 23 December 1994; Committee on Economic, Social and Cultural Rights, General Comment No. 5, Persons with disabilities (Eleventh session, 1994), UN doc. E/C.12/1994/13 (1994); Commission on Human Rights Resolution 1998/31, 'Human rights of persons with disabilities', UN doc. E/CN.4/1998/31 (1998); Inter-American Convention on the Elimination of All Forms of Discrimination against Persons with Disabilities, 1999, below, p.1002.

In 2001, the General Assembly decided to establish an *Ad Hoc* Committee, 'to consider proposals for a comprehensive and integral international convention to promote and protect the rights and dignity of persons with disabilities, based on the holistic approach in the work done in the fields of social development, human rights and non-discrimination and taking into account the recommendations of the Commission on Human Rights and the Commission for Social Development': General Assembly Resolution 56/168, 19 December 2001. The first session took place in 2002, and in 2003 the *Ad Hoc* Committee set up a Working Group to draft a convention on the rights of persons with disabilities, as a basis for negotiation by Member States. Following General Assembly Resolution 58/246, 23 December 2003, the *Ad Hoc* Committee started negotiations at its Third Session in 2004, which resulted in adoption of the Convention on the Rights of Persons with Disabilities in 2006; see below, p.518.

Further reading

OWEN, F. and GRIFFITHS, D., *Challenges to the Human Rights of People with Intellectual Disabilities*, London: Jessica Kingsley Publishers, 2009.

TEXT

The General Assembly,

Mindful of the pledge made by Member States, under the Charter of the United Nations to take joint and separate action in co-operation with the Organization to promote higher standards of living, full employment and conditions of economic and social progress and development,

Reaffirming its faith in human rights and fundamental freedoms and in the principles of peace, of the dignity and worth of the human person and of social justice proclaimed in the Charter,

Recalling the principles of the Universal Declaration of Human Rights, the International Covenants on Human Rights, the Declaration of the Rights of the Child and the Declaration on the Rights of Mentally Retarded Persons, as well as the standards already set for social progress in the constitutions, conventions, recommendations and resolutions of the International Labour Organization, the United Nations Educational, Scientific and Cultural Organization, the World Health Organization, the United Nations Children's Fund and other organizations concerned,

Recalling also Economic and Social Council resolution 1921 (LVIII) of 6 May 1975 on the prevention of disability and the rehabilitation of disabled persons,

Emphasizing that the Declaration on Social Progress and Development has proclaimed the necessity of protecting the rights and assuring the welfare and rehabilitation of the physically and mentally disadvantaged,

Bearing in mind the necessity of preventing physical and mental disabilities and of assisting disabled persons to develop their abilities in the most varied fields of activities and of promoting their integration as far as possible in normal life,

Aware that certain countries, at their present stage of development, can devote only limited efforts to this end,

Proclaims this Declaration on the Rights of Disabled Persons and calls for national and international action to ensure that it will be used as a common basis and frame of reference for the protection of these rights:

1. The term 'disabled person' means any person unable to ensure by himself or herself, wholly or partly, the necessities of a normal individual and/or social life, as a result of deficiency, either congenital or not, in his or her physical or mental capabilities.

2. Disabled persons shall enjoy all the rights set forth in this Declaration. These rights shall be granted to all disabled persons without any exception whatsoever and without distinction or discrimination on the basis of race, colour, sex, language, religion, political or other opinions, national or social origin, state of wealth, birth or any other situation applying either to the disabled person himself or herself or to his or her family.

3. Disabled persons have the inherent right to respect for their human dignity. Disabled persons, whatever the origin, nature and seriousness of their handicaps and disabilities, have the same fundamental rights as their fellow-citizens of the same age, which implies first and foremost the right to enjoy a decent life, as normal and full as possible.

4. Disabled persons have the same civil and political rights as other human beings; paragraph 7 of the Declaration on the Rights of Mentally Retarded Persons applies to any possible limitation or suppression of those rights for mentally disabled persons.

5. Disabled persons are entitled to the measures designed to enable them to become as self-reliant as possible.

6. Disabled persons have the right to medical, psychological and functional treatment, including prosthetic and orthetic appliances, to medical and social rehabilitation, education, vocational training and rehabilitation, aid, counselling, placement services and other services which will enable them to develop their capabilities and skills to the maximum and will hasten the processes of their social integration or reintegration.

7. Disabled persons have the right to economic and social security and to a decent level of living. They have the right, according to their capabilities, to secure and retain employment or to engage in a useful, productive and remunerative occupation and to join trade unions.

8. Disabled persons are entitled to have their special needs taken into consideration at all stages of economic and social planning.

9. Disabled persons have the right to live with their families or with foster parents and to participate in all social, creative or recreational activities. No disabled person shall be subjected, as far as his or her residence is concerned, to differential treatment other than that required by his or her condition or by the improvement which he or she may derive therefrom. If the stay of a disabled person in a specialized establishment is

indispensable, the environment and living conditions therein shall be as close as possible to those of the normal life of a person of his or her age.

10. Disabled persons shall be protected against all exploitation, all regulations and all treatment of a discriminatory, abusive or degrading nature.

11. Disabled persons shall be able to avail themselves of qualified legal aid when such aid proves indispensable for the protection of their persons and property. If judicial proceedings are instituted against them, the legal procedure applied shall take their physical and mental condition fully into account.

12. Organizations of disabled persons may be usefully consulted in all matters regarding the rights of disabled persons.

13. Disabled persons, their families and communities shall be fully informed, by all appropriate means, of the rights contained in this Declaration.

13. DECLARATION ON THE ELIMINATION OF ALL FORMS OF INTOLERANCE AND OF DISCRIMINATION BASED ON RELIGION OR BELIEF, 1981

This Declaration was adopted without a vote by the General Assembly in Resolution 36/55 on 25 November 1981. For the background, see *Yearbook of the United Nations*, 1981, 879–83. The Declaration was prepared by the Commission on Human Rights. For an earlier proposal of a draft Convention on the subject, see the second edition of this work, p. 111. In 1986, the Commission on Human Rights decided to appoint a Special Rapporteur on freedom of religion or belief (resolution 1986/20, subsequently renewed). The Special Rapporteur (Asthma Jahangir, 2008–; Abdelfattah Amor, 1993–2004, Angelo d'Almeida Ribeiro, 1986–93) submits annual reports; see, among others, UN doc. A/HRC/10/8, 6 January 2009; Commission on Human Rights Resolution 2003/54; **http://www2.ohchr.org/english/issues/religion/index.htm**.

Further reading

DAVIS, D. H., 'The Evolution of Religious Freedom as a Universal Human Right: Examining the Role of the 1981 United Nations Declaration on the Elimination of All Forms of Intolerance and of Discrimination Based on Religion or Belief', (2002) *Brigham Young University Law Review* 217.

DICKSON, B., 'The United Nations and Freedom of Religion', (1995) 44 *ICLQ* 327–57.

EVANS, C., 'Time for a Treaty? The Legal Sufficiency of the Declaration on the Elimination of All Forms of Intolerance and Discrimination', (2007) *Brigham Young University Law Review* 617.

GHANEA, N., STEPHENS, A. and WALDEN, R., eds., *Does God Believe in Human Rights? Essays on Religion and Human Rights*, Leiden: Martinus Nijhoff, 2007.

JANIS, M. W. and EVANS, C., *Religion and International Law*, Leiden: Martinus Nijhoff, rev'd edn., 2004.

LERNER, N., *Religion, Secular Beliefs and Human Rights: 25 Years after the 1981 Declaration*, Leiden: Martinus Nijhoff, 2006.

McGOLDRICK, D., *Human Rights and Religion: The Islamic Headscarf Debate in Europe*, Oxford: Hart Publishing, 2006.

WIENER, M., 'The Mandate of the Special Rapporteur on Freedom of Religion or Belief—Institutional, Procedural and Substantive Legal Issues', (2007) 2 *Religion and Human Rights* 3.

TEXT

The General Assembly,

Considering that one of the basic principles of the Charter of the United Nations is that of the dignity and equality inherent in all human beings, and that all Member States have pledged themselves to take joint and separate action in co-operation with the Organization to promote and encourage universal respect for and observance of human rights and fundamental freedoms for all, without distinction as to race, sex, language or religion,

Considering that the Universal Declaration of Human Rights and the International Covenants on Human Rights proclaim the principles of non-discrimination and equality before the law and the right to freedom of thought, conscience, religion and belief,

Considering that the disregard and infringement of human rights and fundamental freedoms, in particular of the right to freedom of thought, conscience, religion or whatever belief, have brought, directly or indirectly, wars and great suffering to mankind, especially where they serve as a means of foreign interference in the internal affairs of other States and amount to kindling hatred between peoples and nations,

Considering that religion or belief, for anyone who professes either, is one of the fundamental elements in his conception of life and that freedom of religion or belief should be fully respected and guaranteed,

Considering that it is essential to promote understanding, tolerance and respect in matters relating to freedom of religion and belief and to ensure that the use of religion or belief for ends inconsistent with the Charter of the United Nations, other relevant instruments of the United Nations and the purposes and principles of the present Declaration is inadmissible,

Convinced that freedom of religion and belief should also contribute to the attainment of the goals of world peace, social justice and friendship among peoples and to the elimination of ideologies or practices of colonialism and racial discrimination,

Noting with satisfaction the adoption of several, and the coming into force of some, conventions, under the aegis of the United Nations and of the specialized agencies, for the elimination of various forms of discrimination,

Concerned by manifestations of intolerance and by the existence of discrimination in matters of religion or belief still in evidence in some areas of the world,

Resolved to adopt all necessary measures for the speedy elimination of such intolerance in all its forms and manifestations and to prevent and combat discrimination on the ground of religion or belief,

Proclaims this Declaration on the Elimination of All Forms of Intolerance and of Discrimination Based on Religion or Belief:

Article 1

1. Everyone shall have the right to freedom of thought, conscience and religion. This right shall include freedom to have a religion or whatever belief of his choice, and freedom, either individually or in community with others and in public or private, to manifest his religion or belief in worship, observance, practice and teaching.

2. No one shall be subject to coercion which would impair his freedom to have a religion or belief of his choice.

3. Freedom to manifest one's religion or belief may be subject only to such limitations as are prescribed by law and are necessary to protect public safety, order, health or morals or the fundamental rights and freedoms of others.

Article 2

1. No one shall be subject to discrimination by any State, institution, group of persons, or person on the grounds of religion or other belief.

2. For the purposes of the present Declaration, the expression 'intolerance and discrimination based on religion or belief' means any distinction, exclusion, restriction or preference based on religion or belief and having as its purpose or as its effect nullification or impairment of the recognition, enjoyment or exercise of human rights and fundamental freedoms on an equal basis.

Article 3

Discrimination between human beings on the grounds of religion or belief constitutes an affront to human dignity and a disavowal of the principles of the Charter of the United Nations, and shall be condemned as a violation of the human rights and fundamental freedoms proclaimed in the Universal Declaration of Human Rights and enunciated in detail in the International Covenants on Human Rights, and as an obstacle to friendly and peaceful relations between nations.

Article 4

1. All States shall take effective measures to prevent and eliminate discrimination on the grounds of religion or belief in the recognition, exercise and enjoyment of human rights and fundamental freedoms in all fields of civil, economic, political, social and cultural life.

2. All States shall make all efforts to enact or rescind legislation where necessary to prohibit any such discrimination, and to take all appropriate measures to combat intolerance on the grounds of religion or other beliefs in this matter.

Article 5

1. The parents or, as the case may be, the legal guardians of the child have the right to organize the life within the family in accordance with their religion or belief and bearing in mind the moral education in which they believe the child should be brought up.

2. Every child shall enjoy the right to have access to education in the matter of religion or belief in accordance with the wishes of his parents or, as the case may be, legal guardians, and shall not be compelled to receive teaching on religion or belief against the wishes of his parents or legal guardians, the best interests of the child being the guiding principle.

3. The child shall be protected from any form of discrimination on the ground of religion or belief. He shall be brought up in a spirit of understanding, tolerance, friendship among peoples, peace and universal brotherhood, respect for freedom of religion or belief of others, and in full consciousness that his energy and talents should be devoted to the service of his fellow men.

4. In the case of a child who is not under the care either of his parents or of legal guardians, due account shall be taken of their expressed wishes or of any other proof of their wishes in the matter of religion or belief, the best interests of the child being the guiding principle.

5. Practices of a religion or belief in which a child is brought up must not be injurious to his physical or mental health or to his full development, taking into account Article 1, paragraph 3, of the present Declaration.

Article 6

In accordance with Article 1 of the present Declaration, and subject to the provisions of Article 1, paragraph 3, the right to freedom of thought, conscience, religion or belief shall include, *inter alia*, the following freedoms:

    (a) To worship or assemble in connection with a religion or belief, and to establish and maintain places for these purposes;

    (b) To establish and maintain appropriate charitable or humanitarian institutions;

    (c)   To make, acquire and use to an adequate extent the necessary articles and materials related to the rites or customs of a religion or belief;

    (d)   To write, issue and disseminate relevant publications in these areas;

    (e)   To teach a religion or belief in places suitable for these purposes;

    (f)   To solicit and receive voluntary financial and other contributions from individuals and institutions;

    (g)   To train, appoint, elect or designate by succession appropriate leaders called for by the requirements and standards of any religion or belief;

    (h)   To observe days of rest and to celebrate holidays and ceremonies in accordance with the precepts of one's religion or belief;

    (i)   To establish and maintain communications with individuals and communities in matters of religion and belief at the national and international levels.

Article 7

The rights and freedoms set forth in the present Declaration shall be accorded in national legislation in such a manner that everyone shall be able to avail himself of such rights and freedoms in practice.

Article 8

Nothing in the present Declaration shall be construed as restricting or derogating from any right defined in the Universal Declaration of Human Rights and the International Covenants on Human Rights.

14. PRINCIPLES OF MEDICAL ETHICS, 1982

The principles set out below were adopted by the General Assembly in Resolution 37/194 on 18 December 1982. They represent a continuation of efforts to combat torture following the adoption of the 1975 Declaration (see above, p.82). As the preamble notes, action was also being taken by the World Health Organization, while already in October 1975, the World Medical Association had adopted Guidelines for medical doctors concerning torture: **http://www.wma.net**.

Further reading

BRUIN, R., RENEMAN, M. and BLOEMEN, E., eds., *Care Full. Medico-legal Reports and the Istanbul Protocol in Asylum Procedures*, Amsterdam: Pharos, Amnesty International, Dutch Council for Refugees, 2006.

MILES, S. and FREEDMAN, A., 'Medical ethics and torture: revising the Declaration of Tokyo', (2009) 373 *The Lancet*, Issue 9660, 344–8.

RUBENSTEIN, L. S. and ANNAS, G. J., 'Medical ethics at Guantanamo Bay detention centre and in the US military: a time for reform' (2009)374 *The Lancet*, Issue 9686, 353–5.

UNITED NATIONS HIGH COMMISSIONER FOR HUMAN RIGHTS, *Istanbul Protocol: Manual on the Effective Investigation and Documentation of Torture and Other Cruel, Inhuman or Degrading Treatment or Punishment*, New York and Geneva: United Nations, 2004.

TEXT

The General Assembly,

Recalling its resolution 31/85 of 13 December 1976, in which it invited the World Health Organization to prepare a draft code of medical ethics relevant to the protection of persons subjected to any form of detention or imprisonment against torture and other cruel, inhuman or degrading treatment or punishment,

Expressing once again its appreciation to the Executive Board of the World Health Organization which, at its sixty-third session, in January 1979, decided to endorse the principles set forth in a report entitled 'Development of codes of medical ethics' containing, in an annex, a draft body of principles prepared by the Council for International Organizations of Medical Sciences and entitled 'Principles of medical ethics relevant to the role of health personnel in the protection of persons against torture and other cruel, inhuman or degrading treatment or punishment',

Bearing in mind Economic and Social Council resolution 1981/27 of 6 May 1981, in which the Council recommended that the General Assembly should take measures to finalize the draft Principles of Medical Ethics at its thirty-sixth session,

Recalling its resolution 36/61 of 25 November 1981, in which it decided to consider the draft Principles of Medical Ethics at its thirty-seventh session with a view to adopting them,

Alarmed that not infrequently members of the medical profession or other health personnel are engaged in activities which are difficult to reconcile with medical ethics,

Recognizing that throughout the world significant medical activities are increasingly being performed by health personnel not licensed or trained as physicians, such as physician-assistants, paramedics, physical therapists and nurse practitioners,

Recalling with appreciation the Declaration of Tokyo of the World Medical Association, containing the Guidelines for Medical Doctors concerning Torture and Other Cruel, Inhuman or Degrading Treatment or Punishment in relation to Detention and Imprisonment, adopted by the twenty-ninth World Medical Assembly, held at Tokyo in October 1975,

Noting that in accordance with the Declaration of Tokyo measures should be taken by States and by professional associations and other bodies, as appropriate, against any attempt to subject health personnel or members of their families to threats or reprisals resulting from a refusal by such personnel to condone the use of torture or other forms of cruel, inhuman or degrading treatment,

Reaffirming the Declaration on the Protection of All Persons from Being Subjected to Torture and Other Cruel, Inhuman or Degrading Treatment or Punishment, unanimously adopted by the General Assembly in its resolution 3452 (XXX) of 9 December 1975, in which it declared any act of torture or other cruel, inhuman or degrading treatment or punishment an offence to human dignity, a denial of the purposes of the Charter of the United Nations and a violation of the Universal Declaration of Human Rights,

Recalling that, in accordance with article 7 of the Declaration adopted in resolution 3452 (XXX), each State shall ensure that the commission of all acts of torture, as defined in article 1 of that Declaration, or participation in, complicity in, incitement to or attempt to commit torture are offences under its criminal law,

Convinced that under no circumstances should a person be punished for carrying out medical activities compatible with medical ethics, regardless of the person benefiting therefrom, or be compelled to perform acts or to carry out work in contravention of medical ethics, but that, at the same time, contravention of medical ethics for which health personnel, particularly physicians, can be held responsible should entail accountability,

Desirous of setting further standards in this field which ought to be implemented by health personnel, particularly physicians, and by Government officials,

1. *Adopts* the Principles of Medical Ethics relevant to the role of health personnel, particularly physicians, in the protection of prisoners and detainees against torture and other cruel, inhuman or degrading treatment or punishment, set forth in the annex to the present resolution;

2. *Calls upon* all Governments to give the Principles of Medical Ethics, together with the present resolution, the widest possible distribution, in particular among medical and paramedical associations and institutions of detention or imprisonment, in an official language of the State;

3. *Invites* all relevant intergovernmental organizations, in particular the World Health Organization, and non-governmental organizations concerned to bring the Principles of Medical Ethics to the attention of the widest possible group of individuals, especially those active in the medical and paramedical field.

ANNEX

Principles of Medical Ethics relevant to the role of health personnel, particularly physicians, in the protection of prisoners and detainees against torture and other cruel, inhuman or degrading treatment of punishment

Principle 1

Health personnel, particularly physicians, charged with the medical care of prisoners and detainees have a duty to provide them with protection of their physical and mental health and treatment of disease of the same quality and standard as is afforded to those who are not imprisoned or detained.

Principle 2

It is a gross contravention of medical ethics, as well as an offence under applicable international instruments, for health personnel, particularly physicians, to engage, actively or passively, in acts which constitute participation in, complicity in, incitement to or attempts to commit torture or other cruel, inhuman or degrading treatment or punishment.

Principle 3

It is a contravention of medical ethics for health personnel, particularly physicians, to be involved in any professional relationship with prisoners or detainees the purpose of which is not solely to evaluate, protect or improve their physical and mental health.

Principle 4

It is a contravention of medical ethics for health personnel, particularly physicians:

(a) To apply their knowledge and skills in order to assist in the interrogation of prisoners and detainees in a manner that may adversely affect the physical or mental health or condition of such prisoners or detainees and which is not in accordance with the relevant international instruments;

(b) To certify, or to participate in the certification of, the fitness of prisoners or detainees for any form of treatment or punishment that may adversely affect their physical or mental health and which is not in accordance with the relevant international instruments, or to participate in any way in the infliction of any such treatment or punishment which is not in accordance with the relevant international instruments.

Principle 5

It is a contravention of medical ethics for health personnel, particularly physicians, to participate in any procedure for restraining a prisoner or detainee unless such a procedure is determined in accordance with purely medical criteria as being necessary for the protection of the physical or mental health or the safety of the prisoner or detainee himself, of his fellow prisoners or detainees, or of his guardians, and presents no hazard to his physical or mental health.

Principle 6

There may be no derogation from the foregoing principles on any ground whatsoever, including public emergency.

15. DECLARATION ON THE RIGHT OF
PEOPLES TO PEACE, 1984

Approved by General Assembly Resolution 39/11, 12 November 1984 on a recorded vote of ninety-two in favour, none against, and thirty-four abstentions. For critical comments, see Alston, P., 'Peoples' Rights: Their Rise and Fall', in Alston, P., ed., *Peoples' Rights*, Oxford: Oxford University Press, 2001, 279–80; Higgins, R., *Problems and Process: International Law and How We Use It*, Oxford: Oxford University Press, 102–3.

TEXT

The General Assembly,

Reaffirming that the principal aim of the United Nations is the maintenance of international peace and security,

Bearing in mind the fundamental principles of international law set forth in the Charter of the United Nations,

Expressing the will and the aspirations of all peoples to eradicate war from the life of mankind and, above all, to avert a world-wide nuclear catastrophe,

Convinced that life without war serves as the primary international prerequisite for the material well-being, development and progress of countries, and for the full implementation of the rights and fundamental human freedoms proclaimed by the United Nations,

Aware that in the nuclear age the establishment of a lasting peace on Earth represents the primary condition for the preservation of human civilization and the survival of mankind,

Recognizing that the maintenance of a peaceful life for peoples is the sacred duty of each State,

1. *Solemnly proclaims* that the peoples of our planet have a sacred right to peace;

2. *Solemnly declares* that the preservation of the right of peoples to peace and the promotion of its implementation constitute a fundamental obligation of each State;

3. *Emphasizes* that ensuring the exercise of the right of peoples to peace demands that the policies of States be directed towards the elimination of the threat of war, particularly nuclear war, the renunciation of the use of force in international relations and the settlement of international disputes by peaceful means on the basis of the Charter of the United Nations;

4. *Appeals* to all States and international organizations to do their utmost to assist in implementing the right of peoples to peace through the adoption of appropriate measures at both the national and the international level.

16. DECLARATION ON THE HUMAN RIGHTS OF INDIVIDUALS WHO ARE NOT NATIONALS OF THE COUNTRY IN WHICH THEY LIVE, 1985

This Declaration was adopted by General Assembly Resolution 40/144 without a vote on 13 December 1985; UN doc. A/40/53 (1985). In 1999, the Commission on Human Rights established the mandate of the Special Rapporteur on the Human Rights of Migrants, (Jorge A. Bustamante, 2005–, Gabriela Rodríguez Pizarro, 1999–2005): see resolution 1999/44; in 2005, it was extended for a further three years by resolution 2005/47. For recent reports, see UN docs. A/HRC/11/7, 14 May 2009 and A/HRC/7/12, 25 February 2008. See also International Convention on the Protection of the Rights of All Migrant Workers and their Families, 1990, below, p. 487; European Convention on the Legal Status of Migrant Workers, 1977, below, p. 773, and generally, **http://www2.ohchr.org/english/issues/migration/rapporteur/**.

For recent judicial notice of the Declaration, see *A and others v Secretary of State for the Home Department* [2004] UKHL 56, [2005] AC 68, paras. 58, 69 (Lord Bingham).

Further reading

CHOLEWINSKI, R., PERRUCHOUD, R. and MACDONALD, E., eds., *International Migration Law: Developing Paradigms and Key Challenges*, The Hague: T. M. C. Asser Press, 2007

CHOLEWINSKI, R., *Migrant Workers in International Human Rights Law: Their Protection in Countries of Employment*, Oxford: Clarendon Press, 1997.

LILLICH, R. B., *The Human Rights of Aliens in Contemporary International Law*, Manchester: Manchester University Press, 1984.

OFFICE OF THE UNITED NATIONS HIGH COMMISSIONER FOR HUMAN RIGHTS, *The Rights of Non-Citizens*, New York, Geneva: United Nations, 2006.

WEISSBRODT, D., *The Human Rights of Non-Citizens*, Oxford: Oxford University Press, 2008.

TEXT

The General Assembly,

Considering that the Charter of the United Nations encourages universal respect for and observance of the human rights and fundamental freedoms of all human beings, without distinction as to race, sex, language or religion,

Considering that the Universal Declaration of Human Rights proclaims that all human beings are born free and equal in dignity and rights and that everyone is entitled to all the rights and freedoms set forth in that Declaration, without distinction of any kind, such as race, colour, sex, language, religion, political or other opinion, national or social origin, property, birth or other status,

Considering that the Universal Declaration of Human Rights proclaims further that everyone has the right to recognition everywhere as a person before the law, that all are equal before the law and entitled without any discrimination to equal protection of the law, and that all are entitled to equal protection against any discrimination in violation of that Declaration and against any incitement to such discrimination,

Being aware that the States Parties to the International Covenants on Human Rights undertake to guarantee that the rights enunciated in these Covenants will be exercised without discrimination of any kind as to race, colour, sex, language, religion, political or other opinion, national or social origin, property, birth or other status,

Conscious that, with improving communications and the development of peaceful and friendly relations among countries, individuals increasingly live in countries of which they are not nationals,

Reaffirming the purposes and principles of the Charter of the United Nations,

Recognizing that the protection of human rights and fundamental freedoms provided for in international instruments should also be ensured for individuals who are not nationals of the country in which they live,

Proclaims this Declaration:

Article 1

For the purposes of this Declaration, the term 'alien' shall apply, with due regard to qualifications made in subsequent articles, to any individual who is not a national of the State in which he or she is present.

Article 2

1. Nothing in this Declaration shall be interpreted as legitimizing the illegal entry into and presence in a State of any alien, nor shall any provision be interpreted as restricting the right of any State to promulgate laws and regulations concerning the entry of aliens and the terms and conditions of their stay or to establish differences between nationals and aliens. However, such laws and regulations shall not be incompatible with the international legal obligations of that State, including those in the field of human rights.

2. This Declaration shall not prejudice the enjoyment of the rights accorded by domestic law and of the rights which under international law a State is obliged to accord to aliens, even where this Declaration does not recognize such rights or recognizes them to a lesser extent.

Article 3

Every State shall make public its national legislation or regulations affecting aliens.

Article 4

Aliens shall observe the laws of the State in which they reside or are present and regard with respect the customs and traditions of the people of that State.

Article 5

1. Aliens shall enjoy, in accordance with domestic law and subject to the relevant international obligation of the State in which they are present, in particular the following rights:

   (a) The right to life and security of person; no alien shall be subjected to arbitrary arrest or detention; no alien shall be deprived of his or her liberty except on such grounds and in accordance with such procedures as are established by law;

   (b) The right to protection against arbitrary or unlawful interference with privacy, family, home or correspondence;

   (c) The right to be equal before the courts, tribunals and all other organs and authorities administering justice and, when necessary, to free assistance of an interpreter in criminal proceedings and, when prescribed by law, other proceedings;

   (d) The right to choose a spouse, to marry, to found a family;

   (e) The right to freedom of thought, opinion, conscience and religion; the right to manifest their religion or beliefs, subject only to such limitations as are prescribed by law and are necessary to protect public safety, order, health or morals or the fundamental rights and freedoms of others;

  (f) The right to retain their own language, culture and tradition;

  (g) The right to transfer abroad earnings, savings or other personal monetary assets, subject to domestic currency regulations.

2. Subject to such restrictions as are prescribed by law and which are necessary in a democratic society to protect national security, public safety, public order, public health or morals or the rights and freedoms of others, and which are consistent with the other rights recognized in the relevant international instruments and those set forth in this Declaration, aliens shall enjoy the following rights:

  (a) The right to leave the country;

  (b) The right to freedom of expression;

  (c) The right to peaceful assembly;

  (d) The right to own property alone as well as in association with others, subject to domestic law.

3. Subject to the provisions referred to in paragraph 2, aliens lawfully in the territory of a State shall enjoy the right to liberty of movement and freedom to choose their residence within the borders of the State.

4. Subject to national legislation and due authorization, the spouse and minor or dependent children of an alien lawfully residing in the territory of a State shall be admitted to accompany, join and stay with the alien.

Article 6

No alien shall be subjected to torture or to cruel, inhuman or degrading treatment or punishment and, in particular, no alien shall be subjected without his or her free consent to medical or scientific experimentation.

Article 7

An alien lawfully in the territory of a State may be expelled therefrom only in pursuance of a decision reached in accordance with law and shall, except where compelling reasons of national security otherwise require, be allowed to submit the reasons why he or she should not be expelled and to have the case reviewed by, and be represented for the purpose before, the competent authority or a person or persons specially designated by the competent authority. Individual or collective expulsion of such aliens on grounds of race, colour, religion, culture, descent or national or ethnic origin is prohibited.

Article 8

1. Aliens lawfully residing in the territory of a State shall also enjoy, in accordance with the national laws, the following rights, subject to their obligations under Article 4:

  (a) The right to safe and healthy working conditions, to fair wages and equal remuneration for work of equal value without distinction of any kind, in particular, women being guaranteed conditions of work not inferior to those enjoyed by men, with equal pay for equal work;

  (b) The right to join trade unions and other organizations or associations of their choice and to participate in their activities. No restrictions may be placed on the exercise of this right other than those prescribed by law and which are necessary, in a democratic society, in the interests of national security or public order or for the protection of the rights and freedoms of others;

(c) The right to health protection, medical care, social security, social services, education, rest and leisure, provided that they fulfil the requirements under the relevant regulations for participation and that undue strain is not placed on the resources of the State.

2. With a view to protecting the rights of aliens carrying on lawful paid activities in the country in which they are present, such rights may be specified by the Governments concerned in multilateral or bilateral conventions.

Article 9

No alien shall be arbitrarily deprived of his or her lawfully acquired assets.

Article 10

Any alien shall be free at any time to communicate with the consulate or diplomatic mission of the State of which he or she is a national or, in the absence thereof, with the consulate or diplomatic mission of any other State entrusted with the protection of the interests of the State of which he or she is a national in the State where he or she resides.

17. DECLARATION ON THE RIGHT TO DEVELOPMENT, 1986

Adopted by General Assembly Resolution 41/128 on 4 December 1986, by a vote of 146 to one against (United States), with eight abstentions, including Germany, Japan and the United Kingdom. For later developments, see UNGA Resolutions 50/184, 22 December 1995, 'Right to development' (adopted without a vote); 51/240, 20 June 1997, 'Agenda for Development' (adopted without a vote); 52/136, 12 December 1997, 'Right to development' (adopted by a vote of 129–12–32); 53/155, 9 December 1998, 'Right to development' (125–1–42); 54/175, 17 December 1999, 'The right to development' (119–10–38); 55/108, 4 December 2000, 'The right to development', (adopted without a vote); 56/150, 19 December 2001, 'The right to development' (123–4–44); 57/223, 18 December 2002, 'The right to development' (133–4–47); 58/172, 23 December 2003, 'The right to development' (173–3–5); 59/185, December 2004, 'The right to development', (181–2–4); 60/157, 'The right to development', 16 December 2005 (134–53–0); 61/169, 'The right to development', 19 December 2006 (134–53–0); 62/161, 'The right to development', 18 December 2007 (182–4–2); 63/178, 'The right to development', 18 December 2008 (182–4–2).

See also the United Nations Millennium Declaration, below p.241, and the 2005 World Summit Outcome, adopted by General Assembly Resolution 60/1, 16 September 2005, which form part of the background to the eight 'Millennium Development Goals' (MDGs): **http://www.un.org/ millenniumgoals/**.

Further reading

ALSTON, P. and ROBINSON, M., *Human Rights and Development: Towards Mutual Reinforcement*, Oxford: Oxford University Press, 2005.

BOUTROS-GHALI, B., *An Agenda for Development*, New York: United Nations, 1995.

BROWNLIE, I., *The Human Right to Development*, London: Commonwealth Secretariat, 1989.

CENTRE FOR DEVELOPMENT AND HUMAN RIGHTS, *The Right to Development: A Primer*, New Delhi: Sage Publications, 2004.

CORDONNIER SEGGER, M.-C. and KHALFAN, A., *Sustainable Development: Principles, Practices and Prospects*, Oxford: Oxford University Press, 2004.

DARROW, M. and ARBOUR, L., 'The Glass Pillar: Human Rights in the Development Operations of the United Nations', (2009) 103 *AJIL* 446.

FRENCH, D., *International Law and Policy of Sustainable Development*, Manchester: Manchester University Press, 2005.

HEY, E., 'Sustainable development, normative development and the legitimacy of decision making', (2003) 34 *Netherlands Yearbook of International Law* 3.

MCINERNEY-LANKFORD, S., 'Human Rights and Development: A Comment on Challenges and Opportunities from a Legal Perspective', (2009) 1 *Journal of Human Rights Practice* 51.

NAGLE, G. and SPENCER, K., *Sustainable Development*, London: Hodder and Stoughton, 1997.

SALOMON, M. E. and SENGUPTA, A., *The Right to Development: Obligations of States and the Rights of Minorities and Indigenous Peoples*, London: Minority Rights Group International, 2003.

SARKAR, R., *International Development Law: Rule of Law, Human Rights, and Global Finance*, Oxford: Oxford University Press, 2009.

SCHRIJVER, N., *The Evolution of Sustainable Development in International Law: Inception, Meaning and Status*, Leiden: Martinus Nijhoff, 2008.

—— and WEISS, F., eds., *International Law and Sustainable Development: Principles and Practice*, Leiden: Martinus Nijhoff, 2004.

SENGUPTA, A., 'On the Theory and Practice of the Right to Development', (2 0 0 2) 24 *Human Rights Quarterly* 8 3 7.

SINHA, M. K., 'Development at the crossroads—Is right to development a human right', (2 0 0 2) 4 2 *Indian Journal of International Law* 5 1 2.

'Special Issue: Millennium Development Goals and Human Rights', (2 0 0 9) 13 *International Journal of Human Rights*, No. 1.

VOIGT, C., *Sustainable Development as a Principle of International Law*, Leiden: Martinus Nijhoff, 2 0 0 9.

TEXT

The General Assembly,

Bearing in mind the purposes and principles of the Charter of the United Nations relating to the achievement of international co-operation in solving international problems of an economic, social, cultural or humanitarian nature, and in promoting and encouraging respect for human rights and fundamental freedoms for all without distinction as to race, sex, language or religion,

Recognizing that development is a comprehensive economic, social, cultural and political process, which aims at the constant improvement of the well-being of the entire population and of all individuals on the basis of their active, free and meaningful participation in development and in the fair distribution of benefits resulting therefrom,

Considering that under the provisions of the Universal Declaration of Human Rights everyone is entitled to a social and international order in which the rights and freedoms set forth in that Declaration can be fully realized,

Recalling the provisions of the International Covenant on Economic, Social and Cultural Rights and of the International Covenant on Civil and Political Rights,

Recalling further the relevant agreements, conventions, resolutions, recommendations and other instruments of the United Nations and its specialized agencies concerning the integral development of the human being, economic and social progress and development of all peoples, including those instruments concerning decolonization, the prevention of discrimination, respect for and observance of, human rights and fundamental freedoms, the maintenance of international peace and security and the further promotion of friendly relations and co-operation among States in accordance with the Charter,

Recalling the right of peoples to self-determination, by virtue of which they have the right freely to determine their political status and to pursue their economic, social and cultural development,

Recalling also the right of peoples to exercise, subject to the relevant provisions of both International Covenants on Human Rights, full and complete sovereignty over all their natural wealth and resources,

Mindful of the obligation of States under the Charter to promote universal respect for and observance of human rights and fundamental freedoms for all without distinction of any kind such as race, colour, sex, language, religion, political or other opinion, national or social origin, property, birth or other status,

Considering that the elimination of the massive and flagrant violations of the human rights of the peoples and individuals affected by situations such as those resulting from colonialism, neo-colonialism, apartheid, all forms of racism and racial discrimination, foreign domination and occupation, aggression and threats against national sovereignty, national unity and territorial integrity and threats of war would contribute to the establishment of circumstances propitious to the development of a great part of mankind,

Concerned at the existence of serious obstacles to development, as well as to the complete fulfilment of human beings and of peoples, constituted, *inter alia*, by the denial of civil, political, economic, social and cultural rights, and considering that all human rights and fundamental freedoms are indivisible and interdependent and that, in order to promote development, equal attention and urgent consideration should be given to the implementation, promotion and protection of civil, political, economic, social and cultural rights and that, accordingly, the promotion of, respect for and enjoyment of certain human rights and fundamental freedoms cannot justify the denial of other human rights and fundamental freedoms,

Considering that international peace and security are essential elements for the realization of the right to development,

Reaffirming that there is a close relationship between disarmament and development and that progress in the field of disarmament would considerably promote progress in the field of development and that resources released through disarmament measures should be devoted to the economic and social development and well-being of all peoples and, in particular, those of the developing countries,

Recognizing that the human person is the central subject of the development process and that development policy should therefore make the human being the main participant and beneficiary of development,

Recognizing that the creation of conditions favourable to the development of peoples and individuals is the primary responsibility of their States,

Aware that efforts at the international level to promote and protect human rights should be accompanied by efforts to establish a new international economic order,

Confirming that the right to development is an inalienable human right and that equality of opportunity for development is a prerogative both of nations and of individuals who make up nations,

Proclaims the following Declaration on the Right to Development:

Article 1

1. The right to development is an inalienable human right by virtue of which every human person and all peoples are entitled to participate in, contribute to, and enjoy economic, social, cultural and political development, in which all human rights and fundamental freedoms can be fully realized.

2. The human right to development also implies the full realization of the right of peoples to self-determination, which includes, subject to the relevant provisions of both International Covenants on Human Rights, the exercise of their inalienable right to full sovereignty over all their natural wealth and resources.

Article 2

1. The human person is the central subject of development and should be the active participant and beneficiary of the right to development.

2. All human beings have a responsibility for development, individually and collectively, taking into account the need for full respect for their human rights and fundamental freedoms as well as their duties to the community, which alone can ensure the free and

complete fulfilment of the human being, and they should therefore promote and protect an appropriate political, social and economic order for development.

3. States have the right and the duty to formulate appropriate national development policies that aim at the constant improvement of the well-being of the entire population and of all individuals, on the basis of their active, free and meaningful participation in development and in the fair distribution of the benefits resulting therefrom.

Article 3

1. States have the primary responsibility for the creation of national and international conditions favourable to the realization of the right to development.

2. The realization of the right to development requires full respect for the principles of international law concerning friendly relations and co-operation among States in accordance with the Charter of the United Nations.

3. States have the duty to co-operate with each other in ensuring development and eliminating obstacles to development. States should realize their rights and fulfil their duties in such a manner as to promote a new international economic order based on sovereign equality, interdependence, mutual interest and co-operation among all States, as well as to encourage the observance and realization of human rights.

Article 4

1. States have the duty to take steps, individually and collectively, to formulate international development policies with a view to facilitating the full realization of the right to development.

2. Sustained action is required to promote more rapid development of developing countries. As a complement to the efforts of developing countries, effective international co-operation is essential in providing these countries with appropriate means and facilities to foster their comprehensive development.

Article 5

States shall take resolute steps to eliminate the massive and flagrant violations of the human rights of peoples and human beings affected by situations such as those resulting from apartheid, all forms of racism and racial discrimination, colonialism, foreign domination and occupation, aggression, foreign interference and threats against national sovereignty, national unity and territorial integrity, threats of war and refusal to recognize the fundamental right of peoples to self-determination.

Article 6

1. All States should co-operate with a view to promoting, encouraging and strengthening universal respect for and observance of all human rights and fundamental freedoms for all without any distinction as to race, sex, language or religion.

2. All human rights and fundamental freedoms are indivisible and interdependent; equal attention and urgent consideration should be given to the implementation, promotion and protection of civil, political, economic, social and cultural rights.

3. States should take steps to eliminate obstacles to development resulting from failure to observe civil and political rights, as well as economic social and cultural rights.

Article 7

All States should promote the establishment, maintenance and strengthening of international peace and security and, to that end, should do their utmost to achieve general and complete disarmament under effective international control, as well as to ensure that the resources released by effective disarmament measures are used for comprehensive development, in particular that of the developing countries.

Article 8

1. States should undertake, at the national level, all necessary measures for the realization of the right to development and shall ensure, *inter alia*, equality of opportunity for all in their access to basic resources, education, health services, food, housing, employment and the fair distribution of income. Effective measures should be undertaken to ensure that women have an active role in the development process. Appropriate economic and social reforms should be carried out with a view to eradicating all social injustices.

2. States should encourage popular participation in all spheres as an important factor in development and in the full realization of all human rights.

Article 9

1. All the aspects of the right to development set forth in the present Declaration are indivisible and interdependent and each of them should be considered in the context of the whole.

2. Nothing in the present Declaration shall be construed as being contrary to the purposes and principles of the United Nations, or as implying that any State, group or person has a right to engage in any activity or to perform any act aimed at the violation of the rights set forth in the Universal Declaration of Human Rights and in the International Covenants on Human Rights.

Article 10

Steps should be taken to ensure the full exercise and progressive enhancement of the right to development, including the formulation, adoption and implementation of policy, legislative and other measures at the national and international levels.

18. BODY OF PRINCIPLES FOR THE PROTECTION OF ALL PERSONS UNDER ANY FORM OF DETENTION OR IMPRISONMENT, 1988

These principles are annexed to General Assembly Resolution 43/173, adopted without a vote on 9 December 1988.

Further reading

CASSELL, D., 'Pretrial and Preventive Detention of Suspected Terrorists: Options and Constraints under International Law', (2008) 98 *Journal of Criminal Law and Criminology* 811.

GENSER, J. M. AND WINTERKORN-MEIKLE, M. K., 'The Intersection of Politics and International Law: The United Nations Working Group on Arbitrary Detention in Theory and Practice', (2007–2008) 39 *Columbia Human Rights Law Review* 687.

RODLEY, N. S. and POLLARD, M., *The Treatment of Prisoners under International Law*, Oxford: Clarendon Press, 3rd edn., 2009.

TEXT

The General Assembly,

Recalling its resolution 35/177 of 15 December 1980, in which it referred the task of elaborating the draft Body of Principles for the Protection of All Persons under Any Form of Detention or Imprisonment to the Sixth Committee and decided to establish an open-ended working group for that purpose,

    Taking note of the report of the Working Group on the Draft Body of Principles for the Protection of All Persons under Any Form of Detention or Imprisonment, which met during the forty-third session of the General Assembly and completed the elaboration of the draft Body of Principles,

    Considering that the Working Group decided to submit the text of the draft Body of Principles to the Sixth Committee for its consideration and adoption,

    Convinced that the adoption of the draft Body of Principles would make an important contribution to the protection of human rights,

    Considering the need to ensure the wide dissemination of the text of the Body of Principles,

1. *Approves* the Body of Principles for the Protection of All Persons under Any Form of Detention or Imprisonment, the text of which is annexed to the present resolution;

2. *Expresses* its appreciation to the Working Group on the Draft Body of Principles for the Protection of All Persons under Any Form of Detention or Imprisonment for its important contribution to the elaboration of the Body of Principles;

3. *Requests* the Secretary-General to inform the States Members of the United Nations or members of specialized agencies of the adoption of the Body of Principles;

4. *Urges* that every effort be made so that the Body of Principles becomes generally known and respected.

ANNEX
BODY OF PRINCIPLES FOR THE PROTECTION OF ALL PERSONS UNDER ANY FORM OF DETENTION OR IMPRISONMENT

Scope of the Body of Principles

These principles apply for the protection of all persons under any form of detention or imprisonment.

Use of terms

For the purposes of the Body of Principles:

    (a) 'Arrest' means the act of apprehending a person for the alleged commission of an offence or by the action of an authority;

    (b) 'Detained person' means any person deprived of personal liberty except as a result of conviction for an offence;

    (c) 'Imprisoned person' means any person deprived of personal liberty as a result of conviction for an offence;

    (d) 'Detention' means the condition of detained persons as defined above;

    (e) 'Imprisonment' means the condition of imprisoned persons as defined above;

    (f) The words 'a judicial or other authority' mean a judicial or other authority under the law whose status and tenure should afford the strongest possible guarantees of competence, impartiality and independence.

Principle 1

All persons under any form of detention or imprisonment shall be treated in a humane manner and with respect for the inherent dignity of the human person.

Principle 2

Arrest, detention or imprisonment shall only be carried out strictly in accordance with the provisions of the law and by competent officials or persons authorized for that purpose.

Principle 3

There shall be no restriction upon or derogation from any of the human rights of persons under any form of detention or imprisonment recognized or existing in any State pursuant to law, conventions, regulations or custom on the pretext that this Body of Principles does not recognize such rights or that it recognizes them to a lesser extent.

Principle 4

Any form of detention or imprisonment and all measures affecting the human rights of a person under any form of detention or imprisonment shall be ordered by, or be subject to the effective control of, a judicial or other authority.

Principle 5

1. These principles shall be applied to all persons within the territory of any given State, without distinction of any kind, such as race, colour, sex, language, religion or religious belief, political or other opinion, national, ethnic or social origin, property, birth or other status.

2. Measures applied under the law and designed solely to protect the rights and special status of women, especially pregnant women and nursing mothers, children and juveniles, aged, sick or handicapped persons shall not be deemed to be discriminatory. The need for, and the application of, such measures shall always be subject to review by a judicial or other authority.

Principle 6

No person under any form of detention or imprisonment shall be subjected to torture or to cruel, inhuman or degrading treatment or punishment.* No circumstance whatever may be invoked as a justification for torture or other cruel, inhuman or degrading treatment or punishment.

Principle 7

1. States should prohibit by law any act contrary to the rights and duties contained in these principles, make any such act subject to appropriate sanctions and conduct impartial investigations upon complaints.

2. Officials who have reason to believe that a violation of this Body of Principles has occurred or is about to occur shall report the matter to their superior authorities and, where necessary, to other appropriate authorities or organs vested with reviewing or remedial powers.

3. Any other person who has ground to believe that a violation of this Body of Principles has occurred or is about to occur shall have the right to report the matter to the superiors of the officials involved as well as to other appropriate authorities or organs vested with reviewing or remedial powers.

Principle 8

Persons in detention shall be subject to treatment appropriate to their unconvicted status. Accordingly, they shall, whenever possible, be kept separate from imprisoned persons.

Principle 9

The authorities which arrest a person, keep him under detention or investigate the case shall exercise only the powers granted to them under the law and the exercise of these powers shall be subject to recourse to a judicial or other authority.

Principle 10

Anyone who is arrested shall be informed at the time of his arrest of the reason for his arrest and shall be promptly informed of any charges against him.

Principle 11

1. A person shall not be kept in detention without being given an effective opportunity to be heard promptly by a judicial or other authority. A detained person shall have the right to defend himself or to be assisted by counsel as prescribed by law.

---

* The term 'cruel, inhuman or degrading treatment or punishment' should be interpreted so as to extend the widest possible protection against abuses, whether physical or mental, including the holding of a detained or imprisoned person in conditions which deprive him, temporarily or permanently, of the use of any of his natural senses, such as sight or hearing, or of his awareness of place and the passing of time.

2. A detained person and his counsel, if any, shall receive prompt and full communication of any order of detention, together with the reasons therefor.

3. A judicial or other authority shall be empowered to review as appropriate the continuance of detention.

Principle 12

1. There shall be duly recorded:

  (a) The reasons for the arrest;
  (b) The time of the arrest and the taking of the arrested person to a place of custody as well as that of his first appearance before a judicial or other authority;
  (c) The identity of the law enforcement officials concerned;
  (d) Precise information concerning the place of custody.

2. Such records shall be communicated to the detained person, or his counsel, if any, in the form prescribed by law.

Principle 13

Any person shall, at the moment of arrest and at the commencement of detention or imprisonment, or promptly thereafter, be provided by the authority responsible for his arrest, detention or imprisonment, respectively, with information on and an explanation of his rights and how to avail himself of such rights.

Principle 14

A person who does not adequately understand or speak the language used by the authorities responsible for his arrest, detention or imprisonment is entitled to receive promptly in a language which he understands the information referred to in principle 10, principle 11, paragraph 2, principle 12, paragraph 1, and principle 13 and to have the assistance, free of charge, if necessary, of an interpreter in connection with legal proceedings subsequent to his arrest.

Principle 15

Notwithstanding the exceptions contained in principle 16, paragraph 4, and principle 18, paragraph 3, communication of the detained or imprisoned person with the outside world, and in particular his family or counsel, shall not be denied for more than a matter of days.

Principle 16

1. Promptly after arrest and after each transfer from one place of detention or imprisonment to another, a detained or imprisoned person shall be entitled to notify or to require the competent authority to notify members of his family or other appropriate persons of his choice of his arrest, detention or imprisonment or of the transfer and of the place where he is kept in custody.

2. If a detained or imprisoned person is a foreigner, he shall also be promptly informed of his right to communicate by appropriate means with a consular post or the diplomatic mission of the State of which he is a national or which is otherwise entitled to receive such communication in accordance with international law or with the representative

of the competent international organization, if he is a refugee or is otherwise under the protection of an intergovernmental organization.

3. If a detained or imprisoned person is a juvenile or is incapable of understanding his entitlement, the competent authority shall on its own initiative undertake the notification referred to in the present principle. Special attention shall be given to notifying parents or guardians.

4. Any notification referred to in the present principle shall be made or permitted to be made without delay. The competent authority may however delay a notification for a reasonable period where exceptional needs of the investigation so require.

Principle 17

1. A detained person shall be entitled to have the assistance of a legal counsel. He shall be informed of his right by the competent authority promptly after arrest and shall be provided with reasonable facilities for exercising it.

2. If a detained person does not have a legal counsel of his own choice, he shall be entitled to have a legal counsel assigned to him by a judicial or other authority in all cases where the interests of justice so require and without payment by him if he does not have sufficient means to pay.

Principle 18

1. A detained or imprisoned person shall be entitled to communicate and consult with his legal counsel.

2. A detained or imprisoned person shall be allowed adequate time and facilities for consultations with his legal counsel.

3. The right of a detained or imprisoned person to be visited by and to consult and communicate, without delay or censorship and in full confidentiality, with his legal counsel may not be suspended or restricted save in exceptional circumstances, to be specified by law or lawful regulations, when it is considered indispensable by a judicial or other authority in order to maintain security and good order.

4. Interviews between a detained or imprisoned person and his legal counsel may be within sight, but not within the hearing, of a law enforcement official.

5. Communications between a detained or imprisoned person and his legal counsel mentioned in the present principle shall be inadmissible as evidence against the detained or imprisoned person unless they are connected with a continuing or contemplated crime.

Principle 19

A detained or imprisoned person shall have the right to be visited by and to correspond with, in particular, members of his family and shall be given adequate opportunity to communicate with the outside world, subject to reasonable conditions and restrictions as specified by law or lawful regulations.

Principle 20

If a detained or imprisoned person so requests, he shall if possible be kept in a place of detention or imprisonment reasonably near his usual place of residence.

Principle 21

1. It shall be prohibited to take undue advantage of the situation of a detained or imprisoned person for the purpose of compelling him to confess, to incriminate himself otherwise or to testify against any other person.

2. No detained person while being interrogated shall be subject to violence, threats or methods of interrogation which impair his capacity of decision or his judgement.

Principle 22

No detained or imprisoned person shall, even with his consent, be subjected to any medical or scientific experimentation which may be detrimental to his health.

Principle 23

1. The duration of any interrogation of a detained or imprisoned person and of the intervals between interrogations as well as the identity of the officials who conducted the interrogations and other persons present shall be recorded and certified in such form as may be prescribed by law.

2. A detained or imprisoned person, or his counsel when provided by law, shall have access to the information described in paragraph 1 of the present principle.

Principle 24

A proper medical examination shall be offered to a detained or imprisoned person as promptly as possible after his admission to the place of detention or imprisonment, and thereafter medical care and treatment shall be provided whenever necessary. This care and treatment shall be provided free of charge.

Principle 25

A detained or imprisoned person or his counsel shall, subject only to reasonable conditions to ensure security and good order in the place of detention or imprisonment, have the right to request or petition a judicial or other authority for a second medical examination or opinion.

Principle 26

The fact that a detained or imprisoned person underwent a medical examination, the name of the physician and the results of such an examination shall be duly recorded. Access to such records shall be ensured. Modalities therefor shall be in accordance with relevant rules of domestic law.

Principle 27

Non-compliance with these principles in obtaining evidence shall be taken into account in determining the admissibility of such evidence against a detained or imprisoned person.

Principle 28

A detained or imprisoned person shall have the right to obtain within the limits of available resources, if from public sources, reasonable quantities of educational, cultural and informational material, subject to reasonable conditions to ensure security and good order in the place of detention or imprisonment.

Principle 29

1. In order to supervise the strict observance of relevant laws and regulations, places of detention shall be visited regularly by qualified and experienced persons appointed by, and responsible to, a competent authority distinct from the authority directly in charge of the administration of the place of detention or imprisonment.

2. A detained or imprisoned person shall have the right to communicate freely and in full confidentiality with the persons who visit the places of detention or imprisonment in accordance with paragraph 1 of the present principle, subject to reasonable conditions to ensure security and good order in such places.

Principle 30

1. The types of conduct of the detained or imprisoned person that constitute disciplinary offences during detention or imprisonment, the description and duration of disciplinary punishment that may be inflicted and the authorities competent to impose such punishment shall be specified by law or lawful regulations and duly published.

2. A detained or imprisoned person shall have the right to be heard before disciplinary action is taken. He shall have the right to bring such action to higher authorities for review.

Principle 31

The appropriate authorities shall endeavour to ensure, according to domestic law, assistance when needed to dependent and, in particular, minor members of the families of detained or imprisoned persons and shall devote a particular measure of care to the appropriate custody of children left without supervision.

Principle 32

1. A detained person or his counsel shall be entitled at any time to take proceedings according to domestic law before a judicial or other authority to challenge the lawfulness of his detention in order to obtain his release without delay, if it is unlawful.

2. The proceedings referred to in paragraph 1 of the present principle shall be simple and expeditious and at no cost for detained persons without adequate means. The detaining authority shall produce without unreasonable delay the detained person before the reviewing authority.

Principle 33

1. A detained or imprisoned person or his counsel shall have the right to make a request or complaint regarding his treatment, in particular in case of torture or other cruel, inhuman or degrading treatment, to the authorities responsible for the administration of the place of detention and to higher authorities and, when necessary, to appropriate authorities vested with reviewing or remedial powers.

2. In those cases where neither the detained or imprisoned person nor his counsel has the possibility to exercise his rights under paragraph 1 of the present principle, a member of the family of the detained or imprisoned person or any other person who has knowledge of the case may exercise such rights.

3. Confidentiality concerning the request or complaint shall be maintained if so requested by the complainant.

4. Every request or complaint shall be promptly dealt with and replied to without undue delay. If the request or complaint is rejected or, in case of inordinate delay, the complainant shall be entitled to bring it before a judicial or other authority. Neither the detained or imprisoned person nor any complainant under paragraph 1 of the present principle shall suffer prejudice for making a request or complaint.

Principle 34

Whenever the death or disappearance of a detained or imprisoned person occurs during his detention or imprisonment, an inquiry into the cause of death or disappearance shall be held by a judicial or other authority, either on its own motion or at the instance of a member of the family of such a person or any person who has knowledge of the case. When circumstances so warrant, such an inquiry shall be held on the same procedural basis whenever the death or disappearance occurs shortly after the termination of the detention or imprisonment. The findings of such inquiry or a report thereon shall be made available upon request, unless doing so would jeopardize an ongoing criminal investigation.

Principle 35

1. Damage incurred because of acts or omissions by a public official contrary to the rights contained in these principles shall be compensated according to the applicable rules on liability provided by domestic law.

2. Information required to be recorded under these principles shall be available in accordance with procedures provided by domestic law for use in claiming compensation under the present principle.

Principle 36

1. A detained person suspected of or charged with a criminal offence shall be presumed innocent and shall be treated as such until proved guilty according to law in a public trial at which he has had all the guarantees necessary for his defence.

2. The arrest or detention of such a person pending investigation and trial shall be carried out only for the purposes of the administration of justice on grounds and under conditions and procedures specified by law. The imposition of restrictions upon such a person which are not strictly required for the purpose of the detention or to prevent hindrance to the process of investigation or the administration of justice, or for the maintenance of security and good order in the place of detention shall be forbidden.

Principle 37

A person detained on a criminal charge shall be brought before a judicial or other authority provided by law promptly after his arrest. Such authority shall decide without delay upon the lawfulness and necessity of detention. No person may be kept under detention pending investigation or trial except upon the written order of such an authority. A detained person shall, when brought before such an authority, have the right to make a statement on the treatment received by him while in custody.

Principle 38

A person detained on a criminal charge shall be entitled to trial within a reasonable time or to release pending trial.

Principle 39

Except in special cases provided for by law, a person detained on a criminal charge shall be entitled, unless a judicial or other authority decides otherwise in the interest of the administration of justice, to release pending trial subject to the conditions that may be imposed in accordance with the law. Such authority shall keep the necessity of detention under review.

General clause

Nothing in this Body of Principles shall be construed as restricting or derogating from any right defined in the International Covenant on Civil and Political Rights.

19. BASIC PRINCIPLES FOR THE TREATMENT OF PRISONERS, 1990

These principles are annexed to General Assembly Resolution 45/111, adopted without a vote on 14 December 1990.

Further reading

RODLEY, N. S. and POLLARD, M., *The Treatment of Prisoners under International Law*, Oxford: Clarendon Press, 3rd edn., 2009.
UNITED NATIONS OFFICE ON DRUG AND CRIME, *Handbook for Prison Managers and Policymakers on Women and Imprisonment*, New York: United Nations, 2008.

TEXT

The General Assembly,

Bearing in mind the long-standing concern of the United Nations for the humanization of criminal justice and the protection of human rights,

Bearing in mind also that sound policies of crime prevention and control are essential to viable planning for economic and social development,

Recognizing that the Standard Minimum Rules for the Treatment of Prisoners, adopted by the First United Nations Congress on the Prevention of Crime and the Treatment of Offenders, are of great value and influence in the development of penal policy and practice,

Considering the concern of previous United Nations congresses on the prevention of crime and the treatment of offenders, regarding the obstacles of various kinds that prevent the full implementation of the Standard Minimum Rules,

Believing that the full implementation of the Standard Minimum Rules would be facilitated by the articulation of the basic principles underlying them,

Recalling resolution 10 on the status of prisoners and resolution 17 on the human rights of prisoners, adopted by the Seventh United Nations Congress on the Prevention of Crime and the Treatment of Offenders,

Recalling also the statement submitted at the tenth session of the Committee on Crime Prevention and Control by Caritas Internationalis, the Commission of the Churches on International Affairs of the World Council of Churches, the International Association of Educators for World Peace, the International Council for Adult Education, the International Federation of Human Rights, the International Prisoners' Aid Association, the International Union of Students, the World Alliance of Young Men's Christian Associations and the World Council of Indigenous Peoples, which are non-governmental organizations in consultative status with the Economic and Social Council, category II,

Recalling further the relevant recommendations contained in the report of the Interregional Preparatory Meeting for the Eighth United Nations Congress on the Prevention of Crime and the Treatment of Offenders on topic II, 'Criminal justice policies in relation to problems of imprisonment, other penal sanctions and alternative measures',

Aware that the Eighth Congress coincided with International Literacy Year, proclaimed by the General Assembly in its resolution 42/104 of 7 December 1987,

Desiring to reflect the perspective noted by the Seventh Congress, namely, that the function of the criminal justice system is to contribute to safeguarding the basic values and norms of society,

Recognizing the usefulness of drafting a declaration on the human rights of prisoners,

Affirms the Basic Principles for the Treatment of Prisoners, contained in the annex to the present resolution, and requests the Secretary-General to bring it to the attention of Member States.

ANNEX
BASIC PRINCIPLES FOR THE TREATMENT OF PRISONERS

1. All prisoners shall be treated with the respect due to their inherent dignity and value as human beings.

2. There shall be no discrimination on the grounds of race, colour, sex, language, religion, political or other opinion, national or social origin, property, birth or other status.

3. It is, however, desirable to respect the religious beliefs and cultural precepts of the group to which prisoners belong, whenever local conditions so require.

4. The responsibility of prisons for the custody of prisoners and for the protection of society against crime shall be discharged in keeping with a State's other social objectives and its fundamental responsibilities for promoting the well-being and development of all members of society.

5. Except for those limitations that are demonstrably necessitated by the fact of incarceration, all prisoners shall retain the human rights and fundamental freedoms set out in the Universal Declaration of Human Rights, and, where the State concerned is a party, the International Covenant on Economic, Social and Cultural Rights, and the International Covenant on Civil and Political Rights and the Optional Protocol thereto, as well as such other rights as are set out in other United Nations covenants.

6. All prisoners shall have the right to take part in cultural activities and education aimed at the full development of the human personality.

7. Efforts addressed to the abolition of solitary confinement as a punishment, or to the restriction of its use, should be undertaken and encouraged.

8. Conditions shall be created enabling prisoners to undertake meaningful remunerated employment which will facilitate their reintegration into the country's labour market and permit them to contribute to their own financial support and to that of their families.

9. Prisoners shall have access to the health services available in the country without discrimination on the grounds of their legal situation.

10. With the participation and help of the community and social institution, and with due regard to the interests of victims, favourable conditions shall be created for the reintegration of the ex-prisoner into society under the best possible conditions.

11. The above Principles shall be applied impartially.

20. UNITED NATIONS RULES FOR THE PROTECTION OF JUVENILES DEPRIVED OF THEIR LIBERTY, 1990

Annexed to General Assembly Resolution 45/113, adopted without a vote, 14 December 1990.

See also, the UN Standard Minimum Rules for the Administration of Juvenile Justice, 1985 (the 'Beijing Rules'), adopted by General Assembly Resolution 40/33, 29 November 1985; and the UN Guidelines for the Prevention of Juvenile Delinquency, 1990 (the 'Riyadh Guidelines'), adopted by General Assembly Resolution 45/112 of 14 December 1990.

Further reading

JENSEN, E. L. and JEPSEN, J., eds., *Juvenile Law Violators, Human Rights, and the Development of New Juvenile Justice Systems*, Oxford: Hart Publishing, 2006.
JUNGER-TAS, J. and DECKER, S. H., *International Handbook of Juvenile Justice*, New York, NY: Springer, 2008.

TEXT

I. FUNDAMENTAL PERSPECTIVES

1. The juvenile justice system should uphold the rights and safety and promote the physical and mental well-being of juveniles. Imprisonment should be used as a last resort.

2. Juveniles should only be deprived of their liberty in accordance with the principles and procedures set forth in these Rules and in the United Nations Standard Minimum Rules for the Administration of Juvenile Justice (The Beijing Rules). Deprivation of the liberty of a juvenile should be a disposition of last resort and for the minimum necessary period and should be limited to exceptional cases. The length of the sanction should be determined by the judicial authority, without precluding the possibility of his or her early release.

3. The Rules are intended to establish minimum standards accepted by the United Nations for the protection of juveniles deprived of their liberty in all forms, consistent with human rights and fundamental freedoms, and with a view to counteracting the detrimental effects of all types of detention and to fostering integration in society.

4. The Rules should be applied impartially, without discrimination of any kind as to race, colour, sex, age, language, religion, nationality, political or other opinion, cultural beliefs or practices, property, birth or family status, ethnic or social origin, and disability. The religious and cultural beliefs, practices and moral concepts of the juvenile should be respected.

5. The Rules are designed to serve as convenient standards of reference and to provide encouragement and guidance to professionals involved in the management of the juvenile justice system.

6. The Rules should be made readily available to juvenile justice personnel in their national languages. Juveniles who are not fluent in the language spoken by the personnel of the detention facility should have the right to the services of an interpreter free of charge whenever necessary, in particular during medical examinations and disciplinary proceedings.

7. Where appropriate, States should incorporate the Rules into their legislation or amend it accordingly and provide effective remedies for their breach, including compensation when injuries are inflicted on juveniles. States should also monitor the application of the Rules.

8. The competent authorities should constantly seek to increase the awareness of the public that the care of detained juveniles and preparation for their return to society is a social service of great importance, and to this end active steps should be taken to foster open contacts between the juveniles and the local community.

9. Nothing in the Rules should be interpreted as precluding the application of the relevant United Nations and human rights instruments and standards, recognized by the international community, that are more conducive to ensuring the rights, care and protection of juveniles, children and all young persons.

10. In the event that the practical application of particular Rules contained in sections II to V, inclusive, presents any conflict with the Rules contained in the present section, compliance with the latter shall be regarded as the predominant requirement.

II. SCOPE AND APPLICATION OF THE RULES

11. For the purposes of the Rules, the following definitions should apply:

  (a) A juvenile is every person under the age of 18. The age limit below which it should not be permitted to deprive a child of his or her liberty should be determined by law;

  (b) The deprivation of liberty means any form of detention or imprisonment or the placement of a person in a public or private custodial setting, from which this person is not permitted to leave at will, by order of any judicial, administrative or other public authority.

12. The deprivation of liberty should be effected in conditions and circumstances which ensure respect for the human rights of juveniles. Juveniles detained in facilities should be guaranteed the benefit of meaningful activities and programmes which would serve to promote and sustain their health and self-respect, to foster their sense of responsibility and encourage those attitudes and skills that will assist them in developing their potential as members of society.

13. Juveniles deprived of their liberty shall not for any reason related to their status be denied the civil, economic, political, social or cultural rights to which they are entitled under national or international law, and which are compatible with the deprivation of liberty.

14. The protection of the individual rights of juveniles with special regard to the legality of the execution of the detention measures shall be ensured by the competent authority, while the objectives of social integration should be secured by regular inspections and other means of control carried out, according to international standards, national laws and regulations, by a duly constituted body authorized to visit the juveniles and not belonging to the detention facility.

15. The Rules apply to all types and forms of detention facilities in which juveniles are deprived of their liberty. Sections I, II, IV and V of the Rules apply to all detention facilities and institutional settings in which juveniles are detained, and section III applies specifically to juveniles under arrest or awaiting trial.

16. The Rules shall be implemented in the context of the economic, social and cultural conditions prevailing in each Member State.

III. JUVENILES UNDER ARREST OR AWAITING TRIAL

17. Juveniles who are detained under arrest or awaiting trial ('untried') are presumed innocent and shall be treated as such. Detention before trial shall be avoided to the extent possible and limited to exceptional circumstances. Therefore, all efforts shall be made to apply alternative measures. When preventive detention is nevertheless used, juvenile courts and investigative bodies shall give the highest priority to the most expeditious processing of such cases to ensure the shortest possible duration of detention. Untried detainees should be separated from convicted juveniles.

18. The conditions under which an untried juvenile is detained should be consistent with the rules set out below, with additional specific provisions as are necessary and appropriate, given the requirements of the presumption of innocence, the duration of the detention and the legal status and circumstances of the juvenile. These provisions would include, but not necessarily be restricted to, the following:

(a) Juveniles should have the right of legal counsel and be enabled to apply for free legal aid, where such aid is available, and to communicate regularly with their legal advisers. Privacy and confidentiality shall be ensured for such communications;

(b) Juveniles should be provided, where possible, with opportunities to pursue work, with remuneration, and continue education or training, but should not be required to do so. Work, education or training should not cause the continuation of the detention;

(c) Juveniles should receive and retain materials for their leisure and recreation as are compatible with the interests of the administration of justice.

IV. THE MANAGEMENT OF JUVENILE FACILITIES

A. Records

19. All reports, including legal records, medical records and records of disciplinary proceedings, and all other documents relating to the form, content and details of treatment, should be placed in a confidential individual file, which should be kept up to date, accessible only to authorized persons and classified in such a way as to be easily understood. Where possible, every juvenile should have the right to contest any fact or opinion contained in his or her file so as to permit rectification of inaccurate, unfounded or unfair statements. In order to exercise this right, there should be procedures that allow an appropriate third party to have access to and to consult the file on request. Upon release, the records of juveniles shall be sealed, and, at an appropriate time, expunged.

20. No juvenile should be received in any detention facility without a valid commitment order of a judicial, administrative or other public authority. The details of this order should be immediately entered in the register. No juvenile should be detained in any facility where there is no such register.

B. Admission, registration, movement and transfer

21. In every place where juveniles are detained, a complete and secure record of the following information should be kept concerning each juvenile received:

 (a) Information on the identity of the juvenile;

 (b) The fact of and reasons for commitment and the authority therefor;

 (c) The day and hour of admission, transfer and release;

 (d) Details of the notifications to parents and guardians on every admission, transfer or release of the juvenile in their care at the time of commitment;

 (e) Details of known physical and mental health problems, including drug and alcohol abuse.

22. The information on admission, place, transfer and release should be provided without delay to the parents and guardians or closest relative of the juvenile concerned.

23. As soon as possible after reception, full reports and relevant information on the personal situation and circumstances of each juvenile should be drawn up and submitted to the administration.

24. On admission, all juveniles shall be given a copy of the rules governing the detention facility and a written description of their rights and obligations in a language they can understand, together with the address of the authorities competent to receive complaints, as well as the address of public or private agencies and organizations which provide legal assistance. For those juveniles who are illiterate or who cannot understand the language in the written form, the information should be conveyed in a manner enabling full comprehension.

25. All juveniles should be helped to understand the regulations governing the internal organization of the facility, the goals and methodology of the care provided, the disciplinary requirements and procedures, other authorized methods of seeking information and of making complaints and all such other matters as are necessary to enable them to understand fully their rights and obligations during detention.

26. The transport of juveniles should be carried out at the expense of the administration in conveyances with adequate ventilation and light, in conditions that should in no way subject them to hardship or indignity. Juveniles should not be transferred from one facility to another arbitrarily.

C. Classification and placement

27. As soon as possible after the moment of admission, each juvenile should be interviewed, and a psychological and social report identifying any factors relevant to the specific type and level of care and programme required by the juvenile should be prepared. This report, together with the report prepared by a medical officer who has examined the juvenile upon admission, should be forwarded to the director for purposes of determining the most appropriate placement for the juvenile within the facility and the specific type and level of care and programme required and to be pursued. When special rehabilitative treatment is required, and the length of stay in the facility permits, trained personnel of the facility should prepare a written, individualized treatment plan specifying treatment objectives and time-frame and the means, stages and delays with which the objectives should be approached.

28. The detention of juveniles should only take place under conditions that take full account of their particular needs, status and special requirements according to their age, personality, sex and type of offence, as well as mental and physical health, and which ensure their protection from harmful influences and risk situations. The principal criterion for the separation of different categories of juveniles deprived of their liberty should be the provision of the type of care best suited to the particular needs of the individuals concerned and the protection of their physical, mental and moral integrity and well-being.

29. In all detention facilities juveniles should be separated from adults, unless they are members of the same family. Under controlled conditions, juveniles may be brought together with carefully selected adults as part of a special programme that has been shown to be beneficial for the juveniles concerned.

30. Open detention facilities for juveniles should be established. Open detention facilities are those with no or minimal security measures. The population in such detention facilities should be as small as possible. The number of juveniles detained in closed facilities should be small enough to enable individualized treatment. Detention facilities for juveniles should be decentralized and of such size as to facilitate access and contact between the juveniles and their families. Small-scale detention facilities should be established and integrated into the social, economic and cultural environment of the community.

D. Physical environment and accommodation

31. Juveniles deprived of their liberty have the right to facilities and services that meet all the requirements of health and human dignity.

32. The design of detention facilities for juveniles and the physical environment should be in keeping with the rehabilitative aim of residential treatment, with due regard to the need of the juvenile for privacy, sensory stimuli, opportunities for association with peers and participation in sports, physical exercise and leisure-time activities. The design and structure of juvenile detention facilities should be such as to minimize the risk of fire and to ensure safe evacuation from the premises. There should be an effective alarm system in case of fire, as well as formal and drilled procedures to ensure the safety of the juveniles. Detention facilities should not be located in areas where there are known health or other hazards or risks.

33. Sleeping accommodation should normally consist of small group dormitories or individual bedrooms, while bearing in mind local standards. During sleeping hours there should be regular, unobtrusive supervision of all sleeping areas, including individual rooms and group dormitories, in order to ensure the protection of each juvenile. Every juvenile should, in accordance with local or national standards, be provided with separate and sufficient bedding, which should be clean when issued, kept in good order and changed often enough to ensure cleanliness.

34. Sanitary installations should be so located and of a sufficient standard to enable every juvenile to comply, as required, with their physical needs in privacy and in a clean and decent manner.

35. The possession of personal effects is a basic element of the right to privacy and essential to the psychological well-being of the juvenile. The right of every juvenile to possess personal effects and to have adequate storage facilities for them should be fully recognized and respected. Personal effects that the juvenile does not choose to retain or that

are confiscated should be placed in safe custody. An inventory thereof should be signed by the juvenile. Steps should be taken to keep them in good condition. All such articles and money should be returned to the juvenile on release, except in so far as he or she has been authorized to spend money or send such property out of the facility. If a juvenile receives or is found in possession of any medicine, the medical officer should decide what use should be made of it.

36. To the extent possible juveniles should have the right to use their own clothing. Detention facilities should ensure that each juvenile has personal clothing suitable for the climate and adequate to ensure good health, and which should in no manner be degrading or humiliating. Juveniles removed from or leaving a facility for any purpose should be allowed to wear their own clothing.

37. Every detention facility shall ensure that every juvenile receives food that is suitably prepared and presented at normal meal times and of a quality and quantity to satisfy the standards of dietetics, hygiene and health and, as far as possible, religious and cultural requirements. Clean drinking water should be available to every juvenile at any time.

E. Education, vocational training and work

38. Every juvenile of compulsory school age has the right to education suited to his or her needs and abilities and designed to prepare him or her for return to society. Such education should be provided outside the detention facility in community schools wherever possible and, in any case, by qualified teachers through programmes integrated with the education system of the country so that, after release, juveniles may continue their education without difficulty. Special attention should be given by the administration of the detention facilities to the education of juveniles of foreign origin or with particular cultural or ethnic needs. Juveniles who are illiterate or have cognitive or learning difficulties should have the right to special education.

39. Juveniles above compulsory school age who wish to continue their education should be permitted and encouraged to do so, and every effort should be made to provide them with access to appropriate educational programmes.

40. Diplomas or educational certificates awarded to juveniles while in detention should not indicate in any way that the juvenile has been institutionalized.

41. Every detention facility should provide access to a library that is adequately stocked with both instructional and recreational books and periodicals suitable for the juveniles, who should be encouraged and enabled to make full use of it.

42. Every juvenile should have the right to receive vocational training in occupations likely to prepare him or her for future employment.

43. With due regard to proper vocational selection and to the requirements of institutional administration, juveniles should be able to choose the type of work they wish to perform.

44. All protective national and international standards applicable to child labour and young workers should apply to juveniles deprived of their liberty.

45. Wherever possible, juveniles should be provided with the opportunity to perform remunerated labour, if possible within the local community, as a complement to the vocational training provided in order to enhance the possibility of finding suitable employment when they return to their communities. The type of work should be such as to

provide appropriate training that will be of benefit to the juveniles following release. The organization and methods of work offered in detention facilities should resemble as closely as possible those of similar work in the community, so as to prepare juveniles for the conditions of normal occupational life.

46. Every juvenile who performs work should have the right to an equitable remuneration. The interests of the juveniles and of their vocational training should not be subordinated to the purpose of making a profit for the detention facility or a third party. Part of the earnings of a juvenile should normally be set aside to constitute a savings fund to be handed over to the juvenile on release. The juvenile should have the right to use the remainder of those earnings to purchase articles for his or her own use or to indemnify the victim injured by his or her offence or to send it to his or her family or other persons outside the detention facility.

F. Recreation

47. Every juvenile should have the right to a suitable amount of time for daily free exercise, in the open air whenever weather permits, during which time appropriate recreational and physical training should normally be provided. Adequate space, installations and equipment should be provided for these activities. Every juvenile should have additional time for daily leisure activities, part of which should be devoted, if the juvenile so wishes, to arts and crafts skill development. The detention facility should ensure that each juvenile is physically able to participate in the available programmes of physical education. Remedial physical education and therapy should be offered, under medical supervision, to juveniles needing it.

G. Religion

48. Every juvenile should be allowed to satisfy the needs of his or her religious and spiritual life, in particular by attending the services or meetings provided in the detention facility or by conducting his or her own services and having possession of the necessary books or items of religious observance and instruction of his or her denomination. If a detention facility contains a sufficient number of juveniles of a given religion, one or more qualified representatives of that religion should be appointed or approved and allowed to hold regular services and to pay pastoral visits in private to juveniles at their request. Every juvenile should have the right to receive visits from a qualified representative of any religion of his or her choice, as well as the right not to participate in religious services and freely to decline religious education, counselling or indoctrination.

H. Medical care

49. Every juvenile shall receive adequate medical care, both preventive and remedial, including dental, ophthalmological and mental health care, as well as pharmaceutical products and special diets as medically indicated. All such medical care should, where possible, be provided to detained juveniles through the appropriate health facilities and services of the community in which the detention facility is located, in order to prevent stigmatization of the juvenile and promote self-respect and integration into the community.

50. Every juvenile has a right to be examined by a physician immediately upon admission to a detention facility, for the purpose of recording any evidence of prior ill-treatment and identifying any physical or mental condition requiring medical attention.

51. The medical services provided to juveniles should seek to detect and should treat any physical or mental illness, substance abuse or other condition that may hinder the integration of the juvenile into society. Every detention facility for juveniles should have immediate access to adequate medical facilities and equipment appropriate to the number and requirements of its residents and staff trained in preventive health care and the handling of medical emergencies. Every juvenile who is ill, who complains of illness or who demonstrates symptoms of physical or mental difficulties, should be examined promptly by a medical officer.

52. Any medical officer who has reason to believe that the physical or mental health of a juvenile has been or will be injuriously affected by continued detention, a hunger strike or any condition of detention should report this fact immediately to the director of the detention facility in question and to the independent authority responsible for safeguarding the well-being of the juvenile.

53. A juvenile who is suffering from mental illness should be treated in a specialized institution under independent medical management. Steps should be taken, by arrangement with appropriate agencies, to ensure any necessary continuation of mental health care after release.

54. Juvenile detention facilities should adopt specialized drug abuse prevention and rehabilitation programmes administered by qualified personnel. These programmes should be adapted to the age, sex and other requirements of the juveniles concerned, and detoxification facilities and services staffed by trained personnel should be available to drug- or alcohol-dependent juveniles.

55. Medicines should be administered only for necessary treatment on medical grounds and, when possible, after having obtained the informed consent of the juvenile concerned. In particular, they must not be administered with a view to eliciting information or a confession, as a punishment or as a means of restraint. Juveniles shall never be testers in the experimental use of drugs and treatment. The administration of any drug should always be authorized and carried out by qualified medical personnel.

I. Notification of illness, injury and death

56. The family or guardian of a juvenile and any other person designated by the juvenile have the right to be informed of the state of health of the juvenile on request and in the event of any important changes in the health of the juvenile. The director of the detention facility should notify immediately the family or guardian of the juvenile concerned, or other designated person, in case of death, illness requiring transfer of the juvenile to an outside medical facility, or a condition requiring clinical care within the detention facility for more than 48 hours. Notification should also be given to the consular authorities of the State of which a foreign juvenile is a citizen.

57. Upon the death of a juvenile during the period of deprivation of liberty, the nearest relative should have the right to inspect the death certificate, see the body and determine the method of disposal of the body. Upon the death of a juvenile in detention, there should be an independent inquiry into the causes of death, the report of which should be made accessible to the nearest relative. This inquiry should also be made when the death of a juvenile occurs within six months from the date of his or her release from the detention facility and there is reason to believe that the death is related to the period of detention.

58. A juvenile should be informed at the earliest possible time of the death, serious illness or injury of any immediate family member and should be provided with the opportunity to attend the funeral of the deceased or go to the bedside of a critically ill relative.

J. Contacts with the wider community

59. Every means should be provided to ensure that juveniles have adequate communication with the outside world, which is an integral part of the right to fair and humane treatment and is essential to the preparation of juveniles for their return to society. Juveniles should be allowed to communicate with their families, friends and other persons or representatives of reputable outside organizations, to leave detention facilities for a visit to their home and family and to receive special permission to leave the detention facility for educational, vocational or other important reasons. Should the juvenile be serving a sentence, the time spent outside a detention facility should be counted as part of the period of sentence.

60. Every juvenile should have the right to receive regular and frequent visits, in principle once a week and not less than once a month, in circumstances that respect the need of the juvenile for privacy, contact and unrestricted communication with the family and the defence counsel.

61. Every juvenile should have the right to communicate in writing or by telephone at least twice a week with the person of his or her choice, unless legally restricted, and should be assisted as necessary in order effectively to enjoy this right. Every juvenile should have the right to receive correspondence.

62. Juveniles should have the opportunity to keep themselves informed regularly of the news by reading newspapers, periodicals and other publications, through access to radio and television programmes and motion pictures, and through the visits of the representatives of any lawful club or organization in which the juvenile is interested.

K. Limitations of physical restraint and the use of force

63. Recourse to instruments of restraint and to force for any purpose should be prohibited, except as set forth in rule 64 below.

64. Instruments of restraint and force can only be used in exceptional cases, where all other control methods have been exhausted and failed, and only as explicitly authorized and specified by law and regulation. They should not cause humiliation or degradation, and should be used restrictively and only for the shortest possible period of time. By order of the director of the administration, such instruments might be resorted to in order to prevent the juvenile from inflicting self-injury, injuries to others or serious destruction of property. In such instances, the director should at once consult medical and other relevant personnel and report to the higher administrative authority.

65. The carrying and use of weapons by personnel should be prohibited in any facility where juveniles are detained.

L. Disciplinary procedures

66. Any disciplinary measures and procedures should maintain the interest of safety and an ordered community life and should be consistent with the upholding of the inherent dignity of the juvenile and the fundamental objective of institutional care, namely, instilling a sense of justice, self-respect and respect for the basic rights of every person.

67. All disciplinary measures constituting cruel, inhuman or degrading treatment shall be strictly prohibited, including corporal punishment, placement in a dark cell, closed or solitary confinement or any other punishment that may compromise the physical or mental health of the juvenile concerned. The reduction of diet and the restriction or denial of contact with family members should be prohibited for any purpose. Labour should always be viewed as an educational tool and a means of promoting the self-respect of the juvenile in preparing him or her for return to the community and should not be imposed as a disciplinary sanction. No juvenile should be sanctioned more than once for the same disciplinary infraction. Collective sanctions should be prohibited.

68. Legislation or regulations adopted by the competent administrative authority should establish norms concerning the following, taking full account of the fundamental characteristics, needs and rights of juveniles:

(a) Conduct constituting a disciplinary offence;

(b) Type and duration of disciplinary sanctions that may be inflicted;

(c) The authority competent to impose such sanctions;

(d) The authority competent to consider appeals.

69. A report of misconduct should be presented promptly to the competent authority, which should decide on it without undue delay. The competent authority should conduct a thorough examination of the case.

70. No juvenile should be disciplinarily sanctioned except in strict accordance with the terms of the law and regulations in force. No juvenile should be sanctioned unless he or she has been informed of the alleged infraction in a manner appropriate to the full understanding of the juvenile, and given a proper opportunity of presenting his or her defence, including the right of appeal to a competent impartial authority. Complete records should be kept of all disciplinary proceedings.

71. No juveniles should be responsible for disciplinary functions except in the supervision of specified social, educational or sports activities or in self-government programmes.

M. Inspection and complaints

72. Qualified inspectors or an equivalent duly constituted authority not belonging to the administration of the facility should be empowered to conduct inspections on a regular basis and to undertake unannounced inspections on their own initiative, and should enjoy full guarantees of independence in the exercise of this function. Inspectors should have unrestricted access to all persons employed by or working in any facility where juveniles are or may be deprived of their liberty, to all juveniles and to all records of such facilities.

73. Qualified medical officers attached to the inspecting authority or the public health service should participate in the inspections, evaluating compliance with the rules concerning the physical environment, hygiene, accommodation, food, exercise and medical services, as well as any other aspect or conditions of institutional life that affect the physical and mental health of juveniles. Every juvenile should have the right to talk in confidence to any inspecting officer.

74. After completing the inspection, the inspector should be required to submit a report on the findings. The report should include an evaluation of the compliance of the detention facilities with the present rules and relevant provisions of national law, and recommendations regarding any steps considered necessary to ensure compliance with them.

Any facts discovered by an inspector that appear to indicate that a violation of legal pro-visions concerning the rights of juveniles or the operation of a juvenile detention facility has occurred should be communicated to the competent authorities for investigation and prosecution.

75. Every juvenile should have the opportunity of making requests or complaints to the director of the detention facility and to his or her authorized representative.

76. Every juvenile should have the right to make a request or complaint, without cen-sorship as to substance, to the central administration, the judicial authority or other proper authorities through approved channels, and to be informed of the response with-out delay.

77. Efforts should be made to establish an independent office (ombudsman) to receive and investigate complaints made by juveniles deprived of their liberty and to assist in the achievement of equitable settlements.

78. Every juvenile should have the right to request assistance from family members, legal counsellors, humanitarian groups or others where possible, in order to make a com-plaint. Illiterate juveniles should be provided with assistance should they need to use the services of public or private agencies and organizations which provide legal counsel or which are competent to receive complaints.

N. Return to the community

79. All juveniles should benefit from arrangements designed to assist them in returning to society, family life, education or employment after release. Procedures, including early release, and special courses should be devised to this end.

80. Competent authorities should provide or ensure services to assist juveniles in re-es-tablishing themselves in society and to lessen prejudice against such juveniles. These services should ensure, to the extent possible, that the juvenile is provided with suitable residence, employment, clothing, and sufficient means to maintain himself or herself upon release in order to facilitate successful reintegration. The representatives of agen-cies providing such services should be consulted and should have access to juveniles while detained, with a view to assisting them in their return to the community.

V. PERSONNEL

81. Personnel should be qualified and include a sufficient number of specialists such as educators, vocational instructors, counsellors, social workers, psychiatrists and psycholo-gists. These and other specialist staff should normally be employed on a permanent basis. This should not preclude part-time or volunteer workers when the level of support and training they can provide is appropriate and beneficial. Detention facilities should make use of all remedial, educational, moral, spiritual, and other resources and forms of assist-ance that are appropriate and available in the community, according to the individual needs and problems of detained juveniles.

82. The administration should provide for the careful selection and recruitment of every grade and type of personnel, since the proper management of detention facilities depends on their integrity, humanity, ability and professional capacity to deal with juveniles, as well as personal suitability for the work.

83. To secure the foregoing ends, personnel should be appointed as professional officers with adequate remuneration to attract and retain suitable women and men. The personnel of juvenile detention facilities should be continually encouraged to fulfil their duties and obligations in a humane, committed, professional, fair and efficient manner, to conduct themselves at all times in such a way as to deserve and gain the respect of the juveniles, and to provide juveniles with a positive role model and perspective.

84. The administration should introduce forms of organization and management that facilitate communications between different categories of staff in each detention facility so as to enhance cooperation between the various services engaged in the care of juveniles, as well as between staff and the administration, with a view to ensuring that staff directly in contact with juveniles are able to function in conditions favourable to the efficient fulfilment of their duties.

85. The personnel should receive such training as will enable them to carry out their responsibilities effectively, in particular training in child psychology, child welfare and international standards and norms of human rights and the rights of the child, including the present Rules. The personnel should maintain and improve their knowledge and professional capacity by attending courses of in-service training, to be organized at suitable intervals throughout their career.

86. The director of a facility should be adequately qualified for his or her task, with administrative ability and suitable training and experience, and should carry out his or her duties on a full-time basis.

87. In the performance of their duties, personnel of detention facilities should respect and protect the human dignity and fundamental human rights of all juveniles, in particular, as follows:

  (a) No member of the detention facility or institutional personnel may inflict, instigate or tolerate any act of torture or any form of harsh, cruel, inhuman or degrading treatment, punishment, correction or discipline under any pretext or circumstance whatsoever;

  (b) All personnel should rigorously oppose and combat any act of corruption, reporting it without delay to the competent authorities;

  (c) All personnel should respect the present Rules. Personnel who have reason to believe that a serious violation of the present Rules has occurred or is about to occur should report the matter to their superior authorities or organs vested with reviewing or remedial power;

  (d) All personnel should ensure the full protection of the physical and mental health of juveniles, including protection from physical, sexual and emotional abuse and exploitation, and should take immediate action to secure medical attention whenever required;

  (e) All personnel should respect the right of the juvenile to privacy, and, in particular, should safeguard all confidential matters concerning juveniles or their families learned as a result of their professional capacity;

  (f) All personnel should seek to minimize any differences between life inside and outside the detention facility which tend to lessen due respect for the dignity of juveniles as human beings.

21. UNITED NATIONS PRINCIPLES FOR OLDER PERSONS, 1991

Annexed to General Assembly resolution 46/91, 'Implementation of the International Plan of Action on Ageing and related activities', adopted without a vote, 16 December 1991. See also, the 'Madrid political declaration and international plan of action on ageing', adopted by consensus at the Second World Assembly on Ageing in 2002, and endorsed in General Assembly Resolution 57/167, 18 December 2002.

Further reading

TANG, KWONG LEUNG, 'Taking Older People's Rights Seriously: The Role of International Law', (2008) 20 *Journal of Aging and Social Policy* 99.
—— and LEE, JIK-JOEN, 'Global Social Justice for Older People: The Case for an International Convention on the Rights of Older People', (2005) *British Journal of Social Work* 1.

TEXT

UNITED NATIONS PRINCIPLES FOR OLDER PERSONS: TO ADD LIFE TO THE YEARS THAT HAVE BEEN ADDED TO LIFE

The General Assembly,

Appreciating the contribution that older persons make to their societies,

Recognizing that, in the Charter of the United Nations, the peoples of the United Nations declare, *inter alia*, their determination to reaffirm faith in fundamental human rights, in the dignity and worth of the human person, in the equal rights of men and women and of nations large and small and to promote social progress and better standards of life in larger freedom,

Noting the elaboration of those rights in the Universal Declaration of Human Rights, the International Covenant on Economic, Social and Cultural Rights and the International Covenant on Civil and Political Rights and other declarations to ensure the application of universal standards to particular groups,

In pursuance of the International Plan of Action on Ageing, adopted by the World Assembly on Ageing and endorsed by the General Assembly in its resolution 37/51 of 3 December 1982,

Appreciating the tremendous diversity in the situation of older persons, not only between countries but within countries and between individuals, which requires a variety of policy responses,

Aware that in all countries, individuals are reaching an advanced age in greater numbers and in better health than ever before,

Aware of the scientific research disproving many stereotypes about inevitable and irreversible declines with age,

Convinced that in a world characterized by an increasing number and proportion of older persons, opportunities must be provided for willing and capable older persons to participate in and contribute to the ongoing activities of society,

Mindful that the strains on family life in both developed and developing countries require support for those providing care to frail older persons,

Bearing in mind the standards already set by the International Plan of Action on Ageing and the conventions, recommendations and resolutions of the International Labour Organization, the World Health Organization and other United Nations entities,

Encourages Governments to incorporate the following principles into their national programmes whenever possible:

Independence

1. Older persons should have access to adequate food, water, shelter, clothing and health care through the provision of income, family and community support and self-help.

2. Older persons should have the opportunity to work or to have access to other income-generating opportunities.

3. Older persons should be able to participate in determining when and at what pace withdrawal from the labour force takes place.

4. Older persons should have access to appropriate educational and training programmes.

5. Older persons should be able to live in environments that are safe and adaptable to personal preferences and changing capacities.

Participation

7. Older persons should remain integrated in society, participate actively in the formulation and implementation of policies that directly affect their well-being and share their knowledge and skills with younger generations.

8. Older persons should be able to seek and develop opportunities for service to the community and to serve as volunteers in positions appropriate to their interests and capabilities.

9. Older persons should be able to form movements or associations of older persons.

Care

10. Older persons should benefit from family and community care and protection in accordance with each society's system of cultural values.

11. Older persons should have access to health care to help them to maintain or regain the optimum level of physical, mental and emotional well-being and to prevent or delay the onset of illness.

12. Older persons should have access to social and legal services to enhance their autonomy, protection and care.

13. Older persons should be able to utilize appropriate levels of institutional care providing protection, rehabilitation and social and mental stimulation in a humane and secure environment.

14. Older persons should be able to enjoy human rights and fundamental freedoms when residing in any shelter, care or treatment facility, including full respect for their dignity, beliefs, needs and privacy and for the right to make decisions about their care and the quality of their lives.

Self-fulfilment

15. Older persons should be able to pursue opportunities for the full development of their potential.

16. Older persons should have access to the educational, cultural, spiritual and recreational resources of society.

Dignity

17. Older persons should be able to live in dignity and security and be free of exploitation and physical or mental abuse.

18. Older persons should be treated fairly regardless of age, gender, racial or ethnic background, disability or other status, and be valued independently of their economic contribution.

22. PRINCIPLES FOR THE PROTECTION OF PERSONS WITH MENTAL ILLNESS AND FOR THE IMPROVEMENT OF MENTAL HEALTH CARE, 1991

Annexed to General Assembly Resolution 46/119, adopted without a vote, 17 December 1991.

Further reading

HALE, B., 'Justice and Equality in Mental Health Law: The European Experience', (2007) 30 *International Journal of Law and Psychiatry* 18.

MCSHERRY, B., 'Mental Health and Human Rights: The Role of the Law in Developing a Right to Enjoy the Highest Attainable Standard of Mental Health in Australia', (2008) 15 *Journal of Law and Medicine* 773.

Perlin, M. L., 'International Human Rights Law and Comparative Mental Disability Law: The Universal Factors', (2006–2007) 34 *Syracuse Journal of International Law and Commerce* 333.

Quinn, G., Degener, T., *et al.*, *Human Rights and Disability: The current use and future potential of United Nations human rights instruments in the context of disability*, New York, Geneva: United Nations, 2002.

Zuckerberg, J., 'International Human Rights for Mentally Ill Persons: The Ontario Experience', (2007) 30 *International Journal of Law and Psychiatry* 512.

TEXT

APPLICATION

The present Principles shall be applied without discrimination on any grounds, such as disability, race, colour, sex, language, religion, political or other opinion, national, ethnic or social origin, legal or social status, age, property or birth.

Definitions

In the present Principles:

(a) 'Counsel' means a legal or other qualified representative;

(b) 'Independent authority' means a competent and independent authority prescribed by domestic law;

(c) 'Mental health care' includes analysis and diagnosis of a person's mental condition, and treatment, care and rehabilitation for a mental illness or suspected mental illness;

(d) 'Mental health facility' means any establishment, or any unit of an establishment, which as its primary function provides mental health care;

(e) 'Mental health practitioner' means a medical doctor, clinical psychologist, nurse, social worker or other appropriately trained and qualified person with specific skills relevant to mental health care;

(f) 'Patient' means a person receiving mental health care and includes all persons who are admitted to a mental health facility;

(g) 'Personal representative' means a person charged by law with the duty of representing a patient's interests in any specified respect or of exercising specified rights on the patient's behalf, and includes the parent or legal guardian of a minor unless otherwise provided by domestic law;

(h) 'The review body' means the body established in accordance with principle 17 to review the involuntary admission or retention of a patient in a mental health facility.

General limitation clause

The exercise of the rights set forth in the present Principles may be subject only to such limitations as are prescribed by law and are necessary to protect the health or safety of the person concerned or of others, or otherwise to protect public safety, order, health or morals or the fundamental rights and freedoms of others.

Principle 1: Fundamental freedoms and basic rights

1. All persons have the right to the best available mental health care, which shall be part of the health and social care system.

2. All persons with a mental illness, or who are being treated as such persons, shall be treated with humanity and respect for the inherent dignity of the human person.

3. All persons with a mental illness, or who are being treated as such persons, have the right to protection from economic, sexual and other forms of exploitation, physical or other abuse and degrading treatment.

4. There shall be no discrimination on the grounds of mental illness. 'Discrimination' means any distinction, exclusion or preference that has the effect of nullifying or impairing equal enjoyment of rights. Special measures solely to protect the rights, or secure the advancement, of persons with mental illness shall not be deemed to be discriminatory. Discrimination does not include any distinction, exclusion or preference undertaken in accordance with the provisions of the present Principles and necessary to protect the human rights of a person with a mental illness or of other individuals.

5. Every person with a mental illness shall have the right to exercise all civil, political, economic, social and cultural rights as recognized in the Universal Declaration of Human Rights, the International Covenant on Economic, Social and Cultural Rights, the International Covenant on Civil and Political Rights and in other relevant instruments, such as the Declaration on the Rights of Disabled Persons and the Body of Principles for the Protection of All Persons under Any Form of Detention or Imprisonment.

6. Any decision that, by reason of his or her mental illness, a person lacks legal capacity, and any decision that, in consequence of such incapacity, a personal representative shall be appointed, shall be made only after a fair hearing by an independent and impartial tribunal established by domestic law. The person whose capacity is at issue shall be entitled to be represented by a counsel. If the person whose capacity is at issue does not himself or herself secure such representation, it shall be made available without payment by that person to the extent that he or she does not have sufficient means to pay for it. The counsel shall not in the same proceedings represent a mental health facility or its personnel and shall not also represent a member of the family of the person whose capacity is at issue unless the tribunal is satisfied that there is no conflict of interest. Decisions regarding capacity and the need for a personal representative shall be reviewed at reasonable intervals prescribed by domestic law. The person whose capacity is at issue, his or her

personal representative, if any, and any other interested person shall have the right to appeal to a higher court against any such decision.

7. Where a court or other competent tribunal finds that a person with mental illness is unable to manage his or her own affairs, measures shall be taken, so far as is necessary and appropriate to that person's condition, to ensure the protection of his or her interests.

Principle 2: Protection of minors

Special care should be given within the purposes of the Principles and within the context of domestic law relating to the protection of minors to protect the rights of minors, including, if necessary, the appointment of a personal representative other than a family member.

Principle 3: Life in the community

Every person with a mental illness shall have the right to live and work, to the extent possible, in the community.

Principle 4: Determination of mental illness

1. A determination that a person has a mental illness shall be made in accordance with internationally accepted medical standards.

2. A determination of mental illness shall never be made on the basis of political, economic or social status, or membership in a cultural, racial or religious group, or for any other reason not directly relevant to mental health status.

3. Family or professional conflict, or non-conformity with moral, social, cultural or political values or religious beliefs prevailing in a person's community, shall never be a determining factor in the diagnosis of mental illness.

4. A background of past treatment or hospitalization as a patient shall not of itself justify any present or future determination of mental illness.

5. No person or authority shall classify a person as having, or otherwise indicate that a person has, a mental illness except for purposes directly relating to mental illness or the consequences of mental illness.

Principle 5: Medical examination

No person shall be compelled to undergo medical examination with a view to determining whether or not he or she has a mental illness except in accordance with a procedure authorized by domestic law.

Principle 6: Confidentiality

The right of confidentiality of information concerning all persons to whom the present Principles apply shall be respected.

Principle 7: Role of community and culture

1. Every patient shall have the right to be treated and cared for, as far as possible, in the community in which he or she lives.

2. Where treatment takes place in a mental health facility, a patient shall have the right, whenever possible, to be treated near his or her home or the home of his or her relatives or friends and shall have the right to return to the community as soon as possible.

3. Every patient shall have the right to treatment suited to his or her cultural background.

Principle 8: Standards of care

1. Every patient shall have the right to receive such health and social care as is appropriate to his or her health needs, and is entitled to care and treatment in accordance with the same standards as other ill persons.

2. Every patient shall be protected from harm, including unjustified medication, abuse by other patients, staff or others or other acts causing mental distress or physical discomfort.

Principle 9: Treatment

1. Every patient shall have the right to be treated in the least restrictive environment and with the least restrictive or intrusive treatment appropriate to the patient's health needs and the need to protect the physical safety of others.

2. The treatment and care of every patient shall be based on an individually prescribed plan, discussed with the patient, reviewed regularly, revised as necessary and provided by qualified professional staff.

3. Mental health care shall always be provided in accordance with applicable standards of ethics for mental health practitioners, including internationally accepted standards such as the Principles of Medical Ethics relevant to the role of health personnel, particularly physicians, in the protection of prisoners and detainees against torture and other cruel, inhuman or degrading treatment or punishment, adopted by the United Nations General Assembly. Mental health knowledge and skills shall never be abused.

4. The treatment of every patient shall be directed towards preserving and enhancing personal autonomy.

Principle 10: Medication

1. Medication shall meet the best health needs of the patient, shall be given to a patient only for therapeutic or diagnostic purposes and shall never be administered as a punishment or for the convenience of others. Subject to the provisions of paragraph 15 of principle 11 below, mental health practitioners shall only administer medication of known or demonstrated efficacy.

2. All medication shall be prescribed by a mental health practitioner authorized by law and shall be recorded in the patient's records.

Principle 11: Consent to treatment

1. No treatment shall be given to a patient without his or her informed consent, except as provided for in paragraphs 6, 7, 8, 13 and 15 of the present principle.

2. Informed consent is consent obtained freely, without threats or improper inducements, after appropriate disclosure to the patient of adequate and understandable information in a form and language understood by the patient on:

(a) The diagnostic assessment;

(b) The purpose, method, likely duration and expected benefit of the proposed treatment;

(c) Alternative modes of treatment, including those less intrusive;

(d) Possible pain or discomfort, risks and side-effects of the proposed treatment.

3. A patient may request the presence of a person or persons of the patient's choosing during the procedure for granting consent.

4. A patient has the right to refuse or stop treatment, except as provided for in paragraphs 6, 7, 8, 13 and 15 of the present principle. The consequences of refusing or stopping treatment must be explained to the patient.

5. A patient shall never be invited or induced to waive the right to informed consent. If the patient should seek to do so, it shall be explained to the patient that the treatment cannot be given without informed consent.

6. Except as provided in paragraphs 7, 8, 12, 13, 14 and 15 of the present principle, a proposed plan of treatment may be given to a patient without a patient's informed consent if the following conditions are satisfied:

    (a) The patient is, at the relevant time, held as an involuntary patient;

    (b) An independent authority, having in its possession all relevant information, including the information specified in paragraph 2 of the present principle, is satisfied that, at the relevant time, the patient lacks the capacity to give or withhold informed consent to the proposed plan of treatment or, if domestic legislation so provides, that, having regard to the patient's own safety or the safety of others, the patient unreasonably withholds such consent;

    (c) The independent authority is satisfied that the proposed plan of treatment is in the best interest of the patient's health needs.

7. Paragraph 6 above does not apply to a patient with a personal representative empowered by law to consent to treatment for the patient; but, except as provided in paragraphs 12, 13, 14 and 15 of the present principle, treatment may be given to such a patient without his or her informed consent if the personal representative, having been given the information described in paragraph 2 of the present principle, consents on the patient's behalf.

8. Except as provided in paragraphs 12, 13, 14 and 15 of the present principle, treatment may also be given to any patient without the patient's informed consent if a qualified mental health practitioner authorized by law determines that it is urgently necessary in order to prevent immediate or imminent harm to the patient or to other persons. Such treatment shall not be prolonged beyond the period that is strictly necessary for this purpose.

9. Where any treatment is authorized without the patient's informed consent, every effort shall nevertheless be made to inform the patient about the nature of the treatment and any possible alternatives and to involve the patient as far as practicable in the development of the treatment plan.

10. All treatment shall be immediately recorded in the patient's medical records, with an indication of whether involuntary or voluntary.

11. Physical restraint or involuntary seclusion of a patient shall not be employed except in accordance with the officially approved procedures of the mental health facility and only when it is the only means available to prevent immediate or imminent harm to the patient or others. It shall not be prolonged beyond the period which is strictly necessary for this purpose. All instances of physical restraint or involuntary seclusion, the reasons for them and their nature and extent shall be recorded in the patient's medical record. A patient who is restrained or secluded shall be kept under humane conditions and be under the care and close and regular supervision of qualified members of the staff. A personal representative, if any and if relevant, shall be given prompt notice of any physical restraint or involuntary seclusion of the patient.

12. Sterilization shall never be carried out as a treatment for mental illness.

13. A major medical or surgical procedure may be carried out on a person with mental illness only where it is permitted by domestic law, where it is considered that it would best serve the health needs of the patient and where the patient gives informed consent, except that, where the patient is unable to give informed consent, the procedure shall be authorized only after independent review.

14. Psychosurgery and other intrusive and irreversible treatments for mental illness shall never be carried out on a patient who is an involuntary patient in a mental health facility and, to the extent that domestic law permits them to be carried out, they may be carried out on any other patient only where the patient has given informed consent and an independent external body has satisfied itself that there is genuine informed consent and that the treatment best serves the health needs of the patient.

15. Clinical trials and experimental treatment shall never be carried out on any patient without informed consent, except that a patient who is unable to give informed consent may be admitted to a clinical trial or given experimental treatment, but only with the approval of a competent, independent review body specifically constituted for this purpose.

16. In the cases specified in paragraphs 6, 7, 8, 13, 14 and 15 of the present principle, the patient or his or her personal representative, or any interested person, shall have the right to appeal to a judicial or other independent authority concerning any treatment given to him or her.

Principle 12: Notice of rights

1. A patient in a mental health facility shall be informed as soon as possible after admission, in a form and a language which the patient understands, of all his or her rights in accordance with the present Principles and under domestic law, and the information shall include an explanation of those rights and how to exercise them.

2. If and for so long as a patient is unable to understand such information, the rights of the patient shall be communicated to the personal representative, if any and if appropriate, and to the person or persons best able to represent the patient's interests and willing to do so.

3. A patient who has the necessary capacity has the right to nominate a person who should be informed on his or her behalf, as well as a person to represent his or her interests to the authorities of the facility.

Principle 13: Rights and conditions in mental health facilities

1. Every patient in a mental health facility shall, in particular, have the right to full respect for his or her:

   (a) Recognition everywhere as a person before the law;
   (b) Privacy;
   (c) Freedom of communication, which includes freedom to communicate with other persons in the facility; freedom to send and receive uncensored private communications; freedom to receive, in private, visits from a counsel or personal representative and, at all reasonable times, from other visitors; and freedom of access to postal and telephone services and to newspapers, radio and television;
   (d) Freedom of religion or belief.

2. The environment and living conditions in mental health facilities shall be as close as possible to those of the normal life of persons of similar age and in particular shall include:

(a) Facilities for recreational and leisure activities;

(b) Facilities for education;

(c) Facilities to purchase or receive items for daily living, recreation and communication;

(d) Facilities, and encouragement to use such facilities, for a patient's engagement in active occupation suited to his or her social and cultural background, and for appropriate vocational rehabilitation measures to promote reintegration in the community. These measures should include vocational guidance, vocational training and placement services to enable patients to secure or retain employment in the community.

3. In no circumstances shall a patient be subject to forced labour. Within the limits compatible with the needs of the patient and with the requirements of institutional administration, a patient shall be able to choose the type of work he or she wishes to perform.

4. The labour of a patient in a mental health facility shall not be exploited. Every such patient shall have the right to receive the same remuneration for any work which he or she does as would, according to domestic law or custom, be paid for such work to a non-patient. Every such patient shall, in any event, have the right to receive a fair share of any remuneration which is paid to the mental health facility for his or her work.

Principle 14: Resources for mental health facilities

1. A mental health facility shall have access to the same level of resources as any other health establishment, and in particular:

(a) Qualified medical and other appropriate professional staff in sufficient numbers and with adequate space to provide each patient with privacy and a programme of appropriate and active therapy;

(b) Diagnostic and therapeutic equipment for the patient;

(c) Appropriate professional care;

(d) Adequate, regular and comprehensive treatment, including supplies of medication.

2. Every mental health facility shall be inspected by the competent authorities with sufficient frequency to ensure that the conditions, treatment and care of patients comply with the present Principles.

Principle 15: Admission principles

1. Where a person needs treatment in a mental health facility, every effort shall be made to avoid involuntary admission.

2. Access to a mental health facility shall be administered in the same way as access to any other facility for any other illness.

3. Every patient not admitted involuntarily shall have the right to leave the mental health facility at any time unless the criteria for his or her retention as an involuntary patient, as set forth in principle 16 below, apply, and he or she shall be informed of that right.

Principle 16: Involuntary admission

1. A person may be admitted involuntarily to a mental health facility as a patient or, having already been admitted voluntarily as a patient, be retained as an involuntary

patient in the mental health facility if, and only if, a qualified mental health practitioner authorized by law for that purpose determines, in accordance with principle 4 above, that that person has a mental illness and considers:

(a) That, because of that mental illness, there is a serious likelihood of immediate or imminent harm to that person or to other persons; or

(b) That, in the case of a person whose mental illness is severe and whose judgement is impaired, failure to admit or retain that person is likely to lead to a serious deterioration in his or her condition or will prevent the giving of appropriate treatment that can only be given by admission to a mental health facility in accordance with the principle of the least restrictive alternative.

In the case referred to in subparagraph (b), a second such mental health practitioner, independent of the first, should be consulted where possible. If such consultation takes place, the involuntary admission or retention may not take place unless the second mental health practitioner concurs.

2. Involuntary admission or retention shall initially be for a short period as specified by domestic law for observation and preliminary treatment pending review of the admission or retention by the review body. The grounds of the admission shall be communicated to the patient without delay and the fact of the admission and the grounds for it shall also be communicated promptly and in detail to the review body, to the patient's personal representative, if any, and, unless the patient objects, to the patient's family.

3. A mental health facility may receive involuntarily admitted patients only if the facility has been designated to do so by a competent authority prescribed by domestic law.

Principle 17: Review body

1. The review body shall be a judicial or other independent and impartial body established by domestic law and functioning in accordance with procedures laid down by domestic law. It shall, in formulating its decisions, have the assistance of one or more qualified and independent mental health practitioners and take their advice into account.

2. The initial review of the review body, as required by paragraph 2 of principle 16 above, of a decision to admit or retain a person as an involuntary patient shall take place as soon as possible after that decision and shall be conducted in accordance with simple and expeditious procedures as specified by domestic law.

3. The review body shall periodically review the cases of involuntary patients at reasonable intervals as specified by domestic law.

4. An involuntary patient may apply to the review body for release or voluntary status, at reasonable intervals as specified by domestic law.

5. At each review, the review body shall consider whether the criteria for involuntary admission set out in paragraph 1 of principle 16 above are still satisfied, and, if not, the patient shall be discharged as an involuntary patient.

6. If at any time the mental health practitioner responsible for the case is satisfied that the conditions for the retention of a person as an involuntary patient are no longer satisfied, he or she shall order the discharge of that person as such a patient.

7. A patient or his personal representative or any interested person shall have the right to appeal to a higher court against a decision that the patient be admitted to, or be retained in, a mental health facility.

Principle 18: Procedural safeguards

1. The patient shall be entitled to choose and appoint a counsel to represent the patient as such, including representation in any complaint procedure or appeal. If the patient does not secure such services, a counsel shall be made available without payment by the patient to the extent that the patient lacks sufficient means to pay.

2. The patient shall also be entitled to the assistance, if necessary, of the services of an interpreter. Where such services are necessary and the patient does not secure them, they shall be made available without payment by the patient to the extent that the patient lacks sufficient means to pay.

3. The patient and the patient's counsel may request and produce at any hearing an independent mental health report and any other reports and oral, written and other evidence that are relevant and admissible.

4. Copies of the patient's records and any reports and documents to be submitted shall be given to the patient and to the patient's counsel, except in special cases where it is determined that a specific disclosure to the patient would cause serious harm to the patient's health or put at risk the safety of others. As domestic law may provide, any document not given to the patient should, when this can be done in confidence, be given to the patient's personal representative and counsel. When any part of a document is withheld from a patient, the patient or the patient's counsel, if any, shall receive notice of the withholding and the reasons for it and it shall be subject to judicial review.

5. The patient and the patient's personal representative and counsel shall be entitled to attend, participate and be heard personally in any hearing.

6. If the patient or the patient's personal representative or counsel requests that a particular person be present at a hearing, that person shall be admitted unless it is determined that the person's presence could cause serious harm to the patient's health or put at risk the safety of others.

7. Any decision on whether the hearing or any part of it shall be in public or in private and may be publicly reported shall give full consideration to the patient's own wishes, to the need to respect the privacy of the patient and of other persons and to the need to prevent serious harm to the patient's health or to avoid putting at risk the safety of others.

8. The decision arising out of the hearing and the reasons for it shall be expressed in writing. Copies shall be given to the patient and his or her personal representative and counsel. In deciding whether the decision shall be published in whole or in part, full consideration shall be given to the patient's own wishes, to the need to respect his or her privacy and that of other persons, to the public interest in the open administration of justice and to the need to prevent serious harm to the patient's health or to avoid putting at risk the safety of others.

Principle 19: Access to information

1. A patient (which term in the present Principle includes a former patient) shall be entitled to have access to the information concerning the patient in his or her health and personal records maintained by a mental health facility. This right may be subject to restrictions in order to prevent serious harm to the patient's health and avoid putting at risk the safety of others. As domestic law may provide, any such information not given to the patient should, when this can be done in confidence, be given to the patient's personal

representative and counsel. When any of the information is withheld from a patient, the patient or the patient's counsel, if any, shall receive notice of the withholding and the reasons for it and it shall be subject to judicial review.

2. Any written comments by the patient or the patient's personal representative or counsel shall, on request, be inserted in the patient's file.

Principle 20: Criminal offenders

1. The present Principle applies to persons serving sentences of imprisonment for criminal offences, or who are otherwise detained in the course of criminal proceedings or investigations against them, and who are determined to have a mental illness or who it is believed may have such an illness.

2. All such persons should receive the best available mental health care as provided in principle 1 above. The present Principles shall apply to them to the fullest extent possible, with only such limited modifications and exceptions as are necessary in the circumstances. No such modifications and exceptions shall prejudice the persons' rights under the instruments noted in paragraph 5 of principle 1 above.

3. Domestic law may authorize a court or other competent authority, acting on the basis of competent and independent medical advice, to order that such persons be admitted to a mental health facility.

4. Treatment of persons determined to have a mental illness shall in all circumstances be consistent with principle 11 above.

Principle 21: Complaints

Every patient and former patient shall have the right to make a complaint through procedures as specified by domestic law.

Principle 22: Monitoring and remedies

States shall ensure that appropriate mechanisms are in force to promote compliance with the present Principles, for the inspection of mental health facilities, for the submission, investigation and resolution of complaints and for the institution of appropriate disciplinary or judicial proceedings for professional misconduct or violation of the rights of a patient.

Principle 23: Implementation

1. States should implement the present Principles through appropriate legislative, judicial, administrative, educational and other measures, which they shall review periodically.

2. States shall make the present Principles widely known by appropriate and active means.

Principle 24: Scope of principles relating to mental health facilities

The present Principles apply to all persons who are admitted to a mental health facility.

Principle 25: Saving of existing rights

There shall be no restriction upon or derogation from any existing rights of patients, including rights recognized in applicable international or domestic law, on the pretext that the present Principles do not recognize such rights or that they recognize them to a lesser extent.

23. DECLARATION ON THE PROTECTION OF ALL PERSONS FROM ENFORCED DISAPPEARANCE, 1992

This Declaration is annexed to General Assembly Resolution 47/133, adopted without a vote on 18 December 1992; and see also the International Convention for the Protection of All Persons from Enforced Disappearance, 2006, below, p.543; the Inter-American Convention on Forced Disappearance of Persons, 1994, below, p.997.

For recent judicial notice of the Declaration, see *Lexa v Slovakia*, Application No. 54334/00, European Court of Human Rights, Fourth Section, 23 September 2008, para. 96, *Süheyla Aydin v Turkey*, Application No. 25660/94, European Court of Human Rights, Second Section, 24 May 2005, para. 153.

TEXT

The General Assembly,

Considering that, in accordance with the principles proclaimed in the Charter of the United Nations and other international instruments, recognition of the inherent dignity and of the equal and inalienable rights of all members of the human family is the foundation of freedom, justice and peace in the world,

Bearing in mind the obligation of States under the Charter, in particular Article 55, to promote universal respect for, and observance of, human rights and fundamental freedoms,

Deeply concerned that in many countries, often in a persistent manner, enforced disappearances occur, in the sense that persons are arrested, detained or abducted against their will or otherwise deprived of their liberty by officials of different branches or levels of Government, or by organized groups or private individuals acting on behalf of, or with the support, direct or indirect, consent or acquiescence of the Government, followed by a refusal to disclose the fate or whereabouts of the persons concerned or a refusal to acknowledge the deprivation of their liberty, which places such persons outside the protection of the law,

Considering that enforced disappearance undermines the deepest values of any society committed to respect for the rule of law, human rights and fundamental freedoms, and that the systematic practice of such acts is of the nature of a crime against humanity,

Recalling its resolution 33/173 of 20 December 1978, in which it expressed concern about the reports from various parts of the world relating to enforced or involuntary disappearances, as well as about the anguish and sorrow caused by those disappearances, and called upon Governments to hold law enforcement and security forces legally responsible for excesses which might lead to enforced or involuntary disappearances of persons,

Recalling also the protection afforded to victims of armed conflicts by the Geneva Conventions of 12 August 1949 and the Additional Protocols thereto, of 1977,

Having regard in particular to the relevant articles of the Universal Declaration of Human Rights and the International Covenant on Civil and Political Rights, which protect the right to life, the right to liberty and security of the person, the right not to be subjected to torture and the right to recognition as a person before the law,

Having regard also to the Convention against Torture and Other Cruel, Inhuman or Degrading Treatment or Punishment, which provides that States parties shall take effective measures to prevent and punish acts of torture,

Bearing in mind the Code of Conduct for Law Enforcement Officials, the Basic Principles on the Use of Force and Firearms by Law Enforcement Officials, the Declaration of Basic Principles of Justice for Victims of Crime and Abuse of Power and the Standard Minimum Rules for the Treatment of Prisoners,

Affirming that, in order to prevent enforced disappearances, it is necessary to ensure strict compliance with the Body of Principles for the Protection of All Persons under Any Form of Detention or Imprisonment contained in the annex to its resolution 43/173 of 9 December 1988, and with the Principles on the Effective Prevention and Investigation of Extra-legal, Arbitrary and Summary Executions, set forth in the annex to Economic and Social Council resolution 1989/65 of 24 May 1989 and endorsed by the General Assembly in its resolution 44/162 of 15 December 1989,

Bearing in mind that, while the acts which comprise enforced disappearance constitute a violation of the prohibitions found in the aforementioned international instruments, it is none the less important to devise an instrument which characterizes all acts of enforced disappearance of persons as very serious offences and sets forth standards designed to punish and prevent their commission,

1. *Proclaims* the present Declaration on the Protection of All Persons from Enforced Disappearance, as a body of principles for all States;

2. *Urges* that all efforts be made so that the Declaration becomes generally known and respected;

Article 1

1. Any act of enforced disappearance is an offence to human dignity. It is condemned as a denial of the purposes of the Charter of the United Nations and as a grave and flagrant violation of the human rights and fundamental freedoms proclaimed in the Universal Declaration of Human Rights and reaffirmed and developed in international instruments in this field.

2. Any act of enforced disappearance places the persons subjected thereto outside the protection of the law and inflicts severe suffering on them and their families. It constitutes a violation of the rules of international law guaranteeing, *inter alia*, the right to recognition as a person before the law, the right to liberty and security of the person and the right not to be subjected to torture and other cruel, inhuman or degrading treatment or punishment. It also violates or constitutes a grave threat to the right to life.

Article 2

1. No State shall practise, permit or tolerate enforced disappearances.

2. States shall act at the national and regional levels and in cooperation with the United Nations to contribute by all means to the prevention and eradication of enforced disappearance.

Article 3

Each State shall take effective legislative, administrative, judicial or other measures to prevent and terminate acts of enforced disappearance in any territory under its jurisdiction.

Article 4

1. All acts of enforced disappearance shall be offences under criminal law punishable by appropriate penalties which shall take into account their extreme seriousness.

2. Mitigating circumstances may be established in national legislation for persons who, having participated in enforced disappearances, are instrumental in bringing the victims forward alive or in providing voluntarily information which would contribute to clarifying cases of enforced disappearance.

Article 5

In addition to such criminal penalties as are applicable, enforced disappearances render their perpetrators and the State or State authorities which organize, acquiesce in or tolerate such disappearances liable under civil law, without prejudice to the international responsibility of the State concerned in accordance with the principles of international law.

Article 6

1. No order or instruction of any public authority, civilian, military or other, may be invoked to justify an enforced disappearance. Any person receiving such an order or instruction shall have the right and duty not to obey it.

2. Each State shall ensure that orders or instructions directing, authorizing or encouraging any enforced disappearance are prohibited.

3. Training of law enforcement officials shall emphasize the provisions in paragraphs 1 and 2 of the present article.

Article 7

No circumstances whatsoever, whether a threat of war, a state of war, internal political instability or any other public emergency, may be invoked to justify enforced disappearances.

Article 8

1. No State shall expel, return (*refouler*) or extradite a person to another State where there are substantial grounds to believe that he would be in danger of enforced disappearance.

2. For the purpose of determining whether there are such grounds, the competent authorities shall take into account all relevant considerations including, where applicable, the existence in the State concerned of a consistent pattern of gross, flagrant or mass violations of human rights.

Article 9

1. The right to a prompt and effective judicial remedy as a means of determining the whereabouts or state of health of persons deprived of their liberty and/or identifying the authority ordering or carrying out the deprivation of liberty is required to prevent enforced disappearances under all circumstances, including those referred to in Article 7 above.

2. In such proceedings, competent national authorities shall have access to all places where persons deprived of their liberty are being held and to each part of those places, as well as to any place in which there are grounds to believe that such persons may be found.

3. Any other competent authority entitled under the law of the State or by any international legal instrument to which the State is a party may also have access to such places.

Article 10

1. Any person deprived of liberty shall be held in an officially recognized place of detention and, in conformity with national law, be brought before a judicial authority promptly after detention.

2. Accurate information on the detention of such persons and their place or places of detention, including transfers, shall be made promptly available to their family members, their counsel or to any other persons having a legitimate interest in the information unless a wish to the contrary has been manifested by the persons concerned.

3. An official up-to-date register of all persons deprived of their liberty shall be maintained in every place of detention. Additionally, each State shall take steps to maintain similar centralized registers. The information contained in these registers shall be made available to the persons mentioned in the preceding paragraph, to any judicial or other competent and independent national authority and to any other competent authority entitled under the law of the State concerned or any international legal instrument to which a State concerned is a party, seeking to trace the whereabouts of a detained person.

Article 11

All persons deprived of liberty must be released in a manner permitting reliable verification that they have actually been released and, further, have been released in conditions in which their physical integrity and ability fully to exercise their rights are assured.

Article 12

1. Each State shall establish rules under its national law indicating those officials authorized to order deprivation of liberty, establishing the conditions under which such orders may be given, and stipulating penalties for officials who, without legal justification, refuse to provide information on any detention.

2. Each State shall likewise ensure strict supervision, including a clear chain of command, of all law enforcement officials responsible for apprehensions, arrests, detentions, custody, transfers and imprisonment, and of other officials authorized by law to use force and firearms.

Article 13

1. Each State shall ensure that any person having knowledge or a legitimate interest who alleges that a person has been subjected to enforced disappearance has the right to complain to a competent and independent State authority and to have that complaint promptly, thoroughly and impartially investigated by that authority. Whenever there are reasonable grounds to believe that an enforced disappearance has been committed, the State shall promptly refer the matter to that authority for such an investigation, even if there has been no formal complaint. No measure shall be taken to curtail or impede the investigation.

2. Each State shall ensure that the competent authority shall have the necessary powers and resources to conduct the investigation effectively, including powers to compel attendance of witnesses and production of relevant documents and to make immediate on-site visits.

3. Steps shall be taken to ensure that all involved in the investigation, including the complainant, counsel, witnesses and those conducting the investigation, are protected against ill-treatment, intimidation or reprisal.

4. The findings of such an investigation shall be made available upon request to all persons concerned, unless doing so would jeopardize an ongoing criminal investigation.

5. Steps shall be taken to ensure that any ill-treatment, intimidation or reprisal or any other form of interference on the occasion of the lodging of a complaint or during the investigation procedure is appropriately punished.

6. An investigation, in accordance with the procedures described above, should be able to be conducted for as long as the fate of the victim of enforced disappearance remains unclarified.

Article 14

Any person alleged to have perpetrated an act of enforced disappearance in a particular State shall, when the facts disclosed by an official investigation so warrant, be brought before the competent civil authorities of that State for the purpose of prosecution and trial unless he has been extradited to another State wishing to exercise jurisdiction in accordance with the relevant international agreements in force. All States should take any lawful and appropriate action available to them to bring to justice all persons presumed responsible for an act of enforced disappearance, who are found to be within their jurisdiction or under their control.

Article 15

The fact that there are grounds to believe that a person has participated in acts of an extremely serious nature such as those referred to in Article 4, paragraph 1, above, regardless of the motives, shall be taken into account when the competent authorities of the State decide whether or not to grant asylum.

Article 16

1. Persons alleged to have committed any of the acts referred to in Article 4, paragraph 1, above, shall be suspended from any official duties during the investigation referred to in Article 13 above.

2. They shall be tried only by the competent ordinary courts in each State, and not by any other special tribunal, in particular military courts.

3. No privileges, immunities or special exemptions shall be admitted in such trials, without prejudice to the provisions contained in the Vienna Convention on Diplomatic Relations.

4. The persons presumed responsible for such acts shall be guaranteed fair treatment in accordance with the relevant provisions of the Universal Declaration of Human Rights and other relevant international agreements in force at all stages of the investigation and eventual prosecution and trial.

Article 17

1. Acts constituting enforced disappearance shall be considered a continuing offence as long as the perpetrators continue to conceal the fate and the whereabouts of persons who have disappeared and these facts remain unclarified.

2. When the remedies provided for in Article 2 of the International Covenant on Civil and Political Rights are no longer effective, the statute of limitations relating to acts of enforced disappearance shall be suspended until these remedies are re-established.

3. Statutes of limitations, where they exist, relating to acts of enforced disappearance shall be substantial and commensurate with the extreme seriousness of the offence.

Article 18

1. Persons who have or are alleged to have committed offences referred to in Article 4, paragraph 1, above, shall not benefit from any special amnesty law or similar measures that might have the effect of exempting them from any criminal proceedings or sanction.

2. In the exercise of the right of pardon, the extreme seriousness of acts of enforced disappearance shall be taken into account.

Article 19

The victims of acts of enforced disappearance and their family shall obtain redress and shall have the right to adequate compensation, including the means for as complete a rehabilitation as possible. In the event of the death of the victim as a result of an act of enforced disappearance, their dependants shall also be entitled to compensation.

Article 20

1. States shall prevent and suppress the abduction of children of parents subjected to enforced disappearance and of children born during their mother's enforced disappearance, and shall devote their efforts to the search for and identification of such children and to the restitution of the children to their families of origin.

2. Considering the need to protect the best interests of children referred to in the preceding paragraph, there shall be an opportunity, in States which recognize a system of adoption, for a review of the adoption of such children and, in particular, for annulment of any adoption which originated in enforced disappearance. Such adoption should, however, continue to be in force if consent is given, at the time of the review, by the child's closest relatives.

3. The abduction of children of parents subjected to enforced disappearance or of children born during their mother's enforced disappearance, and the act of altering or suppressing documents attesting to their true identity, shall constitute an extremely serious offence, which shall be punished as such.

4. For these purposes, States shall, where appropriate, conclude bilateral and multilateral agreements.

Article 21

The provisions of the present Declaration are without prejudice to the provisions enunciated in the Universal Declaration of Human Rights or in any other international instrument, and shall not be construed as restricting or derogating from any of those provisions.

24. DECLARATION ON THE RIGHTS OF PERSONS BELONGING TO NATIONAL OR ETHNIC, RELIGIOUS AND LINGUISTIC MINORITIES, 1992

This Declaration was adopted without a vote by General Assembly Resolution 47/135, 18 December 1992; see also Declaration on the Rights of Indigenous Peoples, 2007, below, p.293, and the European Framework Convention for the Protection of National Minorities, 1994, below, p.811.

Further reading

BARTH, W. K., *On Cultural Rights: The Equality of Nations and the Minority Legal Tradition*, Leiden: Martinus Nijhoff, 2008.

DUNBAR, R., 'Minority Language Rights under International Law', (2001) 50 *ICLQ* 90–120.

GHANEA, N. and XANTHAKI, A., eds., *Minorities, Peoples and Self-Determination: Essays in Honour of Patrick Thornberry*, Leiden: Martinus Nijhoff, 2005.

KYMLICKA, W., 'The internationalization of minority rights', (2008) 6 *International Journal of Constitutional Law* 1.

MACKLEM, P., 'Minority rights in international law', (2008) 6 *International Journal of Constitutional Law* 531.

PENTASSUGLIA, G., *Minority Groups and Judicial Discourse in International Law: A Comparative Perspective*, Leiden: Martinus Nijhoff, 2009.

——, 'Evolving Protection of Minority Groups: Global Challenges and the Role of International Jurisprudence', (2009) 11 *International Community Law Review* 185.

——, 'Reforming the UN Human Rights Machinery: What does the Future Hold for the Protection of Minorities and Indigenous Peoples? An Introduction', (2007) 14 *International Journal on Minority and Group Rights* 127.

THORNBERRY, P., *International Law and the Rights of Minorities*, Oxford: Clarendon Press, 1991.

——*Indigenous Peoples and Human Rights*, Manchester: Manchester University Press, 2002.

WELLER, M., *Universal Minority Rights: A Commentary on the Jurisprudence of International Courts and Treaty Bodies*, Oxford: Oxford University Press, 2007.

TEXT

The General Assembly,

Reaffirming that one of the basic aims of the United Nations, as proclaimed in the Charter, is to promote and encourage respect for human rights and for fundamental freedoms for all, without distinction as to race, sex, language or religion,

Reaffirming faith in fundamental human rights, in the dignity and worth of the human person, in the equal rights of men and women and of nations large and small,

Desiring to promote the realization of the principles contained in the Charter, the Universal Declaration of Human Rights, the Convention on the Prevention and Punishment of the Crime of Genocide, the International Convention on the Elimination of All Forms of Racial Discrimination, the International Covenant on Civil and Political Rights, the International Covenant on Economic, Social and Cultural Rights, the Declaration on the Elimination of All Forms of Intolerance and of Discrimination Based on Religion or Belief, and the Convention on the Rights of the Child, as well as other relevant international instruments that have been adopted at the universal or regional level and those concluded between individual States Members of the United Nations,

Inspired by the provisions of article 27 of the International Covenant on Civil and Political Rights concerning the rights of persons belonging to ethnic, religious or linguistic minorities,

Considering that the promotion and protection of the rights of persons belonging to national or ethnic, religious and linguistic minorities contribute to the political and social stability of States in which they live,

Emphasizing that the constant promotion and realization of the rights of persons belonging to national or ethnic, religious and linguistic minorities, as an integral part of the development of society as a whole and within a democratic framework based on the rule of law, would contribute to the strengthening of friendship and cooperation among peoples and States,

Considering that the United Nations has an important role to play regarding the protection of minorities,

Bearing in mind the work done so far within the United Nations system, in particular by the Commission on Human Rights, the Sub-Commission on Prevention of Discrimination and Protection of Minorities and the bodies established pursuant to the International Covenants on Human Rights and other relevant international human rights instruments in promoting and protecting the rights of persons belonging to national or ethnic, religious and linguistic minorities,

Taking into account the important work which is done by intergovernmental and non-governmental organizations in protecting minorities and in promoting and protecting the rights of persons belonging to national or ethnic, religious and linguistic minorities,

Recognizing the need to ensure even more effective implementation of international human rights instruments with regard to the rights of persons belonging to national or ethnic, religious and linguistic minorities,

Proclaims this Declaration on the Rights of Persons Belonging to National or Ethnic, Religious and Linguistic Minorities:

Article 1

1. States shall protect the existence and the national or ethnic, cultural, religious and linguistic identity of minorities within their respective territories and shall encourage conditions for the promotion of that identity.

2. States shall adopt appropriate legislative and other measures to achieve those ends.

Article 2

1. Persons belonging to national or ethnic, religious and linguistic minorities (hereinafter referred to as persons belonging to minorities) have the right to enjoy their own culture, to profess and practise their own religion, and to use their own language, in private and in public, freely and without interference or any form of discrimination.

2. Persons belonging to minorities have the right to participate effectively in cultural, religious, social, economic and public life.

3. Persons belonging to minorities have the right to participate effectively in decisions on the national and, where appropriate, regional level concerning the minority to which they belong or the regions in which they live, in a manner not incompatible with national legislation.

4. Persons belonging to minorities have the right to establish and maintain their own associations.

5. Persons belonging to minorities have the right to establish and maintain, without any discrimination, free and peaceful contacts with other members of their group and with persons belonging to other minorities, as well as contacts across frontiers with citizens of other States to whom they are related by national or ethnic, religious or linguistic ties.

Article 3

1. Persons belonging to minorities may exercise their rights, including those set forth in the present Declaration, individually as well as in community with other members of their group, without any discrimination.

2. No disadvantage shall result for any person belonging to a minority as the consequence of the exercise or non-exercise of the rights set forth in the present Declaration.

Article 4

1. States shall take measures where required to ensure that persons belonging to minorities may exercise fully and effectively all their human rights and fundamental freedoms without any discrimination and in full equality before the law.

2. States shall take measures to create favourable conditions to enable persons belonging to minorities to express their characteristics and to develop their culture, language, religion, traditions and customs, except where specific practices are in violation of national law and contrary to international standards.

3. States should take appropriate measures so that, wherever possible, persons belonging to minorities may have adequate opportunities to learn their mother tongue or to have instruction in their mother tongue.

4. States should, where appropriate, take measures in the field of education, in order to encourage knowledge of the history, traditions, language and culture of the minorities existing within their territory. Persons belonging to minorities should have adequate opportunities to gain knowledge of the society as a whole.

5. States should consider appropriate measures so that persons belonging to minorities may participate fully in the economic progress and development in their country.

Article 5

1. National policies and programmes shall be planned and implemented with due regard for the legitimate interests of persons belonging to minorities.

2. Programmes of co-operation and assistance among States should be planned and implemented with due regard for the legitimate interests of persons belonging to minorities.

Article 6

States should co-operate on questions relating to persons belonging to minorities, *inter alia*, exchanging information and experiences, in order to promote mutual understanding and confidence.

Article 7

States should co-operate in order to promote respect for the rights set forth in the present Declaration.

Article 8

1. Nothing in the present Declaration shall prevent the fulfilment of international obligations of States in relation to persons belonging to minorities. In particular, States shall fulfil in good faith the obligations and commitments they have assumed under international treaties and agreements to which they are parties.

2. The exercise of the rights set forth in the present Declaration shall not prejudice the enjoyment by all persons of universally recognized human rights and fundamental freedoms.

3. Measures taken by States to ensure the effective enjoyment of the rights set forth in the present Declaration shall not prima facie be considered contrary to the principle of equality contained in the Universal Declaration of Human Rights.

4. Nothing in the present Declaration may be construed as permitting any activity contrary to the purposes and principles of the United Nations, including sovereign equality, territorial integrity and political independence of States.

Article 9

The specialized agencies and other organizations of the United Nations system shall contribute to the full realization of the rights and principles set forth in the present Declaration, within their respective fields of competence.

25. WORLD CONFERENCE ON HUMAN RIGHTS: VIENNA DECLARATION AND PROGRAMME OF ACTION, 1993

Adopted by the World Conference on Human Rights on 25 June 1993: UN doc. A/CONF. 157/23, 12 July 1993, the Declaration and Programme of Action were endorsed by General Assembly Resolution 48/121, adopted without a vote, 20 December 1993.

Further reading

BOYLE, K., 'Stock-taking on Human Rights: The World Conference on Human Rights, Vienna 1993', (1995) 43 *Political Studies* 79.

MARKS, S., 'Nightmare and Noble Dream: The 1993 World Conference on Human Rights', (1994) *Cambridge Law Journal* 54.

TEXT

The World Conference on Human Rights,

Considering that the promotion and protection of human rights is a matter of priority for the international community, and that the Conference affords a unique opportunity to carry out a comprehensive analysis of the international human rights system and of the machinery for the protection of human rights, in order to enhance and thus promote a fuller observance of those rights, in a just and balanced manner,

Recognizing and affirming that all human rights derive from the dignity and worth inherent in the human person, and that the human person is the central subject of human rights and fundamental freedoms, and consequently should be the principal beneficiary and should participate actively in the realization of these rights and freedoms,

Reaffirming their commitment to the purposes and principles contained in the Charter of the United Nations and the Universal Declaration of Human Rights,

Reaffirming the commitment contained in Article 56 of the Charter of the United Nations to take joint and separate action, placing proper emphasis on developing effective international cooperation for the realization of the purposes set out in Article 55, including universal respect for, and observance of, human rights and fundamental freedoms for all,

Emphasizing the responsibilities of all States, in conformity with the Charter of the United Nations, to develop and encourage respect for human rights and fundamental freedoms for all, without distinction as to race, sex, language or religion,

Recalling the Preamble to the Charter of the United Nations, in particular the determination to reaffirm faith in fundamental human rights, in the dignity and worth of the human person, and in the equal rights of men and women and of nations large and small,

Recalling also the determination expressed in the Preamble of the Charter of the United Nations to save succeeding generations from the scourge of war, to establish conditions under which justice and respect for obligations arising from treaties and other sources of international law can be maintained, to promote social progress and better standards of life in larger freedom, to practice tolerance and good neighbourliness, and to employ international machinery for the promotion of the economic and social advancement of all peoples,

Emphasizing that the Universal Declaration of Human Rights, which constitutes a common standard of achievement for all peoples and all nations, is the source of inspiration and has been the basis for the United Nations in making advances in standard setting as contained in the existing international human rights instruments, in particular the International Covenant on Civil and Political Rights and the International Covenant on Economic, Social and Cultural Rights.

Considering the major changes taking place on the international scene and the aspirations of all the peoples for an international order based on the principles enshrined in the Charter of the United Nations, including promoting and encouraging respect for human rights and fundamental freedoms for all and respect for the principle of equal rights and self-determination of peoples, peace, democracy, justice, equality, rule of law, pluralism, development, better standards of living and solidarity,

Deeply concerned by various forms of discrimination and violence, to which women continue to be exposed all over the world,

Recognizing that the activities of the United Nations in the field of human rights should be rationalized and enhanced in order to strengthen the United Nations machinery in this field and to further the objectives of universal respect for observance of international human rights standards,

Having taken into account the Declarations adopted by the three regional meetings at Tunis, San José and Bangkok and the contributions made by Governments, and bearing in mind the suggestions made by intergovernmental and non-governmental organizations, as well as the studies prepared by independent experts during the preparatory process leading to the World Conference on Human Rights,

Welcoming the International Year of the World's Indigenous People 1993 as a reaffirmation of the commitment of the international community to ensure their enjoyment of all human rights and fundamental freedoms and to respect the value and diversity of their cultures and identities,

Recognizing also that the international community should devise ways and means to remove the current obstacles and meet challenges to the full realization of all human rights and to prevent the continuation of human rights violations resulting thereof throughout the world,

Invoking the spirit of our age and the realities of our time which call upon the peoples of the world and all States Members of the United Nations to rededicate themselves to the global task of promoting and protecting all human rights and fundamental freedoms so as to secure full and universal enjoyment of these rights,

Determined to take new steps forward in the commitment of the international community with a view to achieving substantial progress in human rights endeavours by an increased and sustained effort of international cooperation and solidarity,

Solemnly adopts the Vienna Declaration and Programme of Action.

I

1. The World Conference on Human Rights reaffirms the solemn commitment of all States to fulfil their obligations to promote universal respect for, and observance and

protection of, all human rights and fundamental freedoms for all in accordance with the Charter of the United Nations, other instruments relating to human rights, and international law. The universal nature of these rights and freedoms is beyond question.

In this framework, enhancement of international cooperation in the field of human rights is essential for the full achievement of the purposes of the United Nations.

Human rights and fundamental freedoms are the birthright of all human beings; their protection and promotion is the first responsibility of Governments.

2. All peoples have the right of self-determination. By virtue of that right they freely determine their political status, and freely pursue their economic, social and cultural development.

Taking into account the particular situation of peoples under colonial or other forms of alien domination or foreign occupation, the World Conference on Human Rights recognizes the right of peoples to take any legitimate action, in accordance with the Charter of the United Nations, to realize their inalienable right of self-determination. The World Conference on Human Rights considers the denial of the right of self-determination as a violation of human rights and underlines the importance of the effective realization of this right.

In accordance with the Declaration on Principles of International Law concerning Friendly Relations and Cooperation Among States in accordance with the Charter of the United Nations, this shall not be construed as authorizing or encouraging any action which would dismember or impair, totally or in part, the territorial integrity or political unity of sovereign and independent States conducting themselves in compliance with the principle of equal rights and self-determination of peoples and thus possessed of a Government representing the whole people belonging to the territory without distinction of any kind.

3. Effective international measures to guarantee and monitor the implementation of human rights standards should be taken in respect of people under foreign occupation, and effective legal protection against the violation of their human rights should be provided, in accordance with human rights norms and international law, particularly the Geneva Convention relative to the Protection of Civilian Persons in Time of War, of 14 August 1949, and other applicable norms of humanitarian law.

4. The promotion and protection of all human rights and fundamental freedoms must be considered as a priority objective of the United Nations in accordance with its purposes and principles, in particular the purpose of international cooperation. In the framework of these purposes and principles, the promotion and protection of all human rights is a legitimate concern of the international community. The organs and specialized agencies related to human rights should therefore further enhance the coordination of their activities based on the consistent and objective application of international human rights instruments.

5. All human rights are universal, indivisible and interdependent and interrelated. The international community must treat human rights globally in a fair and equal manner, on the same footing, and with the same emphasis. While the significance of national and regional particularities and various historical, cultural and religious backgrounds must be borne in mind, it is the duty of States, regardless of their political, economic and cultural systems, to promote and protect all human rights and fundamental freedoms.

6. The efforts of the United Nations system towards the universal respect for, and observance of, human rights and fundamental freedoms for all, contribute to the stability and well-being necessary for peaceful and friendly relations among nations, and to

improved conditions for peace and security as well as social and economic development, in conformity with the Charter of the United Nations.

7. The processes of promoting and protecting human rights should be conducted in conformity with the purposes and principles of the Charter of the United Nations, and international law.

8. Democracy, development and respect for human rights and fundamental freedoms are interdependent and mutually reinforcing. Democracy is based on the freely expressed will of the people to determine their own political, economic, social and cultural systems and their full participation in all aspects of their lives. In the context of the above, the promotion and protection of human rights and fundamental freedoms at the national and international levels should be universal and conducted without conditions attached. The international community should support the strengthening and promoting of democracy, development and respect for human rights and fundamental freedoms in the entire world.

9. The World Conference on Human Rights reaffirms that least developed countries committed to the process of democratization and economic reforms, many of which are in Africa, should be supported by the international community in order to succeed in their transition to democracy and economic development.

10. The World Conference on Human Rights reaffirms the right to development, as established in the Declaration on the Right to Development, as a universal and inalienable right and an integral part of fundamental human rights.

As stated in the Declaration on the Right to Development, the human person is the central subject of development.

While development facilitates the enjoyment of all human rights, the lack of development may not be invoked to justify the abridgement of internationally recognized human rights.

States should cooperate with each other in ensuring development and eliminating obstacles to development. The international community should promote an effective international cooperation for the realization of the right to development and the elimination of obstacles to development.

Lasting progress towards the implementation of the right to development requires effective development policies at the national level, as well as equitable economic relations and a favourable economic environment at the international level.

11. The right to development should be fulfilled so as to meet equitably the developmental and environmental needs of present and future generations. The World Conference on Human Rights recognizes that illicit dumping of toxic and dangerous substances and waste potentially constitutes a serious threat to the human rights to life and health of everyone.

Consequently, the World Conference on Human Rights calls on all States to adopt and vigorously implement existing conventions relating to the dumping of toxic and dangerous products and waste and to cooperate in the prevention of illicit dumping.

Everyone has the right to enjoy the benefits of scientific progress and its applications. The World Conference on Human Rights notes that certain advances, notably in the biomedical and life sciences as well as in information technology, may have potentially adverse consequences for the integrity, dignity and human rights of the individual, and calls for international cooperation to ensure that human rights and dignity are fully respected in this area of universal concern

12. The World Conference on Human Rights calls upon the international community to make all efforts to help alleviate the external debt burden of developing countries, in

order to supplement the efforts of the Governments of such countries to attain the full realization of the economic, social and cultural rights of their people.

13. There is a need for States and international organizations, in cooperation with non-governmental organizations, to create favourable conditions at the national, regional and international levels to ensure the full and effective enjoyment of human rights. States should eliminate all violations of human rights and their causes, as well as obstacles to the enjoyment of these rights.

14. The existence of widespread extreme poverty inhibits the full and effective enjoyment of human rights; its immediate alleviation and eventual elimination must remain a high priority for the international community.

15. Respect for human rights and for fundamental freedoms without distinction of any kind is a fundamental rule of international human rights law. The speedy and comprehensive elimination of all forms of racism and racial discrimination, xenophobia and related intolerance is a priority task for the international community. Governments should take effective measures to prevent and combat them. Groups, institutions, intergovernmental and non-governmental organizations and individuals are urged to intensify their efforts in cooperating and coordinating their activities against these evils.

16. The World Conference on Human Rights welcomes the progress made in dismantling apartheid and calls upon the international community and the United Nations system to assist in this process.

The World Conference on Human Rights also deplores the continuing acts of violence aimed at undermining the quest for a peaceful dismantling of apartheid.

17. The acts, methods and practices of terrorism in all its forms and manifestations as well as linkage in some countries to drug trafficking are activities aimed at the destruction of human rights, fundamental freedoms and democracy, threatening territorial integrity, security of States and destabilizing legitimately constituted Governments. The international community should take the necessary steps to enhance cooperation to prevent and combat terrorism.

18. The human rights of women and of the girl-child are an inalienable, integral and indivisible part of universal human rights. The full and equal participation of women in political, civil, economic, social and cultural life, at the national, regional and international levels, and the eradication of all forms of discrimination on grounds of sex are priority objectives of the international community.

Gender-based violence and all forms of sexual harassment and exploitation, including those resulting from cultural prejudice and international trafficking, are incompatible with the dignity and worth of the human person, and must be eliminated. This can be achieved by legal measures and through national action and international cooperation in such fields as economic and social development, education, safe maternity and health care, and social support.

The human rights of women should form an integral part of the United Nations human rights activities, including the promotion of all human rights instruments relating to women.

The World Conference on Human Rights urges Governments, institutions, intergovernmental and non-governmental organizations to intensify their efforts for the protection and promotion of human rights of women and the girl-child.

19. Considering the importance of the promotion and protection of the rights of persons belonging to minorities and the contribution of such promotion and protection to the political and social stability of the States in which such persons live,

The World Conference on Human Rights reaffirms the obligation of States to ensure that persons belonging to minorities may exercise fully and effectively all human rights and fundamental freedoms without any discrimination and in full equality before the law in accordance with the Declaration on the Rights of Persons Belonging to National or Ethnic, Religious and Linguistic Minorities.

The persons belonging to minorities have the right to enjoy their own culture, to profess and practise their own religion and to use their own language in private and in public, freely and without interference or any form of discrimination.

20. The World Conference on Human Rights recognizes the inherent dignity and the unique contribution of indigenous people to the development and plurality of society and strongly reaffirms the commitment of the international community to their economic, social and cultural well-being and their enjoyment of the fruits of sustainable development. States should ensure the full and free participation of indigenous people in all aspects of society, in particular in matters of concern to them. Considering the importance of the promotion and protection of the rights of indigenous people, and the contribution of such promotion and protection to the political and social stability of the States in which such people live, States should, in accordance with international law, take concerted positive steps to ensure respect for all human rights and fundamental freedoms of indigenous people, on the basis of equality and non-discrimination, and recognize the value and diversity of their distinct identities, cultures and social organization.

21. The World Conference on Human Rights, welcoming the early ratification of the Convention on the Rights of the Child by a large number of States and noting the recognition of the human rights of children in the World Declaration on the Survival, Protection and Development of Children and Plan of Action adopted by the World Summit for Children, urges universal ratification of the Convention by 1995 and its effective implementation by States parties through the adoption of all the necessary legislative, administrative and other measures and the allocation to the maximum extent of the available resources. In all actions concerning children, non-discrimination and the best interest of the child should be primary considerations and the views of the child given due weight. National and international mechanisms and programmes should be strengthened for the defence and protection of children, in particular, the girl-child, abandoned children, street children, economically and sexually exploited children, including through child pornography, child prostitution or sale of organs, children victims of diseases including acquired immunodeficiency syndrome, refugee and displaced children, children in detention, children in armed conflict, as well as children victims of famine and drought and other emergencies. International cooperation and solidarity should be promoted to support the implementation of the Convention and the rights of the child should be a priority in the United Nations system-wide action on human rights.

The World Conference on Human Rights also stresses that the child for the full and harmonious development of his or her personality should grow up in a family environment which accordingly merits broader protection.

22. Special attention needs to be paid to ensuring non-discrimination, and the equal enjoyment of all human rights and fundamental freedoms by disabled persons, including their active participation in all aspects of society.

23. The World Conference on Human Rights reaffirms that everyone, without distinction of any kind, is entitled to the right to seek and to enjoy in other countries asylum from persecution, as well as the right to return to one's own country. In this respect it stresses the

importance of the Universal Declaration of Human Rights, the 1951 Convention relating to the Status of Refugees, its 1967 Protocol and regional instruments. It expresses its appreciation to States that continue to admit and host large numbers of refugees in their territories, and to the Office of the United Nations High Commissioner for Refugees for its dedication to its task. It also expresses its appreciation to the United Nations Relief and Works Agency for Palestine Refugees in the Near East.

The World Conference on Human Rights recognizes that gross violations of human rights, including in armed conflicts, are among the multiple and complex factors leading to displacement of people.

The World Conference on Human Rights recognizes that, in view of the complexities of the global refugee crisis and in accordance with the Charter of the United Nations, relevant international instruments and international solidarity and in the spirit of burden-sharing, a comprehensive approach by the international community is needed in coordination and cooperation with the countries concerned and relevant organizations, bearing in mind the mandate of the United Nations High Commissioner for Refugees. This should include the development of strategies to address the root causes and effects of movements of refugees and other displaced persons, the strengthening of emergency preparedness and response mechanisms, the provision of effective protection and assistance, bearing in mind the special needs of women and children, as well as the achievement of durable solutions, primarily through the preferred solution of dignified and safe voluntary repatriation, including solutions such as those adopted by the international refugee conferences. The World Conference on Human Rights underlines the responsibilities of States, particularly as they relate to the countries of origin.

In the light of the comprehensive approach, the World Conference on Human Rights emphasizes the importance of giving special attention including through intergovernmental and humanitarian organizations and finding lasting solutions to questions related to internally displaced persons including their voluntary and safe return and rehabilitation.

In accordance with the Charter of the United Nations and the principles of humanitarian law, the World Conference on Human Rights further emphasizes the importance of and the need for humanitarian assistance to victims of all natural and man-made disasters.

24. Great importance must be given to the promotion and protection of the human rights of persons belonging to groups which have been rendered vulnerable, including migrant worke rs, the elimination of all forms of discrimination against them, and the strengthening and more effective implementation of existing human rights instruments. States have an obligation to create and maintain adequate measures at the national level, in particular in the fields of education, health and social support, for the promotion and protection of the rights of persons in vulnerable sectors of their populations and to ensure the participation of those among them who are interested in finding a solution to their own problems.

25. The World Conference on Human Rights affirms that extreme poverty and social exclusion constitute a violation of human dignity and that urgent steps are necessary to achieve better knowledge of extreme poverty and its causes, including those related to the problem of development, in order to promote the human rights of the poorest, and to put an end to extreme poverty and social exclusion and to promote the enjoyment of the fruits of social progress. It is essential for States to foster participation by the poorest

people in the decision-making process by the community in which they live, the promotion of human rights and efforts to combat extreme poverty.

26. The World Conference on Human Rights welcomes the progress made in the codification of human rights instruments, which is a dynamic and evolving process, and urges the universal ratification of human rights treaties. All States are encouraged to accede to these international instruments; all States are encouraged to avoid, as far as possible, the resort to reservations.

27. Every State should provide an effective framework of remedies to redress human rights grievances or violations. The administration of justice, including law enforcement and prosecutorial agencies and, especially, an independent judiciary and legal profession in full conformity with applicable standards contained in international human rights instruments, are essential to the full and non-discriminatory realization of human rights and indispensable to the processes of democracy and sustainable development. In this context, institutions concerned with the administration of justice should be properly funded, and an increased level of both technical and financial assistance should be provided by the international community. It is incumbent upon the United Nations to make use of special programmes of advisory services on a priority basis for the achievement of a strong and independent administration of justice.

28. The World Conference on Human Rights expresses its dismay at massive violations of human rights especially in the form of genocide, 'ethnic cleansing' and systematic rape of women in war situations, creating mass exodus of refugees and displaced persons. While strongly condemning such abhorrent practices it reiterates the call that perpetrators of such crimes be punished and such practices immediately stopped.

29. The World Conference on Human Rights expresses grave concern about continuing human rights violations in all parts of the world in disregard of standards as contained in international human rights instruments and international humanitarian law and about the lack of sufficient and effective remedies for the victims.

The World Conference on Human Rights is deeply concerned about violations of human rights during armed conflicts, affecting the civilian population, especially women, children, the elderly and the disabled. The Conference therefore calls upon States and all parties to armed conflicts strictly to observe international humanitarian law, as set forth in the Geneva Conventions of 1949 and other rules and principles of international law, as well as minimum standards for protection of human rights, as laid down in international conventions.

The World Conference on Human Rights reaffirms the right of the victims to be assisted by humanitarian organizations, as set forth in the Geneva Conventions of 1949 and other relevant instruments of international humanitarian law, and calls for the safe and timely access for such assistance.

30. The World Conference on Human Rights also expresses its dismay and condemnation that gross and systematic violations and situations that constitute serious obstacles to the full enjoyment of all human rights continue to occur in different parts of the world. Such violations and obstacles include, as well as torture and cruel, inhuman and degrading treatment or punishment, summary and arbitrary executions, disappearances, arbitrary detentions, all forms of racism, racial discrimination and apartheid, foreign occupation and alien domination, xenophobia, poverty, hunger and other denials of economic, social and cultural rights, religious intolerance, terrorism, discrimination against women and lack of the rule of law.

31. The World Conference on Human Rights calls upon States to refrain from any unilateral measure not in accordance with international law and the Charter of the United Nations that creates obstacles to trade relations among States and impedes the full realization of the human rights set forth in the Universal Declaration of Human Rights and international human rights instruments, in particular the rights of everyone to a standard of living adequate for their health and well-being, including food and medical care, housing and the necessary social services. The World Conference on Human Rights affirms that food should not be used as a tool for political pressure.

32. The World Conference on Human Rights reaffirms the importance of ensuring the universality, objectivity and non-selectivity of the consideration of human rights issues.

33. The World Conference on Human Rights reaffirms that States are duty-bound, as stipulated in the Universal Declaration of Human Rights and the International Covenant on Economic, Social and Cultural Rights and in other international human rights instruments, to ensure that education is aimed at strengthening the respect of human rights and fundamental freedoms. The World Conference on Human Rights emphasizes the importance of incorporating the subject of human rights education programmes and calls upon States to do so. Education should promote understanding, tolerance, peace and friendly relations between the nations and all racial or religious groups and encourage the development of United Nations activities in pursuance of these objectives. Therefore, education on human rights and the dissemination of proper information, both theoretical and practical, play an important role in the promotion and respect of human rights with regard to all individuals without distinction of any kind such as race, sex, language or religion, and this should be integrated in the education policies at the national as well as international levels. The World Conference on Human Rights notes that resource constraints and institutional inadequacies may impede the immediate realization of these objectives.

34. Increased efforts should be made to assist countries which so request to create the conditions whereby each individual can enjoy universal human rights and fundamental freedoms. Governments, the United Nations system as well as other multilateral organizations are urged to increase considerably the resources allocated to programmes aiming at the establishment and strengthening of national legislation, national institutions and related infrastructures which uphold the rule of law and democracy, electoral assistance, human rights awareness through training, teaching and education, popular participation and civil society.

The programmes of advisory services and technical cooperation under the Centre for Human Rights should be strengthened as well as made more efficient and transparent and thus become a major contribution to improving respect for human rights. States are called upon to increase their contributions to these programmes, both through promoting a larger allocation from the United Nations regular budget, and through voluntary contributions.

35. The full and effective implementation of United Nations activities to promote and protect human rights must reflect the high importance accorded to human rights by the Charter of the United Nations and the demands of the United Nations human rights activities, as mandated by Member States. To this end, United Nations human rights activities should be provided with increased resources.

36. The World Conference on Human Rights reaffirms the important and constructive role played by national institutions for the promotion and protection of human rights, in particular in their advisory capacity to the competent authorities, their role in remedying

human rights violations, in the dissemination of human rights information, and education in human rights.

The World Conference on Human Rights encourages the establishment and strengthening of national institutions, having regard to the 'Principles relating to the status of national institutions' and recognizing that it is the right of each State to choose the framework which is best suited to its particular needs at the national level.

37. Regional arrangements play a fundamental role in promoting and protecting human rights. They should reinforce universal human rights standards, as contained in international human rights instruments, and their protection. The World Conference on Human Rights endorses efforts under way to strengthen these arrangements and to increase their effectiveness, while at the same time stressing the importance of cooperation with the United Nations human rights activities.

The World Conference on Human Rights reiterates the need to consider the possibility of establishing regional and subregional arrangements for the promotion and protection of human rights where they do not already exist.

38. The World Conference on Human Rights recognizes the important role of non-governmental organizations in the promotion of all human rights and in humanitarian activities at national, regional and international levels. The World Conference on Human Rights appreciates their contribution to increasing public awareness of human rights issues, to the conduct of education, training and research in this field, and to the promotion and protection of all human rights and fundamental freedoms. While recognizing that the primary responsibility for standard-setting lies with States, the conference also appreciates the contribution of non-governmental organizations to this process. In this respect, the World Conference on Human Rights emphasizes the importance of continued dialogue and cooperation between Governments and non-governmental organizations. Non-governmental organizations and their members genuinely involved in the field of human rights should enjoy the rights and freedoms recognized in the Universal Declaration of Human Rights, and the protection of the national law. These rights and freedoms may not be exercised contrary to the purposes and principles of the United Nations. Non-governmental organizations should be free to carry out their human rights activities, without interference, within the framework of national law and the Universal Declaration of Human Rights.

39. Underlining the importance of objective, responsible and impartial information about human rights and humanitarian issues, the World Conference on Human Rights encourages the increased involvement of the media, for whom freedom and protection should be guaranteed within the framework of national law.

II

A. INCREASED COORDINATION ON HUMAN RIGHTS WITHIN THE UNITED NATIONS SYSTEM

1. The World Conference on Human Rights recommends increased coordination in support of human rights and fundamental freedoms within the United Nations system. To this end, the World Conference on Human Rights urges all United Nations organs, bodies and the specialized agencies whose activities deal with human rights to cooperate in order to strengthen, rationalize and streamline their activities, taking into account

the need to avoid unnecessary duplication. The World Conference on Human Rights also recommends to the Secretary-General that high-level officials of relevant United Nations bodies and specialized agencies at their annual meeting, besides coordinating their activities, also assess the impact of their strategies and policies on the enjoyment of all human rights.

2. Furthermore, the World Conference on Human Rights calls on regional organizations and prominent international and regional finance and development institutions to assess also the impact of their policies and programmes on the enjoyment of human rights.

3. The World Conference on Human Rights recognizes that relevant specialized agencies and bodies and institutions of the United Nations system as well as other relevant intergovernmental organizations whose activities deal with human rights play a vital role in the formulation, promotion and implementation of human rights standards, within their respective mandates, and should take into account the outcome of the World Conference on Human Rights within their fields of competence.

4. The World Conference on Human Rights strongly recommends that a concerted effort be made to encourage and facilitate the ratification of and accession or succession to international human rights treaties and protocols adopted within the framework of the United Nations system with the aim of universal acceptance. The Secretary-General, in consultation with treaty bodies, should consider opening a dialogue with States not having acceded to these human rights treaties, in order to identify obstacles and to seek ways of overcoming them.

5. The World Conference on Human Rights encourages States to consider limiting the extent of any reservations they lodge to international human rights instruments, formulate any reservations as precisely and narrowly as possible, ensure that none is incompatible with the object and purpose of the relevant treaty and regularly review any reservations with a view to withdrawing them.

6. The World Conference on Human Rights, recognizing the need to maintain consistency with the high quality of existing international standards and to avoid proliferation of human rights instruments, reaffirms the guidelines relating to the elaboration of new international instruments contained in General Assembly resolution 41/120 of 4 December 1986 and calls on the United Nations human rights bodies, when considering the elaboration of new international standards, to keep those guidelines in mind, to consult with human rights treaty bodies on the necessity for drafting new standards and to request the Secretariat to carry out technical reviews of proposed new instruments.

7. The World Conference on Human Rights recommends that human rights officers be assigned if and when necessary to regional offices of the United Nations Organization with the purpose of disseminating information and offering training and other technical assistance in the field of human rights upon the request of concerned Member States. Human rights training for international civil servants who are assigned to work relating to human rights should be organized.

8. The World Conference on Human Rights welcomes the convening of emergency sessions of the Commission on Human Rights as a positive initiative and that other ways of responding to acute violations of human rights be considered by the relevant organs of the United Nations system.

Resources

9. The World Conference on Human Rights, concerned by the growing disparity between the activities of the Centre for Human Rights and the human, financial and

other resources available to carry them out, and bearing in mind the resources needed for other important United Nations programmes, requests the Secretary-General and the General Assembly to take immediate steps to increase substantially the resources for the human rights programme from within the existing and future regular budgets of the United Nations, and to take urgent steps to seek increased extrabudgetary resources.

10.   Within this framework, an increased proportion of the regular budget should be allocated directly to the Centre for Human Rights to cover its costs and all other costs borne by the Centre for Human Rights, including those related to the United Nations human rights bodies. Voluntary funding of the Centre's technical cooperation activities should reinforce this enhanced budget; the World Conference on Human Rights calls for generous contributions to the existing trust funds.

11.   The World Conference on Human Rights requests the Secretary-General and the General Assembly to provide sufficient human, financial and other resources to the Centre for Human Rights to enable it effectively, efficiently and expeditiously to carry out its activities.

12.   The World Conference on Human Rights, noting the need to ensure that human and financial resources are available to carry out the human rights activities, as mandated by intergovernmental bodies, urges the Secretary-General, in accordance with Article 101 of the Charter of the United Nations, and Member States to adopt a coherent approach aimed at securing that resources commensurate to the increased mandates are allocated to the Secretariat. The World Conference on Human Rights invites the Secretary-General to consider whether adjustments to procedures in the programme budget cycle would be necessary or helpful to ensure the timely and effective implementation of human rights activities as mandated by Member States.

Centre for Human Rights

13.   The World Conference on Human Rights stresses the importance of strengthening the United Nations Centre for Human Rights.

14.   The Centre for Human Rights should play an important role in coordinating system-wide attention for human rights. The focal role of the Centre can best be realized if it is enabled to cooperate fully with other United Nations bodies and organs. The coordinating role of the Centre for Human Rights also implies that the office of the Centre for Human Rights in New York is strengthened.

15.   The Centre for Human Rights should be assured adequate means for the system of thematic and country rapporteurs, experts, working groups and treaty bodies. Follow-up on recommendations should become a priority matter for consideration by the Commission on Human Rights.

16.   The Centre for Human Rights should assume a larger role in the promotion of human rights. This role could be given shape through cooperation with Member States and by an enhanced programme of advisory services and technical assistance. The existing voluntary funds will have to be expanded substantially for these purposes and should be managed in a more efficient and coordinated way. All activities should follow strict and transparent project management rules and regular programme and project evaluations should be held periodically. To this end, the results of such evaluation exercises and other relevant information should be made available regularly. The Centre should, in particular, organize at least once a year information meetings open to all Member States and organizations directly involved in these projects and programmes.

Adaptation and strengthening of the United Nations machinery for human rights, including the question of the establishment of a United Nations High Commissioner for Human Rights

17.   The World Conference on Human Rights recognizes the necessity for a continuing adaptation of the United Nations human rights machinery to the current and future needs in the promotion and protection of human rights, as reflected in the present Declaration and within the framework of a balanced and sustainable development for all people. In particular, the United Nations human rights organs should improve their coordination, efficiency and effectiveness.

18.   The World Conference on Human Rights recommends to the General Assembly that when examining the report of the Conference at its forty-eighth session, it begin, as a matter of priority, consideration of the question of the establishment of a High Commissioner for Human Rights for the promotion and protection of all human rights.

B. EQUALITY, DIGNITY AND TOLERANCE

1. Racism, racial discrimination, xenophobia and other forms of intolerance

19.   The World Conference on Human Rights considers the elimination of racism and racial discrimination, in particular in their institutionalized forms such as apartheid or resulting from doctrines of racial superiority or exclusivity or contemporary forms and manifestations of racism, as a primary objective for the international community and a worldwide promotion programme in the field of human rights. United Nations organs and agencies should strengthen their efforts to implement such a programme of action related to the third decade to combat racism and racial discrimination as well as subsequent mandates to the same end. The World Conference on Human Rights strongly appeals to the international community to contribute generously to the Trust Fund for the Programme for the Decade for Action to Combat Racism and Racial Discrimination.

20.   The World Conference on Human Rights urges all Governments to take immediate measures and to develop strong policies to prevent and combat all forms and manifestations of racism, xenophobia or related intolerance, where necessary by enactment of appropriate legislation, including penal measures, and by the establishment of national institutions to combat such phenomena.

21.   The World Conference on Human Rights welcomes the decision of the Commission on Human Rights to appoint a Special Rapporteur on contemporary forms of racism, racial discrimination, xenophobia and related intolerance. The World Conference on Human Rights also appeals to all States parties to the International Convention on the Elimination of All Forms of Racial Discrimination to consider making the declaration under article 14 of the Convention.

22.   The World Conference on Human Rights calls upon all Governments to take all appropriate measures in compliance with their international obligations and with due regard to their respective legal systems to counter intolerance and related violence based on religion or belief, including practices of discrimination against women and including the desecration of religious sites, recognizing that every individual has the right to freedom of thought, conscience, expression and religion. The Conference also invites

all States to put into practice the provisions of the Declaration on the Elimination of All Forms of Intolerance and of Discrimination Based on Religion or Belief.

23. The World Conference on Human Rights stresses that all persons who perpetrate or authorize criminal acts associated with ethnic cleansing are individually responsible and accountable for such human rights violations, and that the international community should exert every effort to bring those legally responsible for such violations to justice.

24. The World Conference on Human Rights calls on all States to take immediate measures, individually and collectively, to combat the practice of ethnic cleansing to bring it quickly to an end. Victims of the abhorrent practice of ethnic cleansing are entitled to appropriate and effective remedies.

2. Persons belonging to national or ethnic, religious and linguistic minorities

25. The World Conference on Human Rights calls on the Commission on Human Rights to examine ways and means to promote and protect effectively the rights of persons belonging to minorities as set out in the Declaration on the Rights of Persons belonging to National or Ethnic, Religious and Linguistic Minorities. In this context, the World Conference on Human Rights calls upon the Centre for Human Rights to provide, at the request of Governments concerned and as part of its programme of advisory services and technical assistance, qualified expertise on minority issues and human rights, as well as on the prevention and resolution of disputes, to assist in existing or potential situations involving minorities.

26. The World Conference on Human Rights urges States and the international community to promote and protect the rights of persons belonging to national or ethnic, religious and linguistic minorities in accordance with the Declaration on the Rights of Persons belonging to National or Ethnic, Religious and Linguistic Minorities.

27. Measures to be taken, where appropriate, should include facilitation of their full participation in all aspects of the political, economic, social, religious and cultural life of society and in the economic progress and development in their country.

Indigenous people

28. The World Conference on Human Rights calls on the Working Group on Indigenous Populations of the Sub-Commission on Prevention of Discrimination and Protection of Minorities to complete the drafting of a declaration on the rights of indigenous people at its eleventh session.

29. The World Conference on Human Rights recommends that the Commission on Human Rights consider the renewal and updating of the mandate of the Working Group on Indigenous Populations upon completion of the drafting of a declaration on the rights of indigenous people.

30. The World Conference on Human Rights also recommends that advisory services and technical assistance programmes within the United Nations system respond positively to requests by States for assistance which would be of direct benefit to indigenous people. The World Conference on Human Rights further recommends that adequate human and financial resources be made available to the Centre for Human Rights within the overall framework of strengthening the Centre's activities as envisaged by this document.

31. The World Conference on Human Rights urges States to ensure the full and free participation of indigenous people in all aspects of society, in particular in matters of concern to them.

32. The World Conference on Human Rights recommends that the General Assembly proclaim an international decade of the world's indigenous people, to begin from January 1994, including action-orientated programmes, to be decided upon in partnership with indigenous people. An appropriate voluntary trust fund should be set up for this purpose. In the framework of such a decade, the establishment of a permanent forum for indigenous people in the United Nations system should be considered.

Migrant workers

33. The World Conference on Human Rights urges all States to guarantee the protection of the human rights of all migrant workers and their families.

34. The World Conference on Human Rights considers that the creation of conditions to foster greater harmony and tolerance between migrant workers and the rest of the society of the State in which they reside is of particular importance.

35. The World Conference on Human Rights invites States to consider the possibility of signing and ratifying, at the earliest possible time, the International Convention on the Rights of All Migrant Workers and Members of Their Families.

3. The equal status and human rights of women

36. The World Conference on Human Rights urges the full and equal enjoyment by women of all human rights and that this be a priority for Governments and for the United Nations. The World Conference on Human Rights also underlines the importance of the integration and full participation of women as both agents and beneficiaries in the development process, and reiterates the objectives established on global action for women towards sustainable and equitable development set forth in the Rio Declaration on Environment and Development and chapter 24 of Agenda 21, adopted by the United Nations Conference on Environment and Development (Rio de Janeiro, Brazil, 3–14 June 1992).

37. The equal status of women and the human rights of women should be integrated into the mainstream of United Nations system-wide activity. These issues should be regularly and systematically addressed throughout relevant United Nations bodies and mechanisms. In particular, steps should be taken to increase cooperation and promote further integration of objectives and goals between the Commission on the Status of Women, the Commission on Human Rights, the Committee for the Elimination of Discrimination against Women, the United Nations Development Fund for Women, the United Nations Development Programme and other United Nations agencies. In this context, cooperation and coordination should be strengthened between the Centre for Human Rights and the Division for the Advancement of Women.

38. In particular, the World Conference on Human Rights stresses the importance of working towards the elimination of violence against women in public and private life, the elimination of all forms of sexual harassment, exploitation and trafficking in women, the elimination of gender bias in the administration of justice and the eradication of any conflicts which may arise between the rights of women and the harmful effects of certain traditional or customary practices, cultural prejudices and religious extremism.

The World Conference on Human Rights calls upon the General Assembly to adopt the draft declaration on violence against women and urges States to combat violence against women in accordance with its provisions. Violations of the human rights of women in situations of armed conflict are violations of the fundamental principles of international human rights and humanitarian law. All violations of this kind, including in particular murder, systematic rape, sexual slavery, and forced pregnancy, require a particularly effective response.

39. The World Conference on Human Rights urges the eradication of all forms of discrimination against women, both hidden and overt. The United Nations should encourage the goal of universal ratification by all States of the Convention on the Elimination of All Forms of Discrimination against Women by the year 2000. Ways and means of addressing the particularly large number of reservations to the Convention should be encouraged. *Inter alia*, the Committee on the Elimination of Discrimination against Women should continue its review of reservations to the Convention. States are urged to withdraw reservations that are contrary to the object and purpose of the Convention or which are otherwise incompatible with international treaty law.

40. Treaty monitoring bodies should disseminate necessary information to enable women to make more effective use of existing implementation procedures in their pursuits of full and equal enjoyment of human rights and non-discrimination. New procedures should also be adopted to strengthen implementation of the commitment to women's equality and the human rights of women. The Commission on the Status of Women and the Committee on the Elimination of Discrimination against Women should quickly examine the possibility of introducing the right of petition through the preparation of an optional protocol to the Convention on the Elimination of All Forms of Discrimination against Women. The World Conference on Human Rights welcomes the decision of the Commission on Human Rights to consider the appointment of a special rapporteur on violence against women at its fiftieth session.

41. The World Conference on Human Rights recognizes the importance of the enjoyment by women of the highest standard of physical and mental health throughout their life span. In the context of the World Conference on Women and the Convention on the Elimination of All Forms of Discrimination against Women, as well as the Proclamation of Tehran of 1968, the World Conference on Human Rights reaffirms, on the basis of equality between women and men, a woman's right to accessible and adequate health care and the widest range of family planning services, as well as equal access to education at all levels.

42. Treaty monitoring bodies should include the status of women and the human rights of women in their deliberations and findings, making use of gender-specific data. States should be encouraged to supply information on the situation of women *de jure* and *de facto* in their reports to treaty monitoring bodies. The World Conference on Human Rights notes with satisfaction that the Commission on Human Rights adopted at its forty-ninth session resolution 1993/46 of 8 March 1993 stating that rapporteurs and working groups in the field of human rights should also be encouraged to do so. Steps should also be taken by the Division for the Advancement of Women in cooperation with other United Nations bodies, specifically the Centre for Human Rights, to ensure that the human rights activities of the United Nations regularly address violations of women's human rights, including gender-specific abuses. Training for United Nations human rights and humanitarian relief personnel to assist them to recognize and deal with human rights

abuses particular to women and to carry out their work without gender bias should be encouraged.

43. The World Conference on Human Rights urges Governments and regional and international organizations to facilitate the access of women to decision-making posts and their greater participation in the decision-making process. It encourages further steps within the United Nations Secretariat to appoint and promote women staff members in accordance with the Charter of the United Nations, and encourages other principal and subsidiary organs of the United Nations to guarantee the participation of women under conditions of equality.

44. The World Conference on Human Rights welcomes the World Conference on Women to be held in Beijing in 1995 and urges that human rights of women should play an important role in its deliberations, in accordance with the priority themes of the World Conference on Women of equality, development and peace.

4. The rights of the child

45. The World Conference on Human Rights reiterates the principle of 'First Call for Children' and, in this respect, underlines the importance of major national and international efforts, especially those of the United Nations Children's Fund, for promoting respect for the rights of the child to survival, protection, development and participation.

46. Measures should be taken to achieve universal ratification of the Convention on the Rights of the Child by 1995 and the universal signing of the World Declaration on the Survival, Protection and Development of Children and Plan of Action adopted by the World Summit for Children, as well as their effective implementation. The World Conference on Human Rights urges States to withdraw reservations to the Convention on the Rights of the Child contrary to the object and purpose of the Convention or otherwise contrary to international treaty law.

47. The World Conference on Human Rights urges all nations to undertake measures to the maximum extent of their available resources, with the support of international cooperation, to achieve the goals in the World Summit Plan of Action. The Conference calls on States to integrate the Convention on the Rights of the Child into their national action plans. By means of these national action plans and through international efforts, particular priority should be placed on reducing infant and maternal mortality rates, reducing malnutrition and illiteracy rates and providing access to safe drinking water and to basic education. Whenever so called for, national plans of action should be devised to combat devastating emergencies resulting from natural disasters and armed conflicts and the equally grave problem of children in extreme poverty.

48. The World Conference on Human Rights urges all States, with the support of international cooperation, to address the acute problem of children under especially difficult circumstances. Exploitation and abuse of children should be actively combated, including by addressing their root causes. Effective measures are required against female infanticide, harmful child labour, sale of children and organs, child prostitution, child pornography, as well as other forms of sexual abuse.

49. The World Conference on Human Rights supports all measures by the United Nations and its specialized agencies to ensure the effective protection and promotion of human rights of the girl child. The World Conference on Human Rights urges States to repeal existing laws and regulations and remove customs and practices which discriminate against and cause harm to the girl child.

50. The World Conference on Human Rights strongly supports the proposal that the Secretary-General initiate a study into means of improving the protection of children in armed conflicts. Humanitarian norms should be implemented and measures taken in order to protect and facilitate assistance to children in war zones. Measures should include protection for children against indiscriminate use of all weapons of war, especially anti-personnel mines. The need for aftercare and rehabilitation of children traumatized by war must be addressed urgently. The Conference calls on the Committee on the Rights of the Child to study the question of raising the minimum age of recruitment into armed forces.

51. The World Conference on Human Rights recommends that matters relating to human rights and the situation of children be regularly reviewed and monitored by all relevant organs and mechanisms of the United Nations system and by the supervisory bodies of the specialized agencies in accordance with their mandates.

52. The World Conference on Human Rights recognizes the important role played by non-governmental organizations in the effective implementation of all human rights instruments and, in particular, the Convention on the Rights of the Child.

53. The World Conference on Human Rights recommends that the Committee on the Rights of the Child, with the assistance of the Centre for Human Rights, be enabled expeditiously and effectively to meet its mandate, especially in view of the unprecedented extent of ratification and subsequent submission of country reports.

5. Freedom from torture

54. The World Conference on Human Rights welcomes the ratification by many Member States of the Convention against Torture and Other Cruel, Inhuman or Degrading Treatment or Punishment and encourages its speedy ratification by all other Member States.

55. The World Conference on Human Rights emphasizes that one of the most atrocious violations against human dignity is the act of torture, the result of which destroys the dignity and impairs the capability of victims to continue their lives and their activities.

56. The World Conference on Human Rights reaffirms that under human rights law and international humanitarian law, freedom from torture is a right which must be protected under all circumstances, including in times of internal or international disturbance or armed conflicts.

57. The World Conference on Human Rights therefore urges all States to put an immediate end to the practice of torture and eradicate this evil forever through full implementation of the Universal Declaration of Human Rights as well as the relevant conventions and, where necessary, strengthening of existing mechanisms. The World Conference on Human Rights calls on all States to cooperate fully with the Special Rapporteur on the question of torture in the fulfilment of his mandate.

58. Special attention should be given to ensure universal respect for, and effective implementation of, the Principles of Medical Ethics relevant to the Role of Health Personnel, particularly Physicians, in the Protection of Prisoners and Detainees against Torture and other Cruel, Inhuman or Degrading Treatment or Punishment adopted by the General Assembly of the United Nations.

59. The World Conference on Human Rights stresses the importance of further concrete action within the framework of the United Nations with the view to providing assistance to victims of torture and ensure more effective remedies for their physical,

psychological and social rehabilitation. Providing the necessary resources for this purpose should be given high priority, *inter alia*, by additional contributions to the United Nations Voluntary Fund for the Victims of Torture.

60. States should abrogate legislation leading to impunity for those responsible for grave violations of human rights such as torture and prosecute such violations, thereby providing a firm basis for the rule of law.

61. The World Conference on Human Rights reaffirms that efforts to eradicate torture should, first and foremost, be concentrated on prevention and, therefore, calls for the early adoption of an optional protocol to the Convention against Torture and Other Cruel, Inhuman and Degrading Treatment or Punishment, which is intended to establish a preventive system of regular visits to places of detention.

Enforced disappearances

62. The World Conference on Human Rights, welcoming the adoption by the General Assembly of the Declaration on the Protection of All Persons from Enforced Disappearance, calls upon all States to take effective legislative, administrative, judicial or other measures to prevent, terminate and punish acts of enforced disappearances. The World Conference on Human Rights reaffirms that it is the duty of all States, under any circumstances, to make investigations whenever there is reason to believe that an enforced disappearance has taken place on a territory under their jurisdiction and, if allegations are confirmed, to prosecute its perpetrators.

6. The rights of the disabled person

63. The World Conference on Human Rights reaffirms that all human rights and fundamental freedoms are universal and thus unreservedly include persons with disabilities. Every person is born equal and has the same rights to life and welfare, education and work, living independently and active participation in all aspects of society. Any direct discrimination or other negative discriminatory treatment of a disabled person is therefore a violation of his or her rights. The World Conference on Human Rights calls on Governments, where necessary, to adopt or adjust legislation to assure access to these and other rights for disabled persons.

64. The place of disabled persons is everywhere. Persons with disabilities should be guaranteed equal opportunity through the elimination of all socially determined barriers, be they physical, financial, social or psychological, which exclude or restrict full participation in society.

65. Recalling the World Programme of Action concerning Disabled Persons, adopted by the General Assembly at its thirty-seventh session, the World Conference on Human Rights calls upon the General Assembly and the Economic and Social Council to adopt the draft standard rules on the equalization of opportunities for persons with disabilities, at their meetings in 1993.

C. COOPERATION, DEVELOPMENT AND STRENGTHENING OF HUMAN RIGHTS

66. The World Conference on Human Rights recommends that priority be given to national and international action to promote democracy, development and human rights.

67. Special emphasis should be given to measures to assist in the strengthening and building of institutions relating to human rights, strengthening of a pluralistic civil society and the protection of groups which have been rendered vulnerable. In this context, assistance provided upon the request of Governments for the conduct of free and fair elections, including assistance in the human rights aspects of elections and public information about elections, is of particular importance. Equally important is the assistance to be given to the strengthening of the rule of law, the promotion of freedom of expression and the administration of justice, and to the real and effective participation of the people in the decision-making processes.

68. The World Conference on Human Rights stresses the need for the implementation of strengthened advisory services and technical assistance activities by the Centre for Human Rights. The Centre should make available to States upon request assistance on specific human rights issues, including the preparation of reports under human rights treaties as well as for the implementation of coherent and comprehensive plans of action for the promotion and protection of human rights. Strengthening the institutions of human rights and democracy, the legal protection of human rights, training of officials and others, broad-based education and public information aimed at promoting respect for human rights should all be available as components of these programmes.

69. The World Conference on Human Rights strongly recommends that a comprehensive programme be established within the United Nations in order to help States in the task of building and strengthening adequate national structures which have a direct impact on the overall observance of human rights and the maintenance of the rule of law. Such a programme, to be coordinated by the Centre for Human Rights, should be able to provide, upon the request of the interested Government, technical and financial assistance to national projects in reforming penal and correctional establishments, education and training of lawyers, judges and security forces in human rights, and any other sphere of activity relevant to the good functioning of the rule of law. That programme should make available to States assistance for the implementation of plans of action for the promotion and protection of human rights.

70. The World Conference on Human Rights requests the Secretary-General of the United Nations to submit proposals to the United Nations General Assembly, containing alternatives for the establishment, structure, operational modalities and funding of the proposed programme.

71. The World Conference on Human Rights recommends that each State consider the desirability of drawing up a national action plan identifying steps whereby that State would improve the promotion and protection of human rights.

72. The World Conference on Human Rights reaffirms that the universal and inalienable right to development, as established in the Declaration on the Right to Development, must be implemented and realized. In this context, the World Conference on Human Rights welcomes the appointment by the Commission on Human Rights of a thematic working group on the right to development and urges that the Working Group, in consultation and cooperation with other organs and agencies of the United Nations system, promptly formulate, for early consideration by the United Nations General Assembly, comprehensive and effective measures to eliminate obstacles to the implementation and realization of the Declaration on the Right to Development and recommending ways and means towards the realization of the right to development by all States.

73. The World Conference on Human Rights recommends that non-governmental and other grass-roots organizations active in development and/or human rights should be enabled to play a major role on the national and international levels in the debate, activities and implementation relating to the right to development and, in cooperation with Governments, in all relevant aspects of development cooperation.

74. The World Conference on Human Rights appeals to Governments, competent agencies and institutions to increase considerably the resources devoted to building well-functioning legal systems able to protect human rights, and to national institutions working in this area. Actors in the field of development cooperation should bear in mind the mutually reinforcing interrelationship between development, democracy and human rights. Cooperation should be based on dialogue and transparency. The World Conference on Human Rights also calls for the establishment of comprehensive programmes, including resource banks of information and personnel with expertise relating to the strengthening of the rule of law and of democratic institutions.

75. The World Conference on Human Rights encourages the Commission on Human Rights, in cooperation with the Committee on Economic, Social and Cultural Rights, to continue the examination of optional protocols to the International Covenant on Economic, Social and Cultural Rights.

76. The World Conference on Human Rights recommends that more resources be made available for the strengthening or the establishment of regional arrangements for the promotion and protection of human rights under the programmes of advisory services and technical assistance of the Centre for Human Rights. States are encouraged to request assistance for such purposes as regional and subregional workshops, seminars and information exchanges designed to strengthen regional arrangements for the promotion and protection of human rights in accord with universal human rights standards as contained in international human rights instruments.

77. The World Conference on Human Rights supports all measures by the United Nations and its relevant specialized agencies to ensure the effective promotion and protection of trade union rights, as stipulated in the International Covenant on Economic, Social and Cultural Rights and other relevant international instruments. It calls on all States to abide fully by their obligations in this regard contained in international instruments.

D. HUMAN RIGHTS EDUCATION

78. The World Conference on Human Rights considers human rights education, training and public information essential for the promotion and achievement of stable and harmonious relations among communities and for fostering mutual understanding, tolerance and peace.

79. States should strive to eradicate illiteracy and should direct education towards the full development of the human personality and to the strengthening of respect for human rights and fundamental freedoms. The World Conference on Human Rights calls on all States and institutions to include human rights, humanitarian law, democracy and rule of law as subjects in the curricula of all learning institutions in formal and non-formal settings.

80. Human rights education should include peace, democracy, development and social justice, as set forth in international and regional human rights instruments, in order to

achieve common understanding and awareness with a view to strengthening universal commitment to human rights.

81. Taking into account the World Plan of Action on Education for Human Rights and Democracy, adopted in March 1993 by the International Congress on Education for Human Rights and Democracy of the United Nations Educational, Scientific and Cultural Organization, and other human rights instruments, the World Conference on Human Rights recommends that States develop specific programmes and strategies for ensuring the widest human rights education and the dissemination of public information, taking particular account of the human rights needs of women.

82. Governments, with the assistance of intergovernmental organizations, national institutions and non-governmental organizations, should promote an increased awareness of human rights and mutual tolerance. The World Conference on Human Rights underlines the importance of strengthening the World Public Information Campaign for Human Rights carried out by the United Nations. They should initiate and support education in human rights and undertake effective dissemination of public information in this field. The advisory services and technical assistance programmes of the United Nations system should be able to respond immediately to requests from States for educational and training activities in the field of human rights as well as for special education concerning standards as contained in international human rights instruments and in humanitarian law and their application to special groups such as military forces, law enforcement personnel, police and the health profession. The proclamation of a United Nations decade for human rights education in order to promote, encourage and focus these educational activities should be considered.

E. IMPLEMENTATION AND MONITORING METHODS

83. The World Conference on Human Rights urges Governments to incorporate standards as contained in international human rights instruments in domestic legislation and to strengthen national structures, institutions and organs of society which play a role in promoting and safeguarding human rights.

84. The World Conference on Human Rights recommends the strengthening of United Nations activities and programmes to meet requests for assistance by States which want to establish or strengthen their own national institutions for the promotion and protection of human rights.

85. The World Conference on Human Rights also encourages the strengthening of cooperation between national institutions for the promotion and protection of human rights, particularly through exchanges of information and experience, as well as cooperation with regional organizations and the United Nations.

86. The World Conference on Human Rights strongly recommends in this regard that representatives of national institutions for the promotion and protection of human rights convene periodic meetings under the auspices of the Centre for Human Rights to examine ways and means of improving their mechanisms and sharing experiences.

87. The World Conference on Human Rights recommends to the human rights treaty bodies, to the meetings of chairpersons of the treaty bodies and to the meetings of States parties that they continue to take steps aimed at coordinating the multiple reporting requirements and guidelines for preparing State reports under the respective human

rights conventions and study the suggestion that the submission of one overall report on treaty obligations undertaken by each State would make these procedures more effective and increase their impact.

88. The World Conference on Human Rights recommends that the States parties to international human rights instruments, the General Assembly and the Economic and Social Council should consider studying the existing human rights treaty bodies and the various thematic mechanisms and procedures with a view to promoting greater efficiency and effectiveness through better coordination of the various bodies, mechanisms and procedures, taking into account the need to avoid unnecessary duplication and overlapping of their mandates and tasks.

89. The World Conference on Human Rights recommends continued work on the improvement of the functioning, including the monitoring tasks, of the treaty bodies, taking into account multiple proposals made in this respect, in particular those made by the treaty bodies themselves and by the meetings of the chairpersons of the treaty bodies. The comprehensive national approach taken by the Committee on the Rights of the Child should also be encouraged.

90. The World Conference on Human Rights recommends that States parties to human rights treaties consider accepting all the available optional communication procedures.

91. The World Conference on Human Rights views with concern the issue of impunity of perpetrators of human rights violations, and supports the efforts of the Commission on Human Rights and the Sub-Commission on Prevention of Discrimination and Protection of Minorities to examine all aspects of the issue.

92. The World Conference on Human Rights recommends that the Commission on Human Rights examine the possibility for better implementation of existing human rights instruments at the international and regional levels and encourages the International Law Commission to continue its work on an international criminal court.

93. The World Conference on Human Rights appeals to States which have not yet done so to accede to the Geneva Conventions of 12 August 1949 and the Protocols thereto, and to take all appropriate national measures, including legislative ones, for their full implementation.

94. The World Conference on Human Rights recommends the speedy completion and adoption of the draft declaration on the right and responsibility of individuals, groups and organs of society to promote and protect universally recognized human rights and fundamental freedoms.

95. The World Conference on Human Rights underlines the importance of preserving and strengthening the system of special procedures, rapporteurs, representatives, experts and working groups of the Commission on Human Rights and the Sub-Commission on the Prevention of Discrimination and Protection of Minorities, in order to enable them to carry out their mandates in all countries throughout the world, providing them with the necessary human and financial resources. The procedures and mechanisms should be enabled to harmonize and rationalize their work through periodic meetings. All States are asked to cooperate fully with these procedures and mechanisms.

96. The World Conference on Human Rights recommends that the United Nations assume a more active role in the promotion and protection of human rights in ensuring full respect for international humanitarian law in all situations of armed conflict, in accordance with the purposes and principles of the Charter of the United Nations.

97. The World Conference on Human Rights, recognizing the important role of human rights components in specific arrangements concerning some peace-keeping operations by the United Nations, recommends that the Secretary-General take into account the reporting, experience and capabilities of the Centre for Human Rights and human rights mechanisms, in conformity with the Charter of the United Nations.

98. To strengthen the enjoyment of economic, social and cultural rights, additional approaches should be examined, such as a system of indicators to measure progress in the realization of the rights set forth in the International Covenant on Economic, Social and Cultural Rights. There must be a concerted effort to ensure recognition of economic, social and cultural rights at the national, regional and international levels.

F. FOLLOW-UP TO THE WORLD CONFERENCE ON HUMAN RIGHTS

99. The World Conference on Human Rights recommends that the General Assembly, the Commission on Human Rights and other organs and agencies of the United Nations system related to human rights consider ways and means for the full implementation, without delay, of the recommendations contained in the present Declaration, including the possibility of proclaiming a United Nations decade for human rights. The World Conference on Human Rights further recommends that the Commission on Human Rights annually review the progress towards this end.

100. The World Conference on Human Rights requests the Secretary-General of the United Nations to invite on the occasion of the fiftieth anniversary of the Universal Declaration of Human Rights all States, all organs and agencies of the United Nations system related to human rights, to report to him on the progress made in the implementation of the present Declaration and to submit a report to the General Assembly at its fifty-third session, through the Commission on Human Rights and the Economic and Social Council. Likewise, regional and, as appropriate, national human rights institutions, as well as non-governmental organizations, may present their views to the Secretary-General on the progress made in the implementation of the present Declaration. Special attention should be paid to assessing the progress towards the goal of universal ratification of international human rights treaties and protocols adopted within the framework of the United Nations system.

26. STANDARD RULES ON THE EQUALIZATION OF OPPORTUNITIES FOR PERSONS WITH DISABILITIES, 1993

These rules were annexed to General Assembly Resolution 48/96, adopted without a vote on 20 December 1993.

In March 1994, the Secretary-General appointed the first Special Rapporteur on Disability of the Commission for Social Development, and the mandate has since been regularly renewed; see 'Monitoring of the Implementation of the Standard Rules on the Equalization of Opportunities for Persons with Disabilities. Note by the Secretary-General', and 'Report of the Special Rapporteur on Disability of the Commission for Social Development': UN doc. E/CN.5/2009/6, 17 November 2008.

The Commission on Human Rights also established the mandate of the Special Rapporteur on the right of everyone to the enjoyment of the highest attainable standard of physical and mental health by resolution 2002/31. This mandate of the Special Rapporteur (Anand Grover, 2008- ; Paul Hunt, 2002-2008) was endorsed and extended by the Human Rights Council in resolution 6/29 of 14 December 2007. See 'The right to health. Note by the Secretary-General' and 'Report of the Special Rapporteur on the right of everyone to the enjoyment of the highest attainable standard of physical and mental health': UN doc. A/63/263, 11 August 2008. See further **http://www.un.org/disabilities/** and **http://www2.ohchr.org/english/issues/health/right/**.

Further reading

HUNT, P. and MESQUITA, J., 'Mental Disabilities and the Human Right to the Highest Attainable Standard of Health', (2006) 28 *Human Rights Quarterly* 332.

STEIN, M. A., 'Disability Human Rights', (2007) 95 *California Law Review* 75.

UNITED NATIONS, OFFICE OF THE UN HIGH COMMISSIONER FOR HUMAN RIGHTS, INTER-PARLIAMENTARY UNION, *From Exclusion to Equality: Realizing the rights of persons with disabilities*, (Handbook for Parliamentarians on the Convention on the Rights of Persons with Disabilities and its Optional Protocol), Geneva: United Nations, 2007.

UNITED NATIONS *ENABLE* – RIGHTS AND DIGNITY OF PERSONS WITH DISABILITIES: **http://www.un.org/disabilities/**.

TEXT

INTRODUCTION

Background and current needs

1. There are persons with disabilities in all parts of the world and at all levels in every society. The number of persons with disabilities in the world is large and is growing.

2. Both the causes and the consequences of disability vary throughout the world. Those variations are the result of different socio-economic circumstances and of the different provisions that States make for the well-being of their citizens.

3. Present disability policy is the result of developments over the past 200 years. In many ways it reflects the general living conditions and social and economic policies of different

times. In the disability field, however, there are also many specific circumstances that have influenced the living conditions of persons with disabilities. Ignorance, neglect, superstition and fear are social factors that throughout the history of disability have isolated persons with disabilities and delayed their development.

4. Over the years disability policy developed from elementary care at institutions to education for children with disabilities and rehabilitation for persons who became disabled during adult life. Through education and rehabilitation, persons with disabilities became more active and a driving force in the further development of disability policy. Organizations of persons with disabilities, their families and advocates were formed, which advocated better conditions for persons with disabilities. After the Second World War the concepts of integration and normalization were introduced, which reflected a growing awareness of the capabilities of persons with disabilities.

5. Towards the end of the 1960s organizations of persons with disabilities in some countries started to formulate a new concept of disability. That new concept indicated the close connection between the limitation experienced by individuals with disabilities, the design and structure of their environments and the attitude of the general population. At the same time the problems of disability in developing countries were more and more highlighted. In some of those countries the percentage of the population with disabilities was estimated to be very high and, for the most part, persons with disabilities were extremely poor.

Previous international action

6. The rights of persons with disabilities have been the subject of much attention in the United Nations and other international organizations over a long period of time. The most important outcome of the International Year of Disabled Persons, 1981, was the World Programme of Action concerning Disabled Persons, adopted by the General Assembly by its resolution 37/52 of 3 December 1982. The Year and the World Programme of Action provided a strong impetus for progress in the field. They both emphasized the right of persons with disabilities to the same opportunities as other citizens and to an equal share in the improvements in living conditions resulting from economic and social development. There also, for the first time, handicap was defined as a function of the relationship between persons with disabilities and their environment.

7. The Global Meeting of Experts to Review the Implementation of the World Programme of Action concerning Disabled Persons at the Mid-Point of the United Nations Decade of Disabled Persons was held at Stockholm in 1987. It was suggested at the Meeting that a guiding philosophy should be developed to indicate the priorities for action in the years ahead. The basis of that philosophy should be the recognition of the rights of persons with disabilities.

8. Consequently, the Meeting recommended that the General Assembly convene a special conference to draft an international convention on the elimination of all forms of discrimination against persons with disabilities, to be ratified by States by the end of the Decade.

9. A draft outline of the convention was prepared by Italy and presented to the General Assembly at its forty-second session. Further presentations concerning a draft convention were made by Sweden at the forty-fourth session of the Assembly. However, on both occasions, no consensus could be reached on the suitability of such a convention. In the opinion of many representatives, existing human rights documents seemed to guarantee persons with disabilities the same rights as other persons.

Towards standard rules

10. Guided by the deliberations in the General Assembly, the Economic and Social Council, at its first regular session of 1990, finally agreed to concentrate on the elaboration of an international instrument of a different kind. By its resolution 1990/26 of 24 May 1990, the Council authorized the Commission for Social Development to consider, at its thirty-second session, the establishment of an ad hoc open-ended working group of government experts, funded by voluntary contributions, to elaborate standard rules on the equalization of opportunities for disabled children, youth and adults, in close collaboration with the specialized agencies, other intergovernmental bodies and non-governmental organizations, especially organizations of disabled persons. The Council also requested the Commission to finalize the text of those rules for consideration in 1993 and for submission to the General Assembly at its forty-eighth session.

11. The subsequent discussions in the Third Committee of the General Assembly at the forty-fifth session showed that there was wide support for the new initiative to elaborate standard rules on the equalization of opportunities for persons with disabilities.

12. At the thirty-second session of the Commission for Social Development, the initiative for standard rules received the support of a large number of representatives and discussions led to the adoption of resolution 32/2 of 20 February 1991, in which the Commission decided to establish an ad hoc open-ended working group in accordance with Economic and Social Council resolution 1990/26.

Purpose and content of the standard rules on the equalization of opportunities for persons with disabilities

13. The Standard Rules on the Equalization of Opportunities for Persons with Disabilities have been developed on the basis of the experience gained during the United Nations Decade of Disabled Persons (1983–1992). The International Bill of Human Rights, comprising the Universal Declaration of Human Rights, the International Covenant on Economic, Social and Cultural Rights and the International Covenant on Civil and Political Rights, the Convention on the Rights of the Child and the Convention on the Elimination of All Forms of Discrimination against Women, as well as the World Programme of Action concerning Disabled Persons, constitute the political and moral foundation for the Rules.

14. Although the Rules are not compulsory, they can become international customary rules when they are applied by a great number of States with the intention of respecting a rule in international law. They imply a strong moral and political commitment on behalf of States to take action for the equalization of opportunities for persons with disabilities. Important principles for responsibility, action and cooperation are indicated. Areas of decisive importance for the quality of life and for the achievement of full participation and equality are pointed out. The Rules offer an instrument for policy-making and action to persons with disabilities and their organizations. They provide a basis for technical and economic cooperation among States, the United Nations and other international organizations.

15. The purpose of the Rules is to ensure that girls, boys, women and men with disabilities, as members of their societies, may exercise the same rights and obligations as others. In all societies of the world there are still obstacles preventing persons with disabilities from exercising their rights and freedoms and making it difficult for them to participate fully in the activities of their societies. It is the responsibility of States to

take appropriate action to remove such obstacles. Persons with disabilities and their organizations should play an active role as partners in this process. The equalization of opportunities for persons with disabilities is an essential contribution in the general and worldwide effort to mobilize human resources. Special attention may need to be directed towards groups such as women, children, the elderly, the poor, migrant workers, persons with dual or multiple disabilities, indigenous people and ethnic minorities. In addition, there are a large number of refugees with disabilities who have special needs requiring attention.

Fundamental concepts in disability policy

16. The concepts set out below appear throughout the Rules. They are essentially built on the concepts in the World Programme of Action concerning Disabled Persons. In some cases they reflect the development that has taken place during the United Nations Decade of Disabled Persons.

Disability and handicap

17. The term 'disability' summarizes a great number of different functional limitations occurring in any population in any country of the world. People may be disabled by physical, intellectual or sensory impairment, medical conditions or mental illness. Such impairments, conditions or illnesses may be permanent or transitory in nature.

18. The term 'handicap' means the loss or limitation of opportunities to take part in the life of the community on an equal level with others. It describes the encounter between the person with a disability and the environment. The purpose of this term is to emphasize the focus on the shortcomings in the environment and in many organized activities in society, for example, information, communication and education, which prevent persons with disabilities from participating on equal terms.

19. The use of the two terms 'disability' and 'handicap', as defined in paragraphs 17 and 18 above, should be seen in the light of modern disability history. During the 1970s there was a strong reaction among representatives of organizations of persons with disabilities and professionals in the field of disability against the terminology of the time. The terms 'disability' and 'handicap' were often used in an unclear and confusing way, which gave poor guidance for policy-making and for political action. The terminology reflected a medical and diagnostic approach, which ignored the imperfections and deficiencies of the surrounding society.

20. In 1980, the World Health Organization adopted an international classification of impairments, disabilities and handicaps, which suggested a more precise and at the same time relativistic approach. The International Classification of Impairments, Disabilities, and Handicaps makes a clear distinction between 'impairment', 'disability' and 'handicap'. It has been extensively used in areas such as rehabilitation, education, statistics, policy, legislation, demography, sociology, economics and anthropology. Some users have expressed concern that the Classification, in its definition of the term 'handicap', may still be considered too medical and too centred on the individual, and may not adequately clarify the interaction between societal conditions or expectations and the abilities of the individual. Those concerns, and others expressed by users during the 12 years since its publication, will be addressed in forthcoming revisions of the Classification.

21. As a result of experience gained in the implementation of the World Programme of Action and of the general discussion that took place during the United Nations Decade of Disabled Persons, there was a deepening of knowledge and extension of understanding concerning disability issues and the terminology used. Current terminology recognizes the necessity of addressing both the individual needs (such as rehabilitation and technical aids) and the shortcomings of the society (various obstacles for participation).

Prevention

22. The term 'prevention' means action aimed at preventing the occurrence of physical, intellectual, psychiatric or sensory impairments (primary prevention) or at preventing impairments from causing a permanent functional limitation or disability (secondary prevention). Prevention may include many different types of action, such as primary health care, prenatal and postnatal care, education in nutrition, immunization campaigns against communicable diseases, measures to control endemic diseases, safety regulations, programmes for the prevention of accidents in different environments, including adaptation of workplaces to prevent occupational disabilities and diseases, and prevention of disability resulting from pollution of the environment or armed conflict.

Rehabilitation

23. The term 'rehabilitation' refers to a process aimed at enabling persons with disabilities to reach and maintain their optimal physical, sensory, intellectual, psychiatric and/or social functional levels, thus providing them with the tools to change their lives towards a higher level of independence. Rehabilitation may include measures to provide and/or restore functions, or compensate for the loss or absence of a function or for a functional limitation. The rehabilitation process does not involve initial medical care. It includes a wide range of measures and activities from more basic and general rehabilitation to goal-oriented activities, for instance vocational rehabilitation.

Equalization of opportunities

24. The term 'equalization of opportunities' means the process through which the various systems of society and the environment, such as services, activities, information and documentation, are made available to all, particularly to persons with disabilities.

25. The principle of equal rights implies that the needs of each and every individual are of equal importance, that those needs must be made the basis for the planning of societies and that all resources must be employed in such a way as to ensure that every individual has equal opportunity for participation.

26. Persons with disabilities are members of society and have the right to remain within their local communities. They should receive the support they need within the ordinary structures of education, health, employment and social services.

27. As persons with disabilities achieve equal rights, they should also have equal obligations. As those rights are being achieved, societies should raise their expectations of persons with disabilities. As part of the process of equal opportunities, provision should be made to assist persons with disabilities to assume their full responsibility as members of society.

PREAMBLE

States,

Mindful of the pledge made, under the Charter of the United Nations, to take joint and separate action in cooperation with the Organization to promote higher standards of living, full employment, and conditions of economic and social progress and development,

Reaffirming the commitment to human rights and fundamental freedoms, social justice and the dignity and worth of the human person proclaimed in the Charter,

Recalling in particular the international standards on human rights, which have been laid down in the Universal Declaration of Human Rights, the International Covenant on Economic, Social and Cultural Rights and the International Covenant on Civil and Political Rights,

Underlining that those instruments proclaim that the rights recognized therein should be ensured equally to all individuals without discrimination,

Recalling the Convention on the Rights of the Child, which prohibits discrimination on the basis of disability and requires special measures to ensure the rights of children with disabilities, and the International Convention on the Protection of the Rights of All Migrant Workers and Members of Their Families, which provides for some protective measures against disability,

Recalling also the provisions in the Convention on the Elimination of All Forms of Discrimination against Women to ensure the rights of girls and women with disabilities,

Having regard to the Declaration on the Rights of Disabled Persons, the Declaration on the Rights of Mentally Retarded Persons, the Declaration on Social Progress and Development, the Principles for the Protection of Persons with Mental Illness and for the Improvement of Mental Health Care and other relevant instruments adopted by the General Assembly,

Also having regard to the relevant conventions and recommendations adopted by the International Labour Organization, with particular reference to participation in employment without discrimination for persons with disabilities,

Mindful of the relevant recommendations and work of the United Nations Educational, Scientific and Cultural Organization, in particular the World Declaration on Education for All, the World Health Organization, the United Nations Children's Fund and other concerned organizations,

Having regard to the commitment made by States concerning the protection of the environment,

Mindful of the devastation caused by armed conflict and deploring the use of scarce resources in the production of weapons,

Recognizing that the World Programme of Action concerning Disabled Persons and the definition therein of equalization of opportunities represent earnest ambitions on the part of the international community to render those various international instruments and recommendations of practical and concrete significance,

Acknowledging that the objective of the United Nations Decade of Disabled Persons (1983–1992) to implement the World Programme of Action is still valid and requires urgent and continued action,

Recalling that the World Programme of Action is based on concepts that are equally valid in developing and industrialized countries,

Convinced that intensified efforts are needed to achieve the full and equal enjoyment of human rights and participation in society by persons with disabilities,

Re-emphasizing that persons with disabilities, and their parents, guardians, advocates and organizations, must be active partners with States in the planning and implementation of all measures affecting their civil, political, economic, social and cultural rights,

In pursuance of Economic and Social Council resolution 1990/26, and basing themselves on the specific measures required for the attainment by persons with disabilities of equality with others, enumerated in detail in the World Programme of Action,

Have adopted the Standard Rules on the Equalization of Opportunities for Persons with Disabilities outlined below, in order:

(a) To stress that all action in the field of disability presupposes adequate knowledge and experience of the conditions and special needs of persons with disabilities;

(b) To emphasize that the process through which every aspect of societal organization is made accessible to all is a basic objective of socio-economic development;

(c) To outline crucial aspects of social policies in the field of disability, including, as appropriate, the active encouragement of technical and economic cooperation;

(d) To provide models for the political decision-making process required for the attainment of equal opportunities, bearing in mind the widely differing technical and economic levels, the fact that the process must reflect keen understanding of the cultural context within which it takes place and the crucial role of persons with disabilities in it;

(e) To propose national mechanisms for close collaboration among States, the organs of the United Nations system, other intergovernmental bodies and organizations of persons with disabilities;

(f) To propose an effective machinery for monitoring the process by which States seek to attain the equalization of opportunities for persons with disabilities.

I. PRECONDITIONS FOR EQUAL PARTICIPATION

Rule 1—Awareness-raising

States should take action to raise awareness in society about persons with disabilities, their rights, their needs, their potential and their contribution.

1. States should ensure that responsible authorities distribute up-to-date information on available programmes and services to persons with disabilities, their families, professionals in the field and the general public. Information to persons with disabilities should be presented in accessible form.

2. States should initiate and support information campaigns concerning persons with disabilities and disability policies, conveying the message that persons with disabilities are citizens with the same rights and obligations as others, thus justifying measures to remove all obstacles to full participation.

3. States should encourage the portrayal of persons with disabilities by the mass media in a positive way; organizations of persons with disabilities should be consulted on this matter.

4. States should ensure that public education programmes reflect in all their aspects the principle of full participation and equality.

5. States should invite persons with disabilities and their families and organizations to participate in public education programmes concerning disability matters.

6. States should encourage enterprises in the private sector to include disability issues in all aspects of their activity.

7. States should initiate and promote programmes aimed at raising the level of awareness of persons with disabilities concerning their rights and potential. Increased self-reliance and empowerment will assist persons with disabilities to take advantage of the opportunities available to them.

8. Awareness-raising should be an important part of the education of children with disabilities and in rehabilitation programmes. Persons with disabilities could also assist one another in awareness-raising through the activities of their own organizations.

9. Awareness-raising should be part of the education of all children and should be a component of teacher-training courses and training of all professionals.

Rule 2—Medical care

States should ensure the provision of effective medical care to persons with disabilities.

1. States should work towards the provision of programmes run by multidisciplinary teams of professionals for early detection, assessment and treatment of impairment. This could prevent, reduce or eliminate disabling effects. Such programmes should ensure the full participation of persons with disabilities and their families at the individual level, and of organizations of persons with disabilities at the planning and evaluation level.

2. Local community workers should be trained to participate in areas such as early detection of impairments, the provision of primary assistance and referral to appropriate services.

3. States should ensure that persons with disabilities, particularly infants and children, are provided with the same level of medical care within the same system as other members of society.

4. States should ensure that all medical and paramedical personnel are adequately trained and equipped to give medical care to persons with disabilities and that they have access to relevant treatment methods and technology.

5. States should ensure that medical, paramedical and related personnel are adequately trained so that they do not give inappropriate advice to parents, thus restricting options for their children. This training should be an ongoing process and should be based on the latest information available.

6. States should ensure that persons with disabilities are provided with any regular treatment and medicines they may need to preserve or improve their level of functioning.

Rule 3—Rehabilitation*

States should ensure the provision of rehabilitation services to persons with disabilities in order for them to reach and sustain their optimum level of independence and functioning.

---

* Rehabilitation is a fundamental concept in disability policy and is defined above in paragraph 23 of the introduction.

1. States should develop national rehabilitation programmes for all groups of persons with disabilities. Such programmes should be based on the actual individual needs of persons with disabilities and on the principles of full participation and equality.

2. Such programmes should include a wide range of activities, such as basic skills training to improve or compensate for an affected function, counselling of persons with disabilities and their families, developing self-reliance, and occasional services such as assessment and guidance.

3. All persons with disabilities, including persons with severe and/or multiple disabilities, who require rehabilitation should have access to it.

4. Persons with disabilities and their families should be able to participate in the design and organization of rehabilitation services concerning themselves.

5. All rehabilitation services should be available in the local community where the person with disabilities lives. However, in some instances, in order to attain a certain training objective, special time-limited rehabilitation courses may be organized, where appropriate, in residential form.

6. Persons with disabilities and their families should be encouraged to involve themselves in rehabilitation, for instance as trained teachers, instructors or counsellors.

7. States should draw upon the expertise of organizations of persons with disabilities when formulating or evaluating rehabilitation programmes.

Rule 4—Support services

States should ensure the development and supply of support services, including assistive devices for persons with disabilities, to assist them to increase their level of independence in their daily living and to exercise their rights.

1. States should ensure the provision of assistive devices and equipment, personal assistance and interpreter services, according to the needs of persons with disabilities, as important measures to achieve the equalization of opportunities.

2. States should support the development, production, distribution and servicing of assistive devices and equipment and the dissemination of knowledge about them.

3. To achieve this, generally available technical know-how should be utilized. In States where high-technology industry is available, it should be fully utilized to improve the standard and effectiveness of assistive devices and equipment. It is important to stimulate the development and production of simple and inexpensive devices, using local material and local production facilities when possible. Persons with disabilities themselves could be involved in the production of those devices.

4. States should recognize that all persons with disabilities who need assistive devices should have access to them as appropriate, including financial accessibility. This may mean that assistive devices and equipment should be provided free of charge or at such a low price that persons with disabilities or their families can afford to buy them.

5. In rehabilitation programmes for the provision of assistive devices and equipment, States should consider the special requirements of girls and boys with disabilities concerning the design, durability and age-appropriateness of assistive devices and equipment.

6. States should support the development and provision of personal assistance programmes and interpretation services, especially for persons with severe and/or multiple disabilities. Such programmes would increase the level of participation of persons with disabilities in everyday life at home, at work, in school and during leisure-time activities.

7. Personal assistance programmes should be designed in such a way that the persons with disabilities using the programmes have a decisive influence on the way in which the programmes are delivered.

II. TARGET AREAS FOR EQUAL PARTICIPATION

Rule 5—Accessibility

States should recognize the overall importance of accessibility in the process of the equalization of opportunities in all spheres of society. For persons with disabilities of any kind, States should (a) introduce programmes of action to make the physical environment accessible; and (b) undertake measures to provide access to information and communication.

(a) Access to the physical environment

1. States should initiate measures to remove the obstacles to participation in the physical environment. Such measures should be to develop standards and guidelines and to consider enacting legislation to ensure accessibility to various areas in society, such as housing, buildings, public transport services and other means of transportation, streets and other outdoor environments.

2. States should ensure that architects, construction engineers and others who are professionally involved in the design and construction of the physical environment have access to adequate information on disability policy and measures to achieve accessibility.

3. Accessibility requirements should be included in the design and construction of the physical environment from the beginning of the designing process.

4. Organizations of persons with disabilities should be consulted when standards and norms for accessibility are being developed. They should also be involved locally from the initial planning stage when public construction projects are being designed, thus ensuring maximum accessibility.

(b) Access to information and communication

5. Persons with disabilities and, where appropriate, their families and advocates should have access to full information on diagnosis, rights and available services and programmes, at all stages. Such information should be presented in forms accessible to persons with disabilities.

6. States should develop strategies to make information services and documentation accessible for different groups of persons with disabilities. Braille, tape services, large print and other appropriate technologies should be used to provide access to written information and documentation for persons with visual impairments. Similarly, appropriate technologies should be used to provide access to spoken information for persons with auditory impairments or comprehension difficulties.

7. Consideration should be given to the use of sign language in the education of deaf children, in their families and communities. Sign language interpretation services should also be provided to facilitate the communication between deaf persons and others.

8. Consideration should also be given to the needs of people with other communication disabilities.

9. States should encourage the media, especially television, radio and newspapers, to make their services accessible.

10. States should ensure that new computerized information and service systems offered to the general public are either made initially accessible or are adapted to be made accessible to persons with disabilities.

11. Organizations of persons with disabilities should be consulted when measures to make information services accessible are being developed.

Rule 6—Education

States should recognize the principle of equal primary, secondary and tertiary educational opportunities for children, youth and adults with disabilities, in integrated settings. They should ensure that the education of persons with disabilities is an integral part of the educational system.

1. General educational authorities are responsible for the education of persons with disabilities in integrated settings. Education for persons with disabilities should form an integral part of national educational planning, curriculum development and school organization.

2. Education in mainstream schools presupposes the provision of interpreter and other appropriate support services. Adequate accessibility and support services, designed to meet the needs of persons with different disabilities, should be provided.

3. Parent groups and organizations of persons with disabilities should be involved in the education process at all levels.

4. In States where education is compulsory it should be provided to girls and boys with all kinds and all levels of disabilities, including the most severe.

5. Special attention should be given in the following areas:

    (a) Very young children with disabilities;

    (b) Pre-school children with disabilities;

    (c) Adults with disabilities, particularly women.

6. To accommodate educational provisions for persons with disabilities in the mainstream, States should:

    (a) Have a clearly stated policy, understood and accepted at the school level and by the wider community;

    (b) Allow for curriculum flexibility, addition and adaptation;

    (c) Provide for quality materials, ongoing teacher training and support teachers.

7. Integrated education and community-based programmes should be seen as complementary approaches in providing cost-effective education and training for persons with disabilities. National community-based programmes should encourage communities to use and develop their resources to provide local education to persons with disabilities.

8. In situations where the general school system does not yet adequately meet the needs of all persons with disabilities, special education may be considered. It should be aimed at preparing students for education in the general school system. The quality of such education should reflect the same standards and ambitions as general education and should be closely linked to it. At a minimum, students with disabilities should be afforded the same portion of educational resources as students without disabilities. States should aim

for the gradual integration of special education services into mainstream education. It is acknowledged that in some instances special education may currently be considered to be the most appropriate form of education for some students with disabilities.

9. Owing to the particular communication needs of deaf and deaf/blind persons, their education may be more suitably provided in schools for such persons or special classes and units in mainstream schools. At the initial stage, in particular, special attention needs to be focused on culturally sensitive instruction that will result in effective communication skills and maximum independence for people who are deaf or deaf/blind.

Rule 7—Employment

States should recognize the principle that persons with disabilities must be empowered to exercise their human rights, particularly in the field of employment. In both rural and urban areas they must have equal opportunities for productive and gainful employment in the labour market.

1. Laws and regulations in the employment field must not discriminate against persons with disabilities and must not raise obstacles to their employment.

2. States should actively support the integration of persons with disabilities into open employment. This active support could occur through a variety of measures, such as vocational training, incentive-oriented quota schemes, reserved or designated employment, loans or grants for small business, exclusive contracts or priority production rights, tax concessions, contract compliance or other technical or financial assistance to enterprises employing workers with disabilities. States should also encourage employers to make reasonable adjustments to accommodate persons with disabilities.

3. States' action programmes should include:

    (a) Measures to design and adapt workplaces and work premises in such a way that they become accessible to persons with different disabilities;

    (b) Support for the use of new technologies and the development and production of assistive devices, tools and equipment and measures to facilitate access to such devices and equipment for persons with disabilities to enable them to gain and maintain employment;

    (c) Provision of appropriate training and placement and ongoing support such as personal assistance and interpreter services.

4. States should initiate and support public awareness-raising campaigns designed to overcome negative attitudes and prejudices concerning workers with disabilities.

5. In their capacity as employers, States should create favourable conditions for the employment of persons with disabilities in the public sector.

6. States, workers' organizations and employers should cooperate to ensure equitable recruitment and promotion policies, employment conditions, rates of pay, measures to improve the work environment in order to prevent injuries and impairments and measures for the rehabilitation of employees who have sustained employment-related injuries.

7. The aim should always be for persons with disabilities to obtain employment in the open labour market. For persons with disabilities whose needs cannot be met in open employment, small units of sheltered or supported employment may be an alternative. It is important that the quality of such programmes be assessed in terms of their relevance and sufficiency in providing opportunities for persons with disabilities to gain employment in the labour market.

8. Measures should be taken to include persons with disabilities in training and employment programmes in the private and informal sectors.

9. States, workers' organizations and employers should cooperate with organizations of persons with disabilities concerning all measures to create training and employment opportunities, including flexible hours, part-time work, job-sharing, self-employment and attendant care for persons with disabilities.

Rule 8—Income maintenance and social security

States are responsible for the provision of social security and income maintenance for persons with disabilities.

1. States should ensure the provision of adequate income support to persons with disabilities who, owing to disability or disability-related factors, have temporarily lost or received a reduction in their income or have been denied employment opportunities. States should ensure that the provision of support takes into account the costs frequently incurred by persons with disabilities and their families as a result of the disability.

2. In countries where social security, social insurance or other social welfare schemes exist or are being developed for the general population, States should ensure that such systems do not exclude or discriminate against persons with disabilities.

3. States should also ensure the provision of income support and social security protection to individuals who undertake the care of a person with a disability.

4. Social security systems should include incentives to restore the income-earning capacity of persons with disabilities. Such systems should provide or contribute to the organization, development and financing of vocational training. They should also assist with placement services.

5. Social security programmes should also provide incentives for persons with disabilities to seek employment in order to establish or re-establish their income-earning capacity.

6. Income support should be maintained as long as the disabling conditions remain in a manner that does not discourage persons with disabilities from seeking employment. It should only be reduced or terminated when persons with disabilities achieve adequate and secure income.

7. States, in countries where social security is to a large extent provided by the private sector, should encourage local communities, welfare organizations and families to develop self-help measures and incentives for employment or employment-related activities for persons with disabilities.

Rule 9—Family life and personal integrity

States should promote the full participation of persons with disabilities in family life. They should promote their right to personal integrity and ensure that laws do not discriminate against persons with disabilities with respect to sexual relationships, marriage and parenthood.

1. Persons with disabilities should be enabled to live with their families. States should encourage the inclusion in family counselling of appropriate modules regarding disability and its effects on family life. Respite-care and attendant-care services should be made available to families which include a person with disabilities. States should remove all unnecessary obstacles to persons who want to foster or adopt a child or adult with disabilities.

2. Persons with disabilities must not be denied the opportunity to experience their sexuality, have sexual relationships and experience parenthood. Taking into account that persons with disabilities may experience difficulties in getting married and setting up a family, States should encourage the availability of appropriate counselling. Persons with disabilities must have the same access as others to family-planning methods, as well as to information in accessible form on the sexual functioning of their bodies.

3. States should promote measures to change negative attitudes towards marriage, sexuality and parenthood of persons with disabilities, especially of girls and women with disabilities, which still prevail in society. The media should be encouraged to play an important role in removing such negative attitudes.

4. Persons with disabilities and their families need to be fully informed about taking precautions against sexual and other forms of abuse. Persons with disabilities are particularly vulnerable to abuse in the family, community or institutions and need to be educated on how to avoid the occurrence of abuse, recognize when abuse has occurred and report on such acts.

Rule 10—Culture

States will ensure that persons with disabilities are integrated into and can participate in cultural activities on an equal basis.

1. States should ensure that persons with disabilities have the opportunity to utilize their creative, artistic and intellectual potential, not only for their own benefit, but also for the enrichment of their community, be they in urban or rural areas. Examples of such activities are dance, music, literature, theatre, plastic arts, painting and sculpture. Particularly in developing countries, emphasis should be placed on traditional and contemporary art forms, such as puppetry, recitation and story-telling.

2. States should promote the accessibility to and availability of places for cultural performances and services, such as theatres, museums, cinemas and libraries, to persons with disabilities.

3. States should initiate the development and use of special technical arrangements to make literature, films and theatre accessible to persons with disabilities.

Rule 11—Recreation and sports

States will take measures to ensure that persons with disabilities have equal opportunities for recreation and sports.

1. States should initiate measures to make places for recreation and sports, hotels, beaches, sports arenas, gym halls, etc., accessible to persons with disabilities. Such measures should encompass support for staff in recreation and sports programmes, including projects to develop methods of accessibility, and participation, information and training programmes.

2. Tourist authorities, travel agencies, hotels, voluntary organizations and others involved in organizing recreational activities or travel opportunities should offer their services to all, taking into account the special needs of persons with disabilities. Suitable training should be provided to assist that process.

3. Sports organizations should be encouraged to develop opportunities for participation by persons with disabilities in sports activities. In some cases, accessibility measures could be enough to open up opportunities for participation. In other cases, special

arrangements or special games would be needed. States should support the participation of persons with disabilities in national and international events.

4. Persons with disabilities participating in sports activities should have access to instruction and training of the same quality as other participants.

5. Organizers of sports and recreation should consult with organizations of persons with disabilities when developing their services for persons with disabilities.

Rule 12—Religion

States will encourage measures for equal participation by persons with disabilities in the religious life of their communities.

1. States should encourage, in consultation with religious authorities, measures to eliminate discrimination and make religious activities accessible to persons with disabilities.

2. States should encourage the distribution of information on disability matters to religious institutions and organizations. States should also encourage religious authorities to include information on disability policies in the training for religious professions, as well as in religious education programmes.

3. They should also encourage the accessibility of religious literature to persons with sensory impairments.

4. States and/or religious organizations should consult with organizations of persons with disabilities when developing measures for equal participation in religious activities.

III. IMPLEMENTATION MEASURES

Rule 13—Information and research

States assume the ultimate responsibility for the collection and dissemination of information on the living conditions of persons with disabilities and promote comprehensive research on all aspects, including obstacles that affect the lives of persons with disabilities.

1. States should, at regular intervals, collect gender-specific statistics and other information concerning the living conditions of persons with disabilities. Such data collection could be conducted in conjunction with national censuses and household surveys and could be undertaken in close collaboration, *inter alia*, with universities, research institutes and organizations of persons with disabilities. The data collection should include questions on programmes and services and their use.

2. States should consider establishing a data bank on disability, which would include statistics on available services and programmes as well as on the different groups of persons with disabilities. They should bear in mind the need to protect individual privacy and personal integrity.

3. States should initiate and support programmes of research on social, economic and participation issues that affect the lives of persons with disabilities and their families. Such research should include studies on the causes, types and frequencies of disabilities, the availability and efficacy of existing programmes and the need for development and evaluation of services and support measures.

4. States should develop and adopt terminology and criteria for the conduct of national surveys, in cooperation with organizations of persons with disabilities.

5. States should facilitate the participation of persons with disabilities in data collection and research. To undertake such research States should particularly encourage the recruitment of qualified persons with disabilities.

6. States should support the exchange of research findings and experiences.

7. States should take measures to disseminate information and knowledge on disability to all political and administration levels within national, regional and local spheres.

Rule 14—Policy-making and planning

States will ensure that disability aspects are included in all relevant policy-making and national planning.

1. States should initiate and plan adequate policies for persons with disabilities at the national level, and stimulate and support action at regional and local levels.

2. States should involve organizations of persons with disabilities in all decision-making relating to plans and programmes concerning persons with disabilities or affecting their economic and social status.

3. The needs and concerns of persons with disabilities should be incorporated into general development plans and not be treated separately.

4. The ultimate responsibility of States for the situation of persons with disabilities does not relieve others of their responsibility. Anyone in charge of services, activities or the provision of information in society should be encouraged to accept responsibility for making such programmes available to persons with disabilities.

5. States should facilitate the development by local communities of programmes and measures for persons with disabilities. One way of doing this could be to develop manuals or check-lists and provide training programmes for local staff.

Rule 15—Legislation

States have a responsibility to create the legal bases for measures to achieve the objectives of full participation and equality for persons with disabilities.

1. National legislation, embodying the rights and obligations of citizens, should include the rights and obligations of persons with disabilities. States are under an obligation to enable persons with disabilities to exercise their rights, including their human, civil and political rights, on an equal basis with other citizens. States must ensure that organizations of persons with disabilities are involved in the development of national legislation concerning the rights of persons with disabilities, as well as in the ongoing evaluation of that legislation.

2. Legislative action may be needed to remove conditions that may adversely affect the lives of persons with disabilities, including harassment and victimization. Any discriminatory provisions against persons with disabilities must be eliminated. National legislation should provide for appropriate sanctions in case of violations of the principles of non-discrimination.

3. National legislation concerning persons with disabilities may appear in two different forms. The rights and obligations may be incorporated in general legislation or contained in special legislation. Special legislation for persons with disabilities may be established in several ways:

   (a) By enacting separate legislation, dealing exclusively with disability matters;

   (b) By including disability matters within legislation on particular topics;

   (c) By mentioning persons with disabilities specifically in the texts that serve to interpret existing legislation.

A combination of those different approaches might be desirable. Affirmative action provisions may also be considered.

4. States may consider establishing formal statutory complaints mechanisms in order to
protect the interests of persons with disabilities.

Rule 16—Economic policies

States have the financial responsibility for national programmes and measures to create
equal opportunities for persons with disabilities.

1. States should include disability matters in the regular budgets of all national, regional
and local government bodies.

2. States, non-governmental organizations and other interested bodies should interact to
determine the most effective ways of supporting projects and measures relevant to persons with disabilities.

3. States should consider the use of economic measures (loans, tax exemptions, ear-
marked grants, special funds, and so on) to stimulate and support equal participation by
persons with disabilities in society.

4. In many States it may be advisable to establish a disability development fund,
which could support various pilot projects and self-help programmes at the grass-
roots level.

Rule 17—Coordination of work

States are responsible for the establishment and strengthening of national coordinating
committees, or similar bodies, to serve as a national focal point on disability matters.

1. The national coordinating committee or similar bodies should be permanent and
based on legal as well as appropriate administrative regulation.

2. A combination of representatives of private and public organizations is most likely to
achieve an intersectoral and multidisciplinary composition. Representatives could be
drawn from concerned government ministries, organizations of persons with disabilities
and non-governmental organizations.

3. Organizations of persons with disabilities should have considerable influence in the
national coordinating committee in order to ensure proper feedback of their concerns.

4. The national coordinating committee should be provided with sufficient autonomy
and resources to fulfil its responsibilities in relation to its decision-making capacities.
It should report to the highest governmental level.

Rule 18—Organizations of persons with disabilities

States should recognize the right of the organizations of persons with disabilities to represent persons with disabilities at national, regional and local levels. States should also recognize the advisory role of organizations of persons with disabilities in decision-making
on disability matters.

1. States should encourage and support economically and in other ways the formation and strengthening of organizations of persons with disabilities, family members and/or advocates. States should recognize that those organizations have a role to play in the development of disability policy.

2. States should establish ongoing communication with organizations of persons with disabilities and ensure their participation in the development of government policies.

3. The role of organizations of persons with disabilities could be to identify needs and priorities, to participate in the planning, implementation and evaluation of services and measures concerning the lives of persons with disabilities, and to contribute to public awareness and to advocate change.

4. As instruments of self-help, organizations of persons with disabilities provide and promote opportunities for the development of skills in various fields, mutual support among members and information sharing.

5. Organizations of persons with disabilities could perform their advisory role in many different ways such as having permanent representation on boards of government-funded agencies, serving on public commissions and providing expert knowledge on different projects.

6. The advisory role of organizations of persons with disabilities should be ongoing in order to develop and deepen the exchange of views and information between the State and the organizations.

7. Organizations should be permanently represented on the national coordinating committee or similar bodies.

8. The role of local organizations of persons with disabilities should be developed and strengthened to ensure that they influence matters at the community level.

Rule 19—Personnel training

States are responsible for ensuring the adequate training of personnel, at all levels, involved in the planning and provision of programmes and services concerning persons with disabilities.

1. States should ensure that all authorities providing services in the disability field give adequate training to their personnel.

2. In the training of professionals in the disability field, as well as in the provision of information on disability in general training programmes, the principle of full participation and equality should be appropriately reflected.

3. States should develop training programmes in consultation with organizations of persons with disabilities, and persons with disabilities should be involved as teachers, instructors or advisers in staff training programmes.

4. The training of community workers is of great strategic importance, particularly in developing countries. It should involve persons with disabilities and include the development of appropriate values, competence and technologies as well as skills which can be practised by persons with disabilities, their parents, families and members of the community.

Rule 20—National monitoring and evaluation of disability programmes in the implementation of the Rules

States are responsible for the continuous monitoring and evaluation of the implementation of national programmes and services concerning the equalization of opportunities for persons with disabilities.

1. States should periodically and systematically evaluate national disability programmes and disseminate both the bases and the results of the evaluations.

2. States should develop and adopt terminology and criteria for the evaluation of disability-related programmes and services.

3. Such criteria and terminology should be developed in close cooperation with organizations of persons with disabilities from the earliest conceptual and planning stages.

4. States should participate in international cooperation in order to develop common standards for national evaluation in the disability field. States should encourage national coordinating committees to participate also.

5. The evaluation of various programmes in the disability field should be built in at the planning stage, so that the overall efficacy in fulfilling their policy objectives can be evaluated.

Rule 21—Technical and economic cooperation

States, both industrialized and developing, have the responsibility to cooperate in and take measures for the improvement of the living conditions of persons with disabilities in developing countries.

1. Measures to achieve the equalization of opportunities of persons with disabilities, including refugees with disabilities, should be integrated into general development programmes.

2. Such measures must be integrated into all forms of technical and economic cooperation, bilateral and multilateral, governmental and non-governmental. States should bring up disability issues in discussions on such cooperation with their counterparts.

3. When planning and reviewing programmes of technical and economic cooperation, special attention should be given to the effects of such programmes on the situation of persons with disabilities. It is of the utmost importance that persons with disabilities and their organizations are consulted on any development projects designed for persons with disabilities. They should be directly involved in the development, implementation and evaluation of such projects.

4. Priority areas for technical and economic cooperation should include:

   (a) The development of human resources through the development of skills, abilities and potentials of persons with disabilities and the initiation of employment-generating activities for and of persons with disabilities;

   (b) The development and dissemination of appropriate disability-related technologies and know-how.

5. States are also encouraged to support the formation and strengthening of organizations of persons with disabilities.

6. States should take measures to improve the knowledge of disability issues among staff involved at all levels in the administration of technical and economic cooperation programmes.

Rule 22—International cooperation

States will participate actively in international cooperation concerning policies for the equalization of opportunities for persons with disabilities.

1. Within the United Nations, the specialized agencies and other concerned intergovernmental organizations, States should participate in the development of disability policy.

2. Whenever appropriate, States should introduce disability aspects in general negotiations concerning standards, information exchange, development programmes, etc.

3. States should encourage and support the exchange of knowledge and experience among:

    (a) Non-governmental organizations concerned with disability issues;

    (b) Research institutions and individual researchers involved in disability issues;

    (c) Representatives of field programmes and of professional groups in the disability field;

    (d) Organizations of persons with disabilities;

    (e) National coordinating committees.

4. States should ensure that the United Nations and the specialized agencies, as well as all intergovernmental and interparliamentary bodies, at global and regional levels, include in their work the global and regional organizations of persons with disabilities.

IV. MONITORING MECHANISM

1. The purpose of a monitoring mechanism is to further the effective implementation of the Rules. It will assist each State in assessing its level of implementation of the Rules and in measuring its progress. The monitoring should identify obstacles and suggest suitable measures that would contribute to the successful implementation of the Rules. The monitoring mechanism will recognize the economic, social and cultural features existing in individual States. An important element should also be the provision of advisory services and the exchange of experience and information between States.

2. The Rules shall be monitored within the framework of the sessions of the Commission for Social Development. A Special Rapporteur with relevant and extensive experience in disability issues and international organizations shall be appointed, if necessary, funded by extrabudgetary resources, for three years to monitor the implementation of the Rules.

3. International organizations of persons with disabilities having consultative status with the Economic and Social Council and organizations representing persons with disabilities who have not yet formed their own organizations should be invited to create among themselves a panel of experts, on which organizations of persons with disabilities shall have a majority, taking into account the different kinds of disabilities and necessary equitable geographical distribution, to be consulted by the Special Rapporteur and, when appropriate, by the Secretariat.

4. The panel of experts will be encouraged by the Special Rapporteur to review, advise and provide feedback and suggestions on the promotion, implementation and monitoring of the Rules.

5. The Special Rapporteur shall send a set of questions to States, entities within the United Nations system, and intergovernmental and non-governmental organizations, including organizations of persons with disabilities. The set of questions should address implementation plans for the Rules in States. The questions should be selective in nature and cover a number of specific rules for in-depth evaluation. In preparing the questions the Special Rapporteur should consult with the panel of experts and the Secretariat.

6. The Special Rapporteur shall seek to establish a direct dialogue not only with States but also with local non-governmental organizations, seeking their views and comments on any information intended to be included in the reports. The Special Rapporteur shall provide advisory services on the implementation and monitoring of the Rules and assistance in the preparation of replies to the sets of questions.

7. The Department for Policy Coordination and Sustainable Development of the Secretariat, as the United Nations focal point on disability issues, the United Nations Development Programme and other entities and mechanisms within the United Nations system, such as the regional commissions and specialized agencies and inter-agency meetings, shall cooperate with the Special Rapporteur in the implementation and monitoring of the Rules at the national level.

8. The Special Rapporteur, assisted by the Secretariat, shall prepare reports for submission to the Commission for Social Development at its thirty-fourth and thirty-fifth sessions. In preparing such reports, the Rapporteur should consult with the panel of experts.

9. States should encourage national coordinating committees or similar bodies to participate in implementation and monitoring. As the focal points on disability matters at the national level, they should be encouraged to establish procedures to coordinate the monitoring of the Rules. Organizations of persons with disabilities should be encouraged to be actively involved in the monitoring of the process at all levels.

10. Should extrabudgetary resources be identified, one or more positions of interregional adviser on the Rules should be created to provide direct services to States, including:

    (a) The organization of national and regional training seminars on the content of the Rules;

    (b) The development of guidelines to assist in strategies for implementation of the Rules;

    (c) Dissemination of information about best practices concerning implementation of the Rules.

11. At its thirty-fourth session, the Commission for Social Development should establish an open-ended working group to examine the Special Rapporteur's report and make recommendations on how to improve the application of the Rules. In examining the Special Rapporteur's report, the Commission, through its open-ended working group, shall consult international organizations of persons with disabilities and specialized agencies, in accordance with rules 71 and 76 of the rules of procedure of the functional commissions of the Economic and Social Council.

12. At its session following the end of the Special Rapporteur's mandate, the Commission should examine the possibility of either renewing that mandate, appointing a new Special Rapporteur or considering another monitoring mechanism, and should make appropriate recommendations to the Economic and Social Council.

13. States should be encouraged to contribute to the United Nations Voluntary Fund on Disability in order to further the implementation of the Rules.

27. DECLARATION ON THE ELIMINATION OF VIOLENCE AGAINST WOMEN, 1993

This Declaration was adopted without a vote in General Assembly Resolution 48/104, 20 December 1993; see also General Assembly Resolution 59/167, 'Elimination of all forms of violence against women, including crimes identified in the outcome document of the twenty-third special session of the General Assembly, entitled "Women 2000: gender equality, development and peace for the twenty-first century"', 20 December 2004, adopted without a vote; the Inter-American Convention on the Prevention, Punishment and Eradication of Violence against Women, 1994, below, p. 991; and the Protocol to the African Charter on Human and Peoples' Rights on the Rights of Women in Africa, 2003, below, p. 1038.

In a related development, in March 2009, the UN Deputy Secretary-General, Dr. Asha-Rose Migiro launched the Secretary-General's database on violence against women: **http://webapps01.un.org/vawdatabase/home.action**.

Further reading

MERRY, S. E., 'Rights Talk and the Experience of Law: Implementing Women's Human Rights to Protection from Violence' (2003) 25 *Human Rights Quarterly* 343.

MYERSFIELD, B., 'Domestic Violence, Health, and International Law', (2008) 22 *Emory International Law Review* 61.

TEXT

The General Assembly,

Recognizing the urgent need for the universal application to women of the rights and principles with regard to equality, security, liberty, integrity and dignity of all human beings,

Noting that those rights and principles are enshrined in international instruments, including the Universal Declaration of Human Rights, the International Covenant on Civil and Political Rights, the International Covenant on Economic, Social and Cultural Rights, the Convention on the Elimination of All Forms of Discrimination against Women and the Convention against Torture and Other Cruel, Inhuman or Degrading Treatment or Punishment,

Recognizing that effective implementation of the Convention on the Elimination of All Forms of Discrimination against Women would contribute to the elimination of violence against women and that the Declaration on the Elimination of Violence against Women, set forth in the present resolution, will strengthen and complement that process,

Concerned that violence against women is an obstacle to the achievement of equality, development and peace, as recognized in the Nairobi Forward-looking Strategies for the Advancement of Women, in which a set of measures to combat violence against women was recommended, and to the full implementation of the Convention on the Elimination of All Forms of Discrimination against Women,

Affirming that violence against women constitutes a violation of the rights and fundamental freedoms of women and impairs or nullifies their enjoyment of those rights and freedoms, and concerned about the long-standing failure to protect and promote those rights and freedoms in the case of violence against women,

Recognizing that violence against women is a manifestation of historically unequal power relations between men and women, which have led to domination over and discrimination against women by men and to the prevention of the full advancement of women, and that violence against women is one of the crucial social mechanisms by which women are forced into a subordinate position compared with men,

Concerned that some groups of women, such as women belonging to minority groups, indigenous women, refugee women, migrant women, women living in rural or remote communities, destitute women, women in institutions or in detention, female children, women with disabilities, elderly women and women in situations of armed conflict, are especially vulnerable to violence,

Recalling the conclusion in paragraph 23 of the annex to Economic and Social Council resolution 1990/15 of 24 May 1990 that the recognition that violence against women in the family and society was pervasive and cut across lines of income, class and culture had to be matched by urgent and effective steps to eliminate its incidence,

Recalling also Economic and Social Council resolution 1991/18 of 30 May 1991, in which the Council recommended the development of a framework for an international instrument that would address explicitly the issue of violence against women,

Welcoming the role that women's movements are playing in drawing increasing attention to the nature, severity and magnitude of the problem of violence against women,

Alarmed that opportunities for women to achieve legal, social, political and economic equality in society are limited, inter alia, by continuing and endemic violence,

Convinced that in the light of the above there is a need for a clear and comprehensive definition of violence against women, a clear statement of the rights to be applied to ensure the elimination of violence against women in all its forms, a commitment by States in respect of their responsibilities, and a commitment by the international community at large to the elimination of violence against women,

Solemnly proclaims the following Declaration on the Elimination of Violence against Women and urges that every effort be made so that it becomes generally known and respected:

Article 1

For the purposes of this Declaration, the term 'violence against women' means any act of gender-based violence that results in, or is likely to result in, physical, sexual or psychological harm or suffering to women, including threats of such acts, coercion or arbitrary deprivation of liberty, whether occurring in public or in private life.

Article 2

Violence against women shall be understood to encompass, but not be limited to, the following:

(a) Physical, sexual and psychological violence occurring in the family, including battering, sexual abuse of female children in the household, dowry-related violence, marital rape, female genital mutilation and other traditional practices harmful to women, non-spousal violence and violence related to exploitation;

(b) Physical, sexual and psychological violence occurring within the general community, including rape, sexual abuse, sexual harassment and intimidation at work, in educational institutions and elsewhere, trafficking in women and forced prostitution;

(c) Physical, sexual and psychological violence perpetrated or condoned by the State, wherever it occurs.

Article 3

Women are entitled to the equal enjoyment and protection of all human rights and fundamental freedoms in the political, economic, social, cultural, civil or any other field. These rights include, *inter alia:*

(a) The right to life;

(b) The right to equality;

(c) The right to liberty and security of person;

(d) The right to equal protection under the law;

(e) The right to be free from all forms of discrimination;

(f) The right to the highest standard attainable of physical and mental health;

(g) The right to just and favourable conditions of work;

(h) The right not to be subjected to torture, or other cruel, inhuman or degrading treatment or punishment.

Article 4

States should condemn violence against women and should not invoke any custom, tradition or religious consideration to avoid their obligations with respect to its elimination. States should pursue by all appropriate means and without delay a policy of eliminating violence against women and, to this end, should:

(a) Consider, where they have not yet done so, ratifying or acceding to the Convention on the Elimination of All Forms of Discrimination against Women or withdrawing reservations to that Convention;

(b) Refrain from engaging in violence against women;

(c) Exercise due diligence to prevent, investigate and, in accordance with national legislation, punish acts of violence against women, whether those acts are perpetrated by the State or by private persons;

(d) Develop penal, civil, labour and administrative sanctions in domestic legislation to punish and redress the wrongs caused to women who are subjected to violence; women who are subjected to violence should be provided with access to the mechanisms of justice and, as provided for by national legislation, to just and effective remedies for the harm that they have suffered; States should also inform women of their rights in seeking redress through such mechanisms;

(e) Consider the possibility of developing national plans of action to promote the protection of women against any form of violence, or to include provisions for that purpose in plans already existing, taking into account, as appropriate, such cooperation as can be provided by non-governmental organizations, particularly those concerned with the issue of violence against women;

(f) Develop, in a comprehensive way, preventive approaches and all those measures of a legal, political, administrative and cultural nature that promote the protection of women against any form of violence, and ensure that the re-victimization of women does not occur because of laws insensitive to gender considerations, enforcement practices or other interventions;

(g) Work to ensure, to the maximum extent feasible in the light of their available resources and, where needed, within the framework of international cooperation, that women subjected to violence and, where appropriate, their children have specialized assistance, such as rehabilitation, assistance in child care and maintenance, treatment, counselling, and health and social services, facilities and programmes, as well as support structures, and should take all other appropriate measures to promote their safety and physical and psychological rehabilitation;

(h) Include in government budgets adequate resources for their activities related to the elimination of violence against women;

(i) Take measures to ensure that law enforcement officers and public officials responsible for implementing policies to prevent, investigate and punish violence against women receive training to sensitize them to the needs of women;

(j) Adopt all appropriate measures, especially in the field of education, to modify the social and cultural patterns of conduct of men and women and to eliminate prejudices, customary practices and all other practices based on the idea of the inferiority or superiority of either of the sexes and on stereotyped roles for men and women;

(k) Promote research, collect data and compile statistics, especially concerning domestic violence, relating to the prevalence of different forms of violence against women and encourage research on the causes, nature, seriousness and consequences of violence against women and on the effectiveness of measures implemented to prevent and redress violence against women; those statistics and findings of the research will be made public;

(l) Adopt measures directed towards the elimination of violence against women who are especially vulnerable to violence;

(m) Include, in submitting reports as required under relevant human rights instruments of the United Nations, information pertaining to violence against women and measures taken to implement the present Declaration;

(n) Encourage the development of appropriate guidelines to assist in the implementation of the principles set forth in the present Declaration;

(o) Recognize the important role of the women's movement and non-governmental organizations world wide in raising awareness and alleviating the problem of violence against women;

(p) Facilitate and enhance the work of the women's movement and non-governmental organizations and cooperate with them at local, national and regional levels;

(q) Encourage intergovernmental regional organizations of which they are members to include the elimination of violence against women in their programmes, as appropriate.

Article 5

The organs and specialized agencies of the United Nations system should, within their respective fields of competence, contribute to the recognition and realization of the rights and the principles set forth in the present Declaration and, to this end, should, *inter alia:*

(a) Foster international and regional cooperation with a view to defining regional strategies for combating violence, exchanging experiences and financing programmes relating to the elimination of violence against women;

(b) Promote meetings and seminars with the aim of creating and raising awareness among all persons of the issue of the elimination of violence against women;

(c) Foster coordination and exchange within the United Nations system between human rights treaty bodies to address the issue of violence against women effectively;

(d) Include in analyses prepared by organizations and bodies of the United Nations system of social trends and problems, such as the periodic reports on the world social situation, examination of trends in violence against women;

(e) Encourage coordination between organizations and bodies of the United Nations system to incorporate the issue of violence against women into ongoing programmes, especially with reference to groups of women particularly vulnerable to violence;

(f) Promote the formulation of guidelines or manuals relating to violence against women, taking into account the measures referred to in the present Declaration;

(g) Consider the issue of the elimination of violence against women, as appropriate, in fulfilling their mandates with respect to the implementation of human rights instruments;

(h) Cooperate with non-governmental organizations in addressing the issue of violence against women.

Article 6

Nothing in the present Declaration shall affect any provision that is more conducive to the elimination of violence against women that may be contained in the legislation of a State or in any international convention, treaty or other instrument in force in a State.

28. APPOINTMENT OF A UNITED NATIONS HIGH COMMISSIONER FOR HUMAN RIGHTS, 1993

After many years of discussion, the General Assembly decided in 1993 to appoint a 'High Commissioner for the Promotion and Protection of All Human Rights': UNGA Resolution 48/141, adopted without a vote on 20 December 1993. The first holder of the post was Ayala Lasso (1994–1997), followed by Mary Robinson (1997–2002); Sergio Vieira de Mello (2002–2003); Bertrand Ramcharan (Acting High Commissioner 2003–2004), and Louise Arbour 2004–2008. The Present High Commissioner, Navanethem Pillay, took up her post on 1 September 2008.

Further reading

CLAPHAM, A., 'Creating the High Commissioner for Human Rights: The Outside Story', (1994) 5 *EJIL* 556–68.

HANNUM, H., 'Human Rights in Conflict Resolution: The Role of the Office of the High Commissioner for Human Rights in UN Peacemaking and Peacebuilding', (2006) 28 *Human Rights Quarterly* 1.

RAMCHARAN, B. G., *The United Nations High Commissioner for Human Rights: The Challenges of International Protection*, The Hague: Martinus Nijhoff, 2002.

VAN BOVEN, T., 'The United Nations High Commissioner for Human Rights: The History of a Contested Project', (2007) 20 *Leiden Journal of International Law* 767.

TEXT

The General Assembly,

Reaffirming its commitment to the purposes and principles of the Charter of the United Nations,

Emphasizing the responsibilities of all States, in conformity with the Charter, to promote and encourage respect for all human rights and fundamental freedoms for all, without distinction as to race, sex, language or religion,

Emphasizing the need to observe the Universal Declaration of Human Rights and for the full implementation of the human rights instruments, including the International Covenant on Civil and Political Rights, the International Covenant on Economic, Social and Cultural Rights, as well as the Declaration on the Right to Development,

Reaffirming that the right to development is a universal and inalienable right which is a fundamental part of the rights of the human person,

Considering that the promotion and the protection of all human rights is one of the priorities of the international community,

Recalling that one of the purposes of the United Nations enshrined in the Charter is to achieve international cooperation in promoting and encouraging respect for human rights,

Reaffirming the commitment made under Article 56 of the Charter to take joint and separate action in cooperation with the United Nations for the achievement of the purposes set forth in Article 55 of the Charter,

Emphasizing the need for the promotion and protection of all human rights to be guided by the principles of impartiality, objectivity and non-selectivity, in the spirit of constructive international dialogue and cooperation,

Aware that all human rights are universal, indivisible, interdependent and interrelated and that as such they should be given the same emphasis,

Affirming its commitment to the Vienna Declaration and Programme of Action, adopted by the World Conference on Human Rights, held at Vienna from 14 to 25 June 1993,

Convinced that the World Conference on Human Rights made an important contribution to the cause of human rights and that its recommendations should be implemented through effective action by all States, the competent organs of the United Nations and the specialized agencies, in cooperation with non-governmental organizations,

Acknowledging the importance of strengthening the provision of advisory services and technical assistance by the Centre for Human Rights of the Secretariat and other relevant programmes and bodies of the United Nations system for the purpose of the promotion and protection of all human rights,

Determined to adapt, strengthen and streamline the existing mechanisms to promote and protect all human rights and fundamental freedoms while avoiding unnecessary duplication,

Recognizing that the activities of the United Nations in the field of human rights should be rationalized and enhanced in order to strengthen the United Nations machinery in this field and to further the objectives of universal respect for observance of international human rights standards,

Reaffirming that the General Assembly, the Economic and Social Council and the Commission on Human Rights are the responsible organs for decision- and policy-making for the promotion and protection of all human rights,

Reaffirming the necessity for a continued adaptation of the United Nations human rights machinery to the current and future needs in the promotion and protection of human rights and the need to improve its coordination, efficiency and effectiveness, as reflected in the Vienna Declaration and Programme of Action and within the framework of a balanced and sustainable development for all people,

Having considered the recommendation contained in paragraph 18 of section II of the Vienna Declaration and Programme of Action,

1. Decides to create the post of the High Commissioner for Human Rights;

2. Decides that the High Commissioner for Human Rights shall:

   (a) Be a person of high moral standing and personal integrity and shall possess expertise, including in the field of human rights, and the general knowledge and understanding of diverse cultures necessary for impartial, objective, non-selective and effective performance of the duties of the High Commissioner;

   (b) Be appointed by the Secretary-General of the United Nations and approved by the General Assembly, with due regard to geographical rotation, and have a fixed term of four years with a possibility of one renewal for another fixed term of four years;

   (c) Be of the rank of Under-Secretary-General;

3. Decides that the High Commissioner for Human Rights shall:

   (a) Function within the framework of the Charter of the United Nations, the Universal Declaration of Human Rights, other international instruments of human rights and international law, including the obligations, within this framework, to respect the sovereignty, territorial integrity and domestic jurisdiction of States and to promote the universal respect for and observance of all human rights, in the recognition that, in the framework of the purposes and principles of the Charter, the promotion and protection of all human rights is a legitimate concern of the international community;

(b) Be guided by the recognition that all human rights—civil, cultural, economic, political and social—are universal, indivisible, interdependent and interrelated and that, while the significance of national and regional particularities and various historical, cultural and religious backgrounds must be borne in mind, it is the duty of States, regardless of their political, economic and cultural systems, to promote and protect all human rights and fundamental freedoms;

(c) Recognize the importance of promoting a balanced and sustainable development for all people and of ensuring realization of the right to development, as established in the Declaration on the Right to Development;

4. Decides that the High Commissioner for Human Rights shall be the United Nations official with principal responsibility for United Nations human rights activities under the direction and authority of the Secretary-General; within the framework of the overall competence, authority and decisions of the General Assembly, the Economic and Social Council and the Commission on Human Rights, the High Commissioner's responsibilities shall be:

(a) To promote and protect the effective enjoyment by all of all civil, cultural, economic, political and social rights;

(b) To carry out the tasks assigned to him/her by the competent bodies of the United Nations system in the field of human rights and to make recommendations to them with a view to improving the promotion and protection of all human rights;

(c) To promote and protect the realization of the right to development and to enhance support from relevant bodies of the United Nations system for this purpose;

(d) To provide, through the Centre for Human Rights of the Secretariat and other appropriate institutions, advisory services and technical and financial assistance, at the request of the State concerned and, where appropriate, the regional human rights organizations, with a view to supporting actions and programmes in the field of human rights;

(e) To coordinate relevant United Nations education and public information programmes in the field of human rights;

(f) To play an active role in removing the current obstacles and in meeting the challenges to the full realization of all human rights and in preventing the continuation of human rights violations throughout the world, as reflected in the Vienna Declaration and Programme of Action;

(g) To engage in a dialogue with all Governments in the implementation of his/her mandate with a view to securing respect for all human rights;

(h) To enhance international cooperation for the promotion and protection of all human rights;

(i) To coordinate the human rights promotion and protection activities throughout the United Nations system;

(j) To rationalize, adapt, strengthen and streamline the United Nations machinery in the field of human rights with a view to improving its efficiency and effectiveness;

(k) To carry out overall supervision of the Centre for Human Rights;

5. Requests the High Commissioner for Human Rights to report annually on his/her activities, in accordance with his/her mandate, to the Commission on Human Rights and, through the Economic and Social Council, to the General Assembly;

6. Decides that the Office of the High Commissioner for Human Rights shall be located at Geneva and shall have a liaison office in New York;

7. Requests the Secretary-General to provide appropriate staff and resources, within the existing and future regular budgets of the United Nations, to enable the High Commissioner to fulfil his/her mandate, without diverting resources from the development programmes and activities of the United Nations;

8. Also requests the Secretary-General to report to the General Assembly at its forty-ninth session on the implementation of the present resolution.

29. NATIONAL INSTITUTIONS FOR THE PROMOTION AND PROTECTION OF HUMAN RIGHTS (THE 'PARIS PRINCIPLES'), 1993

The 'Paris Principles' approved by General Assembly Resolution 48/134, without a vote on 20 December 1993, were initially adopted at a conference convened by the French *Commission nationale consultative des droits de l'homme* and the Office of the United Nations High Commissioner for Human Rights. They were thereafter approved by Commission of Human Rights resolution 1992/54 on 3 March 1993 and submitted to the General Assembly. See also General Assembly Resolution 63/172, 'National institutions for the promotion and protection of human rights', 18 December 2008, adopted without a vote; and see generally the National Human Rights Institutions Forum: **http://www.nhri.net/**.

Further reading

OFFICE OF THE UNITED NATIONS HIGH COMMISSIONER FOR HUMAN RIGHTS, 'OHCHR and NHRIs': **http://www.ohchr.org/EN/Countries/NHRI/**.
'Report of the Secretary-General on national institutions for the promotion and protection of human rights', UN doc. A/HRC/7/69, 14 January 2008.
'Regional arrangements for the promotion and protection of human rights. Note by the Secretary-General', UN doc. A/63/486, 16 October 2008.

TEXT

The General Assembly,

Recalling the relevant resolutions concerning national institutions for the protection and promotion of human rights, notably its resolutions 41/129 of 4 December 1986 and 46/124 of 17 December 1991 and Commission on Human Rights resolutions 1987/40 of 10 March 1987, 1988/72 of 10 March 1988, 1989/52 of 7 March 1989, 1990/73 of 7 March 1990, 1991/27 of 5 March 1991 and 1992/54 of 3 March 1992, and taking note of Commission resolution 1993/55 of 9 March 1993,

Emphasizing the importance of the Universal Declaration of Human Rights, the International Covenants on Human Rights and other international instruments for promoting respect for and observance of human rights and fundamental freedoms,

Affirming that priority should be accorded to the development of appropriate arrangements at the national level to ensure the effective implementation of international human rights standards,

Convinced of the significant role that institutions at the national level can play in promoting and protecting human rights and fundamental freedoms and in developing and enhancing public awareness of those rights and freedoms,

Recognizing that the United Nations can play a catalytic role in assisting the development of national institutions by acting as a clearinghouse for the exchange of information and experience,

Mindful in this regard of the guidelines on the structure and functioning of national and local institutions for the promotion and protection of human rights endorsed by the General Assembly in its resolution 33/46 of 14 December 1978,

Welcoming the growing interest shown worldwide in the creation and strengthening of national institutions, expressed during the Regional Meeting for Africa of the World Conference on Human Rights, held at Tunis from 2 to 6 November 1992, the Regional Meeting for Latin America and the Caribbean, held at San José from 18 to 22 January 1993, the Regional Meeting for Asia, held at Bangkok from 29 March to 2 April 1993, the Commonwealth Workshop on National Human Rights Institutions, held at Ottawa from 30 September to 2 October 1992 and the Workshop for the Asia and Pacific Region on Human Rights Issues, held at Jakarta from 26 to 28 January 1993, and manifested in the decisions announced recently by several Member States to establish national institutions for the promotion and protection of human rights,

Bearing in mind the Vienna Declaration and Programme of Action, in which the World Conference on Human Rights reaffirmed the important and constructive role played by national institutions for the promotion and protection of human rights, in particular in their advisory capacity to the competent authorities, their role in remedying human rights violations, in the dissemination of human rights information and in education in human rights,

Noting the diverse approaches adopted throughout the world for the promotion and protection of human rights at the national level, emphasizing the universality, indivisibility and interdependence of all human rights, and emphasizing and recognizing the value of such approaches to promoting universal respect for and observance of human rights and fundamental freedoms,

1. *Takes note* with satisfaction of the updated report of the Secretary-General, prepared in accordance with General Assembly resolution 46/124 of 17 December 1991;

2. *Reaffirms* the importance of developing, in accordance with national legislation, effective national institutions for the promotion and protection of human rights and of ensuring the pluralism of their membership and their independence;

3. *Encourages* Member States to establish or, where they already exist, to strengthen national institutions for the promotion and protection of human rights and to incorporate those elements in national development plans;

4. *Encourages* national institutions for the promotion and protection of human rights established by Member States to prevent and combat all violations of human rights as enumerated in the Vienna Declaration and Programme of Action and relevant international instruments;

5. *Requests* the Centre for Human Rights of the Secretariat to continue its efforts to enhance cooperation between the United Nations and national institutions, particularly in the field of advisory services and technical assistance and of information and education, including within the framework of the World Public Information Campaign for Human Rights;

6. *Also requests* the Centre for Human Rights to establish, upon the request of States concerned, United Nations centres for human rights documentation and training and to do so on the basis of established procedures for the use of available resources within the United Nations Voluntary Fund for Advisory Services and Technical Assistance in the Field of Human Rights;

7. *Requests* the Secretary-General to respond favourably to requests from Member States for assistance in the establishment and strengthening of national institutions for the promotion and protection of human rights as part of the programme of advisory services and technical cooperation in the field of human rights, as well as national centres for human rights documentation and training;

8. *Encourages* all Member States to take appropriate steps to promote the exchange of information and experience concerning the establishment and effective operation of such national institutions;

9. *Affirms* the role of national institutions as agencies for the dissemination of human rights materials and for other public information activities, prepared or organized under the auspices of the United Nations;

10. *Welcomes* the organization under the auspices of the Centre for Human Rights of a follow-up meeting at Tunis in December 1993 with a view, in particular, to examining ways and means of promoting technical assistance for the cooperation and strengthening of national institutions and to continuing to examine all issues relating to the question of national institutions;

11. *Welcomes also* the Principles relating to the status of national institutions, annexed to the present resolution;

12. *Encourages* the establishment and strengthening of national institutions having regard to those principles and recognizing that it is the right of each State to choose the framework that is best suited to its particular needs at the national level;

13. *Requests* the Secretary-General to report to the General Assembly at its fiftieth session on the implementation of the present resolution.

ANNEX
PRINCIPLES RELATING TO THE STATUS OF NATIONAL INSTITUTIONS

Competence and responsibilities

1. A national institution shall be vested with competence to promote and protect human rights.

2. A national institution shall be given as broad a mandate as possible, which shall be clearly set forth in a constitutional or legislative text, specifying its composition and its sphere of competence.

3. A national institution shall, inter alia, have the following responsibilities:

(a) To submit to the Government, Parliament and any other competent body, on an advisory basis either at the request of the authorities concerned or through the exercise of its power to hear a matter without higher referral, opinions, recommendations, proposals and reports on any matters concerning the promotion and protection of human rights; the national institution may decide to publicize them; these opinions, recommendations, proposals and reports, as well as any prerogative of the national institution, shall relate to the following areas:

   (i) Any legislative or administrative provisions, as well as provisions relating to judicial organizations, intended to preserve and extend the protection of human rights; in that connection, the national institution shall examine the legislation and administrative provisions in force, as well as bills and proposals, and shall make such recommendations as it deems appropriate in order to ensure that these provisions conform to the fundamental principles of human rights; it shall, if necessary, recommend the adoption of new legislation, the amendment of legislation in force and the adoption or amendment of administrative measures;

(ii) Any situation of violation of human rights which it decides to take up;

(iii) The preparation of reports on the national situation with regard to human rights in general, and on more specific matters;

(iv) Drawing the attention of the Government to situations in any part of the country where human rights are violated and making proposals to it for initiatives to put an end to such situations and, where necessary, expressing an opinion on the positions and reactions of the Government;

(b) To promote and ensure the harmonization of national legislation regulations and practices with the international human rights instruments to which the State is a party, and their effective implementation;

(c) To encourage ratification of the above-mentioned instruments or accession to those instruments, and to ensure their implementation;

(d) To contribute to the reports which States are required to submit to United Nations bodies and committees, and to regional institutions, pursuant to their treaty obligations and, where necessary, to express an opinion on the subject, with due respect for their independence;

(e) To cooperate with the United Nations and any other organization in the United Nations system, the regional institutions and the national institutions of other countries that are competent in the areas of the promotion and protection of human rights;

(f) To assist in the formulation of programmes for the teaching of, and research into, human rights and to take part in their execution in schools, universities and professional circles;

(g) To publicize human rights and efforts to combat all forms of discrimination, in particular racial discrimination, by increasing public awareness, especially through information and education and by making use of all press organs.

Composition and guarantees of independence and pluralism

1. The composition of the national institution and the appointment of its members, whether by means of an election or otherwise, shall be established in accordance with a procedure which affords all necessary guarantees to ensure the pluralist representation of the social forces (of civilian society) involved in the promotion and protection of human rights, particularly by powers which will enable effective cooperation to be established with, or through the presence of, representatives of:

(a) Non-governmental organizations responsible for human rights and efforts to combat racial discrimination, trade unions, concerned social and professional organizations, for example, associations of lawyers, doctors, journalists and eminent scientists;

(b) Trends in philosophical or religious thought;

(c) Universities and qualified experts;

(d) Parliament;

(e) Government departments (if these are included, their representatives should participate in the deliberations only in an advisory capacity).

2. The national institution shall have an infrastructure which is suited to the smooth conduct of its activities, in particular adequate funding. The purpose of this funding should be to enable it to have its own staff and premises, in order to be independent of the Government and not be subject to financial control which might affect its independence.

3. In order to ensure a stable mandate for the members of the national institution, without which there can be no real independence, their appointment shall be effected by an official act which shall establish the specific duration of the mandate. This mandate may be renewable, provided that the pluralism of the institution's membership is ensured.

Methods of operation

Within the framework of its operation, the national institution shall:

(a) Freely consider any questions falling within its competence, whether they are submitted by the Government or taken up by it without referral to a higher authority, on the proposal of its members or of any petitioner;

(b) Hear any person and obtain any information and any documents necessary for assessing situations falling within its competence;

(c) Address public opinion directly or through any press organ, particularly in order to publicize its opinions and recommendations;

(d) Meet on a regular basis and whenever necessary in the presence of all its members after they have been duly convened;

(e) Establish working groups from among its members as necessary, and set up local or regional sections to assist it in discharging its functions;

(f) Maintain consultation with the other bodies, whether jurisdictional or otherwise, responsible for the promotion and protection of human rights (in particular ombudsmen, mediators and similar institutions);

(g) In view of the fundamental role played by the non-governmental organizations in expanding the work of the national institutions, develop relations with the non-governmental organizations devoted to promoting and protecting human rights, to economic and social development, to combating racism, to protecting particularly vulnerable groups (especially children, migrant workers, refugees, physically and mentally disabled persons) or to specialized areas.

Additional principles concerning the status of commissions with quasi-jurisdictional competence

A national institution may be authorized to hear and consider complaints and petitions concerning individual situations. Cases may be brought before it by individuals, their representatives, third parties, non-governmental organizations, associations of trade unions or any other representative organizations. In such circumstances, and without prejudice to the principles stated above concerning the other powers of the commissions, the functions entrusted to them may be based on the following principles:

(a) Seeking an amicable settlement through conciliation or, within the limits prescribed by the law, through binding decisions or, where necessary, on the basis of confidentiality;

(b) Informing the party who filed the petition of his rights, in particular the remedies available to him, and promoting his access to them;

(c) Hearing any complaints or petitions or transmitting them to any other competent authority within the limits prescribed by the law;

(d) Making recommendations to the competent authorities, especially by proposing amendments or reforms of the laws, regulations and administrative practices, especially if they have created the difficulties encountered by the persons filing the petitions in order to assert their rights.

30. BEIJING DECLARATION AND PLATFORM FOR ACTION, FOURTH WORLD CONFERENCE ON WOMEN: ACTION FOR EQUALITY, DEVELOPMENT AND PEACE, 1995

The Beijing Declaration and Platform for Action was adopted at the Fourth World Conference on Women, held in Beijing from 4–15 September 1995, which recommended also that it be endorsed by the General Assembly; see Resolution 50/203, 20 December 1995, paragraph 2.

Reproduced below are the Declaration and, from Annex II ('Platform for Action'), Chapters I (Mission Statement), II (Global Framework), and III (Critical Areas of Concern). Chapter IV (Strategic objectives and actions), which is omitted for reasons of space, sets out a detailed programme of action to be taken with regard to women and poverty, education and training, health, violence, armed conflict, the economy, women in power and decision-making, institutional mechanisms for advancement, human rights, the media, the environment, and the girl child. The opening paragraphs to Chapter IV explain that,

'45. In each critical area of concern, the problem is diagnosed and strategic objectives are proposed with concrete actions to be taken by various actors in order to achieve those objectives. The strategic objectives are derived from the critical areas of concern and specific actions to be taken to achieve them cut across the boundaries of equality, development and peace—the goals of the Nairobi Forward-looking Strategies for the Advancement of Women—and reflect their interdependence. The objectives and actions are interlinked, of high priority and mutually reinforcing. The Platform for Action is intended to improve the situation of all women, without exception, who often face similar barriers, while special attention should be given to groups that are the most disadvantaged.

'46. The Platform for Action recognizes that women face barriers to full equality and advancement because of such factors as their race, age, language, ethnicity, culture, religion or disability, because they are indigenous women or because of other status. Many women encounter specific obstacles related to their family status, particularly as single parents; and to their socio-economic status, including their living conditions in rural, isolated or impoverished areas. Additional barriers also exist for refugee women, other displaced women, including internally displaced women as well as for immigrant women and migrant women, including women migrant workers. Many women are also particularly affected by environmental disasters, serious and infectious diseases and various forms of violence against women.'

Also omitted are Chapter V, which makes recommendations on institutional arrangements at the national, sub-regional, regional and international level, and Chapter VI, which deals with financial arrangements.

For the full text, see Fourth World Conference on Women 15 September 1995, UN doc. A/CONF.177/20 (1995) and Add.1 (1995); also UN doc. A/CONF.177/20.Rev. 1 (1996).

Two follow-up meetings have been held: Beijing +5, Women 2000: Gender Equality, Development and Peace for the 21st Century, Twenty-third Special Session of the General Assembly, 5–9 June 2000; and Beijing + 10, a review undertaken at the 49th Session of the Commission on the Status of Women from 28 February–11 March 2005. A further follow-up meeting is planned for the Fifty-fourth Session of the Commission on the Status of Women in 2010.

See generally, **http://www.un.org/womenwatch**.

TEXT

ANNEX I
BEIJING DECLARATION

1. We, the Governments participating in the Fourth World Conference on Women,

2. Gathered here in Beijing in September 1995, the year of the fiftieth anniversary of the founding of the United Nations,

3. Determined to advance the goals of equality, development and peace for all women everywhere in the interest of all humanity,

4. Acknowledging the voices of all women everywhere and taking note of the diversity of women and their roles and circumstances, honouring the women who paved the way and inspired by the hope present in the world's youth,

5. Recognize that the status of women has advanced in some important respects in the past decade but that progress has been uneven, inequalities between women and men have persisted and major obstacles remain, with serious consequences for the well-being of all people,

6. Also recognize that this situation is exacerbated by the increasing poverty that is affecting the lives of the majority of the world's people, in particular women and children, with origins in both the national and international domains,

7. Dedicate ourselves unreservedly to addressing these constraints and obstacles and thus enhancing further the advancement and empowerment of women all over the world, and agree that this requires urgent action in the spirit of determination, hope, cooperation and solidarity, now and to carry us forward into the next century.

We reaffirm our commitment to:

8. The equal rights and inherent human dignity of women and men and other purposes and principles enshrined in the Charter of the United Nations, to the Universal Declaration of Human Rights and other international human rights instruments, in particular the Convention on the Elimination of All Forms of Discrimination against Women and the Convention on the Rights of the Child, as well as the Declaration on the Elimination of Violence against Women and the Declaration on the Right to Development;

9. Ensure the full implementation of the human rights of women and of the girl child as an inalienable, integral and indivisible part of all human rights and fundamental freedoms;

10. Build on consensus and progress made at previous United Nations conferences and summits—on women in Nairobi in 1985, on children in New York in 1990, on environment and development in Rio de Janeiro in 1992, on human rights in Vienna in 1993, on population and development in Cairo in 1994 and on social development in Copenhagen in 1995 with the objective of achieving equality, development and peace;

11. Achieve the full and effective implementation of the Nairobi Forward-looking Strategies for the Advancement of Women;

12. The empowerment and advancement of women, including the right to freedom of thought, conscience, religion and belief, thus contributing to the moral, ethical,

spiritual and intellectual needs of women and men, individually or in community with others and thereby guaranteeing them the possibility of realizing their full potential in society and shaping their lives in accordance with their own aspirations.

We are convinced that:

13. Women's empowerment and their full participation on the basis of equality in all spheres of society, including participation in the decision-making process and access to power, are fundamental for the achievement of equality, development and peace;

14. Women's rights are human rights;

15. Equal rights, opportunities and access to resources, equal sharing of responsibilities for the family by men and women, and a harmonious partnership between them are critical to their well-being and that of their families as well as to the consolidation of democracy;

16. Eradication of poverty based on sustained economic growth, social development, environmental protection and social justice requires the involvement of women in economic and social development, equal opportunities and the full and equal participation of women and men as agents and beneficiaries of people-centred sustainable development;

17. The explicit recognition and reaffirmation of the right of all women to control all aspects of their health, in particular their own fertility, is basic to their empowerment;

18. Local, national, regional and global peace is attainable and is inextricably linked with the advancement of women, who are a fundamental force for leadership, conflict resolution and the promotion of lasting peace at all levels;

19. It is essential to design, implement and monitor, with the full participation of women, effective, efficient and mutually reinforcing gender-sensitive policies and programmes, including development policies and programmes, at all levels that will foster the empowerment and advancement of women;

20. The participation and contribution of all actors of civil society, particularly women's groups and networks and other non-governmental organizations and community-based organizations, with full respect for their autonomy, in cooperation with Governments, are important to the effective implementation and follow-up of the Platform for Action;

21. The implementation of the Platform for Action requires commitment from Governments and the international community. By making national and international commitments for action, including those made at the Conference, Governments and the international community recognize the need to take priority action for the empowerment and advancement of women.

We are determined to:

22. Intensify efforts and actions to achieve the goals of the Nairobi Forward-looking Strategies for the Advancement of Women by the end of this century;

23. Ensure the full enjoyment by women and the girl child of all human rights and fundamental freedoms and take effective action against violations of these rights and freedoms;

24. Take all necessary measures to eliminate all forms of discrimination against women and the girl child and remove all obstacles to gender equality and the advancement and empowerment of women;

25. Encourage men to participate fully in all actions towards equality;

26. Promote women's economic independence, including employment, and eradicate the persistent and increasing burden of poverty on women by addressing the structural causes of poverty through changes in economic structures, ensuring equal access for all women, including those in rural areas, as vital development agents, to productive resources, opportunities and public services;

27. Promote people-centred sustainable development, including sustained economic growth, through the provision of basic education, life-long education, literacy and training, and primary health care for girls and women;

28. Take positive steps to ensure peace for the advancement of women and, recognizing the leading role that women have played in the peace movement, work actively towards general and complete disarmament under strict and effective international control, and support negotiations on the conclusion, without delay, of a universal and multilaterally and effectively verifiable comprehensive nuclear-test-ban treaty which contributes to nuclear disarmament and the prevention of the proliferation of nuclear weapons in all its aspects;

29. Prevent and eliminate all forms of violence against women and girls;

30. Ensure equal access to and equal treatment of women and men in education and health care and enhance women's sexual and reproductive health as well as education;

31. Promote and protect all human rights of women and girls;

32. Intensify efforts to ensure equal enjoyment of all human rights and fundamental freedoms for all women and girls who face multiple barriers to their empowerment and advancement because of such factors as their race, age, language, ethnicity, culture, religion, or disability, or because they are indigenous people;

33. Ensure respect for international law, including humanitarian law, in order to protect women and girls in particular;

34. Develop the fullest potential of girls and women of all ages, ensure their full and equal participation in building a better world for all and enhance their role in the development process.

We are determined to:

35. Ensure women's equal access to economic resources, including land, credit, science and technology, vocational training, information, communication and markets, as a means to further the advancement and empowerment of women and girls, including through the enhancement of their capacities to enjoy the benefits of equal access to these resources, *inter alia*, by means of international cooperation;

36. Ensure the success of the Platform for Action, which will require a strong commitment on the part of Governments, international organizations and institutions at all levels. We are deeply convinced that economic development, social development and environmental protection are interdependent and mutually reinforcing components of sustainable development, which is the framework for our efforts to achieve a higher quality of life for all people. Equitable social development that recognizes empowering the poor, particularly women living in poverty, to utilize environmental resources sustainably is a necessary foundation for sustainable development. We also recognize that broad-based and sustained economic growth in the context of sustainable development is necessary to sustain social development and social justice. The success of the Platform for Action will also require adequate mobilization of resources at the national and international

levels as well as new and additional resources to the developing countries from all available funding mechanisms, including multilateral, bilateral and private sources for the advancement of women; financial resources to strengthen the capacity of national, subregional, regional and international institutions; a commitment to equal rights, equal responsibilities and equal opportunities and to the equal participation of women and men in all national, regional and international bodies and policy-making processes; and the establishment or strengthening of mechanisms at all levels for accountability to the world's women;

37. Ensure also the success of the Platform for Action in countries with economies in transition, which will require continued international cooperation and assistance;

38. We hereby adopt and commit ourselves as Governments to implement the following Platform for Action, ensuring that a gender perspective is reflected in all our policies and programmes. We urge the United Nations system, regional and international financial institutions, other relevant regional and international institutions and all women and men, as well as' non-governmental organizations, with full respect for their autonomy, and all sectors of civil society, in cooperation with Governments, to fully commit themselves and contribute to the implementation of this Platform for Action.

ANNEX II
PLATFORM FOR ACTION
CHAPTER I
Mission Statement

1. The Platform for Action is an agenda for women's empowerment. It aims at accelerating the implementation of the Nairobi Forward-looking Strategies for the Advancement of Women and at removing all the obstacles to women's active participation in all spheres of public and private life through a full and equal share in economic, social, cultural and political decision-making. This means that the principle of shared power and responsibility should be established between women and men at home, in the workplace and in the wider national and international communities. Equality between women and men is a matter of human rights and a condition for social justice and is also a necessary and fundamental prerequisite for equality, development and peace. A transformed partnership based on equality between women and men is a condition for people-centred sustainable development. A sustained and long-term commitment is essential, so that women and men can work together for themselves, for their children and for society to meet the challenges of the twenty-first century.

2. The Platform for Action reaffirms the fundamental principle set forth in the Vienna Declaration and Programme of Action, adopted by the World Conference on Human Rights, that the human rights of women and of the girl child are an inalienable, integral and indivisible part of universal human rights. As an agenda for action, the Platform seeks to promote and protect the full enjoyment of all human rights and the fundamental freedoms of all women throughout their life cycle.

3. The Platform for Action emphasizes that women share common concerns that can be addressed only by working together and in partnership with men towards the common

goal of gender* equality around the world. It respects and values the full diversity of women's situations and conditions and recognizes that some women face particular barriers to their empowerment.

4. The Platform for Action requires immediate and concerted action by all to create a peaceful, just and humane world based on human rights and fundamental freedoms, including the principle of equality for all people of all ages and from all walks of life, and to this end, recognizes that broad-based and sustained economic growth in the context of sustainable development is necessary to sustain social development and social justice.

5. The success of the Platform for Action will require a strong commitment on the part of Governments, international organizations and institutions at all levels. It will also require adequate mobilization of resources at the national and international levels as well as new and additional resources to the developing countries from all available funding mechanisms, including multilateral, bilateral and private sources for the advancement of women; financial resources to strengthen the capacity of national, subregional, regional and international institutions; a commitment to equal rights, equal responsibilities and equal opportunities and to the equal participation of women and men in all national, regional and international bodies and policy-making processes; and the establishment or strengthening of mechanisms at all levels for accountability to the world's women.

CHAPTER II

Global Framework

6. The Fourth World Conference on Women is taking place as the world stands poised on the threshold of a new millennium.

7. The Platform for Action upholds the Convention on the Elimination of All Forms of Discrimination against Women and builds upon the Nairobi Forward-looking Strategies for the Advancement of Women, as well as relevant resolutions adopted by the Economic and Social Council and the General Assembly. The formulation of the Platform for Action is aimed at establishing a basic group of priority actions that should be carried out during the next five years.

8. The Platform for Action recognizes the importance of the agreements reached at the World Summit for Children, the United Nations Conference on Environment and Development, the World Conference on Human Rights, the International Conference on Population and Development and the World Summit for Social Development, which set out specific approaches and commitments to fostering sustainable development and international cooperation and to strengthening the role of the United Nations to that end. Similarly, the Global Conference on the Sustainable Development of Small Island Developing States, the International Conference on Nutrition, the International Conference on Primary Health Care and the World Conference on Education for All

---

* For the commonly understood meaning of the term 'gender', see Annex IV to the present report. [Annex IV contains a statement by the President of the Conference, recording the finding of the 'contact group' that (1) the word 'gender' had been commonly used and understood in its ordinary, generally accepted usage in numerous other United Nations forums and conferences; and (2) there was no indication that any new meaning or connotation of the term, different from accepted prior usage, was intended in the Platform for Action. Accordingly, the contact group reaffirmed that the word 'gender' as used in the Platform for Action was intended to be interpreted and understood as it was in ordinary, generally accepted usage—Eds.]

have addressed the various facets of development and human rights, within their specific perspectives, paying significant attention to the role of women and girls. In addition, the International Year for the World's Indigenous People, the International Year of the Family, the United Nations Year for Tolerance, the Geneva Declaration for Rural Women, and the Declaration on the Elimination of Violence against Women have also emphasized the issues of women's empowerment and equality.

9. The objective of the Platform for Action, which is in full conformity with the purposes and principles of the Charter of the United Nations and international law, is the empowerment of all women. The full realization of all human rights and fundamental freedoms of all women is essential for the empowerment of women. While the significance of national and regional particularities and various historical, cultural and religious backgrounds must be borne in mind, it is the duty of States, regardless of their political, economic and cultural systems, to promote and protect all human rights and fundamental freedoms. The implementation of this Platform, including through national laws and the formulation of strategies, policies, programmes and development priorities, is the sovereign responsibility of each State, in conformity with all human rights and fundamental freedoms, and the significance of and full respect for various religious and ethical values, cultural backgrounds and philosophical convictions of individuals and their communities should contribute to the full enjoyment by women of their human rights in order to achieve equality, development and peace.

10. Since the World Conference to Review and Appraise the Achievements of the United Nations Decade for Women: Equality, Development and Peace, held at Nairobi in 1985, and the adoption of the Nairobi Forward-looking Strategies for the Advancement of Women, the world has experienced profound political, economic, social and cultural changes, which have had both positive and negative effects on women. The World Conference on Human Rights recognized that the human rights of women and the girl child are an inalienable, integral and indivisible part of universal human rights. The full and equal participation of women in political, civil, economic, social and cultural life at the national, regional and international levels, and the eradication of all forms of discrimination on the grounds of sex are priority objectives of the international community. The World Conference on Human Rights reaffirmed the solemn commitment of all States to fulfil their obligations to promote universal respect for, and observance and protection of, all human rights and fundamental freedoms for all in accordance with the Charter of the United Nations, other instruments related to human rights and international law. The universal nature of these rights and freedoms is beyond question.

11. The end of the cold war has resulted in international changes and diminished competition between the super-Powers. The threat of a global armed conflict has diminished, while international relations have improved and prospects for peace among nations have increased. Although the threat of global conflict has been reduced, wars of aggression, armed conflicts, colonial or other forms of alien domination and foreign occupation, civil wars, and terrorism continue to plague many parts of the world. Grave violations of the human rights of women occur, particularly in times of armed conflict, and include murder, torture, systematic rape, forced pregnancy and forced abortion, in particular under policies of ethnic cleansing.

12. The maintenance of peace and security at the global, regional and local levels, together with the prevention of policies of aggression and ethnic cleansing and the resolution of armed conflict, is crucial for the protection of the human rights of women and

girl children, as well as for the elimination of all forms of violence against them and of their use as a weapon of war.

13. Excessive military expenditures, including global military expenditures and arms trade or trafficking, and investments for arms production and acquisition have reduced the resources available for social development. As a result of the debt burden and other economic difficulties, many developing countries have undertaken structural adjustment policies. Moreover, there are structural adjustment programmes that have been poorly designed and implemented, with resulting detrimental effects on social development. The number of people living in poverty has increased disproportionately in most developing countries, particularly the heavily indebted countries, during the past decade.

14. In this context, the social dimension of development should be emphasized. Accelerated economic growth, although necessary for social development, does not by itself improve the quality of life of the population. In some cases, conditions can arise which can aggravate social inequality and marginalization. Hence, it is indispensable to search for new alternatives that ensure that all members of society benefit from economic growth based on a holistic approach to all aspects of development: growth, equality between women and men, social justice, conservation and protection of the environment, sustainability, solidarity, participation, peace and respect for human rights.

15. A worldwide movement towards democratization has opened up the political process in many nations, but the popular participation of women in key decision-making as full and equal partners with men, particularly in politics, has not yet been achieved. South Africa's policy of institutionalized racism—apartheid—has been dismantled and a peaceful and democratic transfer of power has occurred. In Central and Eastern Europe the transition to parliamentary democracy has been rapid and has given rise to a variety of experiences, depending on the specific circumstances of each country. While the transition has been mostly peaceful, in some countries this process has been hindered by armed conflict that has resulted in grave violations of human rights.

16. Widespread economic recession, as well as political instability in some regions, has been responsible for setting back development goals in many countries. This has led to the expansion of unspeakable poverty. Of the more than 1 billion people living in abject poverty, women are an overwhelming majority. The rapid process of change and adjustment in all sectors has also led to increased unemployment and underemployment, with particular impact on women. In many cases, structural adjustment programmes have not been designed to minimize their negative effects on vulnerable and disadvantaged groups or on women, nor have they been designed to assure positive effects on those groups by preventing their marginalization in economic and social activities. The Final Act of the Uruguay Round of multilateral trade negotiations underscored the increasing interdependence of national economies, as well as the importance of trade liberalization and access to open, dynamic markets. There has also been heavy military spending in some regions. Despite increases in official development assistance (ODA) by some countries, ODA has recently declined overall.

17. Absolute poverty and the feminization of poverty, unemployment, the increasing fragility of the environment, continued violence against women and the widespread exclusion of half of humanity from institutions of power and governance underscore the need to continue the search for development, peace and security and for ways of assuring people-centred sustainable development. The participation and leadership of the half of humanity that is female is essential to the success of that search. Therefore, only a new

era of international cooperation among Governments and peoples based on a spirit of partnership, an equitable, international social and economic environment, and a radical transformation of the relationship between women and men to one of full and equal partnership will enable the world to meet the challenges of the twenty-first century.

18.   Recent international economic developments have had in many cases a disproportionate impact on women and children, the majority of whom live in developing countries. For those States that have carried a large burden of foreign debt, structural adjustment programmes and measures, though beneficial in the long term, have led to a reduction in social expenditures, thereby adversely affecting women, particularly in Africa and the least developed countries. This is exacerbated when responsibilities for basic social services have shifted from Governments to women.

19.   Economic recession in many developed and developing countries, as well as ongoing restructuring in countries with economies in transition, have had a disproportionately negative impact on women's employment. Women often have no choice but to take employment that lacks long-term job security or involves dangerous working conditions, to work in unprotected home-based production or to be unemployed. Many women enter the labour market in under-remunerated and undervalued jobs, seeking to improve their household income; others decide to migrate for the same purpose. Without any reduction in their other responsibilities, this has increased the total burden of work for women.

20.   Macro and micro-economic policies and programmes, including structural adjustment, have not always been designed to take account of their impact on women and girl children, especially those living in poverty. Poverty has increased in both absolute and relative terms, and the number of women living in poverty has increased in most regions. There are many urban women living in poverty; however, the plight of women living in rural and remote areas deserves special attention given the stagnation of development in such areas. In developing countries, even those in which national indicators have shown improvement, the majority of rural women continue to live in conditions of economic underdevelopment and social marginalization.

21.   Women are key contributors to the economy and to combating poverty through both remunerated and unremunerated work at home, in the community and in the workplace. Growing numbers of women have achieved economic independence through gainful employment.

22.   One fourth of all households world wide are headed by women and many other households are dependent on female income even where men are present. Female-maintained households are very often among the poorest because of wage discrimination, occupational segregation patterns in the labour market and other gender-based barriers. Family disintegration, population movements between urban and rural areas within countries, international migration, war and internal displacements are factors contributing to the rise of female-headed households.

23.   Recognizing that the achievement and maintenance of peace and security are a precondition for economic and social progress, women are increasingly establishing themselves as central actors in a variety of capacities in the movement of humanity for peace. Their full participation in decision-making, conflict prevention and resolution and all other peace initiatives is essential to the realization of lasting peace.

24.   Religion, spirituality and belief play a central role in the lives of millions of women and men, in the way they live and in the aspirations they have for the future. The right

to freedom of thought, conscience and religion is inalienable and must be universally enjoyed. This right includes the freedom to have or to adopt the religion or belief of their choice either individually or in community with others, in public or in private, and to manifest their religion or belief in worship, observance, practice and teaching. In order to realize equality, development and peace, there is a need to respect these rights and freedoms fully. Religion, thought, conscience and belief may, and can, contribute to fulfilling women's and men's moral, ethical and spiritual needs and to realizing their full potential in society. However, it is acknowledged that any form of extremism may have a negative impact on women and can lead to violence and discrimination.

25. The Fourth World Conference on Women should accelerate the process that formally began in 1975, which was proclaimed International Women's Year by the United Nations General Assembly. The Year was a turning-point in that it put women's issues on the agenda. The United Nations Decade for Women (1976–1985) was a worldwide effort to examine the status and rights of women and to bring women into decision-making at all levels. In 1979, the General Assembly adopted the Convention on the Elimination of All Forms of Discrimination against Women, which entered into force in 1981 and set an international standard for what was meant by equality between women and men. In 1985, the World Conference to Review and Appraise the Achievements of the United Nations Decade for Women: Equality, Development and Peace adopted the Nairobi Forward-looking Strategies for the Advancement of Women, to be implemented by the year 2000. There has been important progress in achieving equality between women and men. Many Governments have enacted legislation to promote equality between women and men and have established national machineries to ensure the mainstreaming of gender perspectives in all spheres of society. International agencies have focused greater attention on women's status and roles.

26. The growing strength of the non-governmental sector, particularly women's organizations and feminist groups, has become a driving force for change. Non-governmental organizations have played an important advocacy role in advancing legislation or mechanisms to ensure the promotion of women. They have also become catalysts for new approaches to development. Many Governments have increasingly recognized the important role that non-governmental organizations play and the importance of working with them for progress. Yet, in some countries, Governments continue to restrict the ability of non-governmental organizations to operate freely. Women, through non-governmental organizations, have participated in and strongly influenced community, national, regional and global forums and international debates.

27. Since 1975, knowledge of the status of women and men, respectively, has increased and is contributing to further actions aimed at promoting equality between women and men. In several countries, there have been important changes in the relationships between women and men, especially where there have been major advances in education for women and significant increases in their participation in the paid labour force. The boundaries of the gender division of labour between productive and reproductive roles are gradually being crossed as women have started to enter formerly male-dominated areas of work and men have started to accept greater responsibility for domestic tasks, including child care. However, changes in women's roles have been greater and much more rapid than changes in men's roles. In many countries, the differences between women's and men's achievements and activities are still not recognized as the consequences of socially constructed gender roles rather than immutable biological differences.

28. Moreover, 10 years after the Nairobi Conference, equality between women and men has still not been achieved. On average, women represent a mere 10 per cent of all elected legislators world wide and in most national and international administrative structures, both public and private, they remain underrepresented. The United Nations is no exception. Fifty years after its creation, the United Nations is continuing to deny itself the benefits of women's leadership by their underrepresentation at decision-making levels within the Secretariat and the specialized agencies.

29. Women play a critical role in the family. The family is the basic unit of society and as such should be strengthened. It is entitled to receive comprehensive protection and support. In different cultural, political and social systems, various forms of the family exist. The rights, capabilities and responsibilities of family members must be respected. Women make a great contribution to the welfare of the family and to the development of society, which is still not recognized or considered in its full importance. The social significance of maternity, motherhood and the role of parents in the family and in the upbringing of children should be acknowledged. The upbringing of children requires shared responsibility of parents, women and men and society as a whole. Maternity, motherhood, parenting and the role of women in procreation must not be a basis for discrimination nor restrict the full participation of women in society. Recognition should also be given to the important role often played by women in many countries in caring for other members of their family.

30. While the rate of growth of world population is on the decline, world population is at an all-time high in absolute numbers, with current increments approaching 86 million persons annually. Two other major demographic trends have had profound repercussions on the dependency ratio within families. In many developing countries, 45 to 50 per cent of the population is less than 15 years old, while in industrialized nations both the number and proportion of elderly people are increasing. According to United Nations projections, 72 per cent of the population over 60 years of age will be living in developing countries by the year 2025, and more than half of that population will be women. Care of children, the sick and the elderly is a responsibility that falls disproportionately on women, owing to lack of equality and the unbalanced distribution of remunerated and unremunerated work between women and men.

31. Many women face particular barriers because of various diverse factors in addition to their gender. Often these diverse factors isolate or marginalize such women. They are, *inter alia*, denied their human rights, they lack access or are denied access to education and vocational training, employment, housing and economic self-sufficiency and they are excluded from decision-making processes. Such women are often denied the opportunity to contribute to their communities as part of the mainstream.

32. The past decade has also witnessed a growing recognition of the distinct interests and concerns of indigenous women, whose identity, cultural traditions and forms of social organization enhance and strengthen the communities in which they live. Indigenous women often face barriers both as women and as members of indigenous communities.

33. In the past 20 years, the world has seen an explosion in the field of communications. With advances in computer technology and satellite and cable television, global access to information continues to increase and expand, creating new opportunities for the participation of women in communications and the mass media and for the dissemination of information about women. However, global communication networks have been used to spread stereotyped and demeaning images of women for narrow commercial

and consumerist purposes. Until women participate equally in both the technical and decision-making areas of communications and the mass media, including the arts, they will continue to be misrepresented and awareness of the reality of women's lives will continue to be lacking. The media have a great potential to promote the advancement of women and the equality of women and men by portraying women and men in a non-stereotypical, diverse and balanced manner, and by respecting the dignity and worth of the human person.

34. The continuing environmental degradation that affects all human lives has often a more direct impact on women. Women's health and their livelihood are threatened by pollution and toxic wastes, large-scale deforestation, desertification, drought and depletion of the soil and of coastal and marine resources, with a rising incidence of environmentally related health problems and even death reported among women and girls. Those most affected are rural and indigenous women, whose livelihood and daily subsistence depends directly on sustainable ecosystems.

35. Poverty and environmental degradation are closely interrelated. While poverty results in certain kinds of environmental stress, the major cause of the continued deterioration of the global environment is the unsustainable patterns of consumption and production, particularly in industrialized countries, which are a matter of grave concern and aggravate poverty and imbalances.

36. Global trends have brought profound changes in family survival strategies and structures. Rural to urban migration has increased substantially in all regions. The global urban population is projected to reach 47 per cent of the total population by the year 2000. An estimated 125 million people are migrants, refugees and displaced persons, half of whom live in developing countries. These massive movements of people have profound consequences for family structures and well-being and have unequal consequences for women and men, including in many cases the sexual exploitation of women.

37. According to World Health Organization (WHO) estimates, by the beginning of 1995 the number of cumulative cases of acquired immunodeficiency syndrome (AIDS) was 4.5 million. An estimated 19.5 million men, women and children have been infected with the human immunodeficiency virus (HIV) since it was first diagnosed and it is projected that another 20 million will be infected by the end of the decade. Among new cases, women are twice as likely to be infected as men. In the early stage of the AIDS pandemic, women were not infected in large numbers; however, about 8 million women are now infected. Young women and adolescents are particularly vulnerable. It is estimated that by the year 2000 more than 13 million women will be infected and 4 million women will have died from AIDS-related conditions. In addition, about 250 million new cases of sexually transmitted diseases are estimated to occur every year. The rate of transmission of sexually transmitted diseases, including HIV/AIDS, is increasing at an alarming rate among women and girls, especially in developing countries.

38. Since 1975, significant knowledge and information have been generated about the status of women and the conditions in which they live. Throughout their entire life cycle, women's daily existence and long-term aspirations are restricted by discriminatory attitudes, unjust social and economic structures, and a lack of resources in most countries that prevent their full and equal participation. In a number of countries, the practice of prenatal sex selection, higher rates of mortality among very young girls and lower rates of school enrolment for girls as compared with boys suggest that son preference is curtailing the access of girl children to food, education and health care and even life itself.

Discrimination against women begins at the earliest stages of life and must therefore be addressed from then onwards.

39. The girl child of today is the woman of tomorrow. The skills, ideas and energy of the girl child are vital for full attainment of the goals of equality, development and peace. For the girl child to develop her full potential she needs to be nurtured in an enabling environment, where her spiritual, intellectual and material needs for survival, protection and development are met and her equal rights safeguarded. If women are to be equal partners with men, in every aspect of life and development, now is the time to recognize the human dignity and worth of the girl child and to ensure the full enjoyment of her human rights and fundamental freedoms, including the rights assured by the Convention on the Rights of the Child, universal ratification of which is strongly urged. Yet there exists worldwide evidence that discrimination and violence against girls begin at the earliest stages of life and continue unabated throughout their lives. They often have less access to nutrition, physical and mental health care and education and enjoy fewer rights, opportunities and benefits of childhood and adolescence than do boys. They are often subjected to various forms of sexual and economic exploitation, paedophilia, forced prostitution and possibly the sale of their organs and tissues, violence and harmful practices such as female infanticide and prenatal sex selection, incest, female genital mutilation and early marriage, including child marriage.

40. Half the world's population is under the age of 25 and most of the world's youth— more than 85 per cent—live in developing countries. Policy makers must recognize the implications of these demographic factors. Special measures must be taken to ensure that young women have the life skills necessary for active and effective participation in all levels of social, cultural, political and economic leadership. It will be critical for the international community to demonstrate a new commitment to the future—a commitment to inspiring a new generation of women and men to work together for a more just society. This new generation of leaders must accept and promote a world in which every child is free from injustice, oppression and inequality and free to develop her/his own potential. The principle of equality of women and men must therefore be integral to the socialization process.

CHAPTER III

Critical Areas of Concern

41. The advancement of women and the achievement of equality between women and men are a matter of human rights and a condition for social justice and should not be seen in isolation as a women's issue. They are the only way to build a sustainable, just and developed society. Empowerment of women and equality between women and men are prerequisites for achieving political, social, economic, cultural and environmental security among all peoples.

42. Most of the goals set out in the Nairobi Forward-looking Strategies for the Advancement of Women have not been achieved. Barriers to women's empowerment remain, despite the efforts of Governments, as well as non-governmental organizations and women and men everywhere. Vast political, economic and ecological crises persist in many parts of the world. Among them are wars of aggression, armed conflicts, colonial or other forms of alien domination or foreign occupation, civil wars and terrorism. These

situations, combined with systematic or *de facto* discrimination, violations of and failure to protect all human rights and fundamental freedoms of all women, and their civil, cultural, economic, political and social rights, including the right to development and ingrained prejudicial attitudes towards women and girls are but a few of the impediments encountered since the World Conference to Review and Appraise the Achievements of the United Nations Decade for Women: Equality, Development and Peace, in 1985.

43. A review of progress since the Nairobi Conference highlights special concerns-areas of particular urgency that stand out as priorities for action. All actors should focus action and resources on the strategic objectives relating to the critical areas of concern which are, necessarily, interrelated, interdependent and of high priority. There is a need for these actors to develop and implement mechanisms of accountability for all the areas of concern.

44. To this end, Governments, the international community and civil society, including non-governmental organizations and the private sector, are called upon to take strategic action in the following critical areas of concern:

- The persistent and increasing burden of poverty on women
- Inequalities and inadequacies in and unequal access to education and training
- Inequalities and inadequacies in and unequal access to health care and related services
- Violence against women
- The effects of armed or other kinds of conflict on women, including those living under foreign occupation
- Inequality in economic structures and policies, in all forms of productive activities and in access to resources
- Inequality between men and women in the sharing of power and decision-making at all levels
- Insufficient mechanisms at all levels to promote the advancement of women
- Lack of respect for and inadequate promotion and protection of the human rights of women
- Stereotyping of women and inequality in women's access to and participation in all communication systems, especially in the media
- Gender inequalities in the management of natural resources and in the safeguarding of the environment
- Persistent discrimination against and violation of the rights of the girl child.

31. GUIDING PRINCIPLES ON INTERNAL DISPLACEMENT, 1997

These principles are published in the 'Report of the Representative of the Secretary-General, Mr. Francis M. Deng, submitted to the United Nations Commission on Human Rights, pursuant to Commission resolution 1997/39, Addendum': UN doc. E/CN.4/1998/53/Add.2. The introductory note has been omitted.

The Guiding Principles were 'noted' by the Commission on Human Rights and have been referred to in various General Assembly resolutions. Although many of the principles are based in treaties and customary international law, the precise status of the 'collection' and the process of 'adoption' initially excited some controversy among Governments; see Goodwin-Gill, G. S., 'Note on paragraph 20 of General Assembly resolution 55/74' (2001) 13 *IJRL* 255–8. Recent General Assembly resolutions indicate that they are new widely accepted by States and institutionally within the UN System, even if their application in practice may prove problematic. In 2004, Walter Kälin, who chaired the committee of legal experts which developed the Guiding Principles, was appointed as Representative of the Secretary-General on the human rights of internally displaced persons.

See generally, **http://www2.ohchr.org/english/issues/idp**.

Further reading

COHEN, R., 'The Guiding Principles on Internal Displacement: An Innovation In International Standard-Setting', (2004) *Global Governance*, Vol. 10, No. 4.

—— and DENG, F. M., *Masses in Flight: The Global Crisis of Internal Displacement*, Washington: The Brookings Institution, 1998.

FERRIS, E., 'Internal Displacement and the Right to Seek Asylum', (2008) 27 *Refugee Survey Quarterly* 76.

HAKATA, K., 'Vers une protection plus effective des "personnes déplacées a l'intérieur de leur proper pays"', *Revue générale de droit international public* 106.3, (2002), 619.

KÄLIN, W., 'The *Guiding Principles* on Internal Displacement—Introduction', (1998) 10 *IJRL* 557.

——, *Guiding Principles on Internal Displacement: Annotations*, Washington, DC: American Society of International Law, The Brookings Institution—University of Bern Project on Internal Displacement, revised edn., 2008.

——, *Addressing Internal Displacement: A Framework for National Responsibility*, Washington, DC: The Brookings Institution and the University of Bern, 2005.

LECKIE, S., ed., *Returning Home: Housing and Property Restitution Rights for Refugees and Displaced Persons*, Leiden: Martinus Nijhoff, 2010.

PHUONG, C., *The International Protection of Internally Displaced Persons*, Cambridge: Cambridge University Press, 2005.

WEISS, T. G. and KORN, D. A. *Internal Displacement: Conceptualization and its Consequences*, London: Routledge, 2006.

TEXT

INTRODUCTION: SCOPE AND PURPOSE

1. These Guiding Principles address the specific needs of internally displaced persons worldwide. They identify rights and guarantees relevant to the protection of persons from forced displacement and to their protection and assistance during displacement as well as during return or resettlement and reintegration.

2. For the purposes of these Principles, internally displaced persons are persons or groups of persons who have been forced or obliged to flee or to leave their homes or places of habitual residence, in particular as a result of or in order to avoid the effects of armed conflict, situations of generalized violence, violations of human rights or natural or human-made disasters, and who have not crossed an internationally recognized State border.

3. These Principles reflect and are consistent with international human rights law and international humanitarian law. They provide guidance to:

(a) The Representative of the Secretary-General on internally displaced persons in carrying out his mandate;

(b) States when faced with the phenomenon of internal displacement;

(c) All other authorities, groups and persons in their relations with internally displaced persons; and

(d) Intergovernmental and non-governmental organizations when addressing internal displacement.

4. These Guiding Principles should be disseminated and applied as widely as possible.

SECTION I
General Principles

Principle 1

1. Internally displaced persons shall enjoy, in full equality, the same rights and freedoms under international and domestic law as do other persons in their country. They shall not be discriminated against in the enjoyment of any rights and freedoms on the ground that they are internally displaced.

2. These Principles are without prejudice to individual criminal responsibility under international law, in particular relating to genocide, crimes against humanity and war crimes.

Principle 2

1. These Principles shall be observed by all authorities, groups and persons irrespective of their legal status and applied without any adverse distinction. The observance of these Principles shall not affect the legal status of any authorities, groups or persons involved.

2. These Principles shall not be interpreted as restricting, modifying or impairing the provisions of any international human rights or international humanitarian law instrument or rights granted to persons under domestic law. In particular, these Principles are without prejudice to the right to seek and enjoy asylum in other countries.

Principle 3

1. National authorities have the primary duty and responsibility to provide protection and humanitarian assistance to internally displaced persons within their jurisdiction.

2. Internally displaced persons have the right to request and to receive protection and humanitarian assistance from these authorities. They shall not be persecuted or punished for making such a request.

Principle 4

1. These Principles shall be applied without discrimination of any kind, such as race, colour, sex, language, religion or belief, political or other opinion, national, ethnic or social origin, legal or social status, age, disability, property, birth, or on any other similar criteria.

2. Certain internally displaced persons, such as children, especially unaccompanied minors, expectant mothers, mothers with young children, female heads of household, persons with disabilities and elderly persons, shall be entitled to protection and assistance required by their condition and to treatment which takes into account their special needs.

SECTION II
Principles Relating to Protection from Displacement

Principle 5

All authorities and international actors shall respect and ensure respect for their obligations under international law, including human rights and humanitarian law, in all circumstances, so as to prevent and avoid conditions that might lead to displacement of persons.

Principle 6

1. Every human being shall have the right to be protected against being arbitrarily displaced from his or her home or place of habitual residence.

2. The prohibition of arbitrary displacement includes displacement:

   (a) When it is based on policies of apartheid, 'ethnic cleansing' or similar practices aimed at/or resulting in altering the ethnic, religious or racial composition of the affected population;

   (b) In situations of armed conflict, unless the security of the civilians involved or imperative military reasons so demand;

   (c) In cases of large-scale development projects, which are not justified by compelling and overriding public interests;

   (d) In cases of disasters, unless the safety and health of those affected requires their evacuation; and

   (e) When it is used as a collective punishment.

3. Displacement shall last no longer than required by the circumstances.

Principle 7

1. Prior to any decision requiring the displacement of persons, the authorities concerned shall ensure that all feasible alternatives are explored in order to avoid displacement altogether. Where no alternatives exist, all measures shall be taken to minimize displacement and its adverse effects.

2. The authorities undertaking such displacement shall ensure, to the greatest practicable extent, that proper accommodation is provided to the displaced persons, that such displacements are effected in satisfactory conditions of safety, nutrition, health and hygiene, and that members of the same family are not separated.

3. If displacement occurs in situations other than during the emergency stages of armed conflicts and disasters, the following guarantees shall be complied with:

(a) A specific decision shall be taken by a State authority empowered by law to order such measures;

(b) Adequate measures shall be taken to guarantee to those to be displaced full information on the reasons and procedures for their displacement and, where applicable, on compensation and relocation;

(c) The free and informed consent of those to be displaced shall be sought;

(d) The authorities concerned shall endeavour to involve those affected, particularly women, in the planning and management of their relocation;

(e) Law enforcement measures, where required, shall be carried out by competent legal authorities; and

(f) The right to an effective remedy, including the review of such decisions by appropriate judicial authorities, shall be respected.

Principle 8

Displacement shall not be carried out in a manner that violates the rights to life, dignity, liberty and security of those affected.

Principle 9

States are under a particular obligation to protect against the displacement of indigenous peoples, minorities, peasants, pastoralists and other groups with a special dependency on and attachment to their lands.

SECTION III
Principles Relating to Protection during Displacement

Principle 10

1. Every human being has the inherent right to life which shall be protected by law. No one shall be arbitrarily deprived of his or her life. Internally displaced persons shall be protected in particular against:

(a) Genocide;

(b) Murder;

(c) Summary or arbitrary executions; and

(d) Enforced disappearances, including abduction or unacknowledged detention, threatening or resulting in death.

Threats and incitement to commit any of the foregoing acts shall be prohibited.

2. Attacks or other acts of violence against internally displaced persons who do not or no longer participate in hostilities are prohibited in all circumstances. Internally displaced persons shall be protected, in particular, against:

(a) Direct or indiscriminate attacks or other acts of violence, including the creation of areas wherein attacks on civilians are permitted;

(b) Starvation as a method of combat;

(c) Their use to shield military objectives from attack or to shield, favour or impede military operations;

(d) Attacks against their camps or settlements; and

(e) The use of anti-personnel landmines.

Principle 11

1. Every human being has the right to dignity and physical, mental and moral integrity.

2. Internally displaced persons, whether or not their liberty has been restricted, shall be protected in particular against:

(a) Rape, mutilation, torture, cruel, inhuman or degrading treatment or punishment, and other outrages upon personal dignity, such as acts of gender-specific violence, forced prostitution and any form of indecent assault;

(b) Slavery or any contemporary form of slavery, such as sale into marriage, sexual exploitation, or forced labour of children; and

(c) Acts of violence intended to spread terror among internally displaced persons.

Threats and incitement to commit any of the foregoing acts shall be prohibited.

Principle 12

1. Every human being has the right to liberty and security of person. No one shall be subjected to arbitrary arrest or detention.

2. To give effect to this right for internally displaced persons, they shall not be interned in or confined to a camp. If in exceptional circumstances such internment or confinement is absolutely necessary, it shall not last longer than required by the circumstances.

3. Internally displaced persons shall be protected from discriminatory arrest and detention as a result of their displacement.

4. In no case shall internally displaced persons be taken hostage.

Principle 13

1. In no circumstances shall displaced children be recruited nor be required or permitted to take part in hostilities.

2. Internally displaced persons shall be protected against discriminatory practices of recruitment into any armed forces or groups as a result of their displacement. In particular any cruel, inhuman or degrading practices that compel compliance or punish non-compliance with recruitment are prohibited in all circumstances.

Principle 14

1. Every internally displaced person has the right to liberty of movement and freedom to choose his or her residence.

2. In particular, internally displaced persons have the right to move freely in and out of camps or other settlements.

Principle 15

Internally displaced persons have:

(a) The right to seek safety in another part of the country;

(b) The right to leave their country;

(c) The right to seek asylum in another country; and

(d) The right to be protected against forcible return to or resettlement in any place where their life, safety, liberty and/or health would be at risk.

Principle 16

1. All internally displaced persons have the right to know the fate and whereabouts of missing relatives.

2. The authorities concerned shall endeavour to establish the fate and whereabouts of internally displaced persons reported missing, and cooperate with relevant international organizations engaged in this task. They shall inform the next of kin on the progress of the investigation and notify them of any result.

3. The authorities concerned shall endeavour to collect and identify the mortal remains of those deceased, prevent their despoliation or mutilation, and facilitate the return of those remains to the next of kin or dispose of them respectfully.

4. Grave sites of internally displaced persons should be protected and respected in all circumstances. Internally displaced persons should have the right of access to the grave sites of their deceased relatives.

Principle 17

1. Every human being has the right to respect of his or her family life.

2. To give effect to this right for internally displaced persons, family members who wish to remain together shall be allowed to do so.

3. Families which are separated by displacement should be reunited as quickly as possible. All appropriate steps shall be taken to expedite the reunion of such families, particularly when children are involved. The responsible authorities shall facilitate inquiries made by family members and encourage and cooperate with the work of humanitarian organizations engaged in the task of family reunification.

4. Members of internally displaced families whose personal liberty has been restricted by internment or confinement in camps shall have the right to remain together.

Principle 18

1. All internally displaced persons have the right to an adequate standard of living.

2. At the minimum, regardless of the circumstances, and without discrimination, competent authorities shall provide internally displaced persons with and ensure safe access to:

(a) Essential food and potable water;

(b) Basic shelter and housing;

(c) Appropriate clothing; and

(d) Essential medical services and sanitation.

3. Special efforts should be made to ensure the full participation of women in the planning and distribution of these basic supplies.

Principle 19

1. All wounded and sick internally displaced persons as well as those with disabilities shall receive to the fullest extent practicable and with the least possible delay, the medical care and attention they require, without distinction on any grounds other than medical ones. When necessary, internally displaced persons shall have access to psychological and social services.

2. Special attention should be paid to the health needs of women, including access to female health care providers and services, such as reproductive health care, as well as appropriate counselling for victims of sexual and other abuses.

3. Special attention should also be given to the prevention of contagious and infectious diseases, including AIDS, among internally displaced persons.

Principle 20

1. Every human being has the right to recognition everywhere as a person before the law.

2. To give effect to this right for internally displaced persons, the authorities concerned shall issue to them all documents necessary for the enjoyment and exercise of their legal rights, such as passports, personal identification documents, birth certificates and marriage certificates. In particular, the authorities shall facilitate the issuance of new documents or the replacement of documents lost in the course of displacement, without imposing unreasonable conditions, such as requiring the return to one's area of habitual residence in order to obtain these or other required documents.

3. Women and men shall have equal rights to obtain such necessary documents and shall have the right to have such documentation issued in their own names.

Principle 21

1. No one shall be arbitrarily deprived of property and possessions.

2. The property and possessions of internally displaced persons shall in all circumstances be protected, in particular, against the following acts:

    (a) Pillage;

    (b) Direct or indiscriminate attacks or other acts of violence;

    (c) Being used to shield military operations or objectives;

    (d) Being made the object of reprisal; and

    (e) Being destroyed or appropriated as a form of collective punishment.

3. Property and possessions left behind by internally displaced persons should be protected against destruction and arbitrary and illegal appropriation, occupation or use.

Principle 22

1. Internally displaced persons, whether or not they are living in camps, shall not be discriminated against as a result of their displacement in the enjoyment of the following rights:

    (a) The rights to freedom of thought, conscience, religion or belief, opinion and expression;

    (b) The right to seek freely opportunities for employment and to participate in economic activities;

    (c) The right to associate freely and participate equally in community affairs;

(d) The right to vote and to participate in governmental and public affairs, including the right to have access to the means necessary to exercise this right; and

(e) The right to communicate in a language they understand.

Principle 23

1. Every human being has the right to education.

2. To give effect to this right for internally displaced persons, the authorities concerned shall ensure that such persons, in particular displaced children, receive education which shall be free and compulsory at the primary level. Education should respect their cultural identity, language and religion.

3. Special efforts should be made to ensure the full and equal participation of women and girls in educational programmes.

4. Education and training facilities shall be made available to internally displaced persons, in particular adolescents and women, whether or not living in camps, as soon as conditions permit.

SECTION IV
Principles Relating to Humanitarian Assistance

Principle 24

1. All humanitarian assistance shall be carried out in accordance with the principles of humanity and impartiality and without discrimination.

2. Humanitarian assistance to internally displaced persons shall not be diverted, in particular for political or military reasons.

Principle 25

1. The primary duty and responsibility for providing humanitarian assistance to internally displaced persons lies with national authorities.

2. International humanitarian organizations and other appropriate actors have the right to offer their services in support of the internally displaced. Such an offer shall not be regarded as an unfriendly act or an interference in a State's internal affairs and shall be considered in good faith. Consent thereto shall not be arbitrarily withheld, particularly when authorities concerned are unable or unwilling to provide the required humanitarian assistance.

3. All authorities concerned shall grant and facilitate the free passage of humanitarian assistance and grant persons engaged in the provision of such assistance rapid and unimpeded access to the internally displaced.

Principle 26

Persons engaged in humanitarian assistance, their transport and supplies shall be respected and protected. They shall not be the object of attack or other acts of violence.

Principle 27

1. International humanitarian organizations and other appropriate actors when providing assistance should give due regard to the protection needs and human rights of

internally displaced persons and take appropriate measures in this regard. In so doing, these organizations and actors should respect relevant international standards and codes of conduct.

2. The preceding paragraph is without prejudice to the protection responsibilities of international organizations mandated for this purpose, whose services may be offered or requested by States.

SECTION V
Principles Relating to Return, Resettlement and Reintegration

Principle 28

1. Competent authorities have the primary duty and responsibility to establish conditions, as well as provide the means, which allow internally displaced persons to return voluntarily, in safety and with dignity, to their homes or places of habitual residence, or to resettle voluntarily in another part of the country. Such authorities shall endeavour to facilitate the reintegration of returned or resettled internally displaced persons.

2. Special efforts should be made to ensure the full participation of internally displaced persons in the planning and management of their return or resettlement and reintegration.

Principle 29

1. Internally displaced persons who have returned to their homes or places of habitual residence or who have resettled in another part of the country shall not be discriminated against as a result of their having been displaced. They shall have the right to participate fully and equally in public affairs at all levels and have equal access to public services.

2. Competent authorities have the duty and responsibility to assist returned and/or resettled internally displaced persons to recover, to the extent possible, their property and possessions which they left behind or were dispossessed of upon their displacement. When recovery of such property and possessions is not possible, competent authorities shall provide or assist these persons in obtaining appropriate compensation or another form of just reparation.

Principle 30

All authorities concerned shall grant and facilitate for international humanitarian organizations and other appropriate actors, in the exercise of their respective mandates, rapid and unimpeded access to internally displaced persons to assist in their return or resettlement and reintegration.

32. DECLARATION ON THE RIGHT AND RESPONSIBILITY OF INDIVIDUALS, GROUPS AND ORGANS OF SOCIETY TO PROMOTE AND PROTECT UNIVERSALLY RECOGNIZED HUMAN RIGHTS AND FUNDAMENTAL FREEDOMS, 1998

This Declaration was adopted by the General Assembly in Resolution 53/144 on 9 December 1998, without a vote. While reaffirming many of the rights already established by treaty, the Declaration also emphasizes responsibilities in promoting and protecting the environment in which human rights are to be enjoyed. It recognizes the primary responsibility of States in this regard, but also underlines the role and duties of individuals and non-governmental organizations.

Further reading

CHARNOVITZ, S., 'Nongovernmental Organizations and International Law', (2006) 100 *AJIL* 348.
CLAPHAM, A., *Human Rights Obligations of Non-State Actors*, Oxford: Oxford University Press, 2006.
KNOX, J. H., 'Horizontal Human Rights Law', (2008) 102 *AJIL* 1.
MUTUA, M., 'Standard Setting in Human Rights: Critique and Prognosis', (2007) 29 *Human Rights Quarterly* 547.

TEXT

The General Assembly,

Reaffirming the importance of the observance of the purposes and principles of the Charter of the United Nations for the promotion and protection of all human rights and fundamental freedoms for all persons in all countries of the world,

Taking note of Commission on Human Rights resolution 1998/7 of 3 April 1998, in which the Commission approved the text of the draft declaration on the right and responsibility of individuals, groups and organs of society to promote and protect universally recognized human rights and fundamental freedoms,

Taking note also of Economic and Social Council resolution 1998/33 of 30 July 1998, in which the Council recommended the draft declaration to the General Assembly for adoption,

Conscious of the importance of the adoption of the draft declaration in the context of the fiftieth anniversary of the Universal Declaration of Human Rights,

1. *Adopts* the Declaration on the Right and Responsibility of Individuals, Groups and Organs of Society to Promote and Protect Universally Recognized Human Rights and Fundamental Freedoms, annexed to the present resolution;

2. *Invites* Governments, agencies and organizations of the United Nations system and intergovernmental and non-governmental organizations to intensify their efforts to disseminate the Declaration and to promote universal respect and understanding thereof, and requests the Secretary-General to include the text of the Declaration in the next edition of *Human Rights: A Compilation of International Instruments*.

ANNEX

Declaration on the right and responsibility of individuals, groups and organs of society to promote and protect universally recognized human rights and fundamental freedoms

The General Assembly,

Reaffirming the importance of the observance of the purposes and principles of the Charter of the United Nations for the promotion and protection of all human rights and fundamental freedoms for all persons in all countries of the world,

Reaffirming also the importance of the Universal Declaration of Human Rights and the International Covenants on Human Rights as basic elements of international efforts to promote universal respect for and observance of human rights and fundamental freedoms and the importance of other human rights instruments adopted within the United Nations system, as well as those at the regional level,

Stressing that all members of the international community shall fulfil, jointly and separately, their solemn obligation to promote and encourage respect for human rights and fundamental freedoms for all without distinction of any kind, including distinctions based on race, colour, sex, language, religion, political or other opinion, national or social origin, property, birth or other status, and reaffirming the particular importance of achieving international cooperation to fulfil this obligation according to the Charter,

Acknowledging the important role of international cooperation for, and the valuable work of individuals, groups and associations in contributing to, the effective elimination of all violations of human rights and fundamental freedoms of peoples and individuals, including in relation to mass, flagrant or systematic violations such as those resulting from apartheid, all forms of racial discrimination, colonialism, foreign domination or occupation, aggression or threats to national sovereignty, national unity or territorial integrity and from the refusal to recognize the right of peoples to self-determination and the right of every people to exercise full sovereignty over its wealth and natural resources,

Recognizing the relationship between international peace and security and the enjoyment of human rights and fundamental freedoms, and mindful that the absence of international peace and security does not excuse non-compliance,

Reiterating that all human rights and fundamental freedoms are universal, indivisible, interdependent and interrelated and should be promoted and implemented in a fair and equitable manner, without prejudice to the implementation of each of those rights and freedoms,

Stressing that the prime responsibility and duty to promote and protect human rights and fundamental freedoms lie with the State,

Recognizing the right and the responsibility of individuals, groups and associations to promote respect for and foster knowledge of human rights and fundamental freedoms at the national and international levels,

Declares:

Article 1

Everyone has the right, individually and in association with others, to promote and to strive for the protection and realization of human rights and fundamental freedoms at the national and international levels.

Article 2

1. Each State has a prime responsibility and duty to protect, promote and implement all human rights and fundamental freedoms, *inter alia*, by adopting such steps as may be necessary to create all conditions necessary in the social, economic, political and other fields, as well as the legal guarantees required to ensure that all persons under its jurisdiction, individually and in association with others, are able to enjoy all those rights and freedoms in practice.

2. Each State shall adopt such legislative, administrative and other steps as may be necessary to ensure that the rights and freedoms referred to in the present Declaration are effectively guaranteed.

Article 3

Domestic law consistent with the Charter of the United Nations and other international obligations of the State in the field of human rights and fundamental freedoms is the juridical framework within which human rights and fundamental freedoms should be implemented and enjoyed and within which all activities referred to in the present Declaration for the promotion, protection and effective realization of those rights and freedoms should be conducted.

Article 4

Nothing in the present Declaration shall be construed as impairing or contradicting the purposes and principles of the Charter of the United Nations or as restricting or derogating from the provisions of the Universal Declaration of Human Rights, the International Covenants on Human Rights and other international instruments and commitments applicable in this field.

Article 5

For the purpose of promoting and protecting human rights and fundamental freedoms, everyone has the right, individually and in association with others, at the national and international levels:

- *(a)* To meet or assemble peacefully;
- *(b)* To form, join and participate in non-governmental organizations, associations or groups;
- *(c)* To communicate with non-governmental or intergovernmental organizations.

Article 6

Everyone has the right, individually and in association with others:

- *(a)* To know, seek, obtain, receive and hold information about all human rights and fundamental freedoms, including having access to information as to how those rights and freedoms are given effect in domestic legislative, judicial or administrative systems;
- *(b)* As provided for in human rights and other applicable international instruments, freely to publish, impart or disseminate to others views, information and knowledge on all human rights and fundamental freedoms;

(c) To study, discuss, form and hold opinions on the observance, both in law and in practice, of all human rights and fundamental freedoms and, through these and other appropriate means, to draw public attention to those matters.

Article 7

Everyone has the right, individually and in association with others, to develop and discuss new human rights ideas and principles and to advocate their acceptance.

Article 8

1. Everyone has the right, individually and in association with others, to have effective access, on a non-discriminatory basis, to participation in the government of his or her country and in the conduct of public affairs.

2. This includes, *inter alia*, the right, individually and in association with others, to submit to governmental bodies and agencies and organizations concerned with public affairs criticism and proposals for improving their functioning and to draw attention to any aspect of their work that may hinder or impede the promotion, protection and realization of human rights and fundamental freedoms.

Article 9

1. In the exercise of human rights and fundamental freedoms, including the promotion and protection of human rights as referred to in the present Declaration, everyone has the right, individually and in association with others, to benefit from an effective remedy and to be protected in the event of the violation of those rights.

2. To this end, everyone whose rights or freedoms are allegedly violated has the right, either in person or through legally authorized representation, to complain to and have that complaint promptly reviewed in a public hearing before an independent, impartial and competent judicial or other authority established by law and to obtain from such an authority a decision, in accordance with law, providing redress, including any compensation due, where there has been a violation of that person's rights or freedoms, as well as enforcement of the eventual decision and award, all without undue delay.

3. To the same end, everyone has the right, individually and in association with others, *inter alia*:

    (a) To complain about the policies and actions of individual officials and governmental bodies with regard to violations of human rights and fundamental freedoms, by petition or other appropriate means, to competent domestic judicial, administrative or legislative authorities or any other competent authority provided for by the legal system of the State, which should render their decision on the complaint without undue delay;

    (b) To attend public hearings, proceedings and trials so as to form an opinion on their compliance with national law and applicable international obligations and commitments;

    (c) To offer and provide professionally qualified legal assistance or other relevant advice and assistance in defending human rights and fundamental freedoms.

4. To the same end, and in accordance with applicable international instruments and procedures, everyone has the right, individually and in association with others, to unhindered

access to and communication with international bodies with general or special competence to receive and consider communications on matters of human rights and fundamental freedoms.

5. The State shall conduct a prompt and impartial investigation or ensure that an inquiry takes place whenever there is reasonable ground to believe that a violation of human rights and fundamental freedoms has occurred in any territory under its jurisdiction.

Article 10

No one shall participate, by act or by failure to act where required, in violating human rights and fundamental freedoms and no one shall be subjected to punishment or adverse action of any kind for refusing to do so.

Article 11

Everyone has the right, individually and in association with others, to the lawful exercise of his or her occupation or profession. Everyone who, as a result of his or her profession, can affect the human dignity, human rights and fundamental freedoms of others should respect those rights and freedoms and comply with relevant national and international standards of occupational and professional conduct or ethics.

Article 12

1. Everyone has the right, individually and in association with others, to participate in peaceful activities against violations of human rights and fundamental freedoms.

2. The State shall take all necessary measures to ensure the protection by the competent authorities of everyone, individually and in association with others, against any violence, threats, retaliation, *de facto* or *de jure* adverse discrimination, pressure or any other arbitrary action as a consequence of his or her legitimate exercise of the rights referred to in the present Declaration.

3. In this connection, everyone is entitled, individually and in association with others, to be protected effectively under national law in reacting against or opposing, through peaceful means, activities and acts, including those by omission, attributable to States that result in violations of human rights and fundamental freedoms, as well as acts of violence perpetrated by groups or individuals that affect the enjoyment of human rights and fundamental freedoms.

Article 13

Everyone has the right, individually and in association with others, to solicit, receive and utilize resources for the express purpose of promoting and protecting human rights and fundamental freedoms through peaceful means, in accordance with article 3 of the present Declaration.

Article 14

1. The State has the responsibility to take legislative, judicial, administrative or other appropriate measures to promote the understanding by all persons under its jurisdiction of their civil, political, economic, social and cultural rights.

2. Such measures shall include, *inter alia*:

  (a) The publication and widespread availability of national laws and regulations and of applicable basic international human rights instruments;

(b) Full and equal access to international documents in the field of human rights, including the periodic reports by the State to the bodies established by the international human rights treaties to which it is a party, as well as the summary records of discussions and the official reports of these bodies.

3. The State shall ensure and support, where appropriate, the creation and development of further independent national institutions for the promotion and protection of human rights and fundamental freedoms in all territory under its jurisdiction, whether they be ombudsmen, human rights commissions or any other form of national institution.

Article 15

The State has the responsibility to promote and facilitate the teaching of human rights and fundamental freedoms at all levels of education and to ensure that all those responsible for training lawyers, law enforcement officers, the personnel of the armed forces and public officials include appropriate elements of human rights teaching in their training programme.

Article 16

Individuals, non-governmental organizations and relevant institutions have an important role to play in contributing to making the public more aware of questions relating to all human rights and fundamental freedoms through activities such as education, training and research in these areas to strengthen further, *inter alia*, understanding, tolerance, peace and friendly relations among nations and among all racial and religious groups, bearing in mind the various backgrounds of the societies and communities in which they carry out their activities.

Article 17

In the exercise of the rights and freedoms referred to in the present Declaration, everyone, acting individually and in association with others, shall be subject only to such limitations as are in accordance with applicable international obligations and are determined by law solely for the purpose of securing due recognition and respect for the rights and freedoms of others and of meeting the just requirements of morality, public order and the general welfare in a democratic society.

Article 18

1. Everyone has duties towards and within the community, in which alone the free and full development of his or her personality is possible.

2. Individuals, groups, institutions and non-governmental organizations have an important role to play and a responsibility in safeguarding democracy, promoting human rights and fundamental freedoms and contributing to the promotion and advancement of democratic societies, institutions and processes.

3. Individuals, groups, institutions and non-governmental organizations also have an important role and a responsibility in contributing, as appropriate, to the promotion of the right of everyone to a social and international order in which the rights and freedoms set forth in the Universal Declaration of Human Rights and other human rights instruments can be fully realized.

Article 19

Nothing in the present Declaration shall be interpreted as implying for any individual, group or organ of society or any State the right to engage in any activity or to perform any act aimed at the destruction of the rights and freedoms referred to in the present Declaration.

Article 20

Nothing in the present Declaration shall be interpreted as permitting States to support and promote activities of individuals, groups of individuals, institutions or non-governmental organizations contrary to the provisions of the Charter of the United Nations.

33. UNITED NATIONS MILLENNIUM DECLARATION, 2000

General Assembly Resolution 55/2, adopted without a vote on 8 September 2000.
See generally, **http://www.un.org/millenniumgoals/**.

Further reading

CLEMENS, M.A., KENNY, C. J. and MOSS, T. J., 'The Trouble with the MDGS: Confronting
Expectations of Aid and Development Success', (2007) 35 *World Development* 735.
UNITED NATIONS HIGH COMMISSIONER FOR HUMAN RIGHTS, *Claiming the Millennium Development
Goals: A Human Rights Approach*, New York and Geneva: United Nations, 2008.
'Special Issue: Millennium Development Goals and Human Rights', (2009) 13 *International Journal
of Human Rights*, No.1.

TEXT

The General Assembly,

Adopts the following Declaration:

UNITED NATIONS MILLENNIUM DECLARATION

I. Values and principles

1. We, heads of State and Government, have gathered at United Nations Headquarters
in New York from 6 to 8 September 2000, at the dawn of a new millennium, to reaffirm
our faith in the Organization and its Charter as indispensable foundations of a more
peaceful, prosperous and just world.

2. We recognize that, in addition to our separate responsibilities to our individual societies, we have a collective responsibility to uphold the principles of human dignity, equality and equity at the global level. As leaders we have a duty therefore to all the world's
people, especially the most vulnerable and, in particular, the children of the world, to
whom the future belongs.

3. We reaffirm our commitment to the purposes and principles of the Charter of the
United Nations, which have proved timeless and universal. Indeed, their relevance and
capacity to inspire have increased, as nations and peoples have become increasingly
interconnected and interdependent.

4. We are determined to establish a just and lasting peace all over the world in accordance
with the purposes and principles of the Charter. We rededicate ourselves to support all
efforts to uphold the sovereign equality of all States, respect for their territorial integrity
and political independence, resolution of disputes by peaceful means and in conformity
with the principles of justice and international law, the right to self-determination of peoples which remain under colonial domination and foreign occupation, non-interference

in the internal affairs of States, respect for human rights and fundamental freedoms, respect for the equal rights of all without distinction as to race, sex, language or religion and international cooperation in solving international problems of an economic, social, cultural or humanitarian character.

5. We believe that the central challenge we face today is to ensure that globalization becomes a positive force for all the world's people. For while globalization offers great opportunities, at present its benefits are very unevenly shared, while its costs are unevenly distributed. We recognize that developing countries and countries with economies in transition face special difficulties in responding to this central challenge. Thus, only through broad and sustained efforts to create a shared future, based upon our common humanity in all its diversity, can globalization be made fully inclusive and equitable. These efforts must include policies and measures, at the global level, which correspond to the needs of developing countries and economies in transition and are formulated and implemented with their effective participation.

6. We consider certain fundamental values to be essential to international relations in the twenty-first century. These include:

- **Freedom**. Men and women have the right to live their lives and raise their children in dignity, free from hunger and from the fear of violence, oppression or injustice. Democratic and participatory governance based on the will of the people best assures these rights.

- **Equality**. No individual and no nation must be denied the opportunity to benefit from development. The equal rights and opportunities of women and men must be assured.

- **Solidarity**. Global challenges must be managed in a way that distributes the costs and burdens fairly in accordance with basic principles of equity and social justice. Those who suffer or who benefit least deserve help from those who benefit most.

- **Tolerance**. Human beings must respect one other, in all their diversity of belief, culture and language. Differences within and between societies should be neither feared nor repressed, but cherished as a precious asset of humanity. A culture of peace and dialogue among all civilizations should be actively promoted.

- **Respect for nature**. Prudence must be shown in the management of all living species and natural resources, in accordance with the precepts of sustainable development. Only in this way can the immeasurable riches provided to us by nature be preserved and passed on to our descendants. The current unsustainable patterns of production and consumption must be changed in the interest of our future welfare and that of our descendants.

- **Shared responsibility**. Responsibility for managing worldwide economic and social development, as well as threats to international peace and security, must be shared among the nations of the world and should be exercised multilaterally. As the most universal and most representative organization in the world, the United Nations must play the central role.

7. In order to translate these shared values into actions, we have identified key objectives to which we assign special significance.

II. Peace, security and disarmament

8. We will spare no effort to free our peoples from the scourge of war, whether within or between States, which has claimed more than 5 million lives in the past decade. We will also seek to eliminate the dangers posed by weapons of mass destruction.

9. We resolve therefore:

- To strengthen respect for the rule of law in international as in national affairs and, in particular, to ensure compliance by Member States with the decisions of the International Court of Justice, in compliance with the Charter of the United Nations, in cases to which they are parties.

- To make the United Nations more effective in maintaining peace and security by giving it the resources and tools it needs for conflict prevention, peaceful resolution of disputes, peacekeeping, post-conflict peace-building and reconstruction. In this context, we take note of the report of the Panel on United Nations Peace Operations and request the General Assembly to consider its recommendations expeditiously.

- To strengthen cooperation between the United Nations and regional organizations, in accordance with the provisions of Chapter VIII of the Charter.

- To ensure the implementation, by States Parties, of treaties in areas such as arms control and disarmament and of international humanitarian law and human rights law, and call upon all States to consider signing and ratifying the Rome Statute of the International Criminal Court.

- To take concerted action against international terrorism, and to accede as soon as possible to all the relevant international conventions.

- To redouble our efforts to implement our commitment to counter the world drug problem.

- To intensify our efforts to fight transnational crime in all its dimensions, including trafficking as well as smuggling in human beings and money laundering.

- To minimize the adverse effects of United Nations economic sanctions on innocent populations, to subject such sanctions regimes to regular reviews and to eliminate the adverse effects of sanctions on third parties.

- To strive for the elimination of weapons of mass destruction, particularly nuclear weapons, and to keep all options open for achieving this aim, including the possibility of convening an international conference to identify ways of eliminating nuclear dangers.

- To take concerted action to end illicit traffic in small arms and light weapons, especially by making arms transfers more transparent and supporting regional disarmament measures, taking account of all the recommendations of the forthcoming United Nations Conference on Illicit Trade in Small Arms and Light Weapons.

- To call on all States to consider acceding to the Convention on the Prohibition of the Use, Stockpiling, Production and Transfer of Anti-personnel Mines and on Their Destruction, as well as the amended mines protocol to the Convention on conventional weapons.

10. We urge Member States to observe the Olympic Truce, individually and collectively, now and in the future, and to support the International Olympic Committee in its efforts to promote peace and human understanding through sport and the Olympic Ideal.

III. Development and poverty eradication

11. We will spare no effort to free our fellow men, women and children from the abject and dehumanizing conditions of extreme poverty, to which more than a billion of them are currently subjected. We are committed to making the right to development a reality for everyone and to freeing the entire human race from want.

12. We resolve therefore to create an environment—at the national and global levels alike—which is conducive to development and to the elimination of poverty.

13. Success in meeting these objectives depends, *inter alia*, on good governance within each country. It also depends on good governance at the international level and on transparency in the financial, monetary and trading systems. We are committed to an open, equitable, rule-based, predictable and non-discriminatory multilateral trading and financial system.

14. We are concerned about the obstacles developing countries face in mobilizing the resources needed to finance their sustained development. We will therefore make every effort to ensure the success of the High-level International and Intergovernmental Event on Financing for Development, to be held in 2001.

15. We also undertake to address the special needs of the least developed countries. In this context, we welcome the Third United Nations Conference on the Least Developed Countries to be held in May 2001 and will endeavour to ensure its success. We call on the industrialized countries:

- To adopt, preferably by the time of that Conference, a policy of duty- and quota-free access for essentially all exports from the least developed countries;
- To implement the enhanced programme of debt relief for the heavily indebted poor countries without further delay and to agree to cancel all official bilateral debts of those countries in return for their making demonstrable commitments to poverty reduction; and
- To grant more generous development assistance, especially to countries that are genuinely making an effort to apply their resources to poverty reduction.

16. We are also determined to deal comprehensively and effectively with the debt problems of low- and middle-income developing countries, through various national and international measures designed to make their debt sustainable in the long term.

17. We also resolve to address the special needs of small island developing States, by implementing the Barbados Programme of Action and the outcome of the twenty-second special session of the General Assembly rapidly and in full. We urge the international community to ensure that, in the development of a vulnerability index, the special needs of small island developing States are taken into account.

18. We recognize the special needs and problems of the landlocked developing countries, and urge both bilateral and multilateral donors to increase financial and technical assistance to this group of countries to meet their special development needs and to help them overcome the impediments of geography by improving their transit transport systems.

19. We resolve further:

- To halve, by the year 2015, the proportion of the world's people whose income is less than one dollar a day and the proportion of people who suffer from hunger and, by the same date, to halve the proportion of people who are unable to reach or to afford safe drinking water.

- To ensure that, by the same date, children everywhere, boys and girls alike, will be able to complete a full course of primary schooling and that girls and boys will have equal access to all levels of education.

- By the same date, to have reduced maternal mortality by three quarters, and under-five child mortality by two thirds, of their current rates.

- To have, by then, halted, and begun to reverse, the spread of HIV/AIDS, the scourge of malaria and other major diseases that afflict humanity.

- To provide special assistance to children orphaned by HIV/AIDS.

- By 2020, to have achieved a significant improvement in the lives of at least 100 million slum dwellers as proposed in the 'Cities Without Slums' initiative.

20. We also resolve:

- To promote gender equality and the empowerment of women as effective ways to combat poverty, hunger and disease and to stimulate development that is truly sustainable.

- To develop and implement strategies that give young people everywhere a real chance to find decent and productive work.

- To encourage the pharmaceutical industry to make essential drugs more widely available and affordable by all who need them in developing countries.

- To develop strong partnerships with the private sector and with civil society organizations in pursuit of development and poverty eradication.

- To ensure that the benefits of new technologies, especially information and communication technologies, in conformity with recommendations contained in the ECOSOC 2000 Ministerial Declaration, are available to all.

IV. Protecting our common environment

21. We must spare no effort to free all of humanity, and above all our children and grandchildren, from the threat of living on a planet irredeemably spoilt by human activities, and whose resources would no longer be sufficient for their needs.

22. We reaffirm our support for the principles of sustainable development, including those set out in Agenda 21, agreed upon at the United Nations Conference on Environment and Development.

23. We resolve therefore to adopt in all our environmental actions a new ethic of conservation and stewardship and, as first steps, we resolve:

- To make every effort to ensure the entry into force of the Kyoto Protocol, preferably by the tenth anniversary of the United Nations Conference on Environment and Development in 2002, and to embark on the required reduction in emissions of greenhouse gases.

- To intensify our collective efforts for the management, conservation and sustainable development of all types of forests.

- To press for the full implementation of the Convention on Biological Diversity and the Convention to Combat Desertification in those Countries Experiencing Serious Drought and/or Desertification, particularly in Africa.

- To stop the unsustainable exploitation of water resources by developing water management strategies at the regional, national and local levels, which promote both equitable access and adequate supplies.
- To intensify cooperation to reduce the number and effects of natural and man-made disasters.
- To ensure free access to information on the human genome sequence.

V. Human rights, democracy and good governance

24. We will spare no effort to promote democracy and strengthen the rule of law, as well as respect for all internationally recognized human rights and fundamental freedoms, including the right to development.

25. We resolve therefore:

- To respect fully and uphold the Universal Declaration of Human Rights.
- To strive for the full protection and promotion in all our countries of civil, political, economic, social and cultural rights for all.
- To strengthen the capacity of all our countries to implement the principles and practices of democracy and respect for human rights, including minority rights.
- To combat all forms of violence against women and to implement the Convention on the Elimination of All Forms of Discrimination against Women.
- To take measures to ensure respect for and protection of the human rights of migrants, migrant workers and their families, to eliminate the increasing acts of racism and xenophobia in many societies and to promote greater harmony and tolerance in all societies.
- To work collectively for more inclusive political processes, allowing genuine participation by all citizens in all our countries.
- To ensure the freedom of the media to perform their essential role and the right of the public to have access to information.

VI. Protecting the vulnerable

26. We will spare no effort to ensure that children and all civilian populations that suffer disproportionately the consequences of natural disasters, genocide, armed conflicts and other humanitarian emergencies are given every assistance and protection so that they can resume normal life as soon as possible.

We resolve therefore:

- To expand and strengthen the protection of civilians in complex emergencies, in conformity with international humanitarian law.
- To strengthen international cooperation, including burden sharing in, and the coordination of humanitarian assistance to, countries hosting refugees and to help all refugees and displaced persons to return voluntarily to their homes, in safety and dignity and to be smoothly reintegrated into their societies.
- To encourage the ratification and full implementation of the Convention on the Rights of the Child and its optional protocols on the involvement of children in armed conflict and on the sale of children, child prostitution and child pornography.

VII. Meeting the special needs of Africa

27. We will support the consolidation of democracy in Africa and assist Africans in their struggle for lasting peace, poverty eradication and sustainable development, thereby bringing Africa into the mainstream of the world economy.

28. We resolve therefore:

- To give full support to the political and institutional structures of emerging democracies in Africa.

- To encourage and sustain regional and subregional mechanisms for preventing conflict and promoting political stability, and to ensure a reliable flow of resources for peacekeeping operations on the continent.

- To take special measures to address the challenges of poverty eradication and sustainable development in Africa, including debt cancellation, improved market access, enhanced Official Development Assistance and increased flows of Foreign Direct Investment, as well as transfers of technology.

- To help Africa build up its capacity to tackle the spread of the HIV/AIDS pandemic and other infectious diseases.

VIII. Strengthening the United Nations

29. We will spare no effort to make the United Nations a more effective instrument for pursuing all of these priorities: the fight for development for all the peoples of the world, the fight against poverty, ignorance and disease; the fight against injustice; the fight against violence, terror and crime; and the fight against the degradation and destruction of our common home.

30. We resolve therefore:

- To reaffirm the central position of the General Assembly as the chief deliberative, policy-making and representative organ of the United Nations, and to enable it to play that role effectively.

- To intensify our efforts to achieve a comprehensive reform of the Security Council in all its aspects.

- To strengthen further the Economic and Social Council, building on its recent achievements, to help it fulfil the role ascribed to it in the Charter.

- To strengthen the International Court of Justice, in order to ensure justice and the rule of law in international affairs.

- To encourage regular consultations and coordination among the principal organs of the United Nations in pursuit of their functions.

- To ensure that the Organization is provided on a timely and predictable basis with the resources it needs to carry out its mandates.

- To urge the Secretariat to make the best use of those resources, in accordance with clear rules and procedures agreed by the General Assembly, in the interests of all Member States, by adopting the best management practices and technologies available and by concentrating on those tasks that reflect the agreed priorities of Member States.

- To promote adherence to the Convention on the Safety of United Nations and Associated Personnel.

- To ensure greater policy coherence and better cooperation between the United Nations, its agencies, the Bretton Woods Institutions and the World Trade Organization, as well as other multilateral bodies, with a view to achieving a fully coordinated approach to the problems of peace and development.

- To strengthen further cooperation between the United Nations and national parliaments through their world organization, the Inter-Parliamentary Union, in various fields, including peace and security, economic and social development, international law and human rights and democracy and gender issues.

- To give greater opportunities to the private sector, non-governmental organizations and civil society, in general, to contribute to the realization of the Organization's goals and programmes.

31. We request the General Assembly to review on a regular basis the progress made in implementing the provisions of this Declaration, and ask the Secretary-General to issue periodic reports for consideration by the General Assembly and as a basis for further action.

32. We solemnly reaffirm, on this historic occasion, that the United Nations is the indispensable common house of the entire human family, through which we will seek to realize our universal aspirations for peace, cooperation and development. We therefore pledge our unstinting support for these common objectives and our determination to achieve them.

34. DECLARATION OF ARTICLES ON NATIONALITY OF NATURAL PERSONS IN RELATION TO THE SUCCESSION OF STATES, 2000

The Declaration of articles is annexed to General Assembly Resolution 55/153, 12 December 2000, adopted without a vote on the report of the Sixth Committee: UN doc. A/55/610. It makes a significant contribution to resolving problems of statelessness, which continue to emerge, particularly with the fragmentation of previously existing federations, such as the USSR and the former Yugoslavia. The Declaration is the culmination of the mandate given to the International Law Commission in 1993; see UNGA Resolution 48/31, 9 December 1993. Besides the annual reports of the ILC from 1993–1999, see the reports of the Special Rapporteur from 1995–1998: UN docs. A/CN.4/467, A/CN.4/474. A/CN.4/480 and A/CN.4/489. See also the European Convention on the Avoidance of Statelessness in Relation to State Succession, 2006, below p.867.

Further reading

ADJAMI, M. and HARRINGTON, J., 'The Scope and Content of Article 15 of the Universal Declaration of Human Rights', (2008) 27 *Refugee Survey Quarterly* 93.

RICHARDSON, N., 'Breaking Up Doesn't Have to Be So Hard: Default Rules for Partition and Succession', (2008–2009) 9 *Chicago Journal of International Law* 685.

TEXT

The General Assembly,

Having considered chapter IV of the report of the International Law Commission on the work of its fifty-first session, which contains final draft articles on nationality of natural persons in relation to the succession of States,

Noting that the International Law Commission decided to recommend the draft articles to the General Assembly for their adoption in the form of a declaration,

Recalling its resolution 54/112 of 9 December 1999, in which it decided to consider at its fifty-fifth session the draft articles on nationality of natural persons in relation to the succession of States with a view to their adoption as a declaration,

Considering that the work of the International Law Commission on nationality of natural persons in relation to the succession of States would provide a useful guide for practice in dealing with this issue,

Acknowledging that the work of the International Law Commission on this topic could contribute to the elaboration of a convention or other appropriate instrument in the future, and reiterating its invitation, contained in its resolution 54/112, for Governments to submit comments and observations on the question of a convention on nationality of natural persons in relation to the succession of States,

1. *Expresses* its appreciation to the International Law Commission for its valuable work on nationality of natural persons in relation to the succession of States;

2. *Takes note* of the articles on nationality of natural persons in relation to the succession of States, presented by the International Law Commission in the form of a declaration, the text of which is annexed to the present resolution;

3. *Invites* Governments to take into account, as appropriate, the provisions contained in the articles in dealing with issues of nationality of natural persons in relation to the succession of States;

4. *Recommends* that all efforts be made for the wide dissemination of the text of the articles;

5. *Decides* to include in the provisional agenda of its fifty-ninth session an item entitled 'Nationality of natural persons in relation to the succession of States'.

ANNEX
NATIONALITY OF NATURAL PERSONS IN RELATION TO THE SUCCESSION OF STATES

Preamble

Considering that problems of nationality arising from succession of States concern the international community,

Emphasizing that nationality is essentially governed by internal law within the limits set by international law,

Recognizing that in matters concerning nationality, due account should be taken both of the legitimate interests of States and those of individuals,

Recalling that the Universal Declaration of Human Rights of 1948 proclaimed the right of every person to a nationality,

Recalling also that the International Covenant on Civil and Political Rights of 1966 and the Convention on the Rights of the Child of 1989 recognize the right of every child to acquire a nationality,

Emphasizing that the human rights and fundamental freedoms of persons whose nationality may be affected by a succession of States must be fully respected,

Bearing in mind the provisions of the Convention on the Reduction of Statelessness of 1961, the Vienna Convention on Succession of States in Respect of Treaties of 1978 and the Vienna Convention on Succession of States in Respect of State Property, Archives and Debts of 1983,

Convinced of the need for the codification and progressive development of the rules of international law concerning nationality in relation to the succession of States as a means for ensuring greater juridical security for States and for individuals,

PART I
GENERAL PROVISIONS

Article 1—*Right to a nationality*

Every individual who, on the date of the succession of States, had the nationality of the predecessor State, irrespective of the mode of acquisition of that nationality, has the right to the nationality of at least one of the States concerned, in accordance with the present articles.

Article 2—Use of terms

For the purposes of the present articles:

   (a) 'Succession of States' means the replacement of one State by another in the responsibility for the international relations of territory;

   (b) 'Predecessor State' means the State which has been replaced by another State on the occurrence of a succession of States;

   (c) 'Successor State' means the State which has replaced another State on the occurrence of a succession of States;

   (d) 'State concerned' means the predecessor State or the successor State, as the case may be;

   (e) 'Third State' means any State other than the predecessor State or the successor State;

   (f) 'Person concerned' means every individual who, on the date of the succession of States, had the nationality of the predecessor State and whose nationality may be affected by such succession;

   (g) 'Date of the succession of States' means the date upon which the successor State replaced the predecessor State in the responsibility for the international relations of the territory to which the succession of States relates.

Article 3—Cases of succession of States covered by the present articles

The present articles apply only to the effects of a succession of States occurring in conformity with international law and, in particular, with the principles of international law embodied in the Charter of the United Nations.

Article 4—Prevention of statelessness

States concerned shall take all appropriate measures to prevent persons who, on the date of the succession of States, had the nationality of the predecessor State from becoming stateless as a result of such succession.

Article 5—Presumption of nationality

Subject to the provisions of the present articles, persons concerned having their habitual residence in the territory affected by the succession of States are presumed to acquire the nationality of the successor State on the date of such succession.

Article 6—Legislation on nationality and other connected issues

Each State concerned should, without undue delay, enact legislation on nationality and other connected issues arising in relation to the succession of States consistent with the provisions of the present articles. It should take all appropriate measures to ensure that persons concerned will be apprised, within a reasonable time period, of the effect of its legislation on their nationality, of any choices they may have thereunder, as well as of the consequences that the exercise of such choices will have on their status.

Article 7—Effective date

The attribution of nationality in relation to the succession of States, as well as the acquisition of nationality following the exercise of an option, shall take effect on the date of such succession, if persons concerned would otherwise be stateless during the period between the date of the succession of States and such attribution or acquisition of nationality.

Article 8—Persons concerned having their habitual residence in another State

1. A successor State does not have the obligation to attribute its nationality to persons concerned who have their habitual residence in another State and also have the nationality of that or any other State.

2. A successor State shall not attribute its nationality to persons concerned who have their habitual residence in another State against the will of the persons concerned unless they would otherwise become stateless.

Article 9—Renunciation of the nationality of another State as a condition for attribution of nationality

When a person concerned who is qualified to acquire the nationality of a successor State has the nationality of another State concerned, the former State may make the attribution of its nationality dependent on the renunciation by such person of the nationality of the latter State. However, such requirement shall not be applied in a manner which would result in rendering the person concerned stateless, even if only temporarily.

Article 10—Loss of nationality upon the voluntary acquisition of the nationality of another State

1. A predecessor State may provide that persons concerned who, in relation to the succession of States, voluntarily acquire the nationality of a successor State shall lose its nationality.

2. A successor State may provide that persons concerned who, in relation to the succession of States, voluntarily acquire the nationality of another successor State or, as the case may be, retain the nationality of the predecessor State shall lose its nationality acquired in relation to such succession.

Article 11—Respect for the will of persons concerned

1. States concerned shall give consideration to the will of persons concerned whenever those persons are qualified to acquire the nationality of two or more States concerned.

2. Each State concerned shall grant a right to opt for its nationality to persons concerned who have appropriate connection with that State if those persons would otherwise become stateless as a result of the succession of States.

3. When persons entitled to the right of option have exercised such right, the State whose nationality they have opted for shall attribute its nationality to such persons.

4. When persons entitled to the right of option have exercised such right, the State whose nationality they have renounced shall withdraw its nationality from such persons, unless they would thereby become stateless.

5. States concerned should provide a reasonable time limit for the exercise of the right of option.

Article 12—Unity of a family

Where the acquisition or loss of nationality in relation to the succession of States would impair the unity of a family, States concerned shall take all appropriate measures to allow that family to remain together or to be reunited.

Article 13—Child born after the succession of States

A child of a person concerned, born after the date of the succession of States, who has not acquired any nationality, has the right to the nationality of the State concerned on whose territory that child was born.

Article 14—Status of habitual residents

1. The status of persons concerned as habitual residents shall not be affected by the succession of States.

2. A State concerned shall take all necessary measures to allow persons concerned who, because of events connected with the succession of States, were forced to leave their habitual residence on its territory to return thereto.

Article 15—Non-discrimination

States concerned shall not deny persons concerned the right to retain or acquire a nationality or the right of option upon the succession of States by discriminating on any ground.

Article 16—Prohibition of arbitrary decisions concerning nationality issues

Persons concerned shall not be arbitrarily deprived of the nationality of the predecessor State, or arbitrarily denied the right to acquire the nationality of the successor State or any right of option, to which they are entitled in relation to the succession of States.

Article 17—Procedures relating to nationality issues

Applications relating to the acquisition, retention or renunciation of nationality or to the exercise of the right of option, in relation to the succession of States, shall be processed without undue delay. Relevant decisions shall be issued in writing and shall be open to effective administrative or judicial review.

Article 18—Exchange of information, consultation and negotiation

1. States concerned shall exchange information and consult in order to identify any detrimental effects on persons concerned with respect to their nationality and other connected issues regarding their status as a result of the succession of States.

2. States concerned shall, when necessary, seek a solution to eliminate or mitigate such detrimental effects by negotiation and, as appropriate, through agreement.

Article 19—Other States

1. Nothing in the present articles requires States to treat persons concerned having no effective link with a State concerned as nationals of that State, unless this would result in treating those persons as if they were stateless.

2. Nothing in the present articles precludes States from treating persons concerned, who have become stateless as a result of the succession of States, as nationals of the State concerned whose nationality they would be entitled to acquire or retain, if such treatment is beneficial to those persons.

PART II

PROVISIONS RELATING TO SPECIFIC CATEGORIES OF SUCCESSION OF STATES

Section 1: Transfer of part of the territory

Article 20—Attribution of the nationality of the successor State and withdrawal of the nationality of the predecessor State

When part of the territory of a State is transferred by that State to another State, the successor State shall attribute its nationality to the persons concerned who have their habitual residence in the transferred territory and the predecessor State shall withdraw its nationality from such persons, unless otherwise indicated by the exercise of the right of option which such persons shall be granted. The predecessor State shall not, however, withdraw its nationality before such persons acquire the nationality of the successor State.

Section 2: Unification of States

Article 21—Attribution of the nationality of the successor State

Subject to the provisions of Article 8, when two or more States unite and so form one successor State, irrespective of whether the successor State is a new State or whether its personality is identical to that of one of the States which have united, the successor State shall attribute its nationality to all persons who, on the date of the succession of States, had the nationality of a predecessor State.

Section 3: Dissolution of a State

Article 22—Attribution of the nationality of the successor States

When a State dissolves and ceases to exist and the various parts of the territory of the predecessor State form two or more successor States, each successor State shall, unless otherwise indicated by the exercise of a right of option, attribute its nationality to:

(a) Persons concerned having their habitual residence in its territory; and

(b) Subject to the provisions of Article 8:

  (i) Persons concerned not covered by subparagraph (a) having an appropriate legal connection with a constituent unit of the predecessor State that has become part of that successor State;

  (ii) Persons concerned not entitled to a nationality of any State concerned under subparagraphs (a) and (b) (i) having their habitual residence in a third State, who were born in or, before leaving the predecessor State, had their last habitual residence in what has become the territory of that successor State or having any other appropriate connection with that successor State.

Article 23—Granting of the right of option by the successor States

1. Successor States shall grant a right of option to persons concerned covered by the provisions of Article 22 who are qualified to acquire the nationality of two or more successor States.

2. Each successor State shall grant a right to opt for its nationality to persons concerned who are not covered by the provisions of Article 22.

Section 4: Separation of part or parts of the territory

Article 24—Attribution of the nationality of the successor State

When part or parts of the territory of a State separate from that State and form one or more successor States while the predecessor State continues to exist, a successor State shall, unless otherwise indicated by the exercise of a right of option, attribute its nationality to:

(a) Persons concerned having their habitual residence in its territory; and

(b) Subject to the provisions of Article 8:

(i) Persons concerned not covered by subparagraph (a) having an appropriate legal connection with a constituent unit of the predecessor State that has become part of that successor State;

(ii) Persons concerned not entitled to a nationality of any State concerned under subparagraphs (a) and (b) (i) having their habitual residence in a third State, who were born in or, before leaving the predecessor State, had their last habitual residence in what has become the territory of that successor State or having any other appropriate connection with that successor State.

Article 25—Withdrawal of the nationality of the predecessor State

1. The predecessor State shall withdraw its nationality from persons concerned qualified to acquire the nationality of the successor State in accordance with Article 24. It shall not, however, withdraw its nationality before such persons acquire the nationality of the successor State.

2. Unless otherwise indicated by the exercise of a right of option, the predecessor State shall not, however, withdraw its nationality from persons referred to in paragraph 1 who:

(a) Have their habitual residence in its territory;

(b) Are not covered by subparagraph (a) and have an appropriate legal connection with a constituent unit of the predecessor State that has remained part of the predecessor State;

(c) Have their habitual residence in a third State, and were born in or, before leaving the predecessor State, had their last habitual residence in what has remained part of the territory of the predecessor State or have any other appropriate connection with that State.

Article 26—Granting of the right of option by the predecessor and the successor States

Predecessor and successor States shall grant a right of option to all persons concerned covered by the provisions of Article 24 and paragraph 2 of Article 25 who are qualified to have the nationality of both the predecessor and successor States or of two or more successor States.

35. GENERAL ASSEMBLY DECLARATION OF COMMITMENT ON HIV/AIDS, 2001

This Declaration, sub-headed 'Global Crisis—Global Action', was adopted by Resolution S-26/2 (2001), at the General Assembly Special Session on HIV-AIDS, 25–27 June 2001. See generally, **http://www.un.org/ga/aids/coverage**.

Further reading

GRUSKIN, S., ROSEMAN, M. J. and FERGUSON, L., 'Reproductive Health and HIV: Do International Human Rights Law and Policy Matter?' (2007) 3 *JSDLP-RDPDD (McGill International Journal of Sustainable Development Law and Policy)* 69.

HAOUR-KNIPE, M. and RECTOR, R., eds., *Crossing Borders: Migration, Ethnicity and AIDS*, London: Taylor & Francis, 1996.

JOINT UNITED NATIONS PROGRAMME ON HIV/AIDS: **http://www.unaids.org**

WALKER, E. M., 'The HIV/AIDS Pandemic and Human Rights: A Continuum Approach', (2007) 19 *Florida Journal of International Law* 335.

TEXT

1. We, heads of State and Government and representatives of States and Governments, assembled at the United Nations, from 25 to 27 June 2001, for the twenty-sixth special session of the General Assembly convened in accordance with resolution 55/13 of 3 November 2000, as a matter of urgency, to review and address the problem of HIV/AIDS in all its aspects, as well as to secure a global commitment to enhancing coordination and intensification of national, regional and international efforts to combat it in a comprehensive manner;

2. Deeply concerned that the global HIV/AIDS epidemic, through its devastating scale and impact, constitutes a global emergency and one of the most formidable challenges to human life and dignity, as well as to the effective enjoyment of human rights, which undermines social and economic development throughout the world and affects all levels of society—national, community, family and individual;

3. Noting with profound concern that by the end of the year 2000, 36.1 million people worldwide were living with HIV/AIDS, 90 per cent in developing countries and 75 per cent in sub-Saharan Africa;

4. Noting with grave concern that all people, rich and poor, without distinction as to age, gender or race, are affected by the HIV/AIDS epidemic, further noting that people in developing countries are the most affected and that women, young adults and children, in particular girls, are the most vulnerable;

5. Concerned also that the continuing spread of HIV/AIDS will constitute a serious obstacle to the realization of the global development goals we adopted at the Millennium Summit of the United Nations;

6. Recalling and reaffirming our previous commitments on HIV/AIDS made through:

   • The United Nations Millennium Declaration, of 8 September 2000;

- The political declaration and further actions and initiatives to implement the commitments made at the World Summit for Social Development, of 1 July 2000;
- The political declaration and further action and initiatives to implement the Beijing Declaration and Platform for Action, of 10 June 2000;
- Key actions for the further implementation of the Programme of Action of the International Conference on Population and Development, of 2 July 1999;
- The regional call for action to fight HIV/AIDS in Asia and the Pacific, of 25 April 2001;
- The Abuja Declaration and Framework for Action for the fight against HIV/AIDS, tuberculosis and other related infectious diseases in Africa, of 27 April 2001;
- The Declaration of the Tenth Ibero-America Summit of heads of State, of 18 November 2000;
- The Pan-Caribbean Partnership against HIV/AIDS, of 14 February 2001;
- The European Union Programme for Action: Accelerated action on HIV/AIDS, malaria and tuberculosis in the context of poverty reduction, of 14 May 2001;
- The Baltic Sea Declaration on HIV/AIDS Prevention, of 4 May 2000;
- The Central Asian Declaration on HIV/AIDS, of 18 May 2001;

7. Convinced of the need to have an urgent, coordinated and sustained response to the HIV/AIDS epidemic, which will build on the experience and lessons learned over the past 20 years;

8. Noting with grave concern that Africa, in particular sub-Saharan Africa, is currently the worst affected region where HIV/AIDS is considered a state of emergency, which threatens development, social cohesion, political stability, food security and life expectancy and imposes a devastating economic burden, and that the dramatic situation on the continent needs urgent and exceptional national, regional and international action;

9. Welcoming the commitments of African heads of State or Government at the Abuja special summit in April 2001, particularly their pledge to set a target of allocating at least 15 per cent of their annual national budgets for the improvement of the health sector to help address the HIV/AIDS epidemic; and recognizing that action to reach this target, by those countries whose resources are limited, will need to be complemented by increased international assistance;

10. Recognizing also that other regions are seriously affected and confront similar threats, particularly the Caribbean region, with the second-highest rate of HIV infection after sub-Saharan Africa, the Asia-Pacific region where 7.5 million people are already living with HIV/AIDS, the Latin America region with 1.5 million people living with HIV/AIDS, and the Central and Eastern European region with very rapidly rising infection rates, and that the potential exists for a rapid escalation of the epidemic and its impact throughout the world if no specific measures are taken;

11. Recognizing that poverty, underdevelopment and illiteracy are among the principal contributing factors to the spread of HIV/AIDS, and noting with grave concern that HIV/AIDS is compounding poverty and is now reversing or impeding development in many countries and should therefore be addressed in an integrated manner;

12. Noting that armed conflicts and natural disasters also exacerbate the spread of the epidemic;

13. Noting further that stigma, silence, discrimination, and denial, as well as a lack of confidentiality, undermine prevention, care and treatment efforts and increase the impact of the epidemic on individuals, families, communities and nations and must also be addressed;

14. Stressing that gender equality and the empowerment of women are fundamental elements in the reduction of the vulnerability of women and girls to HIV/AIDS;

15. Recognizing that access to medication in the context of pandemics such as HIV/AIDS is one of the fundamental elements to achieve progressively the full realization of the right of everyone to the enjoyment of the highest attainable standard of physical and mental health;

16. Recognizing that the full realization of human rights and fundamental freedoms for all is an essential element in a global response to the HIV/AIDS pandemic, including in the areas of prevention, care, support and treatment, and that it reduces vulnerability to HIV/AIDS and prevents stigma and related discrimination against people living with or at risk of HIV/AIDS;

17. Acknowledging that prevention of HIV infection must be the mainstay of the national, regional and international response to the epidemic, and that prevention, care, support and treatment for those infected and affected by HIV/AIDS are mutually reinforcing elements of an effective response and must be integrated in a comprehensive approach to combat the epidemic;

18. Recognizing the need to achieve the prevention goals set out in the present Declaration in order to stop the spread of the epidemic, and acknowledging that all countries must continue to emphasize widespread and effective prevention, including awareness-raising campaigns through education, nutrition, information and health-care services;

19. Recognizing that care, support and treatment can contribute to effective prevention through increased acceptance of voluntary and confidential counselling and testing, and by keeping people living with HIV/AIDS and vulnerable groups in close contact with health-care systems and facilitating their access to information, counselling and preventive supplies;

20. Emphasizing the important role of cultural, family, ethical and religious factors in the prevention of the epidemic and in treatment, care and support, taking into account the particularities of each country as well as the importance of respecting all human rights and fundamental freedoms;

21. Noting with concern that some negative economic, social, cultural, political, financial and legal factors are hampering awareness, education, prevention, care, treatment and support efforts;

22. Noting the importance of establishing and strengthening human resources and national health and social infrastructures as imperatives for the effective delivery of prevention, treatment, care and support services;

23. Recognizing that effective prevention, care and treatment strategies will require behavioural changes and increased availability of and non-discriminatory access to, *inter alia*, vaccines, condoms, microbicides, lubricants, sterile injecting equipment, drugs, including anti-retroviral therapy, diagnostics and related technologies, as well as increased research and development;

24. Recognizing also that the cost, availability and affordability of drugs and related technology are significant factors to be reviewed and addressed in all aspects and that there is a need to reduce the cost of these drugs and technologies in close collaboration with the private sector and pharmaceutical companies;

25. Acknowledging that the lack of affordable pharmaceuticals and of feasible supply structures and health systems continues to hinder an effective response to HIV/AIDS in many countries, especially for the poorest people, and recalling efforts to make drugs available at low prices for those in need;

26. Welcoming the efforts of countries to promote innovation and the development of domestic industries consistent with international law in order to increase access to medicines to protect the health of their populations, and noting that the impact of international trade agreements on access to or local manufacturing of essential drugs and on the development of new drugs needs to be evaluated further;

27. Welcoming the progress made in some countries to contain the epidemic, particularly through: strong political commitment and leadership at the highest levels, including community leadership; effective use of available resources and traditional medicines; successful prevention, care, support and treatment strategies; education and information initiatives; working in partnership with communities, civil society, people living with HIV/AIDS and vulnerable groups; and the active promotion and protection of human rights; and recognizing the importance of sharing and building on our collective and diverse experiences, through regional and international cooperation including North/South, South/South cooperation and triangular cooperation;

28. Acknowledging that resources devoted to combating the epidemic both at the national and international levels are not commensurate with the magnitude of the problem;

29. Recognizing the fundamental importance of strengthening national, regional and subregional capacities to address and effectively combat HIV/AIDS and that this will require increased and sustained human, financial and technical resources through strengthened national action and cooperation and increased regional, subregional and international cooperation;

30. Recognizing that external debt and debt-servicing problems have substantially constrained the capacity of many developing countries, as well as countries with economies in transition, to finance the fight against HIV/AIDS;

31. Affirming the key role played by the family in prevention, care, support and treatment of persons affected and infected by HIV/AIDS, bearing in mind that in different cultural, social and political systems various forms of the family exist;

32. Affirming that beyond the key role played by communities, strong partnerships among Governments, the United Nations system, intergovernmental organizations, people living with HIV/AIDS and vulnerable groups, medical, scientific and educational institutions, non-governmental organizations, the business sector including generic and research-based pharmaceutical companies, trade unions, the media, parliamentarians, foundations, community organizations, faith-based organizations and traditional leaders are important;

33. Acknowledging the particular role and significant contribution of people living with HIV/AIDS, young people and civil society actors in addressing the problem of HIV/AIDS in all its aspects, and recognizing that their full involvement and participation in the design, planning, implementation and evaluation of programmes is crucial to the development of effective responses to the HIV/AIDS epidemic;

34. Further acknowledging the efforts of international humanitarian organizations combating the epidemic, including among others the volunteers of the International Federation of Red Cross and Red Crescent Societies in the most affected areas all over the world;

35. Commending the leadership role on HIV/AIDS policy and coordination in the United Nations system of the Programme Coordinating Board of the Joint United Nations Programme on HIV/AIDS; and noting its endorsement in December 2000 of the Global Strategy Framework on HIV/AIDS, which could assist, as appropriate, Member States and relevant civil society actors in the development of HIV/AIDS strategies, taking into account the particular context of the epidemic in different parts of the world;

36. Solemnly declare our commitment to address the HIV/AIDS crisis by taking action as follows, taking into account the diverse situations and circumstances in different regions and countries throughout the world;

LEADERSHIP

Strong leadership at all levels of society is essential for an effective response to the epidemic Leadership by Governments in combating HIV/AIDS is essential and their efforts should be complemented by the full and active participation of civil society, the business community and the private sector Leadership involves personal commitment and concrete actions

At the national level

37. By 2003, ensure the development and implementation of multisectoral national strategies and financing plans for combating HIV/AIDS that address the epidemic in forthright terms; confront stigma, silence and denial; address gender and age-based dimensions of the epidemic; eliminate discrimination and marginalization; involve partnerships with civil society and the business sector and the full participation of people living with HIV/AIDS, those in vulnerable groups and people mostly at risk, particularly women and young people; are resourced to the extent possible from national budgets without excluding other sources, *inter alia* international cooperation; fully promote and protect all human rights and fundamental freedoms, including the right to the highest attainable standard of physical and mental health; integrate a gender perspective; address risk, vulnerability, prevention, care, treatment and support and reduction of the impact of the epidemic; and strengthen health, education and legal system capacity;

38. By 2003, integrate HIV/AIDS prevention, care, treatment and support and impact mitigation priorities into the mainstream of development planning, including in poverty eradication strategies, national budget allocations and sectoral development plans;

At the regional and subregional level

39. Urge and support regional organizations and partners to be actively involved in addressing the crisis; intensify regional, subregional and interregional cooperation and coordination; and develop regional strategies and responses in support of expanded country level efforts;

40. Support all regional and subregional initiatives on HIV/AIDS including: the International Partnership against AIDS in Africa (IPAA) and the ECA-African

Development Forum Consensus and Plan of Action: Leadership to Overcome HIV/ AIDS; the Abuja Declaration and Framework for Action for the Fight Against HIV/AIDS, Tuberculosis and Other Diseases; the CARICOM Pan-Caribbean Partnership Against HIV/AIDS; the ESCAP Regional Call for Action to Fight HIV/AIDS in Asia and the Pacific; the Baltic Sea Initiative and Action Plan; the Horizontal Technical Cooperation Group on HIV/AIDS in Latin America and the Caribbean; the European Union Programme for Action: Accelerated Action on HIV/AIDS, Malaria and Tuberculosis in the context of poverty reduction;

41. Encourage the development of regional approaches and plans to address HIV/AIDS;

42. Encourage and support local and national organizations to expand and strengthen regional partnerships, coalitions and networks;

43. Encourage the United Nations Economic and Social Council to request the regional commissions within their respective mandates and resources to support national efforts in their respective regions in combating HIV/AIDS;

At the global level

44. Support greater action and coordination by all relevant United Nations system organizations, including their full participation in the development and implementation of a regularly updated United Nations strategic plan for HIV/AIDS, guided by the principles contained in this Declaration;

45. Support greater cooperation between relevant United Nations system organizations and international organizations combating HIV/AIDS;

46. Foster stronger collaboration and the development of innovative partnerships between the public and private sectors and by 2003, establish and strengthen mechanisms that involve the private sector and civil society partners and people living with HIV/AIDS and vulnerable groups in the fight against HIV/AIDS;

PREVENTION

Prevention must be the mainstay of our response

47. By 2003, establish time-bound national target to achieve the internationally agreed global prevention goal to reduce by 2005 HIV prevalence among young men and women aged 15 to 24 in the most affected countries by 25 per cent and by 25 per cent globally by 2010, and to intensify efforts to achieve these targets as well as to challenge gender stereotypes and attitudes, and gender inequalities in relation to HIV/AIDS, encouraging the active involvement of men and boys;

48. By 2003, establish national prevention targets, recognizing and addressing factors leading to the spread of the epidemic and increasing people's vulnerability, to reduce HIV incidence for those identifiable groups, within particular local contexts, which currently have high or increasing rates of HIV infection, or which available public health information indicates are at the highest risk for new infection;

49. By 2005, strengthen the response to HIV/AIDS in the world of work by establishing and implementing prevention and care programmes in public, private and informal work sectors and take measures to provide a supportive workplace environment for people living with HIV/AIDS;

50. By 2005, develop and begin to implement national, regional and international strategies that facilitate access to HIV/AIDS prevention programmes for migrants and mobile workers, including the provision of information on health and social services;

51. By 2003, implement universal precautions in health-care settings to prevent transmission of HIV infection;

52. By 2005, ensure: that a wide range of prevention programmes which take account of local circumstances, ethics and cultural values, is available in all countries, particularly the most affected countries, including information, education and communication, in languages most understood by communities and respectful of cultures, aimed at reducing risk-taking behaviour and encouraging responsible sexual behaviour, including abstinence and fidelity; expanded access to essential commodities, including male and female condoms and sterile injecting equipment; harm-reduction efforts related to drug use; expanded access to voluntary and confidential counselling and testing; safe blood supplies; and early and effective treatment of sexually transmittable infections;

53. By 2005, ensure that at least 90 per cent, and by 2010 at least 95 per cent of young men and women aged 15 to 24 have access to the information, education, including peer education and youth-specific HIV education, and services necessary to develop the life skills required to reduce their vulnerability to HIV infection, in full partnership with youth, parents, families, educators and health-care providers;

54. By 2005, reduce the proportion of infants infected with HIV by 20 per cent, and by 50 per cent by 2010, by ensuring that 80 per cent of pregnant women accessing antenatal care have information, counselling and other HIV prevention services available to them, increasing the availability of and providing access for HIV-infected women and babies to effective treatment to reduce mother-to-child transmission of HIV, as well as through effective interventions for HIV-infected women, including voluntary and confidential counselling and testing, access to treatment, especially anti-retroviral therapy and, where appropriate, breast milk substitutes and the provision of a continuum of care;

CARE, SUPPORT AND TREATMENT

Care, support and treatment are fundamental elements of an effective response

55. By 2003, ensure that national strategies, supported by regional and international strategies, are developed in close collaboration with the international community, including Governments and relevant intergovernmental organizations as well as with civil society and the business sector, to strengthen health care systems and address factors affecting the provision of HIV-related drugs, including anti-retroviral drugs, *inter alia*, affordability and pricing, including differential pricing, and technical and health care systems capacity. Also, in an urgent manner make every effort to provide progressively and in a sustainable manner, the highest attainable standard of treatment for HIV/AIDS, including the prevention and treatment of opportunistic infections, and effective use of quality-controlled anti-retroviral therapy in a careful and monitored manner to improve adherence and effectiveness and reduce the risk of developing resistance; to cooperate constructively in strengthening pharmaceutical policies and practices, including those applicable to generic drugs and intellectual property regimes, in order further to promote innovation and the development of domestic industries consistent with international law;

56. By 2005, develop and make significant progress in implementing comprehensive care strategies to: strengthen family and community-based care, including that provided by the informal sector, and health care systems to provide and monitor treatment to people living with HIV/AIDS, including infected children, and to support individuals, households, families and communities affected by HIV/AIDS; and improve the capacity and working conditions of health care personnel, and the effectiveness of supply systems, financing plans and referral mechanisms required to provide access to affordable medicines, including anti-retroviral drugs, diagnostics and related technologies, as well as quality medical, palliative and psycho-social care;

57. By 2003, ensure that national strategies are developed in order to provide psychosocial care for individuals, families, and communities affected by HIV/AIDS;

HIV/AIDS AND HUMAN RIGHTS

*Realization of human rights and fundamental freedoms for all
is essential to reduce vulnerability to HIV/AIDS*

Respect for the rights of people living with HIV/AIDS drives an effective response

58. By 2003, enact, strengthen or enforce as appropriate, legislation, regulations and other measures to eliminate all forms of discrimination against and to ensure the full enjoyment of all human rights and fundamental freedoms by people living with HIV/AIDS and members of vulnerable groups; in particular to ensure their access to *inter alia*, education, inheritance, employment, health care, social and health services, prevention, support, treatment, information and legal protection, while respecting their privacy and confidentiality; and develop strategies to combat stigma and social exclusion connected with the epidemic;

59. By 2005, bearing in mind the context and character of the epidemic and that globally women and girls are disproportionately affected by HIV/AIDS, develop and accelerate the implementation of national strategies that promote the advancement of women and women's full enjoyment of all human rights; promote shared responsibility of men and women to ensure safe sex; empower women to have control over and decide freely and responsibly on matters related to their sexuality to increase their ability to protect themselves from HIV infection;

60. By 2005, implement measures to increase capacities of women and adolescent girls to protect themselves from the risk of HIV infection, principally through the provision of health care and health services, including sexual and reproductive health, and through prevention education that promotes gender equality within a culturally and gender sensitive framework;

61. By 2005, ensure development and accelerated implementation of national strategies for women's empowerment, promotion and protection of women's full enjoyment of all human rights and reduction of their vulnerability of HIV/AIDS through the elimination of all forms of discrimination, as well as all forms of violence against women and girls, including harmful traditional and customary practices, abuse, rape and other forms of sexual violence, battering and trafficking in women and girls;

REDUCING VULNERABILITY

The vulnerable must be given priority in the response

Empowering women is essential for reducing vulnerability

62. By 2003, in order to complement prevention programmes that address activities which place individuals at risk of HIV infection, such as risky and unsafe sexual behaviour and injecting drug use, have in place in all countries strategies, policies and programmes that identify and begin to address those factors that make individuals particularly vulnerable to HIV infection, including underdevelopment, economic insecurity, poverty, lack of empowerment of women, lack of education, social exclusion, illiteracy, discrimination, lack of information and/or commodities for self-protection, all types of sexual exploitation of women, girls and boys, including for commercial reasons. Such strategies, policies and programmes should address the gender dimension of the epidemic, specify the action that will be taken to address vulnerability and set targets for achievement;

63. By 2003, develop and/or strengthen strategies, policies and programmes, which recognize the importance of the family in reducing vulnerability, *inter alia*, in educating and guiding children and take account of cultural, religious and ethical factors, to reduce the vulnerability of children and young people by ensuring access of both girls and boys to primary and secondary education, including HIV/AIDS in curricula for adolescents; ensuring safe and secure environments, especially for young girls; expanding good quality youth-friendly information and sexual health education and counselling services; strengthening reproductive and sexual health programmes; and involving families and young people in planning, implementing and evaluating HIV/AIDS prevention and care programmes, to the extent possible;

64. By 2003, develop and/or strengthen national strategies, policies and programmes, supported by regional and international initiatives, as appropriate, through a participatory approach, to promote and protect the health of those identifiable groups which currently have high or increasing rates of HIV infection or which public health information indicates are at greatest risk of and most vulnerable to new infection as indicated by such factors as the local history of the epidemic, poverty, sexual practices, drug using behaviour, livelihood, institutional location, disrupted social structures and population movements forced or otherwise;

CHILDREN ORPHANED AND MADE VULNERABLE BY HIV/AIDS

Children orphaned and affected by HIV/AIDS need special assistance

65. By 2003, develop and by 2005 implement national policies and strategies to: build and strengthen governmental, family and community capacities to provide a supportive environment for orphans and girls and boys infected and affected by HIV/AIDS, including by providing appropriate counselling and psycho-social support, ensuring their enrolment in school and access to shelter, good nutrition, health and social services on an equal basis with other children; and protect orphans and vulnerable children from all forms of abuse, violence, exploitation, discrimination, trafficking and loss of inheritance;

66. Ensure non-discrimination and full and equal enjoyment of all human rights through the promotion of an active and visible policy of de-stigmatization of children orphaned and made vulnerable by HIV/AIDS;

67. Urge the international community, particularly donor countries, civil society, as well as the private sector, to complement effectively national programmes to support programmes for children orphaned or made vulnerable by HIV/AIDS in affected regions and in countries at high risk and to direct special assistance to sub-Saharan Africa;

ALLEVIATING SOCIAL AND ECONOMIC IMPACT

To address HIV/AIDS is to invest in sustainable development

68. By 2003, evaluate the economic and social impact of the HIV/AIDS epidemic and develop multisectoral strategies to address the impact at the individual, family, community and national levels; develop and accelerate the implementation of national poverty eradication strategies to address the impact of HIV/AIDS on household income, livelihoods and access to basic social services, with special focus on individuals, families and communities severely affected by the epidemic; review the social and economic impact of HIV/AIDS at all levels of society, especially on women and the elderly, particularly in their role as caregivers, and in families affected by HIV/AIDS, and address their special needs; and adjust and adapt economic and social development policies, including social protection policies, to address the impact of HIV/AIDS on economic growth, provision of essential economic services, labour productivity, government revenues, and deficit-creating pressures on public resources;

69. By 2003, develop a national legal and policy framework that protects in the workplace the rights and dignity of persons living with and affected by HIV/AIDS and those at the greatest risk of HIV/AIDS, in consultation with representatives of employers and workers, taking account of established international guidelines on HIV/AIDS in the workplace;

RESEARCH AND DEVELOPMENT

With no cure for HIV/AIDS yet found, further research and development is crucial

70. Increase investment and accelerate research on the development of HIV vaccines, while building national research capacity especially in developing countries, and especially for viral strains prevalent in highly affected regions; in addition, support and encourage increased national and international investment in HIV/AIDS-related research and development, including biomedical, operations, social, cultural and behavioural research and in traditional medicine to improve prevention and therapeutic approaches; accelerate access to prevention, care and treatment and care technologies for HIV/AIDS (and its associated opportunistic infections and malignancies and sexually transmitted diseases), including female controlled methods and microbicides, and in particular, appropriate, safe and affordable HIV vaccines and their delivery, and to diagnostics, tests and methods to prevent mother-to-child transmission; improve our understanding of factors which influence the epidemic and actions which address it, *inter alia*, through increased funding and public/private partnerships; and create a conducive environment for research and ensure that it is based on the highest ethical standards;

71. Support and encourage the development of national and international research infrastructures, laboratory capacity, improved surveillance systems, data collection, processing and dissemination, and the training of basic and clinical researchers, social scientists, health-care providers and technicians, with a focus on the countries most affected by HIV/AIDS, particularly developing countries and those countries experiencing or at risk of rapid expansion of the epidemic;

72. Develop and evaluate suitable approaches for monitoring treatment efficacy, toxicity, side effects, drug interactions and drug resistance, and develop methodologies to monitor the impact of treatment on HIV transmission and risk behaviours;

73. Strengthen international and regional cooperation, in particular North/South, South/South and triangular cooperation, related to the transfer of relevant technologies suitable to the environment in the prevention and care of HIV/AIDS, the exchange of experiences and best practices, researchers and research findings and strengthen the role of UNAIDS in this process. In this context, encourage ownership of the end results of these cooperative research findings and technologies by all parties to the research, reflecting their relevant contribution and dependent upon their providing legal protection to such findings; and affirm that all such research should be free from bias;

74. By 2003, ensure that all research protocols for the investigation of HIV-related treatment, including anti-retroviral therapies and vaccines, based on international guidelines and best practices, are evaluated by independent committees of ethics, in which persons living with HIV/AIDS and caregivers for anti-retroviral therapy participate;

HIV/AIDS IN CONFLICT AND DISASTER AFFECTED REGIONS

Conflicts and disasters contribute to the spread of HIV/AIDS

75. By 2003, develop and begin to implement national strategies that incorporate HIV/AIDS awareness, prevention, care and treatment elements into programmes or actions that respond to emergency situations, recognizing that populations destabilized by armed conflict, humanitarian emergencies and natural disasters, including refugees, internally displaced persons and in particular, women and children, are at increased risk of exposure to HIV infection; and, where appropriate, factor HIV/AIDS components into international assistance programmes;

76. Call on all United Nations agencies, regional and international organizations, as well as non-governmental organizations involved with the provision and delivery of international assistance to countries and regions affected by conflicts, humanitarian crises or natural disasters, to incorporate as a matter of urgency HIV/AIDS prevention, care and awareness elements into their plans and programmes and provide HIV/AIDS awareness and training to their personnel;

77. By 2003, have in place national strategies to address the spread of HIV among national uniformed services, where this is required, including armed forces and civil defence forces, and consider ways of using personnel from these services who are educated and trained in HIV/AIDS awareness and prevention to assist with HIV/AIDS awareness and prevention activities, including participation in emergency, humanitarian, disaster relief and rehabilitation assistance;

78. By 2003, ensure the inclusion of HIV/AIDS awareness and training, including a gender component, into guidelines designed for use by defence personnel and other personnel

involved in international peacekeeping operations, while also continuing with ongoing education and prevention efforts, including pre-deployment orientation, for these personnel;

RESOURCES

The HIV/AIDS challenge cannot be met without new, additional and sustained resources

79. Ensure that the resources provided for the global response to address HIV/AIDS are substantial, sustained and geared towards achieving results;

80. By 2005, through a series of incremental steps, reach an overall target of annual expenditure on the epidemic of between 7 and 10 billion United States dollars in low and middle-income countries and those countries experiencing or at risk of experiencing rapid expansion for prevention, care, treatment, support and mitigation of the impact of HIV/AIDS, and take measures to ensure that the resources needed are made available, particularly from donor countries and also from national budgets, bearing in mind that resources of the most affected countries are seriously limited;

81. Call on the international community, where possible, to provide assistance for HIV/AIDS prevention, care and treatment in developing countries on a grant basis;

82. Increase and prioritize national budgetary allocations for HIV/AIDS programmes as required, and ensure that adequate allocations are made by all ministries and other relevant stakeholders;

83. Urge the developed countries that have not done so to strive to meet the targets of 0.7 per cent of their gross national product for overall official development assistance and the targets of earmarking of 0.15 per cent to 0.20 per cent of gross national product as official development assistance for least developed countries as agreed, as soon as possible, taking into account the urgency and gravity of the HIV/AIDS epidemic;

84. Urge the international community to complement and supplement efforts of developing countries that commit increased national funds to fight the HIV/AIDS epidemic through increased international development assistance, particularly those countries most affected by HIV/AIDS, particularly in Africa, especially in sub-Saharan Africa, the Caribbean, countries at high risk of expansion of the HIV/AIDS epidemic and other affected regions whose resources to deal with the epidemic are seriously limited;

85. Integrate HIV/AIDS actions in development assistance programmes and poverty eradication strategies as appropriate, and encourage the most effective and transparent use of all resources allocated;

86. Call on the international community, and invite civil society and the private sector to take appropriate measures to help alleviate the social and economic impact of HIV/AIDS in the most affected developing countries;

87. Without further delay, implement the enhanced Heavily Indebted Poor Country (HIPC) Initiative and agree to cancel all bilateral official debts of HIPC countries as soon as possible, especially those most affected by HIV/AIDS, in return for their making demonstrable commitments to poverty eradication, and urge the use of debt service savings to finance poverty eradication programmes, particularly for prevention, treatment, care and support for HIV/AIDS and other infections;

88. Call for speedy and concerted action to address effectively the debt problems of least developed countries, low-income developing countries, and middle-income developing

countries, particularly those affected by HIV/AIDS, in a comprehensive, equitable, development-oriented and durable way through various national and international measures designed to make their debt sustainable in the long term and thereby to improve their capacity to deal with the HIV/AIDS epidemic, including, as appropriate, existing orderly mechanisms for debt reduction, such as debt swaps for projects aimed at the prevention, care and treatment of HIV/AIDS;

89. Encourage increased investment in HIV/AIDS-related research nationally, regionally and internationally, in particular for the development of sustainable and affordable prevention technologies, such as vaccines and microbicides, and encourage the proactive preparation of financial and logistic plans to facilitate rapid access to vaccines when they become available;

90. Support the establishment, on an urgent basis, of a global HIV/AIDS and health fund to finance an urgent and expanded response to the epidemic based on an integrated approach to prevention, care, support and treatment and to assist Governments inter alia in their efforts to combat HIV/AIDS with due priority to the most affected countries, notably in sub-Saharan Africa and the Caribbean and to those countries at high risk, and mobilize contributions to the fund from public and private sources with a special appeal to donor countries, foundations, the business community, including pharmaceutical companies, the private sector, philanthropists and wealthy individuals;

91. By 2002, launch a worldwide fund-raising campaign aimed at the general public as well as the private sector, conducted by UNAIDS with the support and collaboration of interested partners at all levels, to contribute to the global HIV/AIDS and health fund;

92. Direct increased funding to national, regional and subregional commissions and organizations to enable them to assist Governments at the national, regional and subregional level in their efforts to respond to the crisis;

93. Provide the UNAIDS co-sponsoring agencies and the UNAIDS secretariat with the resources needed to work with countries in support of the goals of the present Declaration;

FOLLOW-UP

Maintaining the momentum and monitoring progress are essential

At the national level

94. Conduct national periodic reviews involving the participation of civil society, particularly people living with HIV/AIDS, vulnerable groups and caregivers, of progress achieved in realizing these commitments, identify problems and obstacles to achieving progress, and ensure wide dissemination of the results of these reviews;

95. Develop appropriate monitoring and evaluation mechanisms to assist with follow-up in measuring and assessing progress, develop appropriate monitoring and evaluation instruments, with adequate epidemiological data;

96. By 2003, establish or strengthen effective monitoring systems, where appropriate, for the promotion and protection of human rights of people living with HIV/AIDS;

At the regional level

97. Include HIV/AIDS and related public health concerns, as appropriate, on the agenda of regional meetings at the ministerial and head of State and Government level;

98. Support data collection and processing to facilitate periodic reviews by regional commissions and/or regional organizations of progress in implementing regional strategies and addressing regional priorities, and ensure wide dissemination of the results of these reviews;

99. Encourage the exchange between countries of information and experiences in implementing the measures and commitments contained in the present Declaration, and in particular facilitate intensified South-South and triangular cooperation;

At the global level

100. Devote sufficient time and at least one full day of the annual session of the General Assembly to review and debate a report of the Secretary-General on progress achieved in realizing the commitments set out in the present Declaration, with a view to identifying problems and constraints and making recommendations on action needed to make further progress;

101. Ensure that HIV/AIDS issues are included on the agenda of all appropriate United Nations conferences and meetings;

102. Support initiatives to convene conferences, seminars, workshops, training programmes and courses to follow-up issues raised in the present Declaration and in this regard encourage participation in and wide dissemination of the outcomes of the forthcoming Dakar Conference on access to care for HIV infection; the Sixth International Congress on AIDS in Asia and the Pacific; the Twelfth International Conference on AIDS and Sexually Transmitted Infections in Africa; the Fourteenth International Conference on AIDS, Barcelona; the Tenth International Conference on People Living with HIV/AIDS, Port-of-Spain; the Second Forum and Third Conference of the Horizontal Technical Cooperation Group on HIV/AIDS and Sexually Transmitted Infections in Latin America and the Caribbean, Havana; the Fifth International Conference on Home and Community Care for Persons Living with HIV/AIDS, Chiang Mai, Thailand;

103. Explore, with a view to improving equity in access to essential drugs, the feasibility of developing and implementing, in collaboration with non-governmental organizations and other concerned partners, systems for voluntary monitoring and reporting of global drug prices;

We recognize and express our appreciation to those who have led the effort to raise awareness of the HIV/AIDS epidemic and to deal with its complex challenges;

We look forward to strong leadership by Governments, and concerted efforts with the full and active participation of the United Nations, the entire multilateral system, civil society, the business community and private sector;

And finally, we call on all countries to take the necessary steps to implement the present Declaration, in strengthened partnership and cooperation with other multilateral and bilateral partners and with civil society.

36. NORMS ON THE RESPONSIBILITIES OF TRANSNATIONAL CORPORATIONS AND OTHER BUSINESS ENTERPRISES WITH REGARD TO HUMAN RIGHTS, 2003

These norms were adopted by the Sub-Commission on the Promotion and Protection of Human Rights on 13 August 2003, UN doc. E/CN.4/Sub.2/2003/12/Rev.2, 26 August 2003.

The draft norms were discussed by the Commission on Human Rights in April 2004, and while the Commission affirmed that, as a draft proposal, they had no legal standing, it confirmed the importance and priority accorded to the question of the responsibilities of transnational corporations and related business enterprises with regard to human rights. In 2005, the Commission requested the Secretary-General to appoint a Special Representative on Human Rights and Transnational Corporations and other business enterprises; see Resolution 2005/69, adopted on 20 April 2005 by forty-nine votes in favour, three against, and one abstention. Professor John Ruggie was appointed to the post in July 2005, and he provided an interim report to the Commission in 2006 (UN doc. E/CN.4/2006/97; see paras. 56–69, commenting on the norms) and a final report on his initial mandate to the Human Rights Council the following year (UN doc. A/HRC/4/035, 9 February 2007). The Council renewed his mandate for a further three-year period in 2008.

According to paragraph 1 of the above resolution, the role of the Special Representative is, '(a) To identify and clarify standards of corporate responsibility and accountability for transnational corporations and other business enterprises with regard to human rights; (b) To elaborate on the role of States in effectively regulating and adjudicating the role of transnational corporations and other business enterprises with regard to human rights, including through international coopera- tion; (c) To research and clarify the implications for transnational corporations and other business enterprises of concepts such as "complicity" and "sphere of influence"; (d) To develop materials and methodologies for undertaking human rights impact assessments of the activities of transnational corporations and other business enterprises; (e) To compile a compendium of best practices of States and transnational corporations and other business enterprises.'

In his 2008 report to the Human Rights Council, the Special Representative proposed a policy framework for business and human rights based on three pillars: the duty of the State to protect against human rights abuses by third parties, including business; corporate responsibility to respect human rights; and greater access by victims to effective remedies: UN doc. A/HRC/8/5, 7 April 2008. Proposals for 'operationalizing' the framework were made in his 2009 report: UN doc. A/HRC/11/13, 22 April 2009. See generally, **http://www.business-humanrights.org/ SpecialRepPortal/**.

Earlier, in 1974, the UN established the Programme on Transnational Corporations, which is now based with the United Nations Conference on Trade and Development (UNCTAD) in Geneva and implemented by UNCTAD's Division on Investment, Technology and Enterprise Development: **http://unctc.unctad.org/**.

Further reading

BACKER, L. C., 'Multinational Corporations, Transnational Law: The United Nations' Norms on the Responsibilities of Transnational Corporations as a Harbinger of Corporate Social Responsibility in International Law', (2005–2006) 27 *Columbia Human Rights Law Review* 287.

JERBI, S., 'Business and Human Rights at the UN: What Might Happen Next?' (2009) *Human Rights Quarterly* 299.

KINLEY, D. and CHAMBERS, R., 'The UN Human Rights Norms for Corporations: The Private Implications of Public International Law', (2006) 6 *Human Rights Law Review* 447.

MANTILLA, G., 'Emerging International Human Rights Norms for Transnational Corporations', (2009) 15 *Global Governance* 279.

RUGGIE, J., 'Business and Human Rights: The Evolving International Agenda', (2007) 101 *AJIL* 819.

TEXT

Preamble

Bearing in mind the principles and obligations under the Charter of the United Nations, in particular the preamble and Articles 1, 2, 55 and 56, *inter alia* to promote universal respect for, and observance of, human rights and fundamental freedoms,

Recalling that the Universal Declaration of Human Rights proclaims a common standard of achievement for all peoples and all nations, to the end that Governments, other organs of society and individuals shall strive, by teaching and education to promote respect for human rights and freedoms, and, by progressive measures, to secure universal and effective recognition and observance, including of equal rights of women and men and the promotion of social progress and better standards of life in larger freedom,

Recognizing that even though States have the primary responsibility to promote, secure the fulfilment of, respect, ensure respect of and protect human rights, transnational corporations and other business enterprises, as organs of society, are also responsible for promoting and securing the human rights set forth in the Universal Declaration of Human Rights,

Realizing that transnational corporations and other business enterprises, their officers and persons working for them are also obligated to respect generally recognized responsibilities and norms contained in United Nations treaties and other international instruments such as the Convention on the Prevention and Punishment of the Crime of Genocide; the Convention against Torture and Other Cruel, Inhuman or Degrading Treatment or Punishment; the Slavery Convention and the Supplementary Convention on the Abolition of Slavery, the Slave Trade, and Institutions and Practices Similar to Slavery; the International Convention on the Elimination of All Forms of Racial Discrimination; the Convention on the Elimination of All Forms of Discrimination against Women; the International Covenant on Economic, Social and Cultural Rights; the International Covenant on Civil and Political Rights; the Convention on the Rights of the Child; the International Convention on the Protection of the Rights of All Migrant Workers and Members of Their Families; the four Geneva Conventions of 12 August 1949 and two Additional Protocols thereto for the protection of victims of war; the Declaration on the Right and Responsibility of Individuals, Groups and Organs of Society to Promote and Protect Universally Recognized Human Rights and Fundamental Freedoms; the Rome Statute of the International Criminal Court; the United Nations Convention against Transnational Organized Crime; the Convention on Biological Diversity; the International Convention on Civil Liability for Oil Pollution Damage; the Convention on Civil Liability for Damage Resulting from Activities Dangerous to the Environment; the Declaration on the Right to Development; the Rio Declaration on the Environment and Development; the Plan of Implementation of the World Summit on Sustainable Development; the United Nations Millennium Declaration; the Universal Declaration on the Human Genome and Human Rights; the International Code of Marketing of Breast-milk Substitutes adopted by the World Health Assembly; the Ethical Criteria for

Medical Drug Promotion and the 'Health for All in the Twenty-First Century' policy of the World Health Organization; the Convention against Discrimination in Education of the United Nations Educational, Scientific, and Cultural Organization; conventions and recommendations of the International Labour Organization; the Convention and Protocol relating to the Status of Refugees; the African Charter on Human and Peoples' Rights; the American Convention on Human Rights; the European Convention for the Protection of Human Rights and Fundamental Freedoms; the Charter of Fundamental Rights of the European Union; the Convention on Combating Bribery of Foreign Public Officials in International Business Transactions of the Organization for Economic Cooperation and Development; and other instruments,

Taking into account the standards set forth in the Tripartite Declaration of Principles Concerning Multinational Enterprises and Social Policy and the Declaration on Fundamental Principles and Rights at Work of the International Labour Organization,

Aware of the Guidelines for Multinational Enterprises and the Committee on International Investment and Multinational Enterprises of the Organization for Economic Cooperation and Development,

Aware also of the United Nations Global Compact initiative which challenges business leaders to 'embrace and enact' nine basic principles with respect to human rights, including labour rights and the environment,

Conscious of the fact that the Governing Body Subcommittee on Multinational Enterprises and Social Policy, the Governing Body, the Committee of Experts on the Application of Standards, as well as the Committee on Freedom of Association of the International Labour Organization have named business enterprises implicated in States' failure to comply with Conventions No. 87 concerning the Freedom of Association and Protection of the Right to Organize and No. 98 concerning the Application of the Principles of the Right to Organize and Bargain Collectively, and seeking to supplement and assist their efforts to encourage transnational corporations and other business enterprises to protect human rights,

Conscious also of the Commentary on the Norms on the responsibilities of transnational corporations and other business enterprises with regard to human rights, and finding it a useful interpretation and elaboration of the standards contained in the Norms,

Taking note of global trends which have increased the influence of transnational corporations and other business enterprises on the economies of most countries and in international economic relations, and of the growing number of other business enterprises which operate across national boundaries in a variety of arrangements resulting in economic activities beyond the actual capacities of any one national system,

Noting that transnational corporations and other business enterprises have the capacity to foster economic well-being, development, technological improvement and wealth as well as the capacity to cause harmful impacts on the human rights and lives of individuals through their core business practices and operations, including employment practices, environmental policies, relationships with suppliers and consumers, interactions with Governments and other activities,

Noting also that new international human rights issues and concerns are continually emerging and that transnational corporations and other business enterprises often are involved in these issues and concerns, such that further standard-setting and implementation are required at this time and in the future,

Acknowledging the universality, indivisibility, interdependence and interrelatedness of human rights, including the right to development, which entitles every human person and all peoples to participate in, contribute to and enjoy economic, social, cultural and political development in which all human rights and fundamental freedoms can be fully realized,

Reaffirming that transnational corporations and other business enterprises, their officers—including managers, members of corporate boards or directors and other executives—and persons working for them have, *inter alia*, human rights obligations and responsibilities and that these human rights norms will contribute to the making and development of international law as to those responsibilities and obligations,

Solemnly proclaims these Norms on the Responsibilities of Transnational Corporations and Other Business Enterprises with Regard to Human Rights and urges that every effort be made so that they become generally known and respected.

A. General obligations

1. States have the primary responsibility to promote, secure the fulfilment of, respect, ensure respect of and protect human rights recognized in international as well as national law, including ensuring that transnational corporations and other business enterprises respect human rights. Within their respective spheres of activity and influence, transnational corporations and other business enterprises have the obligation to promote, secure the fulfilment of, respect, ensure respect of and protect human rights recognized in international as well as national law, including the rights and interests of indigenous peoples and other vulnerable groups.

B. Right to equal opportunity and non-discriminatory treatment

2. Transnational corporations and other business enterprises shall ensure equality of opportunity and treatment, as provided in the relevant international instruments and national legislation as well as international human rights law, for the purpose of eliminating discrimination based on race, colour, sex, language, religion, political opinion, national or social origin, social status, indigenous status, disability, age—except for children, who may be given greater protection—or other status of the individual unrelated to the inherent requirements to perform the job, or of complying with special measures designed to overcome past discrimination against certain groups.

C. Right to security of persons

3. Transnational corporations and other business enterprises shall not engage in nor benefit from war crimes, crimes against humanity, genocide, torture, forced disappearance, forced or compulsory labour, hostage-taking, extrajudicial, summary or arbitrary executions, other violations of humanitarian law and other international crimes against the human person as defined by international law, in particular human rights and humanitarian law.

4. Security arrangements for transnational corporations and other business enterprises shall observe international human rights norms as well as the laws and professional standards of the country or countries in which they operate.

D. Rights of workers

5. Transnational corporations and other business enterprises shall not use forced or compulsory labour as forbidden by the relevant international instruments and national legislation as well as international human rights and humanitarian law.

6. Transnational corporations and other business enterprises shall respect the rights of children to be protected from economic exploitation as forbidden by the relevant international instruments and national legislation as well as international human rights and humanitarian law.

7. Transnational corporations and other business enterprises shall provide a safe and healthy working environment as set forth in relevant international instruments and national legislation as well as international human rights and humanitarian law.

8. Transnational corporations and other business enterprises shall provide workers with remuneration that ensures an adequate standard of living for them and their families. Such remuneration shall take due account of their needs for adequate living conditions with a view towards progressive improvement.

9. Transnational corporations and other business enterprises shall ensure freedom of association and effective recognition of the right to collective bargaining by protecting the right to establish and, subject only to the rules of the organization concerned, to join organizations of their own choosing without distinction, previous authorization, or interference, for the protection of their employment interests and for other collective bargaining purposes as provided in national legislation and the relevant conventions of the International Labour Organization.

E. Respect for national sovereignty and human rights

10. Transnational corporations and other business enterprises shall recognize and respect applicable norms of international law, national laws and regulations, as well as administrative practices, the rule of law, the public interest, development objectives, social, economic and cultural policies including transparency, accountability and prohibition of corruption, and authority of the countries in which the enterprises operate.

11. Transnational corporations and other business enterprises shall not offer, promise, give, accept, condone, knowingly benefit from, or demand a bribe or other improper advantage, nor shall they be solicited or expected to give a bribe or other improper advantage to any Government, public official, candidate for elective post, any member of the armed forces or security forces, or any other individual or organization. Transnational corporations and other business enterprises shall refrain from any activity which supports, solicits, or encourages States or any other entities to abuse human rights. They shall further seek to ensure that the goods and services they provide will not be used to abuse human rights.

12. Transnational corporations and other business enterprises shall respect economic, social and cultural rights as well as civil and political rights and contribute to their realization, in particular the rights to development, adequate food and drinking water, the highest attainable standard of physical and mental health, adequate housing, privacy, education, freedom of thought, conscience, and religion and freedom of opinion and expression, and shall refrain from actions which obstruct or impede the realization of those rights.

F. Obligations with regard to consumer protection

13. Transnational corporations and other business enterprises shall act in accordance with fair business, marketing and advertising practices and shall take all necessary steps to ensure the safety and quality of the goods and services they provide, including observance of the precautionary principle. Nor shall they produce, distribute, market, or advertise harmful or potentially harmful products for use by consumers.

G. Obligations with regard to environmental protection

14. Transnational corporations and other business enterprises shall carry out their activities in accordance with national laws, regulations, administrative practices and policies relating to the preservation of the environment of the countries in which they operate, as well as in accordance with relevant international agreements, principles, objectives, responsibilities and standards with regard to the environment as well as human rights, public health and safety, bioethics and the precautionary principle, and shall generally conduct their activities in a manner contributing to the wider goal of sustainable development.

H. General provisions of implementation

15. As an initial step towards implementing these Norms, each transnational corporation or other business enterprise shall adopt, disseminate and implement internal rules of operation in compliance with the Norms. Further, they shall periodically report on and take other measures fully to implement the Norms and to provide at least for the prompt implementation of the protections set forth in the Norms. Each transnational corporation or other business enterprise shall apply and incorporate these Norms in their contracts or other arrangements and dealings with contractors, subcontractors, suppliers, licensees, distributors, or natural or other legal persons that enter into any agreement with the transnational corporation or business enterprise in order to ensure respect for and implementation of the Norms.

16. Transnational corporations and other business enterprises shall be subject to periodic monitoring and verification by United Nations, other international and national mechanisms already in existence or yet to be created, regarding application of the Norms. This monitoring shall be transparent and independent and take into account input from stakeholders (including non-governmental organizations) and as a result of complaints of violations of these Norms. Further, transnational corporations and other business enterprises shall conduct periodic evaluations concerning the impact of their own activities on human rights under these Norms.

17. States should establish and reinforce the necessary legal and administrative framework for ensuring that the Norms and other relevant national and international laws are implemented by transnational corporations and other business enterprises.

18. Transnational corporations and other business enterprises shall provide prompt, effective and adequate reparation to those persons, entities and communities that have been adversely affected by failures to comply with these Norms through, *inter alia*, reparations, restitution, compensation and rehabilitation for any damage done or property taken. In connection with determining damages, in regard to criminal sanctions, and in all other respects, these Norms shall be applied by national courts and/or international tribunals, pursuant to national and international law.

19. Nothing in these Norms shall be construed as diminishing, restricting, or adversely affecting the human rights obligations of States under national and international law, nor shall they be construed as diminishing, restricting, or adversely affecting more protective human rights norms, nor shall they be construed as diminishing, restricting, or adversely affecting other obligations or responsibilities of transnational corporations and other business enterprises in fields other than human rights.

I. Definitions

20. The term 'transnational corporation' refers to an economic entity operating in more than one country or a cluster of economic entities operating in two or more countries—whatever their legal form, whether in their home country or country of activity, and whether taken individually or collectively.

21. The phrase 'other business enterprise' includes any business entity, regardless of the international or domestic nature of its activities, including a transnational corporation, contractor, subcontractor, supplier, licensee or distributor; the corporate, partnership, or other legal form used to establish the business entity; and the nature of the ownership of the entity. These Norms shall be presumed to apply, as a matter of practice, if the business enterprise has any relation with a transnational corporation, the impact of its activities is not entirely local, or the activities involve violations of the right to security as indicated in paragraphs 3 and 4.

22. The term 'stakeholder' includes stockholders, other owners, workers and their representatives, as well as any other individual or group that is affected by the activities of transnational corporations or other business enterprises. The term 'stakeholder' shall be interpreted functionally in the light of the objectives of these Norms and include indirect stakeholders when their interests are or will be substantially affected by the activities of the transnational corporation or business enterprise. In addition to parties directly affected by the activities of business enterprises, stakeholders can include parties which are indirectly affected by the activities of transnational corporations or other business enterprises such as consumer groups, customers, Governments, neighbouring communities, indigenous peoples and communities, non-governmental organizations, public and private lending institutions, suppliers, trade associations, and others.

23. The phrases 'human rights' and 'international human rights' include civil, cultural, economic, political and social rights, as set forth in the International Bill of Human Rights and other human rights treaties, as well as the right to development and rights recognized by international humanitarian law, international refugee law, international labour law, and other relevant instruments adopted within the United Nations system.

37. BASIC PRINCIPLES AND GUIDELINES ON THE RIGHT TO A REMEDY AND REPARATION FOR VICTIMS OF GROSS VIOLATIONS OF INTERNATIONAL HUMAN RIGHTS LAW AND SERIOUS VIOLATIONS OF INTERNATIONAL HUMANITARIAN LAW, 2005

These principles have their origin in Commission on Human Rights Resolution 2005/35, adopted on 19 April 2005 by forty votes to none, with thirteen abstentions. On the Commission's recommendation, the Economic and Social Council likewise adopted the principles and recommended in turn that they be adopted also by the General Assembly: ECOSOC Resolution 2005/30, 25 July 2005. See now General Assembly Resolution 60/147, adopted without a vote on 16 December 2005, to which the following 'Basic Principles and Guidelines' are attached.

Further reading

BASSIOUNI, M. C., 'International Recognition of Victims' Rights', (2006) 6 *Human Rights Law Review* 203.

BILDER, R. B., 'The Role of Apology in International Law and Diplomacy', (2005–2006) 46 *Virginia Journal of International Law* 433.

SHELTON, D., *Remedies in International Human Rights Law*, New York: Oxford University Press, 2nd edn., 2005.

DE FEYTER, K., PARMENTIER, S., BOSSUYT, M., LEMMENS, P., eds., *Out of the Ashes: Reparation for Victims of Gross Human Rights Violations*, Antwerp: Intersentia, 2006.

TEXT

ANNEX

Basic Principles and Guidelines on the Right to a Remedy and Reparation for Victims of Gross Violations of International Human Rights Law and Serious Violations of International Humanitarian Law

Preamble

The General Assembly,

Recalling the provisions providing a right to a remedy for victims of violations of international human rights law found in numerous international instruments, in particular the Universal Declaration of Human Rights at article 8, the International Covenant on Civil and Political Rights at article 2, the International Convention on the Elimination of All Forms of Racial Discrimination at article 6, the Convention against Torture and Other Cruel, Inhuman or Degrading Treatment or Punishment at article 14, the Convention on the Rights of the Child at article 39, and of international humanitarian law as found in article 3 of the Hague Convention of 18 October 1907 concerning the Laws and Customs of War and Land (Convention No. IV of 1907), article 91 of Protocol Additional to the Geneva Conventions of 12 August 1949 relating to the Protection of

Victims of International Armed Conflicts (Protocol I), and articles 68 and 75 of the Rome Statute of the International Criminal Court,

Recalling the provisions providing a right to a remedy for victims of violations of international human rights found in regional conventions, in particular the African Charter on Human and Peoples' Rights at article 7, the American Convention on Human Rights at article 25, and the European Convention for the Protection of Human Rights and Fundamental Freedoms at article 13,

Recalling the Declaration of Basic Principles of Justice for Victims of Crime and Abuse of Power emanating from the deliberations of the Seventh United Nations Congress on the Prevention of Crime and the Treatment of Offenders, and resolution 40/34 of 29 November 1985 by which the General Assembly adopted the text recommended by the Congress,

Reaffirming the principles enunciated in the Declaration of Basic Principles of Justice for Victims of Crime and Abuse of Power, including that victims should be treated with compassion and respect for their dignity, have their right to access to justice and redress mechanisms fully respected, and that the establishment, strengthening and expansion of national funds for compensation to victims should be encouraged, together with the expeditious development of appropriate rights and remedies for victims,

Noting that the Rome Statute of the International Criminal Court requires the establishment of 'principles relating to reparation to, or in respect of, victims, including restitution, compensation and rehabilitation' and requires the Assembly of States Parties to establish a trust fund for the benefit of victims of crimes within the jurisdiction of the Court, and of the families of such victims, and mandates the Court 'to protect the safety, physical and psychological well-being, dignity and privacy of victims' and to permit the participation of victims at all 'stages of the proceedings determined to be appropriate by the Court',

Affirming that the Principles and Guidelines contained herein are directed at gross violations of international human rights law and serious violations of international humanitarian law which, by their very grave nature, constitute an affront to human dignity,

Emphasizing that the Principles and Guidelines do not entail new international or domestic legal obligations but identify mechanisms, modalities, procedures and methods for the implementation of existing legal obligations under international human rights law and international humanitarian law which are complementary though different as to their norms,

Recalling that international law contains the obligation to prosecute perpetrators of certain international crimes in accordance with international obligations of States and the requirements of national law or as provided for in the applicable statutes of international judicial organs, and that the duty to prosecute reinforces the international legal obligations to be carried out in accordance with national legal requirements and procedures and supports the concept of complementarity,

Noting further that contemporary forms of victimization, while essentially directed against persons, may nevertheless also be directed against groups of persons who are targeted collectively,

Recognizing that, in honouring the victims' right to benefit from remedies and reparation, the international community keeps faith with the plight of victims, survivors and future human generations, and reaffirms the international legal principles of accountability, justice and the rule of law,

Convinced that, in adopting a victim-oriented perspective, the international community affirms its human solidarity with victims of violations of international law, including violations of international human rights law and international humanitarian law, as well as with humanity at large, in accordance with the following Basic Principles and Guidelines,

Adopts the Following Basic Principles:

I. *Obligation to respect, ensure respect for and implement international human rights law and international humanitarian law*

1. The obligation to respect, ensure respect for and implement international human rights law and international humanitarian law as provided for under the respective bodies of law emanates from:

 (a) Treaties to which a State is a party;

 (b) Customary international law;

 (c) The domestic law of each State.

2. If they have not already done so, States shall, as required under international law, ensure that their domestic law is consistent with their international legal obligations by:

 (a) Incorporating norms of international human rights law and international humanitarian law into their domestic law, or otherwise implementing them in their domestic legal system;

 (b) Adopting appropriate and effective legislative and administrative procedures and other appropriate measures that provide fair, effective and prompt access to justice;

 (c) Making available adequate, effective, prompt, and appropriate remedies, including reparation, as defined below; and

 (d) Ensuring that their domestic law provides at least the same level of protection for victims as required by their international obligations.

II. *Scope of the obligation*

3. The obligation to respect, ensure respect for and implement international human rights law and international humanitarian law as provided for under the respective bodies of law, includes, *inter alia,* the duty to:

 (a) Take appropriate legislative and administrative and other appropriate measures to prevent violations;

 (b) Investigate violations effectively, promptly, thoroughly and impartially and, where appropriate, take action against those allegedly responsible in accordance with domestic and international law;

 (c) Provide those who claim to be victims of a human rights or humanitarian law violation with equal and effective access to justice, as described below, irrespective of who may ultimately be the bearer of responsibility for the violation; and

 (d) Provide effective remedies to victims, including reparation, as described below.

III. *Gross violations of international human rights law and serious violations of international humanitarian law that constitute crimes under international law*

4. In cases of gross violations of international human rights law and serious violations of international humanitarian law constituting crimes under international law, States have the duty to investigate and, if there is sufficient evidence, the duty to submit to

prosecution the person allegedly responsible for the violations and, if found guilty, the duty to punish her or him. Moreover, in these cases, States should, in accordance with international law, cooperate with one another and assist international judicial organs competent in the investigation and prosecution of these violations.

5. To that end, where so provided in an applicable treaty or under other international law obligations, States shall incorporate or otherwise implement within their domestic law appropriate provisions for universal jurisdiction. Moreover, where it is so provided for in an applicable treaty or other international legal obligations, States should facilitate extradition or surrender offenders to other States and to appropriate international judicial bodies and provide judicial assistance and other forms of cooperation in the pursuit of international justice, including assistance to, and protection of, victims and witnesses, consistent with international human rights legal standards and subject to international legal requirements such as those relating to the prohibition of torture and other forms of cruel, inhuman or degrading treatment or punishment.

IV. *Statutes of limitations*

6. Where so provided for in an applicable treaty or contained in other international legal obligations, statutes of limitations shall not apply to gross violations of international human rights law and serious violations of international humanitarian law which constitute crimes under international law.

7. Domestic statutes of limitations for other types of violations that do not constitute crimes under international law, including those time limitations applicable to civil claims and other procedures, should not be unduly restrictive.

V. *Victims of gross violations of international human rights law and serious violations of international humanitarian law*

8. For purposes of this document, victims are persons who individually or collectively suffered harm, including physical or mental injury, emotional suffering, economic loss or substantial impairment of their fundamental rights, through acts or omissions that constitute gross violations of international human rights law, or serious violations of international humanitarian law. Where appropriate, and in accordance with domestic law, the term 'victim' also includes the immediate family or dependants of the direct victim and persons who have suffered harm in intervening to assist victims in distress or to prevent victimization.

9. A person shall be considered a victim regardless of whether the perpetrator of the violation is identified, apprehended, prosecuted, or convicted and regardless of the familial relationship between the perpetrator and the victim.

VI. *Treatment of victims*

10. Victims should be treated with humanity and respect for their dignity and human rights, and appropriate measures should be taken to ensure their safety, physical and psychological well-being and privacy, as well as those of their families. The State should ensure that its domestic laws, to the extent possible, provide that a victim who has suffered violence or trauma should benefit from special consideration and care to avoid his or her re-traumatization in the course of legal and administrative procedures designed to provide justice and reparation.

VII. *Victims' right to remedies*

11. Remedies for gross violations of international human rights law and serious violations of international humanitarian law include the victim's right to the following as provided for under international law:

    (a) Equal and effective access to justice;

    (b) Adequate, effective and prompt reparation for harm suffered; and

    (c) Access to relevant information concerning violations and reparation mechanisms.

VIII. *Access to justice*

12. A victim of a gross violation of international human rights law or of a serious violation of international humanitarian law shall have equal access to an effective judicial remedy as provided for under international law. Other remedies available to the victim include access to administrative and other bodies, as well as mechanisms, modalities and proceedings conducted in accordance with domestic law. Obligations arising under international law to secure the right to access justice and fair and impartial proceedings shall be reflected in domestic laws. To that end, States should:

    (a) Disseminate, through public and private mechanisms, information about all available remedies for gross violations of international human rights law and serious violations of international humanitarian law;

    (b) Take measures to minimize the inconvenience to victims and their representatives, protect against unlawful interference with their privacy as appropriate and ensure their safety from intimidation and retaliation, as well as that of their families and witnesses, before, during and after judicial, administrative, or other proceedings that affect the interests of victims;

    (c) Provide proper assistance to victims seeking access to justice;

    (d) Make available all appropriate legal, diplomatic and consular means to ensure that victims can exercise their rights to remedy for gross violations of international human rights law or serious violations of international humanitarian law.

13. In addition to individual access to justice, States should endeavour to develop procedures to allow groups of victims to present claims for reparation and to receive reparation, as appropriate.

14. An adequate, effective and prompt remedy for gross violations of international human rights law or serious violations of international humanitarian law should include all available and appropriate international processes in which a person may have legal standing and should be without prejudice to any other domestic remedies.

IX. *Reparation for harm suffered*

15. Adequate, effective and prompt reparation is intended to promote justice by redressing gross violations of international human rights law or serious violations of international humanitarian law. Reparation should be proportional to the gravity of the violations and the harm suffered. In accordance with its domestic laws and international legal obligations, a State shall provide reparation to victims for acts or omissions which can be attributed to the State and constitute gross violations of international human rights law or serious violations of international humanitarian law. In cases where a person, a legal person, or other entity is found liable for reparation to a victim, such party

should provide reparation to the victim or compensate the State if the State has already provided reparation to the victim.

16. States should endeavour to establish national programmes for reparation and other assistance to victims in the event that the party liable for the harm suffered is unable or unwilling to meet their obligations.

17. States shall, with respect to claims by victims, enforce domestic judgements for reparation against individuals or entities liable for the harm suffered and endeavour to enforce valid foreign legal judgements for reparation in accordance with domestic law and international legal obligations. To that end, States should provide under their domestic laws effective mechanisms for the enforcement of reparation judgements.

18. In accordance with domestic law and international law, and taking account of individual circumstances, victims of gross violations of international human rights law and serious violations of international humanitarian law should, as appropriate and proportional to the gravity of the violation and the circumstances of each case, be provided with full and effective reparation, as laid out in principles 19 to 23, which include the following forms: restitution, compensation, rehabilitation, satisfaction and guarantees of non-repetition.

19. *Restitution* should, whenever possible, restore the victim to the original situation before the gross violations of international human rights law or serious violations of international humanitarian law occurred. Restitution includes, as appropriate: restoration of liberty, enjoyment of human rights, identity, family life and citizenship, return to one's place of residence, restoration of employment and return of property.

20. *Compensation* should be provided for any economically assessable damage, as appropriate and proportional to the gravity of the violation and the circumstances of each case, resulting from gross violations of international human rights law and serious violations of international humanitarian law, such as:

(a) Physical or mental harm;

(b) Lost opportunities, including employment, education and social benefits;

(c) Material damages and loss of earnings, including loss of earning potential;

(d) Moral damage;

(e) Costs required for legal or expert assistance, medicine and medical services, and psychological and social services.

21. *Rehabilitation* should include medical and psychological care as well as legal and social services.

22. *Satisfaction* should include, where applicable, any or all of the following:

(a) Effective measures aimed at the cessation of continuing violations;

(b) Verification of the facts and full and public disclosure of the truth to the extent that such disclosure does not cause further harm or threaten the safety and interests of the victim, the victim's relatives, witnesses, or persons who have intervened to assist the victim or prevent the occurrence of further violations;

(c) The search for the whereabouts of the disappeared, for the identities of the children abducted, and for the bodies of those killed, and assistance in the recovery, identification and reburial of the bodies in accordance with the expressed or presumed wish of the victims, or the cultural practices of the families and communities;

(d) An official declaration or a judicial decision restoring the dignity, the reputation and the rights of the victim and of persons closely connected with the victim;

(e) Public apology, including acknowledgement of the facts and acceptance of responsibility;

(f) Judicial and administrative sanctions against persons liable for the violations;

(g) Commemorations and tributes to the victims;

(h) Inclusion of an accurate account of the violations that occurred in international human rights law and international humanitarian law training and in educational material at all levels.

23. *Guarantees of non-repetition* should include, where applicable, any or all of the following measures, which will also contribute to prevention:

(a) Ensuring effective civilian control of military and security forces;

(b) Ensuring that all civilian and military proceedings abide by international standards of due process, fairness and impartiality;

(c) Strengthening the independence of the judiciary;

(d) Protecting persons in the legal, medical and health-care professions, the media and other related professions, and human rights defenders;

(e) Providing, on a priority and continued basis, human rights and international humanitarian law education to all sectors of society and training for law enforcement officials as well as military and security forces;

(f) Promoting the observance of codes of conduct and ethical norms, in particular international standards, by public servants, including law enforcement, correctional, media, medical, psychological, social service and military personnel, as well as by economic enterprises;

(g) Promoting mechanisms for preventing and monitoring social conflicts and their resolution;

(h) Reviewing and reforming laws contributing to or allowing gross violations of international human rights law and serious violations of international humanitarian law.

X. *Access to relevant information concerning violations and reparation mechanisms*

24. States should develop means of informing the general public and, in particular, victims of gross violations of international human rights law and serious violations of international humanitarian law of the rights and remedies addressed by these Principles and Guidelines and of all available legal, medical, psychological, social, administrative and all other services to which victims may have a right of access. Moreover, victims and their representatives should be entitled to seek and obtain information on the causes leading to their victimization and on the causes and conditions pertaining to the gross violations of international human rights law and serious violations of international humanitarian law and to learn the truth in regard to these violations.

XI. *Non-discrimination*

25. The application and interpretation of these Principles and Guidelines must be consistent with international human rights law and international humanitarian law and be without any discrimination of any kind or ground, without exception.

XII. *Non-derogation*

26. Nothing in these Principles and Guidelines shall be construed as restricting or derogating from any rights or obligations arising under domestic and international law. In particular, it is understood that the present Principles and Guidelines are without prejudice to the right to a remedy and reparation for victims of all violations of international human rights law and international humanitarian law. It is further understood that these Principles and Guidelines are without prejudice to special rules of international law.

XIII. *Rights of others*

27. Nothing in this document is to be construed as derogating from internationally or nationally protected rights of others, in particular the right of an accused person to benefit from applicable standards of due process.

38. POLITICAL DECLARATION ON HIV/AIDS, 2006

This Declaration was adopted by General Assembly Resolution 60/262 without a vote on 2 June 2006, and following a three-day review and high-level meeting. The link to human rights and the necessity to promote and protect human rights were recurrent themes in the debate preceding adoption of the Declaration; see UNGAOR, Sixtieth Session, 87th Plenary meeting, 2 June 2006: UN doc. A/60/PV.87.

Further reading

PIOT, P., 'AIDS: From crisis management to sustained strategic response', (2006) 368 *The Lancet* 526.

STEMPLE, L., 'Health and Human Rights in Today's Fight against HIV/AIDS', (2008) 22 *AIDS* (Suppl. 2), S113.

UNITED NATIONS HIGH COMMISSIONER FOR HUMAN RIGHTS and UNAIDS, *Handbook on HIV and Human Rights for National Human Rights Institutions*, Geneva: United Nations, 2007.

WALKER, E. M., 'The HIV/AIDS Pandemic and Human Rights: A Continuum Approach', (2007) 19 *Florida Journal of International Law* 335.

TEXT

The General Assembly

Adopts the Political Declaration on HIV/AIDS annexed to the present resolution.

ANNEX
Political Declaration on HIV/AIDS

1. We, Heads of State and Government and representatives of States and Governments participating in the comprehensive review of the progress achieved in realizing the targets set out in the Declaration of Commitment on HIV/AIDS, held on 31 May and 1 June 2006, and the High-Level Meeting, held on 2 June 2006;

2. Note with alarm that we are facing an unprecedented human catastrophe; that a quarter of a century into the pandemic, AIDS has inflicted immense suffering on countries and communities throughout the world; and that more than 65 million people have been infected with HIV, more than 25 million people have died of AIDS, 15 million children have been orphaned by AIDS and millions more made vulnerable, and 40 million people are currently living with HIV, more than 95 per cent of whom live in developing countries;

3. Recognize that HIV/AIDS constitutes a global emergency and poses one of the most formidable challenges to the development, progress and stability of our respective societies and the world at large, and requires an exceptional and comprehensive global response;

4. Acknowledge that national and international efforts have resulted in important progress since 2001 in the areas of funding, expanding access to HIV prevention, treatment,

care and support and in mitigating the impact of AIDS, and in reducing HIV prevalence in a small but growing number of countries, and also acknowledge that many targets contained in the Declaration of Commitment on HIV/AIDS have not yet been met;

5. Commend the Secretariat and the Co-sponsors of the Joint United Nations Programme on HIV/AIDS for their leadership role on HIV/AIDS policy and coordination, and for the support they provide to countries through the Joint Programme;

6. Recognize the contribution of, and the role played by, various donors in combating HIV/AIDS, as well as the fact that one third of resources spent on HIV/AIDS responses in 2005 came from the domestic sources of low- and middle-income countries, and therefore emphasize the importance of enhanced international cooperation and partnership in our responses to HIV/AIDS worldwide;

7. Remain deeply concerned, however, by the overall expansion and feminization of the pandemic and the fact that women now represent 50 per cent of people living with HIV worldwide and nearly 60 per cent of people living with HIV in Africa, and in this regard recognize that gender inequalities and all forms of violence against women and girls increase their vulnerability to HIV/AIDS;

8. Express grave concern that half of all new HIV infections occur among children and young people under the age of 25, and that there is a lack of information, skills and knowledge regarding HIV/AIDS among young people;

9. Remain gravely concerned that 2.3 million children are living with HIV/AIDS today, and recognize that the lack of paediatric drugs in many countries significantly hinders efforts to protect the health of children;

10. Reiterate with profound concern that the pandemic affects every region, that Africa, in particular sub-Saharan Africa, remains the worst-affected region, and that urgent and exceptional action is required at all levels to curb the devastating effects of this pandemic, and recognize the renewed commitment by African Governments and regional institutions to scale up their own HIV/AIDS responses;

11. Reaffirm that the full realization of all human rights and fundamental freedoms for all is an essential element in the global response to the HIV/AIDS pandemic, including in the areas of prevention, treatment, care and support, and recognize that addressing stigma and discrimination is also a critical element in combating the global HIV/AIDS pandemic;

12. Reaffirm also that access to medication in the context of pandemics, such as HIV/AIDS, is one of the fundamental elements to achieve progressively the full realization of the right of everyone to the enjoyment of the highest attainable standard of physical and mental health;

13. Recognize that in many parts of the world, the spread of HIV/AIDS is a cause and consequence of poverty, and that effectively combating HIV/AIDS is essential to the achievement of internationally agreed development goals and objectives, including the Millennium Development Goals;

14. Recognize also that we now have the means to reverse the global pandemic and to avert millions of needless deaths, and that to be effective, we must deliver an intensified, much more urgent and comprehensive response, in partnership with the United Nations system, intergovernmental organizations, people living with HIV and vulnerable groups, medical, scientific and educational institutions, non-governmental organizations, the business sector, including generic and research-based pharmaceutical companies, trade

unions, the media, parliamentarians, foundations, community organizations, faith-based organizations and traditional leaders;

15. Recognize further that to mount a comprehensive response, we must overcome any legal, regulatory, trade and other barriers that block access to prevention, treatment, care and support; commit adequate resources; promote and protect all human rights and fundamental freedoms for all; promote gender equality and empowerment of women; promote and protect the rights of the girl child in order to reduce the vulnerability of the girl child to HIV/AIDS; strengthen health systems and support health workers; support greater involvement of people living with HIV; scale up the use of known effective and comprehensive prevention interventions; do everything necessary to ensure access to life-saving drugs and prevention tools; and develop with equal urgency better tools—drugs, diagnostics and prevention technologies, including vaccines and microbicides—for the future;

16. Convinced that without renewed political will, strong leadership and sustained commitment and concerted efforts on the part of all stakeholders at all levels, including people living with HIV, civil society and vulnerable groups, and without increased resources, the world will not succeed in bringing about the end of the pandemic;

17. Solemnly declare our commitment to address the HIV/AIDS crisis by taking action as follows, taking into account the diverse situations and circumstances in different regions and countries throughout the world;

Therefore, we:

18. Reaffirm our commitment to implement fully the Declaration of Commitment on HIV/AIDS, entitled 'Global Crisis—Global Action', adopted by the General Assembly at its twenty-sixth special session, in 2001; and to achieve the internationally agreed development goals and objectives, including the Millennium Development Goals, in particular the goal to halt and begin to reverse the spread of HIV/AIDS, malaria and other major diseases, the agreements dealing with HIV/AIDS reached at all major United Nations conferences and summits, including the 2005 World Summit and its statement on treatment, and the goal of achieving universal access to reproductive health by 2015, as set out at the International Conference on Population and Development;

19. Recognize the importance, and encourage the implementation, of the recommendations of the inclusive, country-driven processes and regional consultations facilitated by the Secretariat and the Co-sponsors of the Joint United Nations Programme on HIV/AIDS for scaling up HIV prevention, treatment, care and support, and strongly recommend that this approach be continued;

20. Commit ourselves to pursuing all necessary efforts to scale up nationally driven, sustainable and comprehensive responses to achieve broad multisectoral coverage for prevention, treatment, care and support, with full and active participation of people living with HIV, vulnerable groups, most affected communities, civil society and the private sector, towards the goal of universal access to comprehensive prevention programmes, treatment, care and support by 2010;

21. Emphasize the need to strengthen policy and programme linkages and coordination between HIV/AIDS, sexual and reproductive health, national development plans and strategies, including poverty eradication strategies, and to address, where appropriate, the impact of HIV/AIDS on national development plans and strategies;

22. Reaffirm that the prevention of HIV infection must be the mainstay of national, regional and international responses to the pandemic, and therefore commit ourselves

to intensifying efforts to ensure that a wide range of prevention programmes that take account of local circumstances, ethics and cultural values is available in all countries, particularly the most affected countries, including information, education and communication, in languages most understood by communities and respectful of cultures, aimed at reducing risk-taking behaviours and encouraging responsible sexual behaviour, including abstinence and fidelity; expanded access to essential commodities, including male and female condoms and sterile injecting equipment; harm-reduction efforts related to drug use; expanded access to voluntary and confidential counselling and testing; safe blood supplies; and early and effective treatment of sexually transmitted infections;

23. Reaffirm also that prevention, treatment, care and support for those infected and affected by HIV/AIDS are mutually reinforcing elements of an effective response and must be integrated in a comprehensive approach to combat the pandemic;

24. Commit ourselves to overcoming legal, regulatory or other barriers that block access to effective HIV prevention, treatment, care and support, medicines, commodities and services;

25. Pledge to promote, at the international, regional, national and local levels, access to HIV/AIDS education, information, voluntary counselling and testing and related services, with full protection of confidentiality and informed consent, and to promote a social and legal environment that is supportive of and safe for voluntary disclosure of HIV status;

26. Commit ourselves to addressing the rising rates of HIV infection among young people to ensure an HIV-free future generation through the implementation of comprehensive, evidence-based prevention strategies, responsible sexual behaviour, including the use of condoms, evidence- and skills-based, youth-specific HIV education, mass media interventions and the provision of youth-friendly health services;

27. Commit ourselves also to ensuring that pregnant women have access to antenatal care, information, counselling and other HIV services and to increasing the availability of and access to effective treatment to women living with HIV and infants in order to reduce mother-to-child transmission of HIV, as well as to ensuring effective interventions for women living with HIV, including voluntary and confidential counselling and testing, with informed consent, access to treatment, especially life-long antiretroviral therapy and, where appropriate, breast-milk substitutes and the provision of a continuum of care;

28. Resolve to integrate food and nutritional support, with the goal that all people at all times will have access to sufficient, safe and nutritious food to meet their dietary needs and food preferences, for an active and healthy life, as part of a comprehensive response to HIV/AIDS;

29. Commit ourselves to intensifying efforts to enact, strengthen or enforce, as appropriate, legislation, regulations and other measures to eliminate all forms of discrimination against and to ensure the full enjoyment of all human rights and fundamental freedoms by people living with HIV and members of vulnerable groups, in particular to ensure their access to, inter alia, education, inheritance, employment, health care, social and health services, prevention, support and treatment, information and legal protection, while respecting their privacy and confidentiality; and developing strategies to combat stigma and social exclusion connected with the epidemic;

30. Pledge to eliminate gender inequalities, gender-based abuse and violence; increase the capacity of women and adolescent girls to protect themselves from the risk of HIV

infection, principally through the provision of health care and services, including, inter alia, sexual and reproductive health, and the provision of full access to comprehensive information and education; ensure that women can exercise their right to have control over, and decide freely and responsibly on, matters related to their sexuality in order to increase their ability to protect themselves from HIV infection, including their sexual and reproductive health, free of coercion, discrimination and violence; and take all necessary measures to create an enabling environment for the empowerment of women and strengthen their economic independence; and in this context, reiterate the importance of the role of men and boys in achieving gender equality;

31. Commit ourselves to strengthening legal, policy, administrative and other measures for the promotion and protection of women's full enjoyment of all human rights and the reduction of their vulnerability to HIV/AIDS through the elimination of all forms of discrimination, as well as all types of sexual exploitation of women, girls and boys, including for commercial reasons, and all forms of violence against women and girls, including harmful traditional and customary practices, abuse, rape and other forms of sexual violence, battering and trafficking in women and girls;

32. Commit ourselves also to addressing as a priority the vulnerabilities faced by children affected by and living with HIV; providing support and rehabilitation to these children and their families, women and the elderly, particularly in their role as caregivers; promoting child-oriented HIV/AIDS policies and programmes and increased protection for children orphaned and affected by HIV/AIDS; ensuring access to treatment and intensifying efforts to develop new treatments for children; and building, where needed, and supporting the social security systems that protect them;

33. Emphasize the need for accelerated scale-up of collaborative activities on tuberculosis and HIV, in line with the Global Plan to Stop TB 2006–2015, and for investment in new drugs, diagnostics and vaccines that are appropriate for people with TB-HIV co-infection;

34. Commit ourselves to expanding to the greatest extent possible, supported by international cooperation and partnership, our capacity to deliver comprehensive HIV/AIDS programmes in ways that strengthen existing national health and social systems, including by integrating HIV/AIDS intervention into programmes for primary health care, mother and child health, sexual and reproductive health, tuberculosis, hepatitis C, sexually transmitted infections, nutrition, children affected, orphaned or made vulnerable by HIV/AIDS, as well as formal and informal education;

35. Undertake to reinforce, adopt and implement, where needed, national plans and strategies, supported by international cooperation and partnership, to increase the capacity of human resources for health to meet the urgent need for the training and retention of a broad range of health workers, including community-based health workers; improve training and management and working conditions, including treatment for health workers; and effectively govern the recruitment, retention and deployment of new and existing health workers to mount a more effective HIV/AIDS response;

36. Commit ourselves, invite international financial institutions and the Global Fund to Fight AIDS, Tuberculosis and Malaria, according to its policy framework, and encourage other donors, to provide additional resources to low- and middle- income countries for the strengthening of HIV/AIDS programmes and health systems and for addressing human resources gaps, including the development of alternative and simplified service

delivery models and the expansion of the community-level provision of HIV/AIDS prevention, treatment, care and support, as well as other health and social services;

37. Reiterate the need for Governments, United Nations agencies, regional and international organizations and non-governmental organizations involved with the provision and delivery of assistance to countries and regions affected by conflicts, humanitarian emergencies or natural disasters to incorporate HIV/AIDS prevention, care and treatment elements into their plans and programmes;

38. Pledge to provide the highest level of commitment to ensuring that costed, inclusive, sustainable, credible and evidence-based national HIV/AIDS plans are funded and implemented with transparency, accountability and effectiveness, in line with national priorities;

39. Commit ourselves to reducing the global HIV/AIDS resource gap through greater domestic and international funding to enable countries to have access to predictable and sustainable financial resources and ensuring that international funding is aligned with national HIV/AIDS plans and strategies; and in this regard welcome the increased resources that are being made available through bilateral and multilateral initiatives, as well as those that will become available as a result of the establishment of timetables by many developed countries to achieve the targets of 0.7 per cent of gross national product for official development assistance by 2015 and to reach at least 0.5 per cent of gross national product for official development assistance by 2010 as well as, pursuant to the Brussels Programme of Action for the Least Developed Countries for the Decade 2001–2010, 0.15 per cent to 0.20 per cent for the least developed countries no later than 2010, and urge those developed countries that have not yet done so to make concrete efforts in this regard in accordance with their commitments;

40. Recognize that the Joint United Nations Programme on HIV/AIDS has estimated that 20 to 23 billion United States dollars per annum is needed by 2010 to support rapidly scaled-up AIDS responses in low- and middle-income countries, and therefore commit ourselves to taking measures to ensure that new and additional resources are made available from donor countries and also from national budgets and other national sources;

41. Commit ourselves to supporting and strengthening existing financial mechanisms, including the Global Fund to Fight AIDS, Tuberculosis and Malaria, as well as relevant United Nations organizations, through the provision of funds in a sustained manner, while continuing to develop innovative sources of financing, as well as pursuing other efforts, aimed at generating additional funds;

42. Commit ourselves also to finding appropriate solutions to overcome barriers in pricing, tariffs and trade agreements, and to making improvements to legislation, regulatory policy, procurement and supply chain management in order to accelerate and intensify access to affordable and quality HIV/AIDS prevention products, diagnostics, medicines and treatment commodities;

43. Reaffirm that the World Trade Organization's Agreement on Trade-Related Aspects of Intellectual Property Rights does not and should not prevent members from taking measures now and in the future to protect public health. Accordingly, while reiterating our commitment to the TRIPS Agreement, reaffirm that the Agreement can and should be interpreted and implemented in a manner supportive of the right to protect public health and, in particular, to promote access to medicines for all including the

production of generic antiretroviral drugs and other essential drugs for AIDS-related infections. In this connection, we reaffirm the right to use, to the full, the provisions in the TRIPS Agreement, the Doha Declaration on the TRIPS Agreement and Public Health and the World Trade Organization's General Council Decision of 2003 and amendments to Article 31, which provide flexibilities for this purpose;

44. Resolve to assist developing countries to enable them to employ the flexibilities outlined in the TRIPS Agreement, and to strengthen their capacities for this purpose;

45. Commit ourselves to intensifying investment in and efforts towards the research and development of new, safe and affordable HIV/AIDS-related medicines, products and technologies, such as vaccines, female-controlled methods and microbicides, paediatric antiretroviral formulations, including through such mechanisms as Advance Market Commitments, and to encouraging increased investment in HIV/AIDS-related research and development in traditional medicine;

46. Encourage pharmaceutical companies, donors, multilateral organizations and other partners to develop public-private partnerships in support of research and development and technology transfer, and in the comprehensive response to HIV/AIDS;

47. Encourage bilateral, regional and international efforts to promote bulk procurement, price negotiations and licensing to lower prices for HIV prevention products, diagnostics, medicines and treatment commodities, while recognizing that intellectual property protection is important for the development of new medicines and recognizing the concerns about its effects on prices;

48. Recognize the initiative by a group of countries, such as the International Drug Purchase Facility, based on innovative financing mechanisms that aim to provide further drug access at affordable prices to developing countries on a sustainable and predictable basis;

49. Commit ourselves to setting, in 2006, through inclusive, transparent processes, ambitious national targets, including interim targets for 2008 in accordance with the core indicators recommended by the Joint United Nations Programme on HIV/AIDS, that reflect the commitment of the present Declaration and the urgent need to scale up significantly towards the goal of universal access to comprehensive prevention programmes, treatment, care and support by 2010, and to setting up and maintaining sound and rigorous monitoring and evaluation frameworks within their HIV/AIDS strategies;

50. Call upon the Joint United Nations Programme on HIV/AIDS, including its Co-sponsors, to assist national efforts to coordinate the AIDS response, as elaborated in the 'Three Ones' principles and in line with the recommendations of the Global Task Team on Improving AIDS Coordination among Multilateral Institutions and International Donors; assist national and regional efforts to monitor and report on efforts to achieve the targets set out above; and strengthen global coordination on HIV/AIDS, including through the thematic sessions of the Programme Coordinating Board;

51. Call upon Governments, national parliaments, donors, regional and subregional organizations, organizations of the United Nations system, the Global Fund to Fight AIDS, Tuberculosis and Malaria, civil society, people living with HIV, vulnerable groups, the private sector, communities most affected by HIV/AIDS and other stakeholders to work closely together to achieve the targets set out above, and to ensure accountability and transparency at all levels through participatory reviews of responses to HIV/AIDS;

52. Request the Secretary-General of the United Nations, with the support of the Joint United Nations Programme on HIV/AIDS, to include in his annual report to the General Assembly on the status of implementation of the Declaration of Commitment on HIV/AIDS, in accordance with General Assembly resolution S-26/2 of 27 June 2001, the progress achieved in realizing the commitments set out in the present Declaration;

53. Decide to undertake comprehensive reviews in 2008 and 2011, within the annual reviews of the General Assembly, of the progress achieved in realizing the Declaration of Commitment on HIV/AIDS, entitled 'Global Crisis–Global Action', adopted by the General Assembly at its twenty-sixth special session, and the present Declaration.

39. DECLARATION ON THE RIGHTS OF INDIGENOUS PEOPLES, 2007

In 1994, the Sub-Commission on Prevention of Discrimination and Protection of Minorities adopted the draft declaration on the rights of indigenous peoples (Resolution 1994/45, 26 August 1994), which had been completed by the Working Group on Indigenous Populations, chaired by Erica-Irene Daes (Report of the Working Group: UN doc. E/CN.4/Sub.2/1994/30 and Corr.1). The draft was duly submitted to the Commission on Human Rights and the Secretary-General was requested to transmit the text to indigenous peoples and organizations, governments and intergovernmental organizations.

The Commission on Human Rights established an open-ended inter-sessional Working Group in 1995 (see Commission on Human Rights Resolution 1995/32 and ECOSOC Resolution 1995/32), the sole purpose of which was to elaborate a draft declaration on the rights of indigenous peoples. The Working Group was a subsidiary organ of the Commission on Human Rights and composed of representatives of Member States. Non-governmental and indigenous organizations with consultative status with the Economic and Social Council were able to take part in the proceedings, and Commission on Human Rights Resolution 1995/32 also provided for participation by indigenous organizations without consultative status. Issues on which it proved difficult to secure consensus included the term 'indigenous peoples', partly because of its possible implications with respect to self-determination and individual and collective rights; see, for example, the report of the sixth session of the Working Group (20 November–1 December 2000): UN doc. E/CN.4/2001/85.

The Working Group was called upon to consider the draft adopted by the Sub-Commission, (for the text without its accompanying resolution, see *Basic Documents on Human Rights*, 5th edn., p. 195), with a view to it being considered and adopted by the General Assembly during the International Decade of the World's Indigenous People, which had been proclaimed by the General Assembly in December 1993; see Resolution 48/163, 21 December 1993. In Resolution 53/129, 9 December 1998, the General Assembly reaffirmed that the adoption of a declaration on the rights of indigenous people was a major objective of the Decade. That target not having been achieved, it thereupon proclaimed a Second International Decade of the World's Indigenous People, beginning on 1 January 2005; see Resolution 59/174, adopted without a vote, 20 December 2004, in which it also urged all parties involved 'to do their utmost to carry out successfully the mandate of the open-ended intersessional working group established by the Commission on Human Rights in its resolution 1995/32 and to present for adoption as soon as possible a final draft United Nations declaration on the rights of indigenous peoples...' (para. 12).

The draft in question was finally adopted by the Human Rights Council in Resolution 1/2 of 29 June 2006, and submitted to the General Assembly; see 'Report to the General Assembly on the First Session Of the Human Rights Council', UN doc. A/HRC/1/L.10, 30 June 2006, 56–73. The Declaration was adopted by General Assembly Resolution 61/295 on 13 September 2007 by a vote of 143 in favour, four against (Australia, Canada, New Zealand, United States of America), and eleven abstentions (Azerbaijan, Bangladesh, Bhutan, Burundi, Colombia, Georgia, Kenya, Nigeria, Russian Federation, Samoa, Ukraine).

Further reading

CHARTERS, C., 'The Road to the Adoption of the Declaration on the Rights of Indigenous Peoples', (2007) 4 *New Zealand Yearbook of International Law* 121.

——, MALEZER, L. and TAULI-CORPUZ, V., eds., *Indigenous Voices: The UN Declaration on the Rights of Indigenous Peoples*, Oxford: Hart Publishing, 2009.

DAVIS, M., 'Indigenous Struggles in Standard-Setting: The United Nations Declaration on the Rights of Indigenous Peoples', (2008) 9 *Melbourne Journal of International Law* 439.

EIDE, A., 'Rights of Indigenous Peoples—Achievements in International Law during the Last Quarter of a Century', (2006) 37 *Netherlands Yearbook of International Law* 155.

ERRICO, S., 'The Draft UN Declaration on the Rights of Indigenous Peoples: An Overview', (2007) 7 *Human Rights Law Review* 741.

FOSTER, C. E., 'Articulating Self-Determination in the Draft Declaration on the Rights of Indigenous Peoples', (2001) 12 *EJIL* 141.

GHANEA, N. and XANTHAKI, A., eds., *Minorities, Peoples and Self-Determination: Essays in Honour of Patrick Thornberry*, Leiden: Martinus Nijhoff, 2005.

GILBERT, J., 'Indigenous Rights in the Making: The United Nations Declaration on the Rights of Indigenous Peoples', (2007) 14 *International Journal on Minority and Group Rights* 207.

LENZERINI, F., *Reparations for Indigenous Peoples: International and Comparative Perspectives*, Oxford: Oxford University Press, 2009.

PENTASSUGLIA, G., *Minority Groups and Judicial Discourse in International Law: A Comparative Perspective*, Leiden: Martinus Nijhoff, 2009.

RICHARDSON, B. J., IMAI, S. and MCNEIL, K., eds., *Indigenous Peoples and the Law: Comparative and Critical Perspectives*, Oxford: Hart Publishing, 2009.

WELLER, M., *Universal Minority Rights: A Commentary on the Jurisprudence of International Courts and Treaty Bodies*, Oxford: Oxford University Press, 2007.

XANTHAKI, A., *Indigenous Rights and United Nations Standards: Self-Determination, Culture and Land*, Cambridge: Cambridge University Press, 2008.

TEXT

The General Assembly,

Taking note of the recommendation of the Human Rights Council contained in its resolution 1/2 of 29 June 2006,1 by which the Council adopted the text of the United Nations Declaration on the Rights of Indigenous Peoples,

Recalling its resolution 61/178 of 20 December 2006, by which it decided to defer consideration of and action on the Declaration to allow time for further consultations thereon, and also decided to conclude its consideration before the end of the sixty-first session of the General Assembly,

Adopts the United Nations Declaration on the Rights of Indigenous Peoples as contained in the annex to the present resolution.

ANNEX
United Nations Declaration on the Rights of Indigenous Peoples

The General Assembly,

Guided by the purposes and principles of the Charter of the United Nations, and good faith in the fulfilment of the obligations assumed by States in accordance with the Charter,

Affirming that indigenous peoples are equal to all other peoples, while recognizing the right of all peoples to be different, to consider themselves different, and to be respected as such,

Affirming also that all peoples contribute to the diversity and richness of civilizations and cultures, which constitute the common heritage of humankind,

Affirming further that all doctrines, policies and practices based on or advocating superiority of peoples or individuals on the basis of national origin or racial, religious, ethnic or cultural differences are racist, scientifically false, legally invalid, morally condemnable and socially unjust,

Reaffirming that indigenous peoples, in the exercise of their rights, should be free from discrimination of any kind,

Concerned that indigenous peoples have suffered from historic injustices as a result of, inter alia, their colonization and dispossession of their lands, territories and resources, thus preventing them from exercising, in particular, their right to development in accordance with their own needs and interests,

Recognizing the urgent need to respect and promote the inherent rights of indigenous peoples which derive from their political, economic and social structures and from their cultures, spiritual traditions, histories and philosophies, especially their rights to their lands, territories and resources,

Recognizing also the urgent need to respect and promote the rights of indigenous peoples affirmed in treaties, agreements and other constructive arrangements with States,

Welcoming the fact that indigenous peoples are organizing themselves for political, economic, social and cultural enhancement and in order to bring to an end all forms of discrimination and oppression wherever they occur,

Convinced that control by indigenous peoples over developments affecting them and their lands, territories and resources will enable them to maintain and strengthen their institutions, cultures and traditions, and to promote their development in accordance with their aspirations and needs,

Recognizing that respect for indigenous knowledge, cultures and traditional practices contributes to sustainable and equitable development and proper management of the environment,

Emphasizing the contribution of the demilitarization of the lands and territories of indigenous peoples to peace, economic and social progress and development, understanding and friendly relations among nations and peoples of the world,

Recognizing in particular the right of indigenous families and communities to retain shared responsibility for the upbringing, training, education and well-being of their children, consistent with the rights of the child,

Considering that the rights affirmed in treaties, agreements and other constructive arrangements between States and indigenous peoples are, in some situations, matters of international concern, interest, responsibility and character,

Considering also that treaties, agreements and other constructive arrangements, and the relationship they represent, are the basis for a strengthened partnership between indigenous peoples and States,

Acknowledging that the Charter of the United Nations, the International Covenant on Economic, Social and Cultural Rights and the International Covenant on Civil and Political Rights, as well as the Vienna Declaration and Programme of Action, affirm the fundamental importance of the right to self-determination of all peoples, by virtue of which they freely determine their political status and freely pursue their economic, social and cultural development,

Bearing in mind that nothing in this Declaration may be used to deny any peoples their right to self-determination, exercised in conformity with international law,

Convinced that the recognition of the rights of indigenous peoples in this Declaration will enhance harmonious and cooperative relations between the State and indigenous peoples, based on principles of justice, democracy, respect for human rights, non-discrimination and good faith,

Encouraging States to comply with and effectively implement all their obligations as they apply to indigenous peoples under international instruments, in particular those related to human rights, in consultation and cooperation with the peoples concerned,

Emphasizing that the United Nations has an important and continuing role to play in promoting and protecting the rights of indigenous peoples,

Believing that this Declaration is a further important step forward for the recognition, promotion and protection of the rights and freedoms of indigenous peoples and in the development of relevant activities of the United Nations system in this field,

Recognizing and reaffirming that indigenous individuals are entitled without discrimination to all human rights recognized in international law, and that indigenous peoples possess collective rights which are indispensable for their existence, well-being and integral development as peoples,

Recognizing that the situation of indigenous peoples varies from region to region and from country to country and that the significance of national and regional particularities and various historical and cultural backgrounds should be taken into consideration,

Solemnly proclaims the following United Nations Declaration on the Rights of Indigenous Peoples as a standard of achievement to be pursued in a spirit of partnership and mutual respect:

Article 1

Indigenous peoples have the right to the full enjoyment, as a collective or as individuals, of all human rights and fundamental freedoms as recognized in the Charter of the United Nations, the Universal Declaration of Human Rights and international human rights law.

Article 2

Indigenous peoples and individuals are free and equal to all other peoples and individuals and have the right to be free from any kind of discrimination, in the exercise of their rights, in particular that based on their indigenous origin or identity.

Article 3

Indigenous peoples have the right to self-determination. By virtue of that right they freely determine their political status and freely pursue their economic, social and cultural development.

Article 4

Indigenous peoples, in exercising their right to self-determination, have the right to autonomy or self-government in matters relating to their internal and local affairs, as well as ways and means for financing their autonomous functions.

Article 5

Indigenous peoples have the right to maintain and strengthen their distinct political, legal, economic, social and cultural institutions, while retaining their right to participate fully, if they so choose, in the political, economic, social and cultural life of the State.

Article 6

Every indigenous individual has the right to a nationality.

Article 7

1. Indigenous individuals have the rights to life, physical and mental integrity, liberty and security of person.

2. Indigenous peoples have the collective right to live in freedom, peace and security as distinct peoples and shall not be subjected to any act of genocide or any other act of violence, including forcibly removing children of the group to another group.

Article 8

1. Indigenous peoples and individuals have the right not to be subjected to forced assimilation or destruction of their culture.

2. States shall provide effective mechanisms for prevention of, and redress for:

(a) Any action which has the aim or effect of depriving them of their integrity as distinct peoples, or of their cultural values or ethnic identities;

(b) Any action which has the aim or effect of dispossessing them of their lands, territories or resources;

(c) Any form of forced population transfer which has the aim or effect of violating or undermining any of their rights;

(d) Any form of forced assimilation or integration;

(e) Any form of propaganda designed to promote or incite racial or ethnic discrimination directed against them.

Article 9

Indigenous peoples and individuals have the right to belong to an indigenous community or nation, in accordance with the traditions and customs of the community or nation concerned. No discrimination of any kind may arise from the exercise of such a right.

Article 10

Indigenous peoples shall not be forcibly removed from their lands or territories. No relocation shall take place without the free, prior and informed consent of the indigenous peoples concerned and after agreement on just and fair compensation and, where possible, with the option of return.

Article 11

1. Indigenous peoples have the right to practise and revitalize their cultural traditions and customs. This includes the right to maintain, protect and develop the past, present and future manifestations of their cultures, such as archaeological and historical sites, artefacts, designs, ceremonies, technologies and visual and performing arts and literature.

2. States shall provide redress through effective mechanisms, which may include restitution, developed in conjunction with indigenous peoples, with respect to their cultural, intellectual, religious and spiritual property taken without their free, prior and informed consent or in violation of their laws, traditions and customs.

Article 12

1. Indigenous peoples have the right to manifest, practise, develop and teach their spiritual and religious traditions, customs and ceremonies; the right to maintain, protect, and have access in privacy to their religious and cultural sites; the right to the use and control of their ceremonial objects; and the right to the repatriation of their human remains.

2. States shall seek to enable the access and/or repatriation of ceremonial objects and human remains in their possession through fair, transparent and effective mechanisms developed in conjunction with indigenous peoples concerned.

Article 13

1. Indigenous peoples have the right to revitalize, use, develop and transmit to future generations their histories, languages, oral traditions, philosophies, writing systems and literatures, and to designate and retain their own names for communities, places and persons.

2. States shall take effective measures to ensure that this right is protected and also to ensure that indigenous peoples can understand and be understood in political, legal and administrative proceedings, where necessary through the provision of interpretation or by other appropriate means.

Article 14

1. Indigenous peoples have the right to establish and control their educational systems and institutions providing education in their own languages, in a manner appropriate to their cultural methods of teaching and learning.

2. Indigenous individuals, particularly children, have the right to all levels and forms of education of the State without discrimination.

3. States shall, in conjunction with indigenous peoples, take effective measures, in order for indigenous individuals, particularly children, including those living outside their communities, to have access, when possible, to an education in their own culture and provided in their own language.

Article 15

1. Indigenous peoples have the right to the dignity and diversity of their cultures, traditions, histories and aspirations which shall be appropriately reflected in education and public information.

2. States shall take effective measures, in consultation and cooperation with the indigenous peoples concerned, to combat prejudice and eliminate discrimination and to promote tolerance, understanding and good relations among indigenous peoples and all other segments of society.

Article 16

1. Indigenous peoples have the right to establish their own media in their own languages and to have access to all forms of non-indigenous media without discrimination.

2. States shall take effective measures to ensure that State-owned media duly reflect indigenous cultural diversity. States, without prejudice to ensuring full freedom of expression, should encourage privately owned media to adequately reflect indigenous cultural diversity.

Article 17

1. Indigenous individuals and peoples have the right to enjoy fully all rights established under applicable international and domestic labour law.

2. States shall in consultation and cooperation with indigenous peoples take specific measures to protect indigenous children from economic exploitation and from performing any work that is likely to be hazardous or to interfere with the child's education, or to be harmful to the child's health or physical, mental, spiritual, moral or social development, taking into account their special vulnerability and the importance of education for their empowerment.

3. Indigenous individuals have the right not to be subjected to any discriminatory conditions of labour and, inter alia, employment or salary.

Article 18

Indigenous peoples have the right to participate in decision-making in matters which would affect their rights, through representatives chosen by themselves in accordance with their own procedures, as well as to maintain and develop their own indigenous decision-making institutions.

Article 19

States shall consult and cooperate in good faith with the indigenous peoples concerned through their own representative institutions in order to obtain their free, prior and informed consent before adopting and implementing legislative or administrative measures that may affect them.

Article 20

1. Indigenous peoples have the right to maintain and develop their political, economic and social systems or institutions, to be secure in the enjoyment of their own means of subsistence and development, and to engage freely in all their traditional and other economic activities.

2. Indigenous peoples deprived of their means of subsistence and development are entitled to just and fair redress.

Article 21

1. Indigenous peoples have the right, without discrimination, to the improvement of their economic and social conditions, including, inter alia, in the areas of education, employment, vocational training and retraining, housing, sanitation, health and social security.

2. States shall take effective measures and, where appropriate, special measures to ensure continuing improvement of their economic and social conditions. Particular attention shall be paid to the rights and special needs of indigenous elders, women, youth, children and persons with disabilities.

Article 22

1. Particular attention shall be paid to the rights and special needs of indigenous elders, women, youth, children and persons with disabilities in the implementation of this Declaration.

2. States shall take measures, in conjunction with indigenous peoples, to ensure that indigenous women and children enjoy the full protection and guarantees against all forms of violence and discrimination.

Article 23

Indigenous peoples have the right to determine and develop priorities and strategies for exercising their right to development. In particular, indigenous peoples have the right to be actively involved in developing and determining health, housing and other economic and social programmes affecting them and, as far as possible, to administer such programmes through their own institutions.

Article 24

1. Indigenous peoples have the right to their traditional medicines and to maintain their health practices, including the conservation of their vital medicinal plants, animals and minerals. Indigenous individuals also have the right to access, without any discrimination, to all social and health services.

2. Indigenous individuals have an equal right to the enjoyment of the highest attainable standard of physical and mental health. States shall take the necessary steps with a view to achieving progressively the full realization of this right.

Article 25

Indigenous peoples have the right to maintain and strengthen their distinctive spiritual relationship with their traditionally owned or otherwise occupied and used lands, territories, waters and coastal seas and other resources and to uphold their responsibilities to future generations in this regard.

Article 26

1. Indigenous peoples have the right to the lands, territories and resources which they have traditionally owned, occupied or otherwise used or acquired.

2. Indigenous peoples have the right to own, use, develop and control the lands, territories and resources that they possess by reason of traditional ownership or other traditional occupation or use, as well as those which they have otherwise acquired.

3. States shall give legal recognition and protection to these lands, territories and resources. Such recognition shall be conducted with due respect to the customs, traditions and land tenure systems of the indigenous peoples concerned.

Article 27

States shall establish and implement, in conjunction with indigenous peoples concerned, a fair, independent, impartial, open and transparent process, giving due recognition to indigenous peoples' laws, traditions, customs and land tenure systems, to recognize and adjudicate the rights of indigenous peoples pertaining to their lands, territories and resources, including those which were traditionally owned or otherwise occupied or used. Indigenous peoples shall have the right to participate in this process.

Article 28

1. Indigenous peoples have the right to redress, by means that can include restitution or, when this is not possible, just, fair and equitable compensation, for the lands, territories and resources which they have traditionally owned or otherwise occupied or used, and which have been confiscated, taken, occupied, used or damaged without their free, prior and informed consent.

2. Unless otherwise freely agreed upon by the peoples concerned, compensation shall take the form of lands, territories and resources equal in quality, size and legal status or of monetary compensation or other appropriate redress.

Article 29

1. Indigenous peoples have the right to the conservation and protection of the environment and the productive capacity of their lands or territories and resources. States shall establish and implement assistance programmes for indigenous peoples for such conservation and protection, without discrimination.

2. States shall take effective measures to ensure that no storage or disposal of hazardous materials shall take place in the lands or territories of indigenous peoples without their free, prior and informed consent.

3. States shall also take effective measures to ensure, as needed, that programmes for monitoring, maintaining and restoring the health of indigenous peoples, as developed and implemented by the peoples affected by such materials, are duly implemented.

Article 30

1. Military activities shall not take place in the lands or territories of indigenous peoples, unless justified by a relevant public interest or otherwise freely agreed with or requested by the indigenous peoples concerned.

2. States shall undertake effective consultations with the indigenous peoples concerned, through appropriate procedures and in particular through their representative institutions, prior to using their lands or territories for military activities.

Article 31

1. Indigenous peoples have the right to maintain, control, protect and develop their cultural heritage, traditional knowledge and traditional cultural expressions, as well as the manifestations of their sciences, technologies and cultures, including human and genetic resources, seeds, medicines, knowledge of the properties of fauna and flora, oral traditions, literatures, designs, sports and traditional games and visual and performing arts. They also have the right to maintain, control, protect and develop their intellectual property over such cultural heritage, traditional knowledge, and traditional cultural expressions.

2. In conjunction with indigenous peoples, States shall take effective measures to recognize and protect the exercise of these rights.

Article 32

1. Indigenous peoples have the right to determine and develop priorities and strategies for the development or use of their lands or territories and other resources.

2. States shall consult and cooperate in good faith with the indigenous peoples concerned through their own representative institutions in order to obtain their free and informed

consent prior to the approval of any project affecting their lands or territories and other resources, particularly in connection with the development, utilization or exploitation of mineral, water or other resources.

3. States shall provide effective mechanisms for just and fair redress for any such activities, and appropriate measures shall be taken to mitigate adverse environmental, economic, social, cultural or spiritual impact.

Article 33

1. Indigenous peoples have the right to determine their own identity or membership in accordance with their customs and traditions. This does not impair the right of indigenous individuals to obtain citizenship of the States in which they live.

2. Indigenous peoples have the right to determine the structures and to select the membership of their institutions in accordance with their own procedures.

Article 34

Indigenous peoples have the right to promote, develop and maintain their institutional structures and their distinctive customs, spirituality, traditions, procedures, practices and, in the cases where they exist, juridical systems or customs, in accordance with international human rights standards.

Article 35

Indigenous peoples have the right to determine the responsibilities of individuals to their communities.

Article 36

1. Indigenous peoples, in particular those divided by international borders, have the right to maintain and develop contacts, relations and cooperation, including activities for spiritual, cultural, political, economic and social purposes, with their own members as well as other peoples across borders.

2. States, in consultation and cooperation with indigenous peoples, shall take effective measures to facilitate the exercise and ensure the implementation of this right.

Article 37

1. Indigenous peoples have the right to the recognition, observance and enforcement of treaties, agreements and other constructive arrangements concluded with States or their successors and to have States honour and respect such treaties, agreements and other constructive arrangements.

2. Nothing in this Declaration may be interpreted as diminishing or eliminating the rights of indigenous peoples contained in treaties, agreements and other constructive arrangements.

Article 38

States in consultation and cooperation with indigenous peoples, shall take the appropriate measures, including legislative measures, to achieve the ends of this Declaration.

Article 39

Indigenous peoples have the right to have access to financial and technical assistance from States and through international cooperation, for the enjoyment of the rights contained in this Declaration.

Article 40

Indigenous peoples have the right to access to and prompt decision through just and fair procedures for the resolution of conflicts and disputes with States or other parties, as well as to effective remedies for all infringements of their individual and collective rights. Such a decision shall give due consideration to the customs, traditions, rules and legal systems of the indigenous peoples concerned and international human rights.

Article 41

The organs and specialized agencies of the United Nations system and other intergovernmental organizations shall contribute to the full realization of the provisions of this Declaration through the mobilization, inter alia, of financial cooperation and technical assistance. Ways and means of ensuring participation of indigenous peoples on issues affecting them shall be established.

Article 42

The United Nations, its bodies, including the Permanent Forum on Indigenous Issues, and specialized agencies, including at the country level, and States shall promote respect for and full application of the provisions of this Declaration and follow up the effectiveness of this Declaration.

Article 43

The rights recognized herein constitute the minimum standards for the survival, dignity and well-being of the indigenous peoples of the world.

Article 44

All the rights and freedoms recognized herein are equally guaranteed to male and female indigenous individuals.

Article 45

Nothing in this Declaration may be construed as diminishing or extinguishing the rights indigenous peoples have now or may acquire in the future.

Article 46

1. Nothing in this Declaration may be interpreted as implying for any State, people, group or person any right to engage in any activity or to perform any act contrary to the Charter of the United Nations or construed as authorizing or encouraging any action which would dismember or impair, totally or in part, the territorial integrity or political unity of sovereign and independent States.

2. In the exercise of the rights enunciated in the present Declaration, human rights and fundamental freedoms of all shall be respected. The exercise of the rights set forth in this Declaration shall be subject only to such limitations as are determined by law and in accordance with international human rights obligations. Any such limitations shall be non-discriminatory and strictly necessary solely for the purpose of securing due recognition and respect for the rights and freedoms of others and for meeting the just and most compelling requirements of a democratic society.

3. The provisions set forth in this Declaration shall be interpreted in accordance with the principles of justice, democracy, respect for human rights, equality, non-discrimination, good governance and good faith.

40. DECLARATION ON THE SIXTIETH ANNIVERSARY OF THE UNIVERSAL DECLARATION OF HUMAN RIGHTS, 2008

This Declaration was adopted by General Assembly Resolution 63/116 on 10 December 2008, without a vote.

Further reading

JAICHAND, V. and SUKSI, M., eds., *60 Years of the Universal Declaration of Human Rights in Europe*, Mortsel, Belgium: Intersentia, 2009.

MÉNDEZ, J. E., 'The 60th Anniversary of the UDHR' (2008–9) 30 *University of Pennsylvania Journal of International Law* 1157.

PANEL OF EMINENT PERSONS, *Protecting Dignity; An Agenda for Human Rights*, Geneva: Académie de droit international humanitaire et de droits humains, 2009: **http://www.udhr60.ch/**.

VON BERNSTORFF, J., 'The Changing Fortunes of the Universal Declaration of Human Rights: Genesis and Symbolic Dimensions of the Turn to Rights in International Law', (2008) 19 *EJIL* 903.

TEXT

The General Assembly

Adopts the following Declaration:

DECLARATION ON THE SIXTIETH ANNIVERSARY OF THE UNIVERSAL DECLARATION OF HUMAN RIGHTS

We, the States Members of the United Nations, celebrate today the sixtieth anniversary of the adoption of the Universal Declaration of Human Rights, which is a common standard of achievement for all peoples and all nations in the field of human rights. Since its adoption, it has inspired the world and empowered women and men around the globe to assert their inherent dignity and rights without discrimination on any grounds. It is and will remain a source of progressive development of all human rights.

The Universal Declaration of Human Rights calls upon us to recognize and respect the dignity, freedom and equality of all human beings. We applaud the efforts undertaken by States to promote and protect all human rights for all. We must strive to enhance international cooperation and the dialogue among peoples and nations on the basis of mutual respect and understanding towards this goal.

In an ever-changing world, the Universal Declaration of Human Rights remains a relevant ethical compass that guides us in addressing the challenges we face today. The living, driving force of all human rights unites us in our common goal to eradicate the manifold ills that plague our world. We remain committed to development and to the internationally agreed development goals, and are convinced that their fulfillment will be instrumental to the enjoyment of human rights.

We deplore that human rights and fundamental freedoms are not yet fully and universally respected in all parts of the world. In no country or territory can it be claimed that all human rights have been fully realized at all times for all. Human beings continue to suffer from the neglect and violation of their human rights and fundamental freedoms. We laud the courage and commitment of all women and men around the world who have devoted their lives to promoting and protecting human rights.

We all have the duty to step up our efforts to promote and protect all human rights and to prevent, stop and redress all human rights violations. We must give everybody a chance to learn about and better understand all human rights and fundamental freedoms. We must continue to strengthen the human rights pillar of the United Nations, as we undertook with the creation of the Human Rights Council.

Today, we, the States Members of the United Nations, reiterate that we will not shy away from the magnitude of this challenge. We reaffirm our commitment towards the full realization of all human rights for all, which are universal, indivisible, interrelated, interdependent and mutually reinforcing.

IMPLEMENTATION AND STANDARD-SETTING IN CONVENTIONS SPONSORED BY THE UNITED NATIONS

INTRODUCTION

The documents that follow are concerned with standard-setting, and at the same time provide for measures of implementation apart from the ordinary working of the national legal systems of individual States parties to the Conventions.

In 1989, Philip Alston had completed a major review of the treaty supervisory system and on enhancing the long-term effectiveness of the UN human rights treaty system; see UN doc. A/44/668, 9 November 1989; later developments are reported in a note by the UN High Commissioner for Human Rights: UN doc. E/CN.4/2004/98, 11 February 2004.

In his September 2002 report, 'Strengthening of the United Nations: An agenda for further change', the Secretary-General called for improvements in the reporting process, among others (see UN doc. A/57/387, 9 September 2002, paras. 52–4), and a meeting on reform of the system was held in 2003 (see UN doc. A/58/123, 8 July 2003). Subsequently, in his 2005 report, 'In Larger Freedom: towards development, security and human rights for all' (UN doc. A/59/2005, 21 March 2005), the Secretary-General requested that, 'harmonized guidelines on reporting to all treaty bodies should be finalized and implemented so that these bodies can function as a unified system' (para. 147). Among other initiatives, there is now an annual meeting of the chairpersons of human rights treaty bodies, and 'inter-committee' meetings have been held since 2002. See further the collection of documents on the 'Effective implementation of international human rights instruments: Development of the human rights treaty system': **http://www2.ohchr.org/english/bodies/icm-mc/documents-system.htm**.

Further reading

ALSTON, P. and CRAWFORD, J., eds., *The Future of UN Human Rights Treaty Monitoring*, Cambridge: Cambridge University Press, 2000.

BAYEFSKY, A. F., *The UN Human Rights Treaty System: Universality at the Crossroads*, The Hague: Kluwer Law International, 2001.

41. CONVENTION ON THE PREVENTION AND PUNISHMENT OF THE CRIME OF GENOCIDE, 1948

This agreement was adopted and proposed for signature and ratification or accession by General Assembly Resolution 260 A (III) of 9 December 1948; it entered into force on 12 January 1951, in accordance with Article XIII. Among many other countries, the United Kingdom has ratified and effectively incorporated the convention; see the Genocide Act 1969, in force 30 April 1970, now repealed and replaced by the International Criminal Court Act 2001. See also the decision of the International Court of Justice in *Case Concerning the Application of the Convention on the Prevention and Punishment of the Crime of Genocide (Bosnia and Herzegovina v Serbia and Montenegro)* [2007] ICJ *Reports*: **http://www.icj-cij.org**; and of the European Court of Human Rights in *Jorgic v Germany*, Application no. 74613/01, 12 July 2007.

For the text in various languages, see 78 *UNTS* 277.

Further reading

ABTAHI, H. and Webb, P., *Genocide Convention: The Travaux Préparatoires*, Leiden : Brill Academic Publishing, 2008.

ANON, 'Genocide: A Commentary on the Convention', (1949) 58 *Yale Law Journal* 1142.

DIMITRIJEVIČ, V. and MILANOVIČ, M., 'The Strange Story of the Bosnian *Genocide* Case', (2008) 21 *Leiden Journal of International Law* 65.

GAETA, P., *The UN Genocide Convention: A Commentary*, Oxford: Oxford University Press, 2009.

GOLDSTONE, R. J. and HAMILTON, R. J., '*Bosnia v. Serbia*: Lessons from the Encounter of the International Court of Justice with the International Criminal Tribunal for the Former Yugoslavia', (2008) 21 *Leiden Journal of International Law* 95.

KRESS, C., 'The Crime of Genocide under International Law', (2006) 6 *International Criminal Law Review* 461.

LEMKIN, R., *Axis Rule in Occupied Europe: Laws of Occupation, Analysis of Government, Proposals for Redress*, Washington: Carnegie Endowment for International Peace, 1944.

QUIGLEY, J. B., *The Genocide Convention: An International Law Analysis*, Farnham: Ashgate, 2006.

ROBINSON, N., *The Genocide Convention: A Commentary*, New York: Institute of Jewish Affairs, 1960.

SCHABAS, W., *Genocide in International Law: The Crime of Crimes*, Cambridge: Cambridge University Press, 2nd edn., 2009.

'Symposium: Genocide, Human Rights and the ICJ', (2007) 18 *EJIL* 591–713.

'To Prevent and Punish: Commemorating the Sixtieth Anniversary of the Negotiations of the Genocide Convention', (2007–2008) 40 *Case Western Reserve Journal of International Law*, Nos. 1 & 2.

WHITEMAN, M. M., 11 *Digest of International Law*, Washington: US Department of State, 1968, 848–74.

TEXT

The Contracting Parties,

Having considered the declaration made by the General Assembly of the United Nations in its resolution 96 (I) dated 11 December 1946 that genocide is a crime under international law, contrary to the spirit and aims of the United Nations and condemned by the civilized world,

Recognizing that at all periods of history genocide has inflicted great losses on humanity, and

Being convinced that, in order to liberate mankind from such an odious scourge, international co-operation is required,

Hereby agree as hereinafter provided:

Article I

The Contracting Parties confirm that genocide, whether committed in time of peace or in time of war, is a crime under international law which they undertake to prevent and to punish.

Article II

In the present Convention, genocide means any of the following acts committed with intent to destroy, in whole or in part, a national, ethnical, racial or religious group, as such:

(a) Killing members of the group;

(b) Causing serious bodily or mental harm to members of the group;

(c) Deliberately inflicting on the group conditions of life calculated to bring about its physical destruction in whole or in part;

(d) Imposing measures intended to prevent births within the group;

(e) Forcibly transferring children of the group to another group.

Article III

The following acts shall be punishable:

(a) Genocide;

(b) Conspiracy to commit genocide;

(c) Direct and public incitement to commit genocide;

(d) Attempt to commit genocide;

(e) Complicity in genocide.

Article IV

Persons committing genocide or any of the other acts enumerated in Article III shall be punished, whether they are constitutionally responsible rulers, public officials or private individuals.

Article V

The Contracting Parties undertake to enact, in accordance with their respective Constitutions, the necessary legislation to give effect to the provisions of the present Convention, and, in particular, to provide effective penalties for persons guilty of genocide or any of the other acts enumerated in Article III.

Article VI

Persons charged with genocide or any of the other acts enumerated in Article III shall be tried by a competent tribunal of the State in the territory of which the act was committed, or by such international penal tribunal as may have jurisdiction with respect to those Contracting Parties which shall have accepted its jurisdiction.

Article VII

Genocide and the other acts enumerated in Article III shall not be considered as political crimes for the purpose of extradition.

The Contracting Parties pledge themselves in such cases to grant extradition in accordance with their laws and treaties in force.

Article VIII

Any Contracting Party may call upon the competent organs of the United Nations to take such action under the Charter of the United Nations as they consider appropriate for the prevention and suppression of acts of genocide or any of the other acts enumerated in Article III.

Article IX

Disputes between the Contracting Parties relating to the interpretation, application or fulfilment of the present Convention, including those relating to the responsibility of a State for genocide or for any of the other acts enumerated in Article III, shall be submitted to the International Court of Justice at the request of any of the parties to the dispute.

Article X

The present Convention, of which the Chinese, English, French, Russian and Spanish texts are equally authentic, shall bear the date of 9 December 1948.

Article XI

The present Convention shall be open until 31 December 1949 for signature on behalf of any Member of the United Nations and of any non-member State to which an invitation to sign has been addressed by the General Assembly.

The present Convention shall be ratified, and the instruments of ratification shall be deposited with the Secretary-General of the United Nations.

After 1 January 1950, the present Convention may be acceded to on behalf of any Member of the United Nations and of any non-member State which has received an invitation as aforesaid. Instruments of accession shall be deposited with the Secretary-General of the United Nations.

Article XII

Any Contracting Party may at any time, by notification addressed to the Secretary-General of the United Nations, extend the application of the present Convention to all or any of the territories for the conduct of whose foreign relations that Contracting Party is responsible.

Article XIII

On the day when the first twenty instruments of ratification or accession have been deposited, the Secretary-General shall draw up a *procès-verbal* and transmit a copy thereof to each Member of the United Nations and to each of the non-member States contemplated in Article XI.

The present Convention shall come into force on the ninetieth day following the date of deposit of the twentieth instrument of ratification or accession.

Any ratification or accession effected subsequent to the latter date shall become effective on the ninetieth day following the deposit of the instrument of ratification or accession.

Article XIV

The present Convention shall remain in effect for a period of ten years as from the date of its coming into force.

It shall thereafter remain in force for successive periods of five years for such Contracting Parties as have not denounced it at least six months before the expiration of the current period.

Denunciation shall be effected by a written notification addressed to the Secretary-General of the United Nations.

Article XV

If, as a result of denunciations, the number of Parties to the present Convention should become less than sixteen, the Convention shall cease to be in force as from the date on which the last of these denunciations shall become effective.

Article XVI

A request for the revision of the present Convention may be made at any time by any Contracting Party by means of a notification in writing addressed to the Secretary-General.

The General Assembly shall decide upon the steps, if any, to be taken in respect of such request.

Article XVII

The Secretary-General of the United Nations shall notify all Members of the United Nations and the non-member States contemplated in Article XI of the following:

(a) Signatures, ratifications and accessions received in accordance with Article XI;

(b) Notifications received in accordance with Article XII;

(c) The date upon which the present Convention comes into force in accordance with Article XIII;

(d) Denunciations received in accordance with Article XIV;

(e) The abrogation of the Convention in accordance with Article XV;

(f) Notifications received in accordance with Article XVI.

Article XVIII

The original of the present Convention shall be deposited in the archives of the United Nations.

A certified copy of the Convention shall be transmitted to each Member of the United Nations and to each of the non-member States contemplated in Article XI.

Article XIX

The present Convention shall be registered by the Secretary-General of the United Nations on the date of its coming into force.

42. CONVENTION RELATING TO THE STATUS OF REFUGEES, 1951

The Convention was adopted by the UN Conference on the Status of Refugees and Stateless Persons at Geneva on 25 July 1951. The Final Act of the Conference included five recommendations, adopted unanimously; these are not reprinted below, but can be found in GOODWIN-GILL and MCADAM, *The Refugee in International Law*, 571–2. The Convention entered into force on 22 April 1954. For the text in English and French, see 189 *UNTS* 137.

The definition of 'refugee' in the Convention which follows is confined to those who became refugees 'as a result of events occurring before 1 January 1951'. This limitation is removed by the Protocol relating to the Status of Refugees adopted by the UN General Assembly on 16 December 1966; see WEIS, 42 *BYIL* 39 (1967); GOODWIN-GILL and MCADAM, *The Refugee in International Law*, 507–8 (text of Protocol at 588–92). The Protocol came into force on 4 October 1967. For the text in English and French, see 606 *UNTS* 267. The Protocol is not reproduced here; the changes it makes in Article 1A(2) of the Convention are indicated by square brackets, and States parties to the Protocol undertake to apply Articles 2 to 34 inclusive of the Convention, as if the bracketed words were omitted.

The *International Journal of Refugee Law*, Oxford: Oxford University Press, provides regular academic and practitioner comment on the application of the 1951 Convention and on related issues, while the UNHCR website, *Refworld*, offers an extensive database of materials concerned, among others, with the implementation of the Convention in municipal law: **http://www.unhcr.org/cgi-bin/texis/vtx/refworld/rwmain**.

Further reading

FELLER, E., TÜRK, V. and NICHOLSON, F., eds., *Refugee Protection in International Law: UNHCR's Global Consultations on International Protection*, Cambridge: Cambridge University Press, 2003.

FOSTER, M., *International Refugee Law and Socio-Economic Rights*, Cambridge: Cambridge University Press, 2007.

GOODWIN-GILL, G. S., 'The Search for the One, True Meaning . . .', in GOODWIN-GILL, G. S. and LAMBERT, H., eds., *The Limits of Transnational Law*, Cambridge: Cambridge University Press, 2010, 204–41.

—— and MCADAM, J., *The Refugee in International Law*, Oxford: Oxford University Press, 3rd edn., 2007.

GRAHL-MADSEN, A., *The Status of Refugees in International Law*, Leyden: A. W. Sijthoff, 2 vols., 1966, 1972.

HATHAWAY, J., *The Rights of Refugees under International Law*, Cambridge: Cambridge University Press, 2005.

HURWITZ, A., *The Collective Responsibility of States to Protect Refugees*, Oxford: Oxford University Press, 2009.

JACKSON, I. C., *The Refugee Concept in Group Situations*, The Hague: Kluwer Law International, 1999.

KNEEBONE, S. and CURRAN, L., eds., *The Refugees Convention 50 Years On*, Aldershot: Ashgate, 2003.

MCADAM, J., *Complementary Protection in International Refugee Law*, Oxford: Oxford University Press, 2007.

——, ed., *Forced Migration, Human Rights and Security*, Oxford: Hart Publishing, 2008.

NICHOLSON, F. and TWOMEY, P., eds., *Refugee Rights and Realities: Evolving International Concepts and Regimes*, Cambridge: Cambridge University Press, 1999.

WEIS, P., 'Legal Aspects of the Convention of 25 July 1951 relating to the Status of Refugees', (1953) 30 *BYIL* 478-89.

—— 'The 1967 Protocol relating to the Status of Refugees and some Questions of the Law of Treaties', (1967) 42 *BYIL* 39-70.

ZIMMERMANN, A., ed., *The 1951 Convention relating to the Status of Refugees: A Commentary*, Oxford: Oxford University Press, 2010.

TEXT

PREAMBLE

The High Contracting Parties,

Considering that the Charter of the United Nations and the Universal Declaration of Human Rights approved on 10 December 1948 by the General Assembly have affirmed the principle that human beings shall enjoy fundamental rights and freedoms without discrimination,

Considering that the United Nations has, on various occasions, manifested its profound concern for refugees and endeavoured to assure refugees the widest possible exercise of these fundamental rights and freedoms,

Considering that it is desirable to revise and consolidate previous international agreements relating to the status of refugees and to extend the scope of and protection accorded by such instruments by means of a new agreement,

Considering that the grant of asylum may place unduly heavy burdens on certain countries, and that a satisfactory solution of a problem of which the United Nations has recognized the international scope and nature cannot therefore be achieved without international co-operation,

Expressing the wish that all States, recognizing the social and humanitarian nature of the problem of refugees will do everything within their power to prevent this problem from becoming a cause of tension between States,

Noting that the United Nations High Commissioner for Refugees is charged with the task of supervising international conventions providing for the protection of refugees, and recognizing that the effective co-ordination of measures taken to deal with this problem will depend upon the co-operation of States with the High Commissioner,

Have agreed as follows:

CHAPTER I—GENERAL PROVISIONS

Article 1—Definition of the term 'Refugee'

A. For the purposes of the present Convention, the term 'refugee' shall apply to any person who:

(1) Has been considered a refugee under the Arrangements of 12 May 1926 and 30 June 1928 or under the Conventions of 28 October 1933 and 10 February 1938, the Protocol of 14 September 1939 or the Constitution of the International Refugee Organization;

Decisions of non-eligibility taken by the International Refugee Organization during the period of its activities shall not prevent the status of refugee being accorded to persons who fulfil the conditions of paragraph 2 of this section;

(2) [As a result of events occurring before 1 January 1951 and] owing to well-founded fear of being persecuted for reasons of race, religion, nationality, membership of a particular social group or political opinion, is outside the country of his nationality and is unable or,

owing to such fear, is unwilling to avail himself of the protection of that country; or who, not having a nationality and being outside the country of his former habitual residence [as a result of such events], is unable or, owing to such fear, is unwilling to return to it.

In the case of a person who has more than one nationality, the term 'the country of his nationality' shall mean each of the countries of which he is a national, and a person shall not be deemed to be lacking the protection of the country of his nationality if, without any valid reason based on well-founded fear, he has not availed himself of the protection of one of the countries of which he is a national.

B. (1) For the purposes of this Convention, the words 'events occurring before 1 January 1951' in Article 1, Section A, shall be understood to mean either

    (a) 'events occurring in Europe before 1 January 1951'; or

    (b) 'events occurring in Europe or elsewhere before 1 January 1951', and each Contracting State shall make a declaration at the time of signature, ratification or accession, specifying which of these meanings it applies for the purpose of its obligations under this Convention.

(2) Any Contracting State which has adopted alternative (a) may at any time extend its obligations by adopting alternative (b) by means of a notification addressed to the Secretary-General of the United Nations.

C. This Convention shall cease to apply to any person falling under the terms of Section A if:

(1) He has voluntarily re-availed himself of the protection of the country of his nationality; or

(2) Having lost his nationality, he has voluntarily re-acquired it, or

(3) He has acquired a new nationality, and enjoys the protection of the country of his new nationality; or

(4) He has voluntarily re-established himself in the country which he left or outside which he remained owing to fear of persecution; or

(5) He can no longer, because the circumstances in connection with which he has been recognized as a refugee have ceased to exist, continue to refuse to avail himself of the protection of the country of his nationality;

Provided that this paragraph shall not apply to a refugee falling under Section A(1) of this Article who is able to invoke compelling reasons arising out of previous persecution for refusing to avail himself of the protection of the country of nationality;

(6) Being a person who has no nationality he is, because of the circumstances in connection with which he has been recognized as a refugee have ceased to exist, able to return to the country of his former habitual residence;

Provided that this paragraph shall not apply to a refugee falling under section A(1) of this Article who is able to invoke compelling reasons arising out of previous persecution for refusing to return to the country of his former habitual residence.

D. This Convention shall not apply to persons who are at present receiving from organs or agencies of the United Nations other than the United Nations High Commissioner for Refugees protection or assistance.

When such protection or assistance has ceased for any reason, without the position of such persons being definitively settled in accordance with the relevant resolutions adopted by the General Assembly of the United Nations, these persons shall *ipso facto* be entitled to the benefits of this Convention.

E. This Convention shall not apply to a person who is recognized by the competent authorities of the country in which he has taken residence as having the rights and obligations which are attached to the possession of the nationality of that country.

F. The provisions of this Convention shall not apply to any person with respect to whom there are serious reasons for considering that:

(a) he has committed a crime against peace, a war crime, or a crime against humanity, as defined in the international instruments drawn up to make provision in respect of such crimes;

(b) he has committed a serious non-political crime outside the country of refuge prior to his admission to that country as a refugee;

(c) he has been guilty of acts contrary to the purposes and principles of the United Nations.

Article 2—General obligations

Every refugee has duties to the country in which he finds himself, which require in particular that he conform to its laws and regulations as well as to measures taken for the maintenance of public order.

Article 3—Non-discrimination

The Contracting States shall apply the provisions of this Convention to refugees without discrimination as to race, religion or country of origin.

Article 4—Religion

The Contracting States shall accord to refugees within their territories treatment at least as favourable as that accorded to their nationals with respect to freedom to practise their religion and freedom as regards the religious education of their children.

Article 5—Rights granted apart from this Convention

Nothing in this Convention shall be deemed to impair any rights and benefits granted by a Contracting State to refugees apart from this Convention.

Article 6—The term 'in the same circumstances'

For the purposes of this Convention, the term 'in the same circumstances' implies that any requirements (including requirements as to length and conditions of sojourn or residence) which the particular individual would have to fulfil for the enjoyment of the right in question, if he were not a refugee, must be fulfilled by him, with the exception of requirements which by their nature a refugee is incapable of fulfilling.

Article 7—Exemption from reciprocity

1. Except where this Convention contains more favourable provisions, a Contracting State shall accord to refugees the same treatment as is accorded to aliens generally.

2. After a period of three years' residence, all refugees shall enjoy exemption from legislative reciprocity in the territory of the Contracting States.

3. Each Contracting State shall continue to accord to refugees the rights and benefits to which they were already entitled, in the absence of reciprocity, at the date of entry into force of this Convention for that State.

4. The Contracting States shall consider favourably the possibility of according to refugees, in the absence of reciprocity, rights and benefits beyond those to which they are entitled according to paragraphs 2 and 3, and to extending exemption from reciprocity to refugees who do not fulfil the conditions provided for in paragraphs 2 and 3.

5. The provisions of paragraphs 2 and 3 apply both to the rights and benefits referred to in Articles 13, 18, 19, 21 and 22 of this Convention and to rights and benefits for which this Convention does not provide.

Article 8—Exemption from exceptional measures

With regard to exceptional measures which may be taken against the person, property or interests of nationals of a foreign State, the Contracting States shall not apply such measures to a refugee who is formally a national of the said State solely on account of such nationality. Contracting States which, under their legislation, are prevented from applying the general principle expressed in this Article, shall, in appropriate cases, grant exemptions in favour of such refugees.

Article 9—Provisional measures

Nothing in this Convention shall prevent a Contracting State, in time of war or other grave and exceptional circumstances, from taking provisionally measures which it considers to be essential to the national security in the case of a particular person, pending a determination by the Contracting State that that person is in fact a refugee and that the continuance of such measures is necessary in his case in the interests of national security.

Article 10—Continuity of residence

1. Where a refugee has been forcibly displaced during the Second World War and removed to the territory of a Contracting State, and is resident there, the period of such enforced sojourn shall be considered to have been lawful residence within that territory.

2. Where a refugee has been forcibly displaced during the Second World War from the territory of a Contracting State and has, prior to the date of entry into force of this Convention, returned there for the purpose of taking up residence, the period of residence before and after such enforced displacement shall be regarded as one uninterrupted period for any purposes for which uninterrupted residence is required.

Article 11—Refugee seamen

In the case of refugees regularly serving as crew members on board a ship flying the flag of a Contracting State, that State shall give sympathetic consideration to their establishment on its territory and the issue of travel documents to them or their temporary admission to its territory particularly with a view to facilitating their establishment in another country.

CHAPTER II—JURIDICAL STATUS

Article 12—Personal status

1. The personal status of a refugee shall be governed by the law of the country of his domicile or, if he has no domicile, by the law of the country of his residence.

2. Rights previously acquired by a refugee and dependent on personal status, more particularly rights attaching to marriage, shall be respected by a Contracting State, subject to compliance, if this be necessary, with the formalities required by the law of that State, provided that the right in question is one which would have been recognized by the law of that State had he not become a refugee.

Article 13—Movable and immovable property

The Contracting States shall accord to a refugee treatment as favourable as possible and, in any event, not less favourable than that accorded to aliens generally in the same circumstances, as regards the acquisition of movable and immovable property and other rights pertaining thereto, and to leases and other contracts relating to movable and immovable property.

Article 14—Artistic rights and industrial property

In respect of the protection of industrial property, such as inventions, designs or models, trade marks, trade names, and of rights in literary, artistic, and scientific works, a refugee shall be accorded in the country in which he has his habitual residence the same protection as is accorded to nationals of that country. In the territory of any other Contracting State, he shall be accorded the same protection as is accorded in that territory to nationals of the country in which he has his habitual residence.

Article 15—Right of association

As regards non-political and non-profit making associations and trade unions the Contracting States shall accord to refugees lawfully staying in their territory the most favourable treatment accorded to nationals of a foreign country, in the same circumstances.

Article 16—Access to courts

1. A refugee shall have free access to the courts of law on the territory of all Contracting States.

2. A refugee shall enjoy in the Contracting State in which he has his habitual residence the same treatment as a national in matters pertaining to access to the courts, including legal assistance and exemption from *cautio judicatum solvi*.

3. A refugee shall be accorded in the matters referred to in paragraph 2 in countries other than that in which he has his habitual residence the treatment granted to a national of the country of his habitual residence.

CHAPTER III—GAINFUL EMPLOYMENT

Article 17—Wage-earning employment

1. The Contracting States shall accord to refugees lawfully staying in their territory the most favourable treatment accorded to nationals of a foreign country in the same circumstances, as regards the right to engage in wage-earning employment.

2. In any case, restrictive measures imposed on aliens or the employment of aliens for the protection of the national labour market shall not be applied to a refugee who was already exempt from them at the date of entry into force of this Convention for the Contracting State concerned, or who fulfils one of the following conditions:

(a) He has completed three years' residence in the country;

(b) He has a spouse possessing the nationality of the country of residence. A refugee may not invoke the benefits of this provision if he has abandoned his spouse;

(c) He has one or more children possessing the nationality of the country of residence.

3. The Contracting States shall give sympathetic consideration to assimilating the rights of all refugees with regard to wage-earning employment to those of nationals, and in particular of those refugees who have entered their territory pursuant to programmes of labour recruitment or under immigration schemes.

Article 18—Self-employment

The Contracting States shall accord to a refugee lawfully in their territory treatment as favourable as possible and, in any event, not less favourable than that accorded to aliens generally in the same circumstances, as regards the right to engage on his own account in agriculture, industry, handicrafts and commerce and to establish commercial and industrial companies.

Article 19—Liberal professions

1. Each Contracting State shall accord to refugees lawfully staying in their territory who hold diplomas recognized by the competent authorities of that State, and who are desirous of practising a liberal profession, treatment as favourable as possible and, in any event, not less favourable than that accorded to aliens generally in the same circumstances.

2. The Contracting States shall use their best endeavours consistently with their laws and constitutions to secure the settlement of such refugees in the territories, other than the metropolitan territory, for whose international relations they are responsible.

CHAPTER IV—WELFARE

Article 20—Rationing

Where a rationing system exists, which applies to the population at large and regulates the general distribution of products in short supply, refugees shall be accorded the same treatment as nationals.

Article 21—Housing

As regards housing, the Contracting States, in so far as the matter is regulated by laws or regulations or is subject to the control of public authorities, shall accord to refugees lawfully staying in their territory treatment as favourable as possible and, in any event, not less favourable than that accorded to aliens generally in the same circumstances.

Article 22—Public education

1. The Contracting States shall accord to refugees the same treatment as is accorded to nationals with respect to elementary education.

2. The Contracting States shall accord to refugees treatment as favourable as possible, and, in any event, not less favourable than that accorded to aliens generally in the same circumstances, with respect to education other than elementary education and, in particular, as regards access to studies, the recognition of foreign school

certificates, diplomas and degrees, the remission of fees and charges and the award of scholarships.

Article 23—Public relief

The Contracting States shall accord to refugees lawfully staying in their territory the same treatment with respect to public relief and assistance as is accorded to their nationals.

Article 24—Labour legislation and social security

1. The Contracting States shall accord to refugees lawfully staying in their territory the same treatment as is accorded to nationals in respect of the following matters:

(a) In so far as such matters are governed by laws or regulations or are subject to the control of administrative authorities: remuneration, including family allowances where these form part of remuneration, hours of work, overtime arrangements, holidays with pay, restrictions on home work, minimum age of employment, apprenticeship and training, women's work and the work of young persons, and the enjoyment of the benefits of collective bargaining;

(b) Social security (legal provisions in respect of employment injury, occupational diseases, maternity, sickness, disability, old age, death, unemployment, family responsibilities and any other contingency which, according to national laws or regulations, is covered by a social security scheme), subject to the following limitations:

(i) There may be appropriate arrangements for the maintenance of acquired rights and rights in course of acquisition;

(ii) National laws or regulations of the country of residence may prescribe special arrangements concerning benefits or portions of benefits which are payable wholly out of public funds, and concerning allowances paid to persons who do not fulfil the contribution conditions prescribed for the award of a normal pension.

2. The right to compensation for the death of a refugee resulting from employment injury or from occupational disease shall not be affected by the fact that the residence of the beneficiary is outside the territory of the Contracting State.

3. The Contracting States shall extend to refugees the benefits of agreements concluded between them, or which may be concluded between them in the future, concerning the maintenance of acquired rights and rights in the process of acquisition in regard to social security, subject only to the conditions which apply to nationals of the States signatory to the agreements in question.

4. The Contracting States will give sympathetic consideration to extending to refugees so far as possible the benefits of similar agreements which may at any time be in force between such Contracting States and non-contracting States.

CHAPTER V—ADMINISTRATIVE MEASURES

Article 25—Administrative assistance

1. When the exercise of a right by a refugee would normally require the assistance of authorities of a foreign country to whom he cannot have recourse, the Contracting States in whose territory he is residing shall arrange that such assistance be afforded to him by their own authorities or by an international authority.

2. The authority or authorities mentioned in paragraph 1 shall deliver or cause to be delivered under their supervision to refugees such documents or certifications as would normally be delivered to aliens by or through their national authorities.

3. Documents or certifications so delivered shall stand in the stead of the official instruments delivered to aliens by or through their national authorities, and shall be given credence in the absence of proof to the contrary.

4. Subject to such exceptional treatment as may be granted to indigent persons, fees may be charged for the services mentioned herein, but such fees shall be moderate and commensurate with those charged to nationals for similar services.

5. The provisions of this Article shall be without prejudice to Articles 27 and 28.

Article 26—Freedom of movement

Each Contracting State shall accord to refugees lawfully in its territory the right to choose their place of residence and to move freely within its territory, subject to any regulations applicable to aliens generally in the same circumstances.

Article 27—Identity papers

The Contracting States shall issue identity papers to any refugee in their territory who does not possess a valid travel document.

Article 28—Travel documents

1. The Contracting States shall issue to refugees lawfully staying in their territory travel documents for the purpose of travel outside their territory unless compelling reasons of national security or public order otherwise require, and the provisions of the Schedule to this Convention shall apply with respect to such documents. The Contracting States may issue such a travel document to any other refugee in their territory; they shall in particular give sympathetic consideration to the issue of such a travel document to refugees in their territory who are unable to obtain a travel document from the country of their lawful residence.

2. Travel documents issued to refugees under previous international agreements by parties thereto shall be recognized and treated by the Contracting States in the same way as if they had been issued pursuant to this article.

Article 29—Fiscal charges

1. The Contracting States shall not impose upon refugees duties, charges or taxes, of any description whatsoever, other or higher than those which are or may be levied on their nationals in similar situations.

2. Nothing in the above paragraph shall prevent the application to refugees of the laws and regulations concerning charges in respect of the issue to aliens of administrative documents including identity papers.

Article 30—Transfer of assets

1. A Contracting State shall, in conformity with its laws and regulations, permit refugees to transfer assets which they have brought into its territory, to another country where they have been admitted for the purposes of resettlement.

2. A Contracting State shall give sympathetic consideration to the application of refugees for permission to transfer assets wherever they may be and which are necessary for their resettlement in another country to which they have been admitted.

Article 31—Refugees unlawfully in the country of refuge

1. The Contracting States shall not impose penalties, on account of their illegal entry or presence, on refugees who, coming directly from a territory where their life or freedom was threatened in the sense of Article 1, enter or are present in their territory without authorization, provided they present themselves without delay to the authorities and show good cause for their illegal entry or presence.

2. The Contracting States shall not apply to the movements of such refugees restrictions other than those which are necessary and such restrictions shall only be applied until their status in the country is regularized or they obtain admission into another country. The Contracting States shall allow such refugees a reasonable period and all the necessary facilities to obtain admission into another country.

Article 32—Expulsion

1. The Contracting States shall not expel a refugee lawfully in their territory save on grounds of national security or public order.

2. The expulsion of such a refugee shall be only in pursuance of a decision reached in accordance with due process of law. Except where compelling reasons of national security otherwise require, the refugee shall be allowed to submit evidence to clear himself, and to appeal to and be represented for the purpose before competent authority or a person or persons specially designated by the competent authority.

3. The Contracting States shall allow such a refugee a reasonable period within which to seek legal admission into another country. The Contracting States reserve the right to apply during that period such internal measures as they may deem necessary.

Article 33—Prohibition of expulsion or return ('refoulement')

1. No Contracting State shall expel or return ('refouler') a refugee in any manner whatsoever to the frontiers of territories where his life or freedom would be threatened on account of his race, religion, nationality, membership of a particular social group or political opinion.

2. The benefit of the present provision may not, however, be claimed by a refugee whom there are reasonable grounds for regarding as a danger to the security of the country in which he is, or who, having been convicted by a final judgment of a particularly serious crime, constitutes a danger to the community of that country.

Article 34—Naturalization

The Contracting States shall as far as possible facilitate the assimilation and naturalization of refugees. They shall in particular make every effort to expedite naturalization proceedings and to reduce as far as possible the charges and costs of such proceedings.

CHAPTER VI—EXECUTORY AND TRANSITORY PROVISIONS

Article 35—Co-operation of the national authorities with the United Nations

1. The Contracting States undertake to co-operate with the Office of the United Nations High Commissioner for Refugees, or any other agency of the United Nations which may succeed it, in the exercise of its functions, and shall in particular facilitate its duty of supervising the application of the provisions of this Convention.

2. In order to enable the Office of the High Commissioner or any other agency of the United Nations which may succeed it, to make reports to the competent organs of the United Nations, the Contracting States undertake to provide them in the appropriate form with information and statistical data requested concerning:

   (a) the condition of refugees,

   (b) the implementation of this Convention, and

   (c) laws, regulations and decrees which are, or may hereafter be, in force relating to refugees.

Article 36—Information on national legislation

The Contracting States shall communicate to the Secretary-General of the United Nations the laws and regulations which they may adopt to ensure the application of this Convention.

Article 37—Relation to previous conventions

Without prejudice to Article 28, paragraph 2, of this Convention, this Convention replaces, as between parties to it, the Arrangements of 5 July 1922, 31 May 1924, 12 May 1926, 30 June 1928 and 30 July 1935, the Conventions of 28 October 1933 and 10 February 1938, the Protocol of 14 September 1939 and the Agreement of 15 October 1946.

CHAPTER VII—FINAL CLAUSES

Article 38—Settlement of disputes

Any dispute between parties to this Convention relating to its interpretation or application, which cannot be settled by other means, shall be referred to the International Court of Justice at the request of any one of the parties to the dispute.

Article 39—Signature, ratification and accession

1. This Convention shall be opened for signature at Geneva on 28 July 1951 and shall hereafter be deposited with the Secretary-General of the United Nations. It shall be open for signature at the European Office of the United Nations from 28 July to 31 August 1951 and shall be re-opened for signature at the Headquarters of the United Nations from 17 September 1951 to 31 December 1952.

2. This Convention shall be open for signature on behalf of all States Members of the United Nations, and also on behalf of any other State invited to attend the Conference of Plenipotentiaries on the Status of Refugees and Stateless Persons or to which an invitation to sign will have been addressed by the General Assembly. It shall be ratified and the instruments of ratification shall be deposited with the Secretary-General of the United Nations.

3. This Convention shall be open from 28 July 1951 for accession by the States referred to in paragraph 2 of this Article. Accession shall be effected by the deposit of an instrument of accession with the Secretary-General of the United Nations.

Article 40—Territorial application clause

1. Any State may, at the time of signature, ratification or accession, declare that this Convention shall extend to all or any of the territories for the international relations of

which it is responsible. Such a declaration shall take effect when the Convention enters into force for the State concerned.

2. At any time thereafter any such extension shall be made by notification addressed to the Secretary-General of the United Nations and shall take effect as from the ninetieth day after the day of receipt by the Secretary-General of the United Nations of this notification, or as from the date of entry into force of the Convention for the State concerned, whichever is the later.

3. With respect to those territories to which this Convention is not extended at the time of signature, ratification or accession, each State concerned shall consider the possibility of taking the necessary steps in order to extend the application of this Convention to such territories, subject, where necessary for constitutional reasons, to the consent of the governments of such territories.

Article 41—Federal clause

In the case of a Federal or non-unitary State, the following provisions shall apply:

(a) With respect to those Articles of this Convention that come within the legislative jurisdiction of the federal legislative authority, the obligations of the Federal Government shall to this extent be the same as those of Parties which are not Federal States,

(b) With respect to those Articles of this Convention that come within the legislative jurisdiction of constituent States, provinces or cantons which are not, under the constitutional system of the federation, bound to take legislative action, the Federal Government shall bring such Articles with a favourable recommendation to the notice of the appropriate authorities of States, provinces or cantons at the earliest possible moment.

(c) A Federal State Party to this Convention shall, at the request of any other Contracting State transmitted through the Secretary-General of the United Nations, supply a statement of the law and practice of the Federation and its constituent units in regard to any particular provision of the Convention showing the extent to which effect has been given to that provision by legislative or other action.

Article 42—Reservations

1. At the time of signature, ratification or accession, any State may make reservations to articles of the Convention other than to Articles 1, 3, 4, 16(1), 33, 36–46 inclusive.

2. Any State making a reservation in accordance with paragraph 1 of this article may at any time withdraw the reservation by a communication to that effect addressed to the Secretary-General of the United Nations.

Article 43—Entry into force

1. This Convention shall come into force on the ninetieth day following the day of deposit of the sixth instrument of ratification or accession.

2. For each State ratifying or acceding to the Convention after the deposit of the sixth instrument of ratification or accession, the Convention shall enter into force on the ninetieth day following the date of deposit by such State of its instrument of ratification or accession.

Article 44—Denunciation

1. Any Contracting State may denounce this Convention at any time by a notification addressed to the Secretary-General of the United Nations.

2. Such denunciation shall take effect for the Contracting State concerned one year from the date upon which it is received by the Secretary-General of the United Nations.

3. Any State which has made a declaration or notification under Article 40 may, at any time thereafter, by a notification to the Secretary-General of the United Nations, declare that the Convention shall cease to extend to such territory one year after the date of receipt of the notification by the Secretary-General.

Article 45—Revision

1. Any Contracting State may request revision of this Convention at any time by a notification addressed to the Secretary-General of the United Nations.

2. The General Assembly of the United Nations shall recommend the steps, if any, to be taken in respect of such request.

Article 46—Notifications by the Secretary-General of the United Nations

The Secretary-General of the United Nations shall inform all Members of the United Nations and non-member States referred to in Article 39:

    (a) of declarations and notifications in accordance with Section B of Article 1;

    (b) of signatures, ratifications and accessions in accordance with Article 39;

    (c) of declarations and notifications in accordance with Article 40;

    (d) of reservations and withdrawals in accordance with Article 42;

    (e) of the date on which this Convention will come into force in accordance with Article 43;

    (f) of denunciations and notifications in accordance with Article 44;

    (g) of requests for revision in accordance with Article 45.

In faith whereof the undersigned, duly authorized, have signed this Convention on behalf of their respective Governments,

    Done at Geneva, this twenty-eighth day of July, one thousand nine hundred and fifty-one, in a single copy, of which the English and French texts are equally authentic and which shall remain deposited in the archives of the United Nations, and certified true copies of which shall be delivered to all Members of the United Nations and to the non-member States referred to in Article 39.

SCHEDULE

Paragraph 1

1. The travel document referred to in Article 28 of this Convention shall be similar to the specimen annexed hereto.

2. The document shall be made out in at least two languages, one of which shall be English or French.

Paragraph 2

Subject to the regulations obtaining in the country of issue, children may be included in the travel document of a parent or, in exceptional circumstances, of another adult refugee.

Paragraph 3

The fees charged for issue of the document shall not exceed the lowest scale of charges for national passports.

Paragraph 4

Save in special or exceptional cases, the document shall be made valid for the largest possible number of countries.

Paragraph 5

The document shall have a validity of either one or two years, at the discretion of the issuing authority.

Paragraph 6

1. The renewal or extension of the validity of the document is a matter for the authority which issued it, so long as the holder has not established lawful residence in another territory and resides lawfully in the territory of the said authority. The issue of a new document is, under the same conditions, a matter for the authority which issued the former document.

2. Diplomatic or consular authorities, specially authorized for the purpose, shall be empowered to extend, for a period not exceeding six months, the validity of travel documents issued by their Governments.

3. The Contracting States shall give sympathetic consideration to renewing or extending the validity of travel documents or issuing new documents to refugees no longer lawfully resident in their territory who are unable to obtain a travel document from the country of their lawful residence.

Paragraph 7

The Contracting States shall recognize the validity of the documents issued in accordance with the provisions of Article 28 of this Convention.

Paragraph 8

The competent authorities of the country to which the refugee desires to proceed shall, if they are prepared to admit him and if a visa is required, affix a visa on the document of which he is the holder.

Paragraph 9

1. The Contracting States undertake to issue transit visas to refugees who have obtained visas for a territory of final destination.

2. The issue of such visas may be refused on grounds which would justify refusal of a visa to any alien.

Paragraph 10

The fees for the issue of exit, entry or transit visas shall not exceed the lowest scale of charges for visas on foreign passports.

Paragraph 11

When a refugee has lawfully taken up residence in the territory of another Contracting State, the responsibility for the issue of a new document, under the terms and conditions of Article 28, shall be that of the competent authority of that territory, to which the refugee shall be entitled to apply.

Paragraph 12

The authority issuing a new document shall withdraw the old document and shall return it to the country of issue, if it is stated in the document that it should be so returned; otherwise it shall withdraw and cancel the document.

Paragraph 13

1. Each Contracting State undertakes that the holder of a travel document issued by it in accordance with Article 28 of this Convention shall be re-admitted to its territory at any time during the period of its validity.

2. Subject to the provisions of the preceding sub-paragraph, a Contracting State may require the holder of the document to comply with such formalities as may be prescribed in regard to exit from or return to its territory.

3. The Contracting States reserve the right, in exceptional cases, or in cases where the refugee's stay is authorized for a specific period, when issuing the document, to limit the period during which the refugee may return to a period of not less than three months.

Paragraph 14

Subject only to the terms of paragraph 13, the provisions of this Schedule in no way affect the laws and regulations governing the conditions of admission to, transit through, residence and establishment in, and departure from, the territories of the Contracting States.

Paragraph 15

Neither the issue of the document nor the entries made thereon determine or affect the status of the holder, particularly as regards nationality.

Paragraph 16

The issue of the document does not in any way entitle the holder to the protection of the diplomatic or consular authorities of the country of issue, and does not confer on these authorities a right of protection.

[The Annex with details of the Specimen Travel Document is omitted]

43. CONVENTION ON THE POLITICAL RIGHTS OF WOMEN, 1953

The Convention was adopted by General Assembly Resolution 640 (VII) of 20 December 1952, opened for signature on 31 March 1953, and entered into force on 7 July 1954. For the text in various languages, see 193 *UNTS* 135.

See further, *Convention on the Political Rights of Women: History and Commentary*, ST/SOA/27, UN Sales No. 1955, IV, 17; *Yearbook on Human Rights*, 1948, 439 (Bogotá Convention). See also the Beijing Declaration, above, p. 211; Convention on the Elimination of All Forms of Discrimination against Women, below, p. 418.

Further reading

GOODWIN-GILL, G. S., *Free and Fair Elections*, Geneva: Inter-Parliamentary Union, rev'd edn., 2006.
INTER-PARLIAMENTARY UNION AND UNITED NATIONS DIVISION FOR THE ADVANCEMENT OF WOMEN, *Women in Politics: 2008* (Map), Geneva, Inter-Parliamentary Union, 2008.

TEXT

The Contracting Parties,

Desiring to implement the principle of equality of rights for men and women contained in the Charter of the United Nations,

Recognizing that everyone has the right to take part in the government of his country directly or indirectly through freely chosen representatives, and has the right to equal access to public service in his country, and desiring to equalize the status of men and women in the enjoyment and exercise of political rights, in accordance with the provisions of the Charter of the United Nations and of the Universal Declaration of Human Rights,

Having resolved to conclude a Convention for this purpose,

Hereby agree as hereinafter provided:

Article I

Women shall be entitled to vote in all elections on equal terms with men, without any discrimination.

Article II

Women shall be eligible for election to all publicly elected bodies, established by national law, on equal terms with men, without any discrimination.

Article III

Women shall be entitled to hold public office and to exercise all public functions, established by national law, on equal terms with men, without any discrimination.

Article IV

1. This Convention shall be open for signature on behalf of any Member of the United Nations and also on behalf of any other State to which an invitation has been addressed by the General Assembly.

2. This Convention shall be ratified and the instruments of ratification shall be deposited with the Secretary-General of the United Nations.

Article V

1. This Convention shall be open for accession to all States referred to in paragraph 1 of Article IV.

2. Accession shall be effected by the deposit of an instrument of accession with the Secretary-General of the United Nations.

Article VI

1. This Convention shall come into force on the ninetieth day following the date of deposit of the sixth instrument of ratification or accession.

2. For each State ratifying or acceding to the Convention after the deposit of the sixth instrument of ratification or accession the Convention shall enter into force on the ninetieth day after deposit by such State of its instrument of ratification or accession.

Article VII

In the event that any State submits a reservation to any of the articles of this Convention at the time of signature, ratification or accession, the Secretary-General shall communicate the text of the reservation to all States which are or may become Parties to this Convention. Any State which objects to the reservation may, within a period of ninety days from the date of the said communication (or upon the date of its becoming a Party to the Convention), notify the Secretary-General that it does not accept it. In such case, the Convention shall not enter into force as between such State and the State making the reservation.

Article VIII

1. Any State may denounce this Convention by written notification to the Secretary-General of the United Nations. Denunciation shall take effect one year after the date of receipt of the notification by the Secretary-General.

2. This Convention shall cease to be in force as from the date when the denunciation which reduces the number of Parties to less than six becomes effective.

Article IX

Any dispute which may arise between any two or more Contracting States concerning the interpretation or application of this Convention, which is not settled by negotiation, shall at the request of any one of the parties to the dispute be referred to the International Court of Justice for decision, unless they agree to another mode of settlement.

Article X

The Secretary-General of the United Nations shall notify all Members of the United Nations and the non-member States contemplated in paragraph 1 of Article IV of this Convention of the following:

(a) Signatures and instruments of ratification received in accordance with Article IV;

(b) Instruments of accession received in accordance with Article V;

(c) The date upon which this Convention enters into force in accordance with Article VI;

(d) Communications and notifications received in accordance with Article VII;

(e) Notifications of denunciation received in accordance with paragraph 1 of Article VIII;

(f) Abrogation in accordance with paragraph 2 of Article VIII.

Article XI

1. This Convention, of which the Chinese, English, French, Russian and Spanish texts shall be equally authentic, shall be deposited in the archives of the United Nations.

2. The Secretary-General of the United Nations shall transmit a certified copy to all Members of the United Nations and to the non-member States contemplated in paragraph 1 of Article IV.

44. SLAVERY CONVENTION, 1926, AMENDED BY PROTOCOL, 1953

The Slavery Convention was signed on 25 September 1926 and entered into force on 9 March 1927. For the text in various languages, see 60 *LNTS* 253. The Protocol of Amendment was approved by General Assembly Resolution 794 (VIII) of 23 October 1953, opened for signature on 7 December 1953, and the Slavery Convention as amended by the Protocol entered into force on 7 July 1955. For the text in various languages, see 212 *UNTS* 17; the Preamble has been omitted from the text below.

There have been problems in defining slavery and associated practices, and the position has been improved by the Supplementary Convention, below, p. 335. See the decision of the High Court of Australia in the *The Queen v Tang* [2008] HCA 39; also *Hadijatou Mani Koraou v Republic of Niger* (ECOWAS Community Court of Justice judgment on protection from slavery), noted (2009) 103 *AJIL* 311 (ALLAIN, J.); *Siliadin v France*, Application no. 73316/01, European Court of Human Rights, 28 June 2005.

For the ILO Conventions on forced labour, below, pp. 564, 587. For developments, see the European Convention on Action against Trafficking in Human Beings, 2005, below, p. 848.

Further reading

ALLAIN, J., *The Slavery Conventions: The Travaux Préparatories of the 1926 League of Nations Convention and the 1956 United Nations Convention*, Leiden: Martinus Nijhoff, 2008.

——, 'On the Curious Disappearance of Human Servitude from General International Law', (2009) 11 *Journal of the History of International Law* 303.

TEXT

Article 1

For the purpose of the present Convention, the following definitions are agreed upon:

(1) Slavery is the status or condition of a person over whom any or all of the powers attaching to the right of ownership are exercised.

(2) The slave trade includes all acts involved in the capture, acquisition or disposal of a person with intent to reduce him to slavery; all acts involved in the acquisition of a slave with a view to selling or exchanging him; all acts of disposal by sale or exchange of a slave acquired with a view to being sold or exchanged, and, in general, every act of trade or transport in slaves.

Article 2

The High Contracting Parties undertake, each in respect of the territories placed under its sovereignty, jurisdiction, protection, suzerainty or tutelage, so far as they have not already taken the necessary steps:

- *(a)* To prevent and suppress the slave trade;
- *(b)* To bring about, progressively and as soon as possible, the complete abolition of slavery in all its forms.

Article 3

The High Contracting Parties undertake to adopt all appropriate measures with a view to preventing and suppressing the embarkation, disembarkation and transport of slaves in their territorial waters and upon all vessels flying their respective flags.

The High Contracting Parties undertake to negotiate as soon as possible a general Convention with regard to the slave trade which will give them rights and impose upon them duties of the same nature as those provided for in the Convention of June 17th, 1925, relative to the International Trade in Arms (Articles 12, 20, 21, 22, 23, 24, and paragraphs 3, 4 and 5 of Section II of Annex II), with the necessary adaptations, it being understood that this general Convention will not place the ships (even of small tonnage) of any High Contracting Parties in a position different from that of the other High Contracting Parties.

It is also understood that, before or after the coming into force of this general Convention the High Contracting Parties are entirely free to conclude between themselves, without, however, derogating from the principles laid down in the preceding paragraph, such special agreements as, by reason of their peculiar situation, might appear to be suitable in order to bring about as soon as possible the complete disappearance of the slave trade.

Article 4

The High Contracting Parties shall give to one another every assistance with the object of securing the abolition of slavery and the slave trade.

Article 5

The High Contracting Parties recognize that recourse to compulsory or forced labour may have grave consequences and undertake, each in respect of the territories placed under its sovereignty, jurisdiction, protection, suzerainty or tutelage, to take all necessary measures to prevent compulsory or forced labour from developing into conditions analogous to slavery.

It is agreed that:

(1) Subject to the transitional provisions laid down in paragraph (2) below, compulsory or forced labour may only be exacted for public purposes.

(2) In territories in which compulsory or forced labour for other than public purposes still survives, the High Contracting Parties shall endeavour progressively and as soon as possible to put an end to the practice. So long as such forced or compulsory labour exists, this labour shall invariably be of an exceptional character, shall always receive adequate remuneration, and shall not involve the removal of the labourers from their usual place of residence.

(3) In all cases, the responsibility for any recourse to compulsory or forced labour shall rest with the competent central authorities of the territory concerned.

Article 6

Those of the High Contracting Parties whose laws do not at present make adequate provision for the punishment of infractions of laws and regulations enacted with a view to giving effect to the purposes of the present Convention undertake to adopt the necessary measures in order that severe penalties may be imposed in respect of such infractions.

Article 7

The High Contracting Parties undertake to communicate to each other and to the Secretary-General of the League of Nations any laws and regulations which they may enact with a view to the application of the provisions of the present Convention.

Article 8

The High Contracting Parties agree that disputes arising between them relating to the interpretation or application of this Convention shall, if they cannot be settled by direct negotiation, be referred for decision to the Permanent Court of International Justice. In case either or both of the States Parties to such a dispute should not be parties to the Protocol of December 16th, 1920 relating to the Permanent Court of International Justice, the dispute shall be referred, at the choice of the Parties and in accordance with the constitutional procedure of each State either to the Permanent Court of International Justice or to a court of arbitration constituted in accordance with the Convention of October 18th, 1907, for the Pacific Settlement of International Disputes, or to some other court of arbitration.

Article 9

At the time of signature or of ratification or of accession, any High Contracting Party may declare that its acceptance of the present Convention does not bind some or all of the territories placed under its sovereignty, jurisdiction, protection, suzerainty or tutelage in respect of all or any provisions of the Convention; it may subsequently accede separately on behalf of any one of them or in respect of any provision to which any one of them is not a party.

Article 10

In the event of a High Contracting Party wishing to denounce the present Convention, the denunciation shall be notified in writing to the Secretary-General of the League of Nations, who will at once communicate a certified true copy of the notification to all the other High Contracting Parties, informing them of the date on which it was received.

The denunciation shall only have effect in regard to the notifying State, and one year after the notification has reached the Secretary-General of the League of Nations.

Denunciation may also be made separately in respect of any territory placed under its sovereignty, jurisdiction, protection, suzerainty or tutelage.

Article 11

The present Convention, which will bear this day's date and of which the French and English texts are both authentic, will remain open for signature by the States Members of the League of Nations until April 1st, 1927.

The Secretary-General of the League of Nations will subsequently bring the present Convention to the notice of States which have not signed it, including States which are not Members of the League of Nations, and invite them to accede thereto.

A State desiring to accede to the Convention shall notify its intention in writing to the Secretary-General of the League of Nations and transmit to him the instrument of accession, which shall be deposited in the archives of the League.

The Secretary-General shall immediately transmit to all the other High Contracting Parties a certified true copy of the notification and of the instrument of accession, informing them of the date on which he received them.

Article 12

The present Convention will be ratified and the instruments of ratification shall be deposited in the office of the Secretary-General of the League of Nations. The Secretary-General will inform all the High Contracting Parties of such deposit.

The Convention will come into operation for each State on the date of the deposit of its ratification or of its accession.

In faith whereof the Plenipotentiaries have signed the present Convention.

Done at Geneva the twenty-fifth day of September, One thousand nine hundred and twenty-six, in one copy, which will be deposited in the archives of the League of Nations. A certified copy shall be forwarded to each signatory State.

PROTOCOL AMENDING THE SLAVERY CONVENTION, 1953

The States Parties to the present Protocol,

Considering that under the Slavery Convention signed at Geneva on 25 September 1926 (hereinafter called 'the Convention') the League of Nations was invested with certain duties and functions, and

Considering that it is expedient that these duties and functions should be continued by the United Nations,

Have agreed as follows:

Article I

The States Parties to the present Protocol undertake that as between themselves they will, in accordance with the provisions of the Protocol, attribute full legal force and effect to and duly apply the amendments to the Convention set forth in the annex to the Protocol.

Article II

1. The present Protocol shall be open for signature or acceptance by any of the States Parties to the Convention to which the Secretary-General has communicated for this purpose a copy of the Protocol.

2. States may become Parties to the present Protocol by:

   (a) Signature without reservation as to acceptance;

   (b) Signature with reservation as to acceptance, followed by acceptance;

   (c) Acceptance.

3. Acceptance shall be effected by the deposit of a formal instrument with the Secretary-General of the United Nations.

Article III

1. The present Protocol shall come into force on the date on which two States shall have become Parties thereto, and shall thereafter come into force in respect of each State upon the date on which it becomes a Party to the Protocol.

2. The amendments set forth in the annex to the present Protocol shall come into force when twenty-three States shall have become Parties to the Protocol, and consequently

any State becoming a Party to the Convention, after the amendments thereto have come into force, shall become a Party to the Convention as so amended.

Article IV

In accordance with paragraph 1 of Article 102 of the Charter of the United Nations and the regulations pursuant thereto adopted by the General Assembly, the Secretary-General of the United Nations is authorized to effect registration of the present Protocol and of the amendments made in the Convention by the Protocol on the respective dates of their entry into force and to publish the Protocol and the amended text of the Convention as soon as possible after registration.

Article V

The present Protocol, of which the Chinese, English, French, Russian and Spanish texts are equally authentic, shall be deposited in the archives of the United Nations Secretariat. The texts of the Convention to be amended in accordance with the annex being authentic in the English and French languages only, the English and French texts of the annex shall be equally authentic, and the Chinese, Russian and Spanish texts shall be translations. The Secretary-General shall prepare certified copies of the Protocol, including the annex, for communication to States Parties to the Convention, as well as to all other States Members of the United Nations. He shall likewise prepare for communication to States, including States not Members of the United Nations, upon the entry into force of the amendments as provided in article III, certified copies of the Convention as so amended.

ANNEX

In article 7 'the Secretary-General of the United Nations' *shall be substituted for* 'the Secretary-General of the League of Nations'.

In article 8 'the International Court of Justice' *shall be substituted for* 'the Permanent Court of International Justice', and 'the Statute of the International Court of Justice' *shall be substituted for* 'the Protocol of December 16th, 1920, relating to the Permanent Court of International Justice'.

In the first and second paragraphs of article 10 'the United Nations' *shall be substituted for* 'the League of Nations'.

The last three paragraphs of article 11 shall be *deleted* and the following *substituted*:

'The present Convention shall be open to accession by all States, including States which are not Members of the United Nations, to which the Secretary-General of the United Nations shall have communicated a certified copy of the Convention.

'Accession shall be effected by the deposit of a formal instrument with the Secretary-General of the United Nations, who shall give notice thereof to all States Parties to the Convention and to all other States contemplated in the present article, informing them of the date on which each such instrument of accession was received in deposit.'

In article 12 'the United Nations' *shall be substituted for* 'the League of Nations'.

45. SUPPLEMENTARY CONVENTION ON THE ABOLITION OF SLAVERY, THE SLAVE TRADE, AND INSTITUTIONS AND PRACTICES SIMILAR TO SLAVERY, 1956

The Supplementary Convention was adopted on 7 September 1956 by a United Nations Conference, convened by Economic and Social Council resolution 608(XXI) of 30 April 1956; it entered into force on 30 April 1957. For the text in various languages, see 266 *UNTS* 3.

Further reading

ALLAIN, J., *The Slavery Conventions: The Travaux Préparatoires of the 1926 League of Nations Convention and the 1956 United Nations Convention*, Leiden: Martinus Nijhoff, 2008.
GUTTERIDGE, J., 'Supplementary Slavery Convention, 1956', (1957) 6 *ICLQ* 449.
SCHREIBER, M., 'Convention supplémentaire des Nations Unies relative à l'abolition de l'esclavage, la traite des esclaves et des institutions et pratiques analogues à l'esclavage', 3 *Annuaire français de droit international*, 1956, 547–57.

TEXT

Preamble

The States Parties to the present Convention
Considering that freedom is the birthright of every human being;
Mindful that the peoples of the United Nations reaffirmed in the Charter their faith in the dignity and worth of the human person;
Considering that the Universal Declaration of Human Rights, proclaimed by the General Assembly of the United Nations as a common standard of achievement for all peoples and all nations, states that no one shall be held in slavery or servitude and that slavery and the slave trade shall be prohibited in all their forms;
Recognizing that, since the conclusion of the Slavery Convention signed at Geneva on 25 September 1926, which was designed to secure the abolition of slavery and of the slave trade, further progress has been made towards this end;
Having regard to the Forced Labour Convention of 1930 and to subsequent action by the International Labour Organization in regard to forced or compulsory labour;
Being aware, however, that slavery, the slave trade and institutions and practices similar to slavery have not yet been eliminated in all parts of the world;
Having decided, therefore, that the Convention of 1926, which remains operative, should now be augmented by the conclusion of a supplementary convention designed to intensify national as well as international efforts towards the abolition of slavery, the slave trade and institutions and practices similar to slavery;
Have agreed as follows:

SECTION I
INSTITUTIONS AND PRACTICES SIMILAR TO SLAVERY

Article 1

Each of the States Parties to this Convention shall take all practicable and necessary legislative and other measures to bring about progressively and as soon as possible the complete abolition or abandonment of the following institutions and practices, where they still exist and whether or not they are covered by the definition of slavery contained in article 1 of the Slavery Convention signed at Geneva on 25 September 1926:

(a) Debt bondage, that is to say, the status or condition arising from a pledge by a debtor of his personal services or of those of a person under his control as security for a debt, if the value of those services as reasonably assessed is not applied towards the liquidation of the debt or the length and nature of those services are not respectively limited and defined;

(b) Serfdom, that is to say, the condition or status of a tenant who is by law, custom or agreement bound to live and labour on land belonging to another person and to render some determinate service to such other person, whether for reward or not, and is not free to change his status;

(c) Any institution or practice whereby:

   (i) A woman, without the right to refuse, is promised or given in marriage on payment of a consideration in money or in kind to her parents, guardian, family or any other person or group; or

   (ii) The husband of a woman, his family, or his clan, has the right to transfer her to another person for value received or otherwise; or

   (iii) A woman on the death of her husband is liable to be inherited by another person;

(d) Any institution or practice whereby a child or young person under the age of 18 years is delivered by either or both of his natural parents or by his guardian to another person, whether for reward or not, with a view to the exploitation of the child or young person or of his labour.

Article 2

With a view to bringing to an end the institutions and practices mentioned in Article 1 (c) of this Convention, the States Parties undertake to prescribe, where appropriate, suitable minimum ages of marriage, to encourage the use of facilities whereby the consent of both parties to a marriage may be freely expressed in the presence of a competent civil or religious authority, and to encourage the registration of marriages.

SECTION II
THE SLAVE TRADE

Article 3

1. The act of conveying or attempting to convey slaves from one country to another by whatever means of transport, or of being accessory thereto, shall be a criminal offence

under the laws of the States Parties to this Convention and persons convicted thereof shall be liable to very severe penalties.

2. *(a)* The States Parties shall take all effective measures to prevent ships and aircraft authorized to fly their flags from conveying slaves and to punish persons guilty of such acts or of using national flags for that purpose.

   (b) The States Parties shall take all effective measures to ensure that their ports, airfields and coasts are not used for the conveyance of slaves.

3. The States Parties to this Convention shall exchange information in order to ensure the practical co-ordination of the measures taken by them in combating the slave trade and shall inform each other of every case of the slave trade, and of every attempt to commit this criminal offence, which comes to their notice.

Article 4

Any slave who takes refuge on board any vessel of a State Party to this Convention shall *ipso facto* be free.

SECTION III
SLAVERY AND INSTITUTIONS AND PRACTICES
SIMILAR TO SLAVERY

Article 5

In a country where the abolition or abandonment of slavery, or of the institutions or practices mentioned in Article 1 of this Convention, is not yet complete, the act of mutilating, branding or otherwise marking a slave or a person of servile status in order to indicate his status, or as a punishment, or for any other reason, or of being accessory thereto, shall be a criminal offence under the laws of the States Parties to this Convention and persons convicted thereof shall be liable to punishment.

Article 6

1. The act of enslaving another person or of inducing another person to give himself or a person dependent upon him into slavery, or of attempting these acts, or being accessory thereto, or being a party to a conspiracy to accomplish any such acts, shall be a criminal offence under the laws of the States Parties to this Convention and persons convicted thereof shall be liable to punishment.

2. Subject to the provisions of the introductory paragraph of Article 1 of this Convention, the provisions of paragraph 1 of the present article shall also apply to the act of inducing another person to place himself or a person dependent upon him into the servile status resulting from any of the institutions or practices mentioned in Article 1, to any attempt to perform such acts, to bring accessory thereto, and to being a party to a conspiracy to accomplish any such acts.

SECTION IV
DEFINITIONS

Article 7

For the purposes of the present Convention:

(a) 'Slavery' means, as defined in the Slavery Convention of 1926, the status or condition of a person over whom any or all of the powers attaching to the right of ownership are exercised, and 'slave' means a person in such condition or status;

(b) 'A person of servile status' means a person in the condition or status resulting from any of the institutions or practices mentioned in Article 1 of this Convention;

(c) 'Slave trade' means and includes all acts involved in the capture, acquisition or disposal of a person with intent to reduce him to slavery; all acts involved in the acquisition of a slave with a view to selling or exchanging him; all acts of disposal by sale of exchange of a person acquired with a view to being sold or exchanged; and, in general, every act of trade or transport in slaves by whatever means of conveyance.

SECTION V
CO-OPERATION BETWEEN STATES PARTIES AND COMMUNICATION OF INFORMATION

Article 8

1. The States Parties to this Convention undertake to co-operate with each other and with the United Nations to give effect to the foregoing provisions.

2. The Parties undertake to communicate to the Secretary-General of the United Nations copies of any laws, regulations and administrative measures enacted or put into effect to implement the provisions of this Convention.

3. The Secretary-General shall communicate the information received under paragraph 2 of this article to the other Parties and to the Economic and Social Council as part of the documentation for any discussion which the Council might undertake with a view to making further recommendations for the abolition of slavery, the slave trade or the institutions and practices which are the subject of this Convention.

SECTION VI
FINAL CLAUSES

Article 9

No reservations may be made to this Convention.

Article 10

Any dispute between States Parties to this Convention relating to its interpretation or application, which is not settled by negotiation, shall be referred to the International Court of Justice at the request of any one of the parties to the dispute, unless the parties concerned agree on another mode of settlement.

Article 11

1. This Convention shall be open until 1 July 1957 for signature by any State Member of the United Nations or of a specialized agency. It shall be subject to ratification by the signatory States, and the instruments of ratification shall be deposited with the Secretary-General of the United Nations, who shall inform each signatory and acceding State.

2. After 1 July 1957 this Convention shall be open for accession by any State Member of the United Nations or of a specialized agency, or by any other State to which an invitation to accede has been addressed by the General Assembly of the United Nations. Accession shall be effected by the deposit of a formal instrument with the Secretary-General of the United Nations, who shall inform each signatory and acceding State.

Article 12

1. This Convention shall apply to all non-self-governing, trust, colonial and other non-metropolitan territories for the international relations of which any State Party is responsible; the Party concerned shall, subject to the provisions of paragraph 2 of this article, at the time of signature, ratification or accession declare the non-metropolitan territory or territories to which the Convention shall apply *ipso facto* as a result of such signature, ratification or accession.

2. In any case in which the previous consent of a non-metropolitan territory is required by the constitutional laws or practices of the Party or of the non-metropolitan territory, the Party concerned shall endeavour to secure the needed consent of the non-metropolitan territory within the period of twelve months from the date of signature of the Convention by the metropolitan State, and when such consent has been obtained the Party shall notify the Secretary-General. This Convention shall apply to the territory or territories named in such notification from the date of its receipt by the Secretary-General.

3. After the expiry of the twelve month period mentioned in the preceding paragraph, the States Parties concerned shall inform the Secretary-General of the results of the consultations with those non-metropolitan territories for whose international relations they are responsible and whose consent to the application of this Convention may have been withheld.

Article 13

1. This Convention shall enter into force on the date on which two States have become Parties thereto.

2. It shall thereafter enter into force with respect to each State and territory on the date of deposit of the instrument of ratification or accession of that State or notification of application to that territory.

Article 14

1. The application of this Convention shall be divided into successive periods of three years, of which the first shall begin on the date of entry into force of the Convention in accordance with paragraph 1 of Article 13.

2. Any State Party may denounce this Convention by a notice addressed by that State to the Secretary-General not less than six months before the expiration of the current three-year period. The Secretary-General shall notify all other Parties of each such notice and the date of the receipt thereof.

3. Denunciations shall take effect at the expiration of the current three-year period.

4. In cases where, in accordance with the provisions of Article 12, this Convention has become applicable to a non-metropolitan territory of a Party, that Party may at any time thereafter, with the consent of the territory concerned, give notice to the Secretary-General of the United Nations denouncing this Convention separately in respect of that territory. The denunciation shall take effect one year after the date of the receipt of such notice by the Secretary-General, who shall notify all other Parties of such notice and the date of the receipt thereof.

Article 15

This Convention, of which the Chinese, English, French, Russian and Spanish texts are equally authentic, shall be deposited in the archives of the United Nations Secretariat. The Secretary-General shall prepare a certified copy thereof for communication to States Parties to this Convention, as well as to all other States Members of the United Nations and of the specialized agencies.

In witness whereof the undersigned, being duly authorized thereto by their respective Governments, have signed this Convention on the date appearing opposite their respective signatures.

Done at the European Office of the United Nations at Geneva, this seventh day of September one thousand nine hundred and fifty-six.

46. CONVENTION RELATING TO THE STATUS
OF STATELESS PERSONS, 1954

Statelessness continues to be a very serious problem, but measures to reduce its incidence have not readily found favour with States. The persistence of statelessness has necessitated the creation of a regime which will give stateless persons a stable basis of life in host countries. A Protocol relating to the Status of Stateless Persons was intended also to be adopted by the Conference of Plenipotentiaries which agreed the 1951 Convention relating to the Status of Refugees (above, p. 312), but the matter was deferred to a later conference which met in New York from 13–23 September 1954. The Stateless Persons Convention came into force on 6 June 1960. For the text in English and French, see 360 *UNTS* 117. The text below does not include the Schedule on the issue of travel documents to stateless persons under Article 28, which is similar in many details to that included in the 1951 Convention relating to the Status of Refugees, above, p. 324.

See also the Convention on the Reduction of Statelessness, 1961 (below, p. 352); the European Convention on Nationality, 1997 (below, p. 827); and the Declaration of Articles on Nationality of Natural Persons in relation to the Succession of States, 2000 (above, p. 249); and the European Convention on the Avoidance of Statelessness in Relation to State Succession (below, p. 867).

Further reading

BATCHELOR, C., 'Stateless Persons: Some Gaps in International Protection', (1995) 7 *IJRL* 232.
——, 'Statelessness and the Problem of Resolving Nationality Status', (1998) 10 *IJRL* 156.
MANLY, M., 'The Spirit of Geneva—Traditional and New Actors in the Field of Statelessness', (2007) 26 *Refugee Survey Quarterly* 255.
UNITED NATIONS, *A Study of Statelessness*, New York: United Nations, 1949.
WEIS, P., *Nationality and Statelessness in International Law*, London: Stevens, 1956; Alphen aan den Rijn: Sijthoff and Noordhof, 2nd edn., 1979.
—— 'The Status of Stateless Persons', (1961) 10 *ICLQ* 255.
WEISSBRODT, D. and COLLINS, C., 'The human rights of stateless persons', (2006) 28 *Human Rights Quarterly* 245–76.

TEXT

Preamble

The High Contracting Parties,

Considering that the Charter of the United Nations and the Universal Declaration of Human Rights approved on 10 December 1948 by the General Assembly of the United Nations have affirmed the principle that human beings shall enjoy fundamental rights and freedoms without discrimination,

Considering that the United Nations has, on various occasions, manifested its profound concern for stateless persons and endeavoured to assure stateless persons the widest possible exercise of these fundamental rights and freedoms,

Considering that only those stateless persons who are also refugees are covered by the Convention relating to the Status of Refugees of 28 July 1951, and that there are many stateless persons who are not covered by that Convention,

Considering that it is desirable to regulate and improve the status of stateless persons by an international agreement,

Have agreed as follows:

CHAPTER I

General Provisions

Article 1—Definition of the term 'stateless person'

1. For the purpose of this Convention, the term 'stateless person' means a person who is not considered as a national by any State under the operation of its law.

2. This Convention shall not apply:

(i) To persons who are at present receiving from organs or agencies of the United Nations other than the United Nations High Commissioner for Refugees protection or assistance so long as they are receiving such protection or assistance;

(ii) To persons who are recognized by the competent authorities of the country in which they have taken residence as having the rights and obligations which are attached to the possession of the nationality of that country;

(iii) To persons with respect to whom there are serious reasons for considering that:

(a) They have committed a crime against peace, a war crime, or a crime against humanity, as defined in the international instruments drawn up to make provisions in respect of such crimes;

(b) They have committed a serious non-political crime outside the country of their residence prior to their admission to that country;

(c) They have been guilty of acts contrary to the purposes and principles of the United Nations.

Article 2—General obligations

Every stateless person has duties to the country in which he finds himself, which require in particular that he conform to its laws and regulations as well as to measures taken for the maintenance of public order.

Article 3—Non-discrimination

The Contracting States shall apply the provisions of this Convention to stateless persons without discrimination as to race, religion or country of origin.

Article 4—Religion

The Contracting States shall accord to stateless persons within their territories treatment at least as favourable as that accorded to their nationals with respect to freedom to practise their religion and freedom as regards the religious education of their children.

Article 5—Rights granted apart from this Convention

Nothing in this Convention shall be deemed to impair any rights and benefits granted by a Contracting State to stateless persons apart from this Convention.

Article 6—The term 'in the same circumstances'

For the purpose of this Convention, the term ' in the same circumstances' implies that any requirements (including requirements as to length and conditions of sojourn or residence) which the particular individual would have to fulfil for the enjoyment of the right in question, if he were not a stateless person, must be fulfilled by him, with the exception of requirements which by their nature a stateless person is incapable of fulfilling.

Article 7—Exemption from reciprocity

1. Except where this Convention contains more favourable provisions, a Contracting State shall accord to stateless persons the same treatment as is accorded to aliens generally.

2. After a period of three years' residence, all stateless persons shall enjoy exemption from legislative reciprocity in the territory of the Contracting States.

3. Each Contracting State shall continue to accord to stateless persons the rights and benefits to which they were already entitled, in the absence of reciprocity, at the date of entry into force of this Convention for that State.

4. The Contracting States shall consider favourably the possibility of according to stateless persons, in the absence of reciprocity, rights and benefits beyond those to which they are entitled according to paragraphs 2 and 3, and to extending exemption from reciprocity to stateless persons who do not fulfil the conditions provided for in paragraphs 2 and 3.

5. The provisions of paragraphs 2 and 3 apply both to the rights and benefits referred to in Articles 13, 18, 19, 21 and 22 of this Convention and to rights and benefits for which this Convention does not provide.

Article 8—Exemption from exceptional measures

With regard to exceptional measures which may be taken against the person, property or interests of nationals or former nationals of a foreign State, the Contracting States shall not apply such measures to a stateless person solely on account of his having previously possessed the nationality of the foreign State in question. Contracting States which, under their legislation, are prevented from applying the general principle expressed in this article shall, in appropriate cases, grant exemptions in favour of such stateless persons.

Article 9—Provisional measures

Nothing in this Convention shall prevent a Contracting State, in time of war or other grave and exceptional circumstances, from taking provisionally measures which it considers to be essential to the national security in the case of a particular person, pending a determination by the Contracting State that that person is in fact a stateless person and that the continuance of such measures is necessary in his case in the interests of national security.

Article 10—Continuity of residence

1. Where a stateless person has been forcibly displaced during the Second World War and removed to the territory of a Contracting State, and is resident there, the period of such enforced sojourn shall be considered to have been lawful residence within that territory.

2. Where a stateless person has been forcibly displaced during the Second World War from the territory of a Contracting State and has, prior to the date of entry into force of this Convention, returned there for the purpose of taking up residence, the period of residence before and after such enforced displacement shall be regarded as one uninterrupted period for any purposes for which uninterrupted residence is required.

Article 11—Stateless seamen

In the case of stateless persons regularly serving as crew members on board a ship flying the flag of a Contracting State, that State shall give sympathetic consideration to their establishment on its territory and the issue of travel documents to them or their temporary admission to its territory particularly with a view to facilitating their establishment in another country.

CHAPTER II

Juridical Status

Article 12—Personal status

1. The personal status of a stateless person shall be governed by the law of the country of his domicile or, if he has no domicile, by the law of the country of his residence.

2. Rights previously acquired by a stateless person and dependent on personal status, more particularly rights attaching to marriage, shall be respected by a Contracting State, subject to compliance, if this be necessary, with the formalities required by the law of that State, provided that the right in question is one which would have been recognized by the law of that State had he not become stateless.

Article 13—Movable and immovable property

The Contracting States shall accord to a stateless person treatment as favourable as possible and, in any event, not less favourable than that accorded to aliens generally in the same circumstances, as regards the acquisition of movable and immovable property and other rights pertaining thereto, and to leases and other contracts relating to movable and immovable property.

Article 14—Artistic rights and industrial property

In respect of the protection of industrial property, such as inventions, designs or models, trade marks, trade names, and of rights in literary, artistic and scientific works, a stateless person shall be accorded in the country in which he has his habitual residence the same protection as is accorded to nationals of that country. In the territory of any other Contracting State, he shall be accorded the same protection as is accorded in that territory to nationals of the country in which he has his habitual residence.

Article 15—Right of association

As regards non-political and non-profit-making associations and trade unions the Contracting States shall accord to stateless persons lawfully staying in their territory treatment as favourable as possible, and in any event, not less favourable than that accorded to aliens generally in the same circumstances.

Article 16—Access to courts

1. A stateless person shall have free access to the courts of law on the territory of all Contracting States.

2. A stateless person shall enjoy in the Contracting State in which he has his habitual residence the same treatment as a national in matters pertaining to access to the courts, including legal assistance and exemption from *cautio judicatum solvi*.

3. A stateless person shall be accorded in the matters referred to in paragraph 2 in countries other than that in which he has his habitual residence the treatment granted to a national of the country of his habitual residence.

CHAPTER III

Gainful Employment

Article 17—Wage-earning employment

1. The Contracting States shall accord to stateless persons lawfully staying in their territory treatment as favourable as possible and, in any event, not less favourable that that accorded to aliens generally in the same circumstances, as regards the right to engage in wage-earning employment.

2. The Contracting States shall give sympathetic consideration to assimilating the rights of all stateless persons with regard to wage-earning employment to those of nationals, and in particular of those stateless persons who have entered their territory pursuant to programmes of labour recruitment or under immigration schemes.

Article 18—Self-employment

The Contracting States shall accord to a stateless person lawfully in their territory treatment as favourable as possible and, in any event, not less favourable than that accorded to aliens generally in the same circumstances, as regards the right to engage on his own account in agriculture, industry, handicrafts and commerce and to establish commercial and industrial companies.

Article 19—Liberal professions

Each Contracting State shall accord to stateless persons lawfully staying in their territory who hold diplomas recognized by the competent authorities of that State, and who are desirous of practising a liberal profession, treatment as favourable as possible and, in any event, not less favourable than that accorded to aliens generally in the same circumstances.

CHAPTER IV

Welfare

Article 20—Rationing

Where a rationing system exists, which applies to the population at large and regulates the general distribution of products in short supply, stateless persons shall be accorded the same treatment as nationals.

Article 21—Housing

As regards housing, the Contracting States, in so far as the matter is regulated by laws or regulations or is subject to the control of public authorities, shall accord to stateless persons lawfully staying in their territory treatment as favourable as possible and, in any event, not less favourable than that accorded to aliens generally in the same circumstances.

Article 22—Public education

1. The Contracting States shall accord to stateless persons the same treatment as is accorded to nationals with respect to elementary education.

2. The Contracting States shall accord to stateless persons treatment as favourable as possible and, in any event, not less favourable than that accorded to aliens generally in the same circumstances, with respect to education other than elementary education and, in particular, as regards access to studies, the recognition of foreign school certificates, diplomas and degrees, the remission of fees and charges and the award of scholarships.

Article 23—Public relief

The Contracting States shall accord to stateless persons lawfully staying in their territory the same treatment with respect to public relief and assistance as is accorded to their nationals.

Article 24—Labour legislation and social security

1. The Contracting States shall accord to stateless persons lawfully staying in their territory the same treatment as is accorded to nationals in respect of the following matters:

 (a) In so far as such matters are governed by laws or regulations or are subject to the control of administrative authorities; remuneration, including family allowances where these form part of remuneration, hours of work, overtime arrangements, holidays with pay, restrictions on home work, minimum age of employment, apprenticeship and training, women's work and the work of young persons, and the enjoyment of the benefits of collective bargaining;

 (b) Social security (legal provisions in respect of employment injury, occupational diseases, maternity, sickness, disability, old age, death, unemployment, family responsibilities and any other contingency which, according to national laws or regulations, is covered by a social security scheme), subject to the following limitations:

 (i) There may be appropriate arrangements for the maintenance of acquired rights and rights in course of acquisition;

 (ii) National laws or regulations of the country of residence may prescribe special arrangements concerning benefits or portions of benefits which are payable wholly out of public funds, and concerning allowances paid to persons who do not fulfil the contribution conditions prescribed for the award of a normal pension.

2. The right to compensation for the death of a stateless person resulting from employment injury or from occupational disease shall not be affected by the fact that the residence of the beneficiary is outside the territory of the Contracting State.

3. The Contracting States shall extend to stateless persons the benefits of agreements concluded between them, or which may be concluded between them in the future, concerning the maintenance of acquired rights and rights in the process of acquisition in regard to social security, subject only to the conditions which apply to nationals of the States signatory to the agreements in question.

4. The Contracting States will give sympathetic consideration to extending to stateless persons so far as possible the benefits of similar agreements which may at any time be in force between such Contracting States and non-contracting States.

CHAPTER V

Administrative Measures

Article 25—Administrative assistance

1. When the exercise of a right by a stateless person would normally require the assistance of authorities of a foreign country to whom he cannot have recourse, the Contracting State in whose territory he is residing shall arrange that such assistance be afforded to him by their own authorities.

2. The authority or authorities mentioned in paragraph 1 shall deliver or cause to be delivered under their supervision to stateless persons such documents or certifications as would normally be delivered to aliens by or through their national authorities.

3. Documents or certifications so delivered shall stand in the stead of the official instruments delivered to aliens by or through their national authorities and shall be given credence in the absence of proof to the contrary.

4. Subject to such exceptional treatment as may be granted to indigent persons, fees may be charged for the services mentioned herein, but such fees shall be moderate and commensurate with those charged to nationals for similar services.

5. The provisions of this article shall be without prejudice to Articles 27 and 28.

Article 26—Freedom of movement

Each Contracting State shall accord to stateless persons lawfully in its territory the right to choose their place of residence and to move freely within its territory, subject to any regulations applicable to aliens generally in the same circumstances.

Article 27—Identity papers

The Contracting States shall issue identity papers to any stateless person in their territory who does not possess a valid travel document.

Article 28—Travel documents

The Contracting States shall issue to stateless persons lawfully staying in their territory travel documents for the purpose of travel outside their territory, unless compelling reasons of national security or public order otherwise require, and the provisions of the Schedule to this Convention shall apply with respect to such documents. The Contracting States may issue such a travel document to any other stateless person in their territory; they shall in particular give sympathetic consideration to the issue of such a travel document to stateless persons in their territory who are unable to obtain a travel document from the country of their lawful residence.

Article 29—Fiscal charges

1. The Contracting States shall not impose upon stateless persons duties, charges or taxes, of any description whatsoever, other or higher than those which are or may be levied on their nationals in similar situations.

2. Nothing in the above paragraph shall prevent the application to stateless persons of the laws and regulations concerning charges in respect of the issue to aliens of administrative documents including identity papers.

Article 30—Transfer of assets

1. A Contracting State shall, in conformity with its laws and regulations, permit stateless persons to transfer assets which they have brought into its territory, to another country where they have been admitted for the purposes of resettlement.

2. A Contracting State shall give sympathetic consideration to the application of stateless persons for permission to transfer assets wherever they may be and which are necessary for their resettlement in another country to which they have been admitted.

Article 31—Expulsion

1. The Contracting States shall not expel a stateless person lawfully in their territory save on grounds of national security or public order.

2. The expulsion of such a stateless person shall be only in pursuance of a decision reached in accordance with due process of law. Except where compelling reasons of national security otherwise require, the stateless person shall be allowed to submit evidence to clear himself, and to appeal to and be represented for the purpose before competent authority or a person or persons specially designated by the competent authority.

3. The Contracting States shall allow such a stateless person a reasonable period within which to seek legal admission into another country. The Contracting States reserve the right to apply during that period such internal measures as they may deem necessary.

Article 32—Naturalization

The Contracting States shall as far as possible facilitate the assimilation and naturalization of stateless persons. They shall in particular make every effort to expedite naturalization proceedings and to reduce as far as possible the charges and costs of such proceedings.

CHAPTER VI

Final Clauses

Article 33—Information on national legislation

The Contracting States shall communicate to the Secretary-General of the United Nations the laws and regulations which they may adopt to ensure the application of this Convention.

Article 34—Settlement of disputes

Any dispute between Parties to this Convention relating to its interpretation or application, which cannot be settled by other means, shall be referred to the International Court of Justice at the request of any one of the parties to the dispute.

Article 35—*Signature, ratification and accession*

1. This Convention shall be open for signature at the Headquarters of the United Nations until 31 December 1955.

2. It shall be open for signature on behalf of:

   (a) Any State Member of the United Nations;

   (b) Any other State invited to attend the United Nations Conference on the Status of Stateless Persons; and

   (c) Any State to which an invitation to sign or to accede may be addressed by the General Assembly of the United Nations.

3. It shall be ratified and the instruments of ratification shall be deposited with the Secretary-General of the United Nations.

4. It shall be open for accession by the States referred to in paragraph 2 of this article. Accession shall be effected by the deposit of an instrument of accession with the Secretary-General of the United Nations.

Article 36—*Territorial application clause*

1. Any State may, at the time of signature, ratification or accession, declare that this Convention shall extend to all or any of the territories for the international relations of which it is responsible. Such a declaration shall take effect when the Convention enters into force for the State concerned.

2. At any time thereafter any such extension shall be made by notification addressed to the Secretary-General of the United Nations and shall take effect as from the ninetieth day after the day of receipt by the Secretary-General of the United Nations of this notification, or as from the date of entry into force of the Convention for the State concerned, whichever is the later.

3. With respect to those territories to which this Convention is not extended at the time of signature, ratification or accession, each State concerne d shall consider the possibility of taking the necessary steps in order to extend the application of this Convention to such territories, subject, where necessary for constitutional reasons, to the consent of the Governments of such territories.

Article 37—*Federal clause*

In the case of a Federal or non-unitary State, the following provisions shall apply

   (a) With respect to those articles of this Convention that come within the legislative jurisdiction of the federal legislative authority, the obligations of the Federal Government shall to this extent be the same as those of Parties which are not Federal States;

   (b) With respect to those articles of this Convention that come within the legislative jurisdiction of constituent States, provinces or cantons which are not, under the constitutional system of the Federation, bound to take legislative action, the Federal Government shall bring such articles with a favourable recommendation to the notice of the appropriate authorities of States, provinces or cantons at the earliest possible moment;

   (c) A Federal State Party to this Convention shall, at the request of any other Contracting State transmitted through the Secretary-General of the United Nations, supply a statement of the law and practice of the Federation and its constituent units in regard to any particular provision of the Convention showing the extent to which effect has been given to that provision by legislative or other action.

Article 38—Reservations

1. At the time of signature, ratification or accession, any State may make reservations to articles of the Convention other than to Articles 1, 3, 4, 16 (1) and 33 to 42 inclusive.

2. Any State making a reservation in accordance with paragraph 1 of this article may at any time withdraw the reservation by a communication to that effect addressed to the Secretary-General of the United Nations.

Article 39—Entry into force

1. This Convention shall come into force on the ninetieth day following the day of deposit of the sixth instrument of ratification or accession.

2. For each State ratifying or acceding to the Convention after the deposit of the sixth instrument of ratification or accession, the Convention shall enter into force on the ninetieth day following the date of deposit by such State of its instrument of ratification or accession.

Article 40—Denunciation

1. Any Contracting State may denounce this Convention at any time by a notification addressed to the Secretary-General of the United Nations.

2. Such denunciation shall take effect for the Contracting State concerned one year from the date upon which it is received by the Secretary-General of the United Nations.

3. Any State which has made a declaration or notification under Article 36 may, at any time thereafter, by a notification to the Secretary-General of the United Nations, declare that the Convention shall cease to extend to such territory one year after the date of receipt of the notification by the Secretary-General.

Article 41—Revision

1. Any Contracting State may request revision of this Convention at any time by a notification addressed to the Secretary-General of the United Nations.

2. The General Assembly of the United Nations shall recommend the steps, if any, to be taken in respect of such request.

Article 42—Notifications by the Secretary-General of the United Nations

The Secretary-General of the United Nations shall inform all Members of the United Nations and non-member States referred to in Article 35:

   (a) Of signatures, ratifications and accessions in accordance with Article 35;

   (b) Of declarations and notifications in accordance with Article 36;

   (c) Of reservations and withdrawals in accordance with Article 38;

   (d) Of the date on which this Convention will come into force in accordance with Article 39;

    (e)   Of denunciations and notifications in accordance with Article 40;

    (f)   Of request for revision in accordance with Article 41.

In faith whereof the undersigned, duly authorized, have signed this Convention on behalf of their respective Governments.

Done at New York, this twenty-eighth day of September, one thousand nine hundred and fifty-four, in a single copy, of which the English, French and Spanish texts are equally authentic and which shall remain deposited in the archives of the United Nations, and certified true copies of which shall be delivered to all Members of the United Nations and to the non-member States referred to in Article 35.

[Schedule on travel documents omitted]

47. CONVENTION ON THE REDUCTION OF STATELESSNESS, 1961

The Convention was adopted by the UN Conference on the Elimination or Reduction of Future Statelessness, 24 March–18 April 1959 and 15–28 August 1961; it entered into force on 13 December 1975. For the text, see 989 *UNTS* 175. The Office of the United Nations High Commissioner for Refugees has been appointed to undertake the functions foreseen under Article 11; see General Assembly Resolution 3274 (XXIX), 10 December 1974; also, UNHCR Executive Committee, 'Conclusion on the Identification, Prevention and Reduction of Statelessness and Protection of Stateless Persons', *Report* of the 57th Session: UN doc. A/AC.96/1035, 10 October 2006, para. 18.

Further reading

UNITED NATIONS HIGH COMMISSIONER FOR REFUGEES, *Statelessness: An Analytical Framework for Prevention, Reduction and Protection*, Geneva: UNHCR, 2009.

TEXT

The Contracting States,

Acting in pursuance of resolution 896 (IX), adopted by the General Assembly of the United Nations on 4 December 1954,

Considering it desirable to reduce statelessness by international agreement,

Have agreed as follows:

Article 1

1. A Contracting State shall grant its nationality to a person born in its territory who would otherwise be stateless. Such nationality shall be granted:

 (a) At birth, by operation of law, or

 (b) Upon an application being lodged with the appropriate authority, by or on behalf of the person concerned, in the manner prescribed by the national law. Subject to the provisions of paragraph 2 of this article, no such application may be rejected.

 A Contracting State which provides for the grant of its nationality in accordance with subparagraph (b) of this paragraph may also provide for the grant of its nationality by operation of law at such age and subject to such conditions as may be prescribed by the national law.

2. A Contracting State may make the grant of its nationality in accordance with subparagraph (b) of paragraph 1 of this article subject to one or more of the following conditions:

 (a) That the application is lodged during a period, fixed by the Contracting State, beginning not later than at the age of eighteen years and ending not earlier than at the age of twenty-one years, so, however, that the person concerned shall be allowed at least one year during which he may himself make the application without having to obtain legal authorization to do so;

(b) That the person concerned has habitually resided in the territory of the Contracting State for such period as may be fixed by that State, not exceeding five years immediately preceding the lodging of the application nor ten years in all;

(c) That the person concerned has neither been convicted of an offence against national security nor has been sentenced to imprisonment for a term of five years or more on a criminal charge;

(d) That the person concerned has always been stateless.

3. Notwithstanding the provisions of paragraphs 1 (b) and 2 of this article, a child born in wedlock in the territory of a Contracting State, whose mother has the nationality of that State, shall acquire at birth that nationality if it otherwise would be stateless.

4. A Contracting State shall grant its nationality to a person who would otherwise be stateless and who is unable to acquire the nationality of the Contracting State in whose territory he was born because he has passed the age for lodging his application or has not fulfilled the required residence conditions, if the nationality of one of his parents at the time of the person's birth was that of the Contracting State first above-mentioned. If his parents did not possess the same nationality at the time of his birth, the question whether the nationality of the person concerned should follow that of the father or that of the mother shall be determined by the national law of such Contracting State. If application for such nationality is required, the application shall be made to the appropriate authority by or on behalf of the applicant in the manner prescribed by the national law. Subject to the provisions of paragraph 5 of this article, such application shall not be refused.

5. The Contracting State may make the grant of its nationality in accordance with the provisions of paragraph 4 of this article subject to one or more of the following conditions:

(a) That the application is lodged before the applicant reaches an age, being not less than twenty-three years, fixed by the Contracting State;

(b) That the person concerned has habitually resided in the territory of the Contracting State for such period immediately preceding the lodging of the application, not exceeding three years, as may be fixed by that State;

(c) That the person concerned has always been stateless.

Article 2

A foundling found in the territory of a Contracting State shall, in the absence of proof to the contrary, be considered to have been born within that territory of parents possessing the nationality of that State.

Article 3

For the purpose of determining the obligations of Contracting States under this Convention, birth on a ship or in an aircraft shall be deemed to have taken place in the territory of the State whose flag the ship flies or in the territory of the State in which the aircraft is registered, as the case may be.

Article 4

1. A Contracting State shall grant its nationality to a person, not born in the territory of a Contracting State, who would otherwise be stateless, if the nationality of one of his parents at the time of the person's birth was that of that State. If his parents did not possess the same nationality at the time of his birth, the question whether the nationality

of the person concerned should follow that of the father or that of the mother shall be determined by the national law of such Contracting State. Nationality granted in accordance with the provisions of this paragraph shall be granted:

(a) At birth, by operation of law, or

(b) Upon an application being lodged with the appropriate authority, by or on behalf of the person concerned, in the manner prescribed by the national law. Subject to the provisions of paragraph 2 of this article, no such application may be rejected.

2. A Contracting State may make the grant of its nationality in accordance with the provisions of paragraph 1 of this article subject to one or more of the following conditions:

(a) That the application is lodged before the applicant reaches an age, being not less than twenty-three years, fixed by the Contracting State;

(b) That the person concerned has habitually resided in the territory of the Contracting State for such period immediately preceding the lodging of the application, not exceeding three years, as may be fixed by that State;

(c) That the person concerned has not been convicted of an offence against national security;

(d) That the person concerned has always been stateless.

Article 5

1. If the law of a Contracting State entails loss of nationality as a consequence of any change in the personal status of a person such as marriage, termination of marriage, legitimation, recognition or adoption, such loss shall be conditional upon possession or acquisition of another nationality.

2. If, under the law of a Contracting State, a child born out of wedlock loses the nationality of that State in consequence of a recognition of affiliation, he shall be given an opportunity to recover that nationality by written application to the appropriate authority, and the conditions governing such application shall not be more rigorous than those laid down in paragraph 2 of Article 1 of this Convention.

Article 6

If the law of a Contracting State provides for loss of its nationality by a person's spouse or children as a consequence of that person losing or being deprived of that nationality, such loss shall be conditional upon their possession or acquisition of another nationality.

Article 7

1. (a) If the law of a Contracting State entails loss or renunciation of nationality, such renunciation shall not result in loss of nationality unless the person concerned possesses or acquires another nationality;

(b) The provisions of subparagraph (a) of this paragraph shall not apply where their application would be inconsistent with the principles stated in Articles 13 and 14 of the Universal Declaration of Human Rights approved on 10 December 1948 by the General Assembly of the United Nations.

2. A national of a Contracting State who seeks naturalization in a foreign country shall not lose his nationality unless he acquires or has been accorded assurance of acquiring the nationality of that foreign country.

3. Subject to the provisions of paragraphs 4 and 5 of this article, a national of a Contracting State shall not lose his nationality, so as to become stateless, on the ground of departure, residence abroad, failure to register or on any similar ground.

4. A naturalized person may lose his nationality on account of residence abroad for a period, not less than seven consecutive years, specified by the law of the Contracting State concerned if he fails to declare to the appropriate authority his intention to retain his nationality.

5. In the case of a national of a Contracting State, born outside its territory, the law of that State may make the retention of its nationality after the expiry of one year from his attaining his majority conditional upon residence at that time in the territory of the State or registration with the appropriate authority.

6. Except in the circumstances mentioned in this article, a person shall not lose the nationality of a Contracting State, if such loss would render him stateless, notwithstanding that such loss is not expressly prohibited by any other provision of this Convention.

Article 8

1. A Contracting State shall not deprive a person of his nationality if such deprivation would render him stateless.

2. Notwithstanding the provisions of paragraph 1 of this article, a person may be deprived of the nationality of a Contracting State:

    (a) In the circumstances in which, under paragraphs 4 and 5 of Article 7, it is permissible that a person should lose his nationality;

    (b) Where the nationality has been obtained by misrepresentation or fraud.

3. Notwithstanding the provisions of paragraph 1 of this article, a Contracting State may retain the right to deprive a person of his nationality, if at the time of signature, ratification or accession it specifies its retention of such right on one or more of the following grounds, being grounds existing in its national law at that time:

    (a) That, inconsistently with his duty of loyalty to the Contracting State, the person:

        (i) Has, in disregard of an express prohibition by the Contracting State rendered or continued to render services to, or received or continued to receive emoluments from, another State, or

        (ii) Has conducted himself in a manner seriously prejudicial to the vital interests of the State;

    (b) That the person has taken an oath, or made a formal declaration, of allegiance to another State, or given definite evidence of his determination to repudiate his allegiance to the Contracting State.

4. A Contracting State shall not exercise a power of deprivation permitted by paragraphs 2 or 3 of this article except in accordance with law, which shall provide for the person concerned the right to a fair hearing by a court or other independent body.

Article 9

A Contracting State may not deprive any person or group of persons of their nationality on racial, ethnic, religious or political grounds.

Article 10

1. Every treaty between Contracting States providing for the transfer of territory shall include provisions designed to secure that no person shall become stateless as a result of the transfer. A Contracting State shall use its best endeavours to secure that any such treaty made by it with a State which is not a Party to this Convention includes such provisions.

2. In the absence of such provisions a Contracting State to which territory is transferred or which otherwise acquires territory shall confer its nationality on such persons as would otherwise become stateless as a result of the transfer or acquisition.

Article 11

The Contracting States shall promote the establishment within the framework of the United Nations, as soon as may be after the deposit of the sixth instrument of ratification or accession, of a body to which a person claiming the benefit of this Convention may apply for the examination of his claim and for assistance in presenting it to the appropriate authority.

Article 12

1. In relation to a Contracting State which does not, in accordance with the provisions of paragraph 1 of Article 1 or of Article 4 of this Convention, grant its nationality at birth by operation of law, the provisions of paragraph 1 of Article 1 or of Article 4, as the case may be, shall apply to persons born before as well as to persons born after the entry into force of this Convention.

2. The provisions of paragraph 4 of Article 1 of this Convention shall apply to persons born before as well as to persons born after its entry into force.

3. The provisions of Article 2 of this Convention shall apply only to foundlings found in the territory of a Contracting State after the entry into force of the Convention for that State.

Article 13

This Convention shall not be construed as affecting any provisions more conducive to the reduction of statelessness which may be contained in the law of any Contracting State now or hereafter in force, or may be contained in any other convention, treaty or agreement now or hereafter in force between two or more Contracting States.

Article 14

Any dispute between Contracting States concerning the interpretation or application of this Convention which cannot be settled by other means shall be submitted to the International Court of Justice at the request of any one of the parties to the dispute.

Article 15

1. This Convention shall apply to all non-self-governing, trust, colonial and other non-metropolitan territories for the international relations of which any Contracting State is responsible; the Contracting State concerned shall, subject to the provisions of paragraph 2 of this article, at the time of signature, ratification or accession, declare the non-metropolitan territory or territories to which the Convention shall apply *ipso facto* as a result of such signature, ratification or accession.

2. In any case in which, for the purpose of nationality, a non-metropolitan territory is not treated as one with the metropolitan territory, or in any case in which the previous consent of a non-metropolitan territory is required by the constitutional laws or practices of the Contracting State or of the non-metropolitan territory for the application of the Convention to that territory, that Contracting State shall endeavour to secure the needed consent of the non-metropolitan territory within the period of twelve months from the date of signature of the Convention by that Contracting State, and when such consent has been obtained the Contracting State shall notify the Secretary General of the United Nations. This Convention shall apply to the territory or territories named in such notification from the date of its receipt by the Secretary-General.

3. After the expiry of the twelve-month period mentioned in paragraph 2 of this article, the Contracting States concerned shall inform the Secretary-General of the results of the consultations with those non-metropolitan territories for whose international relations they are responsible and whose consent to the application of this Convention may have been withheld.

Article 16

1. This Convention shall be open for signature at the Headquarters of the United Nations from 30 August 1961 to 31 May 1962.

2. This Convention shall be open for signature on behalf of:

   (a) Any State Member of the United Nations;

   (b) Any other State invited to attend the United Nations Conference on the Elimination or Reduction of Future Statelessness;

   (c) Any State to which an invitation to sign or to accede may be addressed by the General Assembly of the United Nations.

3. This Convention shall be ratified and the instruments of ratification shall be deposited with the Secretary-General of the United Nations.

4. This Convention shall be open for accession by the States referred to in paragraph 2 of this article. Accession shall be effected by the deposit of an instrument of accession with the Secretary-General of the United Nations.

Article 17

1. At the time of signature, ratification or accession any State may make a reservation in respect of Articles 11, 14 or 15.

2. No other reservations to this Convention shall be admissible.

Article 18

1. This Convention shall enter into force two years after the date of the deposit of the sixth instrument of ratification or accession.

2. For each State ratifying or acceding to this Convention after the deposit of the sixth instrument of ratification or accession, it shall enter into force on the ninetieth day after the deposit by such State of its instrument of ratification or accession or on the date on which this Convention enters into force in accordance with the provisions of paragraph 1 of this article, whichever is the later.

Article 19

1. Any Contracting State may denounce this Convention at any time by a written notification addressed to the Secretary-General of the United Nations. Such denunciation shall take effect for the Contracting State concerned one year after the date of its receipt by the Secretary-General.

2. In cases where, in accordance with the provisions of Article 15, this Convention has become applicable to a non-metropolitan territory of a Contracting State, that State may at any time thereafter, with the consent of the territory concerned, give notice to the Secretary-General of the United Nations denouncing this Convention separately in respect to that territory. The denunciation shall take effect one year after the date of the receipt of such notice by the Secretary-General, who shall notify all other Contracting States of such notice and the date of receipt thereof.

Article 20

1. The Secretary-General of the United Nations shall notify all Members of the United Nations and the non-member States referred to in Article 16 of the following particulars:

   (a) Signatures, ratifications and accessions under Article 16;

   (b) Reservations under Article 17;

   (c) The date upon which this Convention enters into force in pursuance of Article 18;

   (d) Denunciations under Article 19.

2. The Secretary-General of the United Nations shall, after the deposit of the sixth instrument of ratification or accession at the latest, bring to the attention of the General Assembly the question of the establishment, in accordance with Article 11, of such a body as therein mentioned.

Article 21

This Convention shall be registered by the Secretary-General of the United Nations on the date of its entry into force.

In witness whereof the undersigned Plenipotentiaries have signed this Convention.

   Done at New York, this thirtieth day of August, one thousand nine hundred and sixty-one, in a single copy, of which the Chinese, English, French, Russian and Spanish texts are equally authentic and which shall be deposited in the archives of the United Nations, and certified copies of which shall be delivered by the Secretary-General of the United Nations to all Members of the United Nations and to the non-member States referred to in Article 16 of this Convention.

48. INTERNATIONAL CONVENTION ON THE ELIMINATION OF ALL FORMS OF RACIAL DISCRIMINATION, 1966

Equality is the great theme which pervades the provisions of the UN Charter and other national and international instruments concerned with human rights and civil liberties; see BROWNLIE, I., *Principles of Public International Law*, Oxford: Oxford University Press, 7th edn, 2008, 572–5. This Convention, opened for signature on 7 March 1966, was adopted by General Assembly Resolution 2106 (XX) of 21 December 1965, and entered into force on 4 January 1969. For the text in various languages see 660 *UNTS* 195.

Article 14 provides an individual complaints mechanism, provided the State against which complaint is made has ratified the treaty and declared that it recognizes the competence of the Committee on the Elimination of Racial Discrimination.; the procedure came into operation in 1982. For reports and other information from the Committee, see **http://www2.ohchr.org/english/bodies/cerd/**.

The link between the issue of racial equality and decolonization is established in Resolution 2106 (XX), B, associated with the adoption by the General Assembly of the Convention itself; see also General Assembly Resolution 2547 (XXIV), 15 December 1969.

Further reading

COHEN-JONATHAN, G., 'Le droit de l'homme à la non-discrimination raciale', *Revue trimestrielle de droits de l'homme*, 2001, 665.

DE GOUTTES, R., 'La Convention internationale sur l'élimination de toutes les formes de discrimination raciale en 1996', *Revue trimestrielle de droits de l'homme*, 1996, 515.

—— 'Le rôle du Comité des Nations Unies pour l'élimination de la discrimination raciale', *Revue trimestrielle de droits de l'homme*, 2001, 567.

FELICE, W. F., 'The UN Committee on the Elimination of All Forms of Racial Discrimination: Race, and Economic and Social Human Rights', (2002) 24 *Human Rights Quarterly* 205.

MERON, T., 'The Meaning and Reach of the International Convention on the Elimination of All Forms of Racial Discrimination', (1985) 79 *AJIL* 283.

PARTSCH, K. J., 'The Committee on the Elimination of Racial Discrimination', in ALSTON, P., ed., *The United Nations and Human Rights*, Oxford: Oxford University Press, 1992, 339–68.

SCHWELB, E., 'The International Convention on the Elimination of All Forms of Racial Discrimination', (1966) 15 *ICLQ* 996.

THORNBERRY, P., *The International Convention on the Elimination of All Forms of Racial Discrimination: A Commentary*, Oxford: Oxford University Press, 2010.

——, 'Confronting Racial Discrimination: A CERD Perspective', (2005) 5 *Human Rights Law Review* 239.

TEXT

The States Parties to this Convention,

Considering that the Charter of the United Nations is based on the principles of the dignity and equality inherent in all human beings, and that all Member States have pledged themselves to take joint and separate action, in co-operation with the Organization, for the achievement of one of the purposes of the United Nations which is to promote and encourage universal respect for and observance of human rights and fundamental freedoms for all, without distinction as to race, sex, language or religion,

Considering that the Universal Declaration of Human Rights proclaims that all human beings are born free and equal in dignity and rights and that everyone is entitled to all the rights and freedoms set out therein, without distinction of any kind, in particular as to race, colour or national origin,

Considering that all human beings are equal before the law and are entitled to equal protection of the law against any discrimination and against any incitement to discrimination,

Considering that the United Nations has condemned colonialism and all practices of segregation and discrimination associated therewith, in whatever form and wherever they exist, and that the Declaration on the Granting of Independence to Colonial Countries and Peoples of 14 December 1960 (General Assembly resolution 1514 (XV)) has affirmed and solemnly proclaimed the necessity of bringing them to a speedy and unconditional end,

Considering that the United Nations Declaration on the Elimination of All Forms of Racial Discrimination of 20 November 1963 (General Assembly resolution 1904 (XVIII)) solemnly affirms the necessity of speedily eliminating racial discrimination throughout the world in all its forms and manifestations and of securing understanding of and respect for the dignity of the human person,

Convinced that any doctrine of superiority based on racial differentiation is scientifically false, morally condemnable, socially unjust and dangerous, and that there is no justification for racial discrimination, in theory or in practice, anywhere,

Reaffirming that discrimination between human beings on the grounds of race, colour or ethnic origin is an obstacle to friendly and peaceful relations among nations and is capable of disturbing peace and security among peoples and the harmony of persons living side by side even within one and the same State,

Convinced that the existence of racial barriers is repugnant to the ideals of any human society,

Alarmed by manifestations of racial discrimination still in evidence in some areas of the world and by governmental policies based on racial superiority or hatred, such as policies of apartheid, segregation or separation,

Resolved to adopt all necessary measures for speedily eliminating racial discrimination in all its forms and manifestations, and to prevent and combat racist doctrines and practices in order to promote understanding between races and to build an international community free from all forms of racial segregation and racial discrimination,

Bearing in mind the Convention concerning Discrimination in respect of Employment and Occupation adopted by the International Labour Organization in 1958, and the Convention against Discrimination in Education adopted by the United Nations Educational, Scientific and Cultural Organization in 1960,

Desiring to implement the principles embodied in the United Nations Declaration on the Elimination of All Forms of Racial Discrimination and to secure the earliest adoption of practical measures to that end,

Have agreed as follows:

PART I

Article 1

1. In this Convention, the term 'racial discrimination' shall mean any distinction, exclusion, restriction or preference based on race, colour, descent, or national or ethnic

origin which has the purpose or effect of nullifying or impairing the recognition, enjoyment or exercise, on an equal footing, of human rights and fundamental freedoms in the political, economic, social, cultural or any other field of public life.

2. This Convention shall not apply to distinctions, exclusions, restrictions or preferences made by a State Party to this Convention between citizens and non-citizens.

3. Nothing in this Convention may be interpreted as affecting in any way the legal provisions of States Parties concerning nationality, citizenship or naturalization, provided that such provisions do not discriminate against any particular nationality.

4. Special measures taken for the sole purpose of securing adequate advancement of certain racial or ethnic groups or individuals requiring such protection as may be necessary in order to ensure such groups or individuals equal enjoyment or exercise of human rights and fundamental freedoms shall not be deemed racial discrimination, provided, however, that such measures do not, as a consequence, lead to the maintenance of separate rights for different racial groups and that they shall not be continued after the objectives for which they were taken have been achieved.

Article 2

1. States Parties condemn racial discrimination and undertake to pursue by all appropriate means and without delay a policy of eliminating racial discrimination in all its forms and promoting understanding among all races, and, to this end:

(a) Each State Party undertakes to engage in no act or practice of racial discrimination against persons, groups of persons or institutions and to ensure that all public authorities and public institutions, national and local, shall act in conformity with this obligation;

(b) Each State Party undertakes not to sponsor, defend or support racial discrimination by any persons or organizations;

(c) Each State Party shall take effective measures to review governmental, national and local policies, and to amend, rescind or nullify any laws and regulations which have the effect of creating or perpetuating racial discrimination wherever it exists;

(d) Each State Party shall prohibit and bring to an end, by all appropriate means, including legislation as required by circumstances, racial discrimination by any persons, group or organization;

(e) Each State Party undertakes to encourage, where appropriate, integrationist multiracial organizations and movements and other means of eliminating barriers between races, and to discourage anything which tends to strengthen racial division.

2. States Parties shall, when the circumstances so warrant, take, in the social, economic, cultural and other fields, special and concrete measures to ensure the adequate development and protection of certain racial groups or individuals belonging to them, for the purpose of guaranteeing them the full and equal enjoyment of human rights and fundamental freedoms. These measures shall in no case entail as a consequence the maintenance of unequal or separate rights for different racial groups after the objectives for which they were taken have been achieved.

Article 3

States Parties particularly condemn racial segregation and apartheid and undertake to prevent, prohibit and eradicate all practices of this nature in territories under their jurisdiction.

Article 4

States Parties condemn all propaganda and all organizations which are based on ideas or theories of superiority of one race or group of persons of one colour or ethnic origin, or which attempt to justify or promote racial hatred and discrimination in any form, and undertake to adopt immediate and positive measures designed to eradicate all incitement to, or acts of, such discrimination and, to this end, with due regard to the principles embodied in the Universal Declaration of Human Rights and the rights expressly set forth in Article 5 of this Convention, *inter alia*:

   (a) Shall declare an offence punishable by law all dissemination of ideas based on racial superiority or hatred, incitement to racial discrimination, as well as all acts of violence or incitement to such acts against any race or group of persons of another colour or ethnic origin, and also the provision of any assistance to racist activities, including the financing thereof;

   (b) Shall declare illegal and prohibit organizations, and also organized and all other propaganda activities, which promote and incite racial discrimination, and shall recognize participation in such organizations or activities as an offence punishable by law;

   (c) Shall not permit public authorities or public institutions, national or local, to promote or incite racial discrimination.

Article 5

In compliance with the fundamental obligations laid down in Article 2 of this Convention, States Parties undertake to prohibit and to eliminate racial discrimination in all its forms and to guarantee the right of everyone, without distinction as to race, colour, or national or ethnic origin, to equality before the law, notably in the enjoyment of the following rights:

   (a) The right to equal treatment before the tribunals and all other organs administering justice;

   (b) The right to security of person and protection by the State against violence or bodily harm, whether inflicted by government officials or by any individual group or institution;

   (c) Political rights, in particular the right to participate in elections—to vote and to stand for election—on the basis of universal and equal suffrage, to take part in the Government as well as in the conduct of public affairs at any level and to have equal access to public service;

   (d) Other civil rights, in particular:

      (i) The right to freedom of movement and residence within the border of the State;

      (ii) The right to leave any country, including one's own, and to return to one's country;

      (iii) The right to nationality;

      (iv) The right to marriage and choice of spouse;

      (v) The right to own property alone as well as in association with others;

      (vi) The right to inherit;

      (vii) The right to freedom of thought, conscience and religion;

      (viii) The right to freedom of opinion and expression;

      (ix) The right to freedom of peaceful assembly and association;

(e) Economic, social and cultural rights, in particular:

(i) The rights to work, to free choice of employment, to just and favourable conditions of work, to protection against unemployment, to equal pay for equal work, to just and favourable remuneration;

(ii) The right to form and join trade unions;

(iii) The right to housing;

(iv) The right to public health, medical care, social security and social services;

(v) The right to education and training;

(vi) The right to equal participation in cultural activities;

(f) The right of access to any place or service intended for use by the general public, such as transport, hotels, restaurants, cafés, theatres and parks.

Article 6

States Parties shall assure to everyone within their jurisdiction effective protection and remedies, through the competent national tribunals and other State institutions, against any acts of racial discrimination which violate his human rights and fundamental freedoms contrary to this Convention, as well as the right to seek from such tribunals just and adequate reparation or satisfaction for any damage suffered as a result of such discrimination.

Article 7

States Parties undertake to adopt immediate and effective measures, particularly in the fields of teaching, education, culture and information, with a view to combatting prejudices which lead to racial discrimination and to promoting understanding, tolerance and friendship among nations and racial or ethnical groups, as well as to propagating the purposes and principles of the Charter of the United Nations, the Universal Declaration of Human Rights, the United Nations Declaration on the Elimination of All Forms of Racial Discrimination, and this Convention.

PART II

Article 8

1. There shall be established a Committee on the Elimination of Racial Discrimination (hereinafter referred to as the Committee) consisting of eighteen experts of high moral standing and acknowledged impartiality elected by States Parties from among their nationals, who shall serve in their personal capacity, consideration being given to equitable geographical distribution and to the representation of the different forms of civilization as well as of the principal legal systems.

2. The members of the Committee shall be elected by secret ballot from a list of persons nominated by the States Parties. Each State Party may nominate one person from among its own nationals.

3. The initial election shall be held six months after the date of the entry into force of this Convention. At least three months before the date of each election the Secretary-General of the United Nations shall address a letter to the States Parties inviting them to submit their nominations within two months. The Secretary-General shall prepare a list

in alphabetical order of all persons thus nominated, indicating the States Parties which have nominated them, and shall submit it to the States Parties.

4. Elections of the members of the Committee shall be held at a meeting of States Parties convened by the Secretary-General at United Nations Headquarters. At that meeting, for which two thirds of the States Parties shall constitute a quorum, the persons elected to the Committee shall be nominees who obtain the largest number of votes and an absolute majority of the votes of the representatives of States Parties present and voting.

5. (a) The members of the Committee shall be elected for a term of four years. However, the terms of nine of the members elected at the first election shall expire at the end of two years; immediately after the first election the names of these nine members shall be chosen by lot by the Chairman of the Committee;

(b) For the filling of casual vacancies, the State Party whose expert has ceased to function as a member of the Committee shall appoint another expert from among its nationals, subject to the approval of the Committee.

6. States Parties shall be responsible for the expenses of the members of the Committee while they are in performance of Committee duties.

Article 9

1. States Parties undertake to submit to the Secretary-General of the United Nations, for consideration by the Committee, a report on the legislative, judicial, administrative or other measures which they have adopted and which give effect to the provisions of this Convention:

(a) within one year after the entry into force of the Convention for the State concerned; and

(b) thereafter every two years and whenever the Committee so requests. The Committee may request further information from the States Parties.

2. The Committee shall report annually, through the Secretary-General, to the General Assembly of the United Nations on its activities and may make suggestions and general recommendations based on the examination of the reports and information received from the States Parties. Such suggestions and general recommendations shall be reported to the General Assembly together with comments, if any, from States Parties.

Article 10

1. The Committee shall adopt its own rules of procedure.

2. The Committee shall elect its officers for a term of two years.

3. The secretariat of the Committee shall be provided by the Secretary-General of the United Nations.

4. The meetings of the Committee shall normally be held at United Nations Headquarters.

Article 11

1. If a State Party considers that another State Party is not giving effect to the provisions of this Convention, it may bring the matter to the attention of the Committee. The Committee shall then transmit the communication to the State Party concerned. Within three months, the receiving State shall submit to the Committee written explanations or statements clarifying the matter and the remedy, if any, that may have been taken by that State.

2. If the matter is not adjusted to the satisfaction of both parties, either by bilateral negotiations or by any other procedure open to them, within six months after the receipt by the receiving State of the initial communication, either State shall have the right to refer the matter again to the Committee by notifying the Committee and also the other State.

3. The Committee shall deal with a matter referred to it in accordance with paragraph 2 of this article after it has ascertained that all available domestic remedies have been invoked and exhausted in the case, in conformity with the generally recognized principles of international law. This shall not be the rule where the application of the remedies is unreasonably prolonged.

4. In any matter referred to it, the Committee may call upon the States Parties concerned to supply any other relevant information.

5. When any matter arising out of this article is being considered by the Committee, the States Parties concerned shall be entitled to send a representative to take part in the proceedings of the Committee, without voting rights, while the matter is under consideration.

Article 12

1. *(a)* After the Committee has obtained and collated all the information it deems necessary, the Chairman shall appoint an *ad hoc* Conciliation Commission (hereinafter referred to as the Commission) comprising five persons who may or may not be members of the Committee. The members of the Commission shall be appointed with the unanimous consent of the parties to the dispute, and its good offices shall be made available to the States concerned with a view to an amicable solution of the matter on the basis of respect for this Convention;

   (b) If the States parties to the dispute fail to reach agreement within three months on all or part of the composition of the Commission, the members of the Commission not agreed upon by the States parties to the dispute shall be elected by secret ballot by a two-thirds majority vote of the Committee from among its own members.

2. The members of the Commission shall serve in their personal capacity. They shall not be nationals of the States parties to the dispute or of a State not Party to this Convention.

3. The Commission shall elect its own Chairman and adopt its own rules of procedure.

4. The meetings of the Commission shall normally be held at United Nations Headquarters or at any other convenient place as determined by the Commission.

5. The secretariat provided in accordance with Article 10, paragraph 3, of this Convention shall also service the Commission whenever a dispute among States Parties brings the Commission into being.

6. The States parties to the dispute shall share equally all the expenses of the members of the Commission in accordance with estimates to be provided by the Secretary-General of the United Nations.

7. The Secretary-General shall be empowered to pay the expenses of the members of the Commission, if necessary, before reimbursement by the States parties to the dispute in accordance with paragraph 6 of this article.

8. The information obtained and collated by the Committee shall be made available to the Commission, and the Commission may call upon the States concerned to supply any other relevant information.

Article 13

1. When the Commission has fully considered the matter, it shall prepare and submit to the Chairman of the Committee a report embodying its findings on all questions of fact relevant to the issue between the parties and containing such recommendations as it may think proper for the amicable solution of the dispute.

2. The Chairman of the Committee shall communicate the report of the Commission to each of the States parties to the dispute. These States shall, within three months, inform the Chairman of the Committee whether or not they accept the recommendations contained in the report of the Commission.

3. After the period provided for in paragraph 2 of this article, the Chairman of the Committee shall communicate the report of the Commission and the declarations of the States Parties concerned to the other States Parties to this Convention.

Article 14

1. A State Party may at any time declare that it recognizes the competence of the Committee to receive and consider communications from individuals or groups of individuals within its jurisdiction claiming to be victims of a violation by that State Party of any of the rights set forth in this Convention. No communication shall be received by the Committee if it concerns a State Party which has not made such a declaration.

2. Any State Party which makes a declaration as provided for in paragraph 1 of this article may establish or indicate a body within its national legal order which shall be competent to receive and consider petitions from individuals and groups of individuals within its jurisdiction who claim to be victims of a violation of any of the rights set forth in this Convention and who have exhausted other available local remedies.

3. A declaration made in accordance with paragraph 1 of this article and the name of any body established or indicated in accordance with paragraph 2 of this article shall be deposited by the State Party concerned with the Secretary-General of the United Nations, who shall transmit copies thereof to the other States Parties. A declaration may be withdrawn at any time by notification to the Secretary-General, but such a withdrawal shall not affect communications pending before the Committee.

4. A register of petitions shall be kept by the body established or indicated in accordance with paragraph 2 of this article, and certified copies of the register shall be filed annually through appropriate channels with the Secretary-General on the understanding that the contents shall not be publicly disclosed.

5. In the event of failure to obtain satisfaction from the body established or indicated in accordance with paragraph 2 of this article, the petitioner shall have the right to communicate the matter to the Committee within six months.

6. (a) The Committee shall confidentially bring any communication referred to it to the attention of the State Party alleged to be violating any provision of this Convention, but the identity of the individual or groups of individuals concerned shall not be revealed without his or their express consent. The Committee shall not receive anonymous communications;

   (b) Within three months, the receiving State shall submit to the Committee written explanations or statements clarifying the matter and the remedy, if any, that may have been taken by that State.

7. *(a)* The Committee shall consider communications in the light of all information made available to it by the State Party concerned and by the petitioner. The Committee shall not consider any communication from a petitioner unless it has ascertained that the petitioner has exhausted all available domestic remedies. However, this shall not be the rule where the application of the remedies is unreasonably prolonged;

(b) The Committee shall forward its suggestions and recommendations, if any, to the State Party concerned and to the petitioner.

8. The Committee shall include in its annual report a summary of such communications and, where appropriate, a summary of the explanations and statements of the States Parties concerned and of its own suggestions and recommendations.

9. The Committee shall be competent to exercise the functions provided for in this article only when at least ten States Parties to this Convention are bound by declarations in accordance with paragraph 1 of this article.

Article 15

1. Pending the achievement of the objectives of the Declaration on the Granting of Independence to Colonial Countries and Peoples, contained in General Assembly resolution 1514 (XV) of 14 December 1960, the provisions of this Convention shall in no way limit the right of petition granted to these peoples by other international instruments or by the United Nations and its specialized agencies.

2. *(a)* The Committee established under Article 8, paragraph 1, of this Convention shall receive copies of the petitions from, and submit expressions of opinion and recommendations on these petitions to, the bodies of the United Nations which deal with matters directly related to the principles and objectives of this Convention in their consideration of petitions from the inhabitants of Trust and Non-Self-Governing Territories and all other territories to which General Assembly resolution 1514 (XV) applies, relating to matters covered by this Convention which are before these bodies;

(b) The Committee shall receive from the competent bodies of the United Nations copies of the reports concerning the legislative, judicial, administrative or other measures directly related to the principles and objectives of this Convention applied by the administering Powers within the Territories mentioned in subparagraph (a) of this paragraph, and shall express opinions and make recommendations to these bodies.

3. The Committee shall include in its report to the General Assembly a summary of the petitions and reports it has received from United Nations bodies, and the expressions of opinion and recommendations of the Committee relating to the said petitions and reports.

4. The Committee shall request from the Secretary-General of the United Nations all information relevant to the objectives of this Convention and available to him regarding the Territories mentioned in paragraph 2 (a) of this article.

Article 16

The provisions of this Convention concerning the settlement of disputes or complaints shall be applied without prejudice to other procedures for settling disputes or complaints in the field of discrimination laid down in the constituent instruments of, or conventions adopted by, the United Nations and its specialized agencies, and shall not prevent the States Parties from having recourse to other procedures for settling a dispute in accordance with general or special international agreements in force between them.

PART III

Article 17

1. This Convention is open for signature by any State Member of the United Nations or member of any of its specialized agencies, by any State Party to the Statute of the International Court of Justice, and by any other State which has been invited by the General Assembly of the United Nations to become a Party to this Convention.

2. This Convention is subject to ratification. Instruments of ratification shall be deposited with the Secretary-General of the United Nations.

Article 18

1. This Convention shall be open to accession by any State referred to in Article 17, paragraph 1, of the Convention.

2. Accession shall be effected by the deposit of an instrument of accession with the Secretary-General of the United Nations.

Article 19

1. This Convention shall enter into force on the thirtieth day after the date of the deposit with the Secretary-General of the United Nations of the twenty-seventh instrument of ratification or instrument of accession.

2. For each State ratifying this Convention or acceding to it after the deposit of the twenty-seventh instrument of ratification or instrument of accession, the Convention shall enter into force on the thirtieth day after the date of the deposit of its own instrument of ratification or instrument of accession.

Article 20

1. The Secretary-General of the United Nations shall receive and circulate to all States which are or may become Parties to this Convention reservations made by States at the time of ratification or accession. Any State which objects to the reservation shall, within a period of ninety days from the date of the said communication, notify the Secretary-General that it does not accept it.

2. A reservation incompatible with the object and purpose of this Convention shall not be permitted, nor shall a reservation the effect of which would inhibit the operation of any of the bodies established by this Convention be allowed. A reservation shall be considered incompatible or inhibitive if at least two thirds of the States Parties to this Convention object to it.

3. Reservations may be withdrawn at any time by notification to this effect addressed to the Secretary-General. Such notification shall take effect on the date on which it is received.

Article 21

A State Party may denounce this Convention by written notification to the Secretary-General of the United Nations. Denunciation shall take effect one year after the date of receipt of the notification by the Secretary General.

Article 22

Any dispute between two or more States Parties with respect to the interpretation or application of this Convention, which is not settled by negotiation or by the procedures expressly provided for in this Convention, shall, at the request of any of the parties to the dispute, be referred to the International Court of Justice for decision, unless the disputants agree to another mode of settlement.

Article 23

1. A request for the revision of this Convention may be made at any time by any State Party by means of a notification in writing addressed to the Secretary-General of the United Nations.

2. The General Assembly of the United Nations shall decide upon the steps, if any, to be taken in respect of such a request.

Article 24

The Secretary-General of the United Nations shall inform all States referred to in Article 17, paragraph 1, of this Convention of the following particulars:

    (a) Signatures, ratifications and accessions under Articles 17 and 18;

    (b) The date of entry into force of this Convention under Article 19;

    (c) Communications and declarations received under Articles 14, 20 and 23;

    (d) Denunciations under Article 21.

Article 25

1. This Convention, of which the Chinese, English, French, Russian and Spanish texts are equally authentic, shall be deposited in the archives of the United Nations.

2. The Secretary-General of the United Nations shall transmit certified copies of this Convention to all States belonging to any of the categories mentioned in Article 17, paragraph 1, of the Convention.

49. INTERNATIONAL COVENANT ON ECONOMIC, SOCIAL AND CULTURAL RIGHTS, 1966

This appears in the annex to General Assembly Resolution 2200 A (XXI) of 16 December 1966; for the text in various languages, see 993 *UNTS* 3. The Covenant entered into force on 3 January 1976, in accordance with Article 27. The Committee on Economic, Social and Cultural Rights was established under ECOSOC Resolution 1985/17, 28 May 1985, to carry out the monitoring functions assigned to ECOSOC in Part IV of the Covenant. See **http://www2.ohchr.org/ english/bodies/cescr/index.htm**.

Further reading

BADERIN, M. and McCORQUODALE, R., eds., *Economic, Social, and Cultural Rights in Action*, Oxford: Oxford University Press, 2007.

BARTH, W. K., *On Cultural Rights: The Equality of Nations and the Minority Legal Tradition*, Leiden: Martinus Nijhoff, 2008.

BEITER, K. D., *The Protection of the Right to Education by International Law*, Leiden: Martinus Nijhoff, 2006.

BILCHITZ, D., *Poverty and Fundamental Rights: The Justification and Enforcement of Socio-economic Rights*, Oxford: Oxford University Press, 2008.

CHAPMAN, A. and RUSSELL, S., *Core Obligations: Building a Framework for Economic, Social and Cultural Rights*, Antwerp, New York: Intersentia, Transnational Publishers, 2002.

CRAVEN, M., *The International Covenant on Economic, Social and Cultural Rights: A Perspective on its Development*, Oxford: Clarendon Press, 1995.

DOWELL-JONES, M., *Contextualising the International Covenant on Economic, Social and Cultural Rights: Assessing the Economic Deficit*, Leiden: Martinus Nijhoff, 2004.

FRANCIONI, F. and SCHEININ, M., *Cultural Human Rights*, Leiden: Martinus Nijhoff, 2008.

McGOLDRICK, D., 'Culture, Cultures and Cultural Rights', in BADERIN, M. and McCORQUODALE, R., eds., *Economic, Social and Cultural Rights in Action*, Oxford: Oxford University Press, 2007.

MOTTERSHAW, E., 'Economic, Social and Cultural Rights in Armed Conflict: International Human Rights Law and International Humanitarian Law', (2008) 12 *International Journal of Human Rights* 449.

SACHS, A., 'Enforcement of Social and Economic Rights', (2006–2007) 22 *American University International Law Review* 673.

SCHREIBER, M., 'La pratique récente des Nations Unies dans le domaine de la protection des droits de l'homme', 145 *Recueil des Cours* (1975–II), 299–398.

SEPÚLVEDA, M. M., *The Nature of the Obligations under the International Covenant on Economic, Social and Cultural Rights*, Antwerpen, Oxford: Intersentia, 2003.

SSENYONJO, M., *Economic, Social and Cultural Rights in International Law*, Oxford: Hart Publishing, 2009.

'The Limburg Principles on the Implementation of the International Covenant on Economic, Social and Cultural Rights', (1987) 9 *Human Rights Quarterly* 122.

TEXT

Preamble

The States Parties to the present Covenant,

Considering that, in accordance with the principles proclaimed in the Charter of the United Nations, recognition of the inherent dignity and of the equal and inalienable rights of all members of the human family is the foundation of freedom, justice and peace in the world,

Recognizing that these rights derive from the inherent dignity of the human person,

Recognizing that, in accordance with the Universal Declaration of Human Rights, the ideal of free human beings enjoying freedom from fear and want can only be achieved if conditions are created whereby everyone may enjoy his economic, social and cultural rights, as well as his civil and political rights,

Considering the obligation of States under the Charter of the United Nations to promote universal respect for, and observance of, human rights and freedoms,

Realizing that the individual, having duties to other individuals and to the community to which he belongs, is under a responsibility to strive for the promotion and observance of the rights recognized in the present Covenant,

Agree upon the following articles:

PART I

Article 1

1. All peoples have the right of self-determination. By virtue of that right they freely determine their political status and freely pursue their economic, social and cultural development.

2. All peoples may, for their own ends, freely dispose of their natural wealth and resources without prejudice to any obligations arising out of international economic co-operation, based upon the principle of mutual benefit, and international law. In no case may a people be deprived of its own means of subsistence.

3. The States Parties to the present Covenant, including those having responsibility for the administration of Non-Self-Governing and Trust Territories, shall promote the realization of the right of self-determination, and shall respect that right, in conformity with the provisions of the Charter of the United Nations.

PART II

Article 2

1. Each State Party to the present Covenant undertakes to take steps, individually and through international assistance and co-operation, especially economic and technical,

to the maximum of its available resources, with a view to achieving progressively the full realization of the rights recognized in the present Covenant by all appropriate means, including particularly the adoption of legislative measures.

2. The States Parties to the present Covenant undertake to guarantee that the rights enunciated in the present Covenant will be exercised without discrimination of any kind as to race, colour, sex, language, religion, political or other opinion, national or social origin, property, birth or other status.

3. Developing countries, with due regard to human rights and their national economy, may determine to what extent they would guarantee the economic rights recognized in the present Covenant to non-nationals.

Article 3

The States Parties to the present Covenant undertake to ensure the equal right of men and women to the enjoyment of all economic, social and cultural rights set forth in the present Covenant.

Article 4

The States Parties to the present Covenant recognize that, in the enjoyment of those rights provided by the State in conformity with the present Covenant, the State may subject such rights only to such limitations as are determined by law only in so far as this may be compatible with the nature of these rights and solely for the purpose of promoting the general welfare in a democratic society.

Article 5

1. Nothing in the present Covenant may be interpreted as implying for any State, group or person any right to engage in any activity or to perform any act aimed at the destruction of any of the rights or freedoms recognized herein, or at their limitation to a greater extent than is provided for in the present Covenant.

2. No restriction upon or derogation from any of the fundamental human rights recognized or existing in any country in virtue of law, conventions, regulations or custom shall be admitted on the pretext that the present Covenant does not recognize such rights or that it recognizes them to a lesser extent.

PART III

Article 6

1. The States Parties to the present Covenant recognize the right to work, which includes the right of everyone to the opportunity to gain his living by work which he freely chooses or accepts, and will take appropriate steps to safeguard this right.

2. The steps to be taken by a State Party to the present Covenant to achieve the full realization of this right shall include technical and vocational guidance and training programmes, policies and techniques to achieve steady economic, social and cultural development and full and productive employment under conditions safeguarding fundamental political and economic freedoms to the individual.

Article 7

The States Parties to the present Covenant recognize the right of everyone to the enjoyment of just and favourable conditions of work which ensure, in particular:

(a) Remuneration which provides all workers, as a minimum, with:
   (i) Fair wages and equal remuneration for work of equal value without distinction of any kind, in particular women being guaranteed conditions of work not inferior to those enjoyed by men, with equal pay for equal work;
   (ii) A decent living for themselves and their families in accordance with the provisions of the present Covenant;
(b) Safe and healthy working conditions;
(c) Equal opportunity for everyone to be promoted in his employment to an appropriate higher level, subject to no considerations other than those of seniority and competence;
(d) Rest, leisure and reasonable limitation of working hours and periodic holidays with pay, as well as remuneration for public holidays.

Article 8

1. The States Parties to the present Covenant undertake to ensure:
   (a) The right of everyone to form trade unions and join the trade union of his choice, subject only to the rules of the organization concerned, for the promotion and protection of his economic and social interests. No restrictions may be placed on the exercise of this right other than those prescribed by law and which are necessary in a democratic society in the interests of national security or public order or for the protection of the rights and freedoms of others;
   (b) The right of trade unions to establish national federations or confederations and the right of the latter to form or join international trade-union organizations;
   (c) The right of trade unions to function freely subject to no limitations other than those prescribed by law and which are necessary in a democratic society in the interests of national security or public order or for the protection of the rights and freedoms of others;
   (d) The right to strike, provided that it is exercised in conformity with the laws of the particular country.

2. This article shall not prevent the imposition of lawful restrictions on the exercise of these rights by members of the armed forces or of the police or of the administration of the State.

3. Nothing in this article shall authorize States Parties to the International Labour Organization Convention of 1948 concerning Freedom of Association and Protection of the Right to Organize to take legislative measures which would prejudice, or apply the law in such a manner as would prejudice, the guarantees provided for in that Convention.

Article 9

The States Parties to the present Covenant recognize the right of everyone to social security, including social insurance.

Article 10

The States Parties to the present Covenant recognize that:

1. The widest possible protection and assistance should be accorded to the family, which is the natural and fundamental group unit of society, particularly for its establishment and while it is responsible for the care and education of dependent children. Marriage must be entered into with the free consent of the intending spouses.

2. Special protection should be accorded to mothers during a reasonable period before and after childbirth. During such period working mothers should be accorded paid leave or leave with adequate social security benefits.

3. Special measures of protection and assistance should be taken on behalf of all children and young persons without any discrimination for reasons of parentage or other conditions. Children and young persons should be protected from economic and social exploitation. Their employment in work harmful to their morals or health or dangerous to life or likely to hamper their normal development should be punishable by law. States should also set age limits below which the paid employment of child labour should be prohibited and punishable by law.

Article 11

1. The States Parties to the present Covenant recognize the right of everyone to an adequate standard of living for himself and his family, including adequate food, clothing and housing, and to the continuous improvement of living conditions. The States Parties will take appropriate steps to ensure the realization of this right, recognizing to this effect the essential importance of international co-operation based on free consent.

2. The States Parties to the present Covenant, recognizing the fundamental right of everyone to be free from hunger, shall take, individually and through international co-operation, the measures, including specific programmes, which are needed:

  (a) To improve methods of production, conservation and distribution of food by making full use of technical and scientific knowledge, by disseminating knowledge of the principles of nutrition and by developing or reforming agrarian systems in such a way as to achieve the most efficient development and utilization of natural resources;

  (b) Taking into account the problems of both food-importing and food-exporting countries, to ensure an equitable distribution of world food supplies in relation to need.

Article 12

1. The States Parties to the present Covenant recognize the right of everyone to the enjoyment of the highest attainable standard of physical and mental health.

2. The steps to be taken by the States Parties to the present Covenant to achieve the full realization of this right shall include those necessary for:

  (a) The provision for the reduction of the stillbirth-rate and of infant mortality and for the healthy development of the child;

  (b) The improvement of all aspects of environmental and industrial hygiene;

  (c) The prevention, treatment and control of epidemic, endemic, occupational and other diseases;

(d) The creation of conditions which would assure to all medical service and medical attention in the event of sickness.

Article 13

1. The States Parties to the present Covenant recognize the right of everyone to education. They agree that education shall be directed to the full development of the human personality and the sense of its dignity, and shall strengthen the respect for human rights and fundamental freedoms. They further agree that education shall enable all persons to participate effectively in a free society, promote understanding, tolerance and friendship among all nations and all racial, ethnic or religious groups, and further the activities of the United Nations for the maintenance of peace.

2. The States Parties to the present Covenant recognize that, with a view to achieving the full realization of this right:

(a) Primary education shall be compulsory and available free to all;

(b) Secondary education in its different forms, including technical and vocational secondary education, shall be made generally available and accessible to all by every appropriate means, and in particular by the progressive introduction of free education;

(c) Higher education shall be made equally accessible to all, on the basis of capacity, by every appropriate means, and in particular by the progressive introduction of free education;

(d) Fundamental education shall be encouraged or intensified as far as possible for those persons who have not received or completed the whole period of their primary education;

(e) The development of a system of schools at all levels shall be actively pursued, an adequate fellowship system shall be established, and the material conditions of teaching staff shall be continuously improved.

3. The States Parties to the present Covenant undertake to have respect for the liberty of parents and, when applicable, legal guardians to choose for their children schools, other than those established by the public authorities, which conform to such minimum educational standards as may be laid down or approved by the State and to ensure the religious and moral education of their children in conformity with their own convictions.

4. No part of this article shall be construed so as to interfere with the liberty of individuals and bodies to establish and direct educational institutions, subject always to the observance of the principles set forth in paragraph 1 of this article and to the requirement that the education given in such institutions shall conform to such minimum standards as may be laid down by the State.

Article 14

Each State Party to the present Covenant which, at the time of becoming a Party, has not been able to secure in its metropolitan territory or other territories under its jurisdiction compulsory primary education, free of charge, undertakes, within two years, to work out and adopt a detailed plan of action for the progressive implementation, within a reasonable number of years, to be fixed in the plan, of the principle of compulsory education free of charge for all.

Article 15

1. The States Parties to the present Covenant recognize the right of everyone:

   (a) To take part in cultural life;

   (b) To enjoy the benefits of scientific progress and its applications;

   (c) To benefit from the protection of the moral and material interests resulting from any scientific, literary or artistic production of which he is the author.

2. The steps to be taken by the States Parties to the present Covenant to achieve the full realization of this right shall include those necessary for the conservation, the development and the diffusion of science and culture.

3. The States Parties to the present Covenant undertake to respect the freedom indispensable for scientific research and creative activity.

4. The States Parties to the present Covenant recognize the benefits to be derived from the encouragement and development of international contacts and co-operation in the scientific and cultural fields.

PART IV

Article 16

1. The States Parties to the present Covenant undertake to submit in conformity with this part of the Covenant reports on the measures which they have adopted and the progress made in achieving the observance of the rights recognized herein.

2. *(a)* All reports shall be submitted to the Secretary-General of the United Nations, who shall transmit copies to the Economic and Social Council for consideration in accordance with the provisions of the present Covenant;

   (b) The Secretary-General of the United Nations shall also transmit to the specialized agencies copies of the reports, or any relevant parts therefrom, from States Parties to the present Covenant which are also members of these specialized agencies in so far as these reports, or parts therefrom, relate to any matters which fall within the responsibilities of the said agencies in accordance with their constitutional instruments.

Article 17

1. The States Parties to the present Covenant shall furnish their reports in stages, in accordance with a programme to be established by the Economic and Social Council within one year of the entry into force of the present Covenant after consultation with the States Parties and the specialized agencies concerned.

2. Reports may indicate factors and difficulties affecting the degree of fulfilment of obligations under the present Covenant.

3. Where relevant information has previously been furnished to the United Nations or to any specialized agency by any State Party to the present Covenant, it will not be necessary to reproduce that information, but a precise reference to the information so furnished will suffice.

Article 18

Pursuant to its responsibilities under the Charter of the United Nations in the field of human rights and fundamental freedoms, the Economic and Social Council may make arrangements with the specialized agencies in respect of their reporting to it on the progress made in achieving the observance of the provisions of the present Covenant falling within the scope of their activities. These reports may include particulars of decisions and recommendations on such implementation adopted by their competent organs.

Article 19

The Economic and Social Council may transmit to the Commission on Human Rights for study and general recommendation or, as appropriate, for information the reports concerning human rights submitted by States in accordance with Articles 16 and 17, and those concerning human rights submitted by the specialized agencies in accordance with Article 18.

Article 20

The States Parties to the present Covenant and the specialized agencies concerned may submit comments to the Economic and Social Council on any general recommendation under Article 19 or reference to such general recommendation in any report of the Commission on Human Rights or any documentation referred to therein.

Article 21

The Economic and Social Council may submit from time to time to the General Assembly reports with recommendations of a general nature and a summary of the information received from the States Parties to the present Covenant and the specialized agencies on the measures taken and the progress made in achieving general observance of the rights recognized in the present Covenant.

Article 22

The Economic and Social Council may bring to the attention of other organs of the United Nations, their subsidiary organs and specialized agencies concerned with furnishing technical assistance any matters arising out of the reports referred to in this part of the present Covenant which may assist such bodies in deciding, each within its field of competence, on the advisability of international measures likely to contribute to the effective progressive implementation of the present Covenant.

Article 23

The States Parties to the present Covenant agree that international action for the achievement of the rights recognized in the present Covenant includes such methods as the conclusion of conventions, the adoption of recommendations, the furnishing of technical assistance and the holding of regional meetings and technical meetings for the purpose of consultation and study organized in conjunction with the Governments concerned.

Article 24

Nothing in the present Covenant shall be interpreted as impairing the provisions of the Charter of the United Nations and of the constitutions of the specialized agencies which define the respective responsibilities of the various organs of the United Nations and of the specialized agencies in regard to the matters dealt with in the present Covenant.

Article 25

Nothing in the present Covenant shall be interpreted as impairing the inherent right of all peoples to enjoy and utilize fully and freely their natural wealth and resources.

PART V

Article 26

1. The present Covenant is open for signature by any State Member of the United Nations or member of any of its specialized agencies, by any State Party to the Statute of the International Court of Justice, and by any other State which has been invited by the General Assembly of the United Nations to become a party to the present Covenant.

2. The present Covenant is subject to ratification. Instruments of ratification shall be deposited with the Secretary-General of the United Nations.

3. The present Covenant shall be open to accession by any State referred to in paragraph 1 of this article.

4. Accession shall be effected by the deposit of an instrument of accession with the Secretary-General of the United Nations.

5. The Secretary-General of the United Nations shall inform all States which have signed the present Covenant or acceded to it of the deposit of each instrument of ratification or accession.

Article 27

1. The present Covenant shall enter into force three months after the date of the deposit with the Secretary-General of the United Nations of the thirty-fifth instrument of ratification or instrument of accession.

2. For each State ratifying the present Covenant or acceding to it after the deposit of the thirty-fifth instrument of ratification or instrument of accession, the present Covenant shall enter into force three months after the date of the deposit of its own instrument of ratification or instrument of accession.

Article 28

The provisions of the present Covenant shall extend to all parts of federal States without any limitations or exceptions.

Article 29

1. Any State Party to the present Covenant may propose an amendment and file it with the Secretary-General of the United Nations. The Secretary-General shall thereupon communicate any proposed amendments to the States Parties to the present Covenant with a request that they notify him whether they favour a conference of States Parties for the purpose of considering and voting upon the proposals. In the event that at least one third of the States Parties favours such a conference, the Secretary-General shall convene the conference under the auspices of the United Nations. Any amendment adopted by a majority of the States Parties present and voting at the conference shall be submitted to the General Assembly of the United Nations for approval.

2. Amendments shall come into force when they have been approved by the General Assembly of the United Nations and accepted by a two-thirds majority of the States Parties to the present Covenant in accordance with their respective constitutional processes.

3. When amendments come into force they shall be binding on those States Parties which have accepted them, other States Parties still being bound by the provisions of the present Covenant and any earlier amendment which they have accepted.

Article 30

Irrespective of the notifications made under Article 26, paragraph 5, the Secretary-General of the United Nations shall inform all States referred to in paragraph 1 of the same article of the following particulars:

(a) Signatures, ratifications and accessions under Article 26;

(b) The date of the entry into force of the present Covenant under Article 27 and the date of the entry into force of any amendments under Article 29.

Article 31

1. The present Covenant, of which the Chinese, English, French, Russian and Spanish texts are equally authentic, shall be deposited in the archives of the United Nations.

2. The Secretary-General of the United Nations shall transmit certified copies of the present Covenant to all States referred to in Article 26.

50. OPTIONAL PROTOCOL TO THE INTERNATIONAL COVENANT ON ECONOMIC, SOCIAL AND CULTURAL RIGHTS, 2008

The Optional Protocol was adopted by General Assembly Resolution 63/117 on 10 December 2008, without a vote, and further to Human Rights Council Resolution 8/2 of 18 June 2008. It was opened for signature in New York on 24 September 2009 and will come into force when ratified by ten States. The Optional Protocol will enable individuals to seek justice for the violations of economic, social and cultural rights at the international level for the first time.

Further reading

MAHON, C., 'Progress at the Front: The Draft Optional Protocol to the International Covenant on Economic, Social and Cultural Rights', (2008) 8 *Human Rights Law Review* 617.

SEPÚLVEDA CARMONA, M., 'The obligations of "international assistance and cooperation" under the International Covenant on Economic, Social and Cultural Rights. A possible entry point to a human rights based approach to Millennium Goal 8', (2009) 13 *International Journal of Human Rights* 86.

WILSON, B., 'Quelques réflexions sur l'adoption du Protocole facultatif se rapportant au Pacte international relatif aux droits économiques, sociaux et culturels des Nations Unies', *Revue trimestrielle de droits de l'homme*, 2009, 295.

TEXT

Preamble

The States Parties to the present Protocol,

Considering that, in accordance with the principles proclaimed in the Charter of the United Nations, recognition of the inherent dignity and of the equal and inalienable rights of all members of the human family is the foundation of freedom, justice and peace in the world,

Noting that the Universal Declaration of Human Rights proclaims that all human beings are born free and equal in dignity and rights and that everyone is entitled to all the rights and freedoms set forth therein, without distinction of any kind, such as race, colour, sex, language, religion, political or other opinion, national or social origin, property, birth or other status,

Recalling that the Universal Declaration of Human Rights and the International Covenants on Human Rights recognize that the ideal of free human beings enjoying freedom from fear and want can only be achieved if conditions are created whereby everyone may enjoy civil, cultural, economic, political and social rights,

Reaffirming the universality, indivisibility, interdependence and interrelatedness of all human rights and fundamental freedoms,

Recalling that each State Party to the International Covenant on Economic, Social and Cultural Rights (hereinafter referred to as 'the Covenant') undertakes to take steps, individually and through international assistance and cooperation, especially economic and technical, to the maximum of its available resources, with a view to achieving progressively the full realization of the rights recognized in the Covenant by all appropriate means, including particularly the adoption of legislative measures,

Considering that, in order further to achieve the purposes of the Covenant and the implementation of its provisions, it would be appropriate to enable the Committee on Economic, Social and Cultural Rights (hereinafter referred to as 'the Committee') to carry out the functions provided for in the present Protocol,

Have agreed as follows:

Article 1—*Competence of the Committee to receive and consider communications*

1. A State Party to the Covenant that becomes a Party to the present Protocol recognizes the competence of the Committee to receive and consider communications as provided for by the provisions of the present Protocol.

2. No communication shall be received by the Committee if it concerns a State Party to the Covenant which is not a Party to the present Protocol.

Article 2—*Communications*

Communications may be submitted by or on behalf of individuals or groups of individuals, under the jurisdiction of a State Party, claiming to be victims of a violation of any of the economic, social and cultural rights set forth in the Covenant by that State Party. Where a communication is submitted on behalf of individuals or groups of individuals, this shall be with their consent unless the author can justify acting on their behalf without such consent.

Article 3—*Admissibility*

1. The Committee shall not consider a communication unless it has ascertained that all available domestic remedies have been exhausted. This shall not be the rule where the application of such remedies is unreasonably prolonged.

2. The Committee shall declare a communication inadmissible when:

(a) It is not submitted within one year after the exhaustion of domestic remedies, except in cases where the author can demonstrate that it had not been possible to submit the communication within that time limit;

(b) The facts that are the subject of the communication occurred prior to the entry into force of the present Protocol for the State Party concerned unless those facts continued after that date;

(c) The same matter has already been examined by the Committee or has been or is being examined under another procedure of international investigation or settlement;

(d) It is incompatible with the provisions of the Covenant;

(e) It is manifestly ill-founded, not sufficiently substantiated or exclusively based on reports disseminated by mass media;

(f) It is an abuse of the right to submit a communication; or when

(g) It is anonymous or not in writing.

Article 4—Communications not revealing a clear disadvantage

The Committee may, if necessary, decline to consider a communication where it does not reveal that the author has suffered a clear disadvantage, unless the Committee considers that the communication raises a serious issue of general importance.

Article 5—Interim measures

1. At any time after the receipt of a communication and before a determination on the merits has been reached, the Committee may transmit to the State Party concerned for its urgent consideration a request that the State Party take such interim measures as may be necessary in exceptional circumstances to avoid possible irreparable damage to the victim or victims of the alleged violations.

2. Where the Committee exercises its discretion under paragraph 1 of the present article, this does not imply a determination on admissibility or on the merits of the communication.

Article 6—Transmission of the communication

1. Unless the Committee considers a communication inadmissible without reference to the State Party concerned, the Committee shall bring any communication submitted to it under the present Protocol confidentially to the attention of the State Party concerned.

2. Within six months, the receiving State Party shall submit to the Committee written explanations or statements clarifying the matter and the remedy, if any, that may have been provided by that State Party.

Article 7—Friendly settlement

1. The Committee shall make available its good offices to the parties concerned with a view to reaching a friendly settlement of the matter on the basis of the respect for the obligations set forth in the Covenant.

2. An agreement on a friendly settlement closes consideration of the communication under the present Protocol.

Article 8—Examination of communications

1. The Committee shall examine communications received under article 2 of the present Protocol in the light of all documentation submitted to it, provided that this documentation is transmitted to the parties concerned.

2. The Committee shall hold closed meetings when examining communications under the present Protocol.

3. When examining a communication under the present Protocol, the Committee may consult, as appropriate, relevant documentation emanating from other United Nations bodies, specialized agencies, funds, programmes and mechanisms, and other international organizations, including from regional human rights systems, and any observations or comments by the State Party concerned.

4. When examining communications under the present Protocol, the Committee shall consider the reasonableness of the steps taken by the State Party in accordance with part II of the Covenant. In doing so, the Committee shall bear in mind that the State Party may adopt a range of possible policy measures for the implementation of the rights set forth in the Covenant.

Article 9—Follow-up to the views of the Committee

1. After examining a communication, the Committee shall transmit its views on the communication, together with its recommendations, if any, to the parties concerned.

2. The State Party shall give due consideration to the views of the Committee, together with its recommendations, if any, and shall submit to the Committee, within six months, a written response, including information on any action taken in the light of the views and recommendations of the Committee.

3. The Committee may invite the State Party to submit further information about any measures the State Party has taken in response to its views or recommendations, if any, including as deemed appropriate by the Committee, in the State Party's subsequent reports under articles 16 and 17 of the Covenant.

Article 10—Inter-State communications

1. A State Party to the present Protocol may at any time declare under the present article that it recognizes the competence of the Committee to receive and consider communications to the effect that a State Party claims that another State Party is not fulfilling its obligations under the Covenant. Communications under the present article may be received and considered only if submitted by a State Party that has made a declaration recognizing in regard to itself the competence of the Committee. No communication shall be received by the Committee if it concerns a State Party which has not made such a declaration. Communications received under the present article shall be dealt with in accordance with the following procedure:

(a) If a State Party to the present Protocol considers that another State Party is not fulfilling its obligations under the Covenant, it may, by written communication, bring the matter to the attention of that State Party. The State Party may also inform the Committee of the matter. Within three months after the receipt of the communication, the receiving State shall afford the State that sent the communication an explanation, or any other statement in writing clarifying the matter, which should include, to the extent possible and pertinent, reference to domestic procedures and remedies taken, pending or available in the matter;

(b) If the matter is not settled to the satisfaction of both States Parties concerned within six months after the receipt by the receiving State of the initial communication, either State shall have the right to refer the matter to the Committee, by notice given to the Committee and to the other State;

(c) The Committee shall deal with a matter referred to it only after it has ascertained that all available domestic remedies have been invoked and exhausted in the matter. This shall not be the rule where the application of the remedies is unreasonably prolonged;

(d) Subject to the provisions of subparagraph (c) of the present paragraph, the Committee shall make available its good offices to the States Parties concerned with a view to a friendly solution of the matter on the basis of the respect for the obligations set forth in the Covenant;

(e) The Committee shall hold closed meetings when examining communications under the present article;

(f) In any matter referred to it in accordance with subparagraph (b) of the present paragraph, the Committee may call upon the States Parties concerned, referred to in subparagraph (b), to supply any relevant information;

(g) The States Parties concerned, referred to in subparagraph (b) of the present paragraph, shall have the right to be represented when the matter is being considered by the Committee and to make submissions orally and/or in writing;

(h) The Committee shall, with all due expediency after the date of receipt of notice under subparagraph (b) of the present paragraph, submit a report, as follows:

  (i) If a solution within the terms of subparagraph (d) of the present paragraph is reached, the Committee shall confine its report to a brief statement of the facts and of the solution reached;

  (ii) If a solution within the terms of subparagraph (d) is not reached, the Committee shall, in its report, set forth the relevant facts concerning the issue between the States Parties concerned. The written submissions and record of the oral submissions made by the States Parties concerned shall be attached to the report. The Committee may also communicate only to the States Parties concerned any views that it may consider relevant to the issue between them.

In every matter, the report shall be communicated to the States Parties concerned.

2. A declaration under paragraph 1 of the present article shall be deposited by the States Parties with the Secretary-General of the United Nations, who shall transmit copies thereof to the other States Parties. A declaration may be withdrawn at any time by notification to the Secretary-General. Such a withdrawal shall not prejudice the consideration of any matter that is the subject of a communication already transmitted under the present article; no further communication by any State Party shall be received under the present article after the notification of withdrawal of the declaration has been received by the Secretary-General, unless the State Party concerned has made a new declaration.

Article 11—Inquiry procedure

1. A State Party to the present Protocol may at any time declare that it recognizes the competence of the Committee provided for under the present article.

2. If the Committee receives reliable information indicating grave or systematic violations by a State Party of any of the economic, social and cultural rights set forth in the Covenant, the Committee shall invite that State Party to cooperate in the examination of the information and to this end to submit observations with regard to the information concerned.

3. Taking into account any observations that may have been submitted by the State Party concerned as well as any other reliable information available to it, the Committee may designate one or more of its members to conduct an inquiry and to report urgently to the Committee. Where warranted and with the consent of the State Party, the inquiry may include a visit to its territory.

4. Such an inquiry shall be conducted confidentially and the cooperation of the State Party shall be sought at all stages of the proceedings.

5. After examining the findings of such an inquiry, the Committee shall transmit these findings to the State Party concerned together with any comments and recommendations.

6. The State Party concerned shall, within six months of receiving the findings, comments and recommendations transmitted by the Committee, submit its observations to the Committee.

7. After such proceedings have been completed with regard to an inquiry made in accordance with paragraph 2 of the present article, the Committee may, after consultations

with the State Party concerned, decide to include a summary account of the results of the proceedings in its annual report provided for in article 15 of the present Protocol.

8. Any State Party having made a declaration in accordance with paragraph 1 of the present article may, at any time, withdraw this declaration by notification to the Secretary-General.

Article 12—Follow-up to the inquiry procedure

1. The Committee may invite the State Party concerned to include in its report under articles 16 and 17 of the Covenant details of any measures taken in response to an inquiry conducted under article 11 of the present Protocol.

2. The Committee may, if necessary, after the end of the period of six months referred to in article 11, paragraph 6, invite the State Party concerned to inform it of the measures taken in response to such an inquiry.

Article 13—Protection measures

A State Party shall take all appropriate measures to ensure that individuals under its jurisdiction are not subjected to any form of ill-treatment or intimidation as a consequence of communicating with the Committee pursuant to the present Protocol.

Article 14—International assistance and cooperation

1. The Committee shall transmit, as it may consider appropriate, and with the consent of the State Party concerned, to United Nations specialized agencies, funds and programmes and other competent bodies, its views or recommendations concerning communications and inquiries that indicate a need for technical advice or assistance, along with the State Party's observations and suggestions, if any, on these views or recommendations.

2. The Committee may also bring to the attention of such bodies, with the consent of the State Party concerned, any matter arising out of communications considered under the present Protocol which may assist them in deciding, each within its field of competence, on the advisability of international measures likely to contribute to assisting States Parties in achieving progress in implementation of the rights recognized in the Covenant.

3. A trust fund shall be established in accordance with the relevant procedures of the General Assembly, to be administered in accordance with the Financial Regulations and Rules of the United Nations, with a view to providing expert and technical assistance to States Parties, with the consent of the State Party concerned, for the enhanced implementation of the rights contained in the Covenant, thus contributing to building national capacities in the area of economic, social and cultural rights in the context of the present Protocol.

4. The provisions of the present article are without prejudice to the obligations of each State Party to fulfil its obligations under the Covenant.

Article 15—Annual report

The Committee shall include in its annual report a summary of its activities under the present Protocol.

Article 16—Dissemination and information

Each State Party undertakes to make widely known and to disseminate the Covenant and the present Protocol and to facilitate access to information about the views and recommendations of the Committee, in particular, on matters involving that State Party, and to do so in accessible formats for persons with disabilities.

Article 17—Signature, ratification and accession

1. The present Protocol is open for signature by any State that has signed, ratified or acceded to the Covenant.

2. The present Protocol is subject to ratification by any State that has ratified or acceded to the Covenant. Instruments of ratification shall be deposited with the Secretary-General of the United Nations.

3. The present Protocol shall be open to accession by any State that has ratified or acceded to the Covenant.

4. Accession shall be effected by the deposit of an instrument of accession with the Secretary-General of the United Nations.

Article 18—Entry into force

1. The present Protocol shall enter into force three months after the date of the deposit with the Secretary-General of the United Nations of the tenth instrument of ratification or accession.

2. For each State ratifying or acceding to the present Protocol after the deposit of the tenth instrument of ratification or accession, the Protocol shall enter into force three months after the date of the deposit of its instrument of ratification or accession.

Article 19—Amendments

1. Any State Party may propose an amendment to the present Protocol and submit it to the Secretary-General of the United Nations. The Secretary-General shall communicate any proposed amendments to States Parties, with a request to be notified whether they favour a meeting of States Parties for the purpose of considering and deciding upon the proposals. In the event that, within four months from the date of such communication, at least one third of the States Parties favour such a meeting, the Secretary-General shall convene the meeting under the auspices of the United Nations. Any amendment adopted by a majority of two thirds of the States Parties present and voting shall be submitted by the Secretary-General to the General Assembly for approval and thereafter to all States Parties for acceptance.

2. An amendment adopted and approved in accordance with paragraph 1 of the present article shall enter into force on the thirtieth day after the number of instruments of acceptance deposited reaches two thirds of the number of States Parties at the date of adoption of the amendment. Thereafter, the amendment shall enter into force for any State Party on the thirtieth day following the deposit of its own instrument of acceptance. An amendment shall be binding only on those States Parties which have accepted it.

Article 20—Denunciation

1. Any State Party may denounce the present Protocol at any time by written notification addressed to the Secretary-General of the United Nations. Denunciation shall take effect six months after the date of receipt of the notification by the Secretary-General.

2. Denunciation shall be without prejudice to the continued application of the provisions of the present Protocol to any communication submitted under articles 2 and 10 or to any procedure initiated under article 11 before the effective date of denunciation.

Article 21—Notification by the Secretary-General

The Secretary-General of the United Nations shall notify all States referred to in article 26, paragraph 1, of the Covenant of the following particulars:

- *(a)* Signatures, ratifications and accessions under the present Protocol;
- *(b)* The date of entry into force of the present Protocol and of any amendment under article 19;
- *(c)* Any denunciation under article 20.

Article 22—Official languages

1. The present Protocol, of which the Arabic, Chinese, English, French, Russian and Spanish texts are equally authentic, shall be deposited in the archives of the United Nations.

2. The Secretary-General of the United Nations shall transmit certified copies of the present Protocol to all States referred to in article 26 of the Covenant.

51. INTENATIONAL COVENANT ON CIVIL AND POLITICAL RIGHTS, 1966

This was adopted at the same time as the previous Covenant, and entered into force on 23 March 1976; see General Assembly Resolution 2200A (XXI), UN doc. A/6316 (1966). For the text in various languages, see 999 *UNTS* 171. For reports and other information from the Human Rights Committee—the body of independent experts established under Part IV to monitor implementation—see **http://www2.ohchr.org/english/bodies/hrc/**.

With respect to inter-State complaints under the optional procedure provided for in Article 41, there is an overlap with the procedure under the European Convention on Human Rights, below. However, unlike its European counterpart, the Covenant provision has not so far been employed.

On the extra-territorial application of human rights treaties in general and of the European Convention in particular, see, among others, *Legal Consequences of the Construction of a Wall in the Occupied Palestinian Territory, Advisory Opinion* [2004] ICJ *Reports*, §111; *Case Concerning Armed Activities in the Territory of the Congo (DRC v Uganda)* (Judgment) [2005] ICJ *Reports*, §§216, 219; *R (B) v Secretary of State for Foreign and Commonwealth Affairs* [2005] QB 643; *R (Al-Skeini) v Secretary of State for Defence* [2007] UKHL 26, [2008] 1 AC 153; *R (Al-Saadoon) v Secretary of State for Defence* [2009] EWCA Civ 7; [2008] EWHC 3098 (Admin); *Al-Saadoon and Mufdhi v United Kingdom* (Appl. No. 61498/08), Decision on admissibility, 30 June 2009; *Banković v Belgium and others* (2001) BHRC 435; *Issa v Turkey* (2005) 41 EHRR 27; *Öcalan v Turkey* (2005) 41 EHRR 985.

Further reading

CONTE, A. and BURCHILL, R., *Defining Civil and Political Rights: The Jurisprudence of the United Nations Human Rights Committee*, Farnham: Ashgate, 2nd edn., 2009

COOMANS, F. and KAMMINGA, M., eds., *Extraterritorial Application of Human Rights Treaties*, Antwerp: Intersentia, 2004.

JOSEPH, S., SCHULTZ, J. and CASTAN, M., *The International Covenant on Civil and Political Rights: Cases, Materials, and Commentary*, Oxford: Oxford University Press, 2nd edn., 2004.

KORKELIA, K., 'New Challenges to the Regime of Reservations under the International Covenant on Civil and Political Rights', (2002) 13 *EJIL* 437.

McGOLDRICK, D., *The Human Rights Committee: Its Role in the Development of the International Covenant on Civil and Political Rights*, Oxford: Clarendon Press, 1991.

NOWAK, M., *UN Covenant on Civil and Political Rights, CCPR Commentary*, Kehl, Arlington: N. P. Engel, 2nd edn., 2005.

SCHWELB, E., 'Civil and Political Rights: The International Measures of Implementation', (1968) 62 *AJIL* 827.

TEXT

Preamble

The States Parties to the present Covenant,

Considering that, in accordance with the principles proclaimed in the Charter of the United Nations, recognition of the inherent dignity and of the equal and inalienable rights of all members of the human family is the foundation of freedom, justice and peace in the world,

Recognizing that these rights derive from the inherent dignity of the human person,

Recognizing that, in accordance with the Universal Declaration of Human Rights, the ideal of free human beings enjoying civil and political freedom and freedom from fear and want can only be achieved if conditions are created whereby everyone may enjoy his civil and political rights, as well as his economic, social and cultural rights,

Considering the obligation of States under the Charter of the United Nations to promote universal respect for, and observance of, human rights and freedoms,

Realizing that the individual, having duties to other individuals and to the community to which he belongs, is under a responsibility to strive for the promotion and observance of the rights recognized in the present Covenant,

Agree upon the following articles:

PART I

Article 1

1. All peoples have the right of self-determination. By virtue of that right they freely determine their political status and freely pursue their economic, social and cultural development.

2. All peoples may, for their own ends, freely dispose of their natural wealth and resources without prejudice to any obligations arising out of international economic co-operation, based upon the principle of mutual benefit, and international law. In no case may a people be deprived of its own means of subsistence.

3. The States Parties to the present Covenant, including those having responsibility for the administration of Non-Self-Governing and Trust Territories, shall promote the realization of the right of self-determination, and shall respect that right, in conformity with the provisions of the Charter of the United Nations.

PART II

Article 2

1. Each State Party to the present Covenant undertakes to respect and to ensure to all individuals within its territory and subject to its jurisdiction the rights recognized in the present Covenant, without distinction of any kind, such as race, colour, sex, language, religion, political or other opinion, national or social origin, property, birth or other status.

2. Where not already provided for by existing legislative or other measures, each State Party to the present Covenant undertakes to take the necessary steps, in accordance with its constitutional processes and with the provisions of the present Covenant, to adopt such legislative or other measures as may be necessary to give effect to the rights recognized in the present Covenant.

3. Each State Party to the present Covenant undertakes:

(a) To ensure that any person whose rights or freedoms as herein recognized are violated shall have an effective remedy, notwithstanding that the violation has been committed by persons acting in an official capacity;

(b) To ensure that any person claiming such a remedy shall have his right thereto determined by competent judicial, administrative or legislative authorities, or by any other competent authority provided for by the legal system of the State, and to develop the possibilities of judicial remedy;

(c) To ensure that the competent authorities shall enforce such remedies when granted.

Article 3

The States Parties to the present Covenant undertake to ensure the equal right of men and women to the enjoyment of all civil and political rights set forth in the present Covenant.

Article 4

1. In time of public emergency which threatens the life of the nation and the existence of which is officially proclaimed, the States Parties to the present Covenant may take measures derogating from their obligations under the present Covenant to the extent strictly required by the exigencies of the situation, provided that such measures are not inconsistent with their other obligations under international law and do not involve discrimination solely on the ground of race, colour, sex, language, religion or social origin.

2. No derogation from Articles 6, 7, 8 (paragraphs 1 and 2), 11, 15, 16 and 18 may be made under this provision.

3. Any State Party to the present Covenant availing itself of the right of derogation shall immediately inform the other States Parties to the present Covenant, through the intermediary of the Secretary-General of the United Nations, of the provisions from which it has derogated and of the reasons by which it was actuated. A further communication shall be made, through the same intermediary, on the date on which it terminates such derogation.

Article 5

1. Nothing in the present Covenant may be interpreted as implying for any State, group or person any right to engage in any activity or perform any act aimed at the destruction of any of the rights and freedoms recognized herein or at their limitation to a greater extent than is provided for in the present Covenant.

2. There shall be no restriction upon or derogation from any of the fundamental human rights recognized or existing in any State Party to the present Covenant pursuant to law, conventions, regulations or custom on the pretext that the present Covenant does not recognize such rights or that it recognizes them to a lesser extent.

PART III

Article 6

1. Every human being has the inherent right to life. This right shall be protected by law. No one shall be arbitrarily deprived of his life.

2. In countries which have not abolished the death penalty, sentence of death may be imposed only for the most serious crimes in accordance with the law in force at the time of the commission of the crime and not contrary to the provisions of the present Covenant and to the Convention on the Prevention and Punishment of the Crime of Genocide. This penalty can only be carried out pursuant to a final judgment rendered by a competent court.

3. When deprivation of life constitutes the crime of genocide, it is understood that nothing in this article shall authorize any State Party to the present Covenant to derogate in any way from any obligation assumed under the provisions of the Convention on the Prevention and Punishment of the Crime of Genocide.

4. Anyone sentenced to death shall have the right to seek pardon or commutation of the sentence. Amnesty, pardon or commutation of the sentence of death may be granted in all cases.

5. Sentence of death shall not be imposed for crimes committed by persons below eighteen years of age and shall not be carried out on pregnant women.

6. Nothing in this article shall be invoked to delay or to prevent the abolition of capital punishment by any State Party to the present Covenant.

Article 7

No one shall be subjected to torture or to cruel, inhuman or degrading treatment or punishment. In particular, no one shall be subjected without his free consent to medical or scientific experimentation.

Article 8

1. No one shall be held in slavery; slavery and the slave-trade in all their forms shall be prohibited.

2. No one shall be held in servitude.

3. *(a)* No one shall be required to perform forced or compulsory labour;

   (b) Paragraph 3 (a) shall not be held to preclude, in countries where imprisonment with hard labour may be imposed as a punishment for a crime, the performance of hard labour in pursuance of a sentence to such punishment by a competent court;

   (c) For the purpose of this paragraph the term 'forced or compulsory labour' shall not include:

      (i) Any work or service, not referred to in subparagraph (b), normally required of a person who is under detention in consequence of a lawful order of a court, or of a person during conditional release from such detention;

      (ii) Any service of a military character and, in countries where conscientious objection is recognized, any national service required by law of conscientious objectors;

    (iii) Any service exacted in cases of emergency or calamity threatening the life or well-being of the community;

    (iv) Any work or service which forms part of normal civil obligations.

Article 9

1. Everyone has the right to liberty and security of person. No one shall be subjected to arbitrary arrest or detention. No one shall be deprived of his liberty except on such grounds and in accordance with such procedure as are established by law.

2. Anyone who is arrested shall be informed, at the time of arrest, of the reasons for his arrest and shall be promptly informed of any charges against him.

3. Anyone arrested or detained on a criminal charge shall be brought promptly before a judge or other officer authorized by law to exercise judicial power and shall be entitled to trial within a reasonable time or to release. It shall not be the general rule that persons awaiting trial shall be detained in custody, but release may be subject to guarantees to appear for trial, at any other stage of the judicial proceedings, and, should occasion arise, for execution of the judgment.

4. Anyone who is deprived of his liberty by arrest or detention shall be entitled to take proceedings before a court, in order that that court may decide without delay on the lawfulness of his detention and order his release if the detention is not lawful.

5. Anyone who has been the victim of unlawful arrest or detention shall have an enforceable right to compensation.

Article 10

1. All persons deprived of their liberty shall be treated with humanity and with respect for the inherent dignity of the human person.

2. *(a)* Accused persons shall, save in exceptional circumstances, be segregated from convicted persons and shall be subject to separate treatment appropriate to their status as unconvicted persons;

   (b) Accused juvenile persons shall be separated from adults and brought as speedily as possible for adjudication.

3. The penitentiary system shall comprise treatment of prisoners the essential aim of which shall be their reformation and social rehabilitation. Juvenile offenders shall be segregated from adults and be accorded treatment appropriate to their age and legal status.

Article 11

No one shall be imprisoned merely on the ground of inability to fulfil a contractual obligation.

Article 12

1. Everyone lawfully within the territory of a State shall, within that territory, have the right to liberty of movement and freedom to choose his residence.

2. Everyone shall be free to leave any country, including his own.

3. The above-mentioned rights shall not be subject to any restrictions except those which are provided by law, are necessary to protect national security, public order (*ordre public*), public health or morals or the rights and freedoms of others, and are consistent with the other rights recognized in the present Covenant.

4. No one shall be arbitrarily deprived of the right to enter his own country.

Article 13

An alien lawfully in the territory of a State Party to the present Covenant may be expelled therefrom only in pursuance of a decision reached in accordance with law and shall, except where compelling reasons of national security otherwise require, be allowed to submit the reasons against his expulsion and to have his case reviewed by, and be represented for the purpose before, the competent authority or a person or persons especially designated by the competent authority.

Article 14

1. All persons shall be equal before the courts and tribunals. In the determination of any criminal charge against him, or of his rights and obligations in a suit at law, everyone shall be entitled to a fair and public hearing by a competent, independent and impartial tribunal established by law. The press and the public may be excluded from all or part of a trial for reasons of morals, public order (*ordre public*) or national security in a democratic society, or when the interest of the private lives of the parties so requires, or to the extent strictly necessary in the opinion of the court in special circumstances where publicity would prejudice the interests of justice; but any judgment rendered in a criminal case or in a suit at law shall be made public except where the interest of juvenile persons otherwise requires or the proceedings concern matrimonial disputes or the guardianship of children.

2. Everyone charged with a criminal offence shall have the right to be presumed innocent until proved guilty according to law.

3. In the determination of any criminal charge against him, everyone shall be entitled to the following minimum guarantees, in full equality:

   (a) To be informed promptly and in detail in a language which he understands of the nature and cause of the charge against him;

   (b) To have adequate time and facilities for the preparation of his defence and to communicate with counsel of his own choosing;

   (c) To be tried without undue delay;

   (d) To be tried in his presence, and to defend himself in person or through legal assistance of his own choosing; to be informed, if he does not have legal assistance, of this right; and to have legal assistance assigned to him, in any case where the interests of justice so require, and without payment by him in any such case if he does not have sufficient means to pay for it;

   (e) To examine, or have examined, the witnesses against him and to obtain the attendance and examination of witnesses on his behalf under the same conditions as witnesses against him;

   (f) To have the free assistance of an interpreter if he cannot understand or speak the language used in court;

   (g) Not to be compelled to testify against himself or to confess guilt.

4. In the case of juvenile persons, the procedure shall be such as will take account of their age and the desirability of promoting their rehabilitation.

5. Everyone convicted of a crime shall have the right to his conviction and sentence being reviewed by a higher tribunal according to law.

6. When a person has by a final decision been convicted of a criminal offence and when subsequently his conviction has been reversed or he has been pardoned on the ground that a new or newly discovered fact shows conclusively that there has been a miscarriage of justice, the person who has suffered punishment as a result of such conviction shall be compensated according to law, unless it is proved that the non-disclosure of the unknown fact in time is wholly or partly attributable to him.

7. No one shall be liable to be tried or punished again for an offence for which he has already been finally convicted or acquitted in accordance with the law and penal procedure of each country.

Article 15

1. No one shall be held guilty of any criminal offence on account of any act or omission which did not constitute a criminal offence, under national or international law, at the time when it was committed. Nor shall a heavier penalty be imposed than the one that was applicable at the time when the criminal offence was committed. If, subsequent to the commission of the offence, provision is made by law for the imposition of a lighter penalty, the offender shall benefit thereby.

2. Nothing in this article shall prejudice the trial and punishment of any person for any act or omission which, at the time when it was committed, was criminal according to the general principles of law recognized by the community of nations.

Article 16

Everyone shall have the right to recognition everywhere as a person before the law.

Article 17

1. No one shall be subjected to arbitrary or unlawful interference with his privacy, family, home or correspondence, nor to unlawful attacks on his honour and reputation.

2. Everyone has the right to the protection of the law against such interference or attacks.

Article 18

1. Everyone shall have the right to freedom of thought, conscience and religion. This right shall include freedom to have or to adopt a religion or belief of his choice, and freedom, either individually or in community with others and in public or private, to manifest his religion or belief in worship, observance, practice and teaching.

2. No one shall be subject to coercion which would impair his freedom to have or to adopt a religion or belief of his choice.

3. Freedom to manifest one's religion or beliefs may be subject only to such limitations as are prescribed by law and are necessary to protect public safety, order, health, or morals or the fundamental rights and freedoms of others.

4. The States Parties to the present Covenant undertake to have respect for the liberty of parents and, when applicable, legal guardians to ensure the religious and moral education of their children in conformity with their own convictions.

Article 19

1. Everyone shall have the right to hold opinions without interference.

2. Everyone shall have the right to freedom of expression; this right shall include freedom to seek, receive and impart information and ideas of all kinds, regardless of frontiers,

either orally, in writing or in print, in the form of art, or through any other media of his choice.

3. The exercise of the rights provided for in paragraph 2 of this article carries with it special duties and responsibilities. It may therefore be subject to certain restrictions, but these shall only be such as are provided by law and are necessary:

(a) For respect of the rights or reputations of others;

(b) For the protection of national security or of public order (*ordre public*), or of public health or morals.

Article 20

1. Any propaganda for war shall be prohibited by law.

2. Any advocacy of national, racial or religious hatred that constitutes incitement to discrimination, hostility or violence shall be prohibited by law.

Article 21

The right of peaceful assembly shall be recognized. No restrictions may be placed on the exercise of this right other than those imposed in conformity with the law and which are necessary in a democratic society in the interests of national security or public safety, public order (*ordre public*), the protection of public health or morals or the protection of the rights and freedoms of others.

Article 22

1. Everyone shall have the right to freedom of association with others, including the right to form and join trade unions for the protection of his interests.

2. No restrictions may be placed on the exercise of this right other than those which are prescribed by law and which are necessary in a democratic society in the interests of national security or public safety, public order (*ordre public*), the protection of public health or morals or the protection of the rights and freedoms of others. This article shall not prevent the imposition of lawful restrictions on members of the armed forces and of the police in their exercise of this right.

3. Nothing in this article shall authorize States Parties to the International Labour Organization Convention of 1948 concerning Freedom of Association and Protection of the Right to Organize to take legislative measures which would prejudice, or to apply the law in such a manner as to prejudice, the guarantees provided for in that Convention.

Article 23

1. The family is the natural and fundamental group unit of society and is entitled to protection by society and the State.

2. The right of men and women of marriageable age to marry and to found a family shall be recognized.

3. No marriage shall be entered into without the free and full consent of the intending spouses.

4. States Parties to the present Covenant shall take appropriate steps to ensure equality of rights and responsibilities of spouses as to marriage, during marriage and at its dissolution. In the case of dissolution, provision shall be made for the necessary protection of any children.

Article 24

1. Every child shall have, without any discrimination as to race, colour, sex, language, religion, national or social origin, property or birth, the right to such measures of protection as are required by his status as a minor, on the part of his family, society and the State.

2. Every child shall be registered immediately after birth and shall have a name.

3. Every child has the right to acquire a nationality.

Article 25

Every citizen shall have the right and the opportunity, without any of the distinctions mentioned in Article 2 and without unreasonable restrictions:

    (a) To take part in the conduct of public affairs, directly or through freely chosen representatives;

    (b) To vote and to be elected at genuine periodic elections which shall be by universal and equal suffrage and shall be held by secret ballot, guaranteeing the free expression of the will of the electors;

    (c) To have access, on general terms of equality, to public service in his country.

Article 26

All persons are equal before the law and are entitled without any discrimination to the equal protection of the law. In this respect, the law shall prohibit any discrimination and guarantee to all persons equal and effective protection against discrimination on any ground such as race, colour, sex, language, religion, political or other opinion, national or social origin, property, birth or other status.

Article 27

In those States in which ethnic, religious or linguistic minorities exist, persons belonging to such minorities shall not be denied the right, in community with the other members of their group, to enjoy their own culture, to profess and practise their own religion, or to use their own language.

PART IV

Article 28

1. There shall be established a Human Rights Committee (hereafter referred to in the present Covenant as the Committee). It shall consist of eighteen members and shall carry out the functions hereinafter provided.

2. The Committee shall be composed of nationals of the States Parties to the present Covenant who shall be persons of high moral character and recognized competence in the field of human rights, consideration being given to the usefulness of the participation of some persons having legal experience.

3. The members of the Committee shall be elected and shall serve in their personal capacity.

Article 29

1. The members of the Committee shall be elected by secret ballot from a list of persons possessing the qualifications prescribed in Article 28 and nominated for the purpose by the States Parties to the present Covenant.

2. Each State Party to the present Covenant may nominate not more than two persons. These persons shall be nationals of the nominating State.

3. A person shall be eligible for renomination.

Article 30

1. The initial election shall be held no later than six months after the date of the entry into force of the present Covenant.

2. At least four months before the date of each election to the Committee, other than an election to fill a vacancy declared in accordance with Article 34, the Secretary-General of the United Nations shall address a written invitation to the States Parties to the present Covenant to submit their nominations for membership of the Committee within three months.

3. The Secretary-General of the United Nations shall prepare a list in alphabetical order of all the persons thus nominated, with an indication of the States Parties which have nominated them, and shall submit it to the States Parties to the present Covenant no later than one month before the date of each election.

4. Elections of the members of the Committee shall be held at a meeting of the States Parties to the present Covenant convened by the Secretary-General of the United Nations at the Headquarters of the United Nations. At that meeting, for which two thirds of the States Parties to the present Covenant shall constitute a quorum, the persons elected to the Committee shall be those nominees who obtain the largest number of votes and an absolute majority of the votes of the representatives of States Parties present and voting.

Article 31

1. The Committee may not include more than one national of the same State.

2. In the election of the Committee, consideration shall be given to equitable geographical distribution of membership and to the representation of the different forms of civilization and of the principal legal systems.

Article 32

1. The members of the Committee shall be elected for a term of four years. They shall be eligible for re-election if renominated. However, the terms of nine of the members elected at the first election shall expire at the end of two years; immediately after the first election, the names of these nine members shall be chosen by lot by the Chairman of the meeting referred to in Article 30, paragraph 4.

2. Elections at the expiry of office shall be held in accordance with the preceding articles of this part of the present Covenant.

Article 33

1. If, in the unanimous opinion of the other members, a member of the Committee has ceased to carry out his functions for any cause other than absence of a temporary

character, the Chairman of the Committee shall notify the Secretary-General of the United Nations, who shall then declare the seat of that member to be vacant.

2. In the event of the death or the resignation of a member of the Committee, the Chairman shall immediately notify the Secretary-General of the United Nations, who shall declare the seat vacant from the date of death or the date on which the resignation takes effect.

Article 34

1. When a vacancy is declared in accordance with Article 33 and if the term of office of the member to be replaced does not expire within six months of the declaration of the vacancy, the Secretary-General of the United Nations shall notify each of the States Parties to the present Covenant, which may within two months submit nominations in accordance with Article 29 for the purpose of filling the vacancy.

2. The Secretary-General of the United Nations shall prepare a list in alphabetical order of the persons thus nominated and shall submit it to the States Parties to the present Covenant. The election to fill the vacancy shall then take place in accordance with the relevant provisions of this part of the present Covenant.

3. A member of the Committee elected to fill a vacancy declared in accordance with Article 33 shall hold office for the remainder of the term of the member who vacated the seat on the Committee under the provisions of that article.

Article 35

The members of the Committee shall, with the approval of the General Assembly of the United Nations, receive emoluments from United Nations resources on such terms and conditions as the General Assembly may decide, having regard to the importance of the Committee's responsibilities.

Article 36

The Secretary-General of the United Nations shall provide the necessary staff and facilities for the effective performance of the functions of the Committee under the present Covenant.

Article 37

1. The Secretary-General of the United Nations shall convene the initial meeting of the Committee at the Headquarters of the United Nations.

2. After its initial meeting, the Committee shall meet at such times as shall be provided in its rules of procedure.

3. The Committee shall normally meet at the Headquarters of the United Nations or at the United Nations Office at Geneva.

Article 38

Every member of the Committee shall, before taking up his duties, make a solemn declaration in open committee that he will perform his functions impartially and conscientiously.

Article 39

1. The Committee shall elect its officers for a term of two years. They may be re-elected.

2. The Committee shall establish its own rules of procedure, but these rules shall provide, *inter alia*, that:

  (a) Twelve members shall constitute a quorum;

  (b) Decisions of the Committee shall be made by a majority vote of the members present.

Article 40

1. The States Parties to the present Covenant undertake to submit reports on the measures they have adopted which give effect to the rights recognized herein and on the progress made in the enjoyment of those rights:

  (a) Within one year of the entry into force of the present Covenant for the States Parties concerned;

  (b) Thereafter whenever the Committee so requests.

2. All reports shall be submitted to the Secretary-General of the United Nations, who shall transmit them to the Committee for consideration. Reports shall indicate the factors and difficulties, if any, affecting the implementation of the present Covenant.

3. The Secretary-General of the United Nations may, after consultation with the Committee, transmit to the specialized agencies concerned copies of such parts of the reports as may fall within their field of competence.

4. The Committee shall study the reports submitted by the States Parties to the present Covenant. It shall transmit its reports, and such general comments as it may consider appropriate, to the States Parties. The Committee may also transmit to the Economic and Social Council these comments along with the copies of the reports it has received from States Parties to the present Covenant.

5. The States Parties to the present Covenant may submit to the Committee observations on any comments that may be made in accordance with paragraph 4 of this article.

Article 41

1. A State Party to the present Covenant may at any time declare under this article that it recognizes the competence of the Committee to receive and consider communications to the effect that a State Party claims that another State Party is not fulfilling its obligations under the present Covenant. Communications under this article may be received and considered only if submitted by a State Party which has made a declaration recognizing in regard to itself the competence of the Committee. No communication shall be received by the Committee if it concerns a State Party which has not made such a declaration. Communications received under this article shall be dealt with in accordance with the following procedure:

  (a) If a State Party to the present Covenant considers that another State Party is not giving effect to the provisions of the present Covenant, it may, by written communication, bring the matter to the attention of that State Party. Within three months after the receipt of the communication the receiving State shall afford the State which sent the communication an explanation, or any other statement in writing clarifying the matter which should include, to the extent possible and pertinent, reference to domestic procedures and remedies taken, pending, or available in the matter;

(b) If the matter is not adjusted to the satisfaction of both States Parties concerned within six months after the receipt by the receiving State of the initial communication, either State shall have the right to refer the matter to the Committee, by notice given to the Committee and to the other State;

(c) The Committee shall deal with a matter referred to it only after it has ascertained that all available domestic remedies have been invoked and exhausted in the matter, in conformity with the generally recognized principles of international law. This shall not be the rule where the application of the remedies is unreasonably prolonged;

(d) The Committee shall hold closed meetings when examining communications under this article;

(e) Subject to the provisions of subparagraph (c), the Committee shall make available its good offices to the States Parties concerned with a view to a friendly solution of the matter on the basis of respect for human rights and fundamental freedoms as recognized in the present Covenant;

(f) In any matter referred to it, the Committee may call upon the States Parties concerned, referred to in subparagraph (b), to supply any relevant information;

(g) The States Parties concerned, referred to in subparagraph (b), shall have the right to be represented when the matter is being considered in the Committee and to make submissions orally and/or in writing;

(h) The Committee shall, within twelve months after the date of receipt of notice under subparagraph (b), submit a report:

    (i) If a solution within the terms of subparagraph (e) is reached, the Committee shall confine its report to a brief statement of the facts and of the solution reached;

    (ii) If a solution within the terms of subparagraph (e) is not reached, the Committee shall confine its report to a brief statement of the facts; the written submissions and record of the oral submissions made by the States Parties concerned shall be attached to the report. In every matter, the report shall be communicated to the States Parties concerned.

2. The provisions of this article shall come into force when ten States Parties to the present Covenant have made declarations under paragraph 1 of this article. Such declarations shall be deposited by the States Parties with the Secretary-General of the United Nations, who shall transmit copies thereof to the other States Parties. A declaration may be withdrawn at any time by notification to the Secretary-General. Such a withdrawal shall not prejudice the consideration of any matter which is the subject of a communication already transmitted under this article; no further communication by any State Party shall be received after the notification of withdrawal of the declaration has been received by the Secretary-General, unless the State Party concerned has made a new declaration.

Article 42

1. (a) If a matter referred to the Committee in accordance with Article 41 is not resolved to the satisfaction of the States Parties concerned, the Committee may, with the prior consent of the States Parties concerned, appoint an *ad hoc* Conciliation Commission

(hereinafter referred to as the Commission). The good offices of the Commission shall be made available to the States Parties concerned with a view to an amicable solution of the matter on the basis of respect for the present Covenant;

(b) The Commission shall consist of five persons acceptable to the States Parties concerned. If the States Parties concerned fail to reach agreement within three months on all or part of the composition of the Commission, the members of the Commission concerning whom no agreement has been reached shall be elected by secret ballot by a two-thirds majority vote of the Committee from among its members.

2. The members of the Commission shall serve in their personal capacity. They shall not be nationals of the States Parties concerned, or of a State not Party to the present Covenant, or of a State Party which has not made a declaration under Article 41.

3. The Commission shall elect its own Chairman and adopt its own rules of procedure.

4. The meetings of the Commission shall normally be held at the Headquarters of the United Nations or at the United Nations Office at Geneva. However, they may be held at such other convenient places as the Commission may determine in consultation with the Secretary-General of the United Nations and the States Parties concerned.

5. The secretariat provided in accordance with Article 36 shall also service the commissions appointed under this article.

6. The information received and collated by the Committee shall be made available to the Commission and the Commission may call upon the States Parties concerned to supply any other relevant information.

7. When the Commission has fully considered the matter, but in any event not later than twelve months after having been seized of the matter, it shall submit to the Chairman of the Committee a report for communication to the States Parties concerned:

(a) If the Commission is unable to complete its consideration of the matter within twelve months, it shall confine its report to a brief statement of the status of its consideration of the matter;

(b) If an amicable solution to the matter on the basis of respect for human rights as recognized in the present Covenant is reached, the Commission shall confine its report to a brief statement of the facts and of the solution reached;

(c) If a solution within the terms of subparagraph (b) is not reached, the Commission's report shall embody its findings on all questions of fact relevant to the issues between the States Parties concerned, and its views on the possibilities of an amicable solution of the matter. This report shall also contain the written submissions and a record of the oral submissions made by the States Parties concerned;

(d) If the Commission's report is submitted under subparagraph (c), the States Parties concerned shall, within three months of the receipt of the report, notify the Chairman of the Committee whether or not they accept the contents of the report of the Commission.

8. The provisions of this article are without prejudice to the responsibilities of the Committee under Article 41.

9. The States Parties concerned shall share equally all the expenses of the members of the Commission in accordance with estimates to be provided by the Secretary-General of the United Nations.

10. The Secretary-General of the United Nations shall be empowered to pay the expenses of the members of the Commission, if necessary, before reimbursement by the States Parties concerned, in accordance with paragraph 9 of this article.

Article 43

The members of the Committee, and of the *ad hoc* conciliation commissions which may be appointed under Article 42, shall be entitled to the facilities, privileges and immunities of experts on mission for the United Nations as laid down in the relevant sections of the Convention on the Privileges and Immunities of the United Nations.

Article 44

The provisions for the implementation of the present Covenant shall apply without prejudice to the procedures prescribed in the field of human rights by or under the constituent instruments and the conventions of the United Nations and of the specialized agencies and shall not prevent the States Parties to the present Covenant from having recourse to other procedures for settling a dispute in accordance with general or special international agreements in force between them.

Article 45

The Committee shall submit to the General Assembly of the United Nations, through the Economic and Social Council, an annual report on its activities.

PART V

Article 46

Nothing in the present Covenant shall be interpreted as impairing the provisions of the Charter of the United Nations and of the constitutions of the specialized agencies which define the respective responsibilities of the various organs of the United Nations and of the specialized agencies in regard to the matters dealt with in the present Covenant.

Article 47

Nothing in the present Covenant shall be interpreted as impairing the inherent right of all peoples to enjoy and utilize fully and freely their natural wealth and resources.

PART VI

Article 48

1. The present Covenant is open for signature by any State Member of the United Nations or member of any of its specialized agencies, by any State Party to the Statute of the International Court of Justice, and by any other State which has been invited by the General Assembly of the United Nations to become a Party to the present Covenant.

2. The present Covenant is subject to ratification. Instruments of ratification shall be deposited with the Secretary-General of the United Nations.

3. The present Covenant shall be open to accession by any State referred to in paragraph 1 of this article.

4. Accession shall be effected by the deposit of an instrument of accession with the Secretary-General of the United Nations.

5. The Secretary-General of the United Nations shall inform all States which have signed this Covenant or acceded to it of the deposit of each instrument of ratification or accession.

Article 49

1. The present Covenant shall enter into force three months after the date of the deposit with the Secretary-General of the United Nations of the thirty-fifth instrument of ratification or instrument of accession.

2. For each State ratifying the present Covenant or acceding to it after the deposit of the thirty-fifth instrument of ratification or instrument of accession, the present Covenant shall enter into force three months after the date of the deposit of its own instrument of ratification or instrument of accession.

Article 50

The provisions of the present Covenant shall extend to all parts of federal States without any limitations or exceptions.

Article 51

1. Any State Party to the present Covenant may propose an amendment and file it with the Secretary-General of the United Nations. The Secretary-General of the United Nations shall thereupon communicate any proposed amendments to the States Parties to the present Covenant with a request that they notify him whether they favour a conference of States Parties for the purpose of considering and voting upon the proposals. In the event that at least one third of the States Parties favours such a conference, the Secretary-General shall convene the conference under the auspices of the United Nations. Any amendment adopted by a majority of the States Parties present and voting at the conference shall be submitted to the General Assembly of the United Nations for approval.

2. Amendments shall come into force when they have been approved by the General Assembly of the United Nations and accepted by a two-thirds majority of the States Parties to the present Covenant in accordance with their respective constitutional processes.

3. When amendments come into force, they shall be binding on those States Parties which have accepted them, other States Parties still being bound by the provisions of the present Covenant and any earlier amendment which they have accepted.

Article 52

Irrespective of the notifications made under Article 48, paragraph 5, the Secretary-General of the United Nations shall inform all States referred to in paragraph 1 of the same article of the following particulars:

    (a) Signatures, ratifications and accessions under Article 48;

    (b) The date of the entry into force of the present Covenant under Article 49 and the date of the entry into force of any amendments under Article 51.

Article 53

1. The present Covenant, of which the Chinese, English, French, Russian and Spanish texts are equally authentic, shall be deposited in the archives of the United Nations.

2. The Secretary-General of the United Nations shall transmit certified copies of the present Covenant to all States referred to in Article 48.

52. OPTIONAL PROTOCOL TO THE INTERNATIONAL COVENANT ON CIVIL AND POLITICAL RIGHTS, 1966

The Protocol, which was adopted at the same time as the Covenant, entered into force on 23 March 1976. For the jurisprudence and General Comments of the Committee, see **http://www2.ohchr.org/english/bodies/hrc**.

Further reading

BUTLER, A. S., 'Legal Aid before Human Rights Treaty Monitoring Bodies', (2000) 49 *ICLQ* 360.

MCGOLDRICK, D., *The Human Rights Committee: Its Role in the Development of the International Covenant on Civil and Political Rights*, Oxford: Clarendon Press, 1991.

TEXT

The States Parties to the present Protocol,

Considering that in order further to achieve the purposes of the International Covenant on Civil and Political Rights (hereinafter referred to as the Covenant) and the implementation of its provisions it would be appropriate to enable the Human Rights Committee set up in part IV of the Covenant (hereinafter referred to as the Committee) to receive and consider, as provided in the present Protocol, communications from individuals claiming to be victims of violations of any of the rights set forth in the Covenant,

Have *agreed* as follows:

Article 1

A State Party to the Covenant that becomes a Party to the present Protocol recognizes the competence of the Committee to receive and consider communications from individuals subject to its jurisdiction who claim to be victims of a violation by that State Party of any of the rights set forth in the Covenant. No communication shall be received by the Committee if it concerns a State Party to the Covenant which is not a Party to the present Protocol.

Article 2

Subject to the provisions of Article 1, individuals who claim that any of their rights enumerated in the Covenant have been violated and who have exhausted all available domestic remedies may submit a written communication to the Committee for consideration.

Article 3

The Committee shall consider inadmissible any communication under the present Protocol which is anonymous, or which it considers to be an abuse of the right of submission of such communications or to be incompatible with the provisions of the Covenant.

Article 4

1. Subject to the provisions of Article 3, the Committee shall bring any communications submitted to it under the present Protocol to the attention of the State Party to the present Protocol alleged to be violating any provision of the Covenant.

2. Within six months, the receiving State shall submit to the Committee written explanations or statements clarifying the matter and the remedy, if any, that may have been taken by that State.

Article 5

1. The Committee shall consider communications received under the present Protocol in the light of all written information made available to it by the individual and by the State Party concerned.

2. The Committee shall not consider any communication from an individual unless it has ascertained that:

   (a) The same matter is not being examined under another procedure of international investigation or settlement;

   (b) The individual has exhausted all available domestic remedies. This shall not be the rule where the application of the remedies is unreasonably prolonged.

3. The Committee shall hold closed meetings when examining communications under the present Protocol.

4. The Committee shall forward its views to the State Party concerned and to the individual.

Article 6

The Committee shall include in its annual report under Article 45 of the Covenant a summary of its activities under the present Protocol.

Article 7

Pending the achievement of the objectives of resolution 1514(XV) adopted by the General Assembly of the United Nations on 14 December 1960 concerning the Declaration on the Granting of Independence to Colonial Countries and Peoples, the provisions of the present Protocol shall in no way limit the right of petition granted to these peoples by the Charter of the United Nations and other international conventions and instruments under the United Nations and its specialized agencies.

Article 8

1. The present Protocol is open for signature by any State which has signed the Covenant.

2. The present Protocol is subject to ratification by any State which has ratified or acceded to the Covenant. Instruments of ratification shall be deposited with the Secretary-General of the United Nations.

3. The present Protocol shall be open to accession by any State which has ratified or acceded to the Covenant.

4. Accession shall be effected by the deposit of an instrument of accession with the Secretary-General of the United Nations.

5. The Secretary-General of the United Nations shall inform all States which have signed the present Protocol or acceded to it of the deposit of each instrument of ratification or accession.

Article 9

1. Subject to the entry into force of the Covenant, the present Protocol shall enter into force three months after the date of the deposit with the Secretary-General of the United Nations of the tenth instrument of ratification or instrument of accession.

2. For each State ratifying the present Protocol or acceding to it after the deposit of the tenth instrument of ratification or instrument of accession, the present Protocol shall enter into force three months after the date of the deposit of its own instrument of ratification or instrument of accession.

Article 10

The provisions of the present Protocol shall extend to all parts of federal States without any limitations or exceptions.

Article 11

1. Any State Party to the present Protocol may propose an amendment and file it with the Secretary-General of the United Nations. The Secretary-General shall thereupon communicate any proposed amendments to the States Parties to the present Protocol with a request that they notify him whether they favour a conference of States Parties for the purpose of considering and voting upon the proposal. In the event that at least one third of the States Parties favours such a conference, the Secretary-General shall convene the conference under the auspices of the United Nations. Any amendment adopted by a majority of the States Parties present and voting at the conference shall be submitted to the General Assembly of the United Nations for approval.

2. Amendments shall come into force when they have been approved by the General Assembly of the United Nations and accepted by a two-thirds majority of the States Parties to the present Protocol in accordance with their respective constitutional processes.

3. When amendments come into force, they shall be binding on those States Parties which have accepted them, other States Parties still being bound by the provisions of the present Protocol and any earlier amendment which they have accepted.

Article 12

1. Any State Party may denounce the present Protocol at any time by written notification addressed to the Secretary-General of the United Nations. Denunciation shall take effect three months after the date of receipt of the notification by the Secretary-General.

2. Denunciation shall be without prejudice to the continued application of the provisions of the present Protocol to any communication submitted under Article 2 before the effective date of denunciation.

Article 13

Irrespective of the notifications made under Article 8, paragraph 5, of the present Protocol, the Secretary-General of the United Nations shall inform all States referred to in Article 48, paragraph 1, of the Covenant of the following particulars:

- (a) Signatures, ratifications and accessions under Article 8;
- (b) The date of the entry into force of the present Protocol under Article 9 and the date of the entry into force of any amendments under Article 11;
- (c) Denunciations under Article 12.

Article 14

1. The present Protocol, of which the Chinese, English, French, Russian and Spanish texts are equally authentic, shall be deposited in the archives of the United Nations.

2. The Secretary-General of the United Nations shall transmit certified copies of the present Protocol to all States referred to in Article 48 of the Covenant.

53. SECOND OPTIONAL PROTOCOL TO THE INTERNATIONAL COVENANT ON CIVIL AND POLITICAL RIGHTS, AIMING AT THE ABOLITION OF THE DEATH PENALTY, 1989

The second optional protocol, aiming at the abolition of the death penalty, was adopted by General Assembly Resolution 44/128, 15 December 1989, on a recorded vote of 59 in favour, 26 against, and 48 abstentions; UN doc. A/44/49 (1989); it entered into force on 11 July 1991.

Further reading

HOOD, R. and HOYLE, C., *The Death Penalty: A Worldwide Perspective*, Oxford: Oxford University Press, 4th edn., 2008.

NEUMAYER, E., 'Death Penalty Abolition and the Ratification of the Second Optional Protocol', (2008) 12 *International Journal of Human Rights* 3.

SCHABAS, W. A., *The Abolition of the Death Penalty in International Law*, Cambridge: Cambridge University Press, 3rd edn., 2002.

——, *War Crimes and Human Rights: Essays on the Death Penalty, Justice and Accountability*, London: Cameron May, 2008.

TEXT

The States Parties to the present Protocol,

Believing that abolition of the death penalty contributes to enhancement of human dignity and progressive development of human rights,

Recalling Article 3 of the Universal Declaration of Human Rights, adopted on 10 December 1948, and Article 6 of the International Covenant on Civil and Political Rights, adopted on 16 December 1966,

Noting that Article 6 of the International Covenant on Civil and Political Rights refers to abolition of the death penalty in terms that strongly suggest that abolition is desirable,

Convinced that all measures of abolition of the death penalty should be considered as progress in the enjoyment of the right to life,

Desirous to undertake hereby an international commitment to abolish the death penalty,

Have *agreed* as follows:

Article 1

1. No one within the jurisdiction of a State Party to the present Protocol shall be executed.

2. Each State Party shall take all necessary measures to abolish the death penalty within its jurisdiction.

Article 2

1. No reservation is admissible to the present Protocol, except for a reservation made at the time of ratification or accession that provides for the application of the death penalty in time of war pursuant to a conviction for a most serious crime of a military nature committed during wartime.

2. The State Party making such a reservation shall at the time of ratification or accession communicate to the Secretary-General of the United Nations the relevant provisions of its national legislation applicable during wartime.

3. The State Party having made such a reservation shall notify the Secretary-General of the United Nations of any beginning or ending of a state of war applicable to its territory.

Article 3

The States Parties to the present Protocol shall include in the reports they submit to the Human Rights Committee, in accordance with Article 40 of the Covenant, information on the measures that they have adopted to give effect to the present Protocol.

Article 4

With respect to the States Parties to the Covenant that have made a declaration under Article 41, the competence of the Human Rights Committee to receive and consider communications when a State Party claims that another State Party is not fulfilling its obligations shall extend to the provisions of the present Protocol, unless the State Party concerned has made a statement to the contrary at the moment of ratification or accession.

Article 5

With respect to the States Parties to the first Optional Protocol to the International Covenant on Civil and Political Rights adopted on 16 December 1966, the competence of the Human Rights Committee to receive and consider communications from individuals subject to its jurisdiction shall extend to the provisions of the present Protocol, unless the State Party concerned has made a statement to the contrary at the moment of ratification or accession.

Article 6

1. The provisions of the present Protocol shall apply as additional provisions to the Covenant.

2. Without prejudice to the possibility of a reservation under Article 2 of the present Protocol, the right guaranteed in Article 1, paragraph 1, of the present Protocol shall not be subject to any derogation under Article 4 of the Covenant.

Article 7

1. The present Protocol is open for signature by any State that has signed the Covenant.

2. The present Protocol is subject to ratification by any State that has ratified the Covenant or acceded to it. Instruments of ratification shall be deposited with the Secretary-General of the United Nations.

3. The present Protocol shall be open to accession by any State that has ratified the Covenant or acceded to it.

4. Accession shall be effected by the deposit of an instrument of accession with the Secretary-General of the United Nations.

5. The Secretary-General of the United Nations shall inform all States that have signed the present Protocol or acceded to it of the deposit of each instrument of ratification or accession.

Article 8

1. The present Protocol shall enter into force three months after the date of the deposit with the Secretary-General of the United Nations of the tenth instrument of ratification or accession.

2. For each State ratifying the present Protocol or acceding to it after the deposit of the tenth instrument of ratification or accession, the present Protocol shall enter into force three months after the date of the deposit of its own instrument of ratification or accession.

Article 9

The provisions of the present Protocol shall extend to all parts of federal States without any limitations or exceptions.

Article 10

The Secretary-General of the United Nations shall inform all States referred to in Article 48, paragraph 1, of the Covenant of the following particulars:

  (a) Reservations, communications and notifications under Article 2 of the present Protocol;

  (b) Statements made under Articles 4 or 5 of the present Protocol;

  (c) Signatures, ratifications and accessions under Article 7 of the present Protocol:

  (d) The date of the entry into force of the present Protocol under Article 8 thereof.

Article 11

1. The present Protocol, of which the Arabic, Chinese, English, French, Russian and Spanish texts are equally authentic, shall be deposited in the archives of the United Nations.

2. The Secretary-General of the United Nations shall transmit certified copies of the present Protocol to all States referred to in Article 48 of the Covenant.

54. INTERNATIONAL CONVENTION ON THE SUPPRESSION AND PUNISHMENT OF THE CRIME OF APARTHEID, 1973

This Convention was adopted and opened for signature by General Assembly Resolution 3068 (XXVIII) of 30 November 1973. The Resolution was adopted by 91 votes in favour, 4 against (Portugal, South Africa, the United Kingdom and the United States of America), and 26 abstentions. The basis of the opposition of the United States is set forth in *Digest of United States Practice in International Law*, 1973, 130–2, where it is pointed out that the Convention was 'not necessary in view of the broad, all-inclusive provisions of the International Convention on the Elimination of All Forms of Racial Discrimination'.

The Convention entered into force on 18 July 1976. Notwithstanding the end of apartheid in South Africa, some seven States ratified the Convention during the present decade alone, while Article 7 of the Rome Statute of the International Criminal Court includes the 'crime of apartheid' as a form of crime against humanity. For text, see 1015 *UNTS* 243.

Further reading

DUGARD, J., 'Introductory Note. International Convention on the Suppression and Punishment of the Crime of Apartheid, 1973': **http://www.un.org/law/avl/**.

TEXT

The States Parties to the present Convention,

Recalling the provisions of the Charter of the United Nations, in which all Members pledged themselves to take joint and separate action in co-operation with the Organization for the achievement of universal respect for, and observance of, human rights and fundamental freedoms for all without distinction as to race, sex, language or religion,

Considering the Universal Declaration of Human Rights, which states that all human beings are born free and equal in dignity and rights and that everyone is entitled to all the rights and freedoms set forth in the Declaration, without distinction of any kind, such as race, colour or national origin,

Considering the Declaration on the Granting of Independence to Colonial Countries and Peoples, in which the General Assembly stated that the process of liberation is irresistible and irreversible and that, in the interests of human dignity, progress and justice, an end must be put to colonialism and all practices of segregation and discrimination associated therewith,

Observing that, in accordance with the International Convention on the Elimination of All Forms of Racial Discrimination, States particularly condemn racial segregation and apartheid and undertake to prevent, prohibit and eradicate all practices of this nature in territories under their jurisdiction,

Observing that, in the Convention on the Prevention and Punishment of the Crime of Genocide, certain acts which may also be qualified as acts of apartheid constitute a crime under international law,

Observing that, in the Convention on the Non-Applicability of Statutory Limitations to War Crimes and Crimes against Humanity, 'inhuman acts resulting from the policy of apartheid' are qualified as crimes against humanity,

Observing that the General Assembly of the United Nations has adopted a number of resolutions in which the policies and practices of apartheid are condemned as a crime against humanity,

Observing that the Security Council has emphasized that apartheid and its continued intensification and expansion seriously disturb and threaten international peace and security,

Convinced that an International Convention on the Suppression and Punishment of the Crime of Apartheid would make it possible to take more effective measures at the international and national levels with a view to the suppression and punishment of the crime of apartheid,

Have agreed as follows:

Article I

1. The States Parties to the present Convention declare that apartheid is a crime against humanity and that inhuman acts resulting from the policies and practices of apartheid and similar policies and practices of racial segregation and discrimination, as defined in article II of the Convention, are crimes violating the principles of international law, in particular the purposes and principles of the Charter of the United Nations, and constituting a serious threat to international peace and security.

2. The States Parties to the present Convention declare criminal those organizations, institutions and individuals committing the crime of apartheid.

Article II

For the purpose of the present Convention, the term 'the crime of apartheid', which shall include similar policies and practices of racial segregation and discrimination as practised in southern Africa, shall apply to the following inhuman acts committed for the purpose of establishing and maintaining domination by one racial group of persons over any other racial group of persons and systematically oppressing them:

(a) Denial to a member or members of a racial group or groups of the right to life and liberty of person:

  (i) By murder of members of a racial group or groups;

  (ii) By the infliction upon the members of a racial group or groups of serious bodily or mental harm, by the infringement of their freedom or dignity, or by subjecting them to torture or to cruel, inhuman or degrading treatment or punishment;

  (iii) By arbitrary arrest and illegal imprisonment of the members of a racial group or groups;

(b) Deliberate imposition on a racial group or groups of living conditions calculated to cause its or their physical destruction in whole or in part;

(c) Any legislative measures and other measures calculated to prevent a racial group or groups from participation in the political, social, economic and cultural life of the country and the deliberate creation of conditions preventing the full development of such a group or groups, in particular by denying to members of a racial group or groups basic human rights and freedoms, including the right to work, the right to form recognized trade unions, the right to education, the right to leave and to return to their country, the right to a nationality, the right to freedom of movement and residence, the right to freedom of opinion and expression, and the right to freedom of peaceful assembly and association;

(d) Any measures, including legislative measures, designed to divide the population along racial lines by the creation of separate reserves and ghettos for the members of a racial group or groups, the prohibition of mixed marriages among members of various racial groups, the expropriation of landed property belonging to a racial group or groups or to members thereof;

(e) Exploitation of the labour of the members of a racial group or groups, in particular by submitting them to forced labour;

(f) Persecution of organizations and persons, by depriving them of fundamental rights and freedoms, because they oppose apartheid.

Article III

International criminal responsibility shall apply, irrespective of the motive involved, to individuals, members of organizations and institutions and representatives of the State, whether residing in the territory of the State in which the acts are perpetrated or in some other State, whenever they:

(a) Commit, participate in, directly incite or conspire in the commission of the acts mentioned in Article II of the present Convention;

(b) Directly abet, encourage or co-operate in the commission of the crime of apartheid.

Article IV

The States Parties to the present Convention undertake:

(a) To adopt any legislative or other measures necessary to suppress as well as to prevent any encouragement of the crime of apartheid and similar segregationist policies or their manifestations and to punish persons guilty of that crime;

(b) To adopt legislative, judicial and administrative measures to prosecute, bring to trial and punish in accordance with their jurisdiction persons responsible for, or accused of, the acts defined in Article II of the present Convention, whether or not such persons reside in the territory of the State in which the acts are committed or are nationals of that State or of some other State or are stateless persons.

Article V

Persons charged with the acts enumerated in Article II of the present Convention may be tried by a competent tribunal of any State Party to the Convention which may acquire jurisdiction over the person of the accused or by an international penal tribunal having jurisdiction with respect to those States Parties which shall have accepted its jurisdiction.

Article VI

The States Parties to the present Convention undertake to accept and carry out in accordance with the Charter of the United Nations the decisions taken by the Security Council aimed at the prevention, suppression and punishment of the crime of apartheid, and to co-operate in the implementation of decisions adopted by other competent organs of the United Nations'with a view to achieving the purposes of the Convention.

Article VII

1. The States Parties to the present Convention undertake to submit periodic reports to the group established under Article IX on the legislative, judicial, administrative or other measures that they have adopted and that give effect to the provisions of the Convention.

2. Copies of the reports shall be transmitted through the Secretary-General of the United Nations to the Special Committee on Apartheid.

Article VIII

Any State Party to the present Convention may call upon any competent organ of the United Nations to take such action under the Charter of the United Nations as it considers appropriate for the prevention and suppression of the crime of apartheid.

Article IX

1. The Chairman of the Commission on Human Rights shall appoint a group consisting of three members of the Commission on Human Rights, who are also representatives of States Parties to the present Convention, to consider reports submitted by States Parties in accordance with Article VII.

2. If, among the members of the Commission on Human Rights, there are no representatives of States Parties to the present Convention or if there are fewer than three such representatives, the Secretary-General of the United Nations shall, after consulting all States Parties to the Convention, designate a representative of the State Party or representatives of the States Parties which are not members of the Commission on Human Rights to take part in the work of the group established in accordance with paragraph 1 of this article, until such time as representatives of the States Parties to the Convention are elected to the Commission on Human Rights.

3. The group may meet for a period of not more than five days, either before the opening or after the closing of the session of the Commission on Human Rights, to consider the reports submitted in accordance with Article VII.

Article X

1. The States Parties to the present Convention empower the Commission on Human Rights:

  (a) To request United Nations organs, when transmitting copies of petitions under Article 15 of the International Convention on the Elimination of All Forms of Racial Discrimination, to draw its attention to complaints concerning acts which are enumerated in Article II of the present Convention;

  (b) To prepare, on the basis of reports from competent organs of the United Nations and periodic reports from States Parties to the present Convention, a list of individuals, organizations, institutions and representatives of States which are alleged to be responsible for the crimes enumerated in Article II of the Convention, as well as those against whom legal proceedings have been undertaken by States Parties to the Convention;

(c) To request information from the competent United Nations organs concerning measures taken by the authorities responsible for the administration of Trust and Non-Self-Governing Territories, and all other Territories to which General Assembly resolution 1514 (XV) of 14 December 1960 applies, with regard to such individuals alleged to be responsible for crimes under Article II of the Convention who are believed to be under their territorial and administrative jurisdiction.

2. Pending the achievement of the objectives of the Declaration on the Granting of Independence to Colonial Countries and Peoples, contained in General Assembly resolution 1514 (XV), the provisions of the present Convention shall in no way limit the right of petition granted to those peoples by other international instruments or by the United Nations and its specialized agencies.

Article XI

1. Acts enumerated in Article II of the present Convention shall not be considered political crimes for the purpose of extradition.

2. The States Parties to the present Convention undertake in such cases to grant extradition in accordance with their legislation and with the treaties in force.

Article XII

Disputes between States Parties arising out of the interpretation, application or implementation of the present Convention which have not been settled by negotiation shall, at the request of the States parties to the dispute, be brought before the International Court of Justice, save where the parties to the dispute have agreed on some other form of settlement.

Article XIII

The present Convention is open for signature by all States. Any State which does not sign the Convention before its entry into force may accede to it.

Article XIV

1. The present Convention is subject to ratification. Instruments of ratification shall be deposited with the Secretary-General of the United Nations.

2. Accession shall be effected by the deposit of an instrument of accession with the Secretary-General of the United Nations.

Article XV

1. The present Convention shall enter into force on the thirtieth day after the date of the deposit with the Secretary-General of the United Nations of the twentieth instrument of ratification or accession.

2. For each State ratifying the present Convention or acceding to it after the deposit of the twentieth instrument of ratification or instrument of accession, the Convention shall enter into force on the thirtieth day after the date of the deposit of its own instrument of ratification or instrument of accession.

Article XVI

A State Party may denounce the present Convention by written notification to the Secretary-General of the United Nations. Denunciation shall take effect one year after the date of receipt of the notification by the Secretary-General.

Article XVII

1. A request for the revision of the present Convention may be made at any time by any State Party by means of a notification in writing addressed to the Secretary-General of the United Nations.

2. The General Assembly of the United Nations shall decide upon the steps, if any, to be taken in respect of such request.

Article XVIII

The Secretary-General of the United Nations shall inform all States of the following particulars:

    (a) Signatures, ratifications and accessions under Articles XIII and XIV;

    (b) The date of entry into force of the present Convention under Article XV;

    (c) Denunciations under Article XVI;

    (d) Notifications under Article XVII.

Article XIX

1. The present Convention, of which the Chinese, English, French, Russian and Spanish texts are equally authentic, shall be deposited in the archives of the United Nations.

2. The Secretary-General of the United Nations shall transmit certified copies of the present Convention to all States.

55. CONVENTION ON THE ELIMINATION OF ALL FORMS OF DISCRIMINATION AGAINST WOMEN, 1979

The text which follows was adopted by General Assembly Resolution 34/180 on 18 December 1979 by a vote of 130 in favour, none against, and ten abstentions. The Convention came into force on 3 September 1981; for text, see 1249 *UNTS* 13. The precursor to the Convention was the Declaration on Elimination of Discrimination against Women, adopted unanimously by the General Assembly on 7 December 1967. For the text of the Declaration, see the first edition of the present work, at 183; and on the standard of non-discrimination in general international law, see BROWNLIE, I., *Principles of Public International Law*, Oxford: Oxford University Press, 7th edn., 2008, 572–5.

Reference should also be made to the ILO Convention concerning equal remuneration for men and women workers for work of equal value (see below, p. 583); and generally to **http://www. un.org/womenwatch/**.

Further reading

BYRNES, A., and CONNORS, J., *The International Bill of Rights for Women: The Impact of the CEDAW Convention*, Oxford: Oxford University Press, 2010.

INTER-PARLIAMENTARY UNION, UNITED NATIONS, *The Convention on the Elimination of All Forms of Discrimination against Women and its Optional Protocol: Handbook for Parliamentarians*, Geneva: Inter-Parliamentary Union, 2003.

McDOUGALL, M. S., LASSWELL, H. D., and CHEN, LUNG-CHU, 'Human Rights for Women and World Public Order: The Outlawing of Sex-based Discrimination', (1975) 69 *AJIL* 497.

PRUITT, L. R., 'Migration, Development, and the Promise of CEDAW for Rural Women', (2009) 30 *Michigan Journal of International Law* 707.

REHOF, L. A., *Guide to the Travaux Préparatoires of the United Nations Convention on the Elimination of all Forms of Discrimination against Women*, Leiden: Martinus Nijhoff, 1993.

YAHYAOUI KRIVENKO, E., *Women, Islam and International Law. Within the Context of the Convention on the Elimination of all Forms of Discrimination Against Women*, Geneva: Graduate Institute of International and Development Studies; Leiden-Boston: Martinus Nijhoff–Brill, 2009.

TEXT

The States Parties to the present Convention,

Noting that the Charter of the United Nations reaffirms faith in fundamental human rights, in the dignity and worth of the human person and in the equal rights of men and women,

Noting that the Universal Declaration of Human Rights affirms the principle of the inadmissibility of discrimination and proclaims that all human beings are born free and equal in dignity and rights and that everyone is entitled to all the rights and freedoms set forth therein, without distinction of any kind, including distinction based on sex,

Noting that the States Parties to the International Covenants on Human Rights have the obligation to ensure the equal rights of men and women to enjoy all economic, social, cultural, civil and political rights,

Considering the international conventions concluded under the auspices of the United Nations and the specialized agencies promoting equality of rights of men and women,

Noting also the resolutions, declarations and recommendations adopted by the United Nations and the specialized agencies promoting equality of rights of men and women,

Concerned, however, that despite these various instruments extensive discrimination against women continues to exist,

Recalling that discrimination against women violates the principles of equality of rights and respect for human dignity, is an obstacle to the participation of women, on equal terms with men, in the political, social, economic and cultural life of their countries, hampers the growth of the prosperity of society and the family and makes more difficult the full development of the potentialities of women in the service of their countries and of humanity,

Concerned that in situations of poverty women have the least access to food, health, education, training and opportunities for employment and other needs,

Convinced that the establishment of the new international economic order based on equity and justice will contribute significantly towards the promotion of equality between men and women,

Emphasizing that the eradication of apartheid, all forms of racism, racial discrimination, colonialism, neo-colonialism, aggression, foreign occupation and domination and interference in the internal affairs of States is essential to the full enjoyment of the rights of men and women,

Affirming that the strengthening of international peace and security, the relaxation of international tension, mutual co-operation among all States irrespective of their social and economic systems, general and complete disarmament, in particular nuclear disarmament under strict and effective international control, the affirmation of the principles of justice, equality and mutual benefit in relations among countries and the realization of the right of peoples under alien and colonial domination and foreign occupation to self-determination and independence, as well as respect for national sovereignty and territorial integrity, will promote social progress and development and as a consequence will contribute to the attainment of full equality between men and women,

Convinced that the full and complete development of a country, the welfare of the world and the cause of peace require the maximum participation of women on equal terms with men in all fields,

Bearing in mind the great contribution of women to the welfare of the family and to the development of society, so far not fully recognized, the social significance of maternity and the role of both parents in the family and in the upbringing of children, and aware that the role of women in procreation should not be a basis for discrimination but that the upbringing of children requires a sharing of responsibility between men and women and society as a whole,

Aware that a change in the traditional role of men as well as the role of women in society and in the family is needed to achieve full equality between men and women,

Determined to implement the principles set forth in the Declaration on the Elimination of Discrimination against Women and, for that purpose, to adopt the measures required for the elimination of such discrimination in all its forms and manifestations,

Have agreed on the following:

PART I

Article 1

For the purposes of the present Convention, the term 'discrimination against women' shall mean any distinction, exclusion or restriction made on the basis of sex which has the effect or purpose of impairing or nullifying the recognition, enjoyment or exercise by women, irrespective of their marital status, on a basis of equality of men and women, of human rights and fundamental freedoms in the political, economic, social, cultural, civil or any other field.

Article 2

States Parties condemn discrimination against women in all its forms, agree to pursue by all appropriate means and without delay a policy of eliminating discrimination against women and, to this end, undertake:

(a) To embody the principle of the equality of men and women in their national constitutions or other appropriate legislation if not yet incorporated therein and to ensure, through law and other appropriate means, the practical realization of this principle;

(b) To adopt appropriate legislative and other measures, including sanctions where appropriate, prohibiting all discrimination against women;

(c) To establish legal protection of the rights of women on an equal basis with men and to ensure through competent national tribunals and other public institutions the effective protection of women against any act of discrimination;

(d) To refrain from engaging in any act or practice of discrimination against women and to ensure that public authorities and institutions shall act in conformity with this obligation;

(e) To take all appropriate measures to eliminate discrimination against women by any person, organization or enterprise;

(f) To take all appropriate measures, including legislation, to modify or abolish existing laws, regulations, customs and practices which constitute discrimination against women;

(g) To repeal all national penal provisions which constitute discrimination against women.

Article 3

States Parties shall take in all fields, in particular in the political, social, economic and cultural fields, all appropriate measures, including legislation, to ensure the full development and advancement of women, for the purpose of guaranteeing them the exercise and enjoyment of human rights and fundamental freedoms on a basis of equality with men.

Article 4

1. Adoption by States Parties of temporary special measures aimed at accelerating *de facto* equality between men and women shall not be considered discrimination as defined in the present Convention, but shall in no way entail as a consequence the maintenance of unequal or separate standards; these measures shall be discontinued when the objectives of equality of opportunity and treatment have been achieved.

2. Adoption by States Parties of special measures, including those measures contained in the present Convention, aimed at protecting maternity shall not be considered discriminatory.

Article 5

States Parties shall take all appropriate measures:

(a) To modify the social and cultural patterns of conduct of men and women, with a view to achieving the elimination of prejudices and customary and all other practices which are based on the idea of the inferiority or the superiority of either of the sexes or on stereotyped roles for men and women;

(b) To ensure that family education includes a proper understanding of maternity as a social function and the recognition of the common responsibility of men and women in the upbringing and development of their children, it being understood that the interest of the children is the primordial consideration in all cases.

Article 6

States Parties shall take all appropriate measures, including legislation, to suppress all forms of traffic in women and exploitation of prostitution of women.

PART II

Article 7

States Parties shall take all appropriate measures to eliminate discrimination against women in the political and public life of the country and, in particular, shall ensure to women, on equal terms with men, the right:

(a) To vote in all elections and public referenda and to be eligible for election to all publicly elected bodies;

(b) To participate in the formulation of government policy and the implementation thereof and to hold public office and perform all public functions at all levels of government;

(c) To participate in non-governmental organizations and associations concerned with the public and political life of the country.

Article 8

States Parties shall take all appropriate measures to ensure to women, on equal terms with men and without any discrimination, the opportunity to represent their Governments at the international level and to participate in the work of international organizations.

Article 9

1. States Parties shall grant women equal rights with men to acquire, change or retain their nationality. They shall ensure in particular that neither marriage to an alien nor change of nationality by the husband during marriage shall automatically change the nationality of the wife, render her stateless or force upon her the nationality of the husband.

2. States Parties shall grant women equal rights with men with respect to the nationality of their children.

PART III

Article 10

States Parties shall take all appropriate measures to eliminate discrimination against women in order to ensure to them equal rights with men in the field of education and in particular to ensure, on a basis of equality of men and women:

(a) The same conditions for career and vocational guidance, for access to studies and for the achievement of diplomas in educational establishments of all categories in rural as well as in urban areas; this equality shall be ensured in pre-school, general, technical, professional and higher technical education, as well as in all types of vocational training;

(b) Access to the same curricula, the same examinations, teaching staff with qualifications of the same standard and school premises and equipment of the same quality;

(c) The elimination of any stereotyped concept of the roles of men and women at all levels and in all forms of education by encouraging coeducation and other types of education which will help to achieve this aim and, in particular, by the revision of textbooks and school programmes and the adaptation of teaching methods;

(d) The same opportunities to benefit from scholarships and other study grants;

(e) The same opportunities for access to programmes of continuing education, including adult and functional literacy programmes, particularly those aimed at reducing, at the earliest possible time, any gap in education existing between men and women;

(f) The reduction of female student drop-out rates and the organization of programmes for girls and women who have left school prematurely;

(g) The same opportunities to participate actively in sports and physical education;

(h) Access to specific educational information to help to ensure the health and well-being of families, including information and advice on family planning.

Article 11

1. States Parties shall take all appropriate measures to eliminate discrimination against women in the field of employment in order to ensure, on a basis of equality of men and women, the same rights, in particular:

(a) The right to work as an inalienable right of all human beings;

(b) The right to the same employment opportunities, including the application of the same criteria for selection in matters of employment;

(c) The right to free choice of profession and employment, the right to promotion, job security and all benefits and conditions of service and the right to receive vocational training and retraining, including apprenticeships, advanced vocational training and recurrent training;

(d) The right to equal remuneration, including benefits, and to equal treatment in respect of work of equal value, as well as equality of treatment in the evaluation of the quality of work;

(e) The right to social security, particularly in cases of retirement, unemployment, sickness, invalidity and old age and other incapacity to work, as well as the right to paid leave;

(f) The right to protection of health and to safety in working conditions, including the safeguarding of the function of reproduction.

2. In order to prevent discrimination against women on the grounds of marriage or maternity and to ensure their effective right to work, States Parties shall take appropriate measures:

(a) To prohibit, subject to the imposition of sanctions, dismissal on the grounds of pregnancy or of maternity leave and discrimination in dismissals on the basis of marital status;

(b) To introduce maternity leave with pay or with comparable social benefits without loss of former employment, seniority or social allowances;

(c) To encourage the provision of the necessary supporting social services to enable parents to combine family obligations with work responsibilities and participation in public life, in particular through promoting the establishment and development of a network of child-care facilities;

(d) To provide special protection to women during pregnancy in types of work proved to be harmful to them.

3. Protective legislation relating to matters covered in this article shall be reviewed periodically in the light of scientific and technological knowledge and shall be revised, repealed or extended as necessary.

Article 12

1. States Parties shall take all appropriate measures to eliminate discrimination against women in the field of health care in order to ensure, on a basis of equality of men and women, access to health care services, including those related to family planning.

2. Notwithstanding the provisions of paragraph 1 of this article, States Parties shall ensure to women appropriate services in connection with pregnancy, confinement and the post-natal period, granting free services where necessary, as well as adequate nutrition during pregnancy and lactation.

Article 13

States Parties shall take all appropriate measures to eliminate discrimination against women in other areas of economic and social life in order to ensure, on a basis of equality of men and women, the same rights, in particular:

(a) The right to family benefits;

(b) The right to bank loans, mortgages and other forms of financial credit;

(c) The right to participate in recreational activities, sports and all aspects of cultural life.

Article 14

1. States Parties shall take into account the particular problems faced by rural women and the significant roles which rural women play in the economic survival of their families, including their work in the non-monetized sectors of the economy, and shall take all appropriate measures to ensure the application of the provisions of the present Convention to women in rural areas.

2. States Parties shall take all appropriate measures to eliminate discrimination against women in rural areas in order to ensure, on a basis of equality of men and women, that they participate in and benefit from rural development and, in particular, shall ensure to such women the right:

 (a) To participate in the elaboration and implementation of development planning at all levels;

 (b) To have access to adequate health care facilities, including information, counselling and services in family planning;

 (c) To benefit directly from social security programmes;

 (d) To obtain all types of training and education, formal and non-formal, including that relating to functional literacy, as well as, *inter alia*, the benefit of all community and extension services, in order to increase their technical proficiency;

 (e) To organize self-help groups and co-operatives in order to obtain equal access to economic opportunities through employment or self employment;

 (f) To participate in all community activities;

 (g) To have access to agricultural credit and loans, marketing facilities, appropriate technology and equal treatment in land and agrarian reform as well as in land resettlement schemes;

 (h) To enjoy adequate living conditions, particularly in relation to housing, sanitation, electricity and water supply, transport and communications.

PART IV

Article 15

1. States Parties shall accord to women equality with men before the law.

2. States Parties shall accord to women, in civil matters, a legal capacity identical to that of men and the same opportunities to exercise that capacity. In particular, they shall give women equal rights to conclude contracts and to administer property and shall treat them equally in all stages of procedure in courts and tribunals.

3. States Parties agree that all contracts and all other private instruments of any kind with a legal effect which is directed at restricting the legal capacity of women shall be deemed null and void.

4. States Parties shall accord to men and women the same rights with regard to the law relating to the movement of persons and the freedom to choose their residence and domicile.

Article 16

1. States Parties shall take all appropriate measures to eliminate discrimination against women in all matters relating to marriage and family relations and in particular shall ensure, on a basis of equality of men and women:

 (a) The same right to enter into marriage;

 (b) The same right freely to choose a spouse and to enter into marriage only with their free and full consent;

 (c) The same rights and responsibilities during marriage and at its dissolution;

(d) The same rights and responsibilities as parents, irrespective of their marital status, in matters relating to their children; in all cases the interests of the children shall be paramount;

(e) The same rights to decide freely and responsibly on the number and spacing of their children and to have access to the information, education and means to enable them to exercise these rights;

(f) The same rights and responsibilities with regard to guardianship, wardship, trustee-ship and adoption of children, or similar institutions where these concepts exist in national legislation; in all cases the interests of the children shall be paramount;

(g) The same personal rights as husband and wife, including the right to choose a family name, a profession and an occupation;

(h) The same rights for both spouses in respect of the ownership, acquisition, management, administration, enjoyment and disposition of property, whether free of charge or for a valuable consideration.

2. The betrothal and the marriage of a child shall have no legal effect, and all necessary action, including legislation, shall be taken to specify a minimum age for marriage and to make the registration of marriages in an official registry compulsory.

PART V

Article 17

1. For the purpose of considering the progress made in the implementation of the present Convention, there shall be established a Committee on the Elimination of Discrimination against Women (hereinafter referred to as the Committee) consisting, at the time of entry into force of the Convention, of eighteen and, after ratification of or accession to the Convention by the thirty-fifth State Party, of twenty-three experts of high moral stand-ing and competence in the field covered by the Convention. The experts shall be elected by States Parties from among their nationals and shall serve in their personal capacity, consideration being given to equitable geographical distribution and to the representa-tion of the different forms of civilization as well as the principal legal systems.

2. The members of the Committee shall be elected by secret ballot from a list of persons nominated by States Parties. Each State Party may nominate one person from among its own nationals.

3. The initial election shall be held six months after the date of the entry into force of the present Convention. At least three months before the date of each election the Secretary-General of the United Nations shall address a letter to the States Parties inviting them to submit their nominations within two months. The Secretary-General shall prepare a list in alphabetical order of all persons thus nominated, indicating the States Parties which have nominated them, and shall submit it to the States Parties.

4. Elections of the members of the Committee shall be held at a meeting of States Parties convened by the Secretary-General at United Nations Headquarters. At that meeting, for which two thirds of the States Parties shall constitute a quorum, the persons elected to the Committee shall be those nominees who obtain the largest number of votes and an absolute majority of the votes of the representatives of States Parties present and voting.

5. The members of the Committee shall be elected for a term of four years. However, the terms of nine of the members elected at the first election shall expire at the end of two years; immediately after the first election the names of these nine members shall be chosen by lot by the Chairman of the Committee.

6. The election of the five additional members of the Committee shall be held in accordance with the provisions of paragraphs 2, 3 and 4 of this article, following the thirty-fifth ratification or accession. The terms of two of the additional members elected on this occasion shall expire at the end of two years, the names of these two members having been chosen by lot by the Chairman of the Committee.

7. For the filling of casual vacancies, the State Party whose expert has ceased to function as a member of the Committee shall appoint another expert from among its nationals, subject to the approval of the Committee.

8. The members of the Committee shall, with the approval of the General Assembly, receive emoluments from United Nations resources on such terms and conditions as the Assembly may decide, having regard to the importance of the Committee's responsibilities.

9. The Secretary-General of the United Nations shall provide the necessary staff and facilities for the effective performance of the functions of the Committee under the present Convention.

Article 18

1. States Parties undertake to submit to the Secretary-General of the United Nations, for consideration by the Committee, a report on the legislative, judicial, administrative or other measures which they have adopted to give effect to the provisions of the present Convention and on the progress made in this respect:

   (a) Within one year after the entry into force for the State concerned;

   (b) Thereafter at least every four years and further whenever the Committee so requests.

2. Reports may indicate factors and difficulties affecting the degree of fulfilment of obligations under the present Convention.

Article 19

1. The Committee shall adopt its own rules of procedure.

2. The Committee shall elect its officers for a term of two years.

Article 20

1. The Committee shall normally meet for a period of not more than two weeks annually in order to consider the reports submitted in accordance with Article 18 of the present Convention.

2. The meetings of the Committee shall normally be held at United Nations Headquarters or at any other convenient place as determined by the Committee.

Article 21

1. The Committee shall, through the Economic and Social Council, report annually to the General Assembly of the United Nations on its activities and may make suggestions and general recommendations based on the examination of reports and information received from the States Parties. Such suggestions and general recommendations shall be included in the report of the Committee together with comments, if any, from States Parties.

2. The Secretary-General of the United Nations shall transmit the reports of the Committee to the Commission on the Status of Women for its information.

Article 22

The specialized agencies shall be entitled to be represented at the consideration of the implementation of such provisions of the present Convention as fall within the scope of their activities. The Committee may invite the specialized agencies to submit reports on the implementation of the Convention in areas falling within the scope of their activities.

PART VI

Article 23

Nothing in the present Convention shall affect any provisions that are more conducive to the achievement of equality between men and women which may be contained:

  (a) In the legislation of a State Party; or

  (b) In any other international convention, treaty or agreement in force for that State.

Article 24

States Parties undertake to adopt all necessary measures at the national level aimed at achieving the full realization of the rights recognized in the present Convention.

Article 25

1. The present Convention shall be open for signature by all States.

2. The Secretary-General of the United Nations is designated as the depositary of the present Convention.

3. The present Convention is subject to ratification. Instruments of ratification shall be deposited with the Secretary-General of the United Nations.

4. The present Convention shall be open to accession by all States. Accession shall be effected by the deposit of an instrument of accession with the Secretary-General of the United Nations.

Article 26

1. A request for the revision of the present Convention may be made at any time by any State Party by means of a notification in writing addressed to the Secretary-General of the United Nations.

2. The General Assembly of the United Nations shall decide upon the steps, if any, to be taken in respect of such a request.

Article 27

1. The present Convention shall enter into force on the thirtieth day after the date of deposit with the Secretary-General of the United Nations of the twentieth instrument of ratification or accession.

2. For each State ratifying the present Convention or acceding to it after the deposit of the twentieth instrument of ratification or accession, the Convention shall enter into force on the thirtieth day after the date of the deposit of its own instrument of ratification or accession.

Article 28

1. The Secretary-General of the United Nations shall receive and circulate to all States the text of reservations made by States at the time of ratification or accession.

2. A reservation incompatible with the object and purpose of the present Convention shall not be permitted.

3. Reservations may be withdrawn at any time by notification to this effect addressed to the Secretary-General of the United Nations, who shall then inform all States thereof. Such notification shall take effect on the date on which it is received.

Article 29

1. Any dispute between two or more States Parties concerning the interpretation or application of the present Convention which is not settled by negotiation shall, at the request of one of them, be submitted to arbitration. If within six months from the date of the request for arbitration the parties are unable to agree on the organization of the arbitration, any one of those parties may refer the dispute to the International Court of Justice by request in conformity with the Statute of the Court.

2. Each State Party may at the time of signature or ratification of the present Convention or accession thereto declare that it does not consider itself bound by paragraph 1 of this article. The other States Parties shall not be bound by that paragraph with respect to any State Party which has made such a reservation.

3. Any State Party which has made a reservation in accordance with paragraph 2 of this article may at any time withdraw that reservation by notification to the Secretary-General of the United Nations.

Article 30

The present Convention, the Arabic, Chinese, English, French, Russian and Spanish texts of which are equally authentic, shall be deposited with the Secretary-General of the United Nations.

In witness whereof the undersigned, duly authorized, have signed the present Convention.

56. OPTIONAL PROTOCOL TO THE CONVENTION ON THE ELIMINATION OF ALL FORMS OF DISCRIMINATION AGAINST WOMEN, 1999

This Protocol was adopted and opened for signature by General Assembly Resolution 54/4 on 6 October 1999, without a vote; it entered into force on 22 December 2000. For decisions and views of the Committee on the Elimination of Discrimination against Women, see **http://un.org/womenwatch/daw/cedaw/protocol/dec-views.htm**.

Further reading

BYRNES, A. and BATH, E., 'Violence against Women, the Obligation of Due Diligence, and the Optional Protocol to the Convention on the Elimination of All Forms of Discrimination against Women—Recent Developments', (2008) 8 *Human Rights Law Review* 517.

McQUIGG, R., 'The Responses of States to the Comments of the CEDAW Committee on Domestic Violence', (2007) 11 *International Journal of Human Rights* 461.

TEXT

The States Parties to the present Protocol,

Noting that the Charter of the United Nations reaffirms faith in fundamental human rights, in the dignity and worth of the human person and in the equal rights of men and women,

Also noting that the Universal Declaration of Human Rights proclaims that all human beings are born free and equal in dignity and rights and that everyone is entitled to all the rights and freedoms set forth therein, without distinction of any kind, including distinction based on sex,

Recalling that the International Covenants on Human Rights and other international human rights instruments prohibit discrimination on the basis of sex,

Also recalling the Convention on the Elimination of All Forms of Discrimination against Women ('the Convention'), in which the States Parties thereto condemn discrimination against women in all its forms and agree to pursue by all appropriate means and without delay a policy of eliminating discrimination against women,

Reaffirming their determination to ensure the full and equal enjoyment by women of all human rights and fundamental freedoms and to take effective action to prevent violations of these rights and freedoms,

Have agreed as follows:

Article 1

A State Party to the present Protocol ('State Party') recognizes the competence of the Committee on the Elimination of Discrimination against Women ('the Committee') to receive and consider communications submitted in accordance with Article 2.

Article 2

Communications may be submitted by or on behalf of individuals or groups of individuals, under the jurisdiction of a State Party, claiming to be victims of a violation of any of the rights set forth in the Convention by that State Party. Where a communication is submitted on behalf of individuals or groups of individuals, this shall be with their consent unless the author can justify acting on their behalf without such consent.

Article 3

Communications shall be in writing and shall not be anonymous. No communication shall be received by the Committee if it concerns a State Party to the Convention that is not a party to the present Protocol.

Article 4

1. The Committee shall not consider a communication unless it has ascertained that all available domestic remedies have been exhausted unless the application of such remedies is unreasonably prolonged or unlikely to bring effective relief.

2. The Committee shall declare a communication inadmissible where:

 (a) The same matter has already been examined by the Committee or has been or is being examined under another procedure of international investigation or settlement;

 (b) It is incompatible with the provisions of the Convention;

 (c) It is manifestly ill-founded or not sufficiently substantiated;

 (d) It is an abuse of the right to submit a communication;

 (e) The facts that are the subject of the communication occurred prior to the entry into force of the present Protocol for the State Party concerned unless those facts continued after that date.

Article 5

1. At any time after the receipt of a communication and before a determination on the merits has been reached, the Committee may transmit to the State Party concerned for its urgent consideration a request that the State Party take such interim measures as may be necessary to avoid possible irreparable damage to the victim or victims of the alleged violation.

2. Where the Committee exercises its discretion under paragraph 1 of the present article, this does not imply a determination on admissibility or on the merits of the communication.

Article 6

1. Unless the Committee considers a communication inadmissible without reference to the State Party concerned, and provided that the individual or individuals consent to the disclosure of their identity to that State Party, the Committee shall bring any communication submitted to it under the present Protocol confidentially to the attention of the State Party concerned.

2. Within six months, the receiving State Party shall submit to the Committee written explanations or statements clarifying the matter and the remedy, if any, that may have been provided by that State Party.

Article 7

1. The Committee shall consider communications received under the present Protocol in the light of all information made available to it by or on behalf of individuals or

groups of individuals and by the State Party concerned, provided that this information is transmitted to the parties concerned.

2. The Committee shall hold closed meetings when examining communications under the present Protocol.

3. After examining a communication, the Committee shall transmit its views on the communication, together with its recommendations, if any, to the parties concerned.

4. The State Party shall give due consideration to the views of the Committee, together with its recommendations, if any, and shall submit to the Committee, within six months, a written response, including information on any action taken in the light of the views and recommendations of the Committee.

5. The Committee may invite the State Party to submit further information about any measures the State Party has taken in response to its views or recommendations, if any, including as deemed appropriate by the Committee, in the State Party's subsequent reports under Article 18 of the Convention.

Article 8

1. If the Committee receives reliable information indicating grave or systematic violations by a State Party of rights set forth in the Convention, the Committee shall invite that State Party to cooperate in the examination of the information and to this end to submit observations with regard to the information concerned.

2. Taking into account any observations that may have been submitted by the State Party concerned as well as any other reliable information available to it, the Committee may designate one or more of its members to conduct an inquiry and to report urgently to the Committee. Where warranted and with the consent of the State Party, the inquiry may include a visit to its territory.

3. After examining the findings of such an inquiry, the Committee shall transmit these findings to the State Party concerned together with any comments and recommendations.

4. The State Party concerned shall, within six months of receiving the findings, comments and recommendations transmitted by the Committee, submit its observations to the Committee.

5. Such an inquiry shall be conducted confidentially and the cooperation of the State Party shall be sought at all stages of the proceedings.

Article 9

1. The Committee may invite the State Party concerned to include in its report under Article 18 of the Convention details of any measures taken in response to an inquiry conducted under Article 8 of the present Protocol.

2. The Committee may, if necessary, after the end of the period of six months referred to in Article 8.4, invite the State Party concerned to inform it of the measures taken in response to such an inquiry.

Article 10

1. Each State Party may, at the time of signature or ratification of the present Protocol or accession thereto, declare that it does not recognize the competence of the Committee provided for in Articles 8 and 9.

2. Any State Party having made a declaration in accordance with paragraph 1 of the present article may, at any time, withdraw this declaration by notification to the Secretary-General.

Article 11

A State Party shall take all appropriate steps to ensure that individuals under its jurisdiction are not subjected to ill-treatment or intimidation as a consequence of communicating with the Committee pursuant to the present Protocol.

Article 12

The Committee shall include in its annual report under Article 21 of the Convention a summary of its activities under the present Protocol.

Article 13

Each State Party undertakes to make widely known and to give publicity to the Convention and the present Protocol and to facilitate access to information about the views and recommendations of the Committee, in particular, on matters involving that State Party.

Article 14

The Committee shall develop its own rules of procedure to be followed when exercising the functions conferred on it by the present Protocol.

Article 15

1. The present Protocol shall be open for signature by any State that has signed, ratified or acceded to the Convention.

2. The present Protocol shall be subject to ratification by any State that has ratified or acceded to the Convention. Instruments of ratification shall be deposited with the Secretary-General of the United Nations.

3. The present Protocol shall be open to accession by any State that has ratified or acceded to the Convention.

4. Accession shall be effected by the deposit of an instrument of accession with the Secretary-General of the United Nations.

Article 16

1. The present Protocol shall enter into force three months after the date of the deposit with the Secretary-General of the United Nations of the tenth instrument of ratification or accession.

2. For each State ratifying the present Protocol or acceding to it after its entry into force, the present Protocol shall enter into force three months after the date of the deposit of its own instrument of ratification or accession.

Article 17

No reservations to the present Protocol shall be permitted.

Article 18

1. Any State Party may propose an amendment to the present Protocol and file it with the Secretary-General of the United Nations. The Secretary-General shall thereupon communicate any proposed amendments to the States Parties with a request that they notify her or him whether they favour a conference of States Parties for the purpose of considering and voting on the proposal. In the event that at least one third of the States Parties favour such a conference, the Secretary-General shall convene the conference under the auspices of the United Nations. Any amendment adopted by a majority of the States Parties present and voting at the conference shall be submitted to the General Assembly of the United Nations for approval.

2. Amendments shall come into force when they have been approved by the General Assembly of the United Nations and accepted by a two-thirds majority of the States Parties to the present Protocol in accordance with their respective constitutional processes.

3. When amendments come into force, they shall be binding on those States Parties that have accepted them, other States Parties still being bound by the provisions of the present Protocol and any earlier amendments that they have accepted.

Article 19

1. Any State Party may denounce the present Protocol at any time by written notification addressed to the Secretary-General of the United Nations. Denunciation shall take effect six months after the date of receipt of the notification by the Secretary-General.

2. Denunciation shall be without prejudice to the continued application of the provisions of the present Protocol to any communication submitted under Article 2 or any inquiry initiated under Article 8 before the effective date of denunciation.

Article 20

The Secretary-General of the United Nations shall inform all States of:

(a) Signatures, ratifications and accessions under the present Protocol;

(b) The date of entry into force of the present Protocol and of any amendment under Article 18;

(c) Any denunciation under Article 19.

Article 21

1. The present Protocol, of which the Arabic, Chinese, English, French, Russian and Spanish texts are equally authentic, shall be deposited in the archives of the United Nations.

2. The Secretary-General of the United Nations shall transmit certified copies of the present Protocol to all States referred to in Article 25 of the Convention.

57. CONVENTION AGAINST TORTURE AND OTHER CRUEL, INHUMAN OR DEGRADING TREATMENT OR PUNISHMENT, 1984

This Convention was the sequel to the 1975 Declaration on Protection against Torture (see above, p. 82). The Convention was adopted by General Assembly Resolution 39/46, 10 December 1984, and entered into force on 26 June 1987; for text, see 1465 *UNTS* 85. Amendments have been proposed to Articles 17(7) and 18(5), but have not yet entered into force; see Article 29 and UN doc. CAT/sp/1992/L.1.

See also the European Convention for the Prevention of Torture and Inhuman or Degrading Treatment or Punishment, 1987 (below, p. 785); and the Inter-American Convention to Prevent and Punish Torture, 1985 (below, p. 986).

For judicial consideration of the Convention, see the judgment of the International Criminal Tribunal for the former Yugoslavia: *Furundžija* (IT-95-17/1) (Lašva Valley), 10 December 1998, paras. 144, 147, 151–3, 159–64; the judgments of the European Court of Human Rights in *Demir v Turkey* (2009) 48 EHRR 54, paras. 72–3; *Saadi v Italy* (2009) 49 EHRR 30; *Al-Adsani v United Kingdom* (2002) 34 EHRR 11, para. 29; *Soering v United Kingdom* (1989) 11 EHRR 439, paras. 86, 88, 97; and, in the United Kingdom, the judgments of the House of Lords in *A and Others (No. 2) v Secretary of State for the Home Department* [2005] UKHL 71, [2005] 3 WLR 1249, paras. 31, 35; *R v Bow Street Stipendiary Magistrate, ex parte Pinochet Ugarte (No. 3)* [2000] 1 AC 147, 197–9; *Jones v Ministry of Interior for the Kingdom of Saudi Arabia* [2006] UKHL 26, [2007] 1 AC 270, paras. 15–17.

Further reading

BARRETT, J., 'The Prohibition of Torture under International Law, Part 1: The Institutional Organisation', (2001) 5(1) *International Journal of Human Rights* 1–36; 'Part 2: The Normative Content', (2001) 5(2) *International Journal of Human Rights* 1–29.

BURGERS, H. and DANELIUS, H., *The United Nations Convention against Torture*, Dordrecht: Nijhoff, 1988.

DE WET, E., 'The Prohibition of Torture as an International Norm of *jus cogens* and its Implications for National and Customary Law', (2004) 15 *EJIL* 97.

EVANS, M. D., 'Getting to Grips with Torture', (2002) 51 *ICLQ* 365.

GINBAR, Y., *Why Not Torture Terrorists? Moral, Practical, and Legal Aspects of the 'Ticking Bomb' Justification for Torture*, Oxford: Oxford University Press, 2008.

HALL, C. K., 'The Duty of States Parties to the Convention against Torture to Provide Procedures Permitting Victims to Recover Reparations for Torture Committed Abroad', (2007) 18 *EJIL* 921.

HOPE, D., 'Torture', (2004) 53 *ICLQ* 807.

McGREGOR, L., 'Torture and State Immunity: Deflecting Impunity, Distorting Sovereignty', (2007) *EJIL* 903.

NAGAN, W. P. and ATKINS, L., 'The International Law of Torture: From Universal Proscription to Effective Application and Enforcement', (2001) 14 *Harvard Human Rights Journal* 87.

NOWAK, M., 'What Practices Constitute Torture? US and UN Standards', (2006) 28 *Human Rights Quarterly* 809.

—— and McARTHUR, E., *The United Nations Convention against Torture: A Commentary*, Oxford: Oxford University Press, 2008.

OHLIN, J. D. and FLETCHER, G. P., eds., 'The Law of Cruelty: Torture as an International Crime', (2008) 6 *Journal of International Criminal Justice*, Special Issue, 157.

SCOTT, C., ed., *Torture as Tort: Comparative Perspectives on the Development of Transnational Human Rights Litigation*, Oxford: Hart Publishing, 2001.

'Symposium: "Torture and the War on Terror",' (2006) 37 *Case Western Reserve Journal of International Law* 145.

WEISSBRODT, D. and BERGQUIST, A., 'Extraordinary Rendition and the Torture Convention', (2005–2006) 46 *Virginia Journal of International Law* 585.

TEXT

The States Parties to this Convention,

Considering that, in accordance with the principles proclaimed in the Charter of the United Nations, recognition of the equal and inalienable rights of all members of the human family is the foundation of freedom, justice and peace in the world,

Recognizing that those rights derive from the inherent dignity of the human person,

Considering the obligation of States under the Charter, in particular Article 55, to promote universal respect for, and observance of, human rights and fundamental freedoms,

Having regard to Article 5 of the Universal Declaration of Human Rights and Article 7 of the International Covenant on Civil and Political Rights, both of which provide that no one shall be subjected to torture or to cruel, inhuman or degrading treatment or punishment,

Having regard also to the Declaration on the Protection of All Persons from Being Subjected to Torture and Other Cruel, Inhuman or Degrading Treatment or Punishment, adopted by the General Assembly on 9 December 1975,

Desiring to make more effective the struggle against torture and other cruel, inhuman or degrading treatment or punishment throughout the world,

Have agreed as follows:

PART I

Article 1

1. For the purposes of this Convention, the term 'torture' means any act by which severe pain or suffering, whether physical or mental, is intentionally inflicted on a person for such purposes as obtaining from him or a third person information or a confession, punishing him for an act he or a third person has committed or is suspected of having committed, or intimidating or coercing him or a third person, or for any reason based on discrimination of any kind, when such pain or suffering is inflicted by or at the instigation of or with the consent or acquiescence of a public official or other person acting in an official capacity. It does not include pain or suffering arising only from, inherent in or incidental to lawful sanctions.

2. This article is without prejudice to any international instrument or national legislation which does or may contain provisions of wider application.

Article 2

1. Each State Party shall take effective legislative, administrative, judicial or other measures to prevent acts of torture in any territory under its jurisdiction.

2. No exceptional circumstances whatsoever, whether a state of war or a threat of war, internal political instability or any other public emergency, may be invoked as a justification of torture.

3. An order from a superior officer or a public authority may not be invoked as a justification of torture.

Article 3

1. No State Party shall expel, return (*refouler*) or extradite a person to another State where there are substantial grounds for believing that he would be in danger of being subjected to torture.

2. For the purpose of determining whether there are such grounds, the competent authorities shall take into account all relevant considerations including, where applicable, the existence in the State concerned of a consistent pattern of gross, flagrant or mass violations of human rights.

Article 4

1. Each State Party shall ensure that all acts of torture are offences under its criminal law. The same shall apply to an attempt to commit torture and to an act by any person which constitutes complicity or participation in torture.

2. Each State Party shall make these offences punishable by appropriate penalties which take into account their grave nature.

Article 5

1. Each State Party shall take such measures as may be necessary to establish its jurisdiction over the offences referred to in Article 4 in the following cases:

   (*a*) When the offences are committed in any territory under its jurisdiction or on board a ship or aircraft registered in that State;

   (*b*) When the alleged offender is a national of that State;

   (*c*) When the victim is a national of that State if that State considers it appropriate.

2. Each State Party shall likewise take such measures as may be necessary to establish its jurisdiction over such offences in cases where the alleged offender is present in any territory under its jurisdiction and it does not extradite him pursuant to Article 8 to any of the States mentioned in paragraph 1 of this article.

3. This Convention does not exclude any criminal jurisdiction exercised in accordance with internal law.

Article 6

1. Upon being satisfied, after an examination of information available to it, that the circumstances so warrant, any State Party in whose territory a person alleged to have committed any offence referred to in Article 4 is present shall take him into custody or take other legal measures to ensure his presence. The custody and other legal measures shall be as provided in the law of that State but may be continued only for such time as is necessary to enable any criminal or extradition proceedings to be instituted.

2. Such State shall immediately make a preliminary inquiry into the facts.

3. Any person in custody pursuant to paragraph 1 of this article shall be assisted in communicating immediately with the nearest appropriate representative of the State of

which he is a national, or, if he is a stateless person, with the representative of the State where he usually resides.

4. When a State, pursuant to this article, has taken a person into custody, it shall immediately notify the States referred to in Article 5, paragraph 1, of the fact that such person is in custody and of the circumstances which warrant his detention. The State which makes the preliminary inquiry contemplated in paragraph 2 of this article shall promptly report its findings to the said States and shall indicate whether it intends to exercise jurisdiction.

Article 7

1. The State Party in the territory under whose jurisdiction a person alleged to have committed any offence referred to in Article 4 is found shall in the cases contemplated in Article 5, if it does not extradite him, submit the case to its competent authorities for the purpose of prosecution.

2. These authorities shall take their decision in the same manner as in the case of any ordinary offence of a serious nature under the law of that State. In the cases referred to in Article 5, paragraph 2, the standards of evidence required for prosecution and conviction shall in no way be less stringent than those which apply in the cases referred to in Article 5, paragraph 1.

3. Any person regarding whom proceedings are brought in connection with any of the offences referred to in Article 4 shall be guaranteed fair treatment at all stages of the proceedings.

Article 8

1. The offences referred to in Article 4 shall be deemed to be included as extraditable offences in any extradition treaty existing between States Parties. States Parties undertake to include such offences as extraditable offences in every extradition treaty to be concluded between them.

2. If a State Party which makes extradition conditional on the existence of a treaty receives a request for extradition from another State Party with which it has no extradition treaty, it may consider this Convention as the legal basis for extradition in respect of such offences. Extradition shall be subject to the other conditions provided by the law of the requested State.

3. States Parties which do not make extradition conditional on the existence of a treaty shall recognize such offences as extraditable offences between themselves subject to the conditions provided by the law of the requested State.

4. Such offences shall be treated, for the purpose of extradition between States Parties, as if they had been committed not only in the place in which they occurred but also in the territories of the States required to establish their jurisdiction in accordance with Article 5, paragraph 1.

Article 9

1. States Parties shall afford one another the greatest measure of assistance in connection with criminal proceedings brought in respect of any of the offences referred to in Article 4, including the supply of all evidence at their disposal necessary for the proceedings.

2. States Parties shall carry out their obligations under paragraph 1 of this article in conformity with any treaties on mutual judicial assistance that may exist between them.

Article 10

1. Each State Party shall ensure that education and information regarding the prohibition against torture are fully included in the training of law enforcement personnel, civil or military, medical personnel, public officials and other persons who may be involved in the custody, interrogation or treatment of any individual subjected to any form of arrest, detention or imprisonment.

2. Each State Party shall include this prohibition in the rules or instructions issued in regard to the duties and functions of any such person.

Article 11

Each State Party shall keep under systematic review interrogation rules, instructions, methods and practices as well as arrangements for the custody and treatment of persons subjected to any form of arrest, detention or imprisonment in any territory under its jurisdiction, with a view to preventing any cases of torture.

Article 12

Each State Party shall ensure that its competent authorities proceed to a prompt and impartial investigation, wherever there is reasonable ground to believe that an act of torture has been committed in any territory under its jurisdiction.

Article 13

Each State Party shall ensure that any individual who alleges he has been subjected to torture in any territory under its jurisdiction has the right to complain to, and to have his case promptly and impartially examined by, its competent authorities. Steps shall be taken to ensure that the complainant and witnesses are protected against all ill-treatment or intimidation as a consequence of his complaint or any evidence given.

Article 14

1. Each State Party shall ensure in its legal system that the victim of an act of torture obtains redress and has an enforceable right to fair and adequate compensation, including the means for as full rehabilitation as possible. In the event of the death of the victim as a result of an act of torture, his dependants shall be entitled to compensation.

2. Nothing in this article shall affect any right of the victim or other persons to compensation which may exist under national law.

Article 15

Each State Party shall ensure that any statement which is established to have been made as a result of torture shall not be invoked as evidence in any proceedings, except against a person accused of torture as evidence that the statement was made.

Article 16

1. Each State Party shall undertake to prevent in any territory under its jurisdiction other acts of cruel, inhuman or degrading treatment or punishment which do not amount to torture as defined in Article 1, when such acts are committed by or at the instigation of or with the consent or acquiescence of a public official or other person acting in an official capacity. In particular, the obligations contained in Articles 10, 11, 12 and 13 shall apply with the substitution for references to torture of references to other forms of cruel, inhuman or degrading treatment or punishment.

2. The provisions of this Convention are without prejudice to the provisions of any other international instrument or national law which prohibits cruel, inhuman or degrading treatment or punishment or which relates to extradition or expulsion.

PART II

Article 17

1. There shall be established a Committee against Torture (hereinafter referred to as the Committee) which shall carry out the functions hereinafter provided. The Committee shall consist of ten experts of high moral standing and recognized competence in the field of human rights, who shall serve in their personal capacity. The experts shall be elected by the States Parties, consideration being given to equitable geographical distribution and to the usefulness of the participation of some persons having legal experience.

2. The members of the Committee shall be elected by secret ballot from a list of persons nominated by States Parties. Each State Party may nominate one person from among its own nationals. States Parties shall bear in mind the usefulness of nominating persons who are also members of the Human Rights Committee established under the International Covenant on Civil and Political Rights and who are willing to serve on the Committee against Torture.

3. Elections of the members of the Committee shall be held at biennial meetings of States Parties convened by the Secretary-General of the United Nations. At those meetings, for which two thirds of the States Parties shall constitute a quorum, the persons elected to the Committee shall be those who obtain the largest number of votes and an absolute majority of the votes of the representatives of States Parties present and voting.

4. The initial election shall be held no later than six months after the date of the entry into force of this Convention. At least four months before the date of each election, the Secretary-General of the United Nations shall address a letter to the States Parties inviting them to submit their nominations within three months. The Secretary-General shall prepare a list in alphabetical order of all persons thus nominated, indicating the States Parties which have nominated them, and shall submit it to the States Parties.

5. The members of the Committee shall be elected for a term of four years. They shall be eligible for re-election if renominated. However, the term of five of the members elected at the first election shall expire at the end of two years; immediately after the first election the names of these five members shall be chosen by lot by the Chairman of the meeting referred to in paragraph 3 of this article.

6. If a member of the Committee dies or resigns or for any other cause can no longer perform his Committee duties, the State Party which nominated him shall appoint another expert from among its nationals to serve for the remainder of his term, subject to the approval of the majority of the States Parties. The approval shall be considered given unless half or more of the States Parties respond negatively within six weeks after having been informed by the Secretary-General of the United Nations of the proposed appointment.

7. States Parties shall be responsible for the expenses of the members of the Committee while they are in performance of Committee duties.

Article 18

1. The Committee shall elect its officers for a term of two years. They may be re-elected.

2. The Committee shall establish its own rules of procedure, but these rules shall provide, *inter alia*, that:

   (a) Six members shall constitute a quorum;

   (b) Decisions of the Committee shall be made by a majority vote of the members present.

3. The Secretary-General of the United Nations shall provide the necessary staff and facilities for the effective performance of the functions of the Committee under this Convention.

4. The Secretary-General of the United Nations shall convene the initial meeting of the Committee. After its initial meeting, the Committee shall meet at such times as shall be provided in its rules of procedure.

5. The States Parties shall be responsible for expenses incurred in connection with the holding of meetings of the States Parties and of the Committee, including reimbursement to the United Nations for any expenses, such as the cost of staff and facilities, incurred by the United Nations pursuant to paragraph 3 of this article.

Article 19

1. The States Parties shall submit to the Committee, through the Secretary-General of the United Nations, reports on the measures they have taken to give effect to their undertakings under this Convention, within one year after the entry into force of the Convention for the State Party concerned. Thereafter the States Parties shall submit supplementary reports every four years on any new measures taken and such other reports as the Committee may request.

2. The Secretary-General of the United Nations shall transmit the reports to all States Parties.

3. Each report shall be considered by the Committee which may make such general comments on the report as it may consider appropriate and shall forward these to the State Party concerned. That State Party may respond with any observations it chooses to the Committee.

4. The Committee may, at its discretion, decide to include any comments made by it in accordance with paragraph 3 of this article, together with the observations thereon received from the State Party concerned, in its annual report made in accordance with Article 24. If so requested by the State Party concerned, the Committee may also include a copy of the report submitted under paragraph 1 of this article.

Article 20

1. If the Committee receives reliable information which appears to it to contain well-founded indications that torture is being systematically practised in the territory of a State Party, the Committee shall invite that State Party to co-operate in the examination of the information and to this end to submit observations with regard to the information concerned.

2. Taking into account any observations which may have been submitted by the State Party concerned, as well as any other relevant information available to it, the Committee

may, if it decides that this is warranted, designate one or more of its members to make a confidential inquiry and to report to the Committee urgently.

3. If an inquiry is made in accordance with paragraph 2 of this article, the Committee shall seek the co-operation of the State Party concerned. In agreement with that State Party, such an inquiry may include a visit to its territory.

4. After examining the findings of its member or members submitted in accordance with paragraph 2 of this article, the Commission shall transmit these findings to the State Party concerned together with any comments or suggestions which seem appropriate in view of the situation.

5. All the proceedings of the Committee referred to in paragraphs 1 to 4 of this article shall be confidential, and at all stages of the proceedings the co-operation of the State Party shall be sought. After such proceedings have been completed with regard to an inquiry made in accordance with paragraph 2, the Committee may, after consultations with the State Party concerned, decide to include a summary account of the results of the proceedings in its annual report made in accordance with Article 24.

Article 21

1. A State Party to this Convention may at any time declare under this article that it recognizes the competence of the Committee to receive and consider communications to the effect that a State Party claims that another State Party is not fulfilling its obligations under this Convention. Such communications may be received and considered according to the procedures laid down in this article only if submitted by a State Party which has made a declaration recognizing in regard to itself the competence of the Committee. No communication shall be dealt with by the Committee under this article if it concerns a State Party which has not made such a declaration. Communications received under this article shall be dealt with in accordance with the following procedure;

(a) If a State Party considers that another State Party is not giving effect to the provisions of this Convention, it may, by written communication, bring the matter to the attention of that State Party. Within three months after the receipt of the communication the receiving State shall afford the State which sent the communication an explanation or any other statement in writing clarifying the matter, which should include, to the extent possible and pertinent, reference to domestic procedures and remedies taken, pending or available in the matter;

(b) If the matter is not adjusted to the satisfaction of both States Parties concerned within six months after the receipt by the receiving State of the initial communication, either State shall have the right to refer the matter to the Committee, by notice given to the Committee and to the other State;

(c) The Committee shall deal with a matter referred to it under this article only after it has ascertained that all domestic remedies have been invoked and exhausted in the matter, in conformity with the generally recognized principles of international law. This shall not be the rule where the application of the remedies is unreasonably prolonged or is unlikely to bring effective relief to the person who is the victim of the violation of this Convention;

(d) The Committee shall hold closed meetings when examining communications under this article;

(e) Subject to the provisions of subparagraph (c), the Committee shall make available its good offices to the States Parties concerned with a view to a friendly solution of the matter on the basis of respect for the obligations provided for in this Convention. For this purpose, the Committee may, when appropriate, set up an *ad hoc* conciliation commission;

(f) In any matter referred to it under this article, the Committee may call upon the States Parties concerned, referred to in subparagraph (b), to supply any relevant information;

(g) The States Parties concerned, referred to in subparagraph (b), shall have the right to be represented when the matter is being considered by the Committee and to make submissions orally and/or in writing;

(h) The Committee shall, within twelve months after the date of receipt of notice under subparagraph (b), submit a report:

    (i) If a solution within the terms of subparagraph (e) is reached, the Committee shall confine its report to a brief statement of the facts and of the solution reached;

    (ii) If a solution within the terms of subparagraph (e) is not reached, the Committee shall confine its report to a brief statement of the facts; the written submissions and record of the oral submissions made by the States Parties concerned shall be attached to the report. In every matter, the report shall be communicated to the States Parties concerned.

2. The provisions of this article shall come into force when five States Parties to this Convention have made declarations under paragraph 1 of this article. Such declarations shall be deposited by the States Parties with the Secretary-General of the United Nations, who shall transmit copies thereof to the other States Parties. A declaration may be withdrawn at any time by notification to the Secretary-General. Such a withdrawal shall not prejudice the consideration of any matter which is the subject of a communication already transmitted under this article; no further communication by any State Party shall be received under this article after the notification of withdrawal of the declaration has been received by the Secretary-General, unless the State Party concerned has made a new declaration.

Article 22

1. A State Party to this Convention may at any time declare under this article that it recognizes the competence of the Committee to receive and consider communications from or on behalf of individuals subject to its jurisdiction who claim to be victims of a violation by a State Party of the provisions of the Convention. No communication shall be received by the Committee if it concerns a State Party which has not made such a declaration.

2. The Committee shall consider inadmissible any communication under this article which is anonymous or which it considers to be an abuse of the right of submission of such communications or to be incompatible with the provisions of this Convention.

3. Subject to the provisions of paragraph 2, the Committee shall bring any communications submitted to it under this article to the attention of the State Party to this Convention which has made a declaration under paragraph 1 and is alleged to be violating any provisions of the Convention. Within six months, the receiving State shall submit to the Committee written explanations or statements clarifying the matter and the remedy, if any, that may have been taken by that State.

4. The Committee shall consider communications received under this article in the light of all information made available to it by or on behalf of the individual and by the State Party concerned.

5. The Committee shall not consider any communications from an individual under this article unless it has ascertained that:

(a) The same matter has not been, and is not being, examined under another procedure of international investigation or settlement;

(b) The individual has exhausted all available domestic remedies; this shall not be the rule where the application of the remedies is unreasonably prolonged or is unlikely to bring effective relief to the person who is the victim of the violation of this Convention.

6. The Committee shall hold closed meetings when examining communications under this article.

7. The Committee shall forward its views to the State Party concerned and to the individual.

8. The provisions of this article shall come into force when five States Parties to this Convention have made declarations under paragraph 1 of this article. Such declarations shall be deposited by the States Parties with the Secretary-General of the United Nations, who shall transmit copies thereof to the other States Parties. A declaration may be withdrawn at any time by notification to the Secretary-General. Such a withdrawal shall not prejudice the consideration of any matter which is the subject of a communication already transmitted under this article; no further communication by or on behalf of an individual shall be received under this article after the notification of withdrawal of the declaration has been received by the Secretary General, unless the State Party has made a new declaration.

Article 23

The members of the Committee and of the *ad hoc* conciliation commissions which may be appointed under Article 21, paragraph 1 (e), shall be entitled to the facilities, privileges and immunities of experts on mission for the United Nations as laid down in the relevant sections of the Convention on the Privileges and Immunities of the United Nations.

Article 24

The Committee shall submit an annual report on its activities under this Convention to the States Parties and to the General Assembly of the United Nations.

PART III

Article 25

1. This Convention is open for signature by all States.

2. This Convention is subject to ratification. Instruments of ratification shall be deposited with the Secretary-General of the United Nations.

Article 26

This Convention is open to accession by all States. Accession shall be effected by the deposit of an instrument of accession with the Secretary-General of the United Nations.

Article 27

1. This Convention shall enter into force on the thirtieth day after the date of the deposit with the Secretary-General of the United Nations of the twentieth instrument of ratification or accession.

2. For each State ratifying this Convention or acceding to it after the deposit of the twentieth instrument of ratification or accession, the Convention shall enter into force on the thirtieth day after the date of the deposit of its own instrument of ratification or accession.

Article 28

1. Each State may, at the time of signature or ratification of this Convention or accession thereto, declare that it does not recognize the competence of the Committee provided for in Article 20.

2. Any State Party having made a reservation in accordance with paragraph 1 of this article may, at any time, withdraw this reservation by notification to the Secretary-General of the United Nations.

Article 29

1. Any State Party to this Convention may propose an amendment and file it with the Secretary-General of the United Nations. The Secretary-General shall thereupon communicate the proposed amendment to the States Parties with a request that they notify him whether they favour a conference of States Parties for the purpose of considering and voting upon the proposal. In the event that within four months from the date of such communication at least one third of the States Parties favours such a conference, the Secretary-General shall convene the conference under the auspices of the United Nations. Any amendment adopted by a majority of the States Parties present and voting at the conference shall be submitted by the Secretary-General to all the States Parties for acceptance.

2. An amendment adopted in accordance with paragraph 1 of this article shall enter into force when two thirds of the States Parties to this Convention have notified the Secretary-General of the United Nations that they have accepted it in accordance with their respective constitutional processes.

3. When amendments enter into force, they shall be binding on those States Parties which have accepted them, other States Parties still being bound by the provisions of this Convention and any earlier amendments which they have accepted.

Article 30

1. Any dispute between two or more States Parties concerning the interpretation or application of this Convention which cannot be settled through negotiation shall, at the request of one of them, be submitted to arbitration. If within six months from the date of the request for arbitration the Parties are unable to agree on the organization of the arbitration, any one of those Parties may refer the dispute to the International Court of Justice by request in conformity with the Statute of the Court.

2. Each State may, at the time of signature or ratification of this Convention or accession thereto, declare that it does not consider itself bound by paragraph 1 of this article. The other States Parties shall not be bound by paragraph 1 of this article with respect to any State Party having made such a reservation.

3. Any State Party having made a reservation in accordance with paragraph 2 of this article may at any time withdraw this reservation by notification to the Secretary-General of the United Nations.

Article 31

1. A State Party may denounce this Convention by written notification to the Secretary-General of the United Nations. Denunciation becomes effective one year after the date of receipt of the notification by the Secretary-General.

2. Such a denunciation shall not have the effect of releasing the State Party from its obligations under this Convention in regard to any act or omission which occurs prior to the date at which the denunciation becomes effective, nor shall denunciation prejudice in any way the continued consideration of any matter which is already under consideration by the Committee prior to the date at which the denunciation becomes effective.

3. Following the date at which the denunciation of a State Party becomes effective, the Committee shall not commence consideration of any new matter regarding that State.

Article 32

The Secretary-General of the United Nations shall inform all States Members of the United Nations and all States which have signed this Convention or acceded to it of the following:

   (a) Signatures, ratifications and accessions under Articles 25 and 26;
   (b) The date of entry into force of this Convention under Article 27 and the date of the entry into force of any amendments under Article 29;
   (c) Denunciations under Article 31.

Article 33

1. This Convention, of which the Arabic, Chinese, English, French, Russian and Spanish texts are equally authentic, shall be deposited with the Secretary-General of the United Nations.

2. The Secretary-General of the United Nations shall transmit certified copies of this Convention to all States.

58. OPTIONAL PROTOCOL TO THE CONVENTION AGAINST TORTURE AND OTHER CRUEL, INHUMAN OR DEGRADING TREATMENT OR PUNISHMENT, 2002

The following Protocol was adopted by the General Assembly on 18 December 2002, by a vote of 127 in favour, 4 against, and 42 abstentions; see Resolution 57/199. It entered into force following deposit of the twentieth instrument of ratification on 22 June 2006; see Article 28. Like the European Convention for the Prevention of Torture and Inhuman or Degrading Treatment or Punishment (below, p. 785), it proposes a mechanism for more effective prevention, namely, a system of regular visits to places of detention.

Further reading

EDWARDS, A., 'The Optional Protocol to the Convention against Torture and the Detention of Refugees', (2008) 57 *ICLQ* 789.

TEXT

Preamble

The States Parties to the present Protocol,

Reaffirming that torture and other cruel, inhuman or degrading treatment or punishment are prohibited and constitute serious violations of human rights,

Convinced that further measures are necessary to achieve the purposes of the Convention against Torture and Other Cruel, Inhuman or Degrading Treatment or Punishment (hereinafter referred to as the Convention) and to strengthen the protection of persons deprived of their liberty against torture and other cruel, inhuman or degrading treatment or punishment,

Recalling that articles 2 and 16 of the Convention oblige each State Party to take effective measures to prevent acts of torture and other cruel, inhuman or degrading treatment or punishment in any territory under its jurisdiction,

Recognizing that States have the primary responsibility for implementing those articles, that strengthening the protection of people deprived of their liberty and the full respect for their human rights is a common responsibility shared by all and that international implementing bodies complement and strengthen national measures,

Recalling that the effective prevention of torture and other cruel, inhuman or degrading treatment or punishment requires education and a combination of various legislative, administrative, judicial and other measures,

Recalling also that the World Conference on Human Rights firmly declared that efforts to eradicate torture should first and foremost be concentrated on prevention and called for the adoption of an optional protocol to the Convention, intended to establish a preventive system of regular visits to places of detention,

Convinced that the protection of persons deprived of their liberty against torture and other cruel, inhuman or degrading treatment or punishment can be strengthened by non-judicial means of a preventive nature, based on regular visits to places of detention,

Have agreed as follows:

PART I

General Principles

Article 1

The objective of the present Protocol is to establish a system of regular visits undertaken by independent international and national bodies to places where people are deprived of their liberty, in order to prevent torture and other cruel, inhuman or degrading treatment or punishment.

Article 2

1. A Subcommittee on Prevention of Torture and Other Cruel, Inhuman or Degrading Treatment or Punishment of the Committee against Torture (hereinafter referred to as the Subcommittee on Prevention) shall be established and shall carry out the functions laid down in the present Protocol.

2. The Subcommittee on Prevention shall carry out its work within the framework of the Charter of the United Nations and shall be guided by the purposes and principles thereof, as well as the norms of the United Nations concerning the treatment of people deprived of their liberty.

3. Equally, the Subcommittee on Prevention shall be guided by the principles of confidentiality, impartiality, non-selectivity, universality and objectivity.

4. The Subcommittee on Prevention and the States Parties shall cooperate in the implementation of the present Protocol.

Article 3

Each State Party shall set up, designate or maintain at the domestic level one or several visiting bodies for the prevention of torture and other cruel, inhuman or degrading treatment or punishment (hereinafter referred to as the national preventive mechanism).

Article 4

1. Each State Party shall allow visits, in accordance with the present Protocol, by the mechanisms referred to in articles 2 and 3 to any place under its jurisdiction and control where persons are or may be deprived of their liberty, either by virtue of an order given by a public authority or at its instigation or with its consent or acquiescence (hereinafter referred to as places of detention). These visits shall be undertaken with a view to strengthening, if necessary, the protection of these persons against torture and other cruel, inhuman or degrading treatment or punishment.

2. For the purposes of the present Protocol, deprivation of liberty means any form of detention or imprisonment or the placement of a person in a public or private custodial setting which that person is not permitted to leave at will by order of any judicial, administrative or other authority.

PART II

Subcommittee on Prevention

Article 5

1. The Subcommittee on Prevention shall consist of ten members. After the fiftieth ratification of or accession to the present Protocol, the number of the members of the Subcommittee on Prevention shall increase to twenty-five.

2. The members of the Subcommittee on Prevention shall be chosen from among persons of high moral character, having proven professional experience in the field of the administration of justice, in particular criminal law, prison or police administration, or in the various fields relevant to the treatment of persons deprived of their liberty.

3. In the composition of the Subcommittee on Prevention due consideration shall be given to equitable geographic distribution and to the representation of different forms of civilization and legal systems of the States Parties.

4. In this composition consideration shall also be given to balanced gender representation on the basis of the principles of equality and non-discrimination.

5. No two members of the Subcommittee on Prevention may be nationals of the same State.

6. The members of the Subcommittee on Prevention shall serve in their individual capacity, shall be independent and impartial and shall be available to serve the Subcommittee on Prevention efficiently.

Article 6

1. Each State Party may nominate, in accordance with paragraph 2 of the present article, up to two candidates possessing the qualifications and meeting the requirements set out in article 5, and in doing so shall provide detailed information on the qualifications of the nominees.

2. (a) The nominees shall have the nationality of a State Party to the present Protocol;

   (b) At least one of the two candidates shall have the nationality of the nominating State Party;

   (c) No more than two nationals of a State Party shall be nominated;

   (d) Before a State Party nominates a national of another State Party, it shall seek and obtain the consent of that State Party.

3. At least five months before the date of the meeting of the States Parties during which the elections will be held, the Secretary-General of the United Nations shall address a letter to the States Parties inviting them to submit their nominations within three months. The Secretary-General shall submit a list, in alphabetical order, of all persons thus nominated, indicating the States Parties that have nominated them.

Article 7

1. The members of the Subcommittee on Prevention shall be elected in the following manner:

   (a) Primary consideration shall be given to the fulfilment of the requirements and criteria of article 5 of the present Protocol;

   (b) The initial election shall be held no later than six months after the entry into force of the present Protocol;

(c) The States Parties shall elect the members of the Subcommittee on Prevention by secret ballot;

(d) Elections of the members of the Subcommittee on Prevention shall be held at biennial meetings of the States Parties convened by the Secretary-General of the United Nations. At those meetings, for which two thirds of the States Parties shall constitute a quorum, the persons elected to the Subcommittee on Prevention shall be those who obtain the largest number of votes and an absolute majority of the votes of the representatives of the States Parties present and voting.

2. If during the election process two nationals of a State Party have become eligible to serve as members of the Subcommittee on Prevention, the candidate receiving the higher number of votes shall serve as the member of the Subcommittee on Prevention. Where nationals have received the same number of votes, the following procedure applies:

(a) Where only one has been nominated by the State Party of which he or she is a national, that national shall serve as the member of the Subcommittee on Prevention;

(b) Where both candidates have been nominated by the State Party of which they are nationals, a separate vote by secret ballot shall be held to determine which national shall become the member;

(c) Where neither candidate has been nominated by the State Party of which he or she is a national, a separate vote by secret ballot shall be held to determine which candidate shall be the member.

Article 8

If a member of the Subcommittee on Prevention dies or resigns, or for any cause can no longer perform his or her duties, the State Party that nominated the member shall nominate another eligible person possessing the qualifications and meeting the requirements set out in article 5, taking into account the need for a proper balance among the various fields of competence, to serve until the next meeting of the States Parties, subject to the approval of the majority of the States Parties. The approval shall be considered given unless half or more of the States Parties respond negatively within six weeks after having been informed by the Secretary-General of the United Nations of the proposed appointment.

Article 9

The members of the Subcommittee on Prevention shall be elected for a term of four years. They shall be eligible for re-election once if renominated. The term of half the members elected at the first election shall expire at the end of two years; immediately after the first election the names of those members shall be chosen by lot by the Chairman of the meeting referred to in article 7, paragraph 1(d).

Article 10

1. The Subcommittee on Prevention shall elect its officers for a term of two years. They may be re-elected.

2. The Subcommittee on Prevention shall establish its own rules of procedure. These rules shall provide, *inter alia*, that:

(a) Half the members plus one shall constitute a quorum;

(b) Decisions of the Subcommittee on Prevention shall be made by a majority vote of the members present;

(c) The Subcommittee on Prevention shall meet in camera.

3. The Secretary-General of the United Nations shall convene the initial meeting of the Subcommittee on Prevention. After its initial meeting, the Subcommittee on Prevention shall meet at such times as shall be provided by its rules of procedure. The Subcommittee on Prevention and the Committee against Torture shall hold their sessions simultaneously at least once a year.

PART III

Mandate of the Subcommittee on Prevention

Article 11

The Subcommittee on Prevention shall:

(a) Visit the places referred to in article 4 and make recommendations to States Parties concerning the protection of persons deprived of their liberty against torture and other cruel, inhuman or degrading treatment or punishment;

(b) In regard to the national preventive mechanisms:

   (i) Advise and assist States Parties, when necessary, in their establishment;

   (ii) Maintain direct, and if necessary confidential, contact with the national preventive mechanisms and offer them training and technical assistance with a view to strengthening their capacities;

   (iii) Advise and assist them in the evaluation of the needs and the means necessary to strengthen the protection of persons deprived of their liberty against torture and other cruel, inhuman or degrading treatment or punishment;

   (iv) Make recommendations and observations to the States Parties with a view to strengthening the capacity and the mandate of the national preventive mechanisms for the prevention of torture and other cruel, inhuman or degrading treatment or punishment;

(c) Cooperate, for the prevention of torture in general, with the relevant United Nations organs and mechanisms as well as with the international, regional and national institutions or organizations working towards the strengthening of the protection of all persons against torture and other cruel, inhuman or degrading treatment or punishment.

Article 12

In order to enable the Subcommittee on Prevention to comply with its mandate as laid down in article 11, the States Parties undertake:

(a) To receive the Subcommittee on Prevention in their territory and grant it access to the places of detention as defined in article 4 of the present Protocol;

(b) To provide all relevant information the Subcommittee on Prevention may request to evaluate the needs and measures that should be adopted to strengthen the

protection of persons deprived of their liberty against torture and other cruel, inhuman or degrading treatment or punishment;

(c) To encourage and facilitate contacts between the Subcommittee on Prevention and the national preventive mechanisms;

(d) To examine the recommendations of the Subcommittee on Prevention and enter into dialogue with it on possible implementation measures.

Article 13

1. The Subcommittee on Prevention shall establish, at first by lot, a programme of regular visits to the States Parties in order to fulfil its mandate as established in article 11.

2. After consultations, the Subcommittee on Prevention shall notify the States Parties of its programme in order that they may, without delay, make the necessary practical arrangements for the visits to be conducted.

3. The visits shall be conducted by at least two members of the Subcommittee on Prevention. These members may be accompanied, if needed, by experts of demonstrated professional experience and knowledge in the fields covered by the present Protocol who shall be selected from a roster of experts prepared on the basis of proposals made by the States Parties, the Office of the United Nations High Commissioner for Human Rights and the United Nations Centre for International Crime Prevention. In preparing the roster, the States Parties concerned shall propose no more than five national experts. The State Party concerned may oppose the inclusion of a specific expert in the visit, whereupon the Subcommittee on Prevention shall propose another expert.

4. If the Subcommittee on Prevention considers it appropriate, it may propose a short follow-up visit after a regular visit.

Article 14

1. In order to enable the Subcommittee on Prevention to fulfil its mandate, the States Parties to the present Protocol undertake to grant it:

(a) Unrestricted access to all information concerning the number of persons deprived of their liberty in places of detention as defined in article 4, as well as the number of places and their location;

(b) Unrestricted access to all information referring to the treatment of those persons as well as their conditions of detention;

(c) Subject to paragraph 2 below, unrestricted access to all places of detention and their installations and facilities;

(d) The opportunity to have private interviews with the persons deprived of their liberty without witnesses, either personally or with a translator if deemed necessary, as well as with any other person who the Subcommittee on Prevention believes may supply relevant information;

(e) The liberty to choose the places it wants to visit and the persons it wants to interview.

2. Objection to a visit to a particular place of detention may be made only on urgent and compelling grounds of national defence, public safety, natural disaster or serious disorder in the place to be visited that temporarily prevent the carrying out of such a visit. The existence of a declared state of emergency as such shall not be invoked by a State Party as a reason to object to a visit.

Article 15

No authority or official shall order, apply, permit or tolerate any sanction against any person or organization for having communicated to the Subcommittee on Prevention or to its delegates any information, whether true or false, and no such person or organization shall be otherwise prejudiced in any way.

Article 16

1. The Subcommittee on Prevention shall communicate its recommendations and observations confidentially to the State Party and, if relevant, to the national preventive mechanism.

2. The Subcommittee on Prevention shall publish its report, together with any comments of the State Party concerned, whenever requested to do so by that State Party. If the State Party makes part of the report public, the Subcommittee on Prevention may publish the report in whole or in part. However, no personal data shall be published without the express consent of the person concerned.

3. The Subcommittee on Prevention shall present a public annual report on its activities to the Committee against Torture.

4. If the State Party refuses to cooperate with the Subcommittee on Prevention according to articles 12 and 14, or to take steps to improve the situation in the light of the recommendations of the Subcommittee on Prevention, the Committee against Torture may, at the request of the Subcommittee on Prevention, decide, by a majority of its members, after the State Party has had an opportunity to make its views known, to make a public statement on the matter or to publish the report of the Subcommittee on Prevention.

PART IV

National Preventive Mechanisms

Article 17

Each State Party shall maintain, designate or establish, at the latest one year after the entry into force of the present Protocol or of its ratification or accession, one or several independent national preventive mechanisms for the prevention of torture at the domestic level. Mechanisms established by decentralized units may be designated as national preventive mechanisms for the purposes of the present Protocol if they are in conformity with its provisions.

Article 18

1. The States Parties shall guarantee the functional independence of the national preventive mechanisms as well as the independence of their personnel.

2. The States Parties shall take the necessary measures to ensure that the experts of the national preventive mechanism have the required capabilities and professional knowledge. They shall strive for a gender balance and the adequate representation of ethnic and minority groups in the country.

3. The States Parties undertake to make available the necessary resources for the functioning of the national preventive mechanisms.

4. When establishing national preventive mechanisms, States Parties shall give due consideration to the Principles relating to the status of national institutions for the promotion and protection of human rights.

Article 19

The national preventive mechanisms shall be granted at a minimum the power:

(a) To regularly examine the treatment of the persons deprived of their liberty in places of detention as defined in article 4, with a view to strengthening, if necessary, their protection against torture and other cruel, inhuman or degrading treatment or punishment;

(b) To make recommendations to the relevant authorities with the aim of improving the treatment and the conditions of the persons deprived of their liberty and to prevent torture and other cruel, inhuman or degrading treatment or punishment, taking into consideration the relevant norms of the United Nations;

(c) To submit proposals and observations concerning existing or draft legislation.

Article 20

In order to enable the national preventive mechanisms to fulfil their mandate, the States Parties to the present Protocol undertake to grant them:

(a) Access to all information concerning the number of persons deprived of their liberty in places of detention as defined in article 4, as well as the number of places and their location;

(b) Access to all information referring to the treatment of those persons as well as their conditions of detention;

(c) Access to all places of detention and their installations and facilities;

(d) The opportunity to have private interviews with the persons deprived of their liberty without witnesses, either personally or with a translator if deemed necessary, as well as with any other person who the national preventive mechanism believes may supply relevant information;

(e) The liberty to choose the places they want to visit and the persons they want to interview;

(f) The right to have contacts with the Subcommittee on Prevention, to send it information and to meet with it.

Article 21

1. No authority or official shall order, apply, permit or tolerate any sanction against any person or organization for having communicated to the national preventive mechanism any information, whether true or false, and no such person or organization shall be otherwise prejudiced in any way.

2. Confidential information collected by the national preventive mechanism shall be privileged. No personal data shall be published without the express consent of the person concerned.

Article 22

The competent authorities of the State Party concerned shall examine the recommendations of the national preventive mechanism and enter into a dialogue with it on possible implementation measures.

Article 23

The States Parties to the present Protocol undertake to publish and disseminate the annual reports of the national preventive mechanisms.

PART V

Declaration

Article 24

1. Upon ratification, States Parties may make a declaration postponing the implementation of their obligations under either part III or part IV of the present Protocol.

2. This postponement shall be valid for a maximum of three years. After due representations made by the State Party and after consultation with the Subcommittee on Prevention, the Committee against Torture may extend that period for an additional two years.

PART VI

Financial Provisions

Article 25

1. The expenditure incurred by the Subcommittee on Prevention in the implementation of the present Protocol shall be borne by the United Nations.

2. The Secretary-General of the United Nations shall provide the necessary staff and facilities for the effective performance of the functions of the Subcommittee on Prevention under the present Protocol.

Article 26

1. A Special Fund shall be set up in accordance with the relevant procedures of the General Assembly, to be administered in accordance with the financial regulations and rules of the United Nations, to help finance the implementation of the recommendations made by the Subcommittee on Prevention after a visit to a State Party, as well as education programmes of the national preventive mechanisms.

2. The Special Fund may be financed through voluntary contributions made by Governments, intergovernmental and non-governmental organizations and other private or public entities.

PART VII

Final Provisions

Article 27

1. The present Protocol is open for signature by any State that has signed the Convention.

2. The present Protocol is subject to ratification by any State that has ratified or acceded to the Convention. Instruments of ratification shall be deposited with the Secretary-General of the United Nations.

3. The present Protocol shall be open to accession by any State that has ratified or acceded to the Convention.

4. Accession shall be effected by the deposit of an instrument of accession with the Secretary-General of the United Nations.

5. The Secretary-General of the United Nations shall inform all States that have signed the present Protocol or acceded to it of the deposit of each instrument of ratification or accession.

Article 28

1. The present Protocol shall enter into force on the thirtieth day after the date of deposit with the Secretary-General of the United Nations of the twentieth instrument of ratification or accession.

2. For each State ratifying the present Protocol or acceding to it after the deposit with the Secretary-General of the United Nations of the twentieth instrument of ratification or accession, the present Protocol shall enter into force on the thirtieth day after the date of deposit of its own instrument of ratification or accession.

Article 29

The provisions of the present Protocol shall extend to all parts of federal States without any limitations or exceptions.

Article 30

No reservations shall be made to the present Protocol.

Article 31

The provisions of the present Protocol shall not affect the obligations of States Parties under any regional convention instituting a system of visits to places of detention. The Subcommittee on Prevention and the bodies established under such regional conventions are encouraged to consult and cooperate with a view to avoiding duplication and promoting effectively the objectives of the present Protocol.

Article 32

The provisions of the present Protocol shall not affect the obligations of States Parties to the four Geneva Conventions of 12 August 1949 and the Additional Protocols thereto of 8 June 1977, nor the opportunity available to any State Party to authorize the International

Committee of the Red Cross to visit places of detention in situations not covered by international humanitarian law.

Article 33

1. Any State Party may denounce the present Protocol at any time by written notification addressed to the Secretary-General of the United Nations, who shall thereafter inform the other States Parties to the present Protocol and the Convention. Denunciation shall take effect one year after the date of receipt of the notification by the Secretary-General.

2. Such a denunciation shall not have the effect of releasing the State Party from its obligations under the present Protocol in regard to any act or situation that may occur prior to the date on which the denunciation becomes effective, or to the actions that the Subcommittee on Prevention has decided or may decide to take with respect to the State Party concerned, nor shall denunciation prejudice in any way the continued consideration of any matter already under consideration by the Subcommittee on Prevention prior to the date on which the denunciation becomes effective.

3. Following the date on which the denunciation of the State Party becomes effective, the Subcommittee on Prevention shall not commence consideration of any new matter regarding that State.

Article 34

1. Any State Party to the present Protocol may propose an amendment and file it with the Secretary-General of the United Nations. The Secretary-General shall thereupon communicate the proposed amendment to the States Parties to the present Protocol with a request that they notify him whether they favour a conference of States Parties for the purpose of considering and voting upon the proposal. In the event that within four months from the date of such communication at least one third of the States Parties favour such a conference, the Secretary-General shall convene the conference under the auspices of the United Nations. Any amendment adopted by a majority of two thirds of the States Parties present and voting at the conference shall be submitted by the Secretary-General of the United Nations to all States Parties for acceptance.

2. An amendment adopted in accordance with paragraph 1 of the present article shall come into force when it has been accepted by a two-thirds majority of the States Parties to the present Protocol in accordance with their respective constitutional processes.

3. When amendments come into force, they shall be binding on those States Parties that have accepted them, other States Parties still being bound by the provisions of the present Protocol and any earlier amendment that they have accepted.

Article 35

Members of the Subcommittee on Prevention and of the national preventive mechanisms shall be accorded such privileges and immunities as are necessary for the independent exercise of their functions. Members of the Subcommittee on Prevention shall be accorded the privileges and immunities specified in section 22 of the Convention on the Privileges and Immunities of the United Nations of 13 February 1946, subject to the provisions of section 23 of that Convention.

Article 36

When visiting a State Party, the members of the Subcommittee on Prevention shall, without prejudice to the provisions and purposes of the present Protocol and such privileges and immunities as they may enjoy:

    (a) Respect the laws and regulations of the visited State;

    (b) Refrain from any action or activity incompatible with the impartial and international nature of their duties.

Article 37

1. The present Protocol, of which the Arabic, Chinese, English, French, Russian and Spanish texts are equally authentic, shall be deposited with the Secretary-General of the United Nations.

2. The Secretary-General of the United Nations shall transmit certified copies of the present Protocol to all States.

59. CONVENTION ON THE RIGHTS OF THE CHILD, 1989

The Convention was adopted by General Assembly Resolution 44/25 without vote on 20 November 1989, and entered into force on 2 September 1990, one month after the twentieth State ratified it, in accordance with Article 49(1). For text, see 1577 *UNTS* 3. Article 43(2) has been amended to raise the number of experts on the Committee from ten to eighteen; see General Assemble Resolution 50/155, 21 December 1995; the amendment came into force on 18 November 2002. For the work of the Committee, see **http://www2.ohchr.org/english/bodies/crc/index.htm**.

In 1979 the United Nations Commission on Human Rights began consideration of a Polish proposal for a draft Convention on the Rights of the Child. The precursors of the Convention of 1989 include the Universal Declaration of Human Rights, Articles 2 and 25(2) (see above, p. 39), and the Declaration of the Rights of the Child adopted by the General Assembly on 20 November 1959 (for the text, see the 2nd edition of this work, at 108).

The Convention is an elaboration of human rights standards in respect of the child. However, human rights standards were applicable to the child (as an individual) independently of the new instrument by virtue of the principles of general international law. The rights of the child are also the subject of Article 24 of the International Covenant on Civil and Political Rights (see above, p. 396).

Further reading

ALEN, A., et al., eds., *A Commentary on the United Nations Convention on the Rights of the Child*, Leiden: Brill, 2005- (Series).

ALSTON, P., *The Best Interests of the Child: Reconciling Culture and Human Rights*, Oxford: Clarendon Press, 1994.

BENTLEY, K. A., 'Can there be any universal children's rights?', (2005) 9 *International Journal of Human Rights* 107.

BOUCAUD, P., 'Droit des enfants en droit international – Traités régionaux et droit humanitaire', *Revue trimestrielle de droits de l'homme*, 1992, 447.

COHEN, C. P., 'Introductory Note', (1989) 28 *ILM* 1448.

DAVIS, M. F. and POWELL, R., 'The International Convention on the Rights of the Child: A Catalyst for Innovative Child Care Policies', (2003) 25 *Human Rights Quarterly* 689.

HARRIS-SHORT, S., 'International Human Rights Law: Imperialist, Inept and Ineffective? Cultural Relativism and the UN Convention on the Rights of the Child', (2003) 25 *Human Rights Quarterly* 130.

HODGKIN, R. and NEWELL, P., *Implementation Handbook for the Convention on the Rights of the Child*, New York: UNICEF, 3rd edn., 2007.

LANDGREN, K., 'The Protective Environment: Development Support for Child Protection', (2005) 27 *Human Rights Quarterly* 214.

McGOLDRICK, D., 'The United Nations Convention on the Rights of the Child', (1991) 5 *International Journal of Law and the Family* 132.

PARKES, A., *Children and International Human Rights Law: The Right of the Child to be Heard*, London: Routledge, 2010.

UNICEF, *Protecting the World's Children: Impact of the Convention on the Rights of the Child in Diverse Legal System*, Cambridge: Cambridge University Press, 2007.

UNITED NATIONS HIGH COMMISSIONER FOR HUMAN RIGHTS, *Legislative History of the Convention on the Rights of the Child*, 2 vols., New York and Geneva: United Nations, 2007.

VAN BUEREN, G., *The International Law on the Rights of the Child*, Dordrecht: Martinus Nijhoff, 1995.

TEXT

Preamble

The States Parties to the present Convention,

Considering that, in accordance with the principles proclaimed in the Charter of the United Nations, recognition of the inherent dignity and of the equal and inalienable rights of all members of the human family is the foundation of freedom, justice and peace in the world,

Bearing in mind that the peoples of the United Nations have, in the Charter, reaffirmed their faith in fundamental human rights and in the dignity and worth of the human person, and have determined to promote social progress and better standards of life in larger freedom,

Recognizing that the United Nations has, in the Universal Declaration of Human Rights and in the International Covenants on Human Rights, proclaimed and agreed that everyone is entitled to all the rights and freedoms set forth therein, without distinction of any kind, such as race, colour, sex, language, religion, political or other opinion, national or social origin, property, birth or other status,

Recalling that, in the Universal Declaration of Human Rights, the United Nations has proclaimed that childhood is entitled to special care and assistance,

Convinced that the family, as the fundamental group of society and the natural environment for the growth and well-being of all its members and particularly children, should be afforded the necessary protection and assistance so that it can fully assume its responsibilities within the community,

Recognizing that the child, for the full and harmonious development of his or her personality, should grow up in a family environment, in an atmosphere of happiness, love and understanding,

Considering that the child should be fully prepared to live an individual life in society, and brought up in the spirit of the ideals proclaimed in the Charter of the United Nations, and in particular in the spirit of peace, dignity, tolerance, freedom, equality and solidarity,

Bearing in mind that the need to extend particular care to the child has been stated in the Geneva Declaration of the Rights of the Child of 1924 and in the Declaration of the Rights of the Child adopted by the General Assembly on 20 November 1959 and recognized in the Universal Declaration of Human Rights, in the International Covenant on Civil and Political Rights (in particular in Articles 23 and 24), in the International Covenant on Economic, Social and Cultural Rights (in particular in Article 10) and in the statutes and relevant instruments of specialized agencies and international organizations concerned with the welfare of children,

Bearing in mind that, as indicated in the Declaration of the Rights of the Child, 'the child, by reason of his physical and mental immaturity, needs special safeguards and care, including appropriate legal protection, before as well as after birth',

Recalling the provisions of the Declaration on Social and Legal Principles relating to the Protection and Welfare of Children, with Special Reference to Foster Placement and Adoption Nationally and Internationally; the United Nations Standard Minimum Rules for the Administration of Juvenile Justice (The Beijing Rules); and the Declaration on the Protection of Women and Children in Emergency and Armed Conflict,

Recognizing that, in all countries in the world, there are children living in exceptionally difficult conditions, and that such children need special consideration,

Taking due account of the importance of the traditions and cultural values of each people for the protection and harmonious development of the child,

Recognizing the importance of international co-operation for improving the living conditions of children in every country, in particular in the developing countries,

Have agreed as follows:

PART I

Article 1

For the purposes of the present Convention, a child means every human being below the age of eighteen years unless under the law applicable to the child, majority is attained earlier.

Article 2

1. States Parties shall respect and ensure the rights set forth in the present Convention to each child within their jurisdiction without discrimination of any kind, irrespective of the child's or his or her parent's or legal guardian's race, colour, sex, language, religion, political or other opinion, national, ethnic or social origin, property, disability, birth or other status.

2. States Parties shall take all appropriate measures to ensure that the child is protected against all forms of discrimination or punishment on the basis of the status, activities, expressed opinions, or beliefs of the child's parents, legal guardians, or family members.

Article 3

1. In all actions concerning children, whether undertaken by public or private social welfare institutions, courts of law, administrative authorities or legislative bodies, the best interests of the child shall be a primary consideration.

2. States Parties undertake to ensure the child such protection and care as is necessary for his or her well-being, taking into account the rights and duties of his or her parents, legal guardians, or other individuals legally responsible for him or her, and, to this end, shall take all appropriate legislative and administrative measures.

3. States Parties shall ensure that the institutions, services and facilities responsible for the care or protection of children shall conform with the standards established by competent authorities, particularly in the areas of safety, health, in the number and suitability of their staff, as well as competent supervision.

Article 4

States Parties shall undertake all appropriate legislative, administrative, and other measures for the implementation of the rights recognized in the present Convention. With regard to economic, social and cultural rights, States Parties shall undertake such measures to the maximum extent of their available resources and, where needed, within the framework of international co-operation.

Article 5

States Parties shall respect the responsibilities, rights and duties of parents or, where applicable, the members of the extended family or community as provided for by local custom, legal guardians or other persons legally responsible for the child, to provide, in a manner consistent with the evolving capacities of the child, appropriate direction and guidance in the exercise by the child of the rights recognized in the present Convention.

Article 6

1. States Parties recognize that every child has the inherent right to life.

2. States Parties shall ensure to the maximum extent possible the survival and development of the child.

Article 7

1. The child shall be registered immediately after birth and shall have the right from birth to a name, the right to acquire a nationality and, as far as possible, the right to know and be cared for by his or her parents.

2. States Parties shall ensure the implementation of these rights in accordance with their national law and their obligations under the relevant international instruments in this field, in particular where the child would otherwise be stateless.

Article 8

1. States Parties undertake to respect the right of the child to preserve his or her identity, including nationality, name and family relations as recognized by law without unlawful interference.

2. Where a child is illegally deprived of some or all of the elements of his or her identity, States Parties shall provide appropriate assistance and protection, with a view to re-establishing speedily his or her identity.

Article 9

1. States Parties shall ensure that a child shall not be separated from his or her parents against their will, except when competent authorities subject to judicial review determine, in accordance with applicable law and procedures, that such separation is necessary for the best interests of the child. Such determination may be necessary in a particular case such as one involving abuse or neglect of the child by the parents, or one where the parents are living separately and a decision must be made as to the child's place of residence.

2. In any proceedings pursuant to paragraph 1 of the present article, all interested parties shall be given an opportunity to participate in the proceedings and make their views known.

3. States Parties shall respect the right of the child who is separated from one or both parents to maintain personal relations and direct contact with both parents on a regular basis, except if it is contrary to the child's best interests.

4. Where such separation results from any action initiated by a State Party, such as the detention, imprisonment, exile, deportation or death (including death arising from any cause while the person is in the custody of the State) of one or both parents or of the child, that State Party shall, upon request, provide the parents, the child or, if appropriate, another member of the family with the essential information concerning the whereabouts of the absent member(s) of the family unless the provision of the information would be detrimental to the well-being of the child. States Parties shall further ensure that the submission of such a request shall of itself entail no adverse consequences for the person(s) concerned.

Article 10

1. In accordance with the obligation of States Parties under Article 9, paragraph 1, applications by a child or his or her parents to enter or leave a State Party for the purpose of family reunification shall be dealt with by States Parties in a positive, humane and expeditious manner. States Parties shall further ensure that the submission of such a request shall entail no adverse consequences for the applicants and for the members of their family.

2. A child whose parents reside in different States shall have the right to maintain on a regular basis, save in exceptional circumstances personal relations and direct contacts with both parents. Towards that end and in accordance with the obligation of States Parties under Article 9, paragraph 1, States Parties shall respect the right of the child and his or her parents to leave any country, including their own, and to enter their own country. The right to leave any country shall be subject only to such restrictions as are prescribed by law and which are necessary to protect the national security, public order (*ordre public*), public health or morals or the rights and freedoms of others and are consistent with the other rights recognized in the present Convention.

Article 11

1. States Parties shall take measures to combat the illicit transfer and non-return of children abroad.

2. To this end, States Parties shall promote the conclusion of bilateral or multilateral agreements or accession to existing agreements.

Article 12

1. States Parties shall assure to the child who is capable of forming his or her own views the right to express those views freely in all matters affecting the child, the views of the child being given due weight in accordance with the age and maturity of the child.

2. For this purpose, the child shall in particular be provided the opportunity to be heard in any judicial and administrative proceedings affecting the child, either directly, or through a representative or an appropriate body, in a manner consistent with the procedural rules of national law.

Article 13

1. The child shall have the right to freedom of expression; this right shall include freedom to seek, receive and impart information and ideas of all kinds, regardless of frontiers, either orally, in writing or in print, in the form of art, or through any other media of the child's choice.

2. The exercise of this right may be subject to certain restrictions, but these shall only be such as are provided by law and are necessary:

   (a) For respect of the rights or reputations of others; or

   (b) For the protection of national security or of public order (*ordre public*), or of public health or morals.

Article 14

1. States Parties shall respect the right of the child to freedom of thought, conscience and religion.

2. States Parties shall respect the rights and duties of the parents and, when applicable, legal guardians, to provide direction to the child in the exercise of his or her right in a manner consistent with the evolving capacities of the child.

3. Freedom to manifest one's religion or beliefs may be subject only to such limitations as are prescribed by law and are necessary to protect public safety, order, health or morals, or the fundamental rights and freedoms of others.

Article 15

1. States Parties recognize the rights of the child to freedom of association and to freedom of peaceful assembly.

2. No restrictions may be placed on the exercise of these rights other than those imposed in conformity with the law and which are necessary in a democratic society in the interests of national security or public safety, public order (*ordre public*), the protection of public health or morals or the protection of the rights and freedoms of others.

Article 16

1. No child shall be subjected to arbitrary or unlawful interference with his or her privacy, family, home or correspondence, nor to unlawful attacks on his or her honour and reputation.

2. The child has the right to the protection of the law against such interference or attacks.

Article 17

States Parties recognize the important function performed by the mass media and shall ensure that the child has access to information and material from a diversity of national and international sources, especially those aimed at the promotion of his or her social, spiritual and moral well-being and physical and mental health. To this end, States Parties shall:

  (a) Encourage the mass media to disseminate information and material of social and cultural benefit to the child and in accordance with the spirit of Article 29;

  (b) Encourage international co-operation in the production, exchange and dissemination of such information and material from a diversity of cultural, national and international sources;

  (c) Encourage the production and dissemination of children's books;

  (d) Encourage the mass media to have particular regard to the linguistic needs of the child who belongs to a minority group or who is indigenous;

  (e) Encourage the development of appropriate guidelines for the protection of the child from information and material injurious to his or her well-being, bearing in mind the provisions of Articles 13 and 18.

Article 18

1. States Parties shall use their best efforts to ensure recognition of the principle that both parents have common responsibilities for the upbringing and development of the child. Parents or, as the case may be, legal guardians, have the primary responsibility for the upbringing and development of the child. The best interests of the child will be their basic concern.

2. For the purpose of guaranteeing and promoting the rights set forth in the present Convention, States Parties shall render appropriate assistance to parents and legal guardians in the performance of their child-rearing responsibilities and shall ensure the development of institutions, facilities and services for the care of children.

3. States Parties shall take all appropriate measures to ensure that children of working parents have the right to benefit from child-care services and facilities for which they are eligible.

Article 19

1. States Parties shall take all appropriate legislative, administrative, social and educational measures to protect the child from all forms of physical or mental violence, injury or abuse, neglect or negligent treatment, maltreatment or exploitation, including sexual abuse, while in the care of parent(s), legal guardian(s) or any other person who has the care of the child.

2. Such protective measures should, as appropriate, include effective procedures for the establishment of social programmes to provide necessary support for the child and for those who have the care of the child, as well as for other forms of prevention and for identification, reporting, referral, investigation, treatment and follow-up of instances of child maltreatment described heretofore, and, as appropriate, for judicial involvement.

Article 20

1. A child temporarily or permanently deprived of his or her family environment, or in whose own best interests cannot be allowed to remain in that environment, shall be entitled to special protection and assistance provided by the State.

2. States Parties shall in accordance with their national laws ensure alternative care for such a child.

3. Such care could include, *inter alia*, foster placement, kafalah of Islamic law, adoption or if necessary placement in suitable institutions for the care of children. When considering solutions, due regard shall be paid to the desirability of continuity in a child's upbringing and to the child's ethnic, religious, cultural and linguistic background.

Article 21

States Parties that recognize and/or permit the system of adoption shall ensure that the best interests of the child shall be the paramount consideration and they shall:

(a) Ensure that the adoption of a child is authorized only by competent authorities who determine, in accordance with applicable law and procedures and on the basis of all pertinent and reliable information, that the adoption is permissible in view of the child's status concerning parents, relatives and legal guardians and that, if required, the persons concerned have given their informed consent to the adoption on the basis of such counselling as may be necessary;

(b) Recognize that inter-country adoption may be considered as an alternative means of child's care, if the child cannot be placed in a foster or an adoptive family or cannot in any suitable manner be cared for in the child's country of origin;

(c) Ensure that the child concerned by inter-country adoption enjoys safeguards and standards equivalent to those existing in the case of national adoption;

(d) Take all appropriate measures to ensure that, in inter-country adoption, the placement does not result in improper financial gain for those involved in it;

(e) Promote, where appropriate, the objectives of the present article by concluding bilateral or multilateral arrangements or agreements, and endeavour, within this framework, to ensure that the placement of the child in another country is carried out by competent authorities or organs.

Article 22

1. States Parties shall take appropriate measures to ensure that a child who is seeking refugee status or who is considered a refugee in accordance with applicable international or domestic law and procedures shall, whether unaccompanied or accompanied by his or her parents or by any other person, receive appropriate protection and humanitarian assistance in the enjoyment of applicable rights set forth in the present Convention and in other international human rights or humanitarian instruments to which the said States are Parties.

2. For this purpose, States Parties shall provide, as they consider appropriate, co-operation in any efforts by the United Nations and other competent intergovernmental organizations or non-governmental organizations co-operating with the United Nations to protect and assist such a child and to trace the parents or other members of the family of any refugee child in order to obtain information necessary for reunification with his or her family. In cases where no parents or other members of the family can be found, the child shall be accorded the same protection as any other child permanently or temporarily deprived of his or her family environment for any reason, as set forth in the present Convention.

Article 23

1. States Parties recognize that a mentally or physically disabled child should enjoy a full and decent life, in conditions which ensure dignity, promote self-reliance and facilitate the child's active participation in the community.

2. States Parties recognize the right of the disabled child to special care and shall encourage and ensure the extension, subject to available resources, to the eligible child and those responsible for his or her care, of assistance for which application is made and which is appropriate to the child's condition and to the circumstances of the parents or others caring for the child.

3. Recognizing the special needs of a disabled child, assistance extended in accordance with paragraph 2 of the present article shall be provided free of charge, whenever possible, taking into account the financial resources of the parents or others caring for the child, and shall be designed to ensure that the disabled child has effective access to and receives education, training, health care services, rehabilitation services, preparation for employment and recreation opportunities in a manner conducive to the child's achieving the fullest possible social integration and individual development, including his or her cultural and spiritual development.

4. States Parties shall promote, in the spirit of international cooperation, the exchange of appropriate information in the field of preventive health care and of medical, psychological and functional treatment of disabled children, including dissemination of and access to information concerning methods of rehabilitation, education and vocational services, with the aim of enabling States Parties to improve their capabilities and skills and to widen their experience in these areas. In this regard, particular account shall be taken of the needs of developing countries.

Article 24

1. States Parties recognize the right of the child to the enjoyment of the highest attainable standard of health and to facilities for the treatment of illness and rehabilitation of health. States Parties shall strive to ensure that no child is deprived of his or her right of access to such health care services.

2. States Parties shall pursue full implementation of this right and, in particular, shall take appropriate measures:

  (a) To diminish infant and child mortality;

  (b) To ensure the provision of necessary medical assistance and health care to all children with emphasis on the development of primary health care;

  (c) To combat disease and malnutrition, including within the framework of primary health care, through, *inter alia*, the application of readily available technology and through the provision of adequate nutritious foods and clean drinking-water, taking into consideration the dangers and risks of environmental pollution;

  (d) To ensure appropriate pre-natal and post-natal health care for mothers;

  (e) To ensure that all segments of society, in particular parents and children, are informed, have access to education and are supported in the use of basic knowledge of child health and nutrition, the advantages of breastfeeding, hygiene and environmental sanitation and the prevention of accidents;

  (f) To develop preventive health care, guidance for parents and family planning education and services.

3. States Parties shall take all effective and appropriate measures with a view to abolishing traditional practices prejudicial to the health of children.

4. States Parties undertake to promote and encourage international co-operation with a view to achieving progressively the full realization of the right recognized in the present article. In this regard, particular account shall be taken of the needs of developing countries.

Article 25

States Parties recognize the right of a child who has been placed by the competent authorities for the purposes of care, protection or treatment of his or her physical or mental health, to a periodic review of the treatment provided to the child and all other circumstances relevant to his or her placement.

Article 26

1. States Parties shall recognize for every child the right to benefit from social security, including social insurance, and shall take the necessary measures to achieve the full realization of this right in accordance with their national law.

2. The benefits should, where appropriate, be granted, taking into account the resources and the circumstances of the child and persons having responsibility for the maintenance of the child, as well as any other consideration relevant to an application for benefits made by or on behalf of the child.

Article 27

1. States Parties recognize the right of every child to a standard of living adequate for the child's physical, mental, spiritual, moral and social development.

2. The parent(s) or others responsible for the child have the primary responsibility to secure, within their abilities and financial capacities, the conditions of living necessary for the child's development.

3. States Parties, in accordance with national conditions and within their means, shall take appropriate measures to assist parents and others responsible for the child to implement this right and shall in case of need provide material assistance and support programmes, particularly with regard to nutrition, clothing and housing.

4. States Parties shall take all appropriate measures to secure the recovery of maintenance for the child from the parents or other persons having financial responsibility for the child, both within the State Party and from abroad. In particular, where the person having financial responsibility for the child lives in a State different from that of the child, States Parties shall promote the accession to international agreements or the conclusion of such agreements, as well as the making of other appropriate arrangements.

Article 28

1. States Parties recognize the right of the child to education, and with a view to achieving this right progressively and on the basis of equal opportunity, they shall, in particular:

(a) Make primary education compulsory and available free to all;

(b) Encourage the development of different forms of secondary education, including general and vocational education, make them available and accessible to every child, and take appropriate measures such as the introduction of free education and offering financial assistance in case of need;

(c) Make higher education accessible to all on the basis of capacity by every appropriate means;

(d) Make educational and vocational information and guidance available and accessible to all children;

(e) Take measures to encourage regular attendance at schools and the reduction of drop-out rates.

2. States Parties shall take all appropriate measures to ensure that school discipline is administered in a manner consistent with the child's human dignity and in conformity with the present Convention.

3. States Parties shall promote and encourage international cooperation in matters relating to education, in particular with a view to contributing to the elimination of ignorance and illiteracy throughout the world and facilitating access to scientific and technical knowledge and modern teaching methods. In this regard, particular account shall be taken of the needs of developing countries.

Article 29

1. States Parties agree that the education of the child shall be directed to:

(a) The development of the child's personality, talents and mental and physical abilities to their fullest potential;

(b) The development of respect for human rights and fundamental freedoms, and for the principles enshrined in the Charter of the United Nations;

(c) The development of respect for the child's parents, his or her own cultural identity, language and values, for the national values of the country in which the child is living, the country from which he or she may originate, and for civilizations different from his or her own;

(d) The preparation of the child for responsible life in a free society, in the spirit of understanding, peace, tolerance, equality of sexes, and friendship among all peoples, ethnic, national and religious groups and persons of indigenous origin;

(e) The development of respect for the natural environment.

2. No part of the present article or Article 28 shall be construed so as to interfere with the liberty of individuals and bodies to establish and direct educational institutions, subject always to the observance of the principle set forth in paragraph 1 of the present article and to the requirements that the education given in such institutions shall conform to such minimum standards as may be laid down by the State.

Article 30

In those States in which ethnic, religious or linguistic minorities or persons of indigenous origin exist, a child belonging to such a minority or who is indigenous shall not be denied the right, in community with other members of his or her group, to enjoy his or her own culture, to profess and practise his or her own religion, or to use his or her own language.

Article 31

1. States Parties recognize the right of the child to rest and leisure, to engage in play and recreational activities appropriate to the age of the child and to participate freely in cultural life and the arts.

2. States Parties shall respect and promote the right of the child to participate fully in cultural and artistic life and shall encourage the provision of appropriate and equal opportunities for cultural, artistic, recreational and leisure activity.

Article 32

1. States Parties recognize the right of the child to be protected from economic exploitation and from performing any work that is likely to be hazardous or to interfere with the child's education, or to be harmful to the child's health or physical, mental, spiritual, moral or social development.

2. States Parties shall take legislative, administrative, social and educational measures to ensure the implementation of the present article. To this end, and having regard to the relevant provisions of other international instruments, States Parties shall in particular:

(a) Provide for a minimum age or minimum ages for admission to employment;

(b) Provide for appropriate regulation of the hours and conditions of employment;

(c) Provide for appropriate penalties or other sanctions to ensure the effective enforcement of the present article.

Article 33

States Parties shall take all appropriate measures, including legislative, administrative, social and educational measures, to protect children from the illicit use of narcotic drugs and psychotropic substances as defined in the relevant international treaties, and to prevent the use of children in the illicit production and trafficking of such substances.

Article 34

States Parties undertake to protect the child from all forms of sexual exploitation and sexual abuse. For these purposes, States Parties shall in particular take all appropriate national, bilateral and multilateral measures to prevent:

(a) The inducement or coercion of a child to engage in any unlawful sexual activity;

(b) The exploitative use of children in prostitution or other unlawful sexual practices;

(c) The exploitative use of children in pornographic performances and materials.

Article 35

States Parties shall take all appropriate national, bilateral and multilateral measures to prevent the abduction of, the sale of or traffic in children for any purpose or in any form.

Article 36

States Parties shall protect the child against all other forms of exploitation prejudicial to any aspects of the child's welfare.

Article 37

States Parties shall ensure that:

(a) No child shall be subjected to torture or other cruel, inhuman or degrading treatment or punishment. Neither capital punishment nor life imprisonment without possibility of release shall be imposed for offences committed by persons below eighteen years of age;

(b) No child shall be deprived of his or her liberty unlawfully or arbitrarily. The arrest, detention or imprisonment of a child shall be in conformity with the law and shall be used only as a measure of last resort and for the shortest appropriate period of time;

(c) Every child deprived of liberty shall be treated with humanity and respect for the inherent dignity of the human person, and in a manner which takes into account the needs of persons of his or her age. In particular, every child deprived of liberty shall be separated from adults unless it is considered in the child's best interest not to do so and shall have the right to maintain contact with his or her family through correspondence and visits, save in exceptional circumstances;

(d) Every child deprived of his or her liberty shall have the right to prompt access to legal and other appropriate assistance, as well as the right to challenge the legality of the deprivation of his or her liberty before a court or other competent, independent and impartial authority, and to a prompt decision on any such action.

Article 38

1. States Parties undertake to respect and to ensure respect for rules of international humanitarian law applicable to them in armed conflicts which are relevant to the child.

2. States Parties shall take all feasible measures to ensure that persons who have not attained the age of fifteen years do not take a direct part in hostilities.

3. States Parties shall refrain from recruiting any person who has not attained the age of fifteen years into their armed forces. In recruiting among those persons who have attained the age of fifteen years but who have not attained the age of eighteen years, States Parties shall endeavour to give priority to those who are oldest.

4. In accordance with their obligations under international humanitarian law to protect the civilian population in armed conflicts, States Parties shall take all feasible measures to ensure protection and care of children who are affected by an armed conflict.

Article 39

States Parties shall take all appropriate measures to promote physical and psychological recovery and social reintegration of a child victim of: any form of neglect, exploitation, or abuse; torture or any other form of cruel, inhuman or degrading treatment or punishment; or armed conflicts. Such recovery and reintegration shall take place in an environment which fosters the health, self-respect and dignity of the child.

Article 40

1. States Parties recognize the right of every child alleged as, accused of, or recognized as having infringed the penal law to be treated in a manner consistent with the promotion of the child's sense of dignity and worth, which reinforces the child's respect for the human rights and fundamental freedoms of others and which takes into account the child's age and the desirability of promoting the child's reintegration and the child's assuming a constructive role in society.

2. To this end, and having regard to the relevant provisions of international instruments, States Parties shall, in particular, ensure that:

(a) No child shall be alleged as, be accused of, or recognized as having infringed the penal law by reason of acts or omissions that were not prohibited by national or international law at the time they were committed;

(b) Every child alleged as or accused of having infringed the penal law has at least the following guarantees:

    (i) To be presumed innocent until proven guilty according to law;

    (ii) To be informed promptly and directly of the charges against him or her, and, if appropriate, through his or her parents or legal guardians, and to have legal or other appropriate assistance in the preparation and presentation of his or her defence;

    (iii) To have the matter determined without delay by a competent, independent and impartial authority or judicial body in a fair hearing according to law, in the presence of legal or other appropriate assistance and, unless it is considered not to be in the best interest of the child, in particular, taking into account his or her age or situation, his or her parents or legal guardians;

    (iv) Not to be compelled to give testimony or to confess guilt; to examine or have examined adverse witnesses and to obtain the participation and examination of witnesses on his or her behalf under conditions of equality;

    (v) If considered to have infringed the penal law, to have this decision and any measures imposed in consequence thereof reviewed by a higher competent, independent and impartial authority or judicial body according to law;

    (vi) To have the free assistance of an interpreter if the child cannot understand or speak the language used;

    (vii) To have his or her privacy fully respected at all stages of the proceedings.

3. States Parties shall seek to promote the establishment of laws, procedures, authorities and institutions specifically applicable to children alleged as, accused of, or recognized as having infringed the penal law, and, in particular:

(a) The establishment of a minimum age below which children shall be presumed not to have the capacity to infringe the penal law;

(b) Whenever appropriate and desirable, measures for dealing with such children without resorting to judicial proceedings, providing that human rights and legal safeguards are fully respected.

4. A variety of dispositions, such as care, guidance and supervision orders; counselling; probation; foster care; education and vocational training programmes and other alternatives to institutional care shall be available to ensure that children are dealt with in a manner appropriate to their well-being and proportionate both to their circumstances and the offence.

Article 41

Nothing in the present Convention shall affect any provisions which are more conducive to the realization of the rights of the child and which may be contained in:

  (a) The law of a State party; or

  (b) International law in force for that State.

PART II

Article 42

States Parties undertake to make the principles and provisions of the Convention widely known, by appropriate and active means, to adults and children alike.

Article 43

1. For the purpose of examining the progress made by States Parties in achieving the realization of the obligations undertaken in the present Convention, there shall be established a Committee on the Rights of the Child, which shall carry out the functions hereinafter provided.

2. The Committee shall consist of eighteen experts of high moral standing and recognized competence in the field covered by this Convention. The members of the Committee shall be elected by States Parties from among their nationals and shall serve in their personal capacity, consideration being given to equitable geographical distribution, as well as to the principal legal systems.

3. The members of the Committee shall be elected by secret ballot from a list of persons nominated by States Parties. Each State Party may nominate one person from among its own nationals.

4. The initial election to the Committee shall be held no later than six months after the date of the entry into force of the present Convention and thereafter every second year. At least four months before the date of each election, the Secretary-General of the United Nations shall address a letter to States Parties inviting them to submit their nominations within two months. The Secretary-General shall subsequently prepare a list in alphabetical order of all persons thus nominated, indicating States Parties which have nominated them, and shall submit it to the States Parties to the present Convention.

5. The elections shall be held at meetings of States Parties convened by the Secretary-General at United Nations Headquarters. At those meetings, for which two thirds of States Parties shall constitute a quorum, the persons elected to the Committee shall be those who obtain the largest number of votes and an absolute majority of the votes of the representatives of States Parties present and voting.

6. The members of the Committee shall be elected for a term of four years. They shall be eligible for re-election if renominated. The term of five of the members elected at the first election shall expire at the end of two years; immediately after the first election, the names of these five members shall be chosen by lot by the Chairman of the meeting.

7. If a member of the Committee dies or resigns or declares that for any other cause he or she can no longer perform the duties of the Committee, the State Party which nominated the member shall appoint another expert from among its nationals to serve for the remainder of the term, subject to the approval of the Committee.

8. The Committee shall establish its own rules of procedure.

9. The Committee shall elect its officers for a period of two years.

10. The meetings of the Committee shall normally be held at United Nations Headquarters or at any other convenient place as determined by the Committee. The Committee shall normally meet annually. The duration of the meetings of the Committee shall be determined, and reviewed, if necessary, by a meeting of the States Parties to the present Convention, subject to the approval of the General Assembly.

11. The Secretary-General of the United Nations shall provide the necessary staff and facilities for the effective performance of the functions of the Committee under the present Convention.

12. With the approval of the General Assembly, the members of the Committee established under the present Convention shall receive emoluments from United Nations resources on such terms and conditions as the Assembly may decide.

Article 44

1. States Parties undertake to submit to the Committee, through the Secretary-General of the United Nations, reports on the measures they have adopted which give effect to the rights recognized herein and on the progress made on the enjoyment of those rights:

    (a) Within two years of the entry into force of the Convention for the State Party concerned;

    (b) Thereafter every five years.

2. Reports made under the present article shall indicate factors and difficulties, if any, affecting the degree of fulfilment of the obligations under the present Convention. Reports shall also contain sufficient information to provide the Committee with a comprehensive understanding of the implementation of the Convention in the country concerned.

3. A State Party which has submitted a comprehensive initial report to the Committee need not, in its subsequent reports submitted in accordance with paragraph 1 (b) of the present article, repeat basic information previously provided.

4. The Committee may request from States Parties further information relevant to the implementation of the Convention.

5. The Committee shall submit to the General Assembly, through the Economic and Social Council, every two years, reports on its activities.

6. States Parties shall make their reports widely available to the public in their own countries.

Article 45

In order to foster the effective implementation of the Convention and to encourage international co-operation in the field covered by the Convention:

    (a) The specialized agencies, the United Nations Children's Fund, and other United Nations organs shall be entitled to be represented at the consideration of the implementation of such provisions of the present Convention as fall within the scope of their mandate. The Committee may invite the specialized agencies,

the United Nations Children's Fund and other competent bodies as it may consider appropriate to provide expert advice on the implementation of the Convention in areas falling within the scope of their respective mandates. The Committee may invite the specialized agencies, the United Nations Children's Fund, and other United Nations organs to submit reports on the implementation of the Convention in areas falling within the scope of their activities;

(b) The Committee shall transmit, as it may consider appropriate, to the specialized agencies, the United Nations Children's Fund and other competent bodies, any reports from States Parties that contain a request, or indicate a need, for technical advice or assistance, along with the Committee's observations and suggestions, if any, on these requests or indications;

(c) The Committee may recommend to the General Assembly to request the Secretary-General to undertake on its behalf studies on specific issues relating to the rights of the child;

(d) The Committee may make suggestions and general recommendations based on information received pursuant to Articles 44 and 45 of the present Convention. Such suggestions and general recommendations shall be transmitted to any State Party concerned and reported to the General Assembly, together with comments, if any, from States Parties.

PART III

Article 46

The present Convention shall be open for signature by all States.

Article 47

The present Convention is subject to ratification. Instruments of ratification shall be deposited with the Secretary-General of the United Nations.

Article 48

The present Convention shall remain open for accession by any State. The instruments of accession shall be deposited with the Secretary-General of the United Nations.

Article 49

1. The present Convention shall enter into force on the thirtieth day following the date of deposit with the Secretary-General of the United Nations of the twentieth instrument of ratification or accession.

2. For each State ratifying or acceding to the Convention after the deposit of the twentieth instrument of ratification or accession, the Convention shall enter into force on the thirtieth day after the deposit by such State of its instrument of ratification or accession.

Article 50

1. Any State Party may propose an amendment and file it with the Secretary-General of the United Nations. The Secretary-General shall thereupon communicate the proposed amendment to States Parties, with a request that they indicate whether they favour a conference of States Parties for the purpose of considering and voting upon the proposals.

In the event that, within four months from the date of such communication, at least one third of the States Parties favour such a conference, the Secretary-General shall convene the conference under the auspices of the United Nations. Any amendment adopted by a majority of States Parties present and voting at the conference shall be submitted to the General Assembly for approval.

2. An amendment adopted in accordance with paragraph 1 of the present article shall enter into force when it has been approved by the General Assembly of the United Nations and accepted by a two-thirds majority of States Parties.

3. When an amendment enters into force, it shall be binding on those States Parties which have accepted it, other States Parties still being bound by the provisions of the present Convention and any earlier amendments which they have accepted.

Article 51

1. The Secretary-General of the United Nations shall receive and circulate to all States the text of reservations made by States at the time of ratification or accession.

2. A reservation incompatible with the object and purpose of the present Convention shall not be permitted.

3. Reservations may be withdrawn at any time by notification to that effect addressed to the Secretary-General of the United Nations, who shall then inform all States. Such notification shall take effect on the date on which it is received by the Secretary-General.

Article 52

A State Party may denounce the present Convention by written notification to the Secretary-General of the United Nations. Denunciation becomes effective one year after the date of receipt of the notification by the Secretary-General.

Article 53

The Secretary-General of the United Nations is designated as the depositary of the present Convention.

Article 54

The original of the present Convention, of which the Arabic, Chinese, English, French, Russian and Spanish texts are equally authentic, shall be deposited with the Secretary-General of the United Nations.

In witness thereof the undersigned plenipotentiaries, being duly authorized thereto by their respective governments, have signed the present Convention.

60. OPTIONAL PROTOCOL TO THE CONVENTION ON THE RIGHTS OF THE CHILD ON THE INVOLVEMENT OF CHILDREN IN ARMED CONFLICT, 2000

This Protocol is annexed to General Assembly Resolution 54/263, adopted without a vote on 25 May 2000, and it entered into force on 12 February 2002. See generally, **http://www.un.org/ children/conflict/english/**.

Further reading

ARTS, K. and POPOVSKI, V., eds., *International Criminal Accountability and the Rights of Children*, Cambridge: Cambridge University Press, 2006.

BARSTAD, K., 'Preventing the Recruitment of Child Soldiers: The ICRC Approach', (2009) 27 *Refugee Survey Quarterly* 142

BOUCAUD, P., 'Droit des enfants en droit international—Traités régionaux et droit humanitaire', *Revue trimestrielle de droits de l'homme*, 1992, 447.

BRETT, R. and McCALLIN, M., *Children: The invisible soldiers*, Sweden: Rädda Barnen, Save The Children, 1996.

COHN, I. and GOODWIN-GILL, G. S., *Child Soldiers: The Role of Children in Armed Conflict*, Oxford: Clarendon Press, 1994.

COOMARASWAMY, R., 'Machel Study 10-Year Strategic Review', Report of the Special Representative of the Secretary-General for Children and Armed Conflict, UN doc. A/62/228, 13 August 2007: **http://www.un.org/children/conflict/english/machel10.html**.

GROSSMAN, M., 'Rehabilitation or Revenge: Prosecuting Child Soldiers for Human Rights Violations', (2006-2007) 38 *Georgia Journal of International Law* 323.

HAPPOLD, M., *Child Soldiers in International Law*, Manchester: Manchester University Press, 2005.

MACHEL, G., 'Impact of armed conflict on children. Note by the Secretary-General': UN doc. A/51/306, 26 August 1996: **http://www.un.org/children/conflict/english/ themachelstudy.html**.

TEXT

The States Parties to the present Protocol,

Encouraged by the overwhelming support for the Convention on the Rights of the Child, demonstrating the widespread commitment that exists to strive for the promotion and protection of the rights of the child,

Reaffirming that the rights of children require special protection, and calling for continuous improvement of the situation of children without distinction, as well as for their development and education in conditions of peace and security,

Disturbed by the harmful and widespread impact of armed conflict on children and the long-term consequences it has for durable peace, security and development,

Condemning the targeting of children in situations of armed conflict and direct attacks on objects protected under international law, including places that generally have a significant presence of children, such as schools and hospitals,

Noting the adoption of the Statute of the International Criminal Court and, in particular, its inclusion as a war crime of conscripting or enlisting children under the age of 15 years or using them to participate actively in hostilities in both international and non-international armed conflicts,

Considering, therefore, that to strengthen further the implementation of rights recognized in the Convention on the Rights of the Child there is a need to increase the protection of children from involvement in armed conflict,

Noting that Article 1 of the Convention on the Rights of the Child specifies that, for the purposes of that Convention, a child means every human being below the age of 18 years unless, under the law applicable to the child, majority is attained earlier,

Convinced that an optional protocol to the Convention raising the age of possible recruitment of persons into armed forces and their participation in hostilities will contribute effectively to the implementation of the principle that the best interests of the child are to be a primary consideration in all actions concerning children,

Noting that the twenty-sixth International Conference of the Red Cross and Red Crescent in December 1995 recommended, *inter alia*, that parties to conflict take every feasible step to ensure that children under the age of 18 years do not take part in hostilities,

Welcoming the unanimous adoption, in June 1999, of International Labour Organization Convention No. 182 on the Prohibition and Immediate Action for the Elimination of the Worst Forms of Child Labour, which prohibits, *inter alia*, forced or compulsory recruitment of children for use in armed conflict,

Condemning with the gravest concern the recruitment, training and use within and across national borders of children in hostilities by armed groups distinct from the armed forces of a State, and recognizing the responsibility of those who recruit, train and use children in this regard,

Recalling the obligation of each party to an armed conflict to abide by the provisions of international humanitarian law,

Stressing that this Protocol is without prejudice to the purposes and principles contained in the Charter of the United Nations, including Article 51, and relevant norms of humanitarian law,

Bearing in mind that conditions of peace and security based on full respect of the purposes and principles contained in the Charter and observance of applicable human rights instruments are indispensable for the full protection of children, in particular during armed conflicts and foreign occupation,

Recognizing the special needs of those children who are particularly vulnerable to recruitment or use in hostilities contrary to this Protocol owing to their economic or social status or gender,

Mindful of the necessity of taking into consideration the economic, social and political root causes of the involvement of children in armed conflicts,

Convinced of the need to strengthen international cooperation in the implementation of this Protocol, as well as the physical and psychosocial rehabilitation and social reintegration of children who are victims of armed conflict,

Encouraging the participation of the community and, in particular, children and child victims in the dissemination of informational and educational programmes concerning the implementation of the Protocol,

Have agreed as follows:

Article 1

States Parties shall take all feasible measures to ensure that members of their armed forces who have not attained the age of 18 years do not take a direct part in hostilities.

Article 2

States Parties shall ensure that persons who have not attained the age of 18 years are not compulsorily recruited into their armed forces.

Article 3

1. States Parties shall raise the minimum age for the voluntary recruitment of persons into their national armed forces from that set out in Article 38, paragraph 3, of the Convention on the Rights of the Child, taking account of the principles contained in that article and recognizing that under the Convention persons under 18 are entitled to special protection.

2. Each State Party shall deposit a binding declaration upon ratification of or accession to this Protocol that sets forth the minimum age at which it will permit voluntary recruitment into its national armed forces and a description of the safeguards it has adopted to ensure that such recruitment is not forced or coerced.

3. States Parties that permit voluntary recruitment into their national armed forces under the age of 18 shall maintain safeguards to ensure, as a minimum, that:

  (a) Such recruitment is genuinely voluntary;
  (b) Such recruitment is carried out with the informed consent of the person's parents or legal guardians;
  (c) Such persons are fully informed of the duties involved in such military service;
  (d) Such persons provide reliable proof of age prior to acceptance into national military service.

4. Each State Party may strengthen its declaration at any time by notification to that effect addressed to the Secretary-General of the United Nations, who shall inform all States Parties. Such notification shall take effect on the date on which it is received by the Secretary-General.

5. The requirement to raise the age in paragraph 1 of the present article does not apply to schools operated by or under the control of the armed forces of the States Parties, in keeping with Articles 28 and 29 of the Convention on the Rights of the Child.

Article 4

1. Armed groups that are distinct from the armed forces of a State should not, under any circumstances, recruit or use in hostilities persons under the age of 18 years.

2. States Parties shall take all feasible measures to prevent such recruitment and use, including the adoption of legal measures necessary to prohibit and criminalize such practices.

3. The application of the present article shall not affect the legal status of any party to an armed conflict.

Article 5

Nothing in the present Protocol shall be construed as precluding provisions in the law of a State Party or in international instruments and international humanitarian law that are more conducive to the realization of the rights of the child.

Article 6

1. Each State Party shall take all necessary legal, administrative and other measures to ensure the effective implementation and enforcement of the provisions of this Protocol within its jurisdiction.

2. States Parties undertake to make the principles and provisions of the present Protocol widely known and promoted by appropriate means, to adults and children alike.

3. States Parties shall take all feasible measures to ensure that persons within their jurisdiction recruited or used in hostilities contrary to this Protocol are demobilized or otherwise released from service. States Parties shall, when necessary, accord to such persons all appropriate assistance for their physical and psychological recovery and their social reintegration.

Article 7

1. States Parties shall cooperate in the implementation of the present Protocol, including in the prevention of any activity contrary to the Protocol and in the rehabilitation and social reintegration of persons who are victims of acts contrary to this Protocol, including through technical cooperation and financial assistance. Such assistance and cooperation will be undertaken in consultation with concerned States Parties and relevant international organizations.

2. States Parties in a position to do so shall provide such assistance through existing multilateral, bilateral or other programmes, or, *inter alia*, through a voluntary fund established in accordance with the rules of the General Assembly.

Article 8

1. Each State Party shall submit, within two years following the entry into force of the Protocol for that State Party, a report to the Committee on the Rights of the Child providing comprehensive information on the measures it has taken to implement the provisions of the Protocol, including the measures taken to implement the provisions on participation and recruitment.

2. Following the submission of the comprehensive report, each State Party shall include in the reports it submits to the Committee on the Rights of the Child, in accordance with Article 44 of the Convention, any further information with respect to the implementation of the Protocol. Other States Parties to the Protocol shall submit a report every five years.

3. The Committee on the Rights of the Child may request from States Parties further information relevant to the implementation of this Protocol.

Article 9

1. The present Protocol is open for signature by any State that is a party to the Convention or has signed it.

2. The present Protocol is subject to ratification and is open to accession by any State. Instruments of ratification or accession shall be deposited with the Secretary-General of the United Nations.

3. The Secretary-General, in his capacity as depositary of the Convention and the Protocol, shall inform all States Parties to the Convention and all States that have signed the Convention of each instrument of declaration pursuant to Article 3.

Article 10

1. The present Protocol shall enter into force three months after the deposit of the tenth instrument of ratification or accession.

2. For each State ratifying the present Protocol or acceding to it after its entry into force, the present Protocol shall enter into force one month after the date of the deposit of its own instrument of ratification or accession.

Article 11

1. Any State Party may denounce the present Protocol at any time by written notification to the Secretary-General of the United Nations, who shall thereafter inform the other States Parties to the Convention and all States that have signed the Convention. The denunciation shall take effect one year after the date of receipt of the notification by the Secretary-General. If, however, on the expiry of that year the denouncing State Party is engaged in armed conflict, the denunciation shall not take effect before the end of the armed conflict.

2. Such a denunciation shall not have the effect of releasing the State Party from its obligations under the present Protocol in regard to any act that occurs prior to the date on which the denunciation becomes effective. Nor shall such a denunciation prejudice in any way the continued consideration of any matter that is already under consideration by the Committee on the Rights of the Child prior to the date on which the denunciation becomes effective.

Article 12

1. Any State Party may propose an amendment and file it with the Secretary-General of the United Nations. The Secretary-General shall thereupon communicate the proposed amendment to States Parties, with a request that they indicate whether they favour a conference of States Parties for the purpose of considering and voting upon the proposals. In the event that, within four months from the date of such communication, at least one third of the States Parties favour such a conference, the Secretary-General shall convene the conference under the auspices of the United Nations. Any amendment adopted by a majority of States Parties present and voting at the conference shall be submitted to the General Assembly of the United Nations for approval.

2. An amendment adopted in accordance with paragraph 1 of the present article shall enter into force when it has been approved by the General Assembly and accepted by a two-thirds majority of States Parties.

3. When an amendment enters into force, it shall be binding on those States Parties that have accepted it, other States Parties still being bound by the provisions of the present Protocol and any earlier amendments that they have accepted.

Article 13

1. The present Protocol, of which the Arabic, Chinese, English, French, Russian and Spanish texts are equally authentic, shall be deposited in the archives of the United Nations.

2. The Secretary-General of the United Nations shall transmit certified copies of the present Protocol to all States Parties to the Convention and all States that have signed the Convention.

61. OPTIONAL PROTOCOL TO THE CONVENTION ON THE RIGHTS OF THE CHILD ON THE SALE OF CHILDREN, CHILD PROSTITUTION AND CHILD PORNOGRAPHY, 2000

This Protocol is annexed to General Assembly Resolution 54/263, adopted without a vote on 25 May 2000, and it entered into force on 18 January 2002. See also the European Convention on Actions against Trafficking in Human Beings, 2005, below, p. 848.

Further reading

BUCK, T., ' " International Criminalisation and Child Welfare Protection", the Optional Protocol to the Convention on the Rights of the Child', (2008) 22 *Children and Society* 167.

TEXT

The States Parties to the present Protocol,

Considering that, in order further to achieve the purposes of the Convention on the Rights of the Child and the implementation of its provisions, especially Articles 1, 11, 21, 32, 33, 34, 35 and 36, it would be appropriate to extend the measures that States Parties should undertake in order to guarantee the protection of the child from the sale of children, child prostitution and child pornography,

Considering also that the Convention on the Rights of the Child recognizes the right of the child to be protected from economic exploitation and from performing any work that is likely to be hazardous or to interfere with the child's education, or to be harmful to the child's health or physical, mental, spiritual, moral or social development,

Gravely concerned at the significant and increasing international traffic of children for the purpose of the sale of children, child prostitution and child pornography,

Deeply concerned at the widespread and continuing practice of sex tourism, to which children are especially vulnerable, as it directly promotes the sale of children, child prostitution and child pornography,

Recognizing that a number of particularly vulnerable groups, including girl children, are at greater risk of sexual exploitation and that girl children are disproportionately represented among the sexually exploited,

Concerned about the growing availability of child pornography on the Internet and other evolving technologies, and recalling the International Conference on Combating Child Pornography on the Internet (Vienna, 1999) and, in particular, its conclusion calling for the worldwide criminalization of the production, distribution, exportation, transmission, importation, intentional possession and advertising of child pornography, and stressing the importance of closer cooperation and partnership between Governments and the Internet industry,

Believing that the elimination of the sale of children, child prostitution and child pornography will be facilitated by adopting a holistic approach, addressing the contributing factors, including underdevelopment, poverty, economic disparities, inequitable socio-economic structure, dysfunctioning families, lack of education, urban-rural migration, gender discrimination, irresponsible adult sexual behaviour, harmful traditional practices, armed conflicts and trafficking in children,

Believing that efforts to raise public awareness are needed to reduce consumer demand for the sale of children, child prostitution and child pornography, and also believing in the importance of strengthening global partnership among all actors and of improving law enforcement at the national level,

Noting the provisions of international legal instruments relevant to the protection of children, including the Hague Convention on Protection of Children and Cooperation in Respect of Inter-Country Adoption, the Hague Convention on the Civil Aspects of International Child Abduction, the Hague Convention on Jurisdiction, Applicable Law, Recognition, Enforcement and Cooperation in Respect of Parental Responsibility and Measures for the Protection of Children, and International Labour Organization Convention No. 182 on the Prohibition and Immediate Action for the Elimination of the Worst Forms of Child Labour,

Encouraged by the overwhelming support for the Convention on the Rights of the Child, demonstrating the widespread commitment that exists for the promotion and protection of the rights of the child,

Recognizing the importance of the implementation of the provisions of the Programme of Action for the Prevention of the Sale of Children, Child Prostitution and Child Pornography and the Declaration and Agenda for Action adopted at the World Congress against Commercial Sexual Exploitation of Children, held in Stockholm from 27 to 31 August 1996, and the other relevant decisions and recommendations of pertinent international bodies,

Taking due account of the importance of the traditions and cultural values of each people for the protection and harmonious development of the child,

Have agreed as follows:

Article 1

States Parties shall prohibit the sale of children, child prostitution and child pornography as provided for by the present Protocol.

Article 2

For the purposes of the present Protocol:

- *(a)* Sale of children means any act or transaction whereby a child is transferred by any person or group of persons to another for remuneration or any other consideration;
- *(b)* Child prostitution means the use of a child in sexual activities for remuneration or any other form of consideration;
- *(c)* Child pornography means any representation, by whatever means, of a child engaged in real or simulated explicit sexual activities or any representation of the sexual parts of a child for primarily sexual purposes.

Article 3

1. Each State Party shall ensure that, as a minimum, the following acts and activities are fully covered under its criminal or penal law, whether such offences are committed domestically or transnationally or on an individual or organized basis:

- *(a)* In the context of sale of children as defined in Article 2:

      (i) Offering, delivering or accepting, by whatever means, a child for the purpose of:

         a. Sexual exploitation of the child;

         b. Transfer of organs of the child for profit;

         c. Engagement of the child in forced labour;

     (ii) Improperly inducing consent, as an intermediary, for the adoption of a child in violation of applicable international legal instruments on adoption;

    (b) Offering, obtaining, procuring or providing a child for child prostitution, as defined in Article 2;

    (c) Producing, distributing, disseminating, importing, exporting, offering, selling or possessing for the above purposes child pornography as defined in Article 2.

2. Subject to the provisions of the national law of a State Party, the same shall apply to an attempt to commit any of the said acts and to complicity or participation in any of the said acts.

3. Each State Party shall make such offences punishable by appropriate penalties that take into account their grave nature.

4. Subject to the provisions of its national law, each State Party shall take measures, where appropriate, to establish the liability of legal persons for offences established in paragraph 1 of the present article. Subject to the legal principles of the State Party, such liability of legal persons may be criminal, civil or administrative.

5. States Parties shall take all appropriate legal and administrative measures to ensure that all persons involved in the adoption of a child act in conformity with applicable international legal instruments.

Article 4

1. Each State Party shall take such measures as may be necessary to establish its jurisdiction over the offences referred to in Article 3, paragraph 1, when the offences are committed in its territory or on board a ship or aircraft registered in that State.

2. Each State Party may take such measures as may be necessary to establish its jurisdiction over the offences referred to in Article 3, paragraph 1, in the following cases:

    (a) When the alleged offender is a national of that State or a person who has his habitual residence in its territory;

    (b) When the victim is a national of that State.

3. Each State Party shall also take such measures as may be necessary to establish its jurisdiction over the aforementioned offences when the alleged offender is present in its territory and it does not extradite him or her to another State Party on the ground that the offence has been committed by one of its nationals.

4. This Protocol does not exclude any criminal jurisdiction exercised in accordance with internal law.

Article 5

1. The offences referred to in Article 3, paragraph 1, shall be deemed to be included as extraditable offences in any extradition treaty existing between States Parties and shall be included as extraditable offences in every extradition treaty subsequently concluded between them, in accordance with the conditions set forth in such treaties.

2. If a State Party that makes extradition conditional on the existence of a treaty receives a request for extradition from another State Party with which it has no extradition treaty, it may consider this Protocol as a legal basis for extradition in respect of such offences. Extradition shall be subject to the conditions provided by the law of the requested State.

3. States Parties that do not make extradition conditional on the existence of a treaty shall recognize such offences as extraditable offences between themselves subject to the conditions provided by the law of the requested State.

4. Such offences shall be treated, for the purpose of extradition between States Parties, as if they had been committed not only in the place in which they occurred but also in the territories of the States required to establish their jurisdiction in accordance with Article 4.

5. If an extradition request is made with respect to an offence described in Article 3, paragraph 1, and the requested State Party does not or will not extradite on the basis of the nationality of the offender, that State shall take suitable measures to submit the case to its competent authorities for the purpose of prosecution.

Article 6

1. States Parties shall afford one another the greatest measure of assistance in connection with investigations or criminal or extradition proceedings brought in respect of the offences set forth in Article 3, paragraph 1, including assistance in obtaining evidence at their disposal necessary for the proceedings.

2. States Parties shall carry out their obligations under paragraph 1 of the present article in conformity with any treaties or other arrangements on mutual legal assistance that may exist between them. In the absence of such treaties or arrangements, States Parties shall afford one another assistance in accordance with their domestic law.

Article 7

States Parties shall, subject to the provisions of their national law:

   (a) Take measures to provide for the seizure and confiscation, as appropriate, of:
      (i) Goods, such as materials, assets and other instrumentalities used to commit or facilitate offences under the present protocol;
      (ii) Proceeds derived from such offences;

   (b) Execute requests from another State Party for seizure or confiscation of goods or proceeds referred to in subparagraph (a);

   (c) Take measures aimed at closing, on a temporary or definitive basis, premises used to commit such offences.

Article 8

1. States Parties shall adopt appropriate measures to protect the rights and interests of child victims of the practices prohibited under the present Protocol at all stages of the criminal justice process, in particular by:

   (a) Recognizing the vulnerability of child victims and adapting procedures to recognize their special needs, including their special needs as witnesses;

   (b) Informing child victims of their rights, their role and the scope, timing and progress of the proceedings and of the disposition of their cases;

    (c) Allowing the views, needs and concerns of child victims to be presented and con-
          sidered in proceedings where their personal interests are affected, in a manner
          consistent with the procedural rules of national law;

    (d) Providing appropriate support services to child victims throughout the legal
          process;

    (e) Protecting, as appropriate, the privacy and identity of child victims and taking
          measures in accordance with national law to avoid the inappropriate dissemin-
          ation of information that could lead to the identification of child victims;

    (f) Providing, in appropriate cases, for the safety of child victims, as well as that of
          their families and witnesses on their behalf, from intimidation and retaliation;

    (g) Avoiding unnecessary delay in the disposition of cases and the execution of orders
          or decrees granting compensation to child victims.

2. States Parties shall ensure that uncertainty as to the actual age of the victim shall not
prevent the initiation of criminal investigations, including investigations aimed at establishing the age of the victim.

3. States Parties shall ensure that, in the treatment by the criminal justice system of
children who are victims of the offences described in the present Protocol, the best interest of the child shall be a primary consideration.

4. States Parties shall take measures to ensure appropriate training, in particular legal
and psychological training, for the persons who work with victims of the offences prohibited under the present Protocol.

5. States Parties shall, in appropriate cases, adopt measures in order to protect the safety
and integrity of those persons and/or organizations involved in the prevention and/or
protection and rehabilitation of victims of such offences.

6. Nothing in the present article shall be construed as prejudicial to or inconsistent with
the rights of the accused to a fair and impartial trial.

Article 9

1. States Parties shall adopt or strengthen, implement and disseminate laws, administrative measures, social policies and programmes to prevent the offences referred to in the
present Protocol. Particular attention shall be given to protect children who are especially vulnerable to such practices.

2. States Parties shall promote awareness in the public at large, including children,
through information by all appropriate means, education and training, about the preventive measures and harmful effects of the offences referred to in the present Protocol.
In fulfilling their obligations under this article, States Parties shall encourage the participation of the community and, in particular, children and child victims, in such information and education and training programmes, including at the international level.

3. States Parties shall take all feasible measures with the aim of ensuring all appropriate
assistance to victims of such offences, including their full social reintegration and their
full physical and psychological recovery.

4. States Parties shall ensure that all child victims of the offences described in the
present Protocol have access to adequate procedures to seek, without discrimination,
compensation for damages from those legally responsible.

5. States Parties shall take appropriate measures aimed at effectively prohibiting the production and dissemination of material advertising the offences described in the present Protocol.

Article 10

1. States Parties shall take all necessary steps to strengthen international cooperation by multilateral, regional and bilateral arrangements for the prevention, detection, investigation, prosecution and punishment of those responsible for acts involving the sale of children, child prostitution, child pornography and child sex tourism. States Parties shall also promote international cooperation and coordination between their authorities, national and international non-governmental organizations and international organizations.

2. States Parties shall promote international cooperation to assist child victims in their physical and psychological recovery, social reintegration and repatriation.

3. States Parties shall promote the strengthening of international cooperation in order to address the root causes, such as poverty and underdevelopment, contributing to the vulnerability of children to the sale of children, child prostitution, child pornography and child sex tourism.

4. States Parties in a position to do so shall provide financial, technical or other assistance through existing multilateral, regional, bilateral or other programmes.

Article 11

Nothing in the present Protocol shall affect any provisions that are more conducive to the realization of the rights of the child and that may be contained in:

    (a) The law of a State Party;

    (b) International law in force for that State.

Article 12

1. Each State Party shall submit, within two years following the entry into force of the present Protocol for that State Party, a report to the Committee on the Rights of the Child providing comprehensive information on the measures it has taken to implement the provisions of the Protocol.

2. Following the submission of the comprehensive report, each State Party shall include in the reports they submit to the Committee on the Rights of the Child, in accordance with Article 44 of the Convention, any further information with respect to the implementation of the present Protocol. Other States Parties to the Protocol shall submit a report every five years.

3. The Committee on the Rights of the Child may request from States Parties further information relevant to the implementation of the present Protocol.

Article 13

1. The present Protocol is open for signature by any State that is a party to the Convention or has signed it.

2. The present Protocol is subject to ratification and is open to accession by any State that is a party to the Convention or has signed it. Instruments of ratification or accession shall be deposited with the Secretary-General of the United Nations.

Article 14

1. The present Protocol shall enter into force three months after the deposit of the tenth instrument of ratification or accession.

2. For each State ratifying the present Protocol or acceding to it after its entry into force, the Protocol shall enter into force one month after the date of the deposit of its own instrument of ratification or accession.

Article 15

1. Any State Party may denounce the present Protocol at any time by written notification to the Secretary-General of the United Nations, who shall thereafter inform the other States Parties to the Convention and all States that have signed the Convention. The denunciation shall take effect one year after the date of receipt of the notification by the Secretary-General.

2. Such a denunciation shall not have the effect of releasing the State Party from its obligations under the present Protocol in regard to any offence that occurs prior to the date on which the denunciation becomes effective. Nor shall such a denunciation prejudice in any way the continued consideration of any matter that is already under consideration by the Committee on the Rights of the Child prior to the date on which the denunciation becomes effective.

Article 16

1. Any State Party may propose an amendment and file it with the Secretary-General of the United Nations. The Secretary-General shall thereupon communicate the proposed amendment to States Parties with a request that they indicate whether they favour a conference of States Parties for the purpose of considering and voting upon the proposals. In the event that, within four months from the date of such communication, at least one third of the States Parties favour such a conference, the Secretary-General shall convene the conference under the auspices of the United Nations. Any amendment adopted by a majority of States Parties present and voting at the conference shall be submitted to the General Assembly of the United Nations for approval.

2. An amendment adopted in accordance with paragraph 1 of the present article shall enter into force when it has been approved by the General Assembly and accepted by a two-thirds majority of States Parties.

3. When an amendment enters into force, it shall be binding on those States Parties that have accepted it, other States Parties still being bound by the provisions of the present Protocol and any earlier amendments they have accepted.

Article 17

1. The present Protocol, of which the Arabic, Chinese, English, French, Russian and Spanish texts are equally authentic, shall be deposited in the archives of the United Nations.

2. The Secretary-General of the United Nations shall transmit certified copies of the present Protocol to all States Parties to the Convention and all States that have signed the Convention.

62. INTERNATIONAL CONVENTION ON THE PROTECTION OF THE RIGHTS OF ALL MIGRANT WORKERS AND MEMBERS OF THEIR FAMILIES, 1990

The Convention was adopted without a vote by General Assembly Resolution 45/158 of 18 December 1990, and entered into force on 1 July 2003. It constitutes an elaboration of human rights standards, so that migrant workers will remain protected even in States which do not become parties to the Convention. The Convention provides for the establishment of a committee to monitor its implementation, together with optional procedures for the examination and determination of complaints on behalf of States parties to the Convention, and on behalf of individuals, concerning breaches of the obligations created by the Convention by a State party. The Committee held its first session in March 2004; see generally, **http://www2.ohchr.org/english/bodies/cmw/index.htm**.

Both the negotiating history leading to the adoption of the final text and events since 1990 confirm that major divisions separate migrant-sending from migrant-receiving countries. In 1999, the Commission on Human Rights decided to appoint a Special Rapporteur on the Human Rights of Migrants (Jorge Bustamente, 2005– ; Gabriela Rodríguez Pizarro, 1999–2005); see Resolution 1999/44, 17 April 1999, and UNGA Resolution 54/166, on the protection of migrants, 17 December 1999. The mandate was extended for a further three years by the Commission (Resolution 2005/47), and has been continued by the Human Rights Council (Resolution 8/10).

Further reading

CHETAIL, V., ed., *Mondialisation, migration et droits de l'homme: le droit international en question/Globalization, Migration and Human Rights: International Law under Review*, Bruxelles: Bruylant, Vol. II, 2007.

CHOLEWINSKI, R., *Migrant Workers in International Human Rights Law: Their Protection in Countries of Employment*, Oxford: Clarendon Press, 1997.

—— 'Protecting Migrant Workers in a Globalized World', in CRAIG, JOHN D. R. and LYNK, M., eds., *Globalization and the Future of Labour Law*, Cambridge: Cambridge University Press, 2006, 409–43.

——, PERRUCHOUD, R. and MACDONALD, E., eds., *International Migration Law: Developing Paradigms and Key Challenges*, Cambridge: Cambridge University Press, 2007.

DAUVERGNE, C., *Making People Illegal: What Globalization Means for Migration and Law*, Cambridge: Cambridge University Press, 2008.

GOODWIN-GILL, G. S., 'Migration—International Law and Human Rights', in GHOSH, B., ed., *Managing Migration: Time for a New International Regime?*, Oxford: Oxford University Press, 2000, 160–89.

GHOSH, B., *Elusive Protection, Uncertain Lands: Migrants' Access to Human Rights*, Geneva: International Organization for Migration, 2003.

GLOBAL COMMISSION ON INTERNATIONAL MIGRATION, *Migration in an Interconnected World: New Directions for Action*, Geneva: Global Commission on International Migration, 2005.

TARAN, P. and GERONIMI, E., 'Globalization, Labour and Migration: Protection is Paramount', Geneva: International Labour Office, 2003.

TEXT

Preamble

The States Parties to the present Convention,

Taking into account the principles embodied in the basic instruments of the United Nations concerning human rights, in particular the Universal Declaration of Human Rights, the International Covenant on Economic, Social and Cultural Rights, the International Covenant on Civil and Political Rights, the International Convention on the Elimination of All Forms of Racial Discrimination, the Convention on the Elimination of All Forms of Discrimination against Women and the Convention on the Rights of the Child,

Taking into account also the principles and standards set forth in the relevant instruments elaborated within the framework of the International Labour Organization, especially the Convention concerning Migration for Employment (No. 97), the Convention concerning Migrations in Abusive Conditions and the Promotion of Equality of Opportunity and Treatment of Migrant Workers (No. 143), the Recommendation concerning Migration for Employment (No. 86), the Recommendation concerning Migrant Workers (No. 151), the Convention concerning Forced or Compulsory Labour (No. 29) and the Convention concerning Abolition of Forced Labour (No. 105),

Reaffirming the importance of the principles contained in the Convention against Discrimination in Education of the United Nations Educational, Scientific and Cultural Organization,

Recalling the Convention against Torture and Other Cruel, Inhuman or Degrading Treatment or Punishment, the Declaration of the Fourth United Nations Congress on the Prevention of Crime and the Treatment of Offenders, the Code of Conduct for Law Enforcement Officials, and the Slavery Conventions,

Recalling that one of the objectives of the International Labour Organization, as stated in its Constitution, is the protection of the interests of workers when employed in countries other than their own, and bearing in mind the expertise and experience of that organization in matters related to migrant workers and members of their families,

Recognizing the importance of the work done in connection with migrant workers and members of their families in various organs of the United Nations, in particular in the Commission on Human Rights and the Commission for Social Development, and in the Food and Agriculture Organization of the United Nations, the United Nations Educational, Scientific and Cultural Organization and the World Health Organization, as well as in other international organizations,

Recognizing also the progress made by certain States on a regional or bilateral basis towards the protection of the rights of migrant workers and members of their families, as well as the importance and usefulness of bilateral and multilateral agreements in this field,

Realizing the importance and extent of the migration phenomenon, which involves millions of people and affects a large number of States in the international community,

Aware of the impact of the flows of migrant workers on States and people concerned, and desiring to establish norms which may contribute to the harmonization of the attitudes of States through the acceptance of basic principles concerning the treatment of migrant workers and members of their families,

Considering the situation of vulnerability in which migrant workers and members of their families frequently find themselves owing, among other things, to their absence from their State of origin and to the difficulties they may encounter arising from their presence in the State of employment,

Convinced that the rights of migrant workers and members of their families have not been sufficiently recognized everywhere and therefore require appropriate international protection,

Taking into account the fact that migration is often the cause of serious problems for the members of the families of migrant workers as well as for the workers themselves, in particular because of the scattering of the family,

Bearing in mind that the human problems involved in migration are even more serious in the case of irregular migration and convinced therefore that appropriate action should be encouraged in order to prevent and eliminate clandestine movements and trafficking in migrant workers, while at the same time assuring the protection of their fundamental human rights,

Considering that workers who are non-documented or in an irregular situation are frequently employed under less favourable conditions of work than other workers and that certain employers find this an inducement to seek such labour in order to reap the benefits of unfair competition,

Considering also that recourse to the employment of migrant workers who are in an irregular situation will be discouraged if the fundamental human rights of all migrant workers are more widely recognized and, moreover, that granting certain additional rights to migrant workers and members of their families in a regular situation will encourage all migrants and employers to respect and comply with the laws and procedures established by the States concerned,

Convinced, therefore, of the need to bring about the international protection of the rights of all migrant workers and members of their families, reaffirming and establishing basic norms in a comprehensive convention which could be applied universally,

Have agreed as follows:

PART I
SCOPE AND DEFINITIONS

Article 1

1. The present Convention is applicable, except as otherwise provided hereafter, to all migrant workers and members of their families without distinction of any kind such as sex, race, colour, language, religion or conviction, political or other opinion, national, ethnic or social origin, nationality, age, economic position, property, marital status, birth or other status.

2. The present Convention shall apply during the entire migration process of migrant workers and members of their families, which comprises preparation for migration, departure, transit and the entire period of stay and remunerated activity in the State of employment as well as return to the State of origin or the State of habitual residence.

Article 2

For the purposes of the present Convention:

1. The term 'migrant worker' refers to a person who is to be engaged, is engaged or has been engaged in a remunerated activity in a State of which he or she is not a national.

2. *(a)* The term 'frontier worker' refers to a migrant worker who retains his or her habitual residence in a neighbouring State to which he or she normally returns every day or at least once a week;

(b) The term 'seasonal worker' refers to a migrant worker whose work by its character is dependent on seasonal conditions and is performed only during part of the year;

(c) The term 'seafarer', which includes a fisherman, refers to a migrant worker employed on board a vessel registered in a State of which he or she is not a national;

(d) The term 'worker on an offshore installation' refers to a migrant worker employed on an offshore installation that is under the jurisdiction of a State of which he or she is not a national;

(e) The term 'itinerant worker' refers to a migrant worker who, having his or her habitual residence in one State, has to travel to another State or States for short periods, owing to the nature of his or her occupation;

(f) The term 'project-tied worker' refers to a migrant worker admitted to a State of employment for a defined period to work solely on a specific project being carried out in that State by his or her employer;

(g) The term 'specified-employment worker' refers to a migrant worker:

   (i) Who has been sent by his or her employer for a restricted and defined period of time to a State of employment to undertake a specific assignment or duty; or

   (ii) Who engages for a restricted and defined period of time in work that requires professional, commercial, technical or other highly specialized skill; or

   (iii) Who, upon the request of his or her employer in the State of employment, engages for a restricted and defined period of time in work whose nature is transitory or brief;

and who is required to depart from the State of employment either at the expiration of his or her authorized period of stay, or earlier if he or she no longer undertakes that specific assignment or duty or engages in that work;

(h) The term 'self-employed worker' refers to a migrant worker who is engaged in a remunerated activity otherwise than under a contract of employment and who earns his or her living through this activity normally working alone or together with members of his or her family, and to any other migrant worker recognized as self-employed by applicable legislation of the State of employment or bilateral or multilateral agreements.

Article 3

The present Convention shall not apply to:

(a) Persons sent or employed by international organizations and agencies or persons sent or employed by a State outside its territory to perform official functions, whose admission and status are regulated by general international law or by specific international agreements or conventions;

(b) Persons sent or employed by a State or on its behalf outside its territory who participate in development programmes and other co-operation programmes, whose admission and status are regulated by agreement with the State of employment and who, in accordance with that agreement, are not considered migrant workers;

(c) Persons taking up residence in a State different from their State of origin as investors;

(d) Refugees and stateless persons, unless such application is provided for in the relevant national legislation of, or international instruments in force for, the State Party concerned;

(e) Students and trainees;

(f) Seafarers and workers on an offshore installation who have not been admitted to take up residence and engage in a remunerated activity in the State of employment.

Article 4

For the purposes of the present Convention the term 'members of the family' refers to persons married to migrant workers or having with them a relationship that, according to applicable law, produces effects equivalent to marriage, as well as their dependent children and other dependent persons who are recognized as members of the family by applicable legislation or applicable bilateral or multilateral agreements between the States concerned.

Article 5

For the purposes of the present Convention, migrant workers and members of their families:

(a) Are considered as documented or in a regular situation if they are authorized to enter, to stay and to engage in a remunerated activity in the State of employment pursuant to the law of that State and to international agreements to which that State is a party;

(b) Are considered as non-documented or in an irregular situation if they do not comply with the conditions provided for in subparagraph (a) of the present article.

Article 6

For the purposes of the present Convention:

(a) The term 'State of origin' means the State of which the person concerned is a national;

(b) The term 'State of employment' means a State where the migrant worker is to be engaged, is engaged or has been engaged in a remunerated activity, as the case may be;

(c) The term 'State of transit' means any State through which the person concerned passes on any journey to the State of employment or from the State of employment to the State of origin or the State of habitual residence.

PART II
NON-DISCRIMINATION WITH RESPECT TO RIGHTS

Article 7

States Parties undertake, in accordance with the international instruments concerning human rights, to respect and to ensure to all migrant workers and members of their families within their territory or subject to their jurisdiction the rights provided for in the present Convention without distinction of any kind such as to sex, race, colour, language, religion or conviction, political or other opinion, national, ethnic or social origin, nationality, age, economic position, property, marital status, birth or other status.

PART III

HUMAN RIGHTS OF ALL MIGRANT WORKERS AND MEMBERS OF THEIR FAMILIES

Article 8

1. Migrant workers and members of their families shall be free to leave any State, including their State of origin. This right shall not be subject to any restrictions except those that are provided by law, are necessary to protect national security, public order (*ordre public*), public health or morals or the rights and freedoms of others and are consistent with the other rights recognized in the present part of the Convention.

2. Migrant workers and members of their families shall have the right at any time to enter and remain in their State of origin.

Article 9

The right to life of migrant workers and members of their families shall be protected by law.

Article 10

No migrant worker or member of his or her family shall be subjected to torture or to cruel, inhuman or degrading treatment or punishment.

Article 11

1. No migrant worker or member of his or her family shall be held in slavery or servitude.

2. No migrant worker or member of his or her family shall be required to perform forced or compulsory labour.

3. Paragraph 2 of the present article shall not be held to preclude, in States where imprisonment with hard labour may be imposed as a punishment for a crime, the performance of hard labour in pursuance of a sentence to such punishment by a competent court.

4. For the purpose of the present article the term 'forced or compulsory labour' shall not include:

(a) Any work or service not referred to in paragraph 3 of the present article normally required of a person who is under detention in consequence of a lawful order of a court or of a person during conditional release from such detention;

(b) Any service exacted in cases of emergency or calamity threatening the life or well-being of the community;

(c) Any work or service that forms part of normal civil obligations so far as it is imposed also on citizens of the State concerned.

Article 12

1. Migrant workers and members of their families shall have the right to freedom of thought, conscience and religion. This right shall include freedom to have or to adopt a religion or belief of their choice and freedom either individually or in community with others and in public or private to manifest their religion or belief in worship, observance, practice and teaching.

2. Migrant workers and members of their families shall not be subject to coercion that would impair their freedom to have or to adopt a religion or belief of their choice.

3. Freedom to manifest one's religion or belief may be subject only to such limitations as are prescribed by law and are necessary to protect public safety, order, health or morals or the fundamental rights and freedoms of others.

4. States Parties to the present Convention undertake to have respect for the liberty of parents, at least one of whom is a migrant worker, and, when applicable, legal guardians to ensure the religious and moral education of their children in conformity with their own convictions.

Article 13

1. Migrant workers and members of their families shall have the right to hold opinions without interference.

2. Migrant workers and members of their families shall have the right to freedom of expression; this right shall include freedom to seek, receive and impart information and ideas of all kinds, regardless of frontiers, either orally, in writing or in print, in the form of art or through any other media of their choice.

3. The exercise of the right provided for in paragraph 2 of the present article carries with it special duties and responsibilities. It may therefore be subject to certain restrictions, but these shall only be such as are provided by law and are necessary:

   (a) For respect of the rights or reputation of others;
   (b) For the protection of the national security of the States concerned or of public order (*ordre public*) or of public health or morals;
   (c) For the purpose of preventing any propaganda for war;
   (d) For the purpose of preventing any advocacy of national, racial or religious hatred that constitutes incitement to discrimination, hostility or violence.

Article 14

No migrant worker or member of his or her family shall be subjected to arbitrary or unlawful interference with his or her privacy, family, home, correspondence or other communications, or to unlawful attacks on his or her honour and reputation. Each migrant worker and member of his or her family shall have the right to the protection of the law against such interference or attacks.

Article 15

No migrant worker or member of his or her family shall be arbitrarily deprived of property, whether owned individually or in association with others. Where, under the legislation in force in the State of employment, the assets of a migrant worker or a member of his or her family are expropriated in whole or in part, the person concerned shall have the right to fair and adequate compensation.

Article 16

1. Migrant workers and members of their families shall have the right to liberty and security of person.

2. Migrant workers and members of their families shall be entitled to effective protection by the State against violence, physical injury, threats and intimidation, whether by public officials or by private individuals, groups or institutions.

3. Any verification by law enforcement officials of the identity of migrant workers or members of their families shall be carried out in accordance with procedures established by law.

4. Migrant workers and members of their families shall not be subjected individually or collectively to arbitrary arrest or detention; they shall not be deprived of their liberty except on such grounds and in accordance with such procedures as are established by law.

5. Migrant workers and members of their families who are arrested shall be informed at the time of arrest as far as possible in a language they understand of the reasons for their arrest and they shall be promptly informed in a language they understand of any charges against them.

6. Migrant workers and members of their families who are arrested or detained on a criminal charge shall be brought promptly before a judge or other officer authorized by law to exercise judicial power and shall be entitled to trial within a reasonable time or to release. It shall not be the general rule that while awaiting trial they shall be detained in custody, but release may be subject to guarantees to appear for trial, at any other stage of the judicial proceedings and, should the occasion arise, for the execution of the judgment.

7. When a migrant worker or a member of his or her family is arrested or committed to prison or custody pending trial or is detained in any other manner:

   (a) The consular or diplomatic authorities of his or her State of origin or of a State representing the interests of that State shall, if he or she so requests, be informed without delay of his or her arrest or detention and of the reasons therefor;

   (b) The person concerned shall have the right to communicate with the said authorities. Any communication by the person concerned to the said authorities shall be forwarded without delay, and he or she shall also have the right to receive communications sent by the said authorities without delay;

   (c) The person concerned shall be informed without delay of this right and of rights deriving from relevant treaties, if any, applicable between the States concerned, to correspond and to meet with representatives of the said authorities and to make arrangements with them for his or her legal representation.

8. Migrant workers and members of their families who are deprived of their liberty by arrest or detention shall be entitled to take proceedings before a court, in order that that court may decide without delay on the lawfulness of their detention and order their release if the detention is not lawful. When they attend such proceedings, they shall have the assistance, if necessary without cost to them, of an interpreter, if they cannot understand or speak the language used.

9. Migrant workers and members of their families who have been victims of unlawful arrest or detention shall have an enforceable right to compensation.

Article 17

1. Migrant workers and members of their families who are deprived of their liberty shall be treated with humanity and with respect for the inherent dignity of the human person and for their cultural identity.

2. Accused migrant workers and members of their families shall, save in exceptional circumstances, be separated from convicted persons and shall be subject to separate treatment appropriate to their status as unconvicted persons. Accused juvenile persons shall be separated from adults and brought as speedily as possible for adjudication.

3. Any migrant worker or member of his or her family who is detained in a State of transit or in a State of employment for violation of provisions relating to migration shall be held, in so far as practicable, separately from convicted persons or persons detained pending trial.

4. During any period of imprisonment in pursuance of a sentence imposed by a court of law, the essential aim of the treatment of a migrant worker or a member of his or her family shall be his or her reformation and social rehabilitation. Juvenile offenders shall be separated from adults and be accorded treatment appropriate to their age and legal status.

5. During detention or imprisonment, migrant workers and members of their families shall enjoy the same rights as nationals to visits by members of their families.

6. Whenever a migrant worker is deprived of his or her liberty, the competent authorities of the State concerned shall pay attention to the problems that may be posed for members of his or her family, in particular for spouses and minor children.

7. Migrant workers and members of their families who are subjected to any form of detention or imprisonment in accordance with the law in force in the State of employment or in the State of transit shall enjoy the same rights as nationals of those States who are in the same situation.

8. If a migrant worker or a member of his or her family is detained for the purpose of verifying any infraction of provisions related to migration, he or she shall not bear any costs arising therefrom.

Article 18

1. Migrant workers and members of their families shall have the right to equality with nationals of the State concerned before the courts and tribunals. In the determination of any criminal charge against them or of their rights and obligations in a suit of law, they shall be entitled to a fair and public hearing by a competent, independent and impartial tribunal established by law.

2. Migrant workers and members of their families who are charged with a criminal offence shall have the right to be presumed innocent until proven guilty according to law.

3. In the determination of any criminal charge against them, migrant workers and members of their families shall be entitled to the following minimum guarantees:

   (a) To be informed promptly and in detail in a language they understand of the nature and cause of the charge against them;

   (b) To have adequate time and facilities for the preparation of their defence and to communicate with counsel of their own choosing;

   (c) To be tried without undue delay;

   (d) To be tried in their presence and to defend themselves in person or through legal assistance of their own choosing; to be informed, if they do not have legal assistance, of this right; and to have legal assistance assigned to them, in any case where the interests of justice so require and without payment by them in any such case if they do not have sufficient means to pay;

   (e) To examine or have examined the witnesses against them and to obtain the attendance and examination of witnesses on their behalf under the same conditions as witnesses against them;

   (f) To have the free assistance of an interpreter if they cannot understand or speak the language used in court;

   (g) Not to be compelled to testify against themselves or to confess guilt.

4. In the case of juvenile persons, the procedure shall be such as will take account of their age and the desirability of promoting their rehabilitation.

5. Migrant workers and members of their families convicted of a crime shall have the right to their conviction and sentence being reviewed by a higher tribunal according to law.

6. When a migrant worker or a member of his or her family has, by a final decision, been convicted of a criminal offence and when subsequently his or her conviction has been reversed or he or she has been pardoned on the ground that a new or newly discovered fact shows conclusively that there has been a miscarriage of justice, the person who has suffered punishment as a result of such conviction shall be compensated according to law, unless it is proved that the non-disclosure of the unknown fact in time is wholly or partly attributable to that person.

7. No migrant worker or member of his or her family shall be liable to be tried or punished again for an offence for which he or she has already been finally convicted or acquitted in accordance with the law and penal procedure of the State concerned.

Article 19

1. No migrant worker or member of his or her family shall be held guilty of any criminal offence on account of any act or omission that did not constitute a criminal offence under national or international law at the time when the criminal offence was committed, nor shall a heavier penalty be imposed than the one that was applicable at the time when it was committed. If, subsequent to the commission of the offence, provision is made by law for the imposition of a lighter penalty, he or she shall benefit thereby.

2. Humanitarian considerations related to the status of a migrant worker, in particular with respect to his or her right of residence or work, should be taken into account in imposing a sentence for a criminal offence committed by a migrant worker or a member of his or her family.

Article 20

1. No migrant worker or member of his or her family shall be imprisoned merely on the ground of failure to fulfil a contractual obligation.

2. No migrant worker or member of his or her family shall be deprived of his or her authorization of residence or work permit or expelled merely on the ground of failure to fulfil an obligation arising out of a work contract unless fulfilment of that obligation constitutes a condition for such authorization or permit.

Article 21

It shall be unlawful for anyone, other than a public official duly authorized by law, to confiscate, destroy or attempt to destroy identity documents, documents authorizing entry to or stay, residence or establishment in the national territory or work permits. No authorized confiscation of such documents shall take place without delivery of a detailed receipt. In no case shall it be permitted to destroy the passport or equivalent document of a migrant worker or a member of his or her family.

Article 22

1. Migrant workers and members of their families shall not be subject to measures of collective expulsion. Each case of expulsion shall be examined and decided individually.

2. Migrant workers and members of their families may be expelled from the territory of a State Party only in pursuance of a decision taken by the competent authority in accordance with law.

3. The decision shall be communicated to them in a language they understand. Upon their request where not otherwise mandatory, the decision shall be communicated to them in writing and, save in exceptional circumstances on account of national security, the reasons for the decision likewise stated. The persons concerned shall be informed of these rights before or at the latest at the time the decision is rendered.

4. Except where a final decision is pronounced by a judicial authority, the person concerned shall have the right to submit the reason he or she should not be expelled and to have his or her case reviewed by the competent authority, unless compelling reasons of national security require otherwise. Pending such review, the person concerned shall have the right to seek a stay of the decision of expulsion.

5. If a decision of expulsion that has already been executed is subsequently annulled, the person concerned shall have the right to seek compensation according to law and the earlier decision shall not be used to prevent him or her from re-entering the State concerned.

6. In case of expulsion, the person concerned shall have a reasonable opportunity before or after departure to settle any claims for wages and other entitlements due to him or her and any pending liabilities.

7. Without prejudice to the execution of a decision of expulsion, a migrant worker or a member of his or her family who is subject to such a decision may seek entry into a State other than his or her State of origin.

8. In case of expulsion of a migrant worker or a member of his or her family the costs of expulsion shall not be borne by him or her. The person concerned may be required to pay his or her own travel costs.

9. Expulsion from the State of employment shall not in itself prejudice any rights of a migrant worker or a member of his or her family acquired in accordance with the law of that State, including the right to receive wages and other entitlements due to him or her.

Article 23

Migrant workers and members of their families shall have the right to have recourse to the protection and assistance of the consular or diplomatic authorities of their State of origin or of a State representing the interests of that State whenever the rights recognized in the present Convention are impaired. In particular, in case of expulsion, the person concerned shall be informed of this right without delay and the authorities of the expelling State shall facilitate the exercise of such right.

Article 24

Every migrant worker and every member of his or her family shall have the right to recognition everywhere as a person before the law.

Article 25

1. Migrant workers shall enjoy treatment not less favourable than that which applies to nationals of the State of employment in respect of remuneration and:

 (a) Other conditions of work, that is to say, overtime, hours of work, weekly rest, holidays with pay, safety, health, termination of the employment relationship and any other conditions of work which, according to national law and practice, are covered by these terms;

(b) Other terms of employment, that is to say, minimum age of employment, restriction on home work and any other matters which, according to national law and practice, are considered a term of employment.

2. It shall not be lawful to derogate in private contracts of employment from the principle of equality of treatment referred to in paragraph 1 of the present article.

3. States Parties shall take all appropriate measures to ensure that migrant workers are not deprived of any rights derived from this principle by reason of any irregularity in their stay or employment. In particular, employers shall not be relieved of any legal or contractual obligations, nor shall their obligations be limited in any manner by reason of such irregularity.

Article 26

1. States Parties recognize the right of migrant workers and members of their families:

(a) To take part in meetings and activities of trade unions and of any other associations established in accordance with law, with a view to protecting their economic, social, cultural and other interests, subject only to the rules of the organization concerned;

(b) To join freely any trade union and any such association as aforesaid, subject only to the rules of the organization concerned;

(c) To seek the aid and assistance of any trade union and of any such association as aforesaid.

2. No restrictions may be placed on the exercise of these rights other than those that are prescribed by law and which are necessary in a democratic society in the interests of national security, public order (*ordre public*) or the protection of the rights and freedoms of others.

Article 27

1. With respect to social security, migrant workers and members of their families shall enjoy in the State of employment the same treatment granted to nationals in so far as they fulfil the requirements provided for by the applicable legislation of that State and the applicable bilateral and multilateral treaties. The competent authorities of the State of origin and the State of employment can at any time establish the necessary arrangements to determine the modalities of application of this norm.

2. Where the applicable legislation does not allow migrant workers and members of their families a benefit, the States concerned shall examine the possibility of reimbursing interested persons the amount of contributions made by them with respect to that benefit on the basis of the treatment granted to nationals who are in similar circumstances.

Article 28

Migrant workers and members of their families shall have the right to receive any medical care that is urgently required for the preservation of their life or the avoidance of irreparable harm to their health on the basis of equality of treatment with nationals of the State concerned. Such emergency medical care shall not be refused them by reason of any irregularity with regard to stay or employment.

Article 29

Each child of a migrant worker shall have the right to a name, to registration of birth and to a nationality.

Article 30

Each child of a migrant worker shall have the basic right of access to education on the basis of equality of treatment with nationals of the State concerned. Access to public pre-school educational institutions or schools shall not be refused or limited by reason of the irregular situation with respect to stay or employment of either parent or by reason of the irregularity of the child's stay in the State of employment.

Article 31

1. States Parties shall ensure respect for the cultural identity of migrant workers and members of their families and shall not prevent them from maintaining their cultural links with their State of origin.

2. States Parties may take appropriate measures to assist and encourage efforts in this respect.

Article 32

Upon the termination of their stay in the State of employment, migrant workers and members of their families shall have the right to transfer their earnings and savings and, in accordance with the applicable legislation of the States concerned, their personal effects and belongings.

Article 33

1. Migrant workers and members of their families shall have the right to be informed by the State of origin, the State of employment or the State of transit as the case may be concerning:

  (a) Their rights arising out of the present Convention;
  (b) The conditions of their admission, their rights and obligations under the law and practice of the State concerned and such other matters as will enable them to comply with administrative or other formalities in that State.

2. States Parties shall take all measures they deem appropriate to disseminate the said information or to ensure that it is provided by employers, trade unions or other appropriate bodies or institutions. As appropriate, they shall co-operate with other States concerned.

3. Such adequate information shall be provided upon request to migrant workers and members of their families, free of charge, and, as far as possible, in a language they are able to understand.

Article 34

Nothing in the present part of the Convention shall have the effect of relieving migrant workers and the members of their families from either the obligation to comply with the laws and regulations of any State of transit and the State of employment or the obligation to respect the cultural identity of the inhabitants of such States.

Article 35

Nothing in the present part of the Convention shall be interpreted as implying the regularization of the situation of migrant workers or members of their families who are non-documented or in an irregular situation or any right to such regularization of their situation, nor shall it prejudice the measures intended to ensure sound and equitable conditions for international migration as provided in Part VI of the present Convention.

PART IV

OTHER RIGHTS OF MIGRANT WORKERS AND MEMBERS OF THEIR FAMILIES WHO ARE DOCUMENTED OR IN A REGULAR SITUATION

Article 36

Migrant workers and members of their families who are documented or in a regular situation in the State of employment shall enjoy the rights set forth in the present part of the Convention in addition to those set forth in Part III.

Article 37

Before their departure, or at the latest at the time of their admission to the State of employment, migrant workers and members of their families shall have the right to be fully informed by the State of origin or the State of employment, as appropriate, of all conditions applicable to their admission and particularly those concerning their stay and the remunerated activities in which they may engage as well as of the requirements they must satisfy in the State of employment and the authority to which they must address themselves for any modification of those conditions.

Article 38

1. States of employment shall make every effort to authorize migrant workers and members of the families to be temporarily absent without effect upon their authorization to stay or to work, as the case may be. In doing so, States of employment shall take into account the special needs and obligations of migrant workers and members of their families, in particular in their States of origin.

2. Migrant workers and members of their families shall have the right to be fully informed of the terms on which such temporary absences are authorized.

Article 39

1. Migrant workers and members of their families shall have the right to liberty of movement in the territory of the State of employment and freedom to choose their residence there.

2. The rights mentioned in paragraph 1 of the present article shall not be subject to any restrictions except those that are provided by law, are necessary to protect national security, public order (*ordre public*), public health or morals, or the rights and freedoms of others and are consistent with the other rights recognized in the present Convention.

Article 40

1. Migrant workers and members of their families shall have the right to form associations and trade unions in the State of employment for the promotion and protection of their economic, social, cultural and other interests.

2. No restrictions may be placed on the exercise of this right other than those that are prescribed by law and are necessary in a democratic society in the interests of national security, public order (*ordre public*) or the protection of the rights and freedoms of others.

Article 41

1. Migrant workers and members of their families shall have the right to participate in public affairs of their State of origin and to vote and to be elected at elections of that State, in accordance with its legislation.

2. The States concerned shall, as appropriate and in accordance with their legislation, facilitate the exercise of these rights.

Article 42

1. States Parties shall consider the establishment of procedures or institutions through which account may be taken, both in States of origin and in States of employment, of special needs, aspirations and obligations of migrant workers and members of their families and shall envisage, as appropriate, the possibility for migrant workers and members of their families to have their freely chosen representatives in those institutions.

2. States of employment shall facilitate, in accordance with their national legislation, the consultation or participation of migrant workers and members of their families in decisions concerning the life and administration of local communities.

3. Migrant workers may enjoy political rights in the State of employment if that State, in the exercise of its sovereignty, grants them such rights.

Article 43

1. Migrant workers shall enjoy equality of treatment with nationals of the State of employment in relation to:

(a) Access to educational institutions and services subject to the admission requirements and other regulations of the institutions and services concerned;

(b) Access to vocational guidance and placement services;

(c) Access to vocational training and retraining facilities and institutions;

(d) Access to housing, including social housing schemes, and protection against exploitation in respect of rents;

(e) Access to social and health services, provided that the requirements for participation in the respective schemes are met;

(f) Access to co-operatives and self-managed enterprises, which shall not imply a change of their migration status and shall be subject to the rules and regulations of the bodies concerned;

(g) Access to and participation in cultural life.

2. States Parties shall promote conditions to ensure effective equality of treatment to enable migrant workers to enjoy the rights mentioned in paragraph 1 of the present article whenever the terms of their stay, as authorized by the State of employment, meet the appropriate requirements.

3. States of employment shall not prevent an employer of migrant workers from establishing housing or social or cultural facilities for them. Subject to Article 70 of

the present Convention, a State of employment may make the establishment of such facilities subject to the requirements generally applied in that State concerning their installation.

Article 44

1. States Parties, recognizing that the family is the natural and fundamental group unit of society and is entitled to protection by society and the State, shall take appropriate measures to ensure the protection of the unity of the families of migrant workers.

2. States Parties shall take measures that they deem appropriate and that fall within their competence to facilitate the reunification of migrant workers with their spouses or persons who have with the migrant worker a relationship that, according to applicable law, produces effects equivalent to marriage, as well as with their minor dependent unmarried children.

3. States of employment, on humanitarian grounds, shall favourably consider granting equal treatment, as set forth in paragraph 2 of the present article, to other family members of migrant workers.

Article 45

1. Members of the families of migrant workers shall, in the State of employment, enjoy equality of treatment with nationals of that State in relation to:

- (a) Access to educational institutions and services, subject to the admission requirements and other regulations of the institutions and services concerned;
- (b) Access to vocational guidance and training institutions and services, provided that requirements for participation are met;
- (c) Access to social and health services, provided that requirements for participation in the respective schemes are met;
- (d) Access to and participation in cultural life.

2. States of employment shall pursue a policy, where appropriate in collaboration with the States of origin, aimed at facilitating the integration of children of migrant workers in the local school system, particularly in respect of teaching them the local language.

3. States of employment shall endeavour to facilitate for the children of migrant workers the teaching of their mother tongue and culture and, in this regard, States of origin shall collaborate whenever appropriate.

4. States of employment may provide special schemes of education in the mother tongue of children of migrant workers, if necessary in collaboration with the States of origin.

Article 46

Migrant workers and members of their families shall, subject to the applicable legislation of the States concerned, as well as relevant international agreements and the obligations of the States concerned arising out of their participation in customs unions, enjoy exemption from import and export duties and taxes in respect of their personal and household effects as well as the equipment necessary to engage in the remunerated activity for which they were admitted to the State of employment:

- (a) Upon departure from the State of origin or State of habitual residence;
- (b) Upon initial admission to the State of employment;

(c) Upon final departure from the State of employment;

(d) Upon final return to the State of origin or State of habitual residence.

Article 47

1. Migrant workers shall have the right to transfer their earnings and savings, in particular those funds necessary for the support of their families, from the State of employment to their State of origin or any other State. Such transfers shall be made in conformity with procedures established by applicable legislation of the State concerned and in conformity with applicable international agreements.

2. States concerned shall take appropriate measures to facilitate such transfers.

Article 48

1. Without prejudice to applicable double taxation agreements, migrant workers and members of their families shall, in the matter of earnings in the State of employment:

(a) Not be liable to taxes, duties or charges of any description higher or more onerous than those imposed on nationals in similar circumstances;

(b) Be entitled to deductions or exemptions from taxes of any description and to any tax allowances applicable to nationals in similar circumstances, including tax allowances for dependent members of their families.

2. States Parties shall endeavour to adopt appropriate measures to avoid double taxation of the earnings and savings of migrant workers and members of their families.

Article 49

1. Where separate authorizations to reside and to engage in employment are required by national legislation, the States of employment shall issue to migrant workers authorization of residence for at least the same period of time as their authorization to engage in remunerated activity.

2. Migrant workers who in the State of employment are allowed freely to choose their remunerated activity shall neither be regarded as in an irregular situation nor shall they lose their authorization of residence by the mere fact of the termination of their remunerated activity prior to the expiration of their work permits or similar authorizations.

3. In order to allow migrant workers referred to in paragraph 2 of the present article sufficient time to find alternative remunerated activities, the authorization of residence shall not be withdrawn at least for a period corresponding to that during which they may be entitled to unemployment benefits.

Article 50

1. In the case of death of a migrant worker or dissolution of marriage, the State of employment shall favourably consider granting family members of that migrant worker residing in that State on the basis of family reunion an authorization to stay; the State of employment shall take into account the length of time they have already resided in that State.

2. Members of the family to whom such authorization is not granted shall be allowed before departure a reasonable period of time in order to enable them to settle their affairs in the State of employment.

3. The provisions of paragraphs 1 and 2 of the present article may not be interpreted as adversely affecting any right to stay and work otherwise granted to such family members by the legislation of the State of employment or by bilateral and multilateral treaties applicable to that State.

Article 51

Migrant workers who in the State of employment are not permitted freely to choose their remunerated activity shall neither be regarded as in an irregular situation nor shall they lose their authorization of residence by the mere fact of the termination of their remunerated activity prior to the expiration of their work permit, except where the authorization of residence is expressly dependent upon the specific remunerated activity for which they were admitted. Such migrant workers shall have the right to seek alternative employment, participation in public work schemes and retraining during the remaining period of their authorization to work, subject to such conditions and limitations as are specified in the authorization to work.

Article 52

1. Migrant workers in the State of employment shall have the right freely to choose their remunerated activity, subject to the following restrictions or conditions.

2. For any migrant worker a State of employment may:

(a) Restrict access to limited categories of employment, functions, services or activities where this is necessary in the interests of this State and provided for by national legislation;

(b) Restrict free choice of remunerated activity in accordance with its legislation concerning recognition of occupational qualifications acquired outside its territory. However, States Parties concerned shall endeavour to provide for recognition of such qualifications.

3. For migrant workers whose permission to work is limited in time, a State of employment may also:

(a) Make the right freely to choose their remunerated activities subject to the condition that the migrant worker has resided lawfully in its territory for the purpose of remunerated activity for a period of time prescribed in its national legislation that should not exceed two years;

(b) Limit access by a migrant worker to remunerated activities in pursuance of a policy of granting priority to its nationals or to persons who are assimilated to them for these purposes by virtue of legislation or bilateral or multilateral agreements. Any such limitation shall cease to apply to a migrant worker who has resided lawfully in its territory for the purpose of remunerated activity for a period of time prescribed in its national legislation that should not exceed five years.

4. States of employment shall prescribe the conditions under which a migrant worker who has been admitted to take up employment may be authorized to engage in work on his or her own account. Account shall be taken of the period during which the worker has already been lawfully in the State of employment.

Article 53

1. Members of a migrant worker's family who have themselves an authorization of residence or admission that is without limit of time or is automatically renewable shall be permitted freely to choose their remunerated activity under the same conditions as are applicable to the said migrant worker in accordance with Article 52 of the present Convention.

2. With respect to members of a migrant worker's family who are not permitted freely to choose their remunerated activity, States Parties shall consider favourably granting them priority in obtaining permission to engage in a remunerated activity over other workers who seek admission to the State of employment, subject to applicable bilateral and multilateral agreements.

Article 54

1. Without prejudice to the terms of their authorization of residence or their permission to work and the rights provided for in Articles 25 and 27 of the present Convention, migrant workers shall enjoy equality of treatment with nationals of the State of employment in respect of:

    (a) Protection against dismissal;

    (b) Unemployment benefits;

    (c) Access to public work schemes intended to combat unemployment;

    (d) Access to alternative employment in the event of loss of work or termination of other remunerated activity, subject to Article 52 of the present Convention.

2. If a migrant worker claims that the terms of his or her work contract have been violated by his or her employer, he or she shall have the right to address his or her case to the competent authorities of the State of employment, on terms provided for in Article 18, paragraph 1, of the present Convention.

Article 55

Migrant workers who have been granted permission to engage in a remunerated activity, subject to the conditions attached to such permission, shall be entitled to equality of treatment with nationals of the State of employment in the exercise of that remunerated activity.

Article 56

1. Migrant workers and members of their families referred to in the present part of the Convention may not be expelled from a State of employment, except for reasons defined in the national legislation of that State, and subject to the safeguards established in Part III.

2. Expulsion shall not be resorted to for the purpose of depriving a migrant worker or a member of his or her family of the rights arising out of the authorization of residence and the work permit.

3. In considering whether to expel a migrant worker or a member of his or her family, account should be taken of humanitarian considerations and of the length of time that the person concerned has already resided in the State of employment.

PART V

PROVISIONS APPLICABLE TO PARTICULAR CATEGORIES OF MIGRANT WORKERS AND OF THEIR FAMILIES

Article 57

The particular categories of migrant workers and members of their families specified in the present part of the Convention who are documented or in a regular situation shall enjoy the rights set forth in Part III and, except as modified below, the rights set forth in Part IV.

Article 58

1. Frontier workers, as defined in Article 2, paragraph 2 (a), of the present Convention, shall be entitled to the rights provided for in Part IV that can be applied to them by reason of their presence and work in the territory of the State of employment, taking into account that they do not have their habitual residence in that State.

2. States of employment shall consider favourably granting frontier workers the right freely to choose their remunerated activity after a specified period of time. The granting of that right shall not affect their status as frontier workers.

Article 59

1. Seasonal workers, as defined in Article 2, paragraph 2 (b), of the present Convention, shall be entitled to the rights provided for in Part IV that can be applied to them by reason of their presence and work in the territory of the State of employment and that are compatible with their status in that State as seasonal workers, taking into account the fact that they are present in that State for only part of the year.

2. The State of employment shall, subject to paragraph 1 of the present article, consider granting seasonal workers who have been employed in its territory for a significant period of time the possibility of taking up other remunerated activities and giving them priority over other workers who seek admission to that State, subject to applicable bilateral and multilateral agreements.

Article 60

Itinerant workers, as defined in Article 2, paragraph 2 (e), of the present Convention, shall be entitled to the rights provided for in Part IV that can be granted to them by reason of their presence and work in the territory of the State of employment and that are compatible with their status as itinerant workers in that State.

Article 61

1. Project-tied workers, as defined in Article 2, paragraph 2 (f), of the present Convention, and members of their families shall be entitled to the rights provided for in Part IV except the provisions of Article 43, paragraphs 1 (b) and (c), Article 43, paragraph 1 (d), as it pertains to social housing schemes, Article 45, paragraph 1 (b), and Articles 52 to 55.

2. If a project-tied worker claims that the terms of his or her work contract have been violated by his or her employer, he or she shall have the right to address his or her case to the competent authorities of the State which has jurisdiction over that employer, on terms provided for in Article 18, paragraph 1, of the present Convention.

3. Subject to bilateral or multilateral agreements in force for them, the States Parties concerned shall endeavour to enable project-tied workers to remain adequately protected by the social security systems of their States of origin or habitual residence during their engagement in the project. States Parties concerned shall take appropriate measures with the aim of avoiding any denial of rights or duplication of payments in this respect.

4. Without prejudice to the provisions of Article 47 of the present Convention and to relevant bilateral or multilateral agreements, States Parties concerned shall permit payment of the earnings of project-tied workers in their State of origin or habitual residence.

Article 62

1. Specified-employment workers as defined in Article 2, paragraph 2 (g), of the present Convention, shall be entitled to the rights provided for in Part IV, except the provisions of Article 43, paragraphs 1 (b) and (c), Article 43, paragraph 1 (d), as it pertains to social housing schemes, Article 52, and Article 54, paragraph 1 (d).

2. Members of the families of specified-employment workers shall be entitled to the rights relating to family members of migrant workers provided for in Part IV of the present Convention, except the provisions of Article 53.

Article 63

1. Self-employed workers, as defined in Article 2, paragraph 2 (h), of the present Convention, shall be entitled to the rights provided for in Part IV with the exception of those rights which are exclusively applicable to workers having a contract of employment.

2. Without prejudice to Articles 52 and 79 of the present Convention, the termination of the economic activity of the self-employed workers shall not in itself imply the withdrawal of the authorization for them or for the members of their families to stay or to engage in a remunerated activity in the State of employment except where the authorization of residence is expressly dependent upon the specific remunerated activity for which they were admitted.

PART VI

PROMOTION OF SOUND, EQUITABLE, HUMANE AND LAWFUL CONDITIONS IN CONNECTION WITH INTERNATIONAL MIGRATION OF WORKERS AND MEMBERS OF THEIR FAMILIES

Article 64

1. Without prejudice to Article 79 of the present Convention, the States Parties concerned shall as appropriate consult and co-operate with a view to promoting sound, equitable and humane conditions in connection with international migration of workers and members of their families.

2. In this respect, due regard shall be paid not only to labour needs and resources, but also to the social, economic, cultural and other needs of migrant workers and members of their families involved, as well as to the consequences of such migration for the communities concerned.

Article 65

1. States Parties shall maintain appropriate services to deal with questions concerning international migration of workers and members of their families. Their functions shall include, *inter alia*:

(a) The formulation and implementation of policies regarding such migration;

(b) An exchange of information. consultation and co-operation with the competent authorities of other States Parties involved in such migration;

(c) The provision of appropriate information, particularly to employers, workers and their organizations on policies, laws and regulations relating to migration and employment, on agreements concluded with other States concerning migration and on other relevant matters;

(d) The provision of information and appropriate assistance to migrant workers and members of their families regarding requisite authorizations and formalities and arrangements for departure, travel, arrival, stay, remunerated activities, exit and return, as well as on conditions of work and life in the State of employment and on customs, currency, tax and other relevant laws and regulations.

2. States Parties shall facilitate as appropriate the provision of adequate consular and other services that are necessary to meet the social, cultural and other needs of migrant workers and members of their families.

Article 66

1. Subject to paragraph 2 of the present article, the right to undertake operations with a view to the recruitment of workers for employment in another State shall be restricted to:

(a) Public services or bodies of the State in which such operations take place;

(b) Public services or bodies of the State of employment on the basis of agreement between the States concerned;

(c) A body established by virtue of a bilateral or multilateral agreement.

2. Subject to any authorization, approval and supervision by the public authorities of the States Parties concerned as may be established pursuant to the legislation and practice of those States, agencies, prospective employers or persons acting on their behalf may also be permitted to undertake the said operations.

Article 67

1. States Parties concerned shall co-operate as appropriate in the adoption of measures regarding the orderly return of migrant workers and members of their families to the State of origin when they decide to return or their authorization of residence or employment expires or when they are in the State of employment in an irregular situation.

2. Concerning migrant workers and members of their families in a regular situation, States Parties concerned shall co-operate as appropriate, on terms agreed upon by those States, with a view to promoting adequate economic conditions for their resettlement and to facilitating their durable social and cultural reintegration in the State of origin.

Article 68

1. States Parties, including States of transit, shall collaborate with a view to preventing and eliminating illegal or clandestine movements and employment of migrant workers in an irregular situation. The measures to be taken to this end within the jurisdiction of each State concerned shall include:

(a) Appropriate measures against the dissemination of misleading information relating to emigration and immigration;

(b) Measures to detect and eradicate illegal or clandestine movements of migrant workers and members of their families and to impose effective sanctions on persons, groups or entities which organize, operate or assist in organizing or operating such movements;

(c) Measures to impose effective sanctions on persons, groups or entities which use violence, threats or intimidation against migrant workers or members of their families in an irregular situation.

2. States of employment shall take all adequate and effective measures to eliminate employment in their territory of migrant workers in an irregular situation, including, whenever appropriate, sanctions on employers of such workers. The rights of migrant workers vis-à-vis their employer arising from employment shall not be impaired by these measures.

Article 69

1. States Parties shall, when there are migrant workers and members of their families within their territory in an irregular situation, take appropriate measures to ensure that such a situation does not persist.

2. Whenever States Parties concerned consider the possibility of regularizing the situation of such persons in accordance with applicable national legislation and bilateral or multilateral agreements, appropriate account shall be taken of the circumstances of their entry, the duration of their stay in the States of employment and other relevant considerations, in particular those relating to their family situation.

Article 70

States Parties shall take measures not less favourable than those applied to nationals to ensure that working and living conditions of migrant workers and members of their families in a regular situation are in keeping with the standards of fitness, safety, health and principles of human dignity.

Article 71

1. States Parties shall facilitate, whenever necessary, the repatriation to the State of origin of the bodies of deceased migrant workers or members of their families.

2. As regards compensation matters relating to the death of a migrant worker or a member of his or her family, States Parties shall, as appropriate, provide assistance to the persons concerned with a view to the prompt settlement of such matters. Settlement of these matters shall be carried out on the basis of applicable national law in accordance with the provisions of the present Convention and any relevant bilateral or multilateral agreements.

PART VII
APPLICATION OF THE CONVENTION

Article 72

1. (a) For the purpose of reviewing the application of the present Convention, there shall be established a Committee on the Protection of the Rights of All Migrant Workers and Members of Their Families (hereinafter referred to as 'the Committee');

(b) The Committee shall consist, at the time of entry into force of the present Convention, of ten and, after the entry into force of the Convention for the forty-first State Party, of fourteen experts of high moral standing, impartiality and recognized competence in the field covered by the Convention.

2. *(a)* Members of the Committee shall be elected by secret ballot by the States Parties from a list of persons nominated by the States Parties, due consideration being given to equitable geographical distribution, including both States of origin and States of employment, and to the representation of the principal legal systems. Each State Party may nominate one person from among its own nationals;

(b) Members shall be elected and shall serve in their personal capacity.

3. The initial election shall be held no later than six months after the date of the entry into force of the present Convention and subsequent elections every second year. At least four months before the date of each election, the Secretary-General of the United Nations shall address a letter to all States Parties inviting them to submit their nominations within two months. The Secretary-General shall prepare a list in alphabetical order of all persons thus nominated, indicating the States Parties that have nominated them, and shall submit it to the States Parties not later than one month before the date of the corresponding election, together with the curricula vitae of the persons thus nominated.

4. Elections of members of the Committee shall be held at a meeting of States Parties convened by the Secretary-General at United Nations Headquarters. At that meeting, for which two thirds of the States Parties shall constitute a quorum, the persons elected to the Committee shall be those nominees who obtain the largest number of votes and an absolute majority of the votes of the States Parties present and voting.

5. *(a)* The members of the Committee shall serve for a term of four years. However, the terms of five of the members elected in the first election shall expire at the end of two years; immediately after the first election, the names of these five members shall be chosen by lot by the Chairman of the meeting of States Parties;

(b) The election of the four additional members of the Committee shall be held in accordance with the provisions of paragraphs 2, 3 and 4 of the present article, following the entry into force of the Convention for the forty-first State Party. The term of two of the additional members elected on this occasion shall expire at the end of two years; the names of these members shall be chosen by lot by the Chairman of the meeting of States Parties;

(c) The members of the Committee shall be eligible for re-election if renominated.

6. If a member of the Committee dies or resigns or declares that for any other cause he or she can no longer perform the duties of the Committee, the State Party that nominated the expert shall appoint another expert from among its own nationals for the remaining part of the term. The new appointment is subject to the approval of the Committee.

7. The Secretary-General of the United Nations shall provide the necessary staff and facilities for the effective performance of the functions of the Committee.

8. The members of the Committee shall receive emoluments from United Nations resources on such terms and conditions as the General Assembly may decide.

9. The members of the Committee shall be entitled to the facilities, privileges and immunities of experts on mission for the United Nations as laid down in the relevant sections of the Convention on the Privileges and Immunities of the United Nations.

Article 73

1. States Parties undertake to submit to the Secretary-General of the United Nations for consideration by the Committee a report on the legislative, judicial, administrative and other measures they have taken to give effect to the provisions of the present Convention:

    (a) Within one year after the entry into force of the Convention for the State Party concerned;

    (b) Thereafter every five years and whenever the Committee so requests.

2. Reports prepared under the present article shall also indicate factors and difficulties, if any, affecting the implementation of the Convention and shall include information on the characteristics of migration flows in which the State Party concerned is involved.

3. The Committee shall decide any further guidelines applicable to the content of the reports.

4. States Parties shall make their reports widely available to the public in their own countries.

Article 74

1. The Committee shall examine the reports submitted by each State Party and shall transmit such comments as it may consider appropriate to the State Party concerned. This State Party may submit to the Committee observations on any comment made by the Committee in accordance with the present article. The Committee may request supplementary information from States Parties when considering these reports.

2. The Secretary-General of the United Nations shall, in due time before the opening of each regular session of the Committee, transmit to the Director-General of the International Labour Office copies of the reports submitted by States Parties concerned and information relevant to the consideration of these reports, in order to enable the Office to assist the Committee with the expertise the Office may provide regarding those matters dealt with by the present Convention that fall within the sphere of competence of the International Labour Organization. The Committee shall consider in its deliberations such comments and materials as the Office may provide.

3. The Secretary-General of the United Nations may also, after consultation with the Committee, transmit to other specialized agencies as well as to intergovernmental organizations, copies of such parts of these reports as may fall within their competence.

4. The Committee may invite the specialized agencies and organs of the United Nations, as well as intergovernmental organizations and other concerned bodies to submit, for consideration by the Committee, written information on such matters dealt with in the present Convention as fall within the scope of their activities.

5. The International Labour Office shall be invited by the Committee to appoint representatives to participate, in a consultative capacity, in the meetings of the Committee.

6. The Committee may invite representatives of other specialized agencies and organs of the United Nations, as well as of intergovernmental organizations, to be present and to be heard in its meetings whenever matters falling within their field of competence are considered.

7. The Committee shall present an annual report to the General Assembly of the United Nations on the implementation of the present Convention, containing its own

considerations and recommendations, based, in particular, on the examination of the reports and any observations presented by States Parties.

8. The Secretary-General of the United Nations shall transmit the annual reports of the Committee to the States Parties to the present Convention, the Economic and Social Council, the Commission on Human Rights of the United Nations, the Director-General of the International Labour Office and other relevant organizations.

Article 75

1. The Committee shall adopt its own rules of procedure.

2. The Committee shall elect its officers for a term of two years.

3. The Committee shall normally meet annually.

4. The meetings of the Committee shall normally be held at United Nations Headquarters.

Article 76

1. A State Party to the present Convention may at any time declare under this article that it recognizes the competence of the Committee to receive and consider communications to the effect that a State Party claims that another State Party is not fulfilling its obligations under the present Convention. Communications under this article may be received and considered only if submitted by a State Party that has made a declaration recognizing in regard to itself the competence of the Committee. No communication shall be received by the Committee if it concerns a State Party which has not made such a declaration. Communications received under this article shall be dealt with in accordance with the following procedure:

(a) If a State Party to the present Convention considers that another State Party is not fulfilling its obligations under the present Convention, it may, by written communication, bring the matter to the attention of that State Party. The State Party may also inform the Committee of the matter. Within three months after the receipt of the communication the receiving State shall afford the State that sent the communication an explanation, or any other statement in writing clarifying the matter which should include, to the extent possible and pertinent, reference to domestic procedures and remedies taken, pending or available in the matter;

(b) If the matter is not adjusted to the satisfaction of both States Parties concerned within six months after the receipt by the receiving State of the initial communication, either State shall have the right to refer the matter to the Committee, by notice given to the Committee and to the other State;

(c) The Committee shall deal with a matter referred to it only after it has ascertained that all available domestic remedies have been invoked and exhausted in the matter, in conformity with the generally recognized principles of international law. This shall not be the rule where, in the view of the Committee, the application of the remedies is unreasonably prolonged;

(d) Subject to the provisions of subparagraph (c) of the present paragraph, the Committee shall make available its good offices to the States Parties concerned with a view to a friendly solution of the matter on the basis of the respect for the obligations set forth in the present Convention;

(e) The Committee shall hold closed meetings when examining communications under the present article;

(f) In any matter referred to it in accordance with subparagraph (b) of the present paragraph, the Committee may call upon the States Parties concerned, referred to in subparagraph (b), to supply any relevant information;

(g) The States Parties concerned, referred to in subparagraph (b) of the present paragraph, shall have the right to be represented when the matter is being considered by the Committee and to make submissions orally and/or in writing;

(h) The Committee shall, within twelve months after the date of receipt of notice under subparagraph (b) of the present paragraph, submit a report, as follows:

    (i) If a solution within the terms of subparagraph (d) of the present paragraph is reached, the Committee shall confine its report to a brief statement of the facts and of the solution reached;

    (ii) If a solution within the terms of subparagraph (d) is not reached, the Committee shall, in its report, set forth the relevant facts concerning the issue between the States Parties concerned. The written submissions and record of the oral submissions made by the States Parties concerned shall be attached to the report. The Committee may also communicate only to the States Parties concerned any views that it may consider relevant to the issue between them. In every matter, the report shall be communicated to the States Parties concerned.

2. The provisions of the present article shall come into force when ten States Parties to the present Convention have made a declaration under paragraph 1 of the present article. Such declarations shall be deposited by the States Parties with the Secretary-General of the United Nations, who shall transmit copies thereof to the other States Parties. A declaration may be withdrawn at any time by notification to the Secretary-General. Such a withdrawal shall not prejudice the consideration of any matter that is the subject of a communication already transmitted under the present article; no further communication by any State Party shall be received under the present article after the notification of withdrawal of the declaration has been received by the Secretary-General, unless the State Party concerned has made a new declaration.

Article 77

1. A State Party to the present Convention may at any time declare under the present article that it recognizes the competence of the Committee to receive and consider communications from or on behalf of individuals subject to its jurisdiction who claim that their individual rights as established by the present Convention have been violated by that State Party. No communication shall be received by the Committee if it concerns a State Party that has not made such a declaration.

2. The Committee shall consider inadmissible any communication under the present article which is anonymous or which it considers to be an abuse of the right of submission of such communications or to be incompatible with the provisions of the present Convention.

3. The Committee shall not consider any communication from an individual under the present article unless it has ascertained that:

    (a) The same matter has not been, and is not being, examined under another procedure of international investigation or settlement;

    (b) The individual has exhausted all available domestic remedies; this shall not be the rule where, in the view of the Committee, the application of the remedies is unreasonably prolonged or is unlikely to bring effective relief to that individual.

4. Subject to the provisions of paragraph 2 of the present article, the Committee shall bring any communications submitted to it under this article to the attention of the State Party to the present Convention that has made a declaration under paragraph 1 and is alleged to be violating any provisions of the Convention. Within six months, the receiving State shall submit to the Committee written explanations or statements clarifying the matter and the remedy, if any, that may have been taken by that State.

5. The Committee shall consider communications received under the present article in the light of all information made available to it by or on behalf of the individual and by the State Party concerned.

6. The Committee shall hold closed meetings when examining communications under the present article.

7. The Committee shall forward its views to the State Party concerned and to the individual.

8. The provisions of the present article shall come into force when ten States Parties to the present Convention have made declarations under paragraph 1 of the present article. Such declarations shall be deposited by the States Parties with the Secretary-General of the United Nations, who shall transmit copies thereof to the other States Parties. A declaration may be withdrawn at any time by notification to the Secretary-General. Such a withdrawal shall not prejudice the consideration of any matter that is the subject of a communication already transmitted under the present article; no further communication by or on behalf of an individual shall be received under the present article after the notification of withdrawal of the declaration has been received by the Secretary-General, unless the State Party has made a new declaration.

Article 78

The provisions of Article 76 of the present Convention shall be applied without prejudice to any procedures for settling disputes or complaints in the field covered by the present Convention laid down in the constituent instruments of, or in conventions adopted by, the United Nations and the specialized agencies and shall not prevent the States Parties from having recourse to any procedures for settling a dispute in accordance with international agreements in force between them.

PART VIII
GENERAL PROVISIONS

Article 79

Nothing in the present Convention shall affect the right of each State Party to establish the criteria governing admission of migrant workers and members of their families. Concerning other matters related to their legal situation and treatment as migrant workers and members of their families, States Parties shall be subject to the limitations set forth in the present Convention.

Article 80

Nothing in the present Convention shall be interpreted as impairing the provisions of the Charter of the United Nations and of the constitutions of the specialized agencies which define the respective responsibilities of the various organs of the United Nations and of the specialized agencies in regard to the matters dealt with in the present Convention.

Article 81

1. Nothing in the present Convention shall affect more favourable rights or freedoms granted to migrant workers and members of their families by virtue of:

   (a) The law or practice of a State Party; or

   (b) Any bilateral or multilateral treaty in force for the State Party concerned.

2. Nothing in the present Convention may be interpreted as implying for any State, group or person any right to engage in any activity or perform any act that would impair any of the rights and freedoms as set forth in the present Convention.

Article 82

The rights of migrant workers and members of their families provided for in the present Convention may not be renounced. It shall not be permissible to exert any form of pressure upon migrant workers and members of their families with a view to their relinquishing or foregoing any of the said rights. It shall not be possible to derogate by contract from rights recognized in the present Convention. States Parties shall take appropriate measures to ensure that these principles are respected.

Article 83

Each State Party to the present Convention undertakes:

   (a) To ensure that any person whose rights or freedoms as herein recognized are violated shall have an effective remedy, notwithstanding that the violation has been committed by persons acting in an official capacity;

   (b) To ensure that any persons seeking such a remedy shall have his or her claim reviewed and decided by competent judicial, administrative or legislative authorities, or by any other competent authority provided for by the legal system of the State, and to develop the possibilities of judicial remedy;

   (c) To ensure that the competent authorities shall enforce such remedies when granted.

Article 84

Each State Party undertakes to adopt the legislative and other measures that are necessary to implement the provisions of the present Convention.

PART IX
FINAL PROVISIONS

Article 85

The Secretary-General of the United Nations is designated as the depositary of the present Convention.

Article 86

1. The present Convention shall be open for signature by all States. It is subject to ratification.

2. The present Convention shall be open to accession by any State.

3. Instruments of ratification or accession shall be deposited with the Secretary-General of the United Nations.

Article 87

1. The present Convention shall enter into force on the first day of the month following a period of three months after the date of the deposit of the twentieth instrument of ratification or accession.

2. For each State ratifying or acceding to the present Convention after its entry into force, the Convention shall enter into force on the first day of the month following a period of three months after the date of the deposit of its own instrument of ratification or accession.

Article 88

A State ratifying or acceding to the present Convention may not exclude the application of any Part of it, or, without prejudice to Article 3, exclude any particular category of migrant workers from its application.

Article 89

1. Any State Party may denounce the present Convention, not earlier than five years after the Convention has entered into force for the State concerned, by means of a notification writing addressed to the Secretary-General of the United Nations.

2. Such denunciation shall become effective on the first day of the month following the expiration of a period of twelve months after the date of the receipt of the notification by the Secretary-General of the United Nations.

3. Such a denunciation shall not have the effect of releasing the State Party from its obligations under the present Convention in regard to any act or omission which occurs prior to the date at which the denunciation becomes effective, nor shall denunciation prejudice in any way the continued consideration of any matter which is already under consideration by the Committee prior to the date at which the denunciation becomes effective.

4. Following the date at which the denunciation of a State Party becomes effective, the Committee shall not commence consideration of any new matter regarding that State.

Article 90

1. After five years from the entry into force of the Convention a request for the revision of the Convention may be made at any time by any State Party by means of a notification in writing addressed to the Secretary-General of the United Nations. The Secretary-General shall thereupon communicate any proposed amendments to the States Parties with a request that they notify him whether they favour a conference of States Parties for the purpose of considering and voting upon the proposals. In the event that within four months from the date of such communication at least one third of the States Parties favours such a conference, the Secretary-General shall convene the conference under the auspices of the United Nations. Any amendment adopted by a majority of the States Parties present and voting shall be submitted to the General Assembly for approval.

2. Amendments shall come into force when they have been approved by the General Assembly of the United Nations and accepted by a two-thirds majority of the States Parties in accordance with their respective constitutional processes.

3. When amendments come into force, they shall be binding on those States Parties that have accepted them, other States Parties still being bound by the provisions of the present Convention and any earlier amendment that they have accepted.

Article 91

1. The Secretary-General of the United Nations shall receive and circulate to all States the text of reservations made by States at the time of signature, ratification or accession.

2. A reservation incompatible with the object and purpose of the present Convention shall not be permitted.

3. Reservations may be withdrawn at any time by notification to this effect addressed to the Secretary-General of the United Nations, who shall then inform all States thereof. Such notification shall take effect on the date on which it is received.

Article 92

1. Any dispute between two or more States Parties concerning the interpretation or application of the present Convention that is not settled by negotiation shall, at the request of one of them, be submitted to arbitration. If within six months from the date of the request for arbitration the Parties are unable to agree on the organization of the arbitration, any one of those Parties may refer the dispute to the International Court of Justice by request in conformity with the Statute of the Court.

2. Each State Party may at the time of signature or ratification of the present Convention or accession thereto declare that it does not consider itself bound by paragraph 1 of the present article. The other States Parties shall not be bound by that paragraph with respect to any State Party that has made such a declaration.

3. Any State Party that has made a declaration in accordance with paragraph 2 of the present article may at any time withdraw that declaration by notification to the Secretary-General of the United Nations.

Article 93

1. The present Convention, of which the Arabic, Chinese, English, French, Russian and Spanish texts are equally authentic, shall be deposited with the Secretary-General of the United Nations.

2. The Secretary-General of the United Nations shall transmit certified copies of the present Convention to all States.

In witness whereof the undersigned plenipotentiaries, being duly authorized thereto by their respective Governments, have signed the present Convention.

63. CONVENTION AND OPTIONAL PROTOCOL ON THE RIGHTS OF PERSONS WITH DISABILITIES, 2006

This Convention and Optional Protocol were adopted by General Assembly Resolution 61/106 on 13 December 2006, without a vote.

Further reading

ARNARDÓTTIR, O. M. AND QUINN, G., eds., *The UN Convention on the Rights of Persons with Disabilities: European and Scandinavian Perspectives*, Leiden: Brill, 2009.

HENDRIKS, A., 'UN Convention on the Rights of Persons with Disabilities', (2007) 14 *European Journal of Health Law* 273.

KAYESS, R. and FRENCH, P., 'Out of Darkness into Light? Introducing the Convention on the Rights of Persons with Disabilities', (2008) 8 *Human Rights Law Review* 1.

MÉGRET, F., 'The Disabilities Convention: Towards a Holistic Concept of Rights', (2008) 12 *International Journal of Human Rights* 261.

O'REILLY, A., *The Right to Decent Work of Persons with Disabilities*, Geneva: ILO, 2007.

SYRACUSE UNIVERSITY COLLEGE OF LAW, 'International and Comparative Disability Law Web Resources': **http://www.law.syr.edu/lawlibrary/electronic/humanrights.aspx**.

UNITED NATIONS *Enable*—Rights and Dignity of Persons with Disabilities: **http://www.un.org/disabilities/**.

UNITED NATIONS, OFFICE OF THE HIGH COMMISSIONER FOR HUMAN RIGHTS, INTER-PARLIAMENTARY UNION, *From Exclusion to Equality: Realizing the rights of persons with disabilities* (Handbook for Parliamentarians on the Convention on the Rights of Persons with Disabilities and its Optional Protocol), Geneva: United Nations, 2007.

TEXT

Preamble

The States Parties to the present Convention,

(a) *Recalling* the principles proclaimed in the Charter of the United Nations which recognize the inherent dignity and worth and the equal and inalienable rights of all members of the human family as the foundation of freedom, justice and peace in the world,

(b) *Recognizing* that the United Nations, in the Universal Declaration of Human Rights and in the International Covenants on Human Rights, has proclaimed and agreed that everyone is entitled to all the rights and freedoms set forth therein, without distinction of any kind,

(c) *Reaffirming* the universality, indivisibility, interdependence and interrelatedness of all human rights and fundamental freedoms and the need for persons with disabilities to be guaranteed their full enjoyment without discrimination,

(d) *Recalling* the International Covenant on Economic, Social and Cultural Rights, the International Covenant on Civil and Political Rights, the International Convention on the Elimination of All Forms of Racial Discrimination, the

Convention on the Elimination of All Forms of Discrimination against Women, the Convention against Torture and Other Cruel, Inhuman or Degrading Treatment or Punishment, the Convention on the Rights of the Child, and the International Convention on the Protection of the Rights of All Migrant Workers and Members of Their Families,

(e) *Recognizing* that disability is an evolving concept and that disability results from the interaction between persons with impairments and attitudinal and environmental barriers that hinders their full and effective participation in society on an equal basis with others,

(f) *Recognizing* the importance of the principles and policy guidelines contained in the World Programme of Action concerning Disabled Persons and in the Standard Rules on the Equalization of Opportunities for Persons with Disabilities in influencing the promotion, formulation and evaluation of the policies, plans, programmes and actions at the national, regional and international levels to further equalize opportunities for persons with disabilities,

(g) *Emphasizing* the importance of mainstreaming disability issues as an integral part of relevant strategies of sustainable development,

(h) *Recognizing also* that discrimination against any person on the basis of disability is a violation of the inherent dignity and worth of the human person,

(i) *Recognizing further* the diversity of persons with disabilities,

(j) *Recognizing* the need to promote and protect the human rights of all persons with disabilities, including those who require more intensive support,

(k) *Concerned* that, despite these various instruments and undertakings, persons with disabilities continue to face barriers in their participation as equal members of society and violations of their human rights in all parts of the world,

(l) *Recognizing* the importance of international cooperation for improving the living conditions of persons with disabilities in every country, particularly in developing countries,

(m) *Recognizing* the valued existing and potential contributions made by persons with disabilities to the overall well-being and diversity of their communities, and that the promotion of the full enjoyment by persons with disabilities of their human rights and fundamental freedoms and of full participation by persons with disabilities will result in their enhanced sense of belonging and in significant advances in the human, social and economic development of society and the eradication of poverty,

(n) *Recognizing* the importance for persons with disabilities of their individual autonomy and independence, including the freedom to make their own choices,

(o) *Considering* that persons with disabilities should have the opportunity to be actively involved in decision-making processes about policies and programmes, including those directly concerning them,

(p) *Concerned* about the difficult conditions faced by persons with disabilities who are subject to multiple or aggravated forms of discrimination on the basis of race, colour, sex, language, religion, political or other opinion, national, ethnic, indigenous or social origin, property, birth, age or other status,

(q) *Recognizing* that women and girls with disabilities are often at greater risk, both within and outside the home, of violence, injury or abuse, neglect or negligent treatment, maltreatment or exploitation,

(r)   *Recognizing* that children with disabilities should have full enjoyment of all human rights and fundamental freedoms on an equal basis with other children, and recalling obligations to that end undertaken by States Parties to the Convention on the Rights of the Child,

(s)   *Emphasizing* the need to incorporate a gender perspective in all efforts to promote the full enjoyment of human rights and fundamental freedoms by persons with disabilities,

(t)   *Highlighting* the fact that the majority of persons with disabilities live in conditions of poverty, and in this regard recognizing the critical need to address the negative impact of poverty on persons with disabilities,

(u)   *Bearing in mind* that conditions of peace and security based on full respect for the purposes and principles contained in the Charter of the United Nations and observance of applicable human rights instruments are indispensable for the full protection of persons with disabilities, in particular during armed conflicts and foreign occupation,

(v)   *Recognizing* the importance of accessibility to the physical, social, economic and cultural environment, to health and education and to information and communication, in enabling persons with disabilities to fully enjoy all human rights and fundamental freedoms,

(w)   *Realizing* that the individual, having duties to other individuals and to the community to which he or she belongs, is under a responsibility to strive for the promotion and observance of the rights recognized in the International Bill of Human Rights,

(x)   *Convinced* that the family is the natural and fundamental group unit of society and is entitled to protection by society and the State, and that persons with disabilities and their family members should receive the necessary protection and assistance to enable families to contribute towards the full and equal enjoyment of the rights of persons with disabilities,

(y)   *Convinced* that a comprehensive and integral international convention to promote and protect the rights and dignity of persons with disabilities will make a significant contribution to redressing the profound social disadvantage of persons with disabilities and promote their participation in the civil, political, economic, social and cultural spheres with equal opportunities, in both developing and developed countries,

Have agreed as follows:

Article 1—*Purpose*

The purpose of the present Convention is to promote, protect and ensure the full and equal enjoyment of all human rights and fundamental freedoms by all persons with disabilities, and to promote respect for their inherent dignity. Persons with disabilities include those who have long-term physical, mental, intellectual or sensory impairments which in interaction with various barriers may hinder their full and effective participation in society on an equal basis with others.

Article 2—*Definitions*

For the purposes of the present Convention:

'Communication' includes languages, display of text, Braille, tactile communication, large print, accessible multimedia as well as written, audio, plain language, human-reader and augmentative and alternative modes, means and formats of communication, including accessible information and communication technology;

'Language' includes spoken and signed languages and other forms of non-spoken languages;

'Discrimination on the basis of disability' means any distinction, exclusion or restriction on the basis of disability which has the purpose or effect of impairing or nullifying the recognition, enjoyment or exercise, on an equal basis with others, of all human rights and fundamental freedoms in the political, economic, social, cultural, civil or any other field. It includes all forms of discrimination, including denial of reasonable accommodation;

'Reasonable accommodation' means necessary and appropriate modification and adjustments not imposing a disproportionate or undue burden, where needed in a particular case, to ensure to persons with disabilities the enjoyment or exercise on an equal basis with others of all human rights and fundamental freedoms;

'Universal design' means the design of products, environments, programmes and services to be usable by all people, to the greatest extent possible, without the need for adaptation or specialized design. 'Universal design' shall not exclude assistive devices for particular groups of persons with disabilities where this is needed.

Article 3—General principles

The principles of the present Convention shall be:

(a) Respect for inherent dignity, individual autonomy including the freedom to make one's own choices, and independence of persons;

(b) Non-discrimination;

(c) Full and effective participation and inclusion in society;

(d) Respect for difference and acceptance of persons with disabilities as part of human diversity and humanity;

(e) Equality of opportunity;

(f) Accessibility;

(g) Equality between men and women;

(h) Respect for the evolving capacities of children with disabilities and respect for the right of children with disabilities to preserve their identities.

Article 4—General obligations

1. States Parties undertake to ensure and promote the full realization of all human rights and fundamental freedoms for all persons with disabilities without discrimination of any kind on the basis of disability. To this end, States Parties undertake:

(a) To adopt all appropriate legislative, administrative and other measures for the implementation of the rights recognized in the present Convention;

(b) To take all appropriate measures, including legislation, to modify or abolish existing laws, regulations, customs and practices that constitute discrimination against persons with disabilities;

(c) To take into account the protection and promotion of the human rights of persons with disabilities in all policies and programmes;

(d) To refrain from engaging in any act or practice that is inconsistent with the present Convention and to ensure that public authorities and institutions act in conformity with the present Convention;

(e) To take all appropriate measures to eliminate discrimination on the basis of disability by any person, organization or private enterprise;

(f) To undertake or promote research and development of universally designed goods, services, equipment and facilities, as defined in article 2 of the present Convention, which should require the minimum possible adaptation and the least cost to meet the specific needs of a person with disabilities, to promote their availability and use, and to promote universal design in the development of standards and guidelines;

(g) To undertake or promote research and development of, and to promote the availability and use of new technologies, including information and communications technologies, mobility aids, devices and assistive technologies, suitable for persons with disabilities, giving priority to technologies at an affordable cost;

(h) To provide accessible information to persons with disabilities about mobility aids, devices and assistive technologies, including new technologies, as well as other forms of assistance, support services and facilities;

(i) To promote the training of professionals and staff working with persons with disabilities in the rights recognized in the present Convention so as to better provide the assistance and services guaranteed by those rights.

2. With regard to economic, social and cultural rights, each State Party undertakes to take measures to the maximum of its available resources and, where needed, within the framework of international cooperation, with a view to achieving progressively the full realization of these rights, without prejudice to those obligations contained in the present Convention that are immediately applicable according to international law.

3. In the development and implementation of legislation and policies to implement the present Convention, and in other decision-making processes concerning issues relating to persons with disabilities, States Parties shall closely consult with and actively involve persons with disabilities, including children with disabilities, through their representative organizations.

4. Nothing in the present Convention shall affect any provisions which are more conducive to the realization of the rights of persons with disabilities and which may be contained in the law of a State Party or international law in force for that State. There shall be no restriction upon or derogation from any of the human rights and fundamental freedoms recognized or existing in any State Party to the present Convention pursuant to law, conventions, regulation or custom on the pretext that the present Convention does not recognize such rights or freedoms or that it recognizes them to a lesser extent.

5. The provisions of the present Convention shall extend to all parts of federal States without any limitations or exceptions.

Article 5—Equality and non-discrimination

1. States Parties recognize that all persons are equal before and under the law and are entitled without any discrimination to the equal protection and equal benefit of the law.

2. States Parties shall prohibit all discrimination on the basis of disability and guarantee to persons with disabilities equal and effective legal protection against discrimination on all grounds.

3. In order to promote equality and eliminate discrimination, States Parties shall take all appropriate steps to ensure that reasonable accommodation is provided.

4. Specific measures which are necessary to accelerate or achieve de facto equality of persons with disabilities shall not be considered discrimination under the terms of the present Convention.

Article 6—Women with disabilities

1. States Parties recognize that women and girls with disabilities are subject to multiple discrimination, and in this regard shall take measures to ensure the full and equal enjoyment by them of all human rights and fundamental freedoms.

2. States Parties shall take all appropriate measures to ensure the full development, advancement and empowerment of women, for the purpose of guaranteeing them the exercise and enjoyment of the human rights and fundamental freedoms set out in the present Convention.

Article 7—Children with disabilities

1. States Parties shall take all necessary measures to ensure the full enjoyment by children with disabilities of all human rights and fundamental freedoms on an equal basis with other children.

2. In all actions concerning children with disabilities, the best interests of the child shall be a primary consideration.

3. States Parties shall ensure that children with disabilities have the right to express their views freely on all matters affecting them, their views being given due weight in accordance with their age and maturity, on an equal basis with other children, and to be provided with disability and age-appropriate assistance to realize that right.

Article 8—Awareness-raising

1. States Parties undertake to adopt immediate, effective and appropriate measures:

    (a) To raise awareness throughout society, including at the family level, regarding persons with disabilities, and to foster respect for the rights and dignity of persons with disabilities;

    (b) To combat stereotypes, prejudices and harmful practices relating to persons with disabilities, including those based on sex and age, in all areas of life;

    (c) To promote awareness of the capabilities and contributions of persons with disabilities.

2. Measures to this end include:

    (a) Initiating and maintaining effective public awareness campaigns designed:

        (i) To nurture receptiveness to the rights of persons with disabilities;

        (ii) To promote positive perceptions and greater social awareness towards persons with disabilities;

        (iii) To promote recognition of the skills, merits and abilities of persons with disabilities, and of their contributions to the workplace and the labour market;

    (b) Fostering at all levels of the education system, including in all children from an early age, an attitude of respect for the rights of persons with disabilities;

    (c) Encouraging all organs of the media to portray persons with disabilities in a manner consistent with the purpose of the present Convention;

    (d) Promoting awareness-training programmes regarding persons with disabilities and the rights of persons with disabilities.

Article 9—Accessibility

1. To enable persons with disabilities to live independently and participate fully in all aspects of life, States Parties shall take appropriate measures to ensure to persons with disabilities access, on an equal basis with others, to the physical environment, to transportation, to information and communications, including information and communications technologies and systems, and to other facilities and services open or provided to the public, both in urban and in rural areas. These measures, which shall include the identification and elimination of obstacles and barriers to accessibility, shall apply to, inter alia:

   (a) Buildings, roads, transportation and other indoor and outdoor facilities, including schools, housing, medical facilities and workplaces;

   (b) Information, communications and other services, including electronic services and emergency services.

2. States Parties shall also take appropriate measures:

   (a) To develop, promulgate and monitor the implementation of minimum standards and guidelines for the accessibility of facilities and services open or provided to the public;

   (b) To ensure that private entities that offer facilities and services which are open or provided to the public take into account all aspects of accessibility for persons with disabilities;

   (c) To provide training for stakeholders on accessibility issues facing persons with disabilities;

   (d) To provide in buildings and other facilities open to the public signage in Braille and in easy to read and understand forms;

   (e) To provide forms of live assistance and intermediaries, including guides, readers and professional sign language interpreters, to facilitate accessibility to buildings and other facilities open to the public;

   (f) To promote other appropriate forms of assistance and support to persons with disabilities to ensure their access to information;

   (g) To promote access for persons with disabilities to new information and communications technologies and systems, including the Internet;

   (h) To promote the design, development, production and distribution of accessible information and communications technologies and systems at an early stage, so that these technologies and systems become accessible at minimum cost.

Article 10—Right to life

States Parties reaffirm that every human being has the inherent right to life and shall take all necessary measures to ensure its effective enjoyment by persons with disabilities on an equal basis with others.

Article 11—Situations of risk and humanitarian emergencies

States Parties shall take, in accordance with their obligations under international law, including international humanitarian law and international human rights law, all necessary measures to ensure the protection and safety of persons with disabilities in situations of risk, including situations of armed conflict, humanitarian emergencies and the occurrence of natural disasters.

Article 12—Equal recognition before the law

1. States Parties reaffirm that persons with disabilities have the right to recognition everywhere as persons before the law.

2. States Parties shall recognize that persons with disabilities enjoy legal capacity on an equal basis with others in all aspects of life.

3. States Parties shall take appropriate measures to provide access by persons with disabilities to the support they may require in exercising their legal capacity.

4. States Parties shall ensure that all measures that relate to the exercise of legal capacity provide for appropriate and effective safeguards to prevent abuse in accordance with international human rights law. Such safeguards shall ensure that measures relating to the exercise of legal capacity respect the rights, will and preferences of the person, are free of conflict of interest and undue influence, are proportional and tailored to the person's circumstances, apply for the shortest time possible and are subject to regular review by a competent, independent and impartial authority or judicial body. The safeguards shall be proportional to the degree to which such measures affect the person's rights and interests.

5. Subject to the provisions of this article, States Parties shall take all appropriate and effective measures to ensure the equal right of persons with disabilities to own or inherit property, to control their own financial affairs and to have equal access to bank loans, mortgages and other forms of financial credit, and shall ensure that persons with disabilities are not arbitrarily deprived of their property.

Article 13—Access to justice

1. States Parties shall ensure effective access to justice for persons with disabilities on an equal basis with others, including through the provision of procedural and age-appropriate accommodations, in order to facilitate their effective role as direct and indirect participants, including as witnesses, in all legal proceedings, including at investigative and other preliminary stages.

2. In order to help to ensure effective access to justice for persons with disabilities, States Parties shall promote appropriate training for those working in the field of administration of justice, including police and prison staff.

Article 14—Liberty and security of person

1. States Parties shall ensure that persons with disabilities, on an equal basis with others:

   (a) Enjoy the right to liberty and security of person;

   (b) Are not deprived of their liberty unlawfully or arbitrarily, and that any deprivation of liberty is in conformity with the law, and that the existence of a disability shall in no case justify a deprivation of liberty.

2. States Parties shall ensure that if persons with disabilities are deprived of their liberty through any process, they are, on an equal basis with others, entitled to guarantees in accordance with international human rights law and shall be treated in compliance with the objectives and principles of the present Convention, including by provision of reasonable accommodation.

Article 15—Freedom from torture or cruel, inhuman or degrading treatment or punishment

1. No one shall be subjected to torture or to cruel, inhuman or degrading treatment or punishment. In particular, no one shall be subjected without his or her free consent to medical or scientific experimentation.

2. States Parties shall take all effective legislative, administrative, judicial or other measures to prevent persons with disabilities, on an equal basis with others, from being subjected to torture or cruel, inhuman or degrading treatment or punishment.

Article 16—Freedom from exploitation, violence and abuse

1. States Parties shall take all appropriate legislative, administrative, social, educational and other measures to protect persons with disabilities, both within and outside the home, from all forms of exploitation, violence and abuse, including their gender-based aspects.

2. States Parties shall also take all appropriate measures to prevent all forms of exploitation, violence and abuse by ensuring, inter alia, appropriate forms of gender- and age-sensitive assistance and support for persons with disabilities and their families and caregivers, including through the provision of information and education on how to avoid, recognize and report instances of exploitation, violence and abuse. States Parties shall ensure that protection services are age-, gender- and disability-sensitive.

3. In order to prevent the occurrence of all forms of exploitation, violence and abuse, States Parties shall ensure that all facilities and programmes designed to serve persons with disabilities are effectively monitored by independent authorities.

4. States Parties shall take all appropriate measures to promote the physical, cognitive and psychological recovery, rehabilitation and social reintegration of persons with disabilities who become victims of any form of exploitation, violence or abuse, including through the provision of protection services. Such recovery and reintegration shall take place in an environment that fosters the health, welfare, self-respect, dignity and autonomy of the person and takes into account gender- and age-specific needs.

5. States Parties shall put in place effective legislation and policies, including women- and child-focused legislation and policies, to ensure that instances of exploitation, violence and abuse against persons with disabilities are identified, investigated and, where appropriate, prosecuted.

Article 17—Protecting the integrity of the person

Every person with disabilities has a right to respect for his or her physical and mental integrity on an equal basis with others.

Article 18—Liberty of movement and nationality

1. States Parties shall recognize the rights of persons with disabilities to liberty of movement, to freedom to choose their residence and to a nationality, on an equal basis with others, including by ensuring that persons with disabilities:

 (a) Have the right to acquire and change a nationality and are not deprived of their nationality arbitrarily or on the basis of disability;

 (b) Are not deprived, on the basis of disability, of their ability to obtain, possess and utilize documentation of their nationality or other documentation of identification, or to utilize relevant processes such as immigration proceedings, that may be needed to facilitate exercise of the right to liberty of movement;

(c) Are free to leave any country, including their own;

(d) Are not deprived, arbitrarily or on the basis of disability, of the right to enter their own country.

2. Children with disabilities shall be registered immediately after birth and shall have the right from birth to a name, the right to acquire a nationality and, as far as possible, the right to know and be cared for by their parents.

Article 19—*Living independently and being included in the community*

States Parties to the present Convention recognize the equal right of all persons with disabilities to live in the community, with choices equal to others, and shall take effective and appropriate measures to facilitate full enjoyment by persons with disabilities of this right and their full inclusion and participation in the community, including by ensuring that:

(a) Persons with disabilities have the opportunity to choose their place of residence and where and with whom they live on an equal basis with others and are not obliged to live in a particular living arrangement;

(b) Persons with disabilities have access to a range of in-home, residential and other community support services, including personal assistance necessary to support living and inclusion in the community, and to prevent isolation or segregation from the community;

(c) Community services and facilities for the general population are available on an equal basis to persons with disabilities and are responsive to their needs.

Article 20—*Personal mobility*

States Parties shall take effective measures to ensure personal mobility with the greatest possible independence for persons with disabilities, including by:

(a) Facilitating the personal mobility of persons with disabilities in the manner and at the time of their choice, and at affordable cost;

(b) Facilitating access by persons with disabilities to quality mobility aids, devices, assistive technologies and forms of live assistance and intermediaries, including by making them available at affordable cost;

(c) Providing training in mobility skills to persons with disabilities and to specialist staff working with persons with disabilities;

(d) Encouraging entities that produce mobility aids, devices and assistive technologies to take into account all aspects of mobility for persons with disabilities.

Article 21—*Freedom of expression and opinion, and access to information*

States Parties shall take all appropriate measures to ensure that persons with disabilities can exercise the right to freedom of expression and opinion, including the freedom to seek, receive and impart information and ideas on an equal basis with others and through all forms of communication of their choice, as defined in article 2 of the present Convention, including by:

(a) Providing information intended for the general public to persons with disabilities in accessible formats and technologies appropriate to different kinds of disabilities in a timely manner and without additional cost;

(b) Accepting and facilitating the use of sign languages, Braille, augmentative and alternative communication, and all other accessible means, modes and formats of communication of their choice by persons with disabilities in official interactions;

(c) Urging private entities that provide services to the general public, including through the Internet, to provide information and services in accessible and usable formats for persons with disabilities;

(d) Encouraging the mass media, including providers of information through the Internet, to make their services accessible to persons with disabilities;

(e) Recognizing and promoting the use of sign languages.

Article 22—Respect for privacy

1. No person with disabilities, regardless of place of residence or living arrangements, shall be subjected to arbitrary or unlawful interference with his or her privacy, family, home or correspondence or other types of communication or to unlawful attacks on his or her honour and reputation. Persons with disabilities have the right to the protection of the law against such interference or attacks.

2. States Parties shall protect the privacy of personal, health and rehabilitation information of persons with disabilities on an equal basis with others.

Article 23—Respect for home and the family

1. States Parties shall take effective and appropriate measures to eliminate discrimination against persons with disabilities in all matters relating to marriage, family, parenthood and relationships, on an equal basis with others, so as to ensure that:

(a) The right of all persons with disabilities who are of marriageable age to marry and to found a family on the basis of free and full consent of the intending spouses is recognized;

(b) The rights of persons with disabilities to decide freely and responsibly on the number and spacing of their children and to have access to age-appropriate information, reproductive and family planning education are recognized, and the means necessary to enable them to exercise these rights are provided;

(c) Persons with disabilities, including children, retain their fertility on an equal basis with others.

2. States Parties shall ensure the rights and responsibilities of persons with disabilities, with regard to guardianship, wardship, trusteeship, adoption of children or similar institutions, where these concepts exist in national legislation; in all cases the best interests of the child shall be paramount. States Parties shall render appropriate assistance to persons with disabilities in the performance of their childrearing responsibilities.

3. States Parties shall ensure that children with disabilities have equal rights with respect to family life. With a view to realizing these rights, and to prevent concealment, abandonment, neglect and segregation of children with disabilities, States Parties shall undertake to provide early and comprehensive information, services and support to children with disabilities and their families.

4. States Parties shall ensure that a child shall not be separated from his or her parents against their will, except when competent authorities subject to judicial review determine, in accordance with applicable law and procedures, that such separation is necessary for the best interests of the child. In no case shall a child be separated from parents on the basis of a disability of either the child or one or both of the parents.

5. States Parties shall, where the immediate family is unable to care for a child with disabilities, undertake every effort to provide alternative care within the wider family, and failing that, within the community in a family setting.

Article 24—Education

1. States Parties recognize the right of persons with disabilities to education. With a view to realizing this right without discrimination and on the basis of equal opportunity, States Parties shall ensure an inclusive education system at all levels and lifelong learning directed to:

(a) The full development of human potential and sense of dignity and selfworth, and the strengthening of respect for human rights, fundamental freedoms and human diversity;

(b) The development by persons with disabilities of their personality, talents and creativity, as well as their mental and physical abilities, to their fullest potential;

(c) Enabling persons with disabilities to participate effectively in a free society.

2. In realizing this right, States Parties shall ensure that:

(a) Persons with disabilities are not excluded from the general education system on the basis of disability, and that children with disabilities are not excluded from free and compulsory primary education, or from secondary education, on the basis of disability;

(b) Persons with disabilities can access an inclusive, quality and free primary education and secondary education on an equal basis with others in the communities in which they live;

(c) Reasonable accommodation of the individual's requirements is provided;

(d) Persons with disabilities receive the support required, within the general education system, to facilitate their effective education;

(e) Effective individualized support measures are provided in environments that maximize academic and social development, consistent with the goal of full inclusion.

3. States Parties shall enable persons with disabilities to learn life and social development skills to facilitate their full and equal participation in education and as members of the community. To this end, States Parties shall take appropriate measures, including:

(a) Facilitating the learning of Braille, alternative script, augmentative and alternative modes, means and formats of communication and orientation and mobility skills, and facilitating peer support and mentoring;

(b) Facilitating the learning of sign language and the promotion of the linguistic identity of the deaf community;

(c) Ensuring that the education of persons, and in particular children, who are blind, deaf or deafblind, is delivered in the most appropriate languages and modes and means of communication for the individual, and in environments which maximize academic and social development.

4. In order to help ensure the realization of this right, States Parties shall take appropriate measures to employ teachers, including teachers with disabilities, who are qualified in sign language and/or Braille, and to train professionals and staff who work at all levels of education. Such training shall incorporate disability awareness and the use of

appropriate augmentative and alternative modes, means and formats of communication, educational techniques and materials to support persons with disabilities.

5. States Parties shall ensure that persons with disabilities are able to access general tertiary education, vocational training, adult education and lifelong learning without discrimination and on an equal basis with others. To this end, States Parties shall ensure that reasonable accommodation is provided to persons with disabilities.

Article 25—Health

States Parties recognize that persons with disabilities have the right to the enjoyment of the highest attainable standard of health without discrimination on the basis of disability. States Parties shall take all appropriate measures to ensure access for persons with disabilities to health services that are gender-sensitive, including health-related rehabilitation. In particular, States Parties shall:

(a) Provide persons with disabilities with the same range, quality and standard of free or affordable health care and programmes as provided to other persons, including in the area of sexual and reproductive health and population-based public health programmes;

(b) Provide those health services needed by persons with disabilities specifically because of their disabilities, including early identification and intervention as appropriate, and services designed to minimize and prevent further disabilities, including among children and older persons;

(c) Provide these health services as close as possible to people's own communities, including in rural areas;

(d) Require health professionals to provide care of the same quality to persons with disabilities as to others, including on the basis of free and informed consent by, inter alia, raising awareness of the human rights, dignity, autonomy and needs of persons with disabilities through training and the promulgation of ethical standards for public and private health care;

(e) Prohibit discrimination against persons with disabilities in the provision of health insurance, and life insurance where such insurance is permitted by national law, which shall be provided in a fair and reasonable manner;

(f) Prevent discriminatory denial of health care or health services or food and fluids on the basis of disability.

Article 26— Habilitation and rehabilitation

1. States Parties shall take effective and appropriate measures, including through peer support, to enable persons with disabilities to attain and maintain maximum independence, full physical, mental, social and vocational ability, and full inclusion and participation in all aspects of life. To that end, States Parties shall organize, strengthen and extend comprehensive habilitation and rehabilitation services and programmes, particularly in the areas of health, employment, education and social services, in such a way that these services and programmes:

(a) Begin at the earliest possible stage, and are based on the multidisciplinary assessment of individual needs and strengths;

(b) Support participation and inclusion in the community and all aspects of society, are voluntary, and are available to persons with disabilities as close as possible to their own communities, including in rural areas.

2. States Parties shall promote the development of initial and continuing training for professionals and staff working in habilitation and rehabilitation services.

3. States Parties shall promote the availability, knowledge and use of assistive devices and technologies, designed for persons with disabilities, as they relate to habilitation and rehabilitation.

Article 27—Work and employment

1. States Parties recognize the right of persons with disabilities to work, on an equal basis with others; this includes the right to the opportunity to gain a living by work freely chosen or accepted in a labour market and work environment that is open, inclusive and accessible to persons with disabilities. States Parties shall safeguard and promote the realization of the right to work, including for those who acquire a disability during the course of employment, by taking appropriate steps, including through legislation, to, inter alia:

    (a) Prohibit discrimination on the basis of disability with regard to all matters concerning all forms of employment, including conditions of recruitment, hiring and employment, continuance of employment, career advancement and safe and healthy working conditions;

    (b) Protect the rights of persons with disabilities, on an equal basis with others, to just and favourable conditions of work, including equal opportunities and equal remuneration for work of equal value, safe and healthy working conditions, including protection from harassment, and the redress of grievances;

    (c) Ensure that persons with disabilities are able to exercise their labour and trade union rights on an equal basis with others;

    (d) Enable persons with disabilities to have effective access to general technical and vocational guidance programmes, placement services and vocational and continuing training;

    (e) Promote employment opportunities and career advancement for persons with disabilities in the labour market, as well as assistance in finding, obtaining, maintaining and returning to employment;

    (f) Promote opportunities for self-employment, entrepreneurship, the development of cooperatives and starting one's own business;

    (g) Employ persons with disabilities in the public sector;

    (h) Promote the employment of persons with disabilities in the private sector through appropriate policies and measures, which may include affirmative action programmes, incentives and other measures;

    (i) Ensure that reasonable accommodation is provided to persons with disabilities in the workplace;

    (j) Promote the acquisition by persons with disabilities of work experience in the open labour market;

    (k) Promote vocational and professional rehabilitation, job retention and return -to-work programmes for persons with disabilities.

2. States Parties shall ensure that persons with disabilities are not held in slavery or in servitude, and are protected, on an equal basis with others, from forced or compulsory labour.

Article 28—Adequate standard of living and social protection

1. States Parties recognize the right of persons with disabilities to an adequate standard of living for themselves and their families, including adequate food, clothing and housing,

and to the continuous improvement of living conditions, and shall take appropriate steps
to safeguard and promote the realization of this right without discrimination on the basis
of disability.

2. States Parties recognize the right of persons with disabilities to social protection and
to the enjoyment of that right without discrimination on the basis of disability, and shall
take appropriate steps to safeguard and promote the realization of this right, including
measures:

(a) To ensure equal access by persons with disabilities to clean water services, and to
    ensure access to appropriate and affordable services, devices and other assistance
    for disability-related needs;

(b) To ensure access by persons with disabilities, in particular women and girls with
    disabilities and older persons with disabilities, to social protection programmes
    and poverty reduction programmes;

(c) To ensure access by persons with disabilities and their families living in situations
    of poverty to assistance from the State with disability-related expenses, including
    adequate training, counselling, financial assistance and respite care;

(d) To ensure access by persons with disabilities to public housing programmes;

(e) To ensure equal access by persons with disabilities to retirement benefits and
    programmes.

Article 29—Participation in political and public life

States Parties shall guarantee to persons with disabilities political rights and the opportunity to enjoy them on an equal basis with others, and shall undertake:

(a) To ensure that persons with disabilities can effectively and fully participate in
    political and public life on an equal basis with others, directly or through freely
    chosen representatives, including the right and opportunity for persons with dis-
    abilities to vote and be elected, inter alia, by:
    (i) Ensuring that voting procedures, facilities and materials are appropriate,
        accessible and easy to understand and use;
    (ii) Protecting the right of persons with disabilities to vote by secret ballot in
         elections and public referendums without intimidation, and to stand for elec-
         tions, to effectively hold office and perform all public functions at all levels
         of government, facilitating the use of assistive and new technologies where
         appropriate;
    (iii) Guaranteeing the free expression of the will of persons with disabilities as
          electors and to this end, where necessary, at their request, allowing assistance
          in voting by a person of their own choice;

(b) To promote actively an environment in which persons with disabilities can effec-
    tively and fully participate in the conduct of public affairs, without discrimination
    and on an equal basis with others, and encourage their participation in public
    affairs, including:
    (i) Participation in non-governmental organizations and associations concerned
        with the public and political life of the country, and in the activities and
        administration of political parties;
    (ii) Forming and joining organizations of persons with disabilities to represent
         persons with disabilities at international, national, regional and local levels.

Article 30—Participation in cultural life, recreation, leisure and sport

1. States Parties recognize the right of persons with disabilities to take part on an equal basis with others in cultural life, and shall take all appropriate measures to ensure that persons with disabilities:

    (a) Enjoy access to cultural materials in accessible formats;

    (b) Enjoy access to television programmes, films, theatre and other cultural activities, in accessible formats;

    (c) Enjoy access to places for cultural performances or services, such as theatres, museums, cinemas, libraries and tourism services, and, as far as possible, enjoy access to monuments and sites of national cultural importance.

2. States Parties shall take appropriate measures to enable persons with disabilities to have the opportunity to develop and utilize their creative, artistic and intellectual potential, not only for their own benefit, but also for the enrichment of society.

3. States Parties shall take all appropriate steps, in accordance with international law, to ensure that laws protecting intellectual property rights do not constitute an unreasonable or discriminatory barrier to access by persons with disabilities to cultural materials.

4. Persons with disabilities shall be entitled, on an equal basis with others, to recognition and support of their specific cultural and linguistic identity, including sign languages and deaf culture.

5. With a view to enabling persons with disabilities to participate on an equal basis with others in recreational, leisure and sporting activities, States Parties shall take appropriate measures:

    (a) To encourage and promote the participation, to the fullest extent possible, of persons with disabilities in mainstream sporting activities at all levels;

    (b) To ensure that persons with disabilities have an opportunity to organize, develop and participate in disability-specific sporting and recreational activities and, to this end, encourage the provision, on an equal basis with others, of appropriate instruction, training and resources;

    (c) To ensure that persons with disabilities have access to sporting, recreational and tourism venues;

    (d) To ensure that children with disabilities have equal access with other children to participation in play, recreation and leisure and sporting activities, including those activities in the school system;

    (e) To ensure that persons with disabilities have access to services from those involved in the organization of recreational, tourism, leisure and sporting activities.

Article 31—Statistics and data collection

1. States Parties undertake to collect appropriate information, including statistical and research data, to enable them to formulate and implement policies to give effect to the present Convention. The process of collecting and maintaining this information shall:

    (a) Comply with legally established safeguards, including legislation on data protection, to ensure confidentiality and respect for the privacy of persons with disabilities;

    (b) Comply with internationally accepted norms to protect human rights and fundamental freedoms and ethical principles in the collection and use of statistics.

2. The information collected in accordance with this article shall be disaggregated, as appropriate, and used to help assess the implementation of States Parties' obligations under the present Convention and to identify and address the barriers faced by persons with disabilities in exercising their rights.

3. States Parties shall assume responsibility for the dissemination of these statistics and ensure their accessibility to persons with disabilities and others.

Article 32—International cooperation

1. States Parties recognize the importance of international cooperation and its promotion, in support of national efforts for the realization of the purpose and objectives of the present Convention, and will undertake appropriate and effective measures in this regard, between and among States and, as appropriate, in partnership with relevant international and regional organizations and civil society, in particular organizations of persons with disabilities. Such measures could include, inter alia:

(a) Ensuring that international cooperation, including international development programmes, is inclusive of and accessible to persons with disabilities;

(b) Facilitating and supporting capacity-building, including through the exchange and sharing of information, experiences, training programmes and best practices;

(c) Facilitating cooperation in research and access to scientific and technical knowledge;

(d) Providing, as appropriate, technical and economic assistance, including by facilitating access to and sharing of accessible and assistive technologies, and through the transfer of technologies.

2. The provisions of this article are without prejudice to the obligations of each State Party to fulfil its obligations under the present Convention.

Article 33—National implementation and monitoring

1. States Parties, in accordance with their system of organization, shall designate one or more focal points within government for matters relating to the implementation of the present Convention, and shall give due consideration to the establishment or designation of a coordination mechanism within government to facilitate related action in different sectors and at different levels.

2. States Parties shall, in accordance with their legal and administrative systems, maintain, strengthen, designate or establish within the State Party, a framework, including one or more independent mechanisms, as appropriate, to promote, protect and monitor implementation of the present Convention. When designating or establishing such a mechanism, States Parties shall take into account the principles relating to the status and functioning of national institutions for protection and promotion of human rights.

3. Civil society, in particular persons with disabilities and their representative organizations, shall be involved and participate fully in the monitoring process.

Article 34—Committee on the Rights of Persons with Disabilities

1. There shall be established a Committee on the Rights of Persons with Disabilities (hereafter referred to as 'the Committee'), which shall carry out the functions hereinafter provided.

2. The Committee shall consist, at the time of entry into force of the present Convention, of twelve experts. After an additional sixty ratifications or accessions to the Convention, the membership of the Committee shall increase by six members, attaining a maximum number of eighteen members.

3. The members of the Committee shall serve in their personal capacity and shall be of high moral standing and recognized competence and experience in the field covered by the present Convention. When nominating their candidates, States Parties are invited to give due consideration to the provision set out in article 4, paragraph 3, of the present Convention.

4. The members of the Committee shall be elected by States Parties, consideration being given to equitable geographical distribution, representation of the different forms of civilization and of the principal legal systems, balanced gender representation and participation of experts with disabilities.

5. The members of the Committee shall be elected by secret ballot from a list of persons nominated by the States Parties from among their nationals at meetings of the Conference of States Parties. At those meetings, for which two thirds of States Parties shall constitute a quorum, the persons elected to the Committee shall be those who obtain the largest number of votes and an absolute majority of the votes of the representatives of States Parties present and voting.

6. The initial election shall be held no later than six months after the date of entry into force of the present Convention. At least four months before the date of each election, the Secretary-General of the United Nations shall address a letter to the States Parties inviting them to submit the nominations within two months. The Secretary-General shall subsequently prepare a list in alphabetical order of all persons thus nominated, indicating the State Parties which have nominated them, and shall submit it to the States Parties to the present Convention.

7. The members of the Committee shall be elected for a term of four years. They shall be eligible for re-election once. However, the term of six of the members elected at the first election shall expire at the end of two years; immediately after the first election, the names of these six members shall be chosen by lot by the chairperson of the meeting referred to in paragraph 5 of this article.

8. The election of the six additional members of the Committee shall be held on the occasion of regular elections, in accordance with the relevant provisions of this article.

9. If a member of the Committee dies or resigns or declares that for any other cause she or he can no longer perform her or his duties, the State Party which nominated the member shall appoint another expert possessing the qualifications and meeting the requirements set out in the relevant provisions of this article, to serve for the remainder of the term.

10. The Committee shall establish its own rules of procedure.

11. The Secretary-General of the United Nations shall provide the necessary staff and facilities for the effective performance of the functions of the Committee under the present Convention, and shall convene its initial meeting.

12. With the approval of the General Assembly of the United Nations, the members of the Committee established under the present Convention shall receive emoluments from United Nations resources on such terms and conditions as the Assembly may decide, having regard to the importance of the Committee's responsibilities.

13. The members of the Committee shall be entitled to the facilities, privileges and immunities of experts on mission for the United Nations as laid down in the relevant sections of the Convention on the Privileges and Immunities of the United Nations.

Article 35—Reports by States Parties

1. Each State Party shall submit to the Committee, through the Secretary-General of the United Nations, a comprehensive report on measures taken to give effect to its obligations under the present Convention and on the progress made in that regard, within two years after the entry into force of the present Convention for the State Party concerned.

2. Thereafter, States Parties shall submit subsequent reports at least every four years and further whenever the Committee so requests.

3. The Committee shall decide any guidelines applicable to the content of the reports.

4. A State Party which has submitted a comprehensive initial report to the Committee need not, in its subsequent reports, repeat information previously provided. When preparing reports to the Committee, States Parties are invited to consider doing so in an open and transparent process and to give due consideration to the provision set out in article 4, paragraph 3, of the present Convention.

5. Reports may indicate factors and difficulties affecting the degree of fulfilment of obligations under the present Convention.

Article 36—Consideration of reports

1. Each report shall be considered by the Committee, which shall make such suggestions and general recommendations on the report as it may consider appropriate and shall forward these to the State Party concerned. The State Party may respond with any information it chooses to the Committee. The Committee may request further information from States Parties relevant to the implementation of the present Convention.

2. If a State Party is significantly overdue in the submission of a report, the Committee may notify the State Party concerned of the need to examine the implementation of the present Convention in that State Party, on the basis of reliable information available to the Committee, if the relevant report is not submitted within three months following the notification. The Committee shall invite the State Party concerned to participate in such examination. Should the State Party respond by submitting the relevant report, the provisions of paragraph 1 of this article will apply.

3. The Secretary-General of the United Nations shall make available the reports to all States Parties.

4. States Parties shall make their reports widely available to the public in their own countries and facilitate access to the suggestions and general recommendations relating to these reports.

5. The Committee shall transmit, as it may consider appropriate, to the specialized agencies, funds and programmes of the United Nations, and other competent bodies, reports from States Parties in order to address a request or indication of a need for technical advice or assistance contained therein, along with the Committee's observations and recommendations, if any, on these requests or indications.

Article 37—Cooperation between States Parties and the Committee

1. Each State Party shall cooperate with the Committee and assist its members in the fulfilment of their mandate.

2. In its relationship with States Parties, the Committee shall give due consideration to ways and means of enhancing national capacities for the implementation of the present Convention, including through international cooperation.

Article 38—Relationship of the Committee with other bodies

In order to foster the effective implementation of the present Convention and to encourage international cooperation in the field covered by the present Convention:

(a) The specialized agencies and other United Nations organs shall be entitled to be represented at the consideration of the implementation of such provisions of the present Convention as fall within the scope of their mandate. The Committee may invite the specialized agencies and other competent bodies as it may consider appropriate to provide expert advice on the implementation of the Convention in areas falling within the scope of their respective mandates. The Committee may invite specialized agencies and other United Nations organs to submit reports on the implementation of the Convention in areas falling within the scope of their activities;

(b) The Committee, as it discharges its mandate, shall consult, as appropriate, other relevant bodies instituted by international human rights treaties, with a view to ensuring the consistency of their respective reporting guidelines, suggestions and general recommendations, and avoiding duplication and overlap in the performance of their functions.

Article 39—Report of the Committee

The Committee shall report every two years to the General Assembly and to the Economic and Social Council on its activities, and may make suggestions and general recommendations based on the examination of reports and information received from the States Parties. Such suggestions and general recommendations shall be included in the report of the Committee together with comments, if any, from States Parties.

Article 40—Conference of States Parties

1. The States Parties shall meet regularly in a Conference of States Parties in order to consider any matter with regard to the implementation of the present Convention.

2. No later than six months after the entry into force of the present Convention, the Conference of States Parties shall be convened by the Secretary-General of the United Nations. The subsequent meetings shall be convened by the Secretary-General biennially or upon the decision of the Conference of States Parties.

Article 41—Depositary

The Secretary-General of the United Nations shall be the depositary of the present Convention.

Article 42—Signature

The present Convention shall be open for signature by all States and by regional integration organizations at United Nations Headquarters in New York as of 30 March 2007.

Article 43—Consent to be bound

The present Convention shall be subject to ratification by signatory States and to formal confirmation by signatory regional integration organizations. It shall be open for accession by any State or regional integration organization which has not signed the Convention.

Article 44—Regional integration organizations

1. 'Regional integration organization' shall mean an organization constituted by sovereign States of a given region, to which its member States have transferred competence in respect of matters governed by the present Convention. Such organizations shall declare, in their instruments of formal confirmation or accession, the extent of their competence with respect to matters governed by the present Convention. Subsequently, they shall inform the depositary of any substantial modification in the extent of their competence.

2. References to 'States Parties' in the present Convention shall apply to such organizations within the limits of their competence.

3. For the purposes of article 45, paragraph 1, and article 47, paragraphs 2 and 3, of the present Convention, any instrument deposited by a regional integration organization shall not be counted.

4. Regional integration organizations, in matters within their competence, may exercise their right to vote in the Conference of States Parties, with a number of votes equal to the number of their member States that are Parties to the present Convention. Such an organization shall not exercise its right to vote if any of its member States exercises its right, and vice versa.

Article 45—Entry into force

1. The present Convention shall enter into force on the thirtieth day after the deposit of the twentieth instrument of ratification or accession.

2. For each State or regional integration organization ratifying, formally confirming or acceding to the present Convention after the deposit of the twentieth such instrument, the Convention shall enter into force on the thirtieth day after the deposit of its own such instrument.

Article 46—Reservations

1. Reservations incompatible with the object and purpose of the present Convention shall not be permitted.

2. Reservations may be withdrawn at any time.

Article 47—Amendments

1. Any State Party may propose an amendment to the present Convention and submit it to the Secretary-General of the United Nations. The Secretary-General shall communicate any proposed amendments to States Parties, with a request to be notified whether they favour a conference of States Parties for the purpose of considering and deciding upon the proposals. In the event that, within four months from the date of such communication, at least one third of the States Parties favour such a conference, the Secretary-General shall convene the conference under the auspices of the United Nations. Any amendment adopted by a majority of two thirds of the States Parties present and voting shall be submitted by the Secretary-General to the General Assembly of the United Nations for approval and thereafter to all States Parties for acceptance.

2. An amendment adopted and approved in accordance with paragraph 1 of this article shall enter into force on the thirtieth day after the number of instruments of acceptance

deposited reaches two thirds of the number of States Parties at the date of adoption of the amendment. Thereafter, the amendment shall enter into force for any State Party on the thirtieth day following the deposit of its own instrument of acceptance. An amendment shall be binding only on those States Parties which have accepted it.

3. If so decided by the Conference of States Parties by consensus, an amendment adopted and approved in accordance with paragraph 1 of this article which relates exclusively to articles 34, 38, 39 and 40 shall enter into force for all States Parties on the thirtieth day after the number of instruments of acceptance deposited reaches two thirds of the number of States Parties at the date of adoption of the amendment.

Article 48—Denunciation

A State Party may denounce the present Convention by written notification to the Secretary-General of the United Nations. The denunciation shall become effective one year after the date of receipt of the notification by the Secretary-General.

Article 49—Accessible format

The text of the present Convention shall be made available in accessible formats.

Article 50—Authentic texts

The Arabic, Chinese, English, French, Russian and Spanish texts of the present Convention shall be equally authentic.

IN WITNESS THEREOF the undersigned plenipotentiaries, being duly authorized thereto by their respective Governments, have signed the present Convention.

OPTIONAL PROTOCOL TO THE CONVENTION ON THE RIGHTS OF PERSONS WITH DISABILITIES

The States Parties to the present Protocol have agreed as follows:

Article 1

1. A State Party to the present Protocol ('State Party') recognizes the competence of the Committee on the Rights of Persons with Disabilities ('the Committee') to receive and consider communications from or on behalf of individuals or groups of individuals subject to its jurisdiction who claim to be victims of a violation by that State Party of the provisions of the Convention.

2. No communication shall be received by the Committee if it concerns a State Party to the Convention that is not a party to the present Protocol.

Article 2

The Committee shall consider a communication inadmissible when:

    (a) The communication is anonymous;

    (b) The communication constitutes an abuse of the right of submission of such communications or is incompatible with the provisions of the Convention;

    (c) The same matter has already been examined by the Committee or has been or is being examined under another procedure of international investigation or settlement;

(d) All available domestic remedies have not been exhausted. This shall not be the rule where the application of the remedies is unreasonably prolonged or unlikely to bring effective relief;

(e) It is manifestly ill-founded or not sufficiently substantiated; or when

(f) The facts that are the subject of the communication occurred prior to the entry into force of the present Protocol for the State Party concerned unless those facts continued after that date.

Article 3

Subject to the provisions of article 2 of the present Protocol, the Committee shall bring any communications submitted to it confidentially to the attention of the State Party. Within six months, the receiving State shall submit to the Committee written explanations or statements clarifying the matter and the remedy, if any, that may have been taken by that State.

Article 4

1. At any time after the receipt of a communication and before a determination on the merits has been reached, the Committee may transmit to the State Party concerned for its urgent consideration a request that the State Party take such interim measures as may be necessary to avoid possible irreparable damage to the victim or victims of the alleged violation.

2. Where the Committee exercises its discretion under paragraph 1 of this article, this does not imply a determination on admissibility or on the merits of the communication.

Article 5

The Committee shall hold closed meetings when examining communications under the present Protocol. After examining a communication, the Committee shall forward its suggestions and recommendations, if any, to the State Party concerned and to the petitioner.

Article 6

1. If the Committee receives reliable information indicating grave or systematic violations by a State Party of rights set forth in the Convention, the Committee shall invite that State Party to cooperate in the examination of the information and to this end submit observations with regard to the information concerned.

2. Taking into account any observations that may have been submitted by the State Party concerned as well as any other reliable information available to it, the Committee may designate one or more of its members to conduct an inquiry and to report urgently to the Committee. Where warranted and with the consent of the State Party, the inquiry may include a visit to its territory.

3. After examining the findings of such an inquiry, the Committee shall transmit these findings to the State Party concerned together with any comments and recommendations.

4. The State Party concerned shall, within six months of receiving the findings, comments and recommendations transmitted by the Committee, submit its observations to the Committee.

5. Such an inquiry shall be conducted confidentially and the cooperation of the State Party shall be sought at all stages of the proceedings.

Article 7

1. The Committee may invite the State Party concerned to include in its report under article 35 of the Convention details of any measures taken in response to an inquiry conducted under article 6 of the present Protocol.

2. The Committee may, if necessary, after the end of the period of six months referred to in article 6, paragraph 4, invite the State Party concerned to inform it of the measures taken in response to such an inquiry.

Article 8

Each State Party may, at the time of signature or ratification of the present Protocol or accession thereto, declare that it does not recognize the competence of the Committee provided for in articles 6 and 7.

Article 9

The Secretary-General of the United Nations shall be the depositary of the present Protocol.

Article 10

The present Protocol shall be open for signature by signatory States and regional integration organizations of the Convention at United Nations Headquarters in New York as of 30 March 2007.

Article 11

The present Protocol shall be subject to ratification by signatory States of the present Protocol which have ratified or acceded to the Convention. It shall be subject to formal confirmation by signatory regional integration organizations of the present Protocol which have formally confirmed or acceded to the Convention. It shall be open for accession by any State or regional integration organization which has ratified, formally confirmed or acceded to the Convention and which has not signed the Protocol.

Article 12

1. 'Regional integration organization' shall mean an organization constituted by sovereign States of a given region, to which its member States have transferred competence in respect of matters governed by the Convention and the present Protocol. Such organizations shall declare, in their instruments of formal confirmation or accession, the extent of their competence with respect to matters governed by the Convention and the present Protocol. Subsequently, they shall inform the depositary of any substantial modification in the extent of their competence.

2. References to 'States Parties' in the present Protocol shall apply to such organizations within the limits of their competence.

3. For the purposes of article 13, paragraph 1, and article 15, paragraph 2, of the present Protocol, any instrument deposited by a regional integration organization shall not be counted.

4. Regional integration organizations, in matters within their competence, may exercise their right to vote in the meeting of States Parties, with a number of votes equal to the number of their member States that are Parties to the present Protocol. Such an organization shall not exercise its right to vote if any of its member States exercises its right, and vice versa.

Article 13

1. Subject to the entry into force of the Convention, the present Protocol shall enter into force on the thirtieth day after the deposit of the tenth instrument of ratification or accession.

2. For each State or regional integration organization ratifying, formally confirming or acceding to the present Protocol after the deposit of the tenth such instrument, the Protocol shall enter into force on the thirtieth day after the deposit of its own such instrument.

Article 14

1. Reservations incompatible with the object and purpose of the present Protocol shall not be permitted.

2. Reservations may be withdrawn at any time.

Article 15

1. Any State Party may propose an amendment to the present Protocol and submit it to the Secretary-General of the United Nations. The Secretary-General shall communicate any proposed amendments to States Parties, with a request to be notified whether they favour a meeting of States Parties for the purpose of considering and deciding upon the proposals. In the event that, within four months from the date of such communication, at least one third of the States Parties favour such a meeting, the Secretary-General shall convene the meeting under the auspices of the United Nations. Any amendment adopted by a majority of two thirds of the States Parties present and voting shall be submitted by the Secretary-General to the General Assembly of the United Nations for approval and thereafter to all States Parties for acceptance.

2. An amendment adopted and approved in accordance with paragraph 1 of this article shall enter into force on the thirtieth day after the number of instruments of acceptance deposited reaches two thirds of the number of States Parties at the date of adoption of the amendment. Thereafter, the amendment shall enter into force for any State Party on the thirtieth day following the deposit of its own instrument of acceptance. An amendment shall be binding only on those States Parties which have accepted it.

Article 16

A State Party may denounce the present Protocol by written notification to the Secretary-General of the United Nations. The denunciation shall become effective one year after the date of receipt of the notification by the Secretary-General.

Article 17

The text of the present Protocol shall be made available in accessible formats.

Article 18

The Arabic, Chinese, English, French, Russian and Spanish texts of the present Protocol shall be equally authentic.

IN WITNESS THEREOF the undersigned plenipotentiaries, being duly authorized thereto by their respective Governments, have signed the present Protocol.

64. INTERNATIONAL CONVENTION FOR THE PROTECTION OF ALL PERSONS FROM ENFORCED DISAPPEARANCE, 2006

This Convention was adopted by General Assembly Resolution 61/177 on 20 December 2006, without a vote, following its earlier adoption by the Human Rights Council in Resolution 1/1 of 29 June 2006. In accordance with Article 39, it will enter into force after ratification by twenty States.

Further reading

McCRORY, S., 'The International Convention for the Protection of all Persons from Enforced Disappearance', (2007) 7 *Human Rights Law Review* 545.

WEISSBRODT, D. and BERGQUIST, A., 'Extraordinary Rendition: A Human Rights Analysis', (2006) 19 *Harvard Human Rights Journal* 123.

TEXT

Preamble

The States Parties to this Convention,

Considering the obligation of States under the Charter of the United Nations to promote universal respect for, and observance of, human rights and fundamental freedoms,

Having regard to the Universal Declaration of Human Rights,

Recalling the International Covenant on Economic, Social and Cultural Rights, the International Covenant on Civil and Political Rights and the other relevant international instruments in the fields of human rights, humanitarian law and international criminal law,

Also recalling the Declaration on the Protection of All Persons from Enforced Disappearance adopted by the General Assembly of the United Nations in its resolution 47/133 of 18 December 1992, Aware of the extreme seriousness of enforced disappearance, which constitutes a crime and, in certain circumstances defined in international law, a crime against humanity,

Determined to prevent enforced disappearances and to combat impunity for the crime of enforced disappearance,

Considering the right of any person not to be subjected to enforced disappearance, the right of victims to justice and to reparation,

Affirming the right of any victim to know the truth about the circumstances of an enforced disappearance and the fate of the disappeared person, and the right to freedom to seek, receive and impart information to this end,

Have agreed on the following articles:

PART I

Article 1

1. No one shall be subjected to enforced disappearance.

2. No exceptional circumstances whatsoever, whether a state of war or a threat of war, internal political instability or any other public emergency, may be invoked as a justification for enforced disappearance.

Article 2

For the purposes of this Convention, 'enforced disappearance' is considered to be the arrest, detention, abduction or any other form of deprivation of liberty by agents of the State or by persons or groups of persons acting with the authorization, support or acquiescence of the State, followed by a refusal to acknowledge the deprivation of liberty or by concealment of the fate or whereabouts of the disappeared person, which place such a person outside the protection of the law.

Article 3

Each State Party shall take appropriate measures to investigate acts defined in article 2 committed by persons or groups of persons acting without the authorization, support or acquiescence of the State and to bring those responsible to justice.

Article 4

Each State Party shall take the necessary measures to ensure that enforced disappearance constitutes an offence under its criminal law.

Article 5

The widespread or systematic practice of enforced disappearance constitutes a crime against humanity as defined in applicable international law and shall attract the consequences provided for under such applicable international law.

Article 6

1. Each State Party shall take the necessary measures to hold criminally responsible at least:

   (a) Any person who commits, orders, solicits or induces the commission of, attempts to commit, is an accomplice to or participates in an enforced disappearance;

   (b) A superior who:
   (i) Knew, or consciously disregarded information which clearly indicated, that subordinates under his or her effective authority and control were committing or about to commit a crime of enforced disappearance;
   (ii) Exercised effective responsibility for and control over activities which were concerned with the crime of enforced disappearance; and
   (iii) Failed to take all necessary and reasonable measures within his or her power to prevent or repress the commission of an enforced disappearance or to submit the matter to the competent authorities for investigation and prosecution;

   (c) Subparagraph (b) above is without prejudice to the higher standards of responsibility applicable under relevant international law to a military commander or to a person effectively acting as a military commander.

2. No order or instruction from any public authority, civilian, military or other, may be invoked to justify an offence of enforced disappearance.

Article 7

1. Each State Party shall make the offence of enforced disappearance punishable by appropriate penalties which take into account its extreme seriousness.

2. Each State Party may establish:

   (a) Mitigating circumstances, in particular for persons who, having been implicated in the commission of an enforced disappearance, effectively contribute to bringing the disappeared person forward alive or make it possible to clarify cases of enforced disappearance or to identify the perpetrators of an enforced disappearance;

   (b) Without prejudice to other criminal procedures, aggravating circumstances, in particular in the event of the death of the disappeared person or the commission of an enforced disappearance in respect of pregnant women, minors, persons with disabilities or other particularly vulnerable persons.

Article 8

Without prejudice to article 5,

1. A State Party which applies a statute of limitations in respect of enforced disappearance shall take the necessary measures to ensure that the term of limitation for criminal proceedings:

   (a) Is of long duration and is proportionate to the extreme seriousness of this offence;

   (b) Commences from the moment when the offence of enforced disappearance ceases, taking into account its continuous nature.

2. Each State Party shall guarantee the right of victims of enforced disappearance to an effective remedy during the term of limitation.

Article 9

1. Each State Party shall take the necessary measures to establish its competence to exercise jurisdiction over the offence of enforced disappearance:

   (a) When the offence is committed in any territory under its jurisdiction or on board a ship or aircraft registered in that State;

   (b) When the alleged offender is one of its nationals;

   (c) When the disappeared person is one of its nationals and the State Party considers it appropriate.

2. Each State Party shall likewise take such measures as may be necessary to establish its competence to exercise jurisdiction over the offence of enforced disappearance when the alleged offender is present in any territory under its jurisdiction, unless it extradites or surrenders him or her to another State in accordance with its international obligations or surrenders him or her to an international criminal tribunal whose jurisdiction it has recognized.

3. This Convention does not exclude any additional criminal jurisdiction exercised in accordance with national law.

Article 10

1. Upon being satisfied, after an examination of the information available to it, that the circumstances so warrant, any State Party in whose territory a person suspected of having committed an offence of enforced disappearance is present shall take him or her into custody or take such other legal measures as are necessary to ensure his or her presence. The custody and other legal measures shall be as provided for in the law of that State Party but may be maintained only for such time as is necessary to ensure the person's presence at criminal, surrender or extradition proceedings.

2. A State Party which has taken the measures referred to in paragraph 1 of this article shall immediately carry out a preliminary inquiry or investigations to establish the facts. It shall notify the States Parties referred to in article 9, paragraph 1, of the measures it has taken in pursuance of paragraph 1 of this article, including detention and the circumstances warranting detention, and of the findings of its preliminary inquiry or its investigations, indicating whether it intends to exercise its jurisdiction.

3. Any person in custody pursuant to paragraph 1 of this article may communicate immediately with the nearest appropriate representative of the State of which he or she is a national, or, if he or she is a stateless person, with the representative of the State where he or she usually resides.

Article 11

1. The State Party in the territory under whose jurisdiction a person alleged to have committed an offence of enforced disappearance is found shall, if it does not extradite that person or surrender him or her to another State in accordance with its international obligations or surrender him or her to an international criminal tribunal whose jurisdiction it has recognized, submit the case to its competent authorities for the purpose of prosecution.

2. These authorities shall take their decision in the same manner as in the case of any ordinary offence of a serious nature under the law of that State Party. In the cases referred to in article 9, paragraph 2, the standards of evidence required for prosecution and conviction shall in no way be less stringent than those which apply in the cases referred to in article 9, paragraph 1.

3. Any person against whom proceedings are brought in connection with an offence of enforced disappearance shall be guaranteed fair treatment at all stages of the proceedings. Any person tried for an offence of enforced disappearance shall benefit from a fair trial before a competent, independent and impartial court or tribunal established by law.

Article 12

1. Each State Party shall ensure that any individual who alleges that a person has been subjected to enforced disappearance has the right to report the facts to the competent authorities, which shall examine the allegation promptly and impartially and, where necessary, undertake without delay a thorough and impartial investigation. Appropriate steps shall be taken, where necessary, to ensure that the complainant, witnesses, relatives of the disappeared person and their defence counsel, as well as persons participating in the investigation, are protected against all ill-treatment or intimidation as a consequence of the complaint or any evidence given.

2. Where there are reasonable grounds for believing that a person has been subjected to enforced disappearance, the authorities referred to in paragraph 1 of this article shall undertake an investigation, even if there has been no formal complaint.

3. Each State Party shall ensure that the authorities referred to in paragraph 1 of this article:

(a) Have the necessary powers and resources to conduct the investigation effectively, including access to the documentation and other information relevant to their investigation;

(b) Have access, if necessary with the prior authorization of a judicial authority, which shall rule promptly on the matter, to any place of detention or any other place where there are reasonable grounds to believe that the disappeared person may be present.

4. Each State Party shall take the necessary measures to prevent and sanction acts that hinder the conduct of an investigation. It shall ensure in particular that persons suspected of having committed an offence of enforced disappearance are not in a position to influence the progress of an investigation by means of pressure or acts of intimidation or reprisal aimed at the complainant, witnesses, relatives of the disappeared person or their defence counsel, or at persons participating in the investigation.

Article 13

1. For the purposes of extradition between States Parties, the offence of enforced disappearance shall not be regarded as a political offence or as an offence connected with a political offence or as an offence inspired by political motives. Accordingly, a request for extradition based on such an offence may not be refused on these grounds alone.

2. The offence of enforced disappearance shall be deemed to be included as an extraditable offence in any extradition treaty existing between States Parties before the entry into force of this Convention.

3. States Parties undertake to include the offence of enforced disappearance as an extraditable offence in any extradition treaty subsequently to be concluded between them.

4. If a State Party which makes extradition conditional on the existence of a treaty receives a request for extradition from another State Party with which it has no extradition treaty, it may consider this Convention as the necessary legal basis for extradition in respect of the offence of enforced disappearance.

5. States Parties which do not make extradition conditional on the existence of a treaty shall recognize the offence of enforced disappearance as an extraditable offence between themselves.

6. Extradition shall, in all cases, be subject to the conditions provided for by the law of the requested State Party or by applicable extradition treaties, including, in particular, conditions relating to the minimum penalty requirement for extradition and the grounds upon which the requested State Party may refuse extradition or make it subject to certain conditions.

7. Nothing in this Convention shall be interpreted as imposing an obligation to extradite if the requested State Party has substantial grounds for believing that the request has been made for the purpose of prosecuting or punishing a person on account of that person's sex, race, religion, nationality, ethnic origin, political opinions or membership of

a particular social group, or that compliance with the request would cause harm to that person for any one of these reasons.

Article 14

1. States Parties shall afford one another the greatest measure of mutual legal assistance in connection with criminal proceedings brought in respect of an offence of enforced disappearance, including the supply of all evidence at their disposal that is necessary for the proceedings.

2. Such mutual legal assistance shall be subject to the conditions provided for by the domestic law of the requested State Party or by applicable treaties on mutual legal assistance, including, in particular, the conditions in relation to the grounds upon which the requested State Party may refuse to grant mutual legal assistance or may make it subject to conditions.

Article 15

States Parties shall cooperate with each other and shall afford one another the greatest measure of mutual assistance with a view to assisting victims of enforced disappearance, and in searching for, locating and releasing disappeared persons and, in the event of death, in exhuming and identifying them and returning their remains.

Article 16

1. No State Party shall expel, return ('refouler'), surrender or extradite a person to another State where there are substantial grounds for believing that he or she would be in danger of being subjected to enforced disappearance.

2. For the purpose of determining whether there are such grounds, the competent authorities shall take into account all relevant considerations, including, where applicable, the existence in the State concerned of a consistent pattern of gross, flagrant or mass violations of human rights or of serious violations of international humanitarian law.

Article 17

1. No one shall be held in secret detention.

2. Without prejudice to other international obligations of the State Party with regard to the deprivation of liberty, each State Party shall, in its legislation:

    (a) Establish the conditions under which orders of deprivation of liberty may be given;

    (b) Indicate those authorities authorized to order the deprivation of liberty;

    (c) Guarantee that any person deprived of liberty shall be held solely in officially recognized and supervised places of deprivation of liberty;

    (d) Guarantee that any person deprived of liberty shall be authorized to communicate with and be visited by his or her family, counsel or any other person of his or her choice, subject only to the conditions established by law, or, if he or she is a foreigner, to communicate with his or her consular authorities, in accordance with applicable international law;

    (e) Guarantee access by the competent and legally authorized authorities and institutions to the places where persons are deprived of liberty, if necessary with prior authorization from a judicial authority;

(f) Guarantee that any person deprived of liberty or, in the case of a suspected enforced disappearance, since the person deprived of liberty is not able to exercise this right, any persons with a legitimate interest, such as relatives of the person deprived of liberty, their representatives or their counsel, shall, in all circumstances, be entitled to take proceedings before a court, in order that the court may decide without delay on the lawfulness of the deprivation of liberty and order the person's release if such deprivation of liberty is not lawful.

3. Each State Party shall assure the compilation and maintenance of one or more up-to-date official registers and/or records of persons deprived of liberty, which shall be made promptly available, upon request, to any judicial or other competent authority or institution authorized for that purpose by the law of the State Party concerned or any relevant international legal instrument to which the State concerned is a party. The information contained therein shall include, as a minimum:

(a) The identity of the person deprived of liberty;

(b) The date, time and place where the person was deprived of liberty and the identity of the authority that deprived the person of liberty;

(c) The authority that ordered the deprivation of liberty and the grounds for the deprivation of liberty;

(d) The authority responsible for supervising the deprivation of liberty;

(e) The place of deprivation of liberty, the date and time of admission to the place of deprivation of liberty and the authority responsible for the place of deprivation of liberty;

(f) Elements relating to the state of health of the person deprived of liberty;

(g) In the event of death during the deprivation of liberty, the circumstances and cause of death and the destination of the remains;

(h) The date and time of release or transfer to another place of detention, the destination and the authority responsible for the transfer.

Article 18

1. Subject to articles 19 and 20, each State Party shall guarantee to any person with a legitimate interest in this information, such as relatives of the person deprived of liberty, their representatives or their counsel, access to at least the following information:

(a) The authority that ordered the deprivation of liberty;

(b) The date, time and place where the person was deprived of liberty and admitted to the place of deprivation of liberty;

(c) The authority responsible for supervising the deprivation of liberty;

(d) The whereabouts of the person deprived of liberty, including, in the event of a transfer to another place of deprivation of liberty, the destination and the authority responsible for the transfer;

(e) The date, time and place of release;

(f) Elements relating to the state of health of the person deprived of liberty;

(g) In the event of death during the deprivation of liberty, the circumstances and cause of death and the destination of the remains.

2. Appropriate measures shall be taken, where necessary, to protect the persons referred to in paragraph 1 of this article, as well as persons participating in the investigation, from any ill-treatment, intimidation or sanction as a result of the search for information concerning a person deprived of liberty.

Article 19

1. Personal information, including medical and genetic data, which is collected and/or transmitted within the framework of the search for a disappeared person shall not be used or made available for purposes other than the search for the disappeared person. This is without prejudice to the use of such information in criminal proceedings relating to an offence of enforced disappearance or the exercise of the right to obtain reparation.

2. The collection, processing, use and storage of personal information, including medical and genetic data, shall not infringe or have the effect of infringing the human rights, fundamental freedoms or human dignity of an individual.

Article 20

1. Only where a person is under the protection of the law and the deprivation of liberty is subject to judicial control may the right to information referred to in article 18 be restricted, on an exceptional basis, where strictly necessary and where provided for by law, and if the transmission of the information would adversely affect the privacy or safety of the person, hinder a criminal investigation, or for other equivalent reasons in accordance with the law, and in conformity with applicable international law and with the objectives of this Convention. In no case shall there be restrictions on the right to information referred to in article 18 that could constitute conduct defined in article 2 or be in violation of article 17, paragraph 1.

2. Without prejudice to consideration of the lawfulness of the deprivation of a person's liberty, States Parties shall guarantee to the persons referred to in article 18, paragraph 1, the right to a prompt and effective judicial remedy as a means of obtaining without delay the information referred to in article 18, paragraph 1. This right to a remedy may not be suspended or restricted in any circumstances.

Article 21

Each State Party shall take the necessary measures to ensure that persons deprived of liberty are released in a manner permitting reliable verification that they have actually been released. Each State Party shall also take the necessary measures to assure the physical integrity of such persons and their ability to exercise fully their rights at the time of release, without prejudice to any obligations to which such persons may be subject under national law.

Article 22

Without prejudice to article 6, each State Party shall take the necessary measures to prevent and impose sanctions for the following conduct:

(a) Delaying or obstructing the remedies referred to in article 17, paragraph 2 (f), and article 20, paragraph 2;

(b) Failure to record the deprivation of liberty of any person, or the recording of any information which the official responsible for the official register knew or should have known to be inaccurate;

(c) Refusal to provide information on the deprivation of liberty of a person, or the provision of inaccurate information, even though the legal requirements for providing such information have been met.

Article 23

1. Each State Party shall ensure that the training of law enforcement personnel, civil or military, medical personnel, public officials and other persons who may be involved in the custody or treatment of any person deprived of liberty includes the necessary education and information regarding the relevant provisions of this Convention, in order to:

(a) Prevent the involvement of such officials in enforced disappearances;

(b) Emphasize the importance of prevention and investigations in relation to enforced disappearances;

(c) Ensure that the urgent need to resolve cases of enforced disappearance is recognized.

2. Each State Party shall ensure that orders or instructions prescribing, authorizing or encouraging enforced disappearance are prohibited. Each State Party shall guarantee that a person who refuses to obey such an order will not be punished.

3. Each State Party shall take the necessary measures to ensure that the persons referred to in paragraph 1 of this article who have reason to believe that an enforced disappearance has occurred or is planned report the matter to their superiors and, where necessary, to the appropriate authorities or bodies vested with powers of review or remedy.

Article 24

1. For the purposes of this Convention, 'victim' means the disappeared person and any individual who has suffered harm as the direct result of an enforced disappearance.

2. Each victim has the right to know the truth regarding the circumstances of the enforced disappearance, the progress and results of the investigation and the fate of the disappeared person. Each State Party shall take appropriate measures in this regard.

3. Each State Party shall take all appropriate measures to search for, locate and release disappeared persons and, in the event of death, to locate, respect and return their remains.

4. Each State Party shall ensure in its legal system that the victims of enforced disappearance have the right to obtain reparation and prompt, fair and adequate compensation.

5. The right to obtain reparation referred to in paragraph 4 of this article covers material and moral damages and, where appropriate, other forms of reparation such as:

(a) Restitution;

(b) Rehabilitation;

(c) Satisfaction, including restoration of dignity and reputation;

(d) Guarantees of non-repetition.

6. Without prejudice to the obligation to continue the investigation until the fate of the disappeared person has been clarified, each State Party shall take the appropriate steps with regard to the legal situation of disappeared persons whose fate has not been clarified and that of their relatives, in fields such as social welfare, financial matters, family law and property rights.

7. Each State Party shall guarantee the right to form and participate freely in organizations and associations concerned with attempting to establish the circumstances of enforced disappearances and the fate of disappeared persons, and to assist victims of enforced disappearance.

Article 25

1. Each State Party shall take the necessary measures to prevent and punish under its criminal law:

  (a) The wrongful removal of children who are subjected to enforced disappearance, children whose father, mother or legal guardian is subjected to enforced disappearance or children born during the captivity of a mother subjected to enforced disappearance;

  (b) The falsification, concealment or destruction of documents attesting to the true identity of the children referred to in subparagraph (a) above.

2. Each State Party shall take the necessary measures to search for and identify the children referred to in paragraph 1 (a) of this article and to return them to their families of origin, in accordance with legal procedures and applicable international agreements.

3. States Parties shall assist one another in searching for, identifying and locating the children referred to in paragraph 1 (a) of this article.

4. Given the need to protect the best interests of the children referred to in paragraph 1 *(a)* of this article and their right to preserve, or to have re-established, their identity, including their nationality, name and family relations as recognized by law, States Parties which recognize a system of adoption or other form of placement of children shall have legal procedures in place to review the adoption or placement procedure, and, where appropriate, to annul any adoption or placement of children that originated in an enforced disappearance.

5. In all cases, and in particular in all matters relating to this article, the best interests of the child shall be a primary consideration, and a child who is capable of forming his or her own views shall have the right to express those views freely, the views of the child being given due weight in accordance with the age and maturity of the child.

PART II

Article 26

1. A Committee on Enforced Disappearances (hereinafter referred to as 'the Committee') shall be established to carry out the functions provided for under this Convention. The Committee shall consist of ten experts of high moral character and recognized competence in the field of human rights, who shall serve in their personal capacity and be independent and impartial. The members of the Committee shall be elected by the States Parties according to equitable geographical distribution. Due account shall be taken of the usefulness of the participation in the work of the Committee of persons having relevant legal experience and of balanced gender representation.

2. The members of the Committee shall be elected by secret ballot from a list of persons nominated by States Parties from among their nationals, at biennial meetings of the States

Parties convened by the Secretary-General of the United Nations for this purpose. At those meetings, for which two thirds of the States Parties shall constitute a quorum, the persons elected to the Committee shall be those who obtain the largest number of votes and an absolute majority of the votes of the representatives of States Parties present and voting.

3. The initial election shall be held no later than six months after the date of entry into force of this Convention. Four months before the date of each election, the Secretary-General of the United Nations shall address a letter to the States Parties inviting them to submit nominations within three months. The Secretary-General shall prepare a list in alphabetical order of all persons thus nominated, indicating the State Party which nominated each candidate, and shall submit this list to all States Parties.

4. The members of the Committee shall be elected for a term of four years. They shall be eligible for re-election once. However, the term of five of the members elected at the first election shall expire at the end of two years; immediately after the first election, the names of these five members shall be chosen by lot by the chairman of the meeting referred to in paragraph 2 of this article.

5. If a member of the Committee dies or resigns or for any other reason can no longer perform his or her Committee duties, the State Party which nominated him or her shall, in accordance with the criteria set out in paragraph 1 of this article, appoint another candidate from among its nationals to serve out his or her term, subject to the approval of the majority of the States Parties. Such approval shall be considered to have been obtained unless half or more of the States Parties respond negatively within six weeks of having been informed by the Secretary-General of the United Nations of the proposed appointment.

6. The Committee shall establish its own rules of procedure.

7. The Secretary-General of the United Nations shall provide the Committee with the necessary means, staff and facilities for the effective performance of its functions. The Secretary-General of the United Nations shall convene the initial meeting of the Committee.

8. The members of the Committee shall be entitled to the facilities, privileges and immunities of experts on mission for the United Nations, as laid down in the relevant sections of the Convention on the Privileges and Immunities of the United Nations.

9. Each State Party shall cooperate with the Committee and assist its members in the fulfilment of their mandate, to the extent of the Committee's functions that the State Party has accepted.

Article 27

A Conference of the States Parties will take place at the earliest four years and at the latest six years following the entry into force of this Convention to evaluate the functioning of the Committee and to decide, in accordance with the procedure described in article 44, paragraph 2, whether it is appropriate to transfer to another body—without excluding any possibility—the monitoring of this Convention, in accordance with the functions defined in articles 28 to 36.

Article 28

1. In the framework of the competencies granted by this Convention, the Committee shall cooperate with all relevant organs, offices and specialized agencies and funds of

the United Nations, with the treaty bodies instituted by international instruments, with the special procedures of the United Nations and with the relevant regional intergovernmental organizations or bodies, as well as with all relevant State institutions, agencies or offices working towards the protection of all persons against enforced disappearances.

2. As it discharges its mandate, the Committee shall consult other treaty bodies instituted by relevant international human rights instruments, in particular the Human Rights Committee instituted by the International Covenant on Civil and Political Rights, with a view to ensuring the consistency of their respective observations and recommendations.

Article 29

1. Each State Party shall submit to the Committee, through the Secretary-General of the United Nations, a report on the measures taken to give effect to its obligations under this Convention, within two years after the entry into force of this Convention for the State Party concerned.

2. The Secretary-General of the United Nations shall make this report available to all States Parties.

3. Each report shall be considered by the Committee, which shall issue such comments, observations or recommendations as it may deem appropriate. The comments, observations or recommendations shall be communicated to the State Party concerned, which may respond to them, on its own initiative or at the request of the Committee.

4. The Committee may also request States Parties to provide additional information on the implementation of this Convention.

Article 30

1. A request that a disappeared person should be sought and found may be submitted to the Committee, as a matter of urgency, by relatives of the disappeared person or their legal representatives, their counsel or any person authorized by them, as well as by any other person having a legitimate interest.

2. If the Committee considers that a request for urgent action submitted in pursuance of paragraph 1 of this article:

    (a) Is not manifestly unfounded;

    (b) Does not constitute an abuse of the right of submission of such requests;

    (c) Has already been duly presented to the competent bodies of the State Party concerned, such as those authorized to undertake investigations, where such a possibility exists;

    (d) Is not incompatible with the provisions of this Convention; and

    (e) The same matter is not being examined under another procedure of international investigation or settlement of the same nature; it shall request the State Party concerned to provide it with information on the situation of the persons sought, within a time limit set by the Committee.

3. In the light of the information provided by the State Party concerned in accordance with paragraph 2 of this article, the Committee may transmit recommendations to the State Party, including a request that the State Party should take all the necessary measures, including interim measures, to locate and protect the person concerned in accordance with this Convention and to inform the Committee, within a specified period of time, of measures taken, taking into account the urgency of the situation. The Committee

shall inform the person submitting the urgent action request of its recommendations and of the information provided to it by the State as it becomes available.

4. The Committee shall continue its efforts to work with the State Party concerned for as long as the fate of the person sought remains unresolved. The person presenting the request shall be kept informed.

Article 31

1. A State Party may at the time of ratification of this Convention or at any time afterwards declare that it recognizes the competence of the Committee to receive and consider communications from or on behalf of individuals subject to its jurisdiction claiming to be victims of a violation by this State Party of provisions of this Convention. The Committee shall not admit any communication concerning a State Party which has not made such a declaration.

2. The Committee shall consider a communication inadmissible where:

   (a) The communication is anonymous;

   (b) The communication constitutes an abuse of the right of submission of such communications or is incompatible with the provisions of this Convention;

   (c) The same matter is being examined under another procedure of international investigation or settlement of the same nature; or where

   (d) All effective available domestic remedies have not been exhausted. This rule shall not apply where the application of the remedies is unreasonably prolonged.

3. If the Committee considers that the communication meets the requirements set out in paragraph 2 of this article, it shall transmit the communication to the State Party concerned, requesting it to provide observations and comments within a time limit set by the Committee.

4. At any time after the receipt of a communication and before a determination on the merits has been reached, the Committee may transmit to the State Party concerned for its urgent consideration a request that the State Party will take such interim measures as may be necessary to avoid possible irreparable damage to the victims of the alleged violation. Where the Committee exercises its discretion, this does not imply a determination on admissibility or on the merits of the communication.

5. The Committee shall hold closed meetings when examining communications under the present article. It shall inform the author of a communication of the responses provided by the State Party concerned. When the Committee decides to finalize the procedure, it shall communicate its views to the State Party and to the author of the communication.

Article 32

A State Party to this Convention may at any time declare that it recognizes the competence of the Committee to receive and consider communications in which a State Party claims that another State Party is not fulfilling its obligations under this Convention. The Committee shall not receive communications concerning a State Party which has not made such a declaration, nor communications from a State Party which has not made such a declaration.

Article 33

1. If the Committee receives reliable information indicating that a State Party is seriously violating the provisions of this Convention, it may, after consultation with the State

Party concerned, request one or more of its members to undertake a visit and report back to it without delay.

2. The Committee shall notify the State Party concerned, in writing, of its intention to organize a visit, indicating the composition of the delegation and the purpose of the visit. The State Party shall answer the Committee within a reasonable time.

3. Upon a substantiated request by the State Party, the Committee may decide to postpone or cancel its visit.

4. If the State Party agrees to the visit, the Committee and the State Party concerned shall work together to define the modalities of the visit and the State Party shall provide the Committee with all the facilities needed for the successful completion of the visit.

5. Following its visit, the Committee shall communicate to the State Party concerned its observations and recommendations.

Article 34

If the Committee receives information which appears to it to contain well-founded indications that enforced disappearance is being practised on a widespread or systematic basis in the territory under the jurisdiction of a State Party, it may, after seeking from the State Party concerned all relevant information on the situation, urgently bring the matter to the attention of the General Assembly of the United Nations, through the Secretary-General of the United Nations.

Article 35

1. The Committee shall have competence solely in respect of enforced disappearances which commenced after the entry into force of this Convention.

2. If a State becomes a party to this Convention after its entry into force, the obligations of that State vis-à-vis the Committee shall relate only to enforced disappearances which commenced after the entry into force of this Convention for the State concerned.

Article 36

1. The Committee shall submit an annual report on its activities under this Convention to the States Parties and to the General Assembly of the United Nations.

2. Before an observation on a State Party is published in the annual report, the State Party concerned shall be informed in advance and shall be given reasonable time to answer. This State Party may request the publication of its comments or observations in the report.

PART III

Article 37

Nothing in this Convention shall affect any provisions which are more conducive to the protection of all persons from enforced disappearance and which may be contained in:

  (a) The law of a State Party;
  (b) International law in force for that State.

Article 38

1. This Convention is open for signature by all Member States of the United Nations.

2. This Convention is subject to ratification by all Member States of the United Nations. Instruments of ratification shall be deposited with the Secretary-General of the United Nations.

3. This Convention is open to accession by all Member States of the United Nations. Accession shall be effected by the deposit of an instrument of accession with the Secretary-General.

Article 39

1. This Convention shall enter into force on the thirtieth day after the date of deposit with the Secretary-General of the United Nations of the twentieth instrument of ratification or accession.

2. For each State ratifying or acceding to this Convention after the deposit of the twentieth instrument of ratification or accession, this Convention shall enter into force on the thirtieth day after the date of the deposit of that State's instrument of ratification or accession.

Article 40

The Secretary-General of the United Nations shall notify all States Members of the United Nations and all States which have signed or acceded to this Convention of the following:

(a) Signatures, ratifications and accessions under article 38;

(b) The date of entry into force of this Convention under article 39.

Article 41

The provisions of this Convention shall apply to all parts of federal States without any limitations or exceptions.

Article 42

1. Any dispute between two or more States Parties concerning the interpretation or application of this Convention which cannot be settled through negotiation or by the procedures expressly provided for in this Convention shall, at the request of one of them, be submitted to arbitration. If within six months from the date of the request for arbitration the Parties are unable to agree on the organization of the arbitration, any one of those Parties may refer the dispute to the International Court of Justice by request in conformity with the Statute of the Court.

2. A State may, at the time of signature or ratification of this Convention or accession thereto, declare that it does not consider itself bound by paragraph 1 of this article. The other States Parties shall not be bound by paragraph 1 of this article with respect to any State Party having made such a declaration.

3. Any State Party having made a declaration in accordance with the provisions of paragraph 2 of this article may at any time withdraw this declaration by notification to the Secretary-General of the United Nations.

Article 43

This Convention is without prejudice to the provisions of international humanitarian law, including the obligations of the High Contracting Parties to the four Geneva Conventions of 12 August 1949 and the two Additional Protocols thereto of 8 June 1977, or to the opportunity available to any State Party to authorize the International Committee of the Red Cross to visit places of detention in situations not covered by international humanitarian law.

Article 44

1. Any State Party to this Convention may propose an amendment and file it with the Secretary-General of the United Nations. The Secretary-General shall thereupon communicate the proposed amendment to the States Parties to this Convention with a request that they indicate whether they favour a conference of States Parties for the purpose of considering and voting upon the proposal. In the event that within four months from the date of such communication at least one third of the States Parties favour such a conference, the Secretary-General shall convene the conference under the auspices of the United Nations.

2. Any amendment adopted by a majority of two thirds of the States Parties present and voting at the conference shall be submitted by the Secretary-General of the United Nations to all the States Parties for acceptance.

3. An amendment adopted in accordance with paragraph 1 of this article shall enter into force when two thirds of the States Parties to this Convention have accepted it in accordance with their respective constitutional processes.

4. When amendments enter into force, they shall be binding on those States Parties which have accepted them, other States Parties still being bound by the provisions of this Convention and any earlier amendment which they have accepted.

Article 45

1. This Convention, of which the Arabic, Chinese, English, French, Russian and Spanish texts are equally authentic, shall be deposited with the Secretary-General of the United Nations.

2. The Secretary-General of the United Nations shall transmit certified copies of this Convention to all States referred to in article 38.

PART THREE

CONTRIBUTION OF THE INTERNATIONAL LABOUR ORGANIZATION

INTRODUCTION

The International Labour Organization is one of seventeen Specialized Agencies brought into relationship with the United Nations under Articles 57 and 63 of the United Nations Charter. The Organization started its life in 1919, and it has the distinction of being in advance of other international institutions in that its major concern is social justice. The preamble to the Constitution begins: 'Whereas universal and lasting peace can be established only if it is based upon social justice . . . ' Now, in the era of the United Nations, there is more emphasis on the attainment of social justice as an aim of international co-operation and action. The Constitution of the ILO with various amendments (some of which are not yet in force), can be found at **http://www.ilo.org/ilolex/english/constq.htm**. The aims and purposes of the ILO are set out in the Declaration of Philadelphia adopted by the General Conference in 1944, and printed below.

The ILO has played a prominent and pioneer role in standard-setting in carefully drafted conventions dealing with specific subject matters, and it has now identified eight conventions as being fundamental to the rights of human beings at work, irrespective of the level of development of individual member States. These rights are seen as a precondition for all the others, and can be grouped under the following four rubrics: (a) Freedom of association: Freedom of Association and Protection of the Right to Organize Convention, 1948; and Right to Organize and Collective Bargaining Convention, 1949; (b) Abolition of forced labour: Forced Labour Convention, 1939; and Abolition of Forced Labour Convention, 1957; (c) Equality: Discrimination (Employment and Occupation) Convention, 1958; and Equal Remuneration Convention, 1951; (d) Elimination of child labour: Minimum Age Convention, 1973; and Worst Forms of Child Labour Convention, 1999. Those conventions and other relevant instruments, including the Declaration on Fundamental Principles and Rights at Work, 1998, are included in this Part.

The ILO, along with other Specialized Agencies, submits periodic reports to the United Nations Human Rights Council.

Further reading

CHOLEWINSKI, R., *Migrant Workers in International Human Rights Law: Their Protection in Countries of Employment*, Oxford: Clarendon Press, 1997.

INTERNATIONAL LABOUR CONFERENCE, *Report of the Committee of Experts on the Application of Conventions and Recommendations*, Geneva: International Labour Office, 2009.

JENKS, C. W., *Human Rights and International Labour Standards*, London: Stevens, 1960.

——, *Social Justice in the Law of Nations: The ILO Impact after Fifty Years*, London: Royal Institute of International Affairs; Oxford: Oxford University Press, 1970.

LEARY, V., *International Labour Conventions and National Law: The Effectiveness of the Automatic Incorporation of Treaties in National Legal Systems*, Dordrecht: Martinus Nijhoff, 1982.

MUNDLAK, G., 'The Right to Work: Linking Human Rights and Employment Policy', (2007) 146 *International Labour Review* 189.

RODGERS, G., SWEPSTON, L., LEE, E. and VAN DAELE, J., *The International Labour Organization and the Quest for Social Justice, 1919–2009*, Geneva: ILO, 2009.

RUBIN, N., ed., with KALULA, E. and HEPPLE, B., *Code of International Labour Law: Law, Practice and Jurisprudence*, Cambridge: Cambridge University Press, 3 vols., 2005.

SERVAIS, J.-M., *International Labour Law*, Leiden: Kluwer Law International, 2nd edn., 2008.

TREBILCOCK, A., 'The Development of International Labour Standards' and 'The Implementation of International Labour Standards': **http://untreaty.un.org/cod/avl/lectureseries.html#labour**.

65. DECLARATION CONCERNING THE AIMS AND PURPOSES OF THE INTERNATIONAL LABOUR ORGANIZATION, 1944

As noted above, the ILO Conference adopted the 'Declaration of Philadelphia' in 1944, and it is now annexed to and forms an integral part of the Constitution.

Further reading

LEE, E., 'The Declaration of Philadelphia: Retrospect and prospect', (1944) 133 *International Labour Review* 467.

TEXT

The General Conference of the International Labour Organization meeting in its Twenty-sixth Session in Philadelphia, hereby adopts this tenth day of May in the year nineteen hundred and forty-four, the present Declaration of the aims and purposes of the International Labour Organization and of the principles which should inspire the policy of its Members.

I

The Conference reaffirms the fundamental principles on which the Organization is based and, in particular, that:

(a) labour is not a commodity;

(b) freedom of expression and of association are essential to sustained progress;

(c) poverty anywhere constitutes a danger to prosperity everywhere;

(d) the war against want required to be carried on with unrelenting vigour within each nation, and by continuous and concerted international effort in which the representatives of workers and employers, enjoying equal status with those of Governments, join with them in free discussion and democratic decision with a view to the promotion of the common welfare.

II

Believing that experience has fully demonstrated the truth of the statement in the Constitution of the International Labour Organization that lasting peace can be established only if it is based on social justice, the Conference affirms that:

(a) all human beings, irrespective of race, creed or sex, have the right to pursue both their material well-being and their spiritual development in conditions of freedom and dignity, of economic security and equal opportunity;

(b) the attainment of the conditions in which this shall be possible must constitute the central aim of national and international policy;

(c) all national and international policies and measures, in particular those of an economic and financial character, should be judged in this light and accepted only in so far as they may be held to promote and not to hinder the achievement of this fundamental objective;

(d) it is a responsibility of the International Labour Organization to examine and consider all international economic and financial policies and measures in the light of this fundamental objective;

(e) in discharging the tasks entrusted to it the International Labour Organization, having considered all relevant economic and financial factors, may include in its decisions and recommendations any provisions which it considers appropriate.

III

The Conference recognizes the solemn obligation of the International Labour Organization to further among the nations of the world programmes which will achieve:

(a) full employment and the raising of standards of living;

(b) the employment of workers in the occupations in which they can have the satisfaction of giving the fullest measure of their skill and attainments and make their greatest contribution to the common well-being;

(c) the provision, as a means to the attainment of this end and under adequate guarantees for all concerned, of facilities for training and the transfer of labour, including migration for employment and settlement;

(d) policies in regard to wages and earnings, hours and other conditions of work calculated to ensure a just share of the fruits of progress to all, and a minimum living wage to all employed and in need of such protection;

(e) the effective recognition of the right of collective bargaining, the co-operation of management and labour in the continuous improvement of productive efficiency, and the collaboration of workers and employers in the preparation and application of social and economic measures;

(f) the extension of social security measures to provide a basic income to all in need of such protection and comprehensive medical care;

(g) adequate protection for the life and health of workers in all occupations;

(h) provision for child welfare and maternity protection;

(i) the provision of adequate nutrition, housing and facilities for recreation and culture;

(j) the assurance of equality of educational and vocational opportunity.

IV

Confident that the fuller and broader utilization of the world's productive resources necessary for the achievement of the objectives set forth in this Declaration can be secured by effective international and national action, including measures to expand production and consumption, to avoid severe economic fluctuations, to promote the economic and social advancement of the less developed regions of the world, to assure greater stability in world prices of primary products, and to promote a high and steady volume of international trade, the Conference pledges the full co-operation of the International Labour Organization with such international bodies as may be entrusted with a share of the responsibility for this great task and for the promotion of the health, education and well-being of all peoples.

V

The Conference affirms that the principles set forth in this Declaration are fully applicable to all peoples everywhere and that, while the manner of their application must be determined with due regard to the stage of social and economic development reached by each people, their progressive application to peoples who are still dependent, as well as to those who have already achieved self-government, is a matter of concern to the whole civilized world.

66. CONVENTION CONCERNING FORCED OR COMPULSORY LABOUR, 1930

The Convention (C29) was adopted by the General Conference of the ILO on 10 June 1930, and entered into force on 1 May 1932. The Convention is aimed at practices in colonial countries and certain independent States at a certain stage of development. The focus is thus on forced labour as a form of economic exploitation. For the text in English and French, see 39 *UNTS* 55. The following version is the authentic text of the Convention, as modified by the Final Articles Revision Convention, 1946. The original text of the Convention was authenticated on 25 July 1930 by the signatures of E. Mahaim, President of the Conference, and Albert Thomas, Director of the International Labour Office.

The definition of forced labour is not an easy matter. The technical difficulties are discussed by FAWCETT, J., *The Application of the European Convention on Human Rights*, Oxford: Clarendon Press (2nd edn., 1987), 56–63. Fawcett comments (at 48): 'the margin between the planned use of labour and the direction of labour, between free and compulsory employment, can become almost indiscernibly narrow'.

Further reading

ANDREES, B. and BELSER, P., *Forced Labor: Coercion and Exploitation in the Private Economy*, Geneva: ILO; Boulder, USA: Lynne Rienner, 2009.

AVINS, A., 'Involuntary Servitude in British Commonwealth Law', (1967) 16 *ICLQ* 29–55.

INTERNATIONAL LABOUR CONFERENCE, *A Global Alliance against Forced Labour: Global Report under the Follow-up to the ILO Declaration on Fundamental Principles and Rights at Work*, Report of the Director-General, ILO Conference, 93rd Session, Geneva: International Labour Office, 2005.

TEXT

The General Conference of the International Labour Organization,

Having been convened at Geneva by the Governing Body of the International Labour Office, and having met in its Fourteenth Session on 10 June 1930, and

Having decided upon the adoption of certain proposals with regard to forced or compulsory labour, which is included in the first item on the agenda of the Session, and

Having determined that these proposals shall take the form of an international Convention,

Adopts this twenty-eighth day of June of the year one thousand nine hundred and thirty the following Convention, which may be cited as the Forced Labour Convention, 1930, for ratification by the Members of the International Labour Organization in accordance with the provisions of the Constitution of the International Labour Organization:

Article 1

1. Each Member of the International Labour Organization which ratifies this Convention undertakes to suppress the use of forced or compulsory labour in all its forms within the shortest possible period.

2. With a view to this complete suppression, recourse to forced or compulsory labour may be had, during the transitional period, for public purposes only and as an exceptional measure, subject to the conditions and guarantees hereinafter provided.

3. At the expiration of a period of five years after the coming into force of this Convention, and when the Governing Body of the International Labour Office prepares the report provided for in Article 31 below, the said Governing Body shall consider the possibility of the suppression of forced or compulsory labour in all its forms without a further transitional period and the desirability of placing this question on the agenda of the Conference.

Article 2

1. For the purposes of this Convention the term 'forced or compulsory labour' shall mean all work or service which is exacted from any person under the menace of any penalty and for which the said person has not offered himself voluntarily.

2. Nevertheless, for the purposes of this Convention, the term 'forced or compulsory labour' shall not include—

(a) any work or service exacted in virtue of compulsory military service laws for work of a purely military character;

(b) any work or service which forms part of the normal civic obligations of the citizens of a fully self-governing country;

(c) any work or service exacted from any person as a consequence of a conviction in a court of law, provided that the said work or service is carried out under the supervision and control of a public authority and that the said person is not hired to or placed at the disposal of private individuals, companies or associations;

(d) any work or service exacted in cases of emergency, that is to say, in the event of war or of a calamity or threatened calamity, such as fire, flood, famine, earthquake, violent epidemic or epizootic diseases, invasion by animal, insect or vegetable pests, and in general any circumstance that would endanger the existence or the well-being of the whole or part of the population;

(e) minor communal services of a kind which, being performed by the members of the community in the direct interest of the said community, can therefore be considered as normal civic obligations incumbent upon the members of the community, provided that the members of the community or their direct representatives shall have the right to be consulted in regard to the need for such services.

Article 3

For the purposes of this Convention the term 'competent authority' shall mean either an authority of the metropolitan country or the highest central authority in the territory concerned.

Article 4

1. The competent authority shall not impose or permit the imposition of forced or compulsory labour for the benefit of private individuals, companies or associations.

2. Where such forced or compulsory labour for the benefit of private individuals, companies or associations exists at the date on which a Member's ratification of this Convention is registered by the Director-General of the International Labour Office, the Member shall completely suppress such forced or compulsory labour from the date on which this Convention comes into force for that Member.

Article 5

1. No concession granted to private individuals, companies or associations shall involve any form of forced or compulsory labour for the production or the collection of products which such private individuals, companies or associations utilise or in which they trade.

2. Where concessions exist containing provisions involving such forced or compulsory labour, such provisions shall be rescinded as soon as possible, in order to comply with Article 1 of this Convention.

Article 6

Officials of the administration, even when they have the duty of encouraging the populations under their charge to engage in some form of labour, shall not put constraint upon the said populations or upon any individual members thereof to work for private individuals, companies or associations.

Article 7

1. Chiefs who do not exercise administrative functions shall not have recourse to forced or compulsory labour.

2. Chiefs who exercise administrative functions may, with the express permission of the competent authority, have recourse to forced or compulsory labour, subject to the provisions of Article 10 of this Convention.

3. Chiefs who are duly recognised and who do not receive adequate remuneration in other forms may have the enjoyment of personal services, subject to due regulation and provided that all necessary measures are taken to prevent abuses.

Article 8

1. The responsibility for every decision to have recourse to forced or compulsory labour shall rest with the highest civil authority in the territory concerned.

2. Nevertheless, that authority may delegate powers to the highest local authorities to exact forced or compulsory labour which does not involve the removal of the workers from their place of habitual residence. That authority may also delegate, for such periods and subject to such conditions as may be laid down in the regulations provided for in Article 23 of this Convention, powers to the highest local authorities to exact forced or compulsory labour which involves the removal of the workers from their place of habitual residence for the purpose of facilitating the movement of officials of the administration, when on duty, and for the transport of Government stores.

Article 9

Except as otherwise provided for in Article 10 of this Convention, any authority competent to exact forced or compulsory labour shall, before deciding to have recourse to such labour, satisfy itself—

- (a) that the work to be done or the service to be rendered is of important direct interest for the community called upon to do the work or render the service;
- (b) that the work or service is of present or imminent necessity;
- (c) that it has been impossible to obtain voluntary labour for carrying out the work or rendering the service by the offer of rates of wages and conditions of labour not

less favourable than those prevailing in the area concerned for similar work or service; and

(d) that the work or service will not lay too heavy a burden upon the present population, having regard to the labour available and its capacity to undertake the work.

Article 10

1. Forced or compulsory labour exacted as a tax and forced or compulsory labour to which recourse is had for the execution of public works by chiefs who exercise administrative functions shall be progressively abolished.

2. Meanwhile, where forced or compulsory labour is exacted as a tax, and where recourse is had to forced or compulsory labour for the execution of public works by chiefs who exercise administrative functions, the authority concerned shall first satisfy itself—

(a) that the work to be done or the service to be rendered is of important direct interest for the community called upon to do the work or render the service;

(b) that the work or the service is of present or imminent necessity;

(c) that the work or service will not lay too heavy a burden upon the present population, having regard to the labour available and its capacity to undertake the work;

(d) that the work or service will not entail the removal of the workers from their place of habitual residence;

(e) that the execution of the work or the rendering of the service will be directed in accordance with the exigencies of religion, social life and agriculture.

Article 11

1. Only adult able-bodied males who are of an apparent age of not less than 18 and not more than 45 years may be called upon for forced or compulsory labour. Except in respect of the kinds of labour provided for in Article 10 of this Convention, the following limitations and conditions shall apply:

(a) whenever possible prior determination by a medical officer appointed by the administration that the persons concerned are not suffering from any infectious or contagious disease and that they are physically fit for the work required and for the conditions under which it is to be carried out;

(b) exemption of school teachers and pupils and of officials of the administration in general;

(c) the maintenance in each community of the number of adult able-bodied men indispensable for family and social life;

(d) respect for conjugal and family ties.

2. For the purposes of sub-paragraph (c) of the preceding paragraph, the regulations provided for in Article 23 of this Convention shall fix the proportion of the resident adult able-bodied males who may be taken at any one time for forced or compulsory labour, provided always that this proportion shall in no case exceed 25 per cent. In fixing this proportion the competent authority shall take account of the density of the population, of its social and physical development, of the seasons, and of the work which must be done by the persons concerned on their own behalf in their locality, and, generally, shall have regard to the economic and social necessities of the normal life of the community concerned.

Article 12

1. The maximum period for which any person may be taken for forced or compulsory labour of all kinds in any one period of twelve months shall not exceed sixty days, including the time spent in going to and from the place of work.

2. Every person from whom forced or compulsory labour is exacted shall be furnished with a certificate indicating the periods of such labour which he has completed.

Article 13

1. The normal working hours of any person from whom forced or compulsory labour is exacted shall be the same as those prevailing in the case of voluntary labour, and the hours worked in excess of the normal working hours shall be remunerated at the rates prevailing in the case of overtime for voluntary labour.

2. A weekly day of rest shall be granted to all persons from whom forced or compulsory labour of any kind is exacted and this day shall coincide as far as possible with the day fixed by tradition or custom in the territories or regions concerned.

Article 14

1. With the exception of the forced or compulsory labour provided for in Article 10 of this Convention, forced or compulsory labour of all kinds shall be remunerated in cash at rates not less than those prevailing for similar kinds of work either in the district in which the labour is employed or in the district from which the labour is recruited, whichever may be the higher.

2. In the case of labour to which recourse is had by chiefs in the exercise of their administrative functions, payment of wages in accordance with the provisions of the preceding paragraph shall be introduced as soon as possible.

3. The wages shall be paid to each worker individually and not to his tribal chief or to any other authority.

4. For the purpose of payment of wages the days spent in travelling to and from the place of work shall be counted as working days.

5. Nothing in this Article shall prevent ordinary rations being given as a part of wages, such rations to be at least equivalent in value to the money payment they are taken to represent, but deductions from wages shall not be made either for the payment of taxes or for special food, clothing or accommodation supplied to a worker for the purpose of maintaining him in a fit condition to carry on his work under the special conditions of any employment, or for the supply of tools.

Article 15

1. Any laws or regulations relating to workmen's compensation for accidents or sickness arising out of the employment of the worker and any laws or regulations providing compensation for the dependants of deceased or incapacitated workers which are or shall be in force in the territory concerned shall be equally applicable to persons from whom forced or compulsory labour is exacted and to voluntary workers.

2. In any case it shall be an obligation on any authority employing any worker on forced or compulsory labour to ensure the subsistence of any such worker who, by accident or sickness arising out of his employment, is rendered wholly or partially incapable of providing for himself, and to take measures to ensure the maintenance of any persons

actually dependent upon such a worker in the event of his incapacity or decease arising out of his employment.

Article 16

1. Except in cases of special necessity, persons from whom forced or compulsory labour is exacted shall not be transferred to districts where the food and climate differ so considerably from those to which they have been accustomed as to endanger their health.

2. In no case shall the transfer of such workers be permitted unless all measures relating to hygiene and accommodation which are necessary to adapt such workers to the conditions and to safeguard their health can be strictly applied.

3. When such transfer cannot be avoided, measures of gradual habituation to the new conditions of diet and of climate shall be adopted on competent medical advice.

4. In cases where such workers are required to perform regular work to which they are not accustomed, measures shall be taken to ensure their habituation to it, especially as regards progressive training, the hours of work and the provision of rest intervals, and any increase or amelioration of diet which may be necessary.

Article 17

Before permitting recourse to forced or compulsory labour for works of construction or maintenance which entail the workers remaining at the workplaces for considerable periods, the competent authority shall satisfy itself—

(1) that all necessary measures are taken to safeguard the health of the workers and to guarantee the necessary medical care, and, in particular, (a) that the workers are medically examined before commencing the work and at fixed intervals during the period of service, (b) that there is an adequate medical staff, provided with the dispensaries, infirmaries, hospitals and equipment necessary to meet all requirements, and (c) that the sanitary conditions of the workplaces, the supply of drinking water, food, fuel, and cooking utensils, and, where necessary, of housing and clothing, are satisfactory;

(2) that definite arrangements are made to ensure the subsistence of the families of the workers, in particular by facilitating the remittance, by a safe method, of part of the wages to the family, at the request or with the consent of the workers;

(3) that the journeys of the workers to and from the workplaces are made at the expense and under the responsibility of the administration, which shall facilitate such journeys by making the fullest use of all available means of transport;

(4) that, in case of illness or accident causing incapacity to work of a certain duration, the worker is repatriated at the expense of the administration;

(5) that any worker who may wish to remain as a voluntary worker at the end of his period of forced or compulsory labour is permitted to do so without, for a period of two years, losing his right to repatriation free of expense to himself.

Article 18

1. Forced or compulsory labour for the transport of persons or goods, such as the labour of porters or boatmen, shall be abolished within the shortest possible period. Meanwhile the competent authority shall promulgate regulations determining, *inter alia*, (a) that such labour shall only be employed for the purpose of facilitating the movement of officials of

the administration, when on duty, or for the transport of Government stores, or, in cases of very urgent necessity, the transport of persons other than officials, (b) that the workers so employed shall be medically certified to be physically fit, where medical examination is possible, and that where such medical examination is not practicable the person employing such workers shall be held responsible for ensuring that they are physically fit and not suffering from any infectious or contagious disease, (c) the maximum load which these workers may carry, (d) the maximum distance from their homes to which they may be taken, (e) the maximum number of days per month or other period for which they may be taken, including the days spent in returning to their homes, and (f) the persons entitled to demand this form of forced or compulsory labour and the extent to which they are entitled to demand it.

2. In fixing the maxima referred to under (c), (d) and (e) in the foregoing paragraph, the competent authority shall have regard to all relevant factors, including the physical development of the population from which the workers are recruited, the nature of the country through which they must travel and the climatic conditions.

3. The competent authority shall further provide that the normal daily journey of such workers shall not exceed a distance corresponding to an average working day of eight hours, it being understood that account shall be taken not only of the weight to be carried and the distance to be covered, but also of the nature of the road, the season and all other relevant factors, and that, where hours of journey in excess of the normal daily journey are exacted, they shall be remunerated at rates higher than the normal rates.

Article 19

1. The competent authority shall only authorise recourse to compulsory cultivation as a method of precaution against famine or a deficiency of food supplies and always under the condition that the food or produce shall remain the property of the individuals or the community producing it.

2. Nothing in this Article shall be construed as abrogating the obligation on members of a community, where production is organised on a communal basis by virtue of law or custom and where the produce or any profit accruing from the sale thereof remain the property of the community, to perform the work demanded by the community by virtue of law or custom.

Article 20

Collective punishment laws under which a community may be punished for crimes committed by any of its members shall not contain provisions for forced or compulsory labour by the community as one of the methods of punishment.

Article 21

Forced or compulsory labour shall not be used for work underground in mines.

Article 22

The annual reports that Members which ratify this Convention agree to make to the International Labour Office, pursuant to the provisions of Article 22 of the Constitution of the International Labour Organization, on the measures they have taken to give effect to the provisions of this Convention, shall contain as full information as possible, in respect of each territory concerned, regarding the extent to which recourse has been had to forced or compulsory labour in that territory, the purposes for which it has been employed, the sickness and death rates, hours of work, methods of payment of wages and rates of wages, and any other relevant information.

Article 23

1. To give effect to the provisions of this Convention the competent authority shall issue complete and precise regulations governing the use of forced or compulsory labour.

2. These regulations shall contain, inter alia, rules permitting any person from whom forced or compulsory labour is exacted to forward all complaints relative to the conditions of labour to the authorities and ensuring that such complaints will be examined and taken into consideration.

Article 24

Adequate measures shall in all cases be taken to ensure that the regulations governing the employment of forced or compulsory labour are strictly applied, either by extending the duties of any existing labour inspectorate which has been established for the inspection of voluntary labour to cover the inspection of forced or compulsory labour or in some other appropriate manner. Measures shall also be taken to ensure that the regulations are brought to the knowledge of persons from whom such labour is exacted.

Article 25

The illegal exaction of forced or compulsory labour shall be punishable as a penal offence, and it shall be an obligation on any Member ratifying this Convention to ensure that the penalties imposed by law are really adequate and are strictly enforced.

Article 26

1. Each Member of the International Labour Organization which ratifies this Convention undertakes to apply it to the territories placed under its sovereignty, jurisdiction, protection, suzerainty, tutelage or authority, so far as it has the right to accept obligations affecting matters of internal jurisdiction; provided that, if such Member may desire to take advantage of the provisions of Article 35 of the Constitution of the International Labour Organization, it shall append to its ratification a declaration stating—

   (1) the territories to which it intends to apply the provisions of this Convention without modification;

   (2) the territories to which it intends to apply the provisions of this Convention with modifications, together with details of the said modifications:

   (3) the territories in respect of which it reserves its decision.

2. The aforesaid declaration shall be deemed to be an integral part of the ratification and shall have the force of ratification. It shall be open to any Member, by a subsequent declaration, to cancel in whole or in part the reservations made, in pursuance of the provisions of subparagraphs (2) and (3) of this Article, in the original declaration.

Article 27

The formal ratifications of this Convention under the conditions set forth in the Constitution of the International Labour Organization shall be communicated to the Director-General of the International Labour Office for registration.

Article 28

1. This Convention shall be binding only upon those Members whose ratifications have been registered with the International Labour Office.

2. It shall come into force twelve months after the date on which the ratifications of two Members of the International Labour Organization have been registered with the Director-General.

3. Thereafter, this Convention shall come into force for any Member twelve months after the date on which the ratification has been registered.

Article 29

As soon as the ratifications of two Members of the International Labour Organization have been registered with the International Labour Office, the Director-General of the International Labour Office shall so notify all the Members of the International Labour Organization. He shall likewise notify them of the registration of ratifications which may be communicated subsequently by other Members of the Organization.

Article 30

1. A Member which has ratified this Convention may denounce it after the expiration of ten years from the date on which the Convention first comes into force, by an act communicated to the Director-General of the International Labour Office for registration. Such denunciation shall not take effect until one year after the date on which it is registered with the International Labour Office.

2. Each Member which has ratified this Convention and which does not, within the year following the expiration of the period of ten years mentioned in the preceding paragraph, exercise the right of denunciation provided for in this Article, will be bound for another period of five years and, thereafter, may denounce this Convention at the expiration of each period of five years under the terms provided for in this Article.

Article 31

At the expiration of each period of five years after the coming into force of this Convention, the Governing Body of the International Labour Office shall present to the General Conference a report on the working of this Convention and shall consider the desirability of placing on the agenda of the Conference the question of its revision in whole or in part.

Article 32

1. Should the Conference adopt a new Convention revising this Convention in whole or in part, the ratification by a Member of the new revising Convention shall *ipso jure* involve denunciation of this Convention without any requirement of delay, notwithstanding the provisions of Article 30 above, if and when the new revising Convention shall have come into force.

2. As from the date of the coming into force of the new revising Convention, the present Convention shall cease to be open to ratification by the Members.

3. Nevertheless, this Convention shall remain in force in its actual form and content for those Members which have ratified it but have not ratified the revising Convention.

Article 33

The French and English texts of this Convention shall both be authentic.

67. FREEDOM OF ASSOCIATION AND PROTECTION OF THE RIGHT TO ORGANIZE CONVENTION, 1948

This Convention (C87) was adopted by the General Conference of the ILO on 9 July 1948, and entered into force on 4 July 1950. For the text in various languages, see 68 *UNTS* 17. This Convention and the one which follows (below) protect the major points of trade union activity and power: freedom to organize and freedom to engage in collective bargaining. Similar freedom is provided for employers. See also the Right of Association (Agriculture) Convention, 1921 and the Right of Association (Non-Metropolitan Territories) Convention, 1947: **http://www.ilo.org/ ilolex/english/convdisp1.htm**. It has been pointed out that none of the Conventions recognize in terms the right to strike. For further reference, see INTERNATIONAL LABOUR OFFICE, *The ILO and Human Rights*, Geneva: ILO, 1968, 32–41; and the Collective Agreements Recommendation (R91), adopted by the ILO General Conference on 29 June 1951: **http://www.ilo.org/ilolex/ english/recdisp1.htm**.

In 1950 the ILO Governing Body decided to establish a Fact-finding and Conciliation Commission on Freedom of Association: see the [1949] *Yearbook on Human Rights* 293. This needs the consent of governments before it can act. However, in the case of a ratified convention the complaints procedure under Article 26 of the Constitution of the ILO applies. See 'Reports of the Committee on Freedom of Association—354th Report', ILO Governing Body, doc. 305/5, June 2009.

Further reading

INTERNATIONAL LABOUR CONFERENCE, *Freedom of Association in Practice: Lessons Learned*, Report of the Director-General, ILO Conference, 97th Session, Geneva: International Labour Office, 2008.

WOLF, F., 'Human Rights and the International Labour Organization', in MERON, T., ed., *Human Rights in International Law*, Oxford: Clarendon Press, 1984, vol. II, 273–305, 290–3.

TEXT

The General Conference of the International Labour Organization,

Having been convened at San Francisco by the Governing Body of the International Labour Office, and having met in its Thirty-first Session on 17 June 1948;

Having decided to adopt, in the form of a Convention, certain proposals concerning freedom of association and protection of the right to organize, which is the seventh item on the agenda of the session;

Considering that the Preamble to the Constitution of the International Labour Organization declares recognition of the principle of freedom of association to be a means of improving conditions of labour and of establishing peace;

Considering that the Declaration of Philadelphia reaffirms that freedom of expression and of association are essential to sustained progress;

Considering that the International Labour Conference, at its Thirtieth Session, unanimously adopted the principles which should form the basis for international regulation;

Considering that the General Assembly of the United Nations, at its Second Session, endorsed these principles and requested the International Labour Organization to continue every effort in order that it may be possible to adopt one or several international Conventions;

Adopts the ninth day of July of the year one thousand nine hundred and forty-eight, the following Convention, which may be cited as the Freedom of Association and Protection of the Right to Organize Convention, 1948:

PART I
FREEDOM OF ASSOCIATION

Article 1

Each Member of the International Labour Organization for which this Convention is in force undertakes to give effect to the following provisions.

Article 2

Workers and employers, without distinction whatsoever, shall have the right to establish and, subject only to the rules of the organization concerned, to join organizations of their own choosing without previous authorisation.

Article 3

1. Workers' and employers' organizations shall have the right to draw up their constitutions and rules, to elect their representatives in full freedom, to organize their administration and activities and to formulate their programmes.

2. The public authorities shall refrain from any interference which would restrict this right or impede the lawful exercise thereof.

Article 4

Workers' and employers' organizations shall not be liable to be dissolved or suspended by administrative authority.

Article 5

Workers' and employers' organizations shall have the right to establish and join federations and confederations and any such organization, federation or confederation shall have the right to affiliate with international organizations of workers and employers.

Article 6

The provisions of Articles 2, 3 and 4 hereof apply to federations and confederations of workers' and employers' organizations.

Article 7

The acquisition of legal personality by workers' and employers' organizations, federations and confederations shall not be made subject to conditions of such a character as to restrict the application of the provisions of Articles 2, 3 and 4 hereof.

Article 8

1. In exercising the rights provided for in this Convention workers and employers and their respective organizations, like other persons or organized collectivities, shall respect the law of the land.

2. The law of the land shall not be such as to impair, nor shall it be so applied as to impair, the guarantees provided for in this Convention.

Article 9

1. The extent to which the guarantees provided for in this Convention shall apply to the armed forces and the police shall be determined by national laws or regulations.

2. In accordance with the principle set forth in paragraph 8 of Article 19 of the Constitution of the International Labour Organization the ratification of this Convention by any Member shall not be deemed to affect any existing law, award, custom or agreement in virtue of which members of the armed forces or the police enjoy any right guaranteed by this Convention.

Article 10

In this Convention the term 'organization' means any organization of workers or of employers for furthering and defending the interests of workers or of employers.

PART II
PROTECTION OF THE RIGHT TO ORGANIZE

Article 11

Each Member of the International Labour Organization for which this Convention is in force undertakes to take all necessary and appropriate measures to ensure that workers and employers may exercise freely the right to organize.

PART III
MISCELLANEOUS PROVISIONS

Article 12

1. In respect of the territories referred to in Article 35 of the Constitution of the International Labour Organization as amended by the Constitution of the International Labour Organization Instrument of Amendment 1946, other than the territories referred to in paragraphs 4 and 5 of the said article as so amended, each Member of the Organization which ratifies this Convention shall communicate to the Director-General of the International Labour Office as soon as possible after ratification a declaration stating:

    (a) the territories in respect of which it undertakes that the provisions of the Convention shall be applied without modification;

    (b) the territories in respect of which it undertakes that the provisions of the Convention shall be applied subject to modifications, together with details of the said modifications;

    (c) the territories in respect of which the Convention is inapplicable and in such cases the grounds on which it is inapplicable;

    (d) the territories in respect of which it reserves its decision.

2. The undertakings referred to in subparagraphs (a) and (b) of paragraph 1 of this Article shall be deemed to be an integral part of the ratification and shall have the force of ratification.

3. Any Member may at any time by a subsequent declaration cancel in whole or in part any reservations made in its original declaration in virtue of subparagraphs (b), (c) or (d) of paragraph 1 of this Article.

4. Any Member may, at any time at which the Convention is subject to denunciation in accordance with the provisions of Article 16, communicate to the Director-General a declaration modifying in any other respect the terms of any former declaration and stating the present position in respect of such territories as it may specify.

Article 13

1. Where the subject matter of this Convention is within the self-governing powers of any non-metropolitan territory, the Member responsible for the international relations of that territory may, in agreement with the Government of the territory, communicate to the Director-General of the International Labour Office a declaration accepting on behalf of the territory the obligations of this Convention.

2. A declaration accepting the obligations of this Convention may be communicated to the Director-General of the International Labour Office:

    (a) by two or more Members of the Organization in respect of any territory which is under their joint authority; or

    (b) by any international authority responsible for the administration of any territory, in virtue of the Charter of the United Nations or otherwise, in respect of any such territory.

3. Declarations communicated to the Director-General of the International Labour Office in accordance with the preceding paragraphs of this Article shall indicate whether the provisions of the Convention will be applied in the territory concerned without modifications or subject to modification; when the declaration indicates that the provisions of the Convention will be applied subject to modifications it shall give details of the said modifications.

4. The Member, Members or international authority concerned may at any time by a subsequent declaration renounce in whole or in part the right to have recourse to any modification indicated in any former declaration.

5. The Member, Members or international authority concerned may, at any time at which this Convention is subject to denunciation in accordance with the provisions of Article 16, communicate to the Director-General a declaration modifying in any other respect the terms of any former declaration and stating the present position in respect of the application of the Convention.

PART IV
FINAL PROVISIONS

Article 14

The formal ratifications of this Convention shall be communicated to the Director-General of the International Labour Office for registration.

Article 15

1. This Convention shall be binding only upon those Members of the International Labour Organization whose ratifications have been registered with the Director-General.

2. It shall come into force twelve months after the date on which the ratifications of two Members have been registered with the Director-General.

3. Thereafter, this Convention shall come into force for any Member twelve months after the date on which its ratifications has been registered.

Article 16

1. A Member which has ratified this Convention may denounce it after the expiration of ten years from the date on which the Convention first comes into force, by an Act communicated to the Director-General of the International Labour Office for registration. Such denunciation should not take effect until one year after the date on which it is registered.

2. Each Member which has ratified this Convention and which does not, within the year following the expiration of the period of ten years mentioned in the preceding paragraph, exercise the right of denunciation provided for in this Article, will be bound for another period of ten years and, thereafter, may denounce this Convention at the expiration of each period of ten years under the terms provided for in this Article.

Article 17

1. The Director-General of the International Labour Office shall notify all Members of the International Labour Organization of the registration of all ratifications, declarations and denunciations communicated to him by the Members of the Organization.

2. When notifying the Members of the Organization of the registration of the second ratification communicated to him, the Director-General shall draw the attention of the Members of the Organization to the date upon which the Convention will come into force.

Article 18

The Director-General of the International Labour Office shall communicate to the Secretary-General of the United Nations for registration in accordance with Article 102 of the Charter of the United Nations full particulars of all ratifications and acts of denunciation registered by him in accordance with the provisions of the preceding Articles.

Article 19

At the expiration of each period of ten years after the coming into force of this Convention, the Governing Body of the International Labour Office shall present to the General Conference a report on the working of this Convention and shall examine the desirability of placing on the agenda of the Conference the question of its revision in whole or in part.

Article 20

1. Should the Conference adopt a new Convention revising this Convention in whole or in part, then, unless the new Convention otherwise provides:

   (a) the ratification by a Member of the new revising Convention shall *ipso jure* involve the immediate denunciation of this Convention, notwithstanding the provisions of Article 16 above, if and when the new revising Convention shall have come into force;

(b) as from the date when the new revising Convention comes into force this Convention shall cease to be open to ratification by the Members.

2. This Convention shall in any case remain in force in its actual form and content for those Members which have ratified it but have not ratified the revising Convention.

Article 21

The English and French versions of the text of this Convention are equally authoritative.

68. RIGHT TO ORGANIZE AND COLLECTIVE BARGAINING CONVENTION, 1949

The Convention concerning the Application of the Principles of the Right to Organize and to Bargain Collectively (C98) was adopted by the General Conference of the ILO on 1 July 1949, and entered into force on 18 July 1951. For the text in various languages, see 96 *UNTS* 257. See the introductory note to the previous Convention, at p. 573.

Further reading

INTERNATIONAL LABOUR OFFICE, *Organizing for Social Justice: Global Report under the Follow-up to the ILO Declaration on Fundamental Principles and Rights at Work*. Report of the ILO Conference, 92nd Session, Geneva, 2004.

TEXT

The General Conference of the International Labour Organization,

Having been convened at Geneva by the Governing Body of the International Labour Office, and having met in its Thirty-second Session on 8 June 1949, and

Having decided upon the adoption of certain proposals concerning the application of the principles of the right to organize and to bargain collectively, which is the fourth item on the agenda of the session, and

Having determined that these proposals shall take the form of an international Convention,

Adopts the first day of July of the year one thousand nine hundred and forty-nine, the following Convention, which may be cited as the Right to Organize and Collective Bargaining Convention, 1949:

Article 1

1. Workers shall enjoy adequate protection against acts of anti-union discrimination in respect of their employment.

2. Such protection shall apply more particularly in respect of acts calculated to—

   (a) make the employment of a worker subject to the condition that he shall not join a union or shall relinquish trade union membership;

   (b) cause the dismissal of or otherwise prejudice a worker by reason of union membership or because of participation in union activities outside working hours or, with the consent of the employer, within working hours.

Article 2

1. Workers' and employers' organizations shall enjoy adequate protection against any acts of interference by each other or each other's agents or members in their establishment, functioning or administration.

2. In particular, acts which are designed to promote the establishment of workers' organizations under the domination of employers or employers' organizations, or to support

workers' organizations by financial or other means, with the object of placing such organizations under the control of employers or employers' organizations, shall be deemed to constitute acts of interference within the meaning of this Article.

Article 3

Machinery appropriate to national conditions shall be established, where necessary, for the purpose of ensuring respect for the right to organize as defined in the preceding Articles.

Article 4

Measures appropriate to national conditions shall be taken, where necessary, to encourage and promote the full development and utilisation of machinery for voluntary negotiation between employers or employers' organizations and workers' organizations, with a view to the regulation of terms and conditions of employment by means of collective agreements.

Article 5

1. The extent to which the guarantees provided for in this Convention shall apply to the armed forces and the police shall be determined by national laws or regulations.

2. In accordance with the principle set forth in paragraph 8 of Article 19 of the Constitution of the International Labour Organization the ratification of this Convention by any Member shall not be deemed to affect any existing law, award, custom or agreement in virtue of which members of the armed forces or the police enjoy any right guaranteed by this Convention.

Article 6

This Convention does not deal with the position of public servants engaged in the administration of the State, nor shall it be construed as prejudicing their rights or status in any way.

Article 7

The formal ratifications of this Convention shall be communicated to the Director-General of the International Labour Office for registration.

Article 8

1. This Convention shall be binding only upon those Members of the International Labour Organization whose ratifications have been registered with the Director-General.

2. It shall come into force twelve months after the date on which the ratifications of two Members have been registered with the Director-General.

3. Thereafter, this Convention shall come into force for any Member twelve months after the date on which its ratifications has been registered.

Article 9

1. Declarations communicated to the Director-General of the International Labour Office in accordance with paragraph 2 of Article 35 of the Constitution of the International Labour Organization shall indicate—

(a) the territories in respect of which the Member concerned undertakes that the provisions of the Convention shall be applied without modification;

(b) the territories in respect of which it undertakes that the provisions of the Convention shall be applied subject to modifications, together with details of the said modifications;

(c) the territories in respect of which the Convention is inapplicable and in such cases the grounds on which it is inapplicable;

(d) the territories in respect of which it reserves its decision pending further consideration of the position.

2. The undertakings referred to in subparagraphs (a) and (b) of paragraph 1 of this Article shall be deemed to be an integral part of the ratification and shall have the force of ratification.

3. Any Member may at any time by a subsequent declaration cancel in whole or in part any reservation made in its original declaration in virtue of subparagraph (b), (c) or (d) of paragraph 1 of this Article.

4. Any Member may, at any time at which the Convention is subject to denunciation in accordance with the provisions of Article 11, communicate to the Director-General a declaration modifying in any other respect the terms of any former declaration and stating the present position in respect of such territories as it may specify.

Article 10

1. Declarations communicated to the Director-General of the International Labour Office in accordance with paragraph 4 or 5 of Article 35 of the Constitution of the International Labour Organization shall indicate whether the provisions of the Convention will be applied in the territory concerned without modification or subject to modifications; when the declaration indicates that the provisions of the Convention will be applied subject to modifications, it shall give details of the said modifications.

2. The Member, Members or international authority concerned may at any time by a subsequent declaration renounce in whole or in part the right to have recourse to any modification indicated in any former declaration.

3. The Member, Members or international authority concerned may, at any time at which the Convention is subject to denunciation in accordance with the provisions of Article 11, communicate to the Director-General a declaration modifying in any other respect the terms of any former declaration and stating the present position in respect of the application of the Convention.

Article 11

1. A Member which has ratified this Convention may denounce it after the expiration of ten years from the date on which the Convention first comes into force, by an Act communicated to the Director-General of the International Labour Office for registration. Such denunciation should not take effect until one year after the date on which it is registered.

2. Each Member which has ratified this Convention and which does not, within the year following the expiration of the period of ten years mentioned in the preceding paragraph, exercise the right of denunciation provided for in this Article, will be bound for another period of ten years and, thereafter, may denounce this Convention at the expiration of each period of ten years under the terms provided for in this Article.

Article 12

1. The Director-General of the International Labour Office shall notify all Members of the International Labour Organization of the registration of all ratifications and denunciations communicated to him by the Members of the Organization.

2. When notifying the Members of the Organization of the registration of the second ratification communicated to him, the Director-General shall draw the attention of the Members of the Organization to the date upon which the Convention will come into force.

Article 13

The Director-General of the International Labour Office shall communicate to the Secretary-General of the United Nations for registration in accordance with Article 102 of the Charter of the United Nations full particulars of all ratifications and acts of denunciation registered by him in accordance with the provisions of the preceding Articles.

Article 14

At such times as may consider necessary the Governing Body of the International Labour Office shall present to the General Conference a report on the working of this Convention and shall examine the desirability of placing on the agenda of the Conference the question of its revision in whole or in part.

Article 15

1. Should the Conference adopt a new Convention revising this Convention in whole or in part, then, unless the new Convention otherwise provides:

   (a) the ratification by a Member of the new revising Convention shall *ipso jure* involve the immediate denunciation of this Convention, notwithstanding the provisions of Article 11 above, if and when the new revising Convention shall have come into force;

   (b) as from the date when the new revising Convention comes into force this Convention shall cease to be open to ratification by the Members.

2. This Convention shall in any case remain in force in its actual form and content for those Members which have ratified it but have not ratified the revising Convention.

Article 16

The English and French versions of the text of this Convention are equally authoritative.

69. EQUAL REMUNERATION CONVENTION, 1951

The full title is the Convention concerning Equal Remuneration for Men and Women Workers for Work of Equal Value. The Convention (C100) was adopted by the General Conference of the ILO on 29 June 1951, and entered into force on 23 May 1953. For the text in various languages, see 165 *UNTS* 304. See also the Equal Remuneration Recommendation, 1951, adopted at the same time.

Equality as between the sexes in the matter of wages and salaries has achieved but slow and reluctant recognition, even in the more advanced societies.

Further reading

INTERNATIONAL LABOUR OFFICE, *Time for Equality at Work: Global Report under the Follow-up to the ILO Declaration on Fundamental Principles and Rights at Work.* Report of the ILO Conference, 91st Session, Geneva, 2003.

TEXT

The General Conference of the International Labour Organization,

Having been convened at Geneva by the Governing Body of the International Labour Office, and having met in its Thirty-fourth Session on 6 June 1951, and

Having decided upon the adoption of certain proposals with regard to the principle of equal remuneration for men and women workers for work of equal value, which is the seventh item on the agenda of the session, and

Having determined that these proposals shall take the form of an international Convention,

Adopts the twenty-ninth day of June of the year one thousand nine hundred and fifty-one, the following Convention, which may be cited as the Equal Remuneration Convention, 1951:

Article 1

For the purpose of this Convention:

(a) the term 'remuneration' includes the ordinary, basic or minimum wage or salary and any additional emoluments whatsoever payable directly or indirectly, whether in cash or in kind, by the employer to the worker and arising out of the worker's employment;

(b) the term 'equal remuneration for men and women workers for work of equal value' refers to rates of remuneration established without discrimination based on sex.

Article 2

1. Each Member shall, by means appropriate to the methods in operation for determining rates of remuneration, promote and, in so far as is consistent with such methods, ensure the application to all workers of the principle of equal remuneration for men and women workers for work of equal value.

2. This principle may be applied by means of:

    (a) national laws or regulations;

    (b) legally established or recognised machinery for wage determination;

    (c) collective agreements between employers and workers; or

    (d) a combination of these various means.

Article 3

1. Where such action will assist in giving effect to the provisions of this Convention measures shall be taken to promote objective appraisal of jobs on the basis of the work to be performed.

2. The methods to be followed in this appraisal may be decided upon by the authorities responsible for the determination of rates of remuneration, or, where such rates are determined by collective agreements, by the parties thereto.

3. Differential rates between workers which correspond, without regard to sex, to differences, as determined by such objective appraisal, in the work to be performed shall not be considered as being contrary to the principle of equal remuneration for men and women workers for work of equal value.

Article 4

Each Member shall co-operate as appropriate with the employers' and workers' organizations concerned for the purpose of giving effect to the provisions of this Convention.

Article 5

The formal ratifications of this Convention shall be communicated to the Director-General of the International Labour Office for registration.

Article 6

1. This Convention shall be binding only upon those Members of the International Labour Organization whose ratifications have been registered with the Director-General.

2. It shall come into force twelve months after the date on which the ratifications of two Members have been registered with the Director-General.

3. Thereafter, this Convention shall come into force for any Member twelve months after the date on which its ratifications has been registered.

Article 7

1. Declarations communicated to the Director-General of the International Labour Office in accordance with paragraph 2 of article 35 of the Constitution of the International Labour Organization shall indicate:

    (a) the territories in respect of which the Member concerned undertakes that the provisions of the Convention shall be applied without modification;

    (b) the territories in respect of which it undertakes that the provisions of the Convention shall be applied subject to modifications, together with details of the said modifications;

    (c) the territories in respect of which the Convention is inapplicable and in such cases the grounds on which it is inapplicable;

(d) the territories in respect of which it reserves its decision pending further consideration of the position.

2. The undertakings referred to in subparagraphs (a) and (b) of paragraph 1 of this Article shall be deemed to be an integral part of the ratification and shall have the force of ratification.

3. Any Member may at any time by a subsequent declaration cancel in whole or in part any reservation made in its original declaration in virtue of subparagraph (b), (c) or (d) of paragraph 1 of this Article.

4. Any Member may, at any time at which the Convention is subject to denunciation in accordance with the provisions of Article 9, communicate to the Director-General a declaration modifying in any other respect the terms of any former declaration and stating the present position in respect of such territories as it may specify.

Article 8

1. Declarations communicated to the Director-General of the International Labour Office in accordance with paragraph 4 or 5 of Article 35 of the Constitution of the International Labour Organization shall indicate whether the provisions of the Convention will be applied in the territory concerned without modification or subject to modifications; when the declaration indicates that the provisions of the Convention will be applied subject to modifications, it shall give details of the said modifications.

2. The Member, Members or international authority concerned may at any time by a subsequent declaration renounce in whole or in part the right to have recourse to any modification indicated in any former declaration.

3. The Member, Members or international authority concerned may, at any time at which the Convention is subject to denunciation in accordance with the provisions of Article 9, communicate to the Director-General a declaration modifying in any other respect the terms of any former declaration and stating the present position in respect of the application of the Convention.

Article 9

1. A Member which has ratified this Convention may denounce it after the expiration of ten years from the date on which the Convention first comes into force, by an Act communicated to the Director-General of the International Labour Office for registration. Such denunciation should not take effect until one year after the date on which it is registered.

2. Each Member which has ratified this Convention and which does not, within the year following the expiration of the period of ten years mentioned in the preceding paragraph, exercise the right of denunciation provided for in this Article, will be bound for another period of ten years and, thereafter, may denounce this Convention at the expiration of each period of ten years under the terms provided for in this Article.

Article 10

1. The Director-General of the International Labour Office shall notify all Members of the International Labour Organization of the registration of all ratifications and denunciations communicated to him by the Members of the Organization.

2. When notifying the Members of the Organization of the registration of the second ratification communicated to him, the Director-General shall draw the attention of the

Members of the Organization to the date upon which the Convention will come into force.

Article 11

The Director-General of the International Labour Office shall communicate to the Secretary-General of the United Nations for registration in accordance with Article 102 of the Charter of the United Nations full particulars of all ratifications and acts of denunciation registered by him in accordance with the provisions of the preceding Articles.

Article 12

At such times as may consider necessary the Governing Body of the International Labour Office shall present to the General Conference a report on the working of this Convention and shall examine the desirability of placing on the agenda of the Conference the question of its revision in whole or in part.

Article 13

1. Should the Conference adopt a new Convention revising this Convention in whole or in part, then, unless the new Convention otherwise provides:
    (a) the ratification by a Member of the new revising Convention shall *ipso jure* involve the immediate denunciation of this Convention, notwithstanding the provisions of Article 9 above, if and when the new revising Convention shall have come into force;
    (b) as from the date when the new revising Convention comes into force this Convention shall cease to be open to ratification by the Members.
2. This Convention shall in any case remain in force in its actual form and content for those Members which have ratified it but have not ratified the revising Convention.

Article 14

The English and French versions of the text of this Convention are equally authoritative.

70. CONVENTION CONCERNING THE ABOLITION OF FORCED LABOUR, 1957

This Convention (C105) complements other conventions, including the Slavery Convention, 1926 (above, p. 330), the Supplementary Convention on Abolition of Slavery, etc, 1956 (above, p. 335), and the Forced Labour Convention, 1930 (above, p. 564). It was adopted by the General Conference of the ILO on 25 June 1957, and entered into force on 17 January 1959. For the text in various languages, see 320 *UNTS* 291.

The present Convention is concerned especially with forced labour as a means of political coercion.

Further reading

ALLAIN, J., *The Slavery Conventions: The Travaux Préparatoires of the 1926 League of Nations Convention and the 1956 United Nations Convention*, Leiden: Martinus Nijhoff, 2008.

ANDREES, B. and BELSER, P., *Forced Labor: Coercion and Exploitation in the Private Economy*, Geneva: ILO; Boulder, USA: Lynne Rienner, 2009.

INTERNATIONAL LABOUR CONFERENCE, *A Global Alliance against Forced Labour: Global Report under the Follow-up to the ILO Declaration on Fundamental Principles and Rights at Work*, Report of the Director-General, ILO Conference, 93rd Session, Geneva: International Labour Office, 2005.

TEXT

The General Conference of the International Labour Organization,

Having been convened at Geneva by the Governing Body of the International Labour Office, and having met in its Fortieth Session on 5 June 1957, and

Having considered the question of forced labour, which is the fourth item on the agenda of the session, and

Having noted the provisions of the Forced Labour Convention, 1930, and

Having noted that the Slavery Convention, 1926, provides that all necessary measures shall be taken to prevent compulsory or forced labour from developing into conditions analogous to slavery and that the Supplementary Convention on the Abolition of Slavery, the Slave Trade and Institutions and Practices Similar to Slavery, 1956, provides for the complete abolition of debt bondage and serfdom, and

Having noted that the Protection of Wages Convention, 1949, provides that wages shall be paid regularly and prohibits methods of payment which deprive the worker of a genuine possibility of terminating his employment, and

Having decided upon the adoption of further proposals with regard to the abolition of certain forms of forced or compulsory labour constituting a violation of the rights of man referred to in the Charter of the United Nations and enunciated by the Universal Declaration of Human Rights, and

Having determined that these proposals shall take the form of an international Convention,

Adopts the twenty-fifth day of June of the year one thousand nine hundred and fifty-seven, the following Convention, which may be cited as the Abolition of Forced Labour Convention, 1957:

Article 1

Each Member of the International Labour Organization which ratifies this Convention undertakes to suppress and not to make use of any form of forced or compulsory labour:

   (a) as a means of political coercion or education or as a punishment for holding or expressing political views or views ideologically opposed to the established political, social or economic system;

   (b) as a method of mobilising and using labour for purposes of economic development;

   (c) as a means of labour discipline;

   (d) as a punishment for having participated in strikes;

   (e) as a means of racial, social, national or religious discrimination.

Article 2

Each Member of the International Labour Organization which ratifies this Convention undertakes to take effective measures to secure the immediate and complete abolition of forced or compulsory labour as specified in Article 1 of this Convention.

Article 3

The formal ratifications of this Convention shall be communicated to the Director-General of the International Labour Office for registration.

Article 4

1. This Convention shall be binding only upon those Members of the International Labour Organization whose ratifications have been registered with the Director-General.

2. It shall come into force twelve months after the date on which the ratifications of two Members have been registered with the Director-General.

3. Thereafter, this Convention shall come into force for any Member twelve months after the date on which its ratifications has been registered.

Article 5

1. A Member which has ratified this Convention may denounce it after the expiration of ten years from the date on which the Convention first comes into force, by an Act communicated to the Director-General of the International Labour Office for registration. Such denunciation should not take effect until one year after the date on which it is registered.

2. Each Member which has ratified this Convention and which does not, within the year following the expiration of the period of ten years mentioned in the preceding paragraph, exercise the right of denunciation provided for in this Article, will be bound for another period of ten years and, thereafter, may denounce this Convention at the expiration of each period of ten years under the terms provided for in this Article.

Article 6

1. The Director-General of the International Labour Office shall notify all Members of the International Labour Organization of the registration of all ratifications and denunciations communicated to him by the Members of the Organization.

2. When notifying the Members of the Organization of the registration of the second ratification communicated to him, the Director-General shall draw the attention of the Members of the Organization to the date upon which the Convention will come into force.

Article 7

The Director-General of the International Labour Office shall communicate to the Secretary-General of the United Nations for registration in accordance with Article 102 of the Charter of the United Nations full particulars of all ratifications and acts of denunciation registered by him in accordance with the provisions of the preceding Articles.

Article 8

At such times as it may consider necessary the Governing Body of the International Labour Office shall present to the General Conference a report on the working of this Convention and shall examine the desirability of placing on the agenda of the Conference the question of its revision in whole or in part.

Article 9

1. Should the Conference adopt a new Convention revising this Convention in whole or in part, then, unless the new Convention otherwise provides:

   (a) the ratification by a Member of the new revising Convention shall *ipso jure* involve the immediate denunciation of this Convention, notwithstanding the provisions of Article 5 above, if and when the new revising Convention shall have come into force;

   (b) as from the date when the new revising Convention comes into force this Convention shall cease to be open to ratification by the Members.

2. This Convention shall in any case remain in force in its actual form and content for those Members which have ratified it but have not ratified the revising Convention.

Article 10

The English and French versions of the text of this Convention are equally authoritative.

71. DISCRIMINATION (EMPLOYMENT AND OCCUPATION) CONVENTION, 1958

The most important aspect of this convention (C111) is its application to racial matters, but it is also aimed at other forms of discrimination. The convention was adopted by the General Conference of the ILO on 25 June 1958 and entered into force on 15 June 1960. For the text in various languages, see 363 *UNTS* 31. The relevant Recommendation of the International Labour Conference is reproduced after the text of the convention, below at p. 594.

Further reading

INTERNATIONAL LABOUR OFFICE, *Equality at Work: Tackling the Challenges. Global Report under the Follow-up to the ILO Declaration on Fundamental Principles and Rights at Work.* Report of the Director-General, ILO Conference, 96th Session, Geneva, 2007.

INTERNATIONAL LABOUR OFFICE, *Time for Equality at Work: Global Report under the Follow-up to the ILO Declaration on Fundamental Principles and Rights at Work.* Report of the Director-General, ILO Conference, 91st Session, Geneva, 2003.

NIELSEN, H. K., 'The Concept of Discrimination in I.L.O. Convention No. 111', (1994) 43 *ICLQ* 827–56.

TEXT

The General Conference of the International Labour Organization,

Having been convened at Geneva by the Governing Body of the International Labour Office, and having met in its Forty-second Session on 4 June 1958, and

Having decided upon the adoption of certain proposals with regard to discrimination in the field of employment and occupation, which is the fourth item on the agenda of the session, and

Having determined that these proposals shall take the form of an international Convention, and

Considering that the Declaration of Philadelphia affirms that all human beings, irrespective of race, creed or sex, have the right to pursue both their material well-being and their spiritual development in conditions of freedom and dignity, of economic security and equal opportunity, and

Considering further that discrimination constitutes a violation of rights enunciated by the Universal Declaration of Human Rights,

Adopts the twenty-fifth day of June of the year one thousand nine hundred and fifty-eight, the following Convention, which may be cited as the Discrimination (Employment and Occupation) Convention, 1958:

Article 1

1. For the purpose of this Convention the term 'discrimination' includes:

   (a) any distinction, exclusion or preference made on the basis of race, colour sex, religion, political opinion, national extraction or social origin, which has the effect of nullifying or impairing equality of opportunity or treatment in employment or occupation;

(b)   such other distinction, exclusion or preference which has the effect of nullifying or impairing equality of opportunity or treatment in employment or occupation as may be determined by the Member concerned after consultation with representative employers' and workers' organizations, where such exist, and with other appropriate bodies.

2. Any distinction, exclusion or preference in respect of a particular job based on the inherent requirements thereof shall not be deemed to be discrimination.

3. For the purpose of this Convention the terms 'employment' and 'occupation' include access to vocational training, access to employment and to particular occupations, and terms and conditions of employment.

Article 2

Each Member for which this Convention is in force undertakes to declare and pursue a national policy designed to promote, by methods appropriate to national conditions and practice, equality of opportunity and treatment in respect of employment and occupation, with a view to eliminating any discrimination in respect thereof.

Article 3

Each Member for which this Convention is in force undertakes, by methods appropriate to national conditions and practice:

(a)   to seek the co-operation of employers' and workers' organizations and other appropriate bodies in promoting the acceptance and observance of this policy;

(b)   to enact such legislation and to promote such educational programmes as may be calculated to secure the acceptance and observance of the policy;

(c)   to repeal any statutory provisions and modify any administrative instructions or practices which are inconsistent with the policy;

(d)   to pursue the policy in respect of employment under the direct control of a national authority;

(e)   to ensure observance of the policy in the activities of vocational guidance, vocational training and placement services under the direction of a national authority;

(f)   to indicate in its annual reports on the application of the Convention the action taken in pursuance of the policy and the results secured by such action.

Article 4

Any measures affecting an individual who is justifiably suspected of, or engaged in, activities prejudicial to the security of the State shall not be deemed to be discrimination, provided that the individual concerned shall have the right to appeal to a competent body established in accordance with national practice.

Article 5

1. Special measures of protection or assistance provided for in other Conventions or Recommendations adopted by the International Labour Conference shall not be deemed to be discrimination.

2. Any Member may, after consultation with representative employers' and workers' organizations, where such exist, determine that other special measures designed to meet the particular requirements of persons who, for reasons such as sex, age, disablement,

family responsibilities or social or cultural status, are generally recognized to require special protection or assistance, shall not be deemed to be discrimination.

Article 6

Each Member which ratifies this Convention undertakes to apply it to non-metropolitan territories in accordance with the provisions of the Constitution of the International Labour Organization.

Article 7

The formal ratifications of this Convention shall be communicated to the Director-General of the International Labour Office for registration.

Article 8

1. This Convention shall be binding only upon those Members of the International Labour Organization whose ratifications have been registered with the Director-General.

2. It shall come into force twelve months after the date on which the ratifications of two Members have been registered with the Director-General.

3. Thereafter, this Convention shall come into force for any Member twelve months after the date on which its ratifications has been registered.

Article 9

1. A Member which has ratified this Convention may denounce it after the expiration of ten years from the date on which the Convention first comes into force, by an Act communicated to the Director-General of the International Labour Office for registration. Such denunciation should not take effect until one year after the date on which it is registered.

2. Each Member which has ratified this Convention and which does not, within the year following the expiration of the period of ten years mentioned in the preceding paragraph, exercise the right of denunciation provided for in this Article, will be bound for another period of ten years and, thereafter, may denounce this Convention at the expiration of each period of ten years under the terms provided for in this Article.

Article 10

1. The Director-General of the International Labour Office shall notify all Members of the International Labour Organization of the registration of all ratifications and denunciations communicated to him by the Members of the Organization.

2. When notifying the Members of the Organization of the registration of the second ratification communicated to him, the Director-General shall draw the attention of the Members of the Organization to the date upon which the Convention will come into force.

Article 11

The Director-General of the International Labour Office shall communicate to the Secretary-General of the United Nations for registration in accordance with Article 102 of the Charter of the United Nations full particulars of all ratifications and acts of denunciation registered by him in accordance with the provisions of the preceding Articles.

Article 12

At such times as it may consider necessary the Governing Body of the International Labour Office shall present to the General Conference a report on the working of this Convention and shall examine the desirability of placing on the agenda of the Conference the question of its revision in whole or in part.

Article 13

1. Should the Conference adopt a new Convention revising this Convention in whole or in part, then, unless the new Convention otherwise provides:

(a) the ratification by a Member of the new revising Convention shall *ipso jure* involve the immediate denunciation of this Convention, notwithstanding the provisions of Article 9 above, if and when the new revising Convention shall have come into force;

(b) as from the date when the new revising Convention comes into force this Convention shall cease to be open to ratification by the Members.

2. This Convention shall in any case remain in force in its actual form and content for those Members which have ratified it but have not ratified the revising Convention.

Article 14

The English and French versions of the text of this Convention are equally authoritative.

72. DISCRIMINATION (EMPLOYMENT AND OCCUPATION) RECOMMENDATION, 1958

Adopted 25 June 1958.

TEXT

The General Conference of the International Labour Organization,

Having been convened at Geneva by the Governing Body of the International Labour Office, and having met in its Forty-second Session on 4 June 1958, and

Having decided upon the adoption of certain proposals with regard to discrimination in the field of employment and occupation, which is the fourth item on the agenda of the session, and

Having determined that these proposals shall take the form of a Recommendation supplementing the Discrimination (Employment and Occupation) Convention, 1958,

Adopts this twenty-fifth day of June of the year one thousand nine hundred and fifty-eight, the following Recommendation, which may be cited as the Discrimination (Employment and Occupation) Recommendation, 1958:

The Conference recommends that each Member should apply the following provisions:

I. DEFINITIONS

1. (1) For the purpose of this Recommendation the term 'discrimination' includes:

(a) Any distinction, exclusion or preference made on the basis of race, colour, sex, religion, political opinion, national extraction or social origin, which has the effect of nullifying or impairing equality of opportunity or treatment in employment or occupation;

(b) Such other distinction, exclusion or preference which has the effect of nullifying or impairing equality of opportunity or treatment in employment or occupation as may be determined by the Member concerned after consultation with representative employers' and workers' organizations, where such exist, and with other appropriate bodies.

(2) Any distinction, exclusion or preference in respect of a particular job based on the inherent requirements thereof is not deemed to be discrimination.

(3) For the purpose of this Recommendation the terms 'employment' and 'occupation' include access to vocational training, access to employment and to particular occupations, and terms and conditions of employment.

II. FORMULATION AND APPLICATION OF POLICY

2. Each Member should formulate a national policy for the prevention of discrimination in employment and occupation. This policy should be applied by means of legislative

measures, collective agreements between representative employers' and workers' organizations or in any other manner consistent with national conditions and practice, and should have regard to the following principles:

(a) The promotion of equality of opportunity and treatment in employment and occupation is a matter of public concern;

(b) All persons should, without discrimination, enjoy equality of opportunity and treatment in respect of:

  (i)   Access to vocational guidance and placement services;
  (ii) Access to training and employment of their own choice on the basis of individual suitability for such training or employment;
  (iii) Advancement in accordance with their individual character, experience, ability and diligence;
  (iv) Security of tenure of employment;
  (v)   Remuneration for work of equal value;
  (vi) Conditions of work including hours of work, rest periods, annual holidays with pay, occupational safety and occupational health measures, as well as social security measures and welfare facilities and benefits provided in connection with employment;

(c) Government agencies should apply non-discriminatory employment policies in all their activities;

(d) Employers should not practise or countenance discrimination in engaging or training any person for employment, in advancing or retaining such person in employment, or in fixing terms and conditions of employment; nor should any person or organization obstruct or interfere, either directly or indirectly, with employers in pursuing this principle;

(e) In collective negotiations and industrial relations the parties should respect the principle of equality of opportunity and treatment in employment and occupation, and should ensure that collective agreements contain no provisions of a discriminatory character in respect of access to, training for, advancement in or retention of employment or in respect of the terms and conditions of employment;

(f) Employers' and workers' organizations should not practise or countenance discrimination in respect of admission, retention of membership or participation in their affairs.

3. Each Member should:

(a) Ensure application of the principles of non-discrimination:

  (i)   In respect of employment under the direct control of a national authority;
  (ii) In the activities of vocational guidance, vocational training and placement services under the direction of a national authority;

(b) Promote their observance, where practicable and necessary, in respect of other employment and other vocational guidance, vocational training and placement services by such methods as:

  (i)   Encouraging state, provincial or local government departments or agencies and industries and undertakings operated under public ownership or control to ensure the application of the principles;
  (ii) Making eligibility for contracts involving the expenditure of public funds dependent on observance of the principles;

(iii) Making eligibility for grants to training establishments and for a licence to operate a private employment agency or a private vocational guidance office dependent on observance of the principles.

4. Appropriate agencies, to be assisted where practicable by advisory committees composed of representatives of employers' and workers' organizations, where such exist, and of other interested bodies, should be established for the purpose of promoting application of the policy in all fields of public and private employment, and in particular:

(a) To take all practicable measures to foster public understanding and acceptance of the principles of non-discrimination;

(b) To receive, examine and investigate complaints that the policy is not being observed and, if necessary by conciliation, to secure the correction of any practices regarded as in conflict with the policy; and

(c) To consider further any complaints which cannot be effectively settled by conciliation and to render opinions or issue decisions concerning the manner in which discriminatory practices revealed should be corrected.

5. Each Member should repeal any statutory provisions and modify any administrative instructions or practices which are inconsistent with the policy.

6. Application of the policy should not adversely affect special measures designed to meet the particular requirements of persons who, for reasons such as sex, age, disablement, family responsibilities or social or cultural status are generally recognised to require special protection or assistance.

7. Any measures affecting an individual who is justifiably suspected of, or engaged in, activities prejudicial to the security of the State should not be deemed to be discrimination, provided that the individual concerned has the right to appeal to a competent body established in accordance with national practice.

8. With respect to immigrant workers of foreign nationality and the members of their families, regard should be had to the provisions of the Migration for Employment Convention (Revised), 1949, relating to equality of treatment and the provisions of the Migration for Employment Recommendation (Revised), 1949, relating to the lifting of restrictions on access to employment.

9. There should be continuing co-operation between the competent authorities, representatives of employers and workers and appropriate bodies to consider what further positive measures may be necessary in the light of national conditions to put the principles of non-discrimination into effect.

III. CO-ORDINATION OF MEASURES FOR THE PREVENTION OF DISCRIMINATION IN ALL FIELDS

10. The authorities responsible for action against discrimination in employment and occupation should co-operate closely and continuously with the authorities responsible for action against discrimination in other fields in order that measures taken in all fields may be co-ordinated.

73. MINIMUM AGE CONVENTION, 1973

The Convention concerning Minimum Age for Admission to Employment (C138) was adopted in Geneva on 26 June 1973 and came into force on 19 June 1976. On child labour, see further below, p. 631; also the International Programme on the Elimination of Child Labour: **http://www.ilo. org/ipec/lang-en/index.htm**.

TEXT

The General Conference of the International Labour Organization,

Having been convened at Geneva by the Governing Body of the International Labour Office, and having met in its Fifty-eighth Session on 6 June 1973, and

Having decided upon the adoption of certain proposals with regard to minimum age for admission to employment, which is the fourth item on the agenda of the session, and

Noting the terms of the Minimum Age (Industry) Convention, 1919, the Minimum Age (Sea) Convention, 1920, the Minimum Age (Agriculture) Convention, 1921, the Minimum Age (Trimmers and Stokers) Convention, 1921, the Minimum Age (Non-Industrial Employment) Convention, 1932, the Minimum Age (Sea) Convention (Revised), 1936, the Minimum Age (Industry) Convention (Revised), 1937, the Minimum Age (Non-Industrial Employment) Convention (Revised), 1937, the Minimum Age (Fishermen) Convention, 1959, and the Minimum Age (Underground Work) Convention, 1965, and

Considering that the time has come to establish a general instrument on the subject, which would gradually replace the existing ones applicable to limited economic sectors, with a view to achieving the total abolition of child labour, and

Having determined that these proposals shall take the form of an international Convention,

Adopts the twenty-sixth day of June of the year one thousand nine hundred and seventy-three, the following Convention, which may be cited as the Minimum Age Convention, 1973:

Article 1

Each Member for which this Convention is in force undertakes to pursue a national policy designed to ensure the effective abolition of child labour and to raise progressively the minimum age for admission to employment or work to a level consistent with the fullest physical and mental development of young persons.

Article 2

1. Each Member which ratifies this Convention shall specify, in a declaration appended to its ratification, a minimum age for admission to employment or work within its territory and on means of transport registered in its territory; subject to Articles 4 to 8 of this Convention, no one under that age shall be admitted to employment or work in any occupation.

2. Each Member which has ratified this Convention may subsequently notify the Director-General of the International Labour Office, by further declarations, that it specifies a minimum age higher than that previously specified.

3. The minimum age specified in pursuance of paragraph 1 of this Article shall not be less than the age of completion of compulsory schooling and, in any case, shall not be less than 15 years.

4. Notwithstanding the provisions of paragraph 3 of this Article, a Member whose economy and educational facilities are insufficiently developed may, after consultation with the organizations of employers and workers concerned, where such exist, initially specify a minimum age of 14 years.

5. Each Member which has specified a minimum age of 14 years in pursuance of the provisions of the preceding paragraph shall include in its reports on the application of this Convention submitted under Article 22 of the Constitution of the International Labour Organization a statement:

  (a) that its reason for doing so subsists; or

  (b) that it renounces its right to avail itself of the provisions in question as from a stated date.

Article 3

1. The minimum age for admission to any type of employment or work which by its nature or the circumstances in which it is carried out is likely to jeopardise the health, safety or morals of young persons shall not be less than 18 years.

2. The types of employment or work to which paragraph 1 of this Article applies shall be determined by national laws or regulations or by the competent authority, after consultation with the organizations of employers and workers concerned, where such exist.

3. Notwithstanding the provisions of paragraph 1 of this Article, national laws or regulations or the competent authority may, after consultation with the organizations of employers and workers concerned, where such exist, authorise employment or work as from the age of 16 years on condition that the health, safety and morals of the young persons concerned are fully protected and that the young persons have received adequate specific instruction or vocational training in the relevant branch of activity.

Article 4

1. In so far as necessary, the competent authority, after consultation with the organizations of employers and workers concerned, where such exist, may exclude from the application of this Convention limited categories of employment or work in respect of which special and substantial problems of application arise.

2. Each Member which ratifies this Convention shall list in its first report on the application of the Convention submitted under Article 22 of the Constitution of the International Labour Organization any categories which may have been excluded in pursuance of paragraph 1 of this Article, giving the reasons for such exclusion, and shall state in subsequent reports the position of its law and practice in respect of the categories excluded and the extent to which effect has been given or is proposed to be given to the Convention in respect of such categories.

3. Employment or work covered by Article 3 of this Convention shall not be excluded from the application of the Convention in pursuance of this Article.

Article 5

1. A Member whose economy and administrative facilities are insufficiently developed may, after consultation with the organizations of employers and workers concerned, where such exist, initially limit the scope of application of this Convention.

2. Each Member which avails itself of the provisions of paragraph 1 of this Article shall specify, in a declaration appended to its ratification, the branches of economic activity or types of undertakings to which it will apply the provisions of the Convention.

3. The provisions of the Convention shall be applicable as a minimum to the following: mining and quarrying; manufacturing; construction; electricity, gas and water; sanitary services; transport, storage and communication; and plantations and other agricultural undertakings mainly producing for commercial purposes, but excluding family and small-scale holdings producing for local consumption and not regularly employing hired workers.

4. Any Member which has limited the scope of application of this Convention in pursuance of this Article:

   (a) shall indicate in its reports under Article 22 of the Constitution of the International Labour Organization the general position as regards the employment or work of young persons and children in the branches of activity which are excluded from the scope of application of this Convention and any progress which may have been made towards wider application of the provisions of the Convention;

   (b) may at any time formally extend the scope of application by a declaration addressed to the Director-General of the International Labour Office.

Article 6

This Convention does not apply to work done by children and young persons in schools for general, vocational or technical education or in other training institutions, or to work done by persons at least 14 years of age in undertakings, where such work is carried out in accordance with conditions prescribed by the competent authority, after consultation with the organizations of employers and workers concerned, where such exist, and is an integral part of:

   (a) a course of education or training for which a school or training institution is primarily responsible;

   (b) a programme of training mainly or entirely in an undertaking, which programme has been approved by the competent authority; or

   (c) a programme of guidance or orientation designed to facilitate the choice of an occupation or of a line of training.

Article 7

1. National laws or regulations may permit the employment or work of persons 13 to 15 years of age on light work which is:

   (a) not likely to be harmful to their health or development; and

   (b) not such as to prejudice their attendance at school, their participation in vocational orientation or training programmes approved by the competent authority or their capacity to benefit from the instruction received.

2. National laws or regulations may also permit the employment or work of persons who are at least 15 years of age but have not yet completed their compulsory schooling on work which meets the requirements set forth in sub-paragraphs (a) and (b) of paragraph 1 of this Article.

3. The competent authority shall determine the activities in which employment or work may be permitted under paragraphs 1 and 2 of this Article and shall prescribe the number of hours during which and the conditions in which such employment or work may be undertaken.

4. Notwithstanding the provisions of paragraphs 1 and 2 of this Article, a Member which has availed itself of the provisions of paragraph 4 of Article 2 may, for as long as it continues to do so, substitute the ages 12 and 14 for the ages 13 and 15 in paragraph 1 and the age 14 for the age 15 in paragraph 2 of this Article.

Article 8

1. After consultation with the organizations of employers and workers concerned, where such exist, the competent authority may, by permits granted in individual cases, allow exceptions to the prohibition of employment or work provided for in Article 2 of this Convention, for such purposes as participation in artistic performances.

2. Permits so granted shall limit the number of hours during which and prescribe the conditions in which employment or work is allowed.

Article 9

1. All necessary measures, including the provision of appropriate penalties, shall be taken by the competent authority to ensure the effective enforcement of the provisions of this Convention.

2. National laws or regulations or the competent authority shall define the persons responsible for compliance with the provisions giving effect to the Convention.

3. National laws or regulations or the competent authority shall prescribe the registers or other documents which shall be kept and made available by the employer; such registers or documents shall contain the names and ages or dates of birth, duly certified wherever possible, of persons whom he employs or who work for him and who are less than 18 years of age.

Article 10

1. This Convention revises, on the terms set forth in this Article, the Minimum Age (Industry) Convention, 1919, the Minimum Age (Sea) Convention, 1920, the Minimum Age (Agriculture) Convention, 1921, the Minimum Age (Trimmers and Stokers) Convention, 1921, the Minimum Age (Non-Industrial Employment) Convention, 1932, the Minimum Age (Sea) Convention (Revised), 1936, the Minimum Age (Industry) Convention (Revised), 1937, the Minimum Age (Non-Industrial Employment) Convention (Revised), 1937, the Minimum Age (Fishermen) Convention, 1959, and the Minimum Age (Underground Work) Convention, 1965.

2. The coming into force of this Convention shall not close the Minimum Age (Sea) Convention (Revised), 1936, the Minimum Age (Industry) Convention (Revised), 1937, the Minimum Age (Non-Industrial Employment) Convention (Revised), 1937, the Minimum Age (Fishermen) Convention, 1959, or the Minimum Age (Underground Work) Convention, 1965, to further ratification.

3. The Minimum Age (Industry) Convention, 1919, the Minimum Age (Sea) Convention, 1920, the Minimum Age (Agriculture) Convention, 1921, and the Minimum Age (Trimmers and Stokers) Convention, 1921, shall be closed to further ratification when all the parties thereto have consented to such closing by ratification of this Convention or by a declaration communicated to the Director-General of the International Labour Office.

4. When the obligations of this Convention are accepted:

(a) by a Member which is a party to the Minimum Age (Industry) Convention (Revised), 1937, and a minimum age of not less than 15 years is specified in pursuance of Article 2 of this Convention, this shall *ipso jure* involve the immediate denunciation of that Convention,

(b) in respect of non-industrial employment as defined in the Minimum Age (Non-Industrial Employment) Convention, 1932, by a Member which is a party to that Convention, this shall *ipso jure* involve the immediate denunciation of that Convention,

(c) in respect of non-industrial employment as defined in the Minimum Age (Non-Industrial Employment) Convention (Revised), 1937, by a Member which is a party to that Convention, and a minimum age of not less than 15 years is specified in pursuance of Article 2 of this Convention, this shall *ipso jure* involve the immediate denunciation of that Convention,

(d) in respect of maritime employment, by a Member which is a party to the Minimum Age (Sea) Convention (Revised), 1936, and a minimum age of not less than 15 years is specified in pursuance of Article 2 of this Convention or the Member specifies that Article 3 of this Convention applies to maritime employment, this shall *ipso jure* involve the immediate denunciation of that Convention,

(e) in respect of employment in maritime fishing, by a Member which is a party to the Minimum Age (Fishermen) Convention, 1959, and a minimum age of not less than 15 years is specified in pursuance of Article 2 of this Convention or the Member specifies that Article 3 of this Convention applies to employment in maritime fishing, this shall *ipso jure* involve the immediate denunciation of that Convention,

(f) by a Member which is a party to the Minimum Age (Underground Work) Convention, 1965, and a minimum age of not less than the age specified in pursuance of that Convention is specified in pursuance of Article 2 of this Convention or the Member specifies that such an age applies to employment underground in mines in virtue of Article 3 of this Convention, this shall *ipso jure* involve the immediate denunciation of that Convention, if and when this Convention shall have come into force.

5. Acceptance of the obligations of this Convention:

(a) shall involve the denunciation of the Minimum Age (Industry) Convention, 1919, in accordance with Article 12 thereof,

(b) in respect of agriculture shall involve the denunciation of the Minimum Age (Agriculture) Convention, 1921, in accordance with Article 9 thereof,

(c) in respect of maritime employment shall involve the denunciation of the Minimum Age (Sea) Convention, 1920, in accordance with Article 10 thereof, and of the Minimum Age (Trimmers and Stokers) Convention, 1921, in accordance with Article 12 thereof, if and when this Convention shall have come into force.

Article 11

The formal ratifications of this Convention shall be communicated to the Director-General of the International Labour Office for registration.

Article 12

1. This Convention shall be binding only upon those Members of the International Labour Organization whose ratifications have been registered with the Director-General.

2. It shall come into force twelve months after the date on which the ratifications of two Members have been registered with the Director-General.

3. Thereafter, this Convention shall come into force for any Member twelve months after the date on which its ratifications has been registered.

Article 13

1. A Member which has ratified this Convention may denounce it after the expiration of ten years from the date on which the Convention first comes into force, by an Act communicated to the Director-General of the International Labour Office for registration. Such denunciation should not take effect until one year after the date on which it is registered.

2. Each Member which has ratified this Convention and which does not, within the year following the expiration of the period of ten years mentioned in the preceding paragraph, exercise the right of denunciation provided for in this Article, will be bound for another period of ten years and, thereafter, may denounce this Convention at the expiration of each period of ten years under the terms provided for in this Article.

Article 14

1. The Director-General of the International Labour Office shall notify all Members of the International Labour Organization of the registration of all ratifications and denunciations communicated to him by the Members of the Organization.

2. When notifying the Members of the Organization of the registration of the second ratification communicated to him, the Director-General shall draw the attention of the Members of the Organization to the date upon which the Convention will come into force.

Article 15

The Director-General of the International Labour Office shall communicate to the Secretary-General of the United Nations for registration in accordance with Article 102 of the Charter of the United Nations full particulars of all ratifications and acts of denunciation registered by him in accordance with the provisions of the preceding Articles.

Article 16

At such times as it may consider necessary the Governing Body of the International Labour Office shall present to the General Conference a report on the working of this Convention and shall examine the desirability of placing on the agenda of the Conference the question of its revision in whole or in part.

Article 17

1. Should the Conference adopt a new Convention revising this Convention in whole or in part, then, unless the new Convention otherwise provides:

   (a) the ratification by a Member of the new revising Convention shall *ipso jure* involve the immediate denunciation of this Convention, notwithstanding the provisions of Article 13 above, if and when the new revising Convention shall have come into force;

   (b) as from the date when the new revising Convention comes into force this Convention shall cease to be open to ratification by the Members.

2. This Convention shall in any case remain in force in its actual form and content for those Members which have ratified it but have not ratified the revising Convention.

Article 18

The English and French versions of the text of this Convention are equally authoritative.

74. CONVENTION CONCERNING EMPLOYMENT PROMOTION AND PROTECTION AGAINST UNEMPLOYMENT, 1988

This convention (C168) was adopted on 21 June 1988 and came into force on 17 October 1991.

TEXT

The General Conference of the International Labour Organization,

Having been convened at Geneva by the Governing Body of the International Labour Office, and having met in its Seventy-fifth Session on 1 June 1988, and

Emphasising the importance of work and productive employment in any society not only because of the resources which they create for the community, but also because of the income which they bring to workers, the social role which they confer and the feeling of self-esteem which workers derive from them, and

Recalling the existing international standards in the field of employment and unemployment protection (the Unemployment Provision Convention and Recommendation, 1934, the Unemployment (Young Persons) Recommendation, 1935, the Income Security Recommendation, 1944, the Social Security (Minimum Standards) Convention, 1952, the Employment Policy Convention and Recommendation, 1964, the Human Resources Development Convention and Recommendation, 1975, the Labour Administration Convention and Recommendation, 1978, and the Employment Policy (Supplementary Provisions) Recommendation, 1984), and

Considering the widespread unemployment and underemployment affecting various countries throughout the world at all stages of development and in particular the problems of young people, many of whom are seeking their first employment, and

Considering that, since the adoption of the international instruments concerning protection against unemployment referred to above, there have been important new developments in the law and practice of many Members necessitating the revision of existing standards, in particular the Unemployment Provision Convention, 1934, and the adoption of new international standards concerning the promotion of full, productive and freely chosen employment by all appropriate means, including social security, and

Noting that the provisions concerning unemployment benefit in the Social Security (Minimum Standards) Convention, 1952, lay down a level of protection that has now been surpassed by most of the existing compensation schemes in the industrialised countries and, unlike standards concerning other benefits, have not been followed by higher standards, but that the standards in question can still constitute a target for developing countries that are in a position to set up an unemployment compensation scheme, and

Recognizing that policies leading to stable, sustained, non-inflationary economic growth and a flexible response to change, as well as to creation and promotion of all forms of productive and freely chosen employment including small undertakings, co-operatives, self-employment and local initiatives for employment, even through the re-distribution of resources currently devoted to the financing of purely assistance-oriented activities towards activities which promote employment especially vocational guidance, training and rehabilitation, offer the best protection against the adverse effects of involuntary unemployment, but that involuntary unemployment nevertheless exists and that it is therefore important to ensure that social security systems should provide employment assistance and economic support to those who are involuntarily unemployed, and

Having decided upon the adoption of certain proposals with regard to employment promotion and social security which is the fifth item on the agenda of the session with a view, in particular, to revising the Unemployment Provision Convention, 1934, and

Having determined that these proposals shall take the form of an international Convention,

Adopts this twenty-first day of June of the year one thousand nine hundred and eighty-eight, the following Convention, which may be cited as the Employment Promotion and Protection against Unemployment Convention, 1988:

I. GENERAL PROVISIONS

Article 1

In this Convention:

(a) the term 'legislation' includes any social security rules as well as laws and regulations;

(b) the term 'prescribed' means determined by or in virtue of national legislation.

Article 2

Each Member shall take appropriate steps to co-ordinate its system of protection against unemployment and its employment policy. To this end, it shall seek to ensure that its system of protection against unemployment, and in particular the methods of providing unemployment benefit, contribute to the promotion of full, productive and freely chosen employment, and are not such as to discourage employers from offering and workers from seeking productive employment.

Article 3

The provisions of this Convention shall be implemented in consultation and co-operation with the organizations of employers and workers, in accordance with national practice.

Article 4

1. Each Member which ratifies this Convention may, by a declaration accompanying its ratification, exclude the provisions of Part VII from the obligations accepted by ratification.

2. Each Member which has made a declaration under paragraph 1 above may withdraw it at any time by a subsequent declaration.

Article 5

1. Each Member may avail itself, by a declaration accompanying its ratification, of at most two of the temporary exceptions provided for in Article 10, paragraph 4, Article 11, paragraph 3, Article 15, paragraph 2, Article 18, paragraph 2, Article 19, paragraph 4, Article 23, paragraph 2, Article 24, paragraph 2, and Article 25, paragraph 2. Such a declaration shall state the reasons which justify these exceptions.

2. Notwithstanding the provisions of paragraph 1 above, a Member, where it is justified by the extent of protection of its social security system, may avail itself, by a declaration

accompanying its ratification, of the temporary exceptions provided for in Article 10, paragraph 4, Article 11, paragraph 3, Article 15, paragraph 2, Article 18, paragraph 2, Article 19, paragraph 4, Article 23, paragraph 2, Article 24, paragraph 2 and Article 25, paragraph 2. Such a declaration shall state the reasons which justify these exceptions.

3. Each Member which has made a declaration under paragraph 1 or paragraph 2 shall include in its reports on the application of this Convention submitted under Article 22 of the Constitution of the International Labour Organization a statement in respect of each exception of which it avails itself:

(a) that its reason for doing so subsists; or

(b) that it renounces its right to avail itself of the exception in question as from a stated date.

4. Each Member which has made a declaration under paragraph 1 or paragraph 2 shall, as appropriate to the terms of such declaration and as circumstances permit:

(a) cover the contingency of partial unemployment;

(b) increase the number of persons protected;

(c) increase the amount of the benefits;

(d) reduce the length of the waiting period;

(e) extend the duration of payment of benefits;

(f) adapt statutory social security schemes to the occupational circumstances of part-time workers;

(g) endeavour to ensure the provision of medical care to persons in receipt of unemployment benefit and their dependants;

(h) endeavour to guarantee that the periods during which such benefit is paid will be taken into account for the acquisition of the right to social security benefits and, where appropriate, the calculation of disability, old-age and survivors' benefit.

Article 6

1. Each Member shall ensure equality of treatment for all persons protected, without discrimination on the basis of race, colour, sex, religion, political opinion, national extraction, nationality, ethnic or social origin, disability or age.

2. The provisions of paragraph 1 shall not prevent the adoption of special measures which are justified by the circumstances of identified groups under the schemes referred to in Article 12, paragraph 2, or are designed to meet the specific needs of categories of persons who have particular problems in the labour market, in particular disadvantaged groups, or the conclusion between States of bilateral or multilateral agreements relating to unemployment benefits on the basis of reciprocity.

II. PROMOTION OF PRODUCTIVE EMPLOYMENT

Article 7

Each Member shall declare as a priority objective a policy designed to promote full, productive and freely chosen employment by all appropriate means, including social security. Such means should include, *inter alia*, employment services, vocational training and vocational guidance.

Article 8

1. Each Member shall endeavour to establish, subject to national law and practice, special programmes to promote additional job opportunities and employment assistance and to encourage freely chosen and productive employment for identified categories of disadvantaged persons having or liable to have difficulties in finding lasting employment such as women, young workers, disabled persons, older workers, the long-term unemployed, migrant workers lawfully resident in the country and workers affected by structural change.

2. Each Member shall specify, in its reports under Article 22 of the Constitution of the International Labour Organization, the categories of persons for whom it undertakes to promote employment programmes.

3. Each Member shall endeavour to extend the promotion of productive employment progressively to a greater number of categories than the number initially covered.

Article 9

The measures envisaged in this Part shall be taken in the light of the Human Resources Development Convention and Recommendation, 1975, and the Employment Policy (Supplementary Provisions) Recommendation, 1984.

III. CONTINGENCIES COVERED

Article 10

1. The contingencies covered shall include, under prescribed conditions, full unemployment defined as the loss of earnings due to inability to obtain suitable employment with due regard to the provisions of Article 21, paragraph 2, in the case of a person capable of working, available for work and actually seeking work.

2. Each Member shall endeavour to extend the protection of the Convention, under prescribed conditions, to the following contingencies:

   (a) loss of earnings due to partial unemployment, defined as a temporary reduction in the normal or statutory hours of work; and

   (b) suspension or reduction of earnings due to a temporary suspension of work, without any break in the employment relationship for reasons of, in particular, an economic, technological, structural or similar nature.

3. Each Member shall in addition endeavour to provide the payment of benefits to part-time workers who are actually seeking full-time work. The total of benefits and earnings from their part-time work may be such as to maintain incentives to take up full-time work.

4. Where a declaration made in virtue of Article 5 is in force, the implementation of paragraphs 2 and 3 above may be deferred.

IV. PERSONS PROTECTED

Article 11

1. The persons protected shall comprise prescribed classes of employees, constituting not less than 85 per cent of all employees, including public employees and apprentices.

2. Notwithstanding the provisions of paragraph 1 above, public employees whose employment up to normal retiring age is guaranteed by national laws or regulations may be excluded from protection.

3. Where a declaration made in virtue of Article 5 is in force, the persons protected shall comprise:

  (a) prescribed classes of employees constituting not less than 50 per cent of all employees; or

  (b) where specifically justified by the level of development, prescribed classes of employees constituting not less than 50 per cent of all employees in industrial workplaces employing 20 persons or more.

V. METHODS OF PROTECTION

Article 12

1. Unless it is otherwise provided in this Convention, each Member may determine the method or methods of protection by which it chooses to put into effect the provisions of the Convention, whether by a contributory or non-contributory system, or by a combination of such systems.

2. Nevertheless, if the legislation of a Member protects all residents whose resources, during the contingency, do not exceed prescribed limits, the protection afforded may be limited, in the light of the resources of the beneficiary and his or her family, in accordance with the provisions of Article 16.

VI. BENEFIT TO BE PROVIDED

Article 13

Benefits provided in the form of periodical payments to the unemployed may be related to the methods of protection.

Article 14

In cases of full unemployment, benefits shall be provided in the form of periodical payments calculated in such a way as to provide the beneficiary with partial and transitional wage replacement and, at the same time, to avoid creating disincentives either to work or to employment creation.

Article 15

1. In cases of full unemployment and suspension of earnings due to a temporary suspension of work without any break in the employment relationship, when this contingency is covered, benefits shall be provided in the form of periodical payments, calculated as follows:

  (a) where these benefits are based on the contributions of or on behalf of the person protected or on previous earnings, they shall be fixed at not less than 50 per cent of previous earnings, it being permitted to fix a maximum for the amount of the benefit or for the earnings to be taken into account, which may be related, for example, to the wage of a skilled manual employee or to the average wage of workers in the region concerned;

    (b) where such benefits are not based on contributions or previous earnings, they shall be fixed at not less than 50 per cent of the statutory minimum wage or of the wage of an ordinary labourer, or at a level which provides the minimum essential for basic living expenses, whichever is the highest;

2. Where a declaration made in virtue of Article 5 is in force, the amount of the benefits shall be equal:

    (a) to not less than 45 per cent of the previous earnings; or

    (b) to not less than 45 per cent of the statutory minimum wage or of the wage of an ordinary labourer but no less than a level which provides the minimum essential for basic living expenses.

3. If appropriate, the percentages specified in paragraphs 1 and 2 may be reached by comparing net periodical payments after tax and contributions with net earnings after tax and contributions.

Article 16

Notwithstanding the provisions of Article 15, the benefit provided beyond the initial period specified in Article 19, paragraph 2 (a), as well as benefits paid by a Member in accordance with Article 12, paragraph 2, may be fixed after taking account of other resources, beyond a prescribed limit, available to the beneficiary and his or her family, in accordance with a prescribed scale. In any case, these benefits, in combination with any other benefits to which they may be entitled, shall guarantee them healthy and reasonable living conditions in accordance with national standards.

Article 17

1. Where the legislation of a Member makes the right to unemployment benefit conditional upon the completion of a qualifying period, this period shall not exceed the length deemed necessary to prevent abuse.

2. Each Member shall endeavour to adapt the qualifying period to the occupational circumstances of seasonal workers.

Article 18

1. If the legislation of a Member provides that the payment of benefit in cases of full unemployment should begin only after the expiry of a waiting period, such period shall not exceed seven days.

2. Where a declaration made in virtue of Article 5 is in force, the length of the waiting period shall not exceed ten days.

3. In the case of seasonal workers the waiting period specified in paragraph 1 above may be adapted to their occupational circumstances.

Article 19

1. The benefits provided in cases of full unemployment and suspension of earnings due to a temporary suspension of work without any break in the employment relationship shall be paid throughout these contingencies.

2. Nevertheless, in the case of full unemployment:

(a) the initial duration of payment of the benefit provided for in Article 15 may be limited to 26 weeks in each spell of unemployment, or to 39 weeks over any period of 24 months;

(b) in the event of unemployment continuing beyond this initial period of benefit, the duration of payment of benefit, which may be calculated in the light of the resources of the beneficiary and his or her family in accordance with the provisions of Article 16, may be limited to a prescribed period.

3. If the legislation of a Member provides that the initial duration of payment of the benefit provided for in Article 15 shall vary with the length of the qualifying period, the average duration fixed for the payment of benefits shall be at least 26 weeks.

4. Where a declaration made in virtue of Article 5 is in force, the duration of payment of benefit may be limited to 13 weeks over any periods of 12 months or to an average of 13 weeks if the legislation provides that the initial duration of payment shall vary with the length of the qualifying period.

5. In the cases envisaged in paragraph 2 (b) above each Member shall endeavour to grant appropriate additional assistance to the persons concerned with a view to permitting them to find productive and freely chosen employment, having recourse in particular to the measures specified in Part II.

6. The duration of payment of benefit to seasonal workers may be adapted to their occupational circumstances, without prejudice to the provisions of paragraph 2 (b) above.

Article 20

The benefit to which a protected person would have been entitled in the cases of full or partial unemployment or suspension of earnings due to a temporary suspension of work without any break in the employment relationship may be refused, withdrawn, suspended or reduced to the extent prescribed:

(a) for as long as the person concerned is absent from the territory of the Member;

(b) when it has been determined by the competent authority that the person concerned had deliberately contributed to his or her own dismissal;

(c) when it has been determined by the competent authority that the person concerned has left employment voluntarily without just cause;

(d) during the period of a labour dispute, when the person concerned has stopped work to take part in a labour dispute or when he or she is prevented from working as a direct result of a stoppage of work due to this labour dispute;

(e) when the person concerned has attempted to obtain or has obtained benefits fraudulently;

(f) when the person concerned has failed without just cause to use the facilities available for placement, vocational guidance, training, retraining or redeployment in suitable work;

(g) as long as the person concerned is in receipt of another income maintenance benefit provided for in the legislation of the Member concerned, except a family benefit, provided that the part of the benefit which is suspended does not exceed that other benefit.

Article 21

1. The benefit to which a protected person would have been entitled in the case of full unemployment may be refused, withdrawn, suspended or reduced, to the extent prescribed, when the person concerned refuses to accept suitable employment.

2. In assessing the suitability of employment, account shall be taken, in particular, under prescribed conditions and to an appropriate extent, of the age of unemployed persons, their length of service in their former occupation, their acquired experience, the length of their period of unemployment, the labour market situation, the impact of the employment in question on their personal and family situation and whether the employment is vacant as a direct result of a stoppage of work due to an on-going labour dispute.

Article 22

When protected persons have received directly from their employer or from any other source under national laws or regulations or collective agreements, severance pay, the principal purpose of which is to contribute towards compensating them for the loss of earnings suffered in the event of full unemployment:

   (a) the unemployment benefit to which the persons concerned would be entitled may be suspended for a period corresponding to that during which the severance pay compensates for the loss of earnings suffered; or

   (b) the severance pay may be reduced by an amount corresponding to the value converted into a lump sum of the unemployment benefit to which the persons concerned are entitled for a period corresponding to that during which the severance pay compensates for the loss of earnings suffered, as each Member may decide.

Article 23

1. Each Member whose legislation provides for the right to medical care and makes it directly or indirectly conditional upon occupational activity shall endeavour to ensure, under prescribed conditions, the provision of medical care to persons in receipt of unemployment benefit and to their dependants.

2. Where a declaration made in virtue of Article 5 is in force, the implementation of paragraph 1 above may be deferred.

Article 24

1. Each Member shall endeavour to guarantee to persons in receipt of unemployment benefit, under prescribed conditions, that the periods during which benefits are paid will be taken into consideration:

   (a) for acquisition of the right to and, where appropriate, calculation of disability, old-age and survivors' benefit, and

   (b) for acquisition of the right to medical care and sickness, maternity and family benefit after the end of unemployment, when the legislation of the Member concerned provides for such benefits and makes them directly or indirectly conditional upon occupational activity.

2. Where a declaration made in virtue of Article 5 is in force, the implementation of paragraph 1 above may be deferred.

Article 25

1. Each Member shall ensure that statutory social security schemes which are based on occupational activity are adjusted to the occupational circumstances of part-time workers, unless their hours of work or earnings can be considered, under prescribed conditions, as negligible.

2. Where a declaration made in virtue of Article 5 is in force, the implementation of paragraph 1 above may be deferred.

VII. SPECIAL PROVISIONS FOR NEW APPLICANTS FOR EMPLOYMENT

Article 26

1. Members shall take account of the fact that there are many categories of persons seeking work who have never been, or have ceased to be, recognised as unemployed or have never been, or have ceased to be, covered by schemes for the protection of the unemployed. Consequently, at least three of the following ten categories of persons seeking work shall receive social benefits, in accordance with prescribed terms and conditions:

- *(a)* young persons who have completed their vocational training;
- *(b)* young persons who have completed their studies;
- *(c)* young persons who have completed their compulsory military service;
- *(d)* persons after a period devoted to bringing up a child or caring for someone who is sick, disabled or elderly;
- *(e)* persons whose spouse had died, when they are not entitled to a survivor's benefit;
- *(f)* divorced or separated persons;
- *(g)* released prisoners;
- *(h)* adults, including disabled persons, who have completed a period of training;
- *(i)* migrant workers on return to their home country, except in so far as they have acquired rights under the legislation of the country where they last worked;
- *(j)* previously self-employed persons.

2. Each Member shall specify, in its reports under Article 22 of the Constitution of the International Labour Organization, the categories of persons listed in paragraph 1 above which it undertakes to protect.

3. Each Member shall endeavour to extend protection progressively to a greater number of categories than the number initially protected.

VIII. LEGAL, ADMINISTRATIVE AND FINANCIAL GUARANTEES

Article 27

1. In the event of refusal, withdrawal, suspension or reduction of benefit or dispute as to its amount, claimants shall have the right to present a complaint to the body administering

the benefit scheme and to appeal thereafter to an independent body. They shall be informed in writing of the procedures available, which shall be simple and rapid.

2. The appeal procedure shall enable the claimant, in accordance with national law and practice, to be represented or assisted by a qualified person of the claimant's choice or by a delegate of a representative workers' organization or by a delegate of an organization representative of protected persons.

Article 28

Each Member shall assume general responsibility for the sound administration of the institutions and services entrusted with the application of the Convention.

Article 29

1. When the administration is directly entrusted to a government department responsible to Parliament, representatives of the protected persons and of the employers shall be associated in the administration in an advisory capacity, under prescribed conditions.

2. When the administration is not entrusted to a government department responsible to Parliament:

  (a) representatives of the protected persons shall participate in the administration or be associated therewith in an advisory capacity under prescribed conditions;

  (b) national laws or regulations may also provide for the participation of employers' representatives;

  (c) the laws or regulations may further provide for the participation of representatives of the public authorities.

Article 30

In cases where subsidies are granted by the State or the social security system in order to safeguard employment, Members shall take the necessary steps to ensure that the payments are expended only for the intended purpose and to prevent fraud or abuse by those who receive such payments.

Article 31

This Convention revises the Unemployment Provision Convention, 1934.

Article 32

The formal ratifications of this Convention shall be communicated to the Director-General of the International Labour Office for registration.

Article 33

1. This Convention shall be binding only upon those Members of the International Labour Organization whose ratifications have been registered with the Director-General.

2. It shall come into force twelve months after the date on which the ratifications of two Members have been registered with the Director-General.

3. Thereafter, this Convention shall come into force for any Member twelve months after the date on which its ratification has been registered.

Article 34

1. A Member which has ratified this Convention may denounce it after the expiration of ten years from the date on which the Convention first comes into force, by an act communicated to the Director-General of the International Labour Office for registration. Such denunciation shall not take effect until one year after the date on which it is registered.

2. Each Member which has ratified this Convention and which does not, within the year following the expiration of the period of ten years mentioned in the preceding paragraph, exercise the right of denunciation provided for in this Article, will be bound for another period of ten years and, thereafter, may denounce this Convention at the expiration of each period of ten years under the terms provided for in this Article.

Article 35

1. The Director-General of the International Labour Office shall notify all Members of the International Labour Organization of the registration of all ratifications and denunciations communicated to him by the Members of the Organization.

2. When notifying the members of the Organization of the registration of the second ratification communicated to him, the Director-General shall draw the attention of the Members of the Organization to the date upon which the Convention will come into force.

Article 36

The Director-General of the International Labour Office shall communicate to the Secretary-General of the United Nations for registration in accordance with Article 102 of the Charter of the United Nations full particulars of all ratifications and acts of denunciation registered by him in accordance with the provisions of the preceding Articles.

Article 37

At such times as it may consider necessary the Governing Body of the International Labour Office shall present to the General Conference a report on the working of this Convention and shall examine the desirability of placing on the agenda of the Conference the question of its revision in whole or in part.

Article 38

1. Should the Conference adopt a new Convention revising this Convention in whole or in part, then, unless the new Convention otherwise provides:

   (a) the ratification by a Member of the new revising Convention shall *ipso jure* involve the immediate denunciation of this Convention, notwithstanding the provisions of Article 34 above, if and when the new revising Convention shall have come into force;

   (b) as from the date when the new revising Convention comes into force this Convention shall cease to be open to ratification by the Members.

2. This Convention shall in any case remain in force in its actual form and content for those Members which have ratified it but have not ratified the revising Convention.

Article 39

The English and French versions of the text of this Convention are equally authoritative.

75. CONVENTION CONCERNING INDIGENOUS AND TRIBAL PEOPLES IN INDEPENDENT COUNTRIES, 1989

The Convention (C169) was adopted during the 1989 Session of the ILO. It revises the provisions of the Indigenous and Tribal Populations Convention, 1957 (No. 107), and came into force on 5 September 1991.

See also the UN Declaration on the Rights of Indigenous Peoples, 2007, above p. 293.

Further reading

BENNETT, G. I., 'The ILO Convention on Indigenous and Tribal Populations: The Resolution of a Problem of *Vires*', (1972–73) 46 *BYIL* 382–92.

FEIRING, B., et al., *Indigenous & Tribal People's Rights in Practice: A Guide to ILO Convention No. 169*, Geneva: ILO, 2009.

TEXT

The General Conference of the International Labour Organization,

Having been convened at Geneva by the Governing Body of the International Labour Office, and having met in its 76th Session on 7 June 1989, and

Noting the international standards contained in the Indigenous and Tribal Populations Convention and Recommendation, 1957, and

Recalling the terms of the Universal Declaration of Human Rights, the International Covenant on Economic, Social and Cultural Rights, the International Covenant on Civil and Political Rights, and the many international instruments on the prevention of discrimination, and

Considering that the developments which have taken place in international law since 1957, as well as developments in the situation of indigenous and tribal peoples in all regions of the world, have made it appropriate to adopt new international standards on the subject with a view to removing the assimilationist orientation of the earlier standards, and

Recognising the aspirations of these peoples to exercise control over their own institutions, ways of life and economic development and to maintain and develop their identities, languages and religions, within the framework of the States in which they live, and

Noting that in many parts of the world these peoples are unable to enjoy their fundamental human rights to the same degree as the rest of the population of the States within which they live, and that their laws, values, customs and perspectives have often been eroded, and

Calling attention to the distinctive contributions of indigenous and tribal peoples to the cultural diversity and social and ecological harmony of humankind and to international co-operation and understanding, and

Noting that the following provisions have been framed with the co-operation of the United Nations, the Food and Agriculture Organization of the United Nations, the United Nations Educational, Scientific and Cultural Organization and the World Health Organization, as well as of the Inter-American Indian Institute, at appropriate levels and in their respective fields, and that it is proposed to continue this co-operation in promoting and securing the application of these provisions, and

Having decided upon the adoption of certain proposals with regard to the partial revision of the Indigenous and Tribal Populations Convention, 1957 (No. 107), which is the fourth item on the agenda of the session, and

Having determined that these proposals shall take the form of an international Convention revising the Indigenous and Tribal Populations Convention, 1957;

Adopts the twenty-seventh day of June of the year one thousand nine hundred and eighty-nine, the following Convention, which may be cited as the Indigenous and Tribal Peoples Convention, 1989;

PART I
GENERAL POLICY

Article 1

1. This Convention applies to:

   (a) tribal peoples in independent countries whose social, cultural and economic conditions distinguish them from other sections of the national community, and whose status is regulated wholly or partially by their own customs or traditions or by special laws or regulations;

   (b) peoples in independent countries who are regarded as indigenous on account of their descent from the populations which inhabited the country, or a geographical region to which the country belongs, at the time of conquest or colonisation or the establishment of present state boundaries and who, irrespective of their legal status, retain some or all of their own social, economic, cultural and political institutions.

2. Self-identification as indigenous or tribal shall be regarded as a fundamental criterion for determining the groups to which the provisions of this Convention apply.

3. The use of the term 'peoples' in this Convention shall not be construed as having any implications as regards the rights which may attach to the term under international law.

Article 2

1. Governments shall have the responsibility for developing, with the participation of the peoples concerned, co-ordinated and systematic action to protect the rights of these peoples and to guarantee respect for their integrity.

2. Such action shall include measures for:

   (a) ensuring that members of these peoples benefit on an equal footing from the rights and opportunities which national laws and regulations grant to other members of the population;

   (b) promoting the full realisation of the social, economic and cultural rights of these peoples with respect for their social and cultural identity, their customs and traditions and their institutions;

   (c) assisting the members of the peoples concerned to eliminate socio-economic gaps that may exist between indigenous and other members of the national community, in a manner compatible with their aspirations and ways of life.

Article 3

1. Indigenous and tribal peoples shall enjoy the full measure of human rights and fundamental freedoms without hindrance or discrimination. The provisions of the Convention shall be applied without discrimination to male and female members of these peoples.

2. No form of force or coercion shall be used in violation of the human rights and fundamental freedoms of the peoples concerned, including the rights contained in this Convention.

Article 4

1. Special measures shall be adopted as appropriate for safeguarding the persons, institutions, property, labour, cultures and environment of the peoples concerned.

2. Such special measures shall not be contrary to the freely-expressed wishes of the peoples concerned.

3. Enjoyment of the general rights of citizenship, without discrimination, shall not be prejudiced in any way by such special measures.

Article 5

In applying the provisions of this Convention:

   (a) the social, cultural, religious and spiritual values and practices of these peoples shall be recognised and protected, and due account shall be taken of the nature of the problems which face them both as groups and as individuals;

   (b) the integrity of the values, practices and institutions of these peoples shall be respected;

   (c) policies aimed at mitigating the difficulties experienced by these peoples in facing new conditions of life and work shall be adopted, with the participation and co-operation of the peoples affected.

Article 6

1. In applying the provisions of this Convention, governments shall:

   (a) consult the peoples concerned, through appropriate procedures and in particular through their representative institutions, whenever consideration is being given to legislative or administrative measures which may affect them directly;

   (b) establish means by which these peoples can freely participate, to at least the same extent as other sectors of the population, at all levels of decision-making in elective institutions and administrative and other bodies responsible for policies and programmes which concern them;

   (c) establish means for the full development of these peoples' own institutions and initiatives, and in appropriate cases provide the resources necessary for this purpose.

2. The consultations carried out in application of this Convention shall be undertaken, in good faith and in a form appropriate to the circumstances, with the objective of achieving agreement or consent to the proposed measures.

Article 7

1. The peoples concerned shall have the right to decide their own priorities for the process of development as it affects their lives, beliefs, institutions and spiritual well-being and

the lands they occupy or otherwise use, and to exercise control, to the extent possible, over their own economic, social and cultural development. In addition, they shall participate in the formulation, implementation and evaluation of plans and programmes for national and regional development which may affect them directly.

2. The improvement of the conditions of life and work and levels of health and education of the peoples concerned, with their participation and co-operation, shall be a matter of priority in plans for the overall economic development of areas they inhabit. Special projects for development of the areas in question shall also be so designed as to promote such improvement.

3. Governments shall ensure that, whenever appropriate, studies are carried out, in co-operation with the peoples concerned, to assess the social, spiritual, cultural and environmental impact on them of planned development activities. The results of these studies shall be considered as fundamental criteria for the implementation of these activities.

4. Governments shall take measures, in co-operation with the peoples concerned, to protect and preserve the environment of the territories they inhabit.

Article 8

1. In applying national laws and regulations to the peoples concerned, due regard shall be had to their customs or customary laws.

2. These peoples shall have the right to retain their own customs and institutions, where these are not incompatible with fundamental rights defined by the national legal system and with internationally recognised human rights. Procedures shall be established, whenever necessary, to resolve conflicts which may arise in the application of this principle.

3. The application of paragraphs 1 and 2 of this Article shall not prevent members of these peoples from exercising the rights granted to all citizens and from assuming the corresponding duties.

Article 9

1. To the extent compatible with the national legal system and internationally recognised human rights, the methods customarily practised by the peoples concerned for dealing with offences committed by their members shall be respected.

2. The customs of these peoples in regard to penal matters shall be taken into consideration by the authorities and courts dealing with such cases.

Article 10

1. In imposing penalties laid down by general law on members of these peoples account shall be taken of their economic, social and cultural characteristics.

2. Preference shall be given to methods of punishment other than confinement in prison.

Article 11

The exaction from members of the peoples concerned of compulsory personal services in any form, whether paid or unpaid, shall be prohibited and punishable by law, except in cases prescribed by law for all citizens.

Article 12

The peoples concerned shall be safeguarded against the abuse of their rights and shall be able to take legal proceedings, either individually or through their representative bodies, for the effective protection of these rights. Measures shall be taken to ensure that members of these peoples can understand and be understood in legal proceedings, where necessary through the provision of interpretation or by other effective means.

PART II
LAND

Article 13

1. In applying the provisions of this Part of the Convention governments shall respect the special importance for the cultures and spiritual values of the peoples concerned of their relationship with the lands or territories, or both as applicable, which they occupy or otherwise use, and in particular the collective aspects of this relationship.

2. The use of the term 'lands' in Articles 15 and 16 shall include the concept of territories, which covers the total environment of the areas which the peoples concerned occupy or otherwise use.

Article 14

1. The rights of ownership and possession of the peoples concerned over the lands which they traditionally occupy shall be recognised. In addition, measures shall be taken in appropriate cases to safeguard the right of the peoples concerned to use lands not exclusively occupied by them, but to which they have traditionally had access for their subsistence and traditional activities. Particular attention shall be paid to the situation of nomadic peoples and shifting cultivators in this respect.

2. Governments shall take steps as necessary to identify the lands which the peoples concerned traditionally occupy, and to guarantee effective protection of their rights of ownership and possession.

3. Adequate procedures shall be established within the national legal system to resolve land claims by the peoples concerned.

Article 15

1. The rights of the peoples concerned to the natural resources pertaining to their lands shall be specially safeguarded. These rights include the right of these peoples to participate in the use, management and conservation of these resources.

2. In cases in which the State retains the ownership of mineral or sub-surface resources or rights to other resources pertaining to lands, governments shall establish or maintain procedures through which they shall consult these peoples, with a view to ascertaining whether and to what degree their interests would be prejudiced, before undertaking or permitting any programmes for the exploration or exploitation of such resources pertaining to their lands. The peoples concerned shall wherever possible participate in the benefits of such activities, and shall receive fair compensation for any damages which they may sustain as a result of such activities.

Article 16

1. Subject to the following paragraphs of this Article, the peoples concerned shall not be removed from the lands which they occupy.

2. Where the relocation of these peoples is considered necessary as an exceptional measure, such relocation shall take place only with their free and informed consent. Where their consent cannot be obtained, such relocation shall take place only following appropriate procedures established by national laws and regulations, including public inquiries where appropriate, which provide the opportunity for effective representation of the peoples concerned.

3. Whenever possible, these peoples shall have the right to return to their traditional lands, as soon as the grounds for relocation cease to exist.

4. When such return is not possible, as determined by agreement or, in the absence of such agreement, through appropriate procedures, these peoples shall be provided in all possible cases with lands of quality and legal status at least equal to that of the lands previously occupied by them, suitable to provide for their present needs and future development. Where the peoples concerned express a preference for compensation in money or in kind, they shall be so compensated under appropriate guarantees.

5. Persons thus relocated shall be fully compensated for any resulting loss or injury.

Article 17

1. Procedures established by the peoples concerned for the transmission of land rights among members of these peoples shall be respected.

2. The peoples concerned shall be consulted whenever consideration is being given to their capacity to alienate their lands or otherwise transmit their rights outside their own community.

3. Persons not belonging to these peoples shall be prevented from taking advantage of their customs or of lack of understanding of the laws on the part of their members to secure the ownership, possession or use of land belonging to them.

Article 18

Adequate penalties shall be established by law for unauthorised intrusion upon, or use of, the lands of the peoples concerned, and governments shall take measures to prevent such offences.

Article 19

National agrarian programmes shall secure to the peoples concerned treatment equivalent to that accorded to other sectors of the population with regard to:

   (a) the provision of more land for these peoples when they have not the area necessary for providing the essentials of a normal existence, or for any possible increase in their numbers;

   (b) the provision of the means required to promote the development of the lands which these peoples already possess.

PART III
RECRUITMENT AND CONDITIONS OF EMPLOYMENT

Article 20

1. Governments shall, within the framework of national laws and regulations, and in co-operation with the peoples concerned, adopt special measures to ensure the effective

protection with regard to recruitment and conditions of employment of workers belonging to these peoples, to the extent that they are not effectively protected by laws applicable to workers in general.

2. Governments shall do everything possible to prevent any discrimination between workers belonging to the peoples concerned and other workers, in particular as regards:

(a) admission to employment, including skilled employment, as well as measures for promotion and advancement;

(b) equal remuneration for work of equal value;

(c) medical and social assistance, occupational safety and health, all social security benefits and any other occupationally related benefits, and housing;

(d) the right of association and freedom for all lawful trade union activities, and the right to conclude collective agreements with employers or employers' organizations.

3. The measures taken shall include measures to ensure:

(a) that workers belonging to the peoples concerned, including seasonal, casual and migrant workers in agricultural and other employment, as well as those employed by labour contractors, enjoy the protection afforded by national law and practice to other such workers in the same sectors, and that they are fully informed of their rights under labour legislation and of the means of redress available to them;

(b) that workers belonging to these peoples are not subjected to working conditions hazardous to their health, in particular through exposure to pesticides or other toxic substances;

(c) that workers belonging to these peoples are not subjected to coercive recruitment systems, including bonded labour and other forms of debt servitude;

(d) that workers belonging to these peoples enjoy equal opportunities and equal treatment in employment for men and women, and protection from sexual harassment.

4. Particular attention shall be paid to the establishment of adequate labour inspection services in areas where workers belonging to the peoples concerned undertake wage employment, in order to ensure compliance with the provisions of this Part of this Convention.

PART IV
VOCATIONAL TRAINING, HANDICRAFTS AND RURAL INDUSTRIES

Article 21

Members of the peoples concerned shall enjoy opportunities at least equal to those of other citizens in respect of vocational training measures.

Article 22

1. Measures shall be taken to promote the voluntary participation of members of the peoples concerned in vocational training programmes of general application.

2. Whenever existing programmes of vocational training of general application do not meet the special needs of the peoples concerned, governments shall, with the participation of these peoples, ensure the provision of special training programmes and facilities.

3. Any special training programmes shall be based on the economic environment, social and cultural conditions and practical needs of the peoples concerned. Any studies made in this connection shall be carried out in co-operation with these peoples, who shall be consulted on the organization and operation of such programmes. Where feasible, these peoples shall progressively assume responsibility for the organization and operation of such special training programmes, if they so decide.

Article 23

1. Handicrafts, rural and community-based industries, and subsistence economy and traditional activities of the peoples concerned, such as hunting, fishing, trapping and gathering, shall be recognised as important factors in the maintenance of their cultures and in their economic self-reliance and development. Governments shall, with the participation of these people and whenever appropriate, ensure that these activities are strengthened and promoted.

2. Upon the request of the peoples concerned, appropriate technical and financial assistance shall be provided wherever possible, taking into account the traditional technologies and cultural characteristics of these peoples, as well as the importance of sustainable and equitable development.

PART V
SOCIAL SECURITY AND HEALTH

Article 24

Social security schemes shall be extended progressively to cover the peoples concerned, and applied without discrimination against them.

Article 25

1. Governments shall ensure that adequate health services are made available to the peoples concerned, or shall provide them with resources to allow them to design and deliver such services under their own responsibility and control, so that they may enjoy the highest attainable standard of physical and mental health.

2. Health services shall, to the extent possible, be community-based. These services shall be planned and administered in co-operation with the peoples concerned and take into account their economic, geographic, social and cultural conditions as well as their traditional preventive care, healing practices and medicines.

3. The health care system shall give preference to the training and employment of local community health workers, and focus on primary health care while maintaining strong links with other levels of health care services.

4. The provision of such health services shall be co-ordinated with other social, economic and cultural measures in the country.

PART VI
EDUCATION AND MEANS OF COMMUNICATION

Article 26

Measures shall be taken to ensure that members of the peoples concerned have the opportunity to acquire education at all levels on at least an equal footing with the rest of the national community.

Article 27

1. Education programmes and services for the peoples concerned shall be developed and implemented in co-operation with them to address their special needs, and shall incorporate their histories, their knowledge and technologies, their value systems and their further social, economic and cultural aspirations.

2. The competent authority shall ensure the training of members of these peoples and their involvement in the formulation and implementation of education programmes, with a view to the progressive transfer of responsibility for the conduct of these programmes to these peoples as appropriate.

3. In addition, governments shall recognise the right of these peoples to establish their own educational institutions and facilities, provided that such institutions meet minimum standards established by the competent authority in consultation with these peoples. Appropriate resources shall be provided for this purpose.

Article 28

1. Children belonging to the peoples concerned shall, wherever practicable, be taught to read and write in their own indigenous language or in the language most commonly used by the group to which they belong. When this is not practicable, the competent authorities shall undertake consultations with these peoples with a view to the adoption of measures to achieve this objective.

2. Adequate measures shall be taken to ensure that these peoples have the opportunity to attain fluency in the national language or in one of the official languages of the country.

3. Measures shall be taken to preserve and promote the development and practice of the indigenous languages of the peoples concerned.

Article 29

The imparting of general knowledge and skills that will help children belonging to the peoples concerned to participate fully and on an equal footing in their own community and in the national community shall be an aim of education for these peoples.

Article 30

1. Governments shall adopt measures appropriate to the traditions and cultures of the peoples concerned, to make known to them their rights and duties, especially in regard to labour, economic opportunities, education and health matters, social welfare and their rights deriving from this Convention.

2. If necessary, this shall be done by means of written translations and through the use of mass communications in the languages of these peoples.

Article 31

Educational measures shall be taken among all sections of the national community, and particularly among those that are in most direct contact with the peoples concerned, with the object of eliminating prejudices that they may harbour in respect of these peoples. To this end, efforts shall be made to ensure that history textbooks and other educational materials provide a fair, accurate and informative portrayal of the societies and cultures of these peoples.

PART VII
CONTACTS AND CO-OPERATION ACROSS BORDERS

Article 32

Governments shall take appropriate measures, including by means of international agreements, to facilitate contacts and co-operation between indigenous and tribal peoples across borders, including activities in the economic, social, cultural, spiritual and environmental fields.

PART VIII
ADMINISTRATION

Article 33

1. The governmental authority responsible for the matters covered in this Convention shall ensure that agencies or other appropriate mechanisms exist to administer the programmes affecting the peoples concerned, and shall ensure that they have the means necessary for the proper fulfilment of the functions assigned to them.

2. These programmes shall include:
   (a) the planning, co-ordination, execution and evaluation, in co-operation with the peoples concerned, of the measures provided for in this Convention;
   (b) the proposing of legislative and other measures to the competent authorities and supervision of the application of the measures taken, in co-operation with the peoples concerned.

PART IX
GENERAL PROVISIONS

Article 34

The nature and scope of the measures to be taken to give effect to this Convention shall be determined in a flexible manner, having regard to the conditions characteristic of each country.

Article 35

The application of the provisions of this Convention shall not adversely affect rights and benefits of the peoples concerned pursuant to other Conventions and Recommendations, international instruments, treaties, or national laws, awards, custom or agreements.

PART X
FINAL PROVISIONS

Article 36

This Convention revises the Indigenous and Tribal Populations Convention, 1957.

Article 37

The formal ratifications of this Convention shall be communicated to the Director-General of the International Labour Office for registration.

Article 38

1. This Convention shall be binding only upon those Members of the International Labour Organization whose ratifications have been registered with the Director-General.

2. It shall come into force twelve months after the date on which the ratifications of two Members have been registered with the Director-General.

3. Thereafter, this Convention shall come into force for any Member twelve months after the date on which its ratification has been registered.

Article 39

1. A Member which has ratified this Convention may denounce it after the expiration of ten years from the date on which the Convention first comes into force, by an act communicated to the Director-General of the International Labour Office for registration. Such denunciation shall not take effect until one year after the date on which it is registered.

2. Each Member which has ratified this Convention and which does not, within the year following the expiration of the period of ten years mentioned in the preceding paragraph, exercise the right of denunciation provided for in this Article, will be bound for another period of ten years and, thereafter, may denounce this Convention at the expiration of each period of ten years under the terms provided for in this Article.

Article 40

1. The Director-General of the International Labour Office shall notify all Members of the International Labour Organization of the registration of all ratifications and denunciations communicated to him by the Members of the Organization.

2. When notifying the Members of the Organization of the registration of the second ratification communicated to him, the Director-General shall draw the attention of the Members of the Organization to the date upon which the Convention will come into force.

Article 41

The Director-General of the International Labour Office shall communicate to the Secretary-General of the United Nations for registration in accordance with Article 102 of the Charter of the United Nations full particulars of all ratifications and acts of denunciation registered by him in accordance with the provisions of the preceding Articles.

Article 42

At such times as it may consider necessary the Governing Body of the International Labour Office shall present to the General Conference a report on the working of this Convention and shall examine the desirability of placing on the agenda of the Conference the question of its revision in whole or in part.

Article 43

1. Should the Conference adopt a new Convention revising this Convention in whole or in part, then, unless the new Convention otherwise provides:

   (a) the ratification by a Member of the new revising Convention shall *ipso jure* involve the immediate denunciation of this Convention, notwithstanding the provisions of Article 39 above, if and when the new revising Convention shall have come into force;

   (b) as from the date when the new revising Convention comes into force this Convention shall cease to be open to ratification by the Members.

2. This Convention shall in any case remain in force in its actual form and content for those Members which have ratified it but have not ratified the revising Convention.

Article 44

The English and French versions of the text of this Convention are equally authoritative.

76. DECLARATION ON FUNDAMENTAL PRINCIPLES AND RIGHTS AT WORK, 1998

This Declaration was adopted by the ILO at its 86th Session in Geneva on 18 June 1998, in large measure in response to the challenges of globalization; for text, see 37 *ILM* 1233 (1998) http://www.ilo.org/declaration/lang-en/index.htm. See also the Copenhagen Declaration on Social Development, 1995, in which Heads of State and Government undertook specific commitments to safeguard and promote respect for basic workers' rights: 'Report of the World Summit for Social Development', Copenhagen, 6–12 March 1995, UN doc. A/CONF.166/9, 19 April 1995, paragraph 54(b) (text also in the fourth edition of this work, at 869).

In the case of States party to the various ILO conventions, the existing supervisory machinery already provides the means to assure their application. For non-parties, however, this Declaration breaks new ground, first, by recognizing that ILO Members generally have an obligation to respect 'in good faith and in accordance with the Constitution, the principles concerning the fundamental rights which are the subject of those Conventions'; and secondly, as means of follow-up, by invoking the ILO's Constitutional procedure under which States which have not ratified the 'fundamental conventions' will be asked to report on progress made implementing the principles they contain.

Further reading

INTERNATIONAL LABOUR OFFICE, 'Review of annual reports under the follow-up to the ILO Declaration on Fundamental Principles and Rights at Work', doc. 304/3, Governing Body, 304th Session, March 2009.

MUNDLAK, G., 'The Right to Work: Linking Human Rights and Employment Policy', (2007) 146 *International Labour Review* 189.

O'REILLY, A., *The Right to Decent Work of Persons with Disabilities*, Geneva: ILO, 2007.

TEXT

Whereas the ILO was founded in the conviction that social justice is essential to universal and lasting peace;

Whereas economic growth is essential but not sufficient to ensure equity, social progress and the eradication of poverty, confirming the need for the ILO to promote strong social policies, justice and democratic institutions;

Whereas the ILO should, now more than ever, draw upon all its standard-setting, technical cooperation and research resources in all its areas of competence, in particular employment, vocational training and working conditions, to ensure that, in the context of a global strategy for economic and social development, economic and social policies are mutually reinforcing components in order to create broad-based sustainable development;

Whereas the ILO should give special attention to the problems of persons with special social needs, particularly the unemployed and migrant workers, and mobilize and encourage international, regional and national efforts aimed at resolving their problems, and promote effective policies aimed at job creation;

Whereas, in seeking to maintain the link between social progress and economic growth, the guarantee of Fundamental Principles and Rights at Work is of particular significance in that it enables the persons concerned, to claim freely and on the basis of equality of opportunity, their fair share of the wealth which they have helped to generate, and to achieve fully their human potential;

Whereas the ILO is the constitutionally mandated international organization and the competent body to set and deal with international labour standards, and enjoys universal support and acknowledgement in promoting Fundamental Rights at Work as the expression of its constitutional principles;

Whereas it is urgent, in a situation of growing economic interdependence, to reaffirm the immutable nature of the Fundamental Principles and Rights embodied in the Constitution of the Organization and to promote their universal application;

The International Labour Conference

1. Recalls:

    (a) that in freely joining the ILO, all Members have endorsed the principles and rights set out in its Constitution and in the Declaration of Philadelphia, and have undertaken to work towards attaining the overall objectives of the Organization to the best of their resources and fully in line with their specific circumstances;

    (b) that these principles and rights have been expressed and developed in the form of specific rights and obligations in Conventions recognized as fundamental both inside and outside the Organization.

2. Declares that all Members, even if they have not ratified the Conventions in question, have an obligation arising from the very fact of membership in the Organization to respect, to promote and to realize, in good faith and in accordance with the Constitution, the principles concerning the fundamental rights which are the subject of those Conventions, namely:

    (a) freedom of association and the effective recognition of the right to collective bargaining;

    (b) the elimination of all forms of forced or compulsory labour;

    (c) the effective abolition of child labour; and

    (d) the elimination of discrimination in respect of employment and occupation.

3. Recognizes the obligation on the Organization to assist its Members, in response to their established and expressed needs, in order to attain these objectives by making full use of its constitutional, operational and budgetary resources, including, by the mobilization of external resources and support, as well as by encouraging other international organizations with which the ILO has established relations, pursuant to Article 12 of its Constitution, to support these efforts:

    (a) by offering technical cooperation and advisory services to promote the ratification and implementation of the fundamental Conventions;

    (b) by assisting those Members not yet in a position to ratify some or all of these Conventions in their efforts to respect, to promote and to realize the principles concerning fundamental rights which are the subject of these Conventions; and

    (c) by helping the Members in their efforts to create a climate for economic and social development.

4. Decides that, to give full effect to this Declaration, a promotional follow-up, which is meaningful and effective, shall be implemented in accordance with the measures specified in the annex hereto, which shall be considered as an integral part of this Declaration.

5. Stresses that labour standards should not be used for protectionist trade purposes, and that nothing in this Declaration and its follow-up shall be invoked or otherwise used for

such purposes; in addition, the comparative advantage of any country should in no way be called into question by this Declaration and its follow-up.

ANNEX
FOLLOW-UP TO THE DECLARATION

I. OVERALL PURPOSE

1. The aim of the follow-up described below is to encourage the efforts made by the Members of the Organization to promote the fundamental principles and rights enshrined in the Constitution of the ILO and the Declaration of Philadelphia and reaffirmed in this Declaration.

2. In line with this objective, which is of a strictly promotional nature, this follow-up will allow the identification of areas in which the assistance of the Organization through its technical cooperation activities may prove useful to its Members to help them implement these fundamental principles and rights. It is not a substitute for the established supervisory mechanisms, nor shall it impede their functioning; consequently, specific situations within the purview of those mechanisms shall not be examined or re-examined within the framework of this follow-up.

3. The two aspects of this follow-up, described below, are based on existing procedures: the annual follow-up concerning non-ratified fundamental Conventions will entail merely some adaptation of the present modalities of application of Article 19, paragraph 5(e) of the Constitution; and the global report will serve to obtain the best results from the procedures carried out pursuant to the Constitution.

II. ANNUAL FOLLOW-UP CONCERNING NON-RATIFIED FUNDAMENTAL CONVENTIONS

A. Purpose and scope

1. The purpose is to provide an opportunity to review each year, by means of simplified procedures to replace the four-year review introduced by the Governing Body in 1995, the efforts made in accordance with the Declaration by Members which have not yet ratified all the fundamental Conventions.

2. The follow-up will cover each year the four areas of fundamental principles and rights specified in the Declaration.

B. Modalities

1. The follow-up will be based on reports requested from Members under Article 19, paragraph 5(e) of the Constitution. The report forms will be drawn up so as to obtain information from governments which have not ratified one or more of the fundamental Conventions, on any changes which may have taken place in their law and practice, taking due account of Article 23 of the Constitution and established practice.

2. These reports, as compiled by the Office, will be reviewed by the Governing Body.

3. With a view to presenting an introduction to the reports thus compiled, drawing attention to any aspects which might call for a more in-depth discussion, the Office may call upon a group of experts appointed for this purpose by the Governing Body.

4. Adjustments to the Governing Body's existing procedures should be examined to allow Members which are not represented on the Governing Body to provide, in the most appropriate way, clarifications which might prove necessary or useful during Governing Body discussions to supplement the information contained in their reports.

III. GLOBAL REPORT

A. Purpose and scope

1. The purpose of this report is to provide a dynamic global picture relating to each category of fundamental principles and rights noted during the preceding four-year period, and to serve as a basis for assessing the effectiveness of the assistance provided by the Organization, and for determining priorities for the following period, in the form of action plans for technical cooperation designed in particular to mobilize the internal and external resources necessary to carry them out.

2. The report will cover, each year, one of the four categories of fundamental principles and rights in turn.

B. Modalities

1. The report will be drawn up under the responsibility of the Director-General on the basis of official information, or information gathered and assessed in accordance with established procedures. In the case of States which have not ratified the fundamental Conventions, it will be based in particular on the findings of the aforementioned annual follow-up. In the case of Members which have ratified the Conventions concerned, the report will be based in particular on reports as dealt with pursuant to Article 22 of the Constitution.

2. This report will be submitted to the Conference for tripartite discussion as a report of the Director-General. The Conference may deal with this report separately from reports under Article 12 of its Standing Orders, and may discuss it during a sitting devoted entirely to this report, or in any other appropriate way. It will then be for the Governing Body, at an early session, to draw conclusions from this discussion concerning the priorities and plans of action for technical cooperation to be implemented for the following four-year period.

IV. IT IS UNDERSTOOD THAT

1. Proposals shall be made for amendments to the Standing Orders of the Governing Body and the Conference which are required to implement the preceding provisions.

2. The Conference shall, in due course, review the operation of this follow-up in the light of the experience acquired to assess whether it has adequately fulfilled the overall purpose articulated in Part I.

77. WORST FORMS OF CHILD LABOUR CONVENTION, 1999

The Convention concerning the Prohibition and Immediate Action for the Elimination of the Worst Forms of Child Labour (C182) was adopted on 17 June 1999 and came into force on 19 November 2000. It focuses on the prohibition and elimination of slavery, debt bondage, prostitution, pornography, and other forms of abusive child labour.

Further reading

ARAT, Z. F., 'Analyzing Child Labor as a Human Rights Issue: Its Causes, Aggravating Policies, and Alternative Proposals', (2002) 24 *Human Rights Quarterly* 177.

CULLEN, H., *The Role of International Law in the Elimination of Child Labor*, Leiden: Martinus Nijhoff, 2008.

INTERNATIONAL LABOUR OFFICE, *The end of child labour: Within reach. Global report under the Follow-up to the ILO Declaration on Fundamental Principles and Rights at Work*, Report of the Director-General, International Labour Conference, 95th Session, Geneva, 2006.

——, *A Future without Child Labour: Global Report under the Follow-up to the ILO Declaration on Fundamental Principles and Rights at Work*, Report of the Director-General, International Labour Conference, 90th Session, Geneva, 2002.

NESI, G., NOGLER, L. and PERTILE, M., *Child Labour in a Globalized World: A Legal Analysis of ILO Action*, Farnham: Ashgate, 2008.

TEXT

The General Conference of the International Labour Organization,

Having been convened at Geneva by the Governing Body of the International Labour Office, and having met in its 87th Session on 1 June 1999, and

Considering the need to adopt new instruments for the prohibition and elimination of the worst forms of child labour, as the main priority for national and international action, including international cooperation and assistance, to complement the Convention and the Recommendation concerning Minimum Age for Admission to Employment, 1973, which remain fundamental instruments on child labour, and

Considering that the effective elimination of the worst forms of child labour requires immediate and comprehensive action, taking into account the importance of free basic education and the need to remove the children concerned from all such work and to provide for their rehabilitation and social integration while addressing the needs of their families, and

Recalling the resolution concerning the elimination of child labour adopted by the International Labour Conference at its 83rd Session in 1996, and

Recognizing that child labour is to a great extent caused by poverty and that the long-term solution lies in sustained economic growth leading to social progress, in particular poverty alleviation and universal education, and

Recalling the Convention on the Rights of the Child adopted by the United Nations General Assembly on 20 November 1989, and

Recalling the ILO Declaration on Fundamental Principles and Rights at Work and its Follow-up, adopted by the International Labour Conference at its 86th Session in 1998, and

Recalling that some of the worst forms of child labour are covered by other international instruments, in particular the Forced Labour Convention, 1930, and the United Nations

Supplementary Convention on the Abolition of Slavery, the Slave Trade, and Institutions and Practices Similar to Slavery, 1956, and

Having decided upon the adoption of certain proposals with regard to child labour, which is the fourth item on the agenda of the session, and

Having determined that these proposals shall take the form of an international Convention;

Adopts this seventeenth day of June of the year one thousand nine hundred and ninety-nine the following Convention, which may be cited as the Worst Forms of Child Labour Convention, 1999.

Article 1

Each Member which ratifies this Convention shall take immediate and effective measures to secure the prohibition and elimination of the worst forms of child labour as a matter of urgency.

Article 2

For the purposes of this Convention, the term 'child' shall apply to all persons under the age of 18.

Article 3

For the purposes of this Convention, the term 'the worst forms of child labour' comprises:

(a) all forms of slavery or practices similar to slavery, such as the sale and trafficking of children, debt bondage and serfdom and forced or compulsory labour, including forced or compulsory recruitment of children for use in armed conflict;

(b) the use, procuring or offering of a child for prostitution, for the production of pornography or for pornographic performances;

(c) the use, procuring or offering of a child for illicit activities, in particular for the production and trafficking of drugs as defined in the relevant international treaties;

(d) work which, by its nature or the circumstances in which it is carried out, is likely to harm the health, safety or morals of children.

Article 4

1. The types of work referred to under Article 3(d) shall be determined by national laws or regulations or by the competent authority, after consultation with the organizations of employers and workers concerned, taking into consideration relevant international standards, in particular Paragraphs 3 and 4 of the Worst Forms of Child Labour Recommendation, 1999.

2. The competent authority, after consultation with the organizations of employers and workers concerned, shall identify where the types of work so determined exist.

3. The list of the types of work determined under paragraph 1 of this Article shall be periodically examined and revised as necessary, in consultation with the organizations of employers and workers concerned.

Article 5

Each Member shall, after consultation with employers' and workers' organizations, establish or designate appropriate mechanisms to monitor the implementation of the provisions giving effect to this Convention.

Article 6

1. Each Member shall design and implement programmes of action to eliminate as a priority the worst forms of child labour.

2. Such programmes of action shall be designed and implemented in consultation with relevant government institutions and employers' and workers' organizations, taking into consideration the views of other concerned groups as appropriate.

Article 7

1. Each Member shall take all necessary measures to ensure the effective implementation and enforcement of the provisions giving effect to this Convention including the provision and application of penal sanctions or, as appropriate, other sanctions.

2. Each Member shall, taking into account the importance of education in eliminating child labour, take effective and time-bound measures to:

  (a) prevent the engagement of children in the worst forms of child labour;

  (b) provide the necessary and appropriate direct assistance for the removal of children from the worst forms of child labour and for their rehabilitation and social integration;

  (c) ensure access to free basic education, and, wherever possible and appropriate, vocational training, for all children removed from the worst forms of child labour;

  (d) identify and reach out to children at special risk; and

  (e) take account of the special situation of girls.

3. Each Member shall designate the competent authority responsible for the implementation of the provisions giving effect to this Convention.

Article 8

Members shall take appropriate steps to assist one another in giving effect to the provisions of this Convention through enhanced international cooperation and/or assistance including support for social and economic development, poverty eradication programmes and universal education.

Article 9

The formal ratifications of this Convention shall be communicated to the Director-General of the International Labour Office for registration.

Article 10

1. This Convention shall be binding only upon those Members of the International Labour Organization whose ratifications have been registered with the Director-General of the International Labour Office.

2. It shall come into force 12 months after the date on which the ratifications of two Members have been registered with the Director-General.

3. Thereafter, this Convention shall come into force for any Member 12 months after the date on which its ratification has been registered.

Article 11

1. A Member which has ratified this Convention may denounce it after the expiration of ten years from the date on which the Convention first comes into force, by an act

communicated to the Director-General of the International Labour Office for registration. Such denunciation shall not take effect until one year after the date on which it is registered.

2. Each Member which has ratified this Convention and which does not, within the year following the expiration of the period of ten years mentioned in the preceding paragraph, exercise the right of denunciation provided for in this Article, will be bound for another period of ten years and, thereafter, may denounce this Convention at the expiration of each period of ten years under the terms provided for in this Article.

Article 12

1. The Director-General of the International Labour Office shall notify all Members of the International Labour Organization of the registration of all ratifications and acts of denunciation communicated by the Members of the Organization.

2. When notifying the Members of the Organization of the registration of the second ratification, the Director-General shall draw the attention of the Members of the Organization to the date upon which the Convention shall come into force.

Article 13

The Director-General of the International Labour Office shall communicate to the Secretary-General of the United Nations, for registration in accordance with article 102 of the Charter of the United Nations, full particulars of all ratifications and acts of denunciation registered by the Director-General in accordance with the provisions of the preceding Articles.

Article 14

At such times as it may consider necessary, the Governing Body of the International Labour Office shall present to the General Conference a report on the working of this Convention and shall examine the desirability of placing on the agenda of the Conference the question of its revision in whole or in part.

Article 15

1. Should the Conference adopt a new Convention revising this Convention in whole or in part, then, unless the new Convention otherwise provides:

(a) the ratification by a Member of the new revising Convention shall *ipso jure* involve the immediate denunciation of this Convention, notwithstanding the provisions of Article 11 above, if and when the new revising Convention shall have come into force;

(b) as from the date when the new revising Convention comes into force, this Convention shall cease to be open to ratification by the Members.

2. This Convention shall in any case remain in force in its actual form and content for those Members which have ratified it but have not ratified the revising Convention.

Article 16

The English and French versions of the text of this Convention are equally authoritative.

78. TRIPARTITE DECLARATION OF PRINCIPLES CONCERNING MULTINATIONAL ENTERPRISES AND SOCIAL POLICY, 2000

Adopted by the Governing Body of the International Labour Office ILO at its 204th Session, Geneva, November 1977, and amended at its 279th Session, November 2000 and 295th Session, March 2006; see *Official Bulletin*, Vol. LXXXIII, 2000, Series A, No. 3. Paragraphs 1–7, 8, 10, 25, 26, and 52 (formerly paragraph 51) have been the subject of interpretation under the Procedure for the examination of disputes concerning the application of the Tripartite Declaration of Principles concerning Multinational Enterprises and Social Policy. Copies of interpretations are available from the Bureau of Multinational Enterprise Activities, International Labour Office, 4, route des Morillons, CH-1211 Geneva 22, Switzerland, or at **http://www.ilo.org**.

The Annex and Addendum I, which contain a list of international labour Conventions and Recommendations referred to in the Tripartite Declaration of Principles concerning Multinational Enterprises and Social Policy, are omitted. Addendum I notes, 'In keeping with the voluntary nature of the Declaration, all of its provisions, whether derived from ILO Conventions and Recommendations or other sources, are recommendatory, except of course for provisions in Conventions which are binding on the member States which have ratified them.'

Further reading

INTERNATIONAL LABOUR ORGANIZATION, THE GLOBAL COMPACT, *The Labour Principles of the United Nations Global Compact: A Guide for Business*, Geneva: ILO, 2008.
——, *Codes of Conduct and Multinational Enterprise*, Geneva: ILO, 2002.

TEXT

The Governing Body of the International Labour Office,

Recalling that the International Labour Organization for many years has been involved with certain social issues related to the activities of multinational enterprises;

Noting in particular that various Industrial Committees, Regional Conferences, and the International Labour Conference since the mid-1960s have requested appropriate action by the Governing Body in the field of multinational enterprises and social policy;

Having been informed of the activities of other international bodies, in particular the UN Commission on Transnational Corporations and the Organization for Economic Cooperation and Development (OECD);

Considering that the ILO, with its unique tripartite structure, its competence, and its long-standing experience in the social field, has an essential role to play in evolving principles for the guidance of governments, workers' and employers' organizations, and multinational enterprises themselves;

Recalling that it convened a Tripartite Meeting of Experts on the Relationship between Multinational Enterprises and Social Policy in 1972, which recommended an ILO programme of research and study, and a Tripartite Advisory Meeting on the Relationship of Multinational Enterprises and Social Policy in 1976 for the purpose of reviewing the ILO programme of research and suggesting appropriate ILO action in the social and labour field;

Bearing in mind the deliberations of the World Employment Conference;

Having thereafter decided to establish a tripartite group to prepare a Draft Tripartite Declaration of Principles covering all of the areas of ILO concern which relate to the social aspects of the activities of multinational enterprises, including employment creation in the developing countries, all the while bearing in mind the recommendations made by the Tripartite Advisory Meeting held in 1976;

Having also decided to reconvene the Tripartite Advisory Meeting to consider the Draft Declaration of Principles as prepared by the tripartite group;

Having considered the Report and the Draft Declaration of Principles submitted to it by the reconvened Tripartite Advisory Meeting;

Hereby approves the following Declaration which may be cited as the Tripartite Declaration of Principles concerning Multinational Enterprises and Social Policy, adopted by the Governing Body of the International Labour Office, and invites governments of States Members of the ILO, the employers' and workers' organizations concerned and the multinational enterprises operating in their territories to observe the principles embodied therein.

1. Multinational enterprises play an important part in the economies of most countries and in international economic relations. This is of increasing interest to governments as well as to employers and workers and their respective organizations. Through international direct investment and other means such enterprises can bring substantial benefits to home and host countries by contributing to the more efficient utilization of capital, technology and labour. Within the framework of development policies established by governments, they can also make an important contribution to the promotion of economic and social welfare; to the improvement of living standards and the satisfaction of basic needs; to the creation of employment opportunities, both directly and indirectly; and to the enjoyment of basic human rights, including freedom of association, throughout the world. On the other hand, the advances made by multinational enterprises in organizing their operations beyond the national framework may lead to abuse of concentrations of economic power and to conflicts with national policy objectives and with the interest of the workers. In addition, the complexity of multinational enterprises and the difficulty of clearly perceiving their diverse structures, operations and policies sometimes give rise to concern either in the home or in the host countries, or in both.

2. The aim of this Tripartite Declaration of Principles is to encourage the positive contribution which multinational enterprises can make to economic and social progress and to minimize and resolve the difficulties to which their various operations may give rise, taking into account the United Nations resolutions advocating the establishment of a New International Economic Order, as well as subsequent developments within the United Nations, for example, the Global Compact and the Millennium Development Goals.

3. This aim will be furthered by appropriate laws and policies, measures and actions adopted by the governments and by cooperation among the governments and the employers' and workers' organizations of all countries.

4. The principles set out in this Declaration are commended to the governments, the employers' and workers' organizations of home and host countries and to the multinational enterprises themselves.

5. These principles are intended to guide the governments, the employers' and workers' organizations and the multinational enterprises in taking such measures and actions and adopting such social policies, including those based on the principles laid down in the Constitution and the relevant Conventions and Recommendations of the ILO, as would further social progress.

6. To serve its purpose this Declaration does not require a precise legal definition of multinational enterprises; this paragraph is designed to facilitate the understanding of the Declaration and not to provide such a definition. Multinational enterprises include enterprises, whether they are of public, mixed or private ownership, which own or control production, distribution, services or other facilities outside the country in which they are based. The degree of autonomy of entities within multinational enterprises in relation to each other varies widely from one such enterprise to another, depending on the nature of the links between such entities and their fields of activity and having regard to the great diversity in the form of ownership, in the size, in the nature and location of the operations of the enterprises concerned. Unless otherwise specified, the term 'multinational enterprise' is used in this Declaration to designate the various entities (parent companies or local entities or both or the organization as a whole) according to the distribution of responsibilities among them, in the expectation that they will cooperate and provide assistance to one another as necessary to facilitate observance of the principles laid down in the Declaration.

7. This Declaration sets out principles in the fields of employment, training, conditions of work and life and industrial relations which governments, employers' and workers' organizations and multinational enterprises are recommended to observe on a voluntary basis; its provisions shall not limit or otherwise affect obligations arising out of ratification of any ILO Convention.

GENERAL POLICIES

8. All the parties concerned by this Declaration should respect the sovereign rights of States, obey the national laws and regulations, give due consideration to local practices and respect relevant international standards. They should respect the Universal Declaration of Human Rights and the corresponding International Covenants adopted by the General Assembly of the United Nations as well as the Constitution of the International Labour Organization and its principles according to which freedom of expression and association are essential to sustained progress. They should contribute to the realization of the ILO Declaration on Fundamental Principles and Rights and Work and its Follow-up, adopted in 1998. They should also honour commitments which they have freely entered into, in conformity with the national law and accepted international obligations.

9. Governments of States which have not yet ratified Conventions Nos. 29, 87, 98, 100, 105, 111, 122, 138 and 182 are urged to do so and in any event to apply, to the greatest extent possible, through their national policies, the principles embodied therein and in Recommendations Nos. 35, 90, 111, 119, 122, 146, 169, 189 and 190.[1] Without prejudice

---

[1] Convention (No. 29) concerning Forced or Compulsory Labour; Convention (No. 87) concerning Freedom of Association and Protection of the Right to Organise; Convention (No. 98) concerning the Application of the Principles of the Right to Organise and to Bargain Collectively; Convention (No. 100) concerning Equal Remuneration for Men and Women Workers for Work of Equal Value; Convention (No. 105) concerning the Abolition of Forced Labour; Convention (No. 111) concerning Discrimination in Respect of Employment and Occupation; Convention (No. 122) concerning Employment Policy; Convention (No. 138) concerning Minimum Age for Admission to Employment; Convention (No. 182) concerning the Prohibition and Immediate Action for the Elimination of the Worst Forms of Child Labour; Recommendation (No. 35) concerning Indirect Compulsion to Labour; Recommendation (No. 90) concerning Equal Remuneration for Men and Women Workers for Work of Equal Value; Recommendation (No. 111) concerning Discrimination in Respect of Employment and Occupation; Recommendation (No. 119) concerning Termination of Employment at the Initiative of the Employer; Recommendation (No. 122) concerning Employment Policy; Recommendation (No. 146) concerning Minimum Age for Admission to Employment; Recommendation (No. 169) concerning

to the obligation of governments to ensure compliance with Conventions they have ratified, in countries in which the Conventions and Recommendations cited in this paragraph are not complied with, all parties should refer to them for guidance in their social policy.

10. Multinational enterprises should take fully into account established general policy objectives of the countries in which they operate. Their activities should be in harmony with the development priorities and social aims and structure of the country in which they operate. To this effect, consultations should be held between multinational enterprises, the government and, wherever appropriate, the national employers' and workers' organizations concerned.

11. The principles laid down in this Declaration do not aim at introducing or maintaining inequalities of treatment between multinational and national enterprises. They reflect good practice for all. Multinational and national enterprises, wherever the principles of this Declaration are relevant to both, should be subject to the same expectations in respect of their conduct in general and their social practices in particular.

12. Governments of home countries should promote good social practice in accordance with this Declaration of Principles, having regard to the social and labour law, regulations and practices in host countries as well as to relevant international standards. Both host and home country governments should be prepared to have consultations with each other, whenever the need arises, on the initiative of either.

EMPLOYMENT

Employment promotion

13. With a view to stimulating economic growth and development, raising living standards, meeting manpower requirements and overcoming unemployment and underemployment, governments should declare and pursue, as a major goal, an active policy designed to promote full, productive and freely chosen employment.[2]

14. This is particularly important in the case of host country governments in developing areas of the world where the problems of unemployment and underemployment are at their most serious. In this connection, the general conclusions adopted by the Tripartite World Conference on Employment, Income Distribution and Social Progress and the International Division of Labour (Geneva, June 1976),[3] and the Global Employment Agenda (Geneva, March 2003)[4] should be kept in mind.

15. Paragraphs 13 and 14 above establish the framework within which due attention should be paid, in both home and host countries, to the employment impact of multinational enterprises.

16. Multinational enterprises, particularly when operating in developing countries, should endeavour to increase employment opportunities and standards, taking into

Employment Policy; Recommendation (No. 189) concerning General Conditions to stimulate Job Creation in Small and Medium-Sized Enterprises; Recommendation (No. 190) concerning the Prohibition and Immediate Action for the Elimination of the Worst Forms of Child Labour.

   [2] Convention (No. 122) and Recommendation (No. 122) concerning Employment Policy; Recommendation (No. 169) concerning Employment Policy; and Recommendation (No. 189) concerning General Conditions to stimulate Job Creation in Small and Medium-Sized Enterprises.

   [3] ILO, World Employment Conference, Geneva, 4–17 June 1976.

   [4] ILO Global Employment Agenda, 2003, ILO, Geneva.

account the employment policies and objectives of the governments, as well as security of employment and the long-term development of the enterprise.

17. Before starting operations, multinational enterprises should, wherever appropriate, consult the competent authorities and the national employers' and workers' organizations in order to keep their manpower plans, as far as practicable, in harmony with national social development policies. Such consultation, as in the case of national enterprises, should continue between the multinational enterprises and all parties concerned, including the workers' organizations.

18. Multinational enterprises should give priority to the employment, occupational development, promotion and advancement of nationals of the host country at all levels in cooperation, as appropriate, with representatives of the workers employed by them or of the organizations of these workers and governmental authorities.

19. Multinational enterprises, when investing in developing countries, should have regard to the importance of using technologies which generate employment, both directly and indirectly. To the extent permitted by the nature of the process and the conditions prevailing in the economic sector concerned, they should adapt technologies to the needs and characteristics of the host countries. They should also, where possible, take part in the development of appropriate technology in host countries.

20. To promote employment in developing countries, in the context of an expanding world economy, multinational enterprises, wherever practicable, should give consideration to the conclusion of contracts with national enterprises for the manufacture of parts and equipment, to the use of local raw materials and to the progressive promotion of the local processing of raw materials. Such arrangements should not be used by multinational enterprises to avoid the responsibilities embodied in the principles of this Declaration.

Equality of opportunity and treatment

21. All governments should pursue policies designed to promote equality of opportunity and treatment in employment, with a view to eliminating any discrimination based on race, colour, sex, religion, political opinion, national extraction or social origin.[5]

22. Multinational enterprises should be guided by this general principle throughout their operations without prejudice to the measures envisaged in paragraph 18 or to government policies designed to correct historical patterns of discrimination and thereby to extend equality of opportunity and treatment in employment.[6] Multinational enterprises should accordingly make qualifications, skill and experience the basis for the recruitment, placement, training and advancement of their staff at all levels.

23. Governments should never require or encourage multinational enterprises to discriminate on any of the grounds mentioned in paragraph 21, and continuing guidance from governments, where appropriate, on the avoidance of such discrimination in employment is encouraged.

---

[5] Convention (No. 111) and Recommendation (No. 111) concerning Discrimination in Respect of Employment and Occupation; Convention (No. 100) and Recommendation (No. 90) concerning Equal Remuneration for Men and Women Workers for Work of Equal Value.

[6] See the two following ILO codes of practice: *HIV/AIDS and the world of work*, ILO code of practice, 2001, ILO, Geneva; *Managing disability in the workplace*, ILO code of practice, 2002, ILO, Geneva.

Security of employment

24. Governments should carefully study the impact of multinational enterprises on employment in different industrial sectors. Governments, as well as multinational enterprises themselves, in all countries should take suitable measures to deal with the employment and labour market impacts of the operations of multinational enterprises.

25. Multinational enterprises equally with national enterprises, through active manpower planning, should endeavour to provide stable employment for their employees and should observe freely negotiated obligations concerning employment stability and social security. In view of the flexibility which multinational enterprises may have, they should strive to assume a leading role in promoting security of employment, particularly in countries where the discontinuation of operations is likely to accentuate long-term unemployment.

26. In considering changes in operations (including those resulting from mergers, take-overs or transfers of production) which would have major employment effects, multinational enterprises should provide reasonable notice of such changes to the appropriate government authorities and representatives of the workers in their employment and their organizations so that the implications may be examined jointly in order to mitigate adverse effects to the greatest possible extent. This is particularly important in the case of the closure of an entity involving collective lay-offs or dismissals.

27. Arbitrary dismissal procedures should be avoided.[7]

28. Governments, in cooperation with multinational as well as national enterprises, should provide some form of income protection for workers whose employment has been terminated.[8]

TRAINING

29. Governments, in cooperation with all the parties concerned, should develop national policies for vocational training and guidance, closely linked with employment.[9] This is the framework within which multinational enterprises should pursue their training policies.

30. In their operations, multinational enterprises should ensure that relevant training is provided for all levels of their employees in the host country, as appropriate, to meet the needs of the enterprise as well as the development policies of the country. Such training should, to the extent possible, develop generally useful skills and promote career opportunities. This responsibility should be carried out, where appropriate, in cooperation with the authorities of the country, employers' and workers' organizations and the competent local, national or international institutions.

31. Multinational enterprises operating in developing countries should participate, along with national enterprises, in programmes, including special funds, encouraged by host governments and supported by employers' and workers' organizations. These programmes should have the aim of encouraging skill formation and development as well as providing vocational guidance, and should be jointly administered by the parties

---

[7] Recommendation (No. 119) concerning Termination of Employment at the Initiative of the Employer.

[8] ibid.

[9] Convention (No. 142) concerning Human Resources Development and Recommendation (No. 195) concerning Human Resources Development: Education, Training and Lifelong Learning, recalling the voluntary nature of the substance and levels of collective bargaining.

which support them. Wherever practicable, multinational enterprises should make the services of skilled resource personnel available to help in training programmes organized by governments as part of a contribution to national development.

32. Multinational enterprises, with the cooperation of governments and to the extent consistent with the efficient operation of the enterprise, should afford opportunities within the enterprise as a whole to broaden the experience of local management in suitable fields such as industrial relations.

CONDITIONS OF WORK AND LIFE

Wages, benefits and conditions of work

33. Wages, benefits and conditions of work offered by multinational enterprises should be not less favourable to the workers than those offered by comparable employers in the country concerned.

34. When multinational enterprises operate in developing countries, where comparable employers may not exist, they should provide the best possible wages, benefits and conditions of work, within the framework of government policies.[10] These should be related to the economic position of the enterprise, but should be at least adequate to satisfy basic needs of the workers and their families. Where they provide workers with basic amenities such as housing, medical care or food, these amenities should be of a good standard.[11]

35. Governments, especially in developing countries, should endeavour to adopt suitable measures to ensure that lower income groups and less developed areas benefit as much as possible from the activities of multinational enterprises.

Minimum age

36. Multinational enterprises, as well as national enterprises, should respect the minimum age for admission to employment or work in order to secure the effective abolition of child labour and should take immediate and effective measures within their own competence to secure the prohibition and elimination of the worst forms of child labour as a matter of urgency.[12]

Safety and health

37. Governments should ensure that both multinational and national enterprises provide adequate safety and health standards for their employees. Those governments which have not yet ratified the ILO Conventions on Guarding of Machinery (No. 119), Ionising Radiation (No. 115), Benzene (No. 136) and Occupational Cancer (No. 139) are urged nevertheless to apply to the greatest extent possible the principles embodied in these Conventions and in their related Recommendations (Nos. 118, 114, 144 and 147).

---

[10] Recommendation (No. 116) concerning Reduction of Hours of Work.

[11] Convention (No. 110) and Recommendation (No. 110) concerning Conditions of Employment of Plantation Workers; Recommendation (No. 115) concerning Workers' Housing; Recommendation (No. 69) concerning Medical Care; Convention (No. 130) and Recommendation (No. 134) concerning Medical Care and Sickness Benefits.

[12] Convention No. 138, Article 1; Convention No. 182, Article 1.

The list of occupational diseases and the codes of practice and guides in the current list of ILO publications on occupational safety and health should also be taken into account.[13]

38. Multinational enterprises should maintain the highest standards of safety and health, in conformity with national requirements, bearing in mind their relevant experience within the enterprise as a whole, including any knowledge of special hazards. They should also make available to the representatives of the workers in the enterprise, and upon request, to the competent authorities and the workers' and employers' organizations in all countries in which they operate, information on the safety and health standards relevant to their local operations, which they observe in other countries. In particular, they should make known to those concerned any special hazards and related protective measures associated with new products and processes. They, like comparable domestic enterprises, should be expected to play a leading role in the examination of causes of industrial safety and health hazards and in the application of resulting improvements within the enterprise as a whole.

39. Multinational enterprises should cooperate in the work of international organizations concerned with the preparation and adoption of international safety and health standards.

40. In accordance with national practice, multinational enterprises should cooperate fully with the competent safety and health authorities, the representatives of the workers and their organizations, and established safety and health organizations. Where appropriate, matters relating to safety and health should be incorporated in agreements with the representatives of the workers and their organizations.

INDUSTRIAL RELATIONS

41. Multinational enterprises should observe standards of industrial relations not less favourable than those observed by comparable employers in the country concerned.

Freedom of association and the right to organize

42. Workers employed by multinational enterprises as well as those employed by national enterprises should, without distinction whatsoever, have the right to establish and, subject only to the rules of the organization concerned, to join organizations of their own choosing without previous authorisation.[14] They should also enjoy adequate protection against acts of anti-union discrimination in respect of their employment.[15]

43. Organizations representing multinational enterprises or the workers in their employment should enjoy adequate protection against any acts of interference by each other or each other's agents or members in their establishment, functioning or administration.[16]

---

[13] Recommendation (No. 194) concerning the List of Occupational Diseases and the Recording and Notification of Occupational Accidents and Diseases. The ILO Conventions and Recommendations referred to are listed in the Catalogue of ILO Publications on Occupational Safety and Health, ed. 2000, ILO, Geneva. See also **http://www.ilo.org/public/english/protection/safework/publicat/index.htm.**

[14] Convention No. 87, Article 2.
[15] Convention No. 98, Article 1(1).
[16] Convention No. 98, Article 2(1).

44. Where appropriate, in the local circumstances, multinational enterprises should support representative employers' organizations.

45. Governments, where they do not already do so, are urged to apply the principles of Convention No. 87, Article 5, in view of the importance, in relation to multinational enterprises, of permitting organizations representing such enterprises or the workers in their employment to affiliate with international organizations of employers and workers of their own choosing.

46. Where governments of host countries offer special incentives to attract foreign investment, these incentives should not include any limitation of the workers' freedom of association or the right to organize and bargain collectively.

47. Representatives of the workers in multinational enterprises should not be hindered from meeting for consultation and exchange of views among themselves, provided that the functioning of the operations of the enterprise and the normal procedures which govern relationships with representatives of the workers and their organizations are not thereby prejudiced.

48. Governments should not restrict the entry of representatives of employers' and workers' organizations who come from other countries at the invitation of the local or national organizations concerned for the purpose of consultation on matters of mutual concern, solely on the grounds that they seek entry in that capacity.

Collective bargaining

49. Workers employed by multinational enterprises should have the right, in accordance with national law and practice, to have representative organizations of their own choosing recognized for the purpose of collective bargaining.

50. Measures appropriate to national conditions should be taken, where necessary, to encourage and promote the full development and utilization of machinery for voluntary negotiation between employers or employers' organizations and workers' organizations, with a view to the regulation of terms and conditions of employment by means of collective agreements.[17]

51. Multinational enterprises, as well as national enterprises, should provide workers' representatives with such facilities as may be necessary to assist in the development of effective collective agreements.[18]

52. Multinational enterprises should enable duly authorized representatives of the workers in their employment in each of the countries in which they operate to conduct negotiations with representatives of management who are authorized to take decisions on the matters under negotiation.

53. Multinational enterprises, in the context of bona fide negotiations with the workers' representatives on conditions of employment, or while workers are exercising the right to organize, should not threaten to utilize a capacity to transfer the whole or part of an operating unit from the country concerned in order to influence unfairly those negotiations or to hinder the exercise of the right to organize; nor should they transfer workers from affiliates in foreign countries with a view to undermining bona fide negotiations with the workers' representatives or the workers' exercise of their right to organize.

---

[17] Convention No. 98, Article 4.

[18] Convention (No. 135) concerning Protection and Facilities to be Afforded to Workers' Representatives in the Undertaking.

54. Collective agreements should include provisions for the settlement of disputes arising over their interpretation and application and for ensuring mutually respected rights and responsibilities.

55. Multinational enterprises should provide workers' representatives with information required for meaningful negotiations with the entity involved and, where this accords with local law and practices, should also provide information to enable them to obtain a true and fair view of the performance of the entity or, where appropriate, of the enterprise as a whole.[19]

56. Governments should supply to the representatives of workers' organizations on request, where law and practice so permit, information on the industries in which the enterprise operates, which would help in laying down objective criteria in the collective bargaining process. In this context, multinational as well as national enterprises should respond constructively to requests by governments for relevant information on their operations.

Consultation

57. In multinational as well as in national enterprises, systems devised by mutual agreement between employers and workers and their representatives should provide, in accordance with national law and practice, for regular consultation on matters of mutual concern. Such consultation should not be a substitute for collective bargaining.[20]

Examination of grievances

58. Multinational as well as national enterprises should respect the right of the workers whom they employ to have all their grievances processed in a manner consistent with the following provision: any worker who, acting individually or jointly with other workers, considers that he has grounds for a grievance should have the right to submit such grievance without suffering any prejudice whatsoever as a result, and to have such grievance examined pursuant to an appropriate procedure.[21] This is particularly important whenever the multinational enterprises operate in countries which do not abide by the principles of ILO Conventions pertaining to freedom of association, to the right to organize and bargain collectively, to discrimination, to child labour and to forced labour.[22]

---

[19] Recommendation (No. 129) concerning Communications between Management and Workers within the Undertaking.

[20] Recommendation (No. 94) concerning Consultation and Co-operation between Employers and Workers at the Level of Undertaking; Recommendation (No. 129) concerning Communications within the Undertaking.

[21] Recommendation (No. 130) concerning the Examination of Grievances within the Undertaking with a View to Their Settlement.

[22] Convention (No. 29) concerning Forced or Compulsory Labour; Convention (No. 87) concerning Freedom of Association and Protection of the Right to Organise; Convention (No. 98) concerning the Application of the Principles of the Right to Organise and to Bargain Collectively; Convention (No. 100) concerning Equal Remuneration for Men and Women Workers for Work of Equal Value; Convention (No. 105) concerning the Abolition of Forced Labour; Convention (No. 111) concerning Discrimination in Respect of Employment and Occupation; Convention (No. 138) concerning Minimum Age for Admission to Employment; Convention (No. 182) concerning the Prohibition and Immediate Action for the Elimination of the Worst Forms of Child Labour; Recommendation (No. 35) concerning Indirect Compulsion to Labour; Recommendation (No. 90) concerning Equal Remuneration for Men and Women Workers for Work of Equal Value; Recommendation (No. 111) concerning Discrimination in Respect of Employment and Occupation; Recommendation (No. 146) concerning Minimum Age for Admission to Employment, and Recommendation (No. 190) concerning the Prohibition and Immediate Action for the Elimination of the Worst Forms of Child Labour.

Settlement of industrial disputes

59. Multinational as well as national enterprises jointly with the representatives and organizations of the workers whom they employ should seek to establish voluntary conciliation machinery, appropriate to national conditions, which may include provisions for voluntary arbitration, to assist in the prevention and settlement of industrial disputes between employers and workers. The voluntary conciliation machinery should include equal representation of employers and workers.[23]

[Annex and Addendum I omitted]

ADDENDUM II

adopted by the Governing Body of the International Labour Office at its
277th Session, Geneva, March 2000

The International Labour Conference adopted in June 1998 the ILO Declaration on Fundamental Principles and Rights at Work. By this adoption, Members renewed their commitment to respect, promote and realize the following fundamental principles and rights at work, namely: (a) freedom of association and the effective recognition of the right to collective bargaining; (b) the elimination of all forms of forced or compulsory labour; (c) the effective abolition of child labour; and (d) the elimination of discrimination in respect of employment and occupation. The ILO Declaration on Fundamental Principles and Rights at Work applies to all Members. Nevertheless, the contribution of multinational enterprises to its implementation can prove an important element in the attainment of its objectives. In this context, the interpretation and application of the Tripartite Declaration of Principles concerning Multinational Enterprises and Social Policy should fully take into account the objectives of the ILO Declaration on Fundamental Principles and Rights at Work. This reference does not in any way affect the voluntary character or the meaning of the provisions of the Tripartite Declaration of Principles concerning Multinational Enterprises and Social Policy.

PROCEDURE FOR THE EXAMINATION OF DISPUTES CONCERNING THE APPLICATION OF THE TRIPARTITE DECLARATION OF PRINCIPLES CONCERNING MULTINATIONAL ENTERPRISES AND SOCIAL POLICY BY MEANS OF INTERPRETATION OF ITS PROVISIONS

adopted by the Governing Body of the International Labour Office at its
232nd Session (Geneva, March 1986)[24]

1. The purpose of the procedure is to interpret the provisions of the Declaration when needed to resolve a disagreement on their meaning, arising from an actual situation, between parties to whom the Declaration is commended.

---

[23] Recommendation (No. 92) concerning Voluntary Conciliation and Arbitration.
[24] Official Bulletin (Geneva, ILO), 1986, Vol. LXIX, Series A, No. 3, pp. 196–197 (to replace Part IV of the Procedures adopted by the Governing Body at its 214th Session (November 1980)). See Official Bulletin, 1981, Vol. LXIV, Series A, No. 1, pp. 89–90.

2. The procedure should in no way duplicate or conflict with existing national or ILO procedures. Thus, it cannot be invoked:

- *(a)* in respect of national law and practice;
- *(b)* in respect of international labour Conventions and Recommendations;
- *(c)* in respect of matters falling under the freedom of association procedure

The above means that questions regarding national law and practice should be considered through appropriate national machinery; that questions regarding international labour Conventions and Recommendations should be examined through the various procedures provided for in articles 19, 22, 24 and 26 of the Constitution of the ILO, or through government requests to the Office for informal interpretation; and that questions concerning freedom of association should be considered through the special ILO procedures applicable to that area.

3. When a request for interpretation of the Declaration is received by the International Labour Office, the Office shall acknowledge receipt and bring it before the Officers of the Committee on Multinational Enterprises. The Office will inform the government and the central organizations of employers and workers concerned of any request for interpretation received directly from an organization under paragraph 5(b) and (c).

4. The Officers of the Committee on Multinational Enterprises shall decide unanimously after consultations in the groups whether the request is receivable under the procedure. If they cannot reach agreement the request shall be referred to the full Committee for decision.

5. Requests for interpretation may be addressed to the Office:

- *(a)* as a rule by the government of a member State acting either on its own initiative or at the request of a national organization of employers or workers;
- *(b)* by a national organization of employers or workers, which is representative at the national and/or sectoral level, subject to the conditions set out in paragraph 6. Such requests should normally be channelled through the central organizations in the country concerned;
- *(c)* by an international organization of employers or workers on behalf of a representative national affiliate.

6. In the case of 5(b) and (c), requests may be submitted if it can be demonstrated:

- *(a)* that the government concerned has declined to submit the request to the Office; or
- *(b)* that three months have elapsed since the organization addressed the government without a statement of the government's intention.

7. In the case of receivable requests the Office shall prepare a draft reply in consultation with the Officers of the Committee on Multinational Enterprises. All appropriate sources of information shall be used, including government, employers' and workers' sources in the country concerned. The Officers may ask the Office to indicate a period within which the information should be provided.

8. The draft reply to a receivable request shall be considered and approved by the Committee on Multinational Enterprises prior to submission to the Governing Body for approval.

9. The reply when approved by the Governing Body shall be forwarded to the parties concerned and published in the Official Bulletin of the International Labour Office.

PART FOUR

CONTRIBUTION OF THE UNITED NATIONS EDUCATIONAL, SCIENTIFIC, AND CULTURAL ORGANIZATION

INTRODUCTION

UNESCO is a Specialized Agency associated with the United Nations. Several aspects of its work concern human rights, in particular, problems of illiteracy in many countries, and the production and dissemination of studies which combat racial prejudice.

In 1978 the Executive Board of UNESCO adopted the procedure for examining communications concerning violations of human rights in relation to education, science, culture, and information; see MARKS, S. P., 'The Complaint Procedure of the United Nations Educational, Scientific and Cultural Organization', in HANNUM, H., ed., *Guide to International Human Rights Practice*, Leiden: Martinus Nijhoff, Transnational Publishers, 4th edn., 2004, 107; ROBERTSON, A. H. and MERRILLS, J. G., eds., *Human Rights in the World*, Manchester: Manchester University Press, 4th edn., 1996, 288.

For UNESCO's work on race and racial prejudice, see below, p. 1169; and on the human genome and genetic data, see the *Online Resource Centre*.

Generally, see **http://unesco.org**.

Further reading

FRANCOVITS, A., *The Human Rights-Based Approach and the United Nations System*, UNESCO Strategy on Human Rights, Paris: UNESCO, 2006.
HUMPHREY, J., *No Distant Millennium: The International Law of Human Rights*, Paris: UNESCO, 1989.
SYMONIDES, J., *Human Rights: Concepts and Standards*, Paris: UNESCO, 2000.

79. CONVENTION AGAINST DISCRIMINATION IN EDUCATION, 1960

Adopted by the UNESCO General Conference at its eleventh session in Paris on 14 December 1960, this Convention can be compared with the ILO Convention concerning discrimination in respect of employment and occupation, above, p. 590. The United Nations Sub-Commission on Prevention of Discrimination and Protection of Minorities initiated a study of discrimination in education, and in due course it was decided to ask UNESCO to consider the possibility of drafting and adopting a convention on the subject. The General Conference of UNESCO duly adopted the Convention, which entered into force on 22 May 1962.

For the text in various languages, see 429 *UNTS* 93. See also the Protocol instituting a Conciliation and Good Offices Commission to be responsible for seeking the Settlement of any Disputes which may arise between States Parties to the Convention against Discrimination in Education, adopted in Paris, 10 December 1962. The Protocol entered into force on 24 October 1968.

Further reading

BEITER, K. D., *The Protection of the Right to Education by International Law*, Leiden: Martinus Nijhoff, 2006.

DONDERS, Y. and VOLODIN, V., eds., *Human Rights in Education, Science and Culture*, Farnham: Ashgate; Paris: UNESCO, 2007.

TOMASEVSKI, K., 'Has the right to education a future within the United Nations? A behind-the-scenes account by the Special Rapporteur on the Right to Education 1998–2004', (2005) 5 *Human Rights Law Review* 205.

TEXT

The General Conference of the United Nations Educational, Scientific and Cultural Organization, meeting in Paris from 14 November to 15 December 1960, at its eleventh session,

Recalling that the Universal Declaration of Human Rights asserts the principle of non-discrimination and proclaims that every person has the right to education,

Considering that discrimination in education is a violation of rights enunciated in that Declaration,

Considering that, under the terms of its Constitution, the United Nations Educational, Scientific and Cultural Organization has the purpose of instituting collaboration among the nations with a view to furthering for all universal respect for human rights and equality of educational opportunity,

Recognizing that, consequently, the United Nations Educational, Scientific and Cultural Organization, while respecting the diversity of national educational systems, has the duty not only to proscribe any form of discrimination in education but also to promote equality of opportunity and treatment for all in education,

Having before it proposals concerning the different aspects of discrimination in education, constituting item 17.1.4 of the agenda of the session,

Having decided at its tenth session that this question should be made the subject of an international convention as well as of recommendations to Member States,

Adopts this Convention on the fourteenth day of December 1960.

Article 1

1. For the purposes of this Convention, the term 'discrimination' includes any distinction, exclusion, limitation or preference which, being based on race, colour, sex, language, religion, political or other opinion, national or social origin, economic condition or birth, has the purpose or effect of nullifying or impairing equality of treatment in education and in particular:

  (a) Of depriving any person or group of persons of access to education of any type or at any level;

  (b) Of limiting any person or group of persons to education of an inferior standard;

  (c) Subject to the provisions of Article 2 of this Convention, of establishing or maintaining separate educational systems or institutions for persons or groups of persons; or

  (d) Of inflicting on any person or group of persons conditions which are incompatible with the dignity of man.

2. For the purposes of this Convention, the term 'education' refers to all types and levels of education, and includes access to education, the standard and quality of education, and the conditions under which it is given.

Article 2

When permitted in a State, the following situations shall not be deemed to constitute discrimination, within the meaning of Article 1 of this Convention:

  (a) The establishment or maintenance of separate educational systems or institutions for pupils of the two sexes, if these systems or institutions offer equivalent access to education, provide a teaching staff with qualifications of the same standard as well as school premises and equipment of the same quality, and afford the opportunity to take the same or equivalent courses of study;

  (b) The establishment or maintenance, for religious or linguistic reasons, of separate educational systems or institutions offering an education which is in keeping with the wishes of the pupil's parents or legal guardians, if participation in such systems or attendance at such institutions is optional and if the education provided conforms to such standards as may be laid down or approved by the competent authorities, in particular for education of the same level;

  (c) The establishment or maintenance of private educational institutions, if the object of the institutions is not to secure the exclusion of any group but to provide educational facilities in addition to those provided by the public authorities, if the institutions are conducted in accordance with that object, and if the education provided conforms with such standards as may be laid down or approved by the competent authorities, in particular for education of the same level.

Article 3

In order to eliminate and prevent discrimination within the meaning of this Convention, the States Parties thereto undertake:

  (a) To abrogate any statutory provisions and any administrative instructions and to discontinue any administrative practices which involve discrimination in education;

(b) To ensure, by legislation where necessary, that there is no discrimination in the admission of pupils to educational institutions;

(c) Not to allow any differences of treatment by the public authorities between nationals, except on the basis of merit or need, in the matter of school fees and the grant of scholarships or other forms of assistance to pupils and necessary permits and facilities for the pursuit of studies in foreign countries;

(d) Not to allow, in any form of assistance granted by the public authorities to educational institutions, any restrictions or preference based solely on the ground that pupils belong to a particular group;

(e) To give foreign nationals resident within their territory the same access to education as that given to their own nationals.

Article 4

The States Parties to this Convention undertake furthermore to formulate, develop and apply a national policy which, by methods appropriate to the circumstances and to national usage, will tend to promote equality of opportunity and of treatment in the matter of education and in particular:

(a) To make primary education free and compulsory; make secondary education in its different forms generally available and accessible to all; make higher education equally accessible to all on the basis of individual capacity; assure compliance by all with the obligation to attend school prescribed by law;

(b) To ensure that the standards of education are equivalent in all public educational institutions of the same level, and that the conditions relating to the quality of the education provided are also equivalent;

(c) To encourage and intensify by appropriate methods the education of persons who have not received any primary education or who have not completed the entire primary education course and the continuation of their education on the basis of individual capacity;

(d) To provide training for the teaching profession without discrimination.

Article 5

1. The States Parties to this Convention agree that:

(a) Education shall be directed to the full development of the human personality and to the strengthening of respect for human rights and fundamental freedoms; it shall promote understanding, tolerance and friendship among all nations, racial or religious groups, and shall further the activities of the United Nations for the maintenance of peace;

(b) It is essential to respect the liberty of parents and, where applicable, of legal guardians, firstly to choose for their children institutions other than those maintained by the public authorities but conforming to such minimum educational standards as may be laid down or approved by the competent authorities and, secondly, to ensure in a manner consistent with the procedures followed in the State for the application of its legislation, the religious and moral education of the children in conformity with their own convictions; and no person or group of persons should be compelled to receive religious instruction inconsistent with his or their convictions;

(c) It is essential to recognize the right of members of national minorities to carry on their own educational activities, including the maintenance of schools and, depending on the educational policy of each State, the use or the teaching of their own language, provided however:

  (i) That this right is not exercised in a manner which prevents the members of these minorities from understanding the culture and language of the community as a whole and from participating in its activities, or which prejudices national sovereignty;

  (ii) That the standard of education is not lower than the general standard laid down or approved by the competent authorities; and

  (iii) That attendance at such schools is optional.

2. The States Parties to this Convention undertake to take all necessary measures to ensure the application of the principles enunciated in paragraph 1 of this Article.

Article 6

In the application of this Convention, the States Parties to it undertake to pay the greatest attention to any recommendations hereafter adopted by the General Conference of the United Nations Educational, Scientific and Cultural Organization defining the measures to be taken against the different forms of discrimination in education and for the purpose of ensuring equality of opportunity and treatment in education.

Article 7

The States Parties to this Convention shall in their periodic reports submitted to the General Conference of the United Nations Educational, Scientific and Cultural Organization on dates and in a manner to be determined by it, give information on the legislative and administrative provisions which they have adopted and other action which they have taken for the application of this Convention, including that taken for the formulation and the development of the national policy defined in Article 4 as well as the results achieved and the obstacles encountered in the application of that policy.

Article 8

Any dispute which may arise between any two or more States Parties to this Convention concerning the interpretation or application of this Convention, which is not settled by negotiation shall at the request of the parties to the dispute be referred, failing other means of settling the dispute, to the International Court of Justice for decision.

Article 9

Reservations to this Convention shall not be permitted.

Article 10

This Convention shall not have the effect of diminishing the rights which individuals or groups may enjoy by virtue of agreements concluded between two or more States, where such rights are not contrary to the letter or spirit of this Convention.

Article 11

This Convention is drawn up in English, French, Russian and Spanish, the four texts being equally authoritative.

Article 12

1. This Convention shall be subject to ratification or acceptance by States Members of the United Nations Educational, Scientific and Cultural Organization in accordance with their respective constitutional procedures.

2. The instruments of ratification or acceptance shall be deposited with the Director-General of the United Nations Educational, Scientific and Cultural Organization.

Article 13

1. This Convention shall be open to accession by all States not Members of the United Nations Educational, Scientific and Cultural Organization which are invited to do so by the Executive Board of the Organization.

2. Accession shall be effected by the deposit of an instrument of accession with the Director-General of the United Nations Educational, Scientific and Cultural Organization.

Article 14

This Convention shall enter into force three months after the date of the deposit of the third instrument of ratification, acceptance or accession, but only with respect to those States which have deposited their respective instruments on or before that date. It shall enter into force with respect to any other State three months after the deposit of its instrument of ratification, acceptance or accession.

Article 15

The States Parties to this Convention recognize that the Convention is applicable not only to their metropolitan territory but also to all non-self-governing, trust, colonial and other territories for the international relations of which they are responsible; they undertake to consult, if necessary, the governments or other competent authorities of these territories on or before ratification, acceptance or accession with a view to securing the application of the Convention to those territories, and to notify the Director-General of the United Nations Educational, Scientific and Cultural Organization of the territories to which it is accordingly applied, the notification to take effect three months after the date of its receipt.

Article 16

1. Each State Party to this Convention may denounce the Convention on its own behalf or on behalf of any territory for whose international relations it is responsible.

2. The denunciation shall be notified by an instrument in writing, deposited with the Director-General of the United Nations Educational, Scientific and Cultural Organization.

3. The denunciation shall take effect twelve months after the receipt of the instrument of denunciation.

Article 17

The Director-General of the United Nations Educational, Scientific and Cultural Organization shall inform the States Members of the Organization, the States not members of the Organization which are referred to in Article 13, as well as the United Nations, of the deposit of all the instruments of ratification, acceptance and accession provided for in Articles 12 and 13, and of the notifications and denunciations provided for in Articles 15 and 16 respectively.

Article 18

1. This Convention may be revised by the General Conference of the United Nations Educational, Scientific and Cultural Organization. Any such revision shall, however, bind only the States which shall become Parties to the revising convention.

2. If the General Conference should adopt a new convention revising this Convention in whole or in part, then, unless the new convention otherwise provides, this Convention shall cease to be open to ratification, acceptance or accession as from the date on which the new revising convention enters into force.

Article 19

In conformity with Article 102 of the Charter of the United Nations, this Convention shall be registered with the Secretariat of the United Nations at the request of the Director-General of the United Nations Educational, Scientific and Cultural Organization.

80. DECLARATION OF THE PRINCIPLES OF INTERNATIONAL CULTURAL CO-OPERATION, 1966

Proclaimed by the General Conference of the United Nations Educational, Scientific and Cultural Organization at its fourteenth session on 4 November 1966.

TEXT

The General Conference of the United Nations Educational, Scientific and Cultural Organization, met in Paris for its fourteenth session, this fourth day of November 1966, being the twentieth anniversary of the foundation of the Organization,

Recalling that the Constitution of the Organization declares that 'since wars begin in the minds of men, it is in the minds of men that the defences of peace must be constructed' and that the peace must be founded, if it is not to fail, upon the intellectual and moral solidarity of mankind,

Recalling that the Constitution also states that the wide diffusion of culture and the education of humanity for justice and liberty and peace are indispensable to the dignity of man and constitute a sacred duty which all the nations must fulfil in a spirit of mutual assistance and concern,

Considering that the Organization's Member States, believing in the pursuit of truth and the free exchange of ideas and knowledge, have agreed and determined to develop and to increase the means of communication between their peoples,

Considering that, despite the technical advances which facilitate the development and dissemination of knowledge and ideas, ignorance of the way of life and customs of peoples still presents an obstacle to friendship among the nations, to peaceful co-operation and to the progress of mankind,

Taking account of the Universal Declaration of Human Rights, the Declaration of the Rights of the Child, the Declaration on the Granting of Independence to Colonial Countries and Peoples, the United Nations Declaration on the Elimination of All Forms of Racial Discrimination, the Declaration on the Promotion among Youth of the Ideals of Peace, Mutual Respect and Understanding between Peoples, and the Declaration on the Inadmissibility of Intervention in the Domestic Affairs of States and the Protection of their Independence and Sovereignty, proclaimed successively by the General Assembly of the United Nations,

Convinced by the experience of the Organization's first twenty years that, if international cultural co-operation is to be strengthened, its principles require to be affirmed,

Proclaims this Declaration of the principles of international cultural co-operation, to the end that governments, authorities, organizations, associations and institutions responsible for cultural activities may constantly be guided by these principles; and for the purpose, as set out in the Constitution of the Organization, of advancing, through the educational, scientific and cultural relations of the peoples of the world, the objectives of peace and welfare that are defined in the Charter of the United Nations:

Article 1

1. Each culture has a dignity and value which must be respected and preserved.

2. Every people has the right and the duty to develop its culture.

3. In their rich variety and diversity, and in the reciprocal influences they exert on one another, all cultures form part of the common heritage belonging to all mankind.

Article 2

Nations shall endeavour to develop the various branches of culture side by side and, as far as possible, simultaneously, so as to establish a harmonious balance between technical progress and the intellectual and moral advancement of mankind.

Article 3

International cultural co-operation shall cover all aspects of intellectual and creative activities relating to education, science and culture.

Article 4

The aims of international cultural co-operation in its various forms, bilateral or multilateral, regional or universal, shall be:

   (1) To spread knowledge, to stimulate talent and to enrich cultures;

   (2) To develop peaceful relations and friendship among the peoples and bring about a better understanding of each other's way of life;

   (3) To contribute to the application of the principles set out in the United Nations Declarations that are recalled in the Preamble to this Declaration;

   (4) To enable everyone to have access to knowledge, to enjoy the arts and literature of all peoples, to share in advances made in science in all parts of the world and in the resulting benefits, and to contribute to the enrichment of cultural life;

   (5) To raise the level of the spiritual and material life of man in all parts of the world.

Article 5

Cultural co-operation is a right and a duty for all peoples and all nations, which should share with one another their knowledge and skills.

Article 6

International co-operation, while promoting the enrichment of all cultures through its beneficent action, shall respect the distinctive character of each.

Article 7

1. Broad dissemination of ideas and knowledge, based on the freest exchange and discussion, is essential to creative activity, the pursuit of truth and the development of the personality.

2. In cultural co-operation, stress shall be laid on ideas and values conducive to the creation of a climate of friendship and peace. Any mark of hostility in attitudes and in expression of opinion shall be avoided. Every effort shall be made, in presenting and disseminating information, to ensure its authenticity.

Article 8

Cultural co-operation shall be carried on for the mutual benefit of all the nations practising it. Exchanges to which it gives rise shall be arranged in a spirit of broad reciprocity.

Article 9

Cultural co-operation shall contribute to the establishment of stable, long-term relations between peoples, which should be subjected as little as possible to the strains which may arise in international life.

Article 10

Cultural co-operation shall be specially concerned with the moral and intellectual education of young people in a spirit of friendship, international understanding and peace and shall foster awareness among States of the need to stimulate talent and promote the training of the rising generations in the most varied sectors.

Article 11

1. In their cultural relations, States shall bear in mind the principles of the United Nations. In seeking to achieve international co-operation, they shall respect the sovereign equality of States and shall refrain from intervention in matters which are essentially within the domestic jurisdiction of any State.

2. The principles of this Declaration shall be applied with due regard for human rights and fundamental freedoms.

81. UNIVERSAL DECLARATION ON CULTURAL DIVERSITY, 2001

Adopted by Resolution 5, at the 20th Plenary Meeting on 2 November 2001; see UNESCO, *Report of the General Conference*, 31st Session, Paris, 15 October–3 November 2001, 2002, Vol. 1, Resolutions, 61. The Declaration recognizes cultural diversity as the 'common heritage of humanity' (Article 1), and commits UNESCO to pursue its standard-setting activities in the field (Article 12(c)). See generally, **http://portal.unesco.org/culture/en**.

Further reading

STENOU, K., *UNESCO and the Issue of Cultural Diversity*, 1946–2007, Paris: UNESCO, 2007.
WALKER, S. and POE, S. C., 'Does cultural diversity affect countries' respect for human rights?', (2002) 24 *Human Rights Quarterly* 237.

TEXT

ANNEX I

The General Conference,

Committed to the full implementation of the human rights and fundamental freedoms proclaimed in the Universal Declaration of Human Rights and other universally recognized legal instruments, such as the two International Covenants of 1966 relating respectively to civil and political rights and to economic, social and cultural rights,

Recalling that the Preamble to the Constitution of UNESCO affirms 'that the wide diffusion of culture, and the education of humanity for justice and liberty and peace are indispensable to the dignity of man and constitute a sacred duty which all the nations must fulfil in a spirit of mutual assistance and concern',

Further recalling Article I of the Constitution, which assigns to UNESCO among other purposes that of recommending 'such international agreements as may be necessary to promote the free flow of ideas by word and image',

Referring to the provisions relating to cultural diversity and the exercise of cultural rights in the international instruments enacted by UNESCO,[1]

Reaffirming that culture should be regarded as the set of distinctive spiritual, material, intellectual and emotional features of society or a social group, and that it encompasses, in addition to art and literature, lifestyles, ways of living together, value systems, traditions and beliefs,[2]

---

[1] Among which, in particular, the Florence Agreement of 1950 and its Nairobi Protocol of 1976, the Universal Copyright Convention of 1952, the Declaration of the Principles of International Cultural Cooperation of 1966, the Convention on the Means of Prohibiting and Preventing the Illicit Import, Export and Transfer of Ownership of Cultural Property of 1970, the Convention for the Protection of the World Cultural and Natural Heritage of 1972, the Declaration on Race and Racial Prejudice of 1978, the Recommendation concerning the Status of the Artist of 1980, and the Recommendation on the Safeguarding of Traditional Culture and Folklore of 1989.

[2] This definition is in line with the conclusions of the World Conference on Cultural Policies (MONDIACULT, Mexico City, 1982), of the World Commission on Culture and Development (Our Creative Diversity, 1995), and of the Intergovernmental Conference on Cultural Policies for Development (Stockholm, 1998).

Noting that culture is at the heart of contemporary debates about identity, social cohesion, and the development of a knowledge-based economy,

Affirming that respect for the diversity of cultures, tolerance, dialogue and cooperation, in a climate of mutual trust and understanding are among the best guarantees of international peace and security,

Aspiring to greater solidarity on the basis of recognition of cultural diversity, of awareness of the unity of humankind, and of the development of intercultural exchanges,

Considering that the process of globalization, facilitated by the rapid development of new information and communication technologies, though representing a challenge for cultural diversity, creates the conditions for renewed dialogue among cultures and civilizations,

Aware of the specific mandate which has been entrusted to UNESCO, within the United Nations system, to ensure the preservation and promotion of the fruitful diversity of cultures,

Proclaims the following principles and adopts the present Declaration:

IDENTITY, DIVERSITY AND PLURALISM

Article 1—Cultural diversity: the common heritage of humanity

Culture takes diverse forms across time and space. This diversity is embodied in the uniqueness and plurality of the identities of the groups and societies making up humankind. As a source of exchange, innovation and creativity, cultural diversity is as necessary for humankind as biodiversity is for nature. In this sense, it is the common heritage of humanity and should be recognized and affirmed for the benefit of present and future generations.

Article 2—From cultural diversity to cultural pluralism

In our increasingly diverse societies, it is essential to ensure harmonious interaction among people and groups with plural, varied and dynamic cultural identities as well as their willingness to live together. Policies for the inclusion and participation of all citizens are guarantees of social cohesion, the vitality of civil society and peace. Thus defined, cultural pluralism gives policy expression to the reality of cultural diversity. Indissociable from a democratic framework, cultural pluralism is conducive to cultural exchange and to the flourishing of creative capacities that sustain public life.

Article 3—Cultural diversity as a factor in development

Cultural diversity widens the range of options open to everyone; it is one of the roots of development, understood not simply in terms of economic growth, but also as a means to achieve a more satisfactory intellectual, emotional, moral and spiritual existence.

CULTURAL DIVERSITY AND HUMAN RIGHTS

Article 4—Human rights as guarantees of cultural diversity

The defence of cultural diversity is an ethical imperative, inseparable from respect for human dignity. It implies a commitment to human rights and fundamental freedoms, in particular the rights of persons belonging to minorities and those of indigenous peoples.

No one may invoke cultural diversity to infringe upon human rights guaranteed by international law, nor to limit their scope.

Article 5—Cultural rights as an enabling environment for cultural diversity

Cultural rights are an integral part of human rights, which are universal, indivisible and interdependent. The flourishing of creative diversity requires the full implementation of cultural rights as defined in Article 27 of the Universal Declaration of Human Rights and in Articles 13 and 15 of the International Covenant on Economic, Social and Cultural Rights. All persons have therefore the right to express themselves and to create and disseminate their work in the language of their choice, and particularly in their mother tongue; all persons are entitled to quality education and training that fully respect their cultural identity; and all persons have the right to participate in the cultural life of their choice and conduct their own cultural practices, subject to respect for human rights and fundamental freedoms.

Article 6—Towards access for all to cultural diversity

While ensuring the free flow of ideas by word and image care should be exercised so that all cultures can express themselves and make themselves known. Freedom of expression, media pluralism, multilingualism, equal access to art and to scientific and technological knowledge, including in digital form, and the possibility for all cultures to have access to the means of expression and dissemination are the guarantees of cultural diversity.

CULTURAL DIVERSITY AND CREATIVITY

Article 7—Cultural heritage as the wellspring of creativity

Creation draws on the roots of cultural tradition, but flourishes in contact with other cultures. For this reason, heritage in all its forms must be preserved, enhanced and handed on to future generations as a record of human experience and aspirations, so as to foster creativity in all its diversity and to inspire genuine dialogue among cultures.

Article 8—Cultural goods and services: commodities of a unique kind

In the face of present-day economic and technological change, opening up vast prospects for creation and innovation, particular attention must be paid to the diversity of the supply of creative work, to due recognition of the rights of authors and artists and to the specificity of cultural goods and services which, as vectors of identity, values and meaning, must not be treated as mere commodities or consumer goods.

Article 9—Cultural policies as catalysts of creativity

While ensuring the free circulation of ideas and works, cultural policies must create conditions conducive to the production and dissemination of diversified cultural goods and services through cultural industries that have the means to assert themselves at the local and global level. It is for each State, with due regard to its international obligations, to define its cultural policy and to implement it through the means it considers fit, whether by operational support or appropriate regulations.

CULTURAL DIVERSITY AND INTERNATIONAL SOLIDARITY

Article 10—Strengthening capacities for creation and dissemination worldwide

In the face of current imbalances in flows and exchanges of cultural goods at the global level, it is necessary to reinforce international cooperation and solidarity aimed at enabling all countries, especially developing countries and countries in transition, to establish cultural industries that are viable and competitive at national and international level.

Article 11—Building partnerships between the public sector, the private sector and civil society

Market forces alone cannot guarantee the preservation and promotion of cultural diversity, which is the key to sustainable human development. From this perspective, the pre-eminence of public policy, in partnership with the private sector and civil society, must be reaffirmed.

Article 12—The role of UNESCO

UNESCO, by virtue of its mandate and functions, has the responsibility to:

(a) Promote the incorporation of the principles set out in the present Declaration into the development strategies drawn up within the various intergovernmental bodies;

(b) Serve as a reference point and a forum where States, international governmental and non-governmental organizations, civil society and the private sector may join together in elaborating concepts, objectives and policies in favour of cultural diversity;

(c) Pursue its activities in standard-setting, awareness raising and capacity-building in the areas related to the present Declaration within its fields of competence;

(d) Facilitate the implementation of the Action Plan, the main lines of which are appended to the present Declaration.

ANNEX II
MAIN LINES OF AN ACTION PLAN FOR THE IMPLEMENTATION OF THE UNESCO UNIVERSAL DECLARATION ON CULTURAL DIVERSITY

The Member States commit themselves to taking appropriate steps to disseminate widely the 'UNESCO Universal Declaration on Cultural Diversity' and to encourage its effective application, in particular by cooperating with a view to achieving the following objectives:

1. Deepening the international debate on questions relating to cultural diversity, particularly in respect of its links with development and its impact on policy-making, at both national and international level; taking forward notably consideration of the advisability of an international legal instrument on cultural diversity.

2. Advancing in the definition of principles, standards and practices, on both the national and the international levels, as well as of awareness-raising modalities and patterns of cooperation, that are most conducive to the safeguarding and promotion of cultural diversity.

3. Fostering the exchange of knowledge and best practices in regard to cultural plural-ism with a view to facilitating, in diversified societies, the inclusion and participation of persons and groups from varied cultural backgrounds.

4. Making further headway in understanding and clarifying the content of cultural rights as an integral part of human rights.

5. Safeguarding the linguistic heritage of humanity and giving support to expression, creation and dissemination in the greatest possible number of languages.

6. Encouraging linguistic diversity—while respecting the mother tongue—at all levels of education, wherever possible, and fostering the learning of several languages from the earliest age.

7. Promoting through education an awareness of the positive value of cultural diver-sity and improving to this end both curriculum design and teacher education.

8. Incorporating, where appropriate, traditional pedagogies into the education proc-ess with a view to preserving and making full use of culturally appropriate methods of communication and transmission of knowledge.

9. Encouraging 'digital literacy' and ensuring greater mastery of the new information and communication technologies, which should be seen both as educational disciplines and as pedagogical tools capable of enhancing the effectiveness of educational services.

10. Promoting linguistic diversity in cyberspace and encouraging universal access through the global network to all information in the public domain.

11. Countering the digital divide, in close cooperation in relevant United Nations sys-tem organizations, by fostering access by the developing countries to the new technolo-gies, by helping them to master information technologies and by facilitating the digital dissemination of endogenous cultural products and access by those countries to the edu-cational, cultural and scientific digital resources available worldwide.

12. Encouraging the production, safeguarding and dissemination of diversified con-tents in the media and global information networks and, to that end, promoting the role of public radio and television services in the development of audiovisual productions of good quality, in particular by fostering the establishment of cooperative mechanisms to facilitate their distribution.

13. Formulating policies and strategies for the preservation and enhancement of the cultural and natural heritage, notably the oral and intangible cultural heritage, and com-bating illicit traffic in cultural goods and services.

14. Respecting and protecting traditional knowledge, in particular that of indigenous peoples; recognizing the contribution of traditional knowledge, particularly with regard to environmental protection and the management of natural resources, and fostering synergies between modern science and local knowledge.

15. Fostering the mobility of creators, artists, researchers, scientists and intellectuals and the development of international research programmes and partnerships, while striving to preserve and enhance the creative capacity of developing countries and countries in transition.

16. Ensuring protection of copyright and related rights in the interest of the develop-ment of contemporary creativity and fair remuneration for creative work, while at the same time upholding a public right of access to culture, in accordance with Article 27 of the Universal Declaration of Human Rights.

17. Assisting in the emergence or consolidation of cultural industries in the developing countries and countries in transition and, to this end, cooperating in the development of the necessary infrastructures and skills, fostering the emergence of viable local markets, and facilitating access for the cultural products of those countries to the global market and international distribution networks.

18. Developing cultural policies, including operational support arrangements and/or appropriate regulatory frameworks, designed to promote the principles enshrined in this Declaration, in accordance with the international obligations incumbent upon each State.

19. Involving the various sections of civil society closely in the framing of public policies aimed at safeguarding and promoting cultural diversity.

20 Recognizing and encouraging the contribution that the private sector can make to enhancing cultural diversity and facilitating, to that end, the establishment of forums for dialogue between the public sector and the private sector.

The Member States recommend that the Director-General take the objectives set forth in this Action Plan into account in the implementation of UNESCO's programmes and communicate it to institutions of the United Nations system and to other intergovernmental and non-governmental organizations concerned with a view to enhancing the synergy of actions in favour of cultural diversity.

82. CONVENTION ON THE PROTECTION AND PROMOTION OF THE DIVERSITY OF CULTURAL EXPRESSIONS, 2005

In 2005, the UNESCO General Conference approved the Convention on the Protection and Promotion of the Diversity of Cultural Expressions. Like the preceding Declaration, this Convention is in part a response to the challenges for cultural diversity raised by globalization. It also reflects an understanding of the concept of cultural diversity as raising two questions in particular: 'on the one hand, the links between cultural diversity, human rights and cultural rights; on the other, the links between diversity, creativity and cultural policies': UNESCO, Executive Board, 'Preliminary Study on the Technical and Legal Aspects Relating to the Desirability of a Standard-setting Instrument on Cultural Diversity', doc. 166 EX/28, 12 March 2003, para. 11. Following preliminary examination of the issues, in 2004, the UNESCO Executive Board initiated discussions and the drafting of a convention on the protection of 'the diversity of cultural contents and artistic expressions'. In August 2005, the Director-General submitted the following text to the General Conference where it was adopted on 20 October 2005. For a summary of the background, see 'Preliminary Report by the Director-General Setting out the Situation to Be Regulated and the Possible Scope of the Regulating Action Proposed, Accompanied by the Preliminary Draft of a Convention on the Protection of the Diversity of Cultural Contents and Artistic Expressions', UNESCO General Conference, 33rd Session, Paris, doc. 33 C/23, 4 August 2005. It entered into force on 18 March 2007.

Further reading

FRANCIONI, F., 'Au-delà des traités: l'émergence d'un nouveau droit coutumier pour la protection du patrimoine culturel', *Revue générale de droit international public*, 2007, 19.
—— and SCHEININ, M., *Cultural Human Rights*, Leiden: Martinus Nijhoff, 2008.
GRABER, C. B. and BURRI-NENOVA, M., *Intellectual Property and Traditional Cultural Expressions in a Digital Environment*, Cheltenham: Edward Elgar Publishing, 2007.
LEUPRECHT, P., 'The Difficult Acceptance of Diversity', (2005–2006) 30 *Vermont Law Review* 552.
McGoldrick, D., 'Culture, Cultures and Cultural Rights', in BADERIN, M. and McCorquodale, R., eds., *Economic, Social and Cultural Rights in Action*, Oxford: Oxford University Press, 2007.
PAUWELYN, J., 'The UNESCO Convention on Cultural Diversity, and the WTO: Diversity in International Law-Making?' *ASIL Insights*, 15 November 2005: **http://www.asil.org/insights051115.cfm**.
RUIZ FABRI, H., 'Jeux dans la fragmentation: la Convention sur la promotion et la protection de la diversité des expressions culturelles', *Revue générale de droit international public*, 2007, 43.
STAMATOPOULOU, D., *Cultural Rights in International Law: Article 27 of the Universal Declaration of Human Rights and Beyond*, Leiden: Martinus Nijhoff, 2007.

TEXT

The General Conference of the United Nations Educational, Scientific and Cultural Organization, Meeting in Paris from 3 to 21 October 2005 at its 33rd Session,

Affirming that cultural diversity is a defining characteristic of humanity,

Conscious that cultural diversity forms a common heritage of humanity and should be cherished and preserved for the benefit of all,

Being aware that cultural diversity creates a rich and varied world, which increases the range of choices and nurtures human capacities and values, and therefore is a mainspring for sustainable development for communities, peoples and nations,

Recalling that cultural diversity, flourishing within a framework of democracy, tolerance, social justice and mutual respect between peoples and cultures, is indispensable for peace and security at the local, national and international levels,

Celebrating the importance of cultural diversity for the full realization of human rights and fundamental freedoms proclaimed in the Universal Declaration of Human Rights and other universally recognized instruments,

Emphasizing the need to incorporate culture as a strategic element in national and international development policies, as well as in international development cooperation, taking into account also the United Nations Millennium Declaration (2000) with its special emphasis on poverty eradication,

Taking into account that culture takes diverse forms across time and space and that this diversity is embodied in the uniqueness and plurality of the identities and cultural expressions of the peoples and societies making up humanity,

Recognizing the importance of traditional knowledge as a source of intangible and material wealth, and in particular the knowledge systems of indigenous peoples, and its positive contribution to sustainable development, as well as the need for its adequate protection and promotion,

Recognizing the need to take measures to protect the diversity of cultural expressions, including their contents, especially in situations where cultural expressions may be threatened by the possibility of extinction or serious impairment,

Emphasizing the importance of culture for social cohesion in general, and in particular its potential for the enhancement of the status and role of women in society,

Being aware that cultural diversity is strengthened by the free flow of ideas, and that it is nurtured by constant exchanges and interaction between cultures,

Reaffirming that freedom of thought, expression and information, as well as diversity of the media, enable cultural expressions to flourish within societies,

Recognizing that the diversity of cultural expressions, including traditional cultural expressions, is an important factor that allows individuals and peoples to express and to share with others their ideas and values,

Recalling that linguistic diversity is a fundamental element of cultural diversity, and reaffirming the fundamental role that education plays in the protection and promotion of cultural expressions,

Taking into account the importance of the vitality of cultures, including for persons belonging to minorities and indigenous peoples, as manifested in their freedom to create, disseminate and distribute their traditional cultural expressions and to have access thereto, so as to benefit them for their own development,

Emphasizing the vital role of cultural interaction and creativity, which nurture and renew cultural expressions and enhance the role played by those involved in the development of culture for the progress of society at large,

Recognizing the importance of intellectual property rights in sustaining those involved in cultural creativity,

Being convinced that cultural activities, goods and services have both an economic and a cultural nature, because they convey identities, values and meanings, and must therefore not be treated as solely having commercial value,

Noting that while the processes of globalization, which have been facilitated by the rapid development of information and communication technologies, afford unprecedented conditions for enhanced interaction between cultures, they also represent a challenge for cultural diversity, namely in view of risks of imbalances between rich and poor countries,

Being aware of UNESCO's specific mandate to ensure respect for the diversity of cultures and to recommend such international agreements as may be necessary to promote the free flow of ideas by word and image,

Referring to the provisions of the international instruments adopted by UNESCO relating to cultural diversity and the exercise of cultural rights, and in particular the Universal Declaration on Cultural Diversity of 2001,

Adopts this Convention on 20 October 2005.

I. OBJECTIVES AND GUIDING PRINCIPLES

Article 1—Objectives

The objectives of this Convention are:

 (a) to protect and promote the diversity of cultural expressions;

 (b) to create the conditions for cultures to flourish and to freely interact in a mutually beneficial manner;

 (c) to encourage dialogue among cultures with a view to ensuring wider and balanced cultural exchanges in the world in favour of intercultural respect and a culture of peace;

 (d) to foster interculturality in order to develop cultural interaction in the spirit of building bridges among peoples;

 (e) to promote respect for the diversity of cultural expressions and raise awareness of its value at the local, national and international levels;

 (f) to reaffirm the importance of the link between culture and development for all countries, particularly for developing countries, and to support actions undertaken nationally and internationally to secure recognition of the true value of this link;

 (g) to give recognition to the distinctive nature of cultural activities, goods and services as vehicles of identity, values and meaning;

 (h) to reaffirm the sovereign rights of States to maintain, adopt and implement policies and measures that they deem appropriate for the protection and promotion of the diversity of cultural expressions on their territory;

   (i)   to strengthen international cooperation and solidarity in a spirit of partnership with a view, in particular, to enhancing the capacities of developing countries in order to protect and promote the diversity of cultural expressions.

Article 2—Guiding principles

1. *Principle of respect for human rights and fundamental freedoms*

Cultural diversity can be protected and promoted only if human rights and fundamental freedoms, such as freedom of expression, information and communication, as well as the ability of individuals to choose cultural expressions, are guaranteed. No one may invoke the provisions of this Convention in order to infringe human rights and fundamental freedoms as enshrined in the Universal Declaration of Human Rights or guaranteed by international law, or to limit the scope thereof.

2. *Principle of sovereignty*

States have, in accordance with the Charter of the United Nations and the principles of international law, the sovereign right to adopt measures and policies to protect and promote the diversity of cultural expressions within their territory.

3. *Principle of equal dignity of and respect for all cultures*

The protection and promotion of the diversity of cultural expressions presuppose the recognition of equal dignity of and respect for all cultures, including the cultures of persons belonging to minorities and indigenous peoples.

4. *Principle of international solidarity and cooperation*

International cooperation and solidarity should be aimed at enabling countries, especially developing countries, to create and strengthen their means of cultural expression, including their cultural industries, whether nascent or established, at the local, national and international levels.

5. *Principle of the complementarity of economic and cultural aspects of development*

Since culture is one of the mainsprings of development, the cultural aspects of development are as important as its economic aspects, which individuals and peoples have the fundamental right to participate in and enjoy.

6. *Principle of sustainable development*

Cultural diversity is a rich asset for individuals and societies. The protection, promotion and maintenance of cultural diversity are an essential requirement for sustainable development for the benefit of present and future generations.

7. *Principle of equitable access*

Equitable access to a rich and diversified range of cultural expressions from all over the world and access of cultures to the means of expressions and dissemination constitute important elements for enhancing cultural diversity and encouraging mutual understanding.

8. *Principle of openness and balance*

When States adopt measures to support the diversity of cultural expressions, they should seek to promote, in an appropriate manner, openness to other cultures of the world and to ensure that these measures are geared to the objectives pursued under the present Convention.

II. SCOPE OF APPLICATION

Article 3—Scope of application

This Convention shall apply to the policies and measures adopted by the Parties related to the protection and promotion of the diversity of cultural expressions.

III. DEFINITIONS

Article 4—Definitions

For the purposes of this Convention, it is understood that:

1. *Cultural diversity*

'Cultural diversity' refers to the manifold ways in which the cultures of groups and societies find expression. These expressions are passed on within and among groups and societies.

Cultural diversity is made manifest not only through the varied ways in which the cultural heritage of humanity is expressed, augmented and transmitted through the variety of cultural expressions, but also through diverse modes of artistic creation, production, dissemination, distribution and enjoyment, whatever the means and technologies used.

2. *Cultural content*

'Cultural content' refers to the symbolic meaning, artistic dimension and cultural values that originate from or express cultural identities.

3. *Cultural expressions*

'Cultural expressions' are those expressions that result from the creativity of individuals, groups and societies, and that have cultural content.

4. *Cultural activities, goods and services*

'Cultural activities, goods and services' refers to those activities, goods and services, which at the time they are considered as a specific attribute, use or purpose, embody or convey cultural expressions, irrespective of the commercial value they may have. Cultural activities may be an end in themselves, or they may contribute to the production of cultural goods and services.

5. *Cultural industries*

'Cultural industries' refers to industries producing and distributing cultural goods or services as defined in paragraph 4 above.

6. *Cultural policies and measures*

'Cultural policies and measures' refers to those policies and measures relating to culture, whether at the local, national, regional or international level that are either focused on culture as such or are designed to have a direct effect on cultural expressions of individuals, groups or societies, including on the creation, production, dissemination, distribution of and access to cultural activities, goods and services.

7. *Protection*

'Protection' means the adoption of measures aimed at the preservation, safeguarding and enhancement of the diversity of cultural expressions.

'Protect' means to adopt such measures.

8. *Interculturality*

'Interculturality' refers to the existence and equitable interaction of diverse cultures and the possibility of generating shared cultural expressions through dialogue and mutual respect.

IV. RIGHTS AND OBLIGATIONS OF PARTIES

Article 5—*General rule regarding rights and obligations*

1. The Parties, in conformity with the Charter of the United Nations, the principles of international law and universally recognized human rights instruments, reaffirm their sovereign right to formulate and implement their cultural policies and to adopt measures to protect and promote the diversity of cultural expressions and to strengthen international cooperation to achieve the purposes of this Convention.

2. When a Party implements policies and takes measures to protect and promote the diversity of cultural expressions within its territory, its policies and measures shall be consistent with the provisions of this Convention.

Article 6—*Rights of parties at the national level*

1. Within the framework of its cultural policies and measures as defined in Article 4.6 and taking into account its own particular circumstances and needs, each Party may adopt measures aimed at protecting and promoting the diversity of cultural expressions within its territory.

2. Such measures may include the following:

> (a) regulatory measures aimed at protecting and promoting diversity of cultural expressions;
>
> (b) measures that, in an appropriate manner, provide opportunities for domestic cultural activities, goods and services among all those available within the national territory for the creation, production, dissemination, distribution and enjoyment of such domestic cultural activities, goods and services, including provisions relating to the language used for such activities, goods and services;
>
> (c) measures aimed at providing domestic independent cultural industries and activities in the informal sector effective access to the means of production, dissemination and distribution of cultural activities, goods and services;
>
> (d) measures aimed at providing public financial assistance;
>
> (e) measures aimed at encouraging non-profit organizations, as well as public and private institutions and artists and other cultural professionals, to develop and promote the free exchange and circulation of ideas, cultural expressions and cultural activities, goods and services, and to stimulate both the creative and entrepreneurial spirit in their activities;

(f) measures aimed at establishing and supporting public institutions, as appropriate;

(g) measures aimed at nurturing and supporting artists and others involved in the creation of cultural expressions;

(h) measures aimed at enhancing diversity of the media, including through public service broadcasting.

Article 7—Measures to promote cultural expressions

1. Parties shall endeavour to create in their territory an environment which encourages individuals and social groups:

(a) to create, produce, disseminate, distribute and have access to their own cultural expressions, paying due attention to the special circumstances and needs of women as well as various social groups, including persons belonging to minorities and indigenous peoples;

(b) to have access to diverse cultural expressions from within their territory as well as from other countries of the world.

2. Parties shall also endeavour to recognize the important contribution of artists, others involved in the creative process, cultural communities, and organizations that support their work, and their central role in nurturing the diversity of cultural expressions.

Article 8—Measures to protect cultural expressions

1. Without prejudice to the provisions of Articles 5 and 6, a Party may determine the existence of special situations where cultural expressions on its territory are at risk of extinction, under serious threat, or otherwise in need of urgent safeguarding.

2. Parties may take all appropriate measures to protect and preserve cultural expressions in situations referred to in paragraph 1 in a manner consistent with the provisions of this Convention.

3. Parties shall report to the Intergovernmental Committee referred to in Article 23 all measures taken to meet the exigencies of the situation, and the Committee may make appropriate recommendations.

Article 9—Information sharing and transparency

Parties shall:

(a) provide appropriate information in their reports to UNESCO every four years on measures taken to protect and promote the diversity of cultural expressions within their territory and at the international level;

(b) designate a point of contact responsible for information sharing in relation to this Convention;

(c) share and exchange information relating to the protection and promotion of the diversity of cultural expressions.

Article 10—Education and public awareness

Parties shall:

(a) encourage and promote understanding of the importance of the protection and promotion of the diversity of cultural expressions, inter alia, through educational and greater public awareness programmes;

(b) cooperate with other Parties and international and regional organizations in achieving the purpose of this article;

(c) endeavour to encourage creativity and strengthen production capacities by setting up educational, training and exchange programmes in the field of cultural industries. These measures should be implemented in a manner which does not have a negative impact on traditional forms of production.

Article 11—Participation of civil society

Parties acknowledge the fundamental role of civil society in protecting and promoting the diversity of cultural expressions. Parties shall encourage the active participation of civil society in their efforts to achieve the objectives of this Convention.

Article 12—Promotion of international cooperation

Parties shall endeavour to strengthen their bilateral, regional and international cooperation for the creation of conditions conducive to the promotion of the diversity of cultural expressions, taking particular account of the situations referred to in Articles 8 and 17, notably in order to:

(a) facilitate dialogue among Parties on cultural policy;

(b) enhance public sector strategic and management capacities in cultural public sector institutions, through professional and international cultural exchanges and sharing of best practices;

(c) reinforce partnerships with and among civil society, non-governmental organizations and the private sector in fostering and promoting the diversity of cultural expressions;

(d) promote the use of new technologies, encourage partnerships to enhance information sharing and cultural understanding, and foster the diversity of cultural expressions;

(e) encourage the conclusion of co-production and co-distribution agreements.

Article 13—Integration of culture in sustainable development

Parties shall endeavour to integrate culture in their development policies at all levels for the creation of conditions conducive to sustainable development and, within this framework, foster aspects relating to the protection and promotion of the diversity of cultural expressions.

Article 14—Cooperation for development

Parties shall endeavour to support cooperation for sustainable development and poverty reduction, especially in relation to the specific needs of developing countries, in order to foster the emergence of a dynamic cultural sector by, inter alia, the following means:

(a) the strengthening of the cultural industries in developing countries through:

(i) creating and strengthening cultural production and distribution capacities in developing countries;

(ii) facilitating wider access to the global market and international distribution networks for their cultural activities, goods and services;

(iii) enabling the emergence of viable local and regional markets;

(iv) adopting, where possible, appropriate measures in developed countries with a view to facilitating access to their territory for the cultural activities, goods and services of developing countries;

(v) providing support for creative work and facilitating the mobility, to the extent possible, of artists from the developing world;

(vi) encouraging appropriate collaboration between developed and developing countries in the areas, inter alia, of music and film;

(b) capacity-building through the exchange of information, experience and expertise, as well as the training of human resources in developing countries, in the public and private sector relating to, inter alia, strategic and management capacities, policy development and implementation, promotion and distribution of cultural expressions, small-, medium- and micro-enterprise development, the use of technology, and skills development and transfer;

(c) technology transfer through the introduction of appropriate incentive measures for the transfer of technology and know-how, especially in the areas of cultural industries and enterprises;

(d) financial support through:

(i) the establishment of an International Fund for Cultural Diversity as provided in Article 18;

(ii) the provision of official development assistance, as appropriate, including technical assistance, to stimulate and support creativity;

(iii) other forms of financial assistance such as low interest loans, grants and other funding mechanisms.

Article 15—Collaborative arrangements

Parties shall encourage the development of partnerships, between and within the public and private sectors and non-profit organizations, in order to cooperate with developing countries in the enhancement of their capacities in the protection and promotion of the diversity of cultural expressions. These innovative partnerships shall, according to the practical needs of developing countries, emphasize the further development of infrastructure, human resources and policies, as well as the exchange of cultural activities, goods and services.

Article 16—Preferential treatment for developing countries

Developed countries shall facilitate cultural exchanges with developing countries by granting, through the appropriate institutional and legal frameworks, preferential treatment to artists and other cultural professionals and practitioners, as well as cultural goods and services from developing countries.

Article 17—International cooperation in situations of serious threat to cultural expressions

Parties shall cooperate in providing assistance to each other, and, in particular to developing countries, in situations referred to under Article 8.

Article 18—International Fund for Cultural Diversity

1. An International Fund for Cultural Diversity, hereinafter referred to as 'the Fund', is hereby established.

2. The Fund shall consist of funds-in-trust established in accordance with the Financial Regulations of UNESCO.

3. The resources of the Fund shall consist of:

(a) voluntary contributions made by Parties;

(b) funds appropriated for this purpose by the General Conference of UNESCO;

(c) contributions, gifts or bequests by other States; organizations and programmes of the United Nations system, other regional or international organizations; and public or private bodies or individuals;

(d) any interest due on resources of the Fund;

(e) funds raised through collections and receipts from events organized for the benefit of the Fund;

(f) any other resources authorized by the Fund's regulations.

4. The use of resources of the Fund shall be decided by the Intergovernmental Committee on the basis of guidelines determined by the Conference of Parties referred to in Article 22.

5. The Intergovernmental Committee may accept contributions and other forms of assistance for general and specific purposes relating to specific projects, provided that those projects have been approved by it.

6. No political, economic or other conditions that are incompatible with the objectives of this Convention may be attached to contributions made to the Fund.

7. Parties shall endeavour to provide voluntary contributions on a regular basis towards the implementation of this Convention.

Article 19—Exchange, analysis and dissemination of information

1. Parties agree to exchange information and share expertise concerning data collection and statistics on the diversity of cultural expressions as well as on best practices for its protection and promotion.

2. UNESCO shall facilitate, through the use of existing mechanisms within the Secretariat, the collection, analysis and dissemination of all relevant information, statistics and best practices.

3. UNESCO shall also establish and update a data bank on different sectors and governmental, private and non-profit organizations involved in the area of cultural expressions.

4. To facilitate the collection of data, UNESCO shall pay particular attention to capacity-building and the strengthening of expertise for Parties that submit a request for such assistance.

5. The collection of information identified in this Article shall complement the information collected under the provisions of Article 9.

V. RELATIONSHIP TO OTHER INSTRUMENTS

Article 20—Relationship to other treaties: mutual supportiveness, complementarity and non-subordination

1. Parties recognize that they shall perform in good faith their obligations under this Convention and all other treaties to which they are parties. Accordingly, without subordinating this Convention to any other treaty,

(a) they shall foster mutual supportiveness between this Convention and the other treaties to which they are parties; and

(b) when interpreting and applying the other treaties to which they are parties or when entering into other international obligations, Parties shall take into account the relevant provisions of this Convention.

2. Nothing in this Convention shall be interpreted as modifying rights and obligations of the Parties under any other treaties to which they are parties.

Article 21—International consultation and coordination

Parties undertake to promote the objectives and principles of this Convention in other international forums. For this purpose, Parties shall consult each other, as appropriate, bearing in mind these objectives and principles.

VI. ORGANS OF THE CONVENTION

Article 22—Conference of Parties

1. A Conference of Parties shall be established. The Conference of Parties shall be the plenary and supreme body of this Convention.

2. The Conference of Parties shall meet in ordinary session every two years, as far as possible, in conjunction with the General Conference of UNESCO. It may meet in extraordinary session if it so decides or if the Intergovernmental Committee receives a request to that effect from at least one-third of the Parties.

3. The Conference of Parties shall adopt its own rules of procedure.

4. The functions of the Conference of Parties shall be, inter alia:

    (a) to elect the Members of the Intergovernmental Committee;

    (b) to receive and examine reports of the Parties to this Convention transmitted by the Intergovernmental Committee;

    (c) to approve the operational guidelines prepared upon its request by the Intergovernmental Committee;

    (d) to take whatever other measures it may consider necessary to further the objectives of this Convention.

Article 23—Intergovernmental Committee

1. An Intergovernmental Committee for the Protection and Promotion of the Diversity of Cultural Expressions, hereinafter referred to as 'the Intergovernmental Committee', shall be established within UNESCO. It shall be composed of representatives of 18 States Parties to the Convention, elected for a term of four years by the Conference of Parties upon entry into force of this Convention pursuant to Article 29.

2. The Intergovernmental Committee shall meet annually.

3. The Intergovernmental Committee shall function under the authority and guidance of and be accountable to the Conference of Parties.

4. The Members of the Intergovernmental Committee shall be increased to 24 once the number of Parties to the Convention reaches 50.

5. The election of Members of the Intergovernmental Committee shall be based on the principles of equitable geographical representation as well as rotation.

6. Without prejudice to the other responsibilities conferred upon it by this Convention, the functions of the Intergovernmental Committee shall be:

> *(a)* to promote the objectives of this Convention and to encourage and monitor the implementation thereof;
>
> *(b)* to prepare and submit for approval by the Conference of Parties, upon its request, the operational guidelines for the implementation and application of the provisions of the Convention;
>
> *(c)* to transmit to the Conference of Parties reports from Parties to the Convention, together with its comments and a summary of their contents;
>
> *(d)* to make appropriate recommendations to be taken in situations brought to its attention by Parties to the Convention in accordance with relevant provisions of the Convention, in particular Article 8;
>
> *(e)* to establish procedures and other mechanisms for consultation aimed at promoting the objectives and principles of this Convention in other international forums;
>
> *(f)* to perform any other tasks as may be requested by the Conference of Parties.

7. The Intergovernmental Committee, in accordance with its Rules of Procedure, may invite at any time public or private organizations or individuals to participate in its meetings for consultation on specific issues.

8. The Intergovernmental Committee shall prepare and submit to the Conference of Parties, for approval, its own Rules of Procedure.

Article 24—UNESCO Secretariat

1. The organs of the Convention shall be assisted by the UNESCO Secretariat.

2. The Secretariat shall prepare the documentation of the Conference of Parties and the Intergovernmental Committee as well as the agenda of their meetings and shall assist in and report on the implementation of their decisions.

VII. FINAL CLAUSES

Article 25—Settlement of disputes

1. In the event of a dispute between Parties to this Convention concerning the interpretation or the application of the Convention, the Parties shall seek a solution by negotiation.

2. If the Parties concerned cannot reach agreement by negotiation, they may jointly seek the good offices of, or request mediation by, a third party.

3. If good offices or mediation are not undertaken or if there is no settlement by negotiation, good offices or mediation, a Party may have recourse to conciliation in accordance with the procedure laid down in the Annex of this Convention. The Parties shall consider in good faith the proposal made by the Conciliation Commission for the resolution of the dispute.

4. Each Party may, at the time of ratification, acceptance, approval or accession, declare that it does not recognize the conciliation procedure provided for above. Any Party having made such a declaration may, at any time, withdraw this declaration by notification to the Director-General of UNESCO.

Article 26—Ratification, acceptance, approval or accession by Member States

1. This Convention shall be subject to ratification, acceptance, approval or accession by Member States of UNESCO in accordance with their respective constitutional procedures.

2. The instruments of ratification, acceptance, approval or accession shall be deposited with the Director-General of UNESCO.

Article 27—Accession

1. This Convention shall be open to accession by all States not Members of UNESCO but members of the United Nations, or of any of its specialized agencies, that are invited by the General Conference of UNESCO to accede to it.

2. This Convention shall also be open to accession by territories which enjoy full internal self-government recognized as such by the United Nations, but which have not attained full independence in accordance with General Assembly resolution 1514 (XV), and which have competence over the matters governed by this Convention, including the competence to enter into treaties in respect of such matters.

3. The following provisions apply to regional economic integration organizations:

   (a) This Convention shall also be open to accession by any regional economic integration organization, which shall, except as provided below, be fully bound by the provisions of the Convention in the same manner as States Parties;

   (b) In the event that one or more Member States of such an organization is also Party to this Convention, the organization and such Member State or States shall decide on their responsibility for the performance of their obligations under this Convention. Such distribution of responsibility shall take effect following completion of the notification procedure described in subparagraph (c). The organization and the Member States shall not be entitled to exercise rights under this Convention concurrently. In addition, regional economic integration organizations, in matters within their competence, shall exercise their rights to vote with a number of votes equal to the number of their Member States that are Parties to this Convention. Such an organization shall not exercise its right to vote if any of its Member States exercises its right, and vice-versa;

   (c) A regional economic integration organization and its Member State or States which have agreed on a distribution of responsibilities as provided in subparagraph (b) shall inform the Parties of any such proposed distribution of responsibilities in the following manner:

      (i) in their instrument of accession, such organization shall declare with specificity, the distribution of their responsibilities with respect to matters governed by the Convention;

      (ii) in the event of any later modification of their respective responsibilities, the regional economic integration organization shall inform the depositary of any such proposed modification of their respective responsibilities; the depositary shall in turn inform the Parties of such modification;

   (d) Member States of a regional economic integration organization which become Parties to this Convention shall be presumed to retain competence over all matters in respect of which transfers of competence to the organization have not been specifically declared or informed to the depositary;

(e) 'Regional economic integration organization' means an organization constituted by sovereign States, members of the United Nations or of any of its specialized agencies, to which those States have transferred competence in respect of matters governed by this Convention and which has been duly authorized, in accordance with its internal procedures, to become a Party to it.

4. The instrument of accession shall be deposited with the Director-General of UNESCO.

Article 28—Point of contact

Upon becoming Parties to this Convention, each Party shall designate a point of contact as referred to in Article 9.

Article 29—Entry into force

1. This Convention shall enter into force three months after the date of deposit of the thirtieth instrument of ratification, acceptance, approval or accession, but only with respect to those States or regional economic integration organizations that have deposited their respective instruments of ratification, acceptance, approval, or accession on or before that date. It shall enter into force with respect to any other Party three months after the deposit of its instrument of ratification, acceptance, approval or accession.

2. For the purposes of this Article, any instrument deposited by a regional economic integration organization shall not be counted as additional to those deposited by Member States of the organization.

Article 30—Federal or non-unitary constitutional systems

Recognizing that international agreements are equally binding on Parties regardless of their constitutional systems, the following provisions shall apply to Parties which have a federal or non-unitary constitutional system:

(a) with regard to the provisions of this Convention, the implementation of which comes under the legal jurisdiction of the federal or central legislative power, the obligations of the federal or central government shall be the same as for those Parties which are not federal States;

(b) with regard to the provisions of the Convention, the implementation of which comes under the jurisdiction of individual constituent units such as States, counties, provinces, or cantons which are not obliged by the constitutional system of the federation to take legislative measures, the federal government shall inform, as necessary, the competent authorities of constituent units such as States, counties, provinces or cantons of the said provisions, with its recommendation for their adoption.

Article 31—Denunciation

1. Any Party to this Convention may denounce this Convention.

2. The denunciation shall be notified by an instrument in writing deposited with the Director-General of UNESCO.

3. The denunciation shall take effect 12 months after the receipt of the instrument of denunciation. It shall in no way affect the financial obligations of the Party denouncing the Convention until the date on which the withdrawal takes effect.

Article 32—Depositary functions

The Director-General of UNESCO, as the depositary of this Convention, shall inform the Member States of the Organization, the States not members of the Organization and regional economic integration organizations referred to in Article 27, as well as the United Nations, of the deposit of all the instruments of ratification, acceptance, approval or accession provided for in Articles 26 and 27, and of the denunciations provided for in Article 31.

Article 33—Amendments

1. A Party to this Convention may, by written communication addressed to the Director-General, propose amendments to this Convention. The Director-General shall circulate such communication to all Parties. If, within six months from the date of dispatch of the communication, no less than one half of the Parties reply favourably to the request, the Director-General shall present such proposal to the next session of the Conference of Parties for discussion and possible adoption.

2. Amendments shall be adopted by a two-thirds majority of Parties present and voting.

3. Once adopted, amendments to this Convention shall be submitted to the Parties for ratification, acceptance, approval or accession.

4. For Parties which have ratified, accepted, approved or acceded to them, amendments to this Convention shall enter into force three months after the deposit of the instruments referred to in paragraph 3 of this Article by two-thirds of the Parties. Thereafter, for each Party that ratifies, accepts, approves or accedes to an amendment, the said amendment shall enter into force three months after the date of deposit by that Party of its instrument of ratification, acceptance, approval or accession.

5. The procedure set out in paragraphs 3 and 4 shall not apply to amendments to Article 23 concerning the number of Members of the Intergovernmental Committee. These amendments shall enter into force at the time they are adopted.

6. A State or a regional economic integration organization referred to in Article 27 which becomes a Party to this Convention after the entry into force of amendments in conformity with paragraph 4 of this Article shall, failing an expression of different intention, be considered to be:

(a) Party to this Convention as so amended; and

(b) a Party to the unamended Convention in relation to any Party not bound by the amendments.

Article 34—Authoritative texts

This Convention has been drawn up in Arabic, Chinese, English, French, Russian and Spanish, all six texts being equally authoritative.

Article 35—Registration

In conformity with Article 102 of the Charter of the United Nations, this Convention shall be registered with the Secretariat of the United Nations at the request of the Director-General of UNESCO.

ANNEX—CONCILIATION PROCEDURE

Article 1—Conciliation Commission

A Conciliation Commission shall be created upon the request of one of the Parties to the dispute. The Commission shall, unless the Parties otherwise agree, be composed of five members, two appointed by each Party concerned and a President chosen jointly by those members.

Article 2—Members of the Commission

In disputes between more than two Parties, Parties in the same interest shall appoint their members of the Commission jointly by agreement. Where two or more Parties have separate interests or there is a disagreement as to whether they are of the same interest, they shall appoint their members separately.

Article 3—Appointments

If any appointments by the Parties are not made within two months of the date of the request to create a Conciliation Commission, the Director-General of UNESCO shall, if asked to do so by the Party that made the request, make those appointments within a further two-month period.

Article 4—President of the Commission

If a President of the Conciliation Commission has not been chosen within two months of the last of the members of the Commission being appointed, the Director-General of UNESCO shall, if asked to do so by a Party, designate a President within a further two-month period.

Article 5—Decisions

The Conciliation Commission shall take its decisions by majority vote of its members. It shall, unless the Parties to the dispute otherwise agree, determine its own procedure. It shall render a proposal for resolution of the dispute, which the Parties shall consider in good faith.

Article 6—Disagreement

A disagreement as to whether the Conciliation Commission has competence shall be decided by the Commission.

PART FIVE

EUROPE

INTRODUCTION

The instruments in this Part derive for the most part from the work of the Council of Europe, an organization created in 1949 as a sort of social and ideological counterpart to the military aspects of European co-operation represented in the North Atlantic Treaty Organization. The Council of Europe was inspired partly by interest in the promotion of European unity, and partly by the political desire for solidarity in the face of the ideology of Communism.

The membership of the Council of Europe has expanded considerably; the original ten signatories of the Statute of the Council of Europe were Belgium, Denmark, France, Ireland, Italy, Luxembourg, the Netherlands, Norway, Sweden, and the United Kingdom, later joined by Greece, Turkey, Iceland, the Federal Republic of Germany, Austria, Cyprus, Switzerland, Malta, Portugal, Spain, Liechtenstein, San Marino, and Finland. Following the end of the Cold War, the membership has further grown to forty-seven States (at 31 December 2009).

Belarus applied for full membership in 1993. From 1992 to 1997, it had Guest Status with the Parliamentary Assembly, but this was suspended following the constitutional referendum and parliamentary by-elections in 1996, which the Council of Europe considered undemocratic. In June 2009, the Parliamentary Assembly voted in favour of restoring Guest Status, with a view to 'engaging in political dialogue with the authorities', while supporting 'the strengthening of democratic forces and civil society'. However, this would be conditional on Belarus introducing a moratorium on execution of the death penalty: Parliamentary Assembly Resolution 1671 (2009) and Recommendation 1874 (2009), 23 June 2009.

Kazakhstan is another possible candidate for membership; see Parliamentary Assembly Resolution 1526 (2006), 'Situation in Kazakhstan and relations with the Council of Europe', 17 November 2006; and generally, **http://www.coe.int**.

On a more limited regional level, and after many years of debate, the member States of the European Union adopted a Charter of Fundamental Rights in December 2000. As and when the Treaty of Lisbon is ratified by all Member States, the Charter will have the force of law; it still remains to be seen how extensive will be its effect, but the European Court of Justice has already had occasion to refer to the Charter's reaffirmation of certain basic principles, such as that of effective judicial protection; see Joined Cases C-402/05 P and C-415/05 P, *Yassin Abdullah Kadi and Al Barakaat International*

Foundation v Council of the EU and Commission of the EC, ECJ Judgment, 3 September 2008:
http://curia.europa.eu/jcms/jcms/j_6/.

The promotion of human rights has also figured prominently in the work of the Conference on (later the 'Organization for') Security and Co-operation in Europe (CSCE/OSCE), which emerged after 1975. This mechanism also involves Canada and the United States of America, so that it exceeds the bounds of a strictly regional organization. Included below are the Final Act of the Helsinki Conference, 1975, and the Charter of Paris for a New Europe, 1990. Related documents included in the 5th edition of this volume have been moved to the Online Resource Centre; these include those from the 1989 Vienna Meeting of the CSCE Conference, the 1990 Copenhagen Meeting of the Second Conference on the Human Dimension, the 1991 Moscow Meeting of the Third Conference on the Human Dimension, the 1992 Helsinki Summit Meeting, the 1994 Budapest Summit Meeting, and the 1996 Lisbon Summit Meeting.

Also to be found in the *Online Resource Centre* is the text of the 1995 Commonwealth of Independent States Convention on Human Rights and Fundamental Freedoms. This Convention was opened for signature in Minsk on 26 May 1995, and entered into force on 11 August 1998; at 31 December 2009, it had been ratified by Belarus, the Kyrgyz Republic, the Russian Federation, and Tajikistan, and signed but not ratified by Armenia, Georgia, and Moldova.

The Convention comprises a preamble and thirty-nine articles. Articles 1 to 29 deal with substantive rights and obligations, many of which are framed in terms similar to those used in the European Convention on Human Rights, and the Convention also provides for a Human Rights Commission to monitor implementation. The question of possible incompatibilities between the two Conventions was raised in the Council of Europe, and in Resolution 1249 (2001), 23 May 2001, the Parliamentary Assembly expressed its concern that the CIS Convention offered less protection, both with regard to scope and enforcement (para. 4). It recommended to Council of Europe Member States which were also CIS Members that they not sign or ratify the CIS Convention or, if they were already parties, that they issue a legally-binding declaration confirming that the ECHR50 procedure would not be replaced or weakened in any way through recourse to that set out in the CIS Convention. On the same day, the Parliamentary Assembly adopted Recommendation 1519 (2001), recommending that the Committee of Ministers seek an advisory opinion from the European Court on the interpretation of Article 35(2)(b) ECHR50, and whether the CIS Human Rights Commission could be considered as 'another procedure of international investigation or settlement', such as to render an application submitted to such other procedure inadmissible before the European Court of Human Rights.

In January 2002, the Committee of Ministers of the Council of Europe duly requested the Court to give an advisory opinion (under Article 47 ECHR50), on the issues raised in Parliamentary Assembly Recommendation 1519 (2001). The Court considered that the request was limited to the specific question, whether the CIS system was to be regarded as 'another procedure of international investigation or settlement', rather than a more general question on the co-existence of the two conventions. It held, however, that to give such an advisory opinion was not within its competence, as it related to a question which the Court might have to consider in consequence of proceedings instituted in accordance with the European Convention: *Decision on the Competence of the Court to give an Advisory Opinion*, European Court of Human Rights, 2 June 2004, paras. 24, 34, 35.

5.1 COUNCIL OF EUROPE

83. THE EUROPEAN CONVENTION FOR THE PROTECTION OF HUMAN RIGHTS AND FUNDAMENTAL FREEDOMS, 1950, TOGETHER WITH PROTOCOLS NOS. 1, 4, 6, AND 7, AS AMENDED BY PROTOCOL NO. 11

The European Convention was the first essay in giving specific legal content to human rights in an international agreement, and combining this with the establishment of machinery for supervision and enforcement. It was signed in Rome on 4 November 1950 and entered into force on 3 September 1953. For the text, see *ETS* No. 5.[1] A central feature of this regime is the right of individual and inter-State petition, and at the request of the Committee of Ministers, the European Court of Human Rights may also give advisory opinions on the interpretation of the Convention and the Protocols. The Court came into being in 1959, and gave its 10,000th judgment in September 2008.

The role of the Court (and of the European Commission and Court in the arrangements preceding the entry into force of Protocol No. 11 in 1998) and the Committee of Ministers is that of review, and not that of an appeal court from the decisions of national tribunals. Their task is to ensure that the standards of the Convention and its Protocols are observed by the administrations of the States concerned. The work of these institutions has had important consequences: valuable material has been provided for the elaboration of the provisions on civil liberties; and anomalies have been exposed in national systems of law, often with the result that the relevant national legislation has been changed for the better. Several individual cases have also served effectively as test cases, and/or have raised issues affecting a whole class of persons, for example, a linguistic minority.

Following the entry into force of Protocol No. 11 (*ETS* No. 155) on 1 November 1998, the control machinery was substantially restructured. All alleged violations of human rights are referred directly to the Court. In most cases, the Court thereafter sat in Chambers of seven judges, decided on the admissibility and merits of applications and, if necessary, undertook an investigation. The Court also made itself available to the parties with a view to securing a friendly settlement on the basis of human rights as defined in the Convention and Protocols. The revised system proved inadequate to the task,[2] and further reforms have now been adopted; see Protocol No. 14, below, at p. 709. A temporary impasse in the ratification process led to the adoption of Protocol No. 14*bis* (below, p. 715), but this has now been superseded with the entry into force of Protocol No. 14 on 1 June 2010.

Over the years, the Convention was supplemented and/or amended by some eleven Protocols, many of which have now been effectively superseded following the entry into force of Protocol No. 11 on 1 November 1998. Of the four remaining Protocols, the first entered into force on 18 May 1954; the fourth on 2 May 1968; the sixth on 1 March 1985; and the seventh on 1 November 1988. See also Protocol No. 12 (on non-discrimination, below p. 703), which entered into force on 1 April 2005. The texts of the Protocols follow that of the principal Convention below.

See also below, p. 900, on the relation between the European Convention and the EU Charter of Fundamental Rights.

---

[1] Council of Europe Conventions and agreements opened for signature between 1949 and 2003 were published in the 'European Treaty Series' (*ETS* Nos. 001 to 193 inclusive). From 2004, this Series is continued by the 'Council of Europe Treaty Series' (*CETS* No. 194 and following).

[2] On 1 January 2009, approximately 97,300 application were pending before a decision-making body, more than half of them against one of three countries—Russia, Turkey, or Romania: **http://echr.coe.int/**.

The text of the Convention was amended by Protocol No. 3 (*ETS* No. 45), which entered into force on 21 September 1970, Protocol No. 5 (*ETS* No. 55), which entered into force on 20 December 1971, and Protocol No. 8 (*ETS* No. 118), which entered into force on 1 January 1990. It also comprised the text of Protocol No. 2 (*ETS* No. 44) which, in accordance with Article 5, paragraph 3 thereof, had been an integral part of the Convention since its entry into force on 21 September 1970. All those provisions which had been amended or added by the above Protocols are now replaced by Protocol No. 11. As from the entry into force of Protocol No. 11 on 1 November 1998, Protocol No. 9 (*ETS* No. 140), which entered into force on 1 October 1994, is repealed, and Protocol No. 10 (*ETS* No. 146) has lost its purpose.

The text below reflects these changes. Protocol 11 added the headings to Articles 1–18 and 52–59, added Section II, renumbered Section III, and amended the text of Articles 56(1), 56(2), and 58(4). It also added the headings of articles and amended the text of Protocol No. 1 (*ETS* No. 9), Protocol No. 4 (*ETS* No. 46), Protocol No. 6 (*ETS* No. 114), and Protocol No. 7 (*ETS* No. 117).

Although it has not been formally amended, Article 2(1) of the Convention ('No one shall be deprived of his life intentionally save in the execution of a sentence of a court following his conviction of a crime for which this penalty is provided by law') must now be read in the light of Protocol No. 6 and Protocol No. 13; cf. *Al-Saadoon and Mufdhi v. United Kingdom*, Application no. 61498/08, Fourth Section, Decision on Admissibility, 30 June 2009.

On the extra-territorial application of the European Convention, see, among others, *Al-Saadoon and Mufdhi v United Kingdom*, (Appl. No. 61498/08), Decision on admissibility, 30 June 2009; *Banković v Belgium and others* (2001) BHRC 435; *Issa v Turkey* (2005) 41 EHRR 27; *Öcalan v Turkey* (2005) 41 EHRR 985; and, in the United Kingdom, *R (B) v Secretary of State for Foreign and Commonwealth Affairs* [2005] QB 643; *R (Al-Skeini) v Secretary of State for Defence* [2007] UKHL 26, [2008] 1 AC 153; *R (Al-Saadoon) v Secretary of State for Defence* [2009] EWCA Civ 7; [2008] EWHC 3098 (Admin).

Further reading

BARTLETT, P., LEWIS, O. and THOROLD, O., *Mental Disability and the European Convention on Human Rights*, Leiden: Martinus Nijhoff, 2007.

BATES, E., *The Evolution of the European Convention on Human Rights*, Oxford: Oxford University Press, 2010.

CAFLISCH, L. and CANÇADO TRINDADE, A. A., 'Les conventions américaine et européenne des droits de l'homme et le droit international général', *Revue générale de droit international public* 108.1, 2004, 5–62.

COHEN-JONATHAN, G., 'La journée de réflexion au Palais des droits de l'homme de Strasbourg sur l'efficacité du système de la Convention européenne des droits de l'homme', *Revue trimestrielle de droits de l'homme*, 2000, 637.

GOMIEN, D., HARRIS, D. and ZWAAK, L., *Law and Practice of the European Convention on Human Rights and the European Social Charter*, Strasbourg: Council of Europe, 1996.

GOODWIN-GILL, G. S., 'The Extra-Territorial Reach of Human Rights Obligations: A Brief Perspective on the Link to Jurisdiction', in BOISSON DE CHAZOURNES, L. and KOHEN, M., *Liber Amicorum Vera Gowlland-Debbas*, Leiden: Martinus Nijhoff, 2010, 293.

GREER, S., *The European Convention on Human Rights: Achievements, Problems and Prospects*, Cambridge: Cambridge University Press, 2006.

——— and WILLIAMS, A., 'Human Rights in the Council of Europe and the EU: Towards "Individual", "Constitutional" or "Institutional" Justice?', (2009) 15 *European Law Journal* 462.

HARMSEN, R., 'The European Convention on Human Rights after Enlargement', (2001) 5(4) *International Journal of Human Rights*, 18–43.

HARPAZ, G., 'The European Court of Justice and its Relations with the European Court of Human Rights: The Quest for Enhanced Reliance, Coherence and Legitimacy', (2009) 46 *Common Market Law Review* 105.

HARRIS, D., O'BOYLE, M., WARBRICK, C., BATES, E. and BUCKLEY, C., *Law of the European Convention on Human Rights*, Oxford: Oxford University Press, 2nd edn., 2009.

JANIS, M. W., KAY, R. S. and BRADLEY, A.W., *European Human Rights Law: Text and Materials*, Oxford: Oxford University Press, 3rd edn., 2008.

JANSSEN-PEVTSCHIN, G., 'Le Protocole n° 11 à la Convention européenne des droits de l'homme', *Revue trimestrielle de droits de l'homme*, 1994, 483.

LETSAS, G., *A Theory of Interpretation of the European Convention on Human Rights*, Oxford: Oxford University Press, 2007.

KELLER, H. and STONE SWEET, A., eds., *A Europe of Rights: The Impact of the ECHR on National Legal Systems*, Oxford: Oxford University Press, 2008.

MOWBRAY, A., *Cases and Materials on the European Human Rights Convention*, Oxford: Oxford University Press, 2007.

WHITE, R. AND OVEY, C., *Jacobs, White & Ovey: The European Convention on Human Rights*, Oxford: Clarendon Press, 5th edn., 2010.

TEXT

The Governments signatory hereto, being members of the Council of Europe,

Considering the Universal Declaration of Human Rights proclaimed by the General Assembly of the United Nations on 10th December 1948;

Considering that this Declaration aims at securing the universal and effective recognition and observance of the Rights therein declared;

Considering that the aim of the Council of Europe is the achievement of greater unity between its members and that one of the methods by which that aim is to be pursued is the maintenance and further realization of human rights and fundamental freedoms;

Reaffirming their profound belief in those fundamental freedoms which are the foundation of justice and peace in the world and are best maintained on the one hand by an effective political democracy and on the other by a common understanding and observance of the human rights upon which they depend;

Being resolved, as the governments of European countries which are like-minded and have a common heritage of political traditions, ideals, freedom and the rule of law, to take the first steps for the collective enforcement of certain of the rights stated in the Universal Declaration,

Have agreed as follows:

Article 1—Obligation to respect human rights

The High Contracting Parties shall secure to everyone within their jurisdiction the rights and freedoms defined in Section I of this Convention.

SECTION I—RIGHTS AND FREEDOMS

Article 2—Right to life

1. Everyone's right to life shall be protected by law. No one shall be deprived of his life intentionally save in the execution of a sentence of a court following his conviction of a crime for which this penalty is provided by law.

2. Deprivation of life shall not be regarded as inflicted in contravention of this article when it results from the use of force which is no more than absolutely necessary:

(a) in defence of any person from unlawful violence;

(b) in order to effect a lawful arrest or to prevent the escape of a person lawfully detained;

(c) in action lawfully taken for the purpose of quelling a riot or insurrection.

Article 3—Prohibition of torture

No one shall be subjected to torture or to inhuman or degrading treatment or punishment.

Article 4—Prohibition of slavery and forced labour

1. No one shall be held in slavery or servitude.

2. No one shall be required to perform forced or compulsory labour.

3. For the purpose of this article the term 'forced or compulsory labour' shall not include:

(a) any work required to be done in the ordinary course of detention imposed according to the provisions of Article 5 of this Convention or during conditional release from such detention;

(b) any service of a military character or, in case of conscientious objectors in countries where they are recognized, service exacted instead of compulsory military service;

(c) any service exacted in case of an emergency or calamity threatening the life or well-being of the community;

(d) any work or service which forms part of normal civic obligations.

Article 5—Right to liberty and security

1. Everyone has the right to liberty and security of person. No one shall be deprived of his liberty save in the following cases and in accordance with a procedure prescribed by law:

(a) the lawful detention of a person after conviction by a competent court;

(b) the lawful arrest or detention of a person for non-compliance with the lawful order of a court or in order to secure the fulfilment of any obligation prescribed by law;

(c) the lawful arrest or detention of a person effected for the purpose of bringing him before the competent legal authority on reasonable suspicion of having committed an offence or when it is reasonably considered necessary to prevent his committing an offence or fleeing after having done so;

(d) the detention of a minor by lawful order for the purpose of educational supervision or his lawful detention for the purpose of bringing him before the competent legal authority;

(e) the lawful detention of persons for the prevention of the spreading of infectious diseases, of persons of unsound mind, alcoholics or drug addicts or vagrants;

(f) the lawful arrest or detention of a person to prevent his effecting an unauthorized entry into the country or of a person against whom action is being taken with a view to deportation or extradition.

2. Everyone who is arrested shall be informed promptly, in a language which he understands, of the reasons for his arrest and of any charge against him.

3. Everyone arrested or detained in accordance with the provisions of paragraph 1(c) of this article shall be brought promptly before a judge or other officer authorized by law to exercise judicial power and shall be entitled to trial within a reasonable time or to release pending trial. Release may be conditioned by guarantees to appear for trial.

4. Everyone who is deprived of his liberty by arrest or detention shall be entitled to take proceedings by which the lawfulness of his detention shall be decided speedily by a court and his release ordered if the detention is not lawful.

5. Everyone who has been the victim of arrest or detention in contravention of the provisions of this article shall have an enforceable right to compensation.

Article 6—Right to a fair trial

1. In the determination of his civil rights and obligations or of any criminal charge against him, everyone is entitled to a fair and public hearing within a reasonable time by an independent and impartial tribunal established by law. Judgment shall be pronounced publicly but the press and public may be excluded from all or part of the trial in the interests of morals, public order or national security in a democratic society, where the interests of juveniles or the protection of the private life of the parties so require, or to the extent strictly necessary in the opinion of the court in special circumstances where publicity would prejudice the interests of justice.

2. Everyone charged with a criminal offence shall be presumed innocent until proved guilty according to law.

3. Everyone charged with a criminal offence has the following minimum rights:

   (a) to be informed promptly, in a language which he understands and in detail, of the nature and cause of the accusation against him;

   (b) to have adequate time and facilities for the preparation of his defence;

   (c) to defend himself in person or through legal assistance of his own choosing or, if he has not sufficient means to pay for legal assistance, to be given it free when the interests of justice so require;

   (d) to examine or have examined witnesses against him and to obtain the attendance and examination of witnesses on his behalf under the same conditions as witnesses against him;

   (e) to have the free assistance of an interpreter if he cannot understand or speak the language used in court.

Article 7—No punishment without law

1. No one shall be held guilty of any criminal offence on account of any act or omission which did not constitute a criminal offence under national or international law at the time when it was committed. Nor shall a heavier penalty be imposed than the one that was applicable at the time the criminal offence was committed.

2. This article shall not prejudice the trial and punishment of any person for any act or omission which, at the time when it was committed, was criminal according to the general principles of law recognized by civilised nations.

Article 8—Right to respect for private and family life

1. Everyone has the right to respect for his private and family life, his home and his correspondence.

2. There shall be no interference by a public authority with the exercise of this right except such as is in accordance with the law and is necessary in a democratic society in the interests of national security, public safety or the economic well-being of the country, for the prevention of disorder or crime, for the protection of health or morals, or for the protection of the rights and freedoms of others.

Article 9—Freedom of thought, conscience and religion

1. Everyone has the right to freedom of thought, conscience and religion; this right includes freedom to change his religion or belief and freedom, either alone or in community with others and in public or private, to manifest his religion or belief, in worship, teaching, practice and observance.

2. Freedom to manifest one's religion or beliefs shall be subject only to such limitations as are prescribed by law and are necessary in a democratic society in the interests of public safety, for the protection of public order, health or morals, or for the protection of the rights and freedoms of others.

Article 10—Freedom of expression

1. Everyone has the right to freedom of expression. This right shall include freedom to hold opinions and to receive and impart information and ideas without interference by public authority and regardless of frontiers. This article shall not prevent States from requiring the licensing of broadcasting, television or cinema enterprises.

2. The exercise of these freedoms, since it carries with it duties and responsibilities, may be subject to such formalities, conditions, restrictions or penalties as are prescribed by law and are necessary in a democratic society, in the interests of national security, territorial integrity or public safety, for the prevention of disorder or crime, for the protection of health or morals, for the protection of the reputation or rights of others, for preventing the disclosure of information received in confidence, or for maintaining the authority and impartiality of the judiciary.

Article 11—Freedom of assembly and association

1. Everyone has the right to freedom of peaceful assembly and to freedom of association with others, including the right to form and to join trade unions for the protection of his interests.

2. No restrictions shall be placed on the exercise of these rights other than such as are prescribed by law and are necessary in a democratic society in the interests of national security or public safety, for the prevention of disorder or crime, for the protection of health or morals or for the protection of the rights and freedoms of others. This article shall not prevent the imposition of lawful restrictions on the exercise of these rights by members of the armed forces, of the police or of the administration of the State.

Article 12—Right to marry

Men and women of marriageable age have the right to marry and to found a family, according to the national laws governing the exercise of this right.

Article 13—Right to an effective remedy

Everyone whose rights and freedoms as set forth in this Convention are violated shall have an effective remedy before a national authority notwithstanding that the violation has been committed by persons acting in an official capacity.

Article 14—Prohibition of discrimination

The enjoyment of the rights and freedoms set forth in this Convention shall be secured without discrimination on any ground such as sex, race, colour, language, religion, political or other opinion, national or social origin, association with a national minority, property, birth or other status.

Article 15—Derogation in time of emergency

1. In time of war or other public emergency threatening the life of the nation any High Contracting Party may take measures derogating from its obligations under this Convention to the extent strictly required by the exigencies of the situation, provided that such measures are not inconsistent with its other obligations under international law.

2. No derogation from Article 2, except in respect of deaths resulting from lawful acts of war, or from Articles 3, 4 (paragraph 1) and 7 shall be made under this provision.

3. Any High Contracting Party availing itself of this right of derogation shall keep the Secretary General of the Council of Europe fully informed of the measures which it has taken and the reasons therefor. It shall also inform the Secretary General of the Council of Europe when such measures have ceased to operate and the provisions of the Convention are again being fully executed.

Article 16—Restrictions on political activity of aliens

Nothing in Articles 10, 11 and 14 shall be regarded as preventing the High Contracting Parties from imposing restrictions on the political activity of aliens.

Article 17—Prohibition of abuse of rights

Nothing in this Convention may be interpreted as implying for any State, group or person any right to engage in any activity or perform any act aimed at the destruction of any of the rights and freedoms set forth herein or at their limitation to a greater extent than is provided for in the Convention.

Article 18—Limitation on use of restrictions on rights

The restrictions permitted under this Convention to the said rights and freedoms shall not be applied for any purpose other than those for which they have been prescribed.

SECTION II—EUROPEAN COURT OF HUMAN RIGHTS

Article 19—Establishment of the Court

To ensure the observance of the engagements undertaken by the High Contracting Parties in the Convention and the Protocols thereto, there shall be set up a European Court of Human Rights, hereinafter referred to as 'the Court'. It shall function on a permanent basis.

Article 20—Number of judges

The Court shall consist of a number of judges equal to that of the High Contracting Parties.

Article 21—Criteria for office

1. The judges shall be of high moral character and must either possess the qualifications required for appointment to high judicial office or be jurisconsults of recognised competence.

2. The judges shall sit on the Court in their individual capacity.

3. During their term of office the judges shall not engage in any activity which is incompatible with their independence, impartiality or with the demands of a full-time office; all questions arising from the application of this paragraph shall be decided by the Court.

Article 22—Election of judges

1. The judges shall be elected by the Parliamentary Assembly with respect to each High Contracting Party by a majority of votes cast from a list of three candidates nominated by the High Contracting Party.

2. The same procedure shall be followed to complete the Court in the event of the accession of new High Contracting Parties and in filling casual vacancies.

Article 23—Terms of office

1. The judges shall be elected for a period of six years. They may be re-elected. However, the terms of office of one-half of the judges elected at the first election shall expire at the end of three years.

2. The judges whose terms of office are to expire at the end of the initial period of three years shall be chosen by lot by the Secretary General of the Council of Europe immediately after their election.

3. In order to ensure that, as far as possible, the terms of office of one-half of the judges are renewed every three years, the Parliamentary Assembly may decide, before proceeding to any subsequent election, that the term or terms of office of one or more judges to be elected shall be for a period other than six years but not more than nine and not less than three years.

4. In cases where more than one term of office is involved and where the Parliamentary Assembly applies the preceding paragraph, the allocation of the terms of office shall be effected by a drawing of lots by the Secretary General of the Council of Europe immediately after the election.

5. A judge elected to replace a judge whose term of office has not expired shall hold office for the remainder of his predecessor's term.

6. The terms of office of judges shall expire when they reach the age of 70.

7. The judges shall hold office until replaced. They shall, however, continue to deal with such cases as they already have under consideration.

Article 24—Dismissal

No judge may be dismissed from his office unless the other judges decide by a majority of two-thirds that he has ceased to fulfil the required conditions.

Article 25—Registry and legal secretaries

The Court shall have a registry, the functions and organization of which shall be laid down in the rules of the Court. The Court shall be assisted by legal secretaries.

Article 26—Plenary Court

The plenary Court shall

(a) elect its President and one or two Vice-Presidents for a period of three years; they may be re-elected;

(b) set up Chambers, constituted for a fixed period of time;

(c) elect the Presidents of the Chambers of the Court; they may be re-elected;

(d) adopt the rules of the Court, and

(e) elect the Registrar and one or more Deputy Registrars.

Article 27—Committees, Chambers and Grand Chamber

1. To consider cases brought before it, the Court shall sit in committees of three judges, in Chambers of seven judges and in a Grand Chamber of seventeen judges. The Court's Chambers shall set up committees for a fixed period of time.

2. There shall sit as an *ex officio* member of the Chamber and the Grand Chamber the judge elected in respect of the State Party concerned or, if there is none or if he is unable to sit, a person of its choice who shall sit in the capacity of judge.

3. The Grand Chamber shall also include the President of the Court, the Vice-Presidents, the Presidents of the Chambers and other judges chosen in accordance with the rules of the Court. When a case is referred to the Grand Chamber under Article 43, no judge from the Chamber which rendered the judgment shall sit in the Grand Chamber, with the exception of the President of the Chamber and the judge who sat in respect of the State Party concerned.

Article 28—Declarations of inadmissibility by committees

A committee may, by a unanimous vote, declare inadmissible or strike out of its list of cases an application submitted under Article 34 where such a decision can be taken without further examination. The decision shall be final.

Article 29—Decisions by Chambers on admissibility and merits

1. If no decision is taken under Article 28, a Chamber shall decide on the admissibility and merits of individual applications submitted under Article 34.

2. A Chamber shall decide on the admissibility and merits of inter-State applications submitted under Article 33.

3. The decision on admissibility shall be taken separately unless the Court, in exceptional cases, decides otherwise.

Article 30—Relinquishment of jurisdiction to the Grand Chamber

Where a case pending before a Chamber raises a serious question affecting the interpretation of the Convention or the protocols thereto, or where the resolution of a question before the Chamber might have a result inconsistent with a judgment previously delivered by the Court, the Chamber may, at any time before it has rendered its judgment, relinquish jurisdiction in favour of the Grand Chamber, unless one of the parties to the case objects.

Article 31—Powers of the Grand Chamber

The Grand Chamber shall

(a) determine applications submitted either under Article 33 or Article 34 when a Chamber has relinquished jurisdiction under Article 30 or when the case has been referred to it under Article 43; and

(b) consider requests for advisory opinions submitted under Article 47.

Article 32—Jurisdiction of the Court

1. The jurisdiction of the Court shall extend to all matters concerning the interpretation and application of the Convention and the protocols thereto which are referred to it as provided in Articles 33, 34 and 47.

2. In the event of dispute as to whether the Court has jurisdiction, the Court shall decide.

Article 33—Inter-State cases

Any High Contracting Party may refer to the Court any alleged breach of the provisions of the Convention and the protocols thereto by another High Contracting Party.

Article 34—Individual applications

The Court may receive applications from any person, non-governmental organization or group of individuals claiming to be the victim of a violation by one of the High Contracting Parties of the rights set forth in the Convention or the protocols thereto. The High Contracting Parties undertake not to hinder in any way the effective exercise of this right.

Article 35—Admissibility criteria

1. The Court may only deal with the matter after all domestic remedies have been exhausted, according to the generally recognised rules of international law, and within a period of six months from the date on which the final decision was taken.

2. The Court shall not deal with any application submitted under Article 34 that

(a) is anonymous; or

(b) is substantially the same as a matter that has already been examined by the Court or has already been submitted to another procedure of international investigation or settlement and contains no relevant new information.

3. The Court shall declare inadmissible any individual application submitted under Article 34 which it considers incompatible with the provisions of the Convention or the protocols thereto, manifestly ill-founded, or an abuse of the right of application.

4. The Court shall reject any application which it considers inadmissible under this Article. It may do so at any stage of the proceedings.

Article 36—Third party intervention

1. In all cases before a Chamber or the Grand Chamber, a High Contracting Party one of whose nationals is an applicant shall have the right to submit written comments and to take part in hearings.

2. The President of the Court may, in the interest of the proper administration of justice, invite any High Contracting Party which is not a party to the proceedings or any person concerned who is not the applicant to submit written comments or take part in hearings.

Article 37—Striking out applications

1. The Court may at any stage of the proceedings decide to strike an application out of its list of cases where the circumstances lead to the conclusion that

(a) the applicant does not intend to pursue his application; or

(b) the matter has been resolved; or

(c) for any other reason established by the Court, it is no longer justified to continue the examination of the application.

However, the Court shall continue the examination of the application if respect for human rights as defined in the Convention and the protocols thereto so requires.

2. The Court may decide to restore an application to its list of cases if it considers that the circumstances justify such a course.

Article 38—Examination of the case and friendly settlement proceedings

1. If the Court declares the application admissible, it shall

(a) pursue the examination of the case, together with the representatives of the parties, and if need be, undertake an investigation, for the effective conduct of which the States concerned shall furnish all necessary facilities;

(b) place itself at the disposal of the parties concerned with a view to securing a friendly settlement of the matter on the basis of respect for human rights as defined in the Convention and the protocols thereto.

2. Proceedings conducted under paragraph 1(b) shall be confidential.

Article 39—Finding of a friendly settlement

If a friendly settlement is effected, the Court shall strike the case out of its list by means of a decision which shall be confined to a brief statement of the facts and of the solution reached.

Article 40—Public hearings and access to documents

1. Hearings shall be in public unless the Court in exceptional circumstances decides otherwise.

2. Documents deposited with the Registrar shall be accessible to the public unless the President of the Court decides otherwise.

Article 41—Just satisfaction

If the Court finds that there has been a violation of the Convention or the protocols thereto, and if the internal law of the High Contracting Party concerned allows only partial reparation to be made, the Court shall, if necessary, afford just satisfaction to the injured party.

Article 42—Judgments of Chambers

Judgments of Chambers shall become final in accordance with the provisions of Article 44, paragraph 2.

Article 43—Referral to the Grand Chamber

1. Within a period of three months from the date of the judgment of the Chamber, any party to the case may, in exceptional cases, request that the case be referred to the Grand Chamber.

2. A panel of five judges of the Grand Chamber shall accept the request if the case raises a serious question affecting the interpretation or application of the Convention or the protocols thereto, or a serious issue of general importance.

3. If the panel accepts the request, the Grand Chamber shall decide the case by means of a judgment.

Article 44—Final judgments

1. The judgment of the Grand Chamber shall be final.

2. The judgment of a Chamber shall become final

   (a) when the parties declare that they will not request that the case be referred to the Grand Chamber; or

   (b) three months after the date of the judgment, if reference of the case to the Grand Chamber has not been requested; or

   (c) when the panel of the Grand Chamber rejects the request to refer under Article 43.

3. The final judgment shall be published.

Article 45—Reasons for judgments and decisions

1. Reasons shall be given for judgments as well as for decisions declaring applications admissible or inadmissible.

2. If a judgment does not represent, in whole or in part, the unanimous opinion of the judges, any judge shall be entitled to deliver a separate opinion.

Article 46—Binding force and execution of judgments

1. The High Contracting Parties undertake to abide by the final judgment of the Court in any case to which they are parties.

2. The final judgment of the Court shall be transmitted to the Committee of Ministers, which shall supervise its execution.

Article 47—Advisory opinions

1. The Court may, at the request of the Committee of Ministers, give advisory opinions on legal questions concerning the interpretation of the Convention and the protocols thereto.

2. Such opinions shall not deal with any question relating to the content or scope of the rights or freedoms defined in Section I of the Convention and the protocols thereto, or with any other question which the Court or the Committee of Ministers might have to consider in consequence of any such proceedings as could be instituted in accordance with the Convention.

3. Decisions of the Committee of Ministers to request an advisory opinion of the Court shall require a majority vote of the representatives entitled to sit on the Committee.

Article 48—Advisory jurisdiction of the Court

The Court shall decide whether a request for an advisory opinion submitted by the Committee of Ministers is within its competence as defined in Article 47.

Article 49—Reasons for advisory opinions

1. Reasons shall be given for advisory opinions of the Court.

2. If the advisory opinion does not represent, in whole or in part, the unanimous opinion of the judges, any judge shall be entitled to deliver a separate opinion.

3. Advisory opinions of the Court shall be communicated to the Committee of Ministers.

Article 50—Expenditure on the Court

The expenditure on the Court shall be borne by the Council of Europe.

Article 51—Privileges and immunities of judges

The judges shall be entitled, during the exercise of their functions, to the privileges and immunities provided for in Article 40 of the Statute of the Council of Europe and in the agreements made thereunder.

SECTION III—MISCELLANEOUS PROVISIONS

Article 52—Inquiries by the Secretary General

On receipt of a request from the Secretary General of the Council of Europe any High Contracting Party shall furnish an explanation of the manner in which its internal law ensures the effective implementation of any of the provisions of the Convention.

Article 53—Safeguard for existing human rights

Nothing in this Convention shall be construed as limiting or derogating from any of the human rights and fundamental freedoms which may be ensured under the laws of any High Contracting Party or under any other agreement to which it is a Party.

Article 54—Powers of the Committee of Ministers

Nothing in this Convention shall prejudice the powers conferred on the Committee of Ministers by the Statute of the Council of Europe.

Article 55—Exclusion of other means of dispute settlement

The High Contracting Parties agree that, except by special agreement, they will not avail themselves of treaties, conventions or declarations in force between them for the purpose of submitting, by way of petition, a dispute arising out of the interpretation or application of this Convention to a means of settlement other than those provided for in this Convention.

Article 56—Territorial application

1. Any State may at the time of its ratification or at any time thereafter declare by notification addressed to the Secretary General of the Council of Europe that the present Convention shall, subject to paragraph 4 of this Article, extend to all or any of the territories for whose international relations it is responsible.

2. The Convention shall extend to the territory or territories named in the notification as from the thirtieth day after the receipt of this notification by the Secretary General of the Council of Europe.

3. The provisions of this Convention shall be applied in such territories with due regard, however, to local requirements.

4. Any State which has made a declaration in accordance with paragraph 1 of this article may at any time thereafter declare on behalf of one or more of the territories to which the declaration relates that it accepts the competence of the Court to receive applications from individuals, non-governmental organizations or groups of individuals as provided by Article 34 of the Convention.

Article 57—Reservations

1. Any State may, when signing this Convention or when depositing its instrument of ratification, make a reservation in respect of any particular provision of the Convention to the extent that any law then in force in its territory is not in conformity with the provision. Reservations of a general character shall not be permitted under this article.

2. Any reservation made under this article shall contain a brief statement of the law concerned.

Article 58—Denunciation

1. A High Contracting Party may denounce the present Convention only after the expiry of five years from the date on which it became a party to it and after six months' notice contained in a notification addressed to the Secretary General of the Council of Europe, who shall inform the other High Contracting Parties.

2. Such a denunciation shall not have the effect of releasing the High Contracting Party concerned from its obligations under this Convention in respect of any act which, being capable of constituting a violation of such obligations, may have been performed by it before the date at which the denunciation became effective.

3. Any High Contracting Party which shall cease to be a member of the Council of Europe shall cease to be a Party to this Convention under the same conditions.

4. The Convention may be denounced in accordance with the provisions of the preceding paragraphs in respect of any territory to which it has been declared to extend under the terms of Article 56.

Article 59—Signature and ratification

1. This Convention shall be open to the signature of the members of the Council of Europe. It shall be ratified. Ratifications shall be deposited with the Secretary General of the Council of Europe.

2. The present Convention shall come into force after the deposit of ten instruments of ratification.

3. As regards any signatory ratifying subsequently, the Convention shall come into force at the date of the deposit of its instrument of ratification.

4. The Secretary General of the Council of Europe shall notify all the members of the Council of Europe of the entry into force of the Convention, the names of the High Contracting Parties who have ratified it, and the deposit of all instruments of ratification which may be effected subsequently.

Done at Rome this 4th day of November 1950, in English and French, both texts being equally authentic, in a single copy which shall remain deposited in the archives of the

Council of Europe. The Secretary General shall transmit certified copies to each of the signatories.

PROTOCOLS

Protocol No. 1, as Amended by Protocol No. 11

The Governments signatory hereto, being Members of the Council of Europe,

Being resolved to take steps to ensure the collective enforcement of certain rights and freedoms other than those already included in Section I of the Convention for the Protection of Human Rights and Fundamental Freedoms signed at Rome on 4 November 1950 (hereinafter referred to as 'the Convention'),

Have agreed as follows:

Article 1—Protection of property

Every natural or legal person is entitled to the peaceful enjoyment of his possessions. No one shall be deprived of his possessions except in the public interest and subject to the conditions provided for by law and by the general principles of international law.

The preceding provisions shall not, however, in any way impair the right of a State to enforce such laws as it deems necessary to control the use of property in accordance with the general interest or to secure the payment of taxes or other contributions or penalties.

Article 2—Right to education

No person shall be denied the right to education. In the exercise of any functions which it assumes in relation to education and to teaching, the State shall respect the right of parents to ensure such education and teaching in conformity with their own religious and philosophical convictions.

Article 3—Right to free elections

The High Contracting Parties undertake to hold free elections at reasonable intervals by secret ballot, under conditions which will ensure the free expression of the opinion of the people in the choice of the legislature.

Article 4—Territorial application

Any High Contracting Party may at the time of signature or ratification or at any time thereafter communicate to the Secretary General of the Council of Europe a declaration stating the extent to which it undertakes that the provisions of the present Protocol shall apply to such of the territories for the international relations of which it is responsible as are named therein.

Any High Contracting Party which has communicated a declaration in virtue of the preceding paragraph may from time to time communicate a further declaration modifying the terms of any former declaration or terminating the application of the provisions of this Protocol in respect of any territory.

A declaration made in accordance with this article shall be deemed to have been made in accordance with paragraph 1 of Article 56 of the Convention.

Article 5—Relationship to the Convention

As between the High Contracting Parties the provisions of Articles 1, 2, 3 and 4 of this Protocol shall be regarded as additional articles to the Convention and all the provisions of the Convention shall apply accordingly.

Article 6—Signature and ratification

This Protocol shall be open for signature by the Members of the Council of Europe, who are the signatories of the Convention; it shall be ratified at the same time as or after the ratification of the Convention. It shall enter into force after the deposit of ten instruments of ratification. As regards any signatory ratifying subsequently, the Protocol shall enter into force at the date of the deposit of its instrument of ratification.

The instruments of ratification shall be deposited with the Secretary General of the Council of Europe, who will notify all members of the names of those who have ratified.

Done at Paris on the 20th day of March 1952, in English and French, both texts being equally authentic, in a single copy which shall remain deposited in the archives of the Council of Europe. The Secretary General shall transmit certified copies to each of the signatory Governments.

Protocol No. 4, as Amended by Protocol No. 11

The Governments signatory hereto, being Members of the Council of Europe,

Being resolved to take steps to ensure the collective enforcement of certain rights and freedoms other than those already included in Section 1 of the Convention for the Protection of Human Rights and Fundamental Freedoms signed at Rome on 4th November 1950 (hereinafter referred to as the 'Convention') and in Articles 1 to 3 of the First Protocol to the Convention , signed at Paris on 20th March 1952,

Have agreed as follows:

Article 1—Prohibition of imprisonment for debt

No one shall be deprived of his liberty merely on the ground of inability to fulfil a contractual obligation.

Article 2—Freedom of movement

1. Everyone lawfully within the territory of a State shall, within that territory, have the right to liberty of movement and freedom to choose his residence.

2. Everyone shall be free to leave any country, including his own.

3. No restrictions shall be placed on the exercise of these rights other than such as are in accordance with law and are necessary in a democratic society in the interests of national security or public safety, for the maintenance of *ordre public*, for the prevention of crime, for the protection of health or morals, or for the protection of the rights and freedoms of others.

4. The rights set forth in paragraph 1 may also be subject, in particular areas, to restrictions imposed in accordance with law and justified by the public interest in a democratic society.

Article 3—Prohibition of expulsion of nationals

1. No one shall be expelled, by means either of an individual or of a collective measure, from the territory of the State of which he is a national.

2. No one shall be deprived of the right to enter the territory of the State of which he is a national.

Article 4—Prohibition of collective expulsion of aliens

Collective expulsion of aliens is prohibited.

Article 5—Territorial application

1. Any High Contracting Party may, at the time of signature or ratification of this Protocol, or at any time thereafter, communicate to the Secretary General of the Council of Europe a declaration stating the extent to which it undertakes that the provisions of this Protocol shall apply to such of the territories for the international relations of which it is responsible as are named therein.

2. Any High Contracting Party which has communicated a declaration in virtue of the preceding paragraph may, from time to time, communicate a further declaration modifying the terms of any former declaration or terminating the application of the provisions of this Protocol in respect of any territory.

3. A declaration made in accordance with this article shall be deemed to have been made in accordance with paragraph 1 of Article 56 of the Convention.

4. The territory of any State to which this Protocol applies by virtue of ratification or acceptance by that State, and each territory to which this Protocol is applied by virtue of a declaration by that State under this article, shall be treated as separate territories for the purpose of the references in Articles 2 and 3 to the territory of a State.

5. Any State which has made a declaration in accordance with paragraph 1 or 2 of this Article may at any time thereafter declare on behalf of one or more of the territories to which the declaration relates that it accepts the competence of the Court to receive applications from individuals, non-governmental organizations or groups of individuals as provided in Article 34 of the Convention in respect of all or any of Articles 1 to 4 of this Protocol.

Article 6—Relationship to the Convention

As between the High Contracting Parties the provisions of Articles 1 to 5 of this Protocol shall be regarded as additional articles to the Convention, and all the provisions of the Convention shall apply accordingly.

Article 7—Signature and ratification

1. This Protocol shall be open for signature by the members of the Council of Europe who are the signatories of the Convention; it shall be ratified at the same time as or after the ratification of the Convention. It shall enter into force after the deposit of five instruments of ratification. As regards any signatory ratifying subsequently, the Protocol shall enter into force at the date of the deposit of its instrument of ratification.

2. The instruments of ratification shall be deposited with the Secretary General of the Council of Europe, who will notify all Members of the names of those who have ratified.

In witness whereof the undersigned, being duly authorized thereto, have signed this Protocol.

Done at Strasbourg, this 16th day of September 1963, in English and in French, both texts being equally authoritative, in a single copy which shall remain deposited in the archives of the Council of Europe. The Secretary General shall transmit certified copies to each of the signatory States.

Protocol No. 6, as Amended by Protocol No. 11

The member States of the Council of Europe, signatory to this Protocol to the Convention for the Protection of Human Rights and Fundamental Freedoms, signed at Rome on 4 November 1950 (hereinafter referred to as 'the Convention'),

Considering that the evolution that has occurred in several member States of the Council of Europe expresses a general tendency in favour of abolition of the death penalty,

Have agreed as follows:

Article 1—Abolition of the death penalty

The death penalty shall be abolished. No-one shall be condemned to such penalty or executed.

Article 2—Death penalty in time of war

A State may make provision in its law for the death penalty in respect of acts committed in time of war or of imminent threat of war; such penalty shall be applied only in the instances laid down in the law and in accordance with its provisions. The State shall communicate to the Secretary General of the Council of Europe the relevant provisions of that law.

Article 3—Prohibition of derogations

No derogation from the provisions of this Protocol shall be made under Article 15 of the Convention.

Article 4—Prohibition of reservations

No reservation may be made under Article 57 of the Convention in respect of the provisions of this Protocol.

Article 5—Territorial application

1. Any State may at the time of signature or when depositing its instrument of ratification, acceptance or approval, specify the territory or territories to which this Protocol shall apply.

2. Any State may at any later date, by a declaration addressed to the Secretary General of the Council of Europe, extend the application of this Protocol to any other territory specified in the declaration. In respect of such territory the Protocol shall enter into force on the first day of the month following the date of receipt of such declaration by the Secretary General.

3. Any declaration made under the two preceding paragraphs may, in respect of any territory specified in such declaration, be withdrawn by a notification addressed to the Secretary General. The withdrawal shall become effective on the first day of the month following the date of receipt of such notification by the Secretary General.

Article 6—Relationship to the Convention

As between the States Parties the provisions of Articles 1 and 5 of this Protocol shall be regarded as additional articles to the Convention and all the provisions of the Convention shall apply accordingly.

Article 7—Signature and ratification

The Protocol shall be open for signature by the member States of the Council of Europe, signatories to the Convention. It shall be subject to ratification, acceptance or approval. A member State of the Council of Europe may not ratify, accept or approve this Protocol unless it has, simultaneously or previously, ratified the Convention. Instruments of ratification, acceptance or approval shall be deposited with the Secretary General of the Council of Europe.

Article 8—Entry into force

1. This Protocol shall enter into force on the first day of the month following the date on which five member States of the Council of Europe have expressed their consent to be bound by the Protocol in accordance with the provisions of Article 7.

2. In respect of any member State which subsequently expresses its consent to be bound by it, the Protocol shall enter into force on the first day of the month following the date of the deposit of the instrument of ratification, acceptance or approval.

Article 9—Depositary functions

The Secretary General of the Council of Europe shall notify the member States of the Council of:

    (a) any signature;

    (b) the deposit of any instrument of ratification, acceptance or approval;

    (c) any date of entry into force of this Protocol in accordance with Articles 5 and 8;

    (d) any other act, notification or communication relating to this Protocol.

In witness whereof the undersigned, being duly authorized thereto, have signed this Protocol.

Done at Strasbourg, this 28th day of April 1983, in English and in French, both texts being equally authentic, in a single copy which shall be deposited in the archives of the Council of Europe. The Secretary General of the Council of Europe shall transmit certified copies to each member State of the Council of Europe.

Protocol No. 7, as Amended by Protocol No. 11

The member States of the Council of Europe signatory hereto,

Being resolved to take further steps to ensure the collective enforcement of certain rights and freedoms by means of the Convention for the Protection of Human Rights and Fundamental Freedoms signed at Rome on 4 November 1950 (hereinafter referred to as 'the Convention'),

Have agreed as follows:

Article 1—Procedural safeguards relating to expulsion of aliens

1. An alien lawfully resident in the territory of a State shall not be expelled therefrom except in pursuance of a decision reached in accordance with law and shall be allowed:

> *(a)* to submit reasons against his expulsion,
>
> *(b)* to have his case reviewed, and
>
> *(c)* to be represented for these purposes before the competent authority or a person or persons designated by that authority.

2. An alien may be expelled before the exercise of his rights under paragraph 1(a), (b) and (c) of this Article, when such expulsion is necessary in the interests of public order or is grounded on reasons of national security.

Article 2—Right of appeal in criminal matters

1. Everyone convicted of a criminal offence by a tribunal shall have the right to have his conviction or sentence reviewed by a higher tribunal. The exercise of this right, including the grounds on which it may be exercised, shall be governed by law.

2. This right may be subject to exceptions in regard to offences of a minor character, as prescribed by law, or in cases in which the person concerned was tried in the first instance by the highest tribunal or was convicted following an appeal against acquittal.

Article 3—Compensation for wrongful conviction

When a person has by a final decision been convicted of a criminal offence and when subsequently his conviction has been reversed, or he has been pardoned, on the ground that a new or newly discovered fact shows conclusively that there has been a miscarriage of justice, the person who has suffered punishment as a result of such conviction shall be compensated according to the law or the practice of the State concerned, unless it is proved that the non-disclosure of the unknown fact in time is wholly or partly attributable to him.

Article 4—Right not to be tried or punished twice

1. No one shall be liable to be tried or punished again in criminal proceedings under the jurisdiction of the same State for an offence for which he has already been finally acquitted or convicted in accordance with the law and penal procedure of that State.

2. The provisions of the preceding paragraph shall not prevent the reopening of the case in accordance with the law and penal procedure of the State concerned, if there is evidence of new or newly discovered facts, or if there has been a fundamental defect in the previous proceedings, which could affect the outcome of the case.

3. No derogation from this Article shall be made under Article 15 of the Convention.

Article 5—Equality between spouses

Spouses shall enjoy equality of rights and responsibilities of a private law character between them, and in their relations with their children, as to marriage, during marriage and in the event of its dissolution. This Article shall not prevent States from taking such measures as are necessary in the interests of the children.

Article 6—Territorial application

1. Any State may at the time of signature or when depositing its instrument of ratification, acceptance or approval, specify the territory or territories to which the Protocol shall apply and state the extent to which it undertakes that the provisions of this Protocol shall apply to such territory or territories.

2. Any State may at any later date, by a declaration addressed to the Secretary General of the Council of Europe, extend the application of this Protocol to any other territory specified in the declaration. In respect of such territory the Protocol shall enter into force on the first day of the month following the expiration of a period of two months after the date of receipt by the Secretary General of such declaration.

3. Any declaration made under the two preceding paragraphs may, in respect of any territory specified in such declaration, be withdrawn or modified by a notification addressed to the Secretary General. The withdrawal or modification shall become effective on the first day of the month following the expiration of a period of two months after the date of receipt of such notification by the Secretary General.

4. A declaration made in accordance with this Article shall be deemed to have been made in accordance with paragraph 1 of Article 56 of the Convention.

5. The territory of any State to which this Protocol applies by virtue of ratification, acceptance or approval by that State, and each territory to which this Protocol is applied by virtue of a declaration by that State under this Article, may be treated as separate territories for the purpose of the reference in Article 1 to the territory of a State.

6. Any State which has made a declaration in accordance with paragraph 1 or 2 of this Article may at any time thereafter declare on behalf of one or more of the territories to which the declaration relates that it accepts the competence of the Court to receive applications from individuals, non-governmental organizations or groups of individuals as provided in Article 34 of the Convention in respect of Articles 1 to 5 of this Protocol.

Article 7—Relationship to the Convention

As between the States Parties, the provisions of Articles 1 to 6 of this Protocol shall be regarded as additional Articles to the Convention, and all the provisions of the Convention shall apply accordingly.

Article 8—Signature and ratification

This Protocol shall be open for signature by member States of the Council of Europe which have signed the Convention. It is subject to ratification, acceptance or approval. A member State of the Council of Europe may not ratify, accept or approve this Protocol without previously or simultaneously ratifying the Convention. Instruments of ratification, acceptance or approval shall be deposited with the Secretary General of the Council of Europe.

Article 9—Entry into force

1. This Protocol shall enter into force on the first day of the month following the expiration of a period of two months after the date on which seven member States of the Council of Europe have expressed their consent to be bound by the Protocol in accordance with the provisions of Article 8.

2. In respect of any member State which subsequently expresses its consent to be bound by it, the Protocol shall enter into force on the first day of the month following the expiration of a period of two months after the date of the deposit of the instrument of ratification, acceptance or approval.

Article 10—Depositary functions

The Secretary General of the Council of Europe shall notify all the member States of the Council of Europe of:

(a) any signature;

(b) the deposit of any instrument of ratification, acceptance or approval;

(c) any date of entry into force of this Protocol in accordance with Articles 6 and 9;

(d) any other act, notification or declaration relating to this Protocol.

In witness whereof the undersigned, being duly authorized thereto, have signed this Protocol.

Done at Strasbourg, this 22nd day of November 1984, in English and French, both texts being equally authentic, in a single copy which shall be deposited in the archives of the Council of Europe. The Secretary General of the Council of Europe shall transmit certified copies to each member State of the Council of Europe.

84. PROTOCOL NO. 12 TO THE EUROPEAN CONVENTION FOR THE PROTECTION OF HUMAN RIGHTS AND FUNDAMENTAL FREEDOMS, 2000

This protocol (*ETS* No. 177) was opened for signature on 4 November 2000, and entered into force on 1 April 2005, having received ten ratifications. It provides for a general prohibition of discrimination.

Further reading

WINTEMUTE, R., 'Filling the Article 14 "Gap": Government Ratification and Judicial Control of Protocol 12 ECHR', (2004) 5 *European Human Rights Law Review* 484.

TEXT

The member States of the Council of Europe signatory hereto,

Having regard to the fundamental principle according to which all persons are equal before the law and are entitled to the equal protection of the law;

Being resolved to take further steps to promote the equality of all persons through the collective enforcement of a general prohibition of discrimination by means of the Convention for the Protection of Human Rights and Fundamental Freedoms signed at Rome on 4 November 1950 (hereinafter referred to as 'the Convention');

Reaffirming that the principle of non-discrimination does not prevent States Parties from taking measures in order to promote full and effective equality, provided that there is an objective and reasonable justification for those measures,

Have agreed as follows:

Article 1—General prohibition of discrimination

1. The enjoyment of any right set forth by law shall be secured without discrimination on any ground such as sex, race, colour, language, religion, political or other opinion, national or social origin, association with a national minority, property, birth or other status.

2. No one shall be discriminated against by any public authority on any ground such as those mentioned in paragraph 1.

Article 2—Territorial application

1. Any State may, at the time of signature or when depositing its instrument of ratification, acceptance or approval, specify the territory or territories to which this Protocol shall apply.

2. Any State may at any later date, by a declaration addressed to the Secretary General of the Council of Europe, extend the application of this Protocol to any other territory specified in the declaration. In respect of such territory the Protocol shall enter into force on the first day of the month following the expiration of a period of three months after the date of receipt by the Secretary General of such declaration.

3. Any declaration made under the two preceding paragraphs may, in respect of any territory specified in such declaration, be withdrawn or modified by a notification addressed to the Secretary General of the Council of Europe. The withdrawal or modification shall become effective on the first day of the month following the expiration of a period of three months after the date of receipt of such notification by the Secretary General.

4. A declaration made in accordance with this article shall be deemed to have been made in accordance with paragraph 1 of Article 56 of the Convention.

5. Any State which has made a declaration in accordance with paragraph 1 or 2 of this article may at any time thereafter declare on behalf of one or more of the territories to which the declaration relates that it accepts the competence of the Court to receive applications from individuals, non-governmental organizations or groups of individuals as provided by Article 34 of the Convention in respect of Article 1 of this Protocol.

Article 3—Relationship to the Convention

As between the States Parties, the provisions of Articles 1 and 2 of this Protocol shall be regarded as additional articles to the Convention, and all the provisions of the Convention shall apply accordingly.

Article 4—Signature and ratification

This Protocol shall be open for signature by member States of the Council of Europe which have signed the Convention. It is subject to ratification, acceptance or approval. A member State of the Council of Europe may not ratify, accept or approve this Protocol without previously or simultaneously ratifying the Convention. Instruments of ratification, acceptance or approval shall be deposited with the Secretary General of the Council of Europe.

Article 5—Entry into force

1. This Protocol shall enter into force on the first day of the month following the expiration of a period of three months after the date on which ten member States of the Council of Europe have expressed their consent to be bound by the Protocol in accordance with the provisions of Article 4.

2. In respect of any member State which subsequently expresses its consent to be bound by it, the Protocol shall enter into force on the first day of the month following the expiration of a period of three months after the date of the deposit of the instrument of ratification, acceptance or approval.

Article 6—Depositary functions

The Secretary General of the Council of Europe shall notify all the member States of the Council of Europe of:

(a) any signature;

(b) the deposit of any instrument of ratification, acceptance or approval;

(c) any date of entry into force of this Protocol in accordance with Articles 2 and 5;

(d) any other act, notification or communication relating to this Protocol.

In witness whereof the undersigned, being duly authorized thereto, have signed this Protocol.

Done at Rome, this 4th day of November 2 0 0 0, in English and in French, both texts being equally authentic, in a single copy which shall be deposited in the archives of the Council of Europe. The Secretary General of the Council of Europe shall transmit certified copies to each member State of the Council of Europe.

85. PROTOCOL NO. 13 TO THE CONVENTION FOR THE PROTECTION OF HUMAN RIGHTS AND FUNDAMENTAL FREEDOMS, CONCERNING THE ABOLITION OF THE DEATH PENALTY IN ALL CIRCUMSTANCES, 2002

ETS No. 187; opened for signature at Vilnius, 3 May 2002, and entered into force 1 July 2003. Protocol No. 6 of 1982, which has been ratified by every member State of the Council of Europe other than Russia, was the first legally binding instrument to provide for the abolition of the death penalty in time of peace, without reservation and irrespective of any emergency situation. The Parliamentary Assembly thereafter began in practice to attach commitment to a moratorium and abolition of the death penalty to applications for membership of the Council of Europe, and the aim of universal abolition was endorsed by the Heads of State and Government in 1997. The abolition of the death penalty also in respect of acts committed in time of war or of imminent threat of war was raised by the Parliamentary Assembly in Recommendation 1246 (1994); Protocol No. 13 goes that one step farther, and entered into force on 1 July 2003. As noted above, Article 2(1) of the Convention now requires to be read in the light of these development.

Further reading

EUROPEAN UNION, 'Guidelines to EU Policy toward Third Countries on the Death Penalty', 1998, reviewed June 2008.
——, **http://ec.europe.eu/external_relations/human_rights/adp/**.

TEXT

The member States of the Council of Europe signatory hereto,

Convinced that everyone's right to life is a basic value in a democratic society and that the abolition of the death penalty is essential for the protection of this right and for the full recognition of the inherent dignity of all human beings;

Wishing to strengthen the protection of the right to life guaranteed by the Convention for the Protection of Human Rights and Fundamental Freedoms signed at Rome on 4 November 1950 (hereinafter referred to as 'the Convention');

Noting that Protocol No. 6 to the Convention, concerning the Abolition of the Death Penalty, signed at Strasbourg on 28 April 1983, does not exclude the death penalty in respect of acts committed in time of war or of imminent threat of war;

Being resolved to take the final step in order to abolish the death penalty in all circumstances,

Have agreed as follows:

Article 1—Abolition of the death penalty

The death penalty shall be abolished. No one shall be condemned to such penalty or executed.

Article 2—Prohibition of derogations

No derogation from the provisions of this Protocol shall be made under Article 15 of the Convention.

Article 3—Prohibition of reservations

No reservation may be made under Article 57 of the Convention in respect of the provisions of this Protocol.

Article 4—Territorial application

1. Any State may, at the time of signature or when depositing its instrument of ratification, acceptance or approval, specify the territory or territories to which this Protocol shall apply.

2. Any State may at any later date, by a declaration addressed to the Secretary General of the Council of Europe, extend the application of this Protocol to any other territory specified in the declaration. In respect of such territory the Protocol shall enter into force on the first day of the month following the expiration of a period of three months after the date of receipt of such declaration by the Secretary General.

3. Any declaration made under the two preceding paragraphs may, in respect of any territory specified in such declaration, be withdrawn or modified by a notification addressed to the Secretary General. The withdrawal or modification shall become effective on the first day of the month following the expiration of a period of three months after the date of receipt of such notification by the Secretary General.

Article 5—Relationship to the Convention

As between the States Parties the provisions of Articles 1 to 4 of this Protocol shall be regarded as additional articles to the Convention, and all the provisions of the Convention shall apply accordingly.

Article 6—Signature and ratification

This Protocol shall be open for signature by member States of the Council of Europe which have signed the Convention. It is subject to ratification, acceptance or approval. A member State of the Council of Europe may not ratify, accept or approve this Protocol without previously or simultaneously ratifying the Convention. Instruments of ratification, acceptance or approval shall be deposited with the Secretary General of the Council of Europe.

Article 7—Entry into force

1. This Protocol shall enter into force on the first day of the month following the expiration of a period of three months after the date on which ten member States of the Council of Europe have expressed their consent to be bound by the Protocol in accordance with the provisions of Article 6.

2. In respect of any member State which subsequently expresses its consent to be bound by it, the Protocol shall enter into force on the first day of the month following the expiration of a period of three months after the date of the deposit of the instrument of ratification, acceptance or approval.

Article 8—Depositary functions

The Secretary General of the Council of Europe shall notify all the member States of the Council of Europe of:

   (a) any signature;

   (b) the deposit of any instrument of ratification, acceptance or approval;

(c) any date of entry into force of this Protocol in accordance with Articles 4 and 7;

(d) any other act, notification or communication relating to this Protocol.

In witness whereof the undersigned, being duly authorised thereto, have signed this Protocol.

Done at Vilnius, this 3rd day of May 2 0 0 2, in English and in French, both texts being equally authentic, in a single copy which shall be deposited in the archives of the Council of Europe. The Secretary General of the Council of Europe shall transmit certified copies to each member State of the Council of Europe.

86. PROTOCOL NO. 14 TO THE CONVENTION FOR THE PROTECTION OF HUMAN RIGHTS AND FUNDAMENTAL FREEDOMS, AMENDING THE CONTROL SYSTEM OF THE CONVENTION, 2004

CETS No. 194. Opened for signature at Strasbourg on 13 May 2004, Protocol No. 14 entered into force on 1 June 2010, after having been ratified by all Member States of the Council of Europe.

This Protocol aims further to improve the efficiency of the European Court of Human Rights and to strengthen its capacity to deal with claims. The reforms introduced by Protocol No. 11 have proven inadequate in the face of the increase in the number of individual applications which has resulted, in part, from the enlargement of the Council of Europe. As the *Explanatory Memorandum* points out, 'between the opening of Protocol No. 11 for signature in May 1994 and the adoption of Protocol No. 14, thirteen new States Parties ratified the Convention, extending the protection of its provisions to over 240 million additional individuals'. The number of applications, in turn, has increased exponentially; see *Annual Report 2008 of the European Court of Human Rights*, Council of Europe, Strasbourg, 2009; 'Statistical Information by Year': **http://www.echr.coe.int/ECHR/EN/**.

While no radical changes are made to the system of oversight, the essential purposes of Protocol No. 14 are to reinforce the Court's filtering capacity in respect of the mass of unmeritorious applications (a single judge competent to declare inadmissible or strike out an individual application); to provide a new admissibility criterion concerning cases in which the applicant has not suffered a significant disadvantage (though with two safeguard clauses); and to provide measures for dealing with repetitive cases (three judges empowered to rule in a simplified procedure, both on admissibility and on the merits of an application, where the underlying issue is already covered by well-established case-law).

On the temporary measures introduced to deal with the Russian Federation's initial reluctance to ratify, see Protocol No. 14*bis*, below, p. 715.

Further reading

ADVISORY COMMITTEE ON ISSUES OF PUBLIC INTERNATIONAL LAW, 'Advisory Report on the Application of Protocol No. 14 to the European Convention on Human Rights and Fundamental Freedoms', (2009) 56 *Netherlands International Law Review* 71.

BEERNAERT, M.-A., 'Protocol 14 and New Strasbourg Procedures: Towards Greater Efficiency? And at What Price?', (2004) 5 *European Human Rights Law Review* 544–57.

BOWRING, B., 'Russia and Human Rights: Incompatible Opposites?', (2009) 1 *Göttingen Journal of International Law* 133; available at **http://eprints.bbk.ac.uk**.

CAFLISCH, L., 'The Reform of the European Court of Human Rights: Protocol No. 14 and Beyond', (2006) 6 *Human Rights Law Review* 403.

LEMMENS, P. and VANDENHOLE, W., eds., *Protocol No. 14 and the Reform of the European Court of Human Rights*, Antwerpen: Intersentia, 2005.

TEXT

Preamble

The member States of the Council of Europe, signatories to this Protocol to the Convention for the Protection of Human Rights and Fundamental Freedoms, signed at Rome on 4 November 1950 (hereinafter referred to as 'the Convention'),

Having regard to Resolution No. 1 and the Declaration adopted at the European Ministerial Conference on Human Rights, held in Rome on 3 and 4 November 2000;

Having regard to the Declarations adopted by the Committee of Ministers on 8 November 2001, 7 November 2002 and 15 May 2003, at their 109th, 111th and 112th Sessions, respectively;

Having regard to Opinion No. 251 (2004) adopted by the Parliamentary Assembly of the Council of Europe on 28 April 2004;

Considering the urgent need to amend certain provisions of the Convention in order to maintain and improve the efficiency of the control system for the long term, mainly in the light of the continuing increase in the workload of the European Court of Human Rights and the Committee of Ministers of the Council of Europe;

Considering, in particular, the need to ensure that the Court can continue to play its pre-eminent role in protecting human rights in Europe,

Have agreed as follows:

Article 1

Paragraph 2 of Article 22 of the Convention shall be deleted.

Article 2

Article 23 of the Convention shall be amended to read as follows:

> '*Article 23—Terms of office and dismissal*
> 1. The judges shall be elected for a period of nine years. They may not be re-elected.
> 2. The terms of office of judges shall expire when they reach the age of 70.
> 3. The judges shall hold office until replaced. They shall, however, continue to deal with such cases as they already have under consideration.
> 4. No judge may be dismissed from office unless the other judges decide by a majority of two-thirds that that judge has ceased to fulfil the required conditions.'

Article 3

Article 24 of the Convention shall be deleted.

Article 4

Article 25 of the Convention shall become Article 24 and its text shall be amended to read as follows:

> '*Article 24—Registry and rapporteurs*
> 1. The Court shall have a registry, the functions and organisation of which shall be laid down in the rules of the Court.
> 2. When sitting in a single-judge formation, the Court shall be assisted by rapporteurs who shall function under the authority of the President of the Court. They shall form part of the Court's registry.'

Article 5

Article 26 of the Convention shall become Article 25 ('Plenary Court') and its text shall be amended as follows:

1. At the end of paragraph (d), the comma shall be replaced by a semi-colon and the word 'and' shall be deleted.

2. At the end of paragraph (e), the full stop shall be replaced by a semi-colon.

3. A new paragraph (f) shall be added which shall read as follows: '(f) make any request under Article 26, paragraph 2.'

Article 6

Article 27 of the Convention shall become Article 26 and its text shall be amended to read as follows:

'*Article 26—Single-judge formation, committees, Chambers and Grand Chamber*

1. To consider cases brought before it, the Court shall sit in a single-judge formation, in committees of three judges, in Chambers of seven judges and in a Grand Chamber of seventeen judges. The Court's Chambers shall set up committees for a fixed period of time.

2. At the request of the plenary Court, the Committee of Ministers may, by a unanimous decision and for a fixed period, reduce to five the number of judges of the Chambers.

3. When sitting as a single judge, a judge shall not examine any application against the High Contracting Party in respect of which that judge has been elected.

4. There shall sit as an *ex officio* member of the Chamber and the Grand Chamber the judge elected in respect of the High Contracting Party concerned. If there is none or if that judge is unable to sit, a person chosen by the President of the Court from a list submitted in advance by that Party shall sit in the capacity of judge.

5. The Grand Chamber shall also include the President of the Court, the Vice-Presidents, the Presidents of the Chambers and other judges chosen in accordance with the rules of the Court. When a case is referred to the Grand Chamber under Article 43, no judge from the Chamber which rendered the judgment shall sit in the Grand Chamber, with the exception of the President of the Chamber and the judge who sat in respect of the High Contracting Party concerned.'

Article 7

After the new Article 26, a new Article 27 shall be inserted into the Convention, which shall read as follows:

'*Article 27—Competence of single judges*

1. A single judge may declare inadmissible or strike out of the Court's list of cases an application submitted under Article 34, where such a decision can be taken without further examination.

2. The decision shall be final.

3. If the single judge does not declare an application inadmissible or strike it out, that judge shall forward it to a committee or to a Chamber for further examination.'

Article 8

Article 28 of the Convention shall be amended to read as follows:

'*Article 28—Competence of committees*

1. In respect of an application submitted under Article 34, a committee may, by a unanimous vote,

   (a) declare it inadmissible or strike it out of its list of cases, where such decision can be taken without further examination; or

   (b) declare it admissible and render at the same time a judgment on the merits, if the underlying question in the case, concerning the interpretation or the application of the Convention or the Protocols thereto, is already the subject of well-established case-law of the Court.

2. Decisions and judgments under paragraph 1 shall be final.

3. If the judge elected in respect of the High Contracting Party concerned is not a member of the committee, the committee may at any stage of the proceedings invite that judge to

take the place of one of the members of the committee, having regard to all relevant factors, including whether that Party has contested the application of the procedure under paragraph 1(b).'

Article 9

Article 29 of the Convention shall be amended as follows:

1. Paragraph 1 shall be amended to read as follows: 'If no decision is taken under Article 27 or 28, or no judgment rendered under Article 28, a Chamber shall decide on the admissibility and merits of individual applications submitted under Article 34. The decision on admissibility may be taken separately.'

2. At the end of paragraph 2 a new sentence shall be added which shall read as follows: 'The decision on admissibility shall be taken separately unless the Court, in exceptional cases, decides otherwise.'

3. Paragraph 3 shall be deleted.

Article 10

Article 31 of the Convention shall be amended as follows:

1. At the end of paragraph (a), the word 'and' shall be deleted.

2. Paragraph (b) shall become paragraph (c) and a new paragraph (b) shall be inserted and shall read as follows: '(b) decide on issues referred to the Court by the Committee of Ministers in accordance with Article 46, paragraph 4; and'.

Article 11

Article 32 of the Convention shall be amended as follows:
At the end of paragraph 1, a comma and the number 46 shall be inserted after the number 34.

Article 12

Paragraph 3 of Article 35 of the Convention shall be amended to read as follows:

'3. The Court shall declare inadmissible any individual application submitted under Article 34 if it considers that:

    (a) the application is incompatible with the provisions of the Convention or the Protocols thereto, manifestly ill-founded, or an abuse of the right of individual application; or

    (b) the applicant has not suffered a significant disadvantage, unless respect for human rights as defined in the Convention and the Protocols thereto requires an examination of the application on the merits and provided that no case may be rejected on this ground which has not been duly considered by a domestic tribunal.'

Article 13

A new paragraph 3 shall be added at the end of Article 36 of the Convention, which shall read as follows:

'3. In all cases before a Chamber or the Grand Chamber, the Council of Europe Commissioner for Human Rights may submit written comments and take part in hearings.'

Article 14

Article 38 of the Convention shall be amended to read as follows:

'Article 38—Examination of the case
The Court shall examine the case together with the representatives of the parties and, if need be, undertake an investigation, for the effective conduct of which the High Contracting Parties concerned shall furnish all necessary facilities.'

Article 15

Article 39 of the Convention shall be amended to read as follows:

'Article 39—Friendly settlements
1. At any stage of the proceedings, the Court may place itself at the disposal of the parties concerned with a view to securing a friendly settlement of the matter on the basis of respect for human rights as defined in the Convention and the Protocols thereto.
2. Proceedings conducted under paragraph 1 shall be confidential.
3. If a friendly settlement is effected, the Court shall strike the case out of its list by means of a decision which shall be confined to a brief statement of the facts and of the solution reached.
4. This decision shall be transmitted to the Committee of Ministers, which shall supervise the execution of the terms of the friendly settlement as set out in the decision.'

Article 16

Article 46 of the Convention shall be amended to read as follows:

'Article 46—Binding force and execution of judgments
1. The High Contracting Parties undertake to abide by the final judgment of the Court in any case to which they are parties.
2. The final judgment of the Court shall be transmitted to the Committee of Ministers, which shall supervise its execution.
3. If the Committee of Ministers considers that the supervision of the execution of a final judgment is hindered by a problem of interpretation of the judgment, it may refer the matter to the Court for a ruling on the question of interpretation. A referral decision shall require a majority vote of two thirds of the representatives entitled to sit on the Committee.
4. If the Committee of Ministers considers that a High Contracting Party refuses to abide by a final judgment in a case to which it is a party, it may, after serving formal notice on that Party and by decision adopted by a majority vote of two thirds of the representatives entitled to sit on the Committee, refer to the Court the question whether that Party has failed to fulfil its obligation under paragraph 1.
5. If the Court finds a violation of paragraph 1, it shall refer the case to the Committee of Ministers for consideration of the measures to be taken. If the Court finds no violation of paragraph 1, it shall refer the case to the Committee of Ministers, which shall close its examination of the case.'

Article 17

Article 59 of the Convention shall be amended as follows:
1. A new paragraph 2 shall be inserted which shall read as follows: '2. The European Union may accede to this Convention.'
2. Paragraphs 2, 3 and 4 shall become paragraphs 3, 4 and 5 respectively.

FINAL AND TRANSITIONAL PROVISIONS

Article 18

1. This Protocol shall be open for signature by member States of the Council of Europe signatories to the Convention, which may express their consent to be bound by

(a) signature without reservation as to ratification, acceptance or approval; or

(b) signature subject to ratification, acceptance or approval, followed by ratification, acceptance or approval.

2. The instruments of ratification, acceptance or approval shall be deposited with the Secretary General of the Council of Europe.

Article 19

This Protocol shall enter into force on the first day of the month following the expiration of a period of three months after the date on which all Parties to the Convention have expressed their consent to be bound by the Protocol, in accordance with the provisions of Article 18.

Article 20

1. From the date of the entry into force of this Protocol, its provisions shall apply to all applications pending before the Court as well as to all judgments whose execution is under supervision by the Committee of Ministers.

2. The new admissibility criterion inserted by Article 12 of this Protocol in Article 35, paragraph 3(b) of the Convention, shall not apply to applications declared admissible before the entry into force of the Protocol. In the two years following the entry into force of this Protocol, the new admissibility criterion may only be applied by Chambers and the Grand Chamber of the Court.

Article 21

The term of office of judges serving their first term of office on the date of entry into force of this Protocol shall be extended *ipso jure* so as to amount to a total period of nine years. The other judges shall complete their term of office, which shall be extended *ipso jure* by two years.

Article 22

The Secretary General of the Council of Europe shall notify the member States of the Council of Europe of:

(a) any signature;

(b) the deposit of any instrument of ratification, acceptance or approval;

(c) the date of entry into force of this Protocol in accordance with Article 19; and

(d) any other act, notification or communication relating to this Protocol.

In witness whereof, the undersigned, being duly authorised thereto, have signed this Protocol.

Done at Strasbourg, this 13th day of May 2004, in English and in French, both texts being equally authentic, in a single copy which shall be deposited in the archives of the Council of Europe. The Secretary General of the Council of Europe shall transmit certified copies to each member State of the Council of Europe.

87. PROTOCOL NO. 14*BIS* TO THE CONVENTION FOR THE PROTECTION OF HUMAN RIGHTS AND FUNDAMENTAL FREEDOMS, 2009

CETS No. 204. Protocol No. 14*bis* was adopted by the Committee of Ministers in Madrid on 12 May 2009 and opened for signature at Strasbourg on 27 May 2009. Its aim was to overcome the obstacles to the reform proposed by Protocol No. 14 caused by the opposition of the Russian Federation. It came into force on 1 October 2009, and was applied (very) temporarily until Protocol No. 14 itself came into force on 1 June 2010.

This Protocol employed two procedures taken from Protocol No. 14, with a view to increasing the Court's capacity to deal with applications lodged against those States which ratified it. Thus, a single judge, instead of a committee of three, could reject plainly inadmissible applications, and a three judge committee could declare applications admissible and decide their merits in clearly well-founded cases and those where there was well-established case law (so-called 'repetitive cases'). Such matters were previously dealt with by chambers of seven judges or by the Grand Chamber.

By 1 April 2010, twelve States had ratified this Protocol (Denmark, Georgia, Iceland, Ireland, Luxembourg, Monaco, Norway, San Marino, Slovakia, Slovenia, Sweden and the former Yugoslav Republic of Macedonia), and ten others had signed it prior to ratification (Austria, Cyprus, France, Hungary, Lithuania, Moldova, Poland, Romania, Spain, and Ukraine). A further nine States, (Albania, Belgium, Estonia, Germany, Liechtenstein, Luxembourg, Netherlands, Switzerland and the United Kingdom), had employed an alternative legal approach and made a declaration accepting that the corresponding Protocol No. 14 procedures could be provisionally applied to applications filed against them.

On 18 February 2010, Russia ratified Protocol No. 14, which duly entered into force on 1 June 2010. Protocol No. 14*bis* therefore ceased to be in force or provisionally applied as from that date, and it is included here for its historical interest.

TEXT

Preamble

The member States of the Council of Europe, signatories to this Protocol to the Convention for the Protection of Human Rights and Fundamental Freedoms, signed at Rome on 4 November 1950 (hereinafter referred to as 'the Convention'),

Having regard to Protocol No. 14 to the Convention for the Protection of Human Rights and Fundamental Freedoms, amending the control system of the Convention, opened for signature by the Committee of Ministers of the Council of Europe in Strasbourg on 13 May 2004;

Having regard to Opinion No. 271 (2009), adopted by the Parliamentary Assembly of the Council of Europe on 30 April 2009;

Considering the urgent need to introduce certain additional procedures to the Convention in order to maintain and improve the efficiency of its control system for the long term, in the light of the continuing increase in the workload of the European Court of Human Rights and the Committee of Ministers of the Council of Europe;

Considering, in particular, the need to ensure that the Court can continue to play its pre-eminent role in protecting human rights in Europe,

Have agreed as follows:

Article 1

In relation to High Contracting Parties to the Convention which are bound by this Protocol, the Convention shall read as provided in Articles 2 to 4.

Article 2

1. The title of Article 25 of the Convention shall read as follows:

'Article 25—Registry, legal secretaries and rapporteurs'

2. A new paragraph 2 shall be added at the end of Article 25 of the Convention, which shall read as follows:

'2. When sitting in a single-judge formation, the Court shall be assisted by rapporteurs who shall function under the authority of the President of the Court. They shall form part of the Court's registry.'

Article 3

1. The title of Article 27 of the Convention shall read as follows:

'Article 27—Single-judge formation, committees, Chambers and Grand Chamber'

2. Paragraph 1 of Article 27 of the Convention shall read as follows:

'1. To consider cases brought before it, the Court shall sit in a single-judge formation, in committees of three judges, in Chambers of seven judges and in a Grand Chamber of seventeen judges. The Court's Chambers shall set up committees for a fixed period of time.'

3. A new paragraph 2 shall be inserted in Article 27 of the Convention, which shall read as follows:

'2. When sitting as a single judge, a judge shall not examine any application against the High Contracting Party in respect of which that judge has been elected.'

4. Paragraphs 2 and 3 of Article 27 of the Convention shall become paragraphs 3 and 4 respectively.

Article 4

Article 28 of the Convention shall read as follows:

'Article 28—Competences of single judges and of committees

1. A single judge may declare inadmissible or strike out of the Court's list of cases an application submitted under Article 34, where such a decision can be taken without further examination.

2. The decision shall be final.

3. If the single judge does not declare an application inadmissible or strike it out, that judge shall forward it to a committee or to a Chamber for further examination.

4. In respect of an application submitted under Article 34, a committee may, by a unanimous vote,

  (a) declare it inadmissible or strike it out of its list of cases, where such decision can be taken without further examination; or

  (b) declare it admissible and render at the same time a judgment on the merits, if the underlying question in the case, concerning the interpretation or the application of the Convention or the Protocols thereto, is already the subject of well-established case-law of the Court.

5. Decisions and judgments under paragraph 4 shall be final.

6. If the judge elected in respect of the High Contracting Party concerned is not a member of the committee, the committee may at any stage of the proceedings invite that judge to take the place of one of the members of the committee, having regard to all relevant factors, including whether that Party has contested the application of the procedure under paragraph 4(b).'

Article 5

1. This Protocol shall be open for signature by member States of the Council of Europe signatories to the Convention, which may express their consent to be bound by:

   (a) signature without reservation as to ratification, acceptance or approval; or

   (b) signature subject to ratification, acceptance or approval, followed by ratification, acceptance or approval.

2. The instruments of ratification, acceptance or approval shall be deposited with the Secretary General of the Council of Europe.

Article 6

1. This Protocol shall enter into force on the first day of the month following the expiration of a period of three months after the date on which three High Contracting Parties to the Convention have expressed their consent to be bound by the Protocol in accordance with the provisions of Article 5.

2. In respect of any High Contracting Party to the Convention which subsequently expresses its consent to be bound by this Protocol, the Protocol shall enter into force for that High Contracting Party on the first day of the month following the expiration of a period of three months after the date of expression of its consent to be bound by the Protocol in accordance with the provisions of Article 5.

Article 7

Pending the entry into force of this Protocol according to the conditions set under Article 6, a High Contracting Party to the Convention having signed or ratified the Protocol may, at any moment, declare that the provisions of this Protocol shall apply to it on a provisional basis. Such a declaration shall take effect on the first day of the month following the date of its receipt by the Secretary General of the Council of Europe.

Article 8

1. From the date of the entry into force or application on a provisional basis of this Protocol, its provisions shall apply to all applications pending before the Court with respect to all High Contracting Parties for which it is in force or being applied on a provisional basis.

2. This Protocol shall not apply in respect of any individual application brought against two or more High Contracting Parties unless, in respect of all of them, either the Protocol is in force or applied on a provisional basis, or the relevant corresponding provisions of Protocol No. 14 are applied on a provisional basis.

Article 9

This Protocol shall cease to be in force or applied on a provisional basis from the date of entry into force of Protocol No. 14 to the Convention.

Article 10

The Secretary General of the Council of Europe shall notify the member States of the Council of Europe of:

    (a) any signature;

    (b) the deposit of any instrument of ratification, acceptance or approval;

    (c) the date of entry into force of this Protocol in accordance with Article 6;

    (d) any declaration made under Article 7; and

    (e) any other act, notification or communication relating to this Protocol.

In witness whereof, the undersigned, being duly authorised thereto, have signed this Protocol.

Done at Strasbourg, this 27th day of May 2009, in English and in French, both texts being equally authentic, in a single copy which shall be deposited in the archives of the Council of Europe. The Secretary General of the Council of Europe shall transmit certified copies to each member State of the Council of Europe.

88. EUROPEAN SOCIAL CHARTER, 1961

This Charter was intended to be complementary to the European Convention on Human Rights. It aims to develop and protect social and economic rights, while the Convention is concerned with political and civil rights, although this division is by no means exact.

The Charter was signed at Turin on 18 October 1961, and came into force on 26 February 1965; for text, see *ETS* No. 35; 529 *UNTS* 89. See further the European Code of Social Security, signed at Strasbourg on 16 April 1964, in force in 1968: *ETS* No. 48. The European Committee of Social Rights is responsible for monitoring compliance.

See generally, **http://www.coe.int/t/dghl/monitoring/socialcharter/**.

Further reading

AKANDJI-KOMBÉ, J.-F., 'Actualité de la Charte sociale européenne: mai 2005–décembre 2007', *Revue trimestrielle de droits de l'homme*, 2008, 507.

CHURCHILL, R. R. and KHALIQ, U., 'The collective complaints system of the European Social Charter: An effective mechanism for ensuring compliance with economic and social rights?', (2004) 15 *EJIL* 417.

COUNCIL OF EUROPE, 'Country Factsheets': **http://www.coe.int/t/dghl/monitoring/socialcharter/**.

CULLEN, H., 'The Collective Complaints System of the European Social Charter: Interpretative Methods of the European Committee of Social Rights', (2009) 9 *Human Rights Law Review* 61.

EUROPEAN COMMITTEE OF SOCIAL RIGHTS, *Collective Complaints Procedure: Summaries of Decisions on Admissibility: 1998–2009*, Strasbourg: Council of Europe, 2009.

——, *Collective Complaints Procedure: Summaries of Decisions on the Merits: 1998–2008*, Strasbourg: Council of Europe, 2009.

——, *Digest of the Case Law of the European Committee of Social Rights*, Strasbourg: Council of Europe, 2008.

HARRIS, D., *The European Social Charter*, Charlottesville: University Press of Virginia, 1984.

TEXT

Preamble

The Governments signatory hereto, being Members of the Council of Europe,

Considering that the aim of the Council of Europe is the achievement of greater unity between its members for the purpose of safeguarding and realizing the ideals and principles which are their common heritage and of facilitating their economic and social progress, in particular by the maintenance and further realization of human rights and fundamental freedoms;

Considering that in the European Convention for the Protection of Human Rights and Fundamental Freedoms signed at Rome on 4th November 1950, and the Protocol thereto signed at Paris on 20th March 1952, the member States of the Council of Europe agreed to secure to their populations the civil and political rights and freedoms therein specified;

Considering that the enjoyment of social rights should be secured without discrimination on grounds of race, colour, sex, religion, political opinion, national extraction or social origin;

Being resolved to make every effort in common to improve the standard of living and to promote the social well-being of both their urban and rural populations by means of appropriate institutions and action,

Have agreed as follows:

PART I

The Contracting Parties accept as the aim of their policy, to be pursued by all appropriate means, both national and international in character, the attainment of conditions in which the following rights and principles may be effectively realised:

(1) Everyone shall have the opportunity to earn his living in an occupation freely entered upon.

(2) All workers have the right to just conditions of work.

(3) All workers have the right to safe and healthy working conditions.

(4) All workers have the right to a fair remuneration sufficient for a decent standard of living for themselves and their families.

(5) All workers and employers have the right to freedom of association in national or international organisations for the protection of their economic and social interests.

(6) All workers and employers have the right to bargain collectively.

(7) Children and young persons have the right to a special protection against the physical and moral hazards to which they are exposed.

(8) Employed women, in case of maternity, and other employed women as appropriate, have the right to a special protection in their work.

(9) Everyone has the right to appropriate facilities for vocational guidance with a view to helping him choose an occupation suited to his personal aptitude and interests.

(10) Everyone has the right to appropriate facilities for vocational training.

(11) Everyone has the right to benefit from any measures enabling him to enjoy the highest possible standard of health attainable.

(12) All workers and their dependants have the right to social security.

(13) Anyone without adequate resources has the right to social and medical assistance.

(14) Everyone has the right to benefit from social welfare services.

(15) Disabled persons have the right to vocational training, rehabilitation and resettlement, whatever the origin and nature of their disability.

(16) The family as a fundamental unit of society has the right to appropriate social, legal and economic protection to ensure its full development.

(17) Mothers and children, irrespective of marital status and family relations, have the right to appropriate social and economic protection.

(18) The nationals of any one of the Contracting Parties have the right to engage in any gainful occupation in the territory of any one of the others on a footing of equality with the nationals of the latter, subject to restrictions based on cogent economic or social reasons.

(19) Migrant workers who are nationals of a Contracting Party and their families have the right to protection and assistance in the territory of any other Contracting Party.

PART II

The Contracting Parties undertake, as provided for in Part III, to consider themselves bound by the obligations laid down in the following articles and paragraphs.

Article 1—The right to work

With a view to ensuring the effective exercise of the right to work, the Contracting Parties undertake:

(1) To accept as one of their primary aims and responsibilities the achievement and maintenance of as high and stable a level of employment as possible, with a view to the attainment of full employment;

(2) To protect effectively the right of the worker to earn his living in an occupation freely entered upon;

(3) To establish or maintain free employment services for all workers;

(4) To provide or promote appropriate vocational guidance, training and rehabilitation.

Article 2—The right to just conditions of work

With a view to ensuring the effective exercise of the right to just conditions of work, the Contracting Parties undertake:

(1) To provide for reasonable daily and weekly working hours, the working week to be progressively reduced to the extent that the increase of productivity and other relevant factors permit;

(2) To provide for public holidays with pay;

(3) To provide for a minimum of two weeks annual holiday with pay;

(4) To provide for additional paid holidays or reduced working hours for workers engaged in dangerous or unhealthy occupations as prescribed;

(5) To ensure a weekly rest period which shall, as far as possible, coincide with the day recognised by tradition or custom in the country or region concerned as a day of rest.

Article 3—The right to safe and healthy working conditions

With a view to ensuring the effective exercise of the right to safe and healthy working conditions, the Contracting Parties undertake:

(1) To issue safety and health regulations;

(2) To provide for the enforcement of such regulations by measures of supervision;

(3) To consult, as appropriate, employers' and workers' organisations on measures intended to improve industrial safety and health.

Article 4—The right to a fair remuneration

With a view to ensuring the effective exercise of the right to a fair remuneration, the Contracting Parties undertake:

(1) To recognize the right of workers to a remuneration such as will give them and their families a decent standard of living;

(2) To recognize the right of workers to an increased rate of remuneration for overtime work, subject to exceptions in particular cases;

(3) To recognize the right of men and women workers to equal pay for work of equal value;

(4) To recognize the right of all workers to a reasonable period of notice for termination of employment;

(5) To permit deductions from wages only under conditions and to the extent prescribed by national laws or regulations or fixed by collective agreements or arbitration awards. The exercise of these rights shall be achieved by freely concluded collective agreements, by statutory wage-fixing machinery, or by other means appropriate to national conditions.

Article 5—The right to organize

With a view to ensuring or promoting the freedom of workers and employers to form local, national or international organisations for the protection of their economic and social interests and to join those organizations, the Contracting Parties undertake that national law shall not be such as to impair, nor shall it be so applied as to impair, this freedom. The extent to which the guarantees provided for in this article shall apply to the police shall be determined by national laws or regulations. The principle governing the application to the members of the armed forces of these guarantees and the extent to which they shall apply to persons in this category shall equally be determined by national laws or regulations.

Article 6—The right to bargain collectively

With a view to ensuring the effective exercise of the right to bargain collectively, the Contracting Parties undertake:

(1) To promote joint consultation between workers and employers;

(2) To promote, where necessary and appropriate, machinery for voluntary negotiations between employers or employers' organisations and workers' organisations, with a view to the regulation of terms and conditions of employment by means of collective agreements;

(3) To promote the establishment and use of appropriate machinery for conciliation and voluntary arbitration for the settlement of labour disputes;
and recognize:

(4) The right of workers and employers to collective action in cases of conflicts of interest, including the right to strike, subject to obligations that might arise out of collective agreements previously entered into.

Article 7—The right of children and young persons to protection

With a view to ensuring the effective exercise of the right of children and young persons to protection, the Contracting Parties undertake:

(1) To provide that the minimum age of admission to employment shall be 15 years, subject to exceptions for children employed in prescribed light work without harm to their health, morals or education;

(2) To provide that a higher minimum age of admission to employment shall be fixed with respect to prescribed occupations regarded as dangerous or unhealthy;

(3) To provide that persons who are still subject to compulsory education shall not be employed in such work as would deprive them of the full benefit of their education;

(4) To provide that the working hours of persons under 16 years of age shall be limited in accordance with the needs of their development, and particularly with their need for vocational training;

(5) To recognize the right of young workers and apprentices to a fair wage or other appropriate allowances;

(6) To provide that the time spent by young persons in vocational training during the normal working hours with the consent of the employer shall be treated as forming part of the working day;

(7) To provide that employed persons of under 18 years of age shall be entitled to not less than three weeks' annual holiday with pay;

(8) To provide that persons under 18 years of age shall not be employed in night work with the exception of certain occupations provided for by national laws or regulations;

(9) To provide that persons under 18 years of age employed in occupations prescribed by national laws or regulations shall be subject to regular medical control;

(10) To ensure special protection against physical and moral dangers to which children and young persons are exposed, and particularly against those resulting directly or indirectly from their work.

Article 8—The right of employed women to protection

With a view to ensuring the effective exercise of the right of employed women to protection, the Contracting Parties undertake:

(1) To provide either by paid leave, by adequate social security benefits or by benefits from public funds for women to take leave before and after childbirth up to a total of at least 12 weeks;

(2) To consider it as unlawful for an employer to give a woman notice of dismissal during her absence on maternity leave or to give her notice of dismissal at such a time that the notice would expire during such absence;

(3) To provide that mothers who are nursing their infants shall be entitled to sufficient time off for this purpose;

(4) (a) To regulate the employment of women workers on night work in industrial employment;

  (b) To prohibit the employment of women workers in underground mining, and, as appropriate, on all other work which is unsuitable for them by reason of its dangerous, unhealthy, or arduous nature.

Article 9—The right to vocational guidance

With a view to ensuring the effective exercise of the right to vocational guidance, the Contracting Parties undertake to provide or promote, as necessary, a service which will assist all persons, including the handicapped, to solve problems related to occupational choice and progress, with due regard to the individual's characteristics and their relation to occupational opportunity: this assistance should be available free of charge, both to young persons, including school children, and to adults.

Article 10—The right to vocational training

With a view to ensuring the effective exercise of the right to vocational training, the Contracting Parties undertake:

(1) To provide or promote, as necessary, the technical and vocational training of all persons, including the handicapped, in consultation with employers' and workers'

organizations, and to grant facilities for access to higher technical and university education, based solely on individual aptitude;

(2) To provide or promote a system of apprenticeship and other systematic arrangements for training young boys and girls in their various employments;

(3) To provide or promote, as necessary:

    (a)   adequate and readily available training facilities for adult workers;

    (b)   special facilities for the re-training of adult workers needed as a result of technological development or new trends in employment;

(4) To encourage the full utilisation of the facilities provided by appropriate measures such as:

    (a)   reducing or abolishing any fees or charges;

    (b)   granting financial assistance in appropriate cases;

    (c)   including in the normal working hours time spent on supplementary training taken by the worker, at the request of his employer, during employment;

    (d)   ensuring, through adequate supervision, in consultation with the employers' and workers' organizations, the efficiency of apprenticeship and other training arrangements for young workers, and the adequate protection of young workers generally.

Article 11—The right to protection of health

With a view to ensuring the effective exercise of the right to protection of health, the Contracting Parties undertake, either directly or in co-operation with public or private organizations, to take appropriate measures designed *inter alia*:

(1) To remove as far as possible the causes of ill-health;

(2) To provide advisory and educational facilities for the promotion of health and the encouragement of individual responsibility in matters of health;

(3) To prevent as far as possible epidemic, endemic and other diseases.

Article 12—The right to social security

With a view to ensuring the effective exercise of the right to social security, the Contracting Parties undertake:

(1) To establish or maintain a system of social security;

(2) To maintain the social security system at a satisfactory level at least equal to that required for ratification of International Labour Convention (No. 102) Concerning Minimum Standards of Social Security;

(3) To endeavour to raise progressively the system of social security to a higher level;

(4) To take steps, by the conclusion of appropriate bilateral and multilateral agreements, or by other means, and subject to the conditions laid down in such agreements, in order to ensure:

    (a)   equal treatment with their own nationals of the nationals of other Contracting Parties in respect of social security rights, including the retention of benefits arising out of social security legislation, whatever movements the persons protected may undertake between the territories of the Contracting Parties;

    (b)   the granting, maintenance and resumption of social security rights by such means as the accumulation of insurance or employment periods completed under the legislation of each of the Contracting Parties.

Article 13—The right to social and medical assistance

With a view to ensuring the effective exercise of the right to social and medical assistance, the Contracting Parties undertake:

(1) To ensure that any person who is without adequate resources and who is unable to secure such resources either by his own efforts or from other sources, in particular by benefits under a social security scheme, be granted adequate assistance, and, in case of sickness, the care necessitated by his condition;

(2) To ensure that persons receiving such assistance shall not, for that reason, suffer from a diminution of their political or social rights;

(3) To provide that everyone may receive by appropriate public or private services such advice and personal help as may be required to prevent, to remove, or to alleviate personal or family want;

(4) To apply the provisions referred to in paragraphs 1, 2 and 3 of this article on an equal footing with their nationals to nationals of other Contracting Parties lawfully within their territories, in accordance with their obligations under the European Convention on Social and Medical Assistance, signed at Paris on 11th December 1953.

Article 14—The right to benefit from social welfare services

With a view to ensuring the effective exercise of the right to benefit from social welfare services, the Contracting Parties undertake:

(1) To promote or provide services which, by using methods of social work, would contribute to the welfare and development of both individuals and groups in the community, and to their adjustment to the social environment;

(2) To encourage the participation of individuals and voluntary or other organizations in the establishment and maintenance of such services.

Article 15—The right of physically or mentally disabled persons to vocational training, rehabilitation and social resettlement

With a view to ensuring the effective exercise of the right of the physically or mentally disabled to vocational training, rehabilitation and resettlement, the Contracting Parties undertake:

(1) To take adequate measures for the provision of training facilities, including, where necessary, specialised institutions, public or private;

(2) To take adequate measures for the placing of disabled persons in employment, such as specialised placing services, facilities for sheltered employment and measures to encourage employers to admit disabled persons to employment.

Article 16—The right of the family to social, legal and economic protection

With a view to ensuring the necessary conditions for the full development of the family, which is a fundamental unit of society, the Contracting Parties undertake to promote the economic, legal and social protection of family life by such means as social and family benefits, fiscal arrangements, provision of family housing, benefits for the newly married, and other appropriate means.

Article 17—The right of mothers and children to social and economic protection

With a view to ensuring the effective exercise of the right of mothers and children to social and economic protection, the Contracting Parties will take all appropriate and necessary measures to that end, including the establishment or maintenance of appropriate institutions or services.

Article 18—*The right to engage in a gainful occupation in the territory of other Contracting Parties*

With a view to ensuring the effective exercise of the right to engage in a gainful occupation in the territory of any other Contracting Party, the Contracting Parties undertake:

(1) To apply existing regulations in a spirit of liberality;

(2) To simplify existing formalities and to reduce or abolish chancery dues and other charges payable by foreign workers or their employers;

(3) To liberalise, individually or collectively, regulations governing the employment of foreign workers;

and recognize:

(4) The right of their nationals to leave the country to engage in a gainful occupation in the territories of the other Contracting Parties.

Article 19—*The right of migrant workers and their families to protection and assistance*

With a view to ensuring the effective exercise of the right of migrant workers and their families to protection and assistance in the territory of any other Contracting Party, the Contracting Parties undertake:

(1) To maintain or to satisfy themselves that there are maintained adequate and free services to assist such workers, particularly in obtaining accurate information, and to take all appropriate steps, so far as national laws and regulations permit, against misleading propaganda relating to emigration and immigration;

(2) To adopt appropriate measures within their own jurisdiction to facilitate the departure, journey and reception of such workers and their families, and to provide, within their own jurisdiction, appropriate services for health, medical attention and good hygienic conditions during the journey;

(3) To promote co-operation, as appropriate, between social services, public and private, in emigration and immigration countries;

(4) To secure for such workers lawfully within their territories, insofar as such matters are regulated by law or regulations or are subject to the control of administrative authorities, treatment not less favourable than that of their own nationals in respect of the following matters:

    (a) remuneration and other employment and working conditions;

    (b) membership of trade unions and enjoyment of the benefits of collective bargaining;

    (c) accommodation;

(5) To secure for such workers lawfully within their territories treatment not less favourable than that of their own nationals with regard to employment taxes, dues or contributions payable in respect of employed persons;

(6)   To facilitate as far as possible the reunion of the family of a foreign worker permitted to establish himself in the territory;

(7)   To secure for such workers lawfully within their territories treatment not less favourable than that of their own nationals in respect of legal proceedings relating to matters referred to in this article;

(8)   To secure that such workers lawfully residing within their territories are not expelled unless they endanger national security or offend against public interest or morality;

(9) To permit, within legal limits, the transfer of such parts of the earnings and savings of such workers as they may desire;

(10) To extend the protection and assistance provided for in this article to self-employed migrants insofar as such measures apply.

PART III

Article 20—Undertakings

1. Each of the Contracting Parties undertakes:

   (a) To consider Part I of this Charter as a declaration of the aims which it will pursue by all appropriate means, as stated in the introductory paragraph of that Part;

   (b) To consider itself bound by at least five of the following articles of Part II of this Charter: Articles 1, 5, 6, 12, 13, 16 and 19;

   (c) In addition to the articles selected by it in accordance with the preceding sub-paragraph, to consider itself bound by such a number of articles or numbered paragraphs of Part II of the Charter as it may select, provided that the total number of articles or numbered paragraphs by which it is bound is not less than 10 articles or 45 numbered paragraphs.

2. The articles or paragraphs selected in accordance with sub-paragraphs (b) and (c) of paragraph 1 of this article shall be notified to the Secretary General of the Council of Europe at the time when the instrument of ratification or approval of the Contracting Party concerned is deposited.

3. Any Contracting Party may, at a later date, declare by notification to the Secretary General that it considers itself bound by any articles or any numbered paragraphs of Part II of the Charter which it has not already accepted under the terms of paragraph 1 of this article. Such undertakings subsequently given shall be deemed to be an integral part of the ratification or approval, and shall have the same effect as from the thirtieth day after the date of the notification.

4. The Secretary General shall communicate to all the signatory governments and to the Director General of the International Labour Office any notification which he shall have received pursuant to this part of the Charter.

5. Each Contracting Party shall maintain a system of labour inspection appropriate to national conditions.

PART IV

Article 21—Reports concerning accepted provisions

The Contracting Parties shall send to the Secretary General of the Council of Europe a report at two-yearly intervals, in a form to be determined by the Committee of Ministers, concerning the application of such provisions of Part II of the Charter as they have accepted.

Article 22—Reports concerning provisions which are not accepted

The Contracting Parties shall send to the Secretary General, at appropriate intervals as requested by the Committee of Ministers, reports relating to the provisions of Part II of the Charter which they did not accept at the time of their ratification or approval or in a subsequent notification. The Committee of Ministers shall determine from time to time in respect of which provisions such reports shall be requested and the form of the reports to be provided.

Article 23—Communication of copies

1. Each Contracting Party shall communicate copies of its reports referred to in Articles 21 and 22 to such of its national organisations as are members of the international organisations of employers and trade unions to be invited under Article 27, paragraph 2, to be represented at meetings of the Sub-committee of the Governmental Social Committee.

2. The Contracting Parties shall forward to the Secretary General any comments on the said reports received from these national organisations, if so requested by them.

Article 24—Examination of the reports

The reports sent to the Secretary General in accordance with Articles 21 and 22 shall be examined by a Committee of Experts, who shall have also before them any comments forwarded to the Secretary General in accordance with paragraph 2 of Article 23.

Article 25—Committee of Experts

1. The Committee of Experts shall consist of not more than seven members appointed by the Committee of Ministers from a list of independent experts of the highest integrity and of recognised competence in international social questions, nominated by the Contracting Parties.

2. The members of the committee shall be appointed for a period of six years. They may be reappointed. However, of the members first appointed, the terms of office of two members shall expire at the end of four years.

3. The members whose terms of office are to expire at the end of the initial period of four years shall be chosen by lot by the Committee of Ministers immediately after the first appointment has been made.

4. A member of the Committee of Experts appointed to replace a member whose term of office has not expired shall hold office for the remainder of his predecessor's term.

Article 26—Participation of the International Labour Organization

The International Labour Organization shall be invited to nominate a representative to participate in a consultative capacity in the deliberations of the Committee of Experts.

Article 27—Sub-committee of the Governmental Social Committee

1. The reports of the Contracting Parties and the conclusions of the Committee of Experts shall be submitted for examination to a sub-committee of the Governmental Social Committee of the Council of Europe.

2. The sub-committee shall be composed of one representative of each of the Contracting Parties. It shall invite no more than two international organizations of employers and no more than two international trade union organizations as it may designate to be represented as observers in a consultative capacity at its meetings. Moreover, it may consult no more than two representatives of international non-governmental organizations having consultative status with the Council of Europe, in respect of questions with which the

organizations are particularly qualified to deal, such as social welfare, and the economic and social protection of the family.

3. The sub-committee shall present to the Committee of Ministers a report containing its conclusions and append the report of the Committee of Experts.

Article 28—Consultative Assembly

The Secretary General of the Council of Europe shall transmit to the Consultative Assembly the conclusions of the Committee of Experts. The Consultative Assembly shall communicate its views on these conclusions to the Committee of Ministers.

Article 29—Committee of Ministers

By a majority of two-thirds of the members entitled to sit on the Committee, the Committee of Ministers may, on the basis of the report of the sub-committee, and after consultation with the Consultative Assembly, make to each Contracting Party any necessary recommendations.

PART V

Article 30—Derogations in time of war or public emergency

1. In time of war or other public emergency threatening the life of the nation any Contracting Party may take measures derogating from its obligations under this Charter to the extent strictly required by the exigencies of the situation, provided that such measures are not inconsistent with its other obligations under international law.

2. Any Contracting Party which has availed itself of this right of derogation shall, within a reasonable lapse of time, keep the Secretary General of the Council of Europe fully informed of the measures taken and of the reasons therefor. It shall likewise inform the Secretary General when such measures have ceased to operate and the provisions of the Charter which it has accepted are again being fully executed.

3. The Secretary General shall in turn inform other Contracting Parties and the Director-General of the International Labour Office of all communications received in accordance with paragraph 2 of this article.

Article 31—Restrictions

1. The rights and principles set forth in Part I when effectively realized, and their effective exercise as provided for in Part II, shall not be subject to any restrictions or limitations not specified in those parts, except such as are prescribed by law and are necessary in a democratic society for the protection of the rights and freedoms of others or for the protection of public interest, national security, public health, or morals.

2. The restrictions permitted under this Charter to the rights and obligations set forth herein shall not be applied for any purpose other than that for which they have been prescribed.

Article 32—Relations between the Charter and domestic law or international agreements

The provisions of this Charter shall not prejudice the provisions of domestic law or of any bilateral or multilateral treaties, conventions or agreements which are already in force, or may come into force, under which more favourable treatment would be accorded to the persons protected.

Article 33—Implementation by collective agreements

1. In member States where the provisions of paragraphs 1, 2, 3, 4 and 5 of Article 2, paragraphs 4, 6 and 7 of Article 7 and paragraphs 1, 2, 3 and 4 of Article 10 of Part II of this Charter are matters normally left to agreements between employers or employers' organizations and workers' organizations, or are normally carried out otherwise than by law, the undertakings of those paragraphs may be given and compliance with them shall be treated as effective if their provisions are applied through such agreements or other means to the great majority of the workers concerned.

2. In member States where these provisions are normally the subject of legislation, the undertakings concerned may likewise be given, and compliance with them shall be regarded as effective if the provisions are applied by law to the great majority of the workers concerned.

Article 34—Territorial application

1. This Charter shall apply to the metropolitan territory of each Contracting Party. Each signatory government may, at the time of signature or of the deposit of its instrument of ratification or approval, specify, by declaration addressed to the Secretary General of the Council of Europe, the territory which shall be considered to be its metropolitan territory for this purpose.

2. Any Contracting Party may, at the time of ratification or approval of this Charter or at any time thereafter, declare by notification addressed to the Secretary General of the Council of Europe, that the Charter shall extend in whole or in part to a non-metropolitan territory or territories specified in the said declaration for whose international relations it is responsible or for which it assumes international responsibility. It shall specify in the declaration the articles or paragraphs of Part II of the Charter which it accepts as binding in respect of the territories named in the declaration.

3. The Charter shall extend to the territory or territories named in the aforesaid declaration as from the thirtieth day after the date on which the Secretary General shall have received notification of such declaration.

4. Any Contracting Party may declare at a later date, by notification addressed to the Secretary General of the Council of Europe, that, in respect of one or more of the territories to which the Charter has been extended in accordance with paragraph 2 of this article, it accepts as binding any articles or any numbered paragraphs which it has not already accepted in respect of that territory or territories. Such undertakings subsequently given shall be deemed to be an integral part of the original declaration in respect of the territory concerned, and shall have the same effect as from the thirtieth day after the date of the notification.

5. The Secretary General shall communicate to the other signatory governments and to the Director-General of the International Labour Office any notification transmitted to him in accordance with this article.

Article 35—Signature, ratification and entry into force

1. This Charter shall be open for signature by the members of the Council of Europe. It shall be ratified or approved. Instruments of ratification or approval shall be deposited with the Secretary General of the Council of Europe.

2. This Charter shall come into force as from the thirtieth day after the date of deposit of the fifth instrument of ratification or approval.

3. In respect of any signatory government ratifying subsequently, the Charter shall come into force as from the thirtieth day after the date of deposit of its instrument of ratification or approval.

4. The Secretary General shall notify all the members of the Council of Europe and the Director-General of the International Labour Office of the entry into force of the Charter, the names of the Contracting Parties which have ratified or approved it and the subsequent deposit of any instruments of ratification or approval.

Article 36—Amendments

Any member of the Council of Europe may propose amendments to this Charter in a communication addressed to the Secretary General of the Council of Europe. The Secretary General shall transmit to the other members of the Council of Europe any amendments so proposed, which shall then be considered by the Committee of Ministers and submitted to the Consultative Assembly for opinion. Any amendments approved by the Committee of Ministers shall enter into force as from the thirtieth day after all the Contracting Parties have informed the Secretary General of their acceptance. The Secretary General shall notify all the members of the Council of Europe and the Director-General of the International Labour Office of the entry into force of such amendments.

Article 37—Denunciation

1. Any Contracting Party may denounce this Charter only at the end of a period of five years from the date on which the Charter entered into force for it, or at the end of any successive period of two years, and, in each case, after giving six months notice to the Secretary General of the Council of Europe who shall inform the other Parties and the Director-General of the International Labour Office accordingly. Such denunciation shall not affect the validity of the Charter in respect of the other Contracting Parties provided that at all times there are not less than five such Contracting Parties.

2. Any Contracting Party may, in accordance with the provisions set out in the preceding paragraph, denounce any article or paragraph of Part II of the Charter accepted by it provided that the number of articles or paragraphs by which this Contracting Party is bound shall never be less than 10 in the former case and 45 in the latter and that this number of articles or paragraphs shall continue to include the articles selected by the Contracting Party among those to which special reference is made in Article 20, paragraph 1, sub-paragraph (b).

3. Any Contracting Party may denounce the present Charter or any of the articles or paragraphs of Part II of the Charter, under the conditions specified in paragraph 1 of this article in respect of any territory to which the said Charter is applicable by virtue of a declaration made in accordance with paragraph 2 of Article 34.

Article 38—Appendix

The Appendix to this Charter shall form an integral part of it.

In witness whereof, the undersigned, being duly authorized thereto, have signed this Charter.

Done at Turin, this 18th day of October 1961, in English and French, both texts being equally authoritative, in a single copy which shall be deposited within the archives of the

Council of Europe. The Secretary General shall transmit certified copies to each of the Signatories.

APPENDIX TO THE SOCIAL CHARTER

Scope of the Social Charter in terms of persons protected

1. Without prejudice to Article 12, paragraph 4, and Article 13, paragraph 4, the persons covered by Articles 1 to 17 include foreigners only insofar as they are nationals of other Contracting Parties lawfully resident or working regularly within the territory of the Contracting Party concerned, subject to the understanding that these articles are to be interpreted in the light of the provisions of Articles 18 and 19. This interpretation would not prejudice the extension of similar facilities to other persons by any of the Contracting Parties.

2. Each Contracting Party will grant to refugees as defined in the Convention relating to the Status of Refugees, signed at Geneva on 28th July 1951, and lawfully staying in its territory, treatment as favourable as possible, and in any case not less favourable than under the obligations accepted by the Contracting Party under the said Convention and under any other existing international instruments applicable to those refugees.

PART I, PARAGRAPH 18, AND PART II, ARTICLE 18, PARAGRAPH 1

It is understood that these provisions are not concerned with the question of entry into the territories of the Contracting Parties and do not prejudice the provisions of the European Convention on Establishment, signed at Paris on 13th December 1955.

PART II

Article 1, paragraph 2

This provision shall not be interpreted as prohibiting or authorizing any union security clause or practice.

Article 4, paragraph 4

This provision shall be so understood as not to prohibit immediate dismissal for any serious offence.

Article 4, paragraph 5

It is understood that a Contracting Party may give the undertaking required in this paragraph if the great majority of workers are not permitted to suffer deductions from wages either by law or through collective agreements or arbitration awards, the exceptions being those persons not so covered.

Article 6, paragraph 4

It is understood that each Contracting Party may, insofar as it is concerned, regulate the exercise of the right to strike by law, provided that any further restriction that this might place on the right can be justified under the terms of Article 31.

Article 7, paragraph 8

It is understood that a Contracting Party may give the undertaking required in this paragraph if it fulfils the spirit of the undertaking by providing by law that the great majority of persons under 18 years of age shall not be employed in night work.

Article 12, paragraph 4

The words 'and subject to the conditions laid down in such agreements' in the introduction to this paragraph are taken to imply *inter alia* that with regard to benefits which are available independently of any insurance contribution a Contracting Party may require the completion of a prescribed period of residence before granting such benefits to nationals of other Contracting Parties.

Article 13, paragraph 4

Governments not Parties to the European Convention on Social and Medical Assistance may ratify the Social Charter in respect of this paragraph provided that they grant to nationals of other Contracting Parties a treatment which is in conformity with the provisions of the said Convention.

Article 19, paragraph 6

For the purpose of this provision, the term 'family of a foreign worker' is understood to mean at least his wife and dependent children under the age of 21 years.

PART III

It is understood that the Charter contains legal obligations of an international character, the application of which is submitted solely to the supervision provided for in Part IV thereof.

Article 20, paragraph 1

It is understood that the 'numbered paragraphs' may include articles consisting of only one paragraph.

PART V

Article 30

The term 'in time of war or other public emergency' shall be so understood as to cover also the threat of war.

89. ADDITIONAL PROTOCOL TO THE EUROPEAN SOCIAL CHARTER, 1988

This first Additional Protocol to the European Social Charter (*ETS* No. 128) was opened for signature by the Member States of the Council of Europe who are signatories to the Charter on 5 May 1988; it entered into force on 4 September 1992.

The Additional Protocol aims at extending the protection of the social and economic rights guaranteed by the European Social Charter, particularly the right for workers to equal opportunities and equal treatment in matters of employment and occupation without discrimination on the ground of sex; the right for workers to be informed and consulted within the undertaking; the right for workers to take part in the determination of working conditions and the working environment in the undertaking; and the right for elderly persons to social protection.

TEXT

Preamble

The member States of the Council of Europe signatory hereto,

Resolved to take new measures to extend the protection of the social and economic rights guaranteed by the European Social Charter, opened for signature in Turin on 18 October 1961 (hereinafter referred to as 'the Charter'),

Have agreed as follows:

PART I

The Parties accept as the aim of their policy to be pursued by all appropriate means, both national and international in character, the attainment of conditions in which the following rights and principles may be effectively realised:

1. All workers have the right to equal opportunities and equal treatment in matters of employment and occupation without discrimination on the grounds of sex.

2. Workers have the right to be informed and to be consulted within the undertaking.

3. Workers have the right to take part in the determination and improvement of the working conditions and working environment in the undertaking.

4. Every elderly person has the right to social protection.

PART II

The Parties undertake, as provided for in Part III, to consider themselves bound by the obligations laid down in the following articles:

Article 1—*Right to equal opportunities and equal treatment in matters of employment and occupation without discrimination on the grounds of sex*

1. With a view to ensuring the effective exercise of the right to equal opportunities and equal treatment in matters of employment and occupation without discrimination on

the grounds of sex, the Parties undertake to recognize that right and to take appropriate measures to ensure or promote its application in the following fields:

— access to employment, protection against dismissal and occupational resettlement;
— vocational guidance, training, retraining and rehabilitation;
— terms of employment and working conditions including remuneration;
— career development including promotion.

2. Provisions concerning the protection of women, particularly as regards pregnancy, confinement and the post-natal period, shall not be deemed to be discrimination as referred to in paragraph 1 of this article.

3. Paragraph 1 of this article shall not prevent the adoption of specific measures aimed at removing *de facto* inequalities.

4. Occupational activities which, by reason of their nature or the context in which they are carried out, can be entrusted only to persons of a particular sex may be excluded from the scope of this article or some of its provisions.

Article 2—Right to information and consultation

1. With a view to ensuring the effective exercise of the right of workers to be informed and consulted within the undertaking, the Parties undertake to adopt or encourage measures enabling workers or their representatives, in accordance with national legislation and practice:

(a) to be informed regularly or at the appropriate time and in a comprehensible way about the economic and financial situation of the undertaking employing them, on the understanding that the disclosure of certain information which could be prejudicial to the undertaking may be refused or subject to confidentiality; and

(b) to be consulted in good time on proposed decisions which could substantially affect the interests of workers, particularly on those decisions which could have an important impact on the employment situation in the undertaking.

2. The Parties may exclude from the field of application of paragraph 1 of this article, those undertakings employing less than a certain number of workers to be determined by national legislation or practice.

Article 3—Right to take part in the determination and improvement of the working conditions and working environment

1. With a view to ensuring the effective exercise of the right of workers to take part in the determination and improvement of the working conditions and working environment in the undertaking, the Parties undertake to adopt or encourage measures enabling workers or their representatives, in accordance with national legislation and practice, to contribute:

(a) to the determination and the improvement of the working conditions, work organization and working environment;

(b) to the protection of health and safety within the undertaking;

(c) to the organization of social and socio-cultural services and facilities within the undertaking;

(d) to the supervision of the observance of regulations on these matters.

2. The Parties may exclude from the field of application of paragraph 1 of this article, those undertakings employing less than a certain number of workers to be determined by national legislation or practice.

Article 4—*Right of elderly persons to social protection*

With a view to ensuring the effective exercise of the right of elderly persons to social protection, the Parties undertake to adopt or encourage, either directly or in co-operation with public or private organizations, appropriate measures designed in particular:

1. to enable elderly persons to remain full members of society for as long as possible, by means of:

   (a)   adequate resources enabling them to lead a decent life and play an active part in public, social and cultural life;

   (b)   provision of information about services and facilities available for elderly persons and their opportunities to make use of them;

2. to enable elderly persons to choose their life-style freely and to lead independent lives in their familiar surroundings for as long as they wish and are able, by means of:

   (a)   provision of housing suited to their needs and their state of health or of adequate support for adapting their housing;

   (b)   the health care and the services necessitated by their state;

3. to guarantee elderly persons living in institutions appropriate support, while respecting their privacy, and participation in decisions concerning living conditions in the institution.

PART III

Article 5—*Undertakings*

1. Each of the Parties undertakes:

   (a)   to consider Part I of this Protocol as a declaration of the aims which it will pursue by all appropriate means, as stated in the introductory paragraph of that part;

   (b)   to consider itself bound by one or more articles of Part II of this Protocol.

2. The article or articles selected in accordance with sub-paragraph (b) of paragraph 1 of this article, shall be notified to the Secretary-General of the Council of Europe at the time when the instrument of ratification, acceptance or approval of the Contracting State concerned is deposited.

3. Any Party may, at a later date, declare by notification to the Secretary General that it considers itself bound by any articles of Part II of this Protocol which it has not already accepted under the terms of paragraph 1 of this article. Such undertakings subsequently given shall be deemed to be an integral part of the ratification, acceptance or approval, and shall have the same effect as from the thirtieth day after the date of the notification.

PART IV

Article 6—Supervision of compliance with the undertakings given

The Parties shall submit reports on the application of those provisions of Part II of this Protocol which they have accepted in the reports submitted by virtue of Article 21 of the Charter.

PART V

Article 7—Implementation of the undertakings given

1. The relevant provisions of Articles 1 to 4 of Part II of this Protocol may be implemented by:

  (a) laws or regulations;
  (b) agreements between employers or employers' organizations and workers' organizations;
  (c) a combination of those two methods; or
  (d) other appropriate means.

2. Compliance with the undertakings deriving from Articles 2 and 3 of Part II of this Protocol shall be regarded as effective if the provisions are applied, in accordance with paragraph 1 of this article, to the great majority of the workers concerned.

Article 8—Relations between the Charter and this Protocol

1. The provisions of this Protocol shall not prejudice the provisions of the Charter.

2. Articles 22 to 32 and Article 36 of the Charter shall apply, *mutatis mutandis*, to this Protocol.

Article 9—Territorial application

1. This Protocol shall apply to the metropolitan territory of each Party. Any State may, at the time of signature or when depositing its instrument of ratification, acceptance or approval, specify by declaration addressed to the Secretary General of the Council of Europe, the territory which shall be considered to be its metropolitan territory for this purpose.

2. Any Contracting State may, at the time of ratification, acceptance or approval of this Protocol or at any time thereafter, declare by notification addressed to the Secretary General of the Council of Europe that the Protocol shall extend in whole or in part to a non-metropolitan territory or territories specified in the said declaration for whose international relations it is responsible or for which it assumes international responsibility. It shall specify in the declaration the article or articles of Part II of this Protocol which it accepts as binding in respect of the territories named in the declaration.

3. This Protocol shall enter into force in respect of the territory or territories named in the aforesaid declaration as from the thirtieth day after the date on which the Secretary General shall have notification of such declaration.

4. Any Party may declare at a later date by notification addressed to the Secretary General of the Council of Europe, that, in respect of one or more of the territories to which this Protocol has been extended in accordance with paragraph 2 of this article, it accepts as binding any articles which it has not already accepted in respect of that territory or territories. Such undertakings subsequently given shall be deemed to be an integral part of the original declaration in respect of the territory concerned, and shall have the same effect as from the thirtieth day after the date on which the Secretary General shall have notification of such declaration.

Article 10—Signature, ratification, acceptance, approval and entry into force

1. This Protocol shall be open for signature by member States of the Council of Europe who are signatories to the Charter. It is subject to ratification, acceptance or approval. No member State of the Council of Europe shall ratify, accept or approve this Protocol except at the same time as or after ratification of the Charter. Instruments of ratification, acceptance of approval shall be deposited with the Secretary General of the Council of Europe.

2. This Protocol shall enter into force on the thirtieth day after the date of deposit of the third instrument of ratification, acceptance or approval.

3. In respect of any signatory State ratifying subsequently, this Protocol shall come into force as from the thirtieth day after the date of deposit of its instrument of ratification, acceptance or approval.

Article 11—Denunciation

1. Any Party may denounce this Protocol only at the end of a period of five years from the date on which the Protocol entered into force for it, or at the end of any successive period of two years, and, in each case, after giving six months' notice to the Secretary General of the Council of Europe. Such denunciation shall not affect the validity of the Protocol in respect of the other Parties provided that at all times there are not less than three such Parties.

2. Any Party may, in accordance with the provisions set out in the preceding paragraph, denounce any article of Part II of this Protocol accepted by it, provided that the number of articles by which this Party is bound shall never be less than one.

3. Any Party may denounce this Protocol or any of the articles of Part II of the Protocol, under the conditions specified in paragraph 1 of this article, in respect of any territory to which the Protocol is applicable by virtue of a declaration made in accordance with paragraphs 2 and 4 of Article 9.

4. Any Party bound by the Charter and this Protocol which denounces the Charter in accordance with the provisions of paragraph 1 of Article 37 thereof, will be considered to have denounced the Protocol likewise.

Article 12—Notifications

The Secretary General of the Council of Europe shall notify the member States of the Council and the Director-General of the International Labour Office of:

(a) any signature;
(b) the deposit of any instrument of ratification, acceptance or approval;
(c) any date of entry into force of this Protocol in accordance with Articles 9 and 10;
(d) any other act, notification or communication relating to this Protocol.

Article 13—Appendix

The appendix to this Protocol shall form an integral part of it.

In witness whereof the undersigned, being duly authorized thereto, have signed this Protocol.

Done at Strasbourg, this 5th day of May, 1988, in English and French, both texts being equally authentic, in a single copy which shall be deposited in the archives of the Council of Europe. The Secretary General of the Council in Europe shall transmit certified copies to each member State of the Council of Europe.

APPENDIX TO THE PROTOCOL

Scope of the Protocol in Terms of Persons Protected

1. The persons covered by Articles 1 to 4 include foreigners only insofar as they are nationals of other Parties lawfully resident or working regularly within the territory of the Party concerned subject to the understanding that these articles are to be interpreted in the light of the provisions of Articles 18 and 19 of the Charter. This interpretation would not prejudice the extension of similar facilities to other persons by any of the Parties.

2. Each Party will grant to refugees as defined in the Convention relating to the Status of Refugees, signed at Geneva on 28 July 1951 and in the Protocol of 31 January 1967, and lawfully staying in its territory, treatment as favourable as possible and in any case not less favourable than under the obligations accepted by the Party under the said instruments and under any other existing international instruments applicable to those refugees.

3. Each Party will grant to stateless persons as defined in the Convention on the Status of Stateless Persons done at New York on 28 September 1954 and lawfully staying in its territory, treatment as favourable as possible and in any case not less favourable than under the obligations accepted by the Party under the said instrument and under any other existing international instruments applicable to those stateless persons.

Article 1

It is understood that social security matters, as well as other provisions relating to unemployment benefit, old age benefit and survivor's benefit, may be excluded from the scope of this article.

Article 1, paragraph 4

This provision is not to be interpreted as requiring the Parties to embody in laws or regulations a list of occupations which, by reason of their nature or the context in which they are carried out, may be reserved to persons of a particular sex.

Articles 2 and 3

1. For the purpose of the application of these articles, the term 'workers' representatives' means persons who are recognised as such under national legislation or practice.

2. The term 'national legislation and practice' embraces as the case may be, in addition to laws and regulations, collective agreements, other agreements between employers and workers' representatives, customs, as well as relevant case law.

3. For the purpose of the application of these articles, the term 'undertaking' is understood as referring to a set of tangible and intangible components, with or without legal personality, formed to produce or provide services for financial gain and with power to determine its own market policy.

4. It is understood that religious communities and their institutions may be excluded from the application of these articles, even if these institutions are 'undertakings' within the meaning of paragraph 3. Establishments pursuing activities which are inspired by certain ideals or guided by certain moral concepts, ideals and concepts which are protected by national legislation, may be excluded from the application of these articles to such an extent as is necessary to protect the orientation of the undertaking.

5. It is understood that where in a State the rights set out in Articles 2 and 3 are exercised in the various establishments of the undertaking, the Party concerned is to be considered as fulfilling the obligations deriving from these provisions.

Article 3

This provision affects neither the powers and obligations of States as regards the adoption of health and safety regulations for workplaces, nor the powers and responsibilities of the bodies in charge of monitoring their application. The terms 'social and socio-cultural services and facilities' are understood as referring to the social and/or cultural facilities for workers provided by some undertakings such as welfare assistance, sports fields, rooms for nursing mothers, libraries, children's holiday camps, etc.

Article 4, paragraph 1

For the purpose of the application of this paragraph, the term 'for as long as possible' refers to the elderly person's physical, psychological and intellectual capacities.

Article 7

It is understood that workers excluded in accordance with paragraph 2 of Article 2 and paragraph 2 of Article 3 are not taken into account in establishing the number of workers concerned.

90. PROTOCOL AMENDING THE EUROPEAN SOCIAL CHARTER, 1991

This Protocol (*ETS* No. 142) was opened for signature by the Member States of the Council of Europe signatories to the Charter on 21 October 1991, and will enter into force once it has been ratified by all Parties to the Charter. It seeks to improve the Charter's control machinery, to clarify the functions of two principal organs (the Committee of Independent Experts and the Governmental Committee), and to strengthen the political role of the Committee of Ministers and the Parliamentary Assembly of the Council of Europe.

TEXT

The member States of the Council of Europe, signatory to this Protocol to the European Social Charter, opened for signature in Turin on 18 October 1961 (hereinafter referred to as 'the Charter'),

Being resolved to take some measures to improve the effectiveness of the Charter, and particularly the functioning of its supervisory machinery;

Considering therefore that it is desirable to amend certain provisions of the Charter,

Have agreed as follows:

Article 1

Article 23 of the Charter shall read as follows:

'*Article 23—Communication of copies of reports and comments*

1. When sending to the Secretary General a report pursuant to Articles 21 and 22, each Contracting Party shall forward a copy of that report to such of its national organizations as are members of the international organizations of employers and trade unions invited, under Article 27, paragraph 2, to be represented at meetings of the Governmental Committee. Those organizations shall send to the Secretary General any comments on the reports of the Contracting Parties. The Secretary General shall send a copy of those comments to the Contracting Parties concerned, who might wish to respond.

2. The Secretary General shall forward a copy of the reports of the Contracting Parties to the international non-governmental organizations which have consultative status with the Council of Europe and have particular competence in the matters governed by the present Charter.

3. The reports and comments referred to in Articles 21 and 22 and in the present article shall be made available to the public on request.'

Article 2

Article 24 of the Charter shall read as follows:

'*Article 24—Examination of the reports*

1. The reports sent to the Secretary General in accordance with Articles 21 and 22 shall be examined by a Committee of Independent Experts constituted pursuant to Article 25. The committee shall also have before it any comments forwarded to the

Secretary General in accordance with paragraph 1 of Article 23. On completion of its examination, the Committee of Independent Experts shall draw up a report containing its conclusions.

2. With regard to the reports referred to in Article 21, the Committee of Independent Experts shall assess from a legal standpoint the compliance of national law and practice with the obligations arising from the Charter for the Contracting Parties concerned.

3. The Committee of Independent Experts may address requests for additional information and clarification directly to Contracting Parties. In this connection the Committee of Independent Experts may also hold, if necessary, a meeting with the representatives of a Contracting Party, either on its own initiative or at the request of the Contracting Party concerned. The organizations referred to in paragraph 1 of Article 23 shall be kept informed.

4. The conclusions of the Committee of Independent Experts shall be made public and communicated by the Secretary General to the Governmental Committee, to the Parliamentary Assembly and to the organizations which are mentioned in paragraph 1 of Article 23 and paragraph 2 of Article 27.'

Article 3

Article 25 of the Charter shall read as follows:

'Article 25—Committee of Independent Experts

1. The Committee of Independent Experts shall consist of at least nine members elected by the Parliamentary Assembly by a majority of votes cast from a list of experts of the highest integrity and of recognised competence in national and international social questions, nominated by the Contracting Parties. The exact number of members shall be determined by the Committee of Ministers.

2. The members of the committee shall be elected for a period of six years. They may stand for re-election once.

3. A member of the Committee of Independent Experts elected to replace a member whose term of office has not expired shall hold office for the remainder of his predecessor's term.

4. The members of the committee shall sit in their individual capacity. Throughout their term of office, they may not perform any function incompatible with the requirements of independence, impartiality and availability inherent in their office.'

Article 4

Article 27 of the Charter shall read as follows:

'Article 27—Governmental Committee

1. The reports of the Contracting Parties, the comments and information communicated in accordance with paragraphs 1 of Article 23 and 3 of Article 24, and the reports of the Committee of Independent Experts shall be submitted to a Governmental Committee.

2. The committee shall be composed of one representative of each of the Contracting Parties. It shall invite no more than two international organizations of employers and no more than two international trade union organizations to send observers in a consultative capacity to its meetings. Moreover, it may consult representatives of international non-governmental organizations which have consultative status with the Council of Europe and have particular competence in the matters governed by the present Charter.

3. The Governmental Committee shall prepare the decisions of the Committee of Ministers. In particular, in the light of the reports of the Committee of Independent Experts and of the Contracting Parties, it shall select, giving reasons for its choice, on the basis of social, economic and other policy considerations the situations which should, in its view, be the subject of recommendations to each Contracting Party concerned, in accordance with Article 28 of the Charter. It shall present to the Committee of Ministers a report which shall be made public.

4. On the basis of its findings on the implementation of the Social Charter in general, the Governmental Committee may submit proposals to the Committee of Ministers aiming at studies to be carried out on social issues and on articles of the Charter which possibly might be updated.'

Article 5

Article 28 of the Charter shall read as follows:

'Article 28—Committee of Ministers

1. The Committee of Ministers shall adopt, by a majority of two-thirds of those voting, with entitlement to voting limited to the Contracting Parties, on the basis of the report of the Governmental Committee, a resolution covering the entire supervision cycle and containing individual recommendations to the Contracting Parties concerned.

2. Having regard to the proposals made by the Governmental Committee pursuant to paragraph 4 of Article 27, the Committee of Ministers shall take such decisions as it deems appropriate.'

Article 6

Article 29 of the Charter shall read as follows:

'Article 29—Parliamentary Assembly

The Secretary General of the Council of Europe shall transmit to the Parliamentary Assembly, with a view to the holding of periodical plenary debates, the reports of the Committee of Independent Experts and of the Governmental Committee, as well as the resolutions of the Committee of Ministers.'

Article 7

1. This Protocol shall be open for signature by member States of the Council of Europe signatories to the Charter, which may express their consent to be bound by:

(a) signature without reservation as to ratification, acceptance or approval; or

(b) signature subject to ratification, acceptance or approval, followed by ratification, acceptance or approval.

2. Instruments of ratification, acceptance or approval shall be deposited with the Secretary General of the Council of Europe.

Article 8

This Protocol shall enter into force on the thirtieth day after the date on which all Contracting Parties to the Charter have expressed their consent to be bound by the Protocol in accordance with the provisions of Article 7.

Article 9

The Secretary General of the Council of Europe shall notify the member States of the Council of:

(a) any signature;

(b) the deposit of any instrument of ratification, acceptance or approval;

(c) the date of entry into force of this Protocol in accordance with Article 8;

(d) any other act, notification or communication relating to this Protocol.

In witness whereof the undersigned, being duly authorized thereto, have signed this Protocol.

Done at Turin, this 21st day of October 1991, in English and French, both texts being equally authentic, in a single copy which shall be deposited in the archives of the Council of Europe. The Secretary General of the Council of Europe shall transmit certified copies to each member State of the Council of Europe.

91. ADDITIONAL PROTOCOL TO THE EUROPEAN SOCIAL CHARTER PROVIDING FOR A SYSTEM OF COLLECTIVE COMPLAINTS, 1995

This Protocol was opened for signature on 9 November 1995 and entered into force on 1 July 1998. It is intended to improve effective enforcement of the Charter, and allows social partners and NGOs to submit collective complaints alleging unsatisfactory performance on the part of a State party, with a view to its examination first by a Committee of Independent Experts—the European Committee of Social Rights—and then by the Committee of Ministers. The Protocol also seeks to increase the interest in the Charter of social partners and of non-governmental organizations. For text, see *ETS* No. 158.

Further reading

CULLEN, J., 'The Collective Complaints System of the European Social Charter: Interpretative Methods of the European Committee of Social Rights', (2009) 9 *Human Rights Law Review* 61.

TEXT

Preamble

The member States of the Council of Europe, signatories to this Protocol to the European Social Charter, opened for signature in Turin on 18 October 1961 (hereinafter referred to as 'the Charter'),

Resolved to take new measures to improve the effective enforcement of the social rights guaranteed by the Charter;

Considering that this aim could be achieved in particular by the establishment of a collective complaints procedure, which, *inter alia*, would strengthen the participation of management and labour and of non-governmental organizations,

Have agreed as follows:

Article 1

The Contracting Parties to this Protocol recognize the right of the following organizations to submit complaints alleging unsatisfactory application of the Charter:

(a) international organizations of employers and trade unions referred to in paragraph 2 of Article 27 of the Charter;

(b) other international non-governmental organizations which have consultative status with the Council of Europe and have been put on a list established for this purpose by the Governmental Committee;

(c) representative national organizations of employers and trade unions within the jurisdiction of the Contracting Party against which they have lodged a complaint.

Article 2

1. Any Contracting State may also, when it expresses its consent to be bound by this Protocol, in accordance with the provisions of Article 13, or at any moment thereafter, declare that it recognizes the right of any other representative national non-governmental organization within its jurisdiction which has particular competence in the matters governed by the Charter, to lodge complaints against it.

2. Such declarations may be made for a specific period.

3. The declarations shall be deposited with the Secretary General of the Council of Europe who shall transmit copies thereof to the Contracting Parties and publish them.

Article 3

The international non-governmental organizations and the national non-governmental organizations referred to in Article 1(b) and Article 2 respectively may submit complaints in accordance with the procedure prescribed by the aforesaid provisions only in respect of those matters regarding which they have been recognized as having particular competence.

Article 4

The complaint shall be lodged in writing, relate to a provision of the Charter accepted by the Contracting Party concerned and indicate in what respect the latter has not ensured the satisfactory application of this provision.

Article 5

Any complaint shall be addressed to the Secretary General who shall acknowledge receipt of it, notify it to the Contracting Party concerned and immediately transmit it to the Committee of Independent Experts.

Article 6

The Committee of Independent Experts may request the Contracting Party concerned and the organization which lodged the complaint to submit written information and observations on the admissibility of the complaint within such time-limit as it shall prescribe.

Article 7

1. If it decides that a complaint is admissible, the Committee of Independent Experts shall notify the Contracting Parties to the Charter through the Secretary General. It shall request the Contracting Party concerned and the organization which lodged the complaint to submit, within such time-limit as it shall prescribe, all relevant written explanations or information, and the other Contracting Parties to this Protocol, the comments they wish to submit, within the same time-limit.

2. If the complaint has been lodged by a national organization of employers or a national trade union or by another national or international non-governmental organization, the Committee of Independent Experts shall notify the international organizations of employers or trade unions referred to in paragraph 2 of Article 27 of the Charter, through the Secretary General, and invite them to submit observations within such time-limit as it shall prescribe.

3. On the basis of the explanations, information or observations submitted under paragraphs 1 and 2 above, the Contracting Party concerned and the organization which

lodged the complaint may submit any additional written information or observations within such time-limit as the Committee of Independent Experts shall prescribe.

4. In the course of the examination of the complaint, the Committee of Independent Experts may organize a hearing with the representatives of the parties.

Article 8

1. The Committee of Independent Experts shall draw up a report in which it shall describe the steps taken by it to examine the complaint and present its conclusions as to whether or not the Contracting Party concerned has ensured the satisfactory application of the provision of the Charter referred to in the complaint.

2. The report shall be transmitted to the Committee of Ministers. It shall also be transmitted to the organization that lodged the complaint and to the Contracting Parties to the Charter, which shall not be at liberty to publish it. It shall be transmitted to the Parliamentary Assembly and made public at the same time as the resolution referred to in Article 9 or no later than four months after it has been transmitted to the Committee of Ministers.

Article 9

1. On the basis of the report of the Committee of Independent Experts, the Committee of Ministers shall adopt a resolution by a majority of those voting. If the Committee of Independent Experts finds that the Charter has not been applied in a satisfactory manner, the Committee of Ministers shall adopt, by a majority of two-thirds of those voting, a recommendation addressed to the Contracting Party concerned. In both cases, entitlement to voting shall be limited to the Contracting Parties to the Charter.

2. At the request of the Contracting Party concerned, the Committee of Ministers may decide, where the report of the Committee of Independent Experts raises new issues, by a two-thirds majority of the Contracting Parties to the Charter, to consult the Governmental Committee.

Article 10

The Contracting Party concerned shall provide information on the measures it has taken to give effect to the Committee of Ministers' recommendation, in the next report which it submits to the Secretary General under Article 21 of the Charter.

Article 11

Articles 1 to 10 of this Protocol shall apply also to the articles of Part II of the first Additional Protocol to the Charter in respect of the States Parties to that Protocol, to the extent that these articles have been accepted.

Article 12

The States Parties to this Protocol consider that the first paragraph of the appendix to the Charter, relating to Part III, reads as follows:

'It is understood that the Charter contains legal obligations of an international character, the application of which is submitted solely to the supervision provided for in Part IV thereof and in the provisions of this Protocol.'

Article 13

1. This Protocol shall be open for signature by member States of the Council of Europe signatories to the Charter, which may express their consent to be bound by:

 (a) signature without reservation as to ratification, acceptance or approval; or

 (b) signature subject to ratification, acceptance or approval, followed by ratification, acceptance or approval.

2. A member State of the Council of Europe may not express its consent to be bound by this Protocol without previously or simultaneously ratifying the Charter.

3. Instruments of ratification, acceptance or approval shall be deposited with the Secretary General of the Council of Europe.

Article 14

1. This Protocol shall enter into force on the first day of the month following the expiration of a period of one month after the date on which five member States of the Council of Europe have expressed their consent to be bound by the Protocol in accordance with the provisions of Article 13.

2. In respect of any member State which subsequently expresses its consent to be bound by it, the Protocol shall enter into force on the first day of the month following the expiration of a period of one month after the date of the deposit of the instrument of ratification, acceptance or approval.

Article 15

1. Any Party may at any time denounce this Protocol by means of a notification addressed to the Secretary General of the Council of Europe.

2. Such denunciation shall become effective on the first day of the month following the expiration of a period of twelve months after the date of receipt of such notification by the Secretary General.

Article 16

The Secretary General of the Council of Europe shall notify all the member States of the Council of:

 (a) any signature;

 (b) the deposit of any instrument of ratification, acceptance or approval;

 (c) the date of entry into force of this Protocol in accordance with Article 14;

 (d) any other act, notification or declaration relating to this Protocol.

In witness whereof the undersigned, being duly authorised thereto, have signed this Protocol.

Done at Strasbourg, this 9th day of November 1995, in English and French, both texts being equally authentic, in a single copy which shall be deposited in the archives of the Council of Europe. The Secretary General of the Council of Europe shall transmit certified copies to each member State of the Council of Europe.

92. EUROPEAN SOCIAL CHARTER
(REVISED), 1996

The revised European Social Charter was opened for signature by the member States of the Council of Europe, in Strasbourg, on 3 May 1996, and it entered into force on 1 July 1999. It co-exists with and runs in parallel to the regime established under the 1961 Charter, which it is intended ultimately to replace. The revised Charter does not provide for denunciation of the earlier one, but if a Contracting State accepts the provisions of the revised Charter, the corresponding provisions of the 1961 Charter and its Protocol cease to apply to that State. In this way, States are not simultaneously bound by undertakings at different levels.

The new Charter takes account of the evolution in the understanding and content of social and economic rights since 1961, contains all the rights guaranteed by the original Charter and the 1988 Protocol, and adds the following new rights: right to protection against poverty and social exclusion; right to housing; right to protection in cases of termination of employment; right to protection against sexual harassment in the workplace and other forms of harassment; rights of workers with family responsibilities to equal opportunities and equal treatment; rights of workers' representatives. It also reinforces the principle of non-discrimination, improves gender equality in all fields within the treaty; provides better protection in matters of maternity and social protection of mothers, better social, legal and economic protection of employed children, and better protection of handicapped people.

Enforcement of the new Charter is submitted to the same system of control as the 1961 Charter, as developed by the 1991 Protocol and by the 1995 Protocol, providing a system of collective complaints. For text, see *ETS* No. 163.

Further reading

BERNARD, L., 'Le droit au logemont dans la Charte Social révisée: à propos de la condamnation de la France par le Comité européen des droits sociaux', *Revue trimestrielle de drois de l'homme*, 2009, 1061.

PETTITI, C., 'La Charte sociale européenne révisée', *Revue trimestrielle de droits de l'homme*, 1997, 3.

TEXT

Preamble

The Governments signatory hereto, being Members of the Council of Europe,

Considering that the aim of the Council of Europe is the achievement of greater unity between its members for the purpose of safeguarding and realising the ideals and principles which are their common heritage and of facilitating their economic and social progress, in particular by the maintenance and further realisation of human rights and fundamental freedoms;

Considering that in the Convention for the Protection of Human Rights and Fundamental Freedoms signed at Rome on 4 November 1950, and the Protocols thereto, the member States of the Council of Europe agreed to secure to their populations the civil and political rights and freedoms therein specified;

Considering that in the European Social Charter opened for signature in Turin on 18 October 1961 and the Protocols thereto, the member States of the Council of Europe agreed to secure to their populations the social rights specified therein in order to improve their standard of living and their social well-being;

Recalling that the Ministerial Conference on Human Rights held in Rome on 5 November 1990 stressed the need, on the one hand, to preserve the indivisible nature of all human rights, be they civil, political, economic, social or cultural and, on the other hand, to give the European Social Charter fresh impetus;

Resolved, as was decided during the Ministerial Conference held in Turin on 21 and 22 October 1991, to update and adapt the substantive contents of the Charter in order to take account in particular of the fundamental social changes which have occurred since the text was adopted;

Recognising the advantage of embodying in a Revised Charter, designed progressively to take the place of the European Social Charter, the rights guaranteed by the Charter as amended, the rights guaranteed by the Additional Protocol of 1988 and to add new rights,

Have agreed as follows:

PART I

The Parties accept as the aim of their policy, to be pursued by all appropriate means both national and international in character, the attainment of conditions in which the following rights and principles may be effectively realised:

(1) Everyone shall have the opportunity to earn his living in an occupation freely entered upon.

(2) All workers have the right to just conditions of work.

(3) All workers have the right to safe and healthy working conditions.

(4) All workers have the right to a fair remuneration sufficient for a decent standard of living for themselves and their families.

(5) All workers and employers have the right to freedom of association in national or international organizations for the protection of their economic and social interests.

(6) All workers and employers have the right to bargain collectively.

(7) Children and young persons have the right to a special protection against the physical and moral hazards to which they are exposed.

(8) Employed women, in case of maternity, have the right to a special protection.

(9) Everyone has the right to appropriate facilities for vocational guidance with a view to helping him choose an occupation suited to his personal aptitude and interests.

(10) Everyone has the right to appropriate facilities for vocational training.

(11) Everyone has the right to benefit from any measures enabling him to enjoy the highest possible standard of health attainable.

(12) All workers and their dependants have the right to social security.

(13) Anyone without adequate resources has the right to social and medical assistance.

(14) Everyone has the right to benefit from social welfare services.

(15) Disabled persons have the right to independence, social integration and participation in the life of the community.

(16) The family as a fundamental unit of society has the right to appropriate social, legal and economic protection to ensure its full development.

(17) Children and young persons have the right to appropriate social, legal and economic protection.

(18) The nationals of any one of the Parties have the right to engage in any gainful occupation in the territory of any one of the others on a footing of equality with the nationals of the latter, subject to restrictions based on cogent economic or social reasons.

(19) Migrant workers who are nationals of a Party and their families have the right to protection and assistance in the territory of any other Party.

(20) All workers have the right to equal opportunities and equal treatment in matters of employment and occupation without discrimination on the grounds of sex.

(21) Workers have the right to be informed and to be consulted within the undertaking.

(22) Workers have the right to take part in the determination and improvement of the working conditions and working environment in the undertaking.

(23) Every elderly person has the right to social protection.

(24) All workers have the right to protection in cases of termination of employment.

(25) All workers have the right to protection of their claims in the event of the insolvency of their employer.

(26) All workers have the right to dignity at work.

(27) All persons with family responsibilities and who are engaged or wish to engage in employment have a right to do so without being subject to discrimination and as far as possible without conflict between their employment and family responsibilities.

(28) Workers' representatives in undertakings have the right to protection against acts prejudicial to them and should be afforded appropriate facilities to carry out their functions.

(29) All workers have the right to be informed and consulted in collective redundancy procedures.

(30) Everyone has the right to protection against poverty and social exclusion.

(31) Everyone has the right to housing.

PART II

The Parties undertake, as provided for in Part III, to consider themselves bound by the obligations laid down in the following articles and paragraphs.

Article 1—The right to work

With a view to ensuring the effective exercise of the right to work, the Parties undertake:

(1) to accept as one of their primary aims and responsibilities the achievement and maintenance of as high and stable a level of employment as possible, with a view to the attainment of full employment;

(2) to protect effectively the right of the worker to earn his living in an occupation freely entered upon;

(3) to establish or maintain free employment services for all workers;

(4) to provide or promote appropriate vocational guidance, training and rehabilitation.

Article 2—The right to just conditions of work

With a view to ensuring the effective exercise of the right to just conditions of work, the Parties undertake:

(1) to provide for reasonable daily and weekly working hours, the working week to be progressively reduced to the extent that the increase of productivity and other relevant factors permit;

(2) to provide for public holidays with pay;

(3) to provide for a minimum of four weeks' annual holiday with pay;

(4) to eliminate risks in inherently dangerous or unhealthy occupations, and where it has not yet been possible to eliminate or reduce sufficiently these risks, to provide for either a reduction of working hours or additional paid holidays for workers engaged in such occupations;

(5) to ensure a weekly rest period which shall, as far as possible, coincide with the day recognised by tradition or custom in the country or region concerned as a day of rest;

(6) to ensure that workers are informed in written form, as soon as possible, and in any event not later than two months after the date of commencing their employment, of the essential aspects of the contract or employment relationship;

(7) to ensure that workers performing night work benefit from measures which take account of the special nature of the work.

Article 3—The right to safe and healthy working conditions

With a view to ensuring the effective exercise of the right to safe and healthy working conditions, the Parties undertake, in consultation with employers' and workers' organizations:

(1) to formulate, implement and periodically review a coherent national policy on occupational safety, occupational health and the working environment. The primary aim of this policy shall be to improve occupational safety and health and to prevent accidents and injury to health arising out of, linked with or occurring in the course of work, particularly by minimising the causes of hazards inherent in the working environment;

(2) to issue safety and health regulations;

(3) to provide for the enforcement of such regulations by measures of supervision;

(4) to promote the progressive development of occupational health services for all workers with essentially preventive and advisory functions.

Article 4—The right to a fair remuneration

With a view to ensuring the effective exercise of the right to a fair remuneration, the Parties undertake:

(1) to recognize the right of workers to a remuneration such as will give them and their families a decent standard of living;

(2) to recognize the right of workers to an increased rate of remuneration for overtime work, subject to exceptions in particular cases;

(3) to recognize the right of men and women workers to equal pay for work of equal value;

(4) to recognize the right of all workers to a reasonable period of notice for termination of employment;

(5) to permit deductions from wages only under conditions and to the extent prescribed by national laws or regulations or fixed by collective agreements or arbitration awards.

The exercise of these rights shall be achieved by freely concluded collective agreements, by statutory wage-fixing machinery, or by other means appropriate to national conditions.

Article 5—The right to organize

With a view to ensuring or promoting the freedom of workers and employers to form local, national or international organizations for the protection of their economic and social interests and to join those organizations, the Parties undertake that national law shall not be such as to impair, nor shall it be so applied as to impair, this freedom. The extent to which the guarantees provided for in this article shall apply to the police shall be determined by national laws or regulations. The principle governing the application to the members of the armed forces of these guarantees and the extent to which they shall apply to persons in this category shall equally be determined by national laws or regulations.

Article 6—The right to bargain collectively

With a view to ensuring the effective exercise of the right to bargain collectively, the Parties undertake:

(1) to promote joint consultation between workers and employers;

(2) to promote, where necessary and appropriate, machinery for voluntary negotiations between employers or employers' organizations and workers' organizations, with a view to the regulation of terms and conditions of employment by means of collective agreements;

(3) to promote the establishment and use of appropriate machinery for conciliation and voluntary arbitration for the settlement of labour disputes;

and recognize:

(4) the right of workers and employers to collective action in cases of conflicts of interest, including the right to strike, subject to obligations that might arise out of collective agreements previously entered into.

Article 7—The right of children and young persons to protection

With a view to ensuring the effective exercise of the right of children and young persons to protection, the Parties undertake:

(1) to provide that the minimum age of admission to employment shall be 15 years, subject to exceptions for children employed in prescribed light work without harm to their health, morals or education;

(2) to provide that the minimum age of admission to employment shall be 18 years with respect to prescribed occupations regarded as dangerous or unhealthy;

(3) to provide that persons who are still subject to compulsory education shall not be employed in such work as would deprive them of the full benefit of their education;

(4) to provide that the working hours of persons under 18 years of age shall be limited in accordance with the needs of their development, and particularly with their need for vocational training;

(5) to recognize the right of young workers and apprentices to a fair wage or other appropriate allowances;

(6) to provide that the time spent by young persons in vocational training during the normal working hours with the consent of the employer shall be treated as forming part of the working day;

(7) to provide that employed persons of under 18 years of age shall be entitled to a minimum of four weeks' annual holiday with pay;

(8) to provide that persons under 18 years of age shall not be employed in night work with the exception of certain occupations provided for by national laws or regulations;

(9) to provide that persons under 18 years of age employed in occupations prescribed by national laws or regulations shall be subject to regular medical control;

(10) to ensure special protection against physical and moral dangers to which children and young persons are exposed, and particularly against those resulting directly or indirectly from their work.

Article 8—The right of employed women to protection of maternity

With a view to ensuring the effective exercise of the right of employed women to the protection of maternity, the Parties undertake:

(1) to provide either by paid leave, by adequate social security benefits or by benefits from public funds for employed women to take leave before and after childbirth up to a total of at least fourteen weeks;

(2) to consider it as unlawful for an employer to give a woman notice of dismissal during the period from the time she notifies her employer that she is pregnant until the end of her maternity leave, or to give her notice of dismissal at such a time that the notice would expire during such a period;

(3) to provide that mothers who are nursing their infants shall be entitled to sufficient time off for this purpose;

(4) to regulate the employment in night work of pregnant women, women who have recently given birth and women nursing their infants;

(5) to prohibit the employment of pregnant women, women who have recently given birth or who are nursing their infants in underground mining and all other work which is unsuitable by reason of its dangerous, unhealthy or arduous nature and to take appropriate measures to protect the employment rights of these women.

Article 9—The right to vocational guidance

With a view to ensuring the effective exercise of the right to vocational guidance, the Parties undertake to provide or promote, as necessary, a service which will assist all persons, including the handicapped, to solve problems related to occupational choice and progress, with due regard to the individual's characteristics and their relation to occupational opportunity: this assistance should be available free of charge, both to young persons, including schoolchildren, and to adults.

Article 10—The right to vocational training

With a view to ensuring the effective exercise of the right to vocational training, the Parties undertake:

(1) to provide or promote, as necessary, the technical and vocational training of all persons, including the handicapped, in consultation with employers' and workers' organizations, and to grant facilities for access to higher technical and university education, based solely on individual aptitude;

(2) to provide or promote a system of apprenticeship and other systematic arrangements for training young boys and girls in their various employments;

(3) to provide or promote, as necessary:

   (a) adequate and readily available training facilities for adult workers;

   (b) special facilities for the retraining of adult workers needed as a result of technological development or new trends in employment;

(4) to provide or promote, as necessary, special measures for the retraining and reintegration of the long-term unemployed;

(5) to encourage the full utilisation of the facilities provided by appropriate measures such as:

   (a) reducing or abolishing any fees or charges;

   (b) granting financial assistance in appropriate cases;

   (c) including in the normal working hours time spent on supplementary training taken by the worker, at the request of his employer, during employment;

   (d) ensuring, through adequate supervision, in consultation with the employers' and workers' organizations, the efficiency of apprenticeship and other training arrangements for young workers, and the adequate protection of young workers generally.

Article 11—The right to protection of health

With a view to ensuring the effective exercise of the right to protection of health, the Parties undertake, either directly or in cooperation with public or private organizations, to take appropriate measures designed *inter alia*:

(1) to remove as far as possible the causes of ill-health;

(2) to provide advisory and educational facilities for the promotion of health and the encouragement of individual responsibility in matters of health;

(3) to prevent as far as possible epidemic, endemic and other diseases, as well as accidents.

Article 12—The right to social security

With a view to ensuring the effective exercise of the right to social security, the Parties undertake:

(1) to establish or maintain a system of social security;

(2) to maintain the social security system at a satisfactory level at least equal to that necessary for the ratification of the European Code of Social Security;

(3) to endeavour to raise progressively the system of social security to a higher level;

(4) to take steps, by the conclusion of appropriate bilateral and multilateral agreements or by other means, and subject to the conditions laid down in such agreements, in order to ensure:

    (a) equal treatment with their own nationals of the nationals of other Parties in respect of social security rights, including the retention of benefits arising out of social security legislation, whatever movements the persons protected may undertake between the territories of the Parties;

    (b) the granting, maintenance and resumption of social security rights by such means as the accumulation of insurance or employment periods completed under the legislation of each of the Parties.

Article 13—The right to social and medical assistance

With a view to ensuring the effective exercise of the right to social and medical assistance, the Parties undertake:

(1) to ensure that any person who is without adequate resources and who is unable to secure such resources either by his own efforts or from other sources, in particular by benefits under a social security scheme, be granted adequate assistance, and, in case of sickness, the care necessitated by his condition;

(2) to ensure that persons receiving such assistance shall not, for that reason, suffer from a diminution of their political or social rights;

(3) to provide that everyone may receive by appropriate public or private services such advice and personal help as may be required to prevent, to remove, or to alleviate personal or family want;

(4) to apply the provisions referred to in paragraphs 1, 2 and 3 of this article on an equal footing with their nationals to nationals of other Parties lawfully within their territories, in accordance with their obligations under the European Convention on Social and Medical Assistance, signed at Paris on 11 December 1953.

Article 14—The right to benefit from social welfare services

With a view to ensuring the effective exercise of the right to benefit from social welfare services, the Parties undertake:

(1) to promote or provide services which, by using methods of social work, would contribute to the welfare and development of both individuals and groups in the community, and to their adjustment to the social environment;

(2) to encourage the participation of individuals and voluntary or other organizations in the establishment and maintenance of such services.

Article 15—The right of persons with disabilities to independence, social integration and participation in the life of the community

With a view to ensuring to persons with disabilities, irrespective of age and the nature and origin of their disabilities, the effective exercise of the right to independence, social integration and participation in the life of the community, the Parties undertake, in particular:

(1) to take the necessary measures to provide persons with disabilities with guidance, education and vocational training in the framework of general schemes wherever possible or, where this is not possible, through specialised bodies, public or private;

(2) to promote their access to employment through all measures tending to encourage employers to hire and keep in employment persons with disabilities in the ordinary working environment and to adjust the working conditions to the needs of the disabled or, where this is not possible by reason of the disability, by arranging for or creating sheltered employment according to the level of disability. In certain cases, such measures may require recourse to specialised placement and support services;

(3) to promote their full social integration and participation in the life of the community in particular through measures, including technical aids, aiming to overcome barriers to communication and mobility and enabling access to transport, housing, cultural activities and leisure.

Article 16—The right of the family to social, legal and economic protection

With a view to ensuring the necessary conditions for the full development of the family, which is a fundamental unit of society, the Parties undertake to promote the economic, legal and social protection of family life by such means as social and family benefits, fiscal arrangements, provision of family housing, benefits for the newly married and other appropriate means.

Article 17—The right of children and young persons to social, legal and economic protection

With a view to ensuring the effective exercise of the right of children and young persons to grow up in an environment which encourages the full development of their personality and of their physical and mental capacities, the Parties undertake, either directly or in co-operation with public and private organizations, to take all appropriate and necessary measures designed:

(1) *(a)* to ensure that children and young persons, taking account of the rights and duties of their parents, have the care, the assistance, the education and the training they need, in particular by providing for the establishment or maintenance of institutions and services sufficient and adequate for this purpose;

    (b) to protect children and young persons against negligence, violence or exploitation;

    (c) to provide protection and special aid from the state for children and young persons temporarily or definitively deprived of their family's support;

(2) to provide to children and young persons a free primary and secondary education as well as to encourage regular attendance at schools.

Article 18—The right to engage in a gainful occupation in the territory of other Parties

With a view to ensuring the effective exercise of the right to engage in a gainful occupation in the territory of any other Party, the Parties undertake:

(1) to apply existing regulations in a spirit of liberality;

(2) to simplify existing formalities and to reduce or abolish chancery dues and other charges payable by foreign workers or their employers;

(3) to liberalise, individually or collectively, regulations governing the employment of foreign workers;

and recognise:

(4) the right of their nationals to leave the country to engage in a gainful occupation in the territories of the other Parties.

Article 19—The right of migrant workers and their families to protection and assistance

With a view to ensuring the effective exercise of the right of migrant workers and their families to protection and assistance in the territory of any other Party, the Parties undertake:

(1) to maintain or to satisfy themselves that there are maintained adequate and free services to assist such workers, particularly in obtaining accurate information, and to take all appropriate steps, so far as national laws and regulations permit, against misleading propaganda relating to emigration and immigration;

(2) to adopt appropriate measures within their own jurisdiction to facilitate the departure, journey and reception of such workers and their families, and to provide, within their own jurisdiction, appropriate services for health, medical attention and good hygienic conditions during the journey;

(3) to promote co-operation, as appropriate, between social services, public and private, in emigration and immigration countries;

(4) to secure for such workers lawfully within their territories, insofar as such matters are regulated by law or regulations or are subject to the control of administrative authorities, treatment not less favourable than that of their own nationals in respect of the following matters:

(a) remuneration and other employment and working conditions;

(b) membership of trade unions and enjoyment of the benefits of collective bargaining;

(c) accommodation;

(5) to secure for such workers lawfully within their territories treatment not less favourable than that of their own nationals with regard to employment taxes, dues or contributions payable in respect of employed persons;

(6) to facilitate as far as possible the reunion of the family of a foreign worker permitted to establish himself in the territory;

(7) to secure for such workers lawfully within their territories treatment not less favourable than that of their own nationals in respect of legal proceedings relating to matters referred to in this article;

(8) to secure that such workers lawfully residing within their territories are not expelled unless they endanger national security or offend against public interest or morality;

(9) to permit, within legal limits, the transfer of such parts of the earnings and savings of such workers as they may desire;

(10) to extend the protection and assistance provided for in this article to self-employed migrants insofar as such measures apply;

(11) to promote and facilitate the teaching of the national language of the receiving state or, if there are several, one of these languages, to migrant workers and members of their families;

(12) to promote and facilitate, as far as practicable, the teaching of the migrant worker's mother tongue to the children of the migrant worker.

Article 20—The right to equal opportunities and equal treatment in matters of employment and occupation without discrimination on the grounds of sex

With a view to ensuring the effective exercise of the right to equal opportunities and equal treatment in matters of employment and occupation without discrimination on the grounds of sex, the Parties undertake to recognize that right and to take appropriate measures to ensure or promote its application in the following fields:

 (a) access to employment, protection against dismissal and occupational reintegration;
 (b) vocational guidance, training, retraining and rehabilitation;
 (c) terms of employment and working conditions, including remuneration;
 (d) career development, including promotion.

Article 21—The right to information and consultation

With a view to ensuring the effective exercise of the right of workers to be informed and consulted within the undertaking, the Parties undertake to adopt or encourage measures enabling workers or their representatives, in accordance with national legislation and practice:

 (a) to be informed regularly or at the appropriate time and in a comprehensible way about the economic and financial situation of the undertaking employing them, on the understanding that the disclosure of certain information which could be prejudicial to the undertaking may be refused or subject to confidentiality; and
 (b) to be consulted in good time on proposed decisions which could substantially affect the interests of workers, particularly on those decisions which could have an important impact on the employment situation in the undertaking.

Article 22—The right to take part in the determination and improvement of the working conditions and working environment

With a view to ensuring the effective exercise of the right of workers to take part in the determination and improvement of the working conditions and working environment in the undertaking, the Parties undertake to adopt or encourage measures enabling workers or their representatives, in accordance with national legislation and practice, to contribute:

 (a) to the determination and the improvement of the working conditions, work organization and working environment;
 (b) to the protection of health and safety within the undertaking;
 (c) to the organization of social and socio-cultural services and facilities within the undertaking;
 (d) to the supervision of the observance of regulations on these matters.

Article 23—The right of elderly persons to social protection

With a view to ensuring the effective exercise of the right of elderly persons to social protection, the Parties undertake to adopt or encourage, either directly or in co-operation with public or private organizations, appropriate measures designed in particular:

— to enable elderly persons to remain full members of society for as long as possible, by means of:

 (a) adequate resources enabling them to lead a decent life and play an active part in public, social and cultural life;
 (b) provision of information about services and facilities available for elderly persons and their opportunities to make use of them;

— to enable elderly persons to choose their life-style freely and to lead independent lives in their familiar surroundings for as long as they wish and are able, by means of:

(a) provision of housing suited to their needs and their state of health or of adequate support for adapting their housing;

(b) the health care and the services necessitated by their state;

— to guarantee elderly persons living in institutions appropriate support, while respecting their privacy, and participation in decisions concerning living conditions in the institution.

Article 24—The right to protection in cases of termination of employment

With a view to ensuring the effective exercise of the right of workers to protection in cases of termination of employment, the Parties undertake to recognize:

(a) the right of all workers not to have their employment terminated without valid reasons for such termination connected with their capacity or conduct or based on the operational requirements of the undertaking, establishment or service;

(b) the right of workers whose employment is terminated without a valid reason to adequate compensation or other appropriate relief.

To this end the Parties undertake to ensure that a worker who considers that his employment has been terminated without a valid reason shall have the right to appeal to an impartial body.

Article 25—The right of workers to the protection of their claims in the event of the insolvency of their employer

With a view to ensuring the effective exercise of the right of workers to the protection of their claims in the event of the insolvency of their employer, the Parties undertake to provide that workers' claims arising from contracts of employment or employment relationships be guaranteed by a guarantee institution or by any other effective form of protection.

Article 26—The right to dignity at work

With a view to ensuring the effective exercise of the right of all workers to protection of their dignity at work, the Parties undertake, in consultation with employers' and workers' organizations:

(1) to promote awareness, information and prevention of sexual harassment in the workplace or in relation to work and to take all appropriate measures to protect workers from such conduct;

(2) to promote awareness, information and prevention of recurrent reprehensible or distinctly negative and offensive actions directed against individual workers in the workplace or in relation to work and to take all appropriate measures to protect workers from such conduct.

Article 27—The right of workers with family responsibilities to equal opportunities and equal treatment

With a view to ensuring the exercise of the right to equality of opportunity and treatment for men and women workers with family responsibilities and between such workers and other workers, the Parties undertake:

(1) to take appropriate measures:

  (a) to enable workers with family responsibilities to enter and remain in employment, as well as to reenter employment after an absence due to those responsibilities, including measures in the field of vocational guidance and training;

  (b) to take account of their needs in terms of conditions of employment and social security;

  (c) to develop or promote services, public or private, in particular child daycare services and other childcare arrangements;

(2) to provide a possibility for either parent to obtain, during a period after maternity leave, parental leave to take care of a child, the duration and conditions of which should be determined by national legislation, collective agreements or practice;

(3) to ensure that family responsibilities shall not, as such, constitute a valid reason for termination of employment.

Article 28—The right of workers' representatives to protection in the undertaking and facilities to be accorded to them

With a view to ensuring the effective exercise of the right of workers' representatives to carry out their functions, the Parties undertake to ensure that in the undertaking:

  (a) they enjoy effective protection against acts prejudicial to them, including dismissal, based on their status or activities as workers' representatives within the undertaking;

  (b) they are afforded such facilities as may be appropriate in order to enable them to carry out their functions promptly and efficiently, account being taken of the industrial relations system of the country and the needs, size and capabilities of the undertaking concerned.

Article 29—The right to information and consultation in collective redundancy procedures

With a view to ensuring the effective exercise of the right of workers to be informed and consulted in situations of collective redundancies, the Parties undertake to ensure that employers shall inform and consult workers' representatives, in good time prior to such collective redundancies, on ways and means of avoiding collective redundancies or limiting their occurrence and mitigating their consequences, for example by recourse to accompanying social measures aimed, in particular, at aid for the redeployment or retraining of the workers concerned.

Article 30—The right to protection against poverty and social exclusion

With a view to ensuring the effective exercise of the right to protection against poverty and social exclusion, the Parties undertake:

  (a) to take measures within the framework of an overall and co-ordinated approach to promote the effective access of persons who live or risk living in a situation of social exclusion or poverty, as well as their families, to, in particular, employment, housing, training, education, culture and social and medical assistance;

  (b) to review these measures with a view to their adaptation if necessary.

Article 31—The right to housing

With a view to ensuring the effective exercise of the right to housing, the Parties undertake to take measures designed:

(1) to promote access to housing of an adequate standard;

(2) to prevent and reduce homelessness with a view to its gradual elimination;

(3) to make the price of housing accessible to those without adequate resources.

PART III

Article A—Undertakings

1. Subject to the provisions of Article B below, each of the Parties undertakes:

   (a) to consider Part I of this Charter as a declaration of the aims which it will pursue by all appropriate means, as stated in the introductory paragraph of that part;

   (b) to consider itself bound by at least six of the following nine articles of Part II of this Charter: Articles 1, 5, 6, 7, 12, 13, 16, 19 and 20;

   (c) to consider itself bound by an additional number of articles or numbered paragraphs of Part II of the Charter which it may select, provided that the total number of articles or numbered paragraphs by which it is bound is not less than sixteen articles or sixty-three numbered paragraphs.

2. The articles or paragraphs selected in accordance with sub-paragraphs (b) and (c) of paragraph 1 of this article shall be notified to the Secretary General of the Council of Europe at the time when the instrument of ratification, acceptance or approval is deposited.

3. Any Party may, at a later date, declare by notification addressed to the Secretary General that it considers itself bound by any articles or any numbered paragraphs of Part II of the Charter which it has not already accepted under the terms of paragraph 1 of this article. Such undertakings subsequently given shall be deemed to be an integral part of the ratification, acceptance or approval and shall have the same effect as from the first day of the month following the expiration of a period of one month after the date of the notification.

4. Each Party shall maintain a system of labour inspection appropriate to national conditions.

Article B—Links with the European Social Charter and the 1988 Additional Protocol

1. No Contracting Party to the European Social Charter or Party to the Additional Protocol of 5 May 1988 may ratify, accept or approve this Charter without considering itself bound by at least the provisions corresponding to the provisions of the European Social Charter and, where appropriate, of the Additional Protocol, to which it was bound.

2. Acceptance of the obligations of any provision of this Charter shall, from the date of entry into force of those obligations for the Party concerned, result in the corresponding provision of the European Social Charter and, where appropriate, of its Additional Protocol of 1988 ceasing to apply to the Party concerned in the event of that Party being bound by the first of those instruments or by both instruments.

PART IV

Article C—Supervision of the implementation of the undertakings contained in this Charter

The implementation of the legal obligations contained in this Charter shall be submitted to the same supervision as the European Social Charter.

Article D—Collective complaints

1. The provisions of the Additional Protocol to the European Social Charter providing for a system of collective complaints shall apply to the undertakings given in this Charter for the States which have ratified the said Protocol.

2. Any State which is not bound by the Additional Protocol to the European Social Charter providing for a system of collective complaints may when depositing its instrument of ratification, acceptance or approval of this Charter or at any time thereafter, declare by notification addressed to the Secretary General of the Council of Europe, that it accepts the supervision of its obligations under this Charter following the procedure provided for in the said Protocol.

PART V

Article E—Non-discrimination

The enjoyment of the rights set forth in this Charter shall be secured without discrimination on any ground such as race, colour, sex, language, religion, political or other opinion, national extraction or social origin, health, association with a national minority, birth or other status.

Article F—Derogations in time of war or public emergency

1. In time of war or other public emergency threatening the life of the nation any Party may take measures derogating from its obligations under this Charter to the extent strictly required by the exigencies of the situation, provided that such measures are not inconsistent with its other obligations under international law.

2. Any Party which has availed itself of this right of derogation shall, within a reasonable lapse of time, keep the Secretary General of the Council of Europe fully informed of the measures taken and of the reasons therefor. It shall likewise inform the Secretary General when such measures have ceased to operate and the provisions of the Charter which it has accepted are again being fully executed.

Article G—Restrictions

1. The rights and principles set forth in Part I when effectively realized, and their effective exercise as provided for in Part II, shall not be subject to any restrictions or limitations not specified in those parts, except such as are prescribed by law and are necessary in a democratic society for the protection of the rights and freedoms of others or for the protection of public interest, national security, public health, or morals.

2. The restrictions permitted under this Charter to the rights and obligations set forth herein shall not be applied for any purpose other than that for which they have been prescribed.

Article H—Relations between the Charter and domestic law or international agreements

The provisions of this Charter shall not prejudice the provisions of domestic law or of any bilateral or multilateral treaties, conventions or agreements which are already in force, or may come into force, under which more favourable treatment would be accorded to the persons protected.

Article I—Implementation of the undertakings given

1. Without prejudice to the methods of implementation foreseen in these articles the relevant provisions of Articles 1 to 31 of Part II of this Charter shall be implemented by:

   (a) laws or regulations;
   (b) agreements between employers or employers' organizations and workers' organizations;
   (c) a combination of those two methods;
   (d) other appropriate means.

2. Compliance with the undertakings deriving from the provisions of paragraphs 1, 2, 3, 4, 5 and 7 of Article 2, paragraphs 4, 6 and 7 of Article 7, paragraphs 1, 2, 3 and 5 of Article 10 and Articles 21 and 22 of Part II of this Charter shall be regarded as effective if the provisions are applied, in accordance with paragraph 1 of this article, to the great majority of the workers concerned.

Article J—Amendments

1. Any amendment to Parts I and II of this Charter with the purpose of extending the rights guaranteed in this Charter as well as any amendment to Parts III to VI, proposed by a Party or by the Governmental Committee, shall be communicated to the Secretary General of the Council of Europe and forwarded by the Secretary General to the Parties to this Charter.

2. Any amendment proposed in accordance with the provisions of the preceding paragraph shall be examined by the Governmental Committee which shall submit the text adopted to the Committee of Ministers for approval after consultation with the Parliamentary Assembly. After its approval by the Committee of Ministers this text shall be forwarded to the Parties for acceptance.

3. Any amendment to Part I and to Part II of this Charter shall enter into force, in respect of those Parties which have accepted it, on the first day of the month following the expiration of a period of one month after the date on which three Parties have informed the Secretary General that they have accepted it.

In respect of any Party which subsequently accepts it, the amendment shall enter into force on the first day of the month following the expiration of a period of one month after the date on which that Party has informed the Secretary General of its acceptance.

4. Any amendment to Parts III to VI of this Charter shall enter into force on the first day of the month following the expiration of a period of one month after the date on which all Parties have informed the Secretary General that they have accepted it.

PART VI

Article K—Signature, ratification and entry into force

1. This Charter shall be open for signature by the member States of the Council of Europe. It shall be subject to ratification, acceptance or approval. Instruments of ratification, acceptance or approval shall be deposited with the Secretary General of the Council of Europe.

2. This Charter shall enter into force on the first day of the month following the expiration of a period of one month after the date on which three member States of the Council of Europe have expressed their consent to be bound by this Charter in accordance with the preceding paragraph.

3. In respect of any member State which subsequently expresses its consent to be bound by this Charter, it shall enter into force on the first day of the month following the expiration of a period of one month after the date of the deposit of the instrument of ratification, acceptance or approval.

Article L—Territorial application

1. This Charter shall apply to the metropolitan territory of each Party. Each signatory may, at the time of signature or of the deposit of its instrument of ratification, acceptance or approval, specify, by declaration addressed to the Secretary General of the Council of Europe, the territory which shall be considered to be its metropolitan territory for this purpose.

2. Any signatory may, at the time of signature or of the deposit of its instrument of ratification, acceptance or approval, or at any time thereafter, declare by notification addressed to the Secretary General of the Council of Europe, that the Charter shall extend in whole or in part to a non-metropolitan territory or territories specified in the said declaration for whose international relations it is responsible or for which it assumes international responsibility. It shall specify in the declaration the articles or paragraphs of Part II of the Charter which it accepts as binding in respect of the territories named in the declaration.

3. The Charter shall extend its application to the territory or territories named in the aforesaid declaration as from the first day of the month following the expiration of a period of one month after the date of receipt of the notification of such declaration by the Secretary General.

4. Any Party may declare at a later date by notification addressed to the Secretary General of the Council of Europe that, in respect of one or more of the territories to which the Charter has been applied in accordance with paragraph 2 of this article, it accepts as binding any articles or any numbered paragraphs which it has not already accepted in respect of that territory or territories. Such undertakings subsequently given shall be deemed to be an integral part of the original declaration in respect of the territory concerned, and shall have the same effect as from the first day of the month following the expiration of a period of one month after the date of receipt of such notification by the Secretary General.

Article M—Denunciation

1. Any Party may denounce this Charter only at the end of a period of five years from the date on which the Charter entered into force for it, or at the end of any subsequent period

of two years, and in either case after giving six months' notice to the Secretary General of the Council of Europe who shall inform the other Parties accordingly.

2. Any Party may, in accordance with the provisions set out in the preceding paragraph, denounce any article or paragraph of Part II of the Charter accepted by it provided that the number of articles or paragraphs by which this Party is bound shall never be less than sixteen in the former case and sixty-three in the latter and that this number of articles or paragraphs shall continue to include the articles selected by the Party among those to which special reference is made in Article A, paragraph 1, sub-paragraph (b).

3. Any Party may denounce the present Charter or any of the articles or paragraphs of Part II of the Charter under the conditions specified in paragraph 1 of this article in respect of any territory to which the said Charter is applicable, by virtue of a declaration made in accordance with paragraph 2 of Article L.

Article N—Appendix

The appendix to this Charter shall form an integral part of it.

Article O—Notifications

The Secretary General of the Council of Europe shall notify the member States of the Council and the Director-General of the International Labour Office of:

(a) any signature;

(b) the deposit of any instrument of ratification, acceptance or approval;

(c) any date of entry into force of this Charter in accordance with Article K;

(d) any declaration made in application of Articles A, paragraphs 2 and 3, D, paragraphs 1 and 2, F, paragraph 2, L, paragraphs 1, 2, 3 and 4;

(e) any amendment in accordance with Article J;

(f) any denunciation in accordance with Article M;

(g) any other act, notification or communication relating to this Charter.

In witness whereof, the undersigned, being duly authorized thereto, have signed this revised Charter.

Done at Strasbourg, this 3rd day of May 1996, in English and French, both texts being equally authentic, in a single copy which shall be deposited in the archives of the Council of Europe. The Secretary General of the Council of Europe shall transmit certified copies to each member State of the Council of Europe and to the Director-General of the International Labour Office.

APPENDIX TO THE REVISED EUROPEAN SOCIAL CHARTER
Scope of the Revised European Social Charter in terms of persons protected

1. Without prejudice to Article 12, paragraph 4, and Article 13, paragraph 4, the persons covered by Articles 1 to 17 and 20 to 31 include foreigners only in so far as they are nationals of other Parties lawfully resident or working regularly within the territory of the

Party concerned, subject to the understanding that these articles are to be interpreted in the light of the provisions of Articles 18 and 19.

This interpretation would not prejudice the extension of similar facilities to other persons by any of the Parties.

2. Each Party will grant to refugees as defined in the Convention relating to the Status of Refugees, signed in Geneva on 28 July 1951 and in the Protocol of 31 January 1967, and lawfully staying in its territory, treatment as favourable as possible, and in any case not less favourable than under the obligations accepted by the Party under the said convention and under any other existing international instruments applicable to those refugees.

3. Each Party will grant to stateless persons as defined in the Convention on the Status of Stateless Persons done in New York on 28 September 1954 and lawfully staying in its territory, treatment as favourable as possible and in any case not less favourable than under the obligations accepted by the Party under the said instrument and under any other existing international instruments applicable to those stateless persons.

PART I, PARAGRAPH 18, AND PART II, ARTICLE 18, PARAGRAPH 1

It is understood that these provisions are not concerned with the question of entry into the territories of the Parties and do not prejudice the provisions of the European Convention on Establishment, signed in Paris on 13 December 1955.

PART II

Article 1, paragraph 2

This provision shall not be interpreted as prohibiting or authorizing any union security clause or practice.

Article 2, paragraph 6

Parties may provide that this provision shall not apply:

- (a) to workers having a contract or employment relationship with a total duration not exceeding one month and/or with a working week not exceeding eight hours;
- (b) where the contract or employment relationship is of a casual and/or specific nature, provided, in these cases, that its non-application is justified by objective considerations.

Article 3, paragraph 4

It is understood that for the purposes of this provision the functions, organization and conditions of operation of these services shall be determined by national laws or regulations, collective agreements or other means appropriate to national conditions.

Article 4, paragraph 4

This provision shall be so understood as not to prohibit immediate dismissal for any serious offence.

Article 4, paragraph 5

It is understood that a Party may give the undertaking required in this paragraph if the great majority of workers are not permitted to suffer deductions from wages either by law or through collective agreements or arbitration awards, the exceptions being those persons not so covered.

Article 6, paragraph 4

It is understood that each Party may, insofar as it is concerned, regulate the exercise of the right to strike by law, provided that any further restriction that this might place on the right can be justified under the terms of Article G.

Article 7, paragraph 2

This provision does not prevent Parties from providing in their legislation that young persons not having reached the minimum age laid down may perform work in so far as it is absolutely necessary for their vocational training where such work is carried out in accordance with conditions prescribed by the competent authority and measures are taken to protect the health and safety of these young persons.

Article 7, paragraph 8

It is understood that a Party may give the undertaking required in this paragraph if it fulfils the spirit of the undertaking by providing by law that the great majority of persons under eighteen years of age shall not be employed in night work.

Article 8, paragraph 2

This provision shall not be interpreted as laying down an absolute prohibition. Exceptions could be made, for instance, in the following cases:

- (a) if an employed woman has been guilty of misconduct which justifies breaking off the employment relationship;
- (b) if the undertaking concerned ceases to operate;
- (c) if the period prescribed in the employment contract has expired.

Article 12, paragraph 4

The words 'and subject to the conditions laid down in such agreements' in the introduction to this paragraph are taken to imply *inter alia* that with regard to benefits which are available independently of any insurance contribution, a Party may require the completion of a prescribed period of residence before granting such benefits to nationals of other Parties.

Article 13, paragraph 4

Governments not Parties to the European Convention on Social and Medical Assistance may ratify the Charter in respect of this paragraph provided that they grant to nationals of other Parties a treatment which is in conformity with the provisions of the said convention.

Article 16

It is understood that the protection afforded in this provision covers single-parent families.

Article 17

It is understood that this provision covers all persons below the age of 18 years, unless under the law applicable to the child majority is attained earlier, without prejudice to the other specific provisions provided by the Charter, particularly Article 7.

This does not imply an obligation to provide compulsory education up to the above-mentioned age.

Article 19, paragraph 6

For the purpose of applying this provision, the term 'family of a foreign worker' is understood to mean at least the worker's spouse and unmarried children, as long as the latter are considered to be minors by the receiving State and are dependent on the migrant worker.

Article 20

1. It is understood that social security matters, as well as other provisions relating to unemployment benefit, old age benefit and survivor's benefit, may be excluded from the scope of this article.

2. Provisions concerning the protection of women, particularly as regards pregnancy, confinement and the post-natal period, shall not be deemed to be discrimination as referred to in this article.

3. This article shall not prevent the adoption of specific measures aimed at removing *de facto* inequalities.

4. Occupational activities which, by reason of their nature or the context in which they are carried out, can be entrusted only to persons of a particular sex may be excluded from the scope of this article or some of its provisions. This provision is not to be interpreted as requiring the Parties to embody in laws or regulations a list of occupations which, by reason of their nature or the context in which they are carried out, may be reserved to persons of a particular sex.

Articles 21 and 22

1. For the purpose of the application of these articles, the term 'workers' representatives' means persons who are recognized as such under national legislation or practice.

2. The terms 'national legislation and practice' embrace as the case may be, in addition to laws and regulations, collective agreements, other agreements between employers and workers' representatives, customs as well as relevant case law.

3. For the purpose of the application of these articles, the term 'undertaking' is understood as referring to a set of tangible and intangible components, with or without legal personality, formed to produce goods or provide services for financial gain and with power to determine its own market policy.

4. It is understood that religious communities and their institutions may be excluded from the application of these articles, even if these institutions are 'undertakings' within the meaning of paragraph 3. Establishments pursuing activities which are inspired by certain ideals or guided by certain moral concepts, ideals and concepts which are protected by national legislation, may be excluded from the application of these articles to such an extent as is necessary to protect the orientation of the undertaking.

5. It is understood that where in a state the rights set out in these articles are exercised in the various establishments of the undertaking, the Party concerned is to be considered as fulfilling the obligations deriving from these provisions.

6. The Parties may exclude from the field of application of these articles, those undertakings employing less than a certain number of workers, to be determined by national legislation or practice.

Article 22

1. This provision affects neither the powers and obligations of States as regards the adoption of health and safety regulations for workplaces, nor the powers and responsibilities of the bodies in charge of monitoring their application.

2. The terms 'social and socio-cultural services and facilities' are understood as referring to the social and/or cultural facilities for workers provided by some undertakings such as welfare assistance, sports fields, rooms for nursing mothers, libraries, children's holiday camps, etc.

Article 23, paragraph 1

For the purpose of the application of this paragraph, the term 'for as long as possible' refers to the elderly person's physical, psychological and intellectual capacities.

Article 24

1. It is understood that for the purposes of this article the terms 'termination of employment' and 'terminated' mean termination of employment at the initiative of the employer.

2. It is understood that this article covers all workers but that a Party may exclude from some or all of its protection the following categories of employed persons:

   (a) workers engaged under a contract of employment for a specified period of time or a specified task;

   (b) workers undergoing a period of probation or a qualifying period of employment, provided that this is determined in advance and is of a reasonable duration;

   (c) workers engaged on a casual basis for a short period.

3. For the purpose of this article the following, in particular, shall not constitute valid reasons for termination of employment:

   (a) trade union membership or participation in union activities outside working hours, or, with the consent of the employer, within working hours;

   (b) seeking office as, acting or having acted in the capacity of a workers' representative;

   (c) the filing of a complaint or the participation in proceedings against an employer involving alleged violation of laws or regulations or recourse to competent administrative authorities;

   (d) race, colour, sex, marital status, family responsibilities, pregnancy, religion, political opinion, national extraction or social origin;

   (e) maternity or parental leave;

   (f) temporary absence from work due to illness or injury.

4. It is understood that compensation or other appropriate relief in case of termination of employment without valid reasons shall be determined by national laws or regulations, collective agreements or other means appropriate to national conditions.

Article 25

1. It is understood that the competent national authority may, by way of exemption and after consulting organizations of employers and workers, exclude certain categories of workers from the protection provided in this provision by reason of the special nature of their employment relationship.

2. It is understood that the definition of the term 'insolvency' must be determined by national law and practice.

3. The workers' claims covered by this provision shall include at least:

   (a) the workers' claims for wages relating to a prescribed period, which shall not be less than three months under a privilege system and eight weeks under a guarantee system, prior to the insolvency or to the termination of employment;

   (b) the workers' claims for holiday pay due as a result of work performed during the year in which the insolvency or the termination of employment occurred;

   (c) the workers' claims for amounts due in respect of other types of paid absence relating to a prescribed period, which shall not be less than three months under a privilege system and eight weeks under a guarantee system, prior to the insolvency or the termination of the employment.

4. National laws or regulations may limit the protection of workers' claims to a prescribed amount, which shall be of a socially acceptable level.

Article 26

It is understood that this article does not require that legislation be enacted by the Parties. It is understood that paragraph 2 does not cover sexual harassment.

Article 27

It is understood that this article applies to men and women workers with family responsibilities in relation to their dependent children as well as in relation to other members of their immediate family who clearly need their care or support where such responsibilities restrict their possibilities of preparing for, entering, participating in or advancing in economic activity. The terms 'dependent children' and 'other members of their immediate family who clearly need their care and support' mean persons defined as such by the national legislation of the Party concerned.

Articles 28 and 29

For the purpose of the application of this article, the term 'workers' representatives' means persons who are recognized as such under national legislation or practice.

PART III

It is understood that the Charter contains legal obligations of an international character, the application of which is submitted solely to the supervision provided for in Part IV thereof.

Article A, paragraph 1

It is understood that the numbered paragraphs may include articles consisting of only one paragraph.

Article B, paragraph 2

For the purpose of paragraph 2 of Article B, the provisions of the revised Charter correspond to the provisions of the Charter with the same article or paragraph number with the exception of:

(a) Article 3, paragraph 2, of the revised Charter which corresponds to Article 3, paragraphs 1 and 3, of the Charter;

(b) Article 3, paragraph 3, of the revised Charter which corresponds to Article 3, paragraphs 2 and 3, of the Charter;

(c) Article 10, paragraph 5, of the revised Charter which corresponds to Article 10, paragraph 4, of the Charter;

(d) Article 17, paragraph 1, of the revised Charter which corresponds to Article 17 of the Charter.

PART V

Article E

A differential treatment based on an objective and reasonable justification shall not be deemed discriminatory.

Article F

The terms 'in time of war or other public emergency' shall be so understood as to cover also the threat of war.

Article I

It is understood that workers excluded in accordance with the appendix to Articles 21 and 22 are not taken into account in establishing the number of workers concerned.

Article J

The term 'amendment' shall be extended so as to cover also the addition of new articles to the Charter.

93. EUROPEAN CONVENTION ON THE LEGAL STATUS OF MIGRANT WORKERS, 1977

This convention (*ETS* No. 93) was opened for signature on 24 November 1977 and entered into force on 1 May 1993. It deals with some of the principal aspects of the legal situation of migrant workers, including recruitment, occupational tests, residence permits, work permits, family reunion, working conditions, transfer of social security benefits, and so forth. It does not deal with migration as such, however, and leaves State rights in the matter of admission and expulsion largely unaffected.

Further reading

BOGUSZ, B., CHOLEWINSKI, R., CYGAN, A. and SZYSZCZAK, E., eds., *Irregular Migration and Human Rights: Theoretical, European and International Perspectives*, Leiden: Martinus Nijhoff, 2004.

CHOLEWINSKI, R., *Migrant Workers in International Human Rights Law: Their Protection in Countries of Employment*, Oxford: Clarendon Press, 1997.

—— 'International labour law and the protection of migrant workers: revitalizing the agenda in the era of globalization', in CRAIG, J. D. R. and LYNK, M., eds, *Globalization and the Future of Labour Law*, Cambridge: Cambridge University Press, 2006, 409.

MAGLIVERAS, K. D., 'Protecting the Rights of Migrant Workers in the Euro-Mediterranean Partnership', (2004) 9 *Mediterranean Politics* 459.

TEXT

The member States of the Council of Europe, signatory hereto,

Considering that the aim of the Council of Europe is to achieve a greater unity between its members for the purpose of safeguarding and realizing the ideals and principles which are their common heritage and facilitating their economic and social progress while respecting human rights and fundamental freedoms;

Considering that the legal status of migrant workers who are nationals of Council of Europe member States should be regulated so as to ensure that as far as possible they are treated no less favourably than workers who are nationals of the receiving State in all aspects of living and working conditions;

Being resolved to facilitate the social advancement of migrant workers and members of their families;

Affirming that the rights and privileges which they grant to each other's nationals are conceded by virtue of the close association uniting the member States of the Council of Europe by means of its Statute,

Have agreed as follows:

CHAPTER I

Article 1—Definition

1. For the purpose of this Convention, the term 'migrant worker' shall mean a national of a Contracting Party who has been authorized by another Contracting Party to reside in its territory in order to take up paid employment.

2. This Convention shall not apply to:

   (a) frontier workers;

   (b) artists, other entertainers and sportsmen engaged for a short period and members of a liberal profession;

   (c) seamen;

   (d) persons undergoing training;

   (e) seasonal workers; seasonal migrant workers are those who, being nationals of a Contracting Party, are employed on the territory of another Contracting Party in an activity dependent on the rhythm of the seasons, on the basis of a contract for a specified period or for specified employment;

   (f) workers, who are nationals of a Contracting Party, carrying out specific work in the territory of another Contracting Party on behalf of an undertaking having its registered office outside the territory of that Contracting Party.

CHAPTER II

Article 2—Forms of recruitment

1. The recruitment of prospective migrant workers may be carried out either by named or by unnamed request and in the latter case shall be effected through the intermediary of the official authority in the State of origin if such an authority exists and, where appropriate, through the intermediary of the official authority of the receiving State.

2. The administrative costs of recruitment, introduction and placing, when these operations are carried out by an official authority, shall not be borne by the prospective migrant worker.

Article 3—Medical examinations and vocational test

1. Recruitment of prospective migrant workers may be preceded by a medical examination and a vocational test.

2. The medical examination and the vocational test are intended to establish whether the prospective migrant worker is physically and mentally fit and technically qualified for the job offered to him and to make certain that his state of health does not endanger public health.

3. Arrangements for the reimbursement of expenses connected with medical examination and vocational test shall be laid down when appropriate by bilateral agreements, so as to ensure that such expenses do not fall upon the prospective migrant worker.

4. A migrant worker to whom an individual offer of employment is made shall not be required, otherwise than on grounds of fraud, to undergo a vocational test except at the employer's request.

Article 4—Right of exit—Right to admission—Administrative formalities

1. Each Contracting Party shall guarantee the following rights to migrant workers:

— the right to leave the territory of the Contracting Party of which they are nationals;

— the right to admission to the territory of a Contracting Party in order to take up paid employment after being authorised to do so and obtaining the necessary papers.

2. These rights shall be subject to such limitations as are prescribed by legislation and are necessary for the protection of national security, public order, public health or morals.

3. The papers required of the migrant worker for emigration and immigration shall be issued as expeditiously as possible free of charge or on payment of an amount not exceeding their administrative cost.

Article 5—Formalities and procedure relating to the work contract

Every migrant worker accepted for employment shall be provided prior to departure for the receiving State with a contract of employment or a definite offer of employment, either of which may be drawn up in one or more of the languages in use in the State of origin and in one or more of the languages in use in the receiving State. The use of at least one language of the State of origin and one language of the receiving State shall be compulsory in the case of recruitment by an official authority or an officially recognised employment bureau.

Article 6—Information

1. The Contracting Parties shall exchange and provide for prospective migrants appropriate information on their residence, conditions of and opportunities for family reunion, the nature of the job, the possibility of a new work contract being concluded after the first has lapsed, the qualifications required, working and living conditions (including the cost of living), remuneration, social security, housing, food, the transfer of savings, travel, and on deductions made from wages in respect of contributions for social protection and social security, taxes and other charges. Information may also be provided on the cultural and religious conditions in the receiving State.

2. In the case of recruitment through an official authority of the receiving State, such information shall be provided, before his departure, in a language which the prospective migrant worker can understand, to enable him to take a decision in full knowledge of the facts. The translation, where necessary, of such information into a language that the prospective migrant worker can understand shall be provided as a general rule by the State of origin.

3. Each Contracting Party undertakes to adopt the appropriate steps to prevent misleading propaganda relating to emigration and immigration.

Article 7—Travel

1. Each Contracting Party undertakes to ensure, in the case of official collective recruitment, that the cost of travel to the receiving State shall never be borne by the migrant worker. The arrangements for payment shall be determined under bilateral agreements, which may also extend these measures to families and to workers recruited individually.

2. In the case of migrant workers and their families in transit through the territory of one Contracting Party en route to the receiving State, or on their return journey to the State of origin, all steps shall be taken by the competent authorities of the transit State to expedite their journey and prevent administrative delays and difficulties.

3. Each Contracting Party shall exempt from import duties and taxes at the time of entry into the receiving State and of the final return to the State of origin and in transit:

   (a) the personal effects and movable property of migrant workers and members of their family belonging to their household;

   (b) a reasonable quantity of hand-tools and portable equipment necessary for the occupation to be engaged in.

The exemptions referred to above shall be granted in accordance with the laws or regulations in force in the States concerned.

CHAPTER III

Article 8—Work permit

1. Each Contracting Party which allows a migrant worker to enter its territory to take up paid employment shall issue or renew a work permit for him (unless he is exempt from this requirement), subject to the conditions laid down in its legislation.

2. However, a work permit issued for the first time may not as a rule bind the worker to the same employer or the same locality for a period longer than one year.

3. In case of renewal of the migrant worker's work permit, this should as a general rule be for a period of at least one year, in so far as the current state and development of the employment situation permits.

Article 9—Residence permit

1. Where required by national legislation, each Contracting Party shall issue residence permits to migrant workers who have been authorised to take up paid employment on their territory under conditions laid down in this Convention.

2. The residence permit shall in accordance with the provisions of national legislation be issued and, if necessary, renewed for a period as a general rule at least as long as that of the work permit. When the work permit is valid indefinitely, the residence permit shall as a general rule be issued and, if necessary, renewed for a period of at least one year. It shall be issued and renewed free of charge or for a sum covering administrative costs only.

3. The provisions of this Article shall also apply to members of the migrant worker's family who are authorized to join him in accordance with Article 12 of this Convention.

4. If a migrant worker is no longer in employment, either because he is temporarily incapable of work as a result of illness or accident or because he is involuntarily unemployed, this being duly confirmed by the competent authorities, he shall be allowed for the purpose of the application of Article 25 of this Convention to remain on the territory of the receiving State for a period which should not be less than five months. Nevertheless, no Contracting Party shall be bound, in the case provided for in the above sub-paragraph, to allow a migrant worker to remain for a period exceeding the period of payment of the unemployment allowance.

5. The residence permit, issued in accordance with the provisions of paragraphs 1 to 3 of this Article, may be withdrawn:

    (a) for reasons of national security, public policy or morals;

    (b) if the holder refuses, after having been duly informed of the consequences of such refusal, to comply with the measures prescribed for him by an official medical authority with a view to the protection of public health;

    (c) if a condition essential to its issue or validity is not fulfilled. Each Contracting Party nevertheless undertakes to grant to migrant workers whose residence permits have been withdrawn, an effective right to appeal, in accordance with the procedure for which provision is made in its legislation, to a judicial or administrative authority.

Article 10—Reception

1. After arrival in the receiving State, migrant workers and members of their families shall be given all appropriate information and advice as well as all necessary assistance for their settlement and adaptation.

2. For this purpose, migrant workers and members of their families shall be entitled to help and assistance from the social services of the receiving State or from bodies working in the public interest in the receiving State and to help from the consular authorities of their State or origin. Moreover, migrant workers shall be entitled, on the same basis as national workers, to help and assistance from the employment services. However, each Contracting Party shall endeavour to ensure that special social services are available, whenever the situation so demands, to facilitate or co-ordinate the reception of migrant workers and their families.

3. Each Contracting Party undertakes to ensure that migrant workers and members of their families can worship freely, in accordance with their faith; each Contracting Party shall facilitate such worship, within the limit of available means.

Article 11—Recovery of sums due in respect of maintenance

1. The status of migrant workers must not interfere with the recovery of sums due in respect of maintenance to persons in the State of origin to whom they have maintenance obligations arising from a family relationship, parentage, marriage or affinity, including a maintenance obligation in respect of a child who is not legitimate.

2. Each Contracting Party shall take the steps necessary to ensure the recovery of sums due in respect of such maintenance, making use as far as possible of the form adopted by the Committee of Ministers of the Council of Europe.

3. As far as possible, each Contracting Party shall take steps to appoint a single national or regional authority to receive and despatch applications for sums due in respect of maintenance provided for in paragraph 1 above.

4. This Article shall not affect existing or future bilateral or multilateral agreements.

Article 12—Family reunion

1. The spouse of a migrant worker who is lawfully employed in the territory of a Contracting Party and the unmarried children thereof, as long as they are considered to be minors by the relevant law of the receiving State, who are dependent on the migrant worker, are authorised on conditions analogous to those which this Convention applies to the admission of migrant workers and according to the admission procedure prescribed by such law or by international agreements to join the migrant worker in the territory of a Contracting Party, provided that the latter has available for the family housing considered as normal for national workers in the region where the migrant worker is employed. Each Contracting Party may make the giving of authorisation conditional upon a waiting period which shall not exceed twelve months.

2. Any State may, at any time, by declaration addressed to the Secretary General of the Council of Europe, which shall take effect one month after the date of receipt, make the family reunion referred to in paragraph 1 above further conditional upon the migrant worker having steady resources sufficient to meet the needs of his family.

3. Any State may, at any time, by declaration addressed to the Secretary General of the Council of Europe, which shall take effect one month after the date of its receipt,

derogate temporarily from the obligation to give the authorisation provided for in paragraph 1 above, for one or more parts of its territory which it shall designate in its declaration, on the condition that these measures do not conflict with obligations under other international instruments. The declarations shall state the special reasons justifying the derogation with regard to receiving capacity.

Any State availing itself of this possibility of derogation shall keep the Secretary General of the Council of Europe fully informed of the measures which it has taken and shall ensure that these measures are published as soon as possible. It shall also inform the Secretary General of the Council of Europe when such measures cease to operate and the provisions of the Convention are again being fully executed.

The derogation shall not, as a general rule, affect requests for family reunion submitted to the competent authorities, before the declaration is addressed to the Secretary General, by migrant workers already established in the part of the territory concerned.

Article 13—Housing

1. Each Contracting Party shall accord to migrant workers, with regard to access to housing and rents, treatment not less favourable than that accorded to its own nationals, insofar as this matter is covered by domestic laws and regulations.

2. Each Contracting Party shall ensure that the competent national authorities carry out inspections in appropriate cases in collaboration with the respective consular authorities, acting within their competence, to ensure that standards of fitness of accommodation are kept up for migrant workers as for its own nationals.

3. Each Contracting Party undertakes to protect migrant workers against exploitation in respect of rents, in accordance with its laws and regulations on the matter.

4. Each Contracting Party shall ensure, by the means available to the competent national authorities, that the housing of the migrant worker shall be suitable.

Article 14—Pretraining—Schooling—Linguistic training—Vocational training and retraining

1. Migrant workers and members of their families officially admitted to the territory of a Contracting Party shall be entitled, on the same basis and under the same conditions as national workers, to general education and vocation training and retraining and shall be granted access to higher education according to the general regulations governing admission to respective institutions in the receiving State.

2. To promote access to general and vocational schools and to vocational training centres, the receiving State shall facilitate the teaching of its language or, if there are several, one of its languages to migrant workers and members of their families.

3. For the purpose of the application of paragraphs 1 and 2 above, the granting of scholarships shall be left to the discretion of each Contracting Party which shall make efforts to grant the children of migrant workers living with their families in the receiving State—in accordance with the provisions of Article 12 of this Convention—the same facilities in this respect as the receiving State's nationals.

4. The workers' previous attainments, as well as diplomas and vocational qualifications acquired in the State of origin, shall be recognised by each Contracting Party in accordance with arrangements laid down in bilateral and multilateral agreements.

5. The Contracting Parties concerned, acting in close co-operation shall endeavour to ensure that the vocational training and retraining schemes, within the meaning of this

Article, cater as far as possible for the needs of migrant workers with a view to their return to their State of origin.

Article 15—Teaching of the migrant worker's mother tongue

The Contracting Parties concerned shall take actions by common accord to arrange, so far as practicable, for the migrant worker's children, special courses for the teaching of the migrant worker's mother tongue, to facilitate, *inter alia*, their return to their State of origin.

Article 16—Conditions of work

1. In the matter of conditions of work, migrant workers authorized to take up employment shall enjoy treatment not less favourable than that which applies to national workers by virtue of legislative or administrative provisions, collective labour agreement or custom.

2. It shall not be possible to derogate by individual contract from the principle of equal treatment referred to in the foregoing paragraph.

Article 17—Transfer of savings

1. Each Contracting Party shall permit, according to the agreements laid down by its legislation, the transfer of all or such parts of the earnings and savings of migrant workers as the latter may wish to transfer.

2. This provision shall apply also to the transfer of sums due by migrant workers in respect of maintenance. The transfer of sums due by migrant workers in respect of main-tenance shall on no account be hindered or prevented.

3. Each Contracting Party shall permit, under bilateral agreements or by other means, the transfer of such sums as remain due to migrant workers when they leave the territory of the receiving State.

Article 18—Social Security

1. Each Contracting Party undertakes to grant within its territory, to migrant workers and members of their families, equality of treatment with its own nationals, in the matter of social security, subject to conditions required by national legislation and by bilateral or multilateral agreements already concluded or to be concluded between the Contracting Parties concerned.

2. The Contracting Parties shall moreover endeavour to secure to migrant workers and members of their families the conservation of rights in course of acquisition and acquired rights, as well as provision of benefits abroad, through bilateral and multilateral agreements.

Article 19—Social and Medical Assistance

Each Contracting Party undertakes to grant within its territory, to migrant workers and members of their families who are lawfully present in its territory, social and medi-cal assistance on the same basis as nationals in accordance with the obligations it has assumed by virtue of other international agreements and in particular of the European Convention on Social and Medical Assistance of 1953.

Article 20—Industrial accidents and occupational diseases—Industrial hygiene

1. With regard to the prevention of industrial accidents and occupational diseases and to industrial hygiene, migrant workers shall enjoy the same rights and protection as national

workers, in application of the laws of a Contracting Party and collective agreements and having regard to their particular situation.

2. A migrant worker who is victim of an industrial accident or who has contracted an occupational disease in the territory of the receiving State shall benefit from occupational rehabilitation on the same basis as national workers.

Article 21—Inspection of working conditions

Each Contracting Party shall inspect or provide for inspection of the conditions of work of migrant workers in the same manner as for national workers. Such inspection shall be carried out by the competent bodies or institutions of the receiving State and by any other authority authorised by the receiving State.

Article 22—Death

Each Contracting Party shall take care, within the framework of its laws and, if need be, within the framework of bilateral agreements, that steps are taken to provide all help and assistance necessary for the transport to the State of origin of the bodies of migrant workers deceased as the result of an industrial accident.

Article 23—Taxation on earnings

1. In the matter of earnings and without predjudice to the provisions on double taxation contained in agreements already concluded or which may in future be concluded between Contracting Parties, migrant workers shall not be liable, in the territory of a Contracting Party, to duties, charges, taxes or contributions of any description whatsoever either higher or more burdensome than those imposed on nationals in similar circumstances. In particular, they shall be entitled to deductions or exemptions from taxes or charges and to all allowances, including allowance for dependants.

2. The Contracting Parties shall decide between themselves, by bilateral or multilateral agreements on double taxation, what measures might be taken to avoid double taxation on the earnings of migrant workers.

Article 24—Expiry of contract and discharge

1. On the expiry of a work contract concluded for a special period at the end of the period agreed on and on the case of anticipated cancellation of such a contract or cancellation of a work contract for an unspecified period, migrant workers shall be accorded treatment not less favourable than that accorded to national workers under the provisions of national legislation or collective labour agreements.

2. In the event of individual or collective dismissal, migrant workers shall receive the treatment applicable to national workers under national legislation or collective labour agreements, as regards the form and period of notice, the compensation provided for in legislation or agreements or such as may be due in cases of unwarranted cancellation of their work contracts.

Article 25—Re-employment

1. If a migrant worker loses his job for reasons beyond his control, such as redundancy or prolonged illness, the competent authority of the receiving State shall facilitate his re-employment in accordance with the laws and regulations of that State.

2. To this end the receiving State shall promote the measures necessary to ensure, as far as possible, the vocational retraining and occupational rehabilitation of the migrant worker in question, provided that he intends to continue in employment in the State concerned afterwards.

Article 26—Right of access to the courts and administrative authorities in the receiving State

1. Each Contracting Party shall secure to migrant workers treatment not less favourable than that of its own nationals in respect of legal proceedings. Migrant workers shall be entitled, under the same conditions as nationals, to full legal and judicial protection of their persons property and their right and interests; in particular, they shall have, in the same manner as nationals, the right of access to the competent courts and administrative authorities, in accordance with the law of the receiving State, and the right to obtain the assistance of any person of their choice who is qualified by the law of that State, for instance in disputes with employers, members of their families or third parties. The rules of private international law of the receiving State shall not be affected by this Article.

2. Each Contracting Party shall provide migrant workers with legal assistance on the same conditions as for their own nationals and, in the case of civil or criminal proceedings, the possibility of obtaining the assistance of an interpreter where they cannot understand or speak the language used in court.

Article 27—Use of employment services

Each Contracting Party recognises the right of migrant workers and of the members of their families officially admitted to its territory to make use of employment services under the same conditions as national workers subject to the legal provisions and regulations and administrative practice, including conditions of access, in force in that State.

Article 28—Exercise of the right to organize

Each Contracting Party shall allow to migrant workers the right to organize for the protection of their economic and social interests on the conditions provided for by national legislation for its own nationals.

Article 29—Participation in the affairs of the undertaking

Each Contracting Party shall facilitate as far as possible the participation of migrant workers in the affairs of the undertaking on the same conditions as national workers.

CHAPTER IV

Article 30—Return home

1. Each Contracting Pary shall, as far as possible, take appropriate measures to assist migrant workers and their families on the occasion of their final return to their State of origin, and in particular the steps referred to in paragraphs 2 and 3 of Article 7 of this Convention. The provision of financial assistance shall be left to the discretion of each Contracting Party.

2. To enable migrant workers to know, before they set out on their return journey, the conditions on which they will be able to resettle in their State of origin, this State shall

communicate to the receiving State, which shall keep available for those who request it, information regarding in particular:

— possibilities and conditions of employment in the State of origin;

— financial aid granted for economic reintegration;

— the maintenance of social security rights aquired abroad;

— steps to be taken to facilitate the finding of accommodation;

— equivalence accorded to occupational qualifications obtained abroad and any tests to be passed to secure their official recognition;

— equivalence accorded to educational qualification, so that migrant workers' children can be admitted to schools without down-grading.

CHAPTER V

Article 31—Conservation of acquired rights

No provision of this Convention may be interpreted as justifying less favourable treatment than that enjoyed by migrant workers under the national legislation of the receiving State or under bilateral and multilateral agreements to which that State is a Contracting Party.

Article 32—Relations between this Convention and the laws of the Contracting Parties or international agreements

The provisions of this Convention shall not prejudice the provisions of the laws of the Contracting Parties or of any bilateral or multilateral treaties, conventions, agreements or arrangements, as well as the steps taken to implement them, which are already in force, or may come into force, and under which more favourable treatment has been, or would be, accorded to the persons protected by the Convention.

Article 33—Application of the Convention

1. A Consultative Committee shall be set up within a year of the entry into force of this Convention.

2. Each Contracting Party shall appoint a representative to the Consultative Committee. Any other member State of the Council of Europe may be represented by an observer with the right to speak.

3. The Consultative Committee shall examine any proposals submitted to it by one of the Contracting Parties with a view to facilitating or improving the application of the Convention, as well as any proposal to amend it.

4. The opinions and recommendations of the Consultative Committee shall be adopted by a majority of the members of the Committee; however, proposals to amend the Convention shall be adopted unanimously by the members of the Committee.

5. The opinions, recommendations and proposals of the Consultative Committee referred to above shall be addressed to the Committee of Ministers of the Council of Europe, which shall decide on the action to be taken.

6. The Consultative Committee shall be convened by the Secretary General of the Council of Europe and shall meet, as a general rule, at least once every two years and, in addition, whenever at least two Contracting Parties or the Committee of Ministers so requests. The committee shall also meet at the request of one Contracting Party whenever the provisions of paragraph 3 of Article 12 are applied.

7. The Consultative Committee shall draw up periodically, for the attention of the Committee of Ministers, a report containing information regarding the laws and regulations in force in the territory of the Contracting Parties in respect of matters provided for in this Convention.

CHAPTER VI

Article 34—Signature, ratification and entry into force

1. This Convention shall be open to signature by the member States of the Council of Europe. It shall be subject to ratification, acceptance or approval. Instruments of ratification, acceptance or approval shall be deposited with the Secretary General of the Council of Europe.

2. This Convention shall enter into force on the first day of the third month following the date of the deposit of the fifth instrument of ratification, acceptance or approval.

3. In respect of a signatory State ratifying, approving or accepting subsequently, the Convention shall enter into force on the first day of the third month following the date of the deposit of its instrument of ratification, acceptance or approval.

Article 35—Territorial scope

1. Any State may, at the time of signature or when depositing its instrument of ratification, acceptance or approval or at any later date, by declaration to the Secretary General of the Council of Europe, extend the application of this Convention to all or any of the territories for whose international relations it is responsible or on whose behalf it is authorized to give undertakings.

2. Any declaration made in pursuance of the preceding paragraph may, in respect of any territory mentioned in such declaration, be withdrawn. Such withdrawal shall take effect six months after receipt by the Secretary General of the Council of Europe of the declaration of withdrawal.

Article 36—Reservations

1. Any Contracting Party may, at the time of signature or when depositing its instrument of ratification, acceptance or approval, make one or more reservations which may relate to no more than nine articles of Chapters II to IV inclusive, other than Articles 4, 8, 9, 12, 16, 17, 20, 25, 26.

2. Any Contracting Party may, at any time, wholly or partly withdraw a reservation it has made in accordance with the foregoing paragraph by means of a declaration addressed to the Secretary General of the Council of Europe, which shall become effective as from the date of its receipt.

Article 37—Denunciation of the Convention

1. Each Contracting Party may denounce this Convention by notification addressed to the Secretary General of the Council of Europe, which shall take effect six months after the date of its receipt.

2. No denunciation may be made within five years of the date of the entry into force of the Convention in respect of the Contracting Party concerned.

3. Each Contracting Party which ceases to be a member of the Council of Europe shall cease to be a Party to this Convention six months after the date on which it loses its quality as a member of the Council of Europe.

Article 38—Notifications

The Secretary General of the Council of Europe shall notify the member States of the Council of:

(a) any signature;

(b) the deposit of any instrument of ratification, acceptance or approval;

(c) any notification received in respect of paragraphs 2 and 3 of Article 12;

(d) any date of entry into force of this Convention in accordance with Article 34 thereof;

(e) any declaration received in pursuance of the provisions of Article 35;

(f) any reservation made in pursuance of the provisions of paragraph 1 of Article 36;

(g) withdrawal of any reservation carried out in pursuance of the provisions of paragraph 2 of Article 36;

(h) any notification received in pursuance of the provisions of Article 37 and the date on which denunciation takes place.

In witness whereof, the undersigned, being duly authorized thereto, have signed this Convention.

Done at Strasbourg, this 24th day of November 1977, in English and in French, both texts being equally authoritative, in a single copy which shall remain deposited in the archives of the Council of Europe. The Secretary General of the Council of Europe shall transmit certified copies to each of the signatory States.

94. EUROPEAN CONVENTION FOR THE PREVENTION OF TORTURE AND INHUMAN OR DEGRADING TREATMENT OR PUNISHMENT, 1987

The Convention entered into force on 1 February 1989; for text, see *ETS* No. 126. Two Protocols were adopted in 1993 (*ETS* No. 151 and *ETS* No. 152), the first of which provided that the Committee of Ministers might invite non-member States to accede, and the second made a number of technical amendments. Since their entry into force on 1 March 2002, they are to be regarded as forming an integral part of the Convention itself and the text which follows incorporates the necessary changes.

The Convention originated in the Legal Affairs Committee of the Council of Europe and parallels the Convention against Torture adopted by the UN General Assembly in 1984 (see above, p. 434). However, the regional Convention has a distinctive feature, the constitution of the European Committee for the Prevention of Torture and Inhuman or Degrading Treatment or Punishment. Each party to the Convention is obliged to permit visits by the Committee to any place within its jurisdiction where persons are deprived of their liberty by a public authority (Article 2).[1] In November 2005, for example, a delegation of the Committee carried out a six-day visit to the United Kingdom to examine the treatment and conditions of detention of certain persons detained under the Immigration Act 1971, with a view to deportation. It paid particular attention to the mental health of the individuals concerned (the delegation included two psychiatrists). Visits were paid to various prisons, Broadmoor Special Hospital, and Paddington Green High Security Police Station, and interviews carried out with two persons under house arrest and with others subject to control orders under the Prevention of Terrorism Act 2005. The Government requested publication of the report and its responses (docs. CPT/Inf (2006) 28 and CPT/Inf (2006) 29: **http://www.cpt.coe.int/documents/gbr/2006-28-inf-eng.htm**. Further visits were made in 2007 and 2008: **http://www.cpt.coe.int/en/states/gbr.htm**.

Further reading

EVANS, M. D. and MORGAN, R., *Preventing Torture*, Oxford: Clarendon Press, 1998.
—— 'The European Convention for the Prevention of Torture: Operational Practice', (1992) 41 *ICLQ* 590–614.
LEHALLE, S., LANDREVILLE, P. and CÉRÉ, J.-P., 'Le Comité européen de prévention de la torture: Mécanisme de contrôle des établissements de détention', (2006) *Canadian Journal of Criminology and Justice* 223.

TEXT

The member States of the Council of Europe, signatory hereto,

Having regard to the provisions of the Convention for the Protection of Human Rights and Fundamental Freedoms,

Recalling that, under Article 3 of the same Convention, 'no one shall be subjected to torture or to inhuman or degrading treatment or punishment';

Noting that the machinery provided for in that Convention operates in relation to persons who allege that they are victims of violations of Article 3;

---

[1] As of 14 October 2009, the Committee had made a total of 276 visits (168 periodic visits and 108 ad hoc visits), and published 222 reports.

Convinced that the protection of persons deprived of their liberty against torture and inhuman or degrading treatment or punishment could be strengthened by non-judicial means of a preventive character based on visits,

Have agreed as follows:

CHAPTER I

Article 1

There shall be established a European Committee for the Prevention of Torture and Inhuman or Degrading Treatment or Punishment (hereinafter referred to as the 'Committee'). The Committee shall, by means of visits, examine the treatment of persons deprived of their liberty with a view to strengthening, if necessary, the protection of such persons from torture and from inhuman or degrading treatment or punishment.

Article 2

Each party shall permit visits, in accordance with this Convention, to any place within its jurisdiction where persons are deprived of their liberty by a public authority.

Article 3

In the application of this Convention, the Committee and the competent national authorities of the party concerned shall co-operate with each other.

CHAPTER II

Article 4

1. The Committee shall consist of a number of members equal to that of the Parties.

2. The members of the Committee shall be chosen from among persons of high moral and character, known for their competence in the field of human rights or having professional experiences in the areas covered by this Convention.

3. No two members of the Committee may be nationals of the same State.

4. The members shall serve in their individual capacity, shall be independent and impartial, and shall be available to serve the Committee effectively.

Article 5

1. The members of the Committee shall be elected by the Committee of Ministers of the Council of Europe by an absolute majority of votes, from a list of names drawn up by the Bureau of the Consultative Assembly of the Council of Europe; each national delegation of the Parties in the Consultative Assembly shall put forward three candidates, of whom two at least shall be its nationals.

Where a member is to be elected to the Committee in respect of a non-member State of the Council of Europe, the Bureau of the Consultative Assembly shall invite the Parliament of that State to put forward three candidates, of whom two at least shall be its nationals. The election by the Committee of Ministers shall take place after consultation with the Party concerned.

2. The same procedure shall be followed in filling casual vacancies.

3. The members of the Committee shall be elected for a period of four years. They may be re-elected twice. However, among the members elected at the first election, the terms of three members shall expire at the end of two years. The members whose terms are to expire at the end of the initial period of two years shall be chosen by lot by the Secretary General of the Council of Europe immediately after the first election has been completed.

4. In order to ensure that, as far as possible, one half of the membership of the Committee shall be renewed every two years, the Committee of Ministers may decide, before proceeding to any subsequent election, that the term or terms of office of one or more members to be elected shall be for a period other than four years but not more than six and not less than two years.

5. In cases where more than one term of office is involved and the Committee of Ministers applies the preceding paragraph, the allocation of the terms of office shall be effected by the drawing of lots by the Secretary General, immediately after the election.

Article 6

1. The Committee shall meet in camera. A quorum shall be equal to the majority of its members. The decisions of the Committee shall be taken by a majority of the members present, subject to the provisions of Article 10, paragraph 2.

2. The Committee shall draw up its own rules of procedure.

3. The Secretariat of the Committee shall be provided by the Secretary General of the Council of Europe.

CHAPTER III

Article 7

1. The Committee shall organize visits to places referred to in Article 2. Apart from periodic visits, the Committee may organize such other visits as appear to it to be required in the circumstances.

2. As a general rule, the visits shall be carried out by at least two members of the Committee. The Committee may, if it considers it necessary, be assisted by experts and interpreters.

Article 8

1. The Committee shall notify the Government of the Party concerned of its intention to carry out a visit. After such notification, it may at any time visit any place referred to in Article 2.

2. A Party shall provide the Committee with the following facilities to carry out its task:

   (a) access to its territory and the right to travel without restriction;

   (b) full information on the place where persons deprived of their liberty are being held;

   (c) unlimited access to any place where persons are deprived of their liberty, including the right to move inside such places without restriction;

   (d) other information available to the Party which is necessary for the Committee to carry out its task. In seeking such information, the Committee shall have regard to applicable rules of national law and professional ethics.

3. The Committee may interview in private persons deprived of their liberty.

4. The Committee may communicate freely with any person whom it believes can supply relevant information.

5. If necessary, the Committee may immediately communicate observations to the competent authorities of the Party concerned.

Article 9

1. In exceptional circumstances, the competent authorities of the Party concerned may make representations to the Committee against a visit at the time or to the particular place proposed by the Committee. Such representations may only be made on grounds of national defence, public safety, serious disorder in places where persons are deprived of their liberty, the medical condition of a person or that an urgent interrogation relating to a serious crime is in progress.

2. Following such representations, the Committee and the Party shall immediately enter into consultations in order to clarify the situation and seek agreement on arrangements to enable the Committee to exercise its functions expeditiously. Such arrangements may include the transfer to another place of any person whom the Committee proposed to visit. Until the visit takes place, the Party shall provide information to the Committee about any person concerned.

Article 10

1. After each visit, the Committee shall draw up a report on the facts found during the visit, taking account of any observations which may have been submitted by the Party concerned. It shall transmit to the latter its report containing any recommendations it considers necessary. The Committee may consult with the Party with a view to suggesting, if necessary, improvements in the protection of persons deprived of their liberty.

2. If the Party fails to co-operate or refuses to improve the situation in the light of the Committee's recommendations, the Committee may decide, after the Party has had an opportunity to make known its views, by a majority of two-thirds of its members to make a public statement on the matter.

Article 11

1. The information gathered by the Committee in relation to a visit, its report and its consultations with the Party concerned shall be confidential.

2. The Committee shall publish its report, together with any comments of the Party concerned, whenever requested to do so by that Party.

3. However, no personal data shall be published without the express consent of the person concerned.

Article 12

Subject to the rules of confidentiality in Article 11, the Committee shall every year submit to the Committee of Ministers a general report on its activities which shall be transmitted to the Consultative Assembly and to any non-member State of the Council of Europe which is a party to the Convention, and made public.

Article 13

The members of the Committee, experts and other persons assisting the Committee are required, during and after their terms of office, to maintain the confidentiality of the facts or information of which they have become aware during the discharge of their functions.

Article 14

1. The names of persons assisting the Committee shall be specified in the notification under Article 8, paragraph 1.

2. Experts shall act on the instructions and under the authority of the Committee. They shall have particular knowledge and experience in the areas covered by this Convention and shall be bound by the same duties and independence, impartiality and availability as the members of the Committee.

3. A Party may exceptionally declare that an expert or other person assisting the Committee may not be allowed to take part in a visit to a place within its jurisdiction.

CHAPTER IV

Article 15

Each Party shall inform the Committee of the name and address of the authority competent to receive notifications to its Government, and of any liaison officer it may appoint.

Article 16

The Committee, its members and experts referred to in Article 7, paragraph 2 shall enjoy the privileges and immunities set out in the Annex to this Convention.

Article 17

1. This Convention shall not prejudice the provisions of domestic law or any international agreement which provide greater protection for persons deprived of their liberty.

2. Nothing in this Convention shall be construed as limiting or derogating from the competence of the organs of the European Convention on Human Rights or from the obligations assumed by the Parties under that Convention.

3. The Committee shall not visit places which representatives or delegates of Protecting Powers or the International Committee of the Red Cross effectively visit on a regular basis by virtue of the Geneva Conventions of 12 August 1949 and the Additional Protocols of 8 June 1977 thereto.

CHAPTER V

Article 18

1. The Convention shall be open for signature by the member States of the Council of Europe. It is subject to ratification, acceptance or approval. Instruments of ratification, acceptance or approval shall be deposited with the Secretary General of the Council of Europe.

2. The Committee of Ministers of the Council of Europe may invite any non-member State of the Council of Europe to accede to the Convention.

Article 19

1. This Convention shall enter into force on the first day of the month following the expiration of a period of three months after the date on which seven member States of the Council of Europe have expressed their consent to be bound by the Convention in accordance with the provisions of Article 18.

2. In respect of any State which subsequently expresses its consent to be bound by it, the Convention shall enter into force on the first day of the month following the expiration of a period of three months after the date of the deposit of the instrument of ratification, acceptance, approval or accession.

Article 20

1. Any State may at the time of the signature or when depositing its instrument of ratification, acceptance or approval, specify the territory or territories to which this Convention shall apply.

2. Any State may at any later date, by a declaration addressed to the Secretary General of the Council of Europe, extend the application of this Convention to any other territory specified in the declaration. In respect of such territory the Convention shall enter into force on the first day of the month following the expiration of a period of three months after the date of receipt of such declaration by the Secretary General.

3. Any declaration made under the two preceding paragraphs may, in respect of any territory specified in such declaration, be withdrawn by a notification addressed to the Secretary General. The withdrawal shall become effective on the first day of the month following the expiration of a period of three months after the date of receipt of such notification by the Secretary General.

Article 21

No reservation may be made in respect of the provisions of this Convention.

Article 22

1. Any Party may, at any time, denounce this Convention by means of a notification addressed to the Secretary General of the Council of Europe.

2. Such denunciation shall become effective on the first day of the month following the expiration of a period of twelve months after the date of receipt of the notification by the Secretary General.

Article 23

The Secretary General of the Council of Europe shall notify the member States and any non-member State of the Council of Europe party to the Convention of:

(a) any signature;

(b) the deposit of any instrument of ratification, acceptance, approval or accession;

(c) any date of entry into force of this Convention in accordance with Articles 19 and 20;

(d) any other act, notification or communication relating to this Convention, except for action taken in pursuance of Articles 8 and 10.

In witness whereof, the undersigned, being duly authorized thereto, have signed this Convention.

Done at Strasbourg, the 26 November 1987, in English and French, both texts being equally authentic, in a single copy which shall be deposited in the archives of the Council of Europe. The Secretary General of the Council of Europe shall transmit certified copies to each member State of the Council of Europe.

ANNEX
Privileges and Immunities
(Article 16)

1. For the purpose of this annex, references to members of the Committee shall be deemed to include references to experts mentioned in Article 7, paragraph 2.

2. The members of the Committee shall, while exercising their functions and during journeys made in the exercise of their functions, enjoy the following privileges and immunities:

   (a) immunity from personal arrest or detention and from seizure of their personal baggage and, in respect of words spoken or written and all acts done by them in their official capacity, immunity from legal process of every kind;

   (b) exemption from any restrictions on their freedom of movement on exit from and return to their country of residence, and entry into and exit from the country in which they exercise their functions, and from alien registration in the country which they are visiting or through which they are passing in the exercise of their functions.

3. In the course of journeys undertaken in the exercise of their functions, the members of the Committee shall, in the matter of customs and exchange control, be accorded:

   (a) by their own Government, the same facilities as those accorded to senior officials travelling abroad on temporary official duty;

   (b) by the Government of other Parties, the same facilities as those accorded to representatives of foreign Governments on temporary official duty.

4. Documents and papers of the Committee, in so far as they relate to the business of the Committee, shall be inviolable.

   The official correspondence and other official communications of the Committee may not be held up or subjected to censorship.

5. In order to secure for the members of the Committee complete freedom of speech and complete independence in the discharge of their duties, the immunity from legal process in respect of words spoken or written and all acts done by them in discharging their duties shall continue to be accorded, notwithstanding that the persons concerned are no longer engaged in the discharge of such duties.

6. Privileges and immunities are accorded to the members of the Committee, not for the personal benefit of the individuals themselves but in order to safeguard the independent exercise of their functions. The Committee alone shall be competent to waive the immunity of its members; it has not only the right, but is under a duty, to waive the immunity of one of its members in any case where, in its opinion, the immunity would impede the course of justice, and where it can be waived without prejudice to the purpose for which the immunity is accorded.

95. EUROPEAN CONVENTION ON THE PARTICIPATION OF FOREIGNERS IN PUBLIC LIFE AT LOCAL LEVEL, 1992

ETS No. 144. This Convention was opened for signature on 5 February 1992 and entered into force on 1 May 1997. As its title implies, its purpose is to improve the integration of lawfully resident foreign nationals into the life of the community. The Parties undertake to guarantee to foreign residents, on the same terms as to its own nationals, the traditional political rights, such as freedom of expression, assembly and association, including the right to form trade unions, and also agree to make efforts to involve foreign residents in consultations on local matters. The Convention provides that the Parties may undertake to grant to every foreign resident the right to vote in local elections, after five years of lawful and habitual residence in the host country, and to stand for election.

Further reading

COUNCIL OF EUROPE, *The Participation of Foreign Residents in Public Life at Local Level: Consultative Bodies*, Strasbourg: Council of Europe, 2003.

TEXT

Preamble

The member States of the Council of Europe, signatory hereto,

Considering that the aim of the Council of Europe is to achieve a greater unity between its members for the purpose of safeguarding and realising the ideals and principles which are their common heritage and facilitating their economic and social progress while respecting human rights and fundamental freedoms;

Reaffirming their commitment to the universal and indivisible nature of human rights and fundamental freedoms based on the dignity of all human beings;

Having regard to Articles 10, 11, 16 and 60 of the Convention for the Protection of Human Rights and Fundamental Freedoms;

Considering that the residence of foreigners on the national territory is now a permanent feature of European societies;

Considering that foreign residents generally have the same duties as citizens at local level;

Aware of the active participation of foreign residents in the life of the local community and the development of its prosperity, and convinced of the need to improve their integration into the local community, especially by enhancing the possibilities for them to participate in local public affairs,

Have agreed as follows:

PART I

Article 1

1. Each Party shall apply the provisions of Chapters A, B, and C.

However, any Contracting State may declare, when depositing its instrument of ratification, acceptance, approval or accession, that it reserves the right not to apply the provisions of either Chapter B or Chapter C or both.

2. Each Party which has declared that it will apply one or two chapters only may, at any subsequent time, notify the Secretary General that it agrees to apply the provisions of the chapter or chapters which it had not accepted at the moment of depositing its instrument of ratification, acceptance, approval or accession.

Article 2

For the purposes of this Convention, the term 'foreign residents' means persons who are not nationals of the State and who are lawfully resident on its territory.

CHAPTER A—FREEDOMS OF EXPRESSION, ASSEMBLY AND ASSOCIATION

Article 3

Each Party undertakes, subject to the provisions of Article 9, to guarantee to foreign residents, on the same terms as to its own nationals:

   (a) the right to freedom of expression; this right shall include freedom to hold opinions and to receive and impart information and ideas without interference by public authority and regardless of frontiers. This article shall not prevent States from requiring the licensing of broadcasting, television or cinema enterprises;

   (b) the right to freedom of peaceful assembly and to freedom of association with others, including the right to form and to join trade unions for the protection of their interests. In particular, the right to freedom of association shall imply the right of foreign residents to form local associations of their own for purposes of mutual assistance, maintenance and expression of their cultural identity or defence of their interests in relation to matters falling within the province of the local authority, as well as the right to join any association.

Article 4

Each Party shall endeavour to ensure that reasonable efforts are made to involve foreign residents in public inquiries, planning procedures and other processes of consultation on local matters.

CHAPTER B—CONSULTATIVE BODIES TO REPRESENT FOREIGN RESIDENTS AT LOCAL LEVEL

Article 5

1. Each Party undertakes, subject to the provisions of Article 9, paragraph 1:

   (a) to ensure that there are no legal or other obstacles to prevent local authorities in whose area there is a significant number of foreign residents from setting up

consultative bodies or making other appropriate institutional arrangements designed:

   (i)   to form a link between themselves and such residents,
   (ii) to provide a forum for the discussion and formulation of the opinions, wishes and concerns of foreign residents on matters which particularly affect them in relation to local public life, including the activities and responsibilities of the local authority concerned, and
   (iii) to foster their general integration into the life of the community;

   (b) to encourage and facilitate the establishment of such consultative bodies or the making of other appropriate institutional arrangements for the representation of foreign residents by local authorities in whose area there is a significant number of foreign residents.

2. Each Party shall ensure that representatives of foreign residents participating in the consultative bodies or other institutional arrangements referred to in paragraph 1 can be elected by the foreign residents in the local authority area or appointed by individual associations of foreign residents.

CHAPTER C—RIGHT TO VOTE IN LOCAL AUTHORITY ELECTIONS

Article 6

1. Each Party undertakes, subject to the provisions of Article 9, paragraph 1, to grant to every foreign resident the right to vote and to stand for election in local authority elections, provided that he fulfils the same legal requirements as apply to nationals and furthermore has been a lawful and habitual resident in the State concerned for the 5 years preceding the elections.

2. However, a Contracting State may declare, when depositing its instrument of ratification, acceptance, approval or accession, that it intends to confine the application of paragraph 1 to the right to vote only.

Article 7

Each Party may, either unilaterally or by bilateral or multilateral agreement, stipulate that the residence requirements laid down in Article 6 are satisfied by a shorter period of residence.

PART II

Article 8

Each Party shall endeavour to ensure that information is available to foreign residents concerning their rights and obligations in relation to local public life.

Article 9

1. In time of war or other public emergency threatening the life of the nation, the rights accorded to foreign residents under Part I may be subjected to further restrictions to the

extent strictly required by the exigencies of the situation, provided that such restrictions are not inconsistent with the Party's other obligations under international law.

2. As the right recognised by Article 3(a) carries with it duties and responsibilities, it may be subject to such formalities, conditions, restrictions or penalties as are prescribed by law and are necessary in a democratic society, in the interests of national security, territorial integrity or public safety, for the prevention of disorder or crime, for the protection of health or morals, for the protection of the reputation or rights of others, for preventing the disclosure of information received in confidence, or for maintaining the authority and impartiality of the judiciary.

3. The right recognised by Article 3(b) may not be subject to any restrictions other than such as are prescribed by law and are necessary in a democratic society, in the interests of national security or public safety, for the prevention of disorder or crime, for the protection of health or morals or for the protection of the rights and freedoms of others.

4. Any measure taken in accordance with the present article must be notified to the Secretary General of the Council of Europe, who shall inform the other Parties. The same procedure shall apply when such measures are revoked.

5. Nothing in this Convention shall be construed as limiting or derogating from any of the rights which may be guaranteed under the laws of any Party or under any other treaty to which it is a party.

Article 10

Each Party shall inform the Secretary General of the Council of Europe of any legislative provision or other measure adopted by the competent authorities on its territory which relates to its undertakings under the terms of this Convention.

PART III

Article 11

This Convention shall be open for signature by the member States of the Council of Europe. It is subject to ratification, acceptance or approval. Instruments of ratification, acceptance or approval shall be deposited with the Secretary General of the Council of Europe.

Article 12

1. This Convention shall enter into force on the first day of the month following the expiration of a period of three months after the date on which four member States of the Council of Europe have expressed their consent to be bound by the Convention in accordance with the provisions of Article 11.

2. In respect of any member State which subsequently expresses its consent to be bound by it, the Convention shall enter into force on the first day of the month following the expiration of a period of three months after the date of the deposit of the instrument of ratification, acceptance or approval.

Article 13

1. After the entry into force of this Convention, the Committee of Ministers of the Council of Europe may invite any State not a member of the Council of Europe to accede

to this Convention, by a decision taken by the majority provided for in Article 20(d) of the Statute of the Council of Europe and by the unanimous vote of the representatives of the Contracting States entitled to sit on the Committee.

2. In respect of any acceding State, the Convention shall enter into force on the first day of the month following the expiration of a period of three months after the date of deposit of the instrument of accession with the Secretary General of the Council of Europe.

Article 14

Undertakings subsequently given by Parties to the Convention in accordance with Article 1, paragraph 2, shall be deemed to be an integral part of the ratification, acceptance, approval or accession of the Party so notifying, and shall have the same effect as from the first day of the month following the expiration of a period of three months after the date of the receipt of the notification by the Secretary General.

Article 15

The provisions of this Convention shall apply to all the categories of local authorities existing within the territory of each Party. However, each Contracting State may, when depositing its instrument of ratification, acceptance, approval or accession, specify the categories of territorial authorities to which it intends to confine the scope of this Convention or which it intends to exclude from its scope.

Article 16

1. Any State may at the time of signature or when depositing its instrument of ratification, acceptance, approval or accession, specify the territory or territories to which this Convention shall apply.

2. Any State may at any later date, by a declaration addressed to the Secretary General of the Council of Europe, extend the application of this Convention to any other territory specified in the declaration. In respect of such territory, the Convention shall enter into force on the first day of the month following the expiration of a period of three months after the date of receipt of such declaration by the Secretary General.

3. Any declaration made under the two preceding paragraphs may, in respect of any territory specified in such declaration, be withdrawn by a notification addressed to the Secretary General. The withdrawal shall become effective on the first day of the month following the expiration of a period of six months after the date of receipt of such notification by the Secretary General.

Article 17

No reservation may be made in respect of the provisions of this Convention, other than that mentioned in Article 1, paragraph 1.

Article 18

1. Any Party may at any time denounce this Convention by means of a notification addressed to the Secretary General of the Council of Europe.

2. Such denunciation shall become effective on the first day of the month following the expiration of a period of six months after the date of receipt of the notification by the Secretary General.

Article 19

The Secretary General of the Council of Europe shall notify the member States of the Council and any State which has acceded to this Convention of:

(a) any signature;

(b) the deposit of any instrument of ratification, acceptance, approval or accession;

(c) any date of entry into force of this Convention in accordance with Articles 12, 13 and 16;

(d) any notification received in application of the provisions of Article 1, paragraph 2;

(e) any notification received in application of the provisions of Article 9, paragraph 4;

(f) any other act, notification or communication relating to this Convention.

In witness whereof the undersigned, being duly authorised thereto, have signed this Convention.

Done at Strasbourg, this 5th day of February 1992, in English and French, both texts being equally authentic, in a single copy which shall be deposited in the archives of the Council of Europe. The Secretary General of the Council of Europe shall transmit certified copies to each member State of the Council of Europe and to any State invited to accede to this Convention.

96. EUROPEAN CHARTER FOR REGIONAL OR MINORITY LANGUAGES, 1992

The Charter was opened for signature on 5 November 1992 and entered into force on 1 March 1998; for text, see *ETS* No. 148.

The treaty aims to protect and promote the 'historical regional or minority languages' of Europe, setting objectives and principles, but also various specific measures which States party undertake to implement. See also Article 22, EU Charter of Fundamental Rights, below, p. 904; and **http://ec.europa.eu/education/languages/languages-of-europe**. The EU provides financial support for the European Bureau for Lesser Used Languages: **http://www.eblul.org**. See also the 'Database for the European Charter for Regional or Minority Languages' at **http://languagecharter.eokik.hu/**.

Further reading

COUNCIL OF EUROPE, *From Theory to Practice: The European Charter for Regional or Minority Languages: International Conference*, Strasbourg: Council of Europe, 2002.
—— *The European Charter for Regional or Minority Languages and the French Dilemma: Diversity v. Unicity— Which Language(s) for the Republic?*, Strasbourg: Council of Europe, 2004.
MÄÄTTÄ, S., 'The European Charter for Regional or Minority Languages, French Language Laws, and National Identity', (2005) 4 *Language Policy* 167.
MARTÍN ESTÉBANEZ, M.-A., 'Council of Europe Policies concerning the Protection of Linguistic Minorities and the Justiciability of Minority Rights', in GHANEA, N. and XANTHAKI, A., eds., *Minorities, Peoples and Self-Determination: Essays in Honour of Patrick Thornberry*, Leiden: Martinus Nijhoff, 2005, 269.
VIEYTEZ, R. and JAVIER, E., *Working Together: NGOs and Regional or Minority Languages*, Strasbourg: Council of Europe, 2004.

TEXT

Preamble

The member States of the Council of Europe signatory hereto,

Considering that the aim of the Council of Europe is to achieve a greater unity between its members, particularly for the purpose of safeguarding and realising the ideals and principles which are their common heritage;

Considering that the protection of the historical regional or minority languages of Europe, some of which are in danger of eventual extinction, contributes to the maintenance and development of Europe's cultural wealth and traditions;

Considering that the right to use a regional or minority language in private and public life is an inalienable right conforming to the principles embodied in the United Nations International Covenant on Civil and Political Rights, and according to the spirit of the Council of Europe Convention for the Protection of Human Rights and Fundamental Freedoms;

Having regard to the work carried out within the CSCE and in particular to the Helsinki Final Act of 1975 and the document of the Copenhagen Meeting of 1990;

Stressing the value of interculturalism and multilingualism and considering that the protection and encouragement of regional or minority languages should not be to the detriment of the official languages and the need to learn them;

Realising that the protection and promotion of regional or minority languages in the different countries and regions of Europe represent an important contribution to the building of a Europe based on the principles of democracy and cultural diversity within the framework of national sovereignty and territorial integrity;

Taking into consideration the specific conditions and historical traditions in the different regions of the European States,

Have agreed as follows:

PART I—GENERAL PROVISIONS

Article 1—Definitions

For the purposes of this Charter:

(a) 'regional or minority languages' means languages that are:
   (i) traditionally used within a given territory of a State by nationals of that State who form a group numerically smaller than the rest of the State's population; and
   (ii) different from the official language(s) of that State;

   it does not include either dialects of the official language(s) of the State or the languages of migrants;

(b) 'territory in which the regional or minority language is used' means the geographical area in which the said language is the mode of expression of a number of people justifying the adoption of the various protective and promotional measures provided for in this Charter;

(c) 'non-territorial languages' means languages used by nationals of the State which differ from the language or languages used by the rest of the State's population but which, although traditionally used within the territory of the State, cannot be identified with a particular area thereof.

Article 2—Undertakings

1. Each Party undertakes to apply the provisions of Part II to all the regional or minority languages spoken within its territory and which comply with the definition in Article 1.

2. In respect of each language specified at the time of ratification, acceptance or approval, in accordance with Article 3, each Party undertakes to apply a minimum of thirty-five paragraphs or sub-paragraphs chosen from among the provisions of Part III of the Charter, including at least three chosen from each of the Articles 8 and 12 and one from each of the Articles 9, 10, 11 and 13.

Article 3—Practical arrangements

1. Each Contracting State shall specify in its instrument of ratification, acceptance or approval, each regional or minority language, or official language which is less widely used on the whole or part of its territory, to which the paragraphs chosen in accordance with Article 2, paragraph 2, shall apply.

2. Any Party may, at any subsequent time, notify the Secretary General that it accepts the obligations arising out of the provisions of any other paragraph of the Charter not already specified in its instrument of ratification, acceptance or approval, or that it will apply paragraph 1 of the present article to other regional or minority languages, or to other official languages which are less widely used on the whole or part of its territory.

3. The undertakings referred to in the foregoing paragraph shall be deemed to form an integral part of the ratification, acceptance or approval and will have the same effect as from their date of notification.

Article 4—Existing regimes of protection

1. Nothing in this Charter shall be construed as limiting or derogating from any of the rights guaranteed by the European Convention on Human Rights.

2. The provisions of this Charter shall not affect any more favourable provisions concerning the status of regional or minority languages, or the legal regime of persons belonging to minorities which may exist in a Party or are provided for by relevant bilateral or multilateral international agreements.

Article 5—Existing obligations

Nothing in this Charter may be interpreted as implying any right to engage in any activity or perform any action in contravention of the purposes of the Charter of the United Nations or other obligations under international law, including the principle of the sovereignty and territorial integrity of States.

Article 6—Information

The Parties undertake to see to it that the authorities, organizations and persons concerned are informed of the rights and duties established by this Charter.

PART II—OBJECTIVES AND PRINCIPLES PURSUED IN ACCORDANCE WITH ARTICLE 2, PARAGRAPH 1

Article 7—Objectives and principles

1. In respect of regional or minority languages, within the territories in which such languages are used and according to the situation of each language, the Parties shall base their policies, legislation and practice on the following objectives and principles:

   (a) the recognition of the regional or minority languages as an expression of cultural wealth;

   (b) the respect of the geographical area of each regional or minority language in order to ensure that existing or new administrative divisions do not constitute an obstacle to the promotion of the regional or minority language in question;

   (c) the need for resolute action to promote regional or minority languages in order to safeguard them;

   (d) the facilitation and/or encouragement of the use of regional or minority languages, in speech and writing, in public and private life;

   (e) the maintenance and development of links, in the fields covered by this Charter, between groups using a regional or minority language and other groups in the

State employing a language used in identical or similar form, as well as the establishment of cultural relations with other groups in the State using different languages;

(f) the provision of appropriate forms and means for the teaching and study of regional or minority languages at all appropriate stages;

(g) the provision of facilities enabling non-speakers of a regional or minority language living in the area where it is used to learn it if they so desire;

(h) the promotion of study and research on regional or minority languages at universities or equivalent institutions;

(i) the promotion of appropriate types of transnational exchanges, in the fields covered by this Charter, for regional or minority languages used in identical or similar form in two or more States.

2. The Parties undertake to eliminate, if they have not yet done so, any unjustified distinction, exclusion, restriction or preference relating to the use of a regional or minority language and intended to discourage or endanger the maintenance or development of it. The adoption of special measures in favour of regional or minority languages aimed at promoting equality between the users of these languages and the rest of the population or which take due account of their specific conditions is not considered to be an act of discrimination against the users of more widely-used languages.

3. The Parties undertake to promote, by appropriate measures, mutual understanding between all the linguistic groups of the country and in particular the inclusion of respect, understanding and tolerance in relation to regional or minority languages among the objectives of education and training provided within their countries and encouragement of the mass media to pursue the same objective.

4. In determining their policy with regard to regional or minority languages, the Parties shall take into consideration the needs and wishes expressed by the groups which use such languages. They are encouraged to establish bodies, if necessary, for the purpose of advising the authorities on all matters pertaining to regional or minority languages.

5. The Parties undertake to apply, *mutatis mutandis*, the principles listed in paragraphs 1 to 4 above to non-territorial languages. However, as far as these languages are concerned, the nature and scope of the measures to be taken to give effect to this Charter shall be determined in a flexible manner, bearing in mind the needs and wishes, and respecting the traditions and characteristics, of the groups which use the languages concerned.

PART III—MEASURES TO PROMOTE THE USE OF REGIONAL OR MINORITY LANGUAGES IN PUBLIC LIFE IN ACCORDANCE WITH THE UNDERTAKINGS ENTERED INTO UNDER ARTICLE 2, PARAGRAPH 2

Article 8—Education

1. With regard to education, the Parties undertake, within the territory in which such languages are used, according to the situation of each of these languages, and without prejudice to the teaching of the official language(s) of the State:

(a) (i) to make available pre-school education in the relevant regional or minority languages; or

      (ii) to make available a substantial part of pre-school education in the relevant regional or minority languages; or

      (iii) to apply one of the measures provided for under (i) and (ii) above at least to those pupils whose families so request and whose number is considered sufficient; or

      (iv) if the public authorities have no direct competence in the field of pre-school education, to favour and/or encourage the application of the measures referred to under (i) to (iii) above;

  (b) (i) to make available primary education in the relevant regional or minority languages; or

      (ii) to make available a substantial part of primary education in the relevant regional or minority languages; or

      (iii) to provide, within primary education, for the teaching of the relevant regional or minority languages as an integral part of the curriculum; or

      (iv) to apply one of the measures provided for under (i) to (iii) above at least to those pupils whose families so request and whose number is considered sufficient;

  (c) (i) to make available secondary education in the relevant regional or minority languages; or

      (ii) to make available a substantial part of secondary education in the relevant regional or minority languages; or

      (iii) to provide, within secondary education, for the teaching of the relevant regional or minority languages as an integral part of the curriculum; or

      (iv) to apply one of the measures provided for under (i) to (iii) above at least to those pupils who, or where appropriate whose families, so wish in a number considered sufficient;

  (d) (i) to make available technical and vocational education in the relevant regional or minority languages; or

      (ii) to make available a substantial part of technical and vocational education in the relevant regional or minority languages; or

      (iii) to provide, within technical and vocational education, for the teaching of the relevant regional or minority languages as an integral part of the curriculum; or

      (iv) to apply one of the measures provided for under (i) to (iii) above at least to those pupils who, or where appropriate whose families, so wish in a number considered sufficient;

  (e) (i) to make available university and other higher education in regional or minority languages; or

      (ii) to provide facilities for the study of these languages as university and higher education subjects; or

      (iii) if, by reason of the role of the State in relation to higher education institutions, sub-paragraphs (i) and (ii) cannot be applied, to encourage and/or allow the provision of university or other forms of higher education in regional or minority languages or of facilities for the study of these languages as university or higher education subjects;

  (f) (i) to arrange for the provision of adult and continuing education courses which are taught mainly or wholly in the regional or minority languages; or

      (ii) to offer such languages as subjects of adult and continuing education; or

(iii) if the public authorities have no direct competence in the field of adult education, to favour and/or encourage the offering of such languages as subjects of adult and continuing education;

(g) to make arrangements to ensure the teaching of the history and the culture which is reflected by the regional or minority language;

(h) to provide the basic and further training of the teachers required to implement those of paragraphs (a) to (g) accepted by the Party;

(i) to set up a supervisory body or bodies responsible for monitoring the measures taken and progress achieved in establishing or developing the teaching of regional or minority languages and for drawing up periodic reports of their findings, which will be made public.

2. With regard to education and in respect of territories other than those in which the regional or minority languages are traditionally used, the Parties undertake, if the number of users of a regional or minority language justifies it, to allow, encourage or provide teaching in or of the regional or minority language at all the appropriate stages of education.

Article 9—Judicial authorities

1. The Parties undertake, in respect of those judicial districts in which the number of residents using the regional or minority languages justifies the measures specified below, according to the situation of each of these languages and on condition that the use of the facilities afforded by the present paragraph is not considered by the judge to hamper the proper administration of justice:

(a) in criminal proceedings:
  (i) to provide that the courts, at the request of one of the parties, shall conduct the proceedings in the regional or minority languages; and/or
  (ii) to guarantee the accused the right to use his/her regional or minority language; and/or
  (iii) to provide that requests and evidence, whether written or oral, shall not be considered inadmissible solely because they are formulated in a regional or minority language; and/or
  (iv) to produce, on request, documents connected with legal proceedings in the relevant regional or minority language,
  if necessary by the use of interpreters and translations involving no extra expense for the persons concerned;

(b) in civil proceedings:
  (i) to provide that the courts, at the request of one of the parties, shall conduct the proceedings in the regional or minority languages; and/or
  (ii) to allow, whenever a litigant has to appear in person before a court, that he or she may use his or her regional or minority language without thereby incurring additional expense; and/or
  (iii) to allow documents and evidence to be produced in the regional or minority languages,
  if necessary by the use of interpreters and translations;

(c) in proceedings before courts concerning administrative matters:
  (i) to provide that the courts, at the request of one of the parties, shall conduct the proceedings in the regional or minority languages; and/or

(ii) to allow, whenever a litigant has to appear in person before a court, that he or she may use his or her regional or minority language without thereby incurring additional expense; and/or

(iii) to allow documents and evidence to be produced in the regional or minority languages,

if necessary by the use of interpreters and translations;

(d) to take steps to ensure that the application of sub-paragraphs (i) and (iii) of paragraphs (b) and (c) above and any necessary use of interpreters and translations does not involve extra expense for the persons concerned.

2. The Parties undertake:

(a) not to deny the validity of legal documents drawn up within the State solely because they are drafted in a regional or minority language; or

(b) not to deny the validity, as between the parties, of legal documents drawn up within the country solely because they are drafted in a regional or minority language, and to provide that they can be invoked against interested third parties who are not users of these languages on condition that the contents of the document are made known to them by the person(s) who invoke(s) it; or

(c) not to deny the validity, as between the parties, of legal documents drawn up within the country solely because they are drafted in a regional or minority language.

3. The Parties undertake to make available in the regional or minority languages the most important national statutory texts and those relating particularly to users of these languages, unless they are otherwise provided.

Article 10—Administrative authorities and public services

1. Within the administrative districts of the State in which the number of residents who are users of regional or minority languages justifies the measures specified below and according to the situation of each language, the Parties undertake, as far as this is reasonably possible:

(a) (i) to ensure that the administrative authorities use the regional or minority languages; or

(ii) to ensure that such of their officers as are in contact with the public use the regional or minority languages in their relations with persons applying to them in these languages; or

(iii) to ensure that users of regional or minority languages may submit oral or written applications and receive a reply in these languages; or

(iv) to ensure that users of regional or minority languages may submit oral or written applications in these languages; or

(v) to ensure that users of regional or minority languages may validly submit a document in these languages;

(b) to make available widely used administrative texts and forms for the population in the regional or minority languages or in bilingual versions;

(c) to allow the administrative authorities to draft documents in a regional or minority language.

2. In respect of the local and regional authorities on whose territory the number of residents who are users of regional or minority languages is such as to justify the measures specified below, the Parties undertake to allow and/or encourage:

(a) the use of regional or minority languages within the framework of the regional or local authority;

(b) the possibility for users of regional or minority languages to submit oral or written applications in these languages;

(c) the publication by regional authorities of their official documents also in the relevant regional or minority languages;

(d) the publication by local authorities of their official documents also in the relevant regional or minority languages;

(e) the use by regional authorities of regional or minority languages in debates in their assemblies, without excluding, however, the use of the official language(s) of the State;

(f) the use by local authorities of regional or minority languages in debates in their assemblies, without excluding, however, the use of the official language(s) of the State;

(g) the use or adoption, if necessary in conjunction with the name in the official language(s), of traditional and correct forms of place-names in regional or minority languages.

3. With regard to public services provided by the administrative authorities or other persons acting on their behalf, the Parties undertake, within the territory in which regional or minority languages are used, in accordance with the situation of each language and as far as this is reasonably possible:

(a) to ensure that the regional or minority languages are used in the provision of the service; or

(b) to allow users of regional or minority languages to submit a request and receive a reply in these languages; or

(c) to allow users of regional or minority languages to submit a request in these languages.

4. With a view to putting into effect those provisions of paragraphs 1, 2 and 3 accepted by them, the Parties undertake to take one or more of the following measures:

(a) translation or interpretation as may be required;

(b) recruitment and, where necessary, training of the officials and other public service employees required;

(c) compliance as far as possible with requests from public service employees having a knowledge of a regional or minority language to be appointed in the territory in which that language is used.

5. The Parties undertake to allow the use or adoption of family names in the regional or minority languages, at the request of those concerned.

Article 11—Media

1. The Parties undertake, for the users of the regional or minority languages within the territories in which those languages are spoken, according to the situation of each language, to the extent that the public authorities, directly or indirectly, are competent, have power or play a role in this field, and respecting the principle of the independence and autonomy of the media:

(a) to the extent that radio and television carry out a public service mission:

(i)   to ensure the creation of at least one radio station and one television channel in the regional or minority languages; or

    (ii) to encourage and/or facilitate the creation of at least one radio station and one television channel in the regional or minority languages; or

    (iii) to make adequate provision so that broadcasters offer programmes in the regional or minority languages;

  (b) (i) to encourage and/or facilitate the creation of at least one radio station in the regional or minority languages; or

    (ii) to encourage and/or facilitate the broadcasting of radio programmes in the regional or minority languages on a regular basis;

  (c) (i) to encourage and/or facilitate the creation of at least one television channel in the regional or minority languages; or

    (ii) to encourage and/or facilitate the broadcasting of television programmes in the regional or minority languages on a regular basis;

  (d) to encourage and/or facilitate the production and distribution of audio and audio-visual works in the regional or minority languages;

  (e) (i) to encourage and/or facilitate the creation and/or maintenance of at least one newspaper in the regional or minority languages; or

    (ii) to encourage and/or facilitate the publication of newspaper articles in the regional or minority languages on a regular basis;

  (f) (i) to cover the additional costs of those media which use regional or minority languages, wherever the law provides for financial assistance in general for the media; or

    (ii) to apply existing measures for financial assistance also to audiovisual productions in the regional or minority languages;

  (g) to support the training of journalists and other staff for media using regional or minority languages.

2. The Parties undertake to guarantee freedom of direct reception of radio and television broadcasts from neighbouring countries in a language used in identical or similar form to a regional or minority language, and not to oppose the retransmission of radio and television broadcasts from neighbouring countries in such a language. They further undertake to ensure that no restrictions will be placed on the freedom of expression and free circulation of information in the written press in a language used in identical or similar form to a regional or minority language. The exercise of the above-mentioned freedoms, since it carries with it duties and responsibilities, may be subject to such formalities, conditions, restrictions or penalties as are prescribed by law and are necessary in a democratic society, in the interests of national security, territorial integrity or public safety, for the prevention of disorder or crime, for the protection of health or morals, for the protection of the reputation or rights of others, for preventing disclosure of information received in confidence, or for maintaining the authority and impartiality of the judiciary.

3. The Parties undertake to ensure that the interests of the users of regional or minority languages are represented or taken into account within such bodies as may be established in accordance with the law with responsibility for guaranteeing the freedom and pluralism of the media.

Article 12—Cultural activities and facilities

1. With regard to cultural activities and facilities—especially libraries, video libraries, cultural centres, museums, archives, academies, theatres and cinemas, as well as literary work and film production, vernacular forms of cultural expression, festivals and the culture industries, including *inter alia* the use of new technologies—the Parties undertake,

within the territory in which such languages are used and to the extent that the public authorities are competent, have power or play a role in this field:

   (a) to encourage types of expression and initiative specific to regional or minority languages and foster the different means of access to works produced in these languages;

   (b) to foster the different means of access in other languages to works produced in regional or minority languages by aiding and developing translation, dubbing, post-synchronisation and subtitling activities;

   (c) to foster access in regional or minority languages to works produced in other languages by aiding and developing translation, dubbing, post-synchronisation and subtitling activities;

   (d) to ensure that the bodies responsible for organizing or supporting cultural activities of various kinds make appropriate allowance for incorporating the knowledge and use of regional or minority languages and cultures in the undertakings which they initiate or for which they provide backing;

   (e) to promote measures to ensure that the bodies responsible for organizing or supporting cultural activities have at their disposal staff who have a full command of the regional or minority language concerned, as well as of the language(s) of the rest of the population;

   (f) to encourage direct participation by representatives of the users of a given regional or minority language in providing facilities and planning cultural activities;

   (g) to encourage and/or facilitate the creation of a body or bodies responsible for collecting, keeping a copy of and presenting or publishing works produced in the regional or minority languages;

   (h) if necessary, to create and/or promote and finance translation and terminological research services, particularly with a view to maintaining and developing appropriate administrative, commercial, economic, social, technical or legal terminology in each regional or minority language.

2. In respect of territories other than those in which the regional or minority languages are traditionally used, the Parties undertake, if the number of users of a regional or minority language justifies it, to allow, encourage and/or provide appropriate cultural activities and facilities in accordance with the preceding paragraph.

3. The Parties undertake to make appropriate provision, in pursuing their cultural policy abroad, for regional or minority languages and the cultures they reflect.

Article 13—Economic and social life

1. With regard to economic and social activities, the Parties undertake, within the whole country:

   (a) to eliminate from their legislation any provision prohibiting or limiting without justifiable reasons the use of regional or minority languages in documents relating to economic or social life, particularly contracts of employment, and in technical documents such as instructions for the use of products or installations;

   (b) to prohibit the insertion in internal regulations of companies and private documents of any clauses excluding or restricting the use of regional or minority languages, at least between users of the same language;

   (c) to oppose practices designed to discourage the use of regional or minority languages in connection with economic or social activities;

(d) to facilitate and/or encourage the use of regional or minority languages by means other than those specified in the above sub-paragraphs.

2. With regard to economic and social activities, the Parties undertake, in so far as the public authorities are competent, within the territory in which the regional or minority languages are used, and as far as this is reasonably possible:

(a) to include in their financial and banking regulations provisions which allow, by means of procedures compatible with commercial practice, the use of regional or minority languages in drawing up payment orders (cheques, drafts, etc.) or other financial documents, or, where appropriate, to ensure the implementation of such provisions;

(b) in the economic and social sectors directly under their control (public sector), to organize activities to promote the use of regional or minority languages;

(c) to ensure that social care facilities such as hospitals, retirement homes and hostels offer the possibility of receiving and treating in their own language persons using a regional or minority language who are in need of care on grounds of ill-health, old age or for other reasons;

(d) to ensure by appropriate means that safety instructions are also drawn up in regional or minority languages;

(e) to arrange for information provided by the competent public authorities concerning the rights of consumers to be made available in regional or minority languages.

Article 14—Transfrontier exchanges

The Parties undertake:

(a) to apply existing bilateral and multilateral agreements which bind them with the States in which the same language is used in identical or similar form, or if necessary to seek to conclude such agreements, in such a way as to foster contacts between the users of the same language in the States concerned in the fields of culture, education, information, vocational training and permanent education;

(b) for the benefit of regional or minority languages, to facilitate and/or promote co-operation across borders, in particular between regional or local authorities in whose territory the same language is used in identical or similar form.

PART IV—APPLICATION OF THE CHARTER

Article 15—Periodical reports

1. The Parties shall present periodically to the Secretary General of the Council of Europe, in a form to be prescribed by the Committee of Ministers, a report on their policy pursued in accordance with Part II of this Charter and on the measures taken in application of those provisions of Part III which they have accepted. The first report shall be presented within the year following the entry into force of the Charter with respect to the Party concerned, the other reports at three-yearly intervals after the first report.

2. The Parties shall make their reports public.

Article 16—Examination of the reports

1. The reports presented to the Secretary General of the Council of Europe under Article 15 shall be examined by a committee of experts constituted in accordance with Article 17.

2. Bodies or associations legally established in a Party may draw the attention of the committee of experts to matters relating to the undertakings entered into by that Party under Part III of this Charter. After consulting the Party concerned, the committee of experts may take account of this information in the preparation of the report specified in paragraph 3 below. These bodies or associations can furthermore submit statements concerning the policy pursued by a Party in accordance with Part II.

3. On the basis of the reports specified in paragraph 1 and the information mentioned in paragraph 2, the committee of experts shall prepare a report for the Committee of Ministers. This report shall be accompanied by the comments which the Parties have been requested to make and may be made public by the Committee of Ministers.

4. The report specified in paragraph 3 shall contain in particular the proposals of the committee of experts to the Committee of Ministers for the preparation of such recommendations of the latter body to one or more of the Parties as may be required.

5. The Secretary General of the Council of Europe shall make a two-yearly detailed report to the Parliamentary Assembly on the application of the Charter.

Article 17—Committee of experts

1. The committee of experts shall be composed of one member per Party, appointed by the Committee of Ministers from a list of individuals of the highest integrity and recognised competence in the matters dealt with in the Charter, who shall be nominated by the Party concerned.

2. Members of the committee shall be appointed for a period of six years and shall be eligible for reappointment. A member who is unable to complete a term of office shall be replaced in accordance with the procedure laid down in paragraph 1, and the replacing member shall complete his predecessor's term of office.

3. The committee of experts shall adopt rules of procedure. Its secretarial services shall be provided by the Secretary General of the Council of Europe.

PART V—FINAL PROVISIONS

Article 18

This Charter shall be open for signature by the member States of the Council of Europe. It is subject to ratification, acceptance or approval. Instruments of ratification, acceptance or approval shall be deposited with the Secretary General of the Council of Europe.

Article 19

1. This Charter shall enter into force on the first day of the month following the expiration of a period of three months after the date on which five member States of the Council of Europe have expressed their consent to be bound by the Charter in accordance with the provisions of Article 18.

2. In respect of any member State which subsequently expresses its consent to be bound by it, the Charter shall enter into force on the first day of the month following the expiration of a period of three months after the date of the deposit of the instrument of ratification, acceptance or approval.

Article 20

1. After the entry into force of this Charter, the Committee of Ministers of the Council of Europe may invite any State not a member of the Council of Europe to accede to this Charter.

2. In respect of any acceding State, the Charter shall enter into force on the first day of the month following the expiration of a period of three months after the date of deposit of the instrument of accession with the Secretary General of the Council of Europe.

Article 21

1. Any State may, at the time of signature or when depositing its instrument of ratification, acceptance, approval or accession, make one or more reservations to paragraphs 2 to 5 of Article 7 of this Charter. No other reservation may be made.

2. Any Contracting State which has made a reservation under the preceding paragraph may wholly or partly withdraw it by means of a notification addressed to the Secretary General of the Council of Europe. The withdrawal shall take effect on the date of receipt of such notification by the Secretary General.

Article 22

1. Any Party may at any time denounce this Charter by means of a notification addressed to the Secretary General of the Council of Europe.

2. Such denunciation shall become effective on the first day of the month following the expiration of a period of six months after the date of receipt of the notification by the Secretary General.

Article 23

The Secretary General of the Council of Europe shall notify the member States of the Council and any State which has acceded to this Charter of:

(a) any signature;

(b) the deposit of any instrument of ratification, acceptance, approval or accession;

(c) any date of entry into force of this Charter in accordance with Articles 19 and 20;

(d) any notification received in application of the provisions of Article 3, paragraph 2;

(e) any other act, notification or communication relating to this Charter.

In witness whereof the undersigned, being duly authorized thereto, have signed this Charter.

Done at Strasbourg, this 5th day of November 1992, in English and French, both texts being equally authentic, in a single copy which shall be deposited in the archives of the Council of Europe. The Secretary General of the Council of Europe shall transmit certified copies to each member State of the Council of Europe and to any State invited to accede to this Charter.

97. EUROPEAN FRAMEWORK CONVENTION FOR THE PROTECTION OF NATIONAL MINORITIES, 1995

This Convention was opened for signature on 1 February 1995 and entered into force on 1 February 1998; for text, see *ETS* No. 157. It provides for a monitoring system, with the Committee of Ministers being assisted by an advisory committee; see generally, **http://www.coe.int/t/dghl/monitoring/minorities/**.

Further reading

HOFMANN, R., 'Protecting the Rights of National Minorities in Europe. First Experiences with the Council of Europe Framework Convention for the Protection of National Minorities', (2001) 44 *German Yearbook of International Law* 237–69.

THORNBERRY, P. and MARTÍN ESTÉBANEZ, M. A., *Minority Rights in Europe*, Strasbourg: Council of Europe, 2004.

WELLER, M., *Universal Minority Rights: A Commentary on the Jurisprudence of International Courts and Treaty Bodies*, Oxford: Oxford University Press, 2007.

——, ed., *The Rights of Minorities: Commentary on the European Framework Convention on the Protection of National Minorities*, Oxford: Oxford University Press, 2006.

TEXT

The member States of the Council of Europe and the other States, signatories to the present framework Convention,

Considering that the aim of the Council of Europe is to achieve greater unity between its members for the purpose of safeguarding and realizing the ideals and principles which are their common heritage;

Considering that one of the methods by which that aim is to be pursued is the maintenance and further realization of human rights and fundamental freedoms;

Wishing to follow-up the Declaration of the Heads of State and Government of the member States of the Council of Europe adopted in Vienna on 9 October 1993;

Being resolved to protect within their respective territories the existence of national minorities;

Considering that the upheavals of European history have shown that the protection of national minorities is essential to stability, democratic security and peace in this continent;

Considering that a pluralist and genuinely democratic society should not only respect the ethnic, cultural, linguistic and religious identity of each person belonging to a national minority, but also create appropriate conditions enabling them to express, preserve and develop this identity;

Considering that the creation of a climate of tolerance and dialogue is necessary to enable cultural diversity to be a source and a factor, not of division, but of enrichment for each society;

Considering that the realization of a tolerant and prosperous Europe does not depend solely on co-operation between States but also requires transfrontier co-operation between local and regional authorities without prejudice to the constitution and territorial integrity of each State;

Having regard to the Convention for the Protection of Human Rights and Fundamental Freedoms and the Protocols thereto;

Having regard to the commitments concerning the protection of national minorities in United Nations conventions and declarations and in the documents of the Conference on Security and Co-operation in Europe, particularly the Copenhagen Document of 29 June 1990;

Being resolved to define the principles to be respected and the obligations which flow from them, in order to ensure, in the member States and such other States as may become Parties to the present instrument, the effective protection of national minorities and of the rights and freedoms of persons belonging to those minorities, within the rule of law, respecting the territorial integrity and national sovereignty of States;

Being determined to implement the principles set out in this framework Convention through national legislation and appropriate governmental policies,

Have agreed as follows:

SECTION I

Article 1

The protection of national minorities and of the rights and freedoms of persons belonging to those minorities forms an integral part of the international protection of human rights, and as such falls within the scope of international co-operation.

Article 2

The provisions of this framework Convention shall be applied in good faith, in a spirit of understanding and tolerance and in conformity with the principles of good neighbourliness, friendly relations and co-operation between States.

Article 3

1. Every person belonging to a national minority shall have the right freely to choose to be treated or not to be treated as such and no disadvantage shall result from this choice or from the exercise of the rights which are connected to that choice.

2. Persons belonging to national minorities may exercise the rights and enjoy the freedoms flowing from the principles enshrined in the present framework Convention individually as well as in community with others.

SECTION II

Article 4

1. The Parties undertake to guarantee to persons belonging to national minorities the right of equality before the law and of equal protection of the law. In this respect, any discrimination based on belonging to a national minority shall be prohibited.

2. The Parties undertake to adopt, where necessary, adequate measures in order to promote, in all areas of economic, social, political and cultural life, full and effective equality between persons belonging to a national minority and those belonging to the majority. In

this respect, they shall take due account of the specific conditions of the persons belonging to national minorities.

3. The measures adopted in accordance with paragraph 2 shall not be considered to be an act of discrimination.

Article 5

1. The Parties undertake to promote the conditions necessary for persons belonging to national minorities to maintain and develop their culture, and to preserve the essential elements of their identity, namely their religion, language, traditions and cultural heritage.

2. Without prejudice to measures taken in pursuance of their general integration policy, the Parties shall refrain from policies or practices aimed at assimilation of persons belonging to national minorities against their will and shall protect these persons from any action aimed at such assimilation.

Article 6

1. The Parties shall encourage a spirit of tolerance and intercultural dialogue and take effective measures to promote mutual respect and understanding and co-operation among all persons living on their territory, irrespective of those persons' ethnic, cultural, linguistic or religious identity, in particular in the fields of education, culture and the media.

2. The Parties undertake to take appropriate measures to protect persons who may be subject to threats or acts of discrimination, hostility or violence as a result of their ethnic, cultural, linguistic or religious identity.

Article 7

The Parties shall ensure respect for the right of every person belonging to a national minority to freedom of peaceful assembly, freedom of association, freedom of expression, and freedom of thought, conscience and religion.

Article 8

The Parties undertake to recognize that every person belonging to a national minority has the right to manifest his or her religion or belief and to establish religious institutions, organisations and associations.

Article 9

1. The Parties undertake to recognize that the right to freedom of expression of every person belonging to a national minority includes freedom to hold opinions and to receive and impart information and ideas in the minority language, without interference by public authorities and regardless of frontiers. The Parties shall ensure, within the framework of their legal systems, that persons belonging to a national minority are not discriminated against in their access to the media.

2. Paragraph 1 shall not prevent Parties from requiring the licensing, without discrimination and based on objective criteria, of sound radio and television broadcasting, or cinema enterprises.

3. The Parties shall not hinder the creation and the use of printed media by persons belonging to national minorities. In the legal framework of sound radio and television broadcasting, they shall ensure, as far as possible, and taking into account the provisions

of paragraph 1, that persons belonging to national minorities are granted the possibility of creating and using their own media.

4. In the framework of their legal systems, the Parties shall adopt adequate measures in order to facilitate access to the media for persons belonging to national minorities and in order to promote tolerance and permit cultural pluralism.

Article 10

1. The Parties undertake to recognize that every person belonging to a national minority has the right to use freely and without interference his or her minority language, in private and in public, orally and in writing.

2. In areas inhabited by persons belonging to national minorities traditionally or in substantial numbers, if those persons so request and where such a request corresponds to a real need, the Parties shall endeavour to ensure, as far as possible, the conditions which would make it possible to use the minority language in relations between those persons and the administrative authorities.

3. The Parties undertake to guarantee the right of every person belonging to a national minority to be informed promptly, in a language which he or she understands, of the reasons for his or her arrest, and of the nature and cause of any accusation against him or her, and to defend himself or herself in this language, if necessary with the free assistance of an interpreter.

Article 11

1. The Parties undertake to recognize that every person belonging to a national minority has the right to use his or her surname (patronym) and first names in the minority language and the right to official recognition of them, according to modalities provided for in their legal system.

2. The Parties undertake to recognize that every person belonging to a national minority has the right to display in his or her minority language signs, inscriptions and other information of a private nature visible to the public.

3. In areas traditionally inhabited by substantial numbers of persons belonging to a national minority, the Parties shall endeavour, in the framework of their legal system, including, where appropriate, agreements with other States, and taking into account their specific conditions, to display traditional local names, street names and other topographical indications intended for the public also in the minority language when there is a sufficient demand for such indications.

Article 12

1. The Parties shall, where appropriate, take measures in the fields of education and research to foster knowledge of the culture, history, language and religion of their national minorities and of the majority.

2. In this context the Parties shall *inter alia* provide adequate opportunities for teacher training and access to textbooks, and facilitate contacts among students and teachers of different communities.

3. The Parties undertake to promote equal opportunities for access to education at all levels for persons belonging to national minorities.

Article 13

1. Within the framework of their education systems, the Parties shall recognize that persons belonging to a national minority have the right to set up and to manage their own private educational and training establishments.

2. The exercise of this right shall not entail any financial obligation for the Parties.

Article 14

1. The Parties undertake to recognize that every person belonging to a national minority has the right to learn his or her minority language.

2. In areas inhabited by persons belonging to national minorities traditionally or in substantial numbers, if there is sufficient demand, the Parties shall endeavour to ensure, as far as possible and within the framework of their education systems, that persons belonging to those minorities have adequate opportunities for being taught the minority language or for receiving instruction in this language.

3. Paragraph 2 of this article shall be implemented without prejudice to the learning of the official language or the teaching in this language.

Article 15

The Parties shall create the conditions necessary for the effective participation of persons belonging to national minorities in cultural, social and economic life and in public affairs, in particular those affecting them.

Article 16

The Parties shall refrain from measures which alter the proportions of the population in areas inhabited by persons belonging to national minorities and are aimed at restricting the rights and freedoms flowing from the principles enshrined in the present framework Convention.

Article 17

1. The Parties undertake not to interfere with the right of persons belonging to national minorities to establish and maintain free and peaceful contacts across frontiers with persons lawfully staying in other States, in particular those with whom they share an ethnic, cultural, linguistic or religious identity, or a common cultural heritage.

2. The Parties undertake not to interfere with the right of persons belonging to national minorities to participate in the activities of non-governmental organizations, both at the national and international levels.

Article 18

1. The Parties shall endeavour to conclude, where necessary, bilateral and multilateral agreements with other States, in particular neighbouring States, in order to ensure the protection of persons belonging to the national minorities concerned.

2. Where relevant, the Parties shall take measures to encourage transfrontier co-operation.

Article 19

The Parties undertake to respect and implement the principles enshrined in the present framework Convention making, where necessary, only those limitations, restrictions or derogations which are provided for in international legal instruments, in particular the Convention for the Protection of Human Rights and Fundamental Freedoms, in so far as they are relevant to the rights and freedoms flowing from the said principles.

SECTION III

Article 20

In the exercise of the rights and freedoms flowing from the principles enshrined in the present framework Convention, any person belonging to a national minority shall respect the national legislation and the rights of others, in particular those of persons belonging to the majority or to other national minorities.

Article 21

Nothing in the present framework Convention shall be interpreted as implying any right to engage in any activity or perform any act contrary to the fundamental principles of international law and in particular of the sovereign equality, territorial integrity and political independence of States.

Article 22

Nothing in the present framework Convention shall be construed as limiting or derogating from any of the human rights and fundamental freedoms which may be ensured under the laws of any Contracting Party or under any other agreement to which it is a Party.

Article 23

The rights and freedoms flowing from the principles enshrined in the present framework Convention, in so far as they are the subject of a corresponding provision in the Convention for the Protection of Human Rights and Fundamental Freedoms or in the Protocols thereto, shall be understood so as to conform to the latter provisions.

SECTION IV

Article 24

1. The Committee of Ministers of the Council of Europe shall monitor the implementation of this framework Convention by the Contracting Parties.

2. The Parties which are not members of the Council of Europe shall participate in the implementation mechanism, according to modalities to be determined.

Article 25

1. Within a period of one year following the entry into force of this framework Convention in respect of a Contracting Party, the latter shall transmit to the Secretary General of the Council of Europe full information on the legislative and other measures taken to give effect to the principles set out in this framework Convention.

2. Thereafter, each Party shall transmit to the Secretary General on a periodical basis and whenever the Committee of Ministers so requests any further information of relevance to the implementation of this framework Convention.

3. The Secretary General shall forward to the Committee of Ministers the information transmitted under the terms of this article.

Article 26

1. In evaluating the adequacy of the measures taken by the Parties to give effect to the principles set out in this framework Convention the Committee of Ministers shall be assisted by an advisory committee, the members of which shall have recognised expertise in the field of the protection of national minorities.

2. The composition of this advisory committee and its procedure shall be determined by the Committee of Ministers within a period of one year following the entry into force of this framework Convention.

SECTION V

Article 27

This framework Convention shall be open for signature by the member States of the Council of Europe. Up until the date when the Convention enters into force, it shall also be open for signature by any other State so invited by the Committee of Ministers. It is subject to ratification, acceptance or approval. Instruments of ratification, acceptance or approval shall be deposited with the Secretary General of the Council of Europe.

Article 28

1. This framework Convention shall enter into force on the first day of the month following the expiration of a period of three months after the date on which twelve member States of the Council of Europe have expressed their consent to be bound by the Convention in accordance with the provisions of Article 27.

2. In respect of any member State which subsequently expresses its consent to be bound by it, the framework Convention shall enter into force on the first day of the month following the expiration of a period of three months after the date of the deposit of the instrument of ratification, acceptance or approval.

Article 29

1. After the entry into force of this framework Convention and after consulting the Contracting States, the Committee of Ministers of the Council of Europe may invite to accede to the Convention, by a decision taken by the majority provided for in Article 20.(d) of the Statute of the Council of Europe, any non-member State of the Council of Europe which, invited to sign in accordance with the provisions of Article 27, has not yet done so, and any other non-member State.

2. In respect of any acceding State, the framework Convention shall enter into force on the first day of the month following the expiration of a period of three months after the date of the deposit of the instrument of accession with the Secretary General of the Council of Europe.

Article 30

1. Any State may at the time of signature or when depositing its instrument of ratification, acceptance, approval or accession, specify the territory or territories for whose international relations it is responsible to which this framework Convention shall apply.

2. Any State may at any later date, by a declaration addressed to the Secretary General of the Council of Europe, extend the application of this framework Convention to any other territory specified in the declaration. In respect of such territory the framework Convention shall enter into force on the first day of the month following the expiration of a period of three months after the date of receipt of such declaration by the Secretary General.

3. Any declaration made under the two preceding paragraphs may, in respect of any territory specified in such declaration, be withdrawn by a notification addressed to the Secretary General. The withdrawal shall become effective on the first day of the month following the expiration of a period of three months after the date of receipt of such notification by the Secretary General.

Article 31

1. Any Party may at any time denounce this framework Convention by means of a notification addressed to the Secretary General of the Council of Europe.

2. Such denunciation shall become effective on the first day of the month following the expiration of a period of six months after the date of receipt of the notification by the Secretary General.

Article 32

The Secretary General of the Council of Europe shall notify the member States of the Council, other signatory States and any State which has acceded to this framework Convention, of:

  (a) any signature;

  (b) the deposit of any instrument of ratification, acceptance, approval or accession;

  (c) any date of entry into force of this framework Convention in accordance with Articles 28, 29 and 30;

  (d) any other act, notification or communication relating to this framework Convention.

In witness whereof the undersigned, being duly authorized thereto, have signed this framework Convention.

Done at Strasbourg, this 1st day of February 1995, in English and French, both texts being equally authentic, in a single copy which shall be deposited in the archives of the Council of Europe. The Secretary General of the Council of Europe shall transmit certified copies to each member State of the Council of Europe and to any State invited to sign or accede to this framework Convention.

98. EUROPEAN CONVENTION ON THE EXERCISE OF CHILDREN'S RIGHTS, 1996

This Convention was opened for signature on 25 January 1996 by Council of Europe Member States and non-member States which had participated in its drafting. It entered into force on 1 July 2000; for text, see *ETS* No. 160. The Convention establishes a number of procedural measures to allow children to exercise their rights and a Standing Committee to keep problems under review. See generally, **http://www.coe.int/children**.

TEXT

Preamble

The member States of the Council of Europe and the other States signatory hereto,

Considering that the aim of the Council of Europe is to achieve greater unity between its members;

Having regard to the United Nations Convention on the rights of the child and in particular Article 4 which requires States Parties to undertake all appropriate legislative, administrative and other measures for the implementation of the rights recognised in the said Convention;

Noting the contents of Recommendation 1121 (1990) of the Parliamentary Assembly on the rights of the child;

Convinced that the rights and best interests of children should be promoted and to that end children should have the opportunity to exercise their rights, in particular in family proceedings affecting them;

Recognizing that children should be provided with relevant information to enable such rights and best interests to be promoted and that due weight should be given to the views of children;

Recognizing the importance of the parental role in protecting and promoting the rights and best interests of children and considering that, where necessary, States should also engage in such protection and promotion;

Considering, however, that in the event of conflict it is desirable for families to try to reach agreement before bringing the matter before a judicial authority,

Have agreed as follows:

CHAPTER I
SCOPE AND OBJECT OF THE CONVENTION AND DEFINITIONS

Article 1—Scope and object of the Convention

1. This Convention shall apply to children who have not reached the age of 18 years.

2. The object of the present Convention is, in the best interests of children, to promote their rights, to grant them procedural rights and to facilitate the exercise of these

rights by ensuring that children are, themselves or through other persons or bodies, informed and allowed to participate in proceedings affecting them before a judicial authority.

3. For the purposes of this Convention proceedings before a judicial authority affecting children are family proceedings, in particular those involving the exercise of parental responsibilities such as residence and access to children.

4. Every State shall, at the time of signature or when depositing its instrument of ratification, acceptance, approval or accession, by a declaration addressed to the Secretary General of the Council of Europe, specify at least three categories of family cases before a judicial authority to which this Convention is to apply.

5. Any Party may, by further declaration, specify additional categories of family cases to which this Convention is to apply or provide information concerning the application of Article 5, paragraph 2 of Article 9, paragraph 2 of Article 10 and Article 11.

6. Nothing in this Convention shall prevent Parties from applying rules more favourable to the promotion and the exercise of children's rights.

Article 2—Definitions

For the purposes of this Convention:

 (a) the term 'judicial authority' means a court or an administrative authority having equivalent powers;
 (b) the term 'holders of parental responsibilities' means parents and other persons or bodies entitled to exercise some or all parental responsibilities;
 (c) the term 'representative' means a person, such as a lawyer, or a body appointed to act before a judicial authority on behalf of a child;
 (d) the term 'relevant information' means information which is appropriate to the age and understanding of the child, and which will be given to enable the child to exercise his or her rights fully unless the provision of such information were contrary to the welfare of the child.

CHAPTER II
PROCEDURAL MEASURES TO PROMOTE THE EXERCISE OF CHILDREN'S RIGHTS

A. Procedural rights of a child

Article 3—Right to be informed and to express his or her views in proceedings

A child considered by internal law as having sufficient understanding, in the case of proceedings before a judicial authority affecting him or her, shall be granted, and shall be entitled to request, the following rights:

 (a) to receive all relevant information;
 (b) to be consulted and express his or her views;
 (c) to be informed of the possible consequences of compliance with these views and the possible consequences of any decision.

Article 4—Right to apply for the appointment of a special representative

1. Subject to Article 9, the child shall have the right to apply, in person or through other persons or bodies, for a special representative in proceedings before a judicial authority affecting the child where internal law precludes the holders of parental responsibilities from representing the child as a result of a conflict of interest with the latter.

2. States are free to limit the right in paragraph 1 to children who are considered by internal law to have sufficient understanding.

Article 5—Other possible procedural rights

Parties shall consider granting children additional procedural rights in relation to proceedings before a judicial authority affecting them, in particular:

(a) the right to apply to be assisted by an appropriate person of their choice in order to help them express their views;

(b) the right to apply themselves, or through other persons or bodies, for the appointment of a separate representative, in appropriate cases a lawyer;

(c) the right to appoint their own representative;

(d) the right to exercise some or all of the rights of parties to such proceedings.

B. Role of judicial authorities

Article 6—Decision-making process

In proceedings affecting a child, the judicial authority, before taking a decision, shall:

(a) consider whether it has sufficient information at its disposal in order to take a decision in the best interests of the child and, where necessary, it shall obtain further information, in particular from the holders of parental responsibilities;

(b) in a case where the child is considered by internal law as having sufficient understanding:

(i) ensure that the child has received all relevant information;

(ii) consult the child in person in appropriate cases, if necessary privately, itself or through other persons or bodies, in a manner appropriate to his or her understanding, unless this would be manifestly contrary to the best interests of the child;

(iii) allow the child to express his or her views;

(c) give due weight to the views expressed by the child.

Article 7—Duty to act speedily

In proceedings affecting a child the judicial authority shall act speedily to avoid any unnecessary delay and procedures shall be available to ensure that its decisions are rapidly enforced. In urgent cases the judicial authority shall have the power, where appropriate, to take decisions which are immediately enforceable.

Article 8—Acting on own motion

In proceedings affecting a child the judicial authority shall have the power to act on its own motion in cases determined by internal law where the welfare of a child is in serious danger.

Article 9—Appointment of a representative

1. In proceedings affecting a child where, by internal law, the holders of parental responsibilities are precluded from representing the child as a result of a conflict of interest between them and the child, the judicial authority shall have the power to appoint a special representative for the child in those proceedings.

2. Parties shall consider providing that, in proceedings affecting a child, the judicial authority shall have the power to appoint a separate representative, in appropriate cases a lawyer, to represent the child.

C. Role of representatives

Article 10

1. In the case of proceedings before a judicial authority affecting a child the representative shall, unless this would be manifestly contrary to the best interests of the child:

   (a) provide all relevant information to the child, if the child is considered by internal law as having sufficient understanding;

   (b) provide explanations to the child if the child is considered by internal law as having sufficient understanding, concerning the possible consequences of compliance with his or her views and the possible consequences of any action by the representative;

   (c) determine the views of the child and present these views to the judicial authority.

2. Parties shall consider extending the provisions of paragraph 1 to the holders of parental responsibilities.

D. Extension of certain provisions

Article 11

Parties shall consider extending the provisions of Articles 3, 4 and 9 to proceedings affecting children before other bodies and to matters affecting children which are not the subject of proceedings.

E. National bodies

Article 12

1. Parties shall encourage, through bodies which perform, *inter alia*, the functions set out in paragraph 2, the promotion and the exercise of children's rights.

2. The functions are as follows:

   (a) to make proposals to strengthen the law relating to the exercise of children's rights;

   (b) to give opinions concerning draft legislation relating to the exercise of children's rights;

   (c) to provide general information concerning the exercise of children's rights to the media, the public and persons and bodies dealing with questions relating to children;

   (d) to seek the views of children and provide them with relevant information.

F. Other matters

Article 13—Mediation or other processes to resolve disputes

In order to prevent or resolve disputes or to avoid proceedings before a judicial authority affecting children, Parties shall encourage the provision of mediation or other processes to resolve disputes and the use of such processes to reach agreement in appropriate cases to be determined by Parties.

Article 14—Legal aid and advice

Where internal law provides for legal aid or advice for the representation of children in proceedings before a judicial authority affecting them, such provisions shall apply in relation to the matters covered by Articles 4 and 9.

Article 15—Relations with other international instruments

This Convention shall not restrict the application of any other international instrument which deals with specific issues arising in the context of the protection of children and families, and to which a Party to this Convention is, or becomes, a Party.

CHAPTER III
STANDING COMMITTEE

Article 16—Establishment and functions of the Standing Committee

1. A Standing Committee is set up for the purposes of this Convention.

2. The Standing Committee shall keep under review problems relating to this Convention. It may, in particular:

(a) consider any relevant questions concerning the interpretation or implementation of the Convention. The Standing Committee's conclusions concerning the implementation of the Convention may take the form of a recommendation; recommendations shall be adopted by a three-quarters majority of the votes cast;

(b) propose amendments to the Convention and examine those proposed in accordance with Article 20;

(c) provide advice and assistance to the national bodies having the functions under paragraph 2 of Article 12 and promote international co-operation between them.

Article 17—Composition

1. Each Party may be represented on the Standing Committee by one or more delegates. Each Party shall have one vote.

2. Any State referred to in Article 21, which is not a Party to this Convention, may be represented in the Standing Committee by an observer. The same applies to any other State or to the European Community after having been invited to accede to the Convention in accordance with the provisions of Article 22.

3. Unless a Party has informed the Secretary General of its objection, at least one month before the meeting, the Standing Committee may invite the following to attend as observers at all its meetings or at one meeting or part of a meeting:

(a) any State not referred to in paragraph 2 above;

(b) the United Nations Committee on the Rights of the Child;

(c) the European Community;

(d) any international governmental body;

(e) any international non-governmental body with one or more functions mentioned under paragraph 2 of Article 12;

(f) any national governmental or non-governmental body with one or more functions mentioned under paragraph 2 of Article 12.

4. The Standing Committee may exchange information with relevant organizations dealing with the exercise of children's rights.

Article 18—Meetings

1. At the end of the third year following the date of entry into force of this Convention and, on his or her own initiative, at any time after this date, the Secretary General of the Council of Europe shall invite the Standing Committee to meet.

2. Decisions may only be taken in the Standing Committee if at least one-half of the Parties are present.

3. Subject to Articles 16 and 20 the decisions of the Standing Committee shall be taken by a majority of the members present.

4. Subject to the provisions of this Convention the Standing Committee shall draw up its own rules of procedure and the rules of procedure of any working party it may set up to carry out all appropriate tasks under the Convention.

Article 19—Reports of the Standing Committee

After each meeting, the Standing Committee shall forward to the Parties and the Committee of Ministers of the Council of Europe a report on its discussions and any decisions taken.

CHAPTER IV
AMENDMENTS TO THE CONVENTION

Article 20

1. Any amendment to the articles of this Convention proposed by a Party or the Standing Committee shall be communicated to the Secretary General of the Council of Europe and forwarded by him or her, at least two months before the next meeting of the Standing Committee, to the member States of the Council of Europe, any signatory, any Party, any State invited to sign this Convention in accordance with the provisions of Article 21 and any State or the European Community invited to accede to it in accordance with the provisions of Article 22.

2. Any amendment proposed in accordance with the provisions of the preceding paragraph shall be examined by the Standing Committee which shall submit the text adopted by a three-quarters majority of the votes cast to the Committee of Ministers for approval. After its approval, this text shall be forwarded to the Parties for acceptance.

3. Any amendment shall enter into force on the first day of the month following the expiration of a period of one month after the date on which all Parties have informed the Secretary General that they have accepted it.

CHAPTER V
FINAL CLAUSES

Article 21—Signature, ratification and entry into force

1. This Convention shall be open for signature by the member States of the Council of Europe and the non-member States which have participated in its elaboration.

2. This Convention is subject to ratification, acceptance or approval. Instruments of ratification, acceptance or approval shall be deposited with the Secretary General of the Council of Europe.

3. This Convention shall enter into force on the first day of the month following the expiration of a period of three months after the date on which three States, including at least two member States of the Council of Europe, have expressed their consent to be bound by the Convention in accordance with the provisions of the preceding paragraph.

4. In respect of any signatory which subsequently expresses its consent to be bound by it, the Convention shall enter into force on the first day of the month following the expiration of a period of three months after the date of the deposit of its instrument of ratification, acceptance or approval.

Article 22—Non-member States and the European Community

1. After the entry into force of this Convention, the Committee of Ministers of the Council of Europe may, on its own initiative or following a proposal from the Standing Committee and after consultation of the Parties, invite any non-member State of the Council of Europe, which has not participated in the elaboration of the Convention, as well as the European Community to accede to this Convention by a decision taken by the majority provided for in Article 20, sub-paragraph (d) of the Statute of the Council of Europe, and by the unanimous vote of the representatives of the contracting States entitled to sit on the Committee of Ministers.

2. In respect of any acceding State or the European Community, the Convention shall enter into force on the first day of the month following the expiration of a period of three months after the date of deposit of the instrument of accession with the Secretary General of the Council of Europe.

Article 23—Territorial application

1. Any State may, at the time of signature or when depositing its instrument of ratification, acceptance, approval or accession, specify the territory or territories to which this Convention shall apply.

2. Any Party may, at any later date, by a declaration addressed to the Secretary General of the Council of Europe, extend the application of this Convention to any other territory specified in the declaration and for whose international relations it is responsible or on whose behalf it is authorized to give undertakings. In respect of such territory the Convention shall enter into force on the first day of the month following the expiration of a period of three months after the date of receipt of such declaration by the Secretary General.

3. Any declaration made under the two preceding paragraphs may, in respect of any territory specified in such declaration, be withdrawn by a notification addressed to the Secretary General. The withdrawal shall become effective on the first day of the month following the expiration of a period of three months after the date of receipt of such notification by the Secretary General.

Article 24—Reservations

No reservation may be made to the Convention.

Article 25—Denunciation

1. Any Party may at any time denounce this Convention by means of a notification addressed to the Secretary General of the Council of Europe.

2. Such denunciation shall become effective on the first day of the month following the expiration of a period of three months after the date of receipt of notification by the Secretary General.

Article 26—Notifications

The Secretary General of the Council of Europe shall notify the member States of the Council, any signatory, any Party and any other State or the European Community which has been invited to accede to this Convention of:

- *(a)* any signature;
- *(b)* the deposit of any instrument of ratification, acceptance, approval or accession;
- *(c)* any date of entry into force of this Convention in accordance with Articles 21 or 22;
- *(d)* any amendment adopted in accordance with Article 20 and the date on which such an amendment enters into force;
- *(e)* any declaration made under the provisions of Articles 1 and 23;
- *(f)* any denunciation made in pursuance of the provisions of Article 25;
- *(g)* any other act, notification or communication relating to this Convention.

In witness whereof, the undersigned, being duly authorized thereto, have signed this Convention.

Done at Strasbourg, the 25th January 1996, in English and French, both texts being equally authentic, in a single copy which shall be deposited in the archives of the Council of Europe. The Secretary General of the Council of Europe shall transmit certified copies to each member State of the Council of Europe, to the non-member States which have participated in the elaboration of this Convention, to the European Community and to any State invited to accede to this Convention.

99. EUROPEAN CONVENTION ON NATIONALITY, 1997

Opened for signature by Member States of the Council of Europe and by non-member States which participated in its elaboration on 6 November 1997, this Convention entered into force on 1 March 2000; for text, see *ETS* No. 166. It is intended to make easier the acquisition of a new nationality or the recovery of a former nationality, to ensure that nationality is not arbitrarily withdrawn, and that the risk of statelessness is reduced. See also the Convention relating to the Status of Stateless Persons, 1954 (above, p. 341), the Convention on the Reduction of Statelessness, 1961 (above, p. 352), and the Declaration of Articles on Nationality of Natural Persons in relation to the Succession of States, 2000 (above, p. 249).

Further reading

BATCHELOR, C., 'Statelessness and the Problem of Resolving Nationality Status', (1998) 10 *IJRL* 156.

KNOP, K., 'Relational Nationality: On Gender and Nationality in International Law', in ALEINIKOFF, T. A and KLUSMEYER, D., eds, *Citizenship Today: Global Perspectives and Practices*, Washington DC: Carnegie Endowment for International Peace, 2001, 89.

TEXT

Preamble

The member States of the Council of Europe and the other States signatory to this Convention,

Considering that the aim of the Council of Europe is to achieve greater unity between its members;

Bearing in mind the numerous international instruments relating to nationality, multiple nationality and statelessness;

Recognising that, in matters concerning nationality, account should be taken both of the legitimate interests of States and those of individuals;

Desiring to promote the progressive development of legal principles concerning nationality, as well as their adoption in internal law and desiring to avoid, as far as possible, cases of statelessness;

Desiring to avoid discrimination in matters relating to nationality;

Aware of the right to respect for family life as contained in Article 8 of the Convention for the Protection of Human Rights and Fundamental Freedoms;

Noting the varied approach of States to the question of multiple nationality and recognizing that each State is free to decide which consequences it attaches in its internal law to the fact that a national acquires or possesses another nationality;

Agreeing on the desirability of finding appropriate solutions to consequences of multiple nationality and in particular as regards the rights and duties of multiple nationals;

Considering it desirable that persons possessing the nationality of two or more States Parties should be required to fulfil their military obligations in relation to only one of those Parties;

Considering the need to promote international co-operation between the national authorities responsible for nationality matters,

Have agreed as follows:

CHAPTER I
General Matters

Article 1—Object of the Convention

This Convention establishes principles and rules relating to the nationality of natural persons and rules regulating military obligations in cases of multiple nationality, to which the internal law of States Parties shall conform.

Article 2—Definitions

For the purpose of this Convention:

(a) 'nationality' means the legal bond between a person and a State and does not indicate the person's ethnic origin;

(b) 'multiple nationality' means the simultaneous possession of two or more nationalities by the same person;

(c) 'child' means every person below the age of 18 years unless, under the law applicable to the child, majority is attained earlier;

(d) 'internal law' means all types of provisions of the national legal system, including the constitution, legislation, regulations, decrees, case-law, customary rules and practice as well as rules deriving from binding international instruments.

CHAPTER II
General Principles Relating
to Nationality

Article 3—Competence of the State

1. Each State shall determine under its own law who are its nationals.
2. This law shall be accepted by other States in so far as it is consistent with applicable international conventions, customary international law and the principles of law generally recognized with regard to nationality.

Article 4—Principles

The rules on nationality of each State Party shall be based on the following principles:

(a) everyone has the right to a nationality;

(b) statelessness shall be avoided;

(c) no one shall be arbitrarily deprived of his or her nationality;

(d) neither marriage nor the dissolution of a marriage between a national of a State Party and an alien, nor the change of nationality by one of the spouses during marriage, shall automatically affect the nationality of the other spouse.

Article 5—Non-discrimination

1. The rules of a State Party on nationality shall not contain distinctions or include any practice which amount to discrimination on the grounds of sex, religion, race, colour or national or ethnic origin.

2. Each State Party shall be guided by the principle of non-discrimination between its nationals, whether they are nationals by birth or have acquired its nationality subsequently.

CHAPTER III
Rules Relating to Nationality

Article 6—Acquisition of nationality

1. Each State Party shall provide in its internal law for its nationality to be acquired *ex lege* by the following persons:

   (a) children one of whose parents possesses, at the time of the birth of these children, the nationality of that State Party, subject to any exceptions which may be provided for by its internal law as regards children born abroad. With respect to children whose parenthood is established by recognition, court order or similar procedures, each State Party may provide that the child acquires its nationality following the procedure determined by its internal law;

   (b) foundlings found in its territory who would otherwise be stateless.

2. Each State Party shall provide in its internal law for its nationality to be acquired by children born on its territory who do not acquire at birth another nationality. Such nationality shall be granted:

   (a) at birth *ex lege*; or

   (b) subsequently, to children who remained stateless, upon an application being lodged with the appropriate authority, by or on behalf of the child concerned, in the manner prescribed by the internal law of the State Party. Such an application may be made subject to the lawful and habitual residence on its territory for a period not exceeding five years immediately preceding the lodging of the application.

3. Each State Party shall provide in its internal law for the possibility of naturalization of persons lawfully and habitually resident on its territory. In establishing the conditions for naturalization, it shall not provide for a period of residence exceeding ten years before the lodging of an application.

4. Each State Party shall facilitate in its internal law the acquisition of its nationality for the following persons:

   (a) spouses of its nationals;

   (b) children of one of its nationals, falling under the exception of Article 6, paragraph 1, sub-paragraph (a);

   (c) children one of whose parents acquires or has acquired its nationality;

   (d) children adopted by one of its nationals;

    (e) persons who were born on its territory and reside there lawfully and habitually;

    (f) persons who are lawfully and habitually resident on its territory for a period of time beginning before the age of 18, that period to be determined by the internal law of the State Party concerned;

    (g) stateless persons and recognized refugees lawfully and habitually resident on its territory.

Article 7—Loss of nationality ex lege or at the initiative of a State Party

1. A State Party may not provide in its internal law for the loss of its nationality *ex lege* or at the initiative of the State Party except in the following cases:

    (a) voluntary acquisition of another nationality;

    (b) acquisition of the nationality of the State Party by means of fraudulent conduct, false information or concealment of any relevant fact attributable to the applicant;

    (c) voluntary service in a foreign military force;

    (d) conduct seriously prejudicial to the vital interests of the State Party;

    (e) lack of a genuine link between the State Party and a national habitually residing abroad;

    (f) where it is established during the minority of a child that the preconditions laid down by internal law which led to the *ex lege* acquisition of the nationality of the State Party are no longer fulfilled;

    (g) adoption of a child if the child acquires or possesses the foreign nationality of one or both of the adopting parents.

2. A State Party may provide for the loss of its nationality by children whose parents lose that nationality except in cases covered by sub-paragraphs (c) and (d) of paragraph 1. However, children shall not lose that nationality if one of their parents retains it.

3. A State Party may not provide in its internal law for the loss of its nationality under paragraphs 1 and 2 of this article if the person concerned would thereby become stateless, with the exception of the cases mentioned in paragraph 1, sub-paragraph (b), of this article.

Article 8—Loss of nationality at the initiative of the individual

1. Each State Party shall permit the renunciation of its nationality provided the persons concerned do not thereby become stateless.

2. However, a State Party may provide in its internal law that renunciation may be effected only by nationals who are habitually resident abroad.

Article 9—Recovery of nationality

Each State Party shall facilitate, in the cases and under the conditions provided for by its internal law, the recovery of its nationality by former nationals who are lawfully and habitually resident on its territory.

CHAPTER IV
Procedures Relating to Nationality

Article 10—Processing of applications

Each State Party shall ensure that applications relating to the acquisition, retention, loss, recovery or certification of its nationality be processed within a reasonable time.

Article 11—Decisions

Each State Party shall ensure that decisions relating to the acquisition, retention, loss, recovery or certification of its nationality contain reasons in writing.

Article 12—Right to a review

Each State Party shall ensure that decisions relating to the acquisition, retention, loss, recovery or certification of its nationality be open to an administrative or judicial review in conformity with its internal law.

Article 13—Fees

1. Each State Party shall ensure that the fees for the acquisition, retention, loss, recovery or certification of its nationality be reasonable.

2. Each State Party shall ensure that the fees for an administrative or judicial review be not an obstacle for applicants.

CHAPTER V
Multiple Nationality

Article 14—Cases of multiple nationality ex lege

1. A State Party shall allow:

    (a) children having different nationalities acquired automatically at birth to retain these nationalities;

    (b) its nationals to possess another nationality where this other nationality is automatically acquired by marriage.

2. The retention of the nationalities mentioned in paragraph 1 is subject to the relevant provisions of Article 7 of this Convention.

Article 15—Other possible cases of multiple nationality

The provisions of this Convention shall not limit the right of a State Party to determine in its internal law whether:

    (a) its nationals who acquire or possess the nationality of another State retain its nationality or lose it;

    (b) the acquisition or retention of its nationality is subject to the renunciation or loss of another nationality.

Article 16—Conservation of previous nationality

A State Party shall not make the renunciation or loss of another nationality a condition for the acquisition or retention of its nationality where such renunciation or loss is not possible or cannot reasonably be required.

Article 17—Rights and duties related to multiple nationality

1. Nationals of a State Party in possession of another nationality shall have, in the territory of that State Party in which they reside, the same rights and duties as other nationals of that State Party.

2. The provisions of this chapter do not affect:

    (a) the rules of international law concerning diplomatic or consular protection by a State Party in favour of one of its nationals who simultaneously possesses another nationality;

    (b) the application of the rules of private international law of each State Party in cases of multiple nationality.

CHAPTER VI
State Succession and Nationality

Article 18—Principles

1. In matters of nationality in cases of State succession, each State Party concerned shall respect the principles of the rule of law, the rules concerning human rights and the principles contained in Articles 4 and 5 of this Convention and in paragraph 2 of this article, in particular in order to avoid statelessness.

2. In deciding on the granting or the retention of nationality in cases of State succession, each State Party concerned shall take account in particular of:

    (a) the genuine and effective link of the person concerned with the State;

    (b) the habitual residence of the person concerned at the time of State succession;

    (c) the will of the person concerned;

    (d) the territorial origin of the person concerned.

3. Where the acquisition of nationality is subject to the loss of a foreign nationality, the provisions of Article 16 of this Convention shall apply.

Article 19—Settlement by international agreement

In cases of State succession, States Parties concerned shall endeavour to regulate matters relating to nationality by agreement amongst themselves and, where applicable, in their relationship with other States concerned. Such agreements shall respect the principles and rules contained or referred to in this chapter.

Article 20—Principles concerning non-nationals

1. Each State Party shall respect the following principles:

    (a) nationals of a predecessor State habitually resident in the territory over which sovereignty is transferred to a successor State and who have not acquired its nationality shall have the right to remain in that State;

(b) persons referred to in sub-paragraph (a) shall enjoy equality of treatment with nationals of the successor State in relation to social and economic rights.

2. Each State Party may exclude persons considered under paragraph 1 from employment in the public service involving the exercise of sovereign powers.

CHAPTER VII
Military Obligations in Cases of Multiple Nationality

Article 21—Fulfilment of military obligations

1. Persons possessing the nationality of two or more States Parties shall be required to fulfil their military obligations in relation to one of those States Parties only.

2. The modes of application of paragraph 1 may be determined by special agreements between any of the States Parties.

3. Except where a special agreement which has been, or may be, concluded provides otherwise, the following provisions are applicable to persons possessing the nationality of two or more States Parties:

(a) Any such person shall be subject to military obligations in relation to the State Party in whose territory they are habitually resident. Nevertheless, they shall be free to choose, up to the age of 19 years, to submit themselves to military obligations as volunteers in relation to any other State Party of which they are also nationals for a total and effective period at least equal to that of the active military service required by the former State Party;

(b) Persons who are habitually resident in the territory of a State Party of which they are not nationals or in that of a State which is not a State Party may choose to perform their military service in the territory of any State Party of which they are nationals;

(c) Persons who, in accordance with the rules laid down in paragraphs (a) and (b), shall fulfil their military obligations in relation to one State Party, as prescribed by the law of that State Party, shall be deemed to have fulfilled their military obligations in relation to any other State Party or States Parties of which they are also nationals;

(d) Persons who, before the entry into force of this Convention between the States Parties of which they are nationals, have, in relation to one of those States Parties, fulfilled their military obligations in accordance with the law of that State Party, shall be deemed to have fulfilled the same obligations in relation to any other State Party or States Parties of which they are also nationals;

(e) Persons who, in conformity with paragraph (a), have performed their active military service in relation to one of the States Parties of which they are nationals, and subsequently transfer their habitual residence to the territory of the other State Party of which they are nationals, shall be liable to military service in the reserve only in relation to the latter State Party;

(f) The application of this article shall not prejudice, in any respect, the nationality of the persons concerned;

(g) In the event of mobilisation by any State Party, the obligations arising under this article shall not be binding upon that State Party.

Article 22—Exemption from military obligations or alternative civil service

Except where a special agreement which has been, or may be, concluded provides otherwise, the following provisions are also applicable to persons possessing the nationality of two or more States Parties:

(a) Article 21, paragraph 3, sub-paragraph (c), of this Convention shall apply to persons who have been exempted from their military obligations or have fulfilled civil service as an alternative;

(b) persons who are nationals of a State Party which does not require obligatory military service shall be considered as having satisfied their military obligations when they have their habitual residence in the territory of that State Party. Nevertheless, they should be deemed not to have satisfied their military obligations in relation to a State Party or States Parties of which they are equally nationals and where military service is required unless the said habitual residence has been maintained up to a certain age, which each State Party concerned shall notify at the time of signature or when depositing its instruments of ratification, acceptance or accession;

(c) also persons who are nationals of a State Party which does not require obligatory military service shall be considered as having satisfied their military obligations when they have enlisted voluntarily in the military forces of that Party for a total and effective period which is at least equal to that of the active military service of the State Party or States Parties of which they are also nationals without regard to where they have their habitual residence.

CHAPTER VIII
Co-operation between the States Parties

Article 23—Co-operation between the States Parties

1. With a view to facilitating co-operation between the States Parties, their competent authorities shall:

(a) provide the Secretary General of the Council of Europe with information about their internal law relating to nationality, including instances of statelessness and multiple nationality, and about developments concerning the application of the Convention;

(b) provide each other upon request with information about their internal law relating to nationality and about developments concerning the application of the Convention.

2. States Parties shall co-operate amongst themselves and with other member States of the Council of Europe within the framework of the appropriate intergovernmental body of the Council of Europe in order to deal with all relevant problems and to promote the progressive development of legal principles and practice concerning nationality and related matters.

Article 24—Exchange of information

Each State Party may at any time declare that it shall inform any other State Party, having made the same declaration, of the voluntary acquisition of its nationality by nationals of the other State Party, subject to applicable laws concerning data protection. Such a declaration may indicate the conditions under which the State Party will give such information. The declaration may be withdrawn at any time.

CHAPTER IX
Application of the Convention

Article 25—Declarations concerning the application of the Convention

1. Each State may declare, at the time of signature or when depositing its instrument of ratification, acceptance, approval or accession, that it will exclude Chapter VII from the application of the Convention.

2. The provisions of Chapter VII shall be applicable only in the relations between States Parties for which it is in force.

3. Each State Party may, at any subsequent time, notify the Secretary General of the Council of Europe that it will apply the provisions of Chapter VII excluded at the time of signature or in its instrument of ratification, acceptance, approval or accession. This notification shall become effective as from the date of its receipt.

Article 26—Effects of this Convention

1. The provisions of this Convention shall not prejudice the provisions of internal law and binding international instruments which are already in force or may come into force, under which more favourable rights are or would be accorded to individuals in the field of nationality.

2. This Convention does not prejudice the application of:

   (a) the 1963 Convention on the Reduction of Cases of Multiple Nationality and Military Obligations in Cases of Multiple Nationality and its Protocols;

   (b) other binding international instruments in so far as such instruments are compatible with this Convention,

in the relationship between the States Parties bound by these instruments.

CHAPTER X
Final Clauses

Article 27—Signature and entry into force

1. This Convention shall be open for signature by the member States of the Council of Europe and the non-member States which have participated in its elaboration. Such States may express their consent to be bound by:

   (a) signature without reservation as to ratification, acceptance or approval; or

   (b) signature subject to ratification, acceptance or approval, followed by ratification, acceptance or approval.

Instruments of ratification, acceptance or approval shall be deposited with the Secretary General of the Council of Europe.

2. This Convention shall enter into force, for all States having expressed their consent to be bound by the Convention, on the first day of the month following the expiration of a period of three months after the date on which three member States of the Council of Europe have expressed their consent to be bound by this Convention in accordance with the provisions of the preceding paragraph.

3. In respect of any State which subsequently expresses its consent to be bound by it, the Convention shall enter into force on the first day of the month following the expiration of a period of three months after the date of signature or of the deposit of its instrument of ratification, acceptance or approval.

Article 28—Accession

1. After the entry into force of this Convention, the Committee of Ministers of the Council of Europe may invite any non-member State of the Council of Europe which has not participated in its elaboration to accede to this Convention.

2. In respect of any acceding State, this Convention shall enter into force on the first day of the month following the expiration of a period of three months after the date of deposit of the instrument of accession with the Secretary General of the Council of Europe.

Article 29—Reservations

1. No reservations may be made to any of the provisions contained in Chapters I, II and VI of this Convention. Any State may, at the time of signature or when depositing its instrument of ratification, acceptance, approval or accession, make one or more reservations to other provisions of the Convention so long as they are compatible with the object and purpose of this Convention.

2. Any State which makes one or more reservations shall notify the Secretary General of the Council of Europe of the relevant contents of its internal law or of any other relevant information.

3. A State which has made one or more reservations in accordance with paragraph 1 shall consider withdrawing them in whole or in part as soon as circumstances permit. Such withdrawal shall be made by means of a notification addressed to the Secretary General of the Council of Europe and shall become effective as from the date of its receipt.

4. Any State which extends the application of this Convention to a territory mentioned in the declaration referred to in Article 30, paragraph 2, may, in respect of the territory concerned, make one or more reservations in accordance with the provisions of the preceding paragraphs.

5. A State Party which has made reservations in respect of any of the provisions in Chapter VII of the Convention may not claim application of the said provisions by another State Party save in so far as it has itself accepted these provisions.

Article 30—Territorial application

1. Any State may, at the time of signature or when depositing its instrument of ratification, acceptance, approval or accession, specify the territory or territories to which this Convention shall apply.

2. Any State may, at any later date, by a declaration addressed to the Secretary General of the Council of Europe, extend the application of this Convention to any other territory

specified in the declaration and for whose international relations it is responsible or on whose behalf it is authorized to give undertakings. In respect of such territory, the Convention shall enter into force on the first day of the month following the expiration of a period of three months after the date of receipt of such declaration by the Secretary General.

3. Any declaration made under the two preceding paragraphs may, in respect of any territory specified in such declaration, be withdrawn by a notification addressed to the Secretary General. The withdrawal shall become effective on the first day of the month following the expiration of a period of three months after the date of receipt of such notification by the Secretary General.

Article 31—Denunciation

1. Any State Party may at any time denounce the Convention as a whole or Chapter VII only by means of a notification addressed to the Secretary General of the Council of Europe.

2. Such denunciation shall become effective on the first day of the month following the expiration of a period of three months after the date of receipt of notification by the Secretary General.

Article 32—Notifications by the Secretary General

The Secretary General of the Council of Europe shall notify the member States of the Council of Europe, any Signatory, any Party and any other State which has acceded to this Convention of:

(a) any signature;

(b) the deposit of any instrument of ratification, acceptance, approval or accession;

(c) any date of entry into force of this Convention in accordance with Articles 27 or 28 of this Convention;

(d) any reservation and withdrawal of reservations made in pursuance of the provisions of Article 29 of this Convention;

(e) any notification or declaration made under the provisions of Articles 23, 24, 25, 27, 28, 29, 30 and 31 of this Convention;

(f) any other act, notification or communication relating to this Convention.

In witness whereof the undersigned, being duly authorized thereto, have signed this Convention.

Done at Strasbourg, this sixth day of November 1997, in English and in French, both texts being equally authentic, in a single copy which shall be deposited in the archives of the Council of Europe. The Secretary General of the Council of Europe shall transmit certified copies to each member State of the Council of Europe, to the non-member States which have participated in the elaboration of this Convention and to any State invited to accede to this Convention.

100. EUROPEAN CONVENTION ON CONTACT CONCERNING CHILDREN, 2003

ETS No. 192. Opened for signature at Strasbourg on 15 May 2003 and entered into force on 1 September 2005. This treaty is open to ratification by non-Member States of the Council of Europe.

TEXT

Preamble

The member States of the Council of Europe and the other Signatories hereto,

Taking into account the European Convention on Recognition and Enforcement of Decisions concerning Custody of Children and on Restoration of Custody of Children of 20 May 1980 (ETS No. 105);

Taking into account the Hague Convention of 25 October 1980 on the Civil Aspects of International Child Abduction and the Hague Convention of 19 October 1996 on Jurisdiction, Applicable Law, Recognition, Enforcement and Co-operation in respect of Parental Responsibility and Measures for the Protection of Children;

Taking into account the Council Regulation (EC) No. 1347/2000 of 29 May 2000 on jurisdiction and the recognition and enforcement of judgments in matrimonial matters and in matters of parental responsibility for children of both spouses;

Recognising that, as provided in the different international legal instruments of the Council of Europe as well as in Article 3 of the United Nations Convention on the Rights of the Child of 20 November 1989, the best interests of the child shall be a primary consideration;

Aware of the need for further provisions to safeguard contact between children and their parents and other persons having family ties with children, as protected by Article 8 of the Convention for the Protection of Human Rights and Fundamental Freedoms of 4 November 1950 (ETS No. 5);

Taking into account Article 9 of the United Nations Convention on the Rights of the Child which provides for the right of a child, who is separated from one or both parents, to maintain personal relations and direct contact with both parents on a regular basis, except when this is contrary to the child's best interests;

Taking into account paragraph 2 of Article 10 of the United Nations Convention on the Rights of the Child, which provides for the right of the child whose parents reside in different States to maintain on a regular basis, save in exceptional circumstances, personal relations and direct contacts with both parents;

Aware of the desirability of recognising not only parents but also children as holders of rights;

Agreeing consequently to replace the notion of 'access to children' with the notion of 'contact concerning children';

Taking into account the European Convention on the Exercise of Children's Rights (ETS No. 160) and the desirability of promoting measures to assist children in matters concerning contact with parents and other persons having family ties with children;

Agreeing on the need for children to have contact not only with both parents but also with certain other persons having family ties with children and the importance for parents and those other persons to remain in contact with children, subject to the best interests of the child;

Noting the need to promote the adoption by States of common principles with respect to contact concerning children, in particular in order to facilitate the application of international instruments in this field;

Realising that machinery set up to give effect to foreign orders relating to contact concerning children is more likely to provide satisfactory results where the principles on which these foreign orders are based are similar to the principles in the State giving effect to such foreign orders;

Recognising the need, when children and parents and other persons having family ties with children live in different States, to encourage judicial authorities to make more frequent use of transfrontier contact and to increase the confidence of all persons concerned that the children will be returned at the end of such contact;

Noting that the provision of efficient safeguards and additional guarantees is likely to ensure the return of children, in particular, at the end of transfrontier contact;

Noting that an additional international instrument is necessary to provide solutions relating in particular to transfrontier contact concerning children;

Desiring to establish co-operation between all central authorities and other bodies in order to promote and improve contact between children and their parents, and other persons having family ties with such children, and in particular to promote judicial co-operation in cases concerning transfrontier contact;

Have agreed as follows:

CHAPTER I
Objects of the Convention and Definitions

Article 1—Objects of the Convention

The objects of this Convention are:

(a) to determine general principles to be applied to contact orders;

(b) to fix appropriate safeguards and guarantees to ensure the proper exercise of contact and the immediate return of children at the end of the period of contact;

(c) to establish co-operation between central authorities, judicial authorities and other bodies in order to promote and improve contact between children and their parents, and other persons having family ties with children.

Article 2—Definitions

For the purposes of this Convention:

(a) 'contact' means:
   (i)   the child staying for a limited period of time with or meeting a person mentioned in Articles 4 or 5 with whom he or she is not usually living;
   (ii) any form of communication between the child and such person;
   (iii) the provision of information to such a person about the child or to the child about such a person.

(b) '*contact order*' means a decision of a judicial authority concerning contact, including an agreement concerning contact which has been confirmed by a competent judicial authority or which has been formally drawn up or registered as an authentic instrument and is enforceable;

(c) '*child*' means a person under 18 years of age in respect of whom a contact order may be made or enforced in a State Party;

(d) '*family ties*' means a close relationship such as between a child and his or her grandparents or siblings, based on law or on a *de facto* family relationship;

(e) '*judicial authority*' means a court or an administrative authority having equivalent powers.

CHAPTER II
General Principles to be Applied to Contact Orders

Article 3—Application of principles

States Parties shall adopt such legislative and other measures as may be necessary to ensure that the principles contained in this chapter are applied by judicial authorities when making, amending, suspending or revoking contact orders.

Article 4—Contact between a child and his or her parents

1. A child and his or her parents shall have the right to obtain and maintain regular contact with each other.

2. Such contact may be restricted or excluded only where necessary in the best interests of the child.

3. Where it is not in the best interests of a child to maintain unsupervised contact with one of his or her parents the possibility of supervised personal contact or other forms of contact with this parent shall be considered.

Article 5—Contact between a child and persons other than his or her parents

1. Subject to his or her best interests, contact may be established between the child and persons other than his or her parents having family ties with the child.

2. States Parties are free to extend this provision to persons other than those mentioned in paragraph 1, and where so extended, States may freely decide what aspects of contact, as defined in Article 2 letter *a* shall apply.

Article 6—The right of a child to be informed, consulted and to express his or her views

1. A child considered by internal law as having sufficient understanding shall have the right, unless this would be manifestly contrary to his or her best interests:

— to receive all relevant information;
— to be consulted;
— to express his or her views.

2. Due weight shall be given to those views and to the ascertainable wishes and feelings of the child.

Article 7—Resolving disputes concerning contact

When resolving disputes concerning contact, the judicial authorities shall take all appropriate measures:

(a) to ensure that both parents are informed of the importance for their child and for both of them of establishing and maintaining regular contact with their child;

(b) to encourage parents and other persons having family ties with the child to reach amicable agreements with respect to contact, in particular through the use of family mediation and other processes for resolving disputes;

(c) before taking a decision, to ensure that they have sufficient information at their disposal, in particular from the holders of parental responsibilities, in order to take a decision in the best interests of the child and, where necessary, obtain further information from other relevant bodies or persons.

Article 8—Contact agreements

1. States Parties shall encourage, by means they consider appropriate, parents and other persons having family ties with the child to comply with the principles laid down in Articles 4 to 7 when making or modifying agreements on contact concerning a child. These agreements should preferably be in writing.

2. Upon request, judicial authorities shall, except where internal law otherwise provides, confirm an agreement on contact concerning a child, unless it is contrary to the best interests of the child.

Article 9—The carrying into effect of contact orders

States Parties shall take all appropriate measures to ensure that contact orders are carried into effect.

Article 10—Safeguards and guarantees to be taken concerning contact

1. Each State Party shall provide for and promote the use of safeguards and guarantees. It shall communicate, through its central authorities, to the Secretary General of the Council of Europe, within three months after the entry into force of this Convention for that State Party, at least three categories of safeguards and guarantees available in its internal law in addition to the safeguards and guarantees referred to in paragraph 3 of Article 4 and in letter b of paragraph 1 of Article 14 of this Convention. Changes of available safeguards and guarantees shall be communicated as soon as possible.

2. Where the circumstances of the case so require, judicial authorities may, at any time, make a contact order subject to any safeguards and guarantees both for the purpose of ensuring that the order is carried into effect and that either the child is returned at the end of the period of contact to the place where he or she usually lives or that he or she is not improperly removed.

(a) Safeguards and guarantees for ensuring that the order is carried into effect, may in particular include:
— supervision of contact;
— the obligation for a person to provide for the travel and accommodation expenses of the child and, as may be appropriate, of any other person accompanying the child;

— a security to be deposited by the person with whom the child is usually living to ensure that the person seeking contact with the child is not prevented from having such contact;

— a fine to be imposed on the person with whom the child is usually living, should this person refuse to comply with the contact order.

(b) Safeguards and guarantees for ensuring the return of the child or preventing an improper removal, may in particular include:

— the surrender of passports or identity documents and, where appropriate, a document indicating that the person seeking contact has notified the competent consular authority about such a surrender during the period of contact;

— financial guarantees;

— charges on property;

— undertakings or stipulations to the court;

— the obligation of the person having contact with the child to present himself or herself, with the child regularly before a competent body such as a youth welfare authority or a police station, in the place where contact is to be exercised;

— the obligation of the person seeking contact to present a document issued by the State where contact is to take place, certifying the recognition and declaration of enforceability of a custody or a contact order or both either before a contact order is made or before contact takes place;

— the imposition of conditions in relation to the place where contact is to be exercised and, where appropriate, the registration, in any national or transfrontier information system, of a prohibition preventing the child from leaving the State where contact is to take place.

3. Any such safeguards and guarantees shall be in writing or evidenced in writing and shall form part of the contact order or the confirmed agreement.

4. If safeguards or guarantees are to be implemented in another State Party, the judicial authority shall preferably order such safeguards or guarantees as are capable of implementation in that State Party.

CHAPTER III
Measures to Promote and Improve
Transfrontier Contact

Article 11—Central authorities

1. Each State Party shall appoint a central authority to carry out the functions provided for by this Convention in cases of transfrontier contact.

2. Federal States, States with more than one system of law or States having autonomous territorial units shall be free to appoint more than one central authority and to specify the territorial or personal extent of their functions. Where a State has appointed more than one central authority, it shall designate the central authority to which any communication may be addressed for transmission to the appropriate central authority within that State.

3. The Secretary General of the Council of Europe shall be notified of any appointment under this article.

Article 12—Duties of the central authorities

The central authorities of States Parties shall:

(a) co-operate with each other and promote co-operation between the competent authorities, including judicial authorities, in their respective countries to achieve the purposes of the Convention. They shall act with all necessary despatch;

(b) with a view to facilitating the operation of this Convention, provide each other on request with information concerning their laws relating to parental responsibilities, including contact and any more detailed information concerning safeguards and guarantees in addition to that already provided according to paragraph 1 of Article 10, and their available services (including legal services, publicly funded or otherwise) as well as information concerning any changes in these laws and services;

(c) take all appropriate steps in order to discover the whereabouts of the child;

(d) secure the transmission of requests for information coming from the competent authorities and relating to legal or factual matters concerning pending proceedings;

(e) keep each other informed of any difficulties likely to arise in applying the Convention and, as far as possible, eliminate obstacles to its application.

Article 13—International co-operation

1. The judicial authorities, the central authorities and the social and other bodies of States Parties concerned, acting within their respective competence, shall co-operate in relation to proceedings regarding transfrontier contact.

2. In particular, the central authorities shall assist the judicial authorities of States Parties in communicating with each other and obtaining such information and assistance as may be necessary for them to achieve the objects of this Convention.

3. In transfrontier cases, the central authorities shall assist children, parents and other persons having family ties with the child, in particular, to institute proceedings regarding transfrontier contact.

Article 14—Recognition and enforcement of transfrontier contact orders

1. States Parties shall provide, including where applicable in accordance with relevant international instruments:

(a) a system for the recognition and enforcement of orders made in other States Parties concerning contact and rights of custody;

(b) a procedure whereby orders relating to contact and rights of custody made in other States Parties may be recognised and declared enforceable in advance of contact being exercised within the State addressed.

2. If a State Party makes recognition or enforcement or both of a foreign order conditional on the existence of a treaty or reciprocity, it may consider this Convention as such a legal basis for recognition or enforcement or both of a foreign contact order.

Article 15—Conditions for implementing transfrontier contact orders

The judicial authority of the State Party in which a transfrontier contact order made in another State Party is to be implemented may, when recognising or declaring enforceable such a contact order, or at any later time, fix or adapt the conditions for its implementation, as well as any safeguards or guarantees attaching to it, if necessary for facilitating the exercise of this contact, provided that the essential elements of the order are respected and taking into account, in particular, a change of circumstances and the arrangements made by the persons concerned. In no circumstances may the foreign decision be reviewed as to its substance.

Article 16—Return of a child

1. Where a child at the end of a period of transfrontier contact based on a contact order is not returned, the competent authorities shall, upon request, ensure the child's immediate return, where applicable, by applying the relevant provisions of international instruments, of internal law and by implementing, where appropriate, such safeguards and guarantees as may be provided in the contact order.

2. A decision on the return of the child shall be made, whenever possible, within six weeks of the date of an application for the return.

Article 17—Costs

With the exception of the cost of repatriation, each State Party undertakes not to claim any payment from an applicant in respect of any measures taken under this Convention by the central authority itself of that State on the applicant's behalf.

Article 18—Language requirement

1. Subject to any special agreements made between the central authorities concerned:

   (a) communications to the central authority of the State addressed shall be made in the official language or in one of the official languages of that State or be accompanied by a translation into that language;

   (b) the central authority of the State addressed shall nevertheless accept communications made in English or in French, or accompanied by a translation into one of these languages.

2. Communications coming from the central authority of the State addressed, including the results of enquiries carried out, may be made in the official language or one of the official languages of that State or in English or French.

3. However, a State Party may, by making a declaration addressed to the Secretary General of the Council of Europe, object to the use of either French or English under paragraphs 1 and 2 of this article, in any application, communication or other documents sent to their central authorities.

CHAPTER IV
Relationship with other Instruments

Article 19—Relationship with the European Convention on Recognition and Enforcement of Decisions concerning Custody of Children and on Restoration of Custody of Children

Paragraphs 2 and 3 of Article 11 of the European Convention of 20 May 1980 (ETS No. 105) on Recognition and Enforcement of Decisions concerning Custody of Children and on Restoration of Custody of Children shall not be applied in relations between States Parties which are also States Parties of the present Convention.

Article 20—Relationships with other instruments

1. This Convention shall not affect any international instrument to which States Parties to the present Convention are Parties or shall become Parties and which contains provisions on matters governed by this Convention. In particular, this Convention shall not prejudice the application of the following legal instruments:

    (a) the Hague Convention of 5 October 1961 on the competence of authorities and the applicable law concerning the protection of minors,

    (b) the European Convention on the recognition and enforcement of decisions concerning custody of children and on restoration of custody of children of 20 May 1980, subject to Article 19 above,

    (c) the Hague Convention of 25 October 1980 on the civil aspects of international child abduction,

    (d) the Hague Convention of 19 October 1996 on jurisdiction, applicable law, recognition, enforcement and co-operation in respect of parental responsibility and measures for the protection of children.

2. Nothing in this Convention shall prevent Parties from concluding international agreements completing or developing the provisions of this Convention or extending their field of application.

3. In their mutual relations, States Parties which are members of the European Community shall apply Community rules and shall therefore not apply the rules arising from this Convention, except in so far as there is no Community rule governing the particular subject concerned.

CHAPTER V
Amendments to the Convention

Article 21—Amendments

1. Any proposal for an amendment to this Convention presented by a Party shall be communicated to the Secretary General of the Council of Europe and forwarded by him or her to the member States of the Council of Europe, any signatory, any State Party, the European Community, to any State invited to sign this Convention in accordance with the provisions of Article 22 and to any State invited to accede to this Convention in accordance with the provisions of Article 23.

2. Any amendment proposed by a Party shall be communicated to the European Committee on Legal Co-operation (CDCJ), which shall submit to the Committee of Ministers its opinion on that proposed amendment.

3. The Committee of Ministers shall consider the proposed amendment and the opinion submitted by the CDCJ and, following consultation of the Parties to the Convention, which are not members of the Council of Europe, may adopt the amendment.

4. The text of any amendment adopted by the Committee of Ministers in accordance with paragraph 3 of this article shall be forwarded to the Parties for acceptance.

5. Any amendment adopted in accordance with paragraph 3 of this article shall enter into force on the first day of the month following the expiration of a period of one month after the date on which all Parties have informed the Secretary General that they have accepted it.

CHAPTER VI
Final Clauses

Article 22—Signature and entry into force

1. This Convention shall be open for signature by the member States of the Council of Europe, the non-member States which have participated in its elaboration and the European Community.

2. This Convention is subject to ratification, acceptance or approval. Instruments of ratification, acceptance or approval shall be deposited with the Secretary General of the Council of Europe.

3. This Convention shall enter into force on the first day of the month following the expiration of a period of three months after the date on which three States, including at least two member States of the Council of Europe, have expressed their consent to be bound by the Convention in accordance with the provisions of the preceding paragraph.

4. In respect of any State mentioned in paragraph 1 or the European Community, which subsequently expresses its consent to be bound by it, the Convention shall enter into force on the first day of the month following the expiration of a period of three months after the date of the deposit of its instrument of ratification, acceptance or approval.

Article 23—Accession to the Convention

1. After the entry into force of this Convention, the Committee of Ministers of the Council of Europe may, after consultation of the Parties, invite any non-member State of the Council of Europe, which has not participated in the elaboration of the Convention, to accede to this Convention by a decision taken by the majority provided for in Article 20 (d) of the Statute of the Council of Europe, and by unanimous vote of the representatives of the Contracting States entitled to sit on the Committee of Ministers.

2. In respect of any acceding State, the Convention shall enter into force on the first day of the month following the expiration of a period of three months after the date of deposit of the instrument of accession with the Secretary General of the Council of Europe.

Article 24—Territorial application

1. Any State or the European Community may, at the time of signature or when depositing its instrument of ratification, acceptance, approval or accession, specify the territory or territories to which this Convention shall apply.

2. Any Party may, at any later date, by a declaration addressed to the Secretary General of the Council of Europe, extend the application of this Convention to any other territory specified in the declaration and for whose international relations it is responsible or on whose behalf it is authorised to give undertakings. In respect of such territory, the Convention shall enter into force on the first day of the month following the expiration of a period of three months after the date of receipt of such declaration by the Secretary General.

3. Any declaration made under the two preceding paragraphs may, in respect of any territory specified in such declaration, be withdrawn by a notification addressed to the Secretary General. The withdrawal shall become effective on the first day of the month following the expiration of a period of three months after the date of receipt of such notification by the Secretary General.

Article 25—Reservations

No reservation may be made in respect of any provision of this Convention.

Article 26—Denunciation

1. Any Party may, at any time, denounce this Convention by means of a notification addressed to the Secretary General of the Council of Europe.

2. Such denunciation shall become effective on the first day of the month following the expiration of a period of three months after the date of receipt of the notification by the Secretary General.

Article 27—Notifications

The Secretary General of the Council of Europe shall notify the member States of the Council of Europe, any State signatory, any State Party, the European Community, to any State invited to sign this Convention in accordance with the provisions of Article 22 and to any State invited to accede to this Convention in accordance with the provisions of Article 23 of:

  (a) any signature;

  (b) the deposit of any instrument of ratification, acceptance, approval or accession;

  (c) any date of entry into force of this Convention in accordance with Articles 22 and 23;

  (d) any amendment adopted in accordance with Article 21 and the date on which such an amendment enters into force;

  (e) any declaration made under the provisions of Article 18;

  (f) any denunciation made in pursuance of the provisions of Article 26;

  (g) any other act, notification or communication, in particular relating to Articles 10 and 11 of this Convention.

In witness whereof, the undersigned, being duly authorised thereto, have signed this Convention.

Done at Strasbourg, this 15th day of May 2003, in English and in French, both texts being equally authentic, in a single copy, which shall be deposited in the archives of the Council of Europe. The Secretary General of the Council of Europe shall transmit certified copies to each member State of the Council of Europe, to the non-member States which have participated in the elaboration of this Convention, to the European Community and to any State invited to accede to this Convention.

101. EUROPEAN CONVENTION ON ACTION AGAINST TRAFFICKING IN HUMAN BEINGS, 2005

This Convention (*CETS* No. 197) was opened for signature in Warsaw on 16 May 2005, by the Member States of the Council of Europe, non-member States which participated in its elaboration, and the European Community. It entered into force on 1 Feburary 2008.

The Convention deals not only with preventing trafficking and prosecuting traffickers, but also with the protection of victims of trafficking and their rights. Unlike other instruments, such as the Protocol additional to the UN Convention on Transnational Crime, this Convention applies to all forms of trafficking; whether national or transnational, and whether or not related to organised crime. It adopts the same definition of trafficking as the UN Protocol in Article 4(a), its personal scope includes women, men and children, and it applies no matter what the form of exploitation (sexual exploitation, forced labour or services, etc.).

The Convention's provisions on human rights (see Articles 3, 10–17) also distinguish it from other instruments, which are primarily concerned with the prevention and criminalisation of trafficking. Some of its provisions are rather weak, however; for example, whereas each State party 'shall adopt such legislative or other measures as may be necessary to assist victims...' (Article 12), it is only required to 'consider' the adoption of measures to criminalize the use of services of a victim of trafficking (Article 19). The terms and the language used in the English text are also not always as clear as they might be.

At the European Union level, the European Commission has proposed a Council Framework Decision on preventing and combating trafficking in human beings and protecting victims, repealing Framework Decision 2002/629/JHA of 19 July 2002: *Official Journal* L 203, 01.08.2002; see 'Opinion of the Experts Group on Trafficking in Human Beings of the European Commission', (2009) 21 *IJRL* 508.

In 2004, the UN Commission on Human Rights appointed a Special Rapporteur on trafficking in persons, especially women and children, and the Human Rights Council extended the mandate for a further three years in 2008: Resolution 8/12.

Further reading

COSTER VAN VOORHOUT, J. E. B., 'Human Trafficking for Labour Exploitation: Interpreting the Crime', (2007) 3 *Utrecht Law Review* 44: **http://www.utrechtlawreview.org**.

EUROPEAN UNION AGENCY FOR FUNDAMENTAL RIGHTS, *Child Trafficking in the European Union: Challenges, Perspectives and Good Practices*, Vienna: European Union Agency for Fundamental Rights, 2009: **http://fra.europa.eu**.

GALLAGHER, A. T., 'Recent Legal Developments in the Field of Human Trafficking: A Critical Review of the 2005 European Convention and Related Instruments', (2006) 8 *European Journal of Migration and Law* 163.

OBOKATA, T., 'Smuggling of human beings from a human rights perspective: Obligations of non-State and State actors under international human rights law', (2005) 17 *IJRL* 394.

RIJKEN, C., *Trafficking in Persons: Prosecution from a European Perspective*, The Hague: T. M. C. Asser Press, 2003.

UNITED NATIONS, 'Trafficking in persons, especially women and children', Report of the Special Rapporteur, UN doc. A/64/290, 12 August 2009.

TEXT

Preamble

The member States of the Council of Europe and the other Signatories hereto,

Considering that the aim of the Council of Europe is to achieve a greater unity between its members;

Considering that trafficking in human beings constitutes a violation of human rights and an offence to the dignity and the integrity of the human being;

Considering that trafficking in human beings may result in slavery for victims;

Considering that respect for victims' rights, protection of victims and action to combat trafficking in human beings must be the paramount objectives;

Considering that all actions or initiatives against trafficking in human beings must be non-discriminatory, take gender equality into account as well as a child-rights approach;

Recalling the declarations by the Ministers for Foreign Affairs of the Member States at the 112th (14–15 May 2003) and the 114th (12–13 May 2004) Sessions of the Committee of Ministers calling for reinforced action by the Council of Europe on trafficking in human beings;

Bearing in mind the Convention for the Protection of Human Rights and Fundamental Freedoms (1950) and its protocols;

Bearing in mind the following recommendations of the Committee of Ministers to member States of the Council of Europe: Recommendation No. R (91) 11 on sexual exploitation, pornography and prostitution of, and trafficking in, children and young adults; Recommendation No. R (97) 13 concerning intimidation of witnesses and the rights of the defence; Recommendation No. R (2000) 11 on action against trafficking in human beings for the purpose of sexual exploitation and Recommendation Rec (2001) 16 on the protection of children against sexual exploitation; Recommendation Rec (2002) 5 on the protection of women against violence;

Bearing in mind the following recommendations of the Parliamentary Assembly of the Council of Europe: Recommendation 1325 (1997) on traffic in women and forced prostitution in Council of Europe member States; Recommendation 1450 (2000) on violence against women in Europe; Recommendation 1545 (2002) on a campaign against trafficking in women; Recommendation 1610 (2003) on migration connected with trafficking in women and prostitution; Recommendation 1611 (2003) on trafficking in organs in Europe; Recommendation 1663 (2004) on domestic slavery: servitude, au pairs and mail-order brides;

Bearing in mind the European Union Council Framework Decision of 19 July 2002 on combating trafficking in human beings, the European Union Council Framework Decision of 15 March 2001 on the standing of victims in criminal proceedings and the European Union Council Directive of 29 April 2004 on the residence permit issued to third-country nationals who are victims of trafficking in human beings or who have been the subject of an action to facilitate illegal immigration, who cooperate with the competent authorities;

Taking due account of the United Nations Convention against Transnational Organized Crime and the Protocol thereto to Prevent, Suppress and Punish Trafficking in Persons, Especially Women and Children with a view to improving the protection which they afford and developing the standards established by them;

Taking due account of the other international legal instruments relevant in the field of action against trafficking in human beings;

Taking into account the need to prepare a comprehensive international legal instrument focusing on the human rights of victims of trafficking and setting up a specific monitoring mechanism,

Have agreed as follows:

CHAPTER I
Purposes, Scope, Non-Discrimination Principle and Definitions

Article 1—*Purposes of the Convention*

1. The purposes of this Convention are:
   - *(a)* to prevent and combat trafficking in human beings, while guaranteeing gender equality;
   - *(b)* to protect the human rights of the victims of trafficking, design a comprehensive framework for the protection and assistance of victims and witnesses, while guaranteeing gender equality, as well as to ensure effective investigation and prosecution;
   - *(c)* to promote international cooperation on action against trafficking in human beings.

2. In order to ensure effective implementation of its provisions by the Parties, this Convention sets up a specific monitoring mechanism.

Article 2—*Scope*

This Convention shall apply to all forms of trafficking in human beings, whether national or transnational, whether or not connected with organised crime.

Article 3—*Non-discrimination principle*

The implementation of the provisions of this Convention by Parties, in particular the enjoyment of measures to protect and promote the rights of victims, shall be secured without discrimination on any ground such as sex, race, colour, language, religion, political or other opinion, national or social origin, association with a national minority, property, birth or other status.

Article 4—*Definitions*

For the purposes of this Convention:
   - *(a)* 'Trafficking in human beings' shall mean the recruitment, transportation, transfer, harbouring or receipt of persons, by means of the threat or use of force or other forms of coercion, of abduction, of fraud, of deception, of the abuse of power or of a position of vulnerability or of the giving or receiving of payments or benefits to achieve the consent of a person having control over another person, for the purpose of exploitation. Exploitation shall include, at a minimum, the exploitation of the prostitution of others or other forms of sexual exploitation, forced labour or services, slavery or practices similar to slavery, servitude or the removal of organs;
   - *(b)* The consent of a victim of 'trafficking in human beings' to the intended exploitation set forth in subparagraph (a) of this article shall be irrelevant where any of the means set forth in subparagraph (a) have been used;

(c) The recruitment, transportation, transfer, harbouring or receipt of a child for the purpose of exploitation shall be considered 'trafficking in human beings' even if this does not involve any of the means set forth in subparagraph (a) of this article;

(d) 'Child' shall mean any person under eighteen years of age;

(e) 'Victim' shall mean any natural person who is subject to trafficking in human beings as defined in this article.

CHAPTER II
Prevention, Co-operation and other Measures

Article 5—Prevention of trafficking in human beings

1. Each Party shall take measures to establish or strengthen national co-ordination between the various bodies responsible for preventing and combating trafficking in human beings.

2. Each Party shall establish and/or strengthen effective policies and programmes to prevent trafficking in human beings, by such means as: research, information, awareness raising and education campaigns, social and economic initiatives and training programmes, in particular for persons vulnerable to trafficking and for professionals concerned with trafficking in human beings.

3. Each Party shall promote a Human Rights-based approach and shall use gender mainstreaming and a child-sensitive approach in the development, implementation and assessment of all the policies and programmes referred to in paragraph 2.

4. Each Party shall take appropriate measures, as may be necessary, to enable migration to take place legally, in particular through dissemination of accurate information by relevant offices, on the conditions enabling the legal entry in and stay on its territory.

5. Each Party shall take specific measures to reduce children's vulnerability to trafficking, notably by creating a protective environment for them.

6. Measures established in accordance with this article shall involve, where appropriate, non-governmental organisations, other relevant organisations and other elements of civil society committed to the prevention of trafficking in human beings and victim protection or assistance.

Article 6—Measures to discourage the demand

To discourage the demand that fosters all forms of exploitation of persons, especially women and children, that leads to trafficking, each Party shall adopt or strengthen legislative, administrative, educational, social, cultural or other measures including:

(a) research on best practices, methods and strategies;

(b) raising awareness of the responsibility and important role of media and civil society in identifying the demand as one of the root causes of trafficking in human beings;

(c) target information campaigns involving, as appropriate, *inter alia*, public authorities and policy makers;

(d) preventive measures, including educational programmes for boys and girls during their schooling, which stress the unacceptable nature of discrimination based on sex, and its disastrous consequences, the importance of gender equality and the dignity and integrity of every human being.

Article 7—Border measures

1. Without prejudice to international commitments in relation to the free movement of persons, Parties shall strengthen, to the extent possible, such border controls as may be necessary to prevent and detect trafficking in human beings.

2. Each Party shall adopt legislative or other appropriate measures to prevent, to the extent possible, means of transport operated by commercial carriers from being used in the commission of offences established in accordance with this Convention.

3. Where appropriate, and without prejudice to applicable international conventions, such measures shall include establishing the obligation of commercial carriers, including any transportation company or the owner or operator of any means of transport, to ascertain that all passengers are in possession of the travel documents required for entry into the receiving State.

4. Each Party shall take the necessary measures, in accordance with its internal law, to provide for sanctions in cases of violation of the obligation set forth in paragraph 3 of this article.

5. Each Party shall adopt such legislative or other measures as may be necessary to permit, in accordance with its internal law, the denial of entry or revocation of visas of persons implicated in the commission of offences established in accordance with this Convention.

6. Parties shall strengthen co-operation among border control agencies by, *inter alia*, establishing and maintaining direct channels of communication.

Article 8—Security and control of documents

Each Party shall adopt such measures as may be necessary:

   (a) To ensure that travel or identity documents issued by it are of such quality that they cannot easily be misused and cannot readily be falsified or unlawfully altered, replicated or issued; and

   (b) To ensure the integrity and security of travel or identity documents issued by or on behalf of the Party and to prevent their unlawful creation and issuance.

Article 9—Legitimacy and validity of documents

At the request of another Party, a Party shall, in accordance with its internal law, verify within a reasonable time the legitimacy and validity of travel or identity documents issued or purported to have been issued in its name and suspected of being used for trafficking in human beings.

CHAPTER III
Measures to Protect and Promote the Rights of Victims, Guaranteeing Gender Equality

Article 10—Identification of the victims

1. Each Party shall provide its competent authorities with persons who are trained and qualified in preventing and combating trafficking in human beings, in identifying and helping victims, including children, and shall ensure that the different authorities collaborate with each other as well as with relevant support organisations, so that victims

can be identified in a procedure duly taking into account the special situation of women and child victims and, in appropriate cases, issued with residence permits under the conditions provided for in Article 14 of the present Convention.

2. Each Party shall adopt such legislative or other measures as may be necessary to identify victims as appropriate in collaboration with other Parties and relevant support organisations. Each Party shall ensure that, if the competent authorities have reasonable grounds to believe that a person has been victim of trafficking in human beings, that person shall not be removed from its territory until the identification process as victim of an offence provided for in Article 18 of this Convention has been completed by the competent authorities and shall likewise ensure that that person receives the assistance provided for in Article 12, paragraphs 1 and 2.

3. When the age of the victim is uncertain and there are reasons to believe that the victim is a child, he or she shall be presumed to be a child and shall be accorded special protection measures pending verification of his/her age.

4. As soon as an unaccompanied child is identified as a victim, each Party shall:

(a) provide for representation of the child by a legal guardian, organisation or authority which shall act in the best interests of that child;

(b) take the necessary steps to establish his/her identity and nationality;

(c) make every effort to locate his/her family when this is in the best interests of the child.

Article 11—Protection of private life

1. Each Party shall protect the private life and identity of victims. Personal data regarding them shall be stored and used in conformity with the conditions provided for by the Convention for the Protection of Individuals with regard to Automatic Processing of Personal Data (ETS No. 108).

2. Each Party shall adopt measures to ensure, in particular, that the identity, or details allowing the identification, of a child victim of trafficking are not made publicly known, through the media or by any other means, except, in exceptional circumstances, in order to facilitate the tracing of family members or otherwise secure the well-being and protection of the child.

3. Each Party shall consider adopting, in accordance with Article 10 of the Convention for the Protection of Human Rights and Fundamental Freedoms as interpreted by the European Court of Human Rights, measures aimed at encouraging the media to protect the private life and identity of victims through self-regulation or through regulatory or co-regulatory measures.

Article 12—Assistance to victims

1. Each Party shall adopt such legislative or other measures as may be necessary to assist victims in their physical, psychological and social recovery. Such assistance shall include at least:

(a) standards of living capable of ensuring their subsistence, through such measures as: appropriate and secure accommodation, psychological and material assistance;

(b) access to emergency medical treatment;

(c) translation and interpretation services, when appropriate;

(d) counselling and information, in particular as regards their legal rights and the services available to them, in a language that they can understand;

(e) assistance to enable their rights and interests to be presented and considered at appropriate stages of criminal proceedings against offenders;

(f) access to education for children.

2. Each Party shall take due account of the victim's safety and protection needs.

3. In addition, each Party shall provide necessary medical or other assistance to victims lawfully resident within its territory who do not have adequate resources and need such help.

4. Each Party shall adopt the rules under which victims lawfully resident within its territory shall be authorised to have access to the labour market, to vocational training and education.

5. Each Party shall take measures, where appropriate and under the conditions provided for by its internal law, to co-operate with non-governmental organisations, other relevant organisations or other elements of civil society engaged in assistance to victims.

6. Each Party shall adopt such legislative or other measures as may be necessary to ensure that assistance to a victim is not made conditional on his or her willingness to act as a witness.

7. For the implementation of the provisions set out in this article, each Party shall ensure that services are provided on a consensual and informed basis, taking due account of the special needs of persons in a vulnerable position and the rights of children in terms of accommodation, education and appropriate health care.

Article 13—Recovery and reflection period

1. Each Party shall provide in its internal law a recovery and reflection period of at least 30 days, when there are reasonable grounds to believe that the person concerned is a victim. Such a period shall be sufficient for the person concerned to recover and escape the influence of traffickers and/or to take an informed decision on cooperating with the competent authorities. During this period it shall not be possible to enforce any expulsion order against him or her. This provision is without prejudice to the activities carried out by the competent authorities in all phases of the relevant national proceedings, and in particular when investigating and prosecuting the offences concerned. During this period, the Parties shall authorise the persons concerned to stay in their territory.

2. During this period, the persons referred to in paragraph 1 of this Article shall be entitled to the measures contained in Article 12, paragraphs 1 and 2.

3. The Parties are not bound to observe this period if grounds of public order prevent it or if it is found that victim status is being claimed improperly.

Article 14—Residence permit

1. Each Party shall issue a renewable residence permit to victims, in one or other of the two following situations or in both:

(a) the competent authority considers that their stay is necessary owing to their personal situation;

(b) the competent authority considers that their stay is necessary for the purpose of their co-operation with the competent authorities in investigation or criminal proceedings.

2. The residence permit for child victims, when legally necessary, shall be issued in accordance with the best interests of the child and, where appropriate, renewed under the same conditions.

3. The non-renewal or withdrawal of a residence permit is subject to the conditions provided for by the internal law of the Party.

4. If a victim submits an application for another kind of residence permit, the Party concerned shall take into account that he or she holds, or has held, a residence permit in conformity with paragraph 1.

5. Having regard to the obligations of Parties to which Article 40 of this Convention refers, each Party shall ensure that granting of a permit according to this provision shall be without prejudice to the right to seek and enjoy asylum.

Article 15—Compensation and legal redress

1. Each Party shall ensure that victims have access, as from their first contact with the competent authorities, to information on relevant judicial and administrative proceedings in a language which they can understand.

2. Each Party shall provide, in its internal law, for the right to legal assistance and to free legal aid for victims under the conditions provided by its internal law.

3. Each Party shall provide, in its internal law, for the right of victims to compensation from the perpetrators.

4. Each Party shall adopt such legislative or other measures as may be necessary to guarantee compensation for victims in accordance with the conditions under its internal law, for instance through the establishment of a fund for victim compensation or measures or programmes aimed at social assistance and social integration of victims, which could be funded by the assets resulting from the application of measures provided in Article 23.

Article 16—Repatriation and return of victims

1. The Party of which a victim is a national or in which that person had the right of permanent residence at the time of entry into the territory of the receiving Party shall, with due regard for his or her rights, safety and dignity, facilitate and accept, his or her return without undue or unreasonable delay.

2. When a Party returns a victim to another State, such return shall be with due regard for the rights, safety and dignity of that person and for the status of any legal proceedings related to the fact that the person is a victim, and shall preferably be voluntary.

3. At the request of a receiving Party, a requested Party shall verify whether a person is its national or had the right of permanent residence in its territory at the time of entry into the territory of the receiving Party.

4. In order to facilitate the return of a victim who is without proper documentation, the Party of which that person is a national or in which he or she had the right of permanent residence at the time of entry into the territory of the receiving Party shall agree to issue, at the request of the receiving Party, such travel documents or other authorisation as may be necessary to enable the person to travel to and re-enter its territory.

5. Each Party shall adopt such legislative or other measures as may be necessary to establish repatriation programmes, involving relevant national or international institutions and non-governmental organisations. These programmes aim at avoiding re-victimisation. Each Party should make its best effort to favour the reintegration of victims into the society of the State of return, including reintegration into the education

system and the labour market, in particular through the acquisition and improvement of their professional skills. With regard to children, these programmes should include enjoyment of the right to education and measures to secure adequate care or receipt by the family or appropriate care structures.

6. Each Party shall adopt such legislative or other measures as may be necessary to make available to victims, where appropriate in co-operation with any other Party concerned, contact information of structures that can assist them in the country where they are returned or repatriated, such as law enforcement offices, non-governmental organisations, legal professions able to provide counselling and social welfare agencies.

7. Child victims shall not be returned to a State, if there is indication, following a risk and security assessment, that such return would not be in the best interests of the child.

Article 17—Gender equality

Each Party shall, in applying measures referred to in this chapter, aim to promote gender equality and use gender mainstreaming in the development, implementation and assessment of the measures.

CHAPTER IV
Substantive Criminal Law

Article 18—Criminalisation of trafficking in human beings

Each Party shall adopt such legislative and other measures as may be necessary to establish as criminal offences the conduct contained in article 4 of this Convention, when committed intentionally.

Article 19—Criminalisation of the use of services of a victim

Each Party shall consider adopting such legislative and other measures as may be necessary to establish as criminal offences under its internal law, the use of services which are the object of exploitation as referred to in Article 4 paragraph (a) of this Convention, with the knowledge that the person is a victim of trafficking in human beings.

Article 20—Criminalisation of acts relating to travel or identity documents

Each Party shall adopt such legislative and other measures as may be necessary to establish as criminal offences the following conducts, when committed intentionally and for the purpose of enabling the trafficking in human beings:

- *(a)* forging a travel or identity document;
- *(b)* procuring or providing such a document;
- *(c)* retaining, removing, concealing, damaging or destroying a travel or identity document of another person.

Article 21—Attempt and aiding or abetting

1. Each Party shall adopt such legislative and other measures as may be necessary to establish as criminal offences when committed intentionally, aiding or abetting the

commission of any of the offences established in accordance with Articles 18 and 20 of the present Convention.

2. Each Party shall adopt such legislative and other measures as may be necessary to establish as criminal offences when committed intentionally, an attempt to commit the offences established in accordance with Articles 18 and 20, paragraph (a), of this Convention.

Article 22—Corporate liability

1. Each Party shall adopt such legislative and other measures as may be necessary to ensure that a legal person can be held liable for a criminal offence established in accordance with this Convention, committed for its benefit by any natural person, acting either individually or as part of an organ of the legal person, who has a leading position within the legal person, based on:

   (a) a power of representation of the legal person;

   (b) an authority to take decisions on behalf of the legal person;

   (c) an authority to exercise control within the legal person.

2. Apart from the cases already provided for in paragraph 1, each Party shall take the measures necessary to ensure that a legal person can be held liable where the lack of supervision or control by a natural person referred to in paragraph 1 has made possible the commission of a criminal offence established in accordance with this Convention for the benefit of that legal person by a natural person acting under its authority.

3. Subject to the legal principles of the Party, the liability of a legal person may be criminal, civil or administrative.

4. Such liability shall be without prejudice to the criminal liability of the natural persons who have committed the offence.

Article 23—Sanctions and measures

1. Each Party shall adopt such legislative and other measures as may be necessary to ensure that the criminal offences established in accordance with Articles 18 to 21 are punishable by effective, proportionate and dissuasive sanctions. These sanctions shall include, for criminal offences established in accordance with Article 18 when committed by natural persons, penalties involving deprivation of liberty which can give rise to extradition.

2. Each Party shall ensure that legal persons held liable in accordance with Article 22 shall be subject to effective, proportionate and dissuasive criminal or non-criminal sanctions or measures, including monetary sanctions.

3. Each Party shall adopt such legislative and other measures as may be necessary to enable it to confiscate or otherwise deprive the instrumentalities and proceeds of criminal offences established in accordance with Articles 18 and 20, paragraph (a), of this Convention, or property the value of which corresponds to such proceeds.

4. Each Party shall adopt such legislative or other measures as may be necessary to enable the temporary or permanent closure of any establishment which was used to carry out trafficking in human beings, without prejudice to the rights of *bona fide* third parties or to deny the perpetrator, temporary or permanently, the exercise of the activity in the course of which this offence was committed.

Article 24—Aggravating circumstances

Each Party shall ensure that the following circumstances are regarded as aggravating circumstances in the determination of the penalty for offences established in accordance with Article 18 of this Convention:

(a) the offence deliberately or by gross negligence endangered the life of the victim;

(b) the offence was committed against a child;

(c) the offence was committed by a public official in the performance of her/his duties;

(d) the offence was committed within the framework of a criminal organisation.

Article 25—Previous convictions

Each Party shall adopt such legislative and other measures providing for the possibility to take into account final sentences passed by another Party in relation to offences established in accordance with this Convention when determining the penalty.

Article 26—Non-punishment provision

Each Party shall, in accordance with the basic principles of its legal system, provide for the possibility of not imposing penalties on victims for their involvement in unlawful activities, to the extent that they have been compelled to do so.

CHAPTER V
Investigation, Prosecution and Procedural Law

Article 27—Ex parte and ex officio applications

1. Each Party shall ensure that investigations into or prosecution of offences established in accordance with this Convention shall not be dependent upon the report or accusation made by a victim, at least when the offence was committed in whole or in part on its territory.

2. Each Party shall ensure that victims of an offence in the territory of a Party other than the one where they reside may make a complaint before the competent authorities of their State of residence. The competent authority to which the complaint is made, insofar as it does not itself have competence in this respect, shall transmit it without delay to the competent authority of the Party in the territory in which the offence was committed. The complaint shall be dealt with in accordance with the internal law of the Party in which the offence was committed.

3. Each Party shall ensure, by means of legislative or other measures, in accordance with the conditions provided for by its internal law, to any group, foundation, association or non-governmental organisations which aims at fighting trafficking in human beings or protection of human rights, the possibility to assist and/or support the victim with his or her consent during criminal proceedings concerning the offence established in accordance with Article 18 of this Convention.

Article 28—Protection of victims, witnesses and collaborators with the judicial authorities

1. Each Party shall adopt such legislative or other measures as may be necessary to provide effective and appropriate protection from potential retaliation or intimidation in particular during and after investigation and prosecution of perpetrators, for:

   (a) victims;

   (b) as appropriate, those who report the criminal offences established in accordance with Article 18 of this Convention or otherwise co-operate with the investigating or prosecuting authorities;

   (c) witnesses who give testimony concerning criminal offences established in accordance with Article 18 of this Convention;

   (d) when necessary, members of the family of persons referred to in subparagraphs (a) and (c).

2. Each Party shall adopt such legislative or other measures as may be necessary to ensure and to offer various kinds of protection. This may include physical protection, relocation, identity change and assistance in obtaining jobs.

3. A child victim shall be afforded special protection measures taking into account the best interests of the child.

4. Each Party shall adopt such legislative or other measures as may be necessary to provide, when necessary, appropriate protection from potential retaliation or intimidation in particular during and after investigation and prosecution of perpetrators, for members of groups, foundations, associations or non-governmental organisations which carry out the activities set out in Article 27, paragraph 3.

5. Each Party shall consider entering into agreements or arrangements with other States for the implementation of this article.

Article 29—Specialised authorities and co-ordinating bodies

1. Each Party shall adopt such measures as may be necessary to ensure that persons or entities are specialised in the fight against trafficking and the protection of victims. Such persons or entities shall have the necessary independence in accordance with the fundamental principles of the legal system of the Party, in order for them to be able to carry out their functions effectively and free from any undue pressure. Such persons or the staffs of such entities shall have adequate training and financial resources for their tasks.

2. Each Party shall adopt such measures as may be necessary to ensure co-ordination of the policies and actions of their governments' departments and other public agencies against trafficking in human beings, where appropriate, through setting up co-ordinating bodies.

3. Each Party shall provide or strengthen training for relevant officials in the prevention of and fight against trafficking in human beings, including Human Rights training. The training may be agency-specific and shall, as appropriate, focus on: methods used in preventing such trafficking, prosecuting the traffickers and protecting the rights of the victims, including protecting the victims from the traffickers.

4. Each Party shall consider appointing National Rapporteurs or other mechanisms for monitoring the anti-trafficking activities of State institutions and the implementation of national legislation requirements.

Article 30—Court proceedings

In accordance with the Convention for the Protection of Human Rights and Fundamental Freedoms, in particular Article 6, each Party shall adopt such legislative or other measures as may be necessary to ensure in the course of judicial proceedings:

- *(a)* the protection of victims' private life and, where appropriate, identity;
- *(b)* victims' safety and protection from intimidation,

in accordance with the conditions under its internal law and, in the case of child victims, by taking special care of children's needs and ensuring their right to special protection measures.

Article 31—Jurisdiction

1. Each Party shall adopt such legislative and other measures as may be necessary to establish jurisdiction over any offence established in accordance with this Convention, when the offence is committed:

- *(a)* in its territory; or
- *(b)* on board a ship flying the flag of that Party; or
- *(c)* on board an aircraft registered under the laws of that Party; or
- *(d)* by one of its nationals or by a stateless person who has his or her habitual residence in its territory, if the offence is punishable under criminal law where it was committed or if the offence is committed outside the territorial jurisdiction of any State;
- *(e)* against one of its nationals.

2. Each Party may, at the time of signature or when depositing its instrument of ratification, acceptance, approval or accession, by a declaration addressed to the Secretary General of the Council of Europe, declare that it reserves the right not to apply or to apply only in specific cases or conditions the jurisdiction rules laid down in paragraphs 1 (d) and (e) of this article or any part thereof.

3. Each Party shall adopt such measures as may be necessary to establish jurisdiction over the offences referred to in this Convention, in cases where an alleged offender is present in its territory and it does not extradite him/her to another Party, solely on the basis of his/her nationality, after a request for extradition.

4. When more than one Party claims jurisdiction over an alleged offence established in accordance with this Convention, the Parties involved shall, where appropriate, consult with a view to determining the most appropriate jurisdiction for prosecution.

5. Without prejudice to the general norms of international law, this Convention does not exclude any criminal jurisdiction exercised by a Party in accordance with internal law.

CHAPTER VI
International Co-operation and Co-operation with Civil Society

Article 32—General principles and measures for international co-operation

The Parties shall co-operate with each other, in accordance with the provisions of this Convention, and through application of relevant applicable international and regional instruments, arrangements agreed on the basis of uniform or reciprocal legislation and internal laws, to the widest extent possible, for the purpose of:

— preventing and combating trafficking in human beings;
— protecting and providing assistance to victims;
— investigations or proceedings concerning criminal offences established in accordance with this Convention.

Article 33—Measures relating to endangered or missing persons

1. When a Party, on the basis of the information at its disposal has reasonable grounds to believe that the life, the freedom or the physical integrity of a person referred to in Article 28, paragraph 1, is in immediate danger on the territory of another Party, the Party that has the information shall, in such a case of emergency, transmit it without delay to the latter so as to take the appropriate protection measures.

2. The Parties to this Convention may consider reinforcing their co-operation in the search for missing people, in particular for missing children, if the information available leads them to believe that she/he is a victim of trafficking in human beings. To this end, the Parties may conclude bilateral or multilateral treaties with each other.

Article 34—Information

1. The requested Party shall promptly inform the requesting Party of the final result of the action taken under this chapter. The requested Party shall also promptly inform the requesting Party of any circumstances which render impossible the carrying out of the action sought or are likely to delay it significantly.

2. A Party may, within the limits of its internal law, without prior request, forward to another Party information obtained within the framework of its own investigations when it considers that the disclosure of such information might assist the receiving Party in initiating or carrying out investigations or proceedings concerning criminal offences established in accordance with this Convention or might lead to a request for co-operation by that Party under this chapter.

3. Prior to providing such information, the providing Party may request that it be kept confidential or used subject to conditions. If the receiving Party cannot comply with such request, it shall notify the providing Party, which shall then determine whether the information should nevertheless be provided. If the receiving Party accepts the information subject to the conditions, it shall be bound by them.

4. All information requested concerning Articles 13, 14 and 16, necessary to provide the rights conferred by these articles, shall be transmitted at the request of the Party concerned without delay with due respect to Article 11 of the present Convention.

Article 35—Co-operation with civil society

Each Party shall encourage State authorities and public officials, to co-operate with non-governmental organisations, other relevant organisations and members of civil society, in establishing strategic partnerships with the aim of achieving the purpose of this Convention.

CHAPTER VII
Monitoring Mechanism

Article 36—Group of experts on action against trafficking in human beings

1. The Group of experts on action against trafficking in human beings (hereinafter referred to as 'GRETA'), shall monitor the implementation of this Convention by the Parties.

2. GRETA shall be composed of a minimum of 10 members and a maximum of 15 members, taking into account a gender and geographical balance, as well as a multidisciplinary expertise. They shall be elected by the Committee of the Parties for a term of office of 4 years, renewable once, chosen from amongst nationals of the States Parties to this Convention.

3. The election of the members of GRETA shall be based on the following principles:

(a) they shall be chosen from among persons of high moral character, known for their recognised competence in the fields of Human Rights, assistance and protection of victims and of action against trafficking in human beings or having professional experience in the areas covered by this Convention;

(b) they shall sit in their individual capacity and shall be independent and impartial in the exercise of their functions and shall be available to carry out their duties in an effective manner;

(c) no two members of GRETA may be nationals of the same State;

(d) they should represent the main legal systems.

4. The election procedure of the members of GRETA shall be determined by the Committee of Ministers, after consulting with and obtaining the unanimous consent of the Parties to the Convention, within a period of one year following the entry into force of this Convention. GRETA shall adopt its own rules of procedure.

Article 37—Committee of the Parties

1. The Committee of the Parties shall be composed of the representatives on the Committee of Ministers of the Council of Europe of the member States Parties to the Convention and representatives of the Parties to the Convention, which are not members of the Council of Europe.

2. The Committee of the Parties shall be convened by the Secretary General of the Council of Europe. Its first meeting shall be held within a period of one year following the entry into force of this Convention in order to elect the members of GRETA. It shall subsequently meet whenever one-third of the Parties, the President of GRETA or the Secretary General so requests.

3. The Committee of the Parties shall adopt its own rules of procedure.

Article 38—Procedure

1. The evaluation procedure shall concern the Parties to the Convention and be divided in rounds, the length of which is determined by GRETA. At the beginning of each round GRETA shall select the specific provisions on which the evaluation procedure shall be based.

2. GRETA shall define the most appropriate means to carry out this evaluation. GRETA may in particular adopt a questionnaire for each evaluation round, which may serve as a basis for the evaluation of the implementation by the Parties of the present Convention. Such a questionnaire shall be addressed to all Parties. Parties shall respond to this questionnaire, as well as to any other request of information from GRETA.

3. GRETA may request information from civil society.

4. GRETA may subsidiarily organise, in co-operation with the national authorities and the 'contact person' appointed by the latter, and, if necessary, with the assistance of independent national experts, country visits. During these visits, GRETA may be assisted by specialists in specific fields.

5. GRETA shall prepare a draft report containing its analysis concerning the implementation of the provisions on which the evaluation is based, as well as its suggestions and proposals concerning the way in which the Party concerned may deal with the problems which have been identified. The draft report shall be transmitted for comments to the Party which undergoes the evaluation. Its comments are taken into account by GRETA when establishing its report.

6. On this basis, GRETA shall adopt its report and conclusions concerning the measures taken by the Party concerned to implement the provisions of the present Convention. This report and conclusions shall be sent to the Party concerned and to the Committee of the Parties. The report and conclusions of GRETA shall be made public as from their adoption, together with eventual comments by the Party concerned.

7. Without prejudice to the procedure of paragraphs 1 to 6 of this article, the Committee of the Parties may adopt, on the basis of the report and conclusions of GRETA, recommendations addressed to this Party (a) concerning the measures to be taken to implement the conclusions of GRETA, if necessary setting a date for submitting information on their implementation, and (b) aiming at promoting co-operation with that Party for the proper implementation of the present Convention.

CHAPTER VIII
Relationship with other International Instruments

Article 39—Relationship with the Protocol to prevent, suppress and punish trafficking in persons, especially women and children, supplementing the United Nations Convention against transnational organised crime

This Convention shall not affect the rights and obligations derived from the provisions of the Protocol to prevent, suppress and punish trafficking in persons, especially women and children, supplementing the United Nations Convention against transnational organised crime, and is intended to enhance the protection afforded by it and develop the standards contained therein.

Article 40—Relationship with other international instruments

1. This Convention shall not affect the rights and obligations derived from other international instruments to which Parties to the present Convention are Parties or shall become Parties and which contain provisions on matters governed by this Convention and which ensure greater protection and assistance for victims of trafficking.

2. The Parties to the Convention may conclude bilateral or multilateral agreements with one another on the matters dealt with in this Convention, for purposes of supplementing or strengthening its provisions or facilitating the application of the principles embodied in it.

3. Parties which are members of the European Union shall, in their mutual relations, apply Community and European Union rules in so far as there are Community or

European Union rules governing the particular subject concerned and applicable to the specific case, without prejudice to the object and purpose of the present Convention and without prejudice to its full application with other Parties.[1]

4. Nothing in this Convention shall affect the rights, obligations and responsibilities of States and individuals under international law, including international humanitarian law and international human rights law and, in particular, where applicable, the 1951 Convention and the 1967 Protocol relating to the Status of Refugees and the principle of *non-refoulement* as contained therein.

CHAPTER IX
Amendments to the Convention

Article 41—Amendments

1. Any proposal for an amendment to this Convention presented by a Party shall be communicated to the Secretary General of the Council of Europe and forwarded by him or her to the member States of the Council of Europe, any signatory, any State Party, the European Community, to any State invited to sign this Convention in accordance with the provisions of Article 42 and to any State invited to accede to this Convention in accordance with the provisions of Article 43.

2. Any amendment proposed by a Party shall be communicated to GRETA, which shall submit to the Committee of Ministers its opinion on that proposed amendment.

3. The Committee of Ministers shall consider the proposed amendment and the opinion submitted by GRETA and, following consultation of the Parties to this Convention and after obtaining their unanimous consent, may adopt the amendment.

4. The text of any amendment adopted by the Committee of Ministers in accordance with paragraph 3 of this article shall be forwarded to the Parties for acceptance.

5. Any amendment adopted in accordance with paragraph 3 of this article shall enter into force on the first day of the month following the expiration of a period of one month after the date on which all Parties have informed the Secretary General that they have accepted it.

---

[1] Note by the Secretariat: See the Declaration formulated by the European Community and the Member States of the European Union upon the adoption of the Convention by the Committee of Ministers of the Council of Europe, on 3 May 2005: 'The European Community/European Union and its Member States reaffirm that their objective in requesting the inclusion of a 'disconnection clause' is to take account of the institutional structure of the Union when acceding to international conventions, in particular in case of transfer of sovereign powers from the Member States to the Community. This clause is not aimed at reducing the rights or increasing the obligations of a non-European Union Party vis-à-vis the European Community/European Union and its Member States, inasmuch as the latter are also parties to this Convention. The disconnection clause is necessary for those parts of the Convention which fall within the competence of the Community/Union, in order to indicate that European Union Member States cannot invoke and apply the rights and obligations deriving from the Convention directly among themselves (or between themselves and the European Community/Union). This does not detract from the fact that the Convention applies fully between the European Community/European Union and its Member States on the one hand, and the other Parties to the Convention, on the other; the Community and the European Union Members States will be bound by the Convention and will apply it like any Party to the Convention, if necessary, through Community/Union legislation. They will thus guarantee the full respect of the Convention's provisions vis-à-vis non-European Union Parties.'

CHAPTER X
Final Clauses

Article 42—Signature and entry into force

1. This Convention shall be open for signature by the member States of the Council of Europe, the non member States which have participated in its elaboration and the European Community.

2. This Convention is subject to ratification, acceptance or approval. Instruments of ratification, acceptance or approval shall be deposited with the Secretary General of the Council of Europe.

3. This Convention shall enter into force on the first day of the month following the expiration of a period of three months after the date on which 10 Signatories, including at least 8 member States of the Council of Europe, have expressed their consent to be bound by the Convention in accordance with the provisions of the preceding paragraph.

4. In respect of any State mentioned in paragraph 1 or the European Community, which subsequently expresses its consent to be bound by it, the Convention shall enter into force on the first day of the month following the expiration of a period of three months after the date of the deposit of its instrument of ratification, acceptance or approval.

Article 43—Accession to the Convention

1. After the entry into force of this Convention, the Committee of Ministers of the Council of Europe may, after consultation of the Parties to this Convention and obtaining their unanimous consent, invite any non-member State of the Council of Europe, which has not participated in the elaboration of the Convention, to accede to this Convention by a decision taken by the majority provided for in Article 20(d) of the Statute of the Council of Europe, and by unanimous vote of the representatives of the Contracting States entitled to sit on the Committee of Ministers.

2. In respect of any acceding State, the Convention shall enter into force on the first day of the month following the expiration of a period of three months after the date of deposit of the instrument of accession with the Secretary General of the Council of Europe.

Article 44—Territorial application

1. Any State or the European Community may, at the time of signature or when depositing its instrument of ratification, acceptance, approval or accession, specify the territory or territories to which this Convention shall apply.

2. Any Party may, at any later date, by a declaration addressed to the Secretary General of the Council of Europe, extend the application of this Convention to any other territory specified in the declaration and for whose international relations it is responsible or on whose behalf it is authorised to give undertakings. In respect of such territory, the Convention shall enter into force on the first day of the month following the expiration of a period of three months after the date of receipt of such declaration by the Secretary General.

3. Any declaration made under the two preceding paragraphs may, in respect of any territory specified in such declaration, be withdrawn by a notification addressed to the Secretary General of the Council of Europe. The withdrawal shall become effective on the first day of the month following the expiration of a period of three months after the date of receipt of such notification by the Secretary General.

Article 45—Reservations

No reservation may be made in respect of any provision of this Convention, with the exception of the reservation of Article 31, paragraph 2.

Article 46—Denunciation

1. Any Party may, at any time, denounce this Convention by means of a notification addressed to the Secretary General of the Council of Europe.
2. Such denunciation shall become effective on the first day of the month following the expiration of a period of three months after the date of receipt of the notification by the Secretary General.

Article 47—Notification

The Secretary General of the Council of Europe shall notify the member States of the Council of Europe, any State signatory, any State Party, the European Community, to any State invited to sign this Convention in accordance with the provisions of Article 42 and to any State invited to accede to this Convention in accordance with the provisions of Article 43 of:

 (a) any signature;
 (b) the deposit of any instrument of ratification, acceptance, approval or accession;
 (c) any date of entry into force of this Convention in accordance with Articles 42 and 43;
 (d) any amendment adopted in accordance with Article 41 and the date on which such an amendment enters into force;
 (e) any denunciation made in pursuance of the provisions of Article 46;
 (f) any other act, notification or communication relating to this Convention,
 (g) any reservation made under Article 45.

In witness whereof the undersigned, being duly authorised thereto, have signed this Convention.

Done at Warsaw, this 16th day of May 2005, in English and in French, both texts being equally authentic, in a single copy which shall be deposited in the archives of the Council of Europe. The Secretary General of the Council of Europe shall transmit certified copies to each member State of the Council of Europe, to the non-member States which have participated in the elaboration of this Convention, to the European Community and to any State invited to accede to this Convention.

102. EUROPEAN CONVENTION ON THE AVOIDANCE OF STATELESSNESS IN RELATION TO STATE SUCCESSION, 2006

CETS No. 200. This Convention was opened for signature at Strasbourg on 19 May 2006 and entered into force on 1 May 2009. It builds on Chapter VI of the European Convention on Nationality, above, pp. 832–3, which contains a number of general principles for the avoidance of statelessness in situations of State succession. The present Convention, which does not apply to those who were already stateless before succession, adopts in essence the definition of statelessness in the 1954 Convention relating to the Status of Stateless Persons (above, p. 341). It stresses the fundamental nature of the right to a nationality (Article 1), and requires States to take all appropriate measures to avoid statelessness arising in the context of succession (Article 3). Among other matters, the Convention also emphasizes the importance of co-operation between States, but also with the Council of Europe and the United Nations High Commissioner for Refugees (Article 14).

Further reading

BATCHELOR, C. A., 'Transforming International Legal Principles into National Law: The Right to a Nationality and the Avoidance of Statelessness', (2006) 25 *Refugee Survey Quarterly* 8.

SCHÄRER, R., 'The Council of Europe and the Reduction of Statelessness', (2006) 25 *Refugee Survey Quarterly* 33.

TEXT

Preamble

The member States of the Council of Europe and the other States signatory to this Convention,

Considering that the avoidance of statelessness is one of the main concerns of the international community in the field of nationality;

Noting that State succession remains a major source of cases of statelessness;

Recognising that the European Convention on Nationality (ETS No. 166), opened for signature in Strasbourg on 6 November 1997, contains only general principles and not specific rules on nationality in case of State succession;

Bearing in mind that, with regard to statelessness in relation to State succession, other international instruments either do not have a binding character or do not address some important issues;

Convinced that for the reasons above there is a need for a comprehensive international instrument on State succession and the avoidance of statelessness which should be interpreted and applied, bearing in mind the principles of the European Convention on Nationality;

Taking into account Recommendation No. R (99) 18 of the Committee of Ministers on the Avoidance and Reduction of Statelessness, as well as the practical experience gained in recent years with regard to State succession and statelessness;

Having regard to other binding international instruments, namely the United Nations Conventions relating to the Status of Stateless Persons and on the Reduction of Statelessness, and the Vienna Conventions on Succession of States in respect of Treaties and on Succession of States in respect of State Property, Archives and Debts;

Having also regard to the draft articles on nationality of natural persons in relation to the succession of States, prepared by the United Nations International Law Commission, contained in the Annex to the United Nations General Assembly Resolution 55/153 of 2001 as well as the Declaration of the European Commission for Democracy through Law (Venice Commission) on the Consequences of State Succession for the Nationality of Natural Persons;

Building upon, but without prejudice to, the general principles established in the international instruments and documents mentioned above, by adding specific rules applicable to the particular situation of statelessness in relation to State succession;

In order to give effect to the principles established in the European Convention on Nationality that everyone has the right to a nationality and that the rule of law and human rights, including the prohibition of arbitrary deprivation of nationality and the principle of non-discrimination, must be respected in order to avoid statelessness,

Have agreed as follows:

Article 1—Definitions

For the purposes of this Convention:

- (a) 'State succession' means the replacement of one State by another in the responsibility for the international relations of territory;
- (b) 'State concerned' means the predecessor State or the successor State, as the case may be;
- (c) 'Statelessness' means the situation where a person is not considered as a national by any State under the operation of its internal law;
- (d) 'Habitual residence' means a stable factual residence;
- (e) 'Person concerned' means every individual who, at the time of the State succession, had the nationality of the predecessor State and who has or would become stateless as a result of the State succession.

Article 2—Right to a nationality

Everyone who, at the time of the State succession, had the nationality of the predecessor State and who has or would become stateless as a result of the State succession has the right to the nationality of a State concerned, in accordance with the following articles.

Article 3—Prevention of statelessness

The State concerned shall take all appropriate measures to prevent persons who, at the time of the State succession, had the nationality of the predecessor State, from becoming stateless as a result of the succession.

Article 4—Non-discrimination

When applying this Convention, States concerned shall not discriminate against any person concerned on any ground such as sex, race, colour, language, religion, political or other opinion, national or social origin, association with a national minority, property, birth or other status.

Article 5—Responsibility of the successor State

1. A successor State shall grant its nationality to persons who, at the time of the State succession, had the nationality of the predecessor State, and who have or would become stateless as a result of the State succession if at that time:

(a) they were habitually resident in the territory which has become territory of the successor State, or

(b) they were not habitually resident in any State concerned but had an appropriate connection with the successor State.

2. For the purpose of paragraph 1, sub-paragraph (b), an appropriate connection includes *inter alia*:

(a) a legal bond to a territorial unit of a predecessor State which has become territory of the successor State;

(b) birth on the territory which has become territory of the successor State;

(c) last habitual residence on the territory of the predecessor State which has become territory of the successor State.

Article 6—Responsibility of the predecessor State

A predecessor State shall not withdraw its nationality from its nationals who have not acquired the nationality of a successor State and who would otherwise become stateless as a result of the State succession.

Article 7—Respect for the expressed will of the person concerned

A successor State shall not refuse to grant its nationality under Article 5 paragraph 1, sub-paragraph (b), where such nationality reflects the expressed will of the person concerned, on the grounds that such a person can acquire the nationality of another State concerned on the basis of an appropriate connection with that State.

Article 8—Rules of proof

1. A successor State shall not insist on its standard requirements of proof necessary for the granting of its nationality in the case of persons who have or would become stateless as a result of State succession and where it is not reasonable for such persons to meet the standard requirements.

2. A successor State shall not require proof of non-acquisition of another nationality before granting its nationality to persons who were habitually resident on its territory at the time of the State succession and who have or would become stateless as a result of the State succession.

Article 9—Facilitating the acquisition of nationality by stateless persons

A State concerned shall facilitate the acquisition of its nationality by persons lawfully and habitually residing on its territory who, despite Articles 5 and 6, are stateless as a result of the State succession.

Article 10—Avoiding statelessness at birth

A State concerned shall grant its nationality at birth to a child born following State succession on its territory to a parent who, at the time of State succession, had the nationality of the predecessor State if that child would otherwise be stateless.

Article 11—Information to persons concerned

States concerned shall take all necessary steps to ensure that persons concerned have sufficient information about rules and procedures with regard to the acquisition of their nationality.

Article 12—Procedural guarantees

When applying this Convention, the State concerned shall ensure that in the framework of the procedures relating to nationality:

    (a) the relevant applications be processed within a reasonable time;

    (b) the relevant decisions contain reasons in writing and be open to an administrative or judicial review in conformity with its internal law;

    (c) the fees be reasonable and not an obstacle for applicants.

Article 13—Settlement by international agreement

States concerned shall endeavour to regulate matters relating to nationality, especially with a view to avoiding statelessness, where appropriate by international agreement.

Article 14 – International co-operation

1. In order to adopt appropriate measures to avoid statelessness arising from State succession, States concerned shall co-operate among themselves, including by providing information with regard to the operation of their relevant internal law.

2. For the same purpose as that mentioned in paragraph 1, States concerned shall also co-operate:

    (a) with the Secretary General of the Council of Europe and the United Nations High Commissioner for Refugees (UNHCR) and,

    (b) where appropriate, with other States and international organisations.

Article 15—Application of this Convention

1. This Convention applies in respect of a State succession which has occurred after its entry into force.

2. A State concerned may, however, declare by notification addressed to the Secretary General of the Council of Europe at the time of expressing its consent to be bound by this Convention, or, at any time thereafter, that it will also apply the provisions of this Convention to a State succession occurring before the entry into force of this Convention.

3. If several States concerned make a declaration, as set out in paragraph 2, in respect of the same State succession, this Convention will apply between the States making such declaration.

Article 16—Effects of this Convention

1. The provisions of this Convention shall not prejudice the provisions of internal law and binding international instruments which are already in force or may come into force, under which more favourable rights are or would be accorded to individuals on the avoidance of statelessness.

2. This Convention does not prejudice the application of:

    (a) the European Convention on Nationality, in particular its Chapter VI relating to State succession and nationality;

(b) other binding international instruments in so far as such instruments are compatible with this Convention,

in the relationship between the States Parties bound by these instruments.

Article 17—Settlement of disputes

Any dispute concerning the interpretation or application of this Convention shall primarily be settled through negotiation.

Article 18—Signature and entry into force

1. This Convention shall be open for signature by the member States of the Council of Europe and the non-member States which have participated in its elaboration. Such States may express their consent to be bound by:

(a) signature without reservation as to ratification, acceptance or approval; or

(b) signature subject to ratification, acceptance or approval, followed by ratification, acceptance or approval.

Instruments of ratification, acceptance or approval shall be deposited with the Secretary General of the Council of Europe.

2. This Convention shall enter into force, for all States having expressed their consent to be bound by the Convention, on the first day of the month following the expiration of a period of three months after the date on which three member States of the Council of Europe have expressed their consent to be bound by this Convention in accordance with the provisions of the preceding paragraph.

3. In respect of any State which subsequently expresses its consent to be bound by it, the Convention shall enter into force on the first day of the month following the expiration of a period of three months after the date of signature or of the deposit of its instrument of ratification, acceptance or approval.

Article 19—Accession

1. After the entry into force of this Convention, the Committee of Ministers of the Council of Europe may invite any non-member State of the Council of Europe which has not participated in its elaboration to accede to this Convention.

2. In respect of any acceding State, this Convention shall enter into force on the first day of the month following the expiration of a period of three months after the date of deposit of the instrument of accession with the Secretary General of the Council of Europe.

Article 20—Reservations

1. No reservations may be made to this Convention except in respect of the provisions of Article 7, Article 8, paragraph 2, Article 12 and Article 14, paragraph 2, subparagraph (b).

2. Any reservation made a State in pursuance of paragraph 1 shall be formulated at the time of signature or upon the deposit of its instrument of ratification, acceptance, approval or accession.

3. Any State may wholly or partly withdraw a reservation it has made in accordance with paragraph 1 by means of a declaration addressed to the Secretary General of the Council of Europe which shall become effective as from the date of its receipt.

Article 21—Denunciation

1. Any State Party may at any time denounce this Convention by means of a notification addressed to the Secretary General of the Council of Europe.

2. Such denunciation shall become effective on the first day of the month following the expiration of a period of three months after the date of receipt of notification by the Secretary General.

Article 22—Notifications

The Secretary General of the Council of Europe shall notify the member States of the Council of Europe, any Signatory, any Party and any other State which has acceded to this Convention of:

(a) any signature;

(b) the deposit of any instrument of ratification, acceptance, approval or accession;

(c) any date of entry into force of this Convention in accordance with Articles 18 and 19 of this Convention;

(d) any reservation and withdrawal of reservations made in pursuance of the provisions of Article 20 of this Convention;

(e) any notification or declaration made under the provisions of Articles 15 and 21 of this Convention;

(f) any other act, notification or communication relating to this Convention.

In witness whereof the undersigned, being duly authorised thereto, have signed this Convention.

Done at Strasbourg, this 19th day of May 2006, in English and in French, both texts being equally authentic, in a single copy which shall be deposited in the archives of the Council of Europe. The Secretary General of the Council of Europe shall transmit certified copies to each member State of the Council of Europe, to each non-member State having participated in the elaboration of this Convention and to any State invited to accede to this Convention.

103. EUROPEAN CONVENTION ON THE PROTECTION OF CHILDREN AGAINST SEXUAL EXPLOITATION AND SEXUAL ABUSE, 2007

CETS No. 201. This Convention was opened for signature at Lanzarote on 25 October 2007. It may be signed by Member States, non-Member States which participated in its elaboration, and the European Community (Article 45). It entered into force on 1 July 2010 and will now be open, upon invitation, to accession by other non-Member States (Article 46).

As the Preamble indicates, there is a considerable background of other international instruments in this field, and the basic aims of the present Convention are 'to contribute effectively to the common goal of protecting children against sexual exploitation and sexual abuse, whoever the perpetrator may be, and of providing assistance to victims...' Among other matters, it therefore seeks to encourage preventive measures (Articles 4–9), co-ordination and collaboration (Article 10), and protective and assistance measures in the form of, among others, effective social and intervention programmes (Articles 11–17). In addition, States Parties agree to take the necessary legislative or other steps to criminalize certain types of intentional conduct against children (Articles 18–29).

Inter-State co-operation is called for (Article 38), and a Committee of the Parties established to monitor implementation (Articles 39–41).

TEXT

Preamble

The member States of the Council of Europe and the other signatories hereto;

Considering that the aim of the Council of Europe is to achieve a greater unity between its members;

Considering that every child has the right to such measures of protection as are required by his or her status as a minor, on the part of his or her family, society and the State;

Observing that the sexual exploitation of children, in particular child pornography and prostitution, and all forms of sexual abuse of children, including acts which are committed abroad, are destructive to children's health and psycho-social development;

Observing that the sexual exploitation and sexual abuse of children have grown to worrying proportions at both national and international level, in particular as regards the increased use by both children and perpetrators of information and communication technologies (ICTs), and that preventing and combating such sexual exploitation and sexual abuse of children require international co-operation;

Considering that the well-being and best interests of children are fundamental values shared by all member States and must be promoted without any discrimination;

Recalling the Action Plan adopted at the 3rd Summit of Heads of State and Governments of the Council of Europe (Warsaw, 16–17 May 2005), calling for the elaboration of measures to stop sexual exploitation of children;

Recalling in particular the Committee of Ministers Recommendation No. R (91) 11 concerning sexual exploitation, pornography and prostitution of, and trafficking in, children and young adults, Recommendation Rec(2001)16 on the protection of children against sexual exploitation, and the Convention on Cybercrime (*ETS* No. 185), especially Article 9 thereof, as well as the Council of Europe Convention on Action against Trafficking in Human Beings (*CETS* No. 197);

Bearing in mind the Convention for the Protection of Human Rights and Fundamental Freedoms (1950, *ETS* No. 5), the revised European Social Charter (1996, *ETS* No. 163), and the European Convention on the Exercise of Children's Rights (1996, *ETS* No. 160);

Also bearing in mind the United Nations Convention on the Rights of the Child, especially Article 34 thereof, the Optional Protocol on the sale of children, child prostitution and child pornography, the Protocol to Prevent, Suppress and Punish Trafficking in Persons, Especially Women and Children, supplementing the United Nations Convention against Transnational Organized Crime, as well as the International Labour Organization Convention concerning the Prohibition and Immediate Action for the Elimination of the Worst Forms of Child Labour;

Bearing in mind the Council of the European Union Framework Decision on combating the sexual exploitation of children and child pornography (2004/68/JHA), the Council of the European Union Framework Decision on the standing of victims in criminal proceedings (2001/220/JHA), and the Council of the European Union Framework Decision on combating trafficking in human beings (2002/629/JHA);

Taking due account of other relevant international instruments and programmes in this field, in particular the Stockholm Declaration and Agenda for Action, adopted at the 1st World Congress against Commercial Sexual Exploitation of Children (27–31 August 1996), the Yokohama Global Commitment adopted at the 2nd World Congress against Commercial Sexual Exploitation of Children (17–20 December 2001), the Budapest Commitment and Plan of Action, adopted at the preparatory Conference for the 2nd World Congress against Commercial Sexual Exploitation of Children (20–21 November 2001), the United Nations General Assembly Resolution S–27/2 'A world fit for children' and the three-year programme 'Building a Europe for and with children', adopted following the 3rd Summit and launched by the Monaco Conference (4–5 April 2006);

Determined to contribute effectively to the common goal of protecting children against sexual exploitation and sexual abuse, whoever the perpetrator may be, and of providing assistance to victims;

Taking into account the need to prepare a comprehensive international instrument focusing on the preventive, protective and criminal law aspects of the fight against all forms of sexual exploitation and sexual abuse of children and setting up a specific monitoring mechanism,

Have agreed as follows:

CHAPTER I—PURPOSES, NON-DISCRIMINATION PRINCIPLE AND DEFINITIONS

Article 1—Purposes

1. The purposes of this Convention are to:

    (a) prevent and combat sexual exploitation and sexual abuse of children;

(b) protect the rights of child victims of sexual exploitation and sexual abuse;

(c) promote national and international co-operation against sexual exploitation and sexual abuse of children.

2. In order to ensure effective implementation of its provisions by the Parties, this Convention sets up a specific monitoring mechanism.

Article 2—Non-discrimination principle

The implementation of the provisions of this Convention by the Parties, in particular the enjoyment of measures to protect the rights of victims, shall be secured without discrimination on any ground such as sex, race, colour, language, religion, political or other opinion, national or social origin, association with a national minority, property, birth, sexual orientation, state of health, disability or other status.

Article 3—Definitions

For the purposes of this Convention:

(a) 'child' shall mean any person under the age of 18 years;

(b) 'sexual exploitation and sexual abuse of children' shall include the behaviour as referred to in Articles 18 to 23 of this Convention;

(c) 'victim' shall mean any child subject to sexual exploitation or sexual abuse.

CHAPTER II—PREVENTIVE MEASURES

Article 4—Principles

Each Party shall take the necessary legislative or other measures to prevent all forms of sexual exploitation and sexual abuse of children and to protect children.

Article 5—Recruitment, training and awareness raising of persons working in contact with children

1. Each Party shall take the necessary legislative or other measures to encourage awareness of the protection and rights of children among persons who have regular contacts with children in the education, health, social protection, judicial and law-enforcement sectors and in areas relating to sport, culture and leisure activities.

2. Each Party shall take the necessary legislative or other measures to ensure that the persons referred to in paragraph 1 have an adequate knowledge of sexual exploitation and sexual abuse of children, of the means to identify them and of the possibility mentioned in Article 12, paragraph 1.

3. Each Party shall take the necessary legislative or other measures, in conformity with its internal law, to ensure that the conditions to accede to those professions whose exercise implies regular contacts with children ensure that the candidates to these professions have not been convicted of acts of sexual exploitation or sexual abuse of children.

Article 6—Education for children

Each Party shall take the necessary legislative or other measures to ensure that children, during primary and secondary education, receive information on the risks of sexual exploitation and sexual abuse, as well as on the means to protect themselves, adapted to their evolving capacity. This information, provided in collaboration with parents, where appropriate, shall be given within a more general context of information on sexuality and shall pay special attention to situations of risk, especially those involving the use of new information and communication technologies.

Article 7—Preventive intervention programmes or measures

Each Party shall ensure that persons who fear that they might commit any of the offences established in accordance with this Convention may have access, where appropriate, to effective intervention programmes or measures designed to evaluate and prevent the risk of offences being committed.

Article 8—Measures for the general public

1. Each Party shall promote or conduct awareness raising campaigns addressed to the general public providing information on the phenomenon of sexual exploitation and sexual abuse of children and on the preventive measures which can be taken.

2. Each Party shall take the necessary legislative or other measures to prevent or prohibit the dissemination of materials advertising the offences established in accordance with this Convention.

Article 9—Participation of children, the private sector, the media and civil society

1. Each Party shall encourage the participation of children, according to their evolving capacity, in the development and the implementation of state policies, programmes or others initiatives concerning the fight against sexual exploitation and sexual abuse of children.

2. Each Party shall encourage the private sector, in particular the information and communication technology sector, the tourism and travel industry and the banking and finance sectors, as well as civil society, to participate in the elaboration and implementation of policies to prevent sexual exploitation and sexual abuse of children and to implement internal norms through self-regulation or co-regulation.

3. Each Party shall encourage the media to provide appropriate information concerning all aspects of sexual exploitation and sexual abuse of children, with due respect for the independence of the media and freedom of the press.

4. Each Party shall encourage the financing, including, where appropriate, by the creation of funds, of the projects and programmes carried out by civil society aiming at preventing and protecting children from sexual exploitation and sexual abuse.

CHAPTER III—SPECIALISED AUTHORITIES AND CO-ORDINATING BODIES

Article 10—National measures of co-ordination and collaboration

1. Each Party shall take the necessary measures to ensure the co-ordination on a national or local level between the different agencies in charge of the protection from, the prevention of and the fight against sexual exploitation and sexual abuse of children, notably the education sector, the health sector, the social services and the law-enforcement and judicial authorities.

2. Each Party shall take the necessary legislative or other measures to set up or designate:

(a) independent competent national or local institutions for the promotion and protection of the rights of the child, ensuring that they are provided with specific resources and responsibilities;

(b) mechanisms for data collection or focal points, at the national or local levels and in collaboration with civil society, for the purpose of observing and evaluating the phenomenon of sexual exploitation and sexual abuse of children, with due respect for the requirements of personal data protection.

3. Each Party shall encourage co-operation between the competent state authorities, civil society and the private sector, in order to better prevent and combat sexual exploitation and sexual abuse of children.

CHAPTER IV—PROTECTIVE MEASURES AND ASSISTANCE TO VICTIMS

Article 11—Principles

1. Each Party shall establish effective social programmes and set up multidisciplinary structures to provide the necessary support for victims, their close relatives and for any person who is responsible for their care.

2. Each Party shall take the necessary legislative or other measures to ensure that when the age of the victim is uncertain and there are reasons to believe that the victim is a child, the protection and assistance measures provided for children shall be accorded to him or her pending verification of his or her age.

Article 12—Reporting suspicion of sexual exploitation or sexual abuse

1. Each Party shall take the necessary legislative or other measures to ensure that the confidentiality rules imposed by internal law on certain professionals called upon to work in contact with children do not constitute an obstacle to the possibility, for those professionals, of their reporting to the services responsible for child protection any situation where they have reasonable grounds for believing that a child is the victim of sexual exploitation or sexual abuse.

2. Each Party shall take the necessary legislative or other measures to encourage any person who knows about or suspects, in good faith, sexual exploitation or sexual abuse of children to report these facts to the competent services.

Article 13—Helplines

Each Party shall take the necessary legislative or other measures to encourage and support the setting up of information services, such as telephone or Internet helplines, to provide advice to callers, even confidentially or with due regard for their anonymity.

Article 14—Assistance to victims

1. Each Party shall take the necessary legislative or other measures to assist victims, in the short and long term, in their physical and psycho-social recovery. Measures taken pursuant to this paragraph shall take due account of the child's views, needs and concerns.

2. Each Party shall take measures, under the conditions provided for by its internal law, to co-operate with non-governmental organisations, other relevant organisations or other elements of civil society engaged in assistance to victims.

3. When the parents or persons who have care of the child are involved in his or her sexual exploitation or sexual abuse, the intervention procedures taken in application of Article 11, paragraph 1, shall include:

— the possibility of removing the alleged perpetrator;

— the possibility of removing the victim from his or her family environment. The conditions and duration of such removal shall be determined in accordance with the best interests of the child.

4. Each Party shall take the necessary legislative or other measures to ensure that the persons who are close to the victim may benefit, where appropriate, from therapeutic assistance, notably emergency psychological care.

CHAPTER V—INTERVENTION PROGRAMMES OR MEASURES

Article 15 – General principles

1. Each Party shall ensure or promote, in accordance with its internal law, effective intervention programmes or measures for the persons referred to in Article 16, paragraphs 1 and 2, with a view to preventing and minimising the risks of repeated offences of a sexual nature against children. Such programmes or measures shall be accessible at any time during the proceedings, inside and outside prison, according to the conditions laid down in internal law.

2. Each Party shall ensure or promote, in accordance with its internal law, the development of partnerships or other forms of co-operation between the competent authorities, in particular health-care services and the social services, and the judicial authorities and other bodies responsible for following the persons referred to in Article 16, paragraphs 1 and 2.

3. Each Party shall provide, in accordance with its internal law, for an assessment of the dangerousness and possible risks of repetition of the offences established in accordance with this Convention, by the persons referred to in Article 16, paragraphs 1 and 2, with the aim of identifying appropriate programmes or measures.

4. Each Party shall provide, in accordance with its internal law, for an assessment of the effectiveness of the programmes and measures implemented.

Article 16—Recipients of intervention programmes and measures

1. Each Party shall ensure, in accordance with its internal law, that persons subject to criminal proceedings for any of the offences established in accordance with this Convention may have access to the programmes or measures mentioned in Article 15, paragraph 1, under conditions which are neither detrimental nor contrary to the rights of the defence and to the requirements of a fair and impartial trial, and particularly with due respect for the rules governing the principle of the presumption of innocence.

2. Each Party shall ensure, in accordance with its internal law, that persons convicted of any of the offences established in accordance with this Convention may have access to the programmes or measures mentioned in Article 15, paragraph 1.

3. Each Party shall ensure, in accordance with its internal law, that intervention programmes or measures are developed or adapted to meet the developmental needs of children who sexually offend, including those who are below the age of criminal responsibility, with the aim of addressing their sexual behavioural problems.

Article 17—Information and consent

1. Each Party shall ensure, in accordance with its internal law, that the persons referred to in Article 16 to whom intervention programmes or measures have been proposed are fully informed of the reasons for the proposal and consent to the programme or measure in full knowledge of the facts.

2. Each Party shall ensure, in accordance with its internal law, that persons to whom intervention programmes or measures have been proposed may refuse them and, in the case of convicted persons, that they are made aware of the possible consequences a refusal might have.

CHAPTER VI—SUBSTANTIVE CRIMINAL LAW

Article 18—Sexual abuse

1. Each Party shall take the necessary legislative or other measures to ensure that the following intentional conduct is criminalised:

   (a) engaging in sexual activities with a child who, according to the relevant provisions of national law, has not reached the legal age for sexual activities;

   (b) engaging in sexual activities with a child where:

   — use is made of coercion, force or threats; or

   — abuse is made of a recognised position of trust, authority or influence over the child, including within the family; or

   — abuse is made of a particularly vulnerable situation of the child, notably because of a mental or physical disability or a situation of dependence.

2. For the purpose of paragraph 1 above, each Party shall decide the age below which it is prohibited to engage in sexual activities with a child.

3. The provisions of paragraph 1(a) are not intended to govern consensual sexual activities between minors.

Article 19—Offences concerning child prostitution

1. Each Party shall take the necessary legislative or other measures to ensure that the following intentional conduct is criminalised:

   (a) recruiting a child into prostitution or causing a child to participate in prostitution;

   (b) coercing a child into prostitution or profiting from or otherwise exploiting a child for such purposes;

   (c) having recourse to child prostitution.

2. For the purpose of the present article, the term 'child prostitution' shall mean the fact of using a child for sexual activities where money or any other form of remuneration or

consideration is given or promised as payment, regardless if this payment, promise or consideration is made to the child or to a third person.

Article 20—Offences concerning child pornography

1. Each Party shall take the necessary legislative or other measures to ensure that the following intentional conduct, when committed without right, is criminalised:

    (a) producing child pornography;

    (b) offering or making available child pornography;

    (c) distributing or transmitting child pornography;

    (d) procuring child pornography for oneself or for another person;

    (e) possessing child pornography;

    (f) knowingly obtaining access, through information and communication technologies, to child pornography.

2. For the purpose of the present article, the term 'child pornography' shall mean any material that visually depicts a child engaged in real or simulated sexually explicit conduct or any depiction of a child's sexual organs for primarily sexual purposes.

3. Each Party may reserve the right not to apply, in whole or in part, paragraph 1(a) and (e) to the production and possession of pornographic material:

    — consisting exclusively of simulated representations or realistic images of a non-existent child;

    — involving children who have reached the age set in application of Article 18, paragraph 2, where these images are produced and possessed by them with their consent and solely for their own private use.

4. Each Party may reserve the right not to apply, in whole or in part, paragraph 1(f).

Article 21—Offences concerning the participation of a child in pornographic performances

1. Each Party shall take the necessary legislative or other measures to ensure that the following intentional conduct is criminalised:

    (a) recruiting a child into participating in pornographic performances or causing a child to participate in such performances;

    (b) coercing a child into participating in pornographic performances or profiting from or otherwise exploiting a child for such purposes;

    (c) knowingly attending pornographic performances involving the participation of children.

2. Each Party may reserve the right to limit the application of paragraph 1(c) to cases where children have been recruited or coerced in conformity with paragraph 1(a) or (b).

Article 22—Corruption of children

Each Party shall take the necessary legislative or other measures to criminalise the intentional causing, for sexual purposes, of a child who has not reached the age set in application of Article 18, paragraph 2, to witness sexual abuse or sexual activities, even without having to participate.

Article 23—Solicitation of children for sexual purposes

Each Party shall take the necessary legislative or other measures to criminalise the intentional proposal, through information and communication technologies, of an adult to meet a child who has not reached the age set in application of Article 18, paragraph 2, for the purpose of committing any of the offences established in accordance with Article 18, paragraph 1(a), or Article 20, paragraph 1(a), against him or her, where this proposal has been followed by material acts leading to such a meeting.

Article 24—Aiding or abetting and attempt

1. Each Party shall take the necessary legislative or other measures to establish as criminal offences, when committed intentionally, aiding or abetting the commission of any of the offences established in accordance with this Convention.

2. Each Party shall take the necessary legislative or other measures to establish as criminal offences, when committed intentionally, attempts to commit the offences established in accordance with this Convention.

3. Each Party may reserve the right not to apply, in whole or in part, paragraph 2 to offences established in accordance with Article 20, paragraph 1(b), (d), (e) and (f), Article 21, paragraph 1(c), Article 22 and Article 23.

Article 25—Jurisdiction

1. Each Party shall take the necessary legislative or other measures to establish jurisdiction over any offence established in accordance with this Convention, when the offence is committed:

    (a) in its territory; or

    (b) on board a ship flying the flag of that Party; or

    (c) on board an aircraft registered under the laws of that Party; or

    (d) by one of its nationals; or

    (e) by a person who has his or her habitual residence in its territory.

2. Each Party shall endeavour to take the necessary legislative or other measures to establish jurisdiction over any offence established in accordance with this Convention where the offence is committed against one of its nationals or a person who has his or her habitual residence in its territory.

3. Each Party may, at the time of signature or when depositing its instrument of ratification, acceptance, approval or accession, by a declaration addressed to the Secretary General of the Council of Europe, declare that it reserves the right not to apply or to apply only in specific cases or conditions the jurisdiction rules laid down in paragraph 1(e) of this article.

4. For the prosecution of the offences established in accordance with Articles 18, 19, 20, paragraph 1(a), and 21, paragraph 1(a) and (b), of this Convention, each Party shall take the necessary legislative or other measures to ensure that its jurisdiction as regards paragraph 1(d) is not subordinated to the condition that the acts are criminalised at the place where they were performed.

5. Each Party may, at the time of signature or when depositing its instrument of ratification, acceptance, approval or accession, by a declaration addressed to the Secretary General of the Council of Europe, declare that it reserves the right to limit the application

of paragraph 4 of this article, with regard to offences established in accordance with Article 18, paragraph 1(b), second and third indents, to cases where its national has his or her habitual residence in its territory.

6. For the prosecution of the offences established in accordance with Articles 18, 19, 20, paragraph 1(a), and 21 of this Convention, each Party shall take the necessary legislative or other measures to ensure that its jurisdiction as regards paragraphs 1(d) and (e) is not subordinated to the condition that the prosecution can only be initiated following a report from the victim or a denunciation from the State of the place where the offence was committed.

7. Each Party shall take the necessary legislative or other measures to establish jurisdiction over the offences established in accordance with this Convention, in cases where an alleged offender is present on its territory and it does not extradite him or her to another Party, solely on the basis of his or her nationality.

8. When more than one Party claims jurisdiction over an alleged offence established in accordance with this Convention, the Parties involved shall, where appropriate, consult with a view to determining the most appropriate jurisdiction for prosecution.

9. Without prejudice to the general rules of international law, this Convention does not exclude any criminal jurisdiction exercised by a Party in accordance with its internal law.

Article 26—Corporate liability

1. Each Party shall take the necessary legislative or other measures to ensure that a legal person can be held liable for an offence established in accordance with this Convention, committed for its benefit by any natural person, acting either individually or as part of an organ of the legal person, who has a leading position within the legal person, based on:

    (a) power of representation of the legal person;

    (b) an authority to take decisions on behalf of the legal person;

    (c) an authority to exercise control within the legal person.

2. Apart from the cases already provided for in paragraph 1, each Party shall take the necessary legislative or other measures to ensure that a legal person can be held liable where the lack of supervision or control by a natural person referred to in paragraph 1 has made possible the commission of an offence established in accordance with this Convention for the benefit of that legal person by a natural person acting under its authority.

3. Subject to the legal principles of the Party, the liability of a legal person may be criminal, civil or administrative.

4. Such liability shall be without prejudice to the criminal liability of the natural persons who have committed the offence.

Article 27—Sanctions and measures

1. Each Party shall take the necessary legislative or other measures to ensure that the offences established in accordance with this Convention are punishable by effective, proportionate and dissuasive sanctions, taking into account their seriousness. These sanctions shall include penalties involving deprivation of liberty which can give rise to extradition.

2. Each Party shall take the necessary legislative or other measures to ensure that legal persons held liable in accordance with Article 26 shall be subject to effective, proportionate and dissuasive sanctions which shall include monetary criminal or non-criminal fines and may include other measures, in particular:

(a) exclusion from entitlement to public benefits or aid;

(b) temporary or permanent disqualification from the practice of commercial activities;

(c) placing under judicial supervision;

(d) judicial winding-up order.

3. Each Party shall take the necessary legislative or other measures to:

(a) provide for the seizure and confiscation of:

— goods, documents and other instrumentalities used to commit the offences established in accordance with this Convention or to facilitate their commission;

— proceeds derived from such offences or property the value of which corresponds to such proceeds;

(b) enable the temporary or permanent closure of any establishment used to carry out any of the offences established in accordance with this Convention, without prejudice to the rights of bona fide third parties, or to deny the perpetrator, temporarily or permanently, the exercise of the professional or voluntary activity involving contact with children in the course of which the offence was committed.

4. Each Party may adopt other measures in relation to perpetrators, such as withdrawal of parental rights or monitoring or supervision of convicted persons.

5. Each Party may establish that the proceeds of crime or property confiscated in accordance with this article can be allocated to a special fund in order to finance prevention and assistance programmes for victims of any of the offences established in accordance with this Convention.

Article 28—Aggravating circumstances

Each Party shall take the necessary legislative or other measures to ensure that the following circumstances, in so far as they do not already form part of the constituent elements of the offence, may, in conformity with the relevant provisions of internal law, be taken into consideration as aggravating circumstances in the determination of the sanctions in relation to the offences established in accordance with this Convention:

(a) the offence seriously damaged the physical or mental health of the victim;

(b) the offence was preceded or accompanied by acts of torture or serious violence;

(c) the offence was committed against a particularly vulnerable victim;

(d) the offence was committed by a member of the family, a person cohabiting with the child or a person having abused his or her authority;

(e) the offence was committed by several people acting together;

(f) the offence was committed within the framework of a criminal organisation;

(g) the perpetrator has previously been convicted of offences of the same nature.

Article 29—Previous convictions

Each Party shall take the necessary legislative or other measures to provide for the possibility to take into account final sentences passed by another Party in relation to the offences established in accordance with this Convention when determining the sanctions.

CHAPTER VII—INVESTIGATION, PROSECUTION AND PROCEDURAL LAW

Article 30—Principles

1. Each Party shall take the necessary legislative or other measures to ensure that investigations and criminal proceedings are carried out in the best interests and respecting the rights of the child.

2. Each Party shall adopt a protective approach towards victims, ensuring that the investigations and criminal proceedings do not aggravate the trauma experienced by the child and that the criminal justice response is followed by assistance, where appropriate.

3. Each Party shall ensure that the investigations and criminal proceedings are treated as priority and carried out without any unjustified delay.

4. Each Party shall ensure that the measures applicable under the current chapter are not prejudicial to the rights of the defence and the requirements of a fair and impartial trial, in conformity with Article 6 of the Convention for the Protection of Human Rights and Fundamental Freedoms.

5. Each Party shall take the necessary legislative or other measures, in conformity with the fundamental principles of its internal law:

— to ensure an effective investigation and prosecution of offences established in accordance with this Convention, allowing, where appropriate, for the possibility of covert operations;

— to enable units or investigative services to identify the victims of the offences established in accordance with Article 20, in particular by analysing child pornography material, such as photographs and audiovisual recordings transmitted or made available through the use of information and communication technologies.

Article 31—General measures of protection

1. Each Party shall take the necessary legislative or other measures to protect the rights and interests of victims, including their special needs as witnesses, at all stages of investigations and criminal proceedings, in particular by:

(a) informing them of their rights and the services at their disposal and, unless they do not wish to receive such information, the follow-up given to their complaint, the charges, the general progress of the investigation or proceedings, and their role therein as well as the outcome of their cases;

(b) ensuring, at least in cases where the victims and their families might be in danger, that they may be informed, if necessary, when the person prosecuted or convicted is released temporarily or definitively;

(c) enabling them, in a manner consistent with the procedural rules of internal law, to be heard, to supply evidence and to choose the means of having their views, needs and concerns presented, directly or through an intermediary, and considered;

(d) providing them with appropriate support services so that their rights and interests are duly presented and taken into account;

(e) protecting their privacy, their identity and their image and by taking measures in accordance with internal law to prevent the public dissemination of any information that could lead to their identification;

(f) providing for their safety, as well as that of their families and witnesses on their behalf, from intimidation, retaliation and repeat victimisation;

(g) ensuring that contact between victims and perpetrators within court and law enforcement agency premises is avoided, unless the competent authorities establish otherwise in the best interests of the child or when the investigations or proceedings require such contact.

2. Each Party shall ensure that victims have access, as from their first contact with the competent authorities, to information on relevant judicial and administrative proceedings.

3. Each Party shall ensure that victims have access, provided free of charge where warranted, to legal aid when it is possible for them to have the status of parties to criminal proceedings.

4. Each Party shall provide for the possibility for the judicial authorities to appoint a special representative for the victim when, by internal law, he or she may have the status of a party to the criminal proceedings and where the holders of parental responsibility are precluded from representing the child in such proceedings as a result of a conflict of interest between them and the victim.

5. Each Party shall provide, by means of legislative or other measures, in accordance with the conditions provided for by its internal law, the possibility for groups, foundations, associations or governmental or non-governmental organisations, to assist and/or support the victims with their consent during criminal proceedings concerning the offences established in accordance with this Convention.

6. Each Party shall ensure that the information given to victims in conformity with the provisions of this article is provided in a manner adapted to their age and maturity and in a language that they can understand.

Article 32—Initiation of proceedings

Each Party shall take the necessary legislative or other measures to ensure that investigations or prosecution of offences established in accordance with this Convention shall not be dependent upon the report or accusation made by a victim, and that the proceedings may continue even if the victim has withdrawn his or her statements.

Article 33—Statute of limitation

Each Party shall take the necessary legislative or other measures to ensure that the statute of limitation for initiating proceedings with regard to the offences established in accordance with Articles 18, 19, paragraph 1(a) and (b), and 21, paragraph 1(a) and (b), shall continue for a period of time sufficient to allow the efficient starting of proceedings after the victim has reached the age of majority and which is commensurate with the gravity of the crime in question.

Article 34—Investigations

1. Each Party shall adopt such measures as may be necessary to ensure that persons, units or services in charge of investigations are specialised in the field of combating sexual exploitation and sexual abuse of children or that persons are trained for this purpose. Such units or services shall have adequate financial resources.

2. Each Party shall take the necessary legislative or other measures to ensure that uncertainty as to the actual age of the victim shall not prevent the initiation of criminal investigations.

Article 35—Interviews with the child

1. Each Party shall take the necessary legislative or other measures to ensure that:

   (a) interviews with the child take place without unjustified delay after the facts have been reported to the competent authorities;

   (b) interviews with the child take place, where necessary, in premises designed or adapted for this purpose;

   (c) interviews with the child are carried out by professionals trained for this purpose;

   (d) the same persons, if possible and where appropriate, conduct all interviews with the child;

   (e) the number of interviews is as limited as possible and in so far as strictly necessary for the purpose of criminal proceedings;

   (f) the child may be accompanied by his or her legal representative or, where appropriate, an adult of his or her choice, unless a reasoned decision has been made to the contrary in respect of that person.

2. Each Party shall take the necessary legislative or other measures to ensure that all interviews with the victim or, where appropriate, those with a child witness, may be videotaped and that these videotaped interviews may be accepted as evidence during the court proceedings, according to the rules provided by its internal law.

3. When the age of the victim is uncertain and there are reasons to believe that the victim is a child, the measures established in paragraphs 1 and 2 shall be applied pending verification of his or her age.

Article 36—Criminal court proceedings

1. Each Party shall take the necessary legislative or other measures, with due respect for the rules governing the autonomy of legal professions, to ensure that training on children's rights and sexual exploitation and sexual abuse of children is available for the benefit of all persons involved in the proceedings, in particular judges, prosecutors and lawyers.

2. Each Party shall take the necessary legislative or other measures to ensure, according to the rules provided by its internal law, that:

   (a) the judge may order the hearing to take place without the presence of the public;

   (b) the victim may be heard in the courtroom without being present, notably through the use of appropriate communication technologies.

CHAPTER VIII—RECORDING AND STORING OF DATA

Article 37—Recording and storing of national data on convicted sexual offenders

1. For the purposes of prevention and prosecution of the offences established in accordance with this Convention, each Party shall take the necessary legislative or other measures to collect and store, in accordance with the relevant provisions on the protection of personal data and other appropriate rules and guarantees as prescribed by domestic law, data relating to the identity and to the genetic profile (DNA) of persons convicted of the offences established in accordance with this Convention.

2. Each Party shall, at the time of signature or when depositing its instrument of ratification, acceptance, approval or accession, communicate to the Secretary General of the Council of Europe the name and address of a single national authority in charge for the purposes of paragraph 1.

3. Each Party shall take the necessary legislative or other measures to ensure that the information referred to in paragraph 1 can be transmitted to the competent authority of another Party, in conformity with the conditions established in its internal law and the relevant international instruments.

CHAPTER IX—INTERNATIONAL CO-OPERATION

Article 38—General principles and measures for international co-operation

1. The Parties shall co-operate with each other, in accordance with the provisions of this Convention, and through the application of relevant applicable international and regional instruments, arrangements agreed on the basis of uniform or reciprocal legislation and internal laws, to the widest extent possible, for the purpose of:

- (a) preventing and combating sexual exploitation and sexual abuse of children;
- (b) protecting and providing assistance to victims;
- (c) investigations or proceedings concerning the offences established in accordance with this Convention.

2. Each Party shall take the necessary legislative or other measures to ensure that victims of an offence established in accordance with this Convention in the territory of a Party other than the one where they reside may make a complaint before the competent authorities of their State of residence.

3. If a Party that makes mutual legal assistance in criminal matters or extradition conditional on the existence of a treaty receives a request for legal assistance or extradition from a Party with which it has not concluded such a treaty, it may consider this Convention the legal basis for mutual legal assistance in criminal matters or extradition in respect of the offences established in accordance with this Convention.

4. Each Party shall endeavour to integrate, where appropriate, prevention and the fight against sexual exploitation and sexual abuse of children in assistance programmes for development provided for the benefit of third states.

CHAPTER X—MONITORING MECHANISM

Article 39—Committee of the Parties

1. The Committee of the Parties shall be composed of representatives of the Parties to the Convention.

2. The Committee of the Parties shall be convened by the Secretary General of the Council of Europe. Its first meeting shall be held within a period of one year following the entry into force of this Convention for the tenth signatory having ratified it. It shall subsequently meet whenever at least one third of the Parties or the Secretary General so requests.

3. The Committee of the Parties shall adopt its own rules of procedure.

Article 40—Other representatives

1. The Parliamentary Assembly of the Council of Europe, the Commissioner for Human Rights, the European Committee on Crime Problems (CDPC), as well as other relevant Council of Europe intergovernmental committees, shall each appoint a representative to the Committee of the Parties.

2. The Committee of Ministers may invite other Council of Europe bodies to appoint a representative to the Committee of the Parties after consulting the latter.

3. Representatives of civil society, and in particular non-governmental organisations, may be admitted as observers to the Committee of the Parties following the procedure established by the relevant rules of the Council of Europe.

4. Representatives appointed under paragraphs 1 to 3 above shall participate in meetings of the Committee of the Parties without the right to vote.

Article 41—Functions of the Committee of the Parties

1. The Committee of the Parties shall monitor the implementation of this Convention. The rules of procedure of the Committee of the Parties shall determine the procedure for evaluating the implementation of this Convention.

2. The Committee of the Parties shall facilitate the collection, analysis and exchange of information, experience and good practice between States to improve their capacity to prevent and combat sexual exploitation and sexual abuse of children.

3. The Committee of the Parties shall also, where appropriate:

   (a) facilitate the effective use and implementation of this Convention, including the identification of any problems and the effects of any declaration or reservation made under this Convention;

   (b) express an opinion on any question concerning the application of this Convention and facilitate the exchange of information on significant legal, policy or techno-logical developments.

4. The Committee of the Parties shall be assisted by the Secretariat of the Council of Europe in carrying out its functions pursuant to this article.

5. The European Committee on Crime Problems (CDPC) shall be kept periodically informed regarding the activities mentioned in paragraphs 1, 2 and 3 of this article.

CHAPTER XI—RELATIONSHIP WITH OTHER INTERNATIONAL INSTRUMENTS

Article 42—Relationship with the United Nations Convention on the Rights of the Child and its Optional Protocol on the sale of children, child prostitution and child pornography

This Convention shall not affect the rights and obligations arising from the provisions of the United Nations Convention on the Rights of the Child and its Optional Protocol on the sale of children, child prostitution and child pornography, and is intended to enhance the protection afforded by them and develop and complement the standards contained therein.

Article 43—Relationship with other international instruments

1. This Convention shall not affect the rights and obligations arising from the provisions of other international instruments to which Parties to the present Convention are Parties or shall become Parties and which contain provisions on matters governed by this Convention and which ensure greater protection and assistance for child victims of sexual exploitation or sexual abuse.

2. The Parties to the Convention may conclude bilateral or multilateral agreements with one another on the matters dealt with in this Convention, for purposes of supplementing or strengthening its provisions or facilitating the application of the principles embodied in it.

3. Parties which are members of the European Union shall, in their mutual relations, apply Community and European Union rules in so far as there are Community or European Union rules governing the particular subject concerned and applicable to the specific case, without prejudice to the object and purpose of the present Convention and without prejudice to its full application with other Parties.

CHAPTER XII—AMENDMENTS TO THE CONVENTION

Article 44—Amendments

1. Any proposal for an amendment to this Convention presented by a Party shall be communicated to the Secretary General of the Council of Europe and forwarded by him or her to the member States of the Council of Europe, any signatory, any State Party, the European Community, any State invited to sign this Convention in accordance with the provisions of Article 45, paragraph 1, and any State invited to accede to this Convention in accordance with the provisions of Article 46, paragraph 1.

2. Any amendment proposed by a Party shall be communicated to the European Committee on Crime Problems (CDPC), which shall submit to the Committee of Ministers its opinion on that proposed amendment.

3. The Committee of Ministers shall consider the proposed amendment and the opinion submitted by the CDPC and, following consultation with the non-member States Parties to this Convention, may adopt the amendment.

4. The text of any amendment adopted by the Committee of Ministers in accordance with paragraph 3 of this article shall be forwarded to the Parties for acceptance.

5. Any amendment adopted in accordance with paragraph 3 of this article shall enter into force on the first day of the month following the expiration of a period of one month after the date on which all Parties have informed the Secretary General that they have accepted it.

CHAPTER XIII—FINAL CLAUSES

Article 45—Signature and entry into force

1. This Convention shall be open for signature by the member States of the Council of Europe, the non-member States which have participated in its elaboration as well as the European Community.

2. This Convention is subject to ratification, acceptance or approval. Instruments of ratification, acceptance or approval shall be deposited with the Secretary General of the Council of Europe.

3. This Convention shall enter into force on the first day of the month following the expiration of a period of three months after the date on which 5 signatories, including at least 3 member States of the Council of Europe, have expressed their consent to be bound by the Convention in accordance with the provisions of the preceding paragraph.

4. In respect of any State referred to in paragraph 1 or the European Community, which subsequently expresses its consent to be bound by it, the Convention shall enter into force on the first day of the month following the expiration of a period of three months after the date of the deposit of its instrument of ratification, acceptance or approval.

Article 46—Accession to the Convention

1. After the entry into force of this Convention, the Committee of Ministers of the Council of Europe may, after consultation of the Parties to this Convention and obtaining their unanimous consent, invite any non-member State of the Council of Europe, which has not participated in the elaboration of the Convention, to accede to this Convention by a decision taken by the majority provided for in Article 20(d) of the Statute of the Council of Europe, and by unanimous vote of the representatives of the Contracting States entitled to sit on the Committee of Ministers.

2. In respect of any acceding State, the Convention shall enter into force on the first day of the month following the expiration of a period of three months after the date of deposit of the instrument of accession with the Secretary General of the Council of Europe.

Article 47—Territorial application

1. Any State or the European Community may, at the time of signature or when depositing its instrument of ratification, acceptance, approval or accession, specify the territory or territories to which this Convention shall apply.

2. Any Party may, at any later date, by a declaration addressed to the Secretary General of the Council of Europe, extend the application of this Convention to any other territory specified in the declaration and for whose international relations it is responsible or on whose behalf it is authorised to give undertakings. In respect of such territory, the Convention shall enter into force on the first day of the month following the expiration of a period of three months after the date of receipt of such declaration by the Secretary General.

3. Any declaration made under the two preceding paragraphs may, in respect of any territory specified in such declaration, be withdrawn by a notification addressed to the Secretary General of the Council of Europe. The withdrawal shall become effective on the first day of the month following the expiration of a period of three months after the date of receipt of such notification by the Secretary General.

Article 48—Reservations

No reservation may be made in respect of any provision of this Convention, with the exception of the reservations expressly established. Any reservation may be withdrawn at any time.

Article 49—Denunciation

1. Any Party may, at any time, denounce this Convention by means of a notification addressed to the Secretary General of the Council of Europe.

2. Such denunciation shall become effective on the first day of the month following the expiration of a period of three months after the date of receipt of the notification by the Secretary General.

Article 50—Notification

The Secretary General of the Council of Europe shall notify the member States of the Council of Europe, any State signatory, any State Party, the European Community, any State invited to sign this Convention in accordance with the provisions of Article 45 and any State invited to accede to this Convention in accordance with the provisions of Article 46 of:

(a) any signature;

(b) the deposit of any instrument of ratification, acceptance, approval or accession;

(c) any date of entry into force of this Convention in accordance with Articles 45 and 46;

(d) any amendment adopted in accordance with Article 44 and the date on which such an amendment enters into force;

(e) any reservation made under Article 48;

(f) any denunciation made in pursuance of the provisions of Article 49;

(g) any other act, notification or communication relating to this Convention.

In witness whereof the undersigned, being duly authorised thereto, have signed this Convention.

Done at Lanzarote, this 25th day of October 2007, in English and in French, both texts being equally authentic, in a single copy which shall be deposited in the archives of the Council of Europe. The Secretary General of the Council of Europe shall transmit certified copies to each member State of the Council of Europe, to the non-member States which have participated in the elaboration of this Convention, to the European Community and to any State invited to accede to this Convention.

104. EUROPEAN CONVENTION ON ACCESS TO OFFICIAL DOCUMENTS, 2009

CETS No. 205. This Convention was opened for signature at Tromsø on 18 June 2009. It will enter into force on receiving ten ratifications.

This is the first international convention to recognize a general right of access to official documents held by public authorities. It is intended as a set of minimum standards, applicable to 'public authorities' as defined in Article 2(1)(a) or as further elaborated by the State party. 'Official documents' are also defined broadly, to include information held on any physical medium (Article 2(1)(b)). Access to personal information, however, may be subject to the European Convention for the Protection of Individuals with regard to Automatic Processing of Personal Data, 1981 (*ETS* No. 108), while the use of information obtained may be governed by particular rules, such as those dealing with intellectual property.

The right of access extends to 'everyone', irrespective of motive or intention, and States parties must take the necessary measures in their domestic law to ensure such access (Article 2). Limitations on the general right are exceptional, and must be 'set down precisely in law', necessary in a democratic society, and proportionate to the aim of protecting the rights and interests listed exhaustively in Article 3(1). Article 3(2) provides that access may be refused if disclosure 'would or would be likely to harm any of the interests mentioned in paragraph 1, unless there is an overriding public interest in disclosure'.

Other provisions deal with requests (Article 4), processing (Article 5) and charges (Article 7). Two monitoring bodies are established: first, a 'Group of Specialists on Access to Official Documents' (a technical body of independent experts); and second, the 'Consultation of the Parties', composed of one representative per State party. The latter elects the former, and reviews its reports, opinions and proposals (Articles 11–15).

On access to European Union documents, see STATEWATCH, 'FOI in the EU': **http://www.statewatch.org/foi/foi.htm**.

TEXT

Preamble

The member States of the Council of Europe and the other signatories hereto,

Considering that the aim of the Council of Europe is to achieve greater unity between its members for the purpose of safeguarding and realising the ideals and principles which are their common heritage;

Bearing in mind, in particular, Article 19 of the Universal Declaration of Human Rights, Articles 6, 8 and 10 of the Convention for the Protection of Human Rights and Fundamental Freedoms, the United Nations Convention on Access to Information, Public Participation in Decision-making and Access to Justice in Environmental Matters (Aarhus, 25 June 1998) and the Convention for the Protection of Individuals with regard to Automatic Processing of Personal Data of 28 January 1981 (*ETS* No. 108);

Bearing in mind also the Declaration of the Committee of Ministers of the Council of Europe on the freedom of expression and information, adopted on 29 April 1982, as well as recommendations of the Committee of Ministers to member States No. R (81) 19 on the access to information held by public authorities, No. R (91) 10 on the communication to third parties of personal data held by public bodies, No. R (97) 18 concerning the protection of personal data collected and processed for statistical purposes, No. R (2000) 13 on a European policy on access to archives and Rec(2002)2 on access to official documents;

Considering the importance in a pluralistic, democratic society of transparency of public authorities;

Considering that exercise of a right to access to official documents:

(i) provides a source of information for the public;

(ii) helps the public to form an opinion on the state of society and on public authorities;

(iii) fosters the integrity, efficiency, effectiveness and accountability of public authorities, so helping affirm their legitimacy;

Considering, therefore, that all official documents are in principle public and can be withheld subject only to the protection of other rights and legitimate interests,

Have agreed as follows:

SECTION I

Article 1—*General provisions*

1. The principles set out hereafter should be understood without prejudice to those domestic laws and regulations and to international treaties which recognise a wider right of access to official documents.

2. For the purposes of this Convention:

    (a) (i) 'public authorities' means:

        (1) government and administration at national, regional and local level;

        (2) legislative bodies and judicial authorities insofar as they perform administrative functions according to national law;

        (3) natural or legal persons insofar as they exercise administrative authority.

    (ii) Each Party may, at the time of signature or when depositing its instrument of ratification, acceptance, approval or accession, by a declaration addressed to the Secretary General of the Council of Europe, declare that the definition of 'public authorities' also includes one or more of the following:

        (1) legislative bodies as regards their other activities;

        (2) judicial authorities as regards their other activities;

        (3) natural or legal persons insofar as they perform public functions or operate with public funds, according to national law.

    (b) 'official documents' means all information recorded in any form, drawn up or received and held by public authorities.

Article 2—*Right of access to official documents*

1. Each Party shall guarantee the right of everyone, without discrimination on any ground, to have access, on request, to official documents held by public authorities.

2. Each Party shall take the necessary measures in its domestic law to give effect to the provisions for access to official documents set out in this Convention.

3. These measures shall be taken at the latest at the time of entry into force of this Convention in respect of that Party.

Article 3—Possible limitations to access to official documents

1. Each Party may limit the right of access to official documents. Limitations shall be set down precisely in law, be necessary in a democratic society and be proportionate to the aim of protecting:

- *(a)* national security, defence and international relations;
- *(b)* public safety;
- *(c)* the prevention, investigation and prosecution of criminal activities;
- *(d)* disciplinary investigations;
- *(e)* inspection, control and supervision by public authorities;
- *(f)* privacy and other legitimate private interests;
- *(g)* commercial and other economic interests;
- *(h)* the economic, monetary and exchange rate policies of the State;
- *(i)* the equality of parties in court proceedings and the effective administration of justice;
- *(j)* environment; or
- *(k)* the deliberations within or between public authorities concerning the examination of a matter.

Concerned States may, at the time of signature or when depositing their instrument of ratification, acceptance, approval or accession, by a declaration addressed to the Secretary General of the Council of Europe, declare that communication with the reigning Family and its Household or the Head of State shall also be included among the possible limitations.

2. Access to information contained in an official document may be refused if its disclosure would or would be likely to harm any of the interests mentioned in paragraph 1, unless there is an overriding public interest in disclosure.

3. The Parties shall consider setting time limits beyond which the limitations mentioned in paragraph 1 would no longer apply.

Article 4—Requests for access to official documents

1. An applicant for an official document shall not be obliged to give reasons for having access to the official document.

2. Parties may give applicants the right to remain anonymous except when disclosure of identity is essential in order to process the request.

3. Formalities for requests shall not exceed what is essential in order to process the request.

Article 5—Processing of requests for access to official documents

1. The public authority shall help the applicant, as far as reasonably possible, to identify the requested official document.

2. A request for access to an official document shall be dealt with by any public authority holding the document. If the public authority does not hold the requested official

document or if it is not authorised to process that request, it shall, wherever possible, refer the application or the applicant to the competent public authority.

3. Requests for access to official documents shall be dealt with on an equal basis.

4. A request for access to an official document shall be dealt with promptly. The decision shall be reached, communicated and executed as soon as possible or within a reasonable time limit which has been specified beforehand.

5. A request for access to an official document may be refused:

(i) if, despite the assistance from the public authority, the request remains too vague to allow the official document to be identified; or

(ii) if the request is manifestly unreasonable.

6. A public authority refusing access to an official document wholly or in part shall give the reasons for the refusal. The applicant has the right to receive on request a written justification from this public authority for the refusal.

Article 6—Forms of access to official documents

1. When access to an official document is granted, the applicant has the right to choose whether to inspect the original or a copy, or to receive a copy of it in any available form or format of his or her choice unless the preference expressed is unreasonable.

2. If a limitation applies to some of the information in an official document, the public authority should nevertheless grant access to the remainder of the information it contains. Any omissions should be clearly indicated. However, if the partial version of the document is misleading or meaningless, or if it poses a manifestly unreasonable burden for the authority to release the remainder of the document, such access may be refused.

3. The public authority may give access to an official document by referring the applicant to easily accessible alternative sources.

Article 7—Charges for access to official documents

1. Inspection of official documents on the premises of a public authority shall be free of charge. This does not prevent Parties from laying down charges for services in this respect provided by archives and museums.

2. A fee may be charged to the applicant for a copy of the official document, which should be reasonable and not exceed the actual costs of reproduction and delivery of the document. Tariffs of charges shall be published.

Article 8—Review procedure

1. An applicant whose request for an official document has been denied, expressly or impliedly, whether in part or in full, shall have access to a review procedure before a court or another independent and impartial body established by law.

2. An applicant shall always have access to an expeditious and inexpensive review procedure, involving either reconsideration by a public authority or review in accordance with paragraph 1.

Article 9—Complementary measures

The Parties shall inform the public about its right of access to official documents and how that right may be exercised. They shall also take appropriate measures to:

(a) educate public authorities in their duties and obligations with respect to the implementation of this right;

    (b) provide information on the matters or activities for which they are responsible;

    (c) manage their documents efficiently so that they are easily accessible; and

    (d) apply clear and established rules for the preservation and destruction of their documents.

Article 10—Documents made public at the initiative of the public authorities

At its own initiative and where appropriate, a public authority shall take the necessary measures to make public official documents which it holds in the interest of promoting the transparency and efficiency of public administration and to encourage informed participation by the public in matters of general interest.

SECTION II

Article 11—Group of Specialists on Access to Official Documents

1. A Group of Specialists on Access to Official Documents shall meet at least once a year with a view to monitoring the implementation of this Convention by the Parties, notably:

    (a) reporting on the adequacy of the measures in law and practice taken by the Parties to give effect to the provisions set out in this Convention;

    (b) (i) expressing opinions on any question concerning the application of this Convention;

        (ii) making proposals to facilitate or improve the effective use and implementation of this Convention, including the identification of any problems;

        (iii) exchanging information and reporting on significant legal, policy or technological developments;

        (iv) making proposals to the Consultation of Parties for the amendment of this Convention;

        (v) formulating its opinion on any proposal for the amendment of this Convention made in accordance with Article 19.

2. The Group of Specialists may request information and opinions from civil society.

3. The Group of Specialists shall consist of a minimum of 10 and a maximum of 15 members. The members are elected by the Consultation of Parties for a period of four years, renewable once, from a list of experts, each Party proposing two experts. They shall be chosen from among persons of the highest integrity recognised for their competence in the field of access to official documents. A maximum of one member may be elected from the list proposed by each Party.

4. The members of the Group of Specialists shall sit in their individual capacity, be independent and impartial in the exercise of their functions and shall not receive any instructions from governments.

5. The election procedure of the members of the Group of Specialists shall be determined by the Committee of Ministers, after consulting with and obtaining the unanimous consent of the Parties to the Convention, within a period of one year following the entry into force of this Convention. The Group of Specialists shall adopt its own rules of procedure.

Article 12—Consultation of the Parties

1. The Consultation of the Parties shall be composed of one representative per Party.

2. The Consultation of the Parties shall take place with a view to:

   (a) considering the reports, opinions and proposals of the Group of Specialists;

   (b) making proposals and recommendations to the Parties;

   (c) making proposals for the amendment of this Convention in accordance with Article 19;

   (d) formulating its opinion on any proposal for the amendment of this Convention made in accordance with Article 19.

3. The Consultation of the Parties shall be convened by the Secretary General of the Council of Europe within one year after the entry into force of this Convention in order to elect the members of the Group of Specialists. It shall subsequently meet at least once every 4 years and in any case, when the majority of the Parties, the Committee of Ministers or the Secretary General of the Council of Europe requests its convocation. The Consultation of the Parties shall adopt its own rules of procedure.

4. After each meeting, the Consultation of the Parties shall submit to the Committee of Ministers an activity report.

Article 13—Secretariat

The Consultation of the Parties and the Group of Specialists shall be assisted by the Secretariat of the Council of Europe in carrying out their functions pursuant to this Section.

Article 14—Reporting

1. Within a period of one year following the entry into force of this Convention in respect of a Contracting Party, the latter shall transmit to the Group of Specialists a report containing full information on the legislative and other measures taken to give effect to the provisions of this Convention.

2. Thereafter, each Party shall transmit to the Group of Specialists before each meeting of the Consultation of the Parties an update of the information mentioned in paragraph 1.

3. Each Party shall also transmit to the Group of Specialists any information that it requests to fulfil its tasks.

Article 15—Publication

The reports submitted by Parties to the Group of Specialists, the reports, proposals and opinions of the Group of Specialists and the activity reports of the Consultation of the Parties shall be made public.

SECTION III

Article 16—Signature and entry into force of the Convention

1. This Convention shall be open for signature by the member States of the Council of Europe.

2. This Convention is subject to ratification, acceptance or approval. Instruments of ratification, acceptance or approval shall be deposited with the Secretary General of the Council of Europe.

3. This Convention shall enter into force on the first day of the month following the expiration of a period of three months after the date on which 10 member States of the Council of Europe have expressed their consent to be bound by the Convention in accordance with the provisions of paragraph 2.

4. In respect of any Signatory State which subsequently expresses its consent to be bound by it, the Convention shall enter into force on the first day of the month following the expiration of a period of three months after the date of the expression of its consent to be bound by the Convention in accordance with the provisions of paragraph 2.

Article 17—Accession to the Convention

1. After the entry into force of this Convention, the Committee of Ministers of the Council of Europe may, after consulting the Parties to this Convention and obtaining their unanimous consent, invite any State which is not a member of the Council of Europe or any international organisation to accede to this Convention. The decision shall be taken by the majority provided for in Article 20(d) of the Statute of the Council of Europe and by unanimous vote of the representatives of the Parties entitled to sit on the Committee of Ministers.

2. In respect of any State or international organisation acceding to the Convention under paragraph 1 above, the Convention shall enter into force on the first day of the month following the expiration of a period of three months after the date of deposit of the instrument of accession with the Secretary General of the Council of Europe.

Article 18—Territorial application

1. Any State may at the time of signature or when depositing its instrument of ratification, acceptance, approval or accession, specify the territory or territories to which this Convention shall apply.

2. Any State may, at any later date, by a declaration addressed to the Secretary General of the Council of Europe, extend the application of this Convention to any other territory specified in the declaration for whose international relations it is responsible. In respect of such territory the Convention shall enter into force on the first day of the month following the expiration of a period of three months after the date of receipt of such declaration by the Secretary General.

3. Any declaration made under the two preceding paragraphs may, in respect of any territory specified in such declaration, be withdrawn by a notification addressed to the Secretary General. The withdrawal shall become effective on the first day of the month following the expiration of a period of three months after the date of receipt of such notification by the Secretary General.

Article 19—Amendments to the Convention

1. Amendments to this Convention may be proposed by any Party, the Committee of Ministers of the Council of Europe, the Group of Specialists or the Consultation of the Parties.

2. Any proposal for amendment shall be communicated by the Secretary General of the Council of Europe to the Parties.

3. Any amendment shall be communicated to the Consultation of the Parties, which, after having consulted the Group of Specialists, shall submit to the Committee of Ministers its opinion on the proposed amendment.

4. The Committee of Ministers shall consider the proposed amendment and any opinion submitted by the Consultation of the Parties and may approve the amendment.

5. The text of any amendment approved by the Committee of Ministers in accordance with paragraph 4 shall be forwarded to the Parties for acceptance.

6. Any amendment approved in accordance with paragraph 4 shall come into force on the first day of the month following the expiration of a period of one month after the date on which all Parties have informed the Secretary General that they have accepted it.

Article 20—Declarations

Any Party may, at the time of the signature or when depositing its instrument of ratification, acceptance, approval or accession, make one or more of the declarations provided for in Articles 1(2), 3(1) and 18. It shall notify any changes to this information to the Secretary General of the Council of Europe.

Article 21—Denunciation

1. Any Party may at any time denounce this Convention by means of a notification addressed to the Secretary General of the Council of Europe.

2. Such denunciation shall become effective on the first day of the month following the expiration of a period of six months after the date of receipt of the notification by the Secretary General.

Article 22—Notification

The Secretary General of the Council of Europe shall notify the member States of the Council of Europe and any State and international organisation which has acceded or been invited to accede to this Convention of:

(a) any signature;

(b) the deposit of any instrument of ratification, acceptance, approval or accession;

(c) any date of entry into force of this Convention in accordance with Articles 16 and 17;

(d) any declaration made under Articles 1(2), 3(1) and 18;

(e) any other act, notification or communication relating to this Convention.

In witness whereof the undersigned, being duly authorised thereto, have signed this Convention.

Done at Tromsø, this 18th day of June 2009, in English and French, both texts being equally authentic, in a single copy which shall be deposited in the archives of the Council of Europe. The Secretary General of the Council of Europe shall transmit certified copies to each member State of the Council of Europe and to any State and international organisation invited to accede to this Convention.

5.2 EUROPEAN UNION

105. EUROPEAN UNION CHARTER OF FUNDAMENTAL RIGHTS, 2000

The place of human rights within the European Union was debated over many years. In June 1999, the European Council decided to entrust the drafting of a charter of rights to a Convention, which first met in December of that year, and adopted the draft text on 2 October 2000. This was unanimously approved by the European Council in Biarritz the same month, and forwarded to the European Parliament and the Commission. The Parliament gave its approval on 14 November 2000 and the European Commission on 6 December 2000. At a meeting in Nice on 7 December 2000, the Presidents of the European Parliament, the Council and the Commission signed and proclaimed the Charter on behalf of their institutions. For text, see [2000] *OJEC* C 364/1.

The rights are based, in particular, on those set out in the European Convention on Human Rights and the European Social Charter. There are some notable developments. For example, see Article 18 of the 'right to asylum' and Article 19 on 'Protection in the event of removal, expulsion or extradition'; but see Article 51 on 'Scope'. Although not itself a treaty, the Charter will acquire normative importance with the entry into force of the Treaty of Lisbon. Under Article 6 of the Treaty on European Union, as amended, 'The Union recognises the rights, freedoms and principles set out in the Charter . . . which shall have the same legal value as the Treaties . . .'[1] The European Court of Justice has already taken note of the Charter; see Joined Cases C-402/05 P and C-415/05 P, *Yassin Abdullah Kadi and Al Barakaat International Foundation v Council of the EU and Commission of the EC*, ECJ Judgment, 3 September 2008: **http://curia.europa.eu/jcms/jcms/j_6/**.

In March 2007, the European Union Agency for Fundamental Rights was established as a body of the EU based in Vienna: **http://www.fra.europa.eu**.

Further reading

ALSTON, P., ed., *The EU and Human Rights*, Oxford: Oxford University Press, 1999.

CARRUTHERS, S., 'Beware of Lawyers Bearing Gifts: A Critical Evaluation of the Proposals on Fundamental Rights in the EU Constitutional Treaty', (2004) 4 *European Human Rights Law Review* 424.

DE SCHUTTER, O., *Fundamental Rights in the European Union*, Oxford: Oxford University Press, 2010.

DOUGLAS-SCOTT, S., 'The Charter of Fundamental Rights as a Constitutional Document', (2004) *European Human Rights Law Review* 37.

ERISKEN, E. O., et al., *The Chartering of Europe: The European Charter of Fundamental Rights and its Constitutional Implications*, Baden-Baden: Nomos, 2003.

---

[1] However, note the Protocol on the Application of the Charter of Fundamental Rights of the European Union to Poland and to the United Kingdom, according to Article 1 of which, '1. The Charter does not extend the ability of the Court of Justice of the European Union, or any court or tribunal of Poland or of the United Kingdom, to find that the laws, regulations or administrative provisions, practices or action of Poland or of the United Kingdom are inconsistent with the fundamental rights, freedoms and principles that it reaffirms. 2. In particular, and for the avoidance of doubt, nothing in Title IV of the Charter creates justiciable rights applicable to Poland or the United Kingdom except in so far as Poland or the United Kingdom has provided for such rights in its national law.'

FREDMAN, S., MCCRUDDEN, C. and FREEDLAND, M., 'An EU Charter of Fundamental Rights', [2000] *Public Law* 178.

HARPAZ, G., 'The European Court of Justice and its Relations with the European Court of Human Rights: The Quest for Enhanced Reliance, Coherence and Legitimacy', (2009) 46 *Common Market Law Review* 105.

HERVEY, T. and KENNER, J., eds., *Economic and Social Rights under the EU Charter of Fundamental Rights*, Oxford: Hart Publishing, 2003.

KRÜGER, H. C. and POLAKIEWICZ, J., 'Proposals for a coherent human rights protection system in Europe. The European Convention on Human Rights and the EU Charter on Fundamental Rights', (2001) 22 *Human Rights Law Journal* 1.

LE BOT, O., 'Charte de l'Union européenne et Convention de sauvegarde des droits de l'homme : la co-existence de deux catalogues de droits fondamentaux', *Revue trimestrielle de droits de l'homme*, 2003, 781.

MAHONEY, P., 'The Charter on Fundamental Rights of the European Union and the European Convention on Human Rights from the Perspective of the European Convention', (2002) 23 *Human Rights Law Journal* 307.

PEERS, S. and WARD, A., eds., *The EU Charter of Fundamental Rights*, Oxford: Hart, 2004.

TEXT

Preamble

The peoples of Europe, in creating an ever closer union among them, are resolved to share a peaceful future based on common values.

Conscious of its spiritual and moral heritage, the Union is founded on the indivisible, universal values of human dignity, freedom, equality and solidarity; it is based on the principles of democracy and the rule of law. It places the individual at the heart of its activities, by establishing the citizenship of the Union and by creating an area of freedom, security and justice.

The Union contributes to the preservation and to the development of these common values while respecting the diversity of the cultures and traditions of the peoples of Europe as well as the national identities of the Member States and the organization of their public authorities at national, regional and local levels; it seeks to promote balanced and sustainable development and ensures free movement of persons, goods, services and capital, and the freedom of establishment.

To this end, it is necessary to strengthen the protection of fundamental rights in the light of changes in society, social progress and scientific and technological developments by making those rights more visible in a Charter.

This Charter reaffirms, with due regard for the powers and tasks of the Community and the Union and the principle of subsidiarity, the rights as they result, in particular, from the constitutional traditions and international obligations common to the Member States, the Treaty on European Union, the Community Treaties, the European Convention for the Protection of Human Rights and Fundamental Freedoms, the Social Charters adopted by the Community and by the Council of Europe and the case-law of the Court of Justice of the European Communities and of the European Court of Human Rights.

Enjoyment of these rights entails responsibilities and duties with regard to other persons, to the human community and to future generations.

The Union therefore recognizes the rights, freedoms and principles set out hereafter.

CHAPTER I
DIGNITY

Article 1—Human dignity

Human dignity is inviolable. It must be respected and protected.

Article 2—Right to life

1. Everyone has the right to life.
2. No one shall be condemned to the death penalty, or executed.

Article 3—Right to the integrity of the person

1. Everyone has the right to respect for his or her physical and mental integrity.
2. In the fields of medicine and biology, the following must be respected in particular:

   — the free and informed consent of the person concerned, according to the procedures laid down by law,

   — the prohibition of eugenic practices, in particular those aiming at the selection of persons,

   — the prohibition on making the human body and its parts as such a source of financial gain,

   — the prohibition of the reproductive cloning of human beings.

Article 4—Prohibition of torture and inhuman or degrading treatment or punishment

No one shall be subjected to torture or to inhuman or degrading treatment or punishment.

Article 5—Prohibition of slavery and forced labour

1. No one shall be held in slavery or servitude.
2. No one shall be required to perform forced or compulsory labour.
3. Trafficking in human beings is prohibited.

CHAPTER II
FREEDOMS

Article 6—Right to liberty and security

Everyone has the right to liberty and security of person.

Article 7—Respect for private and family life

Everyone has the right to respect for his or her private and family life, home and communications.

Article 8—Protection of personal data

1. Everyone has the right to the protection of personal data concerning him or her.
2. Such data must be processed fairly for specified purposes and on the basis of the consent of the person concerned or some other legitimate basis laid down by law. Everyone has the right of access to data which has been collected concerning him or her, and the right to have it rectified.

3. Compliance with these rules shall be subject to control by an independent authority.

Article 9—*Right to marry and right to found a family*

The right to marry and the right to found a family shall be guaranteed in accordance with the national laws governing the exercise of these rights.

Article 10—*Freedom of thought, conscience and religion*

1. Everyone has the right to freedom of thought, conscience and religion. This right includes freedom to change religion or belief and freedom, either alone or in community with others and in public or in private, to manifest religion or belief, in worship, teaching, practice and observance.

2. The right to conscientious objection is recognised, in accordance with the national laws governing the exercise of this right.

Article 11—*Freedom of expression and information*

1. Everyone has the right to freedom of expression. This right shall include freedom to hold opinions and to receive and impart information and ideas without interference by public authority and regardless of frontiers.

2. The freedom and pluralism of the media shall be respected.

Article 12—*Freedom of assembly and of association*

1. Everyone has the right to freedom of peaceful assembly and to freedom of association at all levels, in particular in political, trade union and civic matters, which implies the right of everyone to form and to join trade unions for the protection of his or her interests.

2. Political parties at Union level contribute to expressing the political will of the citizens of the Union.

Article 13—*Freedom of the arts and sciences*

The arts and scientific research shall be free of constraint. Academic freedom shall be respected.

Article 14—*Right to education*

1. Everyone has the right to education and to have access to vocational and continuing training.

2. This right includes the possibility to receive free compulsory education.

3. The freedom to found educational establishments with due respect for democratic principles and the right of parents to ensure the education and teaching of their children in conformity with their religious, philosophical and pedagogical convictions shall be respected, in accordance with the national laws governing the exercise of such freedom and right.

Article 15—*Freedom to choose an occupation and right to engage in work*

1. Everyone has the right to engage in work and to pursue a freely chosen or accepted occupation.

2. Every citizen of the Union has the freedom to seek employment, to work, to exercise the right of establishment and to provide services in any Member State.

3. Nationals of third countries who are authorized to work in the territories of the Member States are entitled to working conditions equivalent to those of citizens of the Union.

Article 16—Freedom to conduct a business

The freedom to conduct a business in accordance with Community law and national laws and practices is recognized.

Article 17—Right to property

1. Everyone has the right to own, use, dispose of and bequeath his or her lawfully acquired possessions. No one may be deprived of his or her possessions, except in the public interest and in the cases and under the conditions provided for by law, subject to fair compensation being paid in good time for their loss. The use of property may be regulated by law in so far as is necessary for the general interest.

2. Intellectual property shall be protected.

Article 18—Right to asylum

The right to asylum shall be guaranteed with due respect for the rules of the Geneva Convention of 28 July 1951 and the Protocol of 31 January 1967 relating to the status of refugees and in accordance with the Treaty establishing the European Community.

Article 19—Protection in the event of removal, expulsion or extradition

1. Collective expulsions are prohibited.

2. No one may be removed, expelled or extradited to a State where there is a serious risk that he or she would be subjected to the death penalty, torture or other inhuman or degrading treatment or punishment.

CHAPTER III
EQUALITY

Article 20—Equality before the law

Everyone is equal before the law.

Article 21—Non-discrimination

1. Any discrimination based on any ground such as sex, race, colour, ethnic or social origin, genetic features, language, religion or belief, political or any other opinion, membership of a national minority, property, birth, disability, age or sexual orientation shall be prohibited.

2. Within the scope of application of the Treaty establishing the European Community and of the Treaty on European Union, and without prejudice to the special provisions of those Treaties, any discrimination on grounds of nationality shall be prohibited.

Article 22—Cultural, religious and linguistic diversity

The Union shall respect cultural, religious and linguistic diversity.

Article 23—Equality between men and women

Equality between men and women must be ensured in all areas, including employment, work and pay.

The principle of equality shall not prevent the maintenance or adoption of measures providing for specific advantages in favour of the under-represented sex.

Article 24—The rights of the child

1. Children shall have the right to such protection and care as is necessary for their well-being. They may express their views freely. Such views shall be taken into consideration on matters which concern them in accordance with their age and maturity.

2. In all actions relating to children, whether taken by public authorities or private institutions, the child's best interests must be a primary consideration.

3. Every child shall have the right to maintain on a regular basis a personal relationship and direct contact with both his or her parents, unless that is contrary to his or her interests.

Article 25—The rights of the elderly

The Union recognizes and respects the rights of the elderly to lead a life of dignity and independence and to participate in social and cultural life.

Article 26—Integration of persons with disabilities

The Union recognizes and respects the right of persons with disabilities to benefit from measures designed to ensure their independence, social and occupational integration and participation in the life of the community.

CHAPTER IV
SOLIDARITY

Article 27—Workers' right to information and consultation within the undertaking

Workers or their representatives must, at the appropriate levels, be guaranteed information and consultation in good time in the cases and under the conditions provided for by Community law and national laws and practices.

Article 28—Right of collective bargaining and action

Workers and employers, or their respective organizations, have, in accordance with Community law and national laws and practices, the right to negotiate and conclude collective agreements at the appropriate levels and, in cases of conflicts of interest, to take collective action to defend their interests, including strike action.

Article 29—Right of access to placement services

Everyone has the right of access to a free placement service.

Article 30—Protection in the event of unjustified dismissal

Every worker has the right to protection against unjustified dismissal, in accordance with Community law and national laws and practices.

Article 31—Fair and just working conditions

1. Every worker has the right to working conditions which respect his or her health, safety and dignity.

2. Every worker has the right to limitation of maximum working hours, to daily and weekly rest periods and to an annual period of paid leave.

Article 32—Prohibition of child labour and protection of young people at work

The employment of children is prohibited. The minimum age of admission to employment may not be lower than the minimum school-leaving age, without prejudice to such rules as may be more favourable to young people and except for limited derogations.

Young people admitted to work must have working conditions appropriate to their age and be protected against economic exploitation and any work likely to harm their safety, health or physical, mental, moral or social development or to interfere with their education.

Article 33—Family and professional life

1. The family shall enjoy legal, economic and social protection.

2. To reconcile family and professional life, everyone shall have the right to protection from dismissal for a reason connected with maternity and the right to paid maternity leave and to parental leave following the birth or adoption of a child.

Article 34—Social security and social assistance

1. The Union recognizes and respects the entitlement to social security benefits and social services providing protection in cases such as maternity, illness, industrial accidents, dependency or old age, and in the case of loss of employment, in accordance with the rules laid down by Community law and national laws and practices.

2. Everyone residing and moving legally within the European Union is entitled to social security benefits and social advantages in accordance with Community law and national laws and practices.

3. In order to combat social exclusion and poverty, the Union recognizes and respects the right to social and housing assistance so as to ensure a decent existence for all those who lack sufficient resources, in accordance with the rules laid down by Community law and national laws and practices.

Article 35—Health care

Everyone has the right of access to preventive health care and the right to benefit from medical treatment under the conditions established by national laws and practices. A high level of human health protection shall be ensured in the definition and implementation of all Union policies and activities.

Article 36—Access to services of general economic interest

The Union recognizes and respects access to services of general economic interest as provided for in national laws and practices, in accordance with the Treaty establishing the European Community, in order to promote the social and territorial cohesion of the Union.

Article 37—Environmental protection

A high level of environmental protection and the improvement of the quality of the environment must be integrated into the policies of the Union and ensured in accordance with the principle of sustainable development.

Article 38—Consumer protection

Union policies shall ensure a high level of consumer protection.

CHAPTER V
CITIZENS' RIGHTS

Article 39—Right to vote and to stand as a candidate at elections to the European Parliament

1. Every citizen of the Union has the right to vote and to stand as a candidate at elections to the European Parliament in the Member State in which he or she resides, under the same conditions as nationals of that State.

2. Members of the European Parliament shall be elected by direct universal suffrage in a free and secret ballot.

Article 40—Right to vote and to stand as a candidate at municipal elections

Every citizen of the Union has the right to vote and to stand as a candidate at municipal elections in the Member State in which he or she resides under the same conditions as nationals of that State.

Article 41—Right to good administration

1. Every person has the right to have his or her affairs handled impartially, fairly and within a reasonable time by the institutions and bodies of the Union.

2. This right includes:
   — the right of every person to be heard, before any individual measure which would affect him or her adversely is taken;
   — the right of every person to have access to his or her file, while respecting the legitimate interests of confidentiality and of professional and business secrecy;
   — the obligation of the administration to give reasons for its decisions.

3. Every person has the right to have the Community make good any damage caused by its institutions or by its servants in the performance of their duties, in accordance with the general principles common to the laws of the Member States.

4. Every person may write to the institutions of the Union in one of the languages of the Treaties and must have an answer in the same language.

Article 42—Right of access to documents

Any citizen of the Union, and any natural or legal person residing or having its registered office in a Member State, has a right of access to European Parliament, Council and Commission documents.

Article 43—Ombudsman

Any citizen of the Union and any natural or legal person residing or having its registered office in a Member State has the right to refer to the Ombudsman of the Union cases of maladministration in the activities of the Community institutions or bodies, with the exception of the Court of Justice and the Court of First Instance acting in their judicial role.

Article 44—Right to petition

Any citizen of the Union and any natural or legal person residing or having its registered office in a Member State has the right to petition the European Parliament.

Article 45—Freedom of movement and of residence

1. Every citizen of the Union has the right to move and reside freely within the territory of the Member States.

2. Freedom of movement and residence may be granted, in accordance with the Treaty establishing the European Community, to nationals of third countries legally resident in the territory of a Member State.

Article 46—Diplomatic and consular protection

Every citizen of the Union shall, in the territory of a third country in which the Member State of which he or she is a national is not represented, be entitled to protection by the diplomatic or consular authorities of any Member State, on the same conditions as the nationals of that Member State.

CHAPTER VI
JUSTICE

Article 47—Right to an effective remedy and to a fair trial

Everyone whose rights and freedoms guaranteed by the law of the Union are violated has the right to an effective remedy before a tribunal in compliance with the conditions laid down in this Article.

Everyone is entitled to a fair and public hearing within a reasonable time by an independent and impartial tribunal previously established by law. Everyone shall have the possibility of being advised, defended and represented.

Legal aid shall be made available to those who lack sufficient resources in so far as such aid is necessary to ensure effective access to justice.

Article 48—Presumption of innocence and right of defence

1. Everyone who has been charged shall be presumed innocent until proved guilty according to law.

2. Respect for the rights of the defence of anyone who has been charged shall be guaranteed.

Article 49—Principles of legality and proportionality of criminal offences and penalties

1. No one shall be held guilty of any criminal offence on account of any act or omission which did not constitute a criminal offence under national law or international law at the time when it was committed. Nor shall a heavier penalty be imposed than that which was applicable at the time the criminal offence was committed. If, subsequent to the commission of a criminal offence, the law provides for a lighter penalty, that penalty shall be applicable.

2. This Article shall not prejudice the trial and punishment of any person for any act or omission which, at the time when it was committed, was criminal according to the general principles recognised by the community of nations.

3. The severity of penalties must not be disproportionate to the criminal offence.

Article 50—Right not to be tried or punished twice in criminal proceedings for the same criminal offence

No one shall be liable to be tried or punished again in criminal proceedings for an offence for which he or she has already been finally acquitted or convicted within the Union in accordance with the law.

CHAPTER VII
GENERAL PROVISIONS

Article 51—Scope

1. The provisions of this Charter are addressed to the institutions and bodies of the Union with due regard for the principle of subsidiarity and to the Member States only when they are implementing Union law. They shall therefore respect the rights, observe the principles and promote the application thereof in accordance with their respective powers.

2. This Charter does not establish any new power or task for the Community or the Union, or modify powers and tasks defined by the Treaties.

Article 52—Scope of guaranteed rights

1. Any limitation on the exercise of the rights and freedoms recognised by this Charter must be provided for by law and respect the essence of those rights and freedoms. Subject to the principle of proportionality, limitations may be made only if they are necessary and genuinely meet objectives of general interest recognised by the Union or the need to protect the rights and freedoms of others.

2. Rights recognised by this Charter which are based on the Community Treaties or the Treaty on European Union shall be exercised under the conditions and within the limits defined by those Treaties.

3. In so far as this Charter contains rights which correspond to rights guaranteed by the Convention for the Protection of Human Rights and Fundamental Freedoms, the meaning and scope of those rights shall be the same as those laid down by the said Convention. This provision shall not prevent Union law providing more extensive protection.

Article 53—Level of protection

Nothing in this Charter shall be interpreted as restricting or adversely affecting human rights and fundamental freedoms as recognized, in their respective fields of application, by Union law and international law and by international agreements to which the Union, the Community or all the Member States are party, including the European Convention for the Protection of Human Rights and Fundamental Freedoms, and by the Member States' constitutions.

Article 54—Prohibition of abuse of rights

Nothing in this Charter shall be interpreted as implying any right to engage in any activity or to perform any act aimed at the destruction of any of the rights and freedoms recognised in this Charter or at their limitation to a greater extent than is provided for herein.

5.3 CONFERENCE ON SECURITY AND CO-OPERATION IN EUROPE (CSCE)/ORGANIZATION FOR SECURITY AND CO-OPERATION IN EUROPE (OSCE)

106. FINAL ACT OF THE HELSINKI CONFERENCE, 1975

On 1 August 1975 the Final Act of the Conference on Security and Co-operation in Europe was adopted in Helsinki. This contains a declaration of principles under the heading 'Questions relating to Security in Europe'. The Final Act was signed by representatives of thirty-five States, including Canada, the United States and the USSR, all of which, and their successors, have continued to play a part in the CSCE/OSCE process; in this regard, it is more than a purely regional instrument, considered from a European perspective.

The Final Act constitutes an important statement of intent but the instrument is not a treaty and the understanding of the signatories was that it was not legally binding. See *Digest of United States Practice in International Law* (1975), 7–12, 190–3, 236–8, 271, 325–7, 529–32, 591–4, 679–81, 688–91, 783–8; (1976), 141–6, 178–81.

The declaration of principles includes a section entitled 'Respect for human rights and fundamental freedoms, including the freedom of thought, conscience, religion or belief'. The text contains a commitment to act in conformity with existing obligations in the field of human rights. In a technical and formal sense the Final Act is not at all innovative in respect of human rights and, indeed, the subject-matter is as much related to security and disarmament as it is to human rights, although this was not conveyed to the public in many countries. In January 1992, ten former Soviet republics joined the Conference which, as the OSCE, has since become the largest regional security organization in the world, with fifty-five participating States. For further information, see **http://www.osce.org/**.

The full text of the Final Act appears in the third edition of this book at pp. 391–449, and can be accessed at **http://www.osce.org/documents/chronological.php**; the following extracts deal with the question of security in Europe and co-operation in humanitarian matters. Other documents included in the 5th edition of this work have been moved to the Online Resource Centre (namely, those relating to the 1989 Vienna Meeting of the CSCE Conference, the 1990 Copenhagen Meeting of the Second Conference on the Human Dimension, the 1991 Moscow Meeting of the Third Conference on the Human Dimension, the 1992 Helsinki Summit Meeting, the 1994 Budapest Summit Meeting, and the 1996 Lisbon Summit Meeting).

The OSCE Office for Democratic Institutions and Human Rights, based in Warsaw, is active throughout the OSCE area; see **http://www.osce.org/odihr/**. In addition, the OSCE Parliamentary Assembly often adopts resolutions and declarations relevant to the human dimension: **http://www.oscepa.org/**.

Further reading

DAVY, R., 'Helsinki Myths: Setting the Record Straight on the Final Act of the CSCE, 1975', (2009) 9 *Cold War History* 1.

OFFICE FOR DEMOCRATIC INSTITUTIONS AND HUMAN RIGHTS (ODIHR), *OSCE Human Dimension Commitments: Thematic Compilation*, Vol. 1, Warsaw: OSCE, 2005.

——, *OSCE Human Dimension Commitments: Chronological Compilation*, Vol. 2, Warsaw: OSCE, 2005.

Ruiz-Fabri, H., 'La Conférence de sécurité et de coopération europénne et le règlement des différends: l'élaboration d'une méthode', (1991) 37 *Annuaire Français de droit international* 297.

Russell, H. S., 'The Helsinki Declaration: Brobdingnag or Lilliput?', (1976) 70 *AJIL* 242–72.

Schachter, O., 'The Twilight Existence of Non-Binding International Agreements', (1977) 71 *AJIL* 296–304.

Snyder, S. B., 'The Rise of the Helsinki Network: "A Sort of Lifeline" for Eastern Europe', in Westad, O. A. and Villaume, P., eds., *Perforating the Iron Curtain: European Détente, Transatlantic Relations, and the Cold War, 1965–1985*, Copenhagen: Museum Tusculanum Press, 2010.

——, 'Principles Overwhelming Tanks: Human Rights and the End of the Cold War', in Iriye, A., Goedde, P. and Hitchcock, W., *Human Rights in the Twentieth Century: An International History*, Oxford: Oxford University Press, 2010.

TEXT

The Conference on Security and Co-operation in Europe, which opened at Helsinki on 3 July 1973 and continued at Geneva from 18 September 1973 to 21 July 1975, was concluded at Helsinki on 1 August 1975 by the High Representatives of Austria, Belgium, Bulgaria, Canada, Cyprus, Czechoslovakia, Denmark, Finland, France, the German Democratic Republic, the Federal Republic of Germany, Greece, the Holy See, Hungary, Iceland, Ireland, Italy, Liechtenstein, Luxembourg, Malta, Monaco, the Netherlands, Norway, Poland, Portugal, Romania, San Marino, Spain, Sweden, Switzerland, Turkey, the Union of Soviet Socialist Republics, the United Kingdom, the United States of America and Yugoslavia.

During the opening and closing stages of the Conference the participants were addressed by the Secretary-General of the United Nations as their guest of honour. The Director-General of UNESCO and the Executive Secretary of the United Nations Economic Commission for Europe addressed the Conference during its second stage.

During the meetings of the second stage of the Conference, contributions were received, and statements heard, from the following non-participating Mediterranean States on various agenda items: the Democratic and Popular Republic of Algeria, the Arab Republic of Egypt, Israel, the Kingdom of Morocco, the Syrian Arab Republic, Tunisia.

Motivated by the political will, in the interest of peoples, to improve and intensify their relations and to contribute in Europe to peace, security, justice and co-operation as well as to rapprochement among themselves and with the other States of the world,

Determined, in consequence, to give full effect to the results of the Conference and to assure, among their States and throughout Europe, the benefits deriving from those results and thus to broaden, deepen and make continuing and lasting the process of détente,

The High Representatives of the participating States have solemnly adopted the following:

QUESTIONS RELATING TO SECURITY IN EUROPE

The States participating in the Conference on Security and Co-operation in Europe,

Reaffirming their objective of promoting better relations among themselves and ensuring conditions in which their people can live in true and lasting peace free from any threat to or attempt against their security;

Convinced of the need to exert efforts to make détente both a continuing and an increasingly viable and comprehensive process, universal in scope, and that the implementation of the results of the Conference on Security and Co-operation in Europe will be a major contribution to this process;

Considering that solidarity among peoples, as well as the common purpose of the participating States in achieving the aims as set forth by the Conference on Security and Co-operation in Europe, should lead to the development of better and closer relations among them in all fields and thus to overcoming the confrontation stemming from the character of their past relations, and to better mutual understanding;

Mindful of their common history and recognizing that the existence of elements common to their traditions and values can assist them in developing their relations, and desiring to search, fully taking into account the individuality and diversity of their positions and views, for possibilities of joining their efforts with a view to overcoming distrust and increasing confidence, solving the problems that separate them and cooperating in the interest of mankind;

Recognizing the indivisibility of security in Europe as well as their common interest in the development of co-operation throughout Europe and among themselves and expressing their intention to pursue efforts accordingly;

Recognizing the close link between peace and security in Europe and in the world as a whole and conscious of the need for each of them to make its contribution to the strengthening of world peace and security and to the promotion of fundamental rights, economic and social progress and well-being for all peoples;

Have adopted the following:

(a) Declaration on Principles Guiding Relations between Participating States

The participating States,

Reaffirming their commitment to peace, security and justice and the continuing development of friendly relations and co-operation;

Recognizing that this commitment, which reflects the interest and aspirations of peoples, constitutes for each participating State a present and future responsibility, heightened by experience of the past;

Reaffirming, in conformity with their membership in the United Nations and in accordance with the purposes and principles of the United Nations, their full and active support for the United Nations and for the enhancement of its role and effectiveness in strengthening international peace, security and justice, and in promoting the solution of international problems, as well as the development of friendly relations and co-operation among States;

Expressing their common adherence to the principles which are set forth below and are in conformity with the Charter of the United Nations, as well as their common will to act, in the application of these principles, in conformity with the purposes and principles of the Charter of the United Nations;

Declare their determination to respect and put into practice, each of them in its relations with all other participating States, irrespective of their political, economic or social systems as well as of their size, geographical location or level of economic development, the following principles, which all are of primary significance, guiding their mutual relations:

I. Sovereign Equality, Respect for the Rights Inherent in Sovereignty

The participating States will respect each other's sovereign equality and individuality as well as all the rights inherent in and encompassed by its sovereignty, including in particular the right of every State to juridical equality, to territorial integrity and to freedom and political independence. They will also respect each other's right freely to choose and develop its political, social, economic and cultural systems as well as its right to determine its laws and regulations.

Within the framework of international law, all the participating States have equal rights and duties. They will respect each other's right to define and conduct as it wishes its relations with other States in accordance with international law and in the spirit of the present Declaration. They consider that their frontiers can be changed, in accordance with international law, by peaceful means and by agreement. They also have the right to belong or not to belong to international organizations, to be or not to be a party to bilateral or multilateral treaties including the right to be or not to be a party to treaties of alliance; they also have the right to neutrality.

II. Refraining from the Threat or Use of Force

The participating States will refrain in their mutual relations, as well as in their international relations in general, from the threat or use of force against the territorial integrity or political independence of any State, or in any other manner inconsistent with the purposes of the United Nations and with the present Declaration. No consideration may be invoked to serve to warrant resort to the threat or use of force in contravention of this principle.

Accordingly, the participating States will refrain from any acts constituting a threat of force or direct or indirect use of force against another participating State.

Likewise they will refrain from any manifestation of force for the purpose of inducing another participating State to renounce the full exercise of its sovereign rights. Likewise they will also refrain in their mutual relations from any act of reprisal by force.

No such threat or use of force will be employed as a means of settling disputes, or questions likely to give rise to disputes, between them.

III. Inviolability of Frontiers

The participating States regard as inviolable all one another's frontiers as well as the frontiers of all States in Europe and therefore they will refrain now and in the future from assaulting these frontiers.

Accordingly, they will also refrain from any demand for, or act of, seizure and usurpation of part or all of the territory of any participating State.

IV. Territorial Integrity of States

The participating States will respect the territorial integrity of each of the participating States.

Accordingly, they will refrain from any action inconsistent with the purposes and principles of the Charter of the United Nations against the territorial integrity, political independence or the unity of any participating State, and in particular from any such action constituting a threat or use of force.

The participating States will likewise refrain from making each other's territory the object of military occupation or other direct or indirect measures of force in contravention of international law, or the object of acquisition by means of such measures or the threat of them. No such occupation or acquisition will be recognized as legal.

V. Peaceful Settlement of Disputes

The participating States will settle disputes among them by peaceful means in such a manner as not to endanger international peace and security, and justice.

They will endeavour in good faith and a spirit of co-operation to reach a rapid and equitable solution on the basis of international law.

For this purpose they will use such means as negotiation, enquiry, mediation, conciliation, arbitration, judicial settlement or other peaceful means of their own choice including any settlement procedure agreed to in advance of disputes to which they are parties.

In the event of failure to reach a solution by any of the above peaceful means, the parties to a dispute will continue to seek a mutually agreed way to settle the dispute peacefully.

Participating States, parties to a dispute among them, as well as other participating States, will refrain from any action which might aggravate the situation to such a degree as to endanger the maintenance of international peace and security and thereby make a peaceful settlement of the dispute more difficult.

VI. Non-Intervention in Internal Affairs

The participating States will refrain from any intervention, direct or indirect, individual or collective, in the internal or external affairs falling within the domestic jurisdiction of another participating State, regardless of their mutual relations.

They will accordingly refrain from any form of armed intervention or threat of such intervention against another participating State.

They will likewise in all circumstances refrain from any other act of military, or of political, economic or other coercion designed to subordinate to their own interest the exercise by another participating State of the rights inherent in its sovereignty and thus to secure advantages of any kind.

Accordingly, they will, *inter alia*, refrain from direct or indirect assistance to terrorist activities, or to subversive or other activities directed towards the violent overthrow of the regime of another participating State.

VII. Respect for Human Rights and Fundamental Freedoms, including the Freedom of Thought, Conscience, Religion or Belief

The participating States will respect human rights and fundamental freedoms, including the freedom of thought, conscience, religion or belief, for all without distinct as to race, sex, language or religion.

They will promote and encourage the effective exercise of civil, political, economic, social, cultural and other rights and freedoms all of which derive from the inherent dignity of the human person and are essential for his free and full development.

Within this framework the participating States will recognize and respect the freedom of the individual to profess and practice, alone or in community with others, religion or belief acting in accordance with the dictates of his own conscience.

The participating States on whose territory national minorities exist will respect the right of persons belonging to such minorities to equality before the law, will afford them the full opportunity for the actual enjoyment of human rights and fundamental freedoms and will, in this manner, protect their legitimate interests in this sphere.

The participating States recognize the universal significance of human rights and fundamental freedoms, respect for which is an essential factor for the peace, justice and well-being necessary to ensure the development of friendly relations and co-operation among themselves as among all States.

They will constantly respect these rights and freedoms in their mutual relations and will endeavour jointly and separately, including in co-operation with the United Nations, to promote universal and effective respect for them.

They confirm the right of the individual to know and act upon his rights and duties in this field.

In the field of human rights and fundamental freedoms, the participating States will act in conformity with the purposes and principles of the Charter of the United Nations and with the Universal Declaration of Human Rights. They will also fulfil their obligations as set forth in the international declarations and agreements in this field, including *inter alia* the International Covenants on Human Rights, by which they may be bound.

VIII. Equal Rights and Self-Determination of Peoples

The participating States will respect the equal rights of peoples and their right to self-determination, acting at all times in conformity with the purposes and principles of the Charter of the United Nations and with the relevant norms of international law, including those relating to territorial integrity of States.

By virtue of the principle of equal rights and self-determination of peoples, all peoples always have the right, in full freedom, to determine, when and as they wish, their internal and external political status, without external interference, and to pursue as they wish their political, economic, social and cultural development.

The participating States reaffirm the universal significance of respect for and effective exercise of equal rights and self-determination of peoples for the development of friendly relations among themselves as among all States; they also recall the importance of the elimination of any form of violation of this principle.

IX. Co-operation among States

The participating States will develop their co-operation with one another and with all States in all fields in accordance with the purposes and principles of the Charter of the United Nations. In developing their co-operation the participating States will place special emphasis on the fields as set forth within the framework of the Conference on Security and Co-operation in Europe, with each of them making its contribution in conditions of full equality.

They will endeavour, in developing their co-operation as equals, to promote mutual understanding and confidence, friendly and good-neighbourly relations among themselves, international peace, security and justice. They will equally endeavour, in developing their co-operation, to improve the well-being of peoples and contribute to the fulfilment of their aspirations through, inter alia, the benefits resulting from increased mutual knowledge and from progress and achievement in the economic, scientific, technological, social, cultural and humanitarian fields. They will take steps to promote conditions favourable to making these benefits available to all; they will take into account the interest of all in the narrowing of differences in the levels of economic development, and in particular the interest of developing countries throughout the world.

They confirm that governments, institutions, organizations and persons have a relevant and positive role to play in contributing toward the achievement of these aims of their co-operation.

They will strive, in increasing their co-operation as set forth above, to develop closer relations among themselves on an improved and more enduring basis for the benefit of peoples.

X. Fulfilment in Good Faith of Obligations under International Law

The participating States will fulfil in good faith their obligations under international law, both those obligations arising from the generally recognized principles and rules of international law and those obligations arising from treaties or other agreements, in conformity with international law, to which they are parties.

In exercising their sovereign rights, including the right to determine their laws and regulations, they will conform with their legal obligations under international law; they will furthermore pay due regard to and implement the provisions in the Final Act of the Conference on Security and Cooperation in Europe.

The participating States confirm that in the event of a conflict between the obligations of the members of the United Nations under the Charter of the United Nations and their obligations under any treaty or other international agreement, their obligations under the Charter will prevail, in accordance with Article 103 of the Charter of the United Nations.

All the principles set forth above are of primary significance and, accordingly, they will be equally and unreservedly applied, each of them being interpreted taking into account the others.

The participating States express their determination fully to respect and apply these principles, as set forth in the present Declaration, in all aspects, to their mutual relations and co-operation in order to ensure to each participating State the benefits resulting from the respect and application of these principles by all.

The participating States, paying due regard to the principles above and, in particular, to the first sentence of the tenth principle, 'Fulfilment in good faith of obligations under international law', note that the present Declaration does not affect their rights and obligations, nor the corresponding treaties and other agreements and arrangements.

The participating States express the conviction that respect for these principles will encourage the development of normal and friendly relations and the progress of co-operation among them in all fields. They also express the conviction that respect for these principles will encourage the development of political contacts among them which in time would contribute to better mutual understanding of their positions and views.

The participating States declare their intention to conduct their relations with all other States in the spirit of the principles contained in the present Declaration.

(b) Matters Related to Giving Effect to Certain of the Above Principles

(i) The participating States,
Reaffirming that they will respect and give effect to refraining from the threat or use of force and convinced of the necessity to make it an effective norm of international life,

Declare that they are resolved to respect and carry out, in their relations with one another, *inter alia*, the following provisions which are in conformity with the Declaration on Principles Guiding Relations between Participating States:

— To give effect and expression, by all the ways and forms which they consider appropriate, to the duty to refrain from the threat or use of force in their relations with one another.

— To refrain from any use of armed forces inconsistent with the purposes and principles of the Charter of the United Nations and the provisions of the Declaration on Principles Guiding Relations between Participating States, against another participating State, in particular from invasion of or attack on its territory.

— To refrain from any manifestation of force for the purpose of inducing another participating State to renounce the full exercise of its sovereign rights.

— To refrain from any act of economic coercion designed to subordinate to their own interest the exercise by another participating State of the rights inherent in its sovereignty and thus to secure advantages of any kind.

— To take effective measures which by their scope and by their nature constitute steps towards the ultimate achievement of general and complete disarmament under strict and effective international control.

— To promote, by all means which each of them considers appropriate, a climate of confidence and respect among peoples consonant with their duty to refrain from propaganda for wars of aggression or for any threat or use of force inconsistent with the purposes of the United Nations and with the Declaration on Principles Guiding Relations between Participating States, against another participating State.

— To make every effort to settle exclusively by peaceful means any dispute between them, the continuance of which is likely to endanger the maintenance of international peace and security in Europe, and to seek, first of all, a solution through the peaceful means set forth in Article 33 of the United Nations Charter.

— To refrain from any action which could hinder the peaceful settlement of disputes between the participating States.

(ii) The participating States,

Reaffirming their determination to settle their disputes as set forth in the Principle of Peaceful Settlement of Disputes;

Convinced that the peaceful settlement of disputes is a complement to refraining from the threat or use of force, both being essential though not exclusive factors for the maintenance and consolidation of peace and security;

Desiring to reinforce and to improve the methods at their disposal for the peaceful settlement of disputes;

1. Are resolved to pursue the examination and elaboration of a generally acceptable method for the peaceful settlement of disputes aimed at complementing existing methods, and to continue to this end to work upon the 'Draft Convention on a European System for the Peaceful Settlement of Disputes' submitted by Switzerland during the second stage of the Conference on Security and Co-operation in Europe, as well as other proposals relating to it and directed towards the elaboration of such a method.

2. Decide that, on the invitation of Switzerland, a meeting of experts of all the participating States will be convoked in order to fulfil the mandate described in paragraph 1 above within the framework and under the procedures of the follow-up to the Conference laid down in the chapter 'Follow-up to the Conference'.

3. This meeting of experts will take place after the meeting of the representatives appointed by the Ministers of Foreign Affairs of the participating States, scheduled according to the chapter 'Follow-up to the Conference' for 1977; the results of the work of this meeting of experts will be submitted to Governments.

...

CO-OPERATION IN HUMANITARIAN AND OTHER FIELDS

The participating States,

Desiring to contribute to the strengthening of peace and understanding among peoples and to the spiritual enrichment of the human personality without distinction as to race, sex, language or religion,

Conscious that increased cultural and educational exchanges, broader dissemination of information, contacts between people, and the solution of humanitarian problems will contribute to the attainment of these aims,

Determined therefore to co-operate among themselves, irrespective of their political, economic and social systems, in order to create better conditions in the above fields, to develop and strengthen existing forms of co-operation and to work out new ways and means appropriate to these aims,

Convinced that this co-operation should take place in full respect for the principles guiding relations among participating States as set forth in the relevant document,

Have adopted the following:

1. Human Contacts

The participating States,

Considering the development of contacts to be an important element in the strengthening of friendly relations and trust among peoples,

Affirming, in relation to their present effort to improve conditions in this area, the importance they attach to humanitarian considerations,

Desiring in this spirit to develop, with the continuance of détente, further efforts to achieve continuing progress in this field

And conscious that the questions relevant hereto must be settled by the States concerned under mutually acceptable conditions,

Make it their aim to facilitate freer movement and contacts, individually and collectively, whether privately or officially, among persons, institutions and organizations of the participating States, and to contribute to the solution of the humanitarian problems that arise in that connexion,

Declare their readiness to these ends to take measures which they consider appropriate and to conclude agreements or arrangements among themselves, as may be needed, and

Express their intention now to proceed to the implementation of the following:

(a) Contacts and Regular Meetings on the Basis of Family Ties

In order to promote further development of contacts on the basis of family ties the participating States will favourably consider applications for travel with the purpose of allowing persons to enter or leave their territory temporarily, and on a regular basis if desired, in order to visit members of their families.

Applications for temporary visits to meet members of their families will be dealt with without distinction as to the country of origin or destination: existing requirements for travel documents and visas will be applied in this spirit. The preparation and issue of such documents and visas will be effected within reasonable time limits, cases of urgent necessity—such as serious illness or death—will be given priority treatment. They will take such steps as may be necessary to ensure that the fees for official travel documents and visas are acceptable.

They confirm that the presentation of an application concerning contacts on the basis of family ties will not modify the rights and obligations of the applicant or of members of his family.

(b) Reunification of Families

The participating States will deal in a positive and humanitarian spirit with the applications of persons who wish to be reunited with members of their family, with special attention being given to requests of an urgent character—such as requests submitted by persons who are ill or old.

They will deal with applications in this field as expeditiously as possible.

They will lower where necessary the fees charged in connexion with these applications to ensure that they are at a moderate level.

Applications for the purpose of family reunification which are not granted may be renewed at the appropriate level and will be reconsidered at reasonably short intervals by the authorities of the country of residence or destination, whichever is concerned, under such circumstances fees will be charged only when applications are granted.

Persons whose applications for family reunification are granted may bring with them or ship their household and personal effects; to this end the participating States will use all possibilities provided by existing regulations.

Until members of the same family are reunited meetings and contacts between them may take place in accordance with the modalities for contacts on the basis of family ties.

The participating States will support the efforts of Red Cross and Red Crescent Societies concerned with the problems of family reunification.

They confirm that the presentation of an application concerning family reunification will not modify the rights and obligations of the applicant or of members of his family.

The receiving participating State will take appropriate care with regard to employment for persons from other participating States who take up permanent residence in that State in connexion with family reunification with its citizens and see that they are afforded opportunities equal to those enjoyed by its own citizens for education, medical assistance and social security.

(c) Marriage between Citizens of Different States

The participating States will examine favourably and on the basis of humanitarian considerations requests for exit or entry permits from persons who have decided to marry a citizen from another participating State.

The processing and issuing of the documents required for the above purposes and for the marriage will be in accordance with the provisions accepted for family reunification.

In dealing with requests from couples from different participating States, once married, to enable them and the minor children of their marriage to transfer their permanent residence to a State in which either one is normally a resident, the participating States will also apply the provisions accepted for family reunification.

(d) Travel for Personal or Professional Reasons

The participating States intend to facilitate wider travel by their citizens for personal or professional reasons and to this end they intend in particular:

— gradually to simplify and to administer flexibly the procedures for exit and entry;
— to ease regulations concerning movement of citizens from the other participating States in their territory, with due regard to security requirements.

They will endeavour gradually to lower, where necessary, the fees for visas and official travel documents.

They intend to consider, as necessary, means—including, in so far as appropriate, the conclusion of multilateral or bilateral consular conventions or other relevant agreements or understandings—for the improvement of arrangements to provide consular services, including legal and consular assistance.

* * *

They confirm that religious faiths, institutions and organizations, practising within the constitutional framework of the participating States, and their representatives can, in the field of their activities, have contacts and meetings among themselves and exchange information.

(e) Improvement of Conditions for Tourism on an Individual or Collective Basis

The participating States consider that tourism contributes to a fuller knowledge of the life, culture and history of other countries, to the growth of understanding among peoples, to the improvement of contacts and to the broader use of leisure. They intend to promote the development of tourism, on an individual or collective basis, and, in particular, they intend:

— to promote visits to their respective countries by encouraging the provision of appropriate facilities and the simplification and expediting of necessary formalities relating to such visits;
— to increase, on the basis of appropriate agreements or arrangements where necessary, co-operation in the development of tourism, in particular by considering bilaterally possible ways to increase information relating to travel to other countries and to the reception and service of tourists, and other related questions of mutual interest.

(f) Meetings among Young People

The participating States intend to further the development of contacts and exchanges among young people by encouraging:

— increased exchanges and contacts on a short or long term basis among young people working, training or undergoing education through bilateral or multilateral agreements or regular programmes in all cases where it is possible;

— study by their youth organizations of the question of possible agreements relating to frameworks of multilateral youth co-operation;

— agreements or regular programmes relating to the organization of exchanges of students, of international youth seminars, of courses of professional training and foreign language study;

— the further development of youth tourism and the provision to this end of appropriate facilities;

— the development, where possible, of exchanges, contacts and co-operation on a bilateral or multilateral basis between their organizations which represent wide circles of young people working, training or undergoing education;

— awareness among youth of the importance of developing mutual understanding and of strengthening friendly relations and confidence among peoples.

(g) Sport

In order to expand existing links and co-operation in the field of sport the participating States will encourage contacts and exchanges of this kind, including sports meetings and competitions of all sorts, on the basis of the established international rules, regulations and practice.

(h) Expansion of Contacts

By way of further developing contacts among governmental institutions and non-governmental organizations and associations, including women's organizations, the participating States will facilitate the convening of meetings as well as travel by delegations, groups and individuals.

2. Information

The participating States,

Conscious of the need for an ever wider knowledge and understanding of the various aspects of life in other participating States,

Acknowledging the contribution of this process to the growth of confidence between peoples,

Desiring, with the development of mutual understanding between the participating States and with the further improvement of their relations, to continue further efforts towards progress in this field,

Recognizing the importance of the dissemination of information from the other participating States and of a better acquaintance with such information,

Emphasizing therefore the essential and influential role of the press, radio, television, cinema and news agencies and of the journalists working in these fields,

Make it their aim to facilitate the freer and wider dissemination of information of all kinds, to encourage co-operation in the field of information and the exchange of information with other countries, and. to improve the conditions under which journalists from one participating State exercise their profession in another participating State, and

Express their intention in particular:

(a) Improvement of the Circulation of, Access to, and Exchange of Information

(i) Oral Information

— To facilitate the dissemination of oral information through the encouragement of lectures and lecture tours by personalities and specialists from the other participating States, as well as exchanges of opinions at round table meetings, seminars, symposia, summer schools, congresses and other bilateral and multilateral meetings.

(ii) Printed Information

— To facilitate the improvement of the dissemination, on their territory, of newspapers and printed publications, periodical and non-periodical, from the other participating States. For this purpose:

they will encourage their competent firms and organizations to conclude agreements and contracts designed gradually to increase the quantities and the number of titles of newspapers and publications imported from the other participating States. These agreements and contracts should in particular mention the speediest conditions of delivery and the use of the normal channels existing in each country for the distribution of its own publications and newspapers, as well as forms and means of payment agreed between the parties making it possible to achieve the objectives aimed at by these agreements and contracts;

where necessary, they will take appropriate measures to achieve the above objectives and to implement the provisions contained in the agreements and contracts.

— To contribute to the improvement of access by the public to periodical and non-periodical printed publications imported on the bases indicated above. In particular:

they will encourage an increase in the number of places where these publications are on sale,

they will facilitate the availability of these periodical publications during congresses, conferences, official visits and other international events and to tourists during the season,

they will develop the possibilities for taking out subscriptions according to the modalities particular to each country;

they will improve the opportunities for reading and borrowing these publications in large public libraries and their reading rooms as well as in university libraries.

They intend to improve the possibilities for acquaintance with bulletins of official information issued by diplomatic missions and distributed by those missions on the basis of arrangements acceptable to the interested parties.

(iii) Filmed and Broadcast Information

— To promote the improvement of the dissemination of filmed and broadcast information. To this end:

they will encourage the wider showing and broadcasting of a greater variety of recorded and filmed information from the other participating States, illustrating the various aspects of life in their countries and received on the basis of such agreements or arrangements as may be necessary between the organizations and firms directly concerned;

they will facilitate the import by competent organizations and firms of recorded audio-visual material from the other participating States.

The participating States note the expansion in the dissemination of information broadcast by radio, and express the hope for the continuation of this process, so as to meet the interest of mutual understanding among peoples and the aims set forth by this Conference.

(b) Co-operation in the Field of Information

— To encourage co-operation in the field of information on the basis of short or long term agreements or arrangements. In particular:

they will favour increased co-operation among mass media organizations. including press agencies, as well as among publishing houses and organizations;

they will favour co-operation among public or private, national or international radio and television organizations, in particular through the exchange of both live and recorded radio and television programmes, and through the joint production and the broadcasting and distribution of such programmes;

they will encourage meetings and contacts both between journalists organizations and between journalists from the participating States;

they will view favourably the possibilities of arrangements between periodical publications as well as between newspapers from the participating States, for the purpose of exchanging and publishing articles;

they will encourage the exchange of technical information as well as the organization of joint research and meetings devoted to the exchange of experience and views between experts in the field of the press, radio and television.

(c) Improvement of Working Conditions for Journalists

The participating States, desiring to improve the conditions under which journalists from one participating State exercise their profession in another participating State, intend in particular to:

— examine in a favourable spirit and within a suitable and reasonable time scale requests from journalists for visas;

— grant to permanently accredited journalists of the participating States, on the basis of arrangements, multiple entry and exit visas for specified periods;

— facilitate the issue to accredited journalists of the participating States of permits for stay in their country of temporary residence and, if and when these are necessary, of other official papers which it is appropriate for them to have;

— ease, on a basis of reciprocity, procedures for arranging travel by journalists of the participating States in the country where they are exercising their profession, and to provide progressively greater opportunities for such travel, subject to the observance of regulations relating to the existence of areas closed for security reasons,

— ensure that requests by such journalists for such travel receive, in so far as possible, an expeditious response, taking into account the time scale of the request;

— increase the opportunities for journalists of the participating States to communicate personally with their sources, including organizations and official institutions;

— grant to journalists of the participating States the right to import, subject only to its being taken out again, the technical equipment (photographic, cinematographic, tape recorder, radio and television) necessary for the exercise of their profession;[1]

— enable journalists of the other participating States, whether permanently or temporarily accredited, to transmit completely, normally and rapidly by means recognized by the participating States to the information organs which they represent, the results of their professional activity, including tape recordings and undeveloped film, for the purpose of publication or of broadcasting on the radio or television.

The participating States reaffirm that the legitimate pursuit of their professional activity will neither render journalists liable to expulsion nor otherwise penalize them. If an accredited journalist is expelled, he will be informed of the reasons for this act and may submit an application for re-examination of his case.

3. Co-operation and Exchanges in the Field of Culture

The participating States

Considering that cultural exchanges and co-operation contribute to a better comprehension among people and among peoples, and thus promote a lasting understanding among States,

Confirming the conclusions already formulated in this field at the multilateral level, particularly at the Intergovernmental Conference on Cultural Policies in Europe, organized by UNESCO in Helsinki in June 1972, where interest was manifested in the active participation of the broadest possible social groups in an increasingly diversified cultural life,

Desiring, with the development of mutual confidence and the further improvement of relations between the participating States, to continue further efforts toward progress in this field,

Disposed in this spirit to increase substantially their cultural exchanges, with regard both to persons and to cultural works, and to develop among them an active co-operation, both at the bilateral and the multilateral level, in all the fields of culture,

---

[1] While recognizing that appropriate local personnel are employed by foreign journalists in many instances, the participating States note that the above provisions would be applied, subject to the observance of the appropriate rules, to persons from the other participating States, who are regularly and professionally engaged as technicians, photographers or cameramen of the press, radio, television or cinema.

Convinced that such a development of their mutual relations will contribute to the enrichment of the respective cultures, while respecting the originality of each, as well as to the reinforcement among them of a consciousness of common values, while continuing to develop cultural co-operation with other countries of the world,

Declare that they jointly set themselves the following objectives:

(a) to develop the mutual exchange of information with a view to a better knowledge of respective cultural achievements,

(b) to improve the facilities for the exchange and for the dissemination of cultural property,

(c) to promote access by all to respective cultural achievements,

(d) to develop contacts and co-operation among persons active in the field of culture,

(e) to seek new fields and forms of cultural co-operation,

Thus *give expression to* their common will to take progressive, coherent and long-term action in order to achieve the objectives of the present declaration; and

Express their intention now to proceed to the implementation of the following:

Extension of Relations

To expand and improve at the various levels co-operation and links in the field of culture, in particular by:

— concluding, where appropriate, agreements on a bilateral or multilateral basis, providing for the extension of relations among competent State institutions and non-governmental organizations in the field of culture, as well as among people engaged in cultural activities, taking into account the need both for flexibility and the fullest possible use of existing agreements, and bearing in mind that agreements and also other arrangements constitute important means of developing cultural co-operation and exchanges;

— contributing to the development of direct communication and co-operation among relevant State institutions and non-governmental organizations, including, where necessary, such communication and co-operation carried on the basis of special agreements and arrangements;

— encouraging direct contacts and communications among persons engaged in cultural activities, including, where necessary, such contacts and communications carried out on the basis of special agreements. and arrangements.

Mutual Knowledge

Within their competence to adopt, on a bilateral and multilateral level, appropriate measures which would give their peoples a more comprehensive and complete mutual knowledge of their achievements in the various fields of culture, and among them:

— to examine jointly, if necessary with the assistance of appropriate international organizations, the possible creation in Europe and the structure of a bank of cultural data, which would collect information from the participating countries and make it available to its correspondents on their request, and to convene for this purpose a meeting of experts from interested States;

— to consider, if necessary in conjunction with appropriate international organizations, ways of compiling in Europe an inventory of documentary films of a cultural or scientific nature from the participating States;

— to encourage more frequent book exhibitions and to examine the possibility of organizing periodically in Europe a large-scale exhibition of books from the participating States;

— to promote the systematic exchange, between the institutions concerned and publishing houses, of catalogues of available books as well as of pre-publication material which will include, as far as possible, all forthcoming publications; and also to promote the exchange of material between firms publishing encyclopaedias, with a view to improving the presentation of each country;

— to examine jointly questions of expanding and improving exchanges of information in the various fields of culture, such as theatre, music, library work as well as the conservation and restoration of cultural property.

Exchanges and Dissemination

To contribute to the improvement of facilities for exchanges and the dissemination of cultural property, by appropriate means, in particular by:

— studying the possibilities for harmonizing and reducing the charges relating to international commercial exchanges of books and other cultural materials, and also for new means of insuring works of art in foreign exhibitions and for reducing the risks of damage or loss to which these works are exposed by their movement;

— facilitating the formalities of customs clearance, in good time for programmes of artistic events, of the works of art, materials and accessories appearing on lists agreed upon by the organizers of these events;

— encouraging meetings among representatives of competent organizations and relevant firms to examine measures within their field of activity—such as the simplification of orders, time limits for sending supplies and modalities of payment—which might facilitate international commercial exchanges of books;

— promoting the loan and exchange of films among their film institutes and film libraries;

— encouraging the exchange of information among interested parties concerning events of a cultural character foreseen in the participating States, in fields where this is most appropriate, such as music, theatre and the plastic and graphic arts, with a view to contributing to the compilation and publication of a calendar of such events, with the assistance, where necessary, of the appropriate international organizations;

— encouraging a study of the impact which the foreseeable development, and a possible harmonization among interested parties, of the technical means used for the dissemination of culture might have on the development of cultural co-operation and exchanges, while keeping in view the preservation of the diversity and originality, of their respective cultures;

— encouraging, in the way they deem appropriate, within their cultural policies, the further development of interest in the cultural heritage of the other participating States, conscious of the merits and the value of each culture;

— endeavouring to ensure the full and effective application of the international agreements and conventions on copyrights and on circulation of cultural property to which they are party or to which they may decide in the future to become party.

Access

To promote fuller mutual access by all to the achievements—works, experiences and performing arts—in the various fields of culture of their countries, and to that end to make the best possible efforts, in accordance with their competence, more particularly:

— to promote wider dissemination of books and artistic works, in particular by such means as:

facilitating, while taking full account of the international copyright conventions to which they are party, international contacts and communications between authors and publishing houses as well as other cultural institutions, with a view to a more complete mutual access to cultural achievements;

recommending that, in determining the size of editions, publishing houses take into account also the demand from the other participating States, and that rights of sale in other participating States be granted, where possible, to several sales organizations of the importing countries, by agreement between interested partners;

encouraging competent organizations and relevant firms to conclude agreements and contracts and contributing, by this means, to a gradual increase in the number and diversity of works by authors from the other participating States available in the original and in translation in their libraries and bookshops;

promoting, where deemed appropriate, an increase in the number of sales outlets where books by authors from the other participating States, imported in the original on the basis of agreements and contracts, and in translation, are for sale;

promoting, on a wider scale, the translation of works in the sphere of literature and other fields of cultural activity, produced in the languages of the other participating States, especially from the less widely-spoken languages, and the publication and dissemination of the translated works by such measures as:

encouraging more regular contacts between interested publishing houses;

developing their efforts in the basic and advanced training of translators;

encouraging, by appropriate means, the publishing houses of their countries to publish translations;

facilitating the exchange between publishers and interested institutions of lists of books which might be translated;

promoting between their countries the professional activity and co-operation of translators;

carrying out joint studies on ways of further promoting translations and their dissemination;

improving and expanding exchanges of books, bibliographies and catalogue cards between libraries;

— to envisage other appropriate measures which would permit, where necessary by mutual agreement among interested parties, the facilitation of access to their respective cultural achievements, in particular in the field of books;

— to contribute by appropriate means to the wider use of the mass media in order to improve mutual acquaintance with the cultural life of each;

— to seek to develop the necessary conditions for migrant workers and their families to preserve their links with their national culture, and also to adapt themselves to their new cultural environment;

— to encourage the competent bodies and enterprises to make a wider choice and effect wider distribution of full-length and documentary films from the other participating States, and to promote more frequent non-commercial showings, such as premieres, film weeks and festivals, giving due consideration to films from countries whose cinematographic works are less well known;

— to promote, by appropriate means, the extension of opportunities for specialists from the other participating States to work with materials of a cultural character from film and audio-visual archives, within the framework of the existing rules for work on such archival materials;

— to encourage a joint study by interested bodies, where appropriate with the assistance of the competent international organizations, of the expediency and the conditions for the establishment of a repertory of their recorded television programmes of a cultural nature, as well as of the means of viewing them rapidly in order to facilitate their selection and possible acquisition.

Contacts and Co-operation

To contribute, by appropriate means, to the development of contacts and co-operation in the various fields of culture, especially among creative artists and people engaged in cultural activities, in particular by making efforts to:

— promote for persons active in the field of culture, travel and meetings including, where necessary, those carried out on the basis of agreements, contracts or other special arrangements and which are relevant to their cultural co-operation;

— encourage in this way contacts among creative and performing artists and artistic groups with a view to their working together, making known their works in other participating States or exchanging views on topics relevant to their common activity;

— encourage, where necessary through appropriate arrangements, exchanges of trainee and specialists and the granting of scholarships for basic and advanced training in various fields of culture such as the arts and architecture, museums and libraries, literary studies and translation, and contribute to the creation of favourable conditions of reception in their respective institutions;

— encourage the exchange of experience in the training of organizers of cultural activities as well as of teachers and specialists in fields such as theatre, opera, ballet, music and fine arts;

— continue to encourage the organization of international meetings among creative artists, especially young creative artists, on current questions of artistic and literary creation which are of interest for joint study;

— study other possibilities for developing exchanges and co-operation among persons active in the field of culture, with a view to a better mutual knowledge of the cultural fife of the participating States.

Fields and Forms of Co-operation

To encourage the search for new fields and forms of cultural co-operation, to these ends contributing to the conclusion among interested parties, where necessary, of appropriate agreements and arrangements, and in this context to promote:

— joint studies regarding cultural policies, in particular in their social aspects, and as they relate to planning, town-planning, educational and environmental policies, and the cultural aspects of tourism;

— the exchange of knowledge in the realm of cultural diversity, with a view to contributing thus to a better understanding by interested parties of such diversity where it occurs;

— the exchange of information, and as may be appropriate, meetings of experts, the elaboration and the execution of research programmes and projects, as well as their joint evaluation, and the dissemination of the results, on the subjects indicated above;

— such forms of cultural co-operation and the development of such joint projects as:

international events in the fields of the plastic and graphic arts, cinema, theatre, ballet, music, folklore, etc.; book fairs and exhibitions, joint performances of operatic and dramatic works, as well as performances given by soloists, instrumental ensembles, orchestras, choirs and other artistic groups, including those composed of amateurs, paying due attention to the organization of international cultural youth events and the exchange of young artists;

the inclusion of works by writers and composers from the other participating States in the repertoires of soloists and artistic ensembles;

the preparation, translation and publication of articles, studies and monographs, as well as of low-cost books and of artistic and literary collections, suited to making better known respective cultural achievements, envisaging for this purpose meetings among experts and representatives of publishing houses;

the co-production and the exchange of films and of radio and television programmes, by promoting, in particular, meetings among producers, technicians and representatives of the public authorities with a view to working out favourable conditions for the execution of specific joint projects and by encouraging, in the field of co-production, the establishment of international filming teams;

the organization of competitions for architects and town-planners, bearing in mind the possible implementation of the best projects and the formation, where possible, of international teams;

the implementation of joint projects for conserving, restoring and showing to advantage works of art, historical and archaeological monuments and sites of cultural interest, with the help, in appropriate cases, of international organizations of a governmental or non-governmental character as well as of private institutions—competent and active in these fields—envisaging for this purpose:

periodic meetings of experts of the interested parties to elaborate the necessary proposals, while bearing in mind the need to consider these questions in a wider social and economic context;

the publication in appropriate periodicals of articles designed to make known and to compare, among the participating States, the most significant achievements and innovations;

a joint study with a view to the improvement and possible harmonization of the different systems used to inventory and catalogue the historical monuments and places of cultural interest in their countries;

the study of the possibilities for organizing international courses for the training of specialists in different disciplines relating to restoration.

* * *

National minorities or regional cultures. The participating States, recognizing the contribution that national minorities or regional cultures can make to co-operation among them in various fields of culture, intend, when such minorities or cultures exist within their territory, to facilitate this contribution, taking into account the legitimate interests of their members.

4. Co-operation and Exchanges in the Field of Education

The participating States,

Conscious that the development of relations of an international character in the fields of education and science contributes to a better mutual understanding and is to the advantage of all peoples as well as to the benefit of future generations,

Prepared to facilitate, between organizations, institutions and persons engaged in education and science, the further development of exchanges of knowledge and experience as well as of contacts, on the basis of special arrangements where these are necessary,

Desiring to strengthen the links among educational and scientific establishments and also to encourage their co-operation in sectors of common interest, particularly where the levels of knowledge and resources require efforts to be concerted internationally, and

Convinced that progress in these fields should be accompanied and supported by a wider knowledge of foreign languages,

Express to these ends their intention in particular:

(a) Extension of Relations

To expand and improve at the various levels co-operation and links in the fields of education and science, in particular by:

— concluding, where appropriate, bilateral or multilateral agreements providing for co-operation and exchanges among State institutions, non-governmental bodies and persons engaged in activities in education and science, bearing in mind the need both for flexibility and the fuller use of existing agreements and arrangements;

— promoting the conclusion of direct arrangements between universities and other institutions of higher education and research, in the framework of agreements between governments where appropriate;

— encouraging among persons engaged in education and science direct contacts and communications' including those based on special agreements or arrangements where these are appropriate.

(b) Access and Exchanges

To improve access, under mutually acceptable conditions, for students, teachers and scholars of the participating States to each other's educational, cultural and scientific institutions, and to intensify exchanges among these institutions in all areas of common interest, in particular by:

— increasing the exchange of information on facilities for study and courses open to foreign participants, as well as on the conditions under which they will be admitted and received;

— facilitating travel between the participating States by scholars, teachers and students for purposes of study, teaching and research as well as for improving knowledge of each other's educational, cultural and scientific achievements;

— encouraging the award of scholarships for study, teaching and research in their countries to scholars, teachers and students of other participating States;

— establishing, developing or encouraging programmes providing for the broader exchange of scholars, teachers and students, including the organization of symposia, seminars and collaborative projects, and the exchanges of educational and scholarly information such as university publications and materials from libraries;

— promoting the efficient implementation of such arrangements and programmes by providing scholars, teachers and students in good time with more detailed information about their placing in universities and institutes and the programmes envisaged for them; by granting them the opportunity to use relevant scholarly, scientific and open archival materials; and by facilitating their travel within the receiving State for the purpose of study or research as well as in the form of vacation tours on the basis of the usual procedures;

— promoting a more exact assessment of the problems of comparison and equivalence of academic degrees and diplomas by fostering the exchange of information on the organization, duration and content of studies, the comparison of methods of assessing levels of knowledge, and academic qualifications, and, where feasible, arriving at the mutual recognition of academic degrees and diplomas either through governmental agreements, where necessary, or direct arrangements between universities and other institutions of higher learning and research;

— recommending, moreover, to the appropriate international organizations that they should intensify their efforts to reach a generally acceptable solution to the problems of comparison and equivalence between academic degrees and diplomas.

(c) Science

Within their competence to broaden and improve co-operation and exchanges in the field of science, in particular:

To increase, on a bilateral or multilateral basis, the exchange and dissemination of scientific information and documentation by such means as:

— making this information more widely available to scientists and research workers of the other participating States through, for instance, participation in international information-sharing programmes or through other appropriate arrangements;

— broadening and facilitating the exchange of samples and other scientific materials used particularly for fundamental research in the fields of natural sciences and medicine;

— inviting scientific institutions and universities to keep each other more fully and regularly informed about their current and contemplated research work in fields of common interest.

To facilitate the extension of communications and direct contacts between universities, scientific institutions and associations as well as among scientists and research workers, including those based where necessary on special agreements or arrangements, by such means as:

— further developing exchanges of scientists and research workers and encouraging the organization of preparatory meetings or working groups on research topics of common interest;

— encouraging the creation of joint teams of scientists to pursue research projects under arrangements made by the scientific institutions of several countries;

— assisting the organization and successful functioning of international conferences and seminars and participation in them by their scientists and research workers;

— furthermore envisaging, in the near future, a 'Scientific Forum' in the form of a meeting of leading personalities in science from the participating States to discuss interrelated problems of common interest concerning current and future developments in science, and to promote the expansion of contacts, communications and the exchange of information between scientific institutions and among scientists;

— foreseeing, at an early date, a meeting of experts representing the participating States and their national scientific institutions, in order to prepare such a 'Scientific Forum' in consultation with appropriate international organizations, such as UNESCO and the ECE;

— considering in due course what further steps might be taken with respect to the 'Scientific Forum'.

To develop in the field of scientific research, on a bilateral or multilateral basis, the co-ordination of programmes carried out in the participating States and the organization of joint programmes, especially in the areas mentioned below, which may involve the combined efforts of scientists and in certain cases the use of costly or unique equipment. The list of subjects in these areas is illustrative; and specific projects would have to be determined subsequently by the potential partners in the participating States, taking account of the contribution which could be made by appropriate international organizations and scientific institutions:

— *exact and natural sciences*, in particular fundamental research in such fields as mathematics, physics, theoretical physics, geophysics, chemistry, biology, ecology and astronomy;

— *medicine*, in particular basic research into cancer and cardiovascular diseases, studies on the diseases endemic in the developing countries, as well as medico-social research with special emphasis on occupational diseases, the rehabilitation of the handicapped and the care of mothers, children and the elderly;

— *the humanities and social sciences*, such as history, geography, philosophy, psychology, pedagogical research, linguistics, sociology, the legal, political and economic sciences; comparative studies on social, socioeconomic and cultural phenomena which are of common interest to the participating States, especially the problems of human environment and urban development; and scientific studies on the methods of conserving and restoring monuments and works of art.

(d) Foreign Languages and Civilizations

To encourage the study of foreign languages and civilizations as an important means of expanding communication among peoples for their better acquaintance with the culture of each country, as well as for the strengthening of international co-operation; to this end to stimulate, within their competence, the further development and improvement of foreign language teaching and the diversification of choice of languages taught at various levels, paying due attention to less widely-spread or studied languages, and in particular:

— to intensify co-operation aimed at improving the teaching of foreign languages through exchanges of information and experience concerning the development and application of effective modem teaching methods and technical aids, adapted to the needs of different categories of students, including methods of accelerated teaching; and to consider the possibility of conducting, on a bilateral or multilateral basis, studies of new methods of foreign language teaching;

— to encourage co-operation among experts in the field of lexicography with the aim of defining the necessary terminological equivalents, particularly in the scientific and technical disciplines, in order to facilitate relations among scientific institutions and specialists;

— to promote the wider spread of foreign language study among the different types of secondary education establishments and greater possibilities of choice between an increased number of European languages; and in this context to consider, wherever appropriate, the possibilities for developing the recruitment and training of teachers as well as the organization of the student groups required;

— to encourage co-operation between institutions concerned, on a bilateral or multilateral basis, aimed at exploiting more fully the resources of modern educational technology in language teaching, for example through comparative studies by their specialists and, where agreed, through exchanges or transfers of audio-visual materials, of materials used for preparing textbooks, as well as of information about new types of technical equipment used for teaching languages;

— to promote the exchange of information on the experience acquired in the training of language teachers and to intensify exchanges on a bilateral basis of language teachers and students as well as to facilitate their participation in summer courses in languages and civilizations, wherever these are organized;

— to encourage co-operation among experts in the field of lexicography with the aim of defining the necessary terminological equivalents, particularly in the scientific and technical disciplines, in order to facilitate relations among scientific institutions and specialists;

— to promote the wider spread of foreign language study among the different types of secondary education establishments and greater possibilities of choice between an increased number of European languages; and in this context to consider, wherever appropriate, the possibilities for developing the recruitment and training of teachers as well as the organization of the student groups required;

— to favour, in higher education, a wider choice in the languages offered to language students and greater opportunities for other students to study various foreign languages; also to facilitate, where desirable, the organization of courses in languages and civilizations, on the basis of special arrangements as necessary to be given by foreign lecturers, particularly from European countries having less widely-spread or studied languages;

— to promote, within the framework of adult education, the further development of specialized programmes, adapted to various needs and interests, for teaching foreign languages to their own inhabitants and the languages of host countries to interested adults from other countries; in this context to encourage interested institutions to cooperate, for example, in the elaboration of programmes for teaching by radio and television and by accelerated methods, and also, where desirable, in the definition of study objectives for such programmes, with a view to arriving at comparable levels of language proficiency;

— to encourage the association, where appropriate, of the teaching of foreign languages with the study of the corresponding civilizations and also to make further efforts to stimulate interest in the study of foreign languages, including relevant out-of-class activities.

(e) Teaching Methods

To promote the exchange of experience, on a bilateral or multilateral basis, in teaching methods at all levels of education, including those used in permanent and adult education, as well as the exchange of teaching materials, in particular by:

— further developing various forms of contacts and co-operation in the different fields of pedagogical science, for example through comparative or joint studies carried out by interested institutions or through exchanges of information on the results of teaching experiments;

— intensifying exchanges of information on teaching methods used in various educational systems and on results of research into the processes by which pupils and students acquire knowledge, taking account of relevant experience in different types of specialized education;

— facilitating exchanges of experience concerning the organization and functioning of education intended for adults and recurrent education, the relationships between these and other forms and levels of education, as well as concerning the means of adapting education, including vocational and technical training, to the needs of economic and social development in their countries;

— encouraging exchanges of experience in the education of youth and adults in international understanding, with particular reference to those major problems of mankind whose solution calls for a common approach and wider international co-operation;

— encouraging exchanges of teaching materials—including school textbooks, having in mind the possibility of promoting mutual knowledge and facilitating the presentation of each country in such books—as well as exchanges of information on technical innovations in the field of education.

* * *

National minorities or regional cultures

The participating States, recognizing the contribution that national minorities or regional cultures can make to co-operation among them in various fields of education, intend, when such minorities or cultures exist within their territory, to facilitate this contribution, taking into account the legitimate interests of their members.

FOLLOW-UP TO THE CONFERENCE

The participating States,

Having considered and evaluated the progress made at the Conference on Security and Co-operation in Europe,

Considering further that, within the broader context of the world, the Conference is an important part of the process of improving security and developing co-operation in Europe and that its results will contribute significantly to this process,

Intending to implement the provisions of the Final Act of the Conference in order to give full effect to its results and thus to further the process of improving security and developing co-operation in Europe,

Convinced that, in order to achieve the aims sought by the Conference, they should make further unilateral, bilateral and multilateral efforts and continue, in the appropriate forms set forth below, the multilateral process initiated by the Conference,

1. *Declare their resolve,* in the period following the Conference, to pay due regard to and implement the provisions of the Final Act of the Conference:

  (a) unilaterally, in all cases which lend themselves to such action;

  (b) bilaterally, by negotiations with other participating States;

  (c) multilaterally, by meetings of experts of the participating States, and also within the framework of existing international organizations, such as the United Nations Economic Commission for Europe and UNESCO, with regard to educational, scientific and cultural co-operation;

2. *Declare furthermore their resolve* to continue the multilateral process initiated by the Conference:

  (a) by proceeding to a thorough exchange of views both on the implementation of the provisions of the Final Act and of the tasks defined by the Conference, as well as, in the context of the questions dealt with by the latter, on the deepening of their mutual relations, the improvement of security and the development of co-operation in Europe, and the development of the process of détente in the future;

(b) by organizing to these ends meetings among their representatives, beginning with a meeting at the level of representatives appointed by the Ministers of Foreign Affairs. This meeting will define the appropriate modalities for the holding of other meetings which could include further similar meetings and the possibility of a new Conference;

3. The first of the meetings indicated above will be held at Belgrade in 1977. A preparatory meeting to organize this meeting will be held at Belgrade on 15 June 1977. The preparatory meeting will decide on the date, duration, agenda and other modalities of the meeting of representatives appointed by the Ministers of Foreign Affairs;

4. The rules of procedure, the working methods and the scale of distribution for the expenses of the Conference will, *mutatis mutandis*, be applied to the meetings envisaged in paragraphs 1 (c), 2 and 3 above. All the above-mentioned meetings will be held in the participating States in rotation. The services of a technical secretariat will be provided by the host country.

The original of this Final Act, drawn up in English, French, German, Italian, Russian and Spanish, will be transmitted to the Government of the Republic of Finland, which will retain it in its archives. Each of the participating States will receive from the Government of the Republic of Finland a true copy of this Final Act.

The text of this Final Act will be published in each participating State, which will disseminate it and make it known as widely as possible.

The Government of the Republic of Finland is requested to transmit to the Secretary-General of the United Nations the text of this Final Act, which is not eligible for registration under Article 102 of the Charter of the United Nations, with a view to its circulation to all the members of the Organization as an official document of the United Nations.

The Government of the Republic of Finland is also requested to transmit the text of this Final Act to the Director-General of UNESCO and to the Executive Secretary of the United Nations Economic Commission for Europe.

Wherefore, the undersigned High Representatives of the participating States, mindful of the high political significance which they attach to the results of the Conference, and declaring their determination to act in accordance with the provisions contained in the above texts, have subscribed their signatures below:

Done at Helsinki, on 1st August 1975, in the name of...

107. THE CHARTER OF PARIS FOR
A NEW EUROPE, 1990

In this declaration, adopted on 21 November 1990, the CSCE participating States (then 34 in number following the unification of Germany) reaffirmed their commitment to the principles of the Helsinki Final Act (above p. 910). In particular, the opening section on 'Human Rights, Democracy and the Rule of Law', relates to the protection of national minorities.

In the Helsinki Final Act, the participating States declared their resolve to continue the multilateral process initiated by the first Conference on Security and Co-operation in Europe, and decided to organize follow-up meetings and conferences. In the Charter of Paris for a New Europe (1990), the participating States also laid the foundations for institutionalization. Four summits have been held since (Helsinki, 1992; Budapest, 1994; Lisbon, 1996; and Istanbul, 1999). The 'Ministerial Council' was also established at Paris and is now the central decision-making and governing body of the OSCE; the 16th Ministerial Council met in Helsinki from 4–5 December 2008: **http://www.osce.org/conferences/mc_2008.html**.

Further reading

CLARK, I., 'Paris and Democracy, 1990', in CLARK, I., *International Legitimacy and World Society*, Oxford: Oxford University Press, 2007, 153; available through OXFORD SCHOLARSHIP ONLINE: **http://www.oxfordscholarship.com/**.

GHEBALI, V.-Y. and WARNER, D., eds., 'The Reform of the OSCE 15 Years after the Charter of Paris for a New Europe: Problems, Challenges and Risks', PSIO Occasional Paper 2/2006, Geneva: Graduate Institute of International Studies, 2006.

TEXT

A NEW ERA OF DEMOCRACY, PEACE AND UNITY

We, the Heads of State or Government of the States participating in the Conference on Security and Co-operation in Europe, have assembled in Paris at a time of profound change and historic expectations. The era of confrontation and division of Europe has ended. We declare that henceforth our relations will be founded on respect and co-operation.

Europe is liberating itself from the legacy of the past. The courage of men and women, the strength of the will of the peoples and the power of the ideas of the Helsinki Final Act have opened a new era of democracy, peace and unity in Europe.

Ours is a time for fulfilling the hopes and expectations our peoples have cherished for decades: steadfast commitment to democracy based on human rights and fundamental freedoms; prosperity through economic liberty and social justice; and equal security for all our countries.

The Ten Principles of the Final Act will guide us towards this ambitious future, just as they have lighted our way towards better relations for the past fifteen years. Full implementation of all CSCE commitments must form the basis for the initiatives we are now taking to enable our nations to live in accordance with their aspirations.

Human Rights, Democracy and Rule of Law

We undertake to build, consolidate and strengthen democracy as the only system of government of our nations. In this endeavour, we will abide by the following:

Human rights and fundamental freedoms are the birthright of all human beings, are inalienable and are guaranteed by law. Their protection and promotion is the first responsibility of government. Respect for them is an essential safeguard against an over-mighty State. Their observance and full exercise are the foundation of freedom, justice and peace.

Democratic government is based on the will of the people, expressed regularly through free and fair elections. Democracy has as its foundation respect for the human person and the rule of law. Democracy is the best safeguard of freedom of expression, tolerance of all groups of society, and equality of opportunity for each person.

Democracy, with its representative and pluralist character, entails accountability to the electorate, the obligation of public authorities to comply with the law and justice administered impartially. No one will be above the law.

We affirm that, without discrimination,

every individual has the right to

freedom of thought, conscience and religion or belief,

freedom of expression,

freedom of association and peaceful assembly,

freedom of movement;

no one will be:

subject to arbitrary arrest or detention,

subject to torture or other cruel, inhuman or degrading treatment or   punishment;

everyone also has the right:

to know and act upon his rights,

to participate in free and fair elections,

to fair and public trial if charged with an offence,

to own property alone or in association and to exercise individual enterprise,

to enjoy his economic, social and cultural rights.

We affirm that the ethnic, cultural, linguistic and religious identity of national minorities will be protected and that persons belonging to national minorities have the right freely to express, preserve and develop that identity without any discrimination and in full equality before the law.

We will ensure that everyone will enjoy recourse to effective remedies, national or international, against any violation of his rights.

Full respect for these precepts is the bedrock on which we will seek to construct the new Europe.

Our States will co-operate and support each other with the aim of making democratic gains irreversible.

Economic Liberty and Responsibility

Economic liberty, social justice and environmental responsibility are indispensable for prosperity.

The free will of the individual, exercised in democracy and protected by the rule of law, forms the necessary basis for successful economic and social development. We will promote economic activity which respects and upholds human dignity.

Freedom and political pluralism are necessary elements in our common objective of developing market economies towards sustainable economic growth, prosperity, social justice, expanding employment and efficient use of economic resources. The success of the transition to market economy by countries making efforts to this effect is important and in the interest of us all. It will enable us to share a higher level of prosperity which is our common objective. We will co-operate to this end.

Preservation of the environment is a shared responsibility of all our nations. While supporting national and regional efforts in this field, we must also look to the pressing need for joint action on a wider scale.

Friendly Relations among Participating States

Now that a new era is dawning in Europe, we are determined to expand and strengthen friendly relations and co-operation among the States of Europe, the United States of America and Canada, and to promote friendship among our peoples.

To uphold and promote democracy, peace and unity in Europe, we solemnly pledge our full commitment to the Ten Principles of the Helsinki Final Act. We affirm the continuing validity of the Ten Principles and our determination to put them into practice. All the Principles apply equally and unreservedly, each of them being interpreted taking into account the others. They form the basis for our relations.

In accordance with our obligations under the Charter of the United Nations and commitments under the Helsinki Final Act, we renew our pledge to refrain from the threat or use of force against the territorial integrity or political independence of any State, or from acting in any other manner inconsistent with the principles or purposes of those documents. We recall that non-compliance with obligations under the Charter of the United Nations constitutes a violation of international law.

We reaffirm our commitment to settle disputes by peaceful means. We decide to develop mechanisms for the prevention and resolution of conflicts among the participating States.With the ending of the division of Europe, we will strive for a new quality in our security relations while fully respecting each other's freedom of choice in that respect. Security is indivisible and the security of every participating State is inseparably linked to that of all the others. We therefore pledge to co-operate in strengthening confidence and security among us and in promoting arms control and disarmament.

We welcome the Joint Declaration of Twenty-Two States on the improvement of their relations.

Our relations will rest on our common adherence to democratic values and to human rights and fundamental freedoms. We are convinced that in order to strengthen peace and security among our States, the advancement of democracy, and respect for and effective exercise of human rights, are indispensable. We reaffirm the equal rights of peoples and their right to self-determination in conformity with the Charter of the United Nations and with the relevant norms of international law, including those relating to territorial integrity of States.

We are determined to enhance political consultation and to widen co-operation to solve economic, social, environmental, cultural and humanitarian problems. This common resolve and our growing interdependence will help to overcome the mistrust of decades, to increase stability and to build a united Europe.

We want Europe to be a source of peace, open to dialogue and to co-operation with other countries, welcoming exchanges and involved in the search for common responses to the challenges of the future.

Security

Friendly relations among us will benefit from the consolidation of democracy and improved security.

We welcome the signature of the Treaty on Conventional Armed Forces in Europe by twenty-two participating States, which will lead to lower levels of armed forces. We endorse the adoption of a substantial new set of Confidence- and Security-building Measures which will lead to increased transparency and confidence among all participating States. These are important steps towards enhanced stability and security in Europe.

The unprecedented reduction in armed forces resulting from the Treaty on Conventional Armed Forces in Europe, together with new approaches to security and co-operation within the CSCE process, will lead to a new perception of security in Europe and a new dimension in our relations. In this context we fully recognize the freedom of States to choose their own security arrangements.

Unity

Europe whole and free is calling for a new beginning. We invite our peoples to join in this great endeavour.

We note with great satisfaction the Treaty on the Final Settlement with respect to Germany signed in Moscow on 12 September 1990 and sincerely welcome the fact that the German people have united to become one State in accordance with the principles of the Final Act of the Conference on Security and Co-operation in Europe and in full accord with their neighbours. The establishment of the national unity of Germany is an important contribution to a just and lasting order of peace for a united, democratic Europe aware of its responsibility for stability, peace and co-operation.

The participation of both North American and European States is a fundamental characteristic of the CSCE; it underlies its past achievements and is essential to the future of the CSCE process. An abiding adherence to shared values and our common heritage are the ties which bind us together. With all the rich diversity of our nations, we are united in our commitment to expand our co-operation in all fields. The challenges confronting us can only be met by common action, co-operation and solidarity.

The CSCE and the World

The destiny of our nations is linked to that of all other nations. We support fully the United Nations and the enhancement of its role in promoting international peace, security and justice. We reaffirm our commitment to the principles and purposes of the United Nations as enshrined in the Charter and condemn all violations of these principles. We recognize with satisfaction the growing role of the United Nations in world affairs and its increasing effectiveness, fostered by the improvement in relations among our States.

Aware of the dire needs of a great part of the world, we commit ourselves to solidarity with all other countries. Therefore, we issue a call from Paris today to all the nations of the world. We stand ready to join with any and all States in common efforts to protect and advance the community of fundamental human values.

GUIDELINES FOR THE FUTURE

Proceeding from our firm commitment to the full implementation of all CSCE principles and provisions, we now resolve to give a new impetus to a balanced and comprehensive development of our co-operation in order to address the needs and aspirations of our peoples.

HUMAN DIMENSION

We declare our respect for human rights and fundamental freedoms to be irrevocable. We will fully implement and build upon the provisions relating to the human dimension of the CSCE.

Proceeding from the Document of the Copenhagen Meeting of the Conference on the Human Dimension, we will co-operate to strengthen democratic institutions and to promote the application of the rule of law. To that end, we decide to convene a seminar of experts in Oslo from 4 to 15 November 1991.

Determined to foster the rich contribution of national minorities to the life of our societies, we undertake further to improve their situation. We reaffirm our deep conviction that friendly relations among our peoples, as well as peace, justice, stability and democracy, require that the ethnic, cultural, linguistic and religious identity of national minorities be protected and conditions for the promotion of that identity be created. We declare that questions related to national minorities can only be satisfactorily resolved in a democratic political framework. We further acknowledge that the rights of persons belonging to national minorities must be fully respected as part of universal human rights. Being aware of the urgent need for increased co-operation on, as well as better protection of, national minorities, we decide to convene a meeting of experts on national minorities to be held in Geneva from 1 to 19 July 1991.

We express our determination to combat all forms of racial and ethnic hatred, antisemitism, xenophobia and discrimination against anyone as well as persecution on religious and ideological grounds.

In accordance with our CSCE commitments, we stress that free movement and contacts among our citizens as well as the free flow of information and ideas are crucial for the maintenance and development of free societies and flourishing cultures. We welcome increased tourism and visits among our countries.

The human dimension mechanism has proved its usefulness, and we are consequently determined to expand it to include new procedures involving, *inter alia*, the services of experts or a roster of eminent persons experienced in human rights issues which could be raised under the mechanism. We shall provide, in the context of the mechanism, for individuals to be involved in the protection of their rights. Therefore, we undertake to develop further our commitments in this respect, in particular at the Moscow Meeting of the Conference on the Human Dimension, without prejudice to obligations under existing international instruments to which our States may be parties.

We recognize the important contribution of the Council of Europe to the promotion of human rights and the principles of democracy and the rule of law as well as to the development of cultural co-operation. We welcome moves by several participating States to join the Council of Europe and adhere to its European Convention on Human Rights. We welcome as well the readiness of the Council of Europe to make its experience available to the CSCE.

SECURITY

The changing political and military environment in Europe opens new possibilities for common efforts in the field of military security. We will build on the important achievements attained in the Treaty on Conventional Armed Forces in Europe and in the

Negotiations on Confidence- and Security-building Measures. We undertake to continue the CSBM negotiations under the same mandate, and to seek to conclude them no later than the Follow-up Meeting of the CSCE to be held in Helsinki in 1992. We also welcome the decision of the participating States concerned to continue the CFE negotiation under the same mandate and to seek to conclude it no later than the Helsinki Follow-up Meeting. Following a period for national preparations, we look forward to a more structured co-operation among all participating States on security matters, and to discussions and consultations among the thirty-four participating States aimed at establishing by 1992, from the conclusion of the Helsinki Follow-up Meeting, new negotiations on disarmament and confidence and security building open to all participating States.

We call for the earliest possible conclusion of the Convention on an effectively verifiable, global and comprehensive ban on chemical weapons, and we intend to be original signatories to it.

We reaffirm the importance of the Open Skies initiative and call for the successful conclusion of the negotiations as soon as possible.

Although the threat of conflict in Europe has diminished, other dangers threaten the stability of our societies. We are determined to co-operate in defending democratic institutions against activities which violate the independence, sovereign equality or territorial integrity of the participating States. These include illegal activities involving outside pressure, coercion and subversion.

We unreservedly condemn, as criminal, all acts, methods and practices of terrorism and express our determination to work for its eradication both bilaterally and through multilateral co-operation. We will also join together in combating illicit trafficking in drugs.

Being aware that an essential complement to the duty of States to refrain from the threat or use of force is the peaceful settlement of disputes, both being essential factors for the maintenance and consolidation of international peace and security, we will not only seek effective ways of preventing, through political means, conflicts which may yet emerge, but also define, in conformity with international law, appropriate mechanisms for the peaceful resolution of any disputes which may arise. Accordingly, we undertake to seek new forms of co-operation in this area, in particular a range of methods for the peaceful settlement of disputes, including mandatory third-party involvement. We stress that full use should be made in this context of the opportunity of the Meeting on the Peaceful Settlement of Disputes which will be convened in Valletta at the beginning of 1991. The Council of Ministers for Foreign Affairs will take into account the Report of the Valletta Meeting.

ECONOMIC CO-OPERATION

We stress that economic co-operation based on market economy constitutes an essential element of our relations and will be instrumental in the construction of a prosperous and united Europe. Democratic institutions and economic liberty foster economic and social progress, as recognized in the Document of the Bonn Conference on Economic Co-operation, the results of which we strongly support.

We underline that co-operation in the economic field, science and technology is now an important pillar of the CSCE. The participating States should periodically review progress and give new impulses in these fields.

We are convinced that our overall economic co-operation should be expanded, free enterprise encouraged and trade increased and diversified according to GATT rules. We will promote social justice and progress and further the welfare of our peoples. We recognize in this context the importance of effective policies to address the problem of unemployment.

We reaffirm the need to continue to support democratic countries in transition towards the establishment of market economy and the creation of the basis for self-sustained economic and social growth, as already undertaken by the Group of twenty-four countries. We further underline the necessity of their increased integration, involving the acceptance of disciplines as well as benefits, into the international economic and financial system.

We consider that increased emphasis on economic co-operation within the CSCE process should take into account the interests of developing participating States.

We recall the link between respect for and promotion of human rights and fundamental freedoms and scientific progress. Co-operation in the field of science and technology will play an essential role in economic and social development. Therefore, it must evolve towards a greater sharing of appropriate scientific and technological information and knowledge with a view to overcoming the technological gap which exists among the participating States. We further encourage the participating States to work together in order to develop human potential and the spirit of free enterprise.

We are determined to give the necessary impetus to co-operation among our States in the fields of energy, transport and tourism for economic and social development. We welcome, in particular, practical steps to create optimal conditions for the economic and rational development of energy resources, with due regard for environmental considerations.

We recognize the important role of the European Community in the political and economic development of Europe. International economic organizations such as the United Nations Economic Commission for Europe (ECE), the Bretton Woods Institutions, the Organization for Economic Co-operation and Development (ECD), the European Free Trade Association (EFTA) and the International Chamber of Commerce (ICC) also have a significant task in promoting economic co-operation, which will be further enhanced by the establishment of the European Bank for Reconstruction and Development (EBRD). In order to pursue our objectives, we stress the necessity for effective co-ordination of the activities of these organizations and emphasize the need to find methods for all our States to take part in these activities.

ENVIRONMENT

We recognize the urgent need to tackle the problems of the environment and the importance of individual and co-operative efforts in this area. We pledge to intensify our endeavours to protect and improve our environment in order to restore and maintain a sound ecological balance in air, water and soil. Therefore, we are determined to make full use of the CSCE as a framework for the formulation of common environmental commitments and objectives, and thus to pursue the work reflected in the Report of the Sofia Meeting on the Protection of the Environment.

We emphasize the significant role of a well-informed society in enabling the public and individuals to take initiatives to improve the environment. To this end, we commit ourselves to promoting public awareness and education on the environment as well as the public reporting of the environmental impact of policies, projects and programmes.

We attach priority to the introduction of clean and low-waste technology, being aware of the need to support countries which do not yet have their own means for appropriate measures.

We underline that environmental policies should be supported by appropriate legislative measures and administrative structures to ensure their effective implementation.

We stress the need for new measures providing for the systematic evaluation of compliance with the existing commitments and, moreover, for the development of more ambitious commitments with regard to notification and exchange of information about the state of the environment and potential environmental hazards. We also welcome the creation of the European Environment Agency (EEA).

We welcome the operational activities, problem-oriented studies and policy reviews in various existing international organizations engaged in the protection of the environment, such as the United Nations Environment Programme (UNEP), the United Nations Economic Commission for Europe (ECE) and the Organization for Economic Co-operation and Development (OECD). We emphasize the need for strengthening their co-operation and for their efficient co-ordination.

CULTURE

We recognize the essential contribution of our common European culture and our shared values in overcoming the division of the continent. Therefore, we underline our attachment to creative freedom and to the protection and promotion of our cultural and spiritual heritage, in all its richness and diversity.

In view of the recent changes in Europe, we stress the increased importance of the Cracow Symposium and we look forward to its consideration of guidelines for intensified co-operation in the field of culture. We invite the Council of Europe to contribute to this Symposium.

In order to promote greater familiarity amongst our peoples, we favour the establishment of cultural centres in cities of other participating States as well as increased co-operation in the audio-visual field and wider exchange in music, theatre, literature and the arts.

We resolve to make special efforts in our national policies to promote better understanding, in particular among young people, through cultural exchanges, co-operation in all fields of education and, more specifically, through teaching and training in the languages of other participating States. We intend to consider first results of this action at the Helsinki Follow-up Meeting in 1992.

MIGRANT WORKERS

We recognize that the issues of migrant workers and their families legally residing in host countries have economic, cultural and social aspects as well as their human dimension. We reaffirm that the protection and promotion of their rights, as well as the implementation of relevant international obligations, is our common concern.

MEDITERRANEAN

We consider that the fundamental political changes that have occurred in Europe have a positive relevance to the Mediterranean region. Thus, we will continue efforts to strengthen security and co-operation in the Mediterranean as an important factor for stability in Europe. We welcome the Report of the Palma de Mallorca Meeting on the Mediterranean, the results of which we all support.

We are concerned with the continuing tensions in the region, and renew our determination to intensify efforts towards finding just, viable and lasting solutions, through peaceful means, to outstanding crucial problems, based on respect for the principles of the Final Act.

We wish to promote favourable conditions for a harmonious development and diversification of relations with the non-participating Mediterranean States. Enhanced co-operation with these States will be pursued with the aim of promoting economic and social development and thereby enhancing stability in the region. To this end, we will strive together with these countries towards a substantial narrowing of the prosperity gap between Europe and its Mediterranean neighbours.

NON-GOVERNMENTAL ORGANIZATIONS

We recall the major role that non-governmental organizations, religious and other groups and individuals have played in the achievement of the objectives of the CSCE and will further facilitate their activities for the implementation of the CSCE commitments by the participating States. These organizations, groups and individuals must be involved in an appropriate way in the activities and new structures of the CSCE in order to fulfil their important tasks.

NEW STRUCTURES AND INSTITUTIONS
OF THE CSCE PROCESS

Our common efforts to consolidate respect for human rights, democracy and the rule of law, to strengthen peace and to promote unity in Europe require a new quality of political dialogue and co-operation and thus development of the structures of the CSCE.

The intensification of our consultations at all levels is of prime importance in shaping our future relations. To this end, we decide on the following:

We, the Heads of State or Government, shall meet next time in Helsinki on the occasion of the CSCE Follow-up Meeting 1992. Thereafter, we will meet on the occasion of subsequent follow-up meetings.

Our Ministers for Foreign Affairs will meet, as a Council, regularly and at least once a year. These meetings will provide the central forum for political consultations within the CSCE process. The Council will consider issues relevant to the Conference on Security and Co-operation in Europe and take appropriate decisions.

The first meeting of the Council will take place in Berlin.

A Committee of Senior Officials will prepare the meetings of the Council and carry out its decisions. The Committee will review current issues and may take appropriate decisions, including in the form of recommendations to the Council.

Additional meetings of the representatives of the participating States may be agreed upon to discuss questions of urgent concern.

The Council will examine the development of provisions for convening meetings of the Committee of Senior Officials in emergency situations.

Meetings of other Ministers may also be agreed by the participating States.

In order to provide administrative support for these consultations we establish a Secretariat in Prague.

Follow-up meetings of the participating States will be held, as a rule, every two years to allow the participating States to take stock of developments, review the implementation of their commitments and consider further steps in the CSCE process.

We decide to create a Conflict Prevention Centre in Vienna to assist the Council in reducing the risk of conflict.

We decide to establish an Office for Free Elections in Warsaw to facilitate contacts and the exchange of information on elections within participating States.

Recognizing the important role parliamentarians can play in the CSCE process, we call for greater parliamentary involvement in the CSCE, in particular through the creation of a CSCE parliamentary assembly, involving members of parliaments from all participating States. To this end, we urge that contacts be pursued at parliamentary level to discuss the field of activities, working methods and rules of procedure of such a CSCE parliamentary structure, drawing on existing experience and work already undertaken in this field.

We ask our Ministers for Foreign Affairs to review this matter on the occasion of their first meeting as a Council.

* * *

Procedural and organizational modalities relating to certain provisions contained in the Charter of Paris for a New Europe are set out in the Supplementary Document which is adopted together with the Charter of Paris.

We entrust to the Council the further steps which may be required to ensure the implementation of decisions contained in the present document, as well as in the Supplementary Document, and to consider further efforts for the strengthening of security and co-operation in Europe. The Council may adopt any amendment to the supplementary document which it may deem appropriate.

* * *

The original of the Charter of Paris for a New Europe, drawn up in English, French, German, Italian, Russian and Spanish, will be transmitted to the Government of the French Republic, which will retain it in its archives. Each of the participating States will receive from the Government of the French Republic a true copy of the Charter of Paris.

The text of the Charter of Paris will be published in each participating State, which will disseminate it and make it known as widely as possible.

The Government of the French Republic is requested to transmit to the Secretary-General of the United Nations the text of the Charter of Paris for a New Europe which is not eligible for registration under Article 102 of the Charter of the United Nations, with a view to its circulation to all the members of the Organization as an official document of the United Nations.

The Government of the French Republic is also requested to transmit the text of the Charter of Paris to all the other international organizations mentioned in the text.

Wherefore, we, the undersigned High Representatives of the participating States, mindful of the high political significance we attach to the results of the Summit Meeting, and declaring our determination to act in accordance with the provisions we have adopted, have subscribed our signatures below:

Done at Paris, on 21 November 1990,
in the name of...

PART SIX

AMERICAS

INTRODUCTION

While the United States of America and Canada are commonly identified, more or less, within the same philosophical and doctrinal field as their European allies, certain notable recent exceptions apart, Latin America provides a store of contradictions in the field of human rights. Legal and political sophistication, even if historically linked to certain social elites, has generated a desire to adopt a variety of legal instruments, such as the American Convention on Human Rights (below, p. 955), which is broadly similar to the European Convention (above, p. 681). At the same time social conditions in nearly all of Latin America entail inequalities and deprivation on such a scale that recourse to guarantees of the classical Western political and civil rights is manifestly inadequate. Moreover, with sometimes faltering movement in the direction of general social and economic development, the position relating to civil and political rights has often been precarious.

The position in Latin America nevertheless has special features. Historically, the whole question of human rights has long been bound up with the status of aliens and their property, and powerful foreign corporations may well seek to rely on human rights standards to preserve an economic *status quo* favourable to their interests. More significant is the relation of human rights to the regional security system represented by the Organization of American States. The concept of human rights in Latin America has been employed as a weapon against revolutionary regimes, particularly Cuba, but it has also been an inescapable and powerful factor, nationally and internationally, in the restoration of democratic government. Even so, formal adherence by governments to agreements containing guarantees of human rights helps politicians striving to improve social conditions, and will improve the possibility of reporting abuses.

Further reading

BARAHONA DE BRITO, A., *Human Rights and Democratization in Latin America: Uruguay and Chile*, Oxford: Oxford University Press, 1997; available online at **http://www.oxfordscholarship.com**.
BUERGENTHAL, T., 'The Revised OAS Charter', (1975) 69 *AJIL* 828.
—— and SHELTON, D., eds., *Protecting Human Rights in the Americas*, Kehl: N. P. Engel, 4th edn., 1995.

CAFLISCH, L. and CANÇADO TRINDADE, A. A., 'Les conventions américaine et européenne des droits de l'homme et le droit international général', (2004) 108 *Revue générale de droit international public*, 5.

CARDENAS, S., *Human Rights in Latin America: A Politics of Terror and Hope*, Philadelphia: University of Pennsylvania Press, 2009.

CLEARY, E., *Mobilizing for Human Rights in Latin America*, Bloomfield, CF: Kumarian Press, 2007.

GROS ESPIELL, H., 'Le système interaméricain comme régime régional de protection internationale des droits de l'homme', 145 *Recueil des Cours* (1975–II), 1–55.

HARRIS, D. and LIVINGSTONE, S., eds., *The Inter-American System of Human Rights*, Oxford: Clarendon Press, 1998.

MEDINA QUIROGA, C., *The Battle of Human Rights: Gross, Systematic Violations and the Inter-American System*, Utrecht: Netherlands Institute for Social and Economic Law Research, 1988.

108. AMERICAN DECLARATION OF THE RIGHTS AND DUTIES OF MAN, 1948

The declaration is to be found in the Final Act of the Ninth International Conference of American States, Bogotá, Colombia, held in 1948: *Acta y Documentos*, 297; OAS Res. XXX, adopted by the Ninth International Conference of American States (1948), reprinted in *Basic Documents Pertaining to Human Rights in the Inter-American System*, OEA/Ser.L.V/I.4 rev 12, 31 January 2008: **http://www. cidh.org/Basicos/English/Basic.TOC.htm**. It was based on a revision of a draft first prepared in 1946 by the Inter-American Juridical Committee. The Declaration was not intended to be binding, and its status was that of a recommendation of the Conference. However, in their practice the organs created in accordance with the American Convention on Human Rights (below, p. 955) have given a certain normative effect to the Declaration; see the decision of the Commission in the case of *Roach and Pinkerton*, Resolution No. 3/87, Case 9647, 22 September 1987, *Annual Report of the Inter-American Commission on Human Rights*, 1986–87: **http://www.cidh.org/casos/86.87.eng. htm/**; and the advisory opinion of the Inter-American Court of Human Rights on the *Interpretation of the American Declaration of the Rights and Duties of Man within the Framework of Article 64 of the American Convention on Human Rights*, 14 July 1989 (OC–10/89); Inter-American Court of Human Rights, Series A, Judgments and Opinions, No. 10: **http://www.corteidh.or.cr/buscadores.cfm**.

TEXT

Whereas:

The American peoples have acknowledged the dignity of the individual, and their national constitutions recognize that juridical and political institutions, which regulate life in human society, have as their principal aim the protection of the essential rights of man and the creation of circumstances that will permit him to achieve spiritual and material progress and attain happiness;

The American States have on repeated occasions recognized that the essential rights of man are not derived from the fact that he is a national of a certain State, but are based upon attributes of his human personality;

The international protection of the rights of man should be the principal guide of an evolving American law;

The affirmation of essential human rights by the American States together with the guarantees given by the internal regimes of the States establish the initial system of protection considered by the American States as being suited to the present social and juridical conditions, not without a recognition on their part that they should increasingly strengthen that system in the international field as conditions become more favorable,

The Ninth International Conference of American States

Agrees

To adopt the following

Preamble

All men are born free and equal, in dignity and in rights, and, being endowed by nature with reason and conscience, they should conduct themselves as brothers one to another.

The fulfilment of duty by each individual is a prerequisite to the rights of all. Rights and duties are interrelated in every social and political activity of man. While rights exalt individual liberty, duties express the dignity of that liberty.

Duties of a juridical nature presuppose others of a moral nature which support them in principle and constitute their basis.

Inasmuch as spiritual development is the supreme end of human existence and the highest expression thereof, it is the duty of man to serve that end with all his strength and resources.

Since culture is the highest social and historical expression of that spiritual development, it is the duty of man to preserve, practise and foster culture by every means within his power.

And, since moral conduct constitutes the noblest flowering of culture, it is the duty of every man always to hold it in high respect.

CHAPTER I
RIGHTS

Article I

Every human being has the right to life, liberty and the security of his person.

Article II

All persons are equal before the law and have the rights and duties established in this Declaration, without distinction as to race, sex, language, creed or any other factor.

Article III

Every person has the right freely to profess a religious faith, and to manifest and practise it both in public and in private.

Article IV

Every person has the right to freedom of investigation, of opinion, and of the expression and dissemination of ideas, by any medium whatsoever.

Article V

Every person has the right to the protection of the law against abusive attacks upon his honor, his reputation, and his private and family life.

Article VI

Every person has the right to establish a family, the basic element of society, and to receive protection therefor.

Article VII

All women, during pregnancy and the nursing period, and all children have the right to special protection, care and aid.

Article VIII

Every person has the right to fix his residence within the territory of the State of which he is a national, to move about freely within such territory, and not to leave it except by his own will.

Article IX

Every person has the right to the inviolability of his home.

Article X

Every person has the right to the inviolability and transmission of his correspondence.

Article XI

Every person has the right to the preservation of his health through sanitary and social measures relating to food, clothing, housing and medical care, to the extent permitted by public and community resources.

Article XII

Every person has the right to an education, which should be based on the principles of liberty, morality and human solidarity.

Likewise every person has the right to an education that will prepare him to attain a decent life, to raise his standard of living, and to be a useful member of society.

The right to an education includes the right to equality of opportunity in every case, in accordance with natural talents, merit and the desire to utilize the resources that the State or the community is in a position to provide.

Every person has the right to receive, free, at least a primary education.

Article XIII

Every person has the right to take part in the cultural life of the community, to enjoy the arts, and to participate in the benefits that result from intellectual progress, especially scientific discoveries.

He likewise has the right to the protection of his moral and material interests as regards his inventions or any literary, scientific or artistic works of which he is the author.

Article XIV

Every person has the right to work, under proper conditions, and to follow his vocation freely, insofar as existing conditions of employment permit.

Every person who works has the right to receive such remuneration as will, in proportion to his capacity and skill, assure him a standard of living suitable for himself and for his family.

Article XV

Every person has the right to leisure time, to wholesome recreation, and to the opportunity for advantageous use of his free time to his spiritual, cultural and physical benefit.

Article XVI

Every person has the right to social security which will protect him from the consequences of unemployment, old age, and any disabilities arising from causes beyond his control that make it physically or mentally impossible for him to earn a living.

Article XVII

Every person has the right to be recognized everywhere as a person having rights and obligations, and to enjoy the basic civil rights.

Article XVIII

Every person may resort to the courts to ensure respect for his legal rights. There should likewise be available to him a simple, brief procedure whereby the courts will protect him from acts of authority that, to his prejudice, violate any fundamental constitutional rights.

Article XIX

Every person has the right to the nationality to which he is entitled by law and to change it, if he so wishes, for the nationality of any other country that is willing to grant it to him.

Article XX

Every person having legal capacity is entitled to participate in the government of his country, directly or through his representatives, and to take part in popular elections, which shall be by secret ballot, and shall be honest, periodic and free.

Article XXI

Every person has the right to assemble peaceably with others in a formal public meeting or an informal gathering, in connection with matters of common interest of any nature.

Article XXII

Every person has the right to associate with others to promote, exercise and protect his legitimate interests of a political, economic, religious, social, cultural, professional, labor-union or other nature.

Article XXIII

Every person has a right to own such private property as meets the essential needs of decent living and helps to maintain the dignity of the individual and of the home.

Article XXIV

Every person has the right to submit respectful petitions to any competent authority, for reasons of either general or private interest, and the right to obtain a prompt decision thereon.

Article XXV

No person may be deprived of his liberty except in the cases and according to the procedures established by pre-existing law.

No person may be deprived of liberty for nonfulfillment of obligations of a purely civil character.

Every individual who has been deprived of his liberty has the right to have the legality of his detention ascertained without delay by a court, and the right to be tried without undue delay or, otherwise, to be released. He also has the right to humane treatment during the time he is in custody.

Article XXVI

Every accused person is presumed to be innocent until proved guilty.

Every person accused of an offense has the right to be given an impartial and public hearing, and to be tried by courts previously established in accordance with pre-existing laws, and not to receive cruel, infamous or unusual punishment.

Article XXVII

Every person has the right, in case of pursuit not resulting from ordinary crimes, to seek and receive asylum in foreign territory, in accordance with the laws of each country and with international agreements.

Article XXVIII

The rights of man are limited by the rights of others, by the security of all, and by the just demands of the general welfare and the advancement of democracy.

CHAPTER II
DUTIES

Article XXIX

It is the duty of the individual so to conduct himself in relation to others that each and every one may fully form and develop his personality.

Article XXX

It is the duty of every person to aid, support, educate and protect his minor children, and it is the duty of children to honor their parents always and to aid, support and protect them when they need it.

Article XXXI

It is the duty of every person to acquire at least an elementary education.

Article XXXII

It is the duty of every person to vote in the popular elections of the country of which he is a national, when he is legally capable of doing so.

Article XXXIII

It is the duty of every person to obey the law and other legitimate commands of the authorities of his country and those of the country in which he may be.

Article XXXIV

It is the duty of every able-bodied person to render whatever civil and military service his country may require for its defense and preservation, and, in case of public disaster, to render such services as may be in his power.

It is likewise his duty to hold any public office to which he may be elected by popular vote in the State of which he is a national.

Article XXXV

It is the duty of every person to cooperate with the State and the community with respect to social security and welfare, in accordance with his ability and with existing circumstances.

Article XXXVI

It is the duty of every person to pay the taxes established by law for the support of public services.

Article XXXVII

It is the duty of every person to work, as far as his capacity and possibilities permit, in order to obtain the means of livelihood or to benefit his community.

Article XXXVIII

It is the duty of every person to refrain from taking part in political activities that, according to law, are reserved exclusively to the citizens of the State in which he is an alien.

109. AMERICAN CONVENTION ON HUMAN RIGHTS, 1969

The Bogotá Conference of 1948 had expressed a tentative interest in a proposal that an Inter-American Court be created to guarantee the basic rights of man, but no further development occurred until the Fifth Meeting of Consultation of Ministers of Foreign Affairs at Santiago, Chile, in 1959. The meeting resolved that the Inter-American Council of Jurists should prepare a draft Convention on Human Rights and that a convention should also be prepared on the creation of an Inter-American Court for the Protection of Human Rights.

The same meeting decided that an Inter-American Commission on Human Rights should be organized. The Commission came into being in 1960 as 'an autonomous entity of the Organization of American States, the function of which is to promote respect for human rights'. Its seven members are elected by the OAS General Assembly and act independently, without representing any particular country. For the text of the statute as approved by the OAS General Assembly in Resolution No. 447 in October 1979, see **http://www.cidh.oas.org/Basicos/ English/Basic.TOC.htm**.

The culmination of Latin American interest in human rights was the Inter-American Specialized Conference on Human Rights held at San José, Costa Rica, 7–22 November 1969. The American Convention on Human Rights was signed on 22 November 1969 by the following States: Chile, Colombia, Costa Rica, El Salvador, Ecuador, Guatemala, Honduras, Nicaragua, Panama, Paraguay, Uruguay, and Venezuela; for text, see OAS *Official Records*, OEA/Ser.K/ XVI/1/1. The Convention provides for a Commission and a Court, and bears a general resemblance to the European Convention, above. However, there are significant differences, for example, in the powers of the Commission, which are both broad and vague in the American Convention. The Commission created by the provisions of the Convention coincides with the pre-existing Inter-American Commission except that the Commission retains its previous powers in respect of States which did not ratify the new Convention, see ROBERTSON, A. H. and MERRILLS, J. G. (1996) *Human Rights in the World* (4th edn), 197–237.

The American Convention entered into force on 18 July 1978, and the Inter-American Court of Human Rights was inaugurated on 3 September 1979. The seat of the Court is at San José, Costa Rica.

Further reading

BUERGENTHAL, T., 'The Inter-American Court of Human Rights', (1982) 76 *AJIL* 231.

CAFLISCH, L. and CANÇADO TRINDADE, A. A., 'Les conventions américaine et européenne des droits de l'homme et le droit international général', (2004) 108 *Revue générale de droit international public*, 5.

CERNA, C. M., 'The Structure and Functioning of the Inter-American Court of Human Rights (1979-1992)', (1992) 63 *BYIL* 135.

MARTIN, C., 'Catching Up with the Past: Recent Decisions of the Inter-American Court of Human Rights Addressing Gross Human Rights Violations Perpetrated During the 1970–1980s', (2007) 7 *Human Rights Law Review* 774.

TARDU, M. E., 'The Protocol to the United Nations Covenant on Civil and Political Rights and the Inter-American System: A Study of Co-existing Petition Procedures', (1976) 70 *AJIL* 778.

TIGROUDJA, H., 'La Cour interaméricaine des droits de l'homme au service de « l'humanisation du droit international public ». Propos autour des récents arrêts et avis', (2006) 52 *Annuaire Français de droit international*, 617.

TEXT

Preamble

The American States signatory to the present Convention,

Reaffirming their intention to consolidate in this hemisphere, within the framework of democratic institutions, a system of personal liberty and social justice based on respect for the essential rights of man;

Recognizing that the essential rights of man are not derived from one's being a national of a certain State, but are based upon attributes of the human personality, and that they therefore justify international protection in the form of a convention reinforcing or complementing the protection provided by the domestic law of the American States;

Considering that these principles have been set forth in the Charter of the Organization of American States, in the American Declaration of the Rights and Duties of Man, and in the Universal Declaration of Human Rights, and that they have been reaffirmed and refined in other international instruments, worldwide as well as regional in scope;

Reiterating that, in accordance with the Universal Declaration of Human Rights, the ideal of free men enjoying freedom from fear and want can be achieved only if conditions are created whereby everyone may enjoy his economic, social, and cultural rights, as well as his civil and political rights; and

Considering that the Third Special Inter-American Conference (Buenos Aires, 1967) approved the incorporation into the Charter of the Organization itself of broader standards with respect to economic, social, and educational rights and resolved that an inter-American convention on human rights should determine the structure, competence, and procedure of the organs responsible for these matters,

Have agreed upon the following:

PART I
STATE OBLIGATIONS AND RIGHTS PROTECTED

Chapter I—General Obligations

Article 1—Obligation to Respect Rights

1. The States Parties to this Convention undertake to respect the rights and freedoms recognized herein and to ensure to all persons subject to their jurisdiction the free and full exercise of those rights and freedoms, without any discrimination for reasons of race, color, sex, language, religion, political or other opinion, national or social origin, economic status, birth, or any other social condition.

2. For the purposes of this Convention, 'person' means every human being.

Article 2—Domestic Legal Effects

Where the exercise of any of the rights or freedoms referred to in Article 1 is not already ensured by legislative or other provisions, the States Parties undertake to adopt, in accordance with their constitutional processes and the provisions of this Convention, such legislative or other measures as may be necessary to give effect to those rights or freedoms.

CHAPTER II—CIVIL AND POLITICAL RIGHTS

Article 3—Right to Juridical Personality

Every person has the right to recognition as a person before the law.

Article 4—Right to Life

1. Every person has the right to have his life respected. This right shall be protected by law and, in general, from the moment of conception. No one shall be arbitrarily deprived of his life.

2. In countries that have not abolished the death penalty, it may be imposed only for the most serious crimes and pursuant to a final judgment rendered by a competent court and in accordance with a law establishing such punishment, enacted prior to the commission of the crime. The application of such punishment shall not be extended to crimes to which it does not presently apply.

3. The death penalty shall not be re-established in States that have abolished it.

4. In no case shall capital punishment be inflicted for political offenses or related common crimes.

5. Capital punishment shall not be imposed upon persons who, at the time the crime was committed, were under 18 years of age or over 70 years of age; nor shall it be applied to pregnant women.

6. Every person condemned to death shall have the right to apply for amnesty, pardon, or commutation of sentence, which may be granted in all cases. Capital punishment shall not be imposed while such a petition is pending decision by the competent authority.

Article 5—Right to Humane Treatment

1. Every person has the right to have his physical, mental, and moral integrity respected.

2. No one shall be subjected to torture or to cruel, inhuman, or degrading punishment or treatment. All persons deprived of their liberty shall be treated with respect for the inherent dignity of the human person.

3. Punishment shall not be extended to any person other than the criminal.

4. Accused persons shall, save in exceptional circumstances, be segregated from convicted persons, and shall be subject to separate treatment appropriate to their status as unconvicted persons.

5. Minors while subject to criminal proceedings shall be separated from adults and brought before specialized tribunals, as speedily as possible, so that they may be treated in accordance with their status as minors.

6. Punishments consisting of deprivation of liberty shall have as an essential aim the reform and social readaptation of the prisoners.

Article 6—Freedom from Slavery

1. No one shall be subject to slavery or to involuntary servitude, which are prohibited in all their forms, as are the slave trade and traffic in women.

2. No one shall be required to perform forced or compulsory labor. This provision shall not be interpreted to mean that, in those countries in which the penalty established for certain crimes is deprivation of liberty at forced labor, the carrying out of such a sentence

imposed by a competent court is prohibited. Forced labor shall not adversely affect the dignity or the physical or intellectual capacity of the prisoner.

3. For the purposes of this article, the following do not constitute forced or compulsory labor:

   (a) work or service normally required of a person imprisoned in execution of a sentence or formal decision passed by the competent judicial authority. Such work or service shall be carried out under the supervision and control of public authorities, and any persons performing such work or service shall not be placed at the disposal of any private party, company, or juridical person;

   (b) military service and, in countries in which conscientious objectors are recognized, national service that the law may provide for in lieu of military service;

   (c) service exacted in time of danger or calamity that threatens the existence or the well-being of the community; or

   (d) work or service that forms part of normal civic obligations.

Article 7—Right to Personal Liberty

1. Every person has the right to personal liberty and security.

2. No one shall be deprived of his physical liberty except for the reasons and under the conditions established beforehand by the constitution of the State Party concerned or by a law established pursuant thereto.

3. No one shall be subject to arbitrary arrest or imprisonment.

4. Anyone who is detained shall be informed of the reasons for his detention and shall be promptly notified of the charge or charges against him.

5. Any person detained shall be brought promptly before a judge or other officer authorized by law to exercise judicial power and shall be entitled to trial within a reasonable time or to be released without prejudice to the continuation of the proceedings. His release may be subject to guarantees to assure his appearance for trial.

6. Anyone who is deprived of his liberty shall be entitled to recourse to a competent court, in order that the court may decide without delay on the lawfulness of his arrest or detention and order his release if the arrest or detention is unlawful. In States Parties whose laws provide that anyone who believes himself to be threatened with deprivation of his liberty is entitled to recourse to a competent court in order that it may decide on the lawfulness of such threat, this remedy may not be restricted or abolished. The interested party or another person in his behalf is entitled to seek these remedies.

7. No one shall be detained for debt. This principle shall not limit the orders of a competent judicial authority issued for nonfulfillment of duties of support.

Article 8—Right to a Fair Trial

1. Every person has the right to a hearing, with due guarantees and within a reasonable time, by a competent, independent, and impartial tribunal, previously established by law, in the substantiation of any accusation of a criminal nature made against him or for the determination of his rights and obligations of a civil, labor, fiscal, or any other nature.

2. Every person accused of a criminal offense has the right to be presumed innocent so long as his guilt has not been proven according to law. During the proceedings, every person is entitled, with full equality, to the following minimum guarantees:

(a) the right of the accused to be assisted without charge by a translator or interpreter, if he does not understand or does not speak the language of the tribunal or court;

(b) prior notification in detail to the accused of the charges against him;

(c) adequate time and means for the preparation of his defense;

(d) the right of the accused to defend himself personally or to be assisted by legal counsel of his own choosing, and to communicate freely and privately with his counsel;

(e) the inalienable right to be assisted by counsel provided by the State, paid or not as the domestic law provides, if the accused does not defend himself personally or engage his own counsel within the time period established by law;

(f) the right of the defense to examine witnesses present in the court and to obtain the appearance, as witnesses, of experts or other persons who may throw light on the facts;

(g) the right not to be compelled to be a witness against himself or to plead guilty; and

(h) the right to appeal the judgment to a higher court.

3. A confession of guilt by the accused shall be valid only if it is made without coercion of any kind.

4. An accused person acquitted by a nonappealable judgment shall not be subjected to a new trial for the same cause.

5. Criminal proceedings shall be public, except insofar as may be necessary to protect the interests of justice.

Article 9—Freedom from Ex Post Facto Laws

No one shall be convicted of any act or omission that did not constitute a criminal offense, under the applicable law, at the time it was committed. A heavier penalty shall not be imposed than the one that was applicable at the time the criminal offense was committed. If subsequent to the commission of the offense the law provides for the imposition of a lighter punishment, the guilty person shall benefit therefrom.

Article 10—Right to Compensation

Every person has the right to be compensated in accordance with the law in the event he has been sentenced by a final judgment through a miscarriage of justice.

Article 11—Right to Privacy

1. Everyone has the right to have his honor respected and his dignity recognized.

2. No one may be the object of arbitrary or abusive interference with his private life, his family, his home, or his correspondence, or of unlawful attacks on his honor or reputation.

3. Everyone has the right to the protection of the law against such interference or attacks.

Article 12—Freedom of Conscience and Religion

1. Everyone has the right to freedom of conscience and of religion. This right includes freedom to maintain or to change one's religion or beliefs, and freedom to profess or

disseminate one's religion or beliefs, either individually or together with others, in public or in private.

2. No one shall be subject to restrictions that might impair his freedom to maintain or to change his religion or beliefs.

3. Freedom to manifest one's religion and beliefs may be subject only to the limitations prescribed by law that are necessary to protect public safety, order, health, or morals, or the rights or freedoms of others.

4. Parents or guardians, as the case may be, have the right to provide for the religious and moral education of their children or wards that is in accord with their own convictions.

Article 13—*Freedom of Thought and Expression*

1. Everyone has the right to freedom of thought and expression. This right includes freedom to seek, receive, and impart information and ideas of all kinds, regardless of frontiers, either orally, in writing, in print, in the form of art, or through any other medium of one's choice.

2. The exercise of the right provided for in the foregoing paragraph shall not be subject to prior censorship but shall be subject to subsequent imposition of liability, which shall be expressly established by law to the extent necessary to ensure:

    (a) respect for the rights or reputations of others; or

    (b) the protection of national security, public order, or public health or morals.

3. The right of expression may not be restricted by indirect methods or means, such as the abuse of government or private controls over newsprint, radio broadcasting frequencies, or equipment used in the dissemination of information, or by any other means tending to impede the communication and circulation of ideas and opinions.

4. Notwithstanding the provisions of paragraph 2 above, public entertainments may be subject by law to prior censorship for the sole purpose of regulating access to them for the moral protection of childhood and adolescence.

5. Any propaganda for war and any advocacy of national, racial, or religious hatred that constitute incitements to lawless violence or to any other similar action against any person or group of persons on any grounds including those of race, color, religion, language, or national origin shall be considered as offenses punishable by law.

Article 14—*Right of Reply*

1. Anyone injured by inaccurate or offensive statements or ideas disseminated to the public in general by a legally regulated medium of communication has the right to reply or to make a correction using the same communications outlet, under such conditions as the law may establish.

2. The correction or reply shall not in any case remit other legal liabilities that may have been incurred.

3. For the effective protection of honor and reputation, every publisher, and every newspaper, motion picture, radio, and television company, shall have a person responsible who is not protected by immunities or special privileges.

Article 15—*Right of Assembly*

The right of peaceful assembly, without arms, is recognized. No restrictions may be placed on the exercise of this right other than those imposed in conformity with the law and necessary in a democratic society in the interest of national security, public safety or public order, or to protect public health or morals or the rights or freedom of others.

Article 16—Freedom of Association

1. Everyone has the right to associate freely for ideological, religious, political, economic, labor, social, cultural, sports, or other purposes.

2. The exercise of this right shall be subject only to such restrictions established by law as may be necessary in a democratic society, in the interest of national security, public safety or public order, or to protect public health or morals or the rights and freedoms of others.

3. The provisions of this article do not bar the imposition of legal restrictions, including even deprivation of the exercise of the right of association, on members of the armed forces and the police.

Article 17—Rights of the Family

1. The family is the natural and fundamental group unit of society and is entitled to protection by society and the state.

2. The right of men and women of marriageable age to marry and to raise a family shall be recognized, if they meet the conditions required by domestic laws, insofar as such conditions do not affect the principle of nondiscrimination established in this Convention.

3. No marriage shall be entered into without the free and full consent of the intending spouses.

4. The States Parties shall take appropriate steps to ensure the equality of rights and the adequate balancing of responsibilities of the spouses as to marriage, during marriage, and in the event of its dissolution. In case of dissolution, provision shall be made for the necessary protection of any children solely on the basis of their own best interests.

5. The law shall recognize equal rights for children born out of wedlock and those born in wedlock.

Article 18—Right to a Name

Every person has the right to a given name and to the surnames of his parents or that of one of them. The law shall regulate the manner in which this right shall be ensured for all, by the use of assumed names if necessary.

Article 19—Rights of the Child

Every minor child has the right to the measures of protection required by his condition as a minor on the part of his family, society, and the State.

Article 20—Right to Nationality

1. Every person has the right to a nationality.

2. Every person has the right to the nationality of the State in whose territory he was born if he does not have the right to any other nationality.

3. No one shall be arbitrarily deprived of his nationality or of the right to change it.

Article 21—Right to Property

1. Everyone has the right to the use and enjoyment of his property. The law may subordinate such use and enjoyment to the interest of society.

2. No one shall be deprived of his property except upon payment of just compensation, for reasons of public utility or social interest, and in the cases and according to the forms established by law.

3. Usury and any other form of exploitation of man by man shall be prohibited by law.

Article 22—Freedom of Movement and Residence

1. Every person lawfully in the territory of a State Party has the right to move about in it, and to reside in it subject to the provisions of the law.

2. Every person has the right lo leave any country freely, including his own.

3. The exercise of the foregoing rights may be restricted only pursuant to a law to the extent necessary in a democratic society to prevent crime or to protect national security, public safety, public order, public morals, public health, or the rights or freedoms of others.

4. The exercise of the rights recognized in paragraph 1 may also be restricted by law in designated zones for reasons of public interest.

5. No one can be expelled from the territory of the State of which he is a national or be deprived of the right to enter it.

6. An alien lawfully in the territory of a State Party to this Convention may be expelled from it only pursuant to a decision reached in accordance with law.

7. Every person has the right to seek and be granted asylum in a foreign territory, in accordance with the legislation of the State and international conventions, in the event he is being pursued for political offenses or related common crimes.

8. In no case may an alien be deported or returned to a country, regardless of whether or not it is his country of origin, if in that country his right to life or personal freedom is in danger of being violated because of his race, nationality, religion, social status, or political opinions.

9. The collective expulsion of aliens is prohibited.

Article 23—Right to Participate in Government

1. Every citizen shall enjoy the following rights and opportunities:

   (a) to take part in the conduct of public affairs, directly or through freely chosen representatives;

   (b) to vote and to be elected in genuine periodic elections, which shall be by universal and equal suffrage and by secret ballot that guarantees the free expression of the will of the voters; and

   (c) to have access, under general conditions of equality, to the public service of his country.

2. The law may regulate the exercise of the rights and opportunities referred to in the preceding paragraph only on the basis of age, nationality, residence, language, education, civil and mental capacity, or sentencing by a competent court in criminal proceedings.

Article 24—Right to Equal Protection

All persons are equal before the law. Consequently, they are entitled, without discrimination, to equal protection of the law.

Article 25—Right to Judicial Protection

1. Everyone has the right to simple and prompt recourse, or any other effective recourse, to a competent court or tribunal for protection against acts that violate his fundamental rights recognized by the constitution or laws of the State concerned or by this Convention, even though such violation may have been committed by persons acting in the course of their official duties.

2. The States Parties undertake:

 (a) to ensure that any person claiming such remedy shall have his rights determined by the competent authority provided for by the legal system of the state;

 (b) to develop the possibilities of judicial remedy; and

 (c) to ensure that the competent authorities shall enforce such remedies when granted.

CHAPTER III—ECONOMIC, SOCIAL, AND CULTURAL RIGHTS

Article 26—Progressive Development

The States Parties undertake to adopt measures, both internally and through international cooperation, especially those of an economic and technical nature, with a view to achieving progressively, by legislation or other appropriate means, the full realization of the rights implicit in the economic, social, educational, scientific, and cultural standards set forth in the Charter of the Organization of American States as amended by the Protocol of Buenos Aires.

CHAPTER IV—SUSPENSION OF GUARANTEES, INTERPRETATION, AND APPLICATION

Article 27—Suspension of Guarantees

1. In time of war, public danger, or other emergency that threatens the independence or security of a State Party, it may take measures derogating from its obligations under the present Convention to the extent and for the period of time strictly required by the exigencies of the situation, provided that such measures are not inconsistent with its other obligations under international law and do not involve discrimination on the ground of race, color, sex, language, religion, or social origin.

2. The foregoing provision does not authorize any suspension of the following articles: Article 3 (Right to Juridical Personality), Article 4 (Right to Life), Article 5 (Right to Humane Treatment), Article 6 (Freedom from Slavery), Article 9 (Freedom from *Ex Post Facto* Laws), Article 12 (Freedom of Conscience and Religion), Article 17 (Rights of the Family), Article 18 (Right to a Name), Article 19 (Rights of the Child), Article 20 (Right to Nationality), and Article 23 (Right to Participate in Government), or of the judicial guarantees essential for the protection of such rights.

3. Any State Party availing itself of the right of suspension shall immediately inform the other States Parties, through the Secretary General of the Organization of American States, of the provisions the application of which it has suspended, the reasons that gave rise to the suspension, and the date set for the termination of such suspension.

Article 28—Federal Clause

1. Where a State Party is constituted as a federal State, the national government of such State Party shall implement all the provisions of the Convention over whose subject matter it exercises legislative and judicial jurisdiction.

2. With respect to the provisions over whose subject matter the constituent units of the federal State have jurisdiction, the national government shall immediately take suitable measures, in accordance with its constitution and its laws, to the end that the competent authorities of the constituent units may adopt appropriate provisions for the fulfillment of this Convention.

3. Whenever two or more States Parties agree to form a federation or other type of association, they shall take care that the resulting federal or other compact contains the provisions necessary for continuing and rendering effective the standards of this Convention in the new State that is organized.

Article 29—Restrictions Regarding Interpretation

No provision of this Convention shall be interpreted as:

   (a) permitting any State Party, group, or person to suppress the enjoyment or exercise of the rights and freedoms recognized in this Convention or to restrict them to a greater extent than is provided for herein;

   (b) restricting the enjoyment or exercise of any right or freedom recognized by virtue of the laws of any State Party or by virtue of another convention to which one of the said States is a party;

   (c) precluding other rights or guarantees that are inherent in the human personality or derived from representative democracy as a form of government; or

   (d) excluding or limiting the effect that the American Declaration of the Rights and Duties of Man and other international acts of the same nature may have.

Article 30—Scope of Restrictions

The restrictions that, pursuant to this Convention, may be placed on the enjoyment or exercise of the rights or freedoms recognized herein may not be applied except in accordance with laws enacted for reasons of general interest and in accordance with the purpose for which such restrictions have been established.

Article 31—Recognition of Other Rights

Other rights and freedoms recognized in accordance with the procedures established in Articles 76 and 77 may be included in the system of protection of this Convention.

CHAPTER V—PERSONAL RESPONSIBILITIES

Article 32—Relationship between Duties and Rights

1. Every person has responsibilities to his family, his community, and mankind.

2. The rights of each person are limited by the rights of others, by the security of all, and by the just demands of the general welfare, in a democratic society.

PART II

MEANS OF PROTECTION

Chapter VI—Competent Organs

Article 33

The following organs shall have competence with respect to matters relating to the fulfillment of the commitments made by the States Parties to this Convention:

    (a) the Inter-American Commission on Human Rights, referred to as 'The Commission;' and

    (b) the Inter-American Court of Human Rights, referred to as 'The Court.'

CHAPTER VII—INTER-AMERICAN COMMISSION ON HUMAN RIGHTS

Section 1. Organization

Article 34

The Inter-American Commission on Human Rights shall be composed of seven members, who shall be persons of high moral character and recognized competence in the field of human rights.

Article 35

The Commission shall represent all the member countries of the Organization of American States.

Article 36

1. The members of the Commission shall be elected in a personal capacity by the General Assembly of the Organization from a list of candidates proposed by the governments of the member States.

2. Each of those governments may propose up to three candidates, who may be nationals of the States proposing them or of any other member state of the Organization of American States. When a slate of three is proposed, at least one of the candidates shall be a national of a State other than the one proposing the slate.

Article 37

1. The members of the Commission shall be elected for a term of four years and may be reelected only once, but the terms of three of the members chosen in the first election shall expire at the end of two years. Immediately following that election the General Assembly shall determine the names of those three members by lot.

2. No two nationals of the same State may be members of the Commission.

Article 38

Vacancies that may occur on the Commission for reasons other than the normal expiration of a term shall be filled by the Permanent Council of the Organization in accordance with the provisions of the Statute of the Commission.

Article 39

The Commission shall prepare its Statute, which it shall submit to the General Assembly for approval. It shall establish its own Regulations.

Article 40

Secretariat services for the Commission shall be furnished by the appropriate specialized unit of the General Secretariat of the Organization. This unit shall be provided with the resources required to accomplish the tasks assigned to it by the Commission.

Section 2. Functions

Article 41

The main function of the Commission shall be to promote respect for and defense of human rights. In the exercise of its mandate, it shall have the following functions and powers:

- *(a)* to develop an awareness of human rights among the peoples of America;
- *(b)* to make recommendations to the governments of the member States, when it considers such action advisable, for the adoption of progressive measures in favor of human rights within the framework of their domestic law and constitutional provisions as well as appropriate measures to further the observance of those rights;
- *(c)* to prepare such studies or reports as it considers advisable in the performance of its duties;
- *(d)* to request the governments of the member States to supply it with information on the measures adopted by them in matters of human rights;
- *(e)* to respond, through the General Secretariat of the Organization of American States, to inquiries made by the member States on matters related to human rights and, within the limits of its possibilities, to provide those States with the advisory services they request;
- *(f)* to take action on petitions and other communications pursuant to its authority under the provisions of Articles 44 through 51 of this Convention; and
- *(g)* to submit an annual report to the General Assembly of the Organization of American States.

Article 42

The States Parties shall transmit to the Commission a copy of each of the reports and studies that they submit annually to the Executive Committees of the Inter-American Economic and Social Council and the Inter-American Council for Education, Science, and Culture, in their respective fields, so that the Commission may watch over the promotion of the rights implicit in the economic, social, educational, scientific, and cultural standards set forth in the Charter of the Organization of American States as amended by the Protocol of Buenos Aires.

Article 43

The States Parties undertake to provide the Commission with such information as it may request of them as to the manner in which their domestic law ensures the effective application of any provisions of this Convention.

Section 3. Competence

Article 44

Any person or group of persons, or any nongovernmental entity legally recognized in one or more member States of the Organization, may lodge petitions with the Commission containing denunciations or complaints of violation of this Convention by a State Party.

Article 45

1. Any State Party may, when it deposits its instrument of ratification of or adherence to this Convention, or at any later time, declare that it recognizes the competence of the Commission to receive and examine communications in which a State Party alleges that another State Party has committed a violation of a human right set forth in this Convention.

2. Communications presented by virtue of this article may be admitted and examined only if they are presented by a State Party that has made a declaration recognizing the aforementioned competence of the Commission. The Commission shall not admit any communication against a State Party that has not made such a declaration.

3. A declaration concerning recognition of competence may be made to be valid for an indefinite time, for a specified period, or for a specific case.

4. Declarations shall be deposited with the General Secretariat of the Organization of American States, which shall transmit copies thereof to the member States of that Organization.

Article 46

1. Admission by the Commission of a petition or communication lodged in accordance with Articles 44 or 45 shall be subject to the following requirements:
   (a) that the remedies under domestic law have been pursued and exhausted in accord-ance with generally recognized principles of international law;
   (b) that the petition or communication is lodged within a period of six months from the date on which the party alleging violation of his rights was notified of the final judgment;
   (c) that the subject of the petition or communication is not pending in another inter-national proceeding for settlement; and
   (d) that, in the case of Article 44, the petition contains the name, nationality, profes-sion, domicile, and signature of the person or persons or of the legal representative of the entity lodging the petition.

2. The provisions of paragraphs 1(a) and 1(b) of this article shall not be applicable when:
   (a) the domestic legislation of the State concerned does not afford due process of law for the protection of the right or rights that have allegedly been violated;
   (b) the party alleging violation of his rights has been denied access to the remedies under domestic law or has been prevented from exhausting them; or
   (c) there has been unwarranted delay in rendering a final judgment under the afore-mentioned remedies.

Article 47

The Commission shall consider inadmissible any petition or communication submitted under Articles 44 or 45 if:

- *(a)* any of the requirements indicated in Article 46 has not been met;
- *(b)* the petition or communication does not state facts that tend to establish a violation of the rights guaranteed by this Convention;
- *(c)* the statements of the petitioner or of the State indicate that the petition or communication is manifestly groundless or obviously out of order; or
- *(d)* the petition or communication is substantially the same as one previously studied by the Commission or by another international organization.

Section 4. Procedure

Article 48

1. When the Commission receives a petition or communication alleging violation of any of the rights protected by this Convention, it shall proceed as follows:

- *(a)* If it considers the petition or communication admissible, it shall request information from the government of the State indicated as being responsible for the alleged violations and shall furnish that government a transcript of the pertinent portions of the petition or communication. This information shall be submitted within a reasonable period to be determined by the Commission in accordance with the circumstances of each case.
- *(b)* After the information has been received, or after the period established has elapsed and the information has not been received, the Commission shall ascertain whether the grounds for the petition or communication still exist. If they do not, the Commission shall order the record to be closed.
- *(c)* The Commission may also declare the petition or communication inadmissible or out of order on the basis of information or evidence subsequently received.
- *(d)* If the record has not been closed, the Commission shall, with the knowledge of the parties, examine the matter set forth in the petition or communication in order to verify the facts. If necessary and advisable, the Commission shall carry out an investigation, for the effective conduct of which it shall request, and the States concerned shall furnish to it, all necessary facilities.
- *(e)* The Commission may request the States concerned to furnish any pertinent information and, if so requested, shall hear oral statements or receive written statements from the parties concerned.
- *(f)* The Commission shall place itself at the disposal of the parties concerned with a view to reaching a friendly settlement of the matter on the basis of respect for the human rights recognized in this Convention.

2. However, in serious and urgent cases, only the presentation of a petition or communication that fulfills all the formal requirements of admissibility shall be necessary in order for the Commission to conduct an investigation with the prior consent of the State in whose territory a violation has allegedly been committed.

Article 49

If a friendly settlement has been reached in accordance with paragraph 1 (f) of Article 48, the Commission shall draw up a report, which shall be transmitted to the petitioner and to the States Parties to this Convention, and shall then be communicated to the Secretary General of the Organization of American States for publication. This report shall contain a brief statement of the facts and of the solution reached. If any party in the case so requests, the fullest possible information shall be provided to it.

Article 50

1. If a settlement is not reached, the Commission shall, within the time limit established by its Statute, draw up a report setting forth the facts and stating its conclusions. If the report, in whole or in part, does not represent the unanimous agreement of the members of the Commission, any member may attach to it a separate opinion. The written and oral statements made by the parties in accordance with paragraph 1 (e) of Article 48 shall also be attached to the report.

2. The report shall be transmitted to the States concerned, which shall not be at liberty to publish it.

3. In transmitting the report, the Commission may make such proposals and recommendations as it sees fit.

Article 51

1. If, within a period of three months from the date of the transmittal of the report of the Commission to the States concerned, the matter has not either been settled or submitted by the Commission or by the State concerned to the Court and its jurisdiction accepted, the Commission may, by the vote of an absolute majority of its members, set forth its opinion and conclusions concerning the question submitted for its consideration.

2. Where appropriate, the Commission shall make pertinent recommendations and shall prescribe a period within which the State is to take the measures that are incumbent upon it to remedy the situation examined.

3. When the prescribed period has expired, the Commission shall decide by the vote of an absolute majority of its members whether the State has taken adequate measures and whether to publish its report.

CHAPTER VIII—INTER-AMERICAN COURT OF HUMAN RIGHTS

Section 1. Organization

Article 52

1. The Court shall consist of seven judges, nationals of the member States of the Organization, elected in an individual capacity from among jurists of the highest moral authority and of recognized competence in the field of human rights, who possess the qualifications required for the exercise of the highest judicial functions in conformity with the law of the State of which they are nationals or of the State that proposes them as candidates.

2. No two judges may be nationals of the same State.

Article 53

1. The judges of the Court shall be elected by secret ballot by an absolute majority vote of the States Parties to the Convention, in the General Assembly of the Organization, from a panel of candidates proposed by those States.

2. Each of the States Parties may propose up to three candidates, nationals of the State that proposes them or of any other member State of the Organization of American States. When a slate of three is proposed, at least one of the candidates shall be a national of a State other than the one proposing the slate.

Article 54

1. The judges of the Court shall be elected for a term of six years and may be reelected only once. The term of three of the judges chosen in the first election shall expire at the end of three years. Immediately after the election, the names of the three judges shall be determined by lot in the General Assembly.

2. A judge elected to replace a judge whose term has not expired shall complete the term of the latter.

3. The judges shall continue in office until the expiration of their term. However, they shall continue to serve with regard to cases that they have begun to hear and that are still pending, for which purposes they shall not be replaced by the newly elected judges.

Article 55

1. If a judge is a national of any of the States Parties to a case submitted to the Court, he shall retain his right to hear that case.

2. If one of the judges called upon to hear a case should be a national of one of the States Parties to the case, any other State Party in the case may appoint a person of its choice to serve on the Court as an *ad hoc* judge.

3. If among the judges called upon to hear a case none is a national of any of the States Parties to the case, each of the latter may appoint an *ad hoc* judge.

4. An *ad hoc* judge shall possess the qualifications indicated in Article 52.

5. If several States Parties to the Convention should have the same interest in a case, they shall be considered as a single party for purposes of the above provisions. In case of doubt, the Court shall decide.

Article 56

Five judges shall constitute a quorum for the transaction of business by the Court.

Article 57

The Commission shall appear in all cases before the Court.

Article 58

1. The Court shall have its seat at the place determined by the States Parties to the Convention in the General Assembly of the Organization; however, it may convene in the territory of any member State of the Organization of American States when a majority of the Court considers it desirable, and with the prior consent of the State concerned.

The seat of the Court may be changed by the States Parties to the Convention in the General Assembly by a two-thirds vote.

2. The Court shall appoint its own Secretary.

3. The Secretary shall have his office at the place where the Court has its seat and shall attend the meetings that the Court may hold away from its seat.

Article 59

The Court shall establish its Secretariat, which shall function under the direction of the Secretary of the Court, in accordance with the administrative standards of the General Secretariat of the Organization in all respects not incompatible with the independence of the Court. The staff of the Court's Secretariat shall be appointed by the Secretary General of the Organization, in consultation with the Secretary of the Court.

Article 60

The Court shall draw up its Statute which it shall submit to the General Assembly for approval. It shall adopt its own Rules of Procedure.

Section 2. Jurisdiction and functions

Article 61

1. Only the States Parties and the Commission shall have the right to submit a case to the Court.

2. In order for the Court to hear a case, it is necessary that the procedures set forth in Articles 48 and 50 shall have been completed.

Article 62

1. A State Party may, upon depositing its instrument of ratification or adherence to this Convention, or at any subsequent time, declare that it recognizes as binding, *ipso facto*, and not requiring special agreement, the jurisdiction of the Court on all matters relating to the interpretation or application of this Convention.

2. Such declaration may be made unconditionally, on the condition of reciprocity, for a specified period, or for specific cases. It shall be presented to the Secretary General of the Organization, who shall transmit copies thereof to the other member states of the Organization and to the Secretary of the Court.

3. The jurisdiction of the Court shall comprise all cases concerning the interpretation and application of the provisions of this Convention that are submitted to it, provided that the States Parties to the case recognize or have recognized such jurisdiction, whether by special declaration pursuant to the preceding paragraphs, or by a special agreement.

Article 63

1. If the Court finds that there has been a violation of a right or freedom protected by this Convention, the Court shall rule that the injured party be ensured the enjoyment of his right or freedom that was violated. It shall also rule, if appropriate, that the consequences of the measure or situation that constituted the breach of such right or freedom be remedied and that fair compensation be paid to the injured party.

2. In cases of extreme gravity and urgency, and when necessary to avoid irreparable damage to persons, the Court shall adopt such provisional measures as it deems pertinent in matters it has under consideration. With respect to a case not yet submitted to the Court, it may act at the request of the Commission.

Article 64

1. The member States of the Organization may consult the Court regarding the interpretation of this Convention or of other treaties concerning the protection of human rights in the American States. Within their spheres of competence, the organs listed in Chapter X of the Charter of the Organization of American States, as amended by the Protocol of Buenos Aires, may in like manner consult the Court.

2. The Court, at the request of a member State of the Organization, may provide that State with opinions regarding the compatibility of any of its domestic laws with the aforesaid international instruments.

Article 65

To each regular session of the General Assembly of the Organization of American States the Court shall submit, for the Assembly's consideration, a report on its work during the previous year. It shall specify, in particular, the cases in which a State has not complied with its judgments, making any pertinent recommendations.

Section 3. Procedure

Article 66

1. Reasons shall be given for the judgment of the Court.

2. If the judgment does not represent in whole or in part the unanimous opinion of the judges, any judge shall be entitled to have his dissenting or separate opinion attached to the judgment.

Article 67

The judgment of the Court shall be final and not subject to appeal. In case of disagreement as to the meaning or scope of the judgment, the Court shall interpret it at the request of any of the parties, provided the request is made within ninety days from the date of notification of the judgment.

Article 68

1. The States Parties to the Convention undertake to comply with the judgment of the Court in any case to which they are parties.

2. That part of a judgment that stipulates compensatory damages may be executed in the country concerned in accordance with domestic procedure governing the execution of judgments against the State.

Article 69

The parties to the case shall be notified of the judgment of the Court and it shall be transmitted to the States Parties to the Convention.

CHAPTER IX—COMMON PROVISIONS

Article 70

1. The judges of the Court and the members of the Commission shall enjoy, from the moment of their election and throughout their term of office, the immunities extended to diplomatic agents in accordance with international law. During the exercise of their official function they shall, in addition, enjoy the diplomatic privileges necessary for the performance of their duties.

2. At no time shall the judges of the Court or the members of the Commission be held liable for any decisions or opinions issued in the exercise of their functions.

Article 71

The position of judge of the Court or member of the Commission is incompatible with any other activity that might affect the independence or impartiality of such judge or member, as determined in the respective statutes.

Article 72

The judges of the Court and the members of the Commission shall receive emoluments and travel allowances in the form and under the conditions set forth in their statutes, with due regard for the importance and independence of their office. Such emoluments and travel allowances shall be determined in the budget of the Organization of American States, which shall also include the expenses of the Court and its Secretariat. To this end, the Court shall draw up its own budget and submit it for approval to the General Assembly through the General Secretariat. The latter may not introduce any changes in it.

Article 73

The General Assembly may, only at the request of the Commission or the Court, as the case may be, determine sanctions to be applied against members of the Commission or judges of the Court when there are justifiable grounds for such action as set forth in the respective statutes. A vote of a two-thirds majority of the member States of the Organization shall be required for a decision in the case of members of the Commission and, in the case of judges of the Court, a two-thirds majority vote of the States Parties to the Convention shall also be required.

PART III

GENERAL AND TRANSITORY PROVISIONS

Chapter X—Signature, Ratification, Reservations, Amendments, Protocols, and Denunciation

Article 74

1. This Convention shall be open for signature and ratification by or adherence of any member State of the Organization of American States.

2. Ratification of or adherence to this Convention shall be made by the deposit of an instrument of ratification or adherence with the General Secretariat of the Organization of American States. As soon as eleven States have deposited their instruments of ratification or adherence, the Convention shall enter into force. With respect to any State that ratifies or adheres thereafter, the Convention shall enter into force on the date of the deposit of its instrument of ratification or adherence.

3. The Secretary General shall inform all member States of the Organization of the entry into force of the Convention.

Article 75

This Convention shall be subject to reservations only in conformity with the provisions of the Vienna Convention on the Law of Treaties signed on May 23, 1969.

Article 76

1. Proposals to amend this Convention may be submitted to the General Assembly for the action it deems appropriate by any State Party directly, and by the Commission or the Court through the Secretary General.

2. Amendments shall enter into force for the States ratifying them on the date when two-thirds of the States Parties to this Convention have deposited their respective instruments of ratification. With respect to the other States Parties, the amendments shall enter into force on the dates on which they deposit their respective instruments of ratification.

Article 77

1. In accordance with Article 31, any State Party and the Commission may submit proposed protocols to this Convention for consideration by the States Parties at the General Assembly with a view to gradually including other rights and freedoms within its system of protection.

2. Each protocol shall determine the manner of its entry into force and shall be applied only among the States Parties to it.

Article 78

1. The States Parties may denounce this Convention at the expiration of a five-year period from the date of its entry into force and by means of notice given one year in advance. Notice of the denunciation shall be addressed to the Secretary General of the Organization, who shall inform the other States Parties.

2. Such a denunciation shall not have the effect of releasing the State Party concerned from the obligations contained in this Convention with respect to any act that may constitute a violation of those obligations and that has been taken by that state prior to the effective date of denunciation.

CHAPTER XI—TRANSITORY PROVISIONS

Section 1. Inter-American commission on human rights

Article 79

Upon the entry into force of this Convention, the Secretary General shall, in writing, request each member State of the Organization to present, within ninety days, its candidates for membership on the Inter-American Commission on Human Rights. The Secretary General shall prepare a list in alphabetical order of the candidates presented, and transmit it to the member States of the Organization at least thirty days prior to the next session of the General Assembly.

Article 80

The members of the Commission shall be elected by secret ballot of the General Assembly from the list of candidates referred to in Article 79. The candidates who obtain the largest number of votes and an absolute majority of the votes of the representatives of the member States shall be declared elected. Should it become necessary to have several ballots in order to elect all the members of the Commission, the candidates who receive the smallest number of votes shall be eliminated successively, in the manner determined by the General Assembly.

Section 2. Inter-American court of human rights

Article 81

Upon the entry into force of this Convention, the Secretary General shall, in writing, request each State Party to present, within ninety days, its candidates for membership on the Inter-American Court of Human Rights. The Secretary General shall prepare a list in alphabetical order of the candidates presented and transmit it to the States Parties at least thirty days prior to the next session of the General Assembly.

Article 82

The judges of the Court shall be elected from the list of candidates referred to in Article 81, by secret ballot of the States Parties to the Convention in the General Assembly. The candidates who obtain the largest number of votes and an absolute majority of the votes of the representatives of the States Parties shall be declared elected. Should it become necessary to have several ballots in order to elect all the judges of the Court, the candidates who receive the smallest number of votes shall be eliminated successively, in the manner determined by the States Parties.

[Statements and reservations, etc., omitted]

110. ADDITIONAL PROTOCOL TO THE AMERICAN CONVENTION ON HUMAN RIGHTS IN THE AREA OF ECONOMIC, SOCIAL AND CULTURAL RIGHTS, 1988

The States Parties to the American Convention on Human Rights adopted this Additional Protocol (the Protocol of San Salvador) on 14 November 1988; it came into force on 16 November 1999. For text, see OAS *Treaty Series* No. 69 (1988), signed 17 November 1988, reprinted in *Basic Documents Pertaining to Human Rights in the Inter-American System*, OEA/Ser.L/V/I.4 rev.12, 31 January 2007: **http://www.cidh.oas.org/Basicos/English/Basic.TOC./htm**.

TEXT

Preamble

The States Parties to the American Convention on Human Rights 'Pact San José, Costa Rica',

Reaffirming their intention to consolidate in this hemisphere, within the framework of democratic institutions, a system of personal liberty and social justice based on respect for the essential rights of man;

Recognizing that the essential rights of man are not derived from one's being a national of a certain State, but are based upon attributes of the human person, for which reason they merit international protection in the form of a convention reinforcing or complementing the protection provided by the domestic law of the American States;

Considering the close relationship that exists between economic, social and cultural rights, and civil and political rights, in that the different categories of rights constitute an indivisible whole based on the recognition of the dignity of the human person, for which reason both require permanent protection and promotion if they are to be fully realized, and the violation of some rights in favor of the realization of others can never be justified;

Recognizing the benefits that stem from the promotion and development of cooperation among States and international relations;

Recalling that, in accordance with the Universal Declaration of Human Rights and the American Convention on Human Rights, the ideal of free human beings enjoying freedom from fear and want can only be achieved if conditions are created whereby everyone may enjoy his economic, social and cultural rights as well as his civil and political rights;

Bearing in mind that, although fundamental economic, social and cultural rights have been recognized in earlier international instruments of both world and regional scope, it is essential that those rights be reaffirmed, developed, perfected and protected in order to consolidate in America, on the basis of full respect for the rights of the individual, the democratic representative form of government as well as the right of its peoples to development, self-determination, and the free disposal of their wealth and natural resources; and

Considering that the American Convention on Human Rights provides that draft additional protocols to that Convention may be submitted for consideration to the States

Parties, meeting together on the occasion of the General Assembly of the Organization of American States, for the purpose of gradually incorporating other rights and freedoms into the protective system thereof,

Have agreed upon the following Additional Protocol to the American Convention on Human Rights 'Protocol of San Salvador':

Article 1—Obligation to Adopt Measures

The States Parties to this Additional Protocol to the American Convention on Human Rights undertake to adopt the necessary measures, both domestically and through international cooperation, especially economic and technical, to the extent allowed by their available resources, and taking into account their degree of development, for the purpose of achieving progressively and pursuant to their internal legislations, the full observance of the rights recognized in this Protocol.

Article 2—Obligation to Enact Domestic Legislation

If the exercise of the rights set forth in this Protocol is not already guaranteed by legislative or other provisions, the States Parties undertake to adopt, in accordance with their constitutional processes and the provisions of this Protocol, such legislative or other measures as may be necessary for making those rights a reality.

Article 3—Obligation of Nondiscrimination

The State Parties to this Protocol undertake to guarantee the exercise of the rights set forth herein without discrimination of any kind for reasons related to race, color, sex, language, religion, political or other opinions, national or social origin, economic status, birth or any other social condition.

Article 4—Inadmissibility of Restrictions

A right which is recognized or in effect in a State by virtue of its internal legislation or international conventions may not be restricted or curtailed on the pretext that this Protocol does not recognize the right or recognizes it to a lesser degree.

Article 5—Scope of Restrictions and Limitations

The State Parties may establish restrictions and limitations on the enjoyment and exercise of the rights established herein by means of laws promulgated for the purpose of preserving the general welfare in a democratic society only to the extent that they are not incompatible with the purpose and reason underlying those rights.

Article 6—Right to Work

1. Everyone has the right to work, which includes the opportunity to secure the means for living a dignified and decent existence by performing a freely elected or accepted lawful activity.

2. The State Parties undertake to adopt measures that will make the right to work fully effective, especially with regard to the achievement of full employment, vocational guidance, and the development of technical and vocational training projects, in particular those directed to the disabled. The States Parties also undertake to implement and strengthen programs that help to ensure suitable family care, so that women may enjoy a real opportunity to exercise the right to work.

Article 7—Just, Equitable, and Satisfactory Conditions of Work

The States Parties to this Protocol recognize that the right to work to which the foregoing article refers presupposes that everyone shall enjoy that right under just, equitable, and satisfactory conditions, which the States Parties undertake to guarantee in their internal legislation, particularly with respect to:

(a) Remuneration which guarantees, as a minimum, to all workers dignified and decent living conditions for them and their families and fair and equal wages for equal work, without distinction;

(b) The right of every worker to follow his vocation and to devote himself to the activity that best fulfills his expectations and to change employment in accordance with the pertinent national regulations;

(c) The right of every worker to promotion or upward mobility in his employment, for which purpose account shall be taken of his qualifications, competence, integrity and seniority;

(d) Stability of employment, subject to the nature of each industry and occupation and the causes for just separation. In cases of unjustified dismissal, the worker shall have the right to indemnity or to reinstatement on the job or any other benefits provided by domestic legislation;

(e) Safety and hygiene at work;

(f) The prohibition of night work or unhealthy or dangerous working conditions and, in general, of all work which jeopardizes health, safety, or morals, for persons under 18 years of age. As regards minors under the age of 16, the work day shall be subordinated to the provisions regarding compulsory education and in no case shall work constitute an impediment to school attendance or a limitation on benefitting from education received;

(g) A reasonable limitation of working hours, both daily and weekly. The days shall be shorter in the case of dangerous or unhealthy work or of night work;

(h) Rest, leisure and paid vacations as well as remuneration for national holidays.

Article 8—Trade Union Rights

1. The States Parties shall ensure:

(a) The right of workers to organize trade unions and to join the union of their choice for the purpose of protecting and promoting their interests. As an extension of that right, the States Parties shall permit trade unions to establish national federations or confederations, or to affiliate with those that already exist, as well as to form international trade union organizations and to affiliate with that of their choice. The States Parties shall also permit trade unions, federations and confederations to function freely;

(b) The right to strike.

2. The exercise of the rights set forth above may be subject only to restrictions established by law, provided that such restrictions are characteristic of a democratic society and necessary for safeguarding public order or for protecting public health or morals or the rights and freedoms of others. Members of the armed forces and the police and of other essential public services shall be subject to limitations and restrictions established by law.

3. No one may be compelled to belong to a trade union.

Article 9—Right to Social Security

1. Everyone shall have the right to social security protecting him from the consequences of old age and of disability which prevents him, physically or mentally, from securing the means for a dignified and decent existence. In the event of the death of a beneficiary, social security benefits shall be applied to his dependents.

2. In the case of persons who are employed, the right to social security shall cover at least medical care and an allowance or retirement benefit in the case of work accidents or occupational disease and, in the case of women, paid maternity leave before and after childbirth.

Article 10—Right to Health

1. Everyone shall have the right to health, understood to mean the enjoyment of the highest level of physical, mental and social well-being.

2. In order to ensure the exercise of the right to health, the States Parties agree to recognize health as a public good and, particularly, to adopt the following measures to ensure that right:

(a) Primary health care, that is, essential health care made available to all individuals and families in the community;

(b) Extension of the benefits of health services to all individuals subject to the State's jurisdiction;

(c) Universal immunization against the principal infectious diseases;

(d) Prevention and treatment of endemic, occupational and other diseases;

(e) Education of the population on the prevention and treatment of health problems, and

(f) Satisfaction of the health needs of the highest risk groups and of those whose poverty makes them the most vulnerable.

Article 11—Right to a Healthy Environment

1. Everyone shall have the right to live in a healthy environment and to have access to basic public services.

2. The States Parties shall promote the protection, preservation, and improvement of the environment.

Article 12—Right to Food

1. Everyone has the right to adequate nutrition which guarantees the possibility of enjoying the highest level of physical, emotional and intellectual development.

2. In order to promote the exercise of this right and eradicate malnutrition, the States Parties undertake to improve methods of production, supply and distribution of food, and to this end, agree to promote greater international cooperation in support of the relevant national policies.

Article 13—Right to Education

1. Everyone has the right to education.

2. The States Parties to this Protocol agree that education should be directed towards the full development of the human personality and human dignity and should

strengthen respect for human rights, ideological pluralism, fundamental freedoms, justice and peace. They further agree that education ought to enable everyone to participate effectively in a democratic and pluralistic society and achieve a decent existence and should foster understanding, tolerance and friendship among all nations and all racial, ethnic or religious groups and promote activities for the maintenance of peace.

3. The States Parties to this Protocol recognize that in order to achieve the full exercise of the right to education:

(a) Primary education should be compulsory and accessible to all without cost;

(b) Secondary education in its different forms, including technical and vocational secondary education, should be made generally available and accessible to all by every appropriate means, and in particular, by the progressive introduction of free education;

(c) Higher education should be made equally accessible to all, on the basis of individual capacity, by every appropriate means, and in particular, by the progressive introduction of free education;

(d) Basic education should be encouraged or intensified as far as possible for those persons who have not received or completed the whole cycle of primary instruction;

(e) Programs of special education should be established for the handicapped, so as to provide special instruction and training to persons with physical disabilities or mental deficiencies.

4. In conformity with the domestic legislation of the States Parties, parents should have the right to select the type of education to be given to their children, provided that it conforms to the principles set forth above.

5. Nothing in this Protocol shall be interpreted as a restriction of the freedom of individuals and entities to establish and direct educational institutions in accordance with the domestic legislation of the States Parties.

Article 14—Right to the Benefits of Culture

1. The States Parties to this Protocol recognize the right of everyone:

(a) To take part in the cultural and artistic life of the community;

(b) To enjoy the benefits of scientific and technological progress;

(c) To benefit from the protection of moral and material interests deriving from any scientific, literary or artistic production of which he is the author.

2. The steps to be taken by the States Parties to this Protocol to ensure the full exercise of this right shall include those necessary for the conservation, development and dissemination of science, culture and art.

3. The States Parties to this Protocol undertake to respect the freedom indispensable for scientific research and creative activity.

4. The States Parties to this Protocol recognize the benefits to be derived from the encouragement and development of international cooperation and relations in the fields of science, arts and culture, and accordingly agree to foster greater international cooperation in these fields.

Article 15—Right to the Formation and the Protection of Families

1. The family is the natural and fundamental element of society and ought to be protected by the State, which should see to the improvement of its spiritual and material conditions.

2. Everyone has the right to form a family, which shall be exercised in accordance with the provisions of the pertinent domestic legislation.

3. The States Parties hereby undertake to accord adequate protection to the family unit and in particular:

   (a) To provide special care and assistance to mothers during a reasonable period before and after childbirth;

   (b) To guarantee adequate nutrition for children at the nursing stage and during school attendance years;

   (c) To adopt special measures for the protection of adolescents in order to ensure the full development of their physical, intellectual and moral capacities;

   (d) To undertake special programs of family training so as to help create a stable and positive environment in which children will receive and develop the values of understanding, solidarity, respect and responsibility.

Article 16—Rights of Children

Every child, whatever his parentage, has the right to the protection that his status as a minor requires from his family, society and the State. Every child has the right to grow under the protection and responsibility of his parents; save in exceptional, judicially-recognized circumstances, a child of young age ought not to be separated from his mother. Every child has the right to free and compulsory education, at least in the elementary phase, and to continue his training at higher levels of the educational system.

Article 17—Protection of the Elderly

Everyone has the right to special protection in old age. With this in view the States Parties agree to take progressively the necessary steps to make this right a reality and, particularly, to:

   (a) Provide suitable facilities, as well as food and specialized medical care, for elderly individuals who lack them and are unable to provide them for themselves;

   (b) Undertake work programs specifically designed to give the elderly the opportunity to engage in a productive activity suited to their abilities and consistent with their vocations or desires;

   (c) Foster the establishment of social organizations aimed at improving the quality of life for the elderly.

Article 18—Protection of the Handicapped

Everyone affected by a diminution of his physical or mental capacities is entitled to receive special attention designed to help him achieve the greatest possible development of his personality. The States Parties agree to adopt such measures as may be necessary for this purpose and, especially, to:

   (a) Undertake programs specifically aimed at providing the handicapped with the resources and environment needed for attaining this goal, including work programs consistent with their possibilities and freely accepted by them or their legal representatives, as the case may be;

(b) Provide special training to the families of the handicapped in order to help them solve the problems of coexistence and convert them into active agents in the physical, mental and emotional development of the latter;

(c) Include the consideration of solutions to specific requirements arising from needs of this group as a priority component of their urban development plans;

(d) Encourage the establishment of social groups in which the handicapped can be helped to enjoy a fuller life.

Article 19—Means of Protection

1. Pursuant to the provisions of this article and the corresponding rules to be formulated for this purpose by the General Assembly of the Organization of American States, the States Parties to this Protocol undertake to submit periodic reports on the progressive measures they have taken to ensure due respect for the rights set forth in this Protocol.

2. All reports shall be submitted to the Secretary General of the OAS, who shall transmit them to the Inter-American Economic and Social Council and the Inter-American Council for Education, Science and Culture so that they may examine them in accordance with the provisions of this article. The Secretary General shall send a copy of such reports to the Inter-American Commission on Human Rights.

3. The Secretary General of the Organization of American States shall also transmit to the specialized organizations of the inter-American system of which the States Parties to the present Protocol are members, copies or pertinent portions of the reports submitted, insofar as they relate to matters within the purview of those organizations, as established by their constituent instruments.

4. The specialized organizations of the inter-American system may submit reports to the Inter-American Economic and Social Council and the Inter-American Council for Education, Science and Culture relative to compliance with the provisions of the present Protocol in their fields of activity.

5. The annual reports submitted to the General Assembly by the Inter-American Economic and Social Council and the Inter-American Council for Education, Science and Culture shall contain a summary of the information received from the States Parties to the present Protocol and the specialized organizations concerning the progressive measures adopted in order to ensure respect for the rights acknowledged in the Protocol itself and the general recommendations they consider to be appropriate in this respect.

6. Any instance in which the rights established in paragraph (a) of Article 8 and in Article 13 are violated by action directly attributable to a State Party to this Protocol may give rise, through participation of the Inter-American Commission on Human Rights and, when applicable, of the Inter-American Court of Human Rights, to application of the system of individual petitions governed by Article 44 through 51 and 61 through 69 of the American Convention on Human Rights.

7. Without prejudice to the provisions of the preceding paragraph, the Inter-American Commission on Human Rights may formulate such observations and recommendations as it deems pertinent concerning the status of the economic, social and cultural rights established in the present Protocol in all or some of the States Parties, which it may

include in its Annual Report to the General Assembly or in a special report, whichever it considers more appropriate.

8. The Councils and the Inter-American Commission on Human Rights, in discharging the functions conferred upon them in this article, shall take into account the progressive nature of the observance of the rights subject to protection by this Protocol.

Article 20—Reservations

The States Parties may, at the time of approval, signature, ratification or accession, make reservations to one or more specific provisions of this Protocol, provided that such reservations are not incompatible with the object and purpose of the Protocol.

Article 21—Signature, Ratification or Accession. Entry into Effect

1. This Protocol shall remain open to signature and ratification or accession by any State Party to the American Convention on Human Rights.

2. Ratification of or accession to this Protocol shall be effected by depositing an instrument of ratification or accession with the General Secretariat of the Organization of American States.

3. The Protocol shall enter into effect when eleven States have deposited their respective instruments of ratification or accession.

4. The Secretary General shall notify all the member States of the Organization of American States of the entry of the Protocol into effect.

Article 22—Inclusion of other Rights and Expansion of those Recognized

1. Any State Party and the Inter-American Commission on Human Rights may submit for the consideration of the States Parties meeting on the occasion of the General Assembly proposed amendments to include the recognition of other rights or freedoms or to extend or expand rights or freedoms recognized in this Protocol.

2. Such amendments shall enter into effect for the States that ratify them on the date of deposit of the instrument of ratification corresponding to the number representing two thirds of the States Parties to this Protocol. For all other States Parties they shall enter into effect on the date on which they deposit their respective instrument of ratification.

111. PROTOCOL TO THE AMERICAN CONVENTION ON HUMAN RIGHTS TO ABOLISH THE DEATH PENALTY, 1990

OAS *Treaty Series* No. 73 (1990), adopted 8 June 1990, reprinted in *Basic Documents Pertaining to Human Rights in the Inter-American System*, OEA/Ser.L/V/I.4 rev.12, 31 January 2007: **http://www.cidh.oas.org/Basicos/English/Basic.TOC./htm**.

TEXT

Preamble

The States Parties to this Protocol,

Considering:

That Article 4 of the American Convention on Human Rights recognizes the right to life and restricts the application of the death penalty;

That everyone has the inalienable right to respect for his life, a right that cannot be suspended for any reason;

That the tendency among the American States is to be in favor of abolition of the death penalty;

That application of the death penalty has irrevocable consequences, forecloses the correction of judicial error, and precludes any possibility of changing or rehabilitating those convicted;

That the abolition of the death penalty helps to ensure more effective protection of the right to life;

That an international agreement must be arrived at that will entail a progressive development of the American Convention on Human Rights, and

That States Parties to the American Convention on Human Rights have expressed their intention to adopt an international agreement with a view to consolidating the practice of not applying the death penalty in the Americas,

Have agreed to sign the following Protocol to the American Convention on Human Rights to abolish the death penalty

Article 1

The States Parties to this Protocol shall not apply the death penalty in their territory to any person subject to their jurisdiction.

Article 2

1. No reservations may be made to this Protocol. However, at the time of ratification or accession, the States Parties to this instrument may declare that they reserve the right to apply the death penalty in wartime in accordance with international law, for extremely serious crimes of a military nature.

2. The State Party making this reservation shall, upon ratification or accession, inform the Secretary General of the Organization of American States of the pertinent provisions of its national legislation applicable in wartime, as referred to in the preceding paragraph.

3. Said State Party shall notify the Secretary General of the Organization of American States of the beginning or end of any state of war in effect in its territory.

Article 3

1. This Protocol shall be open for signature and ratification or accession by any State Party to the American Convention on Human Rights.

2. Ratification of this Protocol or accession thereto shall be made through the deposit of an instrument of ratification or accession with the General Secretariat of the Organization of American States.

Article 4

This Protocol shall enter into force among the States that ratify or accede to it when they deposit their respective instruments of ratification or accession with the General Secretariat of the Organization of American States.

112. INTER-AMERICAN CONVENTION TO PREVENT AND PUNISH TORTURE, 1985

The Convention was adopted as part of a resolution adopted at the third plenary session of the Organization of American States held at Cartagena de Indias on 9 December 1985. It came into force on 28 February 1987. The text appears in the OAS *Treaty Series*, No. 67; reprinted in *Basic Documents Pertaining to Human Rights in the Inter-American System*, OEA/Ser.L/V/I.4 rev.12, 31 January 2007: **http://www.cidh.oas.org/Basicos/English/Basic.TOC./htm**.

TEXT

The American States signatory to the present Convention,

Aware of the provision of the American Convention on Human Rights that no one shall be subjected to torture or to cruel, inhuman, or degrading punishment or treatment;

Reaffirming that all acts of torture or any other cruel, inhuman, or degrading treatment or punishment constitute an offense against human dignity and a denial of the principles set forth in the Charter of the Organization of American States and in the Charter of the United Nations and are violations of the fundamental human rights and freedoms proclaimed in the American Declaration of the Rights and Duties of Man and the Universal Declaration of Human Rights;

Noting that, in order for the pertinent rules contained in the aforementioned global and regional instruments to take effect, it is necessary to draft an Inter-American Convention that prevents and punishes torture;

Reaffirming their purpose of consolidating in this hemisphere the conditions that make for recognition of and respect for the inherent dignity of man, and ensure the full exercise of his fundamental rights and freedoms,

Have agreed upon the following:

Article 1

The State Parties undertake to prevent and punish torture in accordance with the terms of this Convention.

Article 2

For the purposes of this Convention, torture shall be understood to be any act intentionally performed whereby physical or mental pain or suffering is inflicted on a person for purposes of criminal investigation, as a means of intimidation, as personal punishment, as a preventive measure, as a penalty, or for any other purpose. Torture shall also be understood to be the use of methods upon a person intended to obliterate the personality of the victim or to diminish his physical or mental capacities, even if they do not cause physical pain or mental anguish.

The concept of torture shall not include physical or mental pain or suffering that is inherent in or solely the consequence of lawful measures, provided that they do not include the performance of the acts or use of the methods referred to in this article.

Article 3

The following shall be held guilty of the crime of torture:

(a) A public servant or employee who acting in that capacity orders, instigates or induces the use of torture, or who directly commits it or who, being able to prevent it, fails to do so.

(b) A person who at the instigation of a public servant or employee mentioned in subparagraph (a) orders, instigates or induces the use of torture, directly commits it or is an accomplice thereto.

Article 4

The fact of having acted under orders of a superior shall not provide exemption from the corresponding criminal liability.

Article 5

The existence of circumstances such as a state of war, threat of war, state of siege or of emergency, domestic disturbance or strife, suspension of constitutional guarantees, domestic political instability, or other public emergencies or disasters shall not be invoked or admitted as justification for the crime of torture.

Neither the dangerous character of the detainee or prisoner, nor the lack of security of the prison establishment or penitentiary shall justify torture.

Article 6

In accordance with the terms of Article 1, the States Parties shall take effective measures to prevent and punish torture within their jurisdiction.

The States Parties shall ensure that all acts of torture and attempts to commit torture are offenses under their criminal law and shall make such acts punishable by severe penalties that take into account their serious nature.

The States Parties likewise shall take effective measures to prevent and punish other cruel, inhuman, or degrading treatment or punishment within their jurisdiction.

Article 7

The States Parties shall take measures so that, in the training of police officers and other public officials responsible for the custody of persons temporarily or definitively deprived of their freedom, special emphasis shall be put on the prohibition of the use of torture in interrogation, detention, or arrest.

The States Parties likewise shall take similar measures to prevent other cruel, inhuman, or degrading treatment or punishment.

Article 8

The States Parties shall guarantee that any person making an accusation of having been subjected to torture within their jurisdiction shall have the right to an impartial examination of his case.

Likewise, if there is an accusation or well-grounded reason to believe that an act of torture has been committed within their jurisdiction, the States Parties shall guarantee that their respective authorities will proceed properly and immediately to conduct an investigation into the case and to initiate, whenever appropriate, the corresponding criminal process.

After all the domestic legal procedures of the respective State and the corresponding appeals have been exhausted, the case may be submitted to the international fora whose competence has been recognized by that State.

Article 9

The States Parties undertake to incorporate into their national laws regulations guaranteeing suitable compensation for victims of torture.

None of the provisions of this article shall affect the right to receive compensation that the victim or other persons may have by virtue of existing national legislation.

Article 10

No statement that is verified as having been obtained through torture shall be admissible as evidence in a legal proceeding, except in a legal action taken against a person or persons accused of having elicited it through acts of torture, and only as evidence that the accused obtained such statement by such means.

Article 11

The States Parties shall take the necessary steps to extradite anyone accused of having committed the crime of torture or sentenced for commission of that crime, in accordance with their respective national laws on extradition and their international commitments on this matter.

Article 12

Every State Party shall take the necessary measures to establish its jurisdiction over the crime described in this Convention in the following cases:

   (a) When torture has been committed within its jurisdiction;

   (b) When the alleged criminal is a national of that State; or

   (c) When the victim is a national of that State and it so deems appropriate.

Every State Party shall also take the necessary measures to establish its jurisdiction over the crime described in this Convention when the alleged criminal is within the area under its jurisdiction and it is not appropriate to extradite him in accordance with Article 11.

This Convention does not exclude criminal jurisdiction exercised in accordance with domestic law.

Article 13

The crime referred to in Article 2 shall be deemed to be included among the extraditable crimes in every extradition treaty entered into between States Parties. The States Parties undertake to include the crime of torture as an extraditable offence in every extradition treaty to be concluded between them.

Every State Party that makes extradition conditional on the existence of a treaty may, if it receives a request for extradition from another State Party with which it has no extradition treaty, consider this Convention as the legal basis for extradition in respect of the crime of torture. Extradition shall be subject to the other conditions that may be required by the law of the requested State.

States Parties which do not make extradition conditional on the existence of a treaty shall recognize such crimes as extraditable offences between themselves, subject to the conditions required by the law of the requested State.

Extradition shall not be granted nor shall the person sought be returned when there are grounds to believe that his life is in danger, that he will be subjected to torture or to cruel, inhuman or degrading treatment, or that he will be tried by special or *ad hoc* courts in the requesting State.

Article 14

When a State Party does not grant the extradition, the case shall be submitted to its competent authorities as if the crime had been committed within its jurisdiction, for the purposes of investigation, and when appropriate, for criminal action, in accordance with its national law. Any decision adopted by these authorities shall be communicated to the State that has requested the extradition.

Article 15

No provision of this Convention may be interpreted as limiting the right of asylum, when appropriate, nor as altering the obligations of the States Parties in the matter of extradition.

Article 16

This Convention shall not limit the provisions of the American Convention on Human Rights, other conventions on the subject, or the Statutes of the Inter-American Commission on Human Rights, with respect to the crime of torture.

Article 17

The States Parties undertake to inform the Inter-American Commission on Human Rights of any legislative, judicial, administrative, or other measures they adopt in application of this Convention.

In keeping with its duties and responsibilities, the Inter-American Commission on Human Rights will endeavor in its annual report to analyze the existing situation in the member states of the Organization of American States in regard to the prevention and elimination of torture.

Article 18

This Convention is open to signature by the member States of the Organization of American States.

Article 19

This Convention is subject to ratification. The instruments of ratification shall be deposited with the General Secretariat of the Organization of American States.

Article 20

This Convention is open to accession by any other American State. The instruments of accession shall be deposited with the General Secretariat of the Organization of American States.

Article 21

The States Parties may, at the time of approval, signature, ratification, or accession, make reservations to this Convention, provided that such reservations are not incompatible with the object and purpose of the Convention and concern one or more specific provisions.

Article 22

This Convention shall enter into force on the thirtieth day following the date on which the second instrument of ratification is deposited. For each State ratifying or acceding to the Convention after the second instrument of ratification has been deposited, the Convention shall enter into force on the thirtieth day following the date on which that State deposits its instrument of ratification or accession.

Article 23

This Convention shall remain in force indefinitely, but may be denounced by any State Party. The instrument of denunciation shall be deposited with the General Secretariat of the Organization of American States. After one year from the date of deposit of the instrument of denunciation, this Convention shall cease to be in effect for the denouncing State but shall remain in force for the remaining States Parties.

Article 24

The original instrument of this Convention, the English, French, Portuguese, and Spanish texts of which are equally authentic, shall be deposited with the General Secretariat of the Organization of American States, which shall send a certified copy to the Secretariat of the United Nations for registration and publication, in accordance with the provisions of Article 102 of the United Nations Charter. The General Secretariat of the Organization of American States shall notify the member States of the Organization and the States that have acceded to the Convention of signatures and of deposits of instruments of ratification, accession, and denunciation, as well as reservations, if any.

113. INTER-AMERICAN CONVENTION ON THE PREVENTION, PUNISHMENT AND ERADICATION OF VIOLENCE AGAINST WOMEN, 1994

The 'Convention of Belém Do Pará' was adopted at Belém do Pará, Brazil, on 9 June 1994, at the twenty fourth regular session of the General Assembly; it entered into force on 5 March 1995. For text, see *Basic Documents Pertaining to Human Rights in the Inter-American System*, OAS/Ser.L/V/I.4 rev.12, 31 January 2007: **http://www.cidh.oas.org/Basicos/English/Basic.TOC./htm**.

TEXT

The States Parties to this Convention,

Recognizing that full respect for human rights has been enshrined in the American Declaration of the Rights and Duties of Man and the Universal Declaration of Human Rights, and reaffirmed in other international and regional instruments;

Affirming that violence against women constitutes a violation of their human rights and fundamental freedoms, and impairs or nullifies the observance, enjoyment and exercise of such rights and freedoms;

Concerned that violence against women is an offense against human dignity and a manifestation of the historically unequal power relations between women and men;

Recalling the Declaration on the Elimination of Violence against Women, adopted by the Twenty-fifth Assembly of Delegates of the Inter-American Commission of Women, and affirming that violence against women pervades every sector of society regardless of class, race or ethnic group, income, culture, level of education, age or religion and strikes at its very foundations:

Convinced that the elimination of violence against women is essential for their individual and social development and their full and equal participation in all walks of life; and

Convinced that the adoption of a convention on the prevention, punishment and eradication of all forms of violence against women within the framework of the Organization of American States is a positive contribution to protecting the rights of women and eliminating violence against them,

Have agreed to the following:

CHAPTER I—DEFINITION AND SCOPE OF APPLICATION

Article 1

For the purposes of this Convention, violence against women shall be understood as any act or conduct, based on gender, which causes death or physical, sexual or psychological harm or suffering to women, whether in the public or the private sphere.

Article 2

Violence against women shall be understood to include physical, sexual and psychological violence:

(a) that occurs within the family or domestic unit or within any other interpersonal relationship, whether or not the perpetrator shares or has shared the same residence with the woman, including, among others, rape, battery and sexual abuse;

(b) that occurs in the community and is perpetrated by any person, including, among others, rape, sexual abuse, torture, trafficking in persons, forced prostitution, kidnapping and sexual harassment in the workplace, as well as in educational institutions, health facilities or any other place; and

(c) that is perpetrated or condoned by the State or its agents regardless of where it occurs.

CHAPTER II—RIGHTS PROTECTED

Article 3

Every woman has the right to be free from violence in both the public and private spheres.

Article 4

Every woman has the right to the recognition, enjoyment, exercise and protection of all human rights and freedoms embodied in regional and international human rights instruments. These rights include, among others:

(a) The right to have her life respected;

(b) The right to have her physical, mental and moral integrity respected;

(c) The right to personal liberty and security;

(d) The right not to be subjected to torture;

(e) The rights to have the inherent dignity of her person respected and her family protected;

(f) The right to equal protection before the law and of the law;

(g) The right to simple and prompt recourse to a competent court for protection against acts that violate her rights;

(h) The right to associate freely;

(i) The right of freedom to profess her religion and beliefs within the law; and

(j) The right to have equal access to the public service of her country and to take part in the conduct of public affairs, including decision-making.

Article 5

Every woman is entitled to the free and full exercise of her civil, political, economic, social and cultural rights, and may rely on the full protection of those rights as embodied in regional and international instruments on human rights. The States Parties recognize that violence against women prevents and nullifies the exercise of these rights.

Article 6

The right of every woman to be free from violence includes, among others:

(a) The right of women to be free from all forms of discrimination; and *(b)* The right of women to be valued and educated free of stereotyped patterns of behavior and social and cultural practices based on concepts of inferiority or subordination.

CHAPTER III—DUTIES OF THE STATES

Article 7

The States Parties condemn all forms of violence against women and agree to pursue, by all appropriate means and without delay, policies to prevent, punish and eradicate such violence and undertake to:

(a) refrain from engaging in any act or practice of violence against women and to ensure that their authorities, officials, personnel, agents, and institutions act in conformity with this obligation;

(b) apply due diligence to prevent, investigate and impose penalties for violence against women;

(c) include in their domestic legislation penal, civil, administrative and any other type of provisions that may be needed to prevent, punish and eradicate violence against women and to adopt appropriate administrative measures where necessary;

(d) adopt legal measures to require the perpetrator to refrain from harassing, intimidating or threatening the woman or using any method that harms or endangers her life or integrity, or damages her property;

(e) take all appropriate measures, including legislative measures, to amend or repeal existing laws and regulations or to modify legal or customary practices which sustain the persistence and tolerance of violence against women;

(f) establish fair and effective legal procedures for women who have been subjected to violence which include, among others, protective measures, a timely hearing and effective access to such procedures;

(g) establish the necessary legal and administrative mechanisms to ensure that women subjected to violence have effective access to restitution, reparations or other just and effective remedies; and

(h) adopt such legislative or other measures as may be necessary to give effect to this Convention.

Article 8

The States Parties agree to undertake progressively specific measures, including programs:

(a) to promote awareness and observance of the right of women to be free from violence, and the right of women to have their human rights respected and protected;

(b) to modify social and cultural patterns of conduct of men and women, including the development of formal and informal educational programs appropriate to every level of the educational process, to counteract prejudices, customs and all other practices which are based on the idea of the inferiority or superiority of either of the sexes or on the stereotyped roles for men and women which legitimize or exacerbate violence against women;

(c) to promote the education and training of all those involved in the administration of justice, police and other law enforcement officers as well as other personnel responsible for implementing policies for the prevention, punishment and eradication of violence against women;

(d) to provide appropriate specialized services for women who have been subjected to violence, through public and private sector agencies, including shelters, counseling services for all family members where appropriate, and care and custody of the affected children;

(e) to promote and support governmental and private sector education designed to raise the awareness of the public with respect to the problems of and remedies for violence against women;

(f) to provide women who are subjected to violence access to effective readjustment and training programs to enable them to fully participate in public, private and social life;

(g) to encourage the communications media to develop appropriate media guidelines in order to contribute to the eradication of violence against women in all its forms, and to enhance respect for the dignity of women;

(h) to ensure research and the gathering of statistics and other relevant information relating to the causes, consequences and frequency of violence against women, in order to assess the effectiveness of measures to prevent, punish and eradicate violence against women and to formulate and implement the necessary changes; and

(i) to foster international cooperation for the exchange of ideas and experiences and the execution of programs aimed at protecting women who are subjected to violence.

Article 9

With respect to the adoption of the measures in this Chapter, the States Parties shall take special account of the vulnerability of women to violence by reason of, among others, their race or ethnic background or their status as migrants, refugees or displaced persons. Similar consideration shall be given to women subjected to violence while pregnant or who are disabled, of minor age, elderly, socioeconomically disadvantaged, affected by armed conflict or deprived of their freedom.

CHAPTER IV—INTER-AMERICAN MECHANISMS OF PROTECTION

Article 10

In order to protect the rights of every woman to be free from violence, the States Parties shall include in their national reports to the Inter-American Commission of Women information on measures adopted to prevent and prohibit violence against women, and to assist women affected by violence, as well as on any difficulties they observe in applying those measures, and the factors that contribute to violence against women.

Article 11

The States Parties to this Convention and the Inter-American Commission of Women may request of the Inter-American Court of Human Rights advisory opinions on the interpretation of this Convention.

Article 12

Any person or group of persons, or any nongovernmental entity legally recognized in one or more member States of the Organization, may lodge petitions with the Inter-American Commission on Human Rights containing denunciations or complaints of violations of Article 7 of this Convention by a State Party, and the Commission shall consider such claims in accordance with the norms and procedures established by the American Convention on Human Rights and the Statutes and Regulations of the Inter-American Commission on Human Rights for lodging and considering petitions.

CHAPTER V—GENERAL PROVISIONS

Article 13

No part of this Convention shall be understood to restrict or limit the domestic law of any State Party that affords equal or greater protection and guarantees of the rights of women and appropriate safeguards to prevent and eradicate violence against women.

Article 14

No part of this Convention shall be understood to restrict or limit the American Convention on Human Rights or any other international convention on the subject that provides for equal or greater protection in this area.

Article 15

This Convention is open to signature by all the member States of the Organization of American States.

Article 16

This Convention is subject to ratification. The instruments of ratification shall be deposited with the General Secretariat of the Organization of American States.

Article 17

This Convention is open to accession by any other State. Instruments of accession shall be deposited with the General Secretariat of the Organization of American States.

Article 18

Any State may, at the time of approval, signature, ratification, or accession, make reservations to this Convention provided that such reservations are:

(a) not incompatible with the object and purpose of the Convention, and
(b) not of a general nature and relate to one or more specific provisions.

Article 19

Any State Party may submit to the General Assembly, through the Inter-American Commission of Women, proposals for the amendment of this Convention.

Amendments shall enter into force for the States ratifying them on the date when two-thirds of the States Parties to this Convention have deposited their respective instruments of ratification. With respect to the other States Parties, the amendments shall enter into force on the dates on which they deposit their respective instruments of ratification.

Article 20

If a State Party has two or more territorial units in which the matters dealt with in this Convention are governed by different systems of law, it may, at the time of signature, ratification or accession, declare that this Convention shall extend to all its territorial units or to only one or more of them.

Such a declaration may be amended at any time by subsequent declarations, which shall expressly specify the territorial unit or units to which this Convention applies. Such subsequent declarations shall be transmitted to the General Secretariat of the Organization of American States, and shall enter into force thirty days after the date of their receipt.

Article 21

This Convention shall enter into force on the thirtieth day after the date of deposit of the second instrument of ratification. For each State that ratifies or accedes to the Convention after the second instrument of ratification is deposited, it shall enter into force thirty days after the date on which that State deposited its instrument of ratification or accession.

Article 22

The Secretary General shall inform all member States of the Organization of American States of the entry into force of this Convention.

Article 23

The Secretary General of the Organization of American States shall present an annual report to the member States of the Organization on the status of this Convention, including the signatures, deposits of instruments of ratification and accession, and declarations, and any reservations that may have been presented by the States Parties, accompanied by a report thereon if needed.

Article 24

This Convention shall remain in force indefinitely, but any of the States Parties may denounce it by depositing an instrument to that effect with the General Secretariat of the Organization of American States. One year after the date of deposit of the instrument of denunciation, this Convention shall cease to be in effect for the denouncing State but shall remain in force for the remaining States Parties.

Article 25

The original instrument of this Convention, the English, French, Portuguese and Spanish texts of which are equally authentic, shall be deposited with the General Secretariat of the Organization of American States, which shall send a certified copy to the Secretariat of the United Nations for registration and publication in accordance with the provisions of Article 102 of the United Nations Charter.

In witness whereof the undersigned Plenipotentiaries, being duly authorized thereto by their respective governments, have signed this Convention, which shall be called the Inter-American Convention on the Prevention, Punishment and Eradication of Violence against Women 'Convention of Belém do Pará.'

Done in the city of Belém do Pará, Brazil, the ninth of June in the year one thousand nine hundred and ninety-four.

114. INTER-AMERICAN CONVENTION ON FORCED DISAPPEARANCE OF PERSONS, 1994

Signed at Belém do Pará, Brazil, on 9 June 1994; in force 28 March 1996. *Basic Documents Pertaining to Human Rights in the Inter-American System*, OEA/Ser.L/V/I.4 rev.12, 31 January 2007: **http://www.cidh.oas.org/Basicos/English/Basic.TOC./htm**.

Further reading

GUEST, I., *Behind the Disappearances: Argentina's Dirty War against Human Rights and the United Nations*, Philadelphia: University of Pennsylvania Press, 1990.

TEXT

Preamble

The Member States of the Organization of American States signatory to the present Convention,

Disturbed by the persistence of the forced disappearance of persons;

Reaffirming that the true meaning of American solidarity and good neighborliness can be none other than that of consolidating in this Hemisphere, in the framework of democratic institutions, a system of individual freedom and social justice based on respect for essential human rights;

Considering that the forced disappearance of persons in an affront to the conscience of the Hemisphere and a grave and abominable offense against the inherent dignity of the human being, and one that contradicts the principles and purposes enshrined in the Charter of the Organization of American States;

Considering that the forced disappearance of persons violates numerous non-derogable and essential human rights enshrined in the American Convention on Human Rights, in the American Declaration of the Rights and Duties of Man, and in the Universal Declaration of Human Rights;

Recalling that the international protection of human rights is in the form of a convention reinforcing or complementing the protection provided by domestic law and is based upon the attributes of the human personality;

Reaffirming that the systematic practice of the forced disappearance of persons constitutes a crime against humanity;

Hoping that this Convention may help to prevent, punish, and eliminate the forced disappearance of persons in the Hemisphere and make a decisive contribution to the protection of human rights and the rule of law,

Resolve to adopt the following Inter-American Convention on Forced Disappearance of Persons:

Article I

The States Parties to this Convention undertake:

(a) Not to practice, permit, or tolerate the forced disappearance of persons, even in states of emergency or suspension of individual guarantees;

(b) To punish within their jurisdictions, those persons who commit or attempt to commit the crime of forced disappearance of persons and their accomplices and accessories;

(c) To cooperate with one another in helping to prevent, punish, and eliminate the forced disappearance of persons;

(d) To take legislative, administrative, judicial, and any other measures necessary to comply with the commitments undertaken in this Convention.

Article II

For the purposes of this Convention, forced disappearance is considered to be the act of depriving a person or persons of his or their freedom, in whatever way, perpetrated by agents of the State or by persons or groups of persons acting with the authorization, support, or acquiescence of the State, followed by an absence of information or a refusal to acknowledge that deprivation of freedom or to give information on the whereabouts of that person, thereby impeding his or her recourse to the applicable legal remedies and procedural guarantees.

Article III

The States Parties undertake to adopt, in accordance with their constitutional procedures, the legislative measures that may be needed to define the forced disappearance of persons as an offense and to impose an appropriate punishment commensurate with its extreme gravity. This offense shall be deemed continuous or permanent as long as the fate or whereabouts of the victim has not been determined.

The States Parties may establish mitigating circumstances for persons who have participated in acts constituting forced disappearance when they help to cause the victim to reappear alive or provide information that sheds light on the forced disappearance of a person.

Article IV

The acts constituting the forced disappearance of persons shall be considered offenses in every State Party. Consequently, each State Party shall take measures to establish its jurisdiction over such cases in the following instances:

(a) When the forced disappearance of persons or any act constituting such offense was committed within its jurisdiction;

(b) When the accused is a national of that State;

(c) When the victim is a national of that State and that State sees fit to do so.

Every State Party shall, moreover, take the necessary measures to establish its jurisdiction over the crime described in this Convention when the alleged criminal is within its territory and it does not proceed to extradite him.

This Convention does not authorize any State Party to undertake, in the territory of another State Party, the exercise of jurisdiction or the performance of functions that are placed within the exclusive purview of the authorities of that other Party by its domestic law.

Article V

The forced disappearance of persons shall not be considered a political offense for purposes of extradition.

The forced disappearance of persons shall be deemed to be included among the extraditable offenses in every extradition treaty entered into between States Parties.

The States Parties undertake to include the offense of forced disappearance as one which is extraditable in every extradition treaty to be concluded between them in the future.

Every State Party that makes extradition conditional on the existence of a treaty and receives a request for extradition from another State Party with which it has no extradition treaty may consider this Convention as the necessary legal basis for extradition with respect to the offense of forced disappearance.

States Parties which do not make extradition conditional on the existence of a treaty shall recognize such offense as extraditable, subject to the conditions imposed by the law of the requested State.

Extradition shall be subject to the provisions set forth in the constitution and other laws of the requested State.

Article VI

When a State Party does not grant the extradition, the case shall be submitted to its competent authorities as if the offense had been committed within its jurisdiction, for the purposes of investigation and when appropriate, for criminal action, in accordance with its national law. Any decision adopted by these authorities shall be communicated to the State that has requested the extradition.

Article VII

Criminal prosecution for the forced disappearance of persons and the penalty judicially imposed on its perpetrator shall not be subject to statutes of limitations.

However, if there should be a norm of a fundamental character preventing application of the stipulation contained in the previous paragraph, the period of limitation shall be equal to that which applies to the gravest crime in the domestic laws of the corresponding State Party.

Article VIII

The defense of due obedience to superior orders or instructions that stipulate, authorize, or encourage forced disappearance shall not be admitted. All persons who receive such orders have the right and duty not to obey them.

The States Parties shall ensure that the training of public law-enforcement personnel or officials includes the necessary education on the offense of forced disappearance of persons.

Article IX

Persons alleged to be responsible for the acts constituting the offense of forced disappearance of persons may be tried only in the competent jurisdictions of ordinary law in each State, to the exclusion of all other special jurisdictions, particularly military jurisdictions.

The acts constituting forced disappearance shall not be deemed to have been committed in the course of military duties.

Privileges, immunities, or special dispensations shall not be admitted in such trials, without prejudice to the provisions set forth in the Vienna Convention on Diplomatic Relations.

Article X

In no case may exceptional circumstances such as a state of war, the threat of war, internal political instability, or any other public emergency be invoked to justify the forced disappearance of persons. In such cases, the right to expeditious and effective judicial procedures and recourse shall be retained as a means of determining the whereabouts or state of health of a person who has been deprived of freedom, or of identifying the official who ordered or carried out such deprivation of freedom.

In pursuing such procedures or recourse, and in keeping with applicable domestic law, the competent judicial authorities shall have free and immediate access to all detention centers and to each of their units, and to all places where there is reason to believe the disappeared person might be found including places that are subject to military jurisdiction.

Article XI

Every person deprived of liberty shall be held in an officially recognized place of detention and be brought before a competent judicial authority without delay, in accordance with applicable domestic law.

The States Parties shall establish and maintain official up-to-date registries of their detainees and, in accordance with their domestic law, shall make them available to relatives, judges, attorneys, any other person having a legitimate interest, and other authorities.

Article XII

The States Parties shall give each other mutual assistance in the search for, identification, location, and return of minors who have been removed to another State or detained therein as a consequence of the forced disappearance of their parents or guardians.

Article XIII

For the purposes of this Convention, the processing of petitions or communications presented to the Inter-American Commission on Human Rights alleging the forced disappearance of persons shall be subject to the procedures established in the American Convention on Human Rights and to the Statute and Regulations of the Inter-American Commission on Human Rights and to the Statute and Rules of Procedure of the Inter-American Court of Human Rights, including the provisions on precautionary measures.

Article XIV

Without prejudice to the provisions of the preceding article, when the Inter-American Commission on Human Rights receives a petition or communication regarding an alleged forced disappearance, its Executive Secretariat shall urgently and confidentially address the respective government, and shall request that government to provide as soon as possible information as to the whereabouts of the allegedly disappeared person together with any other information it considers pertinent, and such request shall be without prejudice as to the admissibility of the petition.

Article XV

None of the provisions of this Convention shall be interpreted as limiting other bilateral or multilateral treaties or other agreements signed by the Parties.

This Convention shall not apply to the international armed conflicts governed by the 1949 Geneva Conventions and their Protocols, concerning protection of wounded, sick, and shipwrecked members of the armed forces; and prisoners of war and civilians in time of war.

Article XVI

This Convention is open for signature by the member States of the Organization of American States.

Article XVII

This Convention is subject to ratification. The instruments of ratification shall be deposited with the General Secretariat of the Organization of American States.

Article XVIII

This Convention shall be open to accession by any other State. The instruments of accession shall be deposited with the General Secretariat of the Organization of American States.

Article XIX

The States may express reservations with respect to this Convention when adopting, signing, ratifying or acceding to it, unless such reservations are incompatible with the object and purpose of the Convention and as long as they refer to one or more specific provisions.

Article XX

This Convention shall enter into force for the ratifying States on the thirtieth day from the date of deposit of the second instrument of ratification.

For each State ratifying or acceding to the Convention after the second instrument of ratification has been deposited, the Convention shall enter into force on the thirtieth day from the date on which that State deposited its instrument of ratification or accession.

Article XXI

This Convention shall remain in force indefinitely, buy may be denounced by any State Party. The instrument of denunciation shall be deposited with the General Secretariat of the Organization of American States. The Convention shall cease to be in effect for the denouncing State and shall remain in force for the other States Parties one year from the date of deposit of the instrument of denunciation.

Article XXII

The original instrument of this Convention, the Spanish, English, Portuguese, and French texts of which are equally authentic, shall be deposited with the General Secretariat of the Organization of American States, which shall forward certified copies thereof to the United Nations Secretariat, for registration and publication, in accordance with Article 102 of the Charter of the United Nations. The General Secretariat of the Organization of American States shall notify member States of the Organization and States acceding to the Convention of the signatures and deposit of instruments of ratification, accession or denunciation, as well as of any reservations that may be expressed.

115. INTER-AMERICAN CONVENTION ON THE ELIMINATION OF ALL FORMS OF DISCRIMINATION AGAINST PERSONS WITH DISABILITIES, 1999

Adopted by the OAS General Assembly, 7 June 1999: AG/RES. 1608 (XXIX-O/99). For text, see *Basic Documents Pertaining to Human Rights in the Inter-American System*, OEA/Ser.L/V/I.4 rev.12, 31 January 2007: **http://www.cidh.oas.org/Basicos/English/Basic.TOC./htm**.

TEXT

The General Assembly,

Having seen the report of the Permanent Council on the draft Inter-American Convention on the Elimination of All Forms of Discrimination against Persons with Disabilities (CP/CAJP–1532/99);

Considering that, during its twenty-sixth regular session, the General Assembly, in resolution AG/RES. 1369 (XXVI-O/96), 'Panama Commitment to Persons with Disabilities in the American Hemisphere,' instructed the Permanent Council to prepare, through the appropriate working group, a 'draft Inter-American Convention on the Elimination of All Forms of Discrimination by Reason of Disability';

Bearing in mind that disability can lead to situations of discrimination, and that it is necessary therefore to encourage actions and measures to bring about a substantial improvement in the situation of persons with disabilities in the Hemisphere;

Recalling that the American Declaration of the Rights and Duties of Man proclaims that all human beings are born free and equal, in dignity and in rights, and that the rights and freedoms of every person must be respected without distinction of any kind;

Taking into consideration that the Additional Protocol to the American Convention on Human Rights in the area of Economic, Social, and Cultural Rights, or 'Protocol of San Salvador,' recognizes that 'everyone affected by a diminution of his physical or mental capacities is entitled to receive special attention designed to help him achieve the greatest possible development of his personality'; and

Noting that resolution AG/RES. 1564 (XXVIII-O/98) reiterates 'the importance of adopting an Inter-American Convention on the Elimination of All Forms of Discrimination against Persons with Disabilities' and, in addition, requests that every necessary effort be made to ensure that this legal instrument is adopted and signed at the twenty-ninth regular session of the General Assembly,

Resolves:

To adopt the following Inter-American Convention on the Elimination of All Forms of Discrimination against Persons with Disabilities:

INTER-AMERICAN CONVENTION ON THE ELIMINATION OF ALL FORMS OF DISCRIMINATION AGAINST PERSONS WITH DISABILITIES

The States Parties to this Convention,

Reaffirming that persons with disabilities have the same human rights and fundamental freedoms as other persons; and that these rights, which include freedom from discrimination based on disability, flow from the inherent dignity and equality of each person;

Considering that the Charter of the Organization of American States, in Article 3.j, establishes the principle that 'social justice and social security are bases of lasting peace';

Concerned by the discrimination to which people are subject based on their disability;

Bearing in mind the agreement of the International Labour Organisation on the vocational rehabilitation and employment of disabled persons (Convention 159); the Declaration of the Rights of Mentally Retarded Persons (UN General Assembly resolution 2856 (XXVI) of December 20, 1971); the Declaration on the Rights of Disabled Persons (UN General Assembly resolution 3447 (XXX) of December 9, 1975); the World Programme of Action concerning Disabled Persons (UN General Assembly resolution 37/52 of December 3, 1982); the Additional Protocol to the American Convention on Human Rights in the area of Economic, Social, and Cultural Rights, 'Protocol of San Salvador' (1988); the Principles for the Protection of Persons with Mental Illness and for the Improvement of Mental Health Care (UN General Assembly resolution 46/119 of December 17, 1991); the Declaration of Caracas of the Pan American Health Organization; resolution AG/RES. 1249 (XXIII-O/93), 'Situation of Persons with Disabilities in the American Hemisphere'; the Standard Rules on the Equalization of Opportunities for Persons with Disabilities (UN General Assembly resolution 48/96 of December 20, 1993); the Declaration of Managua (December 1993); the Vienna Declaration and Programme of Action, adopted by the UN World Conference on Human Rights (157/93); resolution AG/RES. 1356 (XXV-O/95), 'Situation of Persons with Disabilities in the American Hemisphere'; and AG/RES. 1369 (XXVI-O/96), 'Panama Commitment to Persons with Disabilities in the American Hemisphere'; and

Committed to eliminating discrimination, in all its forms and manifestations, against persons with disabilities,

Have agreed as follows:

Article I

For the purposes of this Convention, the following terms are defined:

1. *Disability*

The term 'disability' means a physical, mental, or sensory impairment, whether permanent or temporary, that limits the capacity to perform one or more essential activities of daily life, and which can be caused or aggravated by the economic and social environment.

2. *Discrimination against persons with disabilities*

    (a) The term 'discrimination against persons with disabilities' means any distinction, exclusion, or restriction based on a disability, record of disability, condition resulting from a previous disability, or perception of disability, whether present or past, which has the effect or objective of impairing or nullifying the recognition, enjoyment, or exercise by a person with a disability of his or her human rights and fundamental freedoms.

(b) A distinction or preference adopted by a State party to promote the social integration or personal development of persons with disabilities does not constitute discrimination provided that the distinction or preference does not in itself limit the right of persons with disabilities to equality and that individuals with disabilities are not forced to accept such distinction or preference. If, under a State's internal law, a person can be declared legally incompetent, when necessary and appropriate for his or her well-being, such declaration does not constitute discrimination.

Article II

The objectives of this Convention are to prevent and eliminate all forms of discrimination against persons with disabilities and to promote their full integration into society.

Article III

To achieve the objectives of this Convention, the States parties undertake:

1. To adopt the legislative, social, educational, labor-related, or any other measures needed to eliminate discrimination against persons with disabilities and to promote their full integration into society, including, but not limited to:

(a) Measures to eliminate discrimination gradually and to promote integration by government authorities and/or private entities in providing or making available goods, services, facilities, programs, and activities such as employment, transportation, communications, housing, recreation, education, sports, law enforcement and administration of justice, and political and administrative activities;

(b) Measures to ensure that new buildings, vehicles, and facilities constructed or manufactured within their respective territories facilitate transportation, communications, and access by persons with disabilities;

(c) Measures to eliminate, to the extent possible, architectural, transportation, and communication obstacles to facilitate access and use by persons with disabilities; and

(d) Measures to ensure that persons responsible for applying this Convention and domestic law in this area are trained to do so.

2. To work on a priority basis in the following areas:

(a) Prevention of all forms of preventable disabilities;

(b) Early detection and intervention, treatment, rehabilitation, education, job training, and the provision of comprehensive services to ensure the optimal level of independence and quality of life for persons with disabilities; and

(c) Increasing of public awareness through educational campaigns aimed at eliminating prejudices, stereotypes, and other attitudes that jeopardize the right of persons to live as equals, thus promoting respect for and coexistence with persons with disabilities.

Article IV

To achieve the objectives of this Convention, the States parties undertake to:

1. Cooperate with one another in helping to prevent and eliminate discrimination against persons with disabilities;

2. Collaborate effectively in:

   (a) Scientific and technological research related to the prevention of disabilities and to the treatment, rehabilitation, and integration into society of persons with disabilities; and

   (b) The development of means and resources designed to facilitate or promote the independence, self-sufficiency, and total integration into society of persons with disabilities, under conditions of equality.

Article V

1. To the extent that it is consistent with their respective internal laws, the States parties shall promote participation by representatives of organizations of persons with disabilities, nongovernmental organizations working in this area, or, if such organizations do not exist, persons with disabilities, in the development, execution, and evaluation of measures and policies to implement this Convention.

2. The States parties shall create effective communication channels to disseminate among the public and private organizations working with persons with disabilities the normative and juridical advances that may be achieved in order to eliminate discrimination against persons with disabilities.

Article VI

1. To follow up on the commitments undertaken in this Convention, a Committee for the Elimination of All Forms of Discrimination against Persons with Disabilities, composed of one representative appointed by each State party, shall be established.

2. The committee shall hold its first meeting within the 90 days following the deposit of the 11th instrument of ratification. Said meeting shall be convened by the General Secretariat of the Organization of American States and shall be held at the Organization's headquarters, unless a State party offers to host it.

3. At the first meeting, the States parties undertake to submit a report to the Secretary General of the Organization for transmission to the Committee so that it may be examined and reviewed. Thereafter, reports shall be submitted every four years.

4. The reports prepared under the previous paragraph shall include information on measures adopted by the member States pursuant to this Convention and on any progress made by the States parties in eliminating all forms of discrimination against persons with disabilities. The reports shall indicate any circumstances or difficulties affecting the degree of fulfillment of the obligations arising from this Convention.

5. The Committee shall be the forum for assessment of progress made in the application of the Convention and for the exchange of experience among the States parties. The reports prepared by the committee shall reflect the deliberations; shall include information on any measures adopted by the States parties pursuant to this Convention, on any progress they have made in eliminating all forms of discrimination against persons with disabilities, and on any circumstances or difficulties they have encountered in the implementation of the Convention; and shall include the committee's conclusions, its observations, and its general suggestions for the gradual fulfillment of the Convention.

6. The committee shall draft its rules of procedure and adopt them by a simple majority.

7. The Secretary General shall provide the Committee with the support it requires in order to perform its functions.

Article VII

No provision of this Convention shall be interpreted as restricting, or permitting the restriction by States parties of the enjoyment of the rights of persons with disabilities recognized by customary international law or the international instruments by which a particular State party is bound.

Article VIII

1. This Convention shall be open for signature by all member States in Guatemala City, Guatemala, on June 8, 1999, and, thereafter, shall remain open for signature by all States at the headquarters of the Organization of American States, until its entry into force.

2. This Convention is subject to ratification.

3. This Convention shall enter into force for the ratifying States on the 30th day following the date of deposit of the sixth instrument of ratification by a member State of the Organization of American States.

Article IX

After its entry into force, this Convention shall be open for accession by all States that have not signed it.

Article X

1. The instruments of ratification and accession shall be deposited with the General Secretariat of the Organization of American States.

2. For each State that ratifies or accedes to the Convention after the sixth instrument of ratification has been deposited, the Convention shall enter into force on the 30th day following deposit by that State of its instrument of ratification or accession.

Article XI

1. Any State party may make proposals for amendment of this Convention. Said proposals shall be submitted to the General Secretariat of the OAS for dissemination to the States parties.

2. Amendments shall enter into force for the States ratifying them on the date of deposit of the respective instruments of ratification by two thirds of the member States. For the remaining States parties, they shall enter into force on the date of deposit of their respective instruments of ratification.

Article XII

The states may enter reservations to this Convention when ratifying or acceding to it, provided that such reservations are not incompatible with the aim and purpose of the Convention and relate to one or more specific provisions thereof.

Article XIII

This Convention shall remain in force indefinitely, but any State party may denounce it. The instrument of denunciation shall be deposited with the General Secretariat of the Organization of American States. The Convention shall cease to have force and effect for the denouncing State one year after the date of deposit of the instrument of denunciation, and shall remain in force for the other States parties. Such denunciation shall not exempt the State party from the obligations imposed upon it under this Convention in respect of any action or omission prior to the date on which the denunciation takes effect.

Article XIV

1. The original instrument of this Convention, the English, French, Portuguese, and Spanish texts of which are equally authentic, shall be deposited with the General Secretariat of the Organization of American States, which shall send a certified copy thereof to the United Nations Secretariat for registration and publication pursuant to Article 102 of the United Nations Charter.

2. The General Secretariat of the Organization of American States shall notify the member States of that Organization and the States that have acceded to the Convention of the signatures, deposits of instruments of ratification, accession, and denunciation, and any reservations entered.

116. INTER-AMERICAN DEMOCRATIC CHARTER, 2001

One of the most significant events in the Americas in recent years was the adoption of the Inter-American Democratic Charter by the OAS General Assembly at its Special Session in Lima, Peru, on 11 September 2001. In 1959, the 'Declaration of Santiago de Chile' had attempted to set out some of the characteristics of a democratic system, including that 'the principle of the rule of law must be assured through the separation of powers and review, by judicial bodies of the State, of the legality of acts of government', and that 'the governments of the American republics must be the result of free elections.' In 1991, the OAS General Assembly adopted Resolution 1080 on 'representative democracy', which it characterised as 'an indispensable condition for the stability, peace, and development of the region'. This provided a mechanism for collective action, in the case of 'the sudden or irregular interruption of the democratic political institutional process or of the legitimate exercise of power by the democratically elected government in any of the Organization's member States': (Fifth Plenary Session, 5 June 1991: AG/RES. 1080 (XXI-O/91). The following year, the General Assembly approved the 'Washington Protocol', which established the possibility to suspend a Member State's participation if its democratic government were overthrown by force (OAS, *Official Documents*, OEA/Ser.A/2 Add.3 (SEPF), Series on Treaties 1-E Rev. (1995), in force 25 September 1997; see now Article 9 of the Charter). This was followed in April 2001 by the adoption of a 'democracy clause', which provides that 'any unconstitutional alteration or interruption of the democratic order in a State of the Hemisphere constitutes an insurmountable obstacle to the participation of that State's government in the Summits of the Americas process' (adopted at the Third Summit of the Americas, Québec City, 20–22 April 2001; see now Articles 17–22 of the Charter).

The 2001 Charter, in common with a number of measures adopted in different forums, extends its reach beyond the traditional civil and political rights dimension. Among others, it clearly identifies the linkage between the elimination of extreme poverty and the promotion and consolidation of democracy, and between education and meaningful participation, and calls for measures to defend democracy to be complemented by 'ongoing and creative work to consolidate democracy as well as a continuing effort to prevent and anticipate the very causes of the problems that affect the democratic system of government' (Preamble, Articles 11–16, 26–28).

The rights aspect to elections and representative democracy is by no means ignored. Indeed, the Charter opens with the affirmation that, 'The peoples of the Americas have a right to democracy and their governments have an obligation to promote and defend it' (Article 1); and that 'The effective exercise of representative democracy is the basis for the rule of law and of the constitutional regimes of the Member States' (Article 2).

See also, Organization of American States, Secretariat for Political Affairs: **http://www.oas. org/sap/english/**.

Further reading

CONSEJO PERMANENTE, *Carta Democrática Interamericana: Documentos e interpretaciones*, Washington: Organization of American States, 2003.

FABRY, M., 'The Inter-American Democratic Charter and Governmental Legitimacy in the International Relations of the Western Hemisphere', (2009) 20 *Diplomacy and Statecraft* 107.

GOODWIN-GILL, G. S., *Free and Fair Elections*, Geneva: Inter-Parliamentary Union, 2nd rev. edn., 2006.

INTER-AMERICAN JURIDICAL COMMITTEE, 'Note from the Chair forwarding to the Permanent Council Resolution CJI/Res. 159 (LXXV-O/09), "The Essential and Fundamental Elements of Representative Democracy and their Relation to Collective Action within the Framework

of the Inter-American Democratic Charter",' OAS doc. OEA/Ser.G, CP/INF.5898/09, 4
September 2009.

TEXT

The General Assembly,

Considering that the Charter of the Organization of American States recognizes that
representative democracy is indispensable for the stability, peace, and development of
the region, and that one of the purposes of the OAS is to promote and consolidate representative democracy, with due respect for the principle of nonintervention;

Recognizing the contributions of the OAS and other regional and sub-regional mechanisms to the promotion and consolidation of democracy in the Americas;

Recalling that the Heads of State and Government of the Americas, gathered at the
Third Summit of the Americas, held from April 20 to 22, 2001 in Quebec City, adopted
a democracy clause which establishes that any unconstitutional alteration or interruption of the democratic order in a State of the Hemisphere constitutes an insurmountable
obstacle to the participation of that State's government in the Summits of the Americas
process;

Bearing in mind that existing democratic provisions in regional and subregional mechanisms express the same objectives as the democracy clause adopted by the Heads of State
and Government in Quebec City;

Reaffirming that the participatory nature of democracy in our countries in different
aspects of public life contributes to the consolidation of democratic values and to freedom
and solidarity in the Hemisphere;

Considering that solidarity among and cooperation between American States require
the political organization of those States based on the effective exercise of representative democracy, and that economic growth and social development based on justice and
equity, and democracy are interdependent and mutually reinforcing;

Reaffirming that the fight against poverty, and especially the elimination of extreme
poverty, is essential to the promotion and consolidation of democracy and constitutes a
common and shared responsibility of the American States;

Bearing in mind that the American Declaration on the Rights and Duties of Man and
the American Convention on Human Rights contain the values and principles of liberty,
equality, and social justice that are intrinsic to democracy;

Reaffirming that the promotion and protection of human rights is a basic prerequisite
for the existence of a democratic society, and recognizing the importance of the continuous development and strengthening of the inter-American human rights system for the
consolidation of democracy;

Considering that education is an effective way to promote citizens' awareness concerning their own countries and thereby achieve meaningful participation in the decision-
making process, and reaffirming the importance of human resource development for a
sound democratic system;

Recognizing that a safe environment is essential to the integral development of the
human being, which contributes to democracy and political stability;

Bearing in mind that the Protocol of San Salvador on Economic, Social, and Cultural
Rights emphasizes the great importance of the reaffirmation, development, improvement,

and protection of those rights in order to consolidate the system of representative democratic government;

Recognizing that the right of workers to associate themselves freely for the defense and promotion of their interests is fundamental to the fulfillment of democratic ideals;

Taking into account that, in the Santiago Commitment to Democracy and the Renewal of the Inter-American System, the Ministers of Foreign Affairs expressed their determination to adopt a series of effective, timely, and expeditious procedures to ensure the promotion and defense of representative democracy, with due respect for the principle of nonintervention; and that resolution AG/RES. 1080 (XXI-O/91) therefore established a mechanism for collective action in the case of a sudden or irregular interruption of the democratic political institutional process or of the legitimate exercise of power by the democratically-elected government in any of the Organization's member States, thereby fulfilling a long-standing aspiration of the Hemisphere to be able to respond rapidly and collectively in defense of democracy;

Recalling that, in the Declaration of Nassau [AG/DEC. 1 (XXII-O/92)], it was agreed to develop mechanisms to provide assistance, when requested by a member State, to promote, preserve, and strengthen representative democracy, in order to complement and give effect to the provisions of resolution AG/RES. 1080 (XXI-O/91);

Bearing in mind that, in the Declaration of Managua for the Promotion of Democracy and Development [AG/DEC. 4 (XXIII-O/93)], the member States expressed their firm belief that democracy, peace, and development are inseparable and indivisible parts of a renewed and integral vision of solidarity in the Americas; and that the ability of the Organization to help preserve and strengthen democratic structures in the region will depend on the implementation of a strategy based on the interdependence and complementarity of those values;

Considering that, in the Declaration of Managua for the Promotion of Democracy and Development, the member States expressed their conviction that the Organization's mission is not limited to the defense of democracy wherever its fundamental values and principles have collapsed, but also calls for ongoing and creative work to consolidate democracy as well as a continuing effort to prevent and anticipate the very causes of the problems that affect the democratic system of government;

Bearing in mind that the Ministers of Foreign Affairs of the Americas, at the thirty-first regular session of the General Assembly, held in San Jose, Costa Rica, in keeping with express instructions from the Heads of State and Government gathered at the Third Summit of the Americas, in Quebec City, accepted the base document of the Inter-American Democratic Charter and entrusted the Permanent Council of the Organization with strengthening and expanding the document, in accordance with the OAS Charter, for final adoption at a special session of the General Assembly in Lima, Peru;

Recognizing that all the rights and obligations of member States under the OAS Charter represent the foundation on which democratic principles in the Hemisphere are built; and

Bearing in mind the progressive development of international law and the advisability of clarifying the provisions set forth in the OAS Charter and related basic instruments on the preservation and defense of democratic institutions, according to established practice,

Resolves:

To adopt the following:

INTER-AMERICAN DEMOCRATIC CHARTER

I DEMOCRACY AND THE INTER-AMERICAN SYSTEM

Article 1

The peoples of the Americas have a right to democracy and their governments have an obligation to promote and defend it.

Democracy is essential for the social, political, and economic development of the peoples of the Americas.

Article 2

The effective exercise of representative democracy is the basis for the rule of law and of the constitutional regimes of the member States of the Organization of American States. Representative democracy is strengthened and deepened by permanent, ethical, and responsible participation of the citizenry within a legal framework conforming to the respective constitutional order.

Article 3

Essential elements of representative democracy include, *inter alia*, respect for human rights and fundamental freedoms, access to and the exercise of power in accordance with the rule of law, the holding of periodic, free, and fair elections based on secret balloting and universal suffrage as an expression of the sovereignty of the people, the pluralistic system of political parties and organizations, and the separation of powers and independence of the branches of government.

Article 4

Transparency in government activities, probity, responsible public administration on the part of governments, respect for social rights, and freedom of expression and of the press are essential components of the exercise of democracy.

The constitutional subordination of all state institutions to the legally constituted civilian authority and respect for the rule of law on the part of all institutions and sectors of society are equally essential to democracy.

Article 5

The strengthening of political parties and other political organizations is a priority for democracy. Special attention will be paid to the problems associated with the high cost of election campaigns and the establishment of a balanced and transparent system for their financing.

Article 6

It is the right and responsibility of all citizens to participate in decisions relating to their own development. This is also a necessary condition for the full and effective exercise of democracy. Promoting and fostering diverse forms of participation strengthens democracy.

II DEMOCRACY AND HUMAN RIGHTS

Article 7

Democracy is indispensable for the effective exercise of fundamental freedoms and human rights in their universality, indivisibility and interdependence, embodied in the respective constitutions of States and in inter-American and international human rights instruments.

Article 8

Any person or group of persons who consider that their human rights have been violated may present claims or petitions to the inter-American system for the promotion and protection of human rights in accordance with its established procedures.

Member States reaffirm their intention to strengthen the inter-American system for the protection of human rights for the consolidation of democracy in the Hemisphere.

Article 9

The elimination of all forms of discrimination, especially gender, ethnic and race discrimination, as well as diverse forms of intolerance, the promotion and protection of human rights of indigenous peoples and migrants, and respect for ethnic, cultural and religious diversity in the Americas contribute to strengthening democracy and citizen participation.

Article 10

The promotion and strengthening of democracy requires the full and effective exercise of workers' rights and the application of core labor standards, as recognized in the International Labour Organization (ILO) Declaration on Fundamental Principles and Rights at Work, and its Follow-up, adopted in 1998, as well as other related fundamental ILO conventions. Democracy is strengthened by improving standards in the workplace and enhancing the quality of life for workers in the Hemisphere.

III DEMOCRACY, INTEGRAL DEVELOPMENT, AND COMBATING POVERTY

Article 11

Democracy and social and economic development are interdependent and are mutually reinforcing.

Article 12

Poverty, illiteracy, and low levels of human development are factors that adversely affect the consolidation of democracy. The OAS member States are committed to adopting and implementing all those actions required to generate productive employment, reduce poverty, and eradicate extreme poverty, taking into account the different economic realities and conditions of the countries of the Hemisphere. This shared commitment regarding the problems associated with development and poverty also underscores the importance of maintaining macroeconomic equilibria and the obligation to strengthen social cohesion and democracy.

Article 13

The promotion and observance of economic, social, and cultural rights are inherently linked to integral development, equitable economic growth, and to the consolidation of democracy in the States of the Hemisphere.

Article 14

Member States agree to review periodically the actions adopted and carried out by the Organization to promote dialogue, cooperation for integral development, and the fight against poverty in the Hemisphere, and to take the appropriate measures to further these objectives.

Article 15

The exercise of democracy promotes the preservation and good stewardship of the environment. It is essential that the States of the Hemisphere implement policies and strategies to protect the environment, including application of various treaties and conventions, to achieve sustainable development for the benefit of future generations.

Article 16

Education is key to strengthening democratic institutions, promoting the development of human potential, and alleviating poverty and fostering greater understanding among our peoples. To achieve these ends, it is essential that a quality education be available to all, including girls and women, rural inhabitants, and minorities.

IV STRENGTHENING AND PRESERVATION OF DEMOCRATIC INSTITUTIONS

Article 17

When the government of a member State considers that its democratic political institutional process or its legitimate exercise of power is at risk, it may request assistance from the Secretary General or the Permanent Council for the strengthening and preservation of its democratic system.

Article 18

When situations arise in a member State that may affect the development of its democratic political institutional process or the legitimate exercise of power, the Secretary General or the Permanent Council may, with prior consent of the government concerned, arrange for visits or other actions in order to analyze the situation. The Secretary General will submit a report to the Permanent Council, which will undertake a collective assessment of the situation and, where necessary, may adopt decisions for the preservation of the democratic system and its strengthening.

Article 19

Based on the principles of the Charter of the OAS and subject to its norms, and in accordance with the democracy clause contained in the Declaration of Quebec City, an unconstitutional interruption of the democratic order or an unconstitutional alteration of the constitutional regime that seriously impairs the democratic order in a member State, constitutes, while it persists, an insurmountable obstacle to its government's participation in sessions of the General Assembly, the Meeting of Consultation, the Councils of the Organization, the specialized conferences, the commissions, working groups, and other bodies of the Organization.

Article 20

In the event of an unconstitutional alteration of the constitutional regime that seriously impairs the democratic order in a member State, any member State or the Secretary General may request the immediate convocation of the Permanent Council to undertake a collective assessment of the situation and to take such decisions as it deems appropriate.

The Permanent Council, depending on the situation, may undertake the necessary diplomatic initiatives, including good offices, to foster the restoration of democracy.

If such diplomatic initiatives prove unsuccessful, or if the urgency of the situation so warrants, the Permanent Council shall immediately convene a special session of the General Assembly. The General Assembly will adopt the decisions it deems appropriate, including the undertaking of diplomatic initiatives, in accordance with the Charter of the Organization, international law, and the provisions of this Democratic Charter.

The necessary diplomatic initiatives, including good offices, to foster the restoration of democracy, will continue during the process.

Article 21

When the special session of the General Assembly determines that there has been an unconstitutional interruption of the democratic order of a member State, and that diplomatic initiatives have failed, the special session shall take the decision to suspend said member State from the exercise of its right to participate in the OAS by an affirmative vote of two thirds of the member States in accordance with the Charter of the OAS. The suspension shall take effect immediately.

The suspended member State shall continue to fulfill its obligations to the Organization, in particular its human rights obligations.

Notwithstanding the suspension of the member State, the Organization will maintain diplomatic initiatives to restore democracy in that State.

Article 22

Once the situation that led to suspension has been resolved, any member State or the Secretary General may propose to the General Assembly that suspension be lifted. This decision shall require the vote of two thirds of the member States in accordance with the OAS Charter.

V DEMOCRACY AND ELECTORAL OBSERVATION MISSIONS

Article 23

Member States are responsible for organizing, conducting, and ensuring free and fair electoral processes.

Member States, in the exercise of their sovereignty, may request that the Organization of American States provide advisory services or assistance for strengthening and developing their electoral institutions and processes, including sending preliminary missions for that purpose.

Article 24

The electoral observation missions shall be carried out at the request of the member State concerned. To that end, the government of that State and the Secretary General shall enter into an agreement establishing the scope and coverage of the electoral observation mission in question. The member State shall guarantee conditions of security, free access to information, and full cooperation with the electoral observation mission.

Electoral observation missions shall be carried out in accordance with the principles and norms of the OAS. The Organization shall ensure that these missions are effective and independent and shall provide them with the necessary resources for that purpose. They shall be conducted in an objective, impartial, and transparent manner and with the appropriate technical expertise.

Electoral observation missions shall present a report on their activities in a timely manner to the Permanent Council, through the General Secretariat.

Article 25

The electoral observation missions shall advise the Permanent Council, through the General Secretariat, if the necessary conditions for free and fair elections do not exist.

The Organization may, with the consent of the State concerned, send special missions with a view to creating or improving said conditions.

VI PROMOTION OF A DEMOCRATIC CULTURE

Article 26

The OAS will continue to carry out programs and activities designed to promote democratic principles and practices and strengthen a democratic culture in the Hemisphere, bearing in mind that democracy is a way of life based on liberty and enhancement of economic, social, and cultural conditions for the peoples of the Americas. The OAS will consult and cooperate on an ongoing basis with member States and take into account the contributions of civil society organizations working in those fields.

Article 27

The objectives of the programs and activities will be to promote good governance, sound administration, democratic values, and the strengthening of political institutions and civil society organizations. Special attention shall be given to the development of programs and activities for the education of children and youth as a means of ensuring the continuance of democratic values, including liberty and social justice.

Article 28

States shall promote the full and equal participation of women in the political structures of their countries as a fundamental element in the promotion and exercise of a democratic culture.

PART SEVEN

AFRICA

INTRODUCTION

In a general way, African States have taken, or reacted to, initiatives involving human rights within the framework of the United Nations. The principle of racial equality and the principle of self-determination have been primary but not exclusive concerns. See the material from the first and second Conferences of Independent African States in 1958 and 1960, and the resolutions of the First Assembly of the Heads of State and Government of the Organization of African Unity, 1964, reproduced in the third edition of this work, at 540–50. The Charter of the Organization of African Unity was adopted by a conference of Heads of State and Government in Addis Ababa on 25 May 1963 and the First Assembly of the OAU met in Cairo in July 1964. For the text of the Charter, see BROWNLIE, I., *Basic Documents in International Law*, Oxford: Oxford University Press, 5th edn., 2002, 56.

Within the Organization of African Unity (OAU), the principal objectives were to bring to an end what remained of colonialism and apartheid, to promote unity and solidarity, and to coordinate development. The trend of policy also was to resist forms of intervention by the Organization and the principle of non-intervention was maintained in the face of the notoriously disastrous situations in the Sudan, Equatorial Guinea, Uganda, the Great Lakes region, and elsewhere. Latterly, attention focused more on internal humanitarian crises, including questions of intervention and human rights, in which sub-regional organizations, such as ECOWAS and IGAD, played an increasing role.

Some thirty-six years later, the OAU was succeeded by the African Union. Article 3 of the Constitutive Act of the African Union, signed in Lomé, Togo, on 1 July 2000, establishes the organization's objectives, which include the promotion of popular participation and good governance, while Article 4 affirms the principles underlying the Union, including non-interference in internal affairs and respect for democratic principles, human rights, the rule of law and good governance. The text of the Constitutive Act can be found in BROWNLIE, I., *Basic Documents in International Law*, Oxford: Oxford University Press, 6th edn., 2009, 53.

Among several noteworthy developments can be counted the adoption in 2002 by the Assembly of Heads of State and Government of the AU 'Declaration on the Principles Governing Democratic Elections in Africa': Thirty-Eighth Ordinary Session of the Organization of African Unity, 8 July 2002, Durban, South Africa, AHG/Decisions 171–184 (XXXVIII), AHG/Decl. 1–2 (XXXVIII), Decisions and Declarations. Debate on a Draft Declaration on Elections, Democracy and Governance in Africa began in 2003 and then moved into discussion of a Charter on Democracy, Elections and Governance, which was adopted in 2007 (below, p. 1081). It differs from the Inter-American model, (above, p. 1008), particularly in the priority given to the strengthening of democratic institutions and culture.

Further reading

AKINYEMI, A. B., 'The Organization of African Unity and the Concept of Non-Interference in Internal Affairs', (1972–73) 46 *BYIL* 393.

ELIAS, T., *Africa and the Development of International Law*, Dordrecht: Martinus Nijhoff, 1972; 2nd edn., revised and edited by R. AKINJIDE, 1988.

MURRAY, R., *Human Rights in Africa: From the OAU to the African Union*, Cambridge: Cambridge University Press, 2004.

VILJOEN, F., *International Human Rights Law in Africa*, Oxford: Oxford University Press, 2007.

117. ORGANIZATION OF AFRICAN UNITY CONVENTION ON THE SPECIFIC ASPECTS OF REFUGEE PROBLEMS IN AFRICA, 1969

This Convention was adopted by the Heads of State and Government at the Sixth Ordinary Session of the Organization of African Unity, Addis Ababa, 10 September 1969, and entered into force on 20 June 1974, in accordance with Article XI; for text, see 1000 *UNTS* 46. It is the regional counterpart of the 1951 Convention relating to the Status of Refugees (above, p. 312).

Further reading

EDWARDS, A., 'Refugee Status Determination in Africa', (2006) 14 *Africa Journal of International and Comparative Law*, 204.

OKOTH-OBBO, G., 'Thirty Years On: A Legal Review of the 1969 OAU Convention Governing the Specific Aspects of Refugee Problems in Africa', (2001) 20 *Refugee Survey Quarterly* 79.

OLOKA-ONYANGO, J., 'Human Rights, the OAU Convention and the Refugee Crisis in Africa', (1991) 3 *IJRL* 453.

TEXT

Preamble

We, the Heads of State and Government assembled in the city of Addis Ababa, from 6–10 September 1969,

1. *Noting with concern* the constantly increasing numbers of refugees in Africa and desirous of finding ways and means of alleviating their misery and suffering as well as providing them with a better life and future,

2. *Recognizing* the need for an essentially humanitarian approach towards solving the problems of refugees,

3. *Aware*, however, that refugee problems are a source of friction among many Member States, and desirous of eliminating the source of such discord,

4. *Anxious* to make a distinction between a refugee who seeks a peaceful and normal life and a person fleeing his country for the sole purpose of fomenting subversion from outside,

5. *Determined* that the activities of such subversive elements should be discouraged, in accordance with the Declaration on the Problem of Subversion and Resolution on the Problem of Refugees adopted at Accra in 1965,

6. *Bearing in mind* that the Charter of the United Nations and the Universal Declaration of Human Rights have affirmed the principle that human beings shall enjoy fundamental rights and freedoms without discrimination,

7. *Recalling* Resolution 2312 (XXII) of 14 December 1967 of the United Nations General Assembly, relating to the Declaration on Territorial Asylum,

8. *Convinced* that all the problems of our continent must be solved in the spirit of the Charter of the Organization of African Unity and in the African context,

9. *Recognizing* that the United Nations Convention of 28 July 1951, as modified by the Protocol of 31 January 1967, constitutes the basic and universal instrument relating to the status of refugees and reflects the deep concern of States for refugees and their desire to establish common standards for their treatment,

10. *Recalling* Resolutions 26 and 104 of the OAU Assemblies of Heads of State and Government, calling upon Member States of the Organization who had not already done so to accede to the United Nations Convention of 1951 and to the Protocol of 1967 relating to the Status of Refugees, and meanwhile to apply their provisions to refugees in Africa,

11. *Convinced* that the efficiency of the measures recommended by the present Convention to solve the problem of refugees in Africa necessitates close and continuous collaboration between the Organization of African Unity and the Office of the United Nations High Commissioner for Refugees,

   Have agreed as follows:

Article I—Definition of the term 'Refugee'

1. For the purposes of this Convention, the term 'refugee' shall mean every person who, owing to well-founded fear of being persecuted for reasons of race, religion, nationality, membership of a particular social group or political opinion, is outside the country of his nationality and is unable or, owing to such fear, is unwilling to avail himself of the protection of that country, or who, not having a nationality and being outside the country of his former habitual residence as a result of such events is unable or, owing to such fear, is unwilling to return to it.

2. The term 'refugee' shall also apply to every person who, owing to external aggression, occupation, foreign domination or events seriously disturbing public order in either part or the whole of his country of origin or nationality, is compelled to leave his place of habitual residence in order to seek refuge in another place outside his country of origin or nationality.

3. In the case of a person who has several nationalities, the term 'a country of which he is a national' shall mean each of the countries of which he is a national, and a person shall not be deemed to be lacking the protection of the country of which he is a national if, without any valid reason based on well-founded fear, he has not availed himself of the protection of one of the countries of which he is a national.

4. This Convention shall cease to apply to any refugee if:

   (a) he has voluntarily re-availed himself of the protection of the country of his nationality, or,

   (b) having lost his nationality, he has voluntarily reacquired it, or,

   (c) he has acquired a new nationality, and enjoys the protection of the country of his new nationality, or,

   (d) he has voluntarily re-established himself in the country which he left or outside which he remained owing to fear of persecution, or,

   (e) he can no longer, because the circumstances in connection with which he was recognized as a refugee have ceased to exist, continue to refuse to avail himself of the protection of the country of his nationality, or,

   (f) he has committed a serious non-political crime outside his country of refuge after his admission to that country as a refugee, or,

(g) he has seriously infringed the purposes and objectives of this Convention.

5. The provisions of this Convention shall not apply to any person with respect to whom the country of asylum has serious reasons for considering that:

(a) he has committed a crime against peace, a war crime, or a crime against humanity, as defined in the international instruments drawn up to make provision in respect of such crimes;

(b) he committed a serious non-political crime outside the country of refuge prior to his admission to that country as a refugee;

(c) he has been guilty of acts contrary to the purposes and principles of the Organization of African Unity;

(d) he has been guilty of acts contrary to the purposes and principles of the United Nations.

6. For the purposes of this Convention, the Contracting State of asylum shall determine whether an applicant is a refugee.

Article II—Asylum

1. Member States of the OAU shall use their best endeavours consistent with their respective legislations to receive refugees and to secure the settlement of those refugees who, for well-founded reasons, are unable or unwilling to return to their country of origin or nationality.

2. The grant of asylum to refugees is a peaceful and humanitarian act and shall not be regarded as an unfriendly act by any Member State.

3. No person shall be subjected by a Member State to measures such as rejection at the frontier, return or expulsion, which would compel him to return to or remain in a territory where his life, physical integrity or liberty would be threatened for the reasons set out in Article I, paragraphs 1 and 2.

4. Where a Member State finds difficulty in continuing to grant asylum to refugees, such Member State may appeal directly to other Member States and through the OAU, and such other Member States shall in the spirit of African solidarity and international co-operation take appropriate measures to lighten the burden of the Member State granting asylum.

5. Where a refugee has not received the right to reside in any country of asylum, he may be granted temporary residence in any country of asylum in which he first presented himself as a refugee pending arrangement for his resettlement in accordance with the preceding paragraph.

6. For reasons of security, countries of asylum shall, as far as possible, settle refugees at a reasonable distance from the frontier of their country of origin.

Article III—Prohibition of Subversive Activities

1. Every refugee has duties to the country in which he finds himself, which require in particular that he conforms with its laws and regulations as well as with measures taken for the maintenance of public order. He shall also abstain from any subversive activities against any Member State of the OAU.

2. Signatory States undertake to prohibit refugees residing in their respective territories from attacking any State Member of the OAU, by any activity likely to cause tension between Member States, and in particular by use of arms, through the press, or by radio.

Article IV—Non-Discrimination

Member States undertake to apply the provisions of this Convention to all refugees without discrimination as to race, religion, nationality, membership of a particular social group or political opinions.

Article V—Voluntary Repatriation

1. The essentially voluntary character of repatriation shall be respected in all cases and no refugee shall be repatriated against his will.

2. The country of asylum, in collaboration with the country of origin, shall make adequate arrangements for the safe return of refugees who request repatriation.

3. The country of origin, on receiving back refugees, shall facilitate their resettlement and grant them the full rights and privileges of nationals of the country, and subject them to the same obligations.

4. Refugees who voluntarily return to their country shall in no way be penalized for having left it for any of the reasons giving rise to refugee situations. Whenever necessary, an appeal shall be made through national information media and through the Administrative Secretary-General of the OAU, inviting refugees to return home and giving assurance that the new circumstances prevailing in their country of origin will enable them to return without risk and to take up a normal and peaceful life without fear of being disturbed or punished, and that the text of such appeal should be given to refugees and clearly explained to them by their country of asylum.

5. Refugees who freely decide to return to their homeland, as a result of such assurances or on their own initiative, shall be given every possible assistance by the country of asylum, the country of origin, voluntary agencies and international and intergovernmental organizations, to facilitate their return.

Article VI—Travel Documents

1. Subject to Article III, Member States shall issue to refugees lawfully staying in their territories travel documents in accordance with the United Nations Convention relating to the Status of Refugees and the Schedule and Annex thereto, for the purpose of travel outside their territory, unless compelling reasons of national security or public order otherwise require. Member States may issue such a travel document to any other refugee in their territory.

2. Where an African country of second asylum accepts a refugee from a country of first asylum, the country of first asylum may be dispensed from issuing a document with a return clause.

3. Travel documents issued to refugees under previous international agreements by States Parties thereto shall be recognized and treated by Member States in the same way as if they had been issued to refugees pursuant to this Article.

Article VII—Co-operation of the National Authorities with the Organization of African Unity

In order to enable the Administrative Secretary-General of the Organization of African Unity to make reports to the competent organs of the Organization of African Unity, Member States undertake to provide the Secretariat in the appropriate form with information and statistical data requested concerning:

  (a) the condition of refugees;

(b) the implementation of this Convention, and

(c) laws, regulations and decrees which are, or may hereafter be, in force relating to refugees.

Article VIII—Co-operation with the Office of the United Nations High Commissioner for Refugees

1. Member States shall co-operate with the Office of the United Nations High Commissioner for Refugees.

2. The present Convention shall be the effective regional complement in Africa of the 1951 United Nations Convention on the Status of Refugees.

Article IX—Settlement of Disputes

Any dispute between States signatories to this Convention relating to its interpretation or application, which cannot be settled by other means, shall be referred to the Commission for Mediation, Conciliation and Arbitration of the Organization of African Unity, at the request of any one of the Parties to the dispute.

Article X—Signature and Ratification

1. This Convention is open for signature and accession by all Member States of the Organization of African Unity and shall be ratified by signatory States in accordance with their respective constitutional processes. The instruments of ratification shall be deposited with the Administrative Secretary-General of the Organization of African Unity.

2. The original instrument, done if possible in African languages, and in English and French, all texts being equally authentic, shall be deposited with the Administrative Secretary-General of the Organization of African Unity.

3. Any independent African State, Member of the Organization of African Unity, may at any time notify the Administrative Secretary-General of the Organization of African Unity of its accession to this Convention.

Article XI—Entry into force

This Convention shall come into force upon deposit of instruments of ratification by one-third of the Member States of the Organization of African Unity.

Article XII—Amendment

This Convention may be amended or revised if any Member State makes a written request to the Administrative Secretary-General to that effect, provided however that the proposed amendment shall not be submitted to the Assembly of Heads of State and Government for consideration until all Member States have been duly notified of it and a period of one year has elapsed. Such an amendment shall not be effective unless approved by at least two-thirds of the Member States Parties to the present Convention.

Article XIII—Denunciation

1. Any Member State Party to this Convention may denounce its provisions by a written notification to the Administrative Secretary-General.

2. At the end of one year from the date of such notification, if not withdrawn, the Convention shall cease to apply with respect to the denouncing State.

Article XIV

Upon entry into force of this Convention, the Administrative Secretary-General of the OAU shall register it with the Secretary-General of the United Nations, in accordance with Article 102 of the Charter of the United Nations.

Article XV—Notifications by the Administrative Secretary-General of the Organization of African Unity

The Administrative Secretary-General of the Organization of African Unity shall inform all Members of the Organization:

(a) of signatures, ratifications and accessions in accordance with Article X;

(b) of entry into force, in accordance with Article XI;

(c) of requests for amendments submitted under the terms of Article XII;

(d) of denunciations, in accordance with Article XIII.

In witness whereof we, the Heads of African State and Government, have signed this Convention.

Done in the City of Addis Ababa this 10th day of September 1969.

118. AFRICAN CHARTER ON HUMAN AND PEOPLES' RIGHTS, 1981

The Charter (the 'Banjul Charter') was adopted on 17 June 1981 by the Eighteenth Assembly of the Heads of State and Government of the Organization of African Unity. The treaty entered into force on 21 October 1986. For text, see OAU doc. CAB/LEG/67/3 rev. 5, 21 *ILM* 58 (1982); **http://www.africa-union.org/root/au/Documents/Treaties/treaties.htm**.

See also the African Commission on Human and Peoples' Rights: **http://www.achpr.org/**.

Further reading

ANKUMAH, E. A., *The African Commission on Human and Peoples' Rights: Practice and Procedures*, The Hague: Kluwer Law International, 1996.

BELLO, E. G., 'The African Charter of Human and Peoples' Rights: A Legal Analysis' 194 *Recueil des Cours* (1985–V) 13.

D'SA, R. M., 'The African Charter of Human and Peoples' Rights: Problems And Prospects for Regional Action', (1987) 10 *Australian Yearbook of International Law* 101.

EVANS, M. and MURRAY, R., eds., *The African Charter on Human and Peoples' Rights: The System in Practice, 1986–2000*, Cambridge: Cambridge University Press, 2nd edn., 2008.

FIERENS, J., 'La Charte africaine des droits de l'homme et des peuples', *Revue trimestrielle de droits de l'homme*, 1990, 235.

MBAZIRA, C., 'Enforcing the Economic, Social and Cultural Rights in the African Charter on Human and People's Rights: Twenty Years of Redundancy, Progression and Significant Strides', (2006) 6 *African Human Rights Law Journal* 333.

MURRAY, R., 'Recent Developments in the African Human Rights System 2007', (2008) 8 *Human Rights Law Review* 356.

—— and EVANS, M. D., eds., *Documents of the African Commission on Human and Peoples' Rights*, Oxford: Hart Publishing, 2002; *Documents of the African Commission on Human and Peoples' Rights, Volume II: 1999–2007*, Oxford: Hart Publishing, 2008.

—— and WHEATLEY, S., 'Groups and the African Charter on Human and Peoples' Rights', (2003) 25 *Human Rights Quarterly* 213.

OKAFOR, O. C., 'The African System on Human and Peoples' Rights, quasi-constructivism, and the possibility of peacebuilding within African States', (2004) 8 *International Journal of Human Rights*, 413.

OUGUERGOUZ, F., *The African Charter of Human and Peoples' Rights: A Comprehensive Agenda for Human Dignity and Sustainable Democracy in Africa*, The Hague: Kluwer Law International, 2003.

UMOZURIKE, U. O., *The African Charter of Human and Peoples' Rights*, The Hague: Martinus Nijhoff, 1997.

TEXT

Preamble

The African States members of the Organization of African Unity, parties to the present convention entitled 'African Charter on Human and Peoples' Rights',

Recalling Decision 115 (XVI) of the Assembly of Heads of State and Government at its Sixteenth Ordinary Session held in Monrovia, Liberia, from 17 to 20 July 1979 on the preparation of 'a preliminary draft on an African Charter on Human and Peoples'

Rights providing *inter alia* for the establishment of bodies to promote and protect human and peoples' rights';

Considering the Charter of the Organization of African Unity, which stipulates that 'freedom, equality, justice and dignity are legitimate aspirations of the African peoples';

Reaffirming the pledge they solemnly made in Article 2 of the said Charter to eradicate all forms of colonialism from Africa, to coordinate and intensify their cooperation and efforts to achieve a better life for the peoples' of Africa and to promote international cooperation having due regard to the Charter of the United Nations and the Universal Declaration of Human Rights;

Taking into consideration the virtues of their historical tradition and the values of African civilization which should inspire and characterize their reflection on the concept of human and peoples rights;

Recognizing on the one hand, that fundamental human rights stem from the attributes of human beings, which justifies their international protection and on the other hand that the reality and respect of peoples rights should necessarily guarantee human rights;

Considering that the enjoyment of rights and freedoms also implies the performance of duties on the part of everyone;

Convinced that it is henceforth essential to pay a particular attention to the right to development and that civil and political rights cannot be dissociated from economic, social and cultural rights in their conception as well as universality and that the satisfaction of economic, social and cultural rights is a guarantee for the enjoyment of civil and political rights;

Conscious of their duty to achieve the total liberation of Africa, the peoples of which are still struggling for their dignity and genuine independence, and undertaking to eliminate colonialism, neo-colonialism, apartheid, zionism and to dismantle aggressive foreign military bases and all forms of discrimination, language, religion or political opinions;

Reaffirming their adherence to the principles of human and peoples' rights and freedoms contained in the declarations, conventions and other instruments adopted by the Organization of African Unity, the Movement of Non-Aligned Countries and the United Nations;

Firmly convinced of their duty to promote and protect human and peoples' rights and freedoms taking into account the importance traditionally attached to these rights and freedoms in Africa;

Have agreed as follows:

PART I

RIGHTS AND DUTIES

Chapter I—Human and Peoples' Rights

Article 1

The Member States of the Organization of African Unity parties to the present Charter shall recognize the rights, duties and freedoms enshrined in this Charter and shall undertake to adopt legislative or other measures to give effect to them.

Article 2

Every individual shall be entitled to the enjoyment of the rights and freedoms recognized and guaranteed in the present Charter without distinction of any kind such as race, ethnic group, colour, sex, language, religion, political or any other opinion, national and social origin, fortune, birth or other status.

Article 3

1. Every individual shall be equal before the law.
2. Every individual shall be entitled to equal protection of the law.

Article 4

Human beings are inviolable. Every human being shall be entitled to respect for his life and the integrity of his person. No one may be arbitrarily deprived of this right.

Article 5

Every individual shall have the right to the respect of the dignity inherent in a human being and to the recognition of his legal status. All forms of exploitation and degradation of man particularly slavery, slave trade, torture, cruel, inhuman or degrading punishment and treatment shall be prohibited.

Article 6

Every individual shall have the right to liberty and to the security of his person. No one may be deprived of his freedom except for reasons and conditions previously laid down by law. In particular, no one may be arbitrarily arrested or detained.

Article 7

1. Every individual shall have the right to have his cause heard. This comprises:

   (a) The right to an appeal to competent national organs against acts of violating his fundamental rights as recognized and guaranteed by conventions, laws, regulations and customs in force;

   (b) the right to be presumed innocent until proved guilty by a competent court or tribunal;

   (c) the right to defence, including the right to be defended by counsel of his choice;

   (d) the right to be tried within a reasonable time by an impartial court or tribunal.

2. No one may be condemned for an act or omission which did not constitute a legally punishable offence at the time it was committed. No penalty may be inflicted for an offence for which no provision was made at the time it was committed. Punishment is personal and can be imposed only on the offender.

Article 8

Freedom of conscience, the profession and free practice of religion shall be guaranteed. No one may, subject to law and order, be submitted to measures restricting the exercise of these freedoms.

Article 9

1. Every individual shall have the right to receive information.

2. Every individual shall have the right to express and disseminate his opinions within the law.

Article 10

1. Every individual shall have the right to free association provided that he abides by the law.

2. Subject to the obligation of solidarity provided for in Article 29 no one may be compelled to join an association.

Article 11

Every individual shall have the right to assemble freely with others. The exercise of this right shall be subject only to necessary restrictions provided for by law in particular those enacted in the interest of national security, the safety, health, ethics and rights and freedoms of others.

Article 12

1. Every individual shall have the right to freedom of movement and residence within the borders of a State provided he abides by the law.

2. Every individual shall have the right to leave any country including his own, and to return to his country. This right may only be subject to restrictions, provided for by law for the protection of national security, law and order, public health or morality.

3. Every individual shall have the right, when persecuted, to seek and obtain asylum in other countries in accordance with the law of those countries and international conventions.

4. A non-national legally admitted in a territory of a State Party to the present Charter, may only be expelled from it by virtue of a decision taken in accordance with the law.

5. The mass expulsion of non-nationals shall be prohibited. Mass expulsion shall be that which is aimed at national, racial, ethnic or religious groups.

Article 13

1. Every citizen shall have the right to participate freely in the government of his country, either directly or through freely chosen representatives in accordance with the provisions of the law.

2. Every citizen shall have the right of equal access to the public service of his country.

3. Every individual shall have the right of access to public property and services in strict equality of all persons before the law.

Article 14

The right to property shall be guaranteed. It may only be encroached upon in the interest of public need or in the general interest of the community and in accordance with the provisions of appropriate laws.

Article 15

Every individual shall have the right to work under equitable and satisfactory conditions, and shall receive equal pay for equal work.

Article 16

1. Every individual shall have the right to enjoy the best attainable state of physical and mental health.

2. States Parties to the present Charter shall take the necessary measures to protect the health of their people and to ensure that they receive medical attention when they are sick.

Article 17

1. Every individual shall have the right to education.

2. Every individual may freely, take part in the cultural life of his community.

3. The promotion and protection of morals and traditional values recognized by the community shall be the duty of the State.

Article 18

1. The family shall be the natural unit and basis of society. It shall be protected by the State which shall take care of its physical health and moral.

2. The State shall have the duty to assist the family which is the custodian of morals and traditional values recognized by the community.

3. The State shall ensure the elimination of every discrimination against women and also ensure the protection of the rights of the woman and the child as stipulated in international declarations and conventions.

4. The aged and the disabled shall also have the right to special measures of protection in keeping with their physical or moral needs.

Article 19

All peoples shall be equal; they shall enjoy the same respect and shall have the same rights. Nothing shall justify the domination of a people by another.

Article 20

1. All peoples shall have right to existence. They shall have the unquestionable and inalienable right to self-determination. They shall freely determine their political status and shall pursue their economic and social development according to the policy they have freely chosen.

2. Colonized or oppressed peoples shall have the right to free themselves from the bonds of domination by resorting to any means recognized by the international community.

3. All peoples shall have the right to the assistance of the States Parties to the present Charter in their liberation struggle against foreign domination, be it political, economic or cultural.

Article 21

1. All peoples shall freely dispose of their wealth and natural resources. This right shall be exercised in the exclusive interest of the people. In no case shall a people be deprived of it.

2. In case of spoliation the dispossessed people shall have the right to the lawful recovery of its property as well as to an adequate compensation.

3. The free disposal of wealth and natural resources shall be exercised without prejudice to the obligation of promoting international economic cooperation based on mutual respect, equitable exchange and the principles of international law.

4. States parties to the present Charter shall individually and collectively exercise the right to free disposal of their wealth and natural resources with a view to strengthening African unity and solidarity.

5. States Parties to the present Charter shall undertake to eliminate all forms of foreign economic exploitation particularly that practised by international monopolies so as to enable their peoples to fully benefit from the advantages derived from their national resources.

Article 22

1. All peoples shall have the right to their economic, social and cultural development with due regard to their freedom and identity and in the equal enjoyment of the common heritage of mankind.

2. States shall have the duty, individually or collectively to ensure the exercise of the right to development.

Article 23

1. All peoples shall have the right to national and international peace and security. The principles of solidarity and friendly relations implicitly affirmed by the Charter of the United Nations and reaffirmed by that of the Organization of African Unity shall govern relations between States.

2. For the purpose of strengthening peace, solidarity and friendly relations, States parties to the present Charter shall ensure that:

   (a) any individual enjoying the right of asylum under Article 12 of the present Charter shall not engage in subversive activities against his country of origin or any other State party to the present Charter;

   (b) their territories shall not be used as bases for subversive or terrorist activities against the people of any other State party to the present Charter.

Article 24

All peoples shall have the right to a general satisfactory environment favourable to their development.

Article 25

States parties to the present Charter shall have the duty to promote and ensure through teaching, education and publication, the respect of the rights and freedoms contained in the present Charter and to see to it that these freedoms and rights as well as corresponding obligations and duties are understood.

Article 26

States parties to the present Charter shall have the duty to guarantee the independence of the Courts and shall allow the establishment and improvement of appropriate national institutions entrusted with the promotion and protection of the rights and freedoms guaranteed by the present Charter.

Chapter II—Duties

Article 27

1. Every individual shall have duties towards his family and society, the State and other legally recognised communities and the international community.

2. The rights and freedoms of each individual shall be exercised with due regard to the rights of others, collective security, morality and common interest.

Article 28

Every individual shall have the duty to respect and consider his fellow beings without discrimination, and to maintain relations aimed at promoting, safeguarding and reinforcing mutual respect and tolerance.

Article 29

The individual shall also have the duty:

1. To preserve the harmonious development of the family and to work for the cohesion and respect of the family; to respect, his parents at all times, to maintain them in case of need;

2. To serve his national community by placing his physical and intellectual abilities at its service;

3. Not to compromise the security of the State whose national or resident he is;

4. To preserve and strengthen social and national solidarity, particularly when the latter is threatened;

5. To preserve and strengthen the national independence and the territorial integrity of his country and to contribute to its defence in accordance with the law;

6. To work to the best of his abilities and competence, and to pay taxes imposed by law in the interest of the society;

7. To preserve and strengthen positive African cultural values in his relations with other members of the society, in the spirit of tolerance, dialogue and consultation and, in general, to contribute to the promotion of the moral well being of society;

8. To contribute to the best of his abilities, at all times and at all levels, to the promotion and achievement of African unity.

PART II

MEASURES OF SAFEGUARD

Chapter I—Establishment and Organization of the African Commission on Human and Peoples' Rights

Article 30

An African Commission on Human and Peoples' Rights, hereinafter called 'the Commission', shall be established within the Organization of African Unity to promote human and peoples' rights and ensure their protection in Africa.

Article 31

1. The Commission shall consist of eleven members chosen from amongst African personalities of the highest reputation, known for their high morality, integrity, impartiality and competence in matters of human and peoples' rights; particular consideration being given to persons having legal experience.

2. The members of the Commission shall serve in their personal capacity.

Article 32

The Commission shall not include more than one national of the same State.

Article 33

The members of the Commission shall be elected by secret ballot by the Assembly of Heads of State and Government, from a list of persons nominated by the States parties to the present Charter.

Article 34

Each State party to the present Charter may not nominate more than two candidates. The candidates must have the nationality of one of the States parties to the present Charter. When two candidates are nominated by a State, one of them may not be a national of that State.

Article 35

1. The Secretary-General of the Organization of African Unity shall invite States parties to the present Charter at least four months before the elections to nominate candidates;

2. The Secretary-General of the Organization of African Unity shall make an alphabetical list of the persons thus nominated and communicate it to the Heads of State and Government at least one month before the elections.

Article 36

The members of the Commission shall be elected for a six year period and shall be eligible for re-election. However, the term of office of four of the members elected at the first election shall terminate after two years and the term of office of three others, at the end of four years.

Article 37

Immediately after the first election, the Chairman of the Assembly of Heads of State and Government of the Organization of African Unity shall draw lots to decide the names of those members referred to in Article 36.

Article 38

After their election, the members of the Commission shall make a solemn declaration to discharge their duties impartially and faithfully.

Article 39

1. In case of death or resignation of a member of the Commission the Chairman of the Commission shall immediately inform the Secretary-General of the Organization of African Unity, who shall declare the seat vacant from the date of death or from the date on which the resignation takes effect.

2. If, in the unanimous opinion of other members of the Commission, a member has stopped discharging his duties for any reason other than a temporary absence, the Chairman of the Commission shall inform the Secretary-General of the Organization of African Unity, who shall then declare the seat vacant.

3. In each of the cases anticipated above, the Assembly of Heads of State and Government shall replace the member whose seat became vacant for the remaining period of his term unless the period is less than six months.

Article 40

Every member of the Commission shall be in office until the date his successor assumes office.

Article 41

The Secretary-General of the Organization of African Unity shall appoint the Secretary of the Commission. He shall provide the staff and services necessary for the effective discharge of the duties of the Commission. The Organization of African Unity shall bear cost of the staff and services.

Article 42

1. The Commission shall elect its Chairman and Vice Chairman for a two-year period. They shall be eligible for re-election.

2. The Commission shall lay down its rules of procedure.

3. Seven members shall form the quorum.

4. In case of an equality of votes, the Chairman shall have a casting vote.

5. The Secretary-General may attend the meetings of the Commission. He shall neither participate in deliberations nor shall he be entitled to vote. The Chairman of the Commission may, however, invite him to speak.

Article 43

In discharging their duties, members of the Commission shall enjoy diplomatic privileges and immunities provided for in the General Convention on the Privileges and immunities of the Organization of African Unity.

Article 44

Provision shall be made for the emoluments and allowances of the members of the Commission in the Regular Budget of the Organization of African Unity.

Chapter II—Mandate of the Commission

Article 45

The functions of the Commission shall be:

1. To promote Human and Peoples' Rights and in particular:
    (a) to collect documents, undertake studies and researches on African problems in the field of human and peoples' rights, organize seminars, symposia and conferences, disseminate information, encourage national and local institutions concerned with human and peoples' rights, and should the case arise, give its views or make recommendations to Governments.
    (b) to formulate and lay down, principles and rules aimed at solving legal problems relating to human and peoples' rights and fundamental freedoms upon which African Governments may base their legislation.
    (c) co-operate with other African and international institutions concerned with the promotion and protection of human and peoples' rights.

2. Ensure the protection of human and peoples' rights under conditions laid down by the present Charter.

3. Interpret all the provisions of the present Charter at the request of a State party, an institution of the OAU or an African Organization recognized by the OAU.

4. Perform any other tasks which may be entrusted to it by the Assembly of Heads of State and Government.

Chapter III—Procedure of the Commission

Article 46

The Commission may resort to any appropriate method of investigation; it may hear from the Secretary-General of the Organization of African Unity or any other person capable of enlightening it.

Article 47

If a State party to the present Charter has good reasons to believe that another State Party to this Charter has violated the provisions of the Charter, it may draw, by written communication, the attention of that State to the matter. This communication shall also be addressed to the Secretary-General of the OAU and to the Chairman of the Commission. Within three months of the receipt of the communication, the State to which the communication is addressed shall give the enquiring State, written explanation or statement elucidating the matter. This should include as much as possible relevant information relating to the laws and rules of procedure applied and applicable and the redress already given or course of action available.

Article 48

If within three months from the date on which the original communication is received by the State to which it is addressed, the issue is not settled to the satisfaction of the two States involved through bilateral negotiation or by any other peaceful procedure, either State shall have the right to submit the matter to the Commission through the Chairman and shall notify the other States involved.

Article 49

Notwithstanding the provisions of Article 47, if a State party to the present Charter considers that another State party has violated the provisions of the Charter, it may refer the matter directly to the Commission by addressing a communication to the Chairman, to the Secretary-General of the Organization of African Unity and the State concerned.

Article 50

The Commission can only deal with a matter submitted to it after making sure that all local remedies, if they exist, have been exhausted, unless it is obvious to the Commission that the procedure of achieving these remedies would be unduly prolonged.

Article 51

1. The Commission may ask the States concerned to provide it with all relevant information.

2. When the Commission is considering the matter, States concerned may be represented before it and submit written or oral representation.

Article 52

After having obtained from the States concerned and from other sources all the information it deems necessary and after having tried all appropriate means to reach an amicable solution based on the respect of Human and Peoples' Rights, the Commission shall prepare, within a reasonable period of time from the notification referred to in Article 48, a report to the States concerned and communicated to the Assembly of Heads of State and Government.

Article 53

While transmitting its report, the Commission may make to the Assembly of Heads of State and Government such recommendations as it deems useful.

Article 54

The Commission shall submit to each ordinary Session of the Assembly of Heads of State and Government a report on its activities.

Article 55

1. Before each Session, the Secretary of the Commission shall make a list of the Communications other than those of States parties to the present Charter and transmit them to the Members of the Commission, who shall indicate which communications should be considered by the commission.

2. A communication shall be considered by the Commission if a simple majority of its members so decide.

Article 56

Communication relating to human and peoples' rights referred to in Article 55 received by the commission, shall be considered if they:

1. Indicate their authors even if the latter request anonymity,

2. Are compatible with the Charter of the Organization of African Unity or with the present Charter,

3. Are not written in disparaging or insulting language directed against the State concerned and its institutions or to the Organization of African Unity,

4. Are not based exclusively on news disseminated through the mass media,

5. Are sent after exhausting local remedies, if any, unless it is obvious that this procedure is unduly prolonged,

6. Are submitted within a reasonable period from the time local remedies are exhausted or from the date the Commission is seized with the matter, and

7. Do not deal with cases which have been settled by these States involved in accordance with the principles of the Charter of the United Nations, or the Charter of the Organization of African Unity or the provisions of the present Charter.

Article 57

Prior to any substantive consideration, all communications shall be brought to the knowledge of the State concerned by the Chairman of the Commission.

Article 58

1. When it appears after deliberations of the Commission that one or more communications apparently relate to special cases which reveal the existence of a series

of serious or massive violations of human and peoples' rights, the Commission shall draw the attention of the Assembly of Heads of State and Government to these special cases.

2. The Assembly of Heads of State and Government may then request the Commission to undertake an in-depth study of these cases and make a factual report, accompanied by its finding and recommendations.

3. A case of emergency duly noticed by the Commission shall be submitted by the latter to the Chairman of the Assembly of Heads of State and Government who may request an in-depth study.

Article 59

1. All measures taken within the provisions of the present Chapter shall remain confidential until such a time as the Assembly of Heads of State and Government shall otherwise decide.

2. However, the report shall be published by the Chairman of the Commission upon the decision of the Assembly of Heads of State and Government.

3. The report on the activities of the Commission shall be published by its Chairman after it has been considered by the Assembly of Heads of State and Government.

Chapter IV—Applicable Principles

Article 60

The Commission shall draw inspiration from international law on human and peoples' rights, particularly from the provisions of various African instruments on human and peoples' rights, the Charter of the United Nations, the Charter of the Organization of African Unity, the Universal Declaration of Human Rights, other instruments adopted by the United Nations and by African countries in the field of human and peoples' rights as well as from the provisions of various instruments adopted within the Specialized Agencies of the United Nations of which the parties to the present Charter are members.

Article 61

The Commission shall also take into consideration, as subsidiary measures to determine the principles of law, other general or special international conventions, laying down rules expressly recognized by member States of the Organization of African Unity, African practices consistent with international norms on human and peoples' rights, customs generally accepted as law, general principles of law recognized by African States as well as legal precedents and doctrine.

Article 62

Each State party shall undertake to submit every two years, from the date the present Charter comes into force, a report on the legislative or other measures taken with a view to giving effect to the rights and freedoms recognized and guaranteed by the present Charter.

Article 63

1. The present Charter shall be open to signature, ratification or adherence of the member States of the Organization of African Unity.

2. The instruments of ratification or adherence to the present Charter shall be deposited with the Secretary-General of the Organization of African Unity.

3. The present Charter shall come into force three months after the reception by the Secretary-General of the instruments of ratification or adherence of a simple majority of the member States of the Organization of African Unity.

PART III

GENERAL PROVISIONS

Article 64

1. After the coming into force of the present Charter, members of the Commission shall be elected in accordance with the relevant Articles of the present Charter.

2. The Secretary-General of the Organization of African Unity shall convene the first meeting of the Commission at the Headquarters of the Organization within three months of the constitution of the Commission. Thereafter, the Commission shall be convened by its Chairman whenever necessary but at least once a year.

Article 65

For each of the States that will ratify or adhere to the present Charter after its coming into force, the Charter shall take effect three months after the date of the deposit by that State of its instrument of ratification or adherence.

Article 66

Special protocols or agreements may, if necessary, supplement the provisions of the present Charter.

Article 67

The Secretary-General of the Organization of African Unity shall inform member States of the Organization of the deposit of each instrument of ratification or adherence.

Article 68

The present Charter may be amended if a State party makes a written request to that effect to the Secretary-General of the Organization of African Unity. The Assembly of Heads of State and Government may only consider the draft amendment after all the States parties have been duly informed of it and the Commission has given its opinion on it at the request of the sponsoring State. The amendment shall be approved by a simple majority of the States parties. It shall come into force for each State which has accepted it in accordance with its constitutional procedure three months after the Secretary-General has received notice of the acceptance.

119. PROTOCOL TO THE AFRICAN CHARTER ON HUMAN AND PEOPLES' RIGHTS ON THE RIGHTS OF WOMEN IN AFRICA, 2003

Adopted by the 2nd Ordinary Session of the Assembly of the African Union, Maputo, 11 July 2003: Assembly/AU/Dec.19(II);   **http://www.africa-union.org/root/au/Documents/Treaties/ treaties.htm**.

The Protocol to the African Charter on Human and Peoples' Rights relating to the Rights of Women was adopted at the Maputo Summit, after a lengthy process; it entered into force on 25 November 2005. The present text obliges States parties to 'include in their national constitutions and other legislative instruments…the principle of equality between women and men and ensure its effective application': Article 2.1(a). It also requires States parties to prohibit all forms of female genital mutilation, 'through legislative measures backed by sanctions': Article 5(b), and confirms other basic rights, such as consensual marriage, a minimum age of consent of 18 years for marriage, property rights during marriage, equal rights in case of separation; equal protection by the law; equal representation in political life; promotion of equal remuneration and occupational freedom; and the right to control fertility and method of contraception: Articles 6(a), (b), (j), 7(d), 8, 9, 13(b), (d), 14(1)(a), (c). However, certain countries expressed reservations on the text, some (such as South Africa) arguing that the standards were set too low, others (such as Libya and Egypt) that the Protocol violated Shari'a law, while Kenya was concerned about the legality of customary marriages. The final text was adopted without reservation, and it will be for national legislatures to deal with specific concerns.

Further reading

BANDA, F., *Women, Law and Human Rights: An African Perspective*, Oxford: Hart Publishing, 2005.

NTOMBIZOZUKO, D., 'Protocol on the Rights of Women in Africa: Protection of Women from Sexual Violence during Armed Conflict', (2006) 6 *African Human Rights Law Journal* 166.

QUILLERÉ-MAJZOUB, F., 'Le protocole à la Charte africaine des droits de l'homme et des peuples relatif aux droits de la femme en Afrique: un projet trop ambitieux?', *Revue trimestrielle de droits de l'homme*, 2008, 127.

TEXT

The States Parties to this Protocol,

Considering that Article 66 of the African Charter on Human and Peoples' Rights provides for special protocols or agreements, if necessary, to supplement the provisions of the African Charter, and that the Assembly of Heads of State and Government of the Organization of African Unity meeting in its Thirty-first Ordinary Session in Addis Ababa, Ethiopia, in June 1995, endorsed by resolution AHG/Res.240 (XXXI) the recommendation of the African Commission on Human and Peoples' Rights to elaborate a Protocol on the Rights of Women in Africa;

Considering that Article 2 of the African Charter on Human and Peoples' Rights enshrines the principle of non-discrimination on the grounds of race, ethnic group, colour, sex, language, religion, political or any other opinion, national and social origin, fortune, birth or other status;

Further considering that Article 18 of the African Charter on Human and Peoples' Rights calls on all States Parties to eliminate every discrimination against women and to ensure the protection of the rights of women as stipulated in international declarations and conventions;

Noting that Articles 60 and 61 of the African Charter on Human and Peoples' Rights recognise regional and international human rights instruments and African practices consistent with international norms on human and peoples' rights as being important reference points for the application and interpretation of the African Charter;

Recalling that women's rights have been recognised and guaranteed in all international human rights instruments, notably the Universal Declaration of Human Rights, the International Covenant on Civil and Political Rights, the International Covenant on Economic, Social and Cultural Rights, the Convention on the Elimination of All Forms of Discrimination Against Women and its Optional Protocol, the African Charter on the Rights and Welfare of the Child, and all other international and regional conventions and covenants relating to the rights of women as being inalienable, interdependent and indivisible human rights;

Noting that women's rights and women's essential role in development, have been reaffirmed in the United Nations Plans of Action on the Environment and Development in 1992, on Human Rights in 1993, on Population and Development in 1994 and on Social Development in 1995;

Recalling also United Nations Security Council's Resolution 1325 (2000) on the role of women in promoting peace and security;

Reaffirming the principle of promoting gender equality as enshrined in the Constitutive Act of the African Union as well as the New Partnership for Africa's Development, relevant Declarations, Resolutions and Decisions, which underline the commitment of the African States to ensure the full participation of African women as equal partners in Africa's development;

Further noting that the African Platform for Action and the Dakar Declaration of 1994 and the Beijing Platform for Action of 1995 call on all Member States of the United Nations, which have made a solemn commitment to implement them, to take concrete steps to give greater attention to the human rights of women in order to eliminate all forms of discrimination and of gender-based violence against women;

Recognising the crucial role of women in the preservation of African values based on the principles of equality, peace, freedom, dignity, justice, solidarity and democracy;

Bearing in mind related Resolutions, Declarations, Recommendations, Decisions, Conventions and other Regional and Sub-Regional Instruments aimed at eliminating all forms of discrimination and at promoting equality between women and men;

Concerned that despite the ratification of the African Charter on Human and Peoples' Rights and other international human rights instruments by the majority of States Parties, and their solemn commitment to eliminate all forms of discrimination and harmful practices against women, women in Africa still continue to be victims of discrimination and harmful practices;

Firmly convinced that any practice that hinders or endangers the normal growth and affects the physical and psychological development of women and girls should be condemned and eliminated;

Determined to ensure that the rights of women are promoted, realised and protected in order to enable them to enjoy fully all their human rights;

Have agreed as follows:

Article 1—Definitions

For the purpose of the present Protocol:

(a) 'African Charter' means the African Charter on Human and Peoples' Rights;

(b) 'African Commission' means the African Commission on Human and Peoples' Rights;

(c) 'Assembly' means the Assembly of Heads of State and Government of the African Union;

(d) 'AU' means the African Union;

(e) 'Constitutive Act' means the Constitutive Act of the African Union;

(f) 'Discrimination against women' means any distinction, exclusion or restriction or any differential treatment based on sex and whose objectives or effects compromise or destroy the recognition, enjoyment or the exercise by women, regardless of their marital status, of human rights and fundamental freedoms in all spheres of life;

(g) 'Harmful Practices' means all behaviour, attitudes and/or practices which negatively affect the fundamental rights of women and girls, such as their right to life, health, dignity, education and physical integrity;

(h) 'NEPAD' means the New Partnership for Africa's Development established by the Assembly;

(i) 'States Parties' means the States Parties to this Protocol;

(j) 'Violence against women' means all acts perpetrated against women which cause or could cause them physical, sexual, psychological, and economic harm, including the threat to take such acts; or to undertake the imposition of arbitrary restrictions on or deprivation of fundamental freedoms in private or public life in peace time and during situations of armed conflicts or of war;

(k) 'Women' means persons of female gender, including girls.

Article 2—Elimination of Discrimination Against Women

1. States Parties shall combat all forms of discrimination against women through appropriate legislative, institutional and other measures. In this regard they shall:

(a) include in their national constitutions and other legislative instruments, if not already done, the principle of equality between women and men and ensure its effective application;

(b) enact and effectively implement appropriate legislative or regulatory measures, including those prohibiting and curbing all forms of discrimination particularly those harmful practices which endanger the health and general well-being of women;

(c) integrate a gender perspective in their policy decisions, legislation, development plans, programmes and activities and in all other spheres of life;

(d) take corrective and positive action in those areas where discrimination against women in law and in fact continues to exist;

(e) support the local, national, regional and continental initiatives directed at eradicating all forms of discrimination against women.

2. States Parties shall commit themselves to modify the social and cultural patterns of conduct of women and men through public education, information, education and communication strategies, with a view to achieving the elimination of harmful cultural and traditional practices and all other practices which are based on the idea of the inferiority or the superiority of either of the sexes, or on stereotyped roles for women and men.

Article 3—Right to Dignity

1. Every woman shall have the right to dignity inherent in a human being and to the recognition and protection of her human and legal rights.

2. Every woman shall have the right to respect as a person and to the free development of her personality.

3. States Parties shall adopt and implement appropriate measures to prohibit any exploitation or degradation of women.

4. States Parties shall adopt and implement appropriate measures to ensure the protection of every woman's right to respect for her dignity and protection of women from all forms of violence, particularly sexual and verbal violence.

Article 4—The Rights to Life, Integrity and Security of the Person

1. Every woman shall be entitled to respect for her life and the integrity and security of her person. All forms of exploitation, cruel, inhuman or degrading punishment and treatment shall be prohibited.

2. States Parties shall take appropriate and effective measures to:

   (a) enact and enforce laws to prohibit all forms of violence against women including unwanted or forced sex whether the violence takes place in private or public;

   (b) adopt such other legislative, administrative, social and economic measures as may be necessary to ensure the prevention, punishment and eradication of all forms of violence against women;

   (c) identify the causes and consequences of violence against women and take appropriate measures to prevent and eliminate such violence;

   (d) actively promote peace education through curricula and social communication in order to eradicate elements in traditional and cultural beliefs, practices and stereotypes which legitimise and exacerbate the persistence and tolerance of violence against women;

   (e) punish the perpetrators of violence against women and implement programmes for the rehabilitation of women victims;

   (f) establish mechanisms and accessible services for effective information, rehabilitation and reparation for victims of violence against women;

   (g) prevent and condemn trafficking in women, prosecute the perpetrators of such trafficking and protect those women most at risk;

   (h) prohibit all medical or scientific experiments on women without their informed consent;

   (i) provide adequate budgetary and other resources for the implementation and monitoring of actions aimed at preventing and eradicating violence against women;

   (j) ensure that, in those countries where the death penalty still exists, not to carry out death sentences on pregnant or nursing women;

(k) ensure that women and men enjoy equal rights in terms of access to refugee status determination procedures and that women refugees are accorded the full protection and benefits guaranteed under international refugee law, including their own identity and other documents.

Article 5—Elimination of Harmful Practices

States Parties shall prohibit and condemn all forms of harmful practices which negatively affect the human rights of women and which are contrary to recognised international standards. States Parties shall take all necessary legislative and other measures to eliminate such practices, including:

(a) creation of public awareness in all sectors of society regarding harmful practices through information, formal and informal education and outreach programmes;

(b) prohibition, through legislative measures backed by sanctions, of all forms of female genital mutilation, scarification, medicalisation and para-medicalisation of female genital mutilation and all other practices in order to eradicate them;

(c) provision of necessary support to victims of harmful practices through basic services such as health services, legal and judicial support, emotional and psychological counselling as well as vocational training to make them self-supporting;

(d) protection of women who are at risk of being subjected to harmful practices or all other forms of violence, abuse and intolerance.

Article 6—Marriage

States Parties shall ensure that women and men enjoy equal rights and are regarded as equal partners in marriage. They shall enact appropriate national legislative measures to guarantee that:

(a) no marriage shall take place without the free and full consent of both parties;

(b) the minimum age of marriage for women shall be 18 years;

(c) monogamy is encouraged as the preferred form of marriage and that the rights of women in marriage and family, including in polygamous marital relationships are promoted and protected;

(d) every marriage shall be recorded in writing and registered in accordance with national laws, in order to be legally recognised;

(e) the husband and wife shall, by mutual agreement, choose their matrimonial regime and place of residence;

(f) a married woman shall have the right to retain her maiden name, to use it as she pleases, jointly or separately with her husband's surname;

(g) a woman shall have the right to retain her nationality or to acquire the nationality of her husband;

(h) a woman and a man shall have equal rights, with respect to the nationality of their children except where this is contrary to a provision in national legislation or is contrary to national security interests;

(i) a woman and a man shall jointly contribute to safeguarding the interests of the family, protecting and educating their children;

(j) during her marriage, a woman shall have the right to acquire her own property and to administer and manage it freely.

Article 7—Separation, Divorce and Annulment of Marriage

States Parties shall enact appropriate legislation to ensure that women and men enjoy the same rights in case of separation, divorce or annulment of marriage. In this regard, they shall ensure that:

(a) separation, divorce or annulment of a marriage shall be effected by judicial order;

(b) women and men shall have the same rights to seek separation, divorce or annulment of a marriage;

(c) in case of separation, divorce or annulment of marriage, women and men shall have reciprocal rights and responsibilities towards their children. In any case, the interests of the children shall be given paramount importance;

(d) in case of separation, divorce or annulment of marriage, women and men shall have the right to an equitable sharing of the joint property deriving from the marriage.

Article 8—Access to Justice and Equal Protection before the Law

Women and men are equal before the law and shall have the right to equal protection and benefit of the law. States Parties shall take all appropriate measures to ensure:

(a) effective access by women to judicial and legal services, including legal aid;

(b) support to local, national, regional and continental initiatives directed at providing women access to legal services, including legal aid;

(c) the establishment of adequate educational and other appropriate structures with particular attention to women and to sensitise everyone to the rights of women;

(d) that law enforcement organs at all levels are equipped to effectively interpret and enforce gender equality rights;

(e) that women are represented equally in the judiciary and law enforcement organs;

(f) reform of existing discriminatory laws and practices in order to promote and protect the rights of women.

Article 9—Right to Participation in the Political and Decision-Making Process

1. States Parties shall take specific positive action to promote participative governance and the equal participation of women in the political life of their countries through affirmative action, enabling national legislation and other measures to ensure that:

(a) women participate without any discrimination in all elections;

(b) women are represented equally at all levels with men in all electoral processes;

(c) women are equal partners with men at all levels of development and implementation of State policies and development programmes.

2. States Parties shall ensure increased and effective representation and participation of women at all levels of decision-making.

Article 10—Right to Peace

1. Women have the right to a peaceful existence and the right to participate in the promotion and maintenance of peace.

2. States Parties shall take all appropriate measures to ensure the increased participation of women:

 (a) in programmes of education for peace and a culture of peace;
 (b) in the structures and processes for conflict prevention, management and resolution at local, national, regional, continental and international levels;
 (c) in the local, national, regional, continental and international decision making structures to ensure physical, psychological, social and legal protection of asylum seekers, refugees, returnees and displaced persons, in particular women;
 (d) in all levels of the structures established for the management of camps and settlements for asylum seekers, refugees, returnees and displaced persons, in particular, women;
 (e) in all aspects of planning, formulation and implementation of post-conflict reconstruction and rehabilitation.

3. States Parties shall take the necessary measures to reduce military expenditure significantly in favour of spending on social development in general, and the promotion of women in particular.

Article 11—Protection of Women in Armed Conflicts

1. States Parties undertake to respect and ensure respect for the rules of international humanitarian law applicable in armed conflict situations, which affect the population, particularly women.
2. States Parties shall, in accordance with the obligations incumbent upon them under international humanitarian law, protect civilians including women, irrespective of the population to which they belong, in the event of armed conflict.
3. States Parties undertake to protect asylum seeking women, refugees, returnees and internally displaced persons, against all forms of violence, rape and other forms of sexual exploitation, and to ensure that such acts are considered war crimes, genocide and/or crimes against humanity and that their perpetrators are brought to justice before a competent criminal jurisdiction.
4. States Parties shall take all necessary measures to ensure that no child, especially girls under 18 years of age, take a direct part in hostilities and that no child is recruited as a soldier.

Article 12—Right to Education and Training

1. States Parties shall take all appropriate measures to:

 (a) eliminate all forms of discrimination against women and guarantee equal opportunity and access in the sphere of education and training;
 (b) eliminate all stereotypes in textbooks, syllabuses and the media, that perpetuate such discrimination;
 (c) protect women, especially the girl-child from all forms of abuse, including sexual harassment in schools and other educational institutions and provide for sanctions against the perpetrators of such practices;
 (d) provide access to counselling and rehabilitation services to women who suffer abuses and sexual harassment;

(e) integrate gender sensitisation and human rights education at all levels of education curricula including teacher training.

2. States Parties shall take specific positive action to:

(a) promote literacy among women;

(b) promote education and training for women at all levels and in all disciplines, particularly in the fields of science and technology;

(c) promote the enrolment and retention of girls in schools and other training institutions and the organisation of programmes for women who leave school prematurely.

Article 13—Economic and Social Welfare Rights

States Parties shall adopt and enforce legislative and other measures to guarantee women equal opportunities in work and career advancement and other economic opportunities. In this respect, they shall:

(a) promote equality of access to employment;

(b) promote the right to equal remuneration for jobs of equal value for women and men;

(c) ensure transparency in recruitment, promotion and dismissal of women and combat and punish sexual harassment in the workplace;

(d) guarantee women the freedom to choose their occupation, and protect them from exploitation by their employers violating and exploiting their fundamental rights as recognised and guaranteed by conventions, laws and regulations in force;

(e) create conditions to promote and support the occupations and economic activities of women, in particular, within the informal sector;

(f) establish a system of protection and social insurance for women working in the informal sector and sensitise them to adhere to it;

(g) introduce a minimum age for work and prohibit the employment of children below that age, and prohibit, combat and punish all forms of exploitation of children, especially the girl-child;

(h) take the necessary measures to recognise the economic value of the work of women in the home;

(i) guarantee adequate and paid pre- and post-natal maternity leave in both the private and public sectors;

(j) ensure the equal application of taxation laws to women and men;

(k) recognise and enforce the right of salaried women to the same allowances and entitlements as those granted to salaried men for their spouses and children;

(l) recognise that both parents bear the primary responsibility for the upbringing and development of children and that this is a social function for which the State and the private sector have secondary responsibility;

(m) take effective legislative and administrative measures to prevent the exploitation and abuse of women in advertising and pornography.

Article 14—Health and Reproductive Rights

1. States Parties shall ensure that the right to health of women, including sexual and reproductive health is respected and promoted. This includes:

(a) the right to control their fertility;

(b) the right to decide whether to have children, the number of children and the spacing of children;

(c) the right to choose any method of contraception;

(d) the right to self-protection and to be protected against sexually transmitted infections, including HIV/AIDS;

(e) the right to be informed on one's health status and on the health status of one's partner, particularly if affected with sexually transmitted infections, including HIV/AIDS, in accordance with internationally recognised standards and best practices;

(f) the right to have family planning education.

2. States Parties shall take all appropriate measures to:

(a) provide adequate, affordable and accessible health services, including information, education and communication programmes to women especially those in rural areas;

(b) establish and strengthen existing pre-natal, delivery and post-natal health and nutritional services for women during pregnancy and while they are breast-feeding;

(c) protect the reproductive rights of women by authorising medical abortion in cases of sexual assault, rape, incest, and where the continued pregnancy endangers the mental and physical health of the mother or the life of the mother or the foetus.

Article 15—Right to Food Security

States Parties shall ensure that women have the right to nutritious and adequate food. In this regard, they shall take appropriate measures to:

(a) provide women with access to clean drinking water, sources of domestic fuel, land, and the means of producing nutritious food;

(b) establish adequate systems of supply and storage to ensure food security.

Article 16—Right to Adequate Housing

Women shall have the right to equal access to housing and to acceptable living conditions in a healthy environment. To ensure this right, States Parties shall grant to women, whatever their marital status, access to adequate housing.

Article 17—Right to Positive Cultural Context

1. Women shall have the right to live in a positive cultural context and to participate at all levels in the determination of cultural policies.

2. States Parties shall take all appropriate measures to enhance the participation of women in the formulation of cultural policies at all levels.

Article 18—Right to a Healthy and Sustainable Environment1

1. Women shall have the right to live in a healthy and sustainable environment.

2. States Parties shall take all appropriate measures to:

---

1 A typographical error in the numbering of the sub-paragraphs of Article 18(2) of the text obtained from the African Union has been corrected—Eds.

(a) ensure greater participation of women in the planning, management and preservation of the environment and the sustainable use of natural resources at all levels;

(b) promote research and investment in new and renewable energy sources and appropriate technologies, including information technologies and facilitate women's access to, and participation in their control;

(c) protect and enable the development of women's indigenous knowledge systems;

(d) regulate the management, processing, storage and disposal of domestic waste;

(e) ensure that proper standards are followed for the storage, transportation and disposal of toxic waste.

Article 19—Right to Sustainable Development

Women shall have the right to fully enjoy their right to sustainable development. In this connection, the States Parties shall take all appropriate measures to:

(a) introduce the gender perspective in the national development planning procedures;

(b) ensure participation of women at all levels in the conceptualisation, decision-making, implementation and evaluation of development policies and programmes;

(c) promote women's access to and control over productive resources such as land and guarantee their right to property;

(d) promote women's access to credit, training, skills development and extension services at rural and urban levels in order to provide women with a higher quality of life and reduce the level of poverty among women;

(e) take into account indicators of human development specifically relating to women in the elaboration of development policies and programmes; and

(f) ensure that the negative effects of globalisation and any adverse effects of the implementation of trade and economic policies and programmes are reduced to the minimum for women.

Article 20—Widows' Rights

States Parties shall take appropriate legal measures to ensure that widows enjoy all human rights through the implementation of the following provisions:

(a) that widows are not subjected to inhuman, humiliating or degrading treatment;

(b) that a widow shall automatically become the guardian and custodian of her children, after the death of her husband, unless this is contrary to the interests and the welfare of the children;

(c) that a widow shall have the right to remarry, and in that event, to marry the person of her choice.

Article 21—Right to Inheritance

1. A widow shall have the right to an equitable share in the inheritance of the property of her husband. A widow shall have the right to continue to live in the matrimonial house. In case of remarriage, she shall retain this right if the house belongs to her or she has inherited it.

2. Women and men shall have the right to inherit, in equitable shares, their parents' properties.

Article 22—Special Protection of Elderly Women

The States Parties undertake to:

(a) provide protection to elderly women and take specific measures commensurate with their physical, economic and social needs as well as their access to employment and professional training;

(b) ensure the right of elderly women to freedom from violence, including sexual abuse, discrimination based on age and the right to be treated with dignity.

Article 23—Special Protection of Women with Disabilities

The States Parties undertake to:

(a) ensure the protection of women with disabilities and take specific measures commensurate with their physical, economic and social needs to facilitate their access to employment, professional and vocational training as well as their participation in decision-making;

(b) ensure the right of women with disabilities to freedom from violence, including sexual abuse, discrimination based on disability and the right to be treated with dignity.

Article 24—Special Protection of Women in Distress

The States Parties undertake to:

(a) ensure the protection of poor women and women heads of families including women from marginalized population groups and provide an environment suitable to their condition and their special physical, economic and social needs;

(b) ensure the right of pregnant or nursing women or women in detention by providing them with an environment which is suitable to their condition and the right to be treated with dignity.

Article 25—Remedies

States Parties shall undertake to:

(a) provide for appropriate remedies to any woman whose rights or freedoms, as herein recognised, have been violated;

(b) ensure that such remedies are determined by competent judicial, administrative or legislative authorities, or by any other competent authority provided for by law.

Article 26—Implementation and Monitoring

1. States Parties shall ensure the implementation of this Protocol at national level, and in their periodic reports submitted in accordance with Article 62 of the African Charter, indicate the legislative and other measures undertaken for the full realisation of the rights herein recognised.

2. States Parties undertake to adopt all necessary measures and in particular shall provide budgetary and other resources for the full and effective implementation of the rights herein recognised.

Article 27—Interpretation

The African Court on Human and Peoples' Rights shall be seized with matters of interpretation arising from the application or implementation of this Protocol.

Article 28—Signature, Ratification and Accession

1. This Protocol shall be open for signature, ratification and accession by the States Parties, in accordance with their respective constitutional procedures.

2. The instruments of ratification or accession shall be deposited with the Chairperson of the Commission of the AU.

Article 29—Entry into Force

1. This Protocol shall enter into force thirty (30) days after the deposit of the fifteenth (15) instrument of ratification.

2. For each State Party that accedes to this Protocol after its coming into force, the Protocol shall come into force on the date of deposit of the instrument of accession.

3. The Chairperson of the Commission of the AU shall notify all Member States of the coming into force of this Protocol.

Article 30—Amendment and Revision

1. Any State Party may submit proposals for the amendment or revision of this Protocol.

2. Proposals for amendment or revision shall be submitted, in writing, to the Chairperson of the Commission of the AU who shall transmit the same to the States Parties within thirty (30) days of receipt thereof.

3. The Assembly, upon advice of the African Commission, shall examine these proposals within a period of one (1) year following notification of States Parties, in accordance with the provisions of paragraph 2 of this article.

4. Amendments or revision shall be adopted by the Assembly by a simple majority.

5. The amendment shall come into force for each State Party, which has accepted it thirty (30) days after the Chairperson of the Commission of the AU has received notice of the acceptance.

Article 31—Status of the Present Protocol

None of the provisions of the present Protocol shall affect more favourable provisions for the realisation of the rights of women contained in the national legislation of States Parties or in any other regional, continental or international conventions, treaties or agreements applicable in these States Parties.

Article 32—Transitional Provisions

Pending the establishment of the African Court on Human and Peoples' Rights, the African Commission on Human and Peoples' Rights shall be seized with matters of interpretation arising from the application and implementation of this Protocol.

120. PROTOCOL ON THE STATUTE OF THE AFRICAN COURT OF JUSTICE AND HUMAN RIGHTS, 2008

Experience in Europe and the Americas has shown the value of regional, judicial oversight of the human rights obligations assumed by States, but also of the importance of regional human rights commissions in building the initial basis of trust among governments and among the peoples of particular regions.

The goal of an African Court of Human Rights was actively promoted by, among others, the African Commission on Human and Peoples' Rights, which particularly encouraged States to ratify the 1998 Protocol on the matter; see, for example, Final Communiqué, 27th Ordinary Session of the African Commission on Human and Peoples' Rights, 27 April–11 May 2000, Algiers, Algeria; and for the text of the 1998 Protocol, see the 5th edition of this work, p. 1021. Notwithstanding the entry into force of the Protocol on 24 January 2004, judicial appointments generally and a decision on the location of the Court were delayed and later the same year, the Assembly of Heads of State and Government of the African Union decided to merge the Human and Peoples' Rights Court with the Court of Justice of the African Union in June 2004, which itself was the subject of a 2003 Protocol; the merger was designed to ensure adequate resources to fund a single effective continental court. At the July 2008 African Union Summit, AU Ministers of Justice adopted the instrument set out below; for text, see also **http://www.africa-union.org/root/au/Documents/Treaties/treaties.htm**.

According to Article 7, the 1998 Protocol will remain in force for a transitional period in order to enable the transfer of 'prerogatives, assets, rights and obligations to the African Court of Justice and Human Rights'.

Articles 28 and 29 of the Statute of the Court annexed to the Protocol set out who may submit cases to the new body. This includes State Parties, the African Commission on Human and Peoples' Rights, the African Committee of Experts on the Rights and Welfare of the Child, African inter-governmental organizations and African National Human Rights Institutions. Individuals or 'relevant non-governmental organizations accredited to the African Union or to its organs' can only submit cases in accordance with Article 8 of the Protocol, that is, if the State concerned has made a declaration accepting the competence of the Court.

The literature cited below may be largely of historical interest, although still also of relevance in identifying problems and challenges.

Further reading

KOWOUVIH, S., 'La Cour africaine des droits de l'homme et des peuples: une rectification institu-tionnelle du concept de "spécificité africaine" en matière de droits de l'homme', *Revue trimestrielle de droits de l'homme*, 2004, 757.

NIYUNGEKO, G., 'La Cour africaine des droits de l'homme et des peuples: défis et perspectives', *Revue trimestrielle de droits de l'homme*, 2009, 731.

OUGUERGOUZ, F., 'La Cour africaine des droits de l'homme et des peuples. Gros plan sur le premier organe judiciaire africain à vocation continentale', (2006) 52 *Annuaire Français de droit international*, 213.

TEXT

The Member States of the African Union, Parties to this Protocol,
Recalling the objectives and principles enunciated in the Constitutive Act of the African Union, adopted on 11 July 2000 in Lomé, Togo, in particular the commitment to settle their disputes through peaceful means;

Bearing in mind their commitment to promote peace, security and stability on the Continent and to protect human and peoples' rights in accordance with the African Charter on Human and Peoples' Rights and other relevant instruments relating to human rights;

Considering that the Constitutive Act of the African Union provides for the establishment of a Court of Justice charged with hearing, among other things, all cases relating to interpretation or application of the said Act or of all other Treaties adopted within the framework of the Union;

Further considering Decisions Assembly/AU/Dec.45 (III) and Assembly/AU/Dec.83 (V) of the Assembly of the Union, adopted respectively at its Third (6–8 July 2004, Addis Ababa, Ethiopia) and Fifth (4–5 July 2005, Sirte, Libya), Ordinary Sessions, to merge the African Court on Human and Peoples' Rights and the Court of Justice of the African Union into a single Court,

Firmly convinced that the establishment of an African Court of Justice and Human Rights shall assist in the achievement of the goals pursued by the African Union and that the attainment of the objectives of the African Charter on Human and Peoples' Rights requires the establishment of a judicial organ to supplement and strengthen the mission of the African Commission on Human and Peoples' Rights as well as the African Committee of Experts on the Rights and Welfare of the Child;

Taking due account of the Protocol to the African Charter on Human and Peoples' Rights on the Establishment an African Court on Human and Peoples' Rights, adopted by the Assembly of Heads of States and Governments of the Organization of African Unity on 10 June 1998 at Ouagadougou, Burkina Faso, and which entered into force on 25 January 2004;

Taking due account also of the Protocol of the Court of Justice of the African Union, adopted by the Assembly of the Union on 11 July 2003 in Maputo Mozambique;

Recalling their commitment to take all necessary measures to strengthen their common institutions and to endow them with the necessary powers and resources to carry out their missions effectively;

Cognizant of the Protocol to the African Charter on Human and Peoples' Rights on the Rights of Women in Africa, and the commitments contained in the Solemn Declaration on the gender equality in Africa (Assembly/AU/Decl.12 (III) adopted by the Assembly of the Union respectively at its Second and Third ordinary sessions held in July 2003 and 2004, in Maputo, Mozambique and in Addis Ababa, Ethiopia);

Convinced that the present Protocol shall supplement the mandate and efforts of other continental treaty bodies as well as national institutions in protecting human rights:

Have Agreed as Follows:

CHAPTER I—MERGER OF THE AFRICAN COURT ON HUMAN AND PEOPLES' RIGHTS AND THE COURT OF JUSTICE OF THE AFRICAN UNION

Article 1—Replacement of the 1998 and 2003 Protocols

The Protocol to the African Charter on Human and Peoples' Rights on the Establishment of an African Court on Human and Peoples' Rights, adopted on 10 June 1998 in Ouagadougou, Burkina Faso and which entered into force on 25 January 2004, and the Protocol of the Court of Justice of the African Union, adopted on 11 July 2003 in Maputo, Mozambique, are hereby replaced by the present Protocol and Statute annexed as its integral part hereto, subject to the provisions of Article 5, 7 and 9 of this Protocol.

Article 2—Establishment of a single Court

The African Court on Human and Peoples' Rights established by the Protocol to the African Charter on Human and Peoples' Rights on the Establishment of an African Court on Human and Peoples' Rights and the Court of Justice of the African Union established by the Constitutive Act of the African Union, are hereby merged into a single Court and established as 'The African Court of Justice and Human Rights'.

Article 3—Reference to the single Court in the Constitutive Act

References made to the 'Court of Justice' in the Constitutive Act of the African Union shall be read as references to the 'African Court of Justice and Human Rights' established under Article 2 of this Protocol.

CHAPTER II—TRANSITIONAL PROVISIONS

Article 4—Term of Office of the Judges of the African Court on Human and Peoples' Rights

The term of office of the Judges of the African Court on Human and Peoples' Rights shall end following the election of the Judges of the African Court of Justice and Human Rights. However, the Judges shall remain in office until the newly elected Judges of the African Court of Justice and Human Rights are sworn in.

Article 5—Cases Pending before the African Court on Human and Peoples' Rights

Cases pending before the African Court on Human and Peoples' Rights, that have not been concluded before the entry into force of the present Protocol, shall be transferred to the Human Rights Section of the African Court of Justice and Human Rights on the understanding that such cases shall be dealt with In accordance with the protocol to the ACHPR on the establishment of the African Court on Human and Peoples' Rights.

Article 6—Registry of the Court

The Registrar of the African Court on Human and Peoples' Rights shall remain in office until the appointment of a new Registrar for the African Court of Justice and Human Rights.

Article 7—Provisional validity of the 1998 Protocol

The Protocol to the African Charter on Human and Peoples' Rights on the Establishment of an African Court on Human and Peoples' Rights shall remain in force for a transitional period not exceeding one (1) year or any other period determined by the Assembly, after entry into force of the present Protocol, to enable the African Court on Human and Peoples' Rights to take the necessary measures for the transfer of its prerogatives, assets, rights and obligations to the African Court of Justice and Human Rights.

CHAPTER III—FINAL PROVISIONS

Article 8—Signature, Ratification and Accession

1. The present Protocol shall be open for signature, ratification or accession by Member States, in accordance with their respective constitutional procedures.

2. The instruments of ratification or accession to the present Protocol shall be deposited with the Chairperson of the Commission of the African Union.

3. Any Member State may, at the time of signature or when depositing its instrument of ratification or accession, or at any time thereafter, make a declaration accepting the competence of the Court to receive cases under Article 30 (f) involving a State which has not made such a declaration.

Article 9—Entry into force

1. The present Protocol and the Statute annexed to it shall enter into force thirty (30) days after the deposit of the instruments of ratification by fifteen (15) Member States.

2. For each Member State which shall ratify or accede to it subsequently, the present Protocol shall enter into force on the date on which the instruments of ratification or accession are deposited.

3. The Chairperson of the Commission shall inform all Member States of the entry into force of the present Protocol.

Adopted by the Eleventh Ordinary Session of the Assembly, Held in Sharm El-Sheikh, Egypt, 1st July 2008.

ANNEX
STATUTE OF THE AFRICAN COURT OF JUSTICE
AND HUMAN RIGHTS

Chapter I—General Provisions

Article 1—Definitions

In this Statute, except otherwise indicated, the following shall mean:

'African Charter' means the African Charter on Human and Peoples' Rights;

'African Commission' means the African Commission on Human and Peoples' Rights;

'African Committee of Experts' means the African Committee of Experts on the Rights and Welfare of the Child; 'African Intergovernmental Organisations' means an organisation that has been established with the aim of ensuring socio-economic integration, and to which some Member States have ceded certain competences to act on their behalf, as well as other sub-regional, regional or inter-African Organisations;

'African Non-Governmental Organizations' means Non-Governmental Organizations at the sub-regional, regional or inter-African levels as well as those in the Diaspora as may be defined by the Executive Council;

'Agent' means a person mandated in writing to represent a party in a case before the Court;

'Assembly' means the Assembly of Heads of State and Government of the Union;

'Chamber(s)' means a Chamber established in accordance with Article 19 of the Statute.

'Constitutive Act' means the Constitutive Act of the African Union;

'Commission': means the Commission of the Union;

'Court' means the African Court of Justice and Human Rights as well as its sections and chambers;

'Executive Council' means the Executive Council of Ministers of the Union;

'Full Court' means joint sitting of the General Affairs and Human Rights Sections of the Court;

'Human Rights Section' means the Human and Peoples' Rights Section of the Court;

'Judge' means a judge of the Court;

'Member State' means a Member State of the Union;

'National Human Rights Institutions' means public institutions established by a state to promote and protect human rights;

'President' means the President of the Court elected in accordance with Article 22(1) of the Statute;

'Protocol' means the Protocol to the Statute of the African Court of Justice and Human Rights;

'Registrar' means the person appointed as such in accordance with Article 22 (4) of the Statute;

'Rules' means the Rules of the Court;

'Section' means the General Affairs or the Human Rights Section of the Court;

'Senior Judge' means the person defined as such in the Rules of Court;

'States Parties' means Member States, which have ratified or acceded to this Protocol;

'Statute' means the present Statute;

'Union' means the African Union established by the Constitutive Act;

'Vice President' means the Vice President of the Court elected in accordance with Article 22 (1) of the Statute.

Article 2—Functions of the Court

1. The African Court of Justice and Human Rights shall be the main judicial organ of the African Union.

2. The Court shall be constituted and function in accordance with the provisions of the present Statute.

CHAPTER II—ORGANIZATION OF THE COURT

Article 3—Composition

1. The Court shall consist of sixteen (16) Judges who are nationals of States Parties. Upon recommendation of the Court, the Assembly, may, review the number of Judges.

2. The Court shall not, at any one time, have more than one judge from a single Member State.

3. Each geographical region of the Continent, as determined by the Decisions of the Assembly shall, where possible, be represented by three (3) Judges except the Western Region which shall have four (4) Judges.

Article 4—Qualifications of Judges

The Court shall be composed of impartial and independent Judges elected from among persons of high moral character, who possess the qualifications required in their respective countries for appointment to the highest judicial offices, or are juris-consults of recognized competence and experience in international law and /or, human rights law.

Article 5—Presentation of Candidates

1. As soon as the Protocol to this Statute enters into force, the Chairperson of the Commission shall invite each State Party to submit, in writing, within a period of ninety (90) days, candidatures to the post of judge of the Court.

2. Each State Party may present up to two (2) candidates and shall take into account equitable gender representation in the nomination process.

Article 6—List of candidates

1. For the purpose of election, the Chairperson of the Commission shall establish two alphabetical lists of candidates presented as follows:
   (i) List A containing the names of candidates having recognized competence and experience in International law; and
   (ii) List B containing the names of candidates possessing recognized competence and experience in Human Rights law.

2. States Parties that nominate candidates possessing the competences required on the two lists shall choose the list on which their candidates may be placed.

3. At the first election, eight (8) Judges shall be elected from amongst the candidates of list A and eight (8) from among the candidates of list B. The elections shall be organized in a way as to maintain the same proportion of judges elected on the two lists.

4. The Chairperson of the Commission shall communicate the two lists to Member States, at least thirty (30) days before the Ordinary Session of the Assembly or of the Council, during which the elections shall take place.

Article 7—Election of judges

1. The Judges shall be elected by the Executive Council, and appointed by the Assembly.

2. They shall be elected through secret ballot by a two-thirds majority of Member States with voting rights, from among the candidates provided for in Article 6 of this Statute. 3. Candidates who obtain the two-thirds majority and the highest number of votes shall be elected. However, if several rounds of election are required, the candidates with the least number of votes shall withdraw.

4. The Assembly shall ensure that in the Court as a whole there is equitable representation of the regions and the principal legal traditions of the Continent.

5. In the election of the Judges, the Assembly shall ensure that there is equitable gender representation.

Article 8—Term of Office

1. The Judges shall be elected for a period of six (6) years and may be re-elected only once. However, the term of office of eight (8) judges, four (4) from each section, elected during the first election shall end after four (4) years.

2. The Judges, whose term of office shall end after the initial period of four (4) years, shall be determined for each section, by lot drawn by the Chairperson of the Assembly or the Executive Council, immediately after the first election.

3. A Judge, elected to replace another whose term of office has not expired, shall complete the term of office of his predecessor.

4. All the Judges except the President and the Vice-President, shall perform their functions on a part-time basis.

Article 9—Resignation, Suspension and Removal from Office

1. A Judge may resign his/her position in writing addressed to the President for transmission to the Chairperson of the Assembly through the Chairperson of the Commission.

2. A Judge shall not be suspended or removed from office save, where, on the recommendation of two-thirds majority of the other members, he/she no longer meets the requisite conditions to be a Judge.

3. The President shall communicate the recommendation for the suspension or removal of a Judge to the Chairperson of the Assembly through the Chairperson of the Commission.

4. Such a recommendation of the Court shall become final upon its adoption by the Assembly.

Article 10—Vacancies

1. A vacancy shall arise in the Court under the following circumstances:
   (a) Death;
   (b) Resignation;
   (c) Removal from office.

2. In the case of death or resignation of a Judge, the President shall immediately inform the Chairperson of the Assembly through the Chairperson of the Commission in writing, who shall declare the seat vacant.

3. The same procedure and consideration for the election of a Judge shall also be followed in filling the vacancies.

Article 11—Solemn Declaration

1. After the first election, the Judges shall, at the first session of the Court and in the presence of the Chairperson of the Assembly, make a Solemn Declaration as follows:

   'I, ..., Do solemnly swear (or affirm or declare) that I shall faithfully exercise
   the duties of my office as Judge of the African Court of Justice and Human Rights of the
   African Union impartially and conscientiously, without fear or favour, affection or ill will
   and that I will preserve the integrity of the Court.'

2. The Chairperson of the Assembly or his/her duly authorized representative shall administer the Solemn Declaration.

3. Subsequently, the Solemn Declaration shall be made before the President of the Court.

Article 12—Independence

1. The independence of the judges shall be fully ensured in accordance with international law.

2. The Court shall act impartially, fairly and justly.

3. In performance of the judicial functions and duties, the Court and its Judges shall not be subject to the direction or control of any person or body.

Article 13—Conflict of Interest

1. Functions of a Judge are incompatible with all other activities, which might infringe on the need for independence or impartiality of the judicial profession. In case of doubt, the Court shall decide.

2. A Judge shall not exercise the function of agent, or counsel, or lawyer in any case before the Court.

Article 14—Conditions Governing the Participation of Members in the Settlement of a Specific Case

1. Where a particular judge feels he/she has a conflicting interest in a particular case, he/she shall so declare. In any event, he/she shall not participate in the settlement of a case for which he/she was previously involved as agent, counsel or lawyer of one of the parties, or as a member of a national or international Court or Tribunal, or a Commission of enquiry or in any other capacity.

2. If the President considers that a Judge should not participate in a particular case, he/she shall notify the judge concerned. Such notification from the President shall, after agreement by the Court, exclude that Judge from participating in that particular case.

3. A Judge of the nationality of a State Party to a case before the full Court or one of its Sections shall not have the right to sit on the case.

4. Where there is doubt on these points, the Court shall decide.

Article 15—Privileges and Immunities

1. The Judges shall enjoy, from the time of their election and throughout their term of office, the full privileges and immunities extended to diplomatic agents in accordance with international law.

2. The Judges shall be immune from legal proceedings for any act or omission committed in the discharge of their judicial functions.

3. The Judges shall continue, after they have ceased to hold office, to enjoy immunity in respect of acts performed by them when engaged in their official capacity.

Article 16—Sections of the Court

The Court shall have two (2) Sections; a General Affairs Section composed of eight (8) Judges and a Human Rights Section composed of eight (8) Judges.

Article 17—Assignment of matters to Sections

1. The General Affairs Section shall be competent to hear all cases submitted under Article 28 of this Statute save those concerning human and/or peoples' rights issues.

2. The Human Rights Section shall be competent to hear all cases relating to human and/or peoples rights.

Article 18—Referral of matters to the Full Court

When a Section of the Court is seized with a case, it may, if it deems it necessary refer that case to the Full Court for consideration.

Article 19—Chambers

1. The General Affairs Section and the Human Rights Section may, at any time, constitute one or several chambers. The quorum required to constitute such chambers shall be determined in the Rules of Court.

2. A judgment given by any Section or Chamber shall be considered as rendered by the Court.

Article 20—Sessions

1. The Court shall hold ordinary and extraordinary sessions.

2. The Court shall decide each year on the periods of its ordinary sessions.

3. Extraordinary sessions shall be convened by the President or at the request of the majority of the Judges.

Article 21—Quorum

1. A quorum of nine (9) Judges shall be required for deliberations of the Full Court.

2. A quorum of five (5) Judges shall be required for the deliberations of the General Affairs Section.

3. A quorum of five (5) Judges shall be required for the deliberations of the Human and Peoples' Rights Section.

Article 22—Presidency, Vice-Presidency and Registry

1. At its first ordinary session after the election of the judges, the full Court shall elect its President as well as the Vice-President from the different lists for a period of three (3) years. The President and the Vice-President may be re-elected once.

2. The President shall preside over all sessions of the full Court and those of the Section to which he/she belongs; in the event of being unable to sit, the President shall be replaced by the Vice president for the full Court and by the most Senior Judge for the sessions of his/her Section.

3. The Vice-President shall preside over all sessions of the section to which he/she belongs. In the event of being unable to sit, the Vice-President shall be replaced by the most Senior Judge of that Section.

4. The Court shall appoint a Registrar and may provide for the appointment of such other officers as may be necessary.

5. The President, the Vice-President and the Registrar shall reside at the seat of the Court.

Article 23—Remuneration of Judges

1. The President and the Vice-President shall receive an annual salary and other benefits.

2. The other Judges shall receive a sitting allowance for each day on which he/she exercises his/her functions.

3. These salaries, allowances and compensation shall be determined by the Assembly, on the proposal of the Executive Council. They may not be decreased during the term of office of the Judges.

4. Regulations adopted by the Assembly on the proposal of the Executive Council shall determine the conditions under which retirement pensions shall be given to the Judges as well as the conditions under which their travel expenses shall be paid.

5. The above-mentioned salaries, allowances and compensation shall be free from all taxation.

Article 24—Conditions of Service of the Registrar and Members of the Registry

The salaries and conditions of service of the Registrar and other Court Officials shall be determined by the Assembly on the proposal of the Court, through the Executive Council.

Article 25—Seat and Seal of the Court

1. The Seat of the Court shall be same as the Seat of the African Court on Human and Peoples' Rights. However, the Court may sit in any other Member State, if circumstances warrant, and with the consent of the Member State concerned. The Assembly may change the seat of the Court after due consultations with the Court.

2. The Court shall have a seal bearing the inscription 'The African Court of Justice and Human Rights'.

Article 26—Budget

1. The Court shall prepare its draft annual budget and shall submit it to the Assembly through the Executive Council.

2. The budget of the Court shall be borne by the African Union.

3. The Court shall be accountable for the execution of its budget and shall submit report thereon to the Executive Council in conformity with the Financial Rules and Regulations of the African Union.

Article 27—Rules of Court

1. The Court shall adopt rules for carrying out its functions and the implementation of the present Statute. In particular, it shall lay down its own Rules.

2. In elaborating its Rules, the Court shall bear in mind the complementarity it maintains with the African Commission and the African Committee of Experts.

CHAPTER III—COMPETENCE OF THE COURT

Article 28—Jurisdiction of the Court

The Court shall have jurisdiction over all cases and all legal disputes submitted to it in accordance with the present Statute which relate to:

    (a) the interpretation and application of the Constitutive Act;

    (b) the interpretation, application or validity of other Union Treaties and all subsidiary legal instruments adopted within the framework of the Union or the Organization of African Unity;

    (c) the interpretation and the application of the African Charter, the Charter on the Rights and Welfare of the Child, the Protocol to the African Charter on Human and Peoples' Rights on the Rights of Women in Africa, or any other legal instrument relating to human rights, ratified by the States Parties concerned;

    (d) any question of international law;

    (e) all acts, decisions, regulations and directives of the organs of the Union;

(f) all matters specifically provided for in any other agreements that States Parties may conclude among themselves, or with the Union and which confer jurisdiction on the Court;

(g) the existence of any fact which, if established, would constitute a breach of an obligation owed to a State Party or to the Union;

(h) the nature or extent of the reparation to be made for the breach of an international obligation.

Article 29—Entities Eligible to Submit Cases to the Court

1. The following entities shall be entitled to submit cases to the Court on any issue or dispute provided for in Article 28:

(a) State Parties to the present Protocol;

(b) The Assembly, the Parliament and other organs of the Union authorized by the Assembly;

(c) A staff member of the African Union on appeal, in a dispute and within the limits and under the terms and conditions laid down in the Staff Rules and Regulations of the Union;

2. The Court shall not be open to States, which are not members of the Union. The Court shall also have no jurisdiction to deal with a dispute involving a Member State that has not ratified the Protocol.

Article 30—Other Entities Eligible to Submit Cases to the Court

The following entities shall also be entitled to submit cases to the Court on any violation of a right guaranteed by the African Charter, by the Charter on the Rights and Welfare of the Child, the Protocol to the African Charter on Human and Peoples' Rights on the Rights of Women in Africa, or any other legal instrument relevant to human rights ratified by the States Parties concerned:

(a) State Parties to the present Protocol;

(b) the African Commission on Human and Peoples' Rights;

(c) the African Committee of Experts on the Rights and Welfare of the Child;

(d) African Intergovernmental Organizations accredited to the Union or its organs;

(e) African National Human Rights Institutions;

(f) Individuals or relevant Non-Governmental Organizations accredited to the African Union or to its organs, subject to the provisions of Article 8 of the Protocol.

Article 31—Applicable Law

1. In carrying out its functions, the Court shall have regard to:

(a) The Constitutive Act;

(b) International treaties, whether general or particular, ratified by the contesting States;

(c) International custom, as evidence of a general practice accepted as law;

(d) The general principles of law recognized universally or by African States;

(e) Subject to the provisions of paragraph 1, of Article 46 of the present Statute, judicial decisions and writings of the most highly qualified publicists of various

nations as well as the regulations, directives and decisions of the Union, as subsidiary means for the determination of the rules of law;

(f) Any other law relevant to the determination of the case.

2. This Article shall not prejudice the power of the Court to decide a case *ex aequo et bono*, if the parties agree thereto.

CHAPTER IV—PROCEDURE

Article 32—Official Languages

The official and working languages of the Court shall be those of the Union.

Article 33—Institution of Proceedings before the General Affairs Section

1. Cases brought before the Court by virtue of Article 29 of the present Statute shall be submitted by written application addressed to the Registrar. The subject of the dispute, the applicable law and basis of jurisdiction shall be indicated.

2. The Registrar shall forthwith give notice of the application to the Parties concerned.

3. The Registrar shall also notify, through the Chairperson of the Commission, all Member States and, if necessary, the organs of the Union whose decisions are in dispute.

Article 34—Institution of Proceedings before the Human Rights Section

1. Cases brought before the Court relating to an alleged violation of a human or peoples' right shall be submitted by a written application to the Registrar. The application shall indicate the right (s) alleged to have been violated, and, insofar as it is possible, the provision or provisions of the African Charter on Human and Peoples' Rights, the Charter on the Rights and Welfare of the Child, Protocol to the African Charter on Human and Peoples' Rights on the Rights of Women in Africa or any other relevant human rights instrument, ratified by the State concerned, on which it is based.

2. The Registrar shall forthwith give notice of the application to all parties concerned, as well as the Chairperson of the Commission.

Article 35—Provisional Measures

1. The Court shall have the power, on its own motion or on application by the parties, to indicate, if it considers that circumstances so require any provisional measures which ought to be taken to preserve the respective rights of the parties.

2. Pending the final decision, notice of the provisional measures shall forthwith be given to the parties and the Chairperson of the Commission, who shall inform the Assembly.

Article 36—Representation of Parties

1. The States, parties to a case, shall be represented by agents.

2. They may, if necessary, have the assistance of counsel or advocates before the Court.

3. The organs of the Union entitled to appear before the Court shall be represented by the Chairperson of the Commission or his/her representative.

4. The African Commission, the African Committee of Experts, African Inter-Governmental Organizations accredited to the Union or its organs and African National

Human Rights Institutions entitled to appear before the Court shall be represented by any person they choose for that purpose.

5. Individuals and Non-Governmental Organizations accredited to the Union or its organs may be represented or assisted by a person of their choice.

6. The agents and other representatives of parties before the Court, their counsel or advocates, witnesses, and any other persons whose presence is required at the Court shall enjoy the privileges and immunities necessary to the independent exercise of their duties or the smooth functioning of the Court.

Article 37—Communications and Notices

1. Communications and notices addressed to agents or counsel of parties to a case shall be considered as addressed to the parties.

2. For the service of all communications or notices upon persons other than the agents, counsel or advocates of parties concerned, the Court shall direct its request to the government of the State upon whose territory the communication or notice has to be served.

3. The same provision shall apply whenever steps are to be taken to procure evidence on the spot.

Article 38—Procedure Before the Court

The procedures before the Court shall be laid out in the Rules of Court, taking into account the complementarity between the Court and other treaty bodies of the Union.

Article 39—Public Hearing

The hearing shall be public, unless the Court, on its own motion or upon application by the parties, decides that the session shall be closed.

Article 40—Record of Proceedings

1. A record of proceedings shall be made at each hearing and shall be signed by the Registrar and the presiding Judge of the session.

2. This record alone shall be authentic.

Article 41—Default Judgment

1. Whenever one of the parties does not appear before the Court, or fails to defend the case against it, the Court shall proceed to consider the case and to give its judgment.

2. The Court shall before doing so, satisfy itself, not only that it has jurisdiction in accordance with Articles 28, 29 and 30 of the present Statute, but also that the claim is well founded in fact and law, and that the other party had due notice.

3. An objection by the party concerned may be lodged against the judgment within ninety (90) days of it being notified of the default judgment. Unless there is a decision to the contrary by the Court, the objection shall not have effect of staying the enforcement of the default judgment.

Article 42—Majority Required for Decision of the Court

1. Without prejudice to the provisions of Article 50(4) of the present Statute, the decisions of the Court shall be decided by a majority of the Judges present.

2. In the event of an equality of votes, the presiding Judge shall have a casting vote.

Article 43—Judgments and Decisions

1. The Court shall render its judgment within ninety (90) days of having completed its deliberations.

2. All judgments shall state the reasons on which they are based.

3. The judgment shall contain the names of the Judges who have taken part in the decision.

4. The judgment shall be signed by all the Judges and certified by the Presiding Judge and the Registrar. It shall be read in open session, due notice having been given to the agents.

5. The Parties to the case shall be notified of the judgment of the Court and it shall be transmitted to the Member States and the Commission.

6. The Executive Council shall also be notified of the judgment and shall monitor its execution on behalf of the Assembly.

Article 44—Dissenting Opinion

If the judgment does not represent in whole or in part the unanimous opinion of the Judges, any Judge shall be entitled to deliver a separate or dissenting opinion.

Article 45—Compensation

Without prejudice to its competence to rule on issues of compensation at the request of a party by virtue of paragraph 1(h) of Article 28 of the present Statute, the Court may, if it considers that there was a violation of a human or peoples' right, order any appropriate measures in order to remedy the situation, including granting fair compensation.

Article 46—Binding Force and Execution of Judgments

1. The decision of the Court shall be binding on the parties.

2. Subject to the provisions of paragraph 3, Article 41 of the present Statute, the judgment of the Court is final.

3. The parties shall comply with the judgment made by the Court in any dispute to which they are parties within the time stipulated by the Court and shall guarantee its execution.

4. Where a party has failed to comply with a judgment, the Court shall refer the matter to the Assembly, which shall decide upon measures to be taken to give effect to that judgment.

5. The Assembly may impose sanctions by virtue of paragraph 2 of Article 23 of the Constitutive Act.

Article 47—Interpretation

In the event of any dispute as to the meaning or scope of a judgment, the Court shall construe it upon the request of any party.

Article 48—Revision

1. An application for revision of a judgment may be made to the Court only when it is based upon discovery of a new fact of such nature as to be a decisive factor, which fact was, when the judgment was given, unknown to the Court and also to the party claiming revision, provided that such ignorance was not due to negligence.

2. The proceedings for revision shall be opened by a ruling of the Court expressly recording the existence of the new fact, recognizing that it has such a character as to lay the case open to revision, and declaring the revision admissible on this ground.

3. The Court may require prior compliance with the terms of the judgment before it admits proceedings in revision.

4. The application for revision shall be made within six (6) months of the discovery of the new fact.

5. No application may be made after the lapse of ten (10) years from the date of the judgment.

Article 49—Intervention

1. Should a Member State or organ of the Union consider that it has an interest of a legal nature which may be affected by the decision in the case, it may submit a request to the Court to be permitted to intervene. It shall be for the Court to decide upon this request.

2. If a Member State or organ of the Union should exercise the option offered under paragraph 1 of the present Article, the interpretation contained in the decision shall be equally binding upon it.

3. In the interest of the effective administration of justice, the Court may invite any Member State that is not a party to the case, any organ of the Union or any person concerned other than the claimant, to present written observations or take part in hearings.

Article 50—Intervention in a Case Concerning the Interpretation of the Constitutive Act

1. Whenever the question of interpretation of the Constitutive Act arises, in a case in which Member States other than the parties to the dispute have expressed an interest, the Registrar shall notify all such States and organs of the Union forthwith.

2. Every State Party and organ of the Union so notified has the right to intervene in the proceedings.

3. The decisions of the Court concerning the interpretation and application of the Constitutive Act shall be binding on Member States and organs of the Union, notwithstanding the provisions of paragraph 1 of Article 46 of this Statute.

4. Any decision made by virtue of this Article shall be made by a qualified majority of at least two (2) votes and in the presence of at least two-thirds of the Judges.

Article 51—Intervention in a Case concerning the Interpretation of Other Treaties

1. Whenever the question is that of interpretation of other treaties ratified by Member States other than the parties to a dispute, the Registrar shall notify all such States and the organs of the Union forthwith.

2. Every State Party and organ of the Union so notified has the right to intervene in the proceedings, and if it exercises this right, the interpretation given by the judgment shall be equally binding upon it.

3. This Article shall not be applicable to cases relating to alleged violations of a human or peoples' right, submitted by virtue of Articles 29 or 30 of the present Statute.

Article 52—Costs

1. Unless otherwise decided by the Court, each party shall bear its own costs.

2. Should it be required in the interest of justice, free legal aid may be provided for the person presenting an individual communication, under conditions to be set out in the Rules of Court.

CHAPTER V—ADVISORY OPINION

Article 53—Request for Advisory Opinion

1. The Court may give an advisory opinion on any legal question at the request of the Assembly, the Parliament, the Executive Council, the Peace and Security Council, the Economic, Social and Cultural Council (ECOSOCC), the Financial Institutions or any other organ of the Union as may be authorized by the Assembly.

2. A request for an advisory opinion shall be in writing and shall contain an exact statement of the question upon which the opinion is required and shall be accompanied by all relevant documents.

3. A request for an advisory opinion must not be related to a pending application before the African Commission or the African Committee of Experts.

Article 54—Service of Notice

1. The Registrar shall forthwith give notice of the request for an advisory opinion to all States or organs entitled to appear before the Court by virtue of Article 30 of the present Statute.

2. The Registrar shall also, by means of a special and direct communication, notify any State entitled to appear before the Court or any Intergovernmental Organization considered by the Court, or should it not be sitting, by the President, as likely to be able to furnish information on the question, that the Court will be prepared to receive, within a time limit to be fixed by the President, written statements, or to hear, at a public sitting to be held for the purpose, oral statements relating to the question.

3. Should any such State entitled to appear before the Court have failed to receive the special communication referred to in paragraph 2 of this Article, such State may express the desire to submit a written statement or to be heard, and the Court shall decide.

4. States and organizations having presented written or oral statements or both shall be permitted to comment on the statements made by other States or organizations in the form, to the extent, and within the time limits which the Court, or should it not be sitting, the President, shall decide in each particular case. Accordingly, the Registrar shall in due course communicate any such written statements to States and organizations having submitted similar statements.

Article 55—Delivery of Advisory Opinion

The Court shall deliver its advisory opinion in open court, notice having been given to the Chairperson of the Commission and Member States, and other International Organizations directly concerned.

Article 56—Application by Analogy of the Provisions of the Statute Applicable to Contentious Cases

In the exercise of its advisory functions, the Court shall further be guided by the provisions of the present Statute which apply in contentious cases to the extent to which it recognizes them to be applicable.

CHAPTER VI—REPORT TO THE ASSEMBLY

Article 57—Annual Activity Report

The Court shall submit to the Assembly, an annual report on its work during the previous year. The report shall specify, in particular, the cases in which a party has not complied with the judgment of the Court.

CHAPTER VII—PROCEDURE FOR AMENDMENTS

Article 58—Proposed Amendments from a State Party

1. The present Statute may be amended if a State Party makes a written request to that effect to the Chairperson of the Commission, who shall transmit same to Member States within thirty (30) days of receipt thereof.

2. The Assembly may adopt by a simple majority, the proposed amendment after the Court has given its opinion on it.

Article 59—Proposed Amendments from the Court

The Court may propose such amendments to the present Statute as it may deem necessary, to the Assembly through written communication to the Chairperson of the Commission, for consideration in conformity with the provisions of Article 58 of the present Statute.

Article 60—Entry into Force of Amendments

The amendment shall enter into force for every State which has accepted it in conformity with its Constitutional laws thirty (30) days after the Chairperson of the Commission is notified of this acceptance.

121. AFRICAN CHARTER ON THE RIGHTS AND WELFARE OF THE CHILD, 1990

This Charter, the first regional treaty on the rights of the child, was adopted and opened for signature by the Twenty-Sixth Ordinary Session of the Assembly of Heads of State and Government of the Organization of African Unity, Addis Ababa, Ethiopia, 11 July 1990; it entered into force on 29 November 1999. For text, see OAU doc. CAB/LEG/24.9/49 (1990); **http://www.africa-union.org.root/au/Documents/Treaties/treaties.htm**.

Further reading

KAIME, T., *The African Charter on the Rights and Welfare of the Child: A Socio-Legal Perspective*, Pretoria, South Africa: Pretoria University Law Press, 2010.
——, 'From lofty jargon to durable solutions: Unaccompanied refugee children and the African Charter on the Rights and Welfare of the Child', (2004) 16 *IJRL* 336.
LLOYD, A., 'Evolution of the African Charter on the Rights and Welfare of the Child and the African Committee of Experts: Raising the Gauntlet', (2002) 10 *International Journal of Children's Rights* 179.

TEXT

Preamble

The African Member States of the Organization of African Unity, Parties to the present Charter entitled 'African Charter on the Rights and Welfare of the Child',

Considering that the Charter of the Organization of African Unity recognizes the paramountcy of Human Rights and the African Charter on Human and Peoples' Rights proclaimed and agreed that everyone is entitled to all the rights and freedoms recognized and guaranteed therein, without distinction of any kind such as race, ethnic group, colour, sex, language, religion, political or any other opinion, national and social origin, fortune, birth or other status,

Recalling the Declaration on the Rights and Welfare of the African Child (AHG/ST.4 Rev. 1) adopted by the Assembly of Heads of State and Government of the Organization of African Unity, at its Sixteenth Ordinary Session in Monrovia, Liberia, from 17 to 20 July, 1979 recognized the need to take all appropriate measures to promote and protect the rights and welfare of the African Child,

Noting with concern that the situation of most African children, remains critical due to the unique factors of their socio-economic, cultural, traditional and developmental circumstances, natural disasters, armed conflicts, exploitation and hunger, and on account of the child's physical and mental immaturity he/she needs special safeguards and care,

Recognizing that the child occupies a unique and privileged position in the African society and that for the full harmonious development of his personality, the child should grow up in a family environment in an atmosphere of happiness, love and understanding,

Recognizing that the child, due to the needs of his physical and mental development requires particular care with regard to health, physical, mental, moral and social development, and requires legal protection in conditions of freedom, dignity and security,

Taking into consideration the virtues of their cultural heritage, historical background and the values of the African civilization which should inspire and characterize their reflection on the concept of the rights and welfare of the child,

Considering that the promotion and protection of the rights and welfare of the child also implies the performance of duties on the part of everyone,

Reaffirming adherence to the principles of the rights and welfare of the child contained in the declaration, conventions and other instruments of the Organization of African Unity and in the United Nations and in particular the United Nations Convention on the Rights of the Child; and the OAU Heads of State and Government's Declaration on the Rights and Welfare of the African Child:

Have agreed as follows:

PART I

RIGHTS AND DUTIES

Chapter One—Rights and Welfare of the Child

Article 1—Obligation of States Parties

1. Member States of the Organization of African Unity Parties to the present Charter shall recognize the rights, freedoms and duties enshrined in this Charter and shall undertake the necessary steps, in accordance with their Constitutional processes and with the provisions of the present Charter, to adopt such legislative or other measures as may be necessary to give effect to the provisions of this Charter.

2. Nothing in this Charter shall affect any provisions that are more conductive to the realization of the rights and welfare of the child contained in the law of a State Party or in any other international Convention or agreement in force in that State.

3. Any custom, tradition, cultural or religious practice that is inconsistent with the rights, duties and obligations contained in the present Charter shall to the extent of such inconsistency be discouraged.

Article 2—Definition of a Child

For the purposes of this Charter, a child means every human being below the age of 18 years.

Article 3—Non-Discrimination

Every child shall be entitled to the enjoyment of the rights and freedoms recognized and guaranteed in this Charter irrespective of the child's or his/her parents' or legal guardians' race, ethnic group, colour, sex, language, religion, political or other opinion, national and social origin, fortune, birth or other status.

Article 4—Best Interests of the Child

1. In all actions concerning the child undertaken by any person or authority the best interests of the child shall be the primary consideration.

2. In all judicial or administrative proceedings affecting a child who is capable of communicating his/her own views, an opportunity shall be provided for the views of the child to be heard either directly or through an impartial representative as a party to

the proceedings, and those views shall be taken into consideration by the relevant authority in accordance with the provisions of appropriate law.

Article 5—Survival and Development

1. Every child has an inherent right to life. This right shall be protected by law.

2. States Parties to the present Charter shall ensure, to the maximum extent possible, the survival, protection and development of the child.

3. Death sentence shall not be pronounced for crimes committed by children.

Article 6—Name and Nationality

1. Every child shall have the right from his birth to a name.

2. Every child shall be registered immediately after birth.

3. Every child has the right to acquire a nationality.

4. States Parties to the present Charter shall undertake to ensure that their Constitutional legislation recognize the principles according to which a child shall acquire the nationality of the State in the territory of which he has been born if, at the time of the child's birth, he is not granted nationality by any other State in accordance with its laws.

Article 7—Freedom of Expression

Every child who is capable of communicating his or her own views shall be assured the rights to express his opinions freely in all matters and to disseminate his opinions subject to such restrictions as are prescribed by laws.

Article 8—Freedom of Association

Every child shall have the right to free association and freedom of peaceful assembly in conformity with the law.

Article 9—Freedom of Thought, Conscience and Religion

1. Every child shall have the right to freedom of thought conscience and religion.

2. Parents, and where applicable, legal guardians shall have a duty to provide guidance and direction in the exercise of these rights having regard to the evolving capacities, and best interests of the child.

3. States Parties shall respect the duty of parents and where applicable, legal guardians to provide guidance and direction in the enjoyment of these rights subject to the national laws and policies.

Article 10—Protection of Privacy

No child shall be subject to arbitrary or unlawful interference with his privacy, family home or correspondence, or to the attacks upon his honour or reputation, provided that parents or legal guardians shall have the right to exercise reasonable supervision over the conduct of their children. The child has the right to the protection of the law against such interference or attacks.

Article 11—Education

1. Every child shall have the right to an education.

2. The education of the child shall be directed to:

   (a) the promotion and development of the child's personality, talents and mental and physical abilities to their fullest potential;

(b) fostering respect for human rights and fundamental freedoms with particular reference to those set out in the provisions of various African instruments on human and peoples' rights and international human rights declarations and conventions;

(c) the preservation and strengthening of positive African morals, traditional values and cultures;

(d) the preparation of the child for responsible life in a free society, in the spirit of understanding tolerance, dialogue, mutual respect and friendship among all peoples ethnic, tribal and religious groups;

(e) the preservation of national independence and territorial integrity;

(f) the promotion and achievements of African Unity and Solidarity;

(g) the development of respect for the environment and natural resources;

(h) the promotion of the child's understanding of primary health care.

3. States Parties to the present Charter shall take all appropriate measures with a view to achieving the full realization of this right and shall in particular:

(a) provide free and compulsory basic education:

(b) encourage the development of secondary education in its different forms and to progressively make it free and accessible to all;

(c) make the higher education accessible to all on the basis of capacity and ability by every appropriate means;

(d) take measures to encourage regular attendance at schools and the reduction of drop-out rates;

(e) take special measures in respect of female, gifted and disadvantaged children, to ensure equal access to education for all sections of the community.

4. States Parties to the present Charter shall respect the rights and duties of parents, and where applicable, of legal guardians to choose for their childrens schools, other than those established by public authorities, which conform to such minimum standards as may be approved by the State, to ensure the religious and moral education of the child in a manner with the evolving capacities of the child.

5. States Parties to the present Charter shall take all appropriate measures to ensure that a child who is subjected to schools or parental discipline shall be treated with humanity and with respect for the inherent dignity of the child and in conformity with the present Charter.

6. States Parties to the present Charter shall take all appropriate measures to ensure that children who become pregnant before completing their education shall have an opportunity to continue with their education on the basis of their individual ability.

7. No part of this Article shall be construed as to interfere with the liberty of individuals and bodies to establish and direct educational institutions subject to the observance of the principles set out in paragraph 1 of this Article and the requirement that the education given in such institutions shall conform to such minimum standards as may be laid down by the States.

Article 12—Leisure, Recreation and Cultural Activities

1. States Parties recognize the right of the child to rest and leisure, to engage in play and recreational activities appropriate to the age of the child and to participate freely in cultural life and the arts.

2. States Parties shall respect and promote the right of the child to fully participate in cultural and artistic life and shall encourage the provision of appropriate and equal opportunities for cultural, artistic, recreational and leisure activity.

Article 13—Handicapped Children

1. Every child who is mentally or physically disabled shall have the right to special measures of protection in keeping with his physical and moral needs and under conditions which ensure his dignity, promote his self-reliance and active participation in the community.

2. States Parties to the present Charter shall ensure, subject to available resources, to a disabled child and to those responsible for his care, of assistance for which application is made and which is appropriate to the child's condition and in particular shall ensure that the disabled child has effective access to training, preparation for employment and recreation opportunities in a manner conducive to the child achieving the fullest possible social integration, individual development and his cultural and moral development.

3. The States Parties to the present Charter shall use their available resources with a view to achieving progressively the full convenience of the mentally and physically disabled person to movement and access to public highway buildings and other places to which the disabled may legitimately want to have access to.

Article 14—Health and Health Services

1. Every child shall have the right to enjoy the best attainable state of physical, mental and spiritual health.

2. States Parties to the present Charter shall undertake to pursue the full implementation of this right and in particular shall take measures:

   (a) to reduce infant and child morality rate;

   (b) to ensure the provision of necessary medical assistance and health care to all children with emphasis on the development of primary health care;

   (c) to ensure the provision of adequate nutrition and safe drinking water;

   (d) to combat disease and malnutrition within the framework of primary health care through the application of appropriate technology;

   (e) to ensure appropriate health care for expectant and nursing mothers;

   (f) to develop preventive health care and family life education and provision of service;

   (g) to integrate basic health service programmes in national development plans;

   (h) to ensure that all sectors of the society, in particular, parents, children, community leaders and community workers are informed and supported in the use of basic knowledge of child health and nutrition, the advantages of breastfeeding, hygiene and environmental sanitation and the prevention of domestic and other accidents;

   (i) to ensure the meaningful participation of non-governmental organizations, local communities and the beneficiary population in the planning and management of a basic service programme for children;

   (j) to support through technical and financial means, the mobilization of local community resources in the development of primary health care for children.

Article 15—Child Labour

1. Every child shall be protected from all forms of economic exploitation and from performing any work that is likely to be hazardous or to interfere with the child's physical, mental, spiritual, moral, or social development.

2. States Parties to the present Charter take all appropriate legislative and administrative measures to ensure the full implementation of this Article which covers both the formal and informal sectors of employment and having regard to the relevant provisions of the International Labour Organization's instruments relating to children, States Parties shall in particular:

- *(a)* provide through legislation, minimum wages for admission to every employment;
- *(b)* provide for appropriate regulation of hours and conditions of employment;
- *(c)* provide for appropriate penalties or other sanctions to ensure the effective enforcement of this Article;
- *(d)* promote the dissemination of information on the hazards of child labour to all sectors of the community.

Article 16—Protection against Child Abuse and Torture

1. States Parties to the present Charter shall take specific legislative, administrative, social and educational measures to protect the child from all forms of torture, inhuman or degrading treatment and especially physical or mental injury or abuse, neglect or maltreatment including sexual abuse, while in the care of the child.

2. Protective measures under this Article shall include effective procedures for the establishment of special monitoring units to provide necessary support for the child and for those who have the care of the child, as well as other forms of prevention and for identification, reporting referral investigation, treatment, and follow-up of instances of child abuse and neglect.

Article 17—Administration of Juvenile Justice

1. Every child accused or found guilty of having infringed penal law shall have the right to special treatment in a manner consistent with the child's sense of dignity and worth and which reinforces the child's respect for human rights and fundamental freedoms of others.

2. States Parties to the present Charter shall in particular:

- *(a)* ensure that no child who is detained or imprisoned or otherwise deprived of his/her liberty is subjected to torture, inhuman or degrading treatment or punishment;
- *(b)* ensure that children are separated from adults in their place of detention or imprisonment;
- *(c)* ensure that every child accused of infringing the penal law:
    - (i)   shall be presumed innocent until duly recognized guilty;
    - (ii)   shall be informed promptly in a language that he understands and in detail of the charge against him, and shall be entitled to the assistance of an interpreter if he or she cannot understand the language used;
    - (iii) shall be afforded legal and other appropriate assistance in the preparation and presentation of his defence;
    - (iv)   shall have the matter determined as speedily as possible by an impartial tribunal and if found guilty, be entitled to an appeal by a higher tribunal;
- *(d)* prohibit the press and the public from trial.

3. The essential aim of treatment of every child during the trial and also if found guilty of infringing the penal law shall be his or her reformation, re-integration into his or her family and social rehabilitation.

4. There shall be a minimum age below which children shall be presumed not to have the capacity to infringe the penal law.

Article 18—*Protection of the Family*

1. The family shall be the natural unit and basis of society. It shall enjoy the protection and support of the State for its establishment and development.

2. States Parties to the present Charter shall take appropriate steps to ensure equality of rights and responsibilities of spouses with regard to children during marriage and in the event of its dissolution. In case of the dissolution, provision shall be made for the necessary protection of the child.

3. No child shall be deprived of maintenance by reference to the parents' marital status.

Article 19—*Parent Care and Protection*

1. Every child shall be entitled to the enjoyment of parental care and protection and shall, whenever possible, have the right to reside with his or her parents. No child shall be separated from his parents against his will, except when a judicial authority determines in accordance with the appropriate law, that such separation is in the best interest of the child.

2. Every child who is separated from one or both parents shall have the right to maintain personal relations and direct contact with both parents on a regular basis.

3. Where separation results from the action of a State Party, the State Party shall provide the child, or if appropriate, another member of the family with essential information concerning the whereabouts of the absent member or members of the family. States Parties shall also ensure that the submission of such a request shall not entail any adverse consequences for the person or persons in whose respect it is made.

4. Where a child is apprehended by a State Party, his parents or guardians shall, as soon as possible, be notified of such apprehension by that State Party.

Article 20—*Parental Responsibilities*

1. Parents or other persons responsible for the child shall have the primary responsibility of the upbringing and development of the child and shall have the duty:

   (a) to ensure that the best interests of the child are their basic concern at all times;
   (b) to secure, within their abilities and financial capacities, conditions of living necessary to the child's development; and
   (c) to ensure that domestic discipline is administered with humanity and in a manner consistent with the inherent dignity of the child.

2. States Parties to the present Charter shall in accordance with their means and national conditions take all appropriate measures;

   (a) to assist parents and other persons responsible for the child and in case of need provide material assistance and support programmes particularly with regard to nutrition, health, education, clothing and housing;
   (b) to assist parents and others responsible for the child in the performance of child-rearing and ensure the development of institutions responsible for providing care of children; and

(c) to ensure that the children of working parents are provided with care services and facilities.

Article 21—Protection against Harmful Social and Cultural Practices

1. States Parties to the present Charter shall take all appropriate measures to eliminate harmful social and cultural practices affecting the welfare, dignity, normal growth and development of the child and in particular:

(a) those customs and practices prejudicial to the health or life of the child; and

(b) those customs and practices discriminatory to the child on the grounds of sex or other status.

2. Child marriage and the betrothal of girls and boys shall be prohibited and effective action, including legislation, shall be taken to specify the minimum age of marriage to be 18 years and make registration of all marriages in an official registry compulsory.

Article 22—Armed Conflicts

1. States Parties to this Charter shall undertake to respect and ensure respect for rules of international humanitarian law applicable in armed conflicts which affect the child.

2. States Parties to the present Charter shall take all necessary measures to ensure that no child shall take a direct part in hostilities and refrain in particular, from recruiting any child.

3. States Parties to the present Charter shall, in accordance with their obligations under international humanitarian law, protect the civilian population in armed conflicts and shall take all feasible measures to ensure the protection and care of children who are affected by armed conflicts. Such rules shall also apply to children in situations of internal armed conflicts, tension and strife.

Article 23—Refugee Children

1. States Parties to the present Charter shall take all appropriate measures to ensure that a child who is seeking refugee status or who is considered a refugee in accordance with applicable international or domestic law shall, whether unaccompanied or accompanied by parents, legal guardians or close relatives, receive appropriate protection and humanitarian assistance in the enjoyment of the rights set out in this Charter and other international human rights and humanitarian instruments to which the States are Parties.

2. States Parties shall undertake to cooperate with existing international organizations which protect and assist refugees in their efforts to protect and assist such a child and to trace the parents or other close relatives or an unaccompanied refugee child in order to obtain information necessary for reunification with the family.

3. Where no parents, legal guardians or close relatives can be found, the child shall be accorded the same protection as any other child permanently or temporarily deprived of his family environment for any reason.

4. The provisions of this Article apply *mutatis mutandis* to internally displaced children whether through natural disaster, internal armed conflicts, civil strife, breakdown of economic and social order or howsoever caused.

Article 24—Adoption

States Parties which recognize the system of adoption shall ensure that the best interest of the child shall be the paramount consideration and they shall:

(a) establish competent authorities to determine matters of adoption and ensure that the adoption is carried out in conformity with applicable laws and procedures and on the basis of all relevant and reliable information, that the adoption is permissible in view of the child's status concerning parents, relatives and guardians and that, if necessary, the appropriate persons concerned have given their informed consent to the adoption on the basis of appropriate counselling;

(b) recognize that inter-country adoption in those States who have ratified or adhered to the International Convention on the Rights of the Child or this Charter may, as the last resort, be considered as an alternative means of a child's care, if the child cannot be placed in a foster or an adoptive family or cannot in any suitable manner be cared for in the child's country of origin;

(c) ensure that the child affected by inter-country adoption enjoys safeguards and standards equivalent to those existing in the case of national adoption;

(d) take all appropriate measures to ensure that in inter-country adoption, the placement does not result in trafficking or improper financial gain for those who try to adopt a child;

(e) promote, where appropriate, the objectives of this Article by concluding bilateral or multilateral arrangements or agreements, and endeavour, within this framework to ensure that the placement of the child in another country is carried out by competent authorities or organs;

(f) establish a machinery to monitor the well-being of the adopted child.

Article 25—Separation from Parents

1. Any child who is permanently or temporarily deprived of his family environment for any reason shall be entitled to special protection and assistance.
2. States Parties to the present Charter:

(a) shall ensure that a child who is parentless, or who is temporarily or permanently deprived of his or her family environment, or who in his or her best interest cannot be brought up or allowed to remain in that environment shall be provided with alternative family care, which could include, among others, foster placement, or placement in suitable institutions for the care of children;

(b) shall take all necessary measures to trace and re-unite children with parents or relatives where separation is caused by internal and external displacement arising from armed conflicts or natural disasters.

3. When considering alternative family care of the child and the best interests of the child, due regard shall be paid to the desirability of continuity in a child's up-bringing and to the child's ethnic, religious or linguistic background.

Article 26—Protection against Apartheid and Discrimination

1. States Parties to the present Charter shall individually and collectively undertake to accord the highest priority to the special needs of children living under apartheid and in States subject to military destabilization by the apartheid regime.
2. States Parties to the present Charter shall individually and collectively undertake to accord the highest priority to the special needs of children living under regimes practising racial, ethnic, religious or other forms of discrimination as well as in States subject to military destabilization.

3. States Parties shall undertake to provide whenever possible, material assistance to such children and to direct their efforts towards the elimination of all forms of discrimination and apartheid on the African Continent.

Article 27—Sexual Exploitation

1. States Parties to the present Charter shall undertake to protect the child from all forms of sexual exploitation and sexual abuse and shall in particular take measures to prevent:

(a) the inducement, coercion or encouragement of a child to engage in any sexual activity;

(b) the use of children in prostitution or other sexual practices;

(c) the use of children in pornographic activities, performances and materials.

Article 28—Drug Abuse

States Parties to the present Charter shall take all appropriate measures to protect the child from the use of narcotics and illicit use of psychotropic substances as defined in the relevant international treaties, and to prevent the use of children in the production and trafficking of such substances.

Article 29—Sale, Trafficking and Abduction

States Parties to the present Charter shall take appropriate measures to prevent:

(a) the abduction, the sale of, or traffic in children for any purpose or in any form, by any person including parents or legal guardians of the child;

(b) the use of children in all forms of begging.

Article 30—Children of Imprisoned Mothers

1. States Parties to the present Charter shall undertake to provide special treatment to expectant mothers and to mothers of infants and young children who have been accused or found guilty of infringing the penal law and shall in particular:

(a) ensure that a non-custodial sentence will always be first considered when sentencing such mothers;

(b) establish and promote measures alternative to institutional confinement for the treatment of such mothers;

(c) establish special alternative institutions for holding such mothers;

(d) ensure that a mother shall not be imprisoned with her child;

(e) ensure that a death sentence shall not be imposed on such mothers;

(f) the essential aim of the penitentiary system will be the reformation, the integration of the mother to the family and social rehabilitation.

Article 31—Responsibility of the Child

Every child shall have responsibilities towards his family and society, the State and other legally recognized communities and the international community. The child, subject to his age and ability, and such limitations as may be contained in the present Charter, shall have the duty:

(a) to work for the cohesion of the family, to respect his parents, superiors and elders at all times and to assist them in case of need;

(b) to serve his national community by placing his physical and intellectual abilities at its service;

(c) to preserve and strengthen social and national solidarity;

(d) to preserve and strengthen African cultural values in his relations with other members of the society, in the spirit of tolerance, dialogue and consultation and to contribute to the moral well-being of society;

(e) to preserve and strengthen the independence and the integrity of his country;

(f) to contribute to the best of his abilities. at all times and at all levels, to the promotion and achievement of African Unity.

PART II

Chapter Two—Establishment and Organization of the Committee on the Rights and Welfare of the Child

Article 32—The Committee

An African Committee of Experts on the Rights and Welfare of the Child hereinafter called 'the Committee' shall be established within the Organization of African Unity to promote and protect the rights and welfare of the child.

Article 33—Composition

1. The Committee shall consist of 11 members of high moral standing, integrity, impartiality and competence in matters of the rights and welfare of the child.

2. The members of the Committee shall serve in their personal capacity.

3. The Committee shall not include more than one national of the same State.

Article 34—Election

As soon as this Charter shall enter into force the members of the Committee shall be elected by secret ballot by the Assembly of Heads of State and Government from a list of persons nominated by the States Parties to the present Charter.

Article 35—Candidates

Each State Party to the present Charter may nominate not more than two candidates. The candidates must have one of the nationalities of the States Parties to the present Charter. When two candidates are nominated by a State, one of them shall not be a national of that State.

Article 36

1. The Secretary-General of the Organization of African Unity shall invite States Parties to the present Charter to nominate candidates at least six months before the elections.

2. The Secretary-General of the Organization of African Unity shall draw up in alphabetical order, a list of persons nominated and communicate it to the Heads of State and Government at least two months before the elections.

Article 37—Term of Office

1. The members of the Committee shall be elected for a term of five years and may not be re-elected. However. the term of four of the members elected at the first election shall expire after two years and the term of six others, after four years.

2. Immediately after the first election, the Chairman of the Assembly of Heads of State and Government of the Organization of African Unity shall draw lots to determine the names of those members referred to in sub-paragraph 1 of this Article.

3. The Secretary-General of the Organization of African Unity shall convene the first meeting of Committee at the Headquarters of the Organization within six months of the election of the members of the Committee, and thereafter the Committee shall be convened by its Chairman whenever necessary, at least once a year.

Article 38—Bureau

1. The Committee shall establish its own Rules of Procedure.

2. The Committee shall elect its officers for a period of two years.

3. Seven Committee members shall form the quorum.

4. In case of an equality of votes, the Chairman shall have a casting vote.

5. The working languages of the Committee shall be the official languages of the OAU.

Article 39—Vacancy

If a member of the Committee vacates his office for any reason other than the normal expiration of a term, the State which nominated that member shall appoint another member from among its nationals to serve for the remainder of the term—subject to the approval of the Assembly.

Article 40—Secretariat

The Secretary-General of the Organization of African Unity shall appoint a Secretary for the Committee.

Article 41—Privileges and Immunities

In discharging their duties, members of the Committee shall enjoy the privileges and immunities provided for in the General Convention on the Privileges and Immunities of the Organization of African Unity.

Chapter Three—Mandate and Procedure of the Committee

Article 42—Mandate

The functions of the Committee shall be:

(a) To promote and protect the rights enshrined in this Charter and in particular to:

   (i) collect and document information, commission inter-disciplinary assessment of situations on African problems in the fields of the rights and welfare of the child, organize meetings, encourage national and local institutions concerned with the rights and welfare of the child, and where necessary give its views and make recommendations to Governments;

   (ii) formulate and lay down principles and rules aimed at protecting the rights and welfare of children in Africa;

(iii) cooperate with other African, international and regional Institutions and organizations concerned with the promotion and protection of the rights and welfare of the child.

(b) To monitor the implementation and ensure protection of the rights enshrined in this Charter.

(c) To interpret the provisions of the present Charter at the request of a State Party, an Institution of the Organization of African Unity or any other person or Institution recognized by the Organization of African Unity, or any State Party.

(d) Perform such other task as may be entrusted to it by the Assembly of Heads of State and Government, Secretary-General of the OAU and any other organs of the OAU or the United Nations.

Article 43—Reporting Procedure

1. Every State Party to the present Charter shall undertake to submit to the Committee through the Secretary-General of the Organization of African Unity, reports on the measures they have adopted which give effect to the provisions of this Charter and on the progress made in the enjoyment of these rights:

(a) within two years of the entry into force of the Charter for the State Party concerned: and

(b) thereafter, every three years.

2. Every report made under this Article shall:

(a) contain sufficient information on the implementation of the present Charter to provide the Committee with comprehensive understanding of the implementation of the Charter in the relevant country; and

(b) shall indicate factors and difficulties, if any, affecting the fulfilment of the obligations contained in the Charter.

3. A State Party which has submitted a comprehensive first report to the Committee need not, in its subsequent reports submitted in accordance with paragraph 1 (a) of this Article, repeat the basic information previously provided.

Article 44—Communications

1. The Committee may receive communication, from any person, group or non-governmental organization recognized by the Organization of African Unity, by a Member State, or the United Nations relating to any matter covered by this Charter.

2. Every communication to the Committee shall contain the name and address of the author and shall be treated in confidence.

Article 45—Investigations by the Committee

1. The Committee may resort to any appropriate method of investigating any matter falling within the ambit of the present Charter, request from the States Parties any information relevant to the implementation of the Charter and may also resort to any appropriate method of investigating the measures the State Party has adopted to implement the Charter.

2. The Committee shall submit to each Ordinary Session of the Assembly of Heads of State and Government every two years, a report on its activities and on any communication made under Article 46 [sc. 44] of this Charter.

3. The Committee shall publish its report after it has been considered by the Assembly of Heads of State and Government.

4. States Parties shall make the Committee's reports widely available to the public in their own countries.

Chapter Four—Miscellaneous Provisions

Article 46—Sources of Inspiration

The Committee shall draw inspiration from International Law on Human Rights, particularly from the provisions of the African Charter on Human and Peoples' Rights, the Charter of the Organization of African Unity, the Universal Declaration on Human Rights, the International Convention on the Rights of the Child, and other instruments adopted by the United Nations and by African countries in the field of human rights. and from African values and traditions.

Article 47—Signature, Ratification or Adherence

1. The present Charter shall be open to signature by all the Member States of the Organization of African Unity.

2. The present Charter shall be subject to ratification or adherence by Member States of the Organization of African Unity. The instruments of ratification or adherence to the present Charter shall be deposited with the Secretary-General of the Organization of African Unity.

3. The present Charter shall come into force 30 days after the reception by the Secretary-General of the Organization of African Unity of the instruments of ratification or adherence of 15 Member States of the Organization of African Unity.

Article 48—Amendment and Revision of the Charter

1. The present Charter may be amended or revised if any State Party makes a written request to that effect to the Secretary-General of the Organization of African Unity, provided that the proposed amendment is not submitted to the Assembly of Heads of State and Government for consideration until all the States Parties have been duly notified of it and the Committee has given its opinion on the amendment.

2. An amendment shall be approved by a simple majority of the States Parties.

122. AFRICAN CHARTER ON DEMOCRACY, ELECTIONS AND GOVERNANCE, 2007

The Charter was adopted by the Eighth Ordinary Session of the Assembly of the African Union, in Addis Ababa, Ethiopia, on 30 January 2007; see **http://www.africa-union.org/root/au/ Documents/Treaties/treaties.htm**. For a summary of the background, see GOODWIN-GILL, G. S., *Free and Fair Elections*, Geneva: Inter-Parliamentary Union, 2nd rev'd edn., 2006, 38–41.

Further reading

AJONG MBAPNDAH, L. and NGONJI NJUNGWE, E., 'Applying the African Charter on Democracy, Elections and Governance to Dictatorships: The Cameroonian Experience', (2008) 2 *Cameroon Journal on Democracy and Human Rights* 59; available at **http://www.cjdhr.org**.

KANE, I., 'The Implementation of the African Charter on Democracy, Elections and Governance', (2008) 17 *African Security Review* 43; available at **http://www.iss.co.za**.

TEXT

Preamble

We, the Member States of the African Union (AU);

Inspired by the objectives and principles enshrined in the Constitutive Act of the African Union, particularly Articles 3 and 4, which emphasise the significance of good governance, popular participation, the rule of law and human rights;

Recognising the contributions of the African Union and Regional Economic Communities to the promotion, nurturing, strengthening and consolidation of democracy and governance;

Reaffirming our collective will to work relentlessly to deepen and consolidate the rule of law, peace, security and development in our countries;

Guided by our common mission to strengthen and consolidate institutions for good governance, continental unity and solidarity;

Committed to promote the universal values and principles of democracy, good governance, human rights and the right to development;

Cognizant of the historical and cultural conditions in Africa;

Seeking to entrench in the Continent a political culture of change of power based on the holding of regular, free, fair and transparent elections conducted by competent, independent and impartial national electoral bodies;

Concerned about the unconstitutional changes of governments that are one of the essential causes of insecurity, instability and violent conflict in Africa;

Determined to promote and strengthen good governance through the institutionalization of transparency, accountability and participatory democracy;

Convinced of the need to enhance the election observation missions in the role they play, particularly as they are an important contributory factor to ensuring the regularity, transparency and credibility of elections;

Desirous to enhance the relevant Declarations and Decisions of the OAU/AU (including the 1990 Declaration on the political and socio-economic situation in Africa and the fundamental changes taking place in the world, the 1995 Cairo Agenda for the Re-launch of Africa's Economic and Social Development, the 1999 Algiers Declaration on Unconstitutional Changes of Government, the 2000 Lomé Declaration for an OAU Response to Unconstitutional Changes of Government, the 2002 OAU/AU Declaration on Principles Governing Democratic Elections in Africa, the 2003 Protocol Relating to the Establishment of the Peace and Security Council of the African Union);

Committed to implementing Decision EX.CL/Dec.31(III) adopted in Maputo, Mozambique, in July 2003 and Decision EX.CL/124(V) adopted in Addis Ababa, Ethiopia, in May 2004 respectively, by the adoption of an African Charter on Democracy, Elections and Governance;

Have agreed as follows:

CHAPTER 1—DEFINITIONS

Article 1

In this Charter, unless otherwise stated, the following expressions shall have the following meaning:

'AU' means the African Union;

'African Human Rights Commission' means the African Commission on Human and Peoples' Rights;

'African Peer Review Mechanism' APRM means the African Peer Review Mechanism;

'Assembly' means the Assembly of Heads of State and Government of the African Union;

'Commission' means the Commission of the Union;

'Constitutive Act' means the Constitutive Act of the Union;

'Charter' means the African Charter on Democracy, Elections and Governance;

'Member States' means the Member States of the African Union;

'National Electoral Body' means a competent authority, established by the relevant legal instruments of a State Party, responsible for organizing and supervising elections;

'NEPAD' means the New Partnership for Africa's Development;

'Peace and Security Council' means the Peace and Security Council of the African Union;

'Regional Economic Communities' means the regional integration blocs of the African Union;

'State Party' means any Member State of the African Union which has ratified or acceded to this Charter and deposited the instruments for ratification or accession with the Chairperson of the African Union Commission;

'Union' means the African Union.

CHAPTER 2—OBJECTIVES

Article 2

The objectives of this Charter are to:

1. Promote adherence, by each State Party, to the universal values and principles of democracy and respect for human rights;

2. Promote and enhance adherence to the principle of the rule of law premised upon the respect for, and the supremacy of, the Constitution and constitutional order in the political arrangements of the State Parties;

3. Promote the holding of regular free and fair elections to institutionalize legitimate authority of representative government as well as democratic change of governments;

4. Prohibit, reject and condemn unconstitutional change of government in any Member State as a serious threat to stability, peace, security and development;

5. Promote and protect the independence of the judiciary;

6. Nurture, support and consolidate good governance by promoting democratic culture and practice, building and strengthening governance institutions and inculcating political pluralism and tolerance;

7. Encourage effective coordination and harmonization of governance policies amongst State Parties with the aim of promoting regional and continental integration;

8. Promote State Parties' sustainable development and human security;

9. Promote the fight against corruption in conformity with the provisions of the AU Convention on Preventing and Combating Corruption adopted in Maputo, Mozambique in July 2003;

10. Promote the establishment of the necessary conditions to foster citizen participation, transparency, access to information, freedom of the press and accountability in the management of public affairs;

11. Promote gender balance and equality in the governance and development processes;

12. Enhance cooperation between the Union, Regional Economic Communities and the International Community on democracy, elections and governance; and

13. Promote best practices in the management of elections for purposes of political stability and good governance.

CHAPTER 3—PRINCIPLES

Article 3

State Parties shall implement this Charter in accordance with the following principles:

1. Respect for human rights and democratic principles;

2. Access to and exercise of state power in accordance with the constitution of the State Party and the principle of the rule of law;

3. Promotion of a system of government that is representative;

4. Holding of regular, transparent, free and fair elections;

5. Separation of powers;

6. Promotion of gender equality in public and private institutions;

7. Effective participation of citizens in democratic and development processes and in governance of public affairs;

8. Transparency and fairness in the management of public affairs;

9. Condemnation and rejection of acts of corruption, related offenses and impunity;

10. Condemnation and total rejection of unconstitutional changes of government;

11. Strengthening political pluralism and recognising the role, rights and responsibilities of legally constituted political parties, including opposition political parties, which should be given a status under national law.

CHAPTER 4—DEMOCRACY, RULE OF LAW AND HUMAN RIGHTS

Article 4

1. State Parties shall commit themselves to promote democracy, the principle of the rule of law and human rights.

2. State Parties shall recognize popular participation through universal suffrage as the inalienable right of the people.

Article 5

State Parties shall take all appropriate measures to ensure constitutional rule, particularly constitutional transfer of power.

Article 6

State Parties shall ensure that citizens enjoy fundamental freedoms and human rights taking into account their universality, interdependence and indivisibility.

Article 7

State Parties shall take all necessary measures to strengthen the Organs of the Union that are mandated to promote and protect human rights and to fight impunity and endow them with the necessary resources.

Article 8

1. State Parties shall eliminate all forms of discrimination, especially those based on political opinion, gender, ethnic, religious and racial grounds as well as any other form of intolerance.

2. State Parties shall adopt legislative and administrative measures to guarantee the rights of women, ethnic minorities, migrants, people with disabilities, refugees and displaced persons and other marginalized and vulnerable social groups.

3. State Parties shall respect ethnic, cultural and religious diversity, which contributes to strengthening democracy and citizen participation.

Article 9

State Parties undertake to design and implement social and economic policies and programmes that promote sustainable development and human security.

Article 10

1. State Parties shall entrench the principle of the supremacy of the constitution in the political organization of the State.

2. State Parties shall ensure that the process of amendment or revision of their constitution reposes on national consensus, obtained if need be, through referendum.

3. State Parties shall protect the right to equality before the law and equal protection by the law as a fundamental precondition for a just and democratic society.

CHAPTER 5—THE CULTURE OF DEMOCRACY AND PEACE

Article 11

The State Parties undertake to develop the necessary legislative and policy frameworks to establish and strengthen a culture of democracy and peace.

Article 12

State Parties undertake to implement programmes and carry out activities designed to promote democratic principles and practices as well as consolidate a culture of democracy and peace.

To this end, State Parties shall:

1. Promote good governance by ensuring transparent and accountable administration.

2. Strengthen political institutions to entrench a culture of democracy and peace.

3. Create conducive conditions for civil society organizations to exist and operate within the law.

4. Integrate civic education in their educational curricula and develop appropriate programmes and activities.

Article 13

State Parties shall take measures to ensure and maintain political and social dialogue, as well as public trust and transparency between political leaders and the people, in order to consolidate democracy and peace.

CHAPTER 6—DEMOCRATIC INSTITUTIONS

Article 14

1. State Parties shall strengthen and institutionalize constitutional civilian control over the armed and security forces to ensure the consolidation of democracy and constitutional order.

2. State Parties shall take legislative and regulatory measures to ensure that those who attempt to remove an elected government through unconstitutional means are dealt with in accordance with the law.

3. State Parties shall cooperate with each other to ensure that those who attempt to remove an elected government through unconstitutional means are dealt with in accordance with the law.

Article 15

1. State Parties shall establish public institutions that promote and support democracy and constitutional order.

2. State Parties shall ensure that the independence or autonomy of the said institutions is guaranteed by the constitution.

3. State Parties shall ensure that these institutions are accountable to competent national organs.

4. State Parties shall provide the above-mentioned institutions with resources to perform their assigned missions efficiently and effectively.

Article 16

State Parties shall cooperate at regional and continental levels in building and consolidating democracy through exchange of experiences.

CHAPTER 7—DEMOCRATIC ELECTIONS

Article 17

State Parties re-affirm their commitment to regularly holding transparent, free and fair elections in accordance with the Union's Declaration on the Principles Governing Democratic Elections in Africa.

To this end, State Parties shall:

1. Establish and strengthen independent and impartial national electoral bodies responsible for the management of elections.

2. Establish and strengthen national mechanisms that redress election-related disputes in a timely manner.

3. Ensure fair and equitable access by contesting parties and candidates to state controlled media during elections.

4. Ensure that there is a binding code of conduct governing legally recognized political stakeholders, government and other political actors prior, during and after elections. The code shall include a commitment by political stakeholders to accept the results of the election or challenge them in through exclusively legal channels.

Article 18

1. State Parties may request the Commission, through the Democracy and Electoral Assistance Unit and the Democracy and Electoral Assistance Fund, to provide advisory services or assistance for strengthening and developing their electoral institutions and processes.

2. The Commission may at any time, in consultation with the State Party concerned, send special advisory missions to provide assistance to that State Party for strengthening its electoral institutions and processes.

Article 19

1. Each State Party shall inform the Commission of scheduled elections and invite it to send an electoral observer mission.

2. Each State Party shall guarantee conditions of security, free access to information, non-interference, freedom of movement and full cooperation with the electoral observer mission.

Article 20

The Chairperson of the Commission shall first send an exploratory mission during the period prior to elections. This mission shall obtain any useful information and documentation, and brief the Chairperson, stating whether the necessary conditions have been established and if the environment is conducive to the holding of transparent, free and fair elections in conformity with the principles of the Union governing democratic elections.

Article 21

1. The Commission shall ensure that these missions are independent and shall provide them with the necessary resources for that purpose.

2. Electoral observer missions shall be conducted by appropriate and competent experts in the area of election monitoring, drawn from continental and national institutions such as, but not limited to, the Pan-African Parliament, national electoral bodies, national legislatures and eminent persons taking due cognizance of the principles of regional representation and gender equality.

3. Electoral observer missions shall be conducted in an objective, impartial and transparent manner.

4. All electoral observer missions shall present the report of their activities to the Chairperson of the Commission within a reasonable time.

5. A copy of the report shall be submitted to the State Party concerned within a reasonable time.

Article 22

State Parties shall create a conducive environment for independent and impartial national monitoring or observation mechanisms.

CHAPTER 8—SANCTIONS IN CASES OF UNCONSTITUTIONAL CHANGES OF GOVERNMENT

Article 23

State Parties agree that the use of, *inter alia*, the following illegal means of accessing or maintaining power constitute an unconstitutional change of government and shall draw appropriate sanctions by the Union:

1. Any putsch or coup d'Etat against a democratically elected government.

2. Any intervention by mercenaries to replace a democratically elected government.

3. Any replacement of a democratically elected government by armed dissidents or rebels.

4. Any refusal by an incumbent government to relinquish power to the winning party or candidate after free, fair and regular elections; or

5. Any amendment or revision of the constitution or legal instruments, which is an infringement on the principles of democratic change of government.

Article 24

When a situation arises in a State Party that may affect its democratic political institutional arrangements or the legitimate exercise of power, the Peace and Security Council shall exercise its responsibilities in order to maintain the constitutional order in accordance with relevant provisions of the Protocol Relating to the Establishment of the Peace and Security Council of the African Union, hereinafter referred to as the Protocol.

Article 25

1. When the Peace and Security Council observes that there has been an unconstitutional change of government in a State Party, and that diplomatic initiatives have failed, it shall suspend the said State Party from the exercise of its right to participate in the activities of the Union in accordance with the provisions of articles 30 of the Constitutive Act and 7 (g) of the Protocol. The suspension shall take effect immediately.

2. However, the suspended State Party shall continue to fulfill its obligations to the Union, in particular with regard to those relating to respect of human rights.

3. Notwithstanding the suspension of the State Party, the Union shall maintain diplomatic contacts and take any initiatives to restore democracy in that State Party.

4. The perpetrators of unconstitutional change of government shall not be allowed to participate in elections held to restore the democratic order or hold any position of responsibility in political institutions of their State.

5. Perpetrators of unconstitutional change of government may also be tried before the competent court of the Union.

6. The Assembly shall impose sanctions on any Member State that is proved to have instigated or supported unconstitutional change of government in another state in conformity with Article 23 of the Constitutive Act.

7. The Assembly may decide to apply other forms of sanctions on perpetrators of unconstitutional change of government including punitive economic measures.

8. State Parties shall not harbour or give sanctuary to perpetrators of unconstitutional changes of government.

9. State Parties shall bring to justice the perpetrators of unconstitutional changes of government or take necessary steps to effect their extradition.

10.   State Parties shall encourage conclusion of bilateral extradition agreements as well as the adoption of legal instruments on extradition and mutual legal assistance.

Article 26

The Peace and Security Council shall lift sanctions once the situation that led to the suspension is resolved.

CHAPTER 9—POLITICAL, ECONOMIC AND SOCIAL GOVERNANCE

Article 27

In order to advance political, economic and social governance, State Parties shall commit themselves to:

1. Strengthening the capacity of parliaments and legally recognised political parties to perform their core functions;

2. Fostering popular participation and partnership with civil society organizations;

3. Undertaking regular reforms of the legal and justice systems;

4. Improving public sector management;

5. Improving efficiency and effectiveness of public services and combating corruption;

6. Promoting the development of the private sector through, inter alia, enabling legislative and regulatory framework;

7. Development and utilisation of information and communication technologies;

8. Promoting freedom of expression, in particular freedom of the press and fostering a professional media;

9. Harnessing the democratic values of the traditional institutions; and

10. Preventing the spread and combating the impact of diseases such as Malaria, Tuberculosis, HIV/AIDS, Ebola fever, and Avian Flu.

Article 28

State Parties shall ensure and promote strong partnerships and dialogue between government, civil society and private sector.

Article 29

1. State Parties shall recognize the crucial role of women in development and strengthening of democracy.

2. State Parties shall create the necessary conditions for full and active participation of women in the decision-making processes and structures at all levels as a fundamental element in the promotion and exercise of a democratic culture.

3. State Parties shall take all possible measures to encourage the full and active participation of women in the electoral process and ensure gender parity in representation at all levels, including legislatures.

Article 30

State Parties shall promote citizen participation in the development process through appropriate structures.

Article 31

1. State Parties shall promote participation of social groups with special needs, including the Youth and people with disabilities, in the governance process.

2. State Parties shall ensure systematic and comprehensive civic education in order to encourage full participation of social groups with special needs in democracy and development processes.

Article 32

State Parties shall strive to institutionalize good political governance through:

1. Accountable, efficient and effective public administration;
2. Strengthening the functioning and effectiveness of parliaments;
3. An independent judiciary;
4. Relevant reforms of public institutions including the security sector;
5. Harmonious relationships in society including civil-military relations;
6. Consolidating sustainable multiparty political systems;
7. Organising regular, free and fair elections; and
8. Entrenching and respecting the principle of the rule of law.

Article 33

State Parties shall institutionalize good economic and corporate governance through, *inter alia*:

1. Effective and efficient public sector management;
2. Promoting transparency in public finance management;
3. Preventing and combating corruption and related offences;
4. Efficient management of public debt;
5. Prudent and sustainable utilization of public resources;
6. Equitable allocation of the nation's wealth and natural resources;
7. Poverty alleviation;
8. Enabling legislative and regulatory framework for private sector development;
9. Providing a conducive environment for foreign capital inflows;
10. Developing tax policies that encourage investment;
11. Preventing and combating crime;
12. Elaborating and implementing economic development strategies including private-public sector partnerships;
13. An efficient and effective tax system premised upon transparency and accountability.

Article 34

State Parties shall decentralize power to democratically elected local authorities as provided in national laws.

Article 35

Given the enduring and vital role of traditional authorities, particularly in rural communities, the State Parties shall strive to find appropriate ways and means to increase their integration and effectiveness within the larger democratic system.

Article 36

State Parties shall promote and deepen democratic governance by implementing the principles and core values of the NEPAD Declaration on Democracy, Political, Economic and Corporate Governance and, where applicable, the African Peer Review Mechanism (APRM).

Article 37

State Parties shall pursue sustainable development and human security through achievement of NEPAD objectives and the United Nations Millennium Development Goals (MDGs).

Article 38

1. State Parties shall promote peace, security and stability in their respective countries, regions and in the continent by fostering participatory political systems with well-functioning and, if need be, inclusive institutions;

2. State Parties shall promote solidarity amongst Member States and support the conflict prevention and resolution initiatives that the Union may undertake in conformity with the Protocol establishing the Peace and Security Council.

Article 39

State Parties shall promote a culture of respect, compromise, consensus and tolerance as a means to mitigate conflicts, promote political stability and security, and to harness the creative energies of the African peoples.

Article 40

State Parties shall adopt and implement policies, strategies and programmes required to generate productive employment, mitigate the impact of diseases and alleviate poverty and eradicate extreme poverty and illiteracy.

Article 41

State Parties shall undertake to provide and enable access to basic social services to the people.

Article 42

State Parties shall implement policies and strategies to protect the environment to achieve sustainable development for the benefit of the present and future generations. In this regard, State Parties are encouraged to accede to the relevant treaties and other international legal instruments.

Article 43

1. State Parties shall endeavour to provide free and compulsory basic education to all, especially girls, rural inhabitants, minorities, people with disabilities and other marginalized social groups.

2. In addition, State Parties shall ensure the literacy of citizens above compulsory school age, particularly women, rural inhabitants, minorities, people with disabilities, and other marginalized social groups.

CHAPTER 10—MECHANISMS FOR APPLICATION

Article 44

To give effect to the commitments contained in this Charter:

1. *Individual State Party Level*

State Parties commit themselves to implement the objectives, apply the principles and respect the commitments enshrined in this Charter as follows:

    (a) State Parties shall initiate appropriate measures including legislative, executive and administrative actions to bring State Parties' national laws and regulations into conformity with this Charter;

(b) State Parties shall take all necessary measures in accordance with constitutional provisions and procedures to ensure the wider dissemination of the Charter and all relevant legislation as may be necessary for the implementation of its fundamental principles;

(c) State Parties shall promote political will as a necessary condition for the attainment of the goals set forth in this Charter;

(d) State Parties shall incorporate the commitments and principles of the Charter in their national policies and strategies.

2. *Commission Level*

A. At Continental Level

(a) The Commission shall develop benchmarks for implementation of the commitments and principles of this Charter and evaluate compliance by State Parties;

(b) The Commission shall promote the creation of favourable conditions for democratic governance in the African Continent, in particular by facilitating the harmonization of policies and laws of State Parties;

(c) The Commission shall take the necessary measures to ensure that the Democracy and Electoral Assistance Unit and the Democracy and Electoral Assistance Fund provide the needed assistance and resources to State Parties in support of electoral processes;

(d) The Commission shall ensure that effect is given to the decisions of the Union in regard to unconstitutional change of government on the Continent.

B. At Regional Level

The Commission shall establish a framework for cooperation with Regional Economic Communities on the implementation of the principles of the Charter. In this regard, it shall commit the Regional Economic Communities (RECs) to:

(a) Encourage Member States to ratify or adhere to this Charter.

(b) Designate focal points for coordination, evaluation and monitoring of the implementation of the commitments and principles enshrined in this Charter in order to ensure massive participation of stakeholders, particularly civil society organizations, in the process.

Article 45

The Commission shall:

(a) Act as the central coordinating structure for the implementation of this Charter;

(b) Assist State Parties in implementing the Charter;

(c) Coordinate evaluation on implementation of the Charter with other key organs of the Union including the Pan-African Parliament, the Peace and Security Council, the African Human Rights Commission, the African Court of Justice and Human Rights, the Economic, Social and Cultural Council, the Regional Economic Communities and appropriate national-level structures.

CHAPTER 11—FINAL CLAUSES

Article 46

In conformity with applicable provisions of the Constitutive Act and the Protocol Relating to the Establishment of the Peace and Security Council of the African Union, the Assembly and the Peace and Security Council shall determine the appropriate measures to be imposed on any State Party that violates this Charter.

Article 47

1. This Charter shall be open for signature, ratification and accession by Member States of the Union in accordance with their respective constitutional procedures.

2. The instruments of ratification or accession shall be deposited with the Chairperson of the Commission.

Article 48

This Charter shall enter into force thirty (30) days after the deposit of fifteen (15) Instruments of Ratification.

Article 49

1. State Parties shall submit every two years, from the date the Charter comes into force, a report to the Commission on the legislative or other relevant measures taken with a view to giving effect to the principles and commitments of the Charter;

2. A copy of the report shall be submitted to the relevant organs of the Union for appropriate action within their respective mandates;

3. The Commission shall prepare and submit to the Assembly, through the Executive Council, a synthesized report on the implementation of the Charter;

4. The Assembly shall take appropriate measures aimed at addressing issues raised in the report.

Article 50

1. Any State Party may submit proposals for the amendment or revision of this Charter;

2. Proposals for amendment or revision shall be submitted to the Chairperson of the Commission who shall transmit same to State Parties within thirty (30) days of receipt thereof;

3. The Assembly, upon the advice of the Executive Council, shall examine these proposals at its session following notification, provided all State Parties have been notified at least three (3) months before the beginning of the session;

4. The Assembly shall adopt amendments or revisions by consensus or failing which, by two-thirds majority;

5. The amendments or revisions shall enter into force when approved by two-thirds majority of State Parties.

Article 51

1. The Chairperson of the Commission shall be the depository of this Charter;

2. The Chairperson of the Commission shall inform all Member States of the signature, ratification, accession, entry into force, reservations, requests for amendments and approvals thereof;

3. Upon entry into force of this Charter, the Chairperson of the Commission shall register it with the Secretary General of the United Nations in accordance with Article 102 of the Charter of the United Nations.

Article 52

None of the provisions of the present Charter shall affect more favourable provisions relating to democracy, elections and governance contained in the national legislation of State Parties or in any other regional, continental or international conventions or agreements applicable in these State Parties.

Article 53

This Charter, drawn up in four (4) original texts, in Arabic, English, French and Portuguese languages, all four (4) being equally authentic, shall be deposited with the Chairperson of the Commission who shall transmit certified copies of same to all Member States and the United Nations General Secretariat.

123. AFRICAN UNION CONVENTION FOR THE PROTECTION AND ASSISTANCE OF INTERNALLY DISPLACED PERSONS IN AFRICA, 2009

This Convention (the 'Kampala Convention') was adopted on 22 October 2009 at the AU Special Summit on Refugees, Returnees and Internally Displaced Persons in Africa. Seventeen States signed the Convention, which will enter into force following fifteen ratifications (Article 17).

On the same day, AU Member States adopted the Kampala Declaration on Refugees, Returnees and Internally Displaced Persons in Africa, which calls for a stronger commitment to meeting the challenges of mass displacement. It places strong emphasis, in particular, on the prevention of forced displacement; effective protection for those displaced, 'including full respect for the fundamental principle of *non-refoulement* as recognised in international customary law as enunciated in...' Article 33 of the 1951 Convention (above, p. 312) and Article 2 of the 1969 OAU Convention (above, p. 1019); meeting the special needs of displaced women and children and other vulnerable groups; and reconstructing communities emerging from conflicts and natural disasters. For the text, see AU doc. Ext/Assembly/AU/PA/Draft/Decl.(I), Rev.1; http://www.africa-union.org; also available in the *Online Resource Centre*.

The AU Convention follows an earlier, sub-regional agreement—the Protocol on the Protection and Assistance to Internally Displaced Persons, 2006, concluded under the auspices of the International Conference on the Great Lakes Region and complemented by a Protocol on the Property Rights of Returning Persons, adopted the same day; the text of both instruments is available in the *Online Resource Centre*. The present convention, which States undertake to incorporate into domestic law (Article 3(2)(a)), includes a wide range of obligations dealing with causes, individual responsibility, protection from displacement, and protection and assistance for those displaced.

In its definition of the internally displaced (Article 1(k)), the Convention matches the approach of the Guiding Principles on Internal Displacement, 1997 (above, p. 225), which are also acknowledged in the Preamble. The Convention's significance, of course, lies in its translation of many of these principles to the level of obligation, and in its provisions on monitoring by way of a 'Conference of States Parties' (Article 14). Of interest also is Article 6, on the obligations of international organizations and humanitarian agencies; Article 7 on, among others, the obligations of armed groups; Article 8, on obligations relating to the African Union in the matter of intervention; and Article 9(2)(e) on the obligation of States parties to 'respect and ensure the right [of internally displaced persons] to seek safety in another part of the State and to be protected against forcible return to or resettlement in any place where their life, safety, liberty and/or health would be at risk'.

Further reading

Mulugeta Abebe, A., 'Legal and Institutional Dimensions of Protecting and Assisting Internally Displaced Persons in Africa', (2009) 22 *Journal of Refugee Studies* 155.

TEXT

PREAMBLE

We, the Heads of State and Government of the Member States of the African Union;

Conscious of the gravity of the situation of internally displaced persons as a source of continuing instability and tension for African States;

Also conscious of the suffering and specific vulnerability of internally displaced persons;

Reiterating the inherent African custom and tradition of hospitality by local host communities for persons in distress and support for such communities;

Committed to sharing our common vision of providing durable solutions to situations of internally displaced persons by establishing an appropriate legal framework for their protection and assistance;

Determined to adopt measures aimed at preventing and putting an end to the phenomenon of internal displacement by eradicating the root causes, especially persistent and recurrent conflicts as well as addressing displacement caused by natural disasters, which have a devastating impact on human life, peace, stability, security, and development;

Considering the 2000 Constitutive Act of the African Union and the 1945 Charter of the United Nations;

Reaffirming the principle of the respect of the sovereign equality of States Parties, their territorial integrity and political independence as stipulated in the Constitutive Act of the African Union and the United Nations Charter;

Recalling the 1948 Universal Declaration of Human Rights, the 1948 Convention on the Prevention and Punishment of the Crime of Genocide, the 1949 Four Geneva Conventions and the 1977 Additional Protocols to the Geneva Conventions, the 1951 United Nations Convention Relating to the Status of Refugees and the 1967 Protocol Relating to the Status of Refugees, the 1969 OAU Convention Governing the Specific Aspects of Refugee Problems in Africa, the 1979 Convention on the Elimination of All Forms of Discrimination Against Women, the 1981 African Charter on Human and Peoples' Rights and the 2003 Protocol to the African Charter on Human and Peoples' Rights on the Rights of Women in Africa, the 1990 African Charter on the Rights and Welfare of the Child, the 1994 Addis Ababa Document on Refugees and Forced Population Displacement in Africa, and other relevant United Nations and African Union human rights instruments, and relevant Security Council Resolutions;

Mindful that Member States of the African Union have adopted democratic practices and adhere to the principles of non-discrimination, equality and equal protection of the law under the 1981 African Charter on Human and Peoples' Rights, as well as under other regional and international human rights law instruments;

Recognising the inherent rights of internally displaced persons as provided for and protected in international human rights and humanitarian law and as set out in the 1998 United Nations Guiding Principles on Internal Displacement, which are recognized as an important international framework for the protection of internally displaced persons;

Affirming our primary responsibility and commitment to respect, protect and fulfill the rights to which internally displaced persons are entitled, without discrimination of any kind;

Noting the specific roles of international Organizations and agencies within the framework of the United Nations inter-agency collaborative approach to internally displaced persons, especially the protection expertise of the Office of the United Nations High Commissioner for Refugees (UNHCR) and the invitation extended to it by the Executive Council of the African Union in Decision EX/CL.413 (XIII) of July 2008 at Sharm El Sheikh, Egypt, to continue and reinforce its role in the protection of and assistance to internally displaced persons, within the United Nations coordination mechanism; and noting also the mandate of the International Committee of the Red Cross to protect and assist persons affected by armed conflict and other situations of violence, as well as the work of civil society organizations, in conformity with the laws of the country in which they exercise such roles and mandates;

Recalling the lack of a binding African and international legal and institutional framework specifically, for the prevention of internal displacement and the protection of and assistance to internally displaced persons;

Reaffirming the historical commitment of the AU Member States to the protection of and assistance to refugees and displaced persons and, in particular, the implementation of Executive Council Decision EX/CL/127 of July 2004 in Addis Ababa to collaborate with relevant cooperating partners and other stakeholders to ensure that internally displaced persons are provided with an appropriate legal framework to ensure their adequate protection and assistance as well as with durable solutions;

Convinced that the present Convention for the Protection and Assistance of Internally Displaced Persons presents such a legal framework;

Have Agreed as Follows:

Article 1—Definitions

For the purpose of the present Convention:

(a) 'African Charter' means the African Charter on Human and Peoples' Rights;

(b) 'African Commission' means the African Commission on Human and Peoples' Rights;

(c) 'African Court of Justice and Human Rights' means the African Court of Justice and Human Rights;

(d) 'Arbitrary displacement' means arbitrary displacement as referred to in Article 4 (4) (a) to (h);

(e) 'Armed Groups' means dissident armed forces or other organized armed groups that are distinct from the armed forces of the State;

(f) 'AU' means the African Union;

(g) 'AU Commission' means the Secretariat of the African Union, which is the depository of the regional instruments;

(h) 'Child' means every human being below the age of 18 years;

(i) 'Constitutive Act' means the Constitutive Act of the African Union;

(j) 'Harmful Practices' means all behaviour, attitudes and/or practices which negatively affect the fundamental rights of persons, such as but not limited to their right to life, health, dignity, education, mental and physical integrity and education;

(k) 'Internally Displaced Persons' means persons or groups of persons who have been forced or obliged to flee or to leave their homes or places of habitual residence, in particular as a result of or in order to avoid the effects of armed conflict, situations of generalized violence, violations of human rights or natural or human-made disasters, and who have not crossed an internationally recognized State border;

(l) 'Internal displacement' means the involuntary or forced movement, evacuation or relocation of persons or groups of persons within internationally recognized state borders;

(m) 'Member State' means a Member State of the African Union;

(n) 'Non-State actors' means private actors who are not public officials of the State, including other armed groups not referred to in article 1(d) above, and whose acts cannot be officially attributed to the State;

(o) 'OAU' means the Organization of African Unity;

(p) 'Women' mean persons of the female gender, including girls;

(q) 'Sphere Standards' mean standards for monitoring and evaluating the effectiveness and impact of humanitarian assistance; and

(r) 'States Parties' means African States which have ratified or acceded to this Convention.

Article 2—Objectives

The objectives of this Convention are to:

(a) Promote and strengthen regional and national measures to prevent or mitigate, prohibit and eliminate root causes of internal displacement as well as provide for durable solutions;

(b) Establish a legal framework for preventing internal displacement, and protecting and assisting internally displaced persons in Africa;

(c) Establish a legal framework for solidarity, cooperation, promotion of durable solutions and mutual support between the States Parties in order to combat displacement and address its consequences;

(d) Provide for the obligations and responsibilities of States Parties, with respect to the prevention of internal displacement and protection of, and assistance to, internally displaced persons;

(e) Provide for the respective obligations, responsibilities and roles of armed groups, non-State actors and other relevant actors, including civil society organizations, with respect to the prevention of internal displacement and protection of, and assistance to, internally displaced persons.

Article 3—General Obligations Relating to States Parties

1. States Parties undertake to respect and ensure respect for the present Convention. In particular, States Parties shall:

(a) Refrain from, prohibit and prevent arbitrary displacement of populations;

(b) Prevent political, social, cultural and economic exclusion and marginalisation, that are likely to cause displacement of populations or persons by virtue of their social identity, religion or political opinion;

(c) Respect and ensure respect for the principles of humanity and human dignity of internally displaced persons;

(d) Respect and ensure respect and protection of the human rights of internally displaced persons, including humane treatment, non-discrimination, equality and equal protection of law;

(e) Respect and ensure respect for international humanitarian law regarding the protection of internally displaced persons;

(f) Respect and ensure respect for the humanitarian and civilian character of the protection of and assistance to internally displaced persons, including ensuring that such persons do not engage in subversive activities;

(g) Ensure individual responsibility for acts of arbitrary displacement, in accordance with applicable domestic and international criminal law;

(h) Ensure the accountability of non-State actors concerned, including multinational companies and private military or security companies, for acts of arbitrary displacement or complicity in such acts;

(i) Ensure the accountability of non-State actors involved in the exploration and exploitation of economic and natural resources leading to displacement;

(j) Ensure assistance to internally displaced persons by meeting their basic needs as well as allowing and facilitating rapid and unimpeded access by humanitarian organizations and personnel;

(k) Promote self-reliance and sustainable livelihoods amongst internally displaced persons, provided that such measures shall not be used as a basis for neglecting the protection of and assistance to internally displaced persons, without prejudice to other means of assistance;

2. States Parties shall:

(a) Incorporate their obligations under this Convention into domestic law by enacting or amending relevant legislation on the protection of, and assistance to, internally displaced persons in conformity with their obligations under international law;

(b) Designate an authority or body, where needed, responsible for coordinating activities aimed at protecting and assisting internally displaced persons and assign responsibilities to appropriate organs for protection and assistance, and for cooperating with relevant international organizations or agencies, and civil society organizations, where no such authority or body exists;

(c) Adopt other measures as appropriate, including strategies and policies on internal displacement at national and local levels, taking into account the needs of host communities;

(d) Provide, to the extent possible, the necessary funds for protection and assistance without prejudice to receiving international support;

(e) Endeavour to incorporate the relevant principles contained in this Convention into peace negotiations and agreements for the purpose of finding sustainable solutions to the problem of internal displacement.

Article 4—Obligations of States Parties relating to Protection from Internal Displacement

1. States Parties shall respect and ensure respect for their obligations under international law, including human rights and humanitarian law, so as to prevent and avoid conditions that might lead to the arbitrary displacement of persons.

2. States Parties shall devise early warning systems, in the context of the continental early warning system, in areas of potential displacement, establish and implement disaster risk reduction strategies, emergency and disaster preparedness and management measures and, where necessary, provide immediate protection and assistance to internally displaced persons.

3. States Parties may seek the cooperation of international organizations or humanitarian agencies, civil society organizations and other relevant actors.

4. All persons have a right to be protected against arbitrary displacement. The prohibited categories of arbitrary displacement include but are not limited to:

(a) Displacement based on policies of racial discrimination or other similar practices aimed at/or resulting in altering the ethnic, religious or racial composition of the population;

(b) Individual or mass displacement of civilians in situations of armed conflict, unless the security of the civilians involved or imperative military reasons so demand, in accordance with international humanitarian law;

(c) Displacement intentionally used as a method of warfare or due to other violations of international humanitarian law in situations of armed conflict;

(d) Displacement caused by generalized violence or violations of human rights;

(e) Displacement as a result of harmful practices;

(f) Forced evacuations in cases of natural or human made disasters or other causes if the evacuations are not required by the safety and health of those affected;

(g) Displacement used as a collective punishment;

(h) Displacement caused by any act, event, factor, or phenomenon of comparable gravity to all of the above and which is not justified under international law, including human rights and international humanitarian law.

5. States Parties shall endeavour to protect communities with special attachment to, and dependency, on land due to their particular culture and spiritual values from being displaced from such lands, except for compelling and overriding public interests.

6. States Parties shall declare as offences punishable by law acts of arbitrary displacement that amount to genocide, war crimes or crimes against humanity.

Article 5—Obligations of States Parties relating to Protection and Assistance

1. States Parties shall bear the primary duty and responsibility for providing protection of and humanitarian assistance to internally displaced persons within their territory or jurisdiction without discrimination of any kind.

2. States Parties shall cooperate with each other upon the request of the concerned State Party or the Conference of State Parties in protecting and assisting internally displaced persons.

3. States Parties shall respect the mandates of the African Union and the United Nations, as well as the roles of international humanitarian organizations in providing protection and assistance to internally displaced persons, in accordance with international law.

4. States Parties shall take measures to protect and assist persons who have been internally displaced due to natural or human made disasters, including climate change.

5. States Parties shall assess or facilitate the assessment of the needs and vulnerabilities of internally displaced persons and of host communities, in cooperation with international organizations or agencies.

6. States Parties shall provide sufficient protection and assistance to internally displaced persons, and where available resources are inadequate to enable them to do so, they shall cooperate in seeking the assistance of international organizations and humanitarian agencies, civil society organizations and other relevant actors. Such organizations may offer their services to all those in need.

7. States Parties shall take necessary steps to effectively organize relief action that is humanitarian, and impartial in character, and guarantee security. States Parties shall allow rapid and unimpeded passage of all relief consignments, equipment and personnel

to internally displaced persons. States Parties shall also enable and facilitate the role of local and international organizations and humanitarian agencies, civil society organizations and other relevant actors, to provide protection and assistance to internally displaced persons. States Parties shall have the right to prescribe the technical arrangements under which such passage is permitted.

8. States Parties shall uphold and ensure respect for the humanitarian principles of humanity, neutrality, impartiality and independence of humanitarian actors.

9. States Parties shall respect the right of internally displaced persons to peacefully request or seek protection and assistance, in accordance with relevant national and international laws, a right for which they shall not be persecuted, prosecuted or punished.

10. States Parties shall respect, protect and not attack or otherwise harm humanitarian personnel and resources or other materials deployed for the assistance or benefit of internally displaced persons.

11. States Parties shall take measures aimed at ensuring that armed groups act in conformity with their obligations under Article 7.

12. Nothing in this Article shall prejudice the principles of sovereignty and territorial integrity of States.

Article 6—Obligations Relating to International Organizations and Humanitarian Agencies

1. International organizations and humanitarian agencies shall discharge their obligations under this Convention in conformity with international law and the laws of the country in which they operate.

2. In providing protection and assistance to internally displaced persons, international organizations and humanitarian agencies shall respect the rights of such persons in accordance with international law.

3. International organizations and humanitarian agencies shall be bound by the principles of humanity, neutrality, impartiality and independence of humanitarian actors, and ensure respect for relevant international standards and codes of conduct.

Article 7—Protection and Assistance to Internally Displaced Persons in Situations of Armed Conflict

1. The provisions of this Article shall not, in any way whatsoever, be construed as affording legal status or legitimizing or recognizing armed groups and are without prejudice to the individual criminal responsibility of the members of such groups under domestic or international criminal law.

2. Nothing in this Convention shall be invoked for the purpose of affecting the sovereignty of a State or the responsibility of the Government, by all legitimate means, to maintain or re-establish law and order in the State or to defend the national unity and territorial integrity of the State.

3. The protection and assistance to internally displaced persons under this Article shall be governed by international law and in particular international humanitarian law.

4. Members of armed groups shall be held criminally responsible for their acts which violate the rights of internally displaced persons under international law and national law.

5. Members of armed groups shall be prohibited from:

(a) Carrying out arbitrary displacement;

(b) Hampering the provision of protection and assistance to internally displaced persons under any circumstances;

(c) Denying internally displaced persons the right to live in satisfactory conditions of dignity, security, sanitation, food, water, health and shelter; and separating members of the same family;

(d) Restricting the freedom of movement of internally displaced persons within and outside their areas of residence;

(e) Recruiting children or requiring or permitting them to take part in hostilities under any circumstances;

(f) Forcibly recruiting persons, kidnapping, abduction or hostage taking, engaging in sexual slavery and trafficking in persons especially women and children;

(g) Impeding humanitarian assistance and passage of all relief consignments, equipment and personnel to internally displaced persons;

(h) Attacking or otherwise harming humanitarian personnel and resources or other materials deployed for the assistance or benefit of internally displaced persons and shall not destroy, confiscate or divert such materials; and

(i) Violating the civilian and humanitarian character of the places where internally displaced persons are sheltered and shall not infiltrate such violations.

Article 8—Obligations relating to the African Union

1. The African Union shall have the right to intervene in a Member State pursuant to a decision of the Assembly in accordance with Article 4 (h) of the Constitutive Act in respect of grave circumstances, namely: war crimes, genocide, and crimes against humanity.

2. The African Union shall respect the right of States Parties to request intervention from the Union in order to restore peace and security in accordance with Article 4 (j) of the Constitutive Act and thus contribute to the creation of favourable conditions for finding durable solutions to the problem of internal displacement.

3. The African Union shall support the efforts of the States Parties to protect and assist internally displaced persons under this Convention. In particular, the Union shall:

(a) Strengthen the institutional framework and capacity of the African Union with respect to protection and assistance to internally displaced persons;

(b) Coordinate the mobilisation of resources for protection and assistance to internally displaced persons;

(c) Collaborate with international organizations and humanitarian agencies, civil society organizations and other relevant actors in accordance with their mandates, to support measures taken by States Parties to protect and assist internally displaced persons;

(d) Cooperate directly with African States and international organizations and humanitarian agencies, civil society organizations and other relevant actors, with respect to appropriate measures to be taken in relation to the protection of and assistance to internally displaced persons;

(e) Share information with the African Commission on Human and Peoples' Rights on the situation of displacement, and the protection and assistance accorded to internally displaced persons in Africa; and,

(f) Cooperate with the Special Rapporteur of the African Commission on Human and Peoples' Rights for Refugees, Returnees, IDPs and Asylum Seekers in addressing issues of internally displaced persons.

Article 9—Obligations of States Parties Relating to Protection and Assistance During Internal Displacement

1. States Parties shall protect the rights of internally displaced persons regardless of the cause of displacement by refraining from, and preventing, the following acts, amongst others:

   (a) Discrimination against such persons in the enjoyment of any rights or freedoms on the grounds that they are internally displaced persons;

   (b) Genocide, crimes against humanity, war crimes and other violations of international humanitarian law against internally displaced persons;

   (c) Arbitrary killing, summary execution, arbitrary detention, abduction, enforced disappearance or torture and other forms of cruel, inhuman or degrading treatment or punishment;

   (d) Sexual and gender based violence in all its forms, notably rape, enforced prostitution, sexual exploitation and harmful practices, slavery, recruitment of children and their use in hostilities, forced labour and human trafficking and smuggling; and

   (e) Starvation.

2. States Parties shall:

   (a) Take necessary measures to ensure that internally displaced persons are received, without discrimination of any kind and live in satisfactory conditions of safety, dignity and security;

   (b) Provide internally displaced persons to the fullest extent practicable and with the least possible delay, with adequate humanitarian assistance, which shall include food, water, shelter, medical care and other health services, sanitation, education, and any other necessary social services, and where appropriate, extend such assistance to local and host communities;

   (c) Provide special protection for and assistance to internally displaced persons with special needs, including separated and unaccompanied children, female heads of households, expectant mothers, mothers with young children, the elderly, and persons with disabilities or with communicable diseases;

   (d) Take special measures to protect and provide for the reproductive and sexual health of internally displaced women as well as appropriate psycho-social support for victims of sexual and other related abuses;

   (e) Respect and ensure the right to seek safety in another part of the State and to be protected against forcible return to or resettlement in any place where their life, safety, liberty and/or health would be at risk;

   (f) Guarantee the freedom of movement and choice of residence of internally displaced persons, except where restrictions on such movement and residence are necessary, justified and proportionate to the requirements of ensuring security for internally displaced persons or maintaining public security, public order and public health;

(g) Respect and maintain the civilian and humanitarian character of the places where internally displaced persons are sheltered and safeguard such locations against infiltration by armed groups or elements and disarm and separate such groups or elements from internally displaced persons;

(h) Take necessary measures, including the establishment of specialized mechanisms, to trace and reunify families separated during displacement and otherwise facilitate the re-establishment of family ties;

(i) Take necessary measures to protect individual, collective and cultural property left behind by displaced persons as well as in areas where internally displaced persons are located, either within the jurisdiction of the State Parties, or in areas under their effective control;

(j) Take necessary measures to safeguard against environmental degradation in areas where internally displaced persons are located, either within the jurisdiction of the State Parties, or in areas under their effective control;

(k) States Parties shall consult internally displaced persons and allow them to participate in decisions relating to their protection and assistance;

(l) Take necessary measures to ensure that internally displaced persons who are citizens in their country of nationality can enjoy their civic and political rights, particularly public participation, the right to vote and to be elected to public office; and

(m) Put in place measures for monitoring and evaluating the effectiveness and impact of the humanitarian assistance delivered to internally displaced persons in accordance with relevant practice, including the Sphere Standards.

3. States Parties shall discharge these obligations, where appropriate, with assistance from international organizations and humanitarian agencies, civil society organizations, and other relevant actors.

Article 10—Displacement induced by Projects

1. States Parties, as much as possible, shall prevent displacement caused by projects carried out by public or private actors.

2. States Parties shall ensure that the stakeholders concerned will explore feasible alternatives, with full information and consultation of persons likely to be displaced by projects.

3. States parties shall carry out a socio-economic and environmental impact assessment of a proposed development project prior to undertaking such a project.

Article 11—Obligations of States Parties relating to Sustainable Return, Local Integration or Relocation

1. States Parties shall seek lasting solutions to the problem of displacement by promoting and creating satisfactory conditions for voluntary return, local integration or relocation on a sustainable basis and in circumstances of safety and dignity.

2. States Parties shall enable internally displaced persons to make a free and informed choice on whether to return, integrate locally or relocate by consulting them on these and other options and ensuring their participation in finding sustainable solutions.

3. States Parties shall cooperate, where appropriate, with the African Union and international organizations or humanitarian agencies and civil society organizations, in

providing protection and assistance in the course of finding and implementing solutions for sustainable return, local integration or relocation and long-term reconstruction.

4. States Parties shall establish appropriate mechanisms providing for simplified procedures where necessary, for resolving disputes relating to the property of internally displaced persons.

5. States Parties shall take all appropriate measures, whenever possible, to restore the lands of communities with special dependency and attachment to such lands upon the communities' return, reintegration, and reinsertion.

Article 12—Compensation

1. States Parties shall provide persons affected by displacement with effective remedies.

2. States Parties shall establish an effective legal framework to provide just and fair compensation and other forms of reparations, where appropriate, to internally displaced persons for damage incurred as a result of displacement, in accordance with international standards.

3. A State Party shall be liable to make reparation to internally displaced persons for damage when such a State Party refrains from protecting and assisting internally displaced persons in the event of natural disasters.

Article 13—Registration and Personal Documentation

1. States Parties shall create and maintain an up-dated register of all internally displaced persons within their jurisdiction or effective control. In doing so, States Parties may collaborate with international organizations or humanitarian agencies or civil society organizations.

2. States Parties shall ensure that internally displaced persons shall be issued with relevant documents necessary for the enjoyment and exercise of their rights, such as passports, personal identification documents, civil certificates, birth certificates and marriage certificates.

3. States Parties shall facilitate the issuance of new documents or the replacement of documents lost or destroyed in the course of displacement, without imposing unreasonable conditions, such as requiring return to one's area of habitual residence in order to obtain these or other required documents. The failure to issue internally displaced persons with such documents shall not in any way impair the exercise or enjoyment of their human rights.

4. Women and men as well as separated and unaccompanied children shall have equal rights to obtain such necessary identity documents and shall have the right to have such documentation issued in their own names.

Article 14—Monitoring Compliance

1. States Parties agree to establish a Conference of States Parties to this Convention to monitor and review the implementation of the objectives of this Convention.

2. States Parties shall enhance their capacity for cooperation and mutual support under the auspices of the Conference of the States Parties.

3. States Parties agree that the Conference of the States Parties shall be convened regularly and facilitated by the African Union.

4. States Parties shall, when presenting their reports under Article 62 of the African Charter on Human and Peoples' Rights as well as, where applicable, under the African

Peer Review Mechanism indicate the legislative and other measures that have been taken to give effect to this Convention.

FINAL PROVISIONS

Article 15—Application

1. States Parties agree that except where expressly stated in this Convention, its provisions apply to all situations of internal displacement regardless of its causes.

2. States Parties agree that nothing in this Convention shall be construed as affording legal status or legitimizing or recognizing armed groups and that its provisions are without prejudice to the individual criminal responsibility of their members under domestic or international criminal law.

Article 16—Signature, ratification and membership

1. This Convention shall be open to signature, ratification or accession by Member States of the AU in accordance with their respective constitutional procedures.

2. The instruments of ratification or accession shall be deposited with the Chairperson of the African Union Commission.

Article 17—Entry into force

1. This Convention shall enter into force thirty (30) days after the deposit of the instruments of ratification or accession by fifteen (15) Member States.

2. The Chairperson of the AU Commission shall notify Member States of the coming into force of this Convention.

Article 18—Amendment and Revision

1. States Parties may submit proposals for the amendment or revision of this Convention.

2. Proposals for amendment or revision shall be submitted, in writing, to the Chairperson of the Commission of the AU who shall transmit the same to the States Parties within thirty (30) days of receipt thereof.

3. The Conference of States Parties, upon advice of the Executive Council, shall examine these proposals within a period of one (1) year following notification of States Parties, in accordance with the provisions of paragraph 2 of this Article.

4. Amendments or revision shall be adopted by the Conference of States Parties by a simple majority of the States Parties present and voting.

5. Amendments shall come into force thirty (30) days following the depositing of the fifteenth (15) instrument of ratification by the States Parties with the Chairperson of the AU Commission.

Article 19—Denunciation

1. A State Party may denounce this Convention by sending a written notification addressed to the Chairperson of the AU Commission, while indicating the reasons for such a denunciation.

2. The denunciation shall take effect one (1) year from the date when the notification was received by the Chairperson of the AU Commission, unless a subsequent date has been specified.

Article 20—Saving Clause

1. No provision in this Convention shall be interpreted as affecting or undermining the right of internally displaced persons to seek and be granted asylum within the framework of the African Charter on Human and Peoples' Rights, and to seek protection, as a refugee, within the purview of the 1969 OAU Convention Governing the Specific Aspects of Refugee Problems in Africa or the 1951 UN Convention Relating to the Status of Refugees as well as the 1967 Protocol Relating to the Status of Refugees.

2. This Convention shall be without prejudice to the human rights of internally displaced persons under the African Charter on Human and Peoples' Rights and other applicable instruments of international human rights law or international humanitarian law. Similarly, it shall in no way be understood, construed or interpreted as restricting, modifying or impeding existing protection under any of the instruments mentioned herein.

3. The right of internally displaced persons to lodge a complaint with the African Commission on Human and Peoples' Rights or the African Court of Justice and Human Rights, or any other competent international body shall in no way be affected by this Convention.

4. The provisions of this Convention shall be without prejudice to the individual criminal responsibility of internally displaced persons, within the framework of national or international criminal law and their duties by virtue of the African Charter on Human and Peoples' Rights.

Article 21—Reservations

States Parties shall not make or enter reservations to this Convention that are incompatible with the object and purpose of this Convention.

Article 22—Settlement of Disputes

1. Any dispute or differences arising between the States Parties with regard to the interpretation or application of this Convention shall be settled amicably through direct consultations between the States Parties concerned. In the event of failure to settle the dispute or differences, either State may refer the dispute to the African Court of Justice and Human Rights.

2. Until such time as and when the latter shall have been established, the dispute or differences shall be submitted to the Conference of the States Parties, which will decide by consensus or, failing which, by a two-third (2/3) majority of the States Parties present and voting.

Article 23—Depository

1. This Convention shall be deposited with the Chairperson of the AU Commission, who shall transmit a certified true copy of the Convention to the Government of each signatory State.

2. The Chairperson of the AU Commission shall register this Convention with the United Nations Secretary-General as soon as it comes into force.

3. This Convention is drawn up in four (4) original texts; in the Arabic, English, French and Portuguese languages, all four (4) being equally authentic.

By virtue of which, we, the Heads of State and Government of the African Union (AU), have signed this Convention.

Adopted by the Special Summit of the Union held in Kampala on the 22nd day of October 2009.

PART EIGHT

ARAB AND OTHER ISLAMIC STATES

INTRODUCTION

Agreement on human rights instruments among Arab and Islamic States has been slow in coming. Two of the documents reproduced below are in the form of declarations, while the fate of the revised Arab Charter on Human Rights remains to be seen. The overall situation has prompted concern, particularly among non-governmental organizations; see the 'Casablanca Declaration of the Arab Human Rights Movement', adopted by the First International Conference of the Arab Human Rights Movement, Casablanca, 23–25 April 1999. The Conference, which was organized by the Cairo Institute for Human Rights Studies and hosted by the Moroccan Organization for Human Rights, examined the human rights conditions in the Arab world, and the responsibilities, tasks and prospects of the Arab human rights movement. After extensive discussions, the Conference declared that the only source of reference is international human rights law and the United Nations instruments and declarations. It also emphasized the universality of human rights.

At the same time, there is evidence also of increasing awareness of the importance of attending to human rights issues; see, for example, the 'Sana'a Declaration, 2004', issued by the Inter-Governmental Regional Conference on Democracy, Human Rights and the Role of the International Criminal Court, held in Sana'a, Yemen, on 10–12 January 2004. The Conference was organized by the Government of Yemen and the non-governmental organization 'No Peace Without Justice'; it involved some 820 participants from 52 countries and representatives from regional and international organizations, and from civil society and political parties. See also the 'Tunis Declaration', issued at the 16th Session of the Arab Summit, which was held in Tunis from 22–23 May 2004.

At the Islamic Summit, held in Dakar from 13-14 March 2008, a number of modifications to the Charter of the Islamic Conference were adopted, in particular, concerning respect for human rights; see AL-MIDANI, M. A., 'Les textes de référence, 2008': http://www.aidh.org/txtref/2008/islamo2a.htm. These include changes to the Preamble and purposes and principles, and provision for a new body, the Permanent Independent Commission on Human Rights.

Further reading

AGI, M., ed., *Islam et droits de l'homme*, Paris: Editions des Idées et des Hommes, 2007.

AL-MIDANI, M. A., 'Les récents développements au sein de l'Organisation de la Conférence Islamique et le respect des droits de l'homme', *Point de vue*, June 2009: available at **http://www. aidh.org**.

——, *Les droits de l'homme et l'Islam. Textes des organisations arabes et islamiques*, édité par l'Association des Publications de la Faculté de Théologie Protestante, Université Marc Bloch de Strasbourg, 2003.

——, 'La Déclaration universelle des droits de l'homme et le droit musulman', 2004: **http:// www.aidh.org/Biblio/Txt_Arabe/HP_Arabe.htm**.

AN-NA'IM, A., 'Human Rights in the Arab World: A Regional Perspective', (2001) 23 *Human Rights Quarterly* 701.

BADERIN, M. A., 'Establishing Areas of Common Ground between Islamic Law and International Human Rights', (2001) 5 *International Journal of Human Rights*, 72.

——, *International Human Rights and Islamic Law* , Oxford: Oxford University Press, 2003.

——, 'The Role of Islam in Human Rights and Development in Muslim States', REHMAN, J. and BREAU, S. C., eds., *Religion, Human Rights and International Law*, The Hague: Martinus Nijhoff, 2007, 321.

BERWEEN, M., 'The Fundamental Human Rights: An Islamic Perspective', (2002) 6 *International Journal of Human Rights*, 61.

——, 'International Bills of Human Rights: An Islamic Critique', (2004) 7 *International Journal of Human Rights*, 129.

MAYER, A. E., *Islam and Human Rights: Tradition and Politics*, Boulder: Westview Press, 4th edn., 2006.

OH, I., *The Rights of God: Islam, Human Rights and Comparative Ethics*, Washington DC: Georgetown University Press, 2007.

SACHEDINA, A., *Islam and the Challenge of Human Rights*, Oxford: Oxford University Press, 2009.

124. CAIRO DECLARATION ON HUMAN RIGHTS IN ISLAM, 1990

The Cairo Declaration on Human Rights in Islam was adopted by the Organization of the Islamic Conference, Cairo, 5 August 1990. Text in UN doc. A/45/421-S/21797, 200; A/CONF.157/PC/35; A/CONF.157/PC/62/Add.18, 2.

Further reading

AL-MIDANI, M. A.,'La Déclaration du Caire sur les droits de l'homme en Islam est-elle conforme à la Déclaration universelle des droits de l'homme?' (2004) 60 *Revue Egyptienne de droit international* 31.

ISLAMIC EDUCATIONAL, SCIENTIFIC and CULTURAL ORGANIZATION, Morocco: **http://www.isesco.org.ma/**.

MAYER, A. E., *Islam and Human Rights: Tradition and Politics*, Boulder: Westview, 4th edn., 2006.

TEXT

The Member States of the Organization of the Islamic Conference,

Reaffirming the civilizing and historical role of the Islamic Ummah which God made the best nation that has given mankind a universal and well-balanced civilization in which harmony is established between this life and the hereafter and knowledge is combined with spiritual faith; and the role that this Ummah should play to guide a humanity confused by competing trends and ideologies and to provide solutions to the chronic problems of this materialistic civilization.

Wishing to contribute to the efforts of mankind to assert human rights, to protect man from exploitation and persecution, and to affirm his freedom and right to a dignified life in accordance with the Islamic Shari'ah.

Convinced that mankind which has reached an advanced stage in materialistic science is still, and shall remain, in dire need of faith to support its civilization and of a self motivating force to guard its rights.

Believing that fundamental rights and universal freedoms in Islam are an integral part of the Islamic religion and that no one as a matter of principle has the right to suspend them in whole or in part or violate or ignore them in as much as they are binding divine commandments, which are contained in the Revealed Books of God and were sent through the last of His Prophets to complete the preceding divine messages thereby making their observance and act of worship and their neglect or violation an abominable sin, and accordingly every person is individually responsible—and the Ummah collectively responsible—for their safeguard.

Proceeding from the above-mentioned principles,

Declare the following:

Article 1

(a) All human beings form one family whose members are united by submission to God and descent from Adam. All men are equal in terms of basic human dignity and basic obligations and responsibilities, without any discrimination on the grounds of race, colour, language, sex, religious belief, political affiliation, social status or other considerations. True faith is the guarantee for enhancing such dignity along the path to human perfection.

(b) All human beings are God's subjects, and the most loved by Him are those who are most useful to the rest of His subjects, and no one has superiority over another except on the basis of piety and good deeds.

Article 2

(a) Life is a God-given gift and the right to life is guaranteed to every human being. It is the duty of individuals, societies and states to protect this right from any violation, and it is prohibited to take away life except for a Shari'ah prescribed reason.

(b) It is forbidden to resort to such means as may result in the genocidal annihilation of mankind.

(c) The preservation of human life throughout the term of time willed by God is a duty prescribed by Shari'ah.

(d) Safety from bodily harm is a guaranteed right. It is the duty of the State to safeguard it, and it is prohibited to breach it without a Shari'ah prescribed reason.

Article 3

(a) In the event of the use of force and in case of armed conflict, it is not permissible to kill non-belligerents such as old men, women and children. The wounded and the sick shall have the right to medical treatment; and prisoners of war shall have the right to be fed, sheltered and clothed. It is prohibited to mutilate dead bodies. It is a duty to exchange prisoners of war and to arrange visits or reunions of the families separated by the circumstances of war.

(b) It is prohibited to fell trees, to damage crops or livestock, and to destroy the enemy's civilian buildings and installations by shelling, blasting or any other means.

Article 4

Every human being is entitled to the inviolability and the protection of his good name and honour during his life and after his death. The State and Society shall protect his remains and burial place.

Article 5

(a) The family is the foundation of society, and marriage is the basis of its formation. Men and women have the right to marriage, and no restrictions stemming from race, colour or nationality shall prevent them from enjoying this right.

(b) Society and the State shall remove all obstacles to marriage and shall facilitate marital procedure. They shall ensure family protection and welfare.

Article 6

(a) Woman is equal to man in human dignity, and has rights to enjoy as well as duties to perform; she has her own civil entity and financial independence, and the right to retain her name and lineage.

(b) The husband is responsible for the support and welfare of the family.

Article 7

(a) As of the moment of birth, every child has rights due from the parents, society and the State to be accorded proper nursing, education and material, hygienic and moral care. Both the fetus and the mother must be protected and accorded special care.

(b) Parents and those in such like capacity have the right to choose the type of education they desire for their children, provided they take into consideration the interest and future of the children in accordance with ethical values and the principles of the Shari'ah.

(c) Both parents are entitled to certain rights from their children, and relatives are entitled to rights from their kin, in accordance with the tenets of the Shari'ah.

Article 8

Every human being has the right to enjoy his legal capacity in terms of both obligation and commitment, should this capacity be lost or impaired, he shall be represented by his guardian.

Article 9

(a) The quest for knowledge is an obligation and the provision of education is a duty for society and the State. The State shall ensure the availability of ways and means to acquire education and shall guarantee educational diversity in the interest of Society so as to enable man to be acquainted with the religion of Islam and the facts of the Universe for the benefit of mankind.

(b) Every human being has the right to receive both religious and worldly education from the various institutions of, education and guidance, including the family, the school, the university, the media, etc., and in such an integrated and balanced manner as to develop his personality, strengthen his faith in God and promote his respect for and defence of both rights and obligations.

Article 10

Islam is the religion of unspoiled nature. It is prohibited to exercise any form of compulsion on man or to exploit his poverty or ignorance in order to convert him to another religion or to atheism.

Article 11

(a) Human beings are born free, and no one has the right to enslave, humiliate, oppress or exploit them, and there can be no subjugation but to God the Most-High.

(b) Colonialism of all types being one of the most evil forms of enslavement is totally prohibited. Peoples suffering from colonialism have the full right to freedom and self-determination. It is the duty of all States and peoples to support the struggle of colonized peoples from the liquidation of all forms of colonialism and occupation, and all States and peoples have the right to preserve their independent identity and exercise control over their wealth and natural resources.

Article 12

Every man shall have the right, within the framework of Shari'ah, to free movement and to select his place of residence whether inside or outside his country and if persecuted, is entitled to seek asylum in another country. The country of refuge shall ensure his protection until he reaches safety, unless asylum is motivated by an act which Shari'ah regards as a crime.

Article 13

Work is a right guaranteed by the State and society for each person able to work. Everyone shall be free to choose the work that suits him best and which serves his interests and those of society. The employee shall have the right to safety and security as well as to all other social guarantees. He may neither be assigned work beyond his capacity nor be subjected to compulsion or exploited or harmed in any way. He shall be entitled without any discrimination between males and females to fair wages for his work without delay, as well as to the holidays allowances and promotions which he deserves. For his part, he shall be required to be dedicated and meticulous in his work. Should workers and employers disagree on any matter, the State shall intervene to settle the dispute and have the grievances redressed, the rights confirmed and justice enforced without bias.

Article 14

Everyone shall have the right to legitimate gains without monopolization, deceit or harm to oneself or to others. Usury (riba) is absolutely prohibited.

Article 15

(a)   Everyone shall have the right to own property acquired in a legitimate way, and shall be entitled to the rights of ownership, without prejudice to oneself, others or to society in general. Expropriation is not permissible except for the requirements of public interest and upon payment of immediate and fair compensation.

(b)   Confiscation and seizure of property is prohibited except for a necessity dictated by law.

Article 16

Everyone shall have the right to enjoy the fruits of his scientific, literary, artistic or technical production and the right to protect the moral and material interest stemming therefrom, provided that such production is not contrary to the principles of Shari'ah.

Article 17

(a)   Everyone shall have the right to live in a clean environment, away from vice and moral corruption, an environment that would foster his self-development and it is incumbent upon the State and society in general to afford that right.

(b)   Everyone shall have the right to medical and social care, and to all public amenities provided by society and the State within the limits of their available resources.

(c)   The State shall ensure the right of the individual to a decent living which will enable him to meet all his requirements and those of his dependants, including food, clothing, housing, education, medical care and all other basic needs.

Article 18

(a)   Everyone shall have the right to live in security for himself, his religion, his dependants, his honour and his property.

(b)   Everyone shall have the right to privacy in the conduct of his private affairs, in his home, among his family, with regard to his property and his relationships. It is not permitted to spy on him, to place him under surveillance or to besmirch his good name. The State shall protect him from arbitrary interference.

(c)   A private residence is inviolable in all cases. It will not be entered without permission from its inhabitants or in any unlawful manner, nor shall it be demolished or confiscated and its dwellers evicted.

Article 19

(a)   All individuals are equal before the law, without distinction between ruler and ruled.

(b)   The right to resort to justice is guaranteed to everyone.

(c)   Liability is in essence personal.

(d)   There shall be no crime or punishment except as provided for in the Shari'ah.

(e)   A defendant is innocent until his guilt is proven in a fair trial in which he shall be given all the guarantees of defence.

Article 20

It is not permitted without legitimate reason to arrest an individual, restrict his freedom, to exile or to punish him. It is not permitted to subject him to physical or psychological torture or to any form of humiliation, cruelty or indignity. Nor is it permitted to subject an individual to medical or scientific experimentation without his consent or at the risk of his health or of his life. Nor is it permitted to promulgate emergency laws that would provide executive authority for such actions.

Article 21

Taking hostages under any form or for any purpose is expressly forbidden.

Article 22

(a)   Everyone shall have the right to express his opinion freely in such manner as would not be contrary to the principles of the Shari'ah.

(b)   Everyone shall have the right to advocate what is right, and propagate what is good, and warn against what is wrong and evil according to the norms of Islamic Shari'ah.

(c)   Information is a vital necessity to society. It may not be exploited or misused in such a way as may violate sanctities and the dignity of Prophets, undermine moral and ethical values or disintegrate, corrupt or harm society or weaken its faith.

(d)   It is not permitted to arouse nationalistic or doctrinal hatred or to do anything that may be an incitement to any form of racial discrimination.

Article 23

(a)   Authority is a trust; and abuse or malicious exploitation thereof is absolutely prohibited, so that fundamental human rights may be guaranteed.

(b)   Everyone shall have the right to participate directly or indirectly in the administration of his country's public affairs. He shall also have the right to assume public office in accordance with the provisions of Shari'ah.

Article 24

All the rights and freedoms stipulated in this Declaration are subject to the Islamic Shari'ah.

Article 25

The Islamic Shari'ah is the only source of reference for the explanation or clarification of any of the articles of this Declaration.

125. DECLARATION ON THE PROTECTION OF REFUGEES AND DISPLACED PERSONS IN THE ARAB WORLD, 1992

This Declaration was adopted by a Group of Arab Experts which met in Cairo in November 1992, at the Fourth Arab Seminar on 'Asylum and Refugee Law in the Arab World', organized by the International Institute of Humanitarian Law in collaboration with the Faculty of Law of Cairo University, and under the sponsorship of the United Nations High Commissioner for Refugees.

Further reading

ELMADMAD, K., 'An Arab Convention on Forced Migration: Desirability and Possibilities', (1991) 3 *IJRL* 461.

TAKKENBERG, L., *The Status of Palestinian Refugees in International Law*, Oxford: Clarendon Press, 1998.

TEXT

The Group of Arab Experts, meeting in Cairo, Arab Republic of Egypt, from 16 to 19 November 1992 at the Fourth Arab Seminar on 'Asylum and Refugee Law in the Arab World', organized by the International Institute of Humanitarian Law in collaboration with the Faculty of Law of Cairo University, under the sponsorship of the United Nations High Commissioner for Refugees,

1. *Noting* with deep regret the suffering which the Arab World has endured from large-scale flows of refugees and displaced persons, and also noting with deep concern the continuing outflow of refugees and displaced persons in the Arab World and the human tragedy encountered by them,

2. *Recalling* the humanitarian principles deeply rooted in Islamic Arab traditions and values and the principles and rules of Moslem law (Islamic Sharia), particularly the principles of social solidarity and asylum, which are reflected in the universally recognized principles of international humanitarian law,

3. *Recognizing* the imperative need for a humanitarian approach in solving the problems or refugees and displaced persons, without prejudice to the political rights of the Palestinian people,

4. *Emphasizing* the need for the effective implementation of paragraph 11 of General Assembly Resolution 194 (111) of 11 December 1948, calling for the right of return or compensation for Palestinian refugees,

5. *Considering* that the required solution is the full implementation of the Resolutions of the Security Council and of the United Nations, including Resolutions 181 of 1947 and Resolution 3236 of 1973, which guarantee the right of the Palestinian people to establish its independent State on its national territory,

6. *Deeply concerned* that Palestinians are not receiving effective protection either from the competent international organizations or from the competent authorities of some Arab countries,

7. *Recognizing* that the refugees and displaced persons problems must be addressed in all their aspects, in particular those relating to their causes, means of prevention and appropriate solutions,

8. *Recalling* that the United Nations Charter and the international human rights instruments affirm the principle that human beings shall enjoy fundamental rights and freedoms without discrimination of whatever nature,

9. *Considering* that Asylum and Refugee Law constitute an integral part of Human Rights Law, respect for which should be fully ensured in the Arab World,

10. *Recognizing* that the United Nations Convention of 28 July 1951 and the Protocol of 31 January 1967 constitute the basic universal instruments governing the status of refugees,

11. *Recalling* the importance or regional legal instruments such as the 1969 OAU Convention governing the Specific Aspects of Refugee Problems in Africa and the 1984 Cartagena Declaration on Refugees,

12. *Recognizing* that the fundamental principles of human rights, international humanitarian law and international refugee law represent a common standard to be attained by all peoples and nations; that they should provide constant guidance to all individuals and organs of society; and that competent national authorities should ensure respect for these principles and should endeavour to promote them by means of education and dissemination,

13. *Recalling* the historic role of Islam and its contribution to humanity, and the fact that universal respect for human rights and fundamental freedoms for all constitute an integral part of Arab values and of the principles and rules of Moslem law (Islamic Sharia),

14. *Noting* with appreciation the humanitarian role of the Office of the United Nations High Commissioner for Refugees in providing protection and assistance to refugees and displaced persons,

15. *Recalling* with particular gratitude the efforts of the International Institute of Humanitarian Law for the developing of refugee law in the Arab World and for organizing the four Arab Seminars held for this purpose in San Remo (1984), Tunis (1989), Amman (1991) and Cairo (1992), and,

16. *Recalling* with appreciation the efforts or the International Committee of the Red Cross in protecting refugees and displaced persons in armed conflict situations,

Adopts the following Declaration:

Article 1

Reaffirms the fundamental right of every person to the free movement within his own country, or to leave it for another country and to return to his country of origin;

Article 2

Reaffirms the importance of the principle prohibiting the return or the expulsion of a refugee to a country where his life or his freedom will be in danger and considers this principle as an imperative rule of the international public law;

Article 3

Considers that the granting or asylum should not as such be regarded as an unfriendly act vis-à-vis any other State;

Article 4

Hopes that Arab States which have not yet acceded to the 1951 Convention and the 1967 Protocol relating to the Status of Refugees will do so;

Article 5

In situations which may not be covered by the 1951 Convention, the 1967 Protocol, or any other relevant instrument in force or United Nations General Assembly resolutions, refugees, asylum seekers and displaced persons shall nevertheless be protected by:

  (a) the humanitarian principles of asylum in Islamic law and Arab values,

  (b) the basic human rights rules, established by international and regional organizations,

  (c) other relevant principles or international law;

Article 6

Recommends that, pending the elaboration of an Arab Convention relating to refugees, Arab States adopt a broad concept of 'refugee' and 'displaced person' as well as a minimum standard for their treatment, guided by the provisions of the United Nations instruments relating to human rights and refugees as well as relevant regional instruments;

Article 7

Calls the League of Arab States to reinforce its efforts with a view to adopting an Arab Convention relating to refugees. These efforts will hopefully be brought to fruition within a reasonable period of time;

Article 8

Calls upon Arab States to provide the Secretariat of the League with relevant information and statistical data, in particular concerning:

  (a) the condition of refugees and displaced persons in their territories,

  (b) the extent of their implementation of international instruments relating to the protection of refugees,

  (c) national laws, regulations and decrees in force, relating to refugees and displaced persons;

This will help the League of Arab States in taking an active role in the protection or refugees and displaced persons in cooperation with the competent international organizations;

Article 9

(a) Strongly emphasizes the need to ensure international protection for Palestinian refugees by competent international organizations and, in particular, by the United Nations, without in any way prejudicing the inalienable national rights of the Palestinian people, especially their right to repatriation and self-determination,

(b) Requests the competent organs of the United Nations to extend with due speed the necessary protection to the Palestinian people, in application of Security Council Resolution 681 of 20 December 1990,

(c) Requests the Arab States to apply in its entirety the Protocol relating to the Treatment of Palestinians in Arab States, adopted at Casablanca on 11 September 1965;

Article 10

Emphasizes the need to provide special protection to women and children, as the largest category of refugees and displaced persons, and the most to suffer, as well as the importance of efforts to reunite the families of refugees and displaced persons;

Article 11

Calls for the necessary attention which should be given to the dissemination of refugee law and to the development of the public awareness thereof in the Arab World; and for the establishment of an Arab Institute of International Humanitarian Law, in cooperation with the United Nations High Commissioner for Refugees, the International Committee of the Red Cross and the League of Arab States.

Done at Cairo, on Thursday, the 24th of Joumada al-oula A.H. 1413, the 19th of November A.D. 1992.

FIRST RECOMMENDATION

The Arab Experts, meeting in Cairo at their Fourth Seminar on Asylum and Refugee Law in the Arab World, wish to express their deep appreciation to the International Institute of Humanitarian Law and to the Faculty of Law of Cairo University for their valuable efforts, as well as to the Office of the United Nations High Commissioner for Refugees for its generous sponsorship, all of which led to the success of the Seminar and point to the need for periodically holding similar seminars in other parts or the Arab World in view or the benefits accruing therefrom.

The Arab Experts address their special thanks to the International Institute of Humanitarian Law for publishing the proceedings and synopsis of previous seminars. They note with deep appreciation the intended publication and large-scale dissemination by the Institute of the proceedings and results of their Fourth Seminar, including the Cairo Declaration.

SECOND RECOMMENDATION

The Arab Experts, meeting in Cairo at their Fourth Seminar on Asylum and Refugee Law in the Arab World, express their appreciation to the General Secretariat of the League of Arab States for its effective participation in the work or the Seminar and urge it to continue its constructive efforts with a view to reaching satisfactory solutions to the problems of refugees, including moral and material sponsorship of future meetings on the subject.

They also invite the League to study the feasibility of creating an Arab organism for refugees in the Arab World, within the framework of the specialized agencies of the League, with a view to providing legal and humanitarian protection for the refugees.

126. ARAB CHARTER ON HUMAN RIGHTS, 2004

The first version of the Arab Charter on Human Rights was adopted by the Council of the League of Arab States (Resolution 5437, 102nd regular session) on 15 September 1994, and opened for signature by the twenty-two members of the Arab League (Jordan, United Arab Emirates, Bahrain, Tunisia, Algeria, Djibouti, Saudi Arabia, Sudan, Syrian Arab Republic, Somalia, Iraq, Oman, Palestine, Qatar, Comoros, Kuwait, Lebanon, Libyan Arab Jamahiriya, Egypt, Morocco, Mauritania, Yemen). For text, see the fourth edition of this work (p. 774); (1997) 18 *Human Rights Law Journal* 151; (1996) 56 *ICJ Review* 57.

None of the member States signed the Charter, and in March 2002 the Arab League Council decided to revise it. In 2003, the Council called on the Arab Standing Committee on Human Rights to 'modernise the Arab Charter on Human Rights in the light of comments and suggestions received from Arab States, with the participation of legal and human rights experts'. When initial efforts attracted criticism, independent experts were allowed to participate in the drafting process; assistance was also provided by the Office of the UN High Commissioner for Human Rights (for some of the views of that Office, see OHCHR, Arab Region, Quarterly Reports of Field Offices, 22 September 2004). The final draft was adopted without amendment at the Summit of Heads of Member States of the League in Tunis in May 2004.

On the occasion of the Charter receiving its seventh ratification (on 15 January 2008, so entering into force on 15 March 2008), the UN High Commissioner for Human Rights, Louise Arbour, reiterated the concerns of her Office. While noting 'that regional systems of protection and promotion can help further strengthen the enjoyment of human rights', she called attention also to the incompatibility of some Charter provisions with international norms and standards. These included the approach to the death penalty for children and the rights of women and non-citizens. In addition, she pointed out that, insofar as it equates Zionism with racism, the Charter is not in conformity with General Assembly Resolution 46/86, which rejects the view that Zionism is a form of racism and racial discrimination. Although not endorsing these inconsistencies, the High Commissioner confirmed that her Office would nevertheless 'continue to work with all stakeholders in the region to ensure the implementation of universal human rights norms': UNITED NATIONS, Press Release, Geneva, 30 January 2008.

In March 2009, the Arab Human Rights Committee was established to supervise implementation of the Charter, in accordance with Article 45.

The text below is a revised English translation of the official Arabic text, and was provided by the Office of the United Nations High Commissioner for Human Rights in January 2006. It differs in a number of details, primarily linguistic, from versions published earlier.

Further reading

RISHMAWI, M., 'The Revised Arab Charter on Human Rights: A Step Forward?', (2005) 5 *Human Rights Law Review* 361–76.

TEXT

Based on the faith of the Arab nation in the dignity of the human person whom God has exalted ever since the beginning of creation and in the fact that the Arab homeland is the cradle of religions and civilizations whose lofty human values affirm the human right to a decent life based on freedom, justice and equality,

In furtherance of the eternal principles of fraternity, equality and tolerance among human beings consecrated by the noble Islamic religion and the other divinely-revealed religions,

Being proud of the humanitarian values and principles that the Arab nation has established throughout its long history, which have played a major role in spreading knowledge between East and West, so making the region a point of reference for the whole world and a destination for seekers of knowledge and wisdom,

Believing in the unity of the Arab nation, which struggles for its freedom and defends the right of nations to self-determination, to the preservation of their wealth and to development; believing in the sovereignty of the law and its contribution to the protection of universal and interrelated human rights and convinced that the human person's enjoyment of freedom, justice and equality of opportunity is a fundamental measure of the value of any society,

Rejecting all forms of racism and Zionism, which constitute a violation of human rights and a threat to international peace and security, recognizing the close link that exists between human rights and international peace and security, reaffirming the principles of the Charter of the United Nations, the Universal Declaration of Human Rights and the provisions of the International Covenant on Civil and Political Rights and the International Covenant on Economic, Social and Cultural Rights, and having regard to the Cairo Declaration on Human Rights in Islam,

The States parties to the Charter have agreed as follows:

Article 1

The present Charter seeks, within the context of the national identity of the Arab States and their sense of belonging to a common civilization, to achieve the following aims:

1.   To place human rights at the centre of the key national concerns of Arab States, making them lofty and fundamental ideals that shape the will of the individual in Arab States and enable him to improve his life in accordance with noble human values.

2.   To teach the human person in the Arab States pride in his identity, loyalty to his country, attachment to his land, history and common interests and to instil in him a culture of human brotherhood, tolerance and openness towards others, in accordance with universal principles and values and with those proclaimed in international human rights instruments.

3.   To prepare the new generations in Arab States for a free and responsible life in a civil society that is characterized by solidarity, founded on a balance between awareness of rights and respect for obligations, and governed by the values of equality, tolerance and moderation.

4.   To entrench the principle that all human rights are universal, indivisible, interdependent and interrelated.

Article 2

1.   All peoples have the right of self-determination and to control over their natural wealth and resources, and the right to freely choose their political system and to freely pursue their economic, social and cultural development.

2.   All peoples have the right to national sovereignty and territorial integrity.

3.   All forms of racism, Zionism and foreign occupation and domination constitute an impediment to human dignity and a major barrier to the exercise of the fundamental rights of peoples; all such practices must be condemned and efforts must be deployed for their elimination.

4.   All peoples have the right to resist foreign occupation.

Article 3

1. Each State party to the present Charter undertakes to ensure to all individuals subject to its jurisdiction the right to enjoy the rights and freedoms set forth herein, without distinction on grounds of race, colour, sex, language, religious belief, opinion, thought, national or social origin, wealth, birth or physical or mental disability.

2. The States parties to the present Charter shall take the requisite measures to guarantee effective equality in the enjoyment of all the rights and freedoms enshrined in the present Charter in order to ensure protection against all forms of discrimination based on any of the grounds mentioned in the preceding paragraph.

3. Men and women are equal in respect of human dignity, rights and obligations within the framework of the positive discrimination established in favour of women by the Islamic Shariah, other divine laws and by applicable laws and legal instruments. Accordingly, each State party pledges to take all the requisite measures to guarantee equal opportunities and effective equality between men and women in the enjoyment of all the rights set out in this Charter.

Article 4

1. In exceptional situations of emergency which threaten the life of the nation and the existence of which is officially proclaimed, the States parties to the present Charter may take measures derogating from their obligations under the present Charter, to the extent strictly required by the exigencies of the situation, provided that such measures are not inconsistent with their other obligations under international law and do not involve discrimination solely on the grounds of race, colour, sex, language, religion or social origin.

2. In exceptional situations of emergency, no derogation shall be made from the following articles: article 5, article 8, article 9, article 10, article 13, article 14, paragraph 6, article 15, article 18, article 19, article 20, article 22, article 27, article 28 and article 29 and article 30. In addition, the judicial guarantees required for the protection of the aforementioned rights may not be suspended.

3. Any State party to the present Charter availing itself of the right of derogation shall immediately inform the other States parties, through the intermediary of the Secretary-General of the League of Arab States, of the provisions from which it has derogated and of the reasons by which it was actuated. A further communication shall be made, through the same intermediary, on the date on which it terminates such derogation.

Article 5

1. Every human being has the inherent right to life.

2. This right shall be protected by law. No one shall be arbitrarily deprived of his life.

Article 6

Sentence of death may be imposed only for the most serious crimes in accordance with the laws in force at the time of commission of the crime and pursuant to a final judgement rendered by a competent court. Anyone sentenced to death shall have the right to seek pardon or commutation of the sentence.

Article 7

1.   Sentence of death shall not be imposed on persons under 18 years of age, unless otherwise stipulated in the laws in force at the time of the commission of the crime.

2.   The death penalty shall not be inflicted on a pregnant woman prior to her delivery or on a nursing mother within two years from the date of her delivery; in all cases, the best interests of the infant shall be the primary consideration.

Article 8

1.   No one shall be subjected to physical or psychological torture or to cruel, degrading, humiliating or inhuman treatment.

2.   Each State party shall protect every individual subject to its jurisdiction from such practices and shall take effective measures to prevent them. The commission of, or participation in, such acts shall be regarded as crimes that are punishable by law and not subject to any statute of limitations. Each State party shall guarantee in its legal system redress for any victim of torture and the right to rehabilitation and compensation.

Article 9

No one shall be subjected to medical or scientific experimentation or to the use of his organs without his free consent and full awareness of the consequences and provided that ethical, humanitarian and professional rules are followed and medical procedures are observed to ensure his personal safety pursuant to the relevant domestic laws in force in each State party. Trafficking in human organs is prohibited in all circumstances.

Article 10

1.   All forms of slavery and trafficking in human beings are prohibited and are punishable by law. No one shall be held in slavery and servitude under any circumstances.

2.   Forced labour, trafficking in human beings for the purposes of prostitution or sexual exploitation, the exploitation of the prostitution of others or any other form of exploitation or the exploitation of children in armed conflict are prohibited.

Article 11

All persons are equal before the law and have the right to enjoy its protection without discrimination.

Article 12

All persons are equal before the courts and tribunals. The States parties shall guarantee the independence of the judiciary and protect magistrates against any interference, pressure or threats. They shall also guarantee every person subject to their jurisdiction the right to seek a legal remedy before courts of all levels.

Article 13

1.   Everyone has the right to a fair trial that affords adequate guarantees before a competent, independent and impartial court that has been constituted by law to hear any criminal charge against him or to decide on his rights or his obligations. Each State party shall guarantee to those without the requisite financial resources legal aid to enable them to defend their rights.

2. Trials shall be public, except in exceptional cases that may be warranted by the interests of justice in a society that respects human freedoms and rights.

Article 14

1. Everyone has the right to liberty and security of person. No one shall be subjected to arbitrary arrest, search or detention without a legal warrant.
2. No one shall be deprived of his liberty except on such grounds and in such circumstances as are determined by law and in accordance with such procedure as is established thereby.
3. Anyone who is arrested shall be informed, at the time of arrest, in a language that he understands, of the reasons for his arrest and shall be promptly informed of any charges against him. He shall be entitled to contact his family members.
4. Anyone who is deprived of his liberty by arrest or detention shall have the right to request a medical examination and must be informed of that right.
5. Anyone arrested or detained on a criminal charge shall be brought promptly before a judge or other officer authorized by law to exercise judicial power and shall be entitled to trial within a reasonable time or to release. His release may be subject to guarantees to appear for trial. Pre-trial detention shall in no case be the general rule.
6. Anyone who is deprived of his liberty by arrest or detention shall be entitled to petition a competent court in order that it may decide without delay on the lawfulness of his arrest or detention and order his release if the arrest or detention is unlawful.
7. Anyone who has been the victim of arbitrary or unlawful arrest or detention shall be entitled to compensation.

Article 15

No crime and no penalty can be established without a prior provision of the law. In all circumstances, the law most favourable to the defendant shall be applied.

Article 16

Everyone charged with a criminal offence shall be presumed innocent until proved guilty by a final judgement rendered according to law and, in the course of the investigation and trial, he shall enjoy the following minimum guarantees:
1. The right to be informed promptly, in detail and in a language which he understands, of the charges against him.
2. The right to have adequate time and facilities for the preparation of his defence and to be allowed to communicate with his family.
3. The right to be tried in his presence before an ordinary court and to defend himself in person or through a lawyer of his own choosing with whom he can communicate freely and confidentially.
4. The right to the free assistance of a lawyer who will defend him if he cannot defend himself or if the interests of justice so require, and the right to the free assistance of an interpreter if he cannot understand or does not speak the language used in court.

5.   The right to examine or have his lawyer examine the prosecution witnesses and to summon defence according to the conditions applied to the prosecution witnesses.

6.   The right not to be compelled to testify against himself or to confess guilt.

7.   The right, if convicted of the crime, to file an appeal in accordance with the law before a higher tribunal.

8.   The right to respect for his security of person and his privacy in all circumstances.

Article 17

Each State party shall ensure in particular to any child at risk or any delinquent charged with an offence the right to a special legal system for minors in all stages of investigation, trial and enforcement of sentence, as well as to special treatment that takes account of his age, protects his dignity, facilitates his rehabilitation and reintegration and enables him to play a constructive role in society.

Article 18

No one who is shown by a court to be unable to pay a debt arising from a contractual obligation shall be imprisoned.

Article 19

1.   No one may be tried twice for the same offence. Anyone against whom such proceedings are brought shall have the right to challenge their legality and to demand his release.

2.   Anyone whose innocence is established by a final judgement shall be entitled to compensation for the damage suffered.

Article 20

1.   All persons deprived of their liberty shall be treated with humanity and with respect for the inherent dignity of the human person.

2.   Persons in pre-trial detention shall be separated from convicted persons and shall be treated in a manner consistent with their status as unconvicted persons.

3.   The aim of the penitentiary system shall be to reform prisoners and effect their social rehabilitation.

Article 21

1.   No one shall be subjected to arbitrary or unlawful interference with regard to his privacy, family, home or correspondence, nor to unlawful attacks on his honour or his reputation.

2.   Everyone has the right to the protection of the law against such interference or attacks.

Article 22

Everyone shall have the right to recognition as a person before the law.

Article 23

Each State party to the present Charter undertakes to ensure that any person whose rights or freedoms as herein recognized are violated shall have an effective remedy, notwithstanding that the violation has been committed by persons acting in an official capacity.

Article 24

Every citizen has the right:
1. To freely pursue a political activity.
2. To take part in the conduct of public affairs, directly or through freely chosen representatives.
3. To stand for election or choose his representatives in free and impartial elections, in conditions of equality among all citizens that guarantee the free expression of his will.
4. To the opportunity to gain access, on an equal footing with others, to public office in his country in accordance with the principle of equality of opportunity.
5. To freely form and join associations with others.
6. To freedom of association and peaceful assembly.
7. No restrictions may be placed on the exercise of these rights other than those which are prescribed by law and which are necessary in a democratic society in the interests of national security or public safety, public health or morals or the protection of the rights and freedoms of others.

Article 25

Persons belonging to minorities shall not be denied the right to enjoy their own culture, to use their own language and to practise their own religion. The exercise of these rights shall be governed by law.

Article 26

1. Everyone lawfully within the territory of a State party shall, within that territory, have the right to freedom of movement and to freely choose his residence in any part of that territory in conformity with the laws in force.
2. No State party may expel a person who does not hold its nationality but is lawfully in its territory, other than in pursuance of a decision reached in accordance with law and after that person has been allowed to submit a petition to the competent authority, unless compelling reasons of national security preclude it. Collective expulsion is prohibited under all circumstances.

Article 27

1. No one may be arbitrarily or unlawfully prevented from leaving any country, including his own, nor prohibited from residing, or compelled to reside, in any part of that country.
2. No one may be exiled from his country or prohibited from returning thereto.

Article 28

Everyone has the right to seek political asylum in another country in order to escape persecution. This right may not be invoked by persons facing prosecution for an offence under ordinary law. Political refugees may not be extradited.

Article 29

1. Everyone has the right to nationality. No one shall be arbitrarily or unlawfully deprived of his nationality.
2. States parties shall take such measures as they deem appropriate, in accordance with their domestic laws on nationality, to allow a child to acquire the mother's nationality, having due regard, in all cases, to the best interests of the child.
3. No one shall be denied the right to acquire another nationality, having due regard for the domestic legal procedures in his country.

Article 30

1. Everyone has the right to freedom of thought, conscience and religion and no restrictions may be imposed on the exercise of such freedoms except as provided for by law.
2. The freedom to manifest one's religion or beliefs or to perform religious observances, either alone or in community with others, shall be subject only to such limitations as are prescribed by law and are necessary in a tolerant society that respects human rights and freedoms for the protection of public safety, public order, public health or morals or the fundamental rights and freedoms of others.
3. Parents or guardians have the freedom to provide for the religious and moral education of their children.

Article 31

Everyone has a guaranteed right to own private property, and shall not under any circumstances be arbitrarily or unlawfully divested of all or any part of his property.

Article 32

1. The present Charter guarantees the right to information and to freedom of opinion and expression, as well as the right to seek, receive and impart information and ideas through any medium, regardless of geographical boundaries.
2. Such rights and freedoms shall be exercised in conformity with the fundamental values of society and shall be subject only to such limitations as are required to ensure respect for the rights or reputation of others or the protection of national security, public order and public health or morals.

Article 33

1. The family is the natural and fundamental group unit of society; it is based on marriage between a man and a woman. Men and women of marrying age have the right to marry and to found a family according to the rules and conditions of marriage. No marriage can take place without the full and free consent of both parties. The laws in force regulate the rights and duties of the man and woman as to marriage, during marriage and at its dissolution.
2. The State and society shall ensure the protection of the family, the strengthening of family ties, the protection of its members and the prohibition of all forms of violence or abuse in the relations among its members, and particularly against women and children. They shall also ensure the necessary protection and care for mothers, children, older persons and persons with special needs and shall provide adolescents and young persons with the best opportunities for physical and mental development.

3.   The States parties shall take all necessary legislative, administrative and judicial measures to guarantee the protection, survival, development and well-being of the child in an atmosphere of freedom and dignity and shall ensure, in all cases, that the child's best interests are the basic criterion for all measures taken in his regard, whether the child is at risk of delinquency or is a juvenile offender.

4.   The States parties shall take all the necessary measures to guarantee, particularly to young persons, the right to pursue a sporting activity.

Article 34

1.   The right to work is a natural right of every citizen. The State shall endeavour to provide, to the extent possible, a job for the largest number of those willing to work, while ensuring production, the freedom to choose one's work and equality of opportunity without discrimination of any kind on grounds of race, colour, sex, religion, language, political opinion, membership in a union, national origin, social origin, disability or any other situation.

2.   Every worker has the right to the enjoyment of just and favourable conditions of work which ensure appropriate remuneration to meet his essential needs and those of his family and regulate working hours, rest and holidays with pay, as well as the rules for the preservation of occupational health and safety and the protection of women, children and disabled persons in the place of work.

3.   The States parties recognize the right of the child to be protected from economic exploitation and from being forced to perform any work that is likely to be hazardous or to interfere with the child's education or to be harmful to the child's health or physical, mental, spiritual, moral or social development. To this end, and having regard to the relevant provisions of other international instruments, States parties shall in particular:

(a)   Define a minimum age for admission to employment;
(b)   Establish appropriate regulation of working hours and conditions;
(c)   Establish appropriate penalities or other sanctions to ensure the effective enforcement of these provisions.

4.   There shall be no discrimination between men and women in their enjoyment of the right to effectively benefit from training, employment and job protection and the right to receive equal remuneration for equal work.

5.   Each State party shall ensure to workers who migrate to its territory the requisite protection in accordance with the laws in force.

Article 35

1.   Every individual has the right to freely form trade unions or to join trade unions and to freely pursue trade union activity for the protection of his interests.

2.   No restrictions shall be placed on the exercise of these rights and freedoms except such as are prescribed by the laws in force and that are necessary for the maintenance of national security, public safety or order or for the protection of public health or morals or the rights and freedoms of others.

3.   Every State party to the present Charter guarantees the right to strike within the limits laid down by the laws in force.

Article 36

The States parties shall ensure the right of every citizen to social security, including social insurance.

Article 37

The right to development is a fundamental human right and all States are required to establish the development policies and to take the measures needed to guarantee this right. They have a duty to give effect to the values of solidarity and cooperation among them and at the international level with a view to eradicating poverty and achieving economic, social, cultural and political development. By virtue of this right, every citizen has the right to participate in the realization of development and to enjoy the benefits and fruits thereof.

Article 38

Every person has the right to an adequate standard of living for himself and his family, which ensures their well-being and a decent life, including food, clothing, housing, services and the right to a healthy environment. The States parties shall take the necessary measures commensurate with their resources to guarantee these rights.

Article 39

1. The States parties recognize the right of every member of society to the enjoyment of the highest attainable standard of physical and mental health and the right of the citizen to free basic health-care services and to have access to medical facilities without discrimination of any kind.

2. The measures taken by States parties shall include the following:

    (a) Development of basic health-care services and the guaranteeing of free and easy access to the centres that provide these services, regardless of geographical location or economic status;

    (b) Efforts to control disease by means of prevention and cure in order to reduce the mortality rate;

    (c) Promotion of health awareness and health education;

    (d) Suppression of traditional practices which are harmful to the health of the individual;

    (e) Provision of basic nutrition and safe drinking water for all;

    (f) Combating environmental pollution and providing proper sanitation systems;

    (g) Combating drugs, psychotropic substances, smoking and substances that are damaging to health.

Article 40

1. The States parties undertake to ensure to persons with mental or physical disabilities a decent life that guarantees their dignity, and to enhance their self-reliance and facilitate their active participation in society.

2. The States parties shall provide social services free of charge for all persons with disabilities, shall provide the material support needed by those persons, their families or the families caring for them, and shall also do whatever is needed to avoid placing those persons in institutions. They shall in all cases take account of the best interests of the disabled person.

3. The States parties shall take all necessary measures to curtail the incidence of disabilities by all possible means, including preventive health programmes, awareness raising and education.

4. The States parties shall provide full educational services suited to persons with disabilities, taking into account the importance of integrating these persons in the

educational system and the importance of vocational training and apprenticeship and the creation of suitable job opportunities in the public or private sectors.

5. The States parties shall provide all health services appropriate for persons with disabilities, including the rehabilitation of these persons with a view to integrating them into society.

6. The States parties shall enable persons with disabilities to make use of all public and private services.

Article 41

1. The eradication of illiteracy is a binding obligation upon the State and everyone has the right to education.

2. The States parties shall guarantee their citizens free education at least throughout the primary and basic levels. All forms and levels of primary education shall be compulsory and accessible to all without discrimination of any kind.

3. The States parties shall take appropriate measures in all domains to ensure partnership between men and women with a view to achieving national development goals.

4. The States parties shall guarantee to provide education directed to the full development of the human person and to strengthening respect for human rights and fundamental freedoms.

5. The States parties shall endeavour to incorporate the principles of human rights and fundamental freedoms into formal and informal education curricula and educational and training programmes.

6. The States parties shall guarantee the establishment of the mechanisms necessary to provide ongoing education for every citizen and shall develop national plans for adult education.

Article 42

1. Every person has the right to take part in cultural life and to enjoy the benefits of scientific progress and its application.

2. The States parties undertake to respect the freedom of scientific research and creative activity and to ensure the protection of moral and material interests resulting from scientific, literary and artistic production.

3. The States parties shall work together and enhance cooperation among them at all levels, with the full participation of intellectuals and inventors and their organizations, in order to develop and implement recreational, cultural, artistic and scientific programmes.

Article 43

Nothing in this Charter may be construed or interpreted as impairing the rights and freedoms protected by the domestic laws of the States parties or those set forth in the international and regional human rights instruments which the States parties have adopted or ratified, including the rights of women, the rights of the child and the rights of persons belonging to minorities.

Article 44

The States parties undertake to adopt, in conformity with their constitutional procedures and with the provisions of the present Charter, whatever legislative or non-legislative measures that may be necessary to give effect to the rights set forth herein.

Article 45

1. Pursuant to this Charter, an 'Arab Human Rights Committee', hereinafter referred to as 'the Committee', shall be established. This Committee shall consist of seven members who shall be elected by secret ballot by the States parties to this Charter.
2. The Committee shall consist of nationals of the States parties to the present Charter, who must be highly experienced and competent in the Committee's field of work. The members of the Committee shall serve in their personal capacity and shall be fully independent and impartial.
3. The Committee shall include among its members not more than one national of a State party; such member may be re-elected only once. Due regard shall be given to the rotation principle.
4. The members of the Committee shall be elected for a four-year term, although the mandate of three of the members elected during the first election shall be for two years and shall be renewed by lot.
5. Six months prior to the date of the election, the Secretary-General of the League of Arab States shall invite the States parties to submit their nominations within the following three months. He shall transmit the list of candidates to the States parties two months prior to the date of the election. The candidates who obtain the largest number of votes cast shall be elected to membership of the Committee. If, because two or more candidates have an equal number of votes, the number of candidates with the largest number of votes exceeds the number required, a second ballot will be held between the persons with equal numbers of votes. If the votes are again equal, the member or members shall be selected by lottery. The first election for membership of the Committee shall be held at least six months after the Charter enters into force.
6. The Secretary-General shall invite the States parties to a meeting at the headquarters of the League of Arab States in order to elect the member of the Committee. The presence of the majority of the States parties shall constitute a quorum. If there is no quorum, the Secretary-General shall call another meeting at which at least two thirds of the States parties must be present. If there is still no quorum, the Secretary-General shall call a third meeting, which will be held regardless of the number of States parties present.
7. The Secretary-General shall convene the first meeting of the Committee, during the course of which the Committee shall elect its Chairman from among its members, for a two-year term which may be renewed only once and for an identical period. The Committee shall establish its own rules of procedure and methods of work and shall determine how often it shall meet. The Committee shall hold its meetings at the headquarters of the League of Arab States. It may also meet in any other State party to the present Charter at that party's invitation.

Article 46

1.   The Secretary-General shall declare a seat vacant after being notified by the Chairman of a member's:

    (a)   Death;

    (b)   Resignation; or

    (c)   If, in the unanimous opinion of the other members, a member of the Committee has ceased to perform his functions without offering an acceptable justification or for any reason other than a temporary absence.

2.   If a member's seat is declared vacant pursuant to the provisions of paragraph 1 and the term of office of the member to be replaced does not expire within six months from the date on which the vacancy was declared, the Secretary-General of the League of Arab States shall refer the matter to the States parties to the present Charter, which may, within two months, submit nominations, pursuant to article 45, in order to fill the vacant seat.

3.   The Secretary-General of the League of Arab States shall draw up an alphabetical list of all the duly nominated candidates, which he shall transmit to the States parties to the present Charter. The elections to fill the vacant seat shall be held in accordance with the relevant provisions.

4.   Any member of the Committee elected to fill a seat declared vacant in accordance with the provisions of paragraph 1 shall remain a member of the Committee until the expiry of the remainder of the term of the member whose seat was declared vacant pursuant to the provisions of that paragraph.

5.   The Secretary-General of the League of Arab States shall make provision within the budget of the League of Arab States for all the necessary financial and human resources and facilities that the Committee needs to discharge its functions effectively. The Committee's experts shall be afforded the same treatment with respect to remuneration and reimbursement of expenses as experts of the secretariat of the League of Arab States.

Article 47

The States parties undertake to ensure that members of the Committee shall enjoy the immunities necessary for their protection against any form of harassment or moral or material pressure or prosecution on account of the positions they take or statements they make while carrying out their functions as members of the Committee.

Article 48

1.   The States parties undertake to submit reports to the Secretary-General of the League of Arab States on the measures they have taken to give effect to the rights and freedoms recognized in this Charter and on the progress made towards the enjoyment thereof. The Secretary-General shall transmit these reports to the Committee for its consideration.

2.   Each State party shall submit an initial report to the Committee within one year from the date on which the Charter enters into force and a periodic report every three years thereafter. The Committee may request the States parties to supply it with additional information relating to the implementation of the Charter.

3.   The Committee shall consider the reports submitted by the States parties under paragraph 2 of this article in the presence of the representative of the State party whose report is being considered.

4.   The Committee shall discuss the report, comment thereon and make the necessary recommendations in accordance with the aims of the Charter.

5.   The Committee shall submit an annual report containing its comments and recommendations to the Council of the League, through the intermediary of the Secretary-General.

6.   The Committee's reports, concluding observations and recommendations shall be public documents which the Committee shall disseminate widely.

Article 49

1.   The Secretary-General of the League of Arab States shall submit the present Charter, once it has been approved by the Council of the League, to the States members for signature, ratification or accession.

2.   The present Charter shall enter into effect two months from the date on which the seventh instrument of ratification is deposited with the secretariat of the League of Arab States.

3.   After its entry into force, the present Charter shall become effective for each State two months after the State in question has deposited its instrument of ratification or accession with the secretariat.

4.   The Secretary-General shall notify the States members of the deposit of each instrument of ratification or accession.

Article 50

Any State party may submit written proposals, though the Secretary-General, for the amendment of the present Charter. After these amendments have been circulated among the States members, the Secretary-General shall invite the States parties to consider the proposed amendments before submitting them to the Council of the League for adoption.

Article 51

The amendments shall take effect, with regard to the States parties that have approved them, once they have been approved by two thirds of the States parties.

Article 52

Any State party may propose additional optional protocols to the present Charter and they shall be adopted in accordance with the procedures used for the adoption of amendments to the Charter.

Article 53

1.   Any State party, when signing this Charter, depositing the instruments of ratification or acceding hereto, may make a reservation to any article of the Charter, provided that such reservation does not conflict with the aims and fundamental purposes of the Charter.

2.   Any State party that has made a reservation pursuant to paragraph 1 of this article may withdraw it at any time by addressing a notification to the Secretary-General of the League of Arab States.

3.   The Secretary-General shall notify the States parties of reservations and of requests for their withdrawal.

PART NINE

ASIA

Notwithstanding the fact that respectable numbers of States from Asia and the Pacific are parties to the principal human rights treaties (see the lists of States parties to the *Multilateral Treaties Deposited with the Secretary-General*, Chapter IV, at **http://treaties.un.org/Pages/ParticipationStatus.aspx**), the region has traditionally been viewed as generally inhospitable to 'international' standards and as a field of contest between 'Asian values' and 'Western values'. While it is true that is as yet no human rights protection mechanism comparable to those found elsewhere, the region has nevertheless benefited from the work of scholars, intellectuals and particularly active non-governmental organizations, such as the Asian Centre for Human Rights: **http://www.achrweb.org/**. It remains to be seen whether institutional developments within the Association of South East Asian States described below will bring in progressive change.

Further reading

BAUER, J. R. and BELL, D. A., *The East Asian Challenge for Human Rights*, Cambridge: Cambridge University Press, 1999.

DE VARENNES, F., 'The Fallacies in the "Universalism versus Cultural Relativism" Debate in Human Rights Law', (2006) 7 *Asia Pacific Journal on Human Rights and the Law* 67.

WILLIAMS, C., 'International Human Rights and Confucianism', (2006) 7 *Asia Pacific Journal on Human Rights and the Law* 38.

127. ASEAN INTER-GOVERNMENTAL COMMISSION ON HUMAN RIGHTS—TERMS OF REFERENCE, 2009

Founded in 1967 by Indonesia, Malaysia, the Philippines, Singapore and Thailand, the Association of Southeast Asian Nations (ASEAN) now includes Brunei Darussalam, Myanmar, Cambodia, Laos and Vietnam. Its original aims were the acceleration of economic growth, social progress, cultural development, peace and stability in the region, and to provide a forum for discussion. ASEAN has been criticized in the past for failing to take action, or even a position, on human rights concerns in and among its Member States, but the ASEAN Charter adopted in Singapore in November 2007 now acknowledges adherence to the 'principles of democracy, the rule of law and good governance, respect for and protection of human rights and fundamental freedoms' (Preamble), and these are included among the organization's purposes and principles (see Articles 1 and 2); the Charter entered into force on 15 December 2008. See further **http://www.aseansec.org/**.

In July 2009, the 42nd ASEAN Ministerial Meeting adopted the Terms of Reference below, so initiating the process of establishing a regional human rights body to be called the ASEAN Inter-Governmental Commission on Human Rights. The Commission was duly launched at the 15th ASEAN Summit in Thailand in October 2009, and it was expected to meet in December 2009 to finalize a five-year work plan and set priorities for 2010; see the *ASEAN Bulletin*, October 2009: **http://www.aseansec.org/23112.htm**.

The Terms of Reference stress the principle of non-interference, identify the Commission's functions as essentially consultative and advisory, make no provision for individual complaints, and emphasize that the body is dependent on voluntary funding.

Further reading

SEAH, D., 'The ASEAN Charter', (2009) 58 *ICLQ* 197.

TEXT

Pursuant to Article 14 of the ASEAN Charter, the ASEAN Intergovernmental Commission on Human Rights (AICHR) shall operate in accordance with the following Terms of Reference (TOR):

1. *Purposes*

The purposes of the AICHR are:

   1.1   To promote and protect human rights and fundamental freedoms of the peoples of ASEAN;

   1.2   To uphold the right of the peoples of ASEAN to live in peace, dignity and prosperity;

   1.3   To contribute to the realisation of the purposes of ASEAN as set out in the ASEAN Charter in order to promote stability and harmony in the region, friendship and cooperation among ASEAN Member States, as well as the well-being, livelihood, welfare and participation of ASEAN peoples in the ASEAN Community building process;

1.4 To promote human rights within the regional context, bearing in mind national and regional particularities and mutual respect for different historical, cultural and religious backgrounds, and taking into account the balance between rights and responsibilities;

1.5 To enhance regional cooperation with a view to complementing national and international efforts on the promotion and protection of human rights; and

1.6 To uphold international human rights standards as prescribed by the Universal Declaration of Human Rights, the Vienna Declaration and Programme of Action, and international human rights instruments to which ASEAN Member States are parties.

2. *Principles*

The AICHR shall be guided by the following principles:

2.1 Respect for principles of ASEAN as embodied in Article 2 of the ASEAN Charter, in particular:

 (a) respect for the independence, sovereignty, equality, territorial integrity and national identity of all ASEAN Member States;

 (b) non-interference in the internal affairs of ASEAN Member States;

 (c) respect for the right of every Member State to lead its national existence free from external interference, subversion and coercion;

 (d) adherence to the rule of law, good governance, the principles of democracy and constitutional government;

 (e) respect for fundamental freedoms, the promotion and protection of human rights, and the promotion of social justice;

 (f) upholding the Charter of the United Nations and international law, including international humanitarian law, subscribed to by ASEAN Member States; and

 (g) respect for different cultures, languages and religions of the peoples of ASEAN, while emphasising their common values in the spirit of unity in diversity.

2.2 Respect for international human rights principles, including universality, indivisibility, interdependence and interrelatedness of all human rights and fundamental freedoms, as well as impartiality, objectivity, non-selectivity, non-discrimination, and avoidance of double standards and politicisation;

2.3 Recognition that the primary responsibility to promote and protect human rights and fundamental freedoms rests with each Member State;

2.4 Pursuance of a constructive and non-confrontational approach and cooperation to enhance promotion and protection of human rights; and

2.5 Adoption of an evolutionary approach that would contribute to the development of human rights norms and standards in ASEAN.

3. *Consultative Inter-Governmental Body*

The AICHR is an inter-governmental body and an integral part of the ASEAN organisational structure. It is a consultative body.

4. Mandate and Functions

4.1   To develop strategies for the promotion and protection of human rights and fundamental freedoms to complement the building of the ASEAN Community;

4.2   To develop an ASEAN Human Rights Declaration with a view to establishing a framework for human rights cooperation through various ASEAN conventions and other instruments dealing with human rights;

4.3   To enhance public awareness of human rights among the peoples of ASEAN through education, research and dissemination of information;

4.4   To promote capacity building for the effective implementation of international human rights treaty obligations undertaken by ASEAN Member States;

4.5   To encourage ASEAN Member States to consider acceding to and ratifying international human rights instruments;

4.6   To promote the full implementation of ASEAN instruments related to human rights;

4.7   To provide advisory services and technical assistance on human rights matters to ASEAN sectoral bodies upon request;

4.8   To engage in dialogue and consultation with other ASEAN bodies and entities associated with ASEAN, including civil society organisations and other stakeholders, as provided for in Chapter V of the ASEAN Charter;

4.9   To consult, as may be appropriate, with other national, regional and international institutions and entities concerned with the promotion and protection of human rights;

4.10 To obtain information from ASEAN Member States on the promotion and protection of human rights;

4.11 To develop common approaches and positions on human rights matters of interest to ASEAN;

4.12 To prepare studies on thematic issues of human rights in ASEAN;

4.13 To submit an annual report on its activities, or other reports if deemed necessary, to the ASEAN Foreign Ministers Meeting; and 4.14. To perform any other tasks as may be assigned to it by the ASEAN Foreign Ministers Meeting.

5. Composition

Membership

5.1   The AICHR shall consist of the Member States of ASEAN.

5.2   Each ASEAN Member State shall appoint a Representative to the AICHR who shall be accountable to the appointing Government.

Qualifications

5.3   When appointing their Representatives to the AICHR, Member States shall give due consideration to gender equality, integrity and competence in the field of human rights.

5.4   Member States should consult, if required by their respective internal processes, with appropriate stakeholders in the appointment of their Representatives to the AICHR.

Term of Office

5.5 Each Representative serves a term of three years and may be consecutively re-appointed for only one more term.

5.6 Notwithstanding paragraph 5.5, the appointing Government may decide, at its discretion, to replace its Representative.

Responsibility

5.7 Each Representative, in the discharge of his or her duties, shall act impartially in accordance with the ASEAN Charter and this TOR.

5.8 Representatives shall have the obligation to attend AICHR meetings. If a Representative is unable to attend a meeting due to exceptional circumstances, the Government concerned shall formally notify the Chair of the AICHR of the appointment of a temporary representative with a full mandate to represent the Member State concerned.

Chair of the AICHR

5.9 The Chair of the AICHR shall be the Representative of the Member State holding the Chairmanship of ASEAN.

5.10 The Chair of the AICHR shall exercise his or her role in accordance with this TOR, which shall include:

(a) leading in the preparation of reports of the AICHR and presenting such reports to the ASEAN Foreign Ministers Meeting;

(b) coordinating with the AICHR's Representatives in between meetings of the AICHR and with the relevant ASEAN bodies;

(c) representing the AICHR at regional and international events pertaining to the promotion and protection of human rights as entrusted by the AICHR; and

(d) undertaking other specific functions entrusted by the AICHR in accordance with this TOR. Immunities and Privileges.

5.11 In accordance with Article 19 of the ASEAN Charter, Representatives participating in official activities of the AICHR shall enjoy such immunities and privileges as are necessary for the exercise of their functions.

6. Modalities

Decision-making

6.1 Decision-making in the AICHR shall be based on consultation and consensus in accordance with Article 20 of the ASEAN Charter.

Number of Meetings

6.2 The AICHR shall convene two regular meetings per year. Each meeting shall normally be not more than five days.

6.3 Regular meetings of the AICHR shall be held alternately at the ASEAN Secretariat and the Member State holding the Chair of ASEAN.

6.4 As and when appropriate, the AICHR may hold additional meetings at the ASEAN Secretariat or at a venue to be agreed upon by the Representatives.

6.5 When necessary, the ASEAN Foreign Ministers may instruct the AICHR to
meet.

Line of Reporting

6.6 The AICHR shall submit an annual report and other appropriate reports to the
ASEAN Foreign Ministers Meeting for its consideration.

Public Information

6.7 The AICHR shall keep the public periodically informed of its work and activities
through appropriate public information materials produced by the AICHR.

Relationship with Other Human Rights Bodies within ASEAN

6.8 The AICHR is the overarching human rights institution in ASEAN with overall
responsibility for the promotion and protection of human rights in ASEAN.

6.9 The AICHR shall work with all ASEAN sectoral bodies dealing with human
rights to expeditiously determine the modalities for their ultimate alignment
with the AICHR. To this end, the AICHR shall closely consult, coordinate
and collaborate with such bodies in order to promote synergy and coherence in
ASEAN's promotion and protection of human rights.

7. *Role of the Secretary-General and ASEAN Secretariat*

7.1 The Secretary-General of ASEAN may bring relevant issues to the attention of
the AICHR in accordance with Article 11.2 (a) and (b) of the ASEAN Charter.
In so doing, the Secretary-General of ASEAN shall concurrently inform the
ASEAN Foreign Ministers of these issues.

7.2 The ASEAN Secretariat shall provide the necessary secretarial support to the
AICHR to ensure its effective performance. To facilitate the Secretariat's sup-
port to the AICHR, ASEAN Member States may, with the concurrence of the
Secretary-General of ASEAN, second their officials to the ASEAN Secretariat.

8. *Work Plan and Funding*

8.1 The AICHR shall prepare and submit a Work Plan of programmes and activi-
ties with indicative budget for a cycle of five years to be approved by the ASEAN
Foreign Ministers Meeting, upon the recommendation of the Committee of
Permanent Representatives to ASEAN.

8.2 The AICHR shall also prepare and submit an annual budget to support high pri-
ority programmes and activities, which shall be approved by the ASEAN Foreign
Ministers Meeting, upon the recommendation of the Committee of Permanent
Representatives to ASEAN.

8.3 The annual budget shall be funded on equal sharing basis by ASEAN Member
States.

8.4 The AHRB may also receive resources from any ASEAN Member States for
specific extrabudgetary programmes from the Work Plan.

8.5 The AICHR shall also establish an endowment fund which consists of voluntary
contributions from ASEAN Member States and other sources.

8.6 Funding and other resources from non-ASEAN Member States shall be solely for
human rights promotion, capacity building and education.

8.7 All funds used by the AICHR shall be managed and disbursed in conformity with the general financial rules of ASEAN.

8.8 Secretarial support for the AICHR shall be funded by the ASEAN Secretariat's annual operational budget.

9. *General and Final Provisions*

9.1 This TOR shall come into force upon the approval of the ASEAN Foreign Ministers Meeting.

Amendments

9.2 Any Member State may submit a formal request for an amendment of this TOR.

9.3 The request for amendment shall be considered by the Committee of Permanent Representatives to ASEAN in consultation with the AICHR, and presented to the ASEAN Foreign Ministers Meeting for approval.

9.4 Such amendments shall enter into force upon the approval of the ASEAN Foreign Ministers.

Meeting

9.5 Such amendments shall not prejudice the rights and obligations arising from or based on this TOR before or up to the date of such amendments.

Review

9.6 This TOR shall be initially reviewed five years after its entry into force. This review and subsequent reviews shall be undertaken by the ASEAN Foreign Ministers Meeting, with a view to further enhancing the promotion and protection of human rights within ASEAN.

9.7 In this connection, the AICHR shall assess its work and submit recommendations for the consideration of the ASEAN Foreign Ministers Meeting on future efforts that could be undertaken in the promotion and protection of human rights within ASEAN consistent with the principles and purposes of the ASEAN Charter and this TOR.

Interpretation

9.8 Any difference concerning the interpretation of this TOR which cannot be resolved shall be referred to the ASEAN Foreign Ministers Meeting for a decision.

PART TEN

THE CONCEPT OF EQUALITY

INTRODUCTION

This Part begins with a passage from the Dissenting Opinion of Judge Tanaka, the Japanese member of the International Court of Justice, in the *South West Africa Cases* (Second Phase), 1966. In that case the Court (by the casting vote of the President) failed to deal with the merits of the submissions of the applicant States (Ethiopia and Liberia) that South Africa had violated her international obligations. However, half of the members of the Court, including Judge Tanaka, were prepared to deal with the issues of substance raised by the applications. In the circumstances and given the quality of the exposition the status of the Opinion as a Dissenting Opinion is of little relevance.

The passage reproduced is from the *Reports of Judgments, Advisory Opinions and Orders* of the International Court of Justice, 1966, at 284–316. It contains what is probably the best exposition of the concept of equality in existing literature. Its importance derives from two sources: first, the lack of sound analysis of the concept in the literature at large; and second, the prominence of the principle of equality, or the standard of non-discrimination, in legislation and other instruments concerning human rights.

This Part now also includes the 1978 UNESCO Declaration on Race and Racial Prejudice and the 2001 Durban Declaration and Programme of Action.

Further reading

Advisory Opinion on Minority Schools in Albania, 1935, *Judgments, Orders and Advisory Opinions of the Permanent Court of International Justice*, Series A/B, No. 64.

Ahmad v Inner London Education Authority [1978] 1 QB 36.

Brown v Board of Education 347 US 483 (1954) (US Supreme Court).

Case relating to certain aspects of the laws on the use of languages in education in Belgium (the *Belgian Linguistics* case) European Court of Human Rights, Judgment of 23 July 1968, Series A, 1968 (1979–80) 1 EHRR 252.

Ealing London Borough Council v Race Relations Board [1972] AC 342.

128. DISSENTING OPINION OF JUDGE TANAKA, *SOUTH WEST AFRICA CASES (SECOND PHASE),* 1966

For recent judicial notice of Judge Tanaka's opinion, see *European Roma Rights Center and Others v Immigration Officer, Prague Airport and others* [2005] AC 1, [2004] UKHL 55, particularly per Baroness Hale at paragraphs 98–103; see also, UNITED NATIONS HIGH COMMISSIONER FOR REFUGEES, *Written Case, Intervening in the House of Lords,* 17 *IJRL* 427 (2005) and *Kavanagh v Governor of Mountjoy Prison* [2002] IESC 13 (Supreme Court of Ireland).

TEXT

Now we shall examine Nos. 3 and 4 of the Applicants' final submissions. Submission No. 3 reads as follows:

> 'Respondent, by laws and regulations, and official methods and measures, which are set out in the pleadings herein, has practised apartheid, i.e., has distinguished as to race, colour, national or tribal origin in establishing the rights and duties of the inhabitants of the Territory; that such practice is in violation of its obligations as stated in Article 2 of the Mandate and Article 22 of the Covenant of the League of Nations; and that Respondent has the duty forthwith to cease the practice of apartheid in the Territory;' (Applicants' final submissions, C.R. 65/35, p. 69).

At the same time, Applicants have presented another submission (Submission No. 4) which states as follows:

> 'Respondent, by virtue of economic, political, social and educational policies applied within the Territory, by means of laws and regulations, and official methods and measures, which are set out in the pleadings herein, has, in the light of applicable international standards or international legal norm, or both, failed to promote to the utmost the material and moral well-being and social progress of the inhabitants of the Territory; that its failure to do so is in violation of its obligations as stated in Article 2 of the Mandate and Article 22 of the Covenant; and that Respondent has the duty forthwith to cease its violations as aforesaid and to take all practicable action to fulfil its duties under such Articles;' (Applicants' final submissions, 19 May 1965, C.R. 65/35, pp. 69–70).

The President, Sir Percy Spender, for the purpose of clarification, addressed a question to the Applicants in relation to Submissions 3 and 4 in the Memorials at page 197, which are not fundamentally different from the above-mentioned Final Submissions Nos. 3 and 4. He asked what was the distinction between one (i.e., Submission No. 3) and the other (i.e., Submission No. 4). (C.R. 65/23, 28 April 1965, p. 31).

The response of the Applicants on this point was that the distinction between the two Submissions 3 and 4 was verbal only (19 May 1965, C.R. 65/35 p. 71). This response, being made after the amendment of the Applicants' submissions, may be considered as applicable to the amended Submissions Nos. 3 and 4.

It should be pointed out that the main difference between the original and the Final Submissions Nos. 3 and 4 is that a phrase, namely: 'in the light of applicable international standards or international legal norm, or both' is inserted between 'has' and 'failed to promote to the utmost...' which seems to make clear the substantive identity existing between these two submissions.

Now we shall analyse each of these submissions, which occupy the central issue of the whole of the Applicants' submissions and upon which the greater part of the arguments of the Parties has been focused. This issue is without doubt the question concerning the policy of apartheid which the Respondent as Mandatory is alleged to have practised.

First, we shall deal with the concept of apartheid. The Applicants, in defining apartheid, said: 'Respondent... has distinguished as to race, colour, national or tribal origin in establishing the rights and duties of the inhabitants of the Territory.'

It may be said that, as between the Parties, no divergence of opinion on the concept of apartheid itself exists, notwithstanding that the Respondent prefers to use other terminology, such as 'separate development', instead of 'apartheid'. Anyhow, it seems that there has been no argument concerning the concept of apartheid itself. Furthermore, we can also recognize that the Respondent has never denied its practice of apartheid; but it wants to establish the legality and reasonableness of this policy under the mandates system and its compatibility with the obligations of the Respondent as Mandatory, as well as its necessity to perform these obligations.

Submission No. 3 contends that such practice (i.e., the practice of apartheid) is in violation of its obligations as stated in Article 2 of the Mandate and Article 22 of the Covenant. However, the Applicants' contention is not clear as to whether the violation, by the practice of apartheid, of the Respondent's obligation is conceived from the viewpoint of politics or law. If we consider Submission No. 3, only on the basis of its literal interpretation, it may be considered to be from the viewpoint of politics; this means that the policy of apartheid is not in conformity with the objectives of the Mandate, namely the promotion of well-being and social progress of the inhabitants without regard to any conceivable legal norm or standards. If the Applicants maintain this position, the issue would be a matter of discretion and the case, so far as this point is concerned, would not be justiciable, as the Respondent has contended.

Now the Applicants do not allege the violation of obligations by the Respondent independently of any legal norm or standards. Since the Applicants amended Submission No. 4 in the Memorials and inserted a phrase 'in the light of applicable international standards or international legal norm', the violation of the obligations as stated in Article 2 of the Mandate and Article 22 of the Covenant (Submission No. 3) which is identical with the failure to promote to the utmost the material and moral well-being and social progress of the inhabitants of the Territory (Submission No. 4) has come to possess a special meaning; namely of a juridical character. Applicants' cause is no longer based directly on a violation of the well-being and progress by the practice of apartheid, but on the alleged violation of certain international standards or international legal norm and not directly on the obligation to promote the well-being and social progress of the inhabitants. There is no doubt that, if such standards and norm exist, their observance in itself may constitute a part of Respondent's general obligations to promote the well-being and social progress.

From what is said above, the relationship between the Applicants' Submissions Nos. 3 and 4 may be understood as follows. The two submissions deal with the same subject-matter, namely the illegal character of the policy and practice of apartheid. However, the contents of each submission are not quite the same, consequently the distinction between the two submissions is not verbal only, as Applicants stated in answer to the question of the President; each seems to be supplementary to the other.

Briefly, the Applicants' Submissions Nos. 3 and 4, as newly formulated, rest upon a norm and/or standard. This norm or standard has been added by the Applicants to Submission No. 4. The existence of this norm or standard to be applied to the Mandate relationships, according to the Applicants' allegation, constitutes a legal limitation of the Respondent's discretionary power and makes the practice of apartheid illegal, and accordingly a violation of the obligations incumbent on the Mandatory.

What the Applicants mean by apartheid is as follows:

'Under apartheid, the status, rights, duties, opportunities and burdens of the population are determined and allotted arbitrarily on the basis of race, color and tribe, in a pattern which ignores the needs and capacities of the groups and individuals affected, and subordinates the interests and rights of the great majority of the people to the preferences of a minority...It deals with apartheid in practice, as it actually is and as it actually has been in the life of the people of the Territory...' (Memorials, p. 108.)

The Applicants contend the existence of a norm or standards which prohibit the practice of apartheid. These norm or standards are nothing other than those of non-discrimination or non-separation.

The Respondent denies the existence of a norm or standard to prohibit the practice of apartheid and tries to justify this practice from the discretionary nature of the Mandatory's power. The Respondent emphasizes that the practice of apartheid is only impermissible when it is carried out in bad faith.

From the viewpoint of the Applicants, the existence, and objective validity, of a norm of non-discrimination make the question of the intention or motivation irrelevant for the purposes of determining whether there has been a violation of this norm. The principle that a legal precept, as opposed to a moral one, in so far as it is not specifically provided otherwise, shall be applied objectively, independently of motivation on the part of those concerned and independently of other individual circumstances, may be applicable to the Respondent's defence of *bona fides*.

Here we are concerned with the existence of a legal norm or standards regarding non-discrimination. It is a question which is concerned with the sources of international law, and, at the same time, with the mandate law. Furthermore, the question is intimately related to the essence and nature of fundamental human rights, the promotion and encouragement of respect for which constitute one of the purposes of the United Nations (Article 1, paragraph 3, Charter of the United Nations), in which the principle of equality before the law occupies the most important part—a principle, from the Applicants' view, antithetical to the policy of apartheid.

What is meant by 'international norm or standards' can be understood as being related to the principle of equality before the law.

The question is whether a legal norm on equality before the law exists in the international sphere and whether it has a binding power upon the Respondent's conduct in carrying out its obligations as Mandatory. The question is whether the principle of equality before the law can find its place among the sources of international law which are referred to in Article 38, paragraph 1.

Now we shall examine one by one the sources of international law enumerated by the above-mentioned provision.

First we consider the international conventions (or treaties). Here we are not concerned with 'special' or 'particular' law-making bilateral treaties, but only with law-making multilateral treaties such as the Charter of the United Nations, the Constitution of the International Labour Organization, the Genocide Convention, which have special significance as legislative methods. However, even such law-making treaties bind only signatory States and they do not bind States which are not parties to them.

The question is whether the Charter of the United Nations contains a legal norm of equality before the law and the principle of non-discrimination on account of religion, race, colour, sex, language, political creed, etc. The achievement of international co-operation in 'promoting and encouraging respect for human rights and for fundamental freedoms for all without distinction as to race, sex, language, or religion' constitutes one of the purposes of the United Nations (Article 1, paragraph 3). Next, the General Assembly shall initiate studies and made recommendations for the purpose of '...(b)...and assisting in the realization of human rights and fundamental freedoms without distinction as to race, sex, language, or religion' (Article 13, paragraph 1 (b)). 'Universal respect for, and observance of, human rights and fundamental freedoms for all without distinction as to race, sex, language, or religion' is one of the items which shall be promoted by the United Nations in the field of international economic and social co-operation (Articles 55(c), 56). In this field the Economic and Social Council may make recommendations for the purpose of promoting respect for, and observance of, human rights and fundamental freedoms for all (Article 62, paragraph 2, Charter). Finally, 'to encourage respect for human rights and for fundamental freedoms for all without distinction as to race, sex, language or religion' is indicated as one of the basic objectives of the trusteeship system (Article 76 (c)).

The repeated references in the Charter to the fundamental rights and freedoms— at least four times—presents itself as one of its differences from the Covenant of the League of Nations, in which the existence of intimate relationships between peace and respect for human rights were not so keenly felt as in the Charter of the United Nations. However, the Charter did not go so far as to give the definition to the fundamental rights and freedoms, nor to provide any machinery of implementation for the protection and guarantee of these rights and freedoms. The 'Universal Declaration of Human Rights and Fundamental Freedoms' of 1948 which wanted to formulate each right and freedom and give them concrete content, is no more than a declaration adopted by the General Assembly and not a treaty binding on the member States. The goal of the codification on the matter of human rights and freedoms has until now not been reached save in very limited degree, namely with the European Convention for the Protection of Human Rights and Fundamental Freedoms of 1953, the validity of which is only regional and not universal and with a few special conventions, such as 'genocide' and political rights of women, the application of which is limited to their respective matters.

In view of these situations, can the Applicants contend, as an interpretation of the Charter, that the existence of a legal norm on equality before the law, which prescribes non-discrimination on account of religion, race, colour, etc., accordingly forbids the practice of apartheid? Is what the Charter requires limited only 'to achieve international co-operation...in promoting and encouraging respect for human rights and for fundamental freedoms...' and other matters referred to above?

Under these circumstances it seems difficult to recognize that the Charter expressly imposes on member States any legal obligation with respect to the fundamental human rights and freedoms. On the other hand, we cannot ignore the enormous importance which the Charter attaches to the realization of fundamental human rights and freedoms. Article 56 states: 'All Members pledge themselves to take joint and separate action in co-operation with the Organization for the achievement of the purposes set forth in Article 55.' (Article 55 enumerates the purposes of international economic and social co-operation, in which 'universal respect for, and observance of, human rights and fundamental freedoms' is included.) Well, those who pledge themselves to take action in co-operation with the United Nations in respect of the promotion of universal respect for, and observance of, human rights and fundamental freedoms, cannot violate, without contradiction, these rights and freedoms. How can one, on the one hand, preach respect for human rights to others and, on the other hand, disclaim for oneself the obligation to respect them? From the provisions of the Charter referring to the human rights and fundamental freedoms it can be inferred that the legal obligation to respect human rights and fundamental freedoms is imposed on member States.

Judge Spiropoulos confirmed the binding character of the human rights provisions of the Charter:

> 'As the obligation to respect human rights was placed upon Member States by the Charter, it followed that any violation of human rights was a violation of the provision of the Charter.'
> (G.A., O.R., 3rd Session, 6th Committee, 138th Meeting, 7 December 1948, p. 765.)

Judge Jessup also attributed the same character to the human rights provisions:

> 'Since this book is written *de lege ferenda*, the attempt is made throughout to distinguish between the existing law and the future goals of the law. It is already the law, at least for Members of the United Nations, that respect for human dignity and fundamental human rights is obligatory. The duty is imposed by the Charter.' (Philip C. Jessup, *Modern Law of Nations*, 1948, p. 91.)

Without doubt, under the present circumstances, the international protection of human rights and fundamental freedoms is very imperfect. The work of codification in this field of law has advanced little from the viewpoint of defining each human right and freedom, as well as the machinery for their realization. But there is little doubt of the existence of human rights and freedoms; if not, respect for these is logically inconceivable; the Charter presupposes the existence of human rights and freedoms which shall be respected; the existence of such rights and freedoms is unthinkable without corresponding obligations of persons concerned and a legal norm underlying them. Furthermore, there is no doubt that these obligations are not only moral ones, and that they also have a legal character by the very nature of the subject-matter.

Therefore, the legislative imperfections in the definition of human rights and freedoms and the lack of mechanism for implementation, do not constitute a reason for denying their existence and the need for their legal protection.

Furthermore, it must be pointed out that the Charter provisions, as indicated above, repeatedly emphasize the principle of equality before the law by saying, 'without distinction as to race, sex, language or religion'.

Under the hypothesis that in the United Nations Charter there exists a legal norm or standards of non-discrimination, are the Applicants, referring to this norm, entitled to have recourse to the International Court of Justice according to Article 7, paragraph 2, of the Mandate? The Respondent contends that such an alleged norm does not constitute a part of the mandate agreement, and therefore the question on this norm falls outside the dispute, which, by the compromissory clause, is placed under the jurisdiction of the International Court of Justice. The Applicants' contention would amount to the introduction of a new element into the mandate agreement which is alien to this instrument.

It is evident that, as the Respondent contends, the mandate agreement does not stipulate equality before the law clause, and that this clause does not formally constitute a part of the mandate instrument. Nevertheless, the equality principle, as an integral part of the Charter of the United Nations or as an independent source of general international law, can be directly applied to the matter of the Mandate either as constituting a kind of law of the Mandate *in sensu lato* or, at least in respect of standards, as a principle of interpretation of the mandate agreement. Accordingly, the dispute concerning the legality of apartheid comes within the field of the interpretation and application of the provisions of the Mandate stipulated in Article 7, paragraph 2, of the Mandate.

This conclusion is justified only on the presupposition that the Respondent is bound by the Charter of the United Nations not only as a member State but also as a Mandatory. The Charter, being of the nature of special international law, or the law of the organized international community, must be applied to all matters which come within the purposes and competence of the United Nations and with which member States are concerned, including the matter of the Mandate. Logic requires that, so long as we recognize the unity of personality, the same principle must govern both the conduct of a member State in the United Nations itself and also its conduct as a mandatory, particularly in the matter of the protection and guarantee of human rights and freedoms.

Concerning the Applicants' contention attributing to the norm of non-discrimination or non-separation the character of customary international law, the following points must be noted.

The Applicants enumerate resolutions and declarations of international organs which condemn racial discrimination, segregation, separation and apartheid, and contend that the said resolutions and declarations were adopted by an overwhelming majority, and therefore have binding power in regard to an opposing State, namely the Respondent. Concerning the question whether the consent of all States is required for the creation of a customary international law or not, we consider that the answer must be in the negative for the reason that Article 38, paragraph 1 (b), of the Statute does not exclude the possibility of a few dissidents for the purpose of the creation of a customary international law and that the contrary view of a particular State or States would result in the permission of obstruction by veto, which could not have been expected by the legislator who drafted the said Article.

An important question involved in the Applicants' contention is whether resolutions and declarations of international organs can be recognized as a factor in the custom-generating process in the interpretation of Article 38, paragraph 1 (b), that is to say, as 'evidence of a general practice'.

According to traditional international law, a general practice is the result of the repetition of individual acts of States constituting consensus in regard to a certain content of a rule of law. Such repetition of acts is a historical process extending over a long period of time. The process of the formation of a customary law in this case may be described as individualistic. On the contrary, this process is going to change in adapting itself to changes in the way of international life. The appearance of organizations such as the League of Nations and the United Nations, with their agencies and affiliated institutions, replacing an important part of the traditional individualistic method of international negotiation by the method of 'parliamentary diplomacy' (Judgment on the *South West Africa* cases, *ICJ Reports 1962*, p. 346), is bound to influence the mode of generation of customary international law. A State, instead of pronouncing its view to a few States directly concerned, has the opportunity, through the medium of an organization, to declare its position to all members of the organization and to know immediately their reaction on the same matter. In former days, practice, repetition and *opinio juris sive necessitatis*, which are the ingredients of customary law might be combined together in a very long and slow process extending over centuries. In the contemporary age of highly developed techniques of communication and information, the formation of a custom through the medium of international organizations is greatly facilitated and accelerated; the establishment of such a custom would require no more than one generation or even far less than that. This is one of the examples of the transformation of law inevitably produced by change in the social substratum.

Of course, we cannot admit that individual resolutions, declarations, judgments, decisions, etc., have binding force upon the members of the organization. What is required for customary international law is the repetition of the same practice; accordingly, in this case resolutions, declarations, etc., on the same matter in the same, or diverse, organizations must take place repeatedly.

Parallel with such repetition, each resolution, declaration, etc., being considered as the manifestation of the collective will of individual participant States, the will of the international community can certainly be formulated more quickly and more accurately as compared with the traditional method of the normative process. This collective, cumulative and organic process of custom-generation can be characterized as the middle way between legislation by convention and the traditional process of custom making, and can be seen to have an important role from the viewpoint of the development of international law.

In short, the accumulation of authoritative pronouncements such as resolutions, declarations, decisions, etc., concerning the interpretation of the Charter by the competent organs of the international community can be characterized as evidence of the international custom referred to in Article 38, paragraph 1 (b).

In the present case the Applicants assert the existence of the international norm and standards of non-discrimination and non-separation and refer to this source of international law. They enumerate resolutions of the General Assembly which repeatedly and strongly deny the apartheid policy of racial discrimination as an interpretation of the Charter (General Assembly resolution 1178 (XII) of 26 November 1957; resolution 1248 (XIII) of 30 October 1958; resolution 1375 (XIV) of 17 November 1959; resolution 1598 (XV) of 13 April 1961; and resolutions of the Security Council (with regard to apartheid as practised in the Republic of South Africa); resolution of 7 August 1953 which declares the inconsistency of the policy of the South African Government with the principles contained in the Charter of the United Nations and with its obligations as a member State of the United Nations; resolution of 4 December 1963 which declares '... the policies of apartheid and racial discrimination ... are abhorrent to the conscience of mankind ...'. The Applicants cite also the report of the Committee on South West Africa for 1956).

Moreover, the 11 trust territories agreements, each of them containing a provision concerning the norm of official non-discrimination or non-separation on the basis of membership in a group or race, may be considered as contributions to the development of the universal acceptance of the norm of non-discrimination, in addition to the meaning which each provision possesses in each trusteeship agreement, by virtue of Article 38, paragraph 1 (a), of the Statute.

Furthermore, the Universal Declaration of Human Rights adopted by the General Assembly in 1948, although not binding in itself, constitutes evidence of the interpretation and application of the relevant Charter provisions. The same may be said of the Draft Declaration on Rights and Duties of States adopted by the International Law Commission in 1949, the Draft Covenant on Civil and Political rights, the Draft Covenant on Economic, Social and Cultural rights, the Declaration on the Elimination of all Forms of Racial Discrimination adopted by the General Assembly of the United Nations on 20 November 1963 and of regional treaties and declarations, particularly the European Convention for the Protection of Human Rights and Fundamental Freedoms signed on 3 September 1953, the Charter of the Organization of American States signed on 30 April 1948, the American Declaration of the Rights and Duties of Man, 1948, the Draft Declaration of International Rights and Duties, 1945.

From what has been said above, we consider that the norm of non-discrimination or non-separation on the basis of race has become a rule of customary international law as is contended by the Applicants, and as a result, the Respondent's obligations as Mandatory are governed by this legal norm in its capacity as a member of the United Nations either directly or at least by way of interpretation of Article 2, paragraph 2.

One of the contentions concerning the application of the said legal norm is that, if such a legal norm exists for judging the Respondent's obligations under Article 2, paragraph 2, of the Mandate, it would be the one in existence at the time the Mandate was entrusted to the Respondent. This is evidently a question of inter-temporal law.

The Respondent's position is that of denying the application of a new law to a matter which arose under an old law, namely the negation of retroactivity of a new customary law. The Applicant's argument is based on 'the relevance of the evolving practice and views of States, growth of experience and increasing knowledge in political and social science to the determination of obligations bearing on the nature and purpose of the Mandate in general, and Article 2 paragraph 2'; briefly, it rests on the assertion of the concept of the 'continuous, dynamic and ascending growth' of the obligation of the Mandatory.

Our view on this question is substantially not very different from that of the Applicants. The reason why we recognize the retroactive application of a new customary law to a matter which started more than 40 years ago is as follows.

The matter in question is in reality not that of an old law and a new law, that is to say, it is not a question which arises out of an amendment of a law and which should be decided on the basis of the principle of the protection of *droit acquis* and therefore of non-retroactivity. In the present case, the protection of the acquired rights of the Respondent is not the issue, but its obligations, because the main purposes of the mandate system are ethical and humanitarian. The Respondent has no right to behave in an inhuman way today as well as during these 40 years. Therefore, the recognition of the generation of a new customary international law on the matter of non-discrimination is not to be regarded as detrimental to the Mandatory, but as an authentic interpretation of the already existing provisions of Article 2, paragraph 2, of the Mandate and the Covenant. It is nothing other than a simple clarification of what was not so clear 40 years ago. What ought to have been clear 40 years ago has been revealed by the creation of a new customary law which plays the role of authentic interpretation the effect of which is retroactive.

Briefly, the method of the generation of customary international law is in the stage of transformation from being an individualistic process to being a collectivistic process. This phenomenon can be said to be the adaptation of the traditional creative process of international law to the reality of the growth of the organized international community. It can be characterized, considered from the sociological viewpoint, as a transition from traditional custom-making to international legislation by treaty.

Following the reference to Article 38, paragraph 1 (b), of the Statute, the Applicants base their contention on the legal norm alternatively on Article 38, paragraph 1 (c), of the Statute, namely 'the general principles of law recognized by civilized nations'.

Applicants refer to this source of international law both as an independent ground for the justification of the norm of non-discrimination and as a supplement and reinforcement of the other arguments advanced by them to demonstrate their theory.

The question is whether the legal norm of non-discrimination or non-separation denying the practice of apartheid can be recognized as a principle enunciated in the said provision.

The wording of this provision is very broad and vague; the meaning is not clear. Multiple interpretations ranging from the most strict to the most liberal are possible.

To decide this question we must clarify the meaning of 'general principles of law'. To restrict the meaning to private law principles or principles of procedural law seems from the viewpoint of literal interpretation untenable. So far as the 'general principles of law' are not qualified, the 'law' must be understood to embrace all branches of law, including municipal law, public law, constitutional and administrative law, private law, commercial law, substantive and procedural law, etc. Nevertheless, analogies drawn from these laws should not be made mechanically, that is to say, to borrow the expression of Lord McNair, 'by means of importing private law institutions "lock, stock and barrel" ready-made and fully equipped with a set of rules'. (*ICJ Reports 1950*, p. 148.)

What international law can with advantage borrow from these sources must be from the viewpoint of underlying or guiding 'principles'. These principles, therefore, must not be limited to statutory provisions and institutions of national laws: they must be extended to the fundamental concepts of each branch of law as well as to law in general so far as these can be considered as 'recognized by civilized nations.'

Accordingly, the general principles of law in the sense of Article 38, paragraph 1 (c), are not limited to certain basic principles of law such as the limitation of State sovereignty, third-party judgment, limitation of the right of self-defence, *pacta sunt servanda*, respect for acquired rights, liability for unlawful harm to one's neighbour, the principle of good faith, etc. The word 'general' may be understood to possess the same meaning as in the case of the '*general* theory of law', 'théorie *générale* de droit', 'die *Allgemeine* Rechtslehre', namely common to all branches of law. But the principles themselves are very extensive and can be interpreted to include not only the general theory of law, but the general theories of each branch of municipal law, so far as recognized by civilized nations. They may be conceived, furthermore, as including not only legal principles but the fundamental legal concepts of which the legal norms are composed such as person, right, duty, property, juristic act, contract, tort, succession, etc.

In short, they may include what can be considered as 'juridical truth' (Bin Cheng, *General Principles of Law as Applied by International Courts and Tribunals*, 1953, p. 24).

The question is whether a legal norm of non-discrimination and non-separation has come into existence in international society, as the Applicants contend. It is beyond all doubt that the presence of laws against racial discrimination and segregation in the municipal systems of virtually every State can be established by comparative law studies. The recognition of this norm by civilized nations can be ascertained. If the condition of 'general principles' is fulfilled, namely if we can say that the general principles include the norm concerning the protection of human rights by adopting the wide interpretation of the provision of Article 38, paragraph 1 (c), the norm will find its place among the sources of international law.

In this context we have to consider the relationship between a norm of a human rights nature and international law. Originally, general principles are considered to be certain private law principles found by the comparative law method and applicable by way of analogy to matters of an international character. These principles are of a nature common to all nations, that is of the character of *jus gentium*. These principles, which originally belong to private law and have the character of *jus gentium*, can be incorporated in international law so as to be applied to matters of an international nature by way of analogy, as we see in the case of the application of some rules of contract law to the interpretation of treaties. In the case of the international protection of human rights, on the contrary, what is involved is not the application by analogy of a principle or a norm of private law to a matter of international character, but the recognition of the juridical validity of a similar legal fact without any distinction as between the municipal and the international legal sphere.

In short, human rights which require protection are the same; they are not the product of a particular juridical system in the hierarchy of the legal order, but the same human rights must be recognized, respected and protected everywhere man goes. The uniformity of national laws on the protection of human rights is not derived, as in the cases of the law of contracts and commercial and maritime transactions, from considerations of expediency by the legislative organs or from the creative power of the custom of a community, but it already exists in spite of its more-or-less vague form. This is of nature *jus naturale* in Roman law.

The unified national laws of the character of *jus gentium* and of the law of human rights, which is of the character of *jus naturale* in Roman law, both constituting a part of the law of the world community which may be designated as World Law, Common Law of Mankind (Jenks), Transnational Law (Jessup), etc., at the same time constitute a part of international law through the medium of Article 38, paragraph 1 (c). But there is a difference between these two cases. In the former, the general principles are presented as common elements among diverse national laws; in the latter, only one and the same law exists and this is valid through all kinds of human societies in relationships of hierarchy and co-ordination.

This distinction between the two categories of law of an international character is important in deciding the scope and extent of Article 38, paragraph 1 (c). The Respondent contends that the suggested application by the Applicants of a principle recognized by civilized nations is not a correct analogy and application as contemplated by Article 38, paragraph 1 (c). The Respondent contends that the alleged norm of non-differentiation as between individuals within a State on the basis of membership of a race, class or group could not be transferred by way of analogy to the international relationship, otherwise it would mean that all nations are to be treated equally despite the difference of race, colour, etc.—a conclusion which is absurd. (C.R. 65/47, p. 7.) If we limit the application of Article 38, paragraph 1 (c), to a strict analogical extension of certain principles of municipal law, we must recognize that the contention of the Respondent is well-founded. The said provision, however, does not limit its application to cases of analogy with municipal, or private law which has certainly been a most important instance of the application of this provision. We must include the international protection of human rights in the application of this provision. It must not be regarded as a case of analogy. In reality, there is only one human right which is valid in the international sphere as well as in the domestic sphere.

The question here is not of an 'international', that is to say, inter-State nature, but it is concerned with the question of the international validity of human rights, that is to say, the question whether a State is obliged to protect human rights in the international sphere as it is obliged in the domestic sphere.

The principle of the protection of human rights is derived from the concept of man as a *person* and his relationship with society which cannot be separated from universal human nature. Then existence of human rights does not depend on the will of a State; neither internally on its law or any other legislative measure, nor internationally on treaty or custom, in which the express or tacit will of a State constitutes the essential element.

A State or States are not capable of creating human rights by law or by convention; they can only confirm their existence and give them protection. The role of the State is no more than declaratory. It is exactly the same as the International Court of Justice ruling concerning the *Reservations to the Genocide Convention* case (*ICJ Reports 1951*, p. 23):

> 'The solution of these problems must be found in the special characteristics of the Genocide Convention... The origins of the Convention show that it was the intention of the United Nations to condemn and punish genocide as "a crime under international law" involving a denial of the right of existence of entire human groups, a denial which shocks the conscience of mankind and results in great losses to humanity, and which is contrary to moral law and to the spirit and aims of the United Nations (resolution 96 (I) of the General Assembly, December 11th, 1946). The first consequence arising from this conception is that the principles underlying the Convention are principles which are recognized by civilized nations as binding on States, *even without any conventional obligation*. A second consequence is the universal character both of the condemnation of genocide and of the co-operation required 'in order to liberate mankind from such an odious scourge' (Preamble to the Convention).' (Italics added.)

Human rights have always existed with the human being. They existed independently of, and before, the State. Alien and even stateless persons must not be deprived of them. Belonging to diverse kinds of communities and societies—ranging from family, club, corporation, to State and international community, the human rights of man must be protected everywhere in this social hierarchy, just as copyright is protected domestically and internationally. There must be no legal vacuum in the protection of human rights. Who can believe, as a reasonable man, that the existence of human rights depends upon the internal or international legislative measures, etc., of the State and that accordingly they can be validly abolished or modified by the will of the State?

If a law exists independently of the will of the State and, accordingly, cannot be abolished or modified even by its constitution, because it is deeply rooted in the conscience of mankind and of any reasonable man, it may be called 'natural law' in contrast to 'positive law'.

Provisions of the constitutions of some countries characterize fundamental human rights and freedoms as 'inalienable', 'sacred', 'eternal', 'inviolate', etc. Therefore, the guarantee of fundamental human rights and freedoms possesses a super-constitutional significance.

If we can introduce in the international field a category of law, namely *jus cogens*, recently examined by the International Law Commission, a kind of imperative law which constitutes the contrast to the *jus dispositivum*, capable of being changed by way of agreement between States, surely the law concerning the protection of human rights may be considered to belong to the *jus cogens*.

As an interpretation of Article 38, paragraph 1 (c), we consider that the concept of human rights and of their protection is included in the general principles mentioned in that article.

Such an interpretation would necessarily be open to the criticism of falling into the error of natural law dogma. But it is undeniable that in Article 38, paragraph 1 (c), some natural law elements are inherent. It extends the concept of the source of international law beyond the limit of legal positivism according to which, the States being bound only by their own will, international law is nothing but the law of the consent and auto-limitation of the State. But this viewpoint, we believe, was clearly overruled by Article 38, paragraph 1 (c), by the fact that this provision does not require the consent of States as a condition of the recognition of the general principles. States which do not recognize this principle or even deny its validity are nevertheless subject to its rule. From this kind of source international law could have the foundation of its validity extended beyond the will of States, that is to say, into the sphere of natural law and assume an aspect of its supra-national and supra-positive character.

The above-mentioned character of Article 38, paragraph 1 (c), of the Statute is proved by the process of the drafting of this article by the Committee of Jurists. The original proposal made by Baron Descamps referred to '*la conscience juridique des peuples civilisés*', a concept which clearly indicated an idea originating in natural law. This proposal met with the opposition of the positivist members of the Committee, represented by Mr. Root. The final draft, namely Article 38, paragraph 1 (c), is the product of a compromise between two schools, naturalist and positivist, and therefore the fact that the natural law idea became incorporated therein is not difficult to discover (see particularly Jean Spiropoulos, *Die Allgemeine Rechtsgrundsätze im Völkerrecht*, 1928, pp. 6 off.; Bin Cheng, *op. cit.*, pp. 24–26).

Furthermore, an important role which can be played by Article 38, paragraph 1 (c), in filling in gaps in the positive sources in order to avoid *nonliquet* decisions, can only be derived from the natural law character of this provision. Professor Brierly puts it, 'its inclusion is important as a rejection of the positivistic doctrine, according to which international law consists solely of rules to which States have given their consent' (J. L. Brierly, *The Law of Nations*, 6th ed., p. 63). Mr. Rosenne comments on the general principles of law as follows:

'Having independent existence, their validity as legal norms does not derive from the consent of the parties as such... The Statute places this element on a footing of formal equality with the two positivist elements of custom and treaty, and thus is positivist recognition of the Grotian concept of the co-existence implying no subordination of positive law and the so-called natural law of nations (in the Grotian sense).' (Shabtai Rosenne, *The International Court of Justice*, 1965, Vol. II, p. 610.)

Now the question is whether the alleged norm of non-discrimination and non-separation as a kind of protection of human rights can be considered as recognized by civilized nations and included in the general principles of law.

First the recognition of a principle by civilized nations, as indicated above, does not mean recognition by all civilized nations, nor does it mean recognition by an official act such as a legislative act; therefore the recognition is of a very elastic nature. The principle of equality before the law, however, is stipulated in the list of human rights recognized by the municipal system of virtually every State no matter whether the form of government be republican or monarchical and in spite of any differences in the degree of precision of the relevant provisions. This principle has become an integral part of the constitutions of most of the civilized countries in the world. Common-law countries must be included. (According to *Constitutions of Nations*, 2nd edn., by Amos

J. Peaslee, 1956, Vol. I, p. 7, about 73 per cent of the national constitutions contain clauses respecting equality.)

The manifestation of the recognition of this principle does not need to be limited to the act of legislation as indicated above; it may include the attitude of delegations of member States in cases of participation in resolutions, declarations, etc., against racial discrimination adopted by the organs of the League of Nations, the United Nations and other organizations which, as we have seen above, constitute an important element in the generation of customary international law.

From what we have seen above, the alleged norm of non-discrimination and non-separation, being based on the United Nations Charter, particularly Articles 55(c), 56, and on numerous resolutions and declarations of the General Assembly and other organs of the United Nations, and owing to its nature as a general principle, can be regarded as a source of international law according to the provisions of Article 38, paragraph 1 (a)–(c). In this case three kinds of sources are cumulatively functioning to defend the above-mentioned norm: (1) international convention, (2) international custom and (3) the general principles of law.

Practically the justification of any one of these is enough, but theoretically there may be a difference in the degree of importance among the three. From a positivistic, voluntaristic viewpoint, first the convention, and next the custom, is considered important, and general principles occupy merely a supplementary position. On the contrary, if we take the supra-national objective viewpoint, the general principles would come first and the two others would follow them. If we accept the fact that convention and custom are generally the manifestation and concretization of already existing general principles, we are inclined to attribute to this third source of international law the primary position vis-à-vis the other two.

To sum up, the principle of the protection of human rights has received recognition as a legal norm under three main sources of international law, namely (1) international conventions, (2) international custom and (3) the general principles of law. Now, the principle of equality before the law or equal protection by the law presents itself as a kind of human rights norm. Therefore, what has been said on human rights in general can be applied to the principle of equality. (Cf. Wilfred Jenks, *The Common Law of Mankind*, 1958, p. 121. The author recognizes the principle of respect for human rights including equality before the law as a general principle of law.)

Here we must consider the principle of equality in relationship to the Mandate. The contention of the Applicants is based on this principle as condemning the practice of apartheid. The Applicants contend not only that this practice is in violation of the obligations of the Respondent imposed upon it by Article 2 of the Mandate and Article 22 of the Covenant (Submission No. 3), but that the Respondent, by virtue of economic, political, social and educational policies has, in the light of applicable international standards or international legal norms, or both, failed to promote to the utmost the material and moral well-being and social progress of the inhabitants of the Territory. What the Applicants seek to establish seems to be that the Respondent's practice of apartheid constitutes a violation of international standards and/or an international legal norm, namely the principle of equality and, as a result, a violation of the obligations to promote to the utmost, etc. If the violation of this principle exists, this will be necessarily followed by failure to promote the well-being, etc. The question is whether the principle of equality is applicable to the relationships of the Mandate or not. The Respondent denies that the Mandate includes in its content the principle of equality as to race, colour, etc.

Regarding this point, we would refer to our above-mentioned view concerning the Respondent's contention that the alleged norm of non-discrimination of the Charter does not constitute a part of the mandate agreement, and therefore the question of this norm falls outside the dispute under Article 7, paragraph 2, of the Mandate.

We consider that the principle of equality, although it is not expressly mentioned in the mandate instrument constitutes, by its nature, an integral part of the mandates system and therefore is embodied in the Mandate. From the natural-law character of this principle its inclusion in the Mandate must be justified.

It appears to be a paradox that the inhabitants of the mandated territories are internationally more protected than citizens of States by the application of Article 7, paragraph 2, but this interpretation falls outside the scope of the present proceedings.

Next, we shall consider the content of the principle of equality which must be applied to the question of apartheid.

IV

As we have seen above, the objectives of the mandates system, being the material and moral well-being and social progress of the inhabitants of the territory, are in themselves of a political nature. Their achievement must be measured by the criteria of politics and the method of their realization belongs to the matter of the discretion conferred upon the Mandatory by Article 2, paragraph 1, of the Mandate, and Article 22 of the Covenant of the League.

The discretionary power of the Mandatory, however, is not unlimited. Besides the general rules which prohibit the Mandatory from abusing its power and *mala fides* in performing its obligations, and besides the individual provisions of the Mandate and the Covenant, the Mandatory is subject to the Charter of the United Nations as a member State, the customary international law, general principles of law, and other sources of international law enunciated in Article 38, paragraph 1. According to the contention of the Applicants, the norm and/or standards which prohibit the practice of apartheid, are either immediately or by way of interpretation of the Mandate binding upon the discretionary power of the Mandatory. The Respondent denies the existence of such norm and/or standards.

The divergence of views between the Parties is summarized in the following formula: whether or not the policy of racial discrimination or separate development is *per se* incompatible with the well-being and social progress of the inhabitants, or in other terms, whether the policy of apartheid is illegal (*bona fides* or *mala fides*), the result or effect. From the Respondent's standpoint apartheid is not *per se* prohibited but only a special kind of discrimination which leads to oppression is prohibited.

This divergence of fundamental standpoints between the Parties is reflected in their attitudes as to what extent their contentions depend on the evidence. Contrary to the Applicants' attitude in denying the necessity of calling witnesses and experts and of an inspection *in loco*, the Respondent abundantly utilized numerous witnesses and experts and requested the Court to visit South West Africa, South Africa and other parts of Africa to make an inspection *in loco*.

First, we shall examine the content of the norm and standards of which violation by the Respondents is alleged by the Applicants.

The Applicants contend, as set forth in the Memorials (p. 108) that the Respondent's violation of its obligations under the said paragraph 2 of Article 2 of the Mandate consists in a 'systematic course of positive action which inhibits the well-being, prevents the social progress and thwarts the development of the overwhelming majority' of the inhabitants of the Territory. In pursuit of such course of action, and as a pervasive feature thereof, the Respondent has, by governmental action, installed and maintained the policy of apartheid, or separate development. What is meant by apartheid is as follows:

> 'Under apartheid, the status, rights, duties, opportunities and burdens of the population are determined and allotted arbitrarily on the basis of race, color and tribe, in a pattern which ignores the needs and capacities of the groups and individuals affected, and subordinates the interests and rights of the great majority of the people to the preferences of a minority.' (Memorials, p. 108.)

Such policy, the Applicants contend, 'runs counter to modern conceptions of human rights, dignities and freedom, irrespective of race, colour or creed', which conclusion is denied by the Respondent.

The alleged legal norms of non-discrimination or non-separation by which, by way of interpretation of Article 2, paragraph 2, of the Mandate, apartheid becomes illegal, are defined by the Applicants as follows:

> 'In the following analysis of the relevant legal norms, the terms "non-discrimination" or "non-separation" are used in their prevalent and customary sense: stated negatively, the terms refer to the absence of governmental policies or actions which allot status, rights, duties, privileges or burdens on the basis of membership in a group, class or race rather than on the basis of individual merit, capacity or potential: stated affirmatively, the terms refer to governmental policies and actions the objective of which is to protect equality of opportunity and equal protection of the laws to individual persons as such.' (Reply, p. 274.)

What the Applicants want to establish, are the legal norms of 'non-discrimination' or 'non-separation' which are of a *per se*, non-qualified absolute nature, namely that the decision of observance or otherwise of the norm does not depend upon the motive, result, effect, etc. Therefore from the standpoint of the Applicants, the violation of the norm of non-discrimination is established if there exists a simple fact of discrimination without regard to the intent of oppression on the part of the Mandatory.

On the other hand, the Respondent does not recognize the existence of the norm of non-discrimination of an absolute character and seeks to prove the necessity of group differentiation in the administration of a multi-racial, multi-national, or multi-lingual community. The pleadings and verbatim records are extremely rich in examples of different treatment of diverse population groups in multi-cultural societies in the world. Many examples of different treatment quoted by the Respondent and testified to by the witnesses and experts appear to belong to the system of protection of minority groups in multi-cultural communities and cover not only the field of public law but also of private law.

The doctrine of different treatment of diverse population groups constitutes a fundamental political principle by which 'the Respondent administers not only the Republic of South Africa, but the neighbouring Territory of South West Africa. The geographical, historical, ethnological, economic and cultural differences and varieties between several population groups, according to the contention of the Respondent, have necessitated the adoption of the policy of apartheid or 'separate development'. This policy is said to be required for the purpose of the promotion of the well-being and social progress of the inhabitants of the Territory. The Respondent insists that each population group developing its own characteristics and individuality, to attain self-determination, separate development should be the best way to realize the well-being and social progress of the inhabitants. The other alternative, namely the mixed integral society in the sense of Western democracy would necessarily lead to competition, friction, struggle, chaos, bloodshed, and dictatorship as examples may be found in some other African countries. Therefore, the most appropriate method of administration of the Territory is the principle of indirect rule maintaining and utilizing the merits of tribalism.

Briefly, it seems that the idea underlying the policy of apartheid or separate development is the racial philosophy which is not entirely identical with ideological Nazism but attributes great importance to the racial or ethnological factors in the fields of politics, law, economy and culture. Next, the method of apartheid is of sociological and, therefore, strong deterministic tendency, as we can guess from the fact that at the oral proceedings the standpoint of the Respondent was energetically sustained by many witnesses-experts who were sociologists and ethnologists.

Contrary to the standpoint of the Applicants who condemn the policy of apartheid or separate development of the Respondent as illegal, the latter conceives this policy as something neutral. The Respondent says that it can be utilized as a tool to attain a particular end, good or bad, as a knife can serve a surgeon as well as a murderer.

Before we decide this question, general consideration of the content of the principle of equality before the law is required. Although the existence of this principle is universally recognized as we have seen above, its precise content is not very clear.

This principle has been recognized as one of the fundamental principles of modern democracy and government based on the rule of law. Judge Lauterpacht puts it:

'The claim to equality before the law is in a substantial sense the most fundamental of the rights of man. It occupies the first place in most written constitutions. It is the starting point of all other liberties.' (Sir Hersch Lauterpacht, *An International Bill of the Rights of Man*, 1945, p.115.)

Historically, this principle was derived from the Christian idea of the equality of all men before God. All mankind are children of God, and consequently, brothers and sisters, notwithstanding their natural and social differences, namely man and woman, husband and wife, master and slave, etc. The idea of equality of man is derived from the fact that human beings 'by the common possession of reason' distinguish themselves 'from other living beings'. (Lauterpacht, *op. cit.*, p. 116.) This idea existed already in the Stoic philosophy, and was developed by the scholastic philosophers and treated by natural law scholars and encyclopedists of the seventeenth and eighteenth centuries. It received legislative formulation, however, at the end of the eighteenth century first by the Bills of Rights of some American states, next by the Declaration of the French Revolution, and then in the course of the nineteenth century the equality clause, as we have seen above, became one of the common elements of the constitutions of modern European and other countries.

Examining the principle of equality before the law, we consider that it is philosophically related to the concepts of freedom and justice. The freedom of individual persons, being one of the fundamental ideas of law, is not unlimited and must be restricted by the principle of equality allotting to each individual a sphere of freedom which is due to him. In other words the freedom can exist only under the premise of the equality principle.

In what way is each individual allotted his sphere of freedom by the principle of equality? What is the content of this principle? The principle is that what is equal is to be treated equally and what is different is to be treated differently, namely proportionately to the factual difference. This is what was indicated by Aristotle as *justitia commutativa* and *justitia distributiva*.

The most fundamental point in the equality principle is that all human beings as persons have an equal value in themselves, that they are the aim itself and not means for others, and that, therefore, slavery is denied. The idea of equality of men as persons and equal treatment as such is of a metaphysical nature. It underlies all modern, democratic and humanitarian law systems as a principle of natural law. This idea, however, does not exclude the different treatment of persons from the consideration of the differences of factual circumstances such as sex, age, language, religion, economic condition, education, etc. To treat different matters equally in a mechanical way would be as unjust as to treat equal matters differently.

We know that law serves the concrete requirements of individual human beings and societies. If individuals differ one from another and societies also, their needs will be different, and accordingly, the content of law may not be identical. Hence is derived the relativity of law to individual circumstances.

This historical development of law tells us that, parallel to the trend of generalization the tendency of individualization or differentiation is remarkable as may be exemplified by the appearance of a system of commercial law separate from the general private law in civil law countries, creation of labour law. The acquisition of independent status by commercial and labour law can be conceived as the conferment of a kind of privilege or special treatment to a merchant or labour class. In the field of criminal law the recent tendency of criminal legislative policy is directed towards the individualization of the penalty.

We can say accordingly that the principle of equality before the law does not mean that absolute equality, namely equal treatment of men without regard to individual, concrete circumstances, but it means the relative equality, namely the principle to treat equally what are equal and unequally what are unequal.

The question is, in what case equal treatment or different treatment should exist. If we attach importance to the fact that no man is strictly equal to another and he may have some particularities, the principle of equal treatment could be easily evaded by referring to any factual and legal differences and the existence of this principle would be virtually denied. A different treatment comes into question only when and to the extent that it corresponds to the nature of the difference. To treat unequal matters differently according to their inequality is not only permitted but required. The issue is whether the difference exists. Accordingly, not every different treatment can be justified by the existence of differences, but only such as corresponds to the differences themselves, namely that which is called for by the idea of justice—'the principle to treat equal equally and unequal according to its inequality, constitutes an essential content of the idea of justice' (Goetz Hueck, *Der Grundsatz der Gleichmässigen Behandlung in Privatrecht*, 1958, p. 106) [*translation*].

Briefly, a different treatment is permitted when it can be justified by the criterion of justice. One may replace justice by the concept of reasonableness generally referred to by the Anglo-American school of law.

Justice or reasonableness as a criterion for the different treatment logically excludes arbitrariness. The arbitrariness which is prohibited, means the purely objective fact and not the subjective condition of those concerned. Accordingly, the arbitrariness can be asserted without regard to his motive or purpose.

There is no doubt that the principle of equality is binding upon administrative organs. The discretionary power exercised on considerations of expediency by the administrative organs is restricted by the norm of equality and the infringement of this norm makes an administrative measure illegal. The judicial power also is subjected to this principle. Then, what about the legislative power? Under the constitutions which express this principle in a form such as 'all citizens are equal before the law', there may be doubt whether or not the legislators also are bound by the principle of equality. From the nature of this principle the answer must be in the affirmative. The legislators cannot be permitted to exercise their power arbitrarily and unreasonably. They are bound not only in exercising the ordinary legislative power but also the power to establish the constitution. The reason therefore is that the principle of equality being in the nature of natural law and therefore of a supra-constitutional character, is placed at the summit of hierarchy of the system of law, and that all positive laws including the constitution shall be in conformity with this principle.

The Respondent for the purpose of justifying its policy of apartheid or separate development quotes many examples of different treatment such as minorities treaties, public conveniences (between man and woman), etc. Nobody would object to the different treatment in these cases as a violation of the norm of non-discrimination or non-separation on the hypothesis that such a norm exists. The Applicants contend for the unqualified application of the norm of non-discrimination or non-separation, but even from their point of view it would be impossible to assert that the above-mentioned cases of different treatment constitute a violation of the norm of nondiscrimination.

Then, what is the criterion to distinguish a permissible discrimination from an impermissible one?

In the case of the minorities treaties the norm of non-discrimination as a reverse side of the notion of equality before the law prohibits a State to exclude members of a minority group from participating in rights, interests and opportunities which a majority population group can enjoy. On the other hand, a minority group shall be guaranteed the exercise of their own religious and education activities. This guarantee is conferred on members of a minority group, for the purpose of protection of their interests and not from the motive of discrimination itself. By reason of protection of the minority this protection cannot be imposed upon members of minority groups, and consequently they have the choice to accept it or not.

In any event, in case of a minority, members belonging to this group, enjoying the citizenship on equal terms with members of majority groups, have conferred on them the possibility of cultivating their own religious, educational or linguistic values as a recognition of their fundamental human rights and freedoms.

The spirit of the minorities treaties, therefore, is not negative and prohibitive, but positive and permissive.

Whether the spirit of the policy of apartheid or separate development is common with that of minorities treaties to which the Respondent repeatedly refers, whether the different treatment between man and woman concerning the public conveniences can be referred to for the purpose of justifying the policy of apartheid or not, that is the question.

In the case of apartheid, we cannot deny the existence of reasonableness in some matters that diverse ethnic groups should be treated in certain aspects differently from one another. As we have seen above, differentiation in law and politics is one of the most remarkable tendencies of the modern political society. This tendency is in itself derived from the concept of justice, therefore it cannot be judged as wrong. It is an adaptation of the idea of justice to social realities which, as its structure, is going to be more complicated and multiplicate from the viewpoint of economic, occupational, cultural and other elements.

Therefore, different treatment requires reasonableness to justify it as is stated above. The reason may be the protection of some fundamental human rights and freedoms as we have seen in the case of minorities treaties, or of some other nature such as incapacity of minors to conclude contracts, physical differences between man and woman.

In the case of the protection of minorities, what is protected is not the religious or linguistic group as a whole but the individuals belonging to this group, the former being nothing but a name and not a group. In the case of different treatment of minors or between man and woman, it is clear that minors, disabled persons or men or women in a country do not constitute respectively a group. But whether a racial or ethnic group can be treated in the same way as categories such as minors, disabled persons, men and women, is doubtful. Our conclusion on this point is negative. The reasons therefor are that the scientific and clear-cut definition of race is not established; that what man considers as a matter of common-sense as criteria to distinguish one race from the other, are the appearance, particularly physical characteristics such as colour, hair, etc., which do not constitute in themselves relevant factors as the basis for different political or legal treatment; and that, if there exists the necessity to treat one race differently from another, this necessity is not derived from the physical characteristics or other racial qualifications but other factors, namely religious, linguistic, educational, social, etc., which in themselves are not related to race or colour.

Briefly, in these cases it is possible that the different treatment in certain aspects is reasonably required by the differences of religion, language, education, custom, etc., not by reason of race or colour. Therefore, the Respondent tries in some cases to justify the different treatment of population groups by the concept of cultural population groups. The different treatment would be justified if there really existed the need for it by reason of cultural differences. The different treatment, however, should be condemned if cultural reasons arc referred to for the purpose of dissimulating the underlying racial intention.

In any case, as we have seen above, all human beings are equal before the law and have equal opportunities without regard to religion, race, language, sex, social groups, etc. As persons they have the dignity to be treated as such. This is the principle of equality which constitutes one of the fundamental human rights and freedoms which are universal to all mankind. On the other hand, human beings, being endowed with individuality, living in different surroundings and circumstances are not all alike, and they need in some aspects politically, legally and socially different treatment. Hence the above-mentioned examples of different treatment are derived. Equal treatment is a principle but its mechanical application ignoring all concrete factors engenders injustice. Accordingly, it requires different treatment, taken into consideration, of concrete circumstances of individual cases. The different treatment is permissible and required by the considerations of justice; it does not mean a disregard of justice.

Equality being a principle and different treatment an exception, those who refer to the different treatment must prove its *raison d'être* and its reasonableness.

The Applicants' norm of non-discrimination or non-separation, being conceived as of a *per se* nature, would appear not to permit any exception. The policy of apartheid or separate development which allots status, rights, duties, privileges or burdens on the basis of membership in a group, class or race rather than on the basis of individual merit, capacity or potential is illegal whether the motive be *bona fide* or *mala fide*, oppressive or benevolent;

whether its effect or result be good or bad for the inhabitants. From this viewpoint all protective measures taken in the case of minorities treaties and other matters would be included in the illegal discrimination—a conclusion which might not be expected from the Applicants. These measures, according to the Applicants, would have nothing to do with the question of discrimination. The protection the minorities treaties intended to afford to the inhabitants is concerned with life, liberty and free exercise of religion. On the contrary, the Respondent argues the existence of the same reason in the policy of apartheid—the reason of protective measures in the case of minorities treaties.

We must recognize, on the one hand, the legality of different treatment so far as justice or reasonableness exists in it. On the other hand, we cannot recognize all measures of different treatment as legal, which have been and will be performed in the name of apartheid or separate development. The Respondent tries to prove by the pleadings and the testimony of the witnesses and experts the existence of a trend of differentiation in accordance with different religious, racial, linguistic groups. From the viewpoint of the Applicants, the abundant examples quoted by the Respondent and the testimony of witnesses and experts cannot serve as the justification of the policy of apartheid, because they belong to an entirely different plane from that of apartheid and because they are of a nature quite heterogeneous to the policy of apartheid, which is based on a particular racial philosophy and group sociology.

The important question is whether there exists, from the point of view of the requirements of justice, any necessity for establishing an exception to the principle of equality, and the Respondent must prove this necessity, namely the reasonableness of different treatment.

On the aspect of 'reasonableness' two considerations arise. The one is the consideration whether or not the individual necessity exists to establish an exception to the general principle of equality before the law and equal opportunity. In this sense the necessity may be conceived as of the same nature as in the case of minorities treaties of which the objectives are protective and beneficial. The other is the consideration whether the different treatment does or does not harm the sense of dignity of individual persons.

For instance, if we consider education, on which the Parties argued extensively, we cannot deny the value of vernacular as the medium of instruction and the result thereof would be separate schooling as between children of diverse population groups, particularly between the Whites and the Natives. In this case separate education and schooling may be recognized as reasonable. This is justified by the nature of the matter in question. But even in such a case, by reason of the matter which is related to a delicate racial and ethnic problem, the manner of dealing with this matter should be extremely careful. But, so far as the public use of such facilities as hotels, buses, etc., justification of discriminatory and separate treatment by racial groups cannot be found in the same way as separation between smokers and non-smokers in a train.

We cannot condemn all measures derived from the Respondent's policy of apartheid or separate development, particularly as proposed by the Odendaal Commission, on the ground that they are motivated by the racial concept, and therefore devoid of the reasonableness. There may be some measures which are of the same character as we see in the protection measures in the case of the minorities treaties and others. We cannot approve, however, all measures constituting a kind of different treatment of apartheid policy as reasonable.

One of the characteristics of the policy of apartheid is marked by its restrictive tendency on the basis of racial distinction. The policy includes on the one hand protective measures for the benefit of the Natives as we see in the institutions of reserves and homelands connected with restrictions on land rights; however, on the other hand, several kinds of restrictions of rights and freedoms are alleged to exist regarding those Natives who live and work in the southern sector, namely the White area outside the reserves. These restrictions, if they exist, in many cases presenting themselves as violation of respective human rights and freedoms at the same time, would constitute violation of the principle of equality before the law (particularly concerning the discrimination between the Natives and the Whites).

Here we are not required to give answers exhaustively in respect of the Applicants' allegations of violation by the Respondent of the Mandate concerning the legislation (*largo sensu*) applicable in the Territory. The items enumerated by the Applicants in the Memorials (pp. 118–66) are not included in their submissions. We are not obliged to pronounce our views thereon. By way of illustration we shall examine a few points. What is required from us is a decision on the question of whether the Respondent's policy of apartheid constitutes a violation of Article 2, paragraph 2, of the Mandate or not.

For the purpose of illustration we shall consider freedom of choice of occupations (cf. Memorials, pp. 121, 122 and 136).

In the field of civil service, participation by 'Natives' in the general administration appears, in practice, to be confined to the lowest and least skilled categories, such as messengers and cleaners. This practice of 'job-reservation' for Natives is exemplified by allusion to the territorial budget, which classifies jobs as between 'European' and 'Natives'.

In the mining industry the Natives are excluded from certain occupations, such as those of prospector for precious and base minerals, dealer in unwrought precious metals, manager, assistant manager, sectional or underground manager, etc., in mines owned by persons of 'European' descent, officer in the Police Force. Concerning these occupations, 'ceilings' are put on the promotion of the Natives. The role of the 'Native' is confined to that of unskilled labourer.

In the fishing industry, the enterprises are essentially 'European' owned and operated. The role of the 'Native' is substantially confined to unskilled labour (Memorials, p. 119).

As regards railways and harbours, all graded posts in the Railway and Harbours Administration are reserved to 'Europeans', subject to temporary exceptions. The official policy appears to be that 'non-Europeans' should not be allowed to occupy graded posts.

The question is whether these restrictions are reasonable or not, whether there is a necessity to establish exceptions to the general application of the principle of equality of non-discrimination or not.

The matter of 'ceilings' was dealt with minutely and at length in the oral proceedings by the Parties. The Respondent's defence against the condemnation of arbitrariness, injustice and unreasonableness on the part of the Applicants may be summarized in two points: the one is the reason of social security and the other is the principle of balance or reciprocity.

The Respondent contends that the Whites in general do not desire to serve under the authority of the Natives in the hierarchy of industrial or bureaucratic systems. If this fact be ignored and the Natives occupy leading positions in which they would be able to supervise Whites friction between the two groups necessarily would occur and the social peace would be disturbed. This argument of the Respondent seems to be based on a pessimistic view of the possibility of harmonious coexistence of diverse racial and ethnic elements in an integrated society.

It is not deniable that there may exist certain causes of friction, conflict and animosity between diverse racial and ethnic groups which produce obstacles to their coexistence and co-operation in a friendly political community. We may recognize this as one aspect of reality of human nature and social life. It is, however, no less true that mankind aspires and strives towards the ideal of the achievement of a harmonious society composed of racially heterogeneous elements overcoming difficulties which may result from the primitive instinctive sentiment of racial prejudice and antagonism. Such sentiment must be overcome and not approved. In modern, democratic societies we have to expect this result mainly from the progress of humanitarian education. But the mission of politics and law cannot be said to be less important in minimizing racial prejudice and antagonism and avoiding collapse and tragedy. The State is obliged to educate the people by means of legislative and administrative measures for the same purpose.

To take into consideration the psychological effect upon the Whites who would be subjected to the supervision of the Natives if a ceiling did not exist, that is nothing else but the justification or official recognition of racial prejudice or sentiment of racial superiority on the part of the White population which does harm to the dignity of man.

Furthermore, individuals who could have advanced by their personal merits if there existed no ceiling are unduly deprived of their opportunity for promotion.

It is contended by the Respondent that those who are excluded from the jobs proportionate to their capacity and ability in the White areas, can find the same jobs in their own homelands where no restriction exists in regard to them. But even if they can find jobs in their homelands the conditions may not be substantially the same and, accordingly, in most cases, they may not be inclined to go back to the northern sector, their homelands, and they cannot be forced to do so.

The Respondent probably being aware of the unreasonableness in such hard cases, tries to explain it as a necessary sacrifice which should be paid by individuals for the maintenance of social security. But it is unjust to require a sacrifice for the sake of social security when this sacrifice is of such importance as humiliation of the dignity of the personality.

The establishment of ceilings in regard to certain jobs violates human rights of the Natives in two respects: one is violation of the principle of equality before the law and equal opportunity; the other is violation of the right of free choice of employment.

The Respondent furthermost advocates the establishment of ceilings by the principle of reciprocity or balance between two legal situations, namely one existing in the White areas where certain rights and freedoms of the Natives are restricted and the other situation existing in the Native areas where the corresponding rights and freedoms of the Whites are restricted. The Respondent seeks to prove by this logic that in such circumstances the principle of equality of the Whites and the Natives is observed. Unequal treatment unfavourable to one population group in area A, however, cannot be justified by similar treatment of the other population group in area B. Each unequal treatment constitutes an independent illegal conduct; the one cannot be counter-balanced by the other, as set-off is not permitted between two obligations resulting from illegal acts.

Besides, from the viewpoint of group interest, those of the Natives living in the White area outside the reserves are, owing to the number of the Native population, far bigger than those of the Whites living in the Native areas, the idea of counter–balance is quantitatively unjust.

It is also maintained, in respect of the restrictive policy as regards study to become an engineer by a non-White person, that the underlying purpose of this policy is to prevent the frustration on the part of the individual which he might experience when he could not find White assistants willing to serve under him. The sentiment of frustration on the part of non-White individuals, however, should not be rightly referred to as a reason for establishing a restriction on the educational opportunity of non-Whites, firstly because the question is that the frustration is caused by the racial prejudice on the part of the Whites which in itself must be eliminated and secondly because a more important matter is to open to the non-Whites the future possibility of social promotion. Therefore, the reason of the frustration of non-Whites cannot be justified.

Finally, we wish to make the following conclusive and supplementary remarks on the matter of the Applicant's Submissions Nos. 3 and 4.

1. The principle of equality before the law requires that what are equal are to be treated equally and what are different are to be treated differently. The question arises: what is equal and what is different.

2. All human beings, notwithstanding the differences in their appearance and other minor points, are equal in their dignity as persons. Accordingly, from the point of view of human rights and fundamental freedoms, they must be treated equally.

3. The principle of equality does not mean absolute equality, but recognizes relative equality, namely different treatment proportionate to concrete individual circumstances. Different treatment must not be given arbitrarily; it requires reasonableness, or must be in conformity with justice, as in the treatment of minorities, different treatment of the sexes regarding public conveniences, etc. In these cases, the differentiation is aimed at the protection of those concerned, and it is not detrimental and therefore not against their will.

4. Discrimination according to the criterion of 'race, colour, national or tribal origin' in establishing the rights and duties of the inhabitants of the territory is not considered reasonable and just. Race, colour, etc., do not constitute in themselves factors which can influence the rights and duties of the inhabitants as in the case of sex, age, language, religion, etc. If differentiation be required, it would be derived from the difference of language, religion, custom, etc., not from the racial difference itself. In the policy of apartheid the necessary logical and material link between difference itself and different treatment, which can justify such treatment in the case of sex, minorities, etc., does not exist.

We cannot imagine in what case the distinction between Natives and Whites, namely racial distinction apart from linguistic, cultural or other differences, may necessarily have an influence on the establishment of the rights and duties of the inhabitants of the territory.

5. Consequently, the practice of apartheid is fundamentally unreasonable and unjust. The unreasonableness and injustice do not depend upon the intention or motive of the Mandatory, namely its *mala fides*. Distinction on a racial basis is in itself contrary to the principle of equality which is of the character of natural law, and accordingly illegal.

The above-mentioned contention of the Respondent that the policy of apartheid has a neutral character, as a tool to attain a particular end, is not right. If the policy of apartheid is a means, the axiom that the end cannot justify the means can be applied to this policy.

6. As to the alleged violation by the Respondent of the obligations incumbent upon it under Article 2, paragraph 2, of the Mandate, the policy of apartheid, including in itself elements not consistent with the principle of equality before the law, constitutes a violation of the said article, because the observance of the principle of equality before the law must be considered as a necessary condition of the promotion of the material and moral well-being and the social progress of the inhabitants of the territory.

7. As indicated above, so far as the interpretation of Article 2, paragraph 2, of the Mandate is concerned, only questions of a legal nature belong to the matter upon which

the Court is competent. Diverse activities which the Respondent as Mandatory carries out as a matter of discretion, to achieve the promotion of the material and moral well-being and the social progress of the inhabitants, fall outside the scope of judicial examination as matters of a political and administrative nature.

Accordingly, questions of whether the ultimate goal of the mandates system should be independence or annexation, and in the first alternative whether a unitary or federal system in regard to the local administration is preferable, whether or in what degree the principle of indirect rule or respect for tribal custom may or must be introduced—such questions, which have been very extensively argued in the written proceedings as well as in the oral proceedings, have, despite their substantial connection with the policy of apartheid, no relevance to a decision on the question of apartheid, from the legal viewpoint.

These questions are of a purely political or administrative character, the study and examination of which might have belonged or may belong to competent organs of the League or the United Nations.

8. The Court cannot examine and pronounce the legality or illegality of the policy of apartheid as a whole; it can decide that there exist some elements in the apartheid policy which are not in conformity with the principle of equality before the law or international standard or international norm of non-discrimination and non-separation. The Court can declare if it is requested to examine the laws, proclamations, ordinances and other governmental measures enacted to implement the policy of apartheid in the light of the principle of equality. For the purpose of the present cases, the foregoing consideration of a few points as illustrations may be sufficient to establish the Respondent's violation of the principle of equality, and accordingly its obligations incumbent upon it by Article 2, paragraph 2, of the Mandate and Article 22 of the Covenant.

9. Measures complained of by the Applicants appear in themselves to be violations of some of the human rights and fundamental freedoms such as rights concerning the security of the person, rights of residence, freedom of movement, etc., but such measures, being applied to the 'Natives' only and the 'Whites' being excluded therefrom, these violations, if they exist, may constitute, at the same time, violations of the principle of equality and non-discrimination also.

In short, we interpret the Applicants' Submissions Nos. 3 and 4 in such a way that their complaints include the violation by the Respondent of two kinds of human rights, namely individual human rights and rights to equal protection of the law. There is no doubt that the Respondent as Mandatory is obliged to protect all human rights and fundamental freedoms including rights to equal protection of the law as a necessary prerequisite of the material and moral well-being and the social progress of the inhabitants of the Territory. By this reason, what has been explained above about the principle of equality in connection with Article 38, paragraph 1 (c), is applicable to human rights and fundamental freedoms in general.

10. From the procedural viewpoint, two matters must be considered. The one is concerned with the effect of the Applicants' amendment of the Submissions Nos. 3 and 4 (Memorials, 15 April 1961, pp. 197–9) by the submissions of 19 May 1965 (C.R. 65/35). Since the amendment of the submissions is allowed until the stage of oral proceedings, and the amendment was made within the scope of the claim set forth in the Applications, there is no reason to deny its effectiveness. Furthermore, we wish to mention that the Respondent raised no objection during the course of the oral proceedings regarding the amendment.

The other is concerned with the question of choice by the Court of the reasons underlying its decisions.

Concerning this question, we consider that, although the Court is bound by the submissions of the Parties, it is entirely free to choose the reasons for its decisions. The Parties
may present and develop their own argument as to the interpretation of the provisions of
the Mandate, the Covenant, the Charter, etc., but the Court, so far as legal questions are
concerned, quite unfettered by what has been put forward by the Parties, can exercise its
power of interpretation in approving or rejecting the submissions of the Parties.

For the foregoing reasons, the Applicants' Submissions Nos. 3 and 4 are well-founded.

129. UNESCO DECLARATION ON RACE AND
RACIAL PREJUDICE, 1978

Resolution 3/1.1/2, UNESCO, *Records of the General Conference*, 20th Session, Paris, 24 October–28 November 1978, Vol. 1, *Resolutions* (1979), 60.

TEXT

Preamble

The General Conference of the United, Nations Educational, Scientific and Cultural Organization, meeting at Paris at its twentieth session, from 24 October to 28 November 1978,

Whereas it is stated in the Preamble to the Constitution of UNESCO, adopted on 16 November 1945, that 'the great and terrible war which has now ended was a war made possible by the denial of the democratic principles of the dignity, equality and mutual respect of men, and by the propagation, in their place, through ignorance and prejudice, of the doctrine of the inequality of men and races', and whereas, according to Article I of the said Constitution, the purpose of UNESCO 'is to contribute to peace and security by promoting collaboration among the nations through education, science and culture in order to further universal respect for justice, for the rule of law and for the human rights and fundamental freedoms... which are affirmed for the peoples of the world, without distinction of race, sex, language or religion, by the Charter of the United Nations',

Recognizing that, more than three decades after the founding of UNESCO, these principles are just as significant as they were when they were embodied in its Constitution,

Mindful of the process of decolonization and other historical changes which have led most of the peoples formerly under foreign rule to recover their sovereignty, making the international community a universal and diversified whole and creating new opportunities of eradicating the scourge of racism and of putting an end to its odious manifestations in all aspects of social and political life, both nationally and internationally,

Convinced that the essential unity of the human race and consequently the fundamental equality of all human beings and all peoples, recognized in the loftiest expressions of philosophy, morality and religion, reflect an ideal towards which ethics and science are converging today,

Convinced that all peoples and all human groups, whatever their composition or ethnic origin, contribute according to their own genius to the progress of the civilizations and cultures which, in their plurality and as a result of their interpenetration, constitute the common heritage of mankind,

Confirming its attachment to the principles proclaimed in the United Nations Charter and the Universal Declaration of Human Rights and its determination to promote the implementation of the International Covenants on Human Rights as well as the Declaration on the Establishment of a New International Economic Order,

Determined also to promote the implementation of the United Nations Declaration and the International Convention on the Elimination of all Forms of Racial Discrimination,

Noting the International Convention on the Prevention and Punishment of the Crime of Genocide, the International Convention on the Suppression and Punishment of the Crime of Apartheid and the Convention on the Non-Applicability of Statutory Limitations to War Crimes and Crimes against Humanity,

Recalling also the international instruments already adopted by UNESCO, including in particular the Convention and Recommendation against Discrimination in Education, the Recommendation concerning the Status of Teachers, the Declaration of the Principles of International Cultural Co-operation, the Recommendation concerning Education for International Understanding, Co-operation and Peace and Education relating to Human Rights and Fundamental Freedoms, the Recommendation on the Status of Scientific Researchers, and the Recommendation on participation by the people at large in cultural life and their contribution to it,

Bearing in mind the four statements on the race question adopted by experts convened by UNESCO,

Reaffirming its desire to play a vigorous and constructive part in the implementation of the programme of the Decade for Action to Combat Racism and Racial Discrimination, as defined by the General Assembly of the United Nations at its twenty-eighth session,

Noting with the gravest concern that racism, racial discrimination, colonialism and apartheid continue to afflict the world in ever-changing forms, as a result both of the continuation of legislative provisions and government and administrative practices contrary to the principles of human rights and also of the continued existence of political and social structures, and of relationships and attitudes, characterized by injustice and contempt for human beings and leading to the exclusion, humiliation and exploitation, or to the forced assimilation, of the members of disadvantaged groups,

Expressing its indignation at these offences against human dignity, deploring the obstacles they place in the way of mutual understanding between peoples and alarmed at the danger of their seriously disturbing international peace and security,

Adopts and solemnly proclaims this Declaration on Race and Racial Prejudice:

Article 1

1. All human beings belong to a single species and are descended from a common stock. They are born equal in dignity and rights and all form an integral part of humanity.

2. All individuals and groups have the right to be different, to consider themselves as different and to be regarded as such. However, the diversity of life styles and the right to be different may not, in any circumstances, serve as a pretext for racial prejudice; they may not justify either in law or in fact any discriminatory practice whatsoever, nor provide a ground for the policy of apartheid, which is the extreme form of racism.

3. Identity of origin in no way affects the fact that human beings can and may live differently, nor does it preclude the existence of differences based on cultural, environmental and historical diversity nor the right to maintain cultural identity.

4. All peoples of the world possess equal faculties for attaining the highest level in intellectual, technical, social, economic, cultural and political development.

5. The differences between the achievements of the different peoples are entirely attributable to geographical, historical, political, economic, social and cultural factors. Such differences can in no case serve as a pretext for any rank-ordered classification of nations or peoples.

Article 2

1. Any theory which involves the claim that racial or ethnic groups are inherently superior or inferior, thus implying that some would be entitled to dominate or eliminate others, presumed to be inferior, or which bases value judgments on racial differentiation, has no scientific foundation and is contrary to the moral and ethical principles of humanity.

2. Racism includes racist ideologies, prejudiced attitudes, discriminatory behaviour, structural arrangements and institutionalized practices resulting in racial inequality as well as the fallacious notion that discriminatory relations between groups are morally and scientifically justifiable; it is reflected in discriminatory provisions in legislation or regulations and discriminatory practices as well as in anti-social beliefs and acts; it hinders the development of its victims, perverts those who practice it, divides nations internally, impedes international co-operation and gives rise to political tensions between peoples; it is contrary to the fundamental principles of international law and, consequently, seriously disturbs international peace and security.

3. Racial prejudice, historically linked with inequalities in power, reinforced by economic and social differences between individuals and groups, and still seeking today to justify such inequalities, is totally without justification.

Article 3

Any distinction, exclusion, restriction or preference based on race, colour, ethnic or national origin or religious intolerance motivated by racist considerations, which destroys or compromises the sovereign equality of States and the right of peoples to self-determination, or which limits in an arbitrary or discriminatory manner the right of every human being and group to full development is incompatible with the requirements of an international order which is just and guarantees respect for human rights; the right to full development implies equal access to the means of personal and collective advancement and fulfilment in a climate of respect for the values of civilizations and cultures, both national and world-wide.

Article 4

1. Any restriction on the complete self-fulfilment of human beings and free communication between them which is based on racial or ethnic considerations is contrary to the principle of equality in dignity and rights; it cannot be admitted.

2. One of the most serious violations of this principle is represented by apartheid, which, like genocide, is a crime against humanity, and gravely disturbs international peace and security.

3. Other policies and practices of racial segregation and discrimination constitute crimes against the conscience and dignity of mankind and may lead to political tensions and gravely endanger international peace and security.

Article 5

1. Culture, as a product of all human beings and a common heritage of mankind, and education in its broadest sense, offer men and women increasingly effective means of adaptation, enabling them not only to affirm that they are born equal in dignity and rights, but also to recognize that they should respect the right of all groups to their own cultural identity and the development of their distinctive cultural life within the national and international context, it being understood that it rests with each group to decide in

complete freedom on the maintenance and, if appropriate, the adaptation or enrichment of the values which it regards as essential to its identity.

2. States, in accordance with their constitutional principles and procedures, as well as all other competent authorities and the entire teaching profession, have a responsibility to see that the educational resources of all countries are used to combat racism, more especially by ensuring that curricula and textbooks include scientific and ethical considerations concerning human unity and diversity and that no invidious distinctions are made with regard to any people; by training teachers to achieve these ends; by making the resources of the educational system available to all groups of the population without racial restriction or discrimination; and by taking appropriate steps to remedy the handicaps from which certain racial or ethnic groups suffer with regard to their level of education and standard of living and in particular to prevent such handicaps from being passed on to children.

3. The mass media and those who control or serve them, as well as all organized groups within national communities, are urged—with due regard to the principles embodied in the Universal Declaration of Human Rights, particularly the principle of freedom of expression—to promote understanding, tolerance and friendship among individuals and groups and to contribute to the eradication of racism, racial discrimination and racial prejudice, in particular by refraining from presenting a stereotyped, partial, unilateral or tendentious picture of individuals and of various human groups. Communication between racial and ethnic groups must be a reciprocal process, enabling them to express themselves and to be fully heard without let or hindrance. The mass media should therefore be freely receptive to ideas of individuals and groups which facilitate such communication.

Article 6

1. The State has prime responsibility for ensuring human rights and fundamental freedoms on an entirely equal footing in dignity and rights for all individuals and all groups.

2. So far as its competence extends and in accordance with its constitutional principles and procedures, the State should take all appropriate steps, *inter alia* by legislation, particularly in the spheres of education, culture and communication, to prevent, prohibit and eradicate racism, racist propaganda, racial segregation and apartheid and to encourage the dissemination of knowledge and the findings of appropriate research in natural and social sciences on the causes and prevention of racial prejudice and racist attitudes, with due regard to the principles embodied in the Universal Declaration of Human Rights and in the International Covenant on Civil and Political Rights.

3. Since laws proscribing racial discrimination are not in themselves sufficient, it is also incumbent on States to supplement them by administrative machinery for the systematic investigation of instances of racial discrimination, by a comprehensive framework of legal remedies against acts of racial discrimination, by broadly based education and research programmes designed to combat racial prejudice and racial discrimination and by programmes of positive political, social, educational and cultural measures calculated to promote genuine mutual respect among groups. Where circumstances warrant, special programmes should be undertaken to promote the advancement of disadvantaged groups and, in the case of nationals, to ensure their effective participation in the decision-making processes of the community.

Article 7

In addition to political, economic and social measures, law is one of the principal means of ensuring equality in dignity and rights among individuals, and of curbing any propaganda, any form of organization or any practice which is based on ideas or theories referring to the alleged superiority of racial or ethnic groups or which seeks to justify or encourage racial hatred and discrimination in any form. States should adopt such legislation as is appropriate to this end and see that it is given effect and applied by all their services, with due regard to the principles embodied in the Universal Declaration of Human Rights. Such legislation should form part of a political, economic and social framework conducive to its implementation. Individuals and other legal entities, both public and private, must conform with such legislation and use all appropriate means to help the population as a whole to understand and apply it.

Article 8

1. Individuals, being entitled to an economic, social, cultural and legal order, on the national and international planes, such as to allow them to exercise all their capabilities on a basis of entire equality of rights and opportunities, have corresponding duties towards their fellows, towards the society in which they live and towards the international community. They are accordingly under an obligation to promote harmony among the peoples, to combat racism and racial prejudice and to assist by every means available to them in eradicating racial discrimination in all its forms.

2. In the field of racial prejudice and racist attitudes and practices, specialists in natural and social sciences and cultural studies, as well as scientific organizations and associations, are called upon to undertake objective research on a wide interdisciplinary basis; all States should encourage them to this end.

3. It is, in particular, incumbent upon such specialists to ensure, by all means available to them, that their research findings are not misinterpreted, and also that they assist the public in understanding such findings.

Article 9

1. The principle of the equality in dignity and rights of all human beings and all peoples, irrespective of race, colour and origin, is a generally accepted and recognized principle of international law. Consequently any form of racial discrimination practised by a State constitutes a violation of international law giving rise to its international responsibility.

2. Special measures must be taken to ensure equality in dignity and rights for individuals and groups wherever necessary, while ensuring that they are not such as to appear racially discriminatory. In this respect, particular attention should be paid to racial or ethnic groups which are socially or economically disadvantaged, so as to afford them, on a completely equal footing and without discrimination or restriction, the protection of the laws and regulations and the advantages of the social measures in force, in particular in regard to housing, employment and health; to respect the authenticity of their culture and values; and to facilitate their social and occupational advancement, especially through education.

3. Population groups of foreign origin, particularly migrant workers and their families who contribute to the development of the host country, should benefit from appropriate measures designed to afford them security and respect for their dignity and cultural values and to facilitate their adaptation to the host environment and their professional

advancement with a view to their subsequent reintegration in their country of origin and their contribution to its development; steps should be taken to make it possible for their children to be taught their mother tongue.

4. Existing disequilibria in international economic relations contribute to the exacerbation of racism and racial prejudice; all States should consequently endeavour to contribute to the restructuring of the international economy on a more equitable basis.

Article 10

International organizations, whether universal or regional, governmental or non-governmental, are called upon to co-operate and assist, so far as their respective fields of competence and means allow, in the full and complete implementation of the principles set out in this Declaration, thus contributing to the legitimate struggle of all men, born equal in dignity and rights, against the tyranny and oppression of racism, racial segregation, apartheid and genocide, so that all the peoples of the world may be forever delivered from these scourges.

130. WORLD CONFERENCE AGAINST RACISM, RACIAL DISCRIMINATION, XENOPHOBIA AND RELATED INTOLERANCE: DURBAN DECLARATION AND PROGRAMME OF ACTION, 2001

Text in 'Report of the World Conference Against Racism, Racial Discrimination, Xenophobia and Related Intolerance', UN doc. A/ CONF.189/12 (2001). The Commission on Human Rights established an open-ended inter-governmental working group on the effective implementation of the Durban Declaration and Programme of Action; see Resolution 2002/68, approved by ECOSOC decision 2002/270 of 25 July 2002. It has held seven sessions since 2003: **http://www2.ohchr.org/english/issues/racism/groups/index.htm**. See also the 'Report of the Durban Review Conference', cited below, and UN General Assembly Resolution 63/242, 24 December 2008, adopted by a vote of 109 in favour, 13 against, and 35 abstentions.

Further reading

COMMISSION OF THE EUROPEAN COMMUNITIES, 'European Union action to combat racism: European Commission contribution to the world Conference against Racism, Racial Discrimination, Xenophobia, and Related Intolerance 2001', Luxembourg: European Communities, 2001.

SPECIAL RAPPORTEUR ON CONTEMPORARY FORMS OF RACISM, RACIAL DISCRIMINATION, XENOPHOBIA AND RELATED INTOLERANCE: **http://www2.ohchr.org/english/issues/racism/rapporteur/**.

UNITED NATIONS, 'Report of the Durban Review Conference, Geneva, 20–24 April 2009', UN doc. A/CONF.211/8, Geneva: United Nations, 2009.

TEXT

Having met in Durban, South Africa, from 31 August to 8 September 2001,

Expressing deep appreciation to the Government of South Africa for hosting this World Conference,

Drawing inspiration from the heroic struggle of the people of South Africa against the institutionalized system of apartheid, as well as for equality and justice under democracy, development, the rule of law and respect for human rights, recalling in this context the important contribution to that struggle of the international community and, in particular, the pivotal role of the people and Governments of Africa, and noting the important role that different actors of civil society, including non-governmental organizations, played in that struggle and in ongoing efforts to combat racism, racial discrimination, xenophobia and related intolerance,

Recalling that the Vienna Declaration and Programme of Action, adopted by the World Conference on Human Rights in June 1993, calls for the speedy and comprehensive elimination of all forms of racism, racial discrimination, xenophobia and related intolerance,

Recalling Commission on Human Rights resolution 1997/74 of 18 April 1997, General Assembly resolution 52/111 of 12 December 1997 and subsequent resolutions of those bodies concerning the convening of the World Conference against Racism, Racial Discrimination, Xenophobia and Related Intolerance and recalling also the two World Conferences to Combat Racism and Racial Discrimination, held in Geneva in 1978 and 1983, respectively,

Noting with grave concern that despite the efforts of the international community, the principal objectives of the three Decades to Combat Racism and Racial Discrimination have not been attained and that countless human beings continue to the present day to be victims of racism, racial discrimination, xenophobia and related intolerance,

Recalling that the year 2001 is the International Year of Mobilization against Racism, Racial Discrimination, Xenophobia and Related Intolerance, aimed at drawing the world's attention to the objectives of the World Conference and giving new momentum to the political commitment to eliminate all forms of racism, racial discrimination, xenophobia and related intolerance,

Welcoming the decision of the General Assembly to proclaim the year 2001 as the United Nations Year of Dialogue among Civilizations, which underlines tolerance and respect for diversity and the need to seek common ground among and within civilizations in order to address common challenges to humanity that threaten shared values, universal human rights and the fight against racism, racial discrimination, xenophobia and related intolerance, through cooperation, partnership and inclusion,

Welcoming also the proclamation by the General Assembly of the period 2001–2010 as the Decade for a Culture of Peace and Non-Violence for Children of the World, as well as the adoption by the General Assembly of the Declaration and Plan of Action on a Culture of Peace,

Recognizing that the World Conference against Racism, Racial Discrimination, Xenophobia and Related Intolerance, in conjunction with the International Decade of the World's Indigenous People, presents a unique opportunity to consider the invaluable contributions of indigenous peoples to political, economic, social, cultural and spiritual development throughout the world to our societies, as well as the challenges faced by them, including racism and racial discrimination,

Recalling the United Nations Declaration on the Granting of Independence to Colonial Countries and Peoples of 1960,

Reaffirming our commitment to the purposes and principles contained in the Charter of the United Nations and the Universal Declaration of Human Rights,

Affirming that racism, racial discrimination, xenophobia and related intolerance constitute a negation of the purposes and principles of the Charter of the United Nations,

Reaffirming the principles of equality and non-discrimination in the Universal Declaration of Human Rights and encouraging respect for human rights and fundamental freedoms for all without distinction of any kind such as race, colour, sex, language, religion, political or other opinion, national or social origin, property, birth or other status,

Convinced of the fundamental importance of universal accession to or ratification of and full implementation of our obligations arising under the International Convention on the Elimination of All Forms of Racial Discrimination as the principal international instrument to eliminate racism, racial discrimination, xenophobia and related intolerance,

Recognizing the fundamental importance for States, in combating racism, racial discrimination, xenophobia, and related intolerance, to consider signing, ratifying or acceding to all relevant international human rights instruments, with a view to universal adherence,

Having taken note of the reports of the regional conferences organized at Strasbourg, Santiago, Dakar and Tehran and other inputs from States, as well as the reports of expert seminars, non-governmental organization regional meetings and other meetings organized in preparation for the World Conference,

Noting with appreciation the Vision Statement launched by President Thabo Mbeki of South Africa under the patronage of The Honourable Nelson Mandela, first President of the new South Africa, and at the initiative of the United Nations High Commissioner for Human Rights and Secretary-General of the World Conference, and signed by seventy-four heads of State, heads of Government and dignitaries,

Reaffirming that cultural diversity is a cherished asset for the advancement and welfare of humanity at large and should be valued, enjoyed, genuinely accepted and embraced as a permanent feature which enriches our societies,

Acknowledging that no derogation from the prohibition of racial discrimination, genocide, the crime of apartheid and slavery is permitted, as defined in the obligations under the relevant human rights instruments,

Having listened to the peoples of the world and recognizing their aspirations to justice, to equality of opportunity for all and everyone, to the enjoyment of their human rights, including the right to development, to live in peace and freedom and to equal participation without discrimination in economic, social, cultural, civil and political life,

Recognizing that the equal participation of all individuals and peoples in the formation of just, equitable, democratic and inclusive societies can contribute to a world free from racism, racial discrimination, xenophobia and related intolerance,

Emphasizing the importance of the equitable participation of all, without any discrimination, in domestic as well as global decision-making,

Affirming that racism, racial discrimination, xenophobia and related intolerance, where they amount to racism and racial discrimination, constitute serious violations of and obstacles to the full enjoyment of all human rights and deny the self-evident truth that all human beings are born free and equal in dignity and rights, are an obstacle to friendly and peaceful relations among peoples and nations, and are among the root causes of many internal and international conflicts, including armed conflicts, and the consequent forced displacement of populations,

Recognizing that national and international actions are required to combat racism, racial discrimination, xenophobia and related intolerance, in order to ensure the full enjoyment of all human rights, economic, social, cultural, civil and political, which are universal, indivisible, interdependent and interrelated, and to improve the living conditions of men, women and children of all nations,

Reaffirming the importance of the enhancement of international cooperation for the promotion and protection of human rights and for the achievement of the objectives of the fight against racism, racial discrimination, xenophobia and related intolerance,

Acknowledging that xenophobia, in its different manifestations, is one of the main contemporary sources and forms of discrimination and conflict, combating which requires urgent attention and prompt action by States, as well as by the international community,

Fully aware that, despite efforts undertaken by the international community, Governments and local authorities, the scourge of racism, racial discrimination, xenophobia and related intolerance persists and continues to result in violations of human rights, suffering, disadvantage and violence, which must be combated by all available and appropriate means and as a matter of the highest priority, preferably in cooperation with affected communities,

Noting with concern the continued and violent occurrence of racism, racial discrimination, xenophobia and related intolerance, and that theories of superiority of certain races and cultures over others, promoted and practised during the colonial era, continue to be propounded in one form or another even today,

Alarmed by the emergence and continued occurrence of racism, racial discrimination, xenophobia and related intolerance in their more subtle and contemporary forms and manifestations, as well as by other ideologies and practices based on racial or ethnic discrimination or superiority,

Strongly rejecting any doctrine of racial superiority, along with theories which attempt to determine the existence of so-called distinct human races,

Recognizing that failure to combat and denounce racism, racial discrimination, xenophobia and related intolerance by all, especially by public authorities and politicians at all levels, is a factor encouraging their perpetuation,

Reaffirming that States have the duty to protect and promote the human rights and fundamental freedoms of all victims, and that they should apply a gender1 perspective, recognizing the multiple forms of discrimination which women can face, and that the enjoyment of their civil, political, economic, social and cultural rights is essential for the development of societies throughout the world,

Recognizing both the challenges and opportunities presented by an increasingly globalized world in relation to the struggle to eradicate racism, racial discrimination, xenophobia and related intolerance,

Determined, in an era when globalization and technology have contributed considerably to bringing people together, to materialize the notion of a human family based on equality, dignity and solidarity, and to make the twenty-first century a century of human rights, the eradication of racism, racial discrimination, xenophobia and related intolerance and the realization of genuine equality of opportunity and treatment for all individuals and peoples,

Reaffirming the principles of equal rights and self-determination of peoples and recalling that all individuals are born equal in dignity and rights, stressing that such equality must be protected as a matter of the highest priority and recognizing the duty of States to take prompt, decisive and appropriate measures with a view to eliminating all forms of racism, racial discrimination, xenophobia and related intolerance,

Dedicating ourselves to combating the scourge of racism, racial discrimination, xenophobia and related intolerance fully and effectively as a matter of priority, while drawing lessons from manifestations and past experiences of racism in all parts of the world with a view to avoiding their recurrence,

Joining together in a spirit of renewed political will and commitment to universal equality, justice and dignity, we salute the memory of all victims of racism, racial discrimination, xenophobia and related intolerance all over the world and solemnly adopt the Durban Declaration and Programme of Action,[2]

GENERAL ISSUES

1. We declare that for the purpose of the present Declaration and Programme of Action, the victims of racism, racial discrimination, xenophobia and related intolerance are individuals or groups of individuals who are or have been negatively affected by, subjected to, or targets of these scourges;

2. We recognize that racism, racial discrimination, xenophobia and related intolerance occur on the grounds of race, colour, descent or national or ethnic origin and that victims can suffer multiple or aggravated forms of discrimination based on other related grounds

---

[1] For the purpose of this Declaration and Programme of Action, it was understood that the term 'gender' refers to the two sexes, male and female, within the context of society. The term 'gender' does not indicate any meaning different from the above.

[2] Reference should be made to chapter VII of the report of the Conference, which lists all the reservations to and statements on the Declaration and the Programme of Action.

such as sex, language, religion, political or other opinion, social origin, property, birth or other status;

3. We recognize and affirm that, at the outset of the third millennium, a global fight against racism, racial discrimination, xenophobia and related intolerance and all their abhorrent and evolving forms and manifestations is a matter of priority for the international community, and that this Conference offers a unique and historic opportunity for assessing and identifying all dimensions of those devastating evils of humanity with a view to their total elimination through, *inter alia*, the initiation of innovative and holistic approaches and the strengthening and enhancement of practical and effective measures at the national, regional and international levels;

4. We express our solidarity with the people of Africa in their continuing struggle against racism, racial discrimination, xenophobia and related intolerance and recognize the sacrifices made by them, as well as their efforts in raising international public awareness of these inhuman tragedies;

5. We also affirm the great importance we attach to the values of solidarity, respect, tolerance and multiculturalism, which constitute the moral ground and inspiration for our worldwide struggle against racism, racial discrimination, xenophobia and related intolerance, inhuman tragedies which have affected people throughout the world, especially in Africa, for too long;

6. We further affirm that all peoples and individuals constitute one human family, rich in diversity. They have contributed to the progress of civilizations and cultures that form the common heritage of humanity. Preservation and promotion of tolerance, pluralism and respect for diversity can produce more inclusive societies;

7. We declare that all human beings are born free, equal in dignity and rights and have the potential to contribute constructively to the development and well-being of their societies. Any doctrine of racial superiority is scientifically false, morally condemnable, socially unjust and dangerous, and must be rejected along with theories which attempt to determine the existence of separate human races;

8. We recognize that religion, spirituality and belief play a central role in the lives of millions of women and men, and in the way they live and treat other persons. Religion, spirituality and belief may and can contribute to the promotion of the inherent dignity and worth of the human person and to the eradication of racism, racial discrimination, xenophobia and related intolerance;

9. We note with concern that racism, racial discrimination, xenophobia and related intolerance may be aggravated by, *inter alia*, inequitable distribution of wealth, marginalization and social exclusion;

10. We reaffirm that everyone is entitled to a social and international order in which all human rights can be fully realized for all, without any discrimination;

11. We note that the process of globalization constitutes a powerful and dynamic force which should be harnessed for the benefit, development and prosperity of all countries, without exclusion. We recognize that developing countries face special difficulties in responding to this central challenge. While globalization offers great opportunities, at present its benefits are very unevenly shared, while its costs are unevenly distributed. We thus express our determination to prevent and mitigate the negative effects of globalization. These effects could aggravate, *inter alia*, poverty, underdevelopment, marginalization, social exclusion, cultural homogenization and economic disparities which may occur along racial lines, within and between States, and have an adverse impact. We further

express our determination to maximize the benefits of globalization through, *inter alia*, the strengthening and enhancement of international cooperation to increase equality of opportunities for trade, economic growth and sustainable development, global communications through the use of new technologies and increased intercultural exchange through the preservation and promotion of cultural diversity, which can contribute to the eradication of racism, racial discrimination, xenophobia and related intolerance. Only through broad and sustained efforts to create a shared future based upon our common humanity, and all its diversity, can globalization be made fully inclusive and equitable;

12. We recognize that interregional and intraregional migration has increased as a result of globalization, in particular from the South to the North, and stress that policies towards migration should not be based on racism, racial discrimination, xenophobia and related intolerance;

SOURCES, CAUSES, FORMS AND CONTEMPORARY MANIFESTATIONS OF RACISM, RACIAL DISCRIMINATION, XENOPHOBIA AND RELATED INTOLERANCE

13. We acknowledge that slavery and the slave trade, including the transatlantic slave trade, were appalling tragedies in the history of humanity not only because of their abhorrent barbarism but also in terms of their magnitude, organized nature and especially their negation of the essence of the victims, and further acknowledge that slavery and the slave trade are a crime against humanity and should always have been so, especially the transatlantic slave trade and are among the major sources and manifestations of racism, racial discrimination, xenophobia and related intolerance, and that Africans and people of African descent, Asians and people of Asian descent and indigenous peoples were victims of these acts and continue to be victims of their consequences;

14. We recognize that colonialism has led to racism, racial discrimination, xenophobia and related intolerance, and that Africans and people of African descent, and people of Asian descent and indigenous peoples were victims of colonialism and continue to be victims of its consequences. We acknowledge the suffering caused by colonialism and affirm that, wherever and whenever it occurred, it must be condemned and its reoccurrence prevented. We further regret that the effects and persistence of these structures and practices have been among the factors contributing to lasting social and economic inequalities in many parts of the world today;

15. We recognize that apartheid and genocide in terms of international law constitute crimes against humanity and are major sources and manifestations of racism, racial discrimination, xenophobia and related intolerance, and acknowledge the untold evil and suffering caused by these acts and affirm that wherever and whenever they occurred, they must be condemned and their recurrence prevented;

16. We recognize that xenophobia against non-nationals, particularly migrants, refugees and asylum-seekers, constitutes one of the main sources of contemporary racism and that human rights violations against members of such groups occur widely in the context of discriminatory, xenophobic and racist practices;

17. We note the importance of paying special attention to new manifestations of racism, racial discrimination, xenophobia and related intolerance to which youth and other vulnerable groups might be exposed;

18. We emphasize that poverty, underdevelopment, marginalization, social exclusion and economic disparities are closely associated with racism, racial discrimination, xenophobia and related intolerance, and contribute to the persistence of racist attitudes and practices which in turn generate more poverty;

19. We recognize the negative economic, social and cultural consequences of racism, racial discrimination, xenophobia and related intolerance, which have contributed significantly to the underdevelopment of developing countries and, in particular, of Africa and resolve to free every man, woman and child from the abject and dehumanizing conditions of extreme poverty to which more than one billion of them are currently subjected, to make the right to development a reality for everyone and to free the entire human race from want;

20. We recognize that racism, racial discrimination, xenophobia and related intolerance are among the root causes of armed conflict and very often one of its consequences and recall that non-discrimination is a fundamental principle of international humanitarian law. We underscore the need for all parties to armed conflicts to abide scrupulously by this principle and for States and the international community to remain especially vigilant during periods of armed conflict and continue to combat all forms of racial discrimination;

21. We express our deep concern that socio-economic development is being hampered by widespread internal conflicts which are due, among other causes, to gross violations of human rights, including those arising from racism, racial discrimination, xenophobia and related intolerance, and from lack of democratic, inclusive and participatory governance;

22. We express our concern that in some States political and legal structures or institutions, some of which were inherited and persist today, do not correspond to the multi-ethnic, pluricultural and plurilingual characteristics of the population and, in many cases, constitute an important factor of discrimination in the exclusion of indigenous peoples;

23. We fully recognize the rights of indigenous peoples consistent with the principles of sovereignty and territorial integrity of States, and therefore stress the need to adopt the appropriate constitutional, administrative, legislative and judicial measures, including those derived from applicable international instruments;

24. We declare that the use of the term 'indigenous peoples' in the Declaration and Programme of Action of the World Conference against Racism, Racial Discrimination, Xenophobia and Related Intolerance is in the context of, and without prejudice to the outcome of, ongoing international negotiations on texts that specifically deal with this issue, and cannot be construed as having any implications as to rights under international law;

25. We express our profound repudiation of the racism, racial discrimination, xenophobia and related intolerance that persist in some States in the functioning of the penal systems and in the application of the law, as well as in the actions and attitudes of institutions and individuals responsible for law enforcement, especially where this has contributed to certain groups being over-represented among persons under detention or imprisoned;

26. We affirm the need to put an end to impunity for violations of the human rights and fundamental freedoms of individuals and groups of individuals who are victimized by racism, racial discrimination, xenophobia and related intolerance;

27. We express our concern that, beyond the fact that racism is gaining ground, contemporary forms and manifestations of racism and xenophobia are striving to regain political, moral and even legal recognition in many ways, including through the platforms of some political parties and organizations and the dissemination through modern communication technologies of ideas based on the notion of racial superiority;

28. We recall that persecution against any identifiable group, collectivity or community on racial, national, ethnic or other grounds that are universally recognized as impermissible under international law, as well as the crime of apartheid, constitute serious violations of human rights and, in some cases, qualify as crimes against humanity;

29. We strongly condemn the fact that slavery and slavery-like practices still exist today in parts of the world and urge States to take immediate measures as a matter of priority to end such practices, which constitute flagrant violations of human rights;

30. We affirm the urgent need to prevent, combat and eliminate all forms of trafficking in persons, in particular women and children, and recognize that victims of trafficking are particularly exposed to racism, racial discrimination, xenophobia and related intolerance;

VICTIMS OF RACISM, RACIAL DISCRIMINATION, XENOPHOBIA AND RELATED INTOLERANCE

31. We also express our deep concern whenever indicators in the fields of, *inter alia*, education, employment, health, housing, infant mortality and life expectancy for many peoples show a situation of disadvantage, particularly where the contributing factors include racism, racial discrimination, xenophobia and related intolerance;

32. We recognize the value and diversity of the cultural heritage of Africans and people of African descent and affirm the importance and necessity of ensuring their full integration into social, economic and political life with a view to facilitating their full participation at all levels in the decision-making process;

33. We consider it essential for all countries in the region of the Americas and all other areas of the African Diaspora to recognize the existence of their population of African descent and the cultural, economic, political and scientific contributions made by that population, and recognize the persistence of racism, racial discrimination, xenophobia and related intolerance that specifically affect them, and recognize that, in many countries, their long-standing inequality in terms of access to, *inter alia*, education, health care and housing has been a profound cause of the socio-economic disparities that affect them;

34. We recognize that people of African descent have for centuries been victims of racism, racial discrimination and enslavement and of the denial by history of many of their rights, and assert that they should be treated with fairness and respect for their dignity and should not suffer discrimination of any kind. Recognition should therefore be given to their rights to culture and their own identity; to participate freely and in equal conditions in political, social, economic and cultural life; to development in the context of their own aspirations and customs; to keep, maintain and foster their own forms of organization, their mode of life, culture, traditions and religious expressions; to maintain and use their own languages; to the protection of their traditional knowledge and their cultural and artistic heritage; to the use, enjoyment and conservation of the natural renewable resources of their habitat and to active participation in the design, implementation and development of educational systems and programmes, including those of a specific and characteristic nature; and where applicable to their ancestrally inhabited land;

35. We recognize that in many parts of the world, Africans and people of African descent face barriers as a result of social biases and discrimination prevailing in public

and private institutions and express our commitment to work towards the eradication of all forms of racism, racial discrimination, xenophobia and related intolerance faced by Africans and people of African descent;

36. We recognize that in many parts of the world, Asians and people of Asian descent face barriers as a result of social biases and discrimination prevailing in public and private institutions and express our commitment to work towards the eradication of all forms of racism, racial discrimination, xenophobia and related intolerance faced by Asians and people of Asian descent;

37. We note with appreciation that despite the racism, racial discrimination, xenophobia and related intolerance faced by them for centuries, people of Asian descent have contributed and continue to contribute significantly to the economic, social, political, scientific and cultural life of the countries where they live;

38. We call upon all States to review and, where necessary, revise any immigration policies which are inconsistent with international human rights instruments, with a view to eliminating all discriminatory policies and practices against migrants, including Asians and people of Asian descent;

39. We recognize that the indigenous peoples have been victims of discrimination for centuries and affirm that they are free and equal in dignity and rights and should not suffer any discrimination, particularly on the basis of their indigenous origin and identity, and we stress the continuing need for action to overcome the persistent racism, racial discrimination, xenophobia and related intolerance that affect them;

40. We recognize the value and diversity of the cultures and the heritage of indigenous peoples, whose singular contribution to the development and cultural pluralism of society and full participation in all aspects of society, in particular on issues that are of concern to them, are fundamental for political and social stability, and for the development of the States in which they live;

41. We reiterate our conviction that the full realization by indigenous peoples of their human rights and fundamental freedoms is indispensable for eliminating racism, racial discrimination, xenophobia and related intolerance. We firmly reiterate our determination to promote their full and equal enjoyment of civil, political, economic, social and cultural rights, as well as the benefits of sustainable development, while fully respecting their distinctive characteristics and their own initiatives;

42. We emphasize that, in order for indigenous peoples freely to express their own identity and exercise their rights, they should be free from all forms of discrimination, which necessarily entails respect for their human rights and fundamental freedoms. Efforts are now being made to secure universal recognition for those rights in the negotiations on the draft declaration on the rights of indigenous peoples, including the following: to call themselves by their own names; to participate freely and on an equal footing in their country's political, economic, social and cultural development; to maintain their own forms of organization, lifestyles, cultures and traditions; to maintain and use their own languages; to maintain their own economic structures in the areas where they live; to take part in the development of their educational systems and programmes; to manage their lands and natural resources, including hunting and fishing rights; and to have access to justice on a basis of equality;

43. We also recognize the special relationship that indigenous peoples have with the land as the basis for their spiritual, physical and cultural existence and encourage States,

wherever possible, to ensure that indigenous peoples are able to retain ownership of their lands and of those natural resources to which they are entitled under domestic law;

44. We welcome the decision to create the Permanent Forum on Indigenous Issues within the United Nations system, giving concrete expression to major objectives of the International Decade of the World's Indigenous People and the Vienna Declaration and Programme of Action;

45. We welcome the appointment by the United Nations of the Special Rapporteur on the situation of human rights and fundamental freedoms of indigenous people and express our commitment to cooperate with the Special Rapporteur;

46. We recognize the positive economic, social and cultural contributions made by migrants to both countries of origin and destination;

47. We reaffirm the sovereign right of each State to formulate and apply its own legal framework and policies for migration, and further affirm that these policies should be consistent with applicable human rights instruments, norms and standards, and designed to ensure that they are free of racism, racial discrimination, xenophobia and related intolerance;

48. We note with concern and strongly condemn the manifestations and acts of racism, racial discrimination, xenophobia and related intolerance against migrants and the stereotypes often applied to them; reaffirm the responsibility of States to protect the human rights of migrants under their jurisdiction and reaffirm the responsibility of States to safeguard and protect migrants against illegal or violent acts, in particular acts of racial discrimination and crimes perpetrated with racist or xenophobic motivation by individuals or groups; and stress the need for their fair, just and equitable treatment in society and in the workplace;

49. We highlight the importance of creating conditions conducive to greater harmony, tolerance and respect between migrants and the rest of society in the countries in which they find themselves, in order to eliminate manifestations of racism and xenophobia against migrants. We underline that family reunification has a positive effect on integration and emphasize the need for States to facilitate family reunion;

50. We are mindful of the situation of vulnerability in which migrants frequently find themselves, owing, *inter alia*, to their departure from their countries of origin and to the difficulties they encounter because of differences in language, customs and culture, as well as economic and social difficulties and obstacles to the return of migrants who are undocumented or in an irregular situation;

51. We reaffirm the necessity of eliminating racial discrimination against migrants, including migrant workers, in relation to issues such as employment, social services, including education and health, as well as access to justice, and that their treatment must be in accordance with international human rights instruments, free from racism, racial discrimination, xenophobia and related intolerance;

52. We note with concern that, among other factors, racism, racial discrimination, xenophobia and related intolerance contribute to forced displacement and the movement of people from their countries of origin as refugees and asylum-seekers;

53. We recognize with concern that, despite efforts to combat racism, racial discrimination, xenophobia and related intolerance, instances of various forms of racism, racial discrimination, xenophobia and related intolerance against refugees, asylum-seekers and internally displaced persons, among others, continue;

54. We underline the urgency of addressing the root causes of displacement and of finding durable solutions for refugees and displaced persons, in particular voluntary return in safety and dignity to the countries of origin, as well as resettlement in third countries and local integration, when and where appropriate and feasible;

55. We affirm our commitment to respect and implement humanitarian obligations relating to the protection of refugees, asylum-seekers, returnees and internally displaced persons, and note in this regard the importance of international solidarity, burden-sharing and international cooperation to share responsibility for the protection of refugees, reaffirming that the 1951 Convention relating to the Status of Refugees and its 1967 Protocol remain the foundation of the international refugee regime and recognizing the importance of their full application by States parties;

56. We recognize the presence in many countries of a Mestizo population of mixed ethnic and racial origins and its valuable contribution to the promotion of tolerance and respect in these societies, and we condemn discrimination against them, especially because such discrimination may be denied owing to its subtle nature;

57. We are conscious of the fact that the history of humanity is replete with major atrocities as a result of gross violations of human rights and believe that lessons can be learned through remembering history to avert future tragedies;

58. We recall that the Holocaust must never be forgotten;

59. We recognize with deep concern religious intolerance against certain religious communities, as well as the emergence of hostile acts and violence against such communities because of their religious beliefs and their racial or ethnic origin in various parts of the world which in particular limit their right to freely practise their belief;

60. We also recognize with deep concern the existence in various parts of the world of religious intolerance against religious communities and their members, in particular limitation of their right to practise their beliefs freely, as well as the emergence of increased negative stereotyping, hostile acts and violence against such communities because of their religious beliefs and their ethnic or so-called racial origin;

61. We recognize with deep concern the increase in anti-Semitism and Islamophobia in various parts of the world, as well as the emergence of racial and violent movements based on racism and discriminatory ideas against Jewish, Muslim and Arab communities;

62. We are conscious that humanity's history is replete with terrible wrongs inflicted through lack of respect for the equality of human beings and note with alarm the increase of such practices in various parts of the world, and we urge people, particularly in conflict situations, to desist from racist incitement, derogatory language and negative stereotyping;

63. We are concerned about the plight of the Palestinian people under foreign occupation. We recognize the inalienable right of the Palestinian people to self-determination and to the establishment of an independent State and we recognize the right to security for all States in the region, including Israel, and call upon all States to support the peace process and bring it to an early conclusion;

64. We call for a just, comprehensive and lasting peace in the region in which all peoples shall co-exist and enjoy equality, justice and internationally recognized human rights, and security;

65. We recognize the right of refugees to return voluntarily to their homes and properties in dignity and safety, and urge all States to facilitate such return;

66. We affirm that the ethnic, cultural, linguistic and religious identity of minorities, where they exist, must be protected and that persons belonging to such minorities should be treated equally and enjoy their human rights and fundamental freedoms without discrimination of any kind;

67. We recognize that members of certain groups with a distinct cultural identity face barriers arising from a complex interplay of ethnic, religious and other factors, as well as their traditions and customs, and call upon States to ensure that measures, policies and programmes aimed at eradicating racism, racial discrimination, xenophobia and related intolerance address the barriers that this interplay of factors creates;

68. We recognize with deep concern the ongoing manifestations of racism, racial discrimination, xenophobia and related intolerance, including violence, against Roma/ Gypsies/Sinti/Travellers and recognize the need to develop effective policies and implementation mechanisms for their full achievement of equality;

69. We are convinced that racism, racial discrimination, xenophobia and related intolerance reveal themselves in a differentiated manner for women and girls, and can be among the factors leading to a deterioration in their living conditions, poverty, violence, multiple forms of discrimination, and the limitation or denial of their human rights. We recognize the need to integrate a gender perspective into relevant policies, strategies and programmes of action against racism, racial discrimination, xenophobia and related intolerance in order to address multiple forms of discrimination;

70. We recognize the need to develop a more systematic and consistent approach to evaluating and monitoring racial discrimination against women, as well as the disadvantages, obstacles and difficulties women face in the full exercise and enjoyment of their civil, political, economic, social and cultural rights because of racism, racial discrimination, xenophobia and related intolerance;

71. We deplore attempts to oblige women belonging to certain faiths and religious minorities to forego their cultural and religious identity, or to restrict their legitimate expression, or to discriminate against them with regard to opportunities for education and employment;

72. We note with concern the large number of children and young people, particularly girls, among the victims of racism, racial discrimination, xenophobia and related intolerance and stress the need to incorporate special measures, in accordance with the principle of the best interests of the child and respect for his or her views, in programmes to combat racism, racial discrimination, xenophobia and related intolerance, in order to give priority attention to the rights and the situation of children and young people who are victims of these practices;

73. We recognize that a child belonging to an ethnic, religious or linguistic minority or who is indigenous shall not be denied the right, individually or in community with other members of his or her group, to enjoy his or her own culture, to profess and practise his or her own religion, or to use his or her own language;

74. We recognize that child labour is linked to poverty, lack of development and related socio-economic conditions and could in some cases perpetuate poverty and racial discrimination by disproportionately denying children from affected groups the opportunity to acquire the human capabilities needed in productive life and to benefit from economic growth;

75. We note with deep concern the fact that, in many countries, people infected or affected by HIV/AIDS, as well as those who are presumed to be infected, belong to

groups vulnerable to racism, racial discrimination, xenophobia and related intolerance, which has a negative impact and impedes their access to health care and medication;

MEASURES OF PREVENTION, EDUCATION AND PROTECTION AIMED AT THE ERADICATION OF RACISM, RACIAL DISCRIMINATION, XENOPHOBIA AND RELATED INTOLERANCE AT THE NATIONAL, REGIONAL AND INTERNATIONAL LEVELS

76. We recognize that inequitable political, economic, cultural and social conditions can breed and foster racism, racial discrimination, xenophobia and related intolerance, which in turn exacerbate the inequity. We believe that genuine equality of opportunity for all, in all spheres, including that for development, is fundamental for the eradication of racism, racial discrimination, xenophobia and related intolerance;

77. We affirm that universal adherence to and full implementation of the International Convention on the Elimination of All Forms of Racial Discrimination are of paramount importance for promoting equality and non-discrimination in the world;

78. We affirm the solemn commitment of all States to promote universal respect for, and observance and protection of, all human rights, economic, social, cultural, civil and political, including the right to development, as a fundamental factor in the prevention and elimination of racism, racial discrimination, xenophobia and related intolerance;

79. We firmly believe that the obstacles to overcoming racial discrimination and achieving racial equality mainly lie in the lack of political will, weak legislation and lack of implementation strategies and concrete action by States, as well as the prevalence of racist attitudes and negative stereotyping;

80. We firmly believe that education, development and the faithful implementation of all international human rights norms and obligations, including enactment of laws and political, social and economic policies, are crucial to combat racism, racial discrimination, xenophobia and related intolerance;

81. We recognize that democracy, transparent, responsible, accountable and participatory governance responsive to the needs and aspirations of the people, and respect for human rights, fundamental freedoms and the rule of law are essential for the effective prevention and elimination of racism, racial discrimination, xenophobia and related intolerance. We reaffirm that any form of impunity for crimes motivated by racist and xenophobic attitudes plays a role in weakening the rule of law and democracy and tends to encourage the recurrence of such acts;

82. We affirm that the Dialogue among Civilizations constitutes a process to attain identification and promotion of common grounds among civilizations, recognition and promotion of the inherent dignity and of the equal rights of all human beings and respect for fundamental principles of justice; in this way, it can dispel notions of cultural superiority based on racism, racial discrimination, xenophobia and related intolerance, and facilitate the building of a reconciled world for the human family;

83. We underline the key role that political leaders and political parties can and ought to play in combating racism, racial discrimination, xenophobia and related

intolerance and encourage political parties to take concrete steps to promote solidarity, tolerance and respect;

84. We condemn the persistence and resurgence of neo-Nazism, neo-Fascism and violent nationalist ideologies based on racial or national prejudice, and state that these phenomena can never be justified in any instance or in any circumstances;

85. We condemn political platforms and organizations based on racism, xenophobia or doctrines of racial superiority and related discrimination, as well as legislation and practices based on racism, racial discrimination, xenophobia and related intolerance, as incompatible with democracy and transparent and accountable governance. We reaffirm that racism, racial discrimination, xenophobia and related intolerance condoned by governmental policies violate human rights and may endanger friendly relations among peoples, cooperation among nations and international peace and security;

86. We recall that the dissemination of all ideas based upon racial superiority or hatred shall be declared an offence punishable by law with due regard to the principles embodied in the Universal Declaration of Human Rights and the rights expressly set forth in article 5 of the International Convention on the Elimination of All Forms of Racial Discrimination;

87. We note that article 4, paragraph b, of the International Convention on the Elimination of All Forms of Racial Discrimination places an obligation upon States to be vigilant and to proceed against organizations that disseminate ideas based on racial superiority or hatred, acts of violence or incitement to such acts. These organizations shall be condemned and discouraged;

88. We recognize that the media should represent the diversity of a multicultural society and play a role in fighting racism, racial discrimination, xenophobia and related intolerance. In this regard we draw attention to the power of advertising;

89. We note with regret that certain media, by promoting false images and negative stereotypes of vulnerable individuals or groups of individuals, particularly of migrants and refugees, have contributed to the spread of xenophobic and racist sentiments among the public and in some cases have encouraged violence by racist individuals and groups;

90. We recognize the positive contribution that the exercise of the right to freedom of expression, particularly by the media and new technologies, including the Internet, and full respect for the freedom to seek, receive and impart information can make to the fight against racism, racial discrimination, xenophobia and related intolerance; we reiterate the need to respect the editorial independence and autonomy of the media in this regard;

91. We express deep concern about the use of new information technologies, such as the Internet, for purposes contrary to respect for human values, equality, non-discrimination, respect for others and tolerance, including to propagate racism, racial hatred, xenophobia, racial discrimination and related intolerance, and that, in particular, children and youth having access to this material could be negatively influenced by it;

92. We also recognize the need to promote the use of new information and communication technologies, including the Internet, to contribute to the fight against racism, racial discrimination, xenophobia and related intolerance; new technologies can assist the promotion of tolerance and respect for human dignity, and the principles of equality and non-discrimination;

93. We affirm that all States should recognize the importance of community media that give a voice to victims of racism, racial discrimination, xenophobia and related intolerance;

94. We reaffirm that the stigmatization of people of different origins by acts or omissions of public authorities, institutions, the media, political parties or national or local organizations is not only an act of racial discrimination but can also incite the recurrence of such acts, thereby resulting in the creation of a vicious circle which reinforces racist attitudes and prejudices, and which must be condemned;

95. We recognize that education at all levels and all ages, including within the family, in particular human rights education, is a key to changing attitudes and behaviour based on racism, racial discrimination, xenophobia and related intolerance and to promoting tolerance and respect for diversity in societies; we further affirm that such education is a determining factor in the promotion, dissemination and protection of the democratic values of justice and equity, which are essential to prevent and combat the spread of racism, racial discrimination, xenophobia and related intolerance;

96. We recognize that quality education, the elimination of illiteracy and access to free primary education for all can contribute to more inclusive societies, equity, stable and harmonious relations and friendship among nations, peoples, groups and individuals, and a culture of peace, fostering mutual understanding, solidarity, social justice and respect for all human rights for all;

97. We underline the links between the right to education and the struggle against racism, racial discrimination, xenophobia and related intolerance and the essential role of education, including human rights education and education which is sensitive to and respects cultural diversity, especially amongst children and young people, in the prevention and eradication of all forms of intolerance and discrimination;

PROVISION OF EFFECTIVE REMEDIES, RECOURSE, REDRESS, AND COMPENSATORY AND OTHER MEASURES AT THE NATIONAL, REGIONAL AND INTERNATIONAL LEVELS

98. We emphasize the importance and necessity of teaching about the facts and truth of the history of humankind from antiquity to the recent past, as well as of teaching about the facts and truth of the history, causes, nature and consequences of racism, racial discrimination, xenophobia and related intolerance, with a view to achieving a comprehensive and objective cognizance of the tragedies of the past;

99. We acknowledge and profoundly regret the massive human suffering and the tragic plight of millions of men, women and children caused by slavery, the slave trade, the transatlantic slave trade, apartheid, colonialism and genocide, and call upon States concerned to honour the memory of the victims of past tragedies and affirm that, wherever and whenever these occurred, they must be condemned and their recurrence prevented. We regret that these practices and structures, political, socio-economic and cultural, have led to racism, racial discrimination, xenophobia and related intolerance;

100. We acknowledge and profoundly regret the untold suffering and evils inflicted on millions of men, women and children as a result of slavery, the slave trade, the transatlantic slave trade, apartheid, genocide and past tragedies. We further note that some States have taken the initiative to apologize and have paid reparation, where appropriate, for grave and massive violations committed;

101. With a view to closing those dark chapters in history and as a means of reconciliation and healing, we invite the international community and its members to honour the memory of the victims of these tragedies. We further note that some have taken the initiative of regretting or expressing remorse or presenting apologies, and call on all those who have not yet contributed to restoring the dignity of the victims to find appropriate ways to do so and, to this end, appreciate those countries that have done so;

102. We are aware of the moral obligation on the part of all concerned States and call upon these States to take appropriate and effective measures to halt and reverse the lasting consequences of those practices;

103. We recognize the consequences of past and contemporary forms of racism, racial discrimination, xenophobia and related intolerance as serious challenges to global peace and security, human dignity and the realization of human rights and fundamental freedoms of many people in the world, in particular Africans, people of African descent, people of Asian descent and indigenous peoples;

104. We also strongly reaffirm as a pressing requirement of justice that victims of human rights violations resulting from racism, racial discrimination, xenophobia and related intolerance, especially in the light of their vulnerable situation socially, culturally and economically, should be assured of having access to justice, including legal assistance where appropriate, and effective and appropriate protection and remedies, including the right to seek just and adequate reparation or satisfaction for any damage suffered as a result of such discrimination, as enshrined in numerous international and regional human rights instruments, in particular the Universal Declaration of Human Rights and the International Convention on the Elimination of All Forms of Racial Discrimination;

105. Guided by the principles set out in the Millennium Declaration and the recognition that we have a collective responsibility to uphold the principles of human dignity, equality and equity and to ensure that globalization becomes a positive force for all the world's people, the international community commits itself to working for the beneficial integration of the developing countries into the global economy, resisting their marginalization, determined to achieve accelerated economic growth and sustainable development and to eradicate poverty, inequality and deprivation;

106. We emphasize that remembering the crimes or wrongs of the past, wherever and whenever they occurred, unequivocally condemning its racist tragedies and telling the truth about history are essential elements for international reconciliation and the creation of societies based on justice, equality and solidarity;

STRATEGIES TO ACHIEVE FULL AND EFFECTIVE EQUALITY, INCLUDING INTERNATIONAL COOPERATION AND ENHANCEMENT OF THE UNITED NATIONS AND OTHER INTERNATIONAL MECHANISMS IN COMBATING RACISM, RACIAL DISCRIMINATION, XENOPHOBIA AND RELATED INTOLERANCE

107. We underscore the need to design, promote and implement at the national, regional and international levels strategies, programmes and policies, and adequate legislation, which may include special and positive measures, for furthering equal social

development and the realization of the civil and political, economic, social and cultural rights of all victims of racism, racial discrimination, xenophobia and related intolerance, including through more effective access to the political, judicial and administrative institutions, as well as the need to promote effective access to justice, as well as to guarantee that the benefits of development, science and technology contribute effectively to the improvement of the quality of life for all, without discrimination;

108.   We recognize the necessity for special measures or positive actions for the victims of racism, racial discrimination, xenophobia and related intolerance in order to promote their full integration into society. Those measures for effective action, including social measures, should aim at correcting the conditions that impair the enjoyment of rights and the introduction of special measures to encourage equal participation of all racial and cultural, linguistic and religious groups in all sectors of society and to bring all onto an equal footing. Those measures should include measures to achieve appropriate representation in educational institutions, housing, political parties, parliaments and employment, especially in the judiciary, police, army and other civil services, which in some cases might involve electoral reforms, land reforms and campaigns for equal participation;

109.   We recall the importance of enhancing international cooperation to promote (a) the fight against racism, racial discrimination, xenophobia and related intolerance; (b) the effective implementation by States of international treaties and instruments that forbid these practices; (c) the goals of the Charter of the United Nations in this regard; (d) the achievement of the goals established by the United Nations Conference on Environment and Development held in Rio de Janeiro in 1992, the World Conference on Human Rights held in Vienna in 1993, the International Conference on Population and Development held in Cairo in 1994, the World Summit for Social Development held in Copenhagen in 1995, the Fourth World Conference on Women held in Beijing in 1995, the United Nations Conference on Human Settlements (Habitat II) held in Istanbul in 1996; and the World Food Summit held in Rome in 1996, making sure that such goals encompass with equity all the victims of racism, racial discrimination, xenophobia and related intolerance;

110.   We recognize the importance of cooperation among States, relevant international and regional organizations, the international financial institutions, non-governmental organizations and individuals in the worldwide fight against racism, racial discrimination, xenophobia and related intolerance, and that success in this fight requires specifically taking into consideration the grievances, opinions and demands of the victims of such discrimination;

111.   We reiterate that the international response and policy, including financial assistance, towards refugees and displaced persons in different parts of the world should not be based on discrimination on the grounds of race, colour, descent, or national or ethnic origin of the refugees and displaced persons concerned and, in this context, we urge the international community to provide adequate assistance on an equitable basis to host countries, in particular to host developing countries and countries in transition;

112.   We recognize the importance of independent national human rights institutions conforming to the Principles relating to the status of national institutions for the promotion and protection of human rights, annexed to General Assembly resolution 48/134 of 20 December 1993, and other relevant specialized institutions created by law for the promotion and protection of human rights, including ombudsman institutions, in the struggle against racism, racial discrimination, xenophobia and related intolerance, as

well as for the promotion of democratic values and the rule of law. We encourage States, as appropriate, to establish such institutions and call upon the authorities and society in general in those countries where they are performing their tasks of promotion, protection and prevention to cooperate to the maximum extent possible with these institutions, while respecting their independence;

113.   We recognize the important role relevant regional bodies, including regional associations of national human rights institutions, can play in combating racism, racial discrimination, xenophobia and related intolerance, and the key role they can play in monitoring and raising awareness about intolerance and discrimination at the regional level, and reaffirm support for such bodies where they exist and encourage their establishment;

114.   We recognize the paramount role of parliaments in the fight against racism, racial discrimination, xenophobia and related intolerance in adopting appropriate legislation, overseeing its implementation and allocating the requisite financial resources;

115.   We stress the importance of involving social partners and other non-governmental organizations in the design and implementation of training and development programmes;

116.   We recognize the fundamental role of civil society in the fight against racism, racial discrimination, xenophobia and related intolerance, in particular in assisting States to develop regulations and strategies, in taking measures and action against such forms of discrimination and through follow-up implementation;

117.   We also recognize that promoting greater respect and trust among different groups within society must be a shared but differentiated responsibility of government institutions, political leaders, grass-roots organizations and citizens. We underline that civil society plays an important role in promoting the public interest, especially in combating racism, racial discrimination, xenophobia and related intolerance;

118.   We welcome the catalytic role that non-governmental organizations play in promoting human rights education and raising awareness about racism, racial discrimination, xenophobia and related intolerance. They can also play an important role in raising awareness of such issues in the relevant bodies of the United Nations, based upon their national, regional or international experiences. Bearing in mind the difficulties they face, we commit ourselves to creating an atmosphere conducive to the effective functioning of human rights non-governmental organizations, in particular anti-racist non-governmental organizations, in combating racism, racial discrimination, xenophobia and related intolerance. We recognize the precarious situation of human rights non-governmental organizations, including anti-racist non-governmental organizations, in many parts of the world and express our commitment to adhere to our international obligations and to lift any unlawful barriers to their effective functioning;

119.   We encourage the full participation of non-governmental organizations in the follow-up to the World Conference;

120.   We recognize that international and national exchange and dialogue, and the development of a global network among youth, are important and fundamental elements in building intercultural understanding and respect, and will contribute to the elimination of racism, racial discrimination, xenophobia and related intolerance;

121.   We underline the usefulness of involving youth in the development of forward-looking national, regional and international strategies and in policies to fight racism, racial discrimination, xenophobia and related intolerance;

122. We affirm that our global drive for the total elimination of racism, racial discrimination, xenophobia and related intolerance is undertaken, and that the recommendations contained in the Programme of Action are made, in a spirit of solidarity and international cooperation and are inspired by the purposes and principles of the Charter of the United Nations and other relevant international instruments. These recommendations are made with due consideration for the past, the present and the future, and with a constructive and forward-looking approach. We recognize that the formulation and implementation of these strategies, policies, programmes and actions, which should be carried out efficiently and promptly, are the responsibility of all States, with the full involvement of civil society at the national, regional and international levels.

PROGRAMME OF ACTION

Recognizing the urgent need to translate the objectives of the Declaration into a practical and workable Programme of Action, the World Conference against Racism, Racial Discrimination, Xenophobia and Related Intolerance:

I. SOURCES, CAUSES, FORMS AND CONTEMPORARY MANIFESTATIONS OF RACISM, RACIAL DISCRIMINATION, XENOPHOBIA AND RELATED INTOLERANCE

1. *Urges* States in their national efforts, and in cooperation with other States, regional and international organizations and financial institutions, to promote the use of public and private investment in consultation with the affected communities in order to eradicate poverty, particularly in those areas in which victims of racism, racial discrimination, xenophobia and related intolerance predominantly live;

2. *Urges* States to take all necessary and appropriate measures to end enslavement and contemporary forms of slavery-like practices, to initiate constructive dialogue among States and implement measures with a view to correcting the problems and the damage resulting therefrom;

II. VICTIMS OF RACISM, RACIAL DISCRIMINATION, XENOPHOBIA AND RELATED INTOLERANCE

Victims: general

3. *Urges* States to work nationally and in cooperation with other States and relevant regional and international organizations and programmes to strengthen national mechanisms to promote and protect the human rights of victims of racism, racial discrimination, xenophobia and related intolerance who are infected, or presumably infected, with pandemic diseases such as HIV/AIDS and to take concrete measures, including preventive action, appropriate access to medication and treatment, programmes of education, training and mass media dissemination, to eliminate violence, stigmatization, discrimination, unemployment and other negative consequences arising from these pandemics;

Africans and people of African descent

4. *Urges* States to facilitate the participation of people of African descent in all political, economic, social and cultural aspects of society and in the advancement and economic development of their countries, and to promote a greater knowledge of and respect for their heritage and culture;

5. *Requests* States, supported by international cooperation as appropriate, to consider positively concentrating additional investments in health-care systems, education, public health, electricity, drinking water and environmental control, as well as other affirmative or positive action initiatives, in communities of primarily African descent;

6. *Calls upon* the United Nations, international financial and development institutions and other appropriate international mechanisms to develop capacity-building programmes intended for Africans and people of African descent in the Americas and around the world;

7. *Requests* the Commission on Human Rights to consider establishing a working group or other mechanism of the United Nations to study the problems of racial discrimination faced by people of African descent living in the African Diaspora and make proposals for the elimination of racial discrimination against people of African descent;

8. *Urges* financial and development institutions and the operational programmes and specialized agencies of the United Nations, in accordance with their regular budgets and the procedures of their governing bodies:

(a) To assign particular priority, and allocate sufficient funding, within their areas of competence and budgets, to improving the situation of Africans and people of African descent, while devoting special attention to the needs of these populations in developing countries, *inter alia* through the preparation of specific programmes of action;

(b) To carry out special projects, through appropriate channels and in collaboration with Africans and people of African descent, to support their initiatives at the community level and to facilitate the exchange of information and technical know-how between these populations and experts in these areas;

(c) To develop programmes intended for people of African descent allocating additional investments to health systems, education, housing, electricity, drinking water and environmental control measures and promoting equal opportunities in employment, as well as other affirmative or positive action initiatives;

9. *Requests* States to increase public actions and policies in favour of women and young males of African descent, given that racism affects them more deeply, placing them in a more marginalized and disadvantaged situation;

10. *Urges* States to ensure access to education and promote access to new technologies that would offer Africans and people of African descent, in particular women and children, adequate resources for education, technological development and long-distance learning in local communities, and further urges States to promote the full and accurate inclusion of the history and contribution of Africans and people of African descent in the education curriculum;

11. *Encourages* States to identify factors which prevent equal access to, and the equitable presence of, people of African descent at all levels of the public sector, including the public service, and in particular the administration of justice, and to take appropriate

measures to remove the obstacles identified and also to encourage the private sector to promote equal access to, and the equitable presence of, people of African descent at all levels within their organizations;

12. *Calls upon* States to take specific steps to ensure full and effective access to the justice system for all individuals, particularly those of African descent;

13. *Urges* States, in accordance with international human rights standards and their respective domestic legal framework, to resolve problems of ownership of ancestral lands inhabited for generations by people of African descent and to promote the productive utilization of land and the comprehensive development of these communities, respecting their culture and their specific forms of decision-making;

14. *Urges* States to recognize the particularly severe problems of religious prejudice and intolerance that many people of African descent experience and to implement policies and measures that are designed to prevent and eliminate all such discrimination on the basis of religion and belief, which, when combined with certain other forms of discrimination, constitutes a form of multiple discrimination;

Indigenous peoples

15. *Urges* States:

    (a) To adopt or continue to apply, in concert with them, constitutional, administrative, legislative, judicial and all necessary measures to promote, protect and ensure the enjoyment by indigenous peoples of their rights, as well as to guarantee them the exercise of their human rights and fundamental freedoms on the basis of equality, non-discrimination and full and free participation in all areas of society, in particular in matters affecting or concerning their interests;

    (b) To promote better knowledge of and respect for indigenous cultures and heritage; and welcomes measures already taken by States in these respects;

16. *Urges* States to work with indigenous peoples to stimulate their access to economic activities and increase their level of employment, where appropriate, through the establishment, acquisition or expansion by indigenous peoples of enterprises, and the implementation of measures such as training, the provision of technical assistance and credit facilities;

17. *Urges* States to work with indigenous peoples to establish and implement programmes that provide access to training and services that could benefit the development of their communities;

18. *Requests* States to adopt public policies and give impetus to programmes on behalf of and in concert with indigenous women and girls, with a view to promoting their civil, political, economic, social and cultural rights; to putting an end to their situation of disadvantage for reasons of gender and ethnicity; to dealing with urgent problems affecting them in regard to education, their physical and mental health, economic life and in the matter of violence against them, including domestic violence; and to eliminating the situation of aggravated discrimination suffered by indigenous women and girls on multiple grounds of racism and gender discrimination;

19. *Recommends* that States examine, in conformity with relevant international human rights instruments, norms and standards, their Constitutions, laws, legal systems and policies in order to identify and eradicate racism, racial discrimination, xenophobia and

related intolerance towards indigenous peoples and individuals, whether implicit, explicit or inherent;

2 0. *Calls upon* concerned States to honour and respect their treaties and agreements with indigenous peoples and to accord them due recognition and observance;

2 1. *Calls upon* States to give full and appropriate consideration to the recommendations produced by indigenous peoples in their own forums on the World Conference;

2 2. *Requests* States:

  (a) To develop and, where they already exist, support institutional mechanisms to promote the accomplishment of the objectives and measures relating to indigenous peoples agreed in this Programme of Action;

  (b) To promote, in concert with indigenous organizations, local authorities and non-governmental organizations, actions aimed at overcoming racism, racial discrimination, xenophobia and related intolerance against indigenous peoples and to make regular assessments of the progress achieved in this regard;

  (c) To promote understanding among society at large of the importance of special measures to overcome disadvantages faced by indigenous peoples;

  (d) To consult indigenous representatives in the process of decision-making concerning policies and measures that directly affect them;

2 3. *Calls upon* States to recognize the particular challenges faced by indigenous peoples and individuals living in urban environments and urges States to implement effective strategies to combat the racism, racial discrimination, xenophobia and related intolerance they encounter, paying particular attention to opportunities for their continued practice of their traditional, cultural, linguistic and spiritual ways of life;

Migrants

2 4. *Requests* all States to combat manifestations of a generalized rejection of migrants and actively to discourage all racist demonstrations and acts that generate xenophobic behaviour and negative sentiments towards, or rejection of, migrants;

2 5. *Invites* international and national non-governmental organizations to include monitoring and protection of the human rights of migrants in their programmes and activities and to sensitize Governments and increase public awareness in all States about the need to prevent racist acts and manifestations of discrimination, xenophobia and related intolerance against migrants;

2 6. *Requests* States to promote and protect fully and effectively the human rights and fundamental freedoms of all migrants, in conformity with the Universal Declaration of Human Rights and their obligations under international human rights instruments, regardless of the migrants' immigration status;

2 7. *Encourages* States to promote education on the human rights of migrants and to engage in information campaigns to ensure that the public receives accurate information regarding migrants and migration issues, including the positive contribution of migrants to the host society and the vulnerability of migrants, particularly those who are in an irregular situation;

2 8. *Calls upon* States to facilitate family reunification in an expeditious and effective manner which has a positive effect on integration of migrants, with due regard for the desire of many family members to have an independent status;

29. *Urges* States to take concrete measures that would eliminate racism, racial discrimination, xenophobia and related intolerance in the workplace against all workers, including migrants, and ensure the full equality of all before the law, including labour law, and further urges States to eliminate barriers, where appropriate, to: participating in vocational training, collective bargaining, employment, contracts and trade union activity; accessing judicial and administrative tribunals dealing with grievances; seeking employment in different parts of their country of residence; and working in safe and healthy conditions;

30. *Urges* States:

(a) To develop and implement policies and action plans, and to reinforce and implement preventive measures, in order to foster greater harmony and tolerance between migrants and host societies, with the aim of eliminating manifestations of racism, racial discrimination, xenophobia and related intolerance, including acts of violence, perpetrated in many societies by individuals or groups;

(b) To review and revise, where necessary, their immigration laws, policies and practices so that they are free of racial discrimination and compatible with States' obligations under international human rights instruments;

(c) To implement specific measures involving the host community and migrants in order to encourage respect for cultural diversity, to promote the fair treatment of migrants and to develop programmes, where appropriate, that facilitate their integration into social, cultural, political and economic life;

(d) To ensure that migrants, regardless of their immigration status, detained by public authorities are treated with humanity and in a fair manner, and receive effective legal protection and, where appropriate, the assistance of a competent interpreter in accordance with the relevant norms of international law and human rights standards, particularly during interrogation;

(e) To ensure that the police and immigration authorities treat migrants in a dignified and non-discriminatory manner, in accordance with international standards, through, *inter alia*, organizing specialized training courses for administrators, police officers, immigration officials and other interested groups;

(f) To consider the question of promoting the recognition of the educational, professional and technical credentials of migrants, with a view to maximizing their contribution to their new States of residence;

(g) To take all possible measures to promote the full enjoyment by all migrants of all human rights, including those related to fair wages and equal remuneration for work of equal value without distinction of any kind, and to the right to security in the event of unemployment, sickness, disability, widowhood, old age or other lack of livelihood in circumstances beyond their control, social security, including social insurance, access to education, health care, social services and respect for their cultural identity;

(h) To consider adopting and implementing immigration policies and programmes that would enable immigrants, in particular women and children who are victims of spousal or domestic violence, to free themselves from abusive relationships;

31. *Urges* States, in the light of the increased proportion of women migrants, to place special focus on gender issues, including gender discrimination, particularly when the multiple barriers faced by migrant women intersect; detailed research should be undertaken not

only in respect of human rights violations perpetrated against women migrants, but also on the contribution they make to the economies of their countries of origin and their host countries, and the findings should be included in reports to treaty bodies;

32. *Urges* States to recognize the same economic opportunities and responsibilities to documented long-term migrants as to other members of society;

33. *Recommends* that host countries of migrants consider the provision of adequate social services, in particular in the areas of health, education and adequate housing, as a matter of priority, in cooperation with the United Nations agencies, the regional organizations and international financial bodies; also requests that these agencies provide an adequate response to requests for such services;

Refugees

34. *Urges* States to comply with their obligations under international human rights, refugee and humanitarian law relating to refugees, asylum-seekers and displaced persons, and urges the international community to provide them with protection and assistance in an equitable manner and with due regard to their needs in different parts of the world, in keeping with principles of international solidarity, burden-sharing and international cooperation, to share responsibilities;

35. *Calls upon* States to recognize the racism, racial discrimination, xenophobia and related intolerance that refugees may face as they endeavour to engage in the life of the societies of their host countries and encourages States, in accordance with their international obligations and commitments, to develop strategies to address this discrimination and to facilitate the full enjoyment of the human rights of refugees. States parties should ensure that all measures relating to refugees must be in full accordance with the 1951 Convention relating to the Status of Refugees and its 1967 Protocol;

36. *Urges* States to take effective steps to protect refugee and internally displaced women and girls from violence, to investigate any such violations and to bring those responsible to justice, in collaboration, when appropriate, with the relevant and competent organizations;

Other victims

37. *Urges* States to take all possible measures to ensure that all persons, without any discrimination, are registered and have access to the necessary documentation reflecting their legal identity to enable them to benefit from available legal procedures, remedies and development opportunities, as well as to reduce the incidence of trafficking;

38. *Recognizes* that victims of trafficking are particularly exposed to racism, racial discrimination, xenophobia and related intolerance. States shall ensure that all measures taken against trafficking in persons, in particular those that affect the victims of such trafficking, are consistent with internationally recognized principles of non-discrimination, including the prohibition of racial discrimination and the availability of appropriate legal redress;

39. *Calls upon* States to ensure that Roma/Gypsy/Sinti/Traveller children and youth, especially girls, are given equal access to education and that educational curricula at all levels, including complementary programmes on intercultural education, which might, *inter alia*, include opportunities for them to learn the official languages in the pre-school period and to recruit Roma/Gypsy/Sinti/Traveller teachers and classroom assistants in

order for such children and youth to learn their mother tongue, are sensitive and responsive to their needs;

40. *Encourages* States to adopt appropriate and concrete policies and measures, to develop implementation mechanisms, where these do not already exist, and to exchange experiences, in cooperation with representatives of the Roma/Gypsies/Sinti/Travellers, in order to eradicate discrimination against them, enable them to achieve equality and ensure their full enjoyment of all their human rights, as recommended in the case of the Roma by the Committee on the Elimination of Racial Discrimination in its general recommendation XXVII, so that their needs are met;

41. *Recommends* that the intergovernmental organizations address, as appropriate, in their projects of cooperation with and assistance to various States, the situation of the Roma/Gypsies/Sinti/Travellers and promote their economic, social and cultural advancement;

42. *Calls upon* States and encourages non-governmental organizations to raise awareness about the racism, racial discrimination, xenophobia and related intolerance experienced by the Roma/Gypsies/Sinti/Travellers, and to promote knowledge and respect for their culture and history;

43. *Encourages* the media to promote equal access to and participation in the media for the Roma/Gypsies/Sinti/Travellers, as well as to protect them from racist, stereotypical and discriminatory media reporting, and calls upon States to facilitate the media's efforts in this regard;

44. *Invites* States to design policies aimed at combating racism, racial discrimination, xenophobia and related intolerance that are based on reliable statistical data recognizing the concerns identified in consultation with the Roma/Gypsies/Sinti/Travellers themselves reflecting as accurately as possible their status in society. All such information shall be collected in accordance with provisions on human rights and fundamental freedoms, such as data protection regulations and privacy guarantees, and in consultation with the persons concerned;

45. *Encourages* States to address the problems of racism, racial discrimination, xenophobia and related intolerance against people of Asian descent and urges States to take all necessary measures to eliminate the barriers that such persons face in participating in economic, social, cultural and political life;

46. *Urges* States to ensure within their jurisdiction that persons belonging to national or ethnic, religious and linguistic minorities can exercise fully and effectively all human rights and fundamental freedoms without any discrimination and in full equality before the law, and also urges States and the international community to promote and protect the rights of such persons;

47. *Urges* States to guarantee the rights of persons belonging to national or ethnic, religious and linguistic minorities, individually or in community with other members of their group, to enjoy their own culture, to profess and practise their own religion, and to use their own language, in private and in public, freely and without interference, and to participate effectively in the cultural, social, economic and political life of the country in which they live, in order to protect them from any form of racism, racial discrimination, xenophobia and related intolerance that they are or may be subjected to;

48. *Urges* States to recognize the effect that discrimination, marginalization and social exclusion have had and continue to have on many racial groups living in a numerically based minority situation within a State, and to ensure that persons in such groups can

exercise, as individual members of such groups, fully and effectively, all human rights and fundamental freedoms without distinction and in full equality before the law, and to take, where applicable, appropriate measures in respect of employment, housing and education with a view to preventing racial discrimination;

49. *Urges* States to take, where applicable, appropriate measures to prevent racial discrimination against persons belonging to national or ethnic, religious and linguistic minorities in respect of employment, health care, housing, social services and education, and in this context forms of multiple discrimination should be taken into account;

50. *Urges* States to incorporate a gender perspective in all programmes of action against racism, racial discrimination, xenophobia and related intolerance and to consider the burden of such discrimination which falls particularly on indigenous women, African women, Asian women, women of African descent, women of Asian descent, women migrants and women from other disadvantaged groups, ensuring their access to the resources of production on an equal footing with men, as a means of promoting their participation in the economic and productive development of their communities;

51. *Urges* States to involve women, especially women victims of racism, racial discrimination, xenophobia and related intolerance, in decision-making at all levels when working towards the eradication of such discrimination, and to develop concrete measures to incorporate race and gender analysis in the implementation of all aspects of the Programme of Action and national plans of action, particularly in the fields of employment programmes and services and resource allocation;

52. *Recognizing* that poverty shapes economic and social status and establishes obstacles to the effective political participation of women and men in different ways and to different extents, *urges* States to undertake gender analyses of all economic and social policies and programmes, especially poverty eradication measures, including those designed and implemented to benefit those individuals or groups of individuals who are victims of racism, racial discrimination, xenophobia and related intolerance;

53. *Urges* States and encourages all sectors of society to empower women and girls who are victims of racism, racial discrimination, xenophobia and related intolerance, so that they can fully exercise their rights in all spheres of public and private life, and to ensure the full, equal and effective participation of women in decision-making at all levels, in particular in the design, implementation and evaluation of policies and measures which affect their lives;

54. *Urges* States:

    (a) To recognize that sexual violence which has been systematically used as a weapon of war, sometimes with the acquiescence or at the instigation of the State, is a serious violation of international humanitarian law that, in defined circumstances, constitutes a crime against humanity and/or a war crime, and that the intersection of discrimination on grounds of race and gender makes women and girls particularly vulnerable to this type of violence, which is often related to racism, racial discrimination, xenophobia and related intolerance;

    (b) To end impunity and prosecute those responsible for crimes against humanity and war crimes, including crimes related to sexual and other gender-based violence against women and girls, as well as to ensure that persons in authority who are responsible for such crimes, including by committing, ordering, soliciting, inducing, aiding in, abetting, assisting or in any other way contributing to their

commission or attempted commission, are identified, investigated, prosecuted and punished;

55. *Requests* States, in collaboration where necessary with international organizations, having the best interests of the child as a primary consideration, to provide protection against racism, racial discrimination, xenophobia and related intolerance against children, especially those in circumstances of particular vulnerability, and to pay special attention to the situation of such children when designing relevant policies, strategies and programmes;

56. *Urges* States, in accordance with their national law and their obligations under the relevant international instruments, to take all measures to the maximum extent of their available resources to guarantee, without any discrimination, the equal right of all children to the immediate registration of birth, in order to enable them to exercise their human rights and fundamental freedoms. States shall grant women equal rights with men with respect to nationality;

57. *Urges* States and international and regional organizations, and encourages non-governmental organizations and the private sector, to address the situation of persons with disabilities who are also subject to racism, racial discrimination, xenophobia and related intolerance; also urges States to take necessary measures to ensure their full enjoyment of all human rights and to facilitate their full integration into all fields of life;

III. MEASURES OF PREVENTION, EDUCATION AND PROTECTION AIMED AT THE ERADICATION OF RACISM, RACIAL DISCRIMINATION, XENOPHOBIA AND RELATED INTOLERANCE AT THE NATIONAL, REGIONAL AND INTERNATIONAL LEVELS

58. *Urges* States to adopt and implement, at both the national and international levels, effective measures and policies, in addition to existing anti-discrimination national legislation and relevant international instruments and mechanisms, which encourage all citizens and institutions to take a stand against racism, racial discrimination, xenophobia and related intolerance, and to recognize, respect and maximize the benefits of diversity within and among all nations in working together to build a harmonious and productive future by putting into practice and promoting values and principles such as justice, equality and non-discrimination, democracy, fairness and friendship, tolerance and respect within and between communities and nations, in particular through public information and education programmes to raise awareness and understanding of the benefits of cultural diversity, including programmes where the public authorities work in partnership with international and non-governmental organizations and other sectors of civil society;

59. *Urges* States to mainstream a gender perspective in the design and development of measures of prevention, education and protection aimed at the eradication of racism, racial discrimination, xenophobia and related intolerance at all levels, to ensure that they effectively target the distinct situations of women and men;

60. *Urges* States to adopt or strengthen, as appropriate, national programmes for eradicating poverty and reducing social exclusion which take account of the needs and experiences of individuals or groups of individuals who are victims of racism, racial discrimination, xenophobia and related intolerance, and also urges that they expand their efforts to foster bilateral, regional and international cooperation in implementing those programmes;

61. *Urges* States to work to ensure that their political and legal systems reflect the multicultural diversity within their societies and, where necessary, to improve democratic institutions so that they are more fully participatory and avoid marginalization, exclusion and discrimination against specific sectors of society;

62. *Urges* States to take all necessary measures to address specifically, through policies and programmes, racism and racially motivated violence against women and girls and to increase cooperation, policy responses and effective implementation of national legislation and of their obligations under relevant international instruments, and other protective and preventive measures aimed at the elimination of all forms of racially motivated discrimination and violence against women and girls;

63. *Encourages* the business sector, in particular the tourist industry and Internet providers, to develop codes of conduct, with a view to preventing trafficking in persons and protecting the victims of such traffic, especially those in prostitution, against gender-based and racial discrimination and promoting their rights, dignity and security;

64. *Urges* States to devise, enforce and strengthen effective measures at the national, regional and international levels to prevent, combat and eliminate all forms of trafficking in women and children, in particular girls, through comprehensive anti-trafficking strategies which include legislative measures, prevention campaigns and information exchange. It also urges States to allocate resources, as appropriate, to provide comprehensive programmes designed to provide assistance to, protection for, healing, reintegration into society and rehabilitation of victims. States shall provide or strengthen training for law enforcement, immigration and other relevant officials who deal with victims of trafficking in this regard;

65. *Encourages* the bodies, agencies and relevant programmes of the United Nations system and States to promote and to make use of the Guiding Principles on Internal Displacement (E/CN.4/1998/53/Add.2), particularly those provisions relating to non-discrimination;

A. National level

1. *Legislative, judicial, regulatory, administrative and other measures to prevent and protect against racism, racial discrimination, xenophobia and related intolerance*

66. *Urges* States to establish and implement without delay national policies and action plans to combat racism, racial discrimination, xenophobia and related intolerance, including their gender-based manifestations;

67. *Urges* States to design or reinforce, promote and implement effective legislative and administrative policies, as well as other preventive measures, against the serious situation experienced by certain groups of workers, including migrant workers, who are victims of racism, racial discrimination, xenophobia and related intolerance. Special attention should be given to protecting people engaged in domestic work and trafficked persons from discrimination and violence, as well as to combating prejudice against them;

68. *Urges* States to adopt and implement, or strengthen, national legislation and administrative measures that expressly and specifically counter racism and prohibit racial discrimination, xenophobia and related intolerance, whether direct or indirect, in all spheres of public life, in accordance with their obligations under the International Convention on the Elimination of All Forms of Racial Discrimination, ensuring that their reservations are not contrary to the object and purpose of the Convention;

69. *Urges* States to enact and implement, as appropriate, laws against trafficking in persons, especially women and children, and smuggling of migrants, taking into account practices that endanger human lives or lead to various kinds of servitude and exploitation, such as debt bondage, slavery, sexual exploitation or labour exploitation; also encourages States to create, if they do not already exist, mechanisms to combat such practices and to allocate adequate resources to ensure law enforcement and the protection of the rights of victims, and to reinforce bilateral, regional and international cooperation, including with non-governmental organizations that assist victims, to combat this trafficking in persons and smuggling of migrants;

70. *Urges* States to take all necessary constitutional, legislative and administrative measures to foster equality among individuals and groups of individuals who are victims of racism, racial discrimination, xenophobia and related intolerance, and to review existing measures with a view to amending or repealing national legislation and administrative provisions that may give rise to such forms of discrimination;

71. *Urges* States, including their law enforcement agencies, to design and fully implement effective policies and programmes to prevent, detect and ensure accountability for misconduct by police officers and other law enforcement personnel which is motivated by racism, racial discrimination, xenophobia and related intolerance, and to prosecute perpetrators of such misconduct;

72. *Urges* States to design, implement and enforce effective measures to eliminate the phenomenon popularly known as 'racial profiling' and comprising the practice of police and other law enforcement officers relying, to any degree, on race, colour, descent or national or ethnic origin as the basis for subjecting persons to investigatory activities or for determining whether an individual is engaged in criminal activity;

73. *Urges* States to take measures to prevent genetic research or its applications from being used to promote racism, racial discrimination, xenophobia and related intolerance, to protect the privacy of personal genetic information and to prevent such information from being used for discriminatory or racist purposes;

74. *Urges* States and invites non-governmental organizations and the private sector:

   (a) To create and implement policies that promote a high-quality and diverse police force free from racism, racial discrimination, xenophobia and related intolerance, and recruit actively all groups, including minorities, into public employment, including the police force and other agencies within the criminal justice system (such as prosecutors);

   (b) To work to reduce violence, including violence motivated by racism, racial discrimination, xenophobia and related intolerance, by:

   (i) Developing educational materials to teach young people the importance of tolerance and respect;

   (ii) Addressing bias before it manifests itself in violent criminal activity;

   (iii) Establishing working groups consisting of, among others, local community leaders and national and local law enforcement officials, to improve coordination, community involvement, training, education and data collection, with the aim of preventing such violent criminal activity;

   (iv) Ensuring that civil rights laws that prohibit violent criminal activity are strongly enforced;

   (v) Enhancing data collection regarding violence motivated by racism, racial discrimination, xenophobia and related intolerance;

(vi) Providing appropriate assistance to victims, and public education to prevent future incidents of violence motivated by racism, racial discrimination, xenophobia and related intolerance;

Ratification of and effective implementation of relevant international and regional legal instruments on human rights and non-discrimination

75. *Urges* States that have not yet done so to consider ratifying or acceding to the international human rights instruments which combat racism, racial discrimination, xenophobia and related intolerance, in particular to accede to the International Convention on the Elimination of All Forms of Racial Discrimination as a matter of urgency, with a view to universal ratification by the year 2005, and to consider making the declaration envisaged under article 14, to comply with their reporting obligations, and to publish and act upon the concluding observations of the Committee on the Elimination of Racial Discrimination. It also urges States to withdraw reservations contrary to the object and purpose of that Convention and to consider withdrawing other reservations;

76. *Urges* States to give due consideration to the observations and recommendations of the Committee on the Elimination of Racial Discrimination. To that effect, States should consider setting up appropriate national monitoring and evaluation mechanisms to ensure that all appropriate steps are taken to follow up on these observations and recommendations;

77. *Urges* States that have not yet done so to consider becoming parties to the International Covenant on Economic, Social and Cultural Rights and the International Covenant on Civil and Political Rights, as well as to consider acceding to the Optional Protocols to the International Covenant on Civil and Political Rights;

78. *Urges* those States that have not yet done so to consider signing and ratifying or acceding to the following instruments:

(a) Convention on the Prevention and Punishment of the Crime of Genocide of 1948;

(b) International Labour Organization Migration for Employment Convention (Revised), 1949 (No. 97);

(c) Convention for the Suppression of the Traffic in Persons and of the Exploitation of the Prostitution of Others of 1949;

(d) Convention relating to the Status of Refugees of 1951, and its 1967 Protocol;

(e) International Labour Organization Discrimination (Employment and Occupation) Convention, 1958 (No. 111);

(f) Convention against Discrimination in Education, adopted on 14 December 1960 by the General Conference of the United Nations Educational, Scientific and Cultural Organization;

(g) Convention on the Elimination of All Forms of Discrimination against Women of 1979, with a view to achieving universal ratification within five years, and its Optional Protocol of 1999;

(h) Convention on the Rights of the Child of 1989 and its two Optional Protocols of 2000, and the International Labour Organization Minimum Age Convention, 1973 (No. 138) and Worst Forms of Child Labour Convention, 1999 (No. 182);

(i) International Labour Organization Migrant Workers (Supplementary Provisions) Convention, 1975 (No. 143);

(j) International Labour Organization Indigenous and Tribal Peoples Convention, 1989 (No. 169) and the Convention on Biological Diversity of 1992;

(k) International Convention on the Protection of the Rights of All Migrant Workers and Members of Their Families of 1990;

(l) The Rome Statute of the International Criminal Court of 1998;

(m) United Nations Convention against Transnational Organized Crime, the Protocol to Prevent, Suppress and Punish Trafficking in Persons, Especially Women and Children, supplementing the Convention and the Protocol against the Smuggling of Migrants by Land, Sea and Air, supplementing the Convention of 2000;

It further urges States parties to these instruments to implement them fully;

79. *Calls upon* States to promote and protect the exercise of the rights set out in the Declaration on the Elimination of All Forms of Intolerance and of Discrimination Based on Religion or Belief, proclaimed by the General Assembly in its resolution 36/55 of 25 November 1981, in order to obviate religious discrimination which, when combined with certain other forms of discrimination, constitutes a form of multiple discrimination;

80. *Urges* States to seek full respect for, and compliance with, the Vienna Convention on Consular Relations of 1963, especially as it relates to the right of foreign nationals, regardless of their legal and immigration status, to communicate with a consular officer of their own State in the case of arrest or detention;

81. *Urges* all States to prohibit discriminatory treatment based on race, colour, descent or national or ethnic origin against foreigners and migrant workers, *inter alia*, where appropriate, concerning the granting of work visas and work permits, housing, health care and access to justice;

82. *Underlines* the importance of combating impunity, including for crimes with a racist or xenophobic motivation, also at the international level, noting that impunity for violations of human rights and international humanitarian law is a serious obstacle to a fair and equitable justice system and, ultimately, reconciliation and stability; it also fully supports the work of the existing international criminal tribunals and ratification of the Rome Statute of the International Criminal Court, and urges all States to cooperate with these international criminal tribunals;

83. *Urges* States to make every effort to apply fully the relevant provisions of the International Labour Organization Declaration on Fundamental Principles and Rights at Work of 1998, in order to combat racism, racial discrimination, xenophobia and related intolerance;

Prosecution of perpetrators of racist acts

84. *Urges* States to adopt effective measures to combat criminal acts motivated by racism, racial discrimination, xenophobia and related intolerance, to take measures so that such motivations are considered an aggravating factor for the purposes of sentencing, to prevent these crimes from going unpunished and to ensure the rule of law;

85. *Urges* States to undertake investigations to examine possible links between criminal prosecution, police violence and penal sanctions, on the one hand, and racism, racial discrimination, xenophobia and related intolerance, on the other, so as to have evidence for taking the necessary steps for the eradication of any such links and discriminatory practices;

86. *Calls upon* States to promote measures to deter the emergence of and to counter neo-fascist, violent nationalist ideologies which promote racial hatred and racial discrimination, as well as racist and xenophobic sentiments, including measures to combat the negative influence of such ideologies especially on young people through formal and non-formal education, the media and sport;

87. *Urges* States parties to adopt legislation implementing the obligations they have assumed to prosecute and punish persons who have committed or ordered to be committed grave breaches of the Geneva Conventions of 12 August 1949 and Additional Protocol I thereto and of other serious violations of the laws and customs of war, in particular in relation to the principle of non-discrimination;

88. *Calls upon* States to criminalize all forms of trafficking in persons, in particular women and children, and to condemn and penalize traffickers and intermediaries, while ensuring protection and assistance to the victims of trafficking, with full respect for their human rights;

89. *Urges* States to carry out comprehensive, exhaustive, timely and impartial investigations of all unlawful acts of racism and racial discrimination, to prosecute criminal offences *ex officio*, as appropriate, or initiate or facilitate all appropriate actions arising from offences of a racist or xenophobic nature, to ensure that criminal and civil investigations and prosecutions of offences of a racist or xenophobic nature are given high priority and are actively and consistently undertaken, and to ensure the right to equal treatment before the tribunals and all other organs administering justice. In this regard, the World Conference underlines the importance of fostering awareness and providing training to the various agents in the criminal justice system to ensure fair and impartial application of the law. In this respect, it recommends that anti-discrimination monitoring services be established;

Establishment and reinforcement of independent specialized national institutions and mediation

90. *Urges* States, as appropriate, to establish, strengthen, review and reinforce the effectiveness of independent national human rights institutions, particularly on issues of racism, racial discrimination, xenophobia and related intolerance, in conformity with the Principles relating to the status of national institutions for the promotion and protection of human rights, annexed to General Assembly resolution 48/134 of 20 December 1993, and to provide them with adequate financial resources, competence and capacity for investigation, research, education and public awareness activities to combat these phenomena;

91. *Also urges* States:

(a) To foster cooperation between these institutions and other national institutions;

(b) To take steps to ensure that those individuals or groups of individuals who are victims of racism, racial discrimination, xenophobia and related intolerance can participate fully in these institutions;

(c) To support these institutions and similar bodies, *inter alia* through the publication and circulation of existing national laws and jurisprudence, and cooperation with institutions in other countries, so that knowledge can be gained of the manifestations, functions and mechanisms of these practices and the strategies designed to prevent, combat and eradicate them;

2. *Policies and practices*

Data collection and disaggregation, research and study

92. *Urges* States to collect, compile, analyse, disseminate and publish reliable statistical data at the national and local levels and undertake all other related measures which are necessary to assess regularly the situation of individuals and groups of individuals who are victims of racism, racial discrimination, xenophobia and related intolerance;

    (a) Such statistical data should be disaggregated in accordance with national legislation. Any such information shall, as appropriate, be collected with the explicit consent of the victims, based on their self-identification and in accordance with provisions on human rights and fundamental freedoms, such as data protection regulations and privacy guarantees. This information must not be misused;

    (b) The statistical data and information should be collected with the objective of monitoring the situation of marginalized groups, and the development and evaluation of legislation, policies, practices and other measures aimed at preventing and combating racism, racial discrimination, xenophobia and related intolerance, as well as for the purpose of determining whether any measures have an unintentional disparate impact on victims. To that end, it recommends the development of voluntary, consensual and participatory strategies in the process of collecting, designing and using information;

    (c) The information should take into account economic and social indicators, including, where appropriate, health and health status, infant and maternal mortality, life expectancy, literacy, education, employment, housing, land ownership, mental and physical health care, water, sanitation, energy and communications services, poverty and average disposable income, in order to elaborate social and economic development policies with a view to closing the existing gaps in social and economic conditions;

93. *Invites* States, intergovernmental organizations, non-governmental organizations, academic institutions and the private sector to improve concepts and methods of data collection and analysis; to promote research, exchange experiences and successful practices and develop promotional activities in this area; and to develop indicators of progress and participation of individuals and groups of individuals in society subject to racism, racial discrimination, xenophobia and related intolerance;

94. *Recognizes* that policies and programmes aimed at combating racism, racial discrimination, xenophobia and related intolerance should be based on quantitative and qualitative research, incorporating a gender perspective. Such policies and programmes should take into account priorities identified by individuals and groups of individuals who are victims of, or subject to, racism, racial discrimination, xenophobia and related intolerance;

95. *Urges* States to establish regular monitoring of acts of racism, racial discrimination, xenophobia and related intolerance in the public and private sectors, including those committed by law enforcement officials;

96. *Invites* States to promote and conduct studies and adopt an integral, objective and long-term approach to all phases and aspects of migration which will deal effectively with both its causes and manifestations. These studies and approaches should pay special attention to the root causes of migratory flows, such as lack of full enjoyment of

human rights and fundamental freedoms, and the effects of economic globalization on migration trends;

97. *Recommends* that further studies be conducted on how racism, racial discrimination, xenophobia and related intolerance may be reflected in laws, policies, institutions and practices and how this may have contributed to the victimization and exclusion of migrants, especially women and children;

98. *Recommends* that States include where applicable in their periodic reports to United Nations human rights treaty bodies, in an appropriate form, statistical information relating to individuals, members of groups and communities within their jurisdiction, including statistical data on participation in political life and on their economic, social and cultural situation. All such information shall be collected in accordance with provisions on human rights and fundamental freedoms, such as data protection regulations and privacy guarantees;

Action-oriented policies and action plans, including affirmative action to ensure non-discrimination, in particular as regards access to social services, employment, housing, education, health care, etc.

99. *Recognizes* that combating racism, racial discrimination, xenophobia and related intolerance is a primary responsibility of States. It therefore encourages States to develop or elaborate national action plans to promote diversity, equality, equity, social justice, equality of opportunity and the participation of all. Through, among other things, affirmative or positive actions and strategies, these plans should aim at creating conditions for all to participate effectively in decision-making and realize civil, cultural, economic, political and social rights in all spheres of life on the basis of non-discrimination. The World Conference encourages States, in developing and elaborating such action plans, to establish, or reinforce, dialogue with non-governmental organizations in order to involve them more closely in designing, implementing and evaluating policies and programmes;

100. *Urges* States to establish, on the basis of statistical information, national programmes, including affirmative or positive measures, to promote the access of individuals and groups of individuals who are or may be victims of racial discrimination to basic social services, including primary education, basic health care and adequate housing;

101. *Urges* States to establish programmes to promote the access without discrimination of individuals or groups of individuals who are victims of racism, racial discrimination, xenophobia and related intolerance to health care, and to promote strong efforts to eliminate disparities, *inter alia* in the infant and maternal mortality rates, childhood immunizations, HIV/AIDS, heart diseases, cancer and contagious diseases;

102. *Urges* States to promote residential integration of all members of the society at the planning stage of urban development schemes and other human settlements, as well as while renewing neglected areas of public housing, so as to counter social exclusion and marginalization;

Employment

103. *Urges* States to promote and support where appropriate the organization and operation of enterprises owned by persons who are victims of racism, racial discrimination, xenophobia and related intolerance by promoting equal access to credit and to training programmes;

104. *Urges* States and encourages non-governmental organizations and the private sector:

(a) To support the creation of workplaces free of discrimination through a multifaceted strategy that includes civil rights enforcement, public education and communication within the workplace, and to promote and protect the rights of workers who are subject to racism, racial discrimination, xenophobia and related intolerance;

(b) To foster the creation, growth and expansion of businesses dedicated to improving economic and educational conditions in underserved and disadvantaged areas, by increasing access to capital through, *inter alia*, community development banks, recognizing that new businesses can have a positive, dynamic impact on communities in need, and to work with the private sector to create jobs, help retain existing jobs and stimulate industrial and commercial growth in economically distressed areas;

(c) To improve the prospects of targeted groups facing, *inter alia*, the greatest obstacles in finding, keeping or regaining work, including skilled employment. Particular attention should be paid to persons subject to multiple discrimination;

105. *Urges* States to give special attention, when devising and implementing legislation and policies designed to enhance the protection of workers' rights, to the serious situation of lack of protection, and in some cases exploitation, as in the case of trafficked persons and smuggled migrants, which makes them more vulnerable to ill-treatment such as confinement in the case of domestic workers and also being employed in dangerous and poorly paid jobs;

106. *Urges* States to avoid the negative effects of discriminatory practices, racism and xenophobia in employment and occupation by promoting the application and observance of international instruments and norms on workers' rights;

107. *Calls upon* States and encourages representative trade unions and the business sector to advance non-discriminatory practices in the workplace and protect the rights of workers, including, in particular, the victims of racism, racial discrimination, xenophobia and related intolerance;

108. *Calls upon* States to provide effective access to administrative and legal procedures and other remedial action to victims of racism, racial discrimination, xenophobia and related intolerance in the workplace;

Health, environment

109. *Urges* States, individually and through international cooperation, to enhance measures to fulfil the right of everyone to the enjoyment of the highest attainable standard of physical and mental health, with a view to eliminating disparities in health status, as indicated in standard health indexes, which might result from racism, racial discrimination, xenophobia and related intolerance;

110. *Urges* States and encourages non-governmental organizations and the private sector:

(a) To provide effective mechanisms for monitoring and eliminating racism, racial discrimination, xenophobia and related intolerance in the health-care system, such as the development and enforcement of effective anti-discrimination laws;

(b) To take steps to ensure equal access to comprehensive, quality health care afford-able for all, including primary health care for medically underserved people, facilitate the training of a health workforce that is both diverse and motivated to work in underserved communities, and work to increase diversity in the health-care profession by recruiting on merit and potential women and men from all groups, representing the diversity of their societies, for health-care careers and by retaining them in the health professions;

(c) To work with health-care professionals, community-based health providers, non-governmental organizations, scientific researchers and private industry as a means of improving the health status of marginalized communities, in particular victims of racism, racial discrimination, xenophobia and related intolerance;

(d) To work with health professionals, scientific researchers and international and regional health organizations to study the differential impact of medical treat-ments and health strategies on various communities;

(e) To adopt and implement policies and programmes to improve HIV/AIDS pre-vention efforts in high-risk communities and work to expand availability of HIV/AIDS care, treatment and other support services;

111. *Invites* States to consider non-discriminatory measures to provide a safe and healthy environment for individuals and groups of individuals victims of or subject to racism, racial discrimination, xenophobia and related intolerance, and in particular:

(a) To improve access to public information on health and environment issues;

(b) To ensure that relevant concerns are taken into account in the public process of decision-making on the environment;

(c) To share technology and successful practices to improve human health and envi-ronment in all areas;

(d) To take appropriate remedial measures, as possible, to clean, re-use and redevelop contaminated sites and, where appropriate, relocate those affected on a voluntary basis after consultations;

Equal participation in political, economic, social and cultural decision-making

112. *Urges* States and encourages the private sector and international financial and development institutions, such as the World Bank and regional development banks, to promote participation of individuals and groups of individuals who are victims of rac-ism, racial discrimination, xenophobia and related intolerance in economic, cultural and social decision-making at all stages, particularly in the development and implementation of poverty alleviation strategies, development projects, and trade and market assistance programmes;

113. *Urges* States to promote, as appropriate, effective and equal access of all members of the community, especially those who are victims of racism, racial discrimination, xenophobia and related intolerance, to the decision-making process in society at all levels and in particular at the local level, and also urges States and encourages the private sec-tor to facilitate their effective participation in economic life;

114. *Urges* all multilateral financial and development institutions, in particular the World Bank, the International Monetary Fund, the World Trade Organization and regional development banks, to promote, in accordance with their regular budgets and the procedures of their governing bodies, participation by all members of the international

community in decision-making processes at all stages and levels in order to facilitate development projects and, as appropriate, trade and market access programmes;

Role of politicians and political parties

115. *Underlines* the key role that politicians and political parties can play in combating racism, racial discrimination, xenophobia and related intolerance and encourages political parties to take concrete steps to promote equality, solidarity and non-discrimination in society, *inter alia* by developing voluntary codes of conduct which include internal disciplinary measures for violations thereof, so their members refrain from public statements and actions that encourage or incite racism, racial discrimination, xenophobia and related intolerance;

116. *Invites* the Inter-Parliamentary Union to encourage debate in, and action by, parliaments on various measures, including laws and policies, to combat racism, racial discrimination, xenophobia and related intolerance;

3. Education and awareness-raising measures

117. *Urges* States, where appropriate working with other relevant bodies, to commit financial resources to anti-racism education and to media campaigns promoting the values of acceptance, tolerance, diversity and respect for the cultures of all indigenous peoples living within their national borders. In particular, States should promote an accurate understanding of the histories and cultures of indigenous peoples;

118. *Urges* the United Nations, other appropriate international and regional organizations and States to redress the marginalization of Africa's contribution to world history and civilization by developing and implementing a specific and comprehensive programme of research, education and mass communication to disseminate widely a balanced and objective presentation of Africa's seminal and valuable contribution to humanity;

119. *Invites* States and relevant international organizations and non-governmental organizations to build upon the efforts of the Slave Route Project of the United Nations Educational Scientific and Cultural Organization and its theme of 'Breaking the silence' by developing texts and testimony, slavery multi-media centres and/or programmes that will collect, record, organize, exhibit and publish the existing data relevant to the history of slavery and the trans-Atlantic, Mediterranean and Indian Ocean slave trades, paying particular attention to the thoughts and actions of the victims of slavery and the slave trade, in their quest for freedom and justice;

120. *Salutes* the efforts of the United Nations Educational, Scientific and Cultural Organization made within the framework of the Slave Route Project and requests that the outcome be made available to the international community as soon as possible;

Access to education without discrimination

121. *Urges* States to commit themselves to ensuring access to education, including access to free primary education for all children, both girls and boys, and access for adults to lifelong learning and education, based on respect for human rights, diversity and tolerance, without discrimination of any kind;

122. *Urges* States to ensure equal access to education for all in law and in practice, and to refrain from any legal or any other measures leading to imposed racial segregation in any form in access to schooling;

123. *Urges* States:

(a) To adopt and implement laws that prohibit discrimination on the basis of race, colour, descent or national or ethnic origin at all levels of education, both formal and non-formal;

(b) To take all appropriate measures to eliminate obstacles limiting the access of children to education;

(c) To ensure that all children have access without discrimination to education of good quality;

(d) To establish and implement standardized methods to measure and track the educational performance of disadvantaged children and young people;

(e) To commit resources to eliminate, where they exist, inequalities in educational outcomes for children and young people;

(f) To support efforts to ensure safe school environments, free from violence and harassment motivated by racism, racial discrimination, xenophobia or related intolerance; and

(g) To consider establishing financial assistance programmes designed to enable all students, regardless of race, colour, descent or ethnic or national origin, to attend institutions of higher education;

124. *Urges* States to adopt, where applicable, appropriate measures to ensure that persons belonging to national or ethnic, religious and linguistic minorities have access to education without discrimination of any kind and, where possible, have an opportunity to learn their own language in order to protect them from any form of racism, racial discrimination, xenophobia and related intolerance that they may be subjected to;

Human rights education

125. *Requests* States to include the struggle against racism, racial discrimination, xenophobia and related intolerance among the activities undertaken within the framework of the United Nations Decade for Human Rights Education (1995–2004) and to take into account the recommendations of the mid-term evaluation report of the Decade;

126. *Encourages* all States, in cooperation with the United Nations, the United Nations Educational, Scientific and Cultural Organization and other relevant international organizations, to initiate and develop cultural and educational programmes aimed at countering racism, racial discrimination, xenophobia and related intolerance, in order to ensure respect for the dignity and worth of all human beings and enhance mutual understanding among all cultures and civilizations. It further urges States to support and implement public information campaigns and specific training programmes in the field of human rights, where appropriate formulated in local languages, to combat racism, racial discrimination, xenophobia and related intolerance and promote respect for the values of diversity, pluralism, tolerance, mutual respect, cultural sensitivity, integration and inclusiveness. Such programmes and campaigns should be addressed to all sectors of society, in particular children and young people;

127. *Urges* States to intensify their efforts in the field of education, including human rights education, in order to promote an understanding and awareness of the causes, consequences and evils of racism, racial discrimination, xenophobia and related intolerance, and also urges States, in consultation with educational authorities and the private sector, as appropriate, and encourages educational authorities and the private sector,

as appropriate, to develop educational materials, including textbooks and dictionaries, aimed at combating those phenomena and, in this context, calls upon States to give importance, if appropriate, to textbook and curriculum review and amendment, so as to eliminate any elements that might promote racism, racial discrimination, xenophobia and related intolerance or reinforce negative stereotypes, and to include material that refutes such stereotypes;

128. *Urges* States, if appropriate in cooperation with relevant organizations, including youth organizations, to support and implement public formal and non-formal education programmes designed to promote respect for cultural diversity;

Human rights education for children and youth

129. *Urges* States to introduce and, as applicable, to reinforce anti-discrimination and anti-racism components in human rights programmes in school curricula, to develop and improve relevant educational material, including history and other textbooks, and to ensure that all teachers are effectively trained and adequately motivated to shape attitudes and behavioural patterns, based on the principles of non-discrimination, mutual respect and tolerance;

130. *Calls upon* States to undertake and facilitate activities aimed at educating young people in human rights and democratic citizenship and instilling values of solidarity, respect and appreciation of diversity, including respect for different groups. A special effort to inform and sensitize young people to respect democratic values and human rights should be undertaken or developed to fight against ideologies based on the fallacious theory of racial superiority;

131. *Urges* States to encourage all schools to consider developing educational activities, including extracurricular ones, to raise awareness against racism, racial discrimination, xenophobia and related intolerance, *inter alia* by commemorating the International Day for the Elimination of Racial Discrimination (21 March);

132. *Recommends* that States introduce, or reinforce, human rights education, with a view to combating prejudices which lead to racial discrimination and to promoting understanding, tolerance and friendship between different racial or ethnic groups, in schools and in institutions of higher education, and support public formal and non-formal education programmes designed to promote respect for cultural diversity and the self-esteem of victims;

Human rights education for public officials and professionals

133. *Urges* States to develop and strengthen anti-racist and gender-sensitive human rights training for public officials, including personnel in the administration of justice, particularly in law enforcement, correctional and security services, as well as among health-care, schools and migration authorities;

134. *Urges* States to pay specific attention to the negative impact of racism, racial discrimination, xenophobia and related intolerance on the administration of justice and fair trial, and to conduct nationwide campaigns, amongst other measures, to raise awareness among State organs and public officials concerning their obligations under the International Convention on the Elimination of All Forms of Racial Discrimination and other relevant instruments;

135. *Requests* States, wherever appropriate through cooperation with international organizations, national institutions, non-governmental organizations and the private

sector, to organize and facilitate training activities, including courses or seminars, on international norms prohibiting racial discrimination and their applicability in domestic law, as well as on their international human rights obligations, for prosecutors, members of the judiciary and other public officials;

136. *Calls upon* States to ensure that education and training, especially teacher training, promote respect for human rights and the fight against racism, racial discrimination, xenophobia and related intolerance and that educational institutions implement policies and programmes agreed by the relevant authorities on equal opportunities, anti-racism, gender equality, and cultural, religious and other diversity, with the participation of teachers, parents and students, and follow up their implementation. It further urges all educators, including teachers at all levels of education, religious communities and the print and electronic media, to play an effective role in human rights education, including as a means to combat racism, racial discrimination, xenophobia and related intolerance;

137. *Encourages* States to consider taking measures to increase the recruitment, retention and promotion of women and men belonging to groups which are currently under-represented in the teaching profession as a result of racism, racial discrimination, xenophobia and related intolerance, and to guarantee them effective equality of access to the profession. Particular efforts should be made to recruit women and men who have the ability to interact effectively with all groups;

138. *Urges* States to strengthen the human rights training and awareness-raising activities designed for immigration officials, border police and staff of detention centres and prisons, local authorities and other civil servants in charge of enforcing laws, as well as teachers, with particular attention to the human rights of migrants, refugees and asylum-seekers, in order to prevent acts of racial discrimination and xenophobia and to avoid situations where prejudices lead to decisions based on racism, racial discrimination, xenophobia or related intolerance;

139. *Urges* States to provide or strengthen training for law enforcement, immigration and other relevant officials in the prevention of trafficking in persons. The training should focus on methods used in preventing such trafficking, prosecuting the traffickers and protecting the rights of victims, including protecting the victims from the traffickers. The training should also take into account the need to consider human rights and child- and gender-sensitive issues and it should encourage cooperation with non-governmental organizations, other relevant organizations and other elements of civil society;

4. Information, communication and the media, including new technologies

140. *Welcomes* the positive contribution made by the new information and communications technologies, including the Internet, in combating racism through rapid and wide-reaching communication;

141. *Draws attention* to the potential to increase the use of the new information and communications technologies, including the Internet, to create educational and awareness-raising networks against racism, racial discrimination, xenophobia and related intolerance, both in and out of school, as well as the ability of the Internet to promote universal respect for human rights and also respect for the value of cultural diversity;

142. *Emphasizes* the importance of recognizing the value of cultural diversity and of putting in place concrete measures to encourage the access of marginalized communities to the mainstream and alternative media through, *inter alia*, the presentation of programmes that reflect their cultures and languages;

143. *Expresses concern* at the material progression of racism, racial discrimination, xenophobia and related intolerance, including their contemporary forms and manifestations, such as the use of the new information and communications technologies, including the Internet, to disseminate ideas of racial superiority;

144. *Urges* States and encourages the private sector to promote the development by the media, including the print and electronic media, including the Internet and advertising, taking into account their independence, through their relevant associations and organizations at the national, regional and international levels, of a voluntary ethical code of conduct and self-regulatory measures, and of policies and practices aimed at:

  (a) Combating racism, racial discrimination, xenophobia and related intolerance;

  (b) Promoting the fair, balanced and equitable representation of the diversity of their societies, as well as ensuring that this diversity is reflected among their staff;

  (c) Combating the proliferation of ideas of racial superiority, justification of racial hatred and discrimination in any form;

  (d) Promoting respect, tolerance and understanding among all individuals, peoples, nations and civilizations, for example through assistance in public awareness-raising campaigns;

  (e) Avoiding stereotyping in all its forms, and particularly the promotion of false images of migrants, including migrant workers, and refugees, in order to prevent the spread of xenophobic sentiments among the public and to encourage the objective and balanced portrayal of people, events and history;

145. *Urges* States to implement legal sanctions, in accordance with relevant international human rights law, in respect of incitement to racial hatred through new information and communications technologies, including the Internet, and further urges them to apply all relevant human rights instruments to which they are parties, in particular the International Convention on the Elimination of All Forms of Racial Discrimination, to racism on the Internet;

146. *Urges* States to encourage the media to avoid stereotyping based on racism, racial discrimination, xenophobia and related intolerance;

147. *Calls upon* States to consider the following, taking fully into account existing international and regional standards on freedom of expression, while taking all necessary measures to guarantee the right to freedom of opinion and expression:

  (a) Encouraging Internet service providers to establish and disseminate specific voluntary codes of conduct and self-regulatory measures against the dissemination of racist messages and those that result in racial discrimination, xenophobia or any form of intolerance and discrimination; to that end, Internet providers are encouraged to set up mediating bodies at national and international levels, involving relevant civil society institutions;

  (b) Adopting and applying, to the extent possible, appropriate legislation for prosecuting those responsible for incitement to racial hatred or violence through the new information and communications technologies, including the Internet;

  (c) Addressing the problem of dissemination of racist material through the new information and communications technologies, including the Internet, *inter alia* by imparting training to law enforcement authorities;

(d) Denouncing and actively discouraging the transmission of racist and xeno-phobic messages through all communications media, including new informa-tion and communications technologies, such as the Internet;

(e) Considering a prompt and coordinated international response to the rapidly evolving phenomenon of the dissemination of hate speech and racist material through the new information and communications technologies, including the Internet; and in this context strengthening international cooperation;

(f) Encouraging access and use by all people of the Internet as an international and equal forum, aware that there are disparities in use of and access to the Internet;

(g) Examining ways in which the positive contribution made by the new informa-tion and communications technologies, such as the Internet, can be enhanced through replication of good practices in combating racism, racial discrimina-tion, xenophobia and related intolerance;

(h) Encouraging the reflection of the diversity of societies among the personnel of media organizations and the new information and communications technolo-gies, such as the Internet, by promoting adequate representation of different segments within societies at all levels of their organizational structure;

B. International level

148. *Urges* all actors on the international scene to build an international order based on inclusion, justice, equality and equity, human dignity, mutual understanding and promotion of and respect for cultural diversity and universal human rights, and to reject all doctrines of exclusion based on racism, racial discrimination, xenophobia and related intolerance;

149. *Believes* that all conflicts and disputes should be resolved through peaceful means and political dialogue. The Conference calls on all parties involved in such conflicts to exercise restraint and to respect human rights and international humanitarian law;

150. *Calls upon* States, in opposing all forms of racism, to recognize the need to counter anti-Semitism, anti-Arabism and Islamophobia world-wide, and urges all States to take effective measures to prevent the emergence of movements based on racism and discrimi-natory ideas concerning these communities;

151. As for the situation in the Middle East, *calls for* the end of violence and the swift resumption of negotiations, respect for international human rights and humanitarian law, respect for the principle of self-determination and the end of all suffering, thus allow-ing Israel and the Palestinians to resume the peace process, and to develop and prosper in security and freedom;

152. *Encourages* States, regional and international organizations, including financial institutions, as well as civil society, to address within existing mechanisms, or where neces-sary to put in place and/or develop mechanisms, to address those aspects of globalization which may lead to racism, racial discrimination, xenophobia and related intolerance;

153. *Recommends* that the Department of Peacekeeping Operations of the Secretariat and other concerned United Nations agencies, bodies and programmes strengthen their coordination to discern patterns of serious violations of human rights and humanitarian law with a view to assessing the risk of further deterioration that could lead to genocide, war crimes or crimes against humanity;

154. *Encourages* the World Health Organization and other relevant international organizations to promote and develop activities for the recognition of the impact of racism, racial discrimination, xenophobia and related intolerance as significant social determinants of physical and mental health status, including the HIV/AIDS pandemic, and access to health care, and to prepare specific projects, including research, to ensure equitable health systems for the victims;

155. *Encourages* the International Labour Organization to carry out activities and programmes to combat racism, racial discrimination, xenophobia and related intolerance in the world of work, and to support actions of States, employers' organizations and trade unions in this field;

156. *Urges* the United Nations Educational, Scientific and Cultural Organization to provide support to States in the preparation of teaching materials and tools for promoting teaching, training and educational activities relating to human rights and the struggle against racism, racial discrimination, xenophobia and related intolerance;

IV. PROVISION OF EFFECTIVE REMEDIES, RECOURSE, REDRESS, AND OTHER MEASURES AT THE NATIONAL, REGIONAL AND INTERNATIONAL LEVELS

157. *Recognizes* the efforts of developing countries, in particular the commitment and the determination of the African leaders, to seriously address the challenges of poverty, underdevelopment, marginalization, social exclusion, economic disparities, instability and insecurity, through initiatives such as the New African Initiative and other innovative mechanisms such as the World Solidarity Fund for the Eradication of Poverty, and calls upon developed countries, the United Nations and its specialized agencies, as well as international financial institutions, to provide, through their operational programmes, new and additional financial resources, as appropriate, to support these initiatives;

158. *Recognizes* that these historical injustices have undeniably contributed to the poverty, underdevelopment, marginalization, social exclusion, economic disparities, instability and insecurity that affect many people in different parts of the world, in particular in developing countries. The Conference recognizes the need to develop programmes for the social and economic development of these societies and the Diaspora, within the framework of a new partnership based on the spirit of solidarity and mutual respect, in the following areas:

Debt relief;

Poverty eradication;

Building or strengthening democratic institutions;

Promotion of foreign direct investment;

Market access;

Intensifying efforts to meet the internationally agreed targets for official development assistance transfers to developing countries;

New information and communication technologies bridging the digital divide;

Agriculture and food security;

Transfer of technology;

Transparent and accountable governance;

Investment in health infrastructure tackling HIV/AIDS, tuberculosis and malaria, including through the Global AIDS and Health Fund;

Infrastructure development;

Human resource development, including capacity-building;

Education, training and cultural development;

Mutual legal assistance in the repatriation of illegally obtained and illegally transferred (stashed) funds, in accordance with national and international instruments;

Illicit traffic in small arms and light weapons;

Restitution of art objects, historical artefacts and documents to their countries of origin, in accordance with bilateral agreements or international instruments;

Trafficking in persons, particularly women and children;

Facilitation of welcomed return and resettlement of the descendants of enslaved Africans;

159. *Urges* international financial and development institutions and the operational programmes and specialized agencies of the United Nations to give greater priority to, and allocate appropriate funding for, programmes addressing the development challenges of the affected States and societies, in particular those on the African continent and in the Diaspora;

Legal assistance

160. *Urges* States to take all necessary measures to address, as a matter of urgency, the pressing requirement for justice for the victims of racism, racial discrimination, xenophobia and related intolerance and to ensure that victims have full access to information, support, effective protection and national, administrative and judicial remedies, including the right to seek just and adequate reparation or satisfaction for damage, as well as legal assistance, where required;

161. *Urges* States to facilitate for victims of racial discrimination, including victims of torture and ill-treatment, access to all appropriate legal procedures and free legal assistance in a manner adapted to their specific needs and vulnerability, including through legal representation;

162. *Urges* States to ensure the protection against victimization of complainants and witnesses of acts of racism, racial discrimination, xenophobia and related intolerance, and to consider measures such as, where appropriate, making legal assistance, including legal aid, available to complainants seeking a legal remedy and, if possible, affording the possibility for non-governmental organizations to support complainants of racism, with their consent, in legal procedures;

National legislation and programmes

163. For the purposes of effectively combating racism and racial discrimination, xenophobia and related intolerance in the civil, political, economic, social and cultural fields, the Conference *recommends* to all States that their national legislative framework should expressly and specifically prohibit racial discrimination and provide effective judicial and other remedies or redress, including through the designation of national, independent, specialized bodies;

164. *Urges* States, with regard to the procedural remedies provided for in their domestic law, to bear in mind the following considerations:

(a) Access to such remedies should be widely available, on a non-discriminatory and equal basis;

(b) Existing procedural remedies should be made known in the context of the relevant action, and victims of racial discrimination should be helped to avail themselves of them in accordance with the particular case;

(c) Inquiries into complaints of racial discrimination and the adjudication of such complaints must be carried out as rapidly as possible;

(d) Persons who are victims of racial discrimination should be accorded legal assistance and aid in complaint proceedings, where applicable free of charge, and, where necessary, should be provided with the help of competent interpreters in such complaint proceedings or in any civil or criminal cases arising therefrom or connected thereto;

(e) The creation of competent national bodies to investigate effectively allegations of racial discrimination and to give protection to complainants against intimidation or harassment is a desirable development and should be undertaken; steps should be taken towards the enactment of legislation to prohibit discriminatory practices on grounds of race, colour, descent, or national or ethnic origin, and to provide for the application of appropriate penalties against offenders and remedies, including adequate compensation, for the victims;

(f) Access to legal remedies should be facilitated for victims of discrimination and, in this regard, the innovation of conferring a capacity on national and other institutions, as well as relevant non-governmental organizations, to assist such victims should be seriously considered, and programmes should be developed to enable the most vulnerable groups to have access to the legal system;

(g) New and innovative methods and procedures of conflict resolution, mediation and conciliation between parties involved in conflicts or disputes based on racism, racial discrimination, xenophobia and related intolerance should be explored and, where possible, established;

(h) The development of restorative justice policies and programmes for the benefit of victims of relevant forms of discrimination is desirable and should be seriously considered;

(i) States which have made the declaration under article 14 of the International Convention on the Elimination of All Forms of Racial Discrimination should make increased efforts to inform their public of the existence of the complaints mechanism under article 14;

Remedies, reparations, compensation

165. *Urges* States to reinforce protection against racism, racial discrimination, xenophobia and related intolerance by ensuring that all persons have access to effective and adequate remedies and enjoy the right to seek from competent national tribunals and other national institutions just and adequate reparation and satisfaction for any damage as a result of such discrimination. It further underlines the importance of access to the law and to the courts for complainants of racism and racial discrimination and draws attention to the need for judicial and other remedies to be made widely known, easily accessible, expeditious and not unduly complicated;

166. *Urges* States to adopt the necessary measures, as provided by national law, to ensure the right of victims to seek just and adequate reparation and satisfaction to redress acts of racism, racial discrimination, xenophobia and related intolerance, and to design effective measures to prevent the repetition of such acts;

V. STRATEGIES TO ACHIEVE FULL AND EFFECTIVE EQUALITY, INCLUDING INTERNATIONAL COOPERATION AND ENHANCEMENT OF THE UNITED NATIONS AND OTHER INTERNATIONAL MECHANISMS IN COMBATING RACISM, RACIAL DISCRIMINATION, XENOPHOBIA AND RELATED INTOLERANCE AND FOLLOW-UP

167. *Calls upon* States to apply diligently all commitments undertaken by them in the declarations and plans of action of the regional conferences in which they participated, and to formulate national policies and action plans to combat racism, racial discrimination, xenophobia and related intolerance in compliance with the objectives set forth therein, and as provided for in other relevant instruments and decisions; and further requests that, in cases where such national policies and action plans to combat racism, racial discrimination, xenophobia and related intolerance already exist, States incorporate in them the commitments arising from their regional conferences;

168. *Urges* States that have not yet done so to consider acceding to the Geneva Conventions of 12 August 1949 and their two Additional Protocols of 1977, as well as to other treaties of international humanitarian law, and to enact, with the highest priority, appropriate legislation, taking the measures required to give full effect to their obligations under international humanitarian law, in particular in relation to the rules prohibiting discrimination;

169. *Urges* States to develop cooperation programmes to promote equal opportunities for the benefit of victims of racism, racial discrimination, xenophobia and related intolerance and encourages them to propose the creation of multilateral cooperation programmes with the same objective;

170. *Invites* States to include the subject of the struggle against racism, racial discrimination, xenophobia and related intolerance in the work programmes of the regional integration agencies and of the regional cross-boundary dialogue forums;

171. *Urges* States to recognize the challenges that people of different socially constructed races, colours, descent, national or ethnic origins, religions and languages experience in seeking to live together and to develop harmonious multiracial and multicultural societies; also urges States to recognize that the positive examples of relatively successful multiracial and multicultural societies, such as some of those in the Caribbean region, need to be examined and analysed, and that techniques, mechanisms, policies and programmes for reconciling conflicts based on factors related to race, colour, descent, language, religion, or national or ethnic origin and for developing harmonious multiracial and multicultural societies need to be systematically considered and developed, and therefore requests the United Nations and its relevant specialized agencies to consider establishing an international centre for multiracial and multicultural studies and policy development to undertake this critical work for the benefit of the international community;

172. *Urges* States to protect the national or ethnic, cultural, religious and linguistic identity of minorities within their respective territories and to develop appropriate legislative and other measures to encourage conditions for the promotion of that identity, in order to protect them from any form of racism, racial discrimination, xenophobia and related intolerance. In this context, forms of multiple discrimination should be fully taken into account;

173. *Further urges* States to ensure the equal protection and promotion of the identities of the historically disadvantaged communities in those unique circumstances where this may be appropriate;

174. *Urges* States to take or strengthen measures, including through bilateral or multi-lateral cooperation, to address root causes, such as poverty, underdevelopment and lack of equal opportunity, some of which may be associated with discriminatory practices, that make persons, especially women and children, vulnerable to trafficking, which may give rise to racism, racial discrimination, xenophobia and related intolerance;

175. *Encourages* States, in cooperation with non-governmental organizations, to under-take campaigns aimed at clarifying opportunities, limitations and rights in the event of migration, so as to enable everyone, in particular women, to make informed decisions and to prevent them from becoming victims of trafficking;

176. *Urges* States to adopt and implement social development policies based on reliable statistical data and centred on the attainment, by the year 2015, of the commitments to meet the basic needs of all set forth in paragraph 36 of the Programme of Action of the World Summit for Social Development, held at Copenhagen in 1995, with a view to closing significantly the existing gaps in living conditions faced by victims of rac-ism, racial discrimination, xenophobia and related intolerance, especially regarding the illiteracy rate, universal primary education, infant mortality, under-five child mortality, health, reproductive health care for all and access to safe drinking water. Promotion of gender equality will also be taken into account in the adoption and implementation of these policies;

International legal framework

177. *Urges* States to continue cooperating with the Committee on the Elimination of Racial Discrimination and other human rights treaty monitoring bodies in order to promote, including by means of a constructive and transparent dialogue, the effective implementation of the instruments concerned and proper consideration of the recom-mendations adopted by these bodies with regard to complaints of racism, racial discrimi-nation, xenophobia and related intolerance;

178. *Requests* adequate resources for the Committee on the Elimination of Racial Discrimination in order to enable it to discharge its mandate fully and stresses the impor-tance of providing adequate resources for all the United Nations human rights treaty bodies;

General international instruments

179. *Endorses* efforts of the international community, in particular steps taken under the auspices of the United Nations Educational, Scientific and Cultural Organization, to promote respect for and preserve cultural diversity within and between communities and nations with a view to creating a harmonious multicultural world, including elaboration of a possible international instrument in this respect in a manner consistent with interna-tional human rights instruments;

180. *Invites* the United Nations General Assembly to consider elaborating an integral and comprehensive international convention to protect and promote the rights and dig-nity of disabled people, including, especially, provisions that address the discriminatory practices and treatment affecting them;

Regional/international cooperation

181. *Invites* the Inter-Parliamentary Union to contribute to the activities of the International Year of Mobilization against Racism, Racial Discrimination, Xenophobia and Related

Intolerance by encouraging national parliaments to review progress on the objectives of the Conference;

182. *Encourages* States to participate in regional dialogues on problems of migration and invites them to consider negotiating bilateral and regional agreements on migrant workers and designing and implementing programmes with States of other regions to protect the rights of migrants;

183. *Urges* States, in consultation with civil society, to support or otherwise establish, as appropriate, regional, comprehensive dialogues on the causes and consequences of migration that focus not only on law enforcement and border control, but also on the promotion and protection of the human rights of migrants and on the relationship between migration and development;

184. *Encourages* international organizations having mandates dealing specifically with migration issues to exchange information and coordinate their activities on matters involving racism, racial discrimination, xenophobia and related intolerance against migrants, including migrant workers, with the support of the Office of the United Nations High Commissioner for Human Rights;

185. *Expresses its deep concern* over the severity of the humanitarian suffering of affected civilian populations and the burden carried by many receiving countries, particularly developing countries and countries in transition, and requests the relevant international institutions to ensure that urgent adequate financial and humanitarian assistance is maintained for the host countries to enable them to help the victims and to address, on an equitable basis, difficulties of populations expelled from their homes, and calls for sufficient safeguards to enable refugees to exercise freely their right of return to their countries of origin voluntarily, in safety and dignity;

186. *Encourages* States to conclude bilateral, subregional, regional and international agreements to address the problem of trafficking in women and children, in particular girls, as well as the smuggling of migrants;

187. *Calls upon* States, to promote, as appropriate, exchanges at the regional and international levels among independent national institutions and, as applicable, other relevant independent bodies with a view to enhancing cooperation to combat racism, racial discrimination, xenophobia and related intolerance;

188. *Urges* States to support the activities of regional bodies or centres which combat racism, racial discrimination, xenophobia and related intolerance where they exist in their region, and recommends the establishment of such bodies or centres in all regions where they do not exist. These bodies or centres may undertake the following activities, amongst others: assess and follow up the situation of racism, racial discrimination, xenophobia and related intolerance, and of individuals or groups of individuals who are victims thereof or subject thereto; identify trends, issues and problems; collect, disseminate and exchange information, *inter alia* relevant to the outcome of the regional conferences and the World Conference, and build networks to these ends; highlight examples of good practices; organize awareness-raising campaigns; develop proposals, solutions and preventive measures, where possible and appropriate, through joint efforts by coordinating with the United Nations, regional organizations and States and national human rights institutions;

189. *Urges* international organizations, within their mandates, to contribute to the fight against racism, racial discrimination, xenophobia and related intolerance;

190. *Encourages* financial and development institutions and the operational programmes and specialized agencies of the United Nations, in accordance with their regular budgets and the procedures of their governing bodies:

(a) To assign particular priority and allocate sufficient funding, within their areas of competence and budgets, to improve the situation of victims of racism, racial discrimination, xenophobia and related intolerance in order to combat manifestations of racism, racial discrimination, xenophobia and related intolerance, and to include them in the development and implementation of projects concerning them;

(b) To integrate human rights principles and standards into their policies and programmes;

(c) To consider including in their regular reporting to their boards of governors information on their contribution to promoting the participation of victims of racism, racial discrimination, xenophobia and related intolerance within their programmes and activities, and information on the efforts taken to facilitate such participation and to ensure that these policies and practices contribute to the eradication of racism, racial discrimination, xenophobia and related intolerance;

(d) To examine how their policies and practices affect victims of racism, racial discrimination, xenophobia and related intolerance, and to ensure that these policies and practices contribute to the eradication of racism, racial discrimination, xenophobia and related intolerance;

191. (a) *Calls upon* States to elaborate action plans in consultation with national human rights institutions, other institutions created by law to combat racism, and civil society and to provide the United Nations High Commissioner for Human Rights with such action plans and other relevant materials on the measures undertaken in order to implement provisions of the present Declaration and the Programme of Action;

(b) *Requests* the United Nations High Commissioner for Human Rights, in follow-up to the Conference, to cooperate with five independent eminent experts, one from each region, appointed by the Secretary-General from among candidates proposed by the Chairperson of the Commission on Human Rights, after consultation with the regional groups, to follow the implementation of the provisions of the Declaration and Programme of Action. An annual progress report on the implementation of these provisions will be presented by the High Commissioner to the Commission on Human Rights and to the General Assembly, taking into account information and views provided by States, relevant human rights treaty bodies, special procedures and other mechanisms of the Commission on Human Rights of the United Nations, international, regional and non-governmental organizations and national human rights institutions;

(c) *Welcomes* the intention of the United Nations High Commissioner for Human Rights to establish, within the Office of the High Commissioner for Human Rights, an anti-discrimination unit to combat racism, racial discrimination, xenophobia and related intolerance and to promote equality and non-discrimination, and invites her to consider the inclusion in its mandate of, *inter alia*, the compilation of information on racial discrimination and its development, and on legal and administrative support and advice to victims of racial discrimination and the collection of background materials provided by States, international, regional and non-governmental organizations and national human rights institutions under the follow-up mechanism of the Conference;

(d) *Recommends* that the Office of the High Commissioner for Human Rights, in cooperation with States, international, regional and non-governmental organizations and national human rights institutions, create a database containing information on practical means to address racism, racial discrimination, xenophobia and related intolerance, particularly international and regional instruments and national legislation, including anti-discrimination legislation, as well as legal means to combat racial discrimination; remedies available through international mechanisms to victims of racial discrimination, as well as national remedies; educational and preventive programmes implemented in various countries and regions; best practices to address racism, racial discrimination, xenophobia and related intolerance; opportunities for technical cooperation; and academic studies and specialized documents; and ensure that such a database is as accessible as possible to those in authority and the public at large, through its Web site and by other appropriate means;

192. *Invites* the United Nations and the United Nations Educational, Scientific and Cultural Organization to continue to organize high-level and other meetings on the Dialogue among Civilizations and, for this purpose, to mobilize funds and promote partnerships;

Office of the High Commissioner for Human Rights

193. *Encourages* the United Nations High Commissioner for Human Rights to continue and expand the appointment and designation of goodwill ambassadors in all countries of the world in order, *inter alia*, to promote respect for human rights and a culture of tolerance and to increase the level of awareness about the scourge of racism, racial discrimination, xenophobia and related intolerance;

194. *Calls upon* the Office of the High Commissioner for Human Rights to continue its efforts further to increase awareness of the work of the Committee on the Elimination of Racial Discrimination and the other United Nations human rights treaty bodies;

195. *Invites* the Office of the High Commissioner for Human Rights, in consultation with the United Nations Educational, Scientific and Cultural Organization, and non-governmental organizations active in the field of the promotion and protection of human rights, to undertake regular consultations with them and to encourage research activities aimed at collecting, maintaining and adapting the technical, scientific, educational and information materials produced by all cultures around the world to fight racism;

196. *Requests* the Office of the High Commissioner for Human Rights to pay special attention to violations of the human rights of victims of racism, racial discrimination, xenophobia and related intolerance, in particular migrants, including migrant workers, to promote international cooperation in combating xenophobia and, to this end, to develop programmes which can be implemented in countries on the basis of appropriate cooperation agreements;

197. *Invites* States to assist the Office of the High Commissioner for Human Rights in developing and funding, upon the request of States, specific technical cooperation projects aimed at combating racism, racial discrimination, xenophobia and related intolerance;

198. *(a) Invites* the Commission on Human Rights to include in the mandates of the special rapporteurs and working groups of the Commission, in particular the Special Rapporteur on contemporary forms of racism, racial discrimination, xenophobia and related intolerance, recommendations that they consider the relevant provisions of the Declaration and the Programme of Action while exercising their mandates, in particular reporting to the General Assembly and the Commission on Human Rights, and also to consider any other appropriate means to follow up on the outcome on the Conference;

(b) Calls upon States to cooperate with the relevant special procedures of the Commission on Human Rights and other mechanisms of the United Nations in matters pertaining to racism, racial discrimination, xenophobia and related intolerance, in particular with the special rapporteurs, independent experts and special representatives;

199. *Recommends* that the Commission on Human Rights prepare complementary international standards to strengthen and update international instruments against racism, racial discrimination, xenophobia and related intolerance in all their aspects;

Decades

200. *Urges* States and the international community to support the activities of the Third Decade to Combat Racism and Racial Discrimination;

201. *Recommends* that the General Assembly consider declaring a United Nations year or decade against trafficking in persons, especially in women, youth and children, in order to protect their dignity and human rights;

202. *Urges* States, in close cooperation with the United Nations Educational, Scientific and Cultural Organization, to promote the implementation of the Declaration and Programme of Action on a Culture of Peace and the objectives of the International Decade for a Culture of Peace and Non-Violence for the Children of the World, which started in 2001, and invites the United Nations Educational, Scientific and Cultural Organization to contribute to these activities;

Indigenous peoples

203. *Recommends* that the United Nations Secretary-General conduct an evaluation of the results of the International Decade of the World's Indigenous People (1995–2004) and make recommendations concerning how to mark the end of the Decade, including an appropriate follow-up;

204. *Requests* States to ensure adequate funding for the establishment of an operational framework and a firm basis for the future development of the Permanent Forum on Indigenous Issues within the United Nations system;

205. *Urges* States to cooperate with the work of the Special Rapporteur on the situation of human rights and fundamental freedoms of indigenous people and requests the Secretary-General and the United Nations High Commissioner for Human Rights to

ensure that the Special Rapporteur is provided with all the necessary human, technical and financial resources to fulfil his responsibilities;

206. *Calls upon* States to conclude negotiations on and approve as soon as possible the text of the draft declaration on the rights of indigenous peoples, under discussion by the working group of the Commission on Human Rights to elaborate a draft declaration, in accordance with Commission resolution 1995/32 of 3 March 1995;

207. *Urges* States, in the light of the relationship between racism, racial discrimination, xenophobia and related intolerance and poverty, marginality and social exclusion of peoples and individuals at both the national and international levels, to enhance their policies and measures to reduce income and wealth inequalities and to take appropriate steps, individually and through international cooperation, to promote and protect economic, social and cultural rights on a non-discriminatory basis;

208. *Urges* States and international financial and development institutions to mitigate any negative effects of globalization by examining, *inter alia*, how their policies and practices affect national populations in general and indigenous peoples in particular; by ensuring that their policies and practices contribute to the eradication of racism through the participation of national populations and, in particular, indigenous peoples in development projects; by further democratizing international financial institutions; and by consulting with indigenous peoples on any matter that may affect their physical, spiritual or cultural integrity;

209. *Invites* financial and development institutions and the operational programmes and specialized agencies of the United Nations, in accordance with their regular budgets and the procedures of their governing bodies:

(a) To assign particular priority to and allocate sufficient funding, within their areas of competence, to the improvement of the status of indigenous peoples, with special attention to the needs of these populations in developing countries, including the preparation of specific programmes with a view to achieving the objectives of the International Decade of the World's Indigenous People;

(b) To carry out special projects, through appropriate channels and in collaboration with indigenous peoples, to support their initiatives at the community level and to facilitate the exchange of information and technical know-how between indigenous peoples and experts in these areas;

Civil society

210. *Calls upon* States to strengthen cooperation, develop partnerships and consult regularly with non-governmental organizations and all other sectors of the civil society to harness their experience and expertise, thereby contributing to the development of legislation, policies and other governmental initiatives, as well as involving them more closely in the elaboration and implementation of policies and programmes designed to combat racism, racial discrimination, xenophobia and related intolerance;

211. *Urges* leaders of religious communities to continue to confront racism, racial discrimination, xenophobia and related intolerance through, *inter alia*, promotion and sponsoring of dialogue and partnerships to bring about reconciliation, healing and harmony within and among societies, invites religious communities to participate in promoting economic and social revitalization and encourages religious leaders to foster greater cooperation and contact between diverse racial groups;

212. *Urges* States to establish and strengthen effective partnerships with and provide support, as appropriate, to all relevant actors of civil society, including non-governmental organizations working to promote gender equality and the advancement of women, particularly women subject to multiple discrimination, and to promote an integrated and holistic approach to the elimination of all forms of discrimination against women and girls;

Non-governmental organizations

213. *Urges* States to provide an open and conducive environment to enable non-governmental organizations to function freely and openly within their societies and thereby make an effective contribution to the elimination of racism, racial discrimination, xenophobia and related intolerance throughout the world, and to promote a wider role for grass-roots organizations;

214. *Calls upon* States to explore means to expand the role of non-governmental organizations in society through, in particular, deepening the ties of solidarity amongst citizens and promoting greater trust across racial and social class divides by promoting wider citizen involvement and more voluntary cooperation;

The private sector

215. *Urges* States to take measures, including, where appropriate, legislative measures, to ensure that transnational corporations and other foreign enterprises operating within their national territories conform to precepts and practices of non-racism and non-discrimination, and further encourages the business sector, including transnational corporations and foreign enterprises, to collaborate with trade unions and other relevant sectors of civil society to develop voluntary codes of conduct for all businesses, designed to prevent, address and eradicate racism, racial discrimination, xenophobia and related intolerance;

Youth

216. *Urges* States to encourage the full and active participation of, as well as involve more closely, youth in the elaboration, planning and implementation of activities to fight racism, racial discrimination, xenophobia and related intolerance, and calls upon States, in partnership with non-governmental organizations and other sectors of society, to facilitate both national and international youth dialogue on racism, racial discrimination, xenophobia and related intolerance, through the World Youth Forum of the United Nations system and through the use of new technologies, exchanges and other means;

217. *Urges* States to encourage and facilitate the establishment and maintenance of youth mechanisms, set up by youth organizations and young women and men themselves, in the spirit of combating racism, racial discrimination, xenophobia and related intolerance, through such activities as: disseminating and exchanging information and building networks to these ends; organizing awareness-raising campaigns and participating in multicultural education programmes; developing proposals and solutions, where possible and appropriate; cooperating and consulting regularly with non-governmental organizations and other actors in civil society in developing initiatives and programmes that promote intercultural exchange and dialogue;

218. *Urges* States, in cooperation with intergovernmental organizations, the International Olympic Committee and international and regional sports federations, to intensify the fight against racism in sport by, among other things, educating the youth of the world through sport practised without discrimination of any kind and in the Olympic spirit, which requires human understanding, tolerance, fair play and solidarity;

219. *Recognizes* that the success of this Programme of Action will require political will and adequate funding at the national, regional and international levels, and international cooperation.

INDEX